CW01338166

THE OXFORD HANDBOOK OF
WORD CLASSES

OXFORD HANDBOOKS IN LINGUISTICS

RECENTLY PUBLISHED

THE OXFORD HANDBOOK OF EXPERIMENTAL SEMANTICS AND PRAGMATICS
Edited by Chris Cummins and Napoleon Katsos

THE OXFORD HANDBOOK OF EVENT STRUCTURE
Edited by Robert Truswell

THE OXFORD HANDBOOK OF LANGUAGE ATTRITION
Edited by Monika S. Schmid and Barbara Köpke

THE OXFORD HANDBOOK OF NEUROLINGUISTICS
Edited by Greig I. de Zubicaray and Niels O. Schiller

THE OXFORD HANDBOOK OF ENGLISH GRAMMAR
Edited by Bas Aarts, Jill Bowie, and Gergana Popova

THE OXFORD HANDBOOK OF AFRICAN LANGUAGES
Edited by Rainer Vossen and Gerrit J. Dimmendaal

THE OXFORD HANDBOOK OF NEGATION
Edited by Viviane Déprez and M. Teresa Espinal

THE OXFORD HANDBOOK OF LANGUAGE CONTACT
Edited by Anthony P. Grant

THE OXFORD HANDBOOK OF LANGUAGE AND RACE
Edited by H. Samy Alim, Angela Reyes, and Paul V. Kroskrity

THE OXFORD HANDBOOK OF LANGUAGE PROSODY
Edited by Carlos Gussenhoven and Aoju Chen

THE OXFORD HANDBOOK OF LANGUAGES OF THE CAUCASUS
Edited by Maria Polinsky

THE OXFORD HANDBOOK OF GRAMMATICAL NUMBER
Edited by Patricia Cabredo Hofherr and Jenny Doetjes

THE OXFORD HANDBOOK OF COMPUTATIONAL LINGUISTICS
Second Edition
Edited by Ruslan Mitkov

THE OXFORD HANDBOOK OF THE MENTAL LEXICON
Edited by Anna Papafragou, John C. Trueswell, and Lila R. Gleitman

THE OXFORD HANDBOOK OF ETHIOPIAN LANGUAGES
Edited by Ronny Meyer, Bedilu Wakjira, and Zelealem Leyew

THE OXFORD HANDBOOK OF EXPERIMENTAL SYNTAX
Edited by Jon Sprouse

THE OXFORD HANDBOOK OF WORD CLASSES
Edited by Eva van Lier

For a complete list of Oxford Handbooks in Linguistics please see pp. 1089–1092

THE OXFORD HANDBOOK OF

WORD CLASSES

Edited by
EVA VAN LIER

OXFORD
UNIVERSITY PRESS

OXFORD
UNIVERSITY PRESS

Great Clarendon Street, Oxford, OX2 6DP,
United Kingdom

Oxford University Press is a department of the University of Oxford.
It furthers the University's objective of excellence in research, scholarship,
and education by publishing worldwide. Oxford is a registered trade mark of
Oxford University Press in the UK and in certain other countries

© editorial matter and organization Eva van Lier 2023
© the chapters their several authors 2023

The moral rights of the authors have been asserted

First Edition published in 2023

All rights reserved. No part of this publication may be reproduced, stored in
a retrieval system, or transmitted, in any form or by any means, without the
prior permission in writing of Oxford University Press, or as expressly permitted
by law, by licence or under terms agreed with the appropriate reprographics
rights organization. Enquiries concerning reproduction outside the scope of the
above should be sent to the Rights Department, Oxford University Press, at the
address above

You must not circulate this work in any other form
and you must impose this same condition on any acquirer

Published in the United States of America by Oxford University Press
198 Madison Avenue, New York, NY 10016, United States of America

British Library Cataloguing in Publication Data
Data available

Library of Congress Control Number: 2022945552

ISBN 978–0–19–885288–9

DOI: 10.1093/oxfordhb/9780198852889.001.0001

Printed and bound by
CPI Group (UK) Ltd, Croydon, CR0 4YY

Links to third party websites are provided by Oxford in good faith and
for information only. Oxford disclaims any responsibility for the materials
contained in any third party website referenced in this work.

Contents

Acknowledgements ix
List of figures and tables xi
List of abbreviations xvii
Notes on the contributors xxvii

1. Introduction 1
   EVA VAN LIER

PART I FUNDAMENTAL ISSUES

2. Word-class universals and language-particular analysis 15
   MARTIN HASPELMATH

3. Levels of analysis and word classes (root, stem, word) 41
   WALTER BISANG

4. Lexical vs grammatical words 72
   KASPER BOYE

5. Transcategorial operations 85
   ANDREJ L. MALCHUKOV

6. Word-class systems and other grammatical properties 109
   WILLIAM A. FOLEY

PART II THEORETICAL APPROACHES

7. Word classes in Formal Semantics 137
   YOAD WINTER

8. Word classes in Cognitive Grammar 160
   CRISTIANO BROCCIAS

9. Word classes and gradience 178
   EVELIEN KEIZER

10. Lexeme classes and word classes in Functional Discourse Grammar — 196
J. LACHLAN MACKENZIE

11. Word classes in Radical Construction Grammar — 213
WILLIAM CROFT

12. Word classes in Minimalist Syntax — 231
HEDDE ZEIJLSTRA

13. Lexical categories in Distributed Morphology — 248
JAN DON

14. Word classes in Head-driven Phrase Structure Grammar — 262
FRANK VAN EYNDE

15. Word classes in Lexical Functional Grammar — 281
MARY DALRYMPLE AND IDA TOIVONEN

PART III SPECIFIC WORD CLASSES

16. Verbs — 305
ALEXANDER LETUCHIY

17. Nouns — 339
JAN RIJKHOFF

18. Adjectives — 365
DAVID BECK

19. Adverbs — 383
KEES HENGEVELD

20. Adpositions — 420
BORJA HERCE

21. Demonstratives — 443
HOLGER DIESSEL

22. Ideophones — 466
MARK DINGEMANSE

23. Interjections — 477
MARK DINGEMANSE

PART IV WORD CLASSES IN GENETIC AND AREAL LANGUAGE GROUPS

24. Word classes in Egyptian, Semitic, and Cushitic (Afroasiatic) — 495
 Elsa Oréal and Martine Vanhove

25. Word classes in Mande languages — 516
 Denis Creissels

26. Word classes in Australian languages — 544
 Dana Louagie

27. Word classes in Indo-European languages — 572
 Paolo Ramat

28. Word classes in classical Chinese — 590
 Walter Bisang

29. Word classes in Salish languages — 613
 Donna B. Gerdts and Lauren Schneider

30. Word classes in Iroquoian languages — 651
 Karin Michelson

31. Word classes in Eskimo–Aleut languages — 669
 Marianne Mithun

32. Word classes in Mayan languages — 700
 Valentina Vapnarsky

33. Word classes in Maweti–Guarani languages — 729
 Françoise Rose

34. Word classes in Quechuan languages — 752
 Pieter Muysken

35. Word classes in Austronesian languages — 771
 Ulrike Mosel

36. Word classes in Timor–Alor–Pantar and the Papuan region — 788
 Marian Klamer

37. Word classes in sign languages — 809
 Vadim Kimmelman and Carl Börstell

PART V WORD CLASSES IN LINGUISTIC SUBDISCIPLINES

38. Word classes in corpus linguistics — 833
    NATALIA LEVSHINA

39. Word classes and grammaticalization — 851
    K. AARON SMITH

40. Word classes in first language acquisition — 865
    SABINE STOLL

41. Word classes in second language acquisition — 876
    SETH LINDSTROMBERG AND FRANK BOERS

42. Word classes in language contact — 887
    YARON MATRAS AND EVANGELIA ADAMOU

43. Word classes in psycholinguistics — 899
    PAUL IBBOTSON

44. Word classes in neurolinguistics — 910
    DAVID KEMMERER

45. Word classes in computational linguistics and artificial intelligence — 930
    MELADEL MISTICA, EKATERINA VYLOMOVA, AND FRANCIS BOND

References — 947
Index of languages — 1075
Subject index handbook of word classes — 1083

Acknowledgements

I would like to express my deep gratitude to all the colleagues that contributed to this handbook. It has been an honour and a privilege to collect the valuable work of so many great scholars, and it is my hope that using this handbook will be inspiring and useful for readers, be they students or advanced linguists. The study of word classes offers a fascinating view onto the diversity and unity of human language.

A very special note of thanks goes out to Pieter Muysken, who wrote Chapter 34 on Word classes in Quechuan languages. Sadly, he passed away in 2021, before completion of this handbook. His long career in linguistics represents a true example of diversity in all senses of the word. In the process of examining a wealth of fundamental linguistic questions, Pieter Muysken brought together not only countless different theories, languages, and methodologies, but also many people. This book is dedicated to him.

List of figures and tables

Figures

2.1	Five alignment types of argument markers	20
2.2	Five coexpression types of function indicators	21
3.1	Types of word-class systems	46
5.1	Hierarchy of verbal categories	89
5.2	Hierarchy of nominal categories	89
5.3	The cline of deverbalization	91
5.4	The cline of substantivization	93
5.5	Generalized scale model for nominalizations	96
5.6	Subject Blocking	98
5.7	Object Blocking	98
5.8	Generalized scale model for verbalization	100
5.9	Modifier Blocking in verbalization	101
6.1	Schematic representation of a lexeme	110
6.2	Schema of noun–verb alignment in Latin	111
6.3	Clausal structure predisposed to categorial neutrality	122
7.1	English vs Warlpiri	140
7.2	Intersective modification of nominals	142
7.3	Intersective modification and extrinsic/intrinsic arguments	143
7.4	N-conservativity	147
8.1	The grammar-lexicon continuum	162
8.2	The Cognitive Grammar analysis of grammatical classes	164
8.3	Grouping	165
8.4	Count and mass nouns	165
8.5	The noun *finger*	166
8.6	The process *eat*	168
8.7	The verb *enter* (after Langacker 1987b: 245)	168
8.8	Sequential (a) vs summary scanning (b) (after Langacker 1987b: 144)	169
8.9	Perfective and imperfective verbs	170
8.10	Adjectives, adverbs, and prepositions	171
8.11	The dynamic preposition *into*	172

8.12	Hollmann's (2013) verb network	174
8.13	The determiner *this* as a grounding element	175
8.14	The baseline viewing arrangement	176
9.1	Crystal's representation of nominal subclasses	183
9.2	Aarts's revised version of Figure 9.1	184
9.3	Gradience within and between the categories of noun, verb, and adjective	192
9.4	Langacker's two-level network of categorization	193
10.1	The architecture of FDG (Hengeveld & Mackenzie 2008: 13)	198
12.1	Feature hierarchy proposed by Harley & Ritter (2002)	241
12.2	Feature sets based on Chomsky (1995)	244
12.3	Feature sets based on Chomsky (2002)	245
12.4	Feature sets based on Pesetsky & Torrego (2007)	245
14.1	The part-of-speech inventory	266
14.2	Complementation	267
14.3	Adjunction	268
14.4	A noun phrase	270
14.5	A marked clause	274
14.6	The major vs minor distinction	275
17.1	Nominal subcategories ('*Seinsarten*'; based on Rijkhoff 2004: 54)	346
19.1	Levels in FDG	391
19.2	Scope relations at the Interpersonal and Representational Levels in FDG	391
20.1	Classification of the 52 adpositions for 10 grammatical properties (dark grey = has property, light grey = lacks property)	427
20.2	Some Hungarian adpositions according to four grammatical properties	428
20.3	Grammatical properties of 42 Basque adpositions (Hualde 2002, personal knowledge; Hualde & Ortiz de Urbina 2003)	431
20.4	Classification of 47 German adpositions for 8 grammatical properties	433
20.5	Number of adpositions in different token frequency ranges (COCA)	434
20.6	Frequency (tokens per million words) over time of *instead of me* vs *in my stead* (Google Books Ngram Viewer: http://books.google.com/ngrams)	436
20.7	Properties of 55 Spanish adpositions, with the 19 traditional prepositions darker	436
20.8	Adpositions and grammatical properties, randomly generated	440
31.1	The Eskimo–Aleut (Eskaleut) family (based on Fortescue et al. 2010)	669
31.2	Noun template	671
31.3	Verb template	673
33.1	The Tupi language family	731
34.1	Classification of the parts of speech based on their suffixation possibilities	757
36.1	Location of the Timor–Alor–Pantar languages in Indonesia	789
36.2	The Timor–Alor–Pantar languages	790
36.3	The internal structure of the Timor Alor Pantar family (Kaiping & Klamer 2022: 303)	791

37.1	A sign variant meaning 'good' in Swedish Sign Language (Swedish Sign Language Dictionary online 2020: #12077)	811
37.2	The palm(s)-up gesture/sign (Swedish Sign Language Dictionary online 2020: #18717)	812
37.3	The sign HAMMER in Swedish Sign Language (Swedish Sign Language Dictionary online 2020: #03829)	813
37.4	A list buoy in Swedish Sign Language: three items listed on left hand; right hand points to each in turn before signing a comment about the associated listed referent (Swedish Sign Language Dictionary online 2020: #00074, phrase 2)	814
37.5	The sign ACCESSIBLE^H-E-T ('accessible'+ '–ity' = 'accessibility') in Swedish Sign Language (Swedish Sign Language Dictionary online 2020: #08617)	814
37.6	The sign WHATSAPP in Swedish Sign Language, borrowed from the ASL phrase 'what's up?' (Swedish Sign Language Dictionary online 2020: #04672)	815
37.7	The sign POSS$_1$ ('my') in Swedish Sign Language (Swedish Sign Language Dictionary online 2020: #00187)	817
37.8	The sign POSS$_2$ ('your') in Swedish Sign Language (Swedish Sign Language Dictionary online 2020: #00275)	817
37.9	LIGHTER (2 frames) vs LIGHT.LIGHTER (2 frames) in RSL (from Kimmelman 2009: 172–173)	820
37.10	The RSL signs $_1$HELP$_2$ 'I help you' and $_2$HELP$_1$ 'You help me'	822
37.11	The RSL sign RECTANGULAR.SASS	823
37.12	The sign TO.TRAIN^PERSON ('trainer, coach') in Swedish Sign Language (Swedish Sign Language Dictionary online 2020: #13035)	824
37.13	The sign FLOOR in Swedish Sign Language (Swedish Sign Language Dictionary online 2020: #12253)	827
37.14	The sign DO in Swedish Sign Language (Swedish Sign Language Dictionary online 2020: #00563)	828
38.1	Average entropy scores of Universal POS tags regarding the syntactic dependencies in the Universal Dependencies corpora	842
38.2	Number of corpora in the Universal Dependencies collection that do not have individual universal part-of-speech tags	845
38.3	Number of corpora in the Universal Dependencies collection without individual part-of-speech tags: Indo-European vs Non-Indo-European languages	846
38.4	Absolute log-odds ratios of wordforms in six Universal Dependencies corpora, with the means (dots) and one standard deviation from the mean (black lines)	849
44.1	Major gyri, sulci, and Brodmann areas (numbered) of the human brain shown on left lateral (A) and ventral (B) surfaces	911
44.2	Longitudinal performance of the patient MML on spoken and written tasks (reproduced with permission from Shapiro & Caramazza 2003; original data from Hillis et al. 2002)	915
44.3	Two alternative accounts of the performance profile of patient MML	916
44.4	MEG-based Minimum Norm Estimates (MNEs) for the time windows during which significant differences between visually presented noun phrases (NPs) and verb phrases (VPs) were revealed by cluster analysis (reproduced with permission from Tsigka et al. 2014: 92)	919

44.5	Proportion of correct responses by patient RE for nouns and verbs in a picture-naming (reproduced with permission from Berndt et al. 2002: 361)	920
44.6	Lesion overlap map of patients with left temporal polar damage with impaired retrieval of proper nouns in naming tasks (reproduced with permission from Waldron et al. 2014: 53. See also Belfi & Tranel 2014)	925
45.1	Nouns	934
45.2	Verbs	934
45.3	Representing the word class NN with explicit features as an attribute–value matrix	934
45.4	A toy grammar in Backus–Naur form (commonly referred to as BNF)	935
45.5	Example of relation pattern based on POS tags	940

Tables

2.1	Three propositional act functions and three semantic root classes	16
3.1	Root and stem categoriality (Lehmann 2008: 558–559)	45
3.2	Person agreement markers on action-denoting lexemes and on object-denoting lexemes (adapted from Launey 1994: 10–11)	48
6.1	Determiner clitics across three Southern Wakashan languages	118
6.2	Inflectional Verb classes in Aghu	121
7.1	Different categories with their extrinsic types and intrinsic arguments	139
7.2	Chierchia's cross-linguistic classification of noun meanings	157
7.3	Languages with a productive possessive strategy (FKG 2017: 25–32)	157
9.1	Gradience in the class of adjectives	185
10.1	Primary and secondary uses of Verbs, Nouns, and Adjectives in FG	201
10.2	Lexeme class systems	206
10.3	Typology of dependent clauses	209
10.4	Revised overview of lexeme class systems	210
12.1	Suppletion for comparative vs superlative adjective forms	243
18.1	Semantic class and syntactic function	367
18.2	Adjectives in Venda (Dixon 1982: 4–5)	368
18.3	Semantic class and pragmatic function (based on Croft 1991: 55)	369
18.4	Unidirectional flexibility of modifying words in Upper Necaxa Totonac	380
18.5	Multilateral flexibility of adjectives in Tukang Besi	381
19.1	Layers and operators in FDG	392
19.2	Cross-classification of adverbs	395
19.3	The sample	407
19.4	The existence of adverbs	411
19.5	The existence of adverbs—illustrations	412
19.6	Reduplication as an adverb-forming strategy in the language sample	415

19.7	Flexible modifiers in the language sample	416
20.1	Definite forms of the phrase 'black valley' (*haran* = valley) for six different cases	430
21.1	Word-class typology of demonstratives	445
21.2	Demonstratives in Awa Pit (Curnow 1997: 87)	448
21.3	Demonstratives in Ubykh (Fenwick 2011: 79)	449
21.4	Demonstratives in Lezgian (Haspelmath 1993a: 190)	449
21.5	Spatial demonstrative adverbs in Imonda (Seiler 1985: 43–46)	453
21.6	Demonstratives pronouns and demonstrative adverbs of space and manner in Lezgian (Haspelmath 1993a), Japanese (König 2012), Croatian (Brala-Vukanović 2015), and Korean (Sohn 1994)	454
21.7	Demonstratives in Pohnpeian (Rehg 1981: 150–153)	456
21.8	Demonstratives in Uduk (Killian 2015: 152–162)	457
21.9	Distal demonstratives in Tümpisa Shoshone (Dayley 1989: 137–145)	458
21.10	Demonstrative pronouns and identifiers in Inuktitut (Denny 1982: 364–365)	459
21.11	Demonstratives in Mauwake (Berghäll 2015: 116, 121, 172)	461
22.1	Semantic classes and discourse functions (Hallonsten Halling–Croft model)	474
23.1	Three frequent interactional functions covered by interjections, with examples from Siwu and English translations	483
23.2	Animal-oriented interjections in Lao (Enfield 2007: 315)	485
24.1	The morphogenesis of the 'have-perfect'	499
24.2	Classical Arabic independent and suffix pronouns	504
24.3	Classical Arabic perfective paradigm of *katab* 'write'	505
24.4	Paradigms of Akkadian stative, Ge'ez perfect, and Classical Arabic perfective	505
24.5	Imperfective and preterit in Neo-Syriac	506
24.6	Personal indices in Cushitic languages	510
24.7	Comparison of paradigm of *di* 'say' and verb class 2 inflectional morphemes in Beja	511
24.8	Common case markers in Cushitic	513
25.1	The Mande language family	517
29.1	Inflected forms for some Halkomelem nouns	623
29.2	Halkomelem adjectives inflected for plural and diminutive (Gerdts 2012: 2)	623
29.3	Halkomelem plural and diminutive verbs	624
29.4	Halkomelem plural and diminutive adverbs	625
29.5	Some Halkomelem nominalizing morphemes	630
29.6	Verbs derived from the root √*pqwa*	631
29.7	Halkomelem denominal morphology	633
29.8	Halkomelem plural and diminutive noun bases (Gerdts & Hukari 2008)	633
29.9	Halkomelem imperfective denominal verbs (Gerdts & Hukari 2008)	634
30.1	The internal structure of verbs	655
30.2	Oneida noun prefixes (word-initial forms with stems beginning in a consonant)	658

32.1	Example of exclusive and non-exclusive Positional formations	724
33.1	Function and morphology of verbs and nouns in Maweti–Guarani (generalization)	736
33.2	Comparison of Maweti–Guarani descriptive roots with nouns and verbs	738
33.3	Teko possessive constructions of nouns with or without the relational prefix	742
33.4	Comparison of Maweti–Guarani postpositions with subclasses of nouns and verbs	742
33.5	The 'canonical' hierarchical indexing system of Maweti–Guarani languages	744
34.1	Types of suffixes in Cuzco Quechua (using examples from Cusihuamán 1976)	755
34.2	Syllabic properties of parts of speech in Cuzco Quechua	758
34.3	Colour terms in Salasaca Kichwa (data from Agustín Jerez, cited from Muysken 2019)	761
34.4	Criteria to distinguish clitics from suffixes in Quechua (partly based on Muysken 1981)	767
34.5	Status of some morphemes on the basis of the criteria in Table 34.4 (s = suffix, c = clitic)	768
34.6	First approximation of lexical categories in some Andean languages	769
35.1	Frequencies of prototypical Teop event, object, and property words	775
35.2	Word classes of property words in 12 Oceanic languages	781
35.3	Property words in Mangap-Mbula	782
35.4	Property words in Toqabaqita	783
35.5	Modification in Samoan (Polynesia)	783
35.6	Teop (PNG) content words with juxtaposed modifying content words	784
35.7	Distribution of attributive and adverbial modifiers in Teop (Mosel 2017)	784
35.8	The marking of event and object words in predicate and referential phrases	787
36.1	Numerals 'seven' to 'nine' in AP languages (Schapper & Klamer 2017: 288)	804
36.2	Indonesian nouns borrowed in five or more TAP varieties	805
36.3	Indonesian verbs and adjectives borrowed in three or more TAP varieties	805
38.1	Some frequencies of common nouns as syntactic dependencies in the Afrikaans Universal Dependencies training corpus (v 2.5)	841
38.2	Top ten ambiguity tags in the British National Corpus	843
38.3	Number of unused tags (maximum: 17)	844
44.1	Examples of large (30%+) dissociations between prototypical nouns and verbs in oral picture-naming tasks	912
45.1	The Penn Treebank	932
45.2	Comparison of some universal parts of speech	936

List of Abbreviations

1	first person
1, 2, 3	1st, 2nd, 3rd person
1>2	1st person subject, 2nd person object
A	agent [agent-like argument of canonical transitive verb]
AA	Afroasiatic
ABL	ablative
ABS	absolute/absolutive
ACC	accusative
ACCID	Accidens
ACT	actual/active (voice)
ADESS	adessive (case)
ADJ	adjective
ADJZ	adjectivizer
ADP	Adposition
ADV	adverb[ial]/adverbializer
ADVman	manner adverb
ADVt	temporal adverb
Afr.	Afrikaans
AG	agentive
AGk.	Ancient Greek
AGR	agreement
AGRO	object agreement
AGRS	subject agreement
AGT	agent
ALL	allative [case]
AMB	ambulative
AN	animate
ANR	action nominalizer
ANT	anterior
ANTIP	antipassive [voice]
AOR	aorist
APL	adjectival plural
APPL	applicative
ARG	argument
ART	article
ASP	aspect
ASS	assistive

ASSRT	assertion particle
AT	attested
ATR	attributive
AUG/AUGM	augmentative/augmented
AUX	auxiliary
AV	actor voice
Av.	Avestan
AVER	aversive
B	bound form/set B personal marker
BEN	benefactive
Bulg.	Bulgarian
C.I.COM	shared information
Cast.	Castilian
Cat.	Catalan
CAU[S]	causative
Celt.	Celtic
CERT	certainty [evidential]
CIRC	circumstantial mode
cis	cislocative, towards speaker
CL	[noun]classifier
CL2	class II gender
CLF	classifier
CLOC	cislocative
CN	connector
CNJ	conjunction
CNT	continuative
COLL	collective
COM	comitative
COMP	complementizer
COMPL	completed/completive/complementizer
CONC	(adjectival) concord
COND	conditional
CONJ	conjunction
CONT	continuative/continuous
CONTR	contrastive
CONV	converb
COORD	coordination
COP	copula
CORE	core case
COREF	coreferential
COTEMP	cotemporal clitic
CP[L]	completive [completive verb stem/completive aspect marker]
CS	causative
CTEMP	contemporaneous
CTR	contrastive
CVB	converb

CVB.MNR	manner converb
Cymr.	Cymric (Welsh)
Cze.	Czech
D	definite article/determiner
DAT	dative
DC/DECL	declarative
DEF	definite [article]
DEIC	deictic
DEL	delimitative
DEM	demonstrative
DEM.DIST	distal demonstrative
DEON	deontic
DER	derivation
DESI/DESID	desiderative
DET	determiner/determinative
DEV	develop into, become
DIM	diminutive
DIR	directional [prefix]
DIST	distal
DISTR	distributive
DL	dual number/dualic (duplicative)
DM	demonstrative
DO	direct object
DS	directional suffix/subject different in switch reference
DT	determiner
DU	dual
Du.	Dutch
DUB	dubitative
DUR	durative [aspect]
DV	duplicative
DYN	dynamic
ECOP	equative copula
EFF	effector (demoted agent of passive)
EMOT	emotional particle
EMPH	emphatic [particle]
EN	epenthetic nasal
EPEN	epenthesis/epenthetic vowel
ERG	ergative
EU	euphonic
EV.AFF	affirmative evidential
EVD	evidential [particle]
EX	exclusive [of hearer]
EXAG	exaggerative
EXCL	exclusive
EXIS[T]	existential
EXP	experiencer

EXPR	expressive
F	feminine
FAC/FACT	factive mood/factual
FDG	Functional Discourse Grammar
FI	feminine-indefinite
FIN	finite
FOC	focus marker/focalization marker
Fr.	French
FR.PAST	far past tense
FRUSTR	frustrative
FUT	future [tense]
FZ	feminine-zoic
GC	glide consonant
GEN	genitive
GER	gerund/gerundive
GOAL	goal
Goth.	Gothic
GRAD	[adjectival] gradation
H	hearer/higher object
HAB	habitual [aspect]
HES	hesitation
Hitt.	Hittite
HPSG	Head-driven Phrase-structure Grammar
hs	hearsay
HUM	human
HYP	hypothetical
Ice.	Icelandic
ICP[L]	incompletive
IDENT	identificational marker
IDEO	ideophone
IDPH	ideophone
IF	illocutionary force marker
I–IV	noun classes
IM[P]	imperative [mood]/imperfect
IMPERF	imperfective aspect
IMV	imperative
IN	inclusive [of hearer]
INAN	inanimate
INC[H]	inchoative
INCL	inclusive
IND	Indonesian
IND	indicative [mood]
INDEF	indefinite
INDET	indeterminate state [Akkadian]
INDF	indefinite
INDIC	indicative

INF	infinitive
INFER	inferential
INFL	inflection
INFR	inferential
INS	instrumental
INSTR	instrumental
INT	interrogative
INTENS	intensifier
INTER	interrogative
INTJ	interjection
INTR	intransitive
IPF	imperfective [aspect]
IPFV	imperfective
IRR	irrealis
It.	Italian
I–X	noun classes
JOIN	joiner vowel
K	case marker
LA	borrowed Spanish definiteness marker *la*
Lat.	Latin
LCOP	locative copula
LCTR	limited control transitive
LEST	verbal aversive suffix
LFG	Lexical Functional Grammar
LIM	limitative
LINK	linking vowel or consonant
Lith.	Lithuanian
LK	linker/linking vowel
LNK	linker/adverbial linker
LOC	locative case/locative adposition
LOC.PUNCT	locative punctual
LPFX	lexical prefix
LV	light verb
M	masculine
MABL	modal ablative
Mac.	Macedonian
MAF	manner adverb focus suffix
MASC	masculine
MED	medial/mediopassive
MGk.	Modern Greek
MID	middle
MIN	minimal
MIR	mirative
MOD	modal [adverb]
MODep	adverb with epistemic function
MODi	adverb with illocutionary function

MODIF	modifier
MPROP	modal proprietive
MS	male speaker
MSA	Modern South Arabian
MSD	masdar
N	noun/neuter/nominalizer
N.ASS	non-commitment of speaker
NAME	proper name marker
NB	number
NCLF	nominal classifier
NEG	negation/negative
NEG.EX	negative existential
NEG.IMP	negative imperative
NEU	neuter
NFN	non-finite
NM	nominative particle
NMLZ	nominalization/nominalizer
NOM	nominative
NOMZ	nominalizer
NON.FUT	non-future
NOUN.SUF	noun suffix
NP	noun phrase
NPAST	nonpast
NPS	non-present stem
NPST	non-past
NR	nominalizer
NR.PAST	near past tense
NSF	noun suffix
Ntr	Neutrum
NUM	numeral
NUM/PERS	cross-referencing suffix signifying number and person
NZR	nominalizer
O	object/object prefix
OBJ	object
OBL	oblique
OBulg.	Old Bulgarian
OBV	obviative marker
OCOMP	object of comparison
OIran.	Old Iranian
OPers.	Old Persian
OPT	optative
ORD	ordinal
OST	ostensive
P	patient [patient-like argument of canonical transitive verb]; preposition
PART	particle
PASS	passive [voice]

PAST	past tense
PAT	patient
PERF	perfect/perfective aspect
PFV	perfective (aspect)
PIE	Proto-Indo-European
PL	plural [number]
PLAC	pluractional
PM	predicative marker
PN	proper name
PNC	punctual
Pol.	Polish
Port.	Portuguese
PoS	part(s) of speech
POS	positional/possessive
POSIT	positional suffix
POSS	possessive [marker]/possessor
POSSD	possessed
POSTP	postposition
POT	potential [mood]
PP	prepositional phrase
PR	independent/oblique pronoun; progressive, durative
PRAEDIC	predicative [adverbial]
PRED	predicative/predicate
PREP	preposition
PRES	present [tense]
PRET	preterite [tense]
PRF	perfect; perfective aspect
PRO	pronoun
PROG	progressive
PROH	prohibitive
PROP	proprietive
PROS	prospective
PROX	proximal/proximate
PRS	present [tense]
PST	past [tense]
PTC[P]	particle
PUNCT	punctual aspect [tense]
PURP	purposive
Q	question particle/marker
QLT	qualitative verb
QTV	quotative
QUOT	quotative
R/A	realis/assertive
RE	argument marker/(adverbial) relator
REAL	realis mood
REC	recent (past)

REC	recipient
RECP	reciprocal
RED	reduplication
RED1	monosyllabic reduplication
RED2	bisyllabic reduplication
REF	referential/reflexive
REFL	reflexive
REL	relational prefix/relativizer/relative case/relative pronoun/relational suffix
REL.PERF	perfective relative marker
REM.PST	remote past
REMEMB	recognitional demonstrative
REP	reportative
RES/RESUL	resultative
REST	restrictive
RETR	retrospective mood
REV	reversive
RLS	realis mood
RM.PAST	remote past
Ru.	Russian
Rum.	Rumanian
Run.	Runic Germanic
S	speaker/subject/single argument [of canonical intransitive verb]
Sb-Cr.	Serbo-Croat
SBJ	subject
SBJV	subjunctive
SEM	semblative
SEQ	sequential [clitic]
SG	singular
SH	subject honorific
Skr.	Sanskrit
Slav.	Old Church Slavonic
Slov.	Slovene
SO	point of view of source
SoA(s)	state of affair(s)
Span.	Spanish
SRF	semireflexive
SS	same subject
ST[A]	stative
STAT	stative
STV	stative
SUB	subject/subordinator [clitic]
SUB.DS	subordinator different subjects
SUBST	substantive
SUF	suffix
Swe.	Swedish
TAM	tense–aspect–mood [marker]

TAP	Timor–Alor–Pantar [languages]
TE	tense
TERM	terminative
TOP	topic/topicalizer
TR	transitive [marker]
TRANS	transitive
TRANSL	translative
TRZER	transitivizer
UA	unit augmented
Ukr.	Ukrainian
UP	verbal extension indicating movement
USAT	usative
V	verb
V2	verb class 2
VAL	valency
VB	verb/verb thematic
VBL	verbalizer
VD	verbal dative
VIS	visible
VN	verbal noun
VOC	vocative
VP	verb phrase
VRBZ	verbalizer
X	oblique
Z/N	feminine-zoic/neuter

Notes on the Contributors

Evangelia Adamou is Senior Researcher at the French National Centre for Scientific Research. Her research focuses on language contact and bilingualism based on corpus and experimental data from endangered languages. She is the author of *The Adaptive Bilingual Mind: Insights from Endangered Languages* (CUP, 2021) and *A Corpus-driven Approach to Language Contact* (de Gruyter, 2016); with Yaron Matras she edited *The Routledge Handbook of Language Contact* (Routledge, 2021).

David Beck is a professor in the Department of Linguistics at the University of Alberta with interests in typology, morphosyntax, and grammatical diffusion among the languages of the Pacific Northwest and Mesoamerica. He has worked extensively on Lushootseed, a language of the Salishan family, for which he has produced a two-volume collection of interlinearized texts. Fieldwork with speakers of Upper Necaxa Totonac begun in 1998 led to the publication of a dictionary, a grammatical sketch, and numerous articles on this language. Beck is currently co-editor of the *International Journal of American Linguistics*.

Walter Bisang has been Professor of General and Comparative Linguistics at the University of Mainz (Germany) since 1992. His research interests are linguistic typology, grammaticalization, and language contact with a focus on East and mainland South East Asian languages. He has published on word class, complexity, serial verb constructions, classifier systems, clause combining, and finiteness. His most recent publication together with Andrej Malchukov (2020) is entitled "Grammaticalization Scenarios: Cross-linguistic Variation and Universal Tendencies". He is a member of the Academy of Sciences and Literature at Mainz and of the European Academy. He had a Chair Professorship at Zhejiang University (2018–2020).

Frank Boers is a professor in Applied Linguistics and TESOL at the University of Western Ontario, Canada. His initial research interests (in the 1990s) were semantics and lexicology, with a special focus on metaphor and figurative language. His more recent research interests, however, were sparked by his extensive experience as an EFL teacher and teacher trainer, and since the 2000s he has published mostly on issues of instructed second language acquisition. His latest book is *Evaluating Second Language Vocabulary and Grammar Instruction: A Synthesis of the Research on Teaching Words, Phrases, and Patterns* (Routledge, 2021).

Francis Bond is an associate professor at the Division of Linguistics and Multilingual Studies, Nanyang Technological University, Singapore. His main research interest is in natural language understanding. He has worked in industry (NTT), government research (NCIT), and academia. He is an active member of the Deep Linguistic Processing with HPSG Initiative (DELPH-IN) and the Global WordNet Association. Francis has developed and released large semantic networks for Chinese, Japanese, Malay, and Indonesian and coordinates the Open Multilingual Wordnet.

Carl Börstell is an associate professor of Linguistics at the Department of Linguistic, Literary and Aesthetic Studies at the University of Bergen (Norway). He received his PhD in general linguistics from Stockholm University, Sweden, in 2017 with a dissertation on object marking across signed languages. He has worked on a number of different signed languages of the world, particularly Swedish Sign Language, and published on topics such as object marking, argument structure, word order, iconicity, plurality, and metaphors, using a typological approach and quantitative (corpus) methods.

Kasper Boye is Associate Professor in the Department of Nordic Studies and Linguistics, University of Copenhagen. He focuses on functional and cognitive linguistics, and his research interests include modality, grammaticalization, and complementation. His publications include "A Usage-Based Theory of Grammatical Status and Grammaticalization" (*Language*, 2012); *Language Usage and Language Structure* (with Elisabeth Engberg-Pedersen, Mouton de Gruyter, 2010); *Epistemic Meaning: A Cross-Linguistic and Functional–Cognitive Study* (Mouton de Gruyter, 2012); and *Complementizer Semantics in European Languages* (with Petar Kehayov; Mouton de Gruyter, 2016).

Cristiano Broccias is Full Professor of English Language and Translation at the University of Genoa (Italy). His research focuses on cognitive theories of grammar, in particular Cognitive Grammar, and English syntax, both synchronically and diachronically. His publications include a monograph on change constructions (*The English Change Network: Forcing Changes into Schemas*, 2003) as well as various papers on resultative constructions, simultaneity constructions, adverbs, datives, *-ing* participles, metonymy, and cognitive approaches to grammar.

Denis Creissels retired in 2008 after teaching general linguistics at the universities of Grenoble (1971–1996) and Lyon (1996–2008). His research interests centre on linguistic diversity, the description of less-studied languages, and morphosyntactic typology. He has been engaged in fieldwork on West African languages (Baule, Manding languages, Balant Ganja, Soninke, Jóola Fooñi), Southern Bantu languages (Tswana), and Daghestanian languages (Akhvakh). His publications on Mande languages include among others three grammars (Kita Maninka, Niokolo Maninka, and Mandinka) and several articles dealing with word classes in Manding languages and Soninke.

William Croft received his PhD at Stanford University under Joseph Greenberg. He has taught at the universities of Michigan, Manchester, and New Mexico, visited the Max Planck Institutes of Psycholinguistics in Nijmegen and Evolutionary Anthropology at Leipzig and the Center for Advanced Study in the Behavioral Sciences at Stanford, and given lectures throughout the world. He is the author of dozens of articles and nine books, including *Typology and Universals* (2002), *Radical Construction Grammar* (2001), *Explaining Language Change* (2000), *Cognitive Linguistics* (with Alan Cruse) (2004), *Verbs* (2012), *Ten Lectures on Construction Grammar and Typology* (2020), and *Morphosyntax* (2022). Croft is Professor Emeritus at the University of New Mexico.

Mary Dalrymple has recently retired as Professor of Syntax at the University of Oxford. Her work explores issues in syntax, semantics, and the syntax–semantics interface, often within the theory of Lexical Functional Grammar. Her most recent publication is the *Oxford Reference Guide to Lexical Functional Grammar* (coauthored with John J. Lowe & Louise Mycock, OUP, 2019). In 2021, she was presented with a festschrift titled *Modular Design of Grammar: Linguistics on the Edge* (ed. I. Wayan Arka, Ash Asudeh, & Tracy Holloway King, OUP).

Holger Diessel is Professor of English Linguistics at the Friedrich-Schiller-Universität Jena. He received a PhD in general linguistics from the University of Buffalo and was a postdoctoral researcher at the Max Planck Institute for Evolutionary Anthropology in Leipzig. His research interests include linguistic typology, L1 acquisition, language change, and usage-based construction grammar. He has published more than 50 articles in journals and edited volumes and three monographs: *Demonstratives: Form, Function and Grammaticalization* (1999); *The Acquisition of Complex Sentences* (2004); and *The Grammar Network: How Linguistic Structure Is Shaped by Language Use* (2019).

Mark Dingemanse studies how language is shaped by and for social interaction. His research is informed by fieldwork in West Africa, comparative research on a wide range of languages, and an interdisciplinary orientation that includes linguistic typology, interactional linguistics, and cognitive science. His work on ideophones has helped rekindle interest in iconicity in language, and his work on social interaction has uncovered a number of pragmatic universals. He is Associate Professor of Language and Communication at Radboud University Nijmegen.

Jan Don is an associate professor at the University of Amsterdam. He has published extensively on the morphology of Dutch and morphological theory, focusing on the status of derivational affixes and morphological conversion. In trying to obtain as much and as different empirical evidence as possible for any theoretical claims made, he also worked on morphological processing and the morphology of Dutch dialects. Recently he co-supervised a dissertation on changes in the verbal morphology of Frisian. He is author of *Morphological Theory and the Morphology of English* (EUP, 2014).

William A. Foley is Emeritus Professor of Linguistics at the University of Sydney and Adjunct Professor of Linguistics at Columbia University in the City of New York. He is a specialist on the Papuan languages of New Guinea and also the Austronesian languages of island South East Asia and Oceania and has done very extensive fieldwork on these languages and published several books and many articles on them. He is particularly interested in the dialogue between the insightful description of the often exotic grammatical patterns of these languages and the development and revision of grammatical theory.

Donna B. Gerdts is a professor in the Department of Linguistics and Associate Director of the Indigenous Language Program at Simon Fraser University. She earned her PhD in 1982 from the University of California, San Diego. Her four decades of research on Halkomelem, a First Nations language of British Columbia, Canada, has led to many publications on the morphosyntax of intransitive, transitive, causative, applicative, and lexical suffix constructions. Her current research focuses on Halkomelem narrative, discourse, and rhetorical structure based on a large corpus of old and new texts.

Martin Haspelmath is a senior scientist at the Max Planck Institute for Evolutionary Anthropology (Leipzig) and an honorary professor at Leipzig University. He received his

PhD from the Freie Universität Berlin and also spent time in Vienna, Cologne, Buffalo, Moscow, Bamberg, and Pavia in his earlier career. He joined the institute in Leipzig in 1998 and collaborated mainly with Bernard Comrie. Between 2015 and 2020, he was a member of the Department of Linguistic and Cultural Evolution of the Max Planck Institute for the Science of Human History (Jena). His research interests are primarily in the area of broadly comparative and diachronic morphosyntax (*Indefinite Pronouns*, 1997; *From Space to Time*, 1997; *Understanding Morphology*, 2002) and in language contact (*Loanwords in the World's Languages*, co-edited with Uri Tadmor, 2009). He is one of the editors of OUP's *World Atlas of Language Structures* (2005) and of the *Atlas of Pidgin and Creole Language Structures* (2013).

Kees Hengeveld is Professor of Theoretical Linguistics at the University of Amsterdam. He is a specialist in linguistic typology and in Functional Discourse Grammar and has published widely on these topics. Among his major publications are *Non-Verbal Predication: Theory, Typology, Diachrony* (Berlin, 1992), his edition of Simon C. Dik's two-volume *The Theory of Functional Grammar* (Berlin, 1997), and, with J. Lachlan Mackenzie, *Functional Discourse Grammar: A Typologically Based Model of Language Structure* (OUP, 2008).

Borja Herce is a postdoctoral researcher at the Department of Comparative Language Science at the University of Zurich (Distributional Linguistics Lab). He has previously held positions at the University of the Basque Country and the University of Surrey (Surrey Morphology Group), where obtained his PhD. His expertise revolves around the typological diversity of inflectional morphology (e.g. *The typological diversity of morphomes: A cross-linguistic study of unnatural morphology*, 2023, OUP) and adpositions (Past–future asymmetries in time adverbials and adpositions: A crosslinguistic and diachronic perspective, 2017, *Linguistic Typology*). His research has relied on synchronic and diachronic corpora, databases, and general quantitative approaches, as well as qualitative analyses, to understand the trends and limits of grammatical architecture, and their motivations.

Paul Ibbotson is a senior lecturer in developmental psychology at the Open University (UK) His research interests and expertise lie at the intersection between language and cognition. He has applied this interest to understanding how children learn language. His work reveals the deep connections between the linguistic system and general psychological processes such as attention, inhibition, and memory. These ideas have recently been brought together in *What It Takes to Talk: Exploring Developmental Linguistics* (de Gruyter, 2020) and *Language Acquisition: The Basics* (Routledge, 2022).

Evelien Keizer is Professor of English Linguistics at the University of Vienna. She obtained her PhD in English linguistics from the Vrije Universiteit Amsterdam in 1992; subsequently she held positions at the University of Tilburg, University College London, and the University of Amsterdam. She has published widely on the noun phrase in English (e.g. *The English Noun Phrase: The Nature of Linguistic Categorization*, 2007, CUP) and Dutch (*Syntax of Dutch: The Noun Phrase*, vol. 1, 2012, AUP). She is also the author of *A Functional Discourse Grammar for English* (2015, OUP) and co-editor of several edited volumes and special issues.

David Kemmerer is a professor at Purdue University with a 50/50 joint appointment in the Department of Speech, Language, and Hearing Sciences and the Department of Psychological Sciences. His research focuses on the neural substrates of conceptual knowledge. He is especially interested in the relationships between semantics, grammar, perception, and action, and in cross-linguistic similarities and differences in conceptual representation. He is the author of a monograph called *Concepts in the Brain: The View from Cross-Linguistic Diversity* (OUP, 2019) and a textbook called *Cognitive Neuroscience of Language* (Psychology Press, 1st edn 2015, 2nd edn 2022).

Vadim Kimmelman (University of Bergen, Norway) has worked on various topics related to the grammar and lexicon of various sign languages, with a special focus on Russian Sign Language and Sign Language of the Netherlands. These topics include word classes, word order, information structure, argument structure, iconicity, and metaphor in sign languages. His most recent research projects concern lexical variation and applying Computer Vision to analyse nonmanual prosody in sign languages.

Marian Klamer is Professor of Austronesian and Papuan Linguistics at Leiden University (the Netherlands). Klamer has worked on Austronesian and Papuan languages in Indonesia for some 25 years, and has published on a wide range of topics in morphology, typology, grammaticalization, language contact, and historical reconstruction. She is the author of grammars on two Austronesian languages (Kambera, 1998; Alorese, 2011) and two Papuan languages (Teiwa, 2010; Kaera, 2014). Over the years, Klamer has led numerous research projects studying grammatical variety, historical affiliations, and contact-induced change in Austronesian and Papuan languages as spoken by small-scale communities in eastern Indonesia.

Alexander Letuchiy is a professor at HSE University, Moscow, where he teaches Russian syntax and morphology, Arabic grammar, and research seminars on voice, valency, and polypredication. His main research domains are complex sentences (in 2021, he published a book, *Russkij jazyk o situacijax*, on complement clauses in Russian, based on his doctoral dissertation) and argument structure, particularly transitivity and labile verbs. He has done fieldwork with native speakers of Khakas (Turkic), Adyghe, Kabardian, and Abaza (West Caucasian) and was one of the editors of the volume *Aspekty polisintetizma* on the grammar of the polysynthetic Adyghe language.

Natalia Levshina is a postdoctoral researcher at the Max Planck Institute for Psycholinguistics in Nijmegen. Since obtaining her PhD in linguistics from the University of Leuven in 2011, she has worked in Belgium, Germany, and the Netherlands. One of her main interests is comparative corpus linguistics, which she tries to approach from the perspectives of language processing and interaction. She is also the author of a bestselling statistics manual, *How to Do Linguistics with R: Data Exploration and Statistical Analysis* and of *Communicative Efficiency: Language Structure and Use* (CUP, 2022).

Seth Lindstromberg has a professional background in teaching English as an additional language (L2) and in language-teacher training. He has written or co-written numerous practice-oriented articles and several books on L2 teaching methods. His empirical research focuses on post-childhood instructed learning of L2 vocabulary. Particular interests in this area have been the usefulness of insights from cognitive semantics and ways of facilitating acquisition of multiword items such as figurative idioms, phrasal verbs, and strong collocations. He has been a frequent contributor of research reports to applied linguistic journals.

Dana Louagie is a postdoctoral research fellow with the Fonds de la Recherche Scientifique and is a member of the research unit Lilith (Liège, Literature, Linguistics) at the University of Liège. She is also an affiliated member of the research unit Functional and Cognitive linguistics: grammar and typology at the University of Leuven. Her research focuses on the syntax of nominal expressions and other topics in the nominal domain, both in Australian Aboriginal languages and from a broader typological perspective.

J. Lachlan Mackenzie is Emeritus Professor of Functional Linguistics at VU Amsterdam, having previously been Full Professor of English Language there. With a PhD from the University of Edinburgh (1978), his career was in the Netherlands, working closely with Simon Dik and Kees Hengeveld on the development of Functional Grammar and Functional Discourse Grammar. He is editor of the journal *Functions of Language* with interests ranging from functional linguistics to pragmatics and discourse analysis. He holds an honorary doctorate from UNED (Spain, 2021). Key publications: *Functional Discourse Grammar* (OUP, 2008) and *Pragmatics: Cognition, Context and Culture* (McGraw Hill, 2016).

Andrej L. Malchukov is an invited professor at the University of Mainz and a senior researcher at the St Petersburg Institute for Linguistic Research (Russian Academy of Sciences). Apart from descriptive work on Tungusic languages, he has published extensively on morphosyntactic typology; in particular, he edited *The Oxford Handbook of Case* (with Andrew Spencer; OUP, 2009), *Studies in Ditransitive Constructions: A Comparative Handbook* (with Bernard Comrie and Martin Haspelmath; Mouton de Gruyter, 2010); *Competing Motivations in Grammar and Cognition* (with Brian MacWhinney and Edith Moravcsik; OUP, 2014); *Valency Classes in the World's Languages* (with Bernard Comrie; 2 vols., Mouton de Gruyter, 2015); and *Grammaticalization Scenarios: Cross-Linguistic Variation and Universal Tendencies* (with Walter Bisang; Mouton de Gruyter, 2020, 2 vols.).

Yaron Matras was Professor of Linguistics at the University of Manchester until 2020, where he founded and led the Multilingual Manchester project. He is now Honorary Professor at the Aston Institute for Forensic Linguistics. His research interests include contact linguistics, language documentation, linguistic typology, urban multilingualism, and forensic linguistics (particularly the application of language analysis in asylum procedures). His language specialisms cover Romani, languages of the Middle East, and German dialects. His book publications include *Language Contact* (CUP, 2009/2020); *A Grammar of Domari* (de Gruyter, 2012); *Romani in Britain: The Afterlife of a Language* (EUP, 2010); and *Romani: A Linguistic Introduction* (CUP, 2002).

Karin Michelson is Professor Emerita of Linguistics at the University at Buffalo. Her research has focused on the languages of the Haudenosaunee Confederacy (Iroquoian languages), especially Oneida and Mohawk, and particularly on the accentual phonology, morphology, syntax, and semantics. In collaboration with Jean-Pierre Koenig, she has looked at how meaning interacts with structure, and the ways this interaction is unique to Oneida and how it bears on the architecture of grammars. She has co-authored an Oneida dictionary (with the late Mercy Doxtator) and a volume of texts (with Norma Kennedy and Mercy Doxtator), with a grammar that focuses on syntactic and discourse structures.

Meladel Mistica is a research data specialist with MDAP (Melbourne Data Analytics Platform), University of Melbourne. Her research interests are in natural language processing (NLP) and its application in low-resource scenarios. She has industry experience, working in Dialogue Systems (Intel, USA) and Search (Chegg, USA). Previously, she was a research fellow at the School of Computing and Information Systems, University of Melbourne. In this role, she investigated biases in pre-trained transformer models when applied to NLP tasks. She is involved in projects that enable and encourage computational methods in text analysis, particularly for research in the humanities, arts, and social sciences.

Marianne Mithun is Professor of Linguistics at the University of California, Santa Barbara. Her work investigates issues in morphology, syntax, discourse, prosody, and their interrelations; typology; language contact and language change; and language documentation. A priority is supporting communities who are working to pass their traditional languages on to future generations, particularly Mohawk, Cayuga, Seneca, and Tuscarora (Iroquoian family); Central Pomo (Pomoan); Barbareño Chumash (Chumashan); Central Alaskan Yup'ik (Unangan–Yupik–Inuit); Navajo (Dene); and Kapampangan and Hiligaynon (Austronesian).

Ulrike Mosel, Professor Emerita of General Linguistics at the University of Kiel (Germany), wrote her PhD thesis on Arabic grammaticography (1974, University of Munich), but then became interested in Oceanic languages, linguistic fieldwork, and corpus linguistics. She was one of the initiators of the Documentation of Endangered Languages Programme (DoBeS) of the Volkswagen Foundation and is currently finalizing a Teop reference grammar. Her major publications include *Tolai Syntax and Its Historical Development* (Australian National University Press, 1984), *Samoan Reference Grammar* (with Even Hovdhaugen, Oslo University Press, 1992), and *A Multifunctional Teop–English Dictionary* (Dictionaria 4, 2019).

Pieter Muysken studied Spanish and South American language and culture at the universities of Yale and Amsterdam; his PhD (Amsterdam, 1977) was on Ecuadorian Quechuan. Since 1989 he was Professor of Linguistics in Amsterdam, Leiden, and Nijmegen, consecutively, and he was a member of the Royal Dutch Science Academy. Apart from Andean languages, he has worked on language contact phenomena in Papiamentu, Turkish, and Dutch. He received a variety of grants and prizes, including the Spinoza premium, and an ERC Advanced Grant. He died in 2020 at the age of 70, prior to the publication of this handbook.

Elsa Oréal is an HDR researcher working at the Centre National de la Recherche Scientifique (AOROC-UMR 8546, Paris). She is currently editor of the *Revue d'égyptologie*. She is author of *Les particules en égyptien ancien de l'ancien égyptien à l'égyptien classique* (2011). Her research interests include the history of the Ancient Egyptian verbal system and the analysis of Egyptian and Akkadian common morphological features, aiming at a better understanding of the place of Egyptian within the Afroasiatic languages.

Paolo Ramat holds a PhD in linguistics from the University of Florence (1958). He has worked as a Lektor for Italian Language and Culture at the University of Saarland (1961–1962), as a Professor of Germanic Philology at the universities of Cagliari (1968–1971) and Pavia (1971–1974), and as Professor of Linguistics at the University of Pavia and the Istituto Universitario di Studi Superiori (Pavia), until he retired in 2009. He is a doctor *honoris causa* of the University of Erfurt (2006), a Member of the Accademia dei Lincei (Rome), and an honorary member of the Academia Europaea and the Societas Linguistica Europaea. His research interests include historical linguistics, Indo-European languages, and typology. He has published 10 books and edited 13 volumes.

Jan Rijkhoff is an emeritus associate professor of linguistics at Aarhus University (Denmark). His research is mostly concerned with (semantic, formal, functional) categories, modification, parts of speech, and various aspects of noun phrases (from a functional–typological perspective). Key publications: *The Noun Phrase* (OUP, 2004); *Flexible Word Classes* (co-editor Eva van Lier, OUP, 2013); *The Noun Phrase in Functional Discourse Grammar* (co-editor Daniel García Velasco, de Gruyter Mouton, 2008); "Determiners from a Functional–Typological Perspective" (in the forthcoming *The Oxford Handbook of Determiners*), "Word Order" (in *Encyclopedia of the Social & Behavioral Sciences (Second Edition)*, Elsevier, 2015), and "Crosslinguistic Categories in Morphosyntactic Typology" (*Linguistic Typology*, 2016, 20–22).

Françoise Rose is a research fellow of the National Scientific Research Center of France in Lyon. Her research interests lie primarily in the description of indigenous languages of Amazonia (phonology and morphosyntax). She studies more specifically Teko (aka Emerillon, Tupi-Guarani, French Guiana) and Mojeño Trinitario (Arawak, Bolivia), on the basis of data collected in the field. She has written the first comprehensive grammar of Emerillon/Teko. She is also interested in typological, diachronic, and areal issues.

Lauren Schneider is a PhD candidate in the Department of Linguistics at Simon Fraser University. She earned her MA in linguistics in 2017 from Trinity Western University. She considers it an honour and a privilege to work on the languages of the First Peoples of the land on which she was raised. Her current research is focused on Halkomelem serial verb constructions, as well as other aspects of Salish morphosyntax.

K. Aaron Smith received his PhD in theoretical linguistics from the University of New Mexico in 2002 and has been a professor of linguistics in the English Department of Illinois State University since then. He is the author of several articles and book chapters on language change. He is the co-editor of the book *Functionalist and Usage-based Approaches to the Study of Language: In Honor of Joan L. Bybee* and the co-author of *This Language, a River: A History of English*.

Sabine Stoll is Professor of Psycholinguistics leading the Language, acquisition, diversity Lab, and Head of the Department of Comparative Language Science at the University of Zurich. She is also the director of the Center for the Interdisciplinary Study of Language Evolution at the University of Zurich. Her research centres around first language acquisition in typologically and culturally diverse contexts. She has contributed to questions on how patterns in the input precondition implicit first language learning.

Ida Toivonen is Professor of Linguistics and Cognitive Science at Carleton University, Canada. She has published articles on phonetics, phonology, morphology, syntax, and semantics. She is also the author of *Non-Projecting Words* (2003), co-author of *Lexical-Functional Syntax* (with Joan Bresnan and Ash Asudeh, 2016), and co-editor of *Saami Linguistics* (with Diane Carlita Nelson, 2007) as well as *Structures in the Mind* (with Piroska Csuri and Emile van der Zee, 2015).

Frank Van Eynde is Professor of Formal and Computational Linguistics at the University of Leuven. His main research interests are in formal syntax and semantics, focusing on their application in computational linguistics and language technology. A recent interest concerns the exploration of the potential of annotated corpora, especially treebanks, for research in theoretical linguistics. At the University of Leuven, he founded the Center for

Computational Linguistics in 1991 and the Speech and Language Technology teaching programme in 2000.

Martine Vanhove is a senior researcher at the Centre National de la Recherche Scientifique (Llacan Research Unit), specializing in Semitic (Maltese, Yemeni Arabic) and Cushitic languages (Beja). She has done numerous fieldtrips in Malta, Yemen, and Sudan. Her research interests include syntax, lexical typology, information structure, grammaticalization, language contact, and corpus linguistics. She is the author of a recent grammar of Beja, has (co-)edited a dozen books, and published numerous articles. She was PI or co-PI of six national, European, and Franco-Brazilian research projects.

Eva van Lier is Associate Professor of Linguistics at the University of Amsterdam. She obtained her PhD from the same institute in 2009 with a typological study on word classes and dependent clause constructions. Later, she authored and (co-)edited several publications on (flexible) word classes, especially in Oceanic languages. She also worked on the typology of ditransitive verbs, action nominalizations, and noun incorporation. She currently leads a project on alternating verbs across languages.

Valentina Vapnarsky is Senior Researcher at the CNRS and Director of Studies at the EPHE (France). A linguistic anthropologist, her research focuses on Yucatecan Maya languages and grammar, and the verbal and written practices of its speakers, in everyday, religious, historical, and poetic registers. Based on fieldwork among the Itza (Guatemala) and the Yucatecan Maya (Mexico), her work integrates a comparative and interdisciplinary perspective. She is the co-editor of *Lexical categories and root classes in Amerindian languages* (Peter Lang, 2006) and *Lexical Polycategoriality: Crosslinguistic, Cross-theoretical and Language Acquisition Approaches* (John Benjamins, 2017).

Ekaterina Vylomova is an adjunct lecturer at the University of Melbourne. She graduated with a PhD in natural language processing from the University of Melbourne in 2018. She is one of the founding members of the ACL Special Interest Group on Linguistic Typology. Her research is focused on computational modelling of morphologies of typologically diverse languages. Since 2017, she has been working on the UniMorph project, focusing on the enhancement of the universal morphosyntactic annotation. She co-organized the SIGMORPHON 2017-2021 shared tasks on morphological reinflection that served as a platform to collect and unify language data for the UniMorph.

Yoad Winter is Professor in Semantics and Artificial Intelligence at Utrecht University, the Netherlands. Winter is the author of *Flexibility Principles in Boolean Semantics* (MIT Press, 2001) and *Elements of Formal Semantics* (Edinburgh University Press, 2016), and he is a co-editor of *Compositionality and Concepts in Linguistics and Psychology* (with J. Hampton, Springer, 2017).

Hedde Zeijlstra is a university professor of English linguistics and grammar theory at the University of Göttingen. His main interest is the relation between sentence meaning and form: how does the meaning of a sentence follow from its parts, and why are there so many different ways of expressing the same meaning across languages? He has held guest lecturer appointments at, among others, Cambridge University, MIT, and UCLA. Since 2017 he also has served as an associate editor of *Natural Language & Linguistic Theory*, and since 2018 as general editor of *Linguistic Variation*.

CHAPTER 1

INTRODUCTION

EVA VAN LIER

1.1 AIMS AND SCOPE OF THIS HANDBOOK

THE study of WORD CLASSES (also known as PARTS OF SPEECH or LEXICAL CATEGORIES) in contemporary linguistics can be traced back to antiquity (Dionysius Thrax), and is strongly influenced by the early 20th-century structuralist tradition (Sapir 1921; Bloomfield 1933). These classical works already displayed remarkable differences in focus on the distinct dimensions of word-class definitions—semantic, pragmatic, and morphosyntactic properties—which resonate in various later approaches, many of which arose in the second half of the previous century but are still relevant to current research agendas and theoretical debates.

Despite these differences, word classes are of fundamental importance to any linguistic theory or description, be it formal or functional, be it language-internal analysis or cross-linguistic comparison. As a consequence, word classes are the central concern of countless monographs, edited volumes and special issues, and journal articles.

While word classes thus constitute too vast and diverse a topic for a reference work to be comprehensive, this handbook has two general aims. First, it gives an overview of the fundamental issues and controversies in the field, and includes chapters on a wide variety of theoretical approaches to the study of word classes. Second, this work aims at a very broad empirical coverage in terms of language diversity: it includes data from a large number of areally and genetically distinct languages, including sign languages, as well as data from specific linguistic subdisciplines, such as language acquisition and processing, language change and contact, corpus-based and computational linguistics. Together, all these perspectives on word classes make clear that their centrality to linguistics is undisputed, but their essentials are still subject to deep-rooted debates. This volume seeks to identify, examine, and explain these debates, to look for common ground, and to point out promising ways to move forward.

1.2 STRUCTURE OF THE HANDBOOK

1.2.1 Part I

This handbook consists of five parts: Part I 'Fundamental issues', Part II 'Theoretical approaches', Part III 'Specific word classes', Part IV 'Word classes in genetic and areal language groups', and Part V 'Word classes in linguistic subdisciplines'. In this section, each part and its constituent chapters will be briefly introduced. Along the way, recurrent and overarching themes will be outlined.

Part I addresses a number of fundamental issues pertaining to word classes. They are fundamental in the sense that the distinctions and dimensions touched upon are all couched in cross-linguistic diversity and that they all have important theoretical repercussions. In a way, therefore, these chapters connect to all the subsequent parts of the handbook. Part I thus essentially forms a preamble to the theoretical and empirical material that follows.

This part starts with a contribution by **Martin Haspelmath** (Chapter 2), on the relationship between linguistic universals in the realm of word classes versus language-specific description of word classes. He shows that semantic classes or roots, together with function-indicating morphosyntactic markers, provide a way into cross-linguistic comparison, in the face of rampant diversity. The chapter outlines similarities and differences between Haspelmath's approach and various theories of word classes and, importantly, pinpoints areas where solid typological data is still lacking.

In Chapter 3, **Walter Bisang** discusses the different levels at which categories can be distinguished: the root, the stem, and the word. Bisang's ideas build on earlier proposals by Haig and Lehmann. He takes into consideration a range of languages that have been centre stage in discussions on word-class typology (including Classical Nahuatl, Tagalog, Classical Chinese, and Tongan), and addresses the challenges they pose for various theoretical frameworks. Finally, Bisang argues for a stronger integration of frequency-based data into research on word classes.

Subsequently, in Chapter 4, **Kasper Boye** sheds light on the distinction between lexical and functional words. He points to a number of related but not equivalent distinctions, such as those between content and function words, and between open- and closed-class words. He also shows how various particular types of word classes (verbs, nouns and pronouns, adjectives, and adpositions) behave with respect to these dimensions. Finally, he considers the lexical–grammatical distinction from the perspective of different theoretical approaches, as well as from (impaired) language processing, acquisition, and change.

In Chapter 5, **Andrej L. Malchukov** is concerned with the phenomenon of transcategorial operations, leading to 'mixed' categories through processes of decategorization and recategorization. Malchukov summarizes relevant theoretical and typological work, which often focuses on nominalization, but also applies to verbalization. Against this background, he outlines a model that constrains the feature combinations found in mixed categories within and across languages. He also shows how this model can be formalized in Optimality Theory, and how this relates to other possible theoretical approaches.[1]

---

[1] It may be noted that Optimality Theory is not among the theoretical approaches covered in Part II of this handbook. Apart from Malchukov's use of this framework, I am not aware of any substantial treatment of word classes in this framework.

Finally, in Chapter 6, **William A. Foley** rounds off Part I by again drawing attention to the fundamental differences between languages in terms of their word-class systems, but now relating this to other aspects of their basic architecture, in particular their morphology. Foley does this by means of a comparison between Yimas, a Papuan (Lower Sepik-Ramu) language with a pervasive noun–verb distinction, and various other languages in which this distinction is less pronounced: Southern Wakashan and Northern Iroquoian languages. His chapter closes with observations on cross-linguistic diversity in the realm of adjectives and adpositions.

Before moving on to Part II, it may be noted that the contributions that make up Part I are all deeply informed by linguistic diversity and universal cognitive principles. While the observations made are essentially framework-independent, they ultimately deny the existence of universal lexical categories and hence are more compatible with functionalist than with generative approaches.

In Part II, however, word classes are discussed in terms of a wide range of specific theoretical frameworks. The selection of these frameworks is driven primarily by whether or not the theory in question offers a substantial and explicit proposal regarding the treatment of word classes. In some cases, most notably in Chapter 9 on gradience, an approach to word classes is outlined which plays a role in various related theories.

1.2.2 Part II

The first chapter in Part II (Chapter 7) is on formal semantics. Subsequently, various functionalist frameworks are reviewed (Chapters 8–11), followed by four different formalist theories (Chapters 12–15).

Yoad Winter (Chapter 7) describes the history and current treatment of word classes in FORMAL SEMANTICS, a framework which has focused on the meaning of nouns, for a number of reasons. Nouns are assumed to not take intrinsic semantic arguments, which sets them apart from other word classes, in particular verbs (states/events), gradable adjectives (degrees), and locative prepositions (spatial objects). Winter also describes other distinctive aspects of nouns, including their ability to restrict quantificational domains, to introduce identity criteria, and to refer to kinds and mass substances. These properties are scrutinized against descriptive data from a range of typologically diverse languages.

Cristiano Broccias (Chapter 8) shows that COGNITIVE GRAMMAR (CG) stands out among other theoretical frameworks (including functional ones) in prioritizing the conceptual aspects of word classes, rather than the formal ones. In particular, while CG recognizes the distributional differences between word classes across languages, the focus is instead on the universal representations underlying their use. Another crucial point is that CG does not make a principled difference between lexicon and grammar, so that not only traditional content word classes but also more grammatical classes (e.g. auxiliaries) as well as complex constructions can be accounted for using the same tool set.

In Chapter 9, **Evelien Keizer** outlines the development towards GRADIENCE in word–class distinctions and away from classical Aristotelian discrete categories. She illustrates prototype effects within categories and discusses fuzzy boundaries between categories, using both synchronic and diachronic data. Her chapter contains a concise inventory of the different ways in which (mainly cognitive and functionalist) approaches have dealt with gradience, the difference between them residing in whether they focus on morphosyntactic, semantic, or pragmatic categories, or some combination of those.

J. Lachlan Mackenzie, in Chapter 10, describes the treatment of lexeme and word classes in FUNCTIONAL DISCOURSE GRAMMAR (FDG) and its predecessor, Functional Grammar. The different layers at which categories are defined in this framework have clear ties with other frameworks. Importantly, however, FDG greatly values typological adequacy and has given rise to an explicit typology of word classes. This typology distinguishes between various flexible and rigid word-class systems, which are shown to correlate with other linguistic properties, including word order, morphological classes, and subordination strategies.

In Chapter 11, **William Croft** describes the approach to word classes taken in his own RADICAL CONSTRUCTION GRAMMAR theory, which takes categories (including word classes) to be language- and construction-specific. Yet, it allows for the formulation of universals based on the prototypical meanings and functions of word classes, and their relative markedness when used in non-prototypical functions. As such, it is similar to the typological perspective taken by Haspelmath (Chapter 2). Also, and similar to Bisang (Chapter 3), in this chapter Croft signals the need to shift attention from essentialist to frequency-based methods to study word classes.

Chapter 12, by **Hedde Zeijlstra**, is on word classes in MINIMALIST SYNTAX. The starting point here is that grammatical rules are not sensitive to word classes or grammatical categories per se, but rather to the abstract features underlying them. Zeijlstra discusses a number of theoretical proposals, including Baker's influential theory, which differ in the exact nature of features and their relative ordering in hierarchical structures. This chapter also addresses the traditional generative assumption of universal categories, and evaluates it against critical language data, explaining how different scholars handle this issue.

Jan Don explains in Chapter 13 how DISTRIBUTED MORPHOLOGY views lexical items as universally a-categorical: categorization is a morphosyntactic process. Yet, different proposals have been made as to how this categorization actually happens: through (derivational) affixation, or through 'insertion' of lexemes into syntactic structures. While the idea of multiple layers of categorization in Distributed Morphology is shared by many frameworks, the purely formal approach (to the exclusion of semantic and pragmatic criteria) is akin to mainstream Minimalism.

In Chapter 14 by **Frank Van Eynde**, we see that HEAD-DRIVEN PHRASE STRUCTURE GRAMMAR (HPSG), having evolved out of (Transformational) Generative Approaches, also places most weight on syntactic features of word classes. While there is no explicit questioning of the universality of word classes in this framework, there is discussion as to what constitutes the appropriate word-class inventory. Despite the syntactic focus, the HPSG-style feature bundles also include a semantic part. In addition, different levels of lexical and morphological analysis are acknowledged, and cross-linguistic differences in morphological features are highlighted.

In Chapter 15, **Mary Dalrymple and Ida Toivonen** explain that LEXICAL FUNCTIONAL GRAMMAR (LFG), like HPSG, is based on generative phrase-structural theory, and is highly modular, with a focus on syntactic properties of word classes. A restricted and universal inventory of classes is defined, with 'projecting' categories and some non-projecting ones, such as particles. Yet, it is acknowledged that in individual languages certain categorial distinctions may not be grammatically relevant. A special aspect of LFG is its distinction between c-structure (where phrase structure is handled) and f-structure (where, e.g., grammatical relations are represented). This distinction accommodates some of the 'mismatches' between different types of word-class criteria.

To summarize, the chapters in Part II feature a range of overarching and interrelated theoretical themes. These include:

(i) the status of the lexicon–grammar interface, and layers of categorization more generally;
(ii) the relative importance of specific types of word-class criteria: syntactic, morphological, semantic, and pragmatic. Notably, phonological criteria are strongly underrepresented in the large majority of theories (but see Chapter 13 on Distributed Morphology);
(iii) the (non-)discreteness and inventory of word classes, including the treatment of 'minor' categories; and
(iv) the (non-)universal status of word classes.

Clearly, all theories strike some kind of balance between what is universal and what is language- or construction-specific, but the balance tips in different directions. This depends on how the other fundamental issues (especially those in (i) and (iii) above) are dealt with, and probably also on the empirical backdrop against which particular frameworks have developed.

1.2.3 Part III

In this part of the handbook, each chapter focuses on a single word class, taking a comparative perspective. The approach that these chapters have in common is that they describe the relevant word class as a combination of functional (pragmatic and semantic) and formal (morphosyntactic) traits. As a result of this, they offer both an overview of language- and construction-specific patterns, and are able to pinpoint recurrent cross-linguistic trends.

Importantly, Part III concentrates on the one hand on 'the big four' word classes: verbs, nouns, adjectives, and adverbs. On the other hand, it also contains four chapters on other word classes: two chapters on adpositions and demonstratives, respectively, and two on ideophones and interjections. The reason for integrating the latter four chapters lies in their diachronic and synchronic, as well as their functional and formal ties with major word classes in many languages. Also, like major word classes, the cross-linguistic comparison of these 'minor' categories reveals both a stunning diversity and allows for function-related generalizations.

The first contribution to this part is **Alexander Letuchiy**'s Chapter 16 on VERBS. Defining verbs as the word class that most typically fulfils the predicative function, he addresses a wide range of topics associated with verbs across languages. These include the structure of verbal paradigms, especially person/number marking, and other 'verbal' categories, such as tense, mood/modality, and evidentiality, as well as aspects of argument structure that are associated with verbs rather than other lexical categories. In addition, the issue of (relative) finiteness is discussed and its relation to clausality, including mismatches as found in, e.g., serial verbs constructions, or verbless clauses. Finally, this chapter touches upon various typological parameters linked to verbs, such as valency orientation and pro-drop.

Next comes Chapter 17 on NOUNS, by **Jan Rijkhoff**. He defines nouns as unmarked, underived words used to talk about spatial objects, and he offers a classification of nouns employing two semantic parameters: Shape and Homogeneity. Based on the binary values of these features he divides nouns into various subtypes, including, e.g., count and mass nouns. He also correlates these subtypes with the co-occurrence of functional items like sortal/mensural classifiers and numerals.

Chapter 18, by **David Beck**, is on ADJECTIVES. He shows that, while all languages have lexicalized expressions for property concepts, and all of them recognize a function of adnominal modification, it is not the case that all languages have a word class that could be called 'Adjective'. Also, there are significant differences in the distribution and properties of adjective classes across those languages that do distinguish them.

Kees Hengeveld's contribution (Chapter 19) is on ADVERBS, which are defined as lexical expressions that are used as modifiers of *non*-nominal heads. Hengeveld goes on to further classify adverbs across a variety of languages, based on the semantic–pragmatic domain to which they belong, and their scope properties (described in the framework of Functional Discourse Grammar; see Chapter 10). This typology in turn gives rise to a series of generalizations concerning the formal behaviour of adverb classes.

Chapter 20, by **Borja Herce**, is the first chapter on a word class at the intersection of lexical and grammatical words: ADPOSITIONS. The hybrid position of adpositions is further blurred by the fact that diachronically they stem from different 'major' word classes. Through the lens of three language-specific case studies, Herce illustrates the heterogeneity of adpositions both between and within languages.

Quite similarly, in Chapter 21, **Holger Diessel** describes the profound diversity of DEMONSTRATIVES across languages, but based on a typological sample of 150 languages. Due to their function—creating and manipulating joint attention—demonstratives often take on properties of other (major) word classes. Using a combination of syntactic and morphological criteria, Diessel proposes a division into five demonstrative subclasses: pronouns, determiners, adverbs, identifiers, and verbs.

The final two chapters of Part III are both written by **Mark Dingemanse**. Chapter 22 is on IDEOPHONES. These are vocal depictions, which in many languages (especially of Asia, Africa, and the Americas) form a major class of words, functioning as modifying expressions or predicates. Again, similarly to the perspectives taken by Herce and Diessel, Dingemanse points out both the unique status of ideophones and highlights cross-linguistic patterns, drawing (diachronic) connections with other major word classes.

In Chapter 23 Dingemanse defines INTERJECTIONS as a class of linguistic items that typically function as free-standing utterances. By studying interjections in their 'natural habitat', namely conversations, and by combining both their formal (positional) and functional (interactional) properties, Dingemanse is again able to account for unity and diversity in this special word class.

1.2.4 Part IV

This part of the handbook contains a number of family-specific case studies on word classes. These studies cover all of the five macro-areas, as well as a range of genetically diverse languages. The selection of families, as well as languages within those families, is also based in part on the role that they have played in the history of research on word classes. For example, in Chapter 35 on word classes in Austronesian languages, there is special attention given to languages such as Samoan and Tagalog, which have featured prominently in debates about lexical flexibility and the (non-)universality of the noun–verb distinction. In addition to this, the specific expertise of individual authors has co-determined the focus on specific family members. Moreover, in line with the design of Part III, within each chapter most attention is given to major content word classes. However, there is also room for functional classes, for instance classifiers, in those languages where they play a crucial role in the delineation of word classes. Finally, typologically interesting and/or unusual word-class systems are highlighted and connections to larger genetic and/or areal groups are drawn.

In what follows, I will introduce the chapters per macro-area.

The macro-area AFRICA is represented by two families: Afroasiatic languages (Chapter 24) and Mande languages (Chapter 25).

Elsa Oréal and **Martine Vanhove** focus on three Afroasiatic branches: ANCIENT EGYPTIAN, SEMITIC, AND CUSHITIC. They illustrate different scenarios and outcomes in the development and constellation of word classes. In particular, while all languages show a clear distinction between nouns and verbs, diachronically the two classes are often connected. The properties of adjectival classes vary. There is also variation as concerns the role of non-concatenative morphology, which is famously pervasive in Semitic, but less so in the two other subgroups.

Denis Creissels's chapter is on MANDE languages, spoken in West Africa. He shows how the combination of rigid word order and reduced inflection allows verbs to be used without derivation as nouns (but not vice versa). In addition, he discusses subclasses of nouns and verbs, as well as other word classes, including so-called predicative markers. The latter are a kind of auxiliary that can carry information on a range of categories, such as Tense–Aspect–Mood (TAM), polarity, and grammatical relations.

In Chapter 26, **Dana Louagie** covers the word classes of LANGUAGES OF AUSTRALIA, including both the large Pama–Nyungan family and several smaller families of this macro-area. Australian languages are often described as having a flexible word class that can be used in both nominal and adjectival function. As Louagie shows, however, this picture actually varies across languages, and also depends on which criteria one considers. In addition, some Australian languages display an interesting distinction between inflecting and non-inflecting verb classes.

The first of the two chapters representing the macro-area of EURASIA is **Paolo Ramat**'s Chapter 27 on word classes in INDO-EUROPEAN (IE) LANGUAGES. The set-up is slightly different from most chapters in this part of the handbook, because historical sources and a reconstructed proto-language allow for a diachronic viewpoint. Also, the fact that traditionally research on word classes was based on the systems of classical Latin and Greek motivates a discussion of how word classes in modern IE languages have developed over time. Ramat covers the major word classes, as well as pronouns, adpositions, and conjunctions.

The second contribution in this macro-area is Chapter 28, by **Walter Bisang**, on Word classes in Classical Chinese (Sinitic). This chapter again takes a diachronic perspective, since Classical Chinese has been transmitted in philosophical and historical texts. This language is treated differently in distinct scholarly traditions: most Western approaches advocate a system of complete word-class flexibility, while contemporary Chinese research argues in favour of lexical categorical distinctions. Bisang explains and compares both viewpoints and also integrates the role of reconstructed Old Chinese morphology into the discussion.

Three language families are treated in the macro-area of NORTH AMERICA: Salish, Iroquoian, and Eskimo–Aleut languages.

Chapter 29, by **Donna B. Gerdts** and **Lauren Schneider**, is on word classes in SALISH LANGUAGES. The authors first give an overview of the controversy surrounding word classes in these languages. Then, drawing mainly on data from Halkomelem, they show that nouns and verbs are different in their inflectional possibilities, even though some categories apply to both classes. In addition, this chapter discusses category-changing morphological processes and various modifying word classes.

Chapter 30 by **Karin Michelson** describes the distributional properties of word classes in IROQUOIAN LANGUAGES. Sasse's early idea that morphological nouns in these languages can be used without a copula in predicative function has been refuted by Mithun (2000). However, the reverse situation—the extent to which morphological verbs are being used as referential expressions—makes this language family typologically remarkable. In addition, based on corpus data, Michelson describes the distribution of other morphological types of words, including those with nominal inflection, with mixed inflection, and without inflection.

In Chapter 31, **Marianne Mithun** describes word classes in ESKIMO–ALEUT LANGUAGES. Again, this family has played a key role in word-class research, especially concerning lexical flexibility. Against earlier proposals that all content words in these languages are actually nouns, Mithun shows that there is in fact a clear distinction between nouns and verbs at the root and word levels. Using a wealth of examples, she discusses two key issues in this debate: conversion and de-subordination of nominalizations.

In the macro-area of SOUTH AMERICA, again three families are featured: Mayan languages, Maweti–Guarani languages, and Quechuan languages.

Chapter 32, by **Valentina Vapnarsky**, is on MAYAN LANGUAGES. Being polysynthetic, these languages show a rich array of word formation processes, resulting in complex relationships between root and stem classes. Vapnarsky shows that Mayan languages differ in terms of the type and degree of lexical flexibility that they display, at each level of analysis. In addition to major word classes, minor word classes that are characteristic of the family are discussed. The latter include expressives, positionals, and classifiers.

In Chapter 33, **Françoise Rose** shows that in MAWETI–GUARANI LANGUAGES, the distinction between nouns and verbs is again not clear-cut. This is especially due to the use of object-denoting words in predicative function, but also to distributional overlap with property words and postpositions. Besides, Rose presents the main characteristics of other word classes (adverbs, ideophones, interjections, particles), as well as typologically remarkable features, including hierarchical indexation on predicates. Moreover, the Maweti–Guarani languages are placed in a larger perspective of Amazonian languages.

The final South American language family concerns the QUECHUAN LANGUAGES, in Chapter 34 by **Pieter Muysken**. A typologically salient issue in this family concerns the status of adjectives as a separate category. Also, the morphological status of adpositions, and phrasal enclitics is examined. In line with the previous chapter, Muysken places the Quechuan languages in an areal perspective, comparing them with other Andean languages and with South American languages more generally.

There are two chapters on languages in the macro-area of PAPUNESIA: Austronesian languages and a family of 'Papuan' languages.

Since some AUSTRONESIAN LANGUAGES are known for their lexical flexibility, **Ulrike Mosel** starts Chapter 35 with an explanation of various concepts that have featured in literature on flexible word classes. Furthermore, she discusses various types of diagnostic features that can be relevant for the (potential) identification of word classes in particular Austronesian languages. A separate section is devoted to variation in modifying (adjectival and adverbial) word classes. Also, there is special attention given to word classes in Tagalog, which, as mentioned previously, is one of the languages that has attracted most attention in the history of (flexible) word-class research.

In Chapter 36, **Marian Klamer** describes the word classes of TIMOR–ALOR–PANTAR (TAP) LANGUAGES, which is a family of Papuan (i.e. non-Austronesian) languages. In addition to an overview of the properties of the major word classes, special attention is given to the typologically rare numeral system, as well as to loanwords from Indonesian. Similarities and differences between TAP languages and Papuan languages from mainland Papua New Guinea are also pointed out.

The final chapter (37) of Part IV is dedicated to SIGN LANGUAGES. **Vadim Kimmelman** and **Carl Börstell** give an overview of the criteria that have been used to identify word classes across a number of different sign languages. In addition to morphosyntactic criteria, properties related to the gestural–visual modality are relevant here. Importantly, this chapter also pays ample attention to methodological issues related to studying word classes in sign languages across the world.

1.2.5 Part V

In this final part of the handbook, word classes are discussed from the perspective of a range of linguistic subdisciplines. It is noticeable that in some of these subdisciplines (e.g. corpus linguistics, contact linguistics, and neurolinguistics), word classes are part and parcel of central research questions, which resonate with a number of the theoretical and empirical topics covered in foregoing parts. These concern, for instance, the status of the noun–verb distinction, the relationship between conceptual and distributional aspects of word classes, and subdivisions within major word classes.

Yet, even in research traditions that pay ample attention to word classes, there are differences in focus. It seems, for instance, that for some disciplines the morphosyntactic properties of word classes are most important, while in others the functional (semantic and pragmatic) load of word classes plays a more central role.

In addition, however, there are certain subdisciplines, most notably those concerned with processing and acquisition, which have traditionally been heavily skewed towards research on IE languages. As a result, in acquisition research as well as in neurolinguistics and psycholinguistics research, the study of language diversity in the realm of word classes is a relatively recent development.

In Chapter 38, **Natalia Levshina** describes the central role of word classes in CORPUS LINGUISTICS. In this field, language corpora are often tagged for word class, typically called POS (for 'part of speech'). Levshina explains the different methods and types of tags that are used in this process. Also, she shows how POS tagging raises a number of fundamental issues pertaining to, e.g., cross-linguistic comparability versus language-specific accuracy, fuzzy category boundaries, subclassifications, and lexical flexibility.

K. Aaron Smith, in Chapter 39, discusses the relationship between word classes and GRAMMATICALIZATION. In its 'classic' form, grammaticalization involves the development of a lexical item into a grammatical one. This chapter provides a concise overview of grammaticalization research in this area. It offers ample examples as well as one more detailed case study, which serves to illustrates the role of frequency in language change.

In Chapter 40 **Sabine Stoll** discusses word classes in FIRST LANGUAGE ACQUISITION. She starts by outlining the theoretical spectrum concerning word-class acquisition, which varies from innate abstract categories to bottom-up generalization through statistical learning. The chapter goes on to highlight the influence of input patterns, for nouns and verbs, and displays a wide cross-linguistic variety in terms of relevant features, as well as order of acquisition.

Chapter 41 is on word classes in SECOND LANGUAGE ACQUISITION. **Seth Lindstromberg** and **Frank Boers** scrutinize the question whether there is evidence for word class as an independent factor in adult second language vocabulary learning. They notice a general lack of relevant studies and a strong overrepresentation of English. However, the distinction between content and function words does play a role, and connects to more general factors like frequency, salience, and concreteness of meaning.

Chapter 42, by **Yaron Matras** and **Evangelia Adamou**, concerns word classes in LANGUAGE CONTACT. In particular, this chapter discusses how different word classes behave in terms of the likelihood to be affected by borrowing, as well as to be the locus of language switching in conversation. For both phenomena, the authors also consider the issue of structural integration of words into the receiving or matrix language. Their overall observation is that the relative susceptibility of words to be targeted in language contact scenarios has more to do with their functional (semantic and pragmatic) load than with traditional categories defined by distributional properties.

Paul Ibbotson, in Chapter 43, illuminates word classes in PSYCHOLINGUISTICS, i.e. how word classes are produced, comprehended, and constructed in language development (see also Chapter 40). Ibbotson argues that the functional utility of different word classes, from a processing perspective, resides in enhanced predictability. In addition, he discusses the mental representation of word classes, and the relationship between their conceptual properties and general cognition, with an eye to the debate on the (non-)universal status of word–class distinctions.

In Chapter 44, **David Kemmerer** reviews recent research on word classes in NEUROLINGUISTICS. He observes that most attention has been paid to the neurological underpinnings of the distinction between nouns and verbs, and the problem of confounding meaning and form in these studies. Other well-researched topics in this area include differential impairments of either nouns or verbs, the role of inflection in categorization, and the differences between subclasses, such as verbs of different valency types, or the proper noun–common noun distinction.

The final chapter of this handbook, Chapter 45, is by **Meladel Mistica, Ekaterina Vylomova**, and **Francis Bond**, and concerns word classes in COMPUTATIONAL LINGUISTICS AND ARTIFICIAL INTELLIGENCE. These fields have in common with corpus linguistics (see Chapter 38) that they commonly make use of POS tagging to reach a certain level of abstraction concerning the function and/or distribution of specific groups of words. The authors of this chapter explain which tools, methods, and resources are used for this kind of research. Also, they give examples of how it can be applied to solve a range of problems, such as lexical ambiguity, automatic summarization, and speech recognition by computer applications.

PART I
FUNDAMENTAL ISSUES

CHAPTER 2

WORD-CLASS UNIVERSALS AND LANGUAGE-PARTICULAR ANALYSIS

MARTIN HASPELMATH

2.1 THREE WORD-CLASS UNIVERSALS

THIS chapter considers both how word classes are analysed or described in particular languages (section 2.3), and what we can say in general about major word classes. We will see that these two questions are less directly related than is often thought. We begin with some important word-class universals in this first section, as well as some cross-linguistic macro-types of word-class patterns in section 2.2. Word-class universals are not particularly well known, although many comparative linguists are aware of them and will not be surprised by the Universals 1–3 given below, even if they have not read Croft (1991; 2000).

Much of the comparative literature on word classes asks to what extent the distinction between nouns, verbs, and adjectives is universal (e.g. Sasse 1993; Evans 2000; Baker 2003; Dixon 2010: ch. 11). This question (which I refer to as the 'distinctness question') has no clear answer, so it will be discussed only later (section 2.4), and I first focus on universals (section 2.1) and cross-linguistic macro-types (section 2.2).

Universals 1–3 (due to Croft 1991: ch. 3) are about the occurrence of function indicators, i.e. copulas, attributivizers, and termifiers, in three different propositional act functions: predication, modification, and reference, with three different semantic root classes: action, property, and object roots. All these terms will be explained and discussed further below, and the universals will become clearer once they are exemplified.

Universal 1
If a language has a copula, i.e. a special form that indicates predicative function, it is used with object roots and/or property roots.

Universal 2
If a language has an attributivizer, i.e. a special form that indicates modifying function, it is used with action roots and/or object roots.

Universal 3
If a language has a termifier (= nominalizer or substantivizer), i.e. a special form that indicates referential function, it is used with property roots and/or action roots.

The term triple 'predication/modification/reference' for the propositional act functions is familiar to every linguist, but of the three types of function indicators, only the first has a well-known existing term (*copula*). But the main subtypes of the other function indicators are also well known: relativizers and genitive flags (the two subtypes of attributivizers seen in (3a) and (4a)), as well as action nominalizers and substantivizers (the two subtypes of termifiers seen in (5a) and (6a)).

The reason the universals are formulated in terms of roots, not in terms of 'words', is that there is no general cross-linguistic understanding of what a 'word' is (other than as defined by the conventional orthographic representation). But in many or most languages, many roots can be words (especially nouns like *dog* and adjectives like *big*), and whenever a root cannot occur on its own without an affix (e.g. when tense affixes or person indexes are obligatory in verbs), these obligatory elements are not immediately relevant to Universals 1–3. Thus, formulating the universals in this way makes them generally applicable, and we do not need to worry about 'words'.

The construction types that the three universals make claims about are summarized in Table 2.1, where the boldfaced elements in the examples are the function indicators.

Table 2.1 Three propositional act functions and three semantic root classes

	reference: marked by termifiers	modification: marked by attributivizers	predication: marked by copulas
objects	—	genitive flag ((4a): *the rent of the house*)	object–word copula ((1a): *is a student*)
properties	substantivizer ((5a): *the new one*)	—	property copula ((2a): *is big*)
actions	nominalizer ((6a): *the open-ing*)	relativizer (3a: *the work that they did*)	—

What the function indicators have in common is that they indicate an unusual (unexpected, surprising) propositional act function: a genitive flag indicates that an object root (unexpectedly, surprisingly) has modifying function, a property copula indicates that a property root has predicating function, a nominalizer indicates that an action root (unusually) has referential function,[1] and so on.

After this short overview, let us now consider each of the universals individually. For convenience, the Universals 1–3 are repeated in what follows.

Universal 1
If a language has a copula, i.e. a special form that indicates predicative function, it is used with object roots or property roots.

So, we find many languages which require a copula with object–word predicates as in (1a), though not all languages have them (1b). Likewise, many languages require a copula with property predicates (2a), but some have no copula here (2b).

[1] For action nominalization constructions, see Chapter 5 in this volume.

(1) a. Italian (copula *è*)
 Michele è studente.
 Michele is student
 'Michele is a student.'

 b. Russian (no copula)
 Миша—студент.
 Miša student.
 Misha student
 'Misha is a student.'

(2) a. English (copula *is*)
 Our dog is big.

 b. Mandarin Chinese (no copula)
 我們的狗很大
 Wǒmen de gǒu hěn dà.
 we GEN dog very big
 'Our dog is big.'

While a function indicator is commonly used for predicating object or property roots, it is not always necessary, so Universal 1 must be formulated as an implicational universal. But, crucially, action roots generally do not require a form that indicates predicative function (in fact, they probably never do, as I do not know of a single example).

Universal 2 is analogous to Universal 1:

Universal 2
If a language has an attributivizer, i.e. a special form that indicates modifying function, it is used with action roots or object roots.

The two main types of attributivizers are relativizers (relative markers, including participial affixes) and genitive flags (affixes or adpositions). So, we find many languages which require a relativizer with action modifiers (= relative clauses) as in (3a), though not all languages have them (3b). Likewise, many languages require a genitive flag with object–word modifiers (4a), but some have no marker here (4b).

(3) a. Lezgian (relativizer *-j*) (Haspelmath 1993a: 344)
 awu-nwa-j k'walax-ar
 [do-PRF-REL] work-PL
 'the work that had been done'

 b. Japanese (no relativizer)
 私がした仕事
 watashi ga shi-ta shigoto
 [I NOM do-PST] work
 'the work I did'

(4) a. Cape Verdean Creole (genitive flag *di+*) (Baptista 2013)
    kel   renda   di   kaza
    the   rent   of   house
    'the rent of the house'

   b. Seychelles Creole (Michaelis & Rosalie 2013)
    lakaz   sa   zonm
    house   that   man
    'that man's house'

So, again, the function indicators do not occur universally, but property words are the least likely to require an attributivizer.

Finally, the situation is again completely analogous with indicators of referential function:

Universal 3
If a language has a termifier (= nominalizer or substantivizer), i.e. a special form that indicates referential function, it is used with property roots or action roots.

The two main types of termifiers are substantivizers and nominalizers.[2] So we find some languages which require a substantivizer with property-denoting referential expressions as in (5a), though not all languages have them (5b). Likewise, many languages require a nominalizer with action-denoting referential expressions (6a), but some have no marker here (6b).

(5) a. English (substantivizer +*one*)
    the new one

   b. Spanish (no substantivizer)
    la   nueva
    the   new
    'the new one'

(6) a. German (nominalizer -*ung*)
    die Öffn-ung des Fensters
    the open-NMLZ of.the window
    'the opening of the window'

   b. Malay (no nominalizer) (Yap et al. 2011: 13)
    Makan   lewat   tak   bagus.
    eat   late   not   good
    'Eating late is not good.'

---

[2] The term *termifier* (created for the purposes of this chapter) is derived from *term*, a synonym of *nominal (expression)* (*term* is used, for example, by Dik (1997)). The term *termifier* is probably not really necessary outside of the current comparative context, but it nicely serves to highlight the parallel with attributivizers and copulas (= predicativizers). (As Eva van Lier points out (p.c.), a term such as *referentializer* would also be possible.)

In addition to substantivizers, property roots may also occur with abstract-noun markers, as in English *new-ness*, or Spanish *nov-edad*. Such markers are semantically similar to action nominalizers, as the resulting form refers to the property as such, not to an entity bearing the property. Such markers are left aside in the present chapter for expository reasons, but the main generalizations should apply to them, too.

In the world's languages, the three pairings object–reference, property–modification, and action–predication have no special function indicators corresponding to them (though this would be logically possible). Table 2.1 thus shows dashes for these pairings. Croft (1991) describes these as 'unmarked combinations', and he shows that the lack of special marking is due to frequency differences: The usual pairings are much more frequent in discourse than the unusual pairings (there is thus a kind of form–frequency correspondence here).

Now, crucially, it is logically possible that these pairings might have function indicators as well, so there might be languages that have copulas with all three root classes (as in (7)), attributivizers with all three root classes (as in (8)), and termifiers with all three root classes (as in (9)).

(7) hypothetical all-copula language (copula BE)
   a. Michael BE student.
   b. Dog BE big.
   c. **Penny BE run home.**   (action–predication)

(8) hypothetical all-attributivizer language (attributivizer OF)
   a. house OF man
   b. **house OF new**   (property–modification)
   c. house OF I bought

(9) hypothetical all-referentializer language (termifier ONE)
   a. **I saw the teacher ONE.**   (object–reference)
   b. I saw the new ONE.
   c. I saw Penny's run ONE home.   ('I saw Penny running home.')

The claim of Universals 1–3 is that if a language has such an unlikely function indicator, it will also have the more likely ones.

This may not sound like a very strong claim, but it needs to be formulated in this somewhat weak way because there are many constructions where no function indicators are used, i.e. where the coding is not asymmetric: the (b) cases in (1)–(6). In addition to such cases of symmetric zero coding, as well as symmetric overt coding (as in (7)–(9), and as sometimes actually attested, e.g. in (20)), it is logically also possible to have **counter-asymmetric coding**: a function indicator only in the usual pairings object–reference, property–modification, and action–predication. The latter is what the Universals 1–3 exclude, and this tendency for asymmetric coding can be explained as due to frequency-induced predictability and efficient coding (Haspelmath 2021).

So far, I have not used the terms *noun*, *verb*, or *adjective*. This is deliberate, because the use of these terms in general contexts has led to a lot of confusion in the past (see also Croft 2022: ch. 2). It is worth emphasizing that we do not need them for stating these key observations about grammatical coding and their efficiency-based explanation. In the next section, we will see what role the traditional word-class labels can play in a cross-linguistic context.

2.2 Macro-types: Indicator coexpression patterns

2.2.1 Alignment types and indicator coexpression types

The word-class universals of section 2.1 are similar to the universals of argument marking (flagging and indexing; see Haspelmath 2005; Dryer 2007; Siewierska & Bakker 2009; Bickel 2011).[3] In order to highlight the major types, linguists have set up a tripartite semantic map with different coexpression ('alignment') patterns, as shown in Figure 2.1.

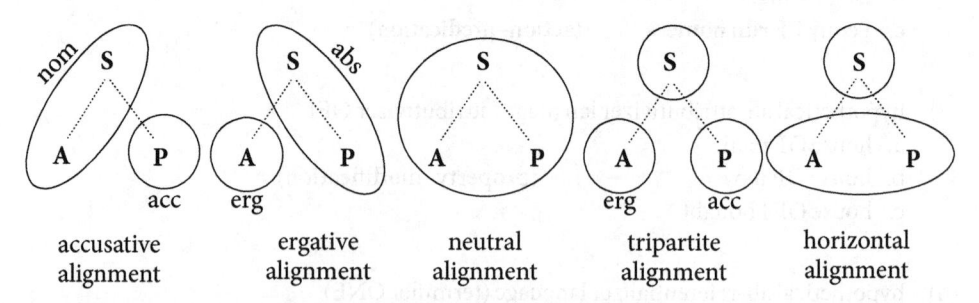

FIGURE 2.1 Five alignment types of argument markers

Labels for the two kinds of argument marker (flags and index sets) usually have terms that are taken from these alignment patterns (accusative case, ergative case, absolutive indexing, etc.), and as shown in Haspelmath (2005; 2015), a very similar approach works well for ditransitive alignment.

For word-class coding patterns, the three elements on the semantic map are the three root classes object (*ob*), action (*ac*), and property (*py*).[4] Figure 2.2 is parallel to Figure 2.1.

---

[3] That the comparison of word classes involves very similar issues as the comparison of syntactic role classes ('grammatical relations') was made particularly clear by Dryer (1997: §2).

[4] The terminology in the literature varies a little; in Haspelmath (2012a), I used *thing* for *object*, and some authors use *event* for *action*. There is no difference in substance here, though actions are generally thought to be subtypes of events. The universals are unaffected by this difference. (The reason I used *thing* instead of *object* was that the latter term is also used prominently for a syntactic role type (*subject*, *object*, *oblique*); but here I use *object*, to conform with Croft's usage.)

WORD-CLASS UNIVERSALS AND LANGUAGE-PARTICULAR ANALYSIS

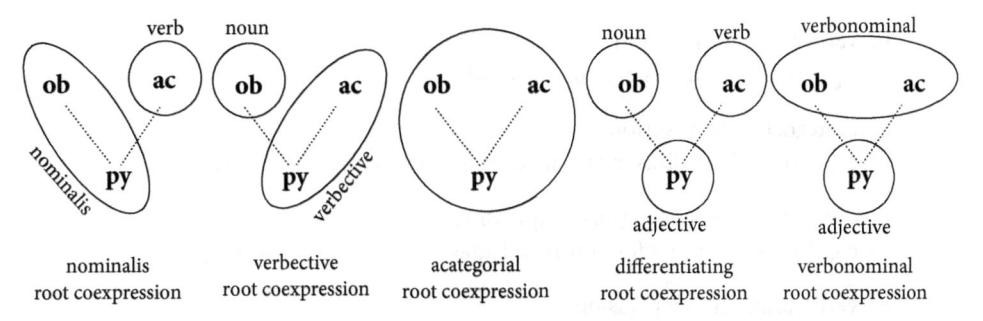

FIGURE 2.2 Five coexpression types of function indicators

The three terms *nominalis*, *verbective*, and *verbonominal* for three of the coexpression patterns are new and perhaps surprising.[5] By contrast, the terms *verb*, *noun*, and *adjective* for non-coexpressing parts of the maps are quite familiar. I did not need them in the statement of the universals in section 2.1, but here we are talking about the ways in which the semantic root classes differ in their coding, so it is here that the old grammatical terms come to play a role (see also section 2.5).

Just as different aspects of argument coding (flagging vs indexing) can have different alignment types (e.g. ergative case marking but accusative indexing), we may have different indicator coexpression patterns for different aspects of coding.[6] In the following sections, we will see examples of the five coexpression types in the three propositional act functions: predicative (section 2.2.2), referential (section 2.2.3), and modifying function (section 2.2.4).

2.2.2 Coexpression types in predicative function

In (10), I give an overview of the five predicative coexpression types, with a few initial examples. They are illustrated further below.[7]

(10) a. nominalis coexpression
         e.g. a nominalis copula, as in English (*be* for both noun and adjective)

---

[5] Alternatively, one could use the terms *anti-verb*, *anti-noun*, and *anti-adjective* (David Gil (p.c.)). They would work quite well, too, and are transparent in the context of the semantic map in Figure 2.2 (though less so if one is not aware of this context).

[6] In alignment patterns of argument markers, the tripartite and horizontal types are very rare because they make unnecessary distinctions (S never cooccurs in the same clause with A or P, so it can be conflated with either or both of them). This motivating factor is absent in the coexpression patterns of function indicators, so there is no a priori reason to expect that only three of the five logically possible patterns are attested.

[7] The second line in (10a–e) is preceded by 'e.g.' because, in each case, there are alternative logical possibilities for the coexpression patterns. However, due to the frequent absence of function indicators in the usual ('unmarked') pairings (as seen in Universals 1–3), the types mentioned here are de facto the only ones.

b. verbective coexpression
e.g. a noun copula, as in Mandarin Chinese (是 shì)

c. acategorial coexpression
e.g. no copula at all, as in Sri Lanka Malay (ex. 12) and Lillooet (ex. 13)

d. differentiating pattern (no coexpression)
e.g. different copulas for nouns and adjectives, as in Buwal (ex. 14)

e. verbonominal coexpression
e.g. copula only for adjectives, but not for nouns (nonexistent?)

The NOMINALIS type has this label because in the earlier Western tradition, the Latin terms *nomen* and *nominalis* were used both for nouns and adjectives (these were regarded as subtypes of the *nomen* class, called *nomen substantivum* and *nomen adjectivum*; see Chapter 27 in this volume). This coexpression type is well known from Indo-European languages like Latin and English, but also occurs elsewhere (Stassen 1997: xxx). It is so well known that no further illustration is needed (see (1a) and (2a)).

The VERBECTIVE type, where event predication and property predication are treated in the same way, is also well known, and is found, for example, in Cantonese (Francis & Matthews 2005: 274), which has an obligatory copula *hai* 'be' for object-word predicates (corresponding to Mandarin *shì*), but no copula with action and property predicates:

(11) Cantonese
 a. *M hai hoksaang.*
    not be student
    'He's not a student.'

 b. *M haam.*
    not cry
    'He's not crying.'

 c. *M hausaang.*
    not young
    'He's not young.'

The ACATEGORIAL type is not so uncommon in predicative position, because there are many languages that lack a copula. In Sri Lanka Malay (Nordhoff 2013: §9.3), for example, there is no nominal copula (12a), and property roots (12b) look even more like action roots (12c) in that they can also be preceded by tense-aspect markers such as *arà-*:

(12) Sri Lanka Malay (Nordhoff 2013: 252, 255, 250)
 a. *Sindbad hatthu Muslim.*
    Sindbad INDEF Muslim
    'Sindbad was a Moor.'

b. *Ruuma arà-kiccil.*
   house NPST-small
   'The houses are getting small.'

c. *Incayang arà-maakang.*
   3SG NPST-eat
   'He is eating.'

Another example of the acategorial type is Lillooet (a Salishan language), where predicative elements are always clause-initial, again without any copula (Davis et al. 2014: 196).

(13) Lillooet
   a. *Šmúɬač ta=kʷúkʷpiʔa.*
      woman DET=chief
      'The chief is a woman.'

   b. *Láχləχ ta=kʷúkʷpiʔa.*
      smart DET=chief
      'The chief is smart.'

   c. *ƛ'iq ta=kʷúkʷpiʔa.*
      arrive DET=chief
      'The chief arrived.'

A similar pattern is found in Southern Wakashan languages such as Nuu-chah-nulth (discussed in Chapter 6 in this volume). For more on Salishan languages, see Chapter 29 in this volume.

The DIFFERENTIATING type would be represented by languages that have two different copulas, one for object roots (nouns) and one for property roots (adjectives). They seem to be quite rare, but the Chadic language Buwal is described in this way by Viljoen (2013): the nominal copula is *ārā*, while the adjectival copula is *ndzā*.

(14) Buwal (Viljoen 2013: 448, 187)
   a. *mbàw ārā dādāwār*
      child COP evil.person
      'The child is an evil person.'

   b. *ā-ndzā bārbār*
      3SG.SBJ-COP hard
      'It is hard.'

Finally, the VERBONOMINAL type would be represented by a language that only has a copula for property words, but such languages do not seem to exist: Stassen (1997) and Pustet (2003) note that if a language has a copula for property word predication, it also has a copula for object word predication.

2.2.3 Coexpression types in referential function

Moving on to the second propositional act function, (15) gives an overview of the coexpression types in referring function, with a few initial examples.

(15) a. nominalis coexpression
e.g. no substantivizer, as in Spanish (*la casa, la nueva* (ex. 5b))

b. verbective coexpression
e.g. identical termifier for properties and actions (nonexistent?)

c. acategorial coexpression
e.g. no termifier, as in Tagalog ((ex. 16))

d. differentiating pattern (no coexpression)
e.g. different substantivizer and nominalizer, as in English
(*the house, the new one, the open-ing*)

e. verbonominal coexpression: unattested
e.g. substantivizer but no nominalizer (nonexistent?)

The NOMINALIS coexpression type is again the type found in the traditional Indo-European languages such as Latin, and also in Spanish and German. Both object roots and property roots (but not action roots) can be used in referring function with an article in these languages, e.g. Spanish *la casa* 'the house', *la nueva* 'the new one' (see (5b); German *das Haus* 'the house', *das neue* 'the new one'. By contrast, action roots in referring function need some kind of relativizer or nominalizer.

The VERBECTIVE type would be represented by a language which uses a general termifier, i.e. the same marker as a substantivizer ('the new-TERM' = the new one) and as a nominalizer ('the open-TERM' = the open-ing). Such languages do not seem to exist.

The ACATEGORIAL type is famously found in Classical Nahuatl and also in Tagalog, as illustrated by the examples in (16) from Gil (1993). Not only object roots as in (16a) and property roots as in (16b), but also action roots as in (16c) can be used in referring function following a role-marking proclitic (in these examples, it is always the Nominative marker *ang*).

(16) Tagalog (Gil 1993: 1140)
a. *Lumabas   ang   bangkero.*
   went.out   NOM   boatman
   'The boatman went out.'

b. *Lumabas   ang   mabait.*
   went.out   NOM   kind
   'The kind one went out.'

c. *Lumabas   ang   bumalik.*
   went.out   NOM   returned
   'The one who returned went out.'

The claim here is that the role marker is not a termifier, and if we say the same about the Lillooet determiner *ta =* in (13), then Lillooet also exemplifies this type (because Lillooet allows reversing all of (13a–c): *kʷúkʷpiʔa ta-láχləχ* 'the smart one is a chief', etc.).

Next, the DIFFERENTIATING type is represented by English, which has two different termifiers: a substantivizer *one* for property roots (*the new one*), and an action nominalizer *-ing* (in *the open-ing*).

Finally, the VERBONOMINAL type would be represented by languages where adjectives need a substantivizer, but verbs do not need a nominalizer. Again, such languages may not exist.

Now before we get to the coexpression types in modifying function in the next section, let us consider the first two propositional act functions together. There are two clear types here: the DOUBLY NOMINALIS type represented by Spanish (coexpression of objects and properties in both functions), and the DOUBLY ACATEGORIAL type represented by Lillooet and Tagalog. These are the kinds of languages that have sometimes been said to lack a noun–verb(–adjective) distinction, though in different ways: in languages like Spanish (and especially in Latin), nouns and verbs have been said to be subclasses of a larger 'nomen' class, also because they have very similar number marking (and in Latin case marking) properties.[8] In Lillooet and Tagalog, the reason for saying that they are acategorial has been that they lack a copula in predicative function. The doubly DIFFERENTIATING TYPE may exist as well, but is much less prominent.

If one focuses one's attention on the two salient types, one may come to the conclusion that Spanish/Latin-type languages have a single ('flexible', or 'merged') noun–adjective class, while languages like Lillooet and Tagalog only have a single noun–verb–adjective class. There is nothing wrong with this, in principle, because one may choose one's types as one pleases, and, at first glance, it seems interesting that the doubly nominalis Spanish type seems to be fairly common, while the doubly acategorial type of Tagalog and Lillooet seems to be quite rare.

But we need to remember that we know nothing about correlations at this point: is the doubly nominalis type more common than expected by chance (i.e. expected on the basis of the combined probabilities of nominalis predication and nominalis referential use)? Is the doubly differentiating type less common than expected by chance? For the doubly acategorial type, we can perhaps exclude this possibility, because acategorial (= copulaless) predication is not uncommon (see Sri Lanka Malay in (12)), whereas acategorial referential use of the Tagalog or Lillooet type is quite uncommon. But we would need more systematic cross-linguistic data before quantitative statements can be made.

Thus, it is too early to make generalizations about 'Spanish-type' languages, let alone 'Tagalog-type' languages. We do not know how common these language types are, and whether these types are significant. Moreover, we should not neglect the modifying function, which we will consider in the next section.

---

[8] The fact that Spanish and Latin use the same copula in predicative function has been less salient in the traditional discussion, but if they used two different copulas (like Buwal in (14)), they would probably not have been lumped together by anyone.

2.2.4 Coexpression types in modifying function

Finally, (17) gives an overview of the coexpression types in modifying function.

(17) a. nominalis coexpression
e.g. relativizer for action modification vs uncoded adjective and uncoded possessor, as in Seychelles Creole (ex. 18)

b. verbective coexpression
e.g. identical attributivizer for action and property modification, as in Archi (ex. 19)

c. acategorial coexpression
e.g. a general attributivizer, as in Mandarin Chinese *de* (ex. 20)

d. differentiating pattern (no coexpression)
e.g. different genitive flag and relativizer, as in English (genitive flag *of* vs relativizer *that*)

e. verbonominal coexpression
e.g. identical relativizer and genitive flag, as in Aramaic (ex. 21)

The NOMINALIS type is found, for example, in Seychelles Creole, where there is no marker for possessive object–word modifiers (18a) or property modifiers (18b), whereas action modifiers (relative clauses) have a relativizer *ki* (18c) (Michaelis & Rosalie 2013).

(18) Seychelles Creole
a. *lakaz   Marcel*
   house   Marcel
   'Marcel's house' (see (4b))

b. *dilo   so*
   water   hot
   'hot water'

c. *sa   zoli   lakaz   ki   ou   annan   la*
   DEM   nice   house   REL   you   have   there
   'this nice house that you have there'

The VERBECTIVE type is found, for example, in Archi, which has an attributive suffix *-t:u* for action and property modifiers, but a Genitive suffix *-n* (Chumakina 2018). Some examples of the attributivizer are given in (19).

(19) Archi (Chumakina 2018: 177)
a. *mu-t:u-b   noʕš*
   beautiful-ATTR-G3   horse(G3)
   'beautiful horse'

b. *kwaršu-t:u-b*   *χabar*
happen-ATTR-G3   story(G3)
'story that happened'

This type seems to be widely represented among the world's languages. The *WALS* chapter by Gil (2005) gives 33 languages from all continents that 'collapse adjectives and relative clauses'.

The ACATEGORIAL type is represented, for example, by Mandarin Chinese, which has an attributivizer *de* that is used with object roots, property roots, and action roots. For example:

(20) a. 父親的房子
     fùqīn   *de*   *fángzi*
     father   ATT   house
     'father's house'

    b. 漂亮的房子
     piàoliang   *de*   *fángzi*
     beautiful   ATT   house
     'beautiful house'

    c. 笑的孩子們
     xiào   *de*   *háizi-men*
     laugh   ATT   child-PL
     'laughing children'

The DIFFERENTIATING type is again represented by English, which has two genitive flags (postclitic *'s*, preposition *of*) for object–word modifiers, no marking for property modifiers, and relativizers (*that*, *-ing*) for action modifiers.

Finally, the VERBONOMINAL type is represented by those languages that have a relativizer with the same shape as the genitive marker, which is not used with property words. Gil (2005) finds this type only in two languages, one of which is a variety of Aramaic. Fassberg (2019) describes Western Aramaic, where a particle *ti* can be used both as a genitive flag and as a relativizer.

(21) Western Aramaic (Fassberg 2019: 648)
     a. *so:ba*   *ti*   *blo:ta*
        mayor   of   village
        'the mayor of the village'

     b. *hanna*   *yamla*   *ti*   *tˤsˤil-le*
        this   camel   that   it.carried-him
        'this camel which carried him'

2.2.5 Coexpression patterns across the three propositional act functions

If we now continue to compare the patterns across the three functions, we do not find much further evidence for a dominant coexpression pattern of function indicators. Recall that we suggested that 'Spanish-type' languages might have a general nominalis type, but at least in Latin, Spanish, and German, this does not extend to the modifying function (which is of the differentiating type, as in English).

Perhaps most strikingly, the acategorial type does not extend even to Tagalog (see Chapter 35 in this volume). Object-word modifiers are indicated by a genitive flag *nang* (22a), while property and action modifiers are indicated by an attributivizer *na/ng* (22b–c).

(22) a. ang   bahay   n(an)g   ama
       NOM   house   GEN   father
       'father's house'

   b. ang   maliit   na   bahay
      NOM   small   ATT   house
      'small house'

   c. ang   babae=ng   nagbabasa   n(an)g   diyaryo
      NOM   woman=ATT   read.IPV   GEN   newspaper
      'the woman who is reading a newspaper'

Thus, as far as we know at this moment, there is no strong tendency for coexpression patterns to cluster beyond the individual propositional act functions. While linguists generally have the feeling that there is something like a 'dominant role alignment' across argument-marking constructions (and we often even say that a language is 'an ergative language'), there is no good evidence, at this point, for a notion of 'dominant coexpression pattern' across propositional act functions. Thus, from the point of view that is adopted in this section, we cannot say (so far) that in general, languages have 'flexible' or 'differentiated' root classes (see Rijkhoff & van Lier 2013).

2.3 LANGUAGE-PARTICULAR ANALYSIS CREATES CONSTRUCTION-BASED CLASSES

There has long been broad agreement that languages differ in interesting ways in the way they group words into word classes (or *parts of speech*, or *lexical categories*). Sapir (1921: 118) wrote: 'Each language has its own scheme [of parts of speech]. Everything depends on the formal demarcations which it recognizes.' And Schachter & Shopen (2007: 1) wrote: 'There are striking differences between languages with respect to both the kind and the number of distinctions.'[9]

---

[9] See also Himmelmann (2008: 259): 'Lexical and syntactic categories are by definition language-specific as they are based on language-specific formal features and the distribution of such features tends to show language-specific idiosyncrasies.'

But what exactly do these authors mean by 'demarcations' or 'distinctions'? This is not immediately clear, because there is a wide variety of ways in which the roots, grammatical markers, and complex expressions are grouped into morphosyntactically relevant classes.

For example, about one-third of verbs and adjectives in Godoberi (a Nakh–Dagestanian language) have an initial gender marker, while two-thirds lack such a marker (Kibrik 1996: 24, 44). So one could set up a word-class 'Gendered Verbective' and another word-class 'Genderless Verbective'.[10] Similarly, for German, one could set up a word-class 'Very-Modifiable' for those verbs and adjectives that can be modified by *sehr* 'very' (e.g. degree adjectives such as *schön*, and 'degree verbs' such as *sich freuen* 'be happy'; but not verbs like *arbeiten* 'work'). Or for Maricopa (a Yuman language), one could distinguish between Pluralizable words (most verbs and some nouns) and Nonpluralizable words (all the others; Gordon 1986: 29, 90).

These examples may appear surprising, but that we can bring them up here simply follows from the logic of grammatical analysis: we formulate general (nonsemantic) regularities that govern the cooccurrence of classes of forms. These nonsemantic rules are called CONSTRUCTIONS,[11] and the classes of forms are FORM CLASSES (Bloomfield 1933: 146). The identification of form-classes is sometimes called distributional analysis (see section 11.2 in this volume).[12] Such form-classes are often cross-classified, as in Godoberi, which has four classes of verbs/adjectives:

(i) Gendered Tense-marked (e.g. *ičā*: 'to sell')
(ii) Gendered Tenseless (e.g. *mik'isi*: 'young')
(iii) Genderless Tense-marked (e.g. *bit'i*: 'to tear')
(iv) Genderless Tenseless (e.g. *q'aruma*: 'greedy')

Which of the classes (Gendered/Genderless or Tense-marked/Tenseless) is taken as the superclass here and which is the subclass is essentially arbitrary, and is determined largely by pedagogical considerations. For reasons of grammatical tradition, linguists will almost always give preference to the labels 'noun', 'verb', and 'adjective' (as was done at the end of the preceding paragraph, and as is done in Kibrik (1996)), but this does not mean that these classes are in fact privileged in the languages.

Many linguists have the feeling that when we consider all the relevant facts, we find again and again that the most important (or privileged) form classes are noun, verb, and adjective, and it may be that this will eventually turn out to be the case. But, in practice, we never consider all the facts—not when we describe the word classes of a single language, and not at all when we compare languages, because the various language-particular constructions are so hard to compare. So de facto, we tend to look for classes that resemble our stereotypical nouns, verbs, and adjectives, and often we find some 'criteria' for identifying classes with these well-known labels in particular languages. But language analysis (= description) is not

---

[10] Recall that 'verbective' as introduced above as a term for classes that neutralize the property vs action distinction.

[11] By *nonsemantic*, I simply mean regularities of cooccurrence that do not follow from semantic (in)compatibility. Thus, #*I will leave yesterday* is semantically ill-formed, but **I will tomorrow leave* is syntactically ill-formed.

[12] The term *distributional analysis* may seem to suggest a specific approach, but in fact this is the basis of all morphological and syntactic analysis. There is no reason to associate it with a particular theoretical or ideological orientation, because it is universally adopted in linguistics.

about finding criteria to identify pre-established classes[13]—it is about creating those classes that we need to describe the constructions of a language.[14] And these classes are very numerous once one considers all the facts (probably many hundreds of classes for all languages; this is also observed by Croft in this volume—see section 11.6).

In reality, we do not know which kinds of classes are 'privileged', either in particular languages or in general. The notion of privileged classes may not mean much for language-particular analysis, where we need a complete picture anyway, and cannot be content with a few major classes. So, apart from pedagogical considerations, it does not really matter how exactly we set up the major classes and their subclasses. And, for comparative purposes, all we can do is focus on particular kinds of differences that happen to be readily comparable, as we did in sections 2.1–2.2. Intuitively, it seems that the distribution of function indicators is the most important criterion for nouns/verbs/adjectives across languages (but see section 2.7 on other markers).

In addition to 'major classes' (for which we use the labels *noun, verb, adjective*), all languages also have forms that do not readily fit into such larger classes, e.g. pronouns, numerals, quantifiers, demonstratives, coordinators, subordinators, as well as adverbs and particles. In the older 'parts of speech' tradition (see Chapter 27 in this volume), seven of these were included as specific parts of speech (numerals, interjections, adverbs, prepositions, conjunctions, pronouns, articles), but here the degree of cross-classification and arbitrariness of decisions is even greater than in the case of nouns, verbs, and adjectives. The reason why these old and plainly unsatisfactory terms are still around is that there is no alternative general set of classes. As Sapir noted: each language has its own classes, and what is general across languages is not kinds of classes, but universals like those in section 2.1.

2.4 WHY THE DISTINCTNESS QUESTION CANNOT BE ANSWERED

In the past, many linguists have asked whether two semantic classes (of the type object, action, property) are 'distinct' or not, either in a particular language or in the world's languages in general. We often find questions such as those quoted in (23).

(23) a. Robins (1952: 296): 'Are we then able to say that there are any universal categories in grammar other than the purely segmental ones?'

---

[13] It is therefore surprising how much effort the general literature tends to invest in 'finding criteria' (e.g. Sasse 1993; Beck 2002), as if we already knew which classes there are and we only had to match these pre-existing classes to language-particular phenomena. But the point of the comments at the beginning of this section was precisely to remind us that there are no pre-existing classes.

[14] It is thus wrong to ask, in a questionnaire for descriptive grammars, whether there are 'operational definitions' of the classes noun, verb, adjective, etc. (Comrie & Smith 1977: §1.16). The operational definitions must be language-particular, and they cannot define general categories.

b. Evans (2000: 720): 'Are there languages which go further [than merging verbs and adjectives], merging nouns and verbs into a single class of predicates?'

c. Chung (2012): 'Are lexical categories universal?' (title of paper)

d. Davis et al. (2014: e195): 'The empirical question addressed in our second case study is: "Do all languages have a distinction between nouns and verbs?"'

e. Sasse (2015: 166): 'The articles in Vogel & Comrie (2000) provide a good overview of the more recent landscape of cross-linguistic word class research and its central controversies and proposals. The most fundamental point in dispute ... is the universality of word classes.'

However, these questions cannot be answered when there are no limits on what can count as a 'distinction' between classes and when at the same time the classes are not defined independently of the language-particular grammatical constructions (the same point is made by Croft in this volume—see section 11.3). The latter point is of course universally recognized: word classes (of particular languages) are defined in terms of grammatical constructions, not in terms of 'notional categories'. The 'traditional notional classes' do not necessarily correspond to grammatical classes in particular languages.[15]

So if word classes are defined in a language-particular way, with reference to different constructions in different languages (as seen in section 2.3), then there is no way to match classes across languages. Rigorous comparative grammar requires uniformly defined yardsticks for 'measurement' (comparative concepts—see Haspelmath 2018), so it is not admissible to apply different criteria in different languages for identifying, say, adjectives or verbs. But this is precisely what Baker (2003) does (as described by Croft 2009: §3), and it is also what Chung (2012) does (as described by Haspelmath 2012b).[16]

The conventional way of hoping to resolve this problem is to say that the classes are set up by language-particular constructional (or distributional) criteria, but are matched across languages by their semantics:

[With reference to 'formal', distributional criteria], we can decide for each word in the language to what syntactic class or classes it belongs. It is true that not all the members of class X [English *boy, woman, grass, atom, tree, cow, truth, beauty* ...] denote persons, places and things ... However, it may still be true that all (or the vast majority) of the lexical items which refer to persons, places and things fall within the class X; and, if this is so, we may call X the class of nouns.

(Lyons 1968: 318)

---

[15] For example, Lyons (1968: 317): 'If the class of nouns is defined in "notional" terms, as that class of lexical items whose members denote places, persons and things ... the definition cannot be applied without circularity to determine the status of such English words as *truth, beauty, electricity*, etc.'

[16] See also Croft & van Lier's (2012) critique of Chung (2012), and Haspelmath's (2014) critique of Davis et al. (2014).

For very similar statements, see Evans (2000: 709) and Schachter & Shopen (2007: 2). But this does not solve the problem, because it merely provides a justification for labelling. Of course, it would not be very reader-friendly to set up a class of nouns and to call it 'Class Y' (this was Garvin's (1951) approach for the North American language Kutenai), but it would highlight the fact that this class is not defined in the same way as the class that we call 'noun' in English. There is no theoretical reason to equate the two classes of words.

As we saw in section 2.3, there are many different ways in which word–size elements can be arranged in classes and subclasses. For example, one might say that English words like *Pat*, *Kim*, or *Lee* are a subclass of the English class 'Noun', or one might say that they constitute a separate class 'Proper Name' (though there would of course have to be a superclass comprising both Nouns and Proper Names). Which of the many different classes that must be created for the purpose of language-particular analysis are to be known by which label is quite arbitrary. This is recognized by some authors,[17] but many still treat it as a substantive question (and they sometimes even claim that word classes are part of an innate grammar blueprint or 'universal grammar').[18]

That there is no substantive question here was clearly recognized by Croft (2000: 65): 'Noun, verb and adjective are not categories of particular languages'. What is general across languages is implicational universals of coding like those seen in sections 2.1–2.2, but not the classes noun, verb, and adjective, and it is not even clear what it would mean for these classes to be universal as grammatical classes.[19] Some cross-linguistic work on word classes has recognized this and has focused on finding generalizations about the various kinds of markers, rather than about the grammatical classes (e.g. Pustet 2003 on copulas; Ye 2021 on markers associated with property words/adjectives).

2.5 NOUNS, VERBS, AND ADJECTIVES AS CONCEPTS OF GENERAL GRAMMAR

We have seen that we do not need the concepts of noun, verb, and adjective for stating universals and distinguishing macro-types (sections 2.1–2.2), and that different languages have a large number of classes that cannot be mapped onto each other because they are based on different language-particular constructions (section 2.3). Such classes can (for mnemonic

---

[17] Schachter & Shopen (2007: 13), after discussing Tagalog and Nuu-chah-nulth word classes, conclude: 'Since this seems to be essentially a matter of terminology, it need not concern us further'.

[18] Matthewson & Demirdache (1995: 69): 'We propose that distinctions between the lexical categories N, V and A ... are a universal property of language ... We claim that it reflects a deep property of the syntax of Universal Grammar'.

[19] Baker (2003: §1.2) also recognizes the problem with the traditional approach exemplified by (23), and after a discussion of the question of the adjective–verb distinction in Mohawk, he observes: 'The unanswerable question, then, is this: do these differences justify positing a separate category of adjectives in Mohawk after all? Or do we continue to say that Mohawk has only verbs, but concede that there are two subtypes of verbs, intransitive stative verbs and other verbs?' But he does not seem to draw any conclusion from this insight.

and pedagogical purposes) be called 'Noun', 'Verb', and 'Adjective', but this labelling convention does not mean that they are concepts of general linguistics.

So, do these terms have a role in general linguistics at all? Or should we use them exclusively as language-particular labels? The answer given by Croft (1991; 2000; 2001) is that the terms *noun*, *verb*, and *adjective* represent 'language universals' or 'typological prototypes':

> Noun, verb and adjective are not categories of particular languages. But noun, verb and adjective are language universals—that is, there are typological prototypes which should be called noun, verb and adjective.
>
> (Croft 2000: 65)

Croft's important insight is that the widespread sense of universality of nouns, verbs, and adjectives (reflected also in recent generative work like Baker 2003; Chung 2012; Davis et al. 2014) is not wrong, but is not manifested at the level of language-particular classes. It is manifested by universals like those seen in section 2.1, and Croft calls these patterns 'prototypes' and relates them to his 'typological markedness theory' (Croft 2003: ch. 4). But it is odd to describe these correct insights by saying that 'noun' and 'verb' are 'language universals', because a language universal is a statement. And Croft's talk of 'prototypes' has often been misunderstood as claiming that there are no sharp boundaries between the classes of particular languages.[20]

In practical terms, there is a clear answer to the question whether we need nouns, verbs, and adjectives as concepts of general grammar: Yes, we do, because we use these terms as general concepts all the time. We make general statements such as those in (24a-c) about the world's languages or about languages of a particular area. Moreover, even when we talk about particular languages, we often make implicitly comparative statements, as in (25a-c).

(24) a. Tense marking on nouns is much rarer than tense marking on verbs.
b. If a language has dominant SOV order and the genitive follows the governing noun, then the adjective likewise follows the noun
(Universal 5 in Greenberg 1963a).
c. In European languages, nouns tend to have obligatory plural marking, whereas plural marking of nouns is often optional in East Asian languages.

(25) a. Japanese has two distinct adjective classes.
b. Verbs do not show person indexing in Modern Swedish.
c. In Yoruba, nouns usually begin with a vowel.

---

[20] For example, Francis & Matthews (2005: 270) say that 'Croft (1991, 2001) defines the prototype for the category "noun" cross-linguistically as a correlation of the semantic class of physical objects with the pragmatic function of reference. Within a given language, some nouns (e.g. those used as modifiers or predicates) may fail to conform to the prototype ...' This sounds as if there were more or less prototypical nouns, but this is not what Croft is saying. He says that when physical object words are used in referring function, they are typologically unmarked, and he calls this a 'typological prototype'. (See also Newmeyer 1998: ch. 4 for a similar misunderstanding.)

The statements in (25a–c) are not as precise as they could be if they were made about language-particular categories (Japanese Verby Adjectives, Nouny Adjectives, Swedish Verbs, Yoruba Nouns), but they are highly informative, and we want to continue talking about particular languages in this implicitly comparative way. Thus, in practice, we treat nouns, verbs, and adjectives as cross-linguistic categories. But what do they refer to? Perhaps surprisingly, I suggest that they can be defined as in (26).[21]

(26) a. A noun is an object-denoting root.
      b. A verb is an action-denoting root.
      d. An adjective is a property-denoting root.

Now one might object that these definitions do not cover everything that we mean by these terms. It may seem that we want to include non-object nouns like *beauty*, non-action verbs like *know*, and maybe non-property adjectives like *royal* as well. In addition, it may seem that we want to include non-root nouns like *play-er*, non-root verbs like *en-large*, and non-root adjectives like *help-ful*.

But while English *know* is a Stative Verb by some English-specific criteria, it is not clear how one could provide a generally applicable (and thus presumably conceptual/semantic) definition that would include it in a general 'verb' category, while not at the same time including many English Adjectives (such as *aware* or *happy*). Thus, it seems that we need to focus on the shared core that all form classes that we generally call 'verbs' have in common: the action meaning. The definitions in (26) give the right results for the universal tendencies in (24) and the language-particular statements in (25), although they are not as informative as one might hope. But since languages differ in many ways, comparative statements are necessarily restricted in scope, and the shared-core definitions in (26a–c) remind us of this.

Now one may grant that the traditional word-class terms are best defined semantically, but one may still ask: couldn't we replace 'root' in (26) by 'lexeme'? Aren't complex words like *play-er*, *en-large*, and *help-ful* object-denoting nouns, action-denoting verbs, and property-denoting adjectives in the same way as roots? Intuitively, this is certainly the case, but there is no clear general understanding of the term 'lexeme', as far as I know. Lexemes are often thought of as abstractions over all forms that only differ in inflectional properties, but since there is no general way of distinguishing between inflection and derivation (e.g. Plank 1994; Spencer 2013),[22] this definition cannot be applied to languages in general. So, it is best to define the traditional word-class terms in terms of roots,

---

[21] A reviewer objected that this terminology will never be adopted in the discipline, and of course it goes against the basic point that word classes are defined grammatically, not semantically (section 2.3–2.4; see n. 12). However, this basic point is valid only for particular languages, and the examples in (24)–(25) are meant to show that in general comparative contexts, linguists actually do use the word-class terms in a notional way.

[22] It is sometimes thought that the difference between inflection and derivation is 'fuzzy', and that this is no different to other distinctions in linguistics (which are all somewhat fuzzy). But there is a crucial difference between a lack of a clear definition and a clear definition with fuzziness. If there is no clear definition, then all we can rely on is stereotypes. I suspect that the inflection–derivation contrast is merely the reflection of traditional ways of describing European languages (in grammars and dictionaries), and has no basis in the structures of languages. For this reason, I do not want to rely on this distinction for the definition of key concepts.

i.e. minimal segmental forms (see Haspelmath 2020 on morphs and their various subtypes, such as affixes and roots).

The definitions in (26) entail that the terms *noun*, *verb*, and *adjective* could alternatively be used in the statement of the universals in section 2.1 and of the macro-types in section 2.2. Thus, we have answered the question raised in these earlier sections about the relevance of these general statements to word classes. They may not be directly relevant to language-particular word classes, but they are highly relevant to the general concepts of noun, verb, and adjective in the sense in which these terms are normally used.

Thus, even though noun, verb, and adjective are (almost by definition)[23] universal semantic types of roots, different languages use different ways of treating such roots in predicative, modifying, and referring functions (as we saw in section 2.2). This is the core of what is generally meant by cross-linguistic word-class variability: languages use function indicators in different ways. But in the next two sections, we will see two further ways in which word classes can be variable: heterosemous root sets (section 2.6) and variation in substantive markers (section 2.7).

2.6 Heterosemous root sets

Many languages have pairs such as those listed in (27)–(30), which I call 'heterosemous root sets' here (following Lichtenberk 1991, who introduced the term *heterosemy*, for different meanings of a single element that are associated with different word classes).

(27) English
a hammer	to hammer
a mother	to mother
a head	to head
a cook	to cook
a ship	to ship
a dance	to dance
a walk	to walk

(28) Yupik (Mithun 2017b: 163–164)
amirlu	'cloud'	'be cloudy'
taqmak/g	'dress'	'put on a dress'
kuvya	'fishnet'	'fish by driftnetting'

---

[23] Not *quite* by definition, because it is logically possible that a language might lack verbs (= action roots) in the sense of only having object-denoting roots, resorting to complex forms to express actions. For example, 'go' would be expressed as 'use legs', 'eat' as 'use mouth', 'speak' as 'use tongue', 'kill' as 'turn into corpse'. Or, vice versa, everything would ultimately be expressed by event-denoting roots, so 'bird' would be expressed as 'flyer', 'dog' as 'barker', 'woman' as 'birthgiver', 'small' as 'having been reduced', and so on. Thus, the fact that all languages have many object-denoting roots, many action-denoting roots, and many property-denoting roots is an interesting language universal which has not received much attention so far (perhaps because the alternative logical possibility seems so far-fetched).

(29) Lao (Enfield 2006: 4)
    kèeng3   'soup'   'to make soup of'
    khua5   'fry'   'to fry'
    tôm4   'dish made by boiling'   'to boil'

(30) Hiw (Oceanic) (François 2017: 333)
    pyë   'a bait'   'to attach a bait'
    veřoye   'a fight'   'to fight'
    togekëse   'a game'   'to play'
    vegevage   'speech, language'   'to speak'

For such cases, one might suggest that a single root can occur 'as different word classes'. For example, one might want to say that English *hammer* is a 'category-neutral' root that may 'become a verb' and then have an action meaning, but it might also 'become a noun' and then have an object meaning. This view is often called the 'precategorial' view of such elements (e.g. Evans & Osada 2005: §2.2).

However, it has often been observed that the semantic relationships in such pairs tend to be quite unpredictable and idiosyncratic. And since many languages have corresponding derivational markers (e.g. Spanish *martillo* 'hammer', *martill-ear* 'to hammer'; German *Mutter* 'mother', *be-muttern* 'to mother'), it has been more common to regard such pairs as created by a derivational operation called ZERO-DERIVATION or CONVERSION (e.g. Bauer & Valera Hernández 2005). Unpredictable and idiosyncratic meaning relationships are also otherwise characteristic of derivational relationships.

The problem with the 'derivation/conversion' view is that it presupposes a particular directionality, which is often not evident at all, and there are no good criteria for establishing the direction of derivation: is *a walk* derived from *to walk*? Is *a dance* derived from *to dance*? Is a *a tango* derived from *to tango*? Such questions arise for all languages. (See also Gil 2013a: §4.5.2 for Riau Indonesian in comparison with English.)

Thus, in order to avoid unmotivated decisions, at least in a comparative context, it is best to treat these pairs simply as what they uncontroversially are: heterosemous root sets, i.e. sets of roots that are related by sharing the same shape and having related meanings.[24] Note that we cannot say that elements like *hammer* are 'heterosemous roots', because the approach taken in this chapter requires that by definition, a root (in the comparative sense) can only be associated with one semantic type (an object, an action, or a property). Thus, English *hammer* is a root set, or it could perhaps be said to be a 'super-root', as long as one remembers that a super-root is not a single root but a set of roots.[25]

---

[24] In some languages, there are heterosemous root sets which have to combine with 'stem markers' that clearly indicate the semantic class, e.g. Latin *tim-e(-o)* '(I) fear', *tim-or* '(the) fear' (Lehmann 2008; see also section 6.2 in this volume). For such cases, one might prefer a 'precategorial root' view to a heterosemous root set view, because the root does not occur without a stem marker.

[25] If the term *multicategoriality* is used (François 2017: 299), it must be understood that what is 'multicategorial' is the super-root, not a root in the comparative sense. (Vapnarsky & Veneziano 2017 use *polycategorial* in the same sense.)

But from a language-particular perspective, a rather different treatment of such heterosemous root sets is of course possible: one might say for English that elements like *hammer* and others in (27) are neither Nouns nor Verbs, but represent a third class, perhaps called 'Nomiverbs'. Thus, English might be said to have Nouns like *city* (which can occur after the definite article *the*), Verbs like *steal* (which can occur before the Present-tense 3rd-Singular suffix *-s*), and Nomiverbs like *hammer* (which can occur in both these contexts). In fact, one might say that 'Nomiverb' is the superordinate class, of which Nouns and Verbs are more restricted subclasses which do not occur in all the contexts where unrestricted Nomiverbs occur. This would be a weird way of looking at English heterosemous root sets, but why is it weird? It seems that the main reason is that in a comparative perspective, a concept like 'nomiverb' makes no sense, because comparison always involves nouns, verbs, and adjectives as defined in (26). And even though we want to be faithful to the language-particular peculiarities, in the end we usually assimilate our ways of describing languages to general patterns after all.

In fact, the existence of a Nomiverb class in English has been argued for by Farrell (2001), who claims that words like those in (27) 'are not inherently associated with the syntactic categories "noun" or "verb". Rather, they are associated with meanings that can manifest as either of these categories, by virtue of being compatible with different contextually imposed profiling scenarios' (2001: 128). Clearly, Farrell is more optimistic about the semantic regularity of the relationships than most other linguists. But whatever the merits of such analyses in terms of a Janus-like third class (or even in terms of a superordinate class of which the others are subclasses), they can hardly be the basis of cross-linguistic comparison. For cross-linguistic comparison, we need semantically defined notions, or notions defined in terms of universal construction types (predication, reference, modification).

2.7 MARKERS OF SEMANTIC SUBSTANCE DIFFERENTIATING BETWEEN THE ROOT CLASSES

Many experienced readers will have wondered why my discussion of grammatical marking of nouns, verbs, and adjectives has been limited to function indicators so far (i.e. termifiers, attributivizers, and copulas; recall Table 2.1). To be sure, differences between these three root types have often been motivated by the kinds of behaviours in predicative, modifying, and referring function that we saw above, but of course the literature is much richer.

For example, Dixon (2004: 16) notes that in Cherokee, verbs take tense suffixes but adjectives do not; in Kamaiurá, adjectives have clitic person indexes, while verbs have person prefixes (in some of the moods); and in Korean, adjectives and verbs have different markers for the indicative mood. Similarly, Chung (2012) reports that in Chamorro, verbs but not adjectives allow 'specific external arguments' (see the overview in Haspelmath 2012b: 94). And we can give a straightforward example from English: in predicative position, nouns and verbs take the same copula, but they do not behave in a completely identical way; we can say *Our dog is a labrador* (using the indefinite article on the noun), but not **Our dog is a big* (see (2a)).

So, in addition to function indicators (copulas, termifiers, attributivizers), words may also fall into different classes because they have different substantive markers, i.e. markers such as those in (31).

(31) substantive markers
 on nouns: articles, plural markers, case markers, possessive indexes, etc.
 on adjectives: comparative markers, degree adverbs, etc.
 on verbs: tense–aspect–mood markers, argument indexes, voice markers, etc.

In many circumstances, these kinds of markers are much more salient for distinguishing nouns, verbs, and adjectives than the function indicators that I focused on in sections 2.1–2.2. For language-particular classification, they are often more immediately relevant than the function indicators. In many languages, nouns are typically accompanied by articles (while verbs and adjectives never are), verbs are obligatorily marked for tense (while nouns never are), and so on.

For example, the English Noun class (excluding the Proper Noun class) can be defined quite easily: a Noun in English is a word that can be preceded by the definite article *the*. This is quite typical, and the literature on word classes is full of such statements. Croft (1991) has a special term for the non-function-indicator markers that can be associated with a class: 'behavioural potential'. Following Ye (2021), I call them *substantive markers* (because they contribute semantic substance, and do not merely point to an atypical propositional act function).

So why did I leave these very important markers aside so far, relegating them to the second-last section? The reason is that they vary too much across languages to be usable for worldwide cross-linguistic comparison. Many languages have articles and plural markers on nouns, but there are also many languages that lack them. Most languages lack comparative marking on adjectives, and verbal marking is very variable, too. Tense marking is quite characteristic of verbs, but there are quite a few languages that only use aspect marking (e.g. Mandarin Chinese), and a few languages do not seem to have tense or aspect marking at all. Thus, we cannot identify word classes across languages in terms of substantive markers, and the same goes for other syntactic properties such as the possibility of 'specific external arguments' in Chamorro.

This issue does not arise for the function indicators, as we saw in section 2.1, and for this reason, they have a privileged role: all languages have predication, modification, and reference, so we can examine how they treat the various semantic root classes in these propositional act functions. As we saw in section 2.2, the classification of words is similar to the classification of argument-marking patterns. Here, too, we have seen a long discussion of universality of syntactic roles like 'subject', and many different criteria have been cited (e.g. occurrence in control constructions, behaviour as reflexive-pronoun antecedents, behaviour in quantifier float constructions). But most of these criteria are not universal, so a general notion of 'subject' must be based on argument marking: The occurrence of flags (ergative or accusative case markers) or of argument indexes, which define A, S, and P, thus allowing us to equate 'subject' with A/S (Haspelmath 2011).

There is thus a solution to the perennial problem of word classes, just as there is a solution to the perennial problem of the subject and other syntactic functions. But the solution implies a deviation from traditional practice, in that we need to focus our attention on the most basic phenomena: only function indicators in the case of word classes, only argument markers (flags and indexes) in the case of syntactic roles. This is not very interesting from a language-particular perspective, but, as we saw in sections 2.3–2.5, we must keep language-particular analyses separate from general comparative linguistics.

2.8 Conclusion

In this chapter, I have drawn some seemingly radical, but unavoidable consequences from an old insight: that different languages have different grammars which are made up of different building blocks. It is obvious to the naked eye that different languages have different words, but once we consider grammatical constructions, one needs a closer look to see that languages also differ in their constructions (maybe less so than in their words, but still quite significantly).

Since we distinguish grammatical classes in a language based on its grammatical constructions, different languages also have different classes, and it is not immediately clear how they can be compared. For example, how should the class of Gendered Tenseless words in Godoberi (section 2.3) be compared with some class of words in Persian, a genderless language, or some class of words in Mandarin, a tenseless language?

The solution to this problem is to base our comparisons not on language-particular constructions or classes (i.e. on language structures), but on comparable forms, with their meanings and shapes (i.e. on conceptual and phonetic substance). As seen in section 2.1, we can formulate universals based on cross-linguistic comparison in terms of object roots (or 'nouns', section 2.5), action roots (or 'verbs'), and property roots (or 'adjectives'). These are defined in terms of universally available concepts, and a root is simply defined as a minimal form (a segment sequence not consisting of other forms, Haspelmath (2020)). In addition, we need the comparative concept of *function indicator* (a cover term for termifiers, attributivizers, and copulas), which is defined as a marker (= a bound form that is not a root) which signals the propositional act function (i.e. predication, modification, reference) of its host. These core comparative concepts are independent of language-particular constructions and allow us to formulate universals (as in section 2.1) and to identify some macro-types in terms of coexpression patterns of function indicators.

There is a long tradition in comparative grammar of identifying some languages as being 'flexible' in their word classes and others as more 'differentiated', but, as we saw in section 2.2, it is quite difficult to make general statements across the three propositional act functions. Clearly, most (or all?) languages are not fully differentiating, but we do not know whether there are implicational links among coexpression patterns of different propositional act functions. Languages that completely lack any function indicators and that are thus fully acategorial do not seem to exist.

Much past work on word classes across languages has not singled out function indicators as I have done in this chapter (following Croft 1991; 2000), but has attempted to take all kinds of properties of different word classes into account. This approach does not work, because it is only function indicators that are comparable across languages (section 2.7). There seem to be some tendencies in some kinds of substantive markers (in particular, tense markers tend to be restricted to action words and similar words), but these do not lend themselves so easily to cross-linguistic generalizations.

Finally, I should note that not all linguists agree with Sapir and others that different languages have different classes (section 2.3). Instead, these linguists think that by examining languages more closely, we will eventually find that they can be described in terms of a universal set of innate building blocks (e.g. Baker 2003; Chung 2012; Davis et al. 2014; Panagiotidis 2014).[26] However, there is nothing close to a consensus on what this set of innate building blocks might be, so, in practice, this approach is difficult to apply to a larger set of languages. Simply hypothesizing that all languages have the categories noun, verb, and adjective because these are part of an innate grammar blueprint ('universal grammar'), as is done by Chung (2012) and others, will not give reliable results as long as we do not know much about what is innate, and it is prone to yielding results that are coloured by expectations based on European languages (Haspelmath 2012b).

---

[26] Gil's (2000) proposal is similar to these generative authors in positing a universal set of building blocks, but with no reference to the usual categories of noun, verb, adjective. Instead, Gil makes reference to simple combinatorial properties that could be applied to a larger set of languages. This is an interesting alternative that is worth considering.

CHAPTER 3

LEVELS OF ANALYSIS AND WORD CLASSES (ROOT, STEM, WORD)

WALTER BISANG

3.1 SETTING THE STAGE: BASIC NOTIONS, CRITERIA, AND CONTENT OF THE CHAPTER

DEFINITIONS of word class, parts of speech, or lexical categories[1] often combine criteria from the domains of meaning and form. Thus, lexical items are divided into different categories on the basis of their semantic denotations to objects, actions, and properties, and their formal distribution in constructions expressing reference, predication, and modification.[2] In a simple English sentence like (1), object-denoting linguistic items like *cats* and *salmon* can only occur in a syntactic position provided by a referential construction as it is associated with nouns, while action-denoting items like *enjoy* take the head position of a predication construction as it is associated with verbs:

(1) *Cats enjoy salmon.*

The combination of meaning and form is crucial for empirical testing, i.e. for providing discovery procedures for word-class identification (Bisang 2011: 282; Baker & Croft 2017: 194) and it is even more important for a chapter which deals with word class from the perspective of word-internal structure with its morphological units of roots, stems, and words (Haig 2006; Lehmann 2008, 2013).[3] The definition of these units adopted in

---

[1] Notice that this chapter does not make any terminological difference between word class, parts of speech, or lexical categories.
[2] This view is by now widely accepted as a kind of compromise across different theories for defining word classes (Baker & Croft 2017) and will be adopted in this chapter. For some of its shortcomings in the context of word-internal structure, see section 3.7.1.
[3] It is for that reason that approaches based mainly on meaning like Langacker's (1987a) semantic view and Hopper & Thompson's (1984) discourse-based view will not be discussed in this chapter.

this chapter is based on classical distributional criteria as they are found in textbooks (Hockett 1958; Katamba 1993: 41–54; Haspelmath & Sims 2010: 21; O'Grady & Guzman 2011). In this context, roots are defined as the smallest unanalysable lexical portion of a word, i.e. they are morphological bases 'which cannot be analyzed any further into constituent morphemes' (Haspelmath & Sims 2010: 21). Thus, *assert* in *assert-ion-s* is a root, while *assert-ion-* is not because it has its internal morphological complexity. Roots are not always readily available for a given syntactic position associated with lexical categories nor are they readily compatible with any type of inflectional marker (e.g. tense, person for verbs vs number, case for nouns). The combination of a root with various types of additional marking in that sense is called a stem, the relevant morphemes serve the purpose of stem formation. Thus, the function of *-ion* in *assert-ion* exactly consists in making the root compatible with nominal morphology and syntax. Similarly, an impressive number of Latin roots need a specific thematic vowel or some additional morphology before being used as nouns or verbs. Thus, the root *am-* 'love' needs suffixation of the thematic vowel (TV) -ā- before being able to function as a verb (*am-ā-b-ō* [love-TV-FUT-1.SG] 'I will love'), while it gets the suffix *-or/ōr* in the function of a noun (*am-ōr-is* [love-SUFF-GEN.SG] 'of love') (on Latin, see section 3.4.3). Suffixes like *-ion* in English are generally called 'derivational morphemes', while it is less clear in the literature what to call thematic vowels in Latin. For this chapter, both types are seen as derivational (see Haig 2006: 44; Lehmann 2008). In fact, there will be a third type of pattern-related derivation introduced in section 3.4.3 on Arabic. Finally, stems can be further extended into words by the addition of inflectional markers. With these definitions, the three levels of root, stem, and word can be schematized as follows:

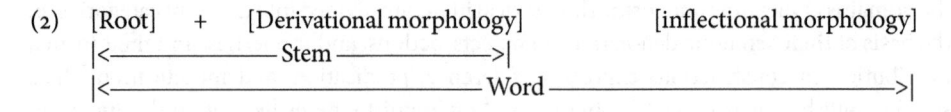

(2) [Root]   +   [Derivational morphology]   [inflectional morphology]
     |<——————————— Stem ———————————>|
     |<———————————————————— Word ————————————————————>|

The word structure given in (2) is a maximal structure. Depending on the language or certain subsystems within it, roots alone can be words (see *salmon* in (1)) or roots can be identical with stems if they are directly attached to inflectional markers (see *cat-s* in (1)).

Even though word class plays an important role in textbook definitions of derivational morphology,[4] typological studies which systematically integrate the three levels of root, stem, and word are extremely rare. There are only Haig (2006) and Lehmann (2008, 2013). While these two authors explicitly focus on a small number of languages which only cover part of the linguistic variation as discussed in the literature (section 3.2), it is the aim of this chapter to analyse a typologically wider spectrum of languages (i) for defining a set of types of morphology-based word-class systems and for using these types, (ii) to check the validity of certain basic assumptions in morphology, and (iii) to point out problems for current models of word-class systems. For that reason, some of the languages selected for this chapter are known for their typologically challenging word-class systems in the literature. The languages

---

[4] See O'Grady & de Guzman (2011: 122) as an example in which change of word class/lexical category is one of the two criteria for defining derivation: 'Derivation is an affixational process that forms a word with a meaning and/or category distinct from that of its base'.

belonging to this category are Classical Nahuatl, Tagalog, Classical Chinese, Tongan, and, as it will turn out, Turkish. Other languages are Latin, Arabic, Khmer, Northern Iroquoian, Yorùbá, Mande, and English.

The morphology-based typology starts out from the question of how flexible or rigid a linguistic item is at the three levels, whereby flexibility means that that item with its marking properties can be assigned to more than a single word class, while rigid means strict limitation to a single word class (Van Lier & Rijkhoff 2013: 1). Thus, the root *enjoy* in (1) is already rigidly determined as a verb. Similarly, the derived stem *enjoy-ment* can only be a noun. In contrast, linguistic items like *work* or *fish* are flexible because they can be verbs or nouns. The different types of morphological word-class systems are defined on the basis of three criteria: (i) what are the different combinations of flexibility and rigidity at the levels of root, stem, and word? (ii) Does a language use a probabilistic calculus for assigning roots to word class [±probabilistic]? (iii) Does a language only have a single word class [±single word class]? (See section 3.2 for details.)

The second aim of checking the validity of certain basic assumptions on morphology is concerned with input–output-oriented hypotheses like Word Formation Rules (WFR) (Aronoff 1976) and Lexeme Formation Rules (LFR) (Aronoff 1994). Even though their status turns out to be problematic in Haig's (2006) and Lehmann's (2008, 2013) research, both authors adopt the input–output model for their generalizations that roots tend to be more flexible than stems and that words tend to be even more rigidly determined than stems for word class.

Finally, the following three models are assessed in terms of aim (iii):

- Hengeveld's (1992b, 2013) model of Functional Discourse Grammar
- Croft's (1991, 2000, 2001) model of Radical Construction Grammar
- Distributed Morphology (DM) as developed by Halle & Marantz (1993, 1994) and Marantz (1997)

On the structure of the chapter: section 3.2 presents eight types of morphological word-class systems based on a critical presentation of Word/LFR and an assessment of Haig's (2006) and Lehmann's (2008, 2013) generalizations based on a broader typological range of languages. Since it is important to provide at least some data from individual languages, the description of the eight types is distributed over four sections from sections 3.3 to 3.6 (for more details, see the end of section 3.2). Finally, section 3.7 discusses some challenges for the above models of word-class systems.

3.2 Flexibility in Roots, Stems, and Words: Haig, Lehmann, and beyond

Haig (2006) and Lehmann (2008, 2013) are both interested in generalizations concerning the morphological level at which words lose their word-class flexibility. A good starting point for introducing both approaches are sequences of morphological derivation in which each morpheme produces a change of word class as in the following example from English:

(3) a. $brain_N > brain\text{-}less_A > brain\text{-}less\text{-}ness_N$
     b. $false_A > fals\text{-}ify_V > fals\text{-}ifi\text{-}able_A > fals\text{-}ifi\text{-}abil\text{-}ity_N$
     c. $operate_V > operat\text{-}ion_N > operat\text{-}ion\text{-}al_A > operat\text{-}ion\text{-}al\text{-}ize_V > operat\text{-}ion\text{-}al\text{-}iz\text{-}ation_N$

Such derivational sequences are not uncommon cross-linguistically (see Turkish, section 3.5.3). Looking at them, one may be tempted into the general assumption that the morphological base always belongs to a single word class and that the derived output form likewise belongs to a different but single word class. In fact, such examples fit nicely with two of Aronoff's (1976, 1994) input–output-related generalizations (WFR in 1976 and LFR in 1994),[5] which are extensively discussed in Haig (2006). The Unitary Base Hypothesis (UBH) states that the input exclusively belongs to a single word class, or, as Aronoff (1976: 48) puts it, '[w]e will assume that the syntactosemantic specification of the base, though it may be more or less complex, is always unique. A WFR will never operate on either this or that.' Analogously, the Principle of Unitary Output (PUO) claims that the output of an LFR uniquely belongs to a single major word class (Aronoff 1976: 49–51).

The problem with these generalizations is that they may be too rigid and that their cross-linguistic validity is questionable even on the basis of the small number of five languages analysed by Haig (2006), who discusses Turkish as an agglutinative language and German, English, Italian, and Latin[6] as fusional/inflectional languages. In spite of this, he takes up the input–output perspective as a fruitful basis for his own typological generalizations. Adopting the model of LFR, he distinguishes the following levels of grammatical structure, starting with radical elements, which I call 'roots' in this chapter for the sake of terminological coherence:

(4) Levels of grammatical structure (Haig 2006: 45):
     roots > input LFR > output LFR > inflection (> syntax)

Based on his detailed analysis, Haig (2006) proposes the following hierarchy with its decreasing flexibility from the root to the higher levels of morphology:

(5) Principle of Successively Increasing Categorization (Haig 2006: 46)
     The extent to which different levels of linguistic structure impose categorial distinctions increases monotonically as we move to the right of the hierarchy in (4).[7]

As Haig (2006: 47) points out, this principle is not new. It follows naturally from Aronoff's (1976) WFR, later LFR (Aronoff 1994). Even under the assumption that the root-level input may be flexible, its outcome at the next higher level must be categorially specified.

Interestingly enough, Lehmann's (2008) empirical study comes up with a similar conclusion. His paper is based on the morphological analysis of samples of words from the semantic field of experience (bodily sensation, emotion, volition, cognition, perception) in six

---

[5] The arguments for this change in terminology are given in Aronoff (1994: 14–15).
[6] Haig (2006) also briefly discusses Tongan as a language which is flexible at all levels (section 3.4.2).
[7] The numeration of the hierarchy is adapted for this chapter.

languages (English, German, Latin, Spanish, Yucatec Maya, Mandarin Chinese). As one can see from comparing the values of categorial flexibility of roots and stems (Table 3.1; higher values reflect lower flexibility), stems are always less flexible than roots.[8]

Table 3.1 Root and stem categoriality (Lehmann 2008: 558–559)

	Root	Stem	Difference
Latin	0.30	0.99	0.69
Spanish	0.59	0.98	0.29
Mandarin	0.60	0.84	0.24
Yucatec	0.76	0.96	0.20
English	0.62	0.77	0.15
German	0.78	0.86	0.08
average	0.61	0.90	0.28

In addition to the observation of increasing word-class determination from root to stem, Lehmann (2008, 2013) addresses the nature of the criteria which determine word class at the lowest level of primary categorization (root) and at the highest level of final categorization (syntax). While the final categorization of a linguistic sign is determined by syntactic function alone, primary categorization must be more flexible 'because a lexical concept must be available for different syntactic functions so that the primary categorization cannot foresee the ultimate use that a sign will be put to' (Lehmann 2008: 550). Given that only the conceptual meaning is available at the root level, the assignment of roots to a specific category can only be based on universal cognitive principles and a 'probability calculus', which tends to interpret it as a referring item if it has high time-stability and as a predicational item if it has low time-stability. In terms of syntax, this means that the probability calculus predicts that a time-stable root concept tends to be a noun, while a concept with low time-stability tends to be a verb. This begs the question of when a lexical concept acquires its specification for a lexical category. Some languages anticipate word class already at the root level, others at a later level. Determining word class at a low level may have its advantages in clarifying the overall syntactic function of a linguistic sign as early as possible but it also comes with the disadvantage 'that much of the lower level categorization may not be what is wanted at higher levels and therefore has to be undone by recategorization operations' (Lehmann 2013: 148). A good example is Turkish with its rigid word-class distinction at the root level and rich derivational morphology with extensive options for recategorization at higher levels (section 3.5.3).

If one applies the method of comparing input–output flexibilities in terms of Haig (2006) and Lehmann (2008, 2013) on a wider range of languages, one can see that their generalizations on the reduction of word-class flexibility from root to stem is only partly borne out. In fact, there are word-class systems consisting only of a single word class which

---

[8] For the methodological details of his calculations, see Lehmann (2008: 556).

clearly outrange that hierarchy. What is characteristic of these languages is that there is no distinction between the predication of action-denoting lexemes and the predication of object-denoting lexemes (sections 3.3 and 3.7.1). This conflation produces two types of languages, omnipredicative languages (type I) like Classical Nahuatl in which all lexical items are treated like verbal predicates (Launey 1994) and nominalistic languages (type II) like Tagalog in which all lexical items behave like nouns in an equational construction (Himmelmann 2008, 2009; Kaufman 2009, 2018). Another type fits with Lehmann's (2008, 2013) observation that roots in languages with little derivational morphology may be directly assigned to the syntactic positions of N and V by a probabilistic calculus. As will be discussed in section 3.4.1, Classical Chinese comes close to this probability-based type (type III). Given the absence of extensive derivational morphology, it is hard to integrate this type into a hierarchy of increasing rigidity from root to word. The other languages of this chapter (types IV–VIII) can be classified according to the level at which their roots, stems, or words are flexible or rigid. Based on the criteria of [±single word class], [±probabilistic] assignment and [flexibility/rigidity at the root, stem, or word level], the above eight types can be represented as in Figure 3.1 (flex = flexible, rig = rigid).

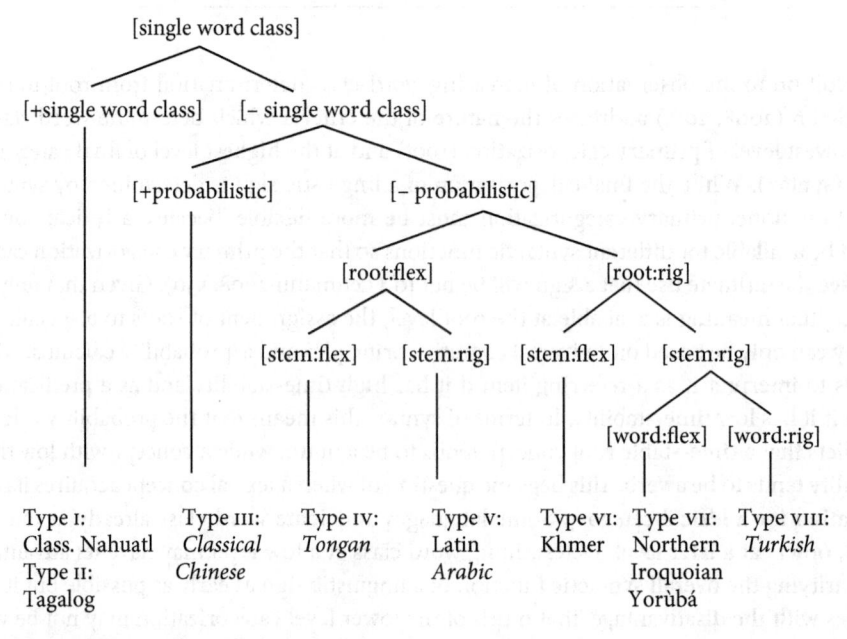

FIGURE 3.1 Types of word-class systems

Remarkably enough, only morphological systems of type VIII fully conform to the UBH and the Unitary Output Hypothesis (Aronoff 1976, 1994). The other types listed below violate one or both LFRs if one does not assume zero-operators for V and N (see sections 3.7.2 and 3.7.3 on problems with this approach in DM):

- UBH: V (root:flex)
- Unitary Output Principle: VI (root:rig/stem:flex), VII (root & stem rigid/word:flex)
- Both: III (probabilistic assignment), IV (root:flex/stem:flex)

The definition of flexibility adopted in this chapter is largely concerned with word-class systems, not with the classification of individual languages even though some types can be highly dominant in individual languages. Thus, the chapter is only partly concerned with statistical criteria in terms of the proportion of vocabulary that belongs to a given type in a language nor does it address the criterion of semantic regularities between input and output. As Croft (2001: 70, 72) rightly points out, these criteria are important for those linguists who try to claim that an individual language belongs to a single type, since neglecting them may lead to 'methodological opportunism' by focusing just on a few examples which happen to confirm that claim. Evans & Osada (2005) advocate even more methodological rigour by proposing the Exhaustiveness Criterion and the Compositionality Criterion. While the former states that flexibility needs to hold for all the relevant words of the lexicon of a language, the latter requires that the semantic differences of a given lexeme in different syntactic positions (e.g. argument or predicate) must be fully attributed to the functions of these positions.

The criteria of Evans & Osada's (2005) clearly have their relevance for classifying entire languages even though they are most likely too rigorous because one would expect a certain percentage of exceptions and cases of lexicalization if individual languages are supposed to be the result of an evolutionary process with a large number of different interacting factors. In the typology suggested in Figure 3.1, both criteria matter for type III in the sense that the rules for predicting the meaning of a given lexical item must be applicable in principle to all lexical items[9] even though processes of lexicalization cannot be excluded. In contrast, these criteria are clearly irrelevant for types IV to VIII if they are seen as systems without any presuppositions concerning exhaustiveness in the lexicon or in semantic regularities. Finally, types I and II differ from all other types because exhaustiveness is intrinsic to them, i.e. lexemes cannot but belong to a single word class in a language of these types. If the Exhaustiveness Criterion applies here, it does so in a different way by referring to the inventory of constructions. It must be shown that the same predication construction is used with all action-denoting and object-denoting lexemes.

Looking at those types for which exhaustiveness is not intrinsic to the system, one can see that several of them are at least almost exhaustive in some languages (see those in italics in Figure 3.1). This applies to Classical Chinese (III), Tongan (IV), Arabic (V) and Turkish (VIII). A closer look at these systems shows that all of them follow the generalizations of Haig (2006) and Lehmann (2008, 2013) in the sense that the higher morphological level is more or equally rigid/flexible than the lower level. The types which are not attested as the only word-class systems of a language (as far as the existing literature goes) are those in which the higher morphological level is more flexible than its lower level, i.e. type VI (root:rig/stem:flex) and type VII (stem:rig/word:flex). Thus, the generalization root > stem > word still seems to hold in a statistical sense if one compares systems which have the potential to be (almost) exhaustive in a language and those that cannot.

Even though this chapter focuses on languages which are notoriously characterized in the literature as belonging (almost) exhaustively to a single type which is assumed to be a

---

[9] As discussed in Chapter 28 on Classical Chinese in this volume, there are rules for predicting the meaning of a given lexical item in an argument-structure construction, depending on semantic classes like, humans, tools, etc.

typological challenge, this does not exclude combinations of different types within a language. Some Mande languages and English will be presented in this chapter. Overall, the different types and languages are presented as follows:

Section 3.3: Single word class type (I: Classical Nahuatl; II: Tagalog)
Section 3.4: Flexible root: III (Classical Chinese), IV (Tongan), V (Latin, Arabic)
Section 3.5: Rigid root: VI (Khmer), VII (Northern Iroquoian, Yorùbá, VIII (Turkish)
Section 3.6: Combinations of types (Mande, English)

3.3 SINGLE WORD CLASS TYPES (I, II)

3.3.1 Type I: Omnipredicativity in Classical Nahuatl

Classical Nahuatl (Uto-Aztecan) was spoken in Mexico and its periphery at the time of the Spanish Conquest (16th century). It is analysed as an omnipredicative language by Launey (1994). An important basis for his analysis is the observation that action-denoting lexemes and object-denoting lexemes take the same agreement morphology as given in Table 3.2.

Table 3.2 Person agreement markers on action-denoting lexemes and on object-denoting lexemes (adapted from Launey 1994: 10–11)

	Action-denoting lexemes			Object-denoting lexemes	
	S/A	U	Reflexive	S	Possessive
1.SG	n(i)-	-nēch-	-n(o)-	n(i)-	-n(o)-
2.SG	t(i)/x(i)-	-mitz-	-m(o)-	t(i)-	-m(o)-
3.SG	ø-	-c-/-qu(i)-	-m(o)-	ø-	ī
1.PL	t(i)-	-tēch-	-t(o)-	t(i)-	-t(o)-
2.PL	aM-/x(i)-	-amēch-	-m(o)-	aM-	-am(o)-
3.PL	ø-	-quiM-	-m(o)-	ø-	īm

Thus, a sentence like the one in (6) with its translation of 'The child is crying' can be analysed as consisting of two predicates with the ø-marker for 3rd person of intransitive constructions (S), i.e. [s/he is crying] and [it is the child]:

(6) Classical Nahuatl (Launey 1994: 42)
ø-chōca   in   ø-piltōntli
3-cry   LNK   3-child
'The child is crying.'

Analogously, the semantic content of 'The child eats the meat' is constructed with the three predicates [s/he eats it], [it's the child], and [it's the meat]:

(7) Launey (1994: 37)
ø-qui-cua   in   piltōntli   in   nacatl.
3.SG:A-3.SG:U-eat LNK   child   LNK   meat
'The child eats the meat.'

Given that the agreement forms of the 3rd person are generally zero, the predicative status of both object-denoting and action-denoting lexemes can only be seen in the context of the whole inflectional paradigm in Table 3.2. Example (8) shows how the omnipredicative analysis works with overt marking of the 1st and 2nd person in the two predicates of [I implore you] and [you are high priests]:

(8) Classical Nahuatl (Launey 1994: 72)
N-*amēch*-tzàtzilia   in   an-tlamacaz-quê.
1.SG:A-2.PL:U-implore   LNK   2.PL:S-high.priest:PL
'I implore you—who are high priests!'

The second important element for understanding Launey's (1994) omnipredicative analysis is the linker (LNK) *in*. With its functions of a demonstrative and a relative-clause marker it serves as a pivot for linking two predicates. It is the argument of one predicate in its demonstrative function and it simultaneously marks the subsequent predicate as a headless relative clause. In example (6), it is the demonstrative of the first predicate in *ø-chōca in* [3-cry LNK] 'that one is crying' and it introduces the headless relative clause *in ø-piltōntli* [LNK 3-child] 'the one who is the child'. With this analysis, the structure of (6) can approximately be analysed in terms of the following translation: 'That one cries, the one who is the child'.

Additional evidence of the omnipredicative character of Classical Nahuatl comes from two observations. The first one is that object-denoting lexemes cannot be used independently for calling somebody. They need extra vocative marking for expressing that non-predicative use. The second one is free word order. The positions of the individual predications of object-denoting (S and O) and action-denoting (V) lexemes are governed purely by information structure. Even though VSO and SVO are the most frequent word orders (Launey 1994: 41), all the other word-order patterns with their corresponding information structures are attested as well.

Even though every content-denoting lexeme functions as a predicate in Classical Nahuatl, there are word-class distinctions at the level of morphology, which clearly separate action-denoting lexemes (including property-denoting lexemes) from object-denoting lexemes. One of them can be seen from the morphological paradigm in Table 3.2. While object-denoting lexemes can only have one argument which corresponds to the agreement set of S/A with action denoting lexemes, the subgroup of transitive action-denoting lexemes can take an additional set for marking undergoer agreement. Moreover, object-denoting lexemes can take a set of possessor markers which is inaccessible to action-denoting lexemes.

Some bound morphemes are exclusively used with action- and property-denoting lexemes, among them the following tense-aspect markers (Launey 1994: 28):

(9)   a. Future marker *-z*:   *chōca-z* 'S/he will cry'
        b. Perfective marker *-c*:   *chōca-c* 'S/he cried'
        c. Completed-action marker *ō*:   *ō chōca* 'S/he has cried'
        d. Imperfective marker *-ya*:   *chōca-ya* 'S/he was crying'
        e. Irrealis marker *-zquiya*:   *chōca-zquiya* 'S/he was about to cry' /
                                                     'S/he almost cried'

Another set of morphological markers only occurs with object-denoting lexemes. The suffix *-tl/-tli* [-ʎ/-ʎi] is the most prominent marker of this type. It occurs exclusively with object-denoting lexemes referring to humans, animals, plants, natural objects, artefacts, abstracts, and processes (Launey 1994: 207–208). There are also some derivational affixes for changing the action-related meaning of a lexeme into an object-related meaning. The most productive form is *tla-* ... *-l-li* as in *tla-cua-l-li* 'food, nourishment' (*-cua-* 'eat') or *tla-chīhua-l-li* 'created object, creature' (from chI@hua 'create') (Launey 1994: 266).

3.3.2 Type II: The nominalistic type and Tagalog

Describing word classes in Tagalog is a challenge since Humboldt (1838). The present chapter takes up the analysis of Tagalog as a language with exclusively nominal roots and exclusively nominal syntax in terms of copular or equational constructions (Himmelmann 2008, 2009; Kaufman 2009, 2018; Bisang 2013: 299–302; see also Chapter 35 in this volume).

The basis for this analysis is the symmetric voice system as a characteristic of Philippine-type Austronesian languages. It is illustrated by example (10) with the root *bili* 'price bought for, buy'. A simple clause in Tagalog starts with the predicate, followed by arguments and adjuncts[10] introduced by elements like *ang*, a determiner expressing specificity (Himmelmann 1997), the genitive marker *ng* (pronounced [naŋ], for further explanations see below) and various prepositions like *sa* for locatives. The elements in the predicate function of (10) carry information on voice, combined with information on aspect and mood. In (10a), the infix <*um*> is expressing actor voice (AV), indicating that the element marked by *ang* has the semantic role of actor. Analogously, the undergoer voice (UV) of the predicate in (10b) indicates that the element in the *ang* phrase is an undergoer, while the locative voice suffix *-han* (LV) in (10c) marks the locative role of the *ang* phrase. The genitive marker *ng* marks actors, undergoers, and certain types of instrumentals whose semantic role is not marked by the voice system.

(10)   Tagalog (Foley & Van Valin 1984: 135)
       a.   B<*um*>ili   ang   lalaki   ng   isda   sa   tindahan.
           PFV:/AV/-buy   SPEC   man   GEN   fish   LOC   store
           'The man bought fish at the store.'

---

[10] On the problem of distinguishing arguments and adjuncts in Tagalog, see Foley & Van Valin (1984), Bisang (2006).

b. B<in>ili-ø   ng   lalaki   ang   isda   sa   tindahan.
/PFV/-buy-UV GEN   man   SPEC   fish   LOC   store
'The man bought *the fish* at the store.'

c. B<in>il-han ng   lalaki   ng   isda   ang   tindahan.
/PFV/-buy-LV GEN   man   GEN   fish   SPEC   store
'The man bought fish *at the store*.'

What is crucial for the analysis of Tagalog clauses is that each content word can either occur in the predicate position or in one of the positions introduced by a function word like *ang*, *ng*, or *sa*, irrespective of whether it carries voice/aspect/mood marking or not. If one puts *lalaki* 'man' of (10a) into the predicate position and the voice-marked form *bumili* into the *ang* phrase, one gets *lalaki ang bumili* 'the one who bought [it] is a man'. It is even possible to find voice-marked forms in the predicate function *and* in the *ang* phrase (Himmelmann 2008: 266). In contrast, voice/aspect/mood marking has clear derivational properties, i.e. 'all voice-marked words in Tagalog, regardless of their base, are members of a single morpho-lexical class and ... this morpho-lexical class is different from all other morpho-lexical classes' (Himmelmann 2008: 285).[11] If a voice marker is added to an object-denoting root, it converts that root into an action word with its specific role orientation. A good example is the root *anak* 'child' with the prefix *i-* denoting that an action is oriented towards a displaced theme in the *ang* phrase. Thus, the derived form *i-anak* has the meaning of 'to give birth to' (Himmelmann 2008: 285). Action-denoting roots without voice marking can have the following three different nominal functions, which partly overlap with individual roots: (i) a 'state which ensues from the successful performance of the action', (ii) 'the result or the typical or cognate object of the action' or (iii) 'the name of the action' (action nominalization) (Himmelmann 2008: 275). If these roots are taking voice morphology, they clearly change their meaning from one of these meanings into an 'actor- or undergoer-oriented action expression' (Himmelmann 2008: 287). This discussion shows that voice marking has clear derivational properties which are further indicated by various root-specific idiosyncrasies of the formal realization of these markers. In spite of all this, what is particularly remarkable is that the products of this derivation can still occur in the predicate position as well as in the *ang* position.

For understanding the hypothesis of the equational structure of Tagalog basic clauses, it is necessary to look at nominal possession as it is expressed by the genitive marker *ng*:

(11)   Tagalog (Himmelmann 2008: 256)
       ang   hari   ng   lamok
       SPEC   king   GEN   mosquito
       'the king of the mosquitos'

If the genitive function of *ng* is transferred to the clauses in (10), the element in the *ng* phrase can be analysed as a modifier of the voice-marked nominal predicate in the sense of 'the buyer of fish' in (10a). Similarly, the PPs introduced by *sa* 'locative' can be interpreted as modifiers of that nominal predicate. What remains is the *ang* phrase, which can be analysed as the

---

[11] The derivational property of voice marking was already pointed out by Bloomfield (1917: 213–215).

subject[12] of an equational clause. Thus, the sentence in (10a) can be roughly analysed as nominal in the sense of the following literal translation: 'the buyer of fish at the shop is the man'.

Of course, the above informal analysis needs further specification. Following Kaufman's (2018) analysis, the constructions in (10) represent a particular type of pseudo-cleft which was first mentioned by Ball (1977) under the heading of TH-cleft. In this type, the relative clause modifies a semantically bleached noun phrase (*the one, the thing*) as in *The one/thing I like is CHAMPAGNE* or, in its inverse form, *CHAMPAGNE is the one/thing I like* (Kaufman 2018: 218). The constructions in (10) basically correspond to this type of cleft, with the difference that they are monoclausal copular or equational clauses with a null copula (Kaufman 2018: 222–223).

3.4 Flexible root types (III–V)

3.4.1 Type III: Classical Chinese and the probabilistic assignment of roots

Classical Chinese as it was written between the fifth and the third century BC is analysed as a precategorial language by various researchers (among them Bisang 2008a, 2008b; Zádrapa 2011; Sun 2020; see also Chapter 28 in this volume). In the following example, we find the lexeme *měi* in its nominal function with the meaning of 'beauty' (12a) and in the verb position of the transitive argument structure construction with the meaning of 'making/considering somebody as beautiful' (12b) (example (2a) in Chapter 28):

(12) Classical Chinese:
    a. Lunyu (6.14)
       宋朝之美
       Sòng Zhāo   zhī   měi
       Song Zhao   POSS   beauty
       'the beauty of Song Zhao'

    b. Zuozhuan, Xiang 25
       見棠姜而美之。
       jiàn   Táng Jiāng   ér   měi   zhī
       see   Tang Jiang   and   beautiful   3.OBJ
       'He saw Tang Jiang and thought her to be beautiful.'

The assignment of *měi* to the word class of noun in (12a) is due to its head in a noun phrase with the possessor and the possessive marker *zhī* preceding it. Analogously, its verbal function in (12b) can be derived from its position in V followed by an object expressed by the object pronoun of the 3rd person.

If one looks more closely at these lexemes, they basically turn out to be roots. As was pointed out by Zádrapa (2011: 96–97), derivational morphology as we find it in example

---

[12] On the subject functions of the *ang* phrase, see Kroeger's (1993) classical analysis and Kaufman's (2017) analysis in terms of nominative or absolutive.

(3) from English (*falsifiability, operationalization*, etc.) is poorly developed in Classical Chinese. Thus, there is simply no equivalent form for abstract nouns corresponding to English *beauty* (12a), or to its French original of *beauté* 'beauty' > *beau* 'beautiful', or to German *Schön-heit* [beautiful-NMLZ] 'beauty', etc. Even though some derivational morphology can be reconstructed for individual roots in Classical Chinese (Chapter 28 in this volume), the majority of its roots remain underived. These are indicators that lexemes generally are identical to roots. Moreover, there is no evidence for the presence of inflectional morphology in Classical Chinese but there are numerous syntactic markers for the expression of inflectional categories which can be used for checking the behavioural potential of roots if they are present (see Croft 2001: §7.1). Since the use of these markers is by no means obligatory, the lexical category of a root in a clause often is only determined by its syntactic position in V or N, depending on the meaning of the roots/words involved.

With these properties, Classical Chinese comes pretty close to a language in which the assignment of roots to the syntactic positions of N and V takes place at the level of primary categorization. According to Lehmann (2008), the assignment of a linguistic sign to word class follows a probabilistic calculus in such a situation (section 3.2). Depending on the time-stability of the concept expressed by a given root, that root will be more likely to be used as a noun or a verb. This basically corresponds to the analysis of precategoriality as discussed earlier by Bisang (2008a, 2008b), who argues that lexical items are flexible and that their assignment to the functions of N and V is determined by pragmatic inference based on the meaning of the root and the construction in which it occurs. As for the criteria that influence pragmatic inference, time-stability clearly matters but it can be further refined to the distinction of [±abstract] and [±animate]. Moreover, the meaning of a lexical item in a given syntactic function can be predicted productively by combining the semantics of the root plus the semantics of the construction in which it occurs (Bisang 2008a, 2008b). In other cases, the interpretation depends on various types of metaphoric inference (Chapter 28 in this volume; Sun 2020).

Classical Chinese differs considerably from Modern Standard Chinese (see the values in Table 3.1), which has developed more elaborate derivational morphology expressed by morphemes, mostly of syllabic size, and has three different types of roots. Some of them can only take the syntactic position of nouns (*qiáng* 'wall', *chē* 'car', *fángwū* 'house'), others only the syntactic position of verbs (*mǎi* 'buy', *sòng* 'send', *chūxiàn* 'materialize, come into sight'), and a third type can occur in both syntactic functions (*yánjiū* 'investigate [V], research [N]'; *dòuzhēng* 'to fight [V], fight [N]') (see Chapter 28 in this volume).

3.4.2 Type IV: root:flex/stem:flex in Tongan

This type is associated with several languages from different families spoken on different continents. It is found in Tongan and Samoan (both Austronesian, Oceanic; see Chapter 35 in this volume), Kharia (Austroasiatic, Munda; Peterson 2006, 2010), Mayan (see Chapter 32 in this volume), and Southern Wakashan in Foley's analysis (Chapter 6 in this volume).[13] This chapter presents Tongan as an example of type IV.

---

[13] This analysis contradicts Croft (1991, 2000, 2001) who argues on the basis of Jacobsen (1979) that there is no flexibility in Wakashan languages.

Tongan is well known in typology for its lexically consistent flexibility even though the extent to which lexical items are found in verbal and nominal function depends to a certain extent on their semantics (Völkel 2017). Tongan has verb-first word order, and the verb is preceded by an obligatory marker of tense–aspect–mood (TAM) as a clear behavioural indicator of verbhood. Similarly, the subsequent nouns are marked for definiteness and case. In the following well-known example from Broschart (1997), the lexicon does not preclassify object-denoting and action-denoting lexical items. Thus, an object-denoting lexeme (*fefine* 'woman') and an action-denoting lexeme (*lele* 'run') can both occur with tense marking as well as with the article *e*:[14]

(13) Tongan (Broschart 1997: 134)
    a. *na'e lele e kau fefiné.*
        PST run ART PL:HUM woman
        'The women were running.'

    b. *na'e fefine kotoa e kau lelé.*
        PST woman all ART PL:HUM run
        'The ones running were all female.'

Lexical items like *lele* 'run' and *fefine* 'woman' are independent words as in Classical Chinese (section 3.4.1). For that reason, they can be treated as roots. In contrast to Classical Chinese, Tongan additionally has its morphology which consists in a set of different morphemes which form a system of what Broschart (1997: 143) calls lexical 'paradigms', i.e. a set of affixes for deriving words with new meanings. A good example for such a paradigm is the suffix *-Canga*,[15] which denotes the overall domain where something takes place. This suffix is flexible, since it can be added to action-denoting roots (*pule* 'govern' > *pule'anga* 'government'), property-denoting roots (*motu'a* 'old' > *motu'a'anga* 'reason for having aged'), and object-denoting roots (*api* 'home' > *apitanga* 'homestead'). Even though these markers may resemble derivational morphemes, they clearly differ from the general type of word-class changing derivational markers inasmuch as the resulting stems or words are still flexible, i.e. they can occur in the clause initial verb position after TAM markers, negation, and subject markers (SUBJ) as well as in one of the nominal positions. In the following example, we find *pule'anga* 'government' as a whole in the verbal position (see also (19) on Kharia and (31) on Samoan):

(14) Tongan (Broschart 1997: 145)
    'oku 'ikai ke pule'anga.
    PRS NEG SUBJ government
    'It does not belong to the government.' (lit. 'It is not that it government-s.')

---

[14] The accent in *fefiné* and *lelé* in (13a) and (13b) indicates definiteness. Definite argument phrases are characterized by an accent shift on their last syllable (Broschart 1997: 132).
[15] C stands for 'consonant'.

3.4.3 Type V: root:flex/stem:rig in Latin and Arabic

Both languages, Latin and Arabic, are characterized by the high degree to which their stems are rigid. This can be seen in Table 3.1 from Lehmann (2008) on Latin (value 0.99) and it is a characteristic of Semitic (Aronoff 1994, 2007). In Latin, this is due to the derivational status of the thematic vowels which appear between the root and its inflectional suffixes associated with the relevant lexical categories (conjugation and declension). In contrast, the flexibility at the root level differs between Latin and Arabic. While not all roots are flexible in Latin (see the value of 0.30 in Table 3.1), Semitic roots are generally flexible (see below for more). This means that Latin cannot be fully described as a type-v language. In fact, we also find two other types which will be briefly presented here (for type v, see examples in section 3.1). In one of them, the root is compatible with a thematic vowel of only one lexical category (e.g. *vēn-ī-* 'to come' (*ī--conjugation*) or *hort-us* 'garden' (*o-declination*)). This type can be treated as an instance of type VIII (root:rig/stem:rig, Turkish). The second alternative to type v is relatively rare and is characterized by flexible stems. One context in which this situation can occur is with roots ending in a consonant. Since these roots have no thematic vowel but maximally an epenthetic vowel in certain phonological environments, there is formal identity of roots and stems when they are directly combined with inflectional morphology. If in such a constellation a consonantal root can occur with nominal and verbal inflectional morphology, we get examples of type IV (root:flex/stem:flex) in Latin. A good example is the root/stem *dūc-* which is nominal if combined with the suffix of the nominative singular as in *dūc-s* 'leader' (written *dūx*) or verbal if combined with the form of the 1st person present as in *dūc-ō* 'I lead'. In an alternative analysis based on the PUO (section 3.1), one may argue that roots are flexible[16] and that there are zero-derivational morphemes (-$\emptyset_N$ and -$\emptyset_V$) for avoiding the problem of flexible output. I will not take a final decision here but what clearly remains is the overall statistical dominance of rigid stems even if there are alternative analyses in terms of flexibility for cases of the *dūc-type*.

The Semitic system of non-concatenative roots and patterns/templates as illustrated by Arabic here needs some previous remarks on the basics of the morphology of these languages. In standard analyses of Arabic (e.g. Fischer 2002; Ryding 2005, 2014), roots consist of a sequence of consonants, most commonly three as in /k-t-b/ 'write', /dʒ-m-ʕ/ 'collect, gather', /k-tˤ-l/ 'kill', and /ʕ-r-f/ 'know'.[17] These roots are integrated into patterns (or templates) consisting of consonants (C) and vowels (V). In some cases, the patterns are further characterized by the gemination of a consonant (CC) or by additional morphemes. In (15a), we find the root /k-t-b/ in the pattern CuCiC as the base for perfective passive forms to which the perfective suffix *-a* of the 3rd person singular masculine

---

[16] Or acategorial as discussed in the context of the acategorial root hypothesis in DM (Marantz 2001) (section 3.7.2).

[17] Notice there are also patterns consisting of two or four consonants and there are special classes of word patterns which are characterized by the occurrence of the consonants *w, j*, and the glottal stop / in one of the three positions for consonants. In his presentation of Hebrew, Aronoff (2007) describes roots showing output alternations depending on the position of specific consonant phonemes within the template as 'alternation classes'. In Arabic, the situation is similar.

is added. In (15b), the same root is integrated into the pattern *CiCaaC* creating a noun with the meaning 'book':

(15) a. CuCiC: *kutib-a* 'it was written'
      b. CiCaaC: *kitaab* 'book'

Seen from the input–output perspective, consonantal roots (e.g. *k-t-b* 'write') are often described as input and patterns as output. This straightforward approach is not completely inadequate and has its attractions, but it also has some shortcomings. Glanville (2018: 8–10) discusses a whole list from which two are picked out here. One of them is mentioned by Heath (2003: 115), who points out that it is not clear why words like *xubz* 'bread', *kabʃ* 'ram', or *hifðˤ* 'preservation' should be seen as a combination of a consonant-based root with a corresponding pattern CVCC, since the insertion of different vowels (*u, a, i*) into this pattern cannot be associated with different functions. The other problem is that many roots occur in many different patterns from which it is hard to derive a single overall meaning. The extent to which a single root can be associated with a single meaning ultimately depends on each individual case and its history of diffusion into different patterns.

To avoid these problems, Glanville (2018) presents a more complex model that integrates form and meaning and is based on the existence of patterns as the diachronic results of the regular use of morphological operations. In his analysis (Glanville 2018: 15), the input is a concrete word belonging to a specific pattern whose consonantal grid (= root) will be extracted for being integrated into the relevant output pattern. The precondition for such an extraction is that output patterns are associated with a specific meaning that motivates such a process.[18]

If one transfers this analysis to the input–output model used in the present context of word class, the input consists of two components: the root with its sequence of consonants on the morphophonological side and the meaning of the input word/pattern on the semantic side. As pointed out above, the root does not necessarily have a single overall meaning. Moreover, it does not belong to a particular word class even if the word that serves as input clearly does. Combining these facts, I would argue that roots as they are extracted from input words are flexible,[19] and can be combined with various rather divergent patterns. The individual patterns themselves have the behavioural potential of being combined either with inflectional morphology expressing tense aspect and agreement (person, number, gender) for verbs or with case, number, and gender for nouns and adjectives. For that reason, patterns correspond to stems which determine the word class or lexical category of a fully fledged word. Taken together, roots are flexible in the sense that they can be integrated into stems/patterns that represent different word classes, while stems/patterns themselves are rigidly associated with a specific word class. Thus, Arabic is not that different from Latin in terms of rigid stems (also see Aronoff 2007 for a similar observation). What is special is the input with its division into a morphophonological and a semantic side.

---

[18] A good example is the pattern ʔaCCaC with its elative/superlative meaning. No matter what the phonological shape of the input word is, its root consonants are inserted into the same pattern as, e.g., in *sahl* 'easy' [CaCC] > *ʔashal* 'easiest', *kabiir* 'big' [CaCiiC] > *ʔakbar* 'biggest', and *dʒaahil* 'ignorant' [CaaCiC] > *adʒhal* 'very/most ignorant' (Glanville 2018: 12; initially from Ratcliff 2006: 76, who combines rule-based and templatic morphology).

[19] On the argument that Semitic roots are generally acategorial, see the discussion in sections 3.7.2 and 3.7.3 on DM.

To illustrate that roots are not necessarily associated with a single meaning and need to be considered together with the input word, let's briefly look at the root /dʒ-m-ʕ/ 'collect, gather' as it is described by Glanville (2018). Arabic has no fewer than 15 verb patterns or stems counted by convention from I to XV[20] for expressing functions like repetition, reflexivity, reciprocity, and causativity with quite some lexical specifics, depending on the root. In the case of our example, some stem meanings can be predicted on the basis of the verbal input *dʒamaʕ-a* [gather-3SG.M. PFV] 'he gathered'[21] as in (16a) with stems II and VII, while the meaning of stem IV can be derived from the adjectival pattern *dʒamiiʕ* 'all, entire' (16b).[22] The profiled meaning of 'a total/a whole' as it matters for stem IV cannot be directly derived from the input meaning of 'to gather' in (16a) (Glanville 2018: 165).

(16) a. Arabic (Glanville (2018: 164))
    a. Stems based on *dʒamaʕ-a* 'he gathered':
       II.   CaCCaC 'repeated action'
           => *dʒammaʕ-a* 'amass, accumulate'
       VIII. iCtaCaC 'reflexive (spontaneous change of state)':
           => *idʒdamaʕ-a* 'meet, come together'
    b. Stem based on *dʒamiiʕ* 'all, entire':
       IV. /aCCaC: activated state verb:
           => *ʔdʒamaʕ-a* 'to agree unanimously on'

More recent experimental studies additionally support the cognitively independent status of roots in Arabic and in Semitic in general (Boudelaa & Marslen-Wilson 2001, 2011; Prunet 2006). Glanville (2018: 11) takes this as additional evidence for his model:

> [R]oots and patterns appear to be discrete morphological objects that have some special status in the minds of native speakers as separate components of words.

As is shown by a recent cross-modal priming experiment (Freynik et al. 2017), even non-native speakers of Arabic whose first language is English develop the ability to discern roots from Arabic words.

3.5 Rigid root types (VI–VIII)

3.5.1 Type VI: root:rig/stem:flex—examples from Khmer

This type contradicts Haig's (2006) and Lehmann's (2008: 560) assumption of increasing specification from root to stem and it also violates Aronoff's (1994) LFR. Even though

---

[20] These patterns or stems are called /awzaan (singular: *wazn*) in Arabic. In Hebrew, the same phenomenon is known as *binyanim* (singular: *binyan*).
[21] Notice that the perfective form of the 3rd person singular masculine is the quotation form.
[22] Stems IV and VIII use additional material beyond the three root consonants. This is because some stems are formed by additional affixation.

there do not seem to be languages which only use this system, it can be found at the lexical level of individual roots if the derivational morpheme is flexible. While the number of such examples is rather small in English (section 3.6), this type is more pervasive in the derivational morphology of the Khmer[23] lexicon (Bisang 2013). The morphology of this language is remarkable in two ways: (i) it has a relatively rich inventory of 28 derivational morphemes (Jenner & Pou 1981/1982) with different degrees of productivity but only a relatively small number of functions (mainly nominalization, causativization/ transitivization and semantic specification of the root concept) and (ii) 22 of its 28 derivational morphemes are flexible in the sense that they produce stems belonging to different word classes, depending on the individual root with which they are combined. The second property, which is more important for this chapter, is illustrated by two relatively frequent markers, the infix -vmn-/-vN-[24] (17) and the prefix prə- in (18). In both cases, the same marker is used for word-class change (17a)/(18a) and for causativization/transitivization in (17b)/(18b). The case of (18a) is of particular interest because the prefix prə- changes a verb into a noun in the first two examples, while it derives a verb from a noun in the last example:

(17) Functions of the syllabic infix -vmn-/-vN- (Bisang 2013: 291)
    a. Nominalization:
        Results: khcɔp 'to pack'   > kɔɲcɔp 'parcel [n.]'
        Instruments: tba:ɲ 'weave [v.]'   > dɔmba:ɲ 'equipment for weaving'
        Abstracts: thŋùən 'be heavy'   > tùmŋùən 'heaviness, weight'
                          lʔɔ: 'be beautiful'   > lùmʔɔ: 'beauty; embellishment'
        Agentives: ta:ŋ 'go in place of'   > dɔma:ŋ 'representative'

    b. Causativization/Transitivization:
        sʔa:t 'be clean(ed)'   > sɔmʔa:t 'to clean'
        thlɛ`ək 'fall'                    > tùmlɛ`ək 'cause to fall, put down'
        slap 'die'   > sɔmlap 'to kill'
        rədɔh 'be freed, free from'   > rùmdɔh 'to free [tr.]'

(18) Functions of the prefix prə- (Bisang 2013: 293–293)
    a. Change of word class:
        cheh 'catch fire, be on fire'   > prəcheh 'wick'
        vɛ`:ŋ 'be long'   > prəvaeŋ 'length'
        yùt(th) 'combat [n.]'   > prəyot(th) 'to fight, attack'

---

[23] Roots are generally rigid. If object-denoting roots occur in predicative function, they occur in the equational construction of the type $N_1 N_2$ 'N$_1$ is identical/belongs to the class of N$_2$'. In general, they cannot be used as transitive verbs as in Classical Chinese (section 3.3). Action-denoting roots occur in the topic position. If they occur as bare heads in an argument position, they remain clausal. To my knowledge, there is no detailed study of this topic.

[24] This infix has several allomorphs. The form -vmn- appears in syllables with only a single consonant in their onsets (e.g. CV(C)). The symbol v represents the two vowels ɔ or u, depending on register. The form -vN- occurs between C_1 and C_2 in syllables of the type C_1C_2VC with a homorganic nasal N depending on C_2.

b. Causativization/Transitivization:
 kaət 'be born'   > *prəkaət* 'cause, produce'
 do:c 'be like'   > *prədo:c* 'compare'
 mù:l 'be round'   > *prəmo:l* 'gather together'
 cùm 'a round, a turnaround'   > *prəcùm* 'assemble [tr. and intr.]'

Khmer has a relatively large number of derivational morphemes in the Mon-Khmer group (Sidwell 2008, who reconstructs six morphemes only) and none of its markers are productive (for more on Khmer, see Jenner & Pou 1981/1982; Bisang 1992: 447–472; 2013: 288–294). These observations indicate that its rich inventory of derivational morphemes is a relatively recent phenomenon that developed at the level of individual lexical items.

These findings from Khmer are in remarkable contrast to Kharia, another Austroasiatic language which belongs to the Munda subfamily. As mentioned in section 3.4.2 based on Peterson (2006), this language belongs to type IV. In analogy to Tongan and Samoan, Kharia also has derivational affixes like the infix *-n-* (sometimes also *-m-*) for producing output which denotes objects (19a), instruments (19b), or locations (19c) and is still open to the functions of noun and verb:

(19)   Kharia (Peterson 2006: 80)
   a. *kuj* 'dance'   >   *ku<nu>i* 'dance'
   b. *joʔ* 'sweep'   >   *jo-no-ʔ* 'broom'
   c. *rab* 'bury'   >   *ra-na-b* 'burial ground'

From a diachronic perspective, one may speculate whether Khmer was flexible in a similar way at earlier times for which we have no written documents.

3.5.2 Type VII: Behavioural mismatch—the case of Northern Iroquoian and Yorùbá

In Northern Iroquoian, nominal and verbal roots are generally distinguished by their behavioural potential (Mithun 2000: 398–401; see also Chapters 6 and 30 in this volume). Object-denoting roots take a suffix indicating their status as nouns and an overt gender prefix in independent use. Action-denoting and property-denoting roots behave like verbs by minimally carrying obligatory marking of a pronominal prefix and an aspect suffix (perfective, imperfective, or stative). With these properties, roots of Northern Iroquoian are similarly rigid as the roots of Turkish (section 3.5.3). In spite of this, there is a set of some 400 fully inflected verbs which are used as nouns denoting a wealth of objects from different domains of life (see Chapter 30, section 30.6.1 in this volume). The following verb form is used for referring to a restaurant:

(20)   Cayuga (Mithun 2000: 412)
   otekhǫnyáʔthaʔ
   ye-ate-khw-ǫni-aʔt-haʔ
   INDEF.AGENT-REFL-meal-make-INSTR-IPFV
   'one makes a meal with it' = 'restaurant'

The indicators of the nominal function of these verbs presented by Mithun (2000: 411–418) are impressive.[25] These are clear indicators of a mismatch between the morphological marking in terms of behavioural potential (aspect and person) and the syntactic occurrence in an argument position. In spite of this, it is obviously not the case that all nouns are like this. The use of fully inflected verb forms as nouns is lexical, even though with different degrees of lexicalization, as can be seen from differences in the extent to which speakers are still aware of their verbal structure (Mithun 2000: 419).

Michelson (section 30.6.1 in this volume) also briefly discusses Chafe's (2003) explanation for this use, which is based on the presence of bound pronominals 'for specifying a participant in an event'. The function of reference to a participant serves as a bridge for the referential use of the verb form as a holistic unit. To what extent this explanation can be generalized remains an open question. Interestingly enough, Yorùbá (Niger Congo: Atlantic Congo Volta: Benue–Congo: Congo Defoid) uses entire clauses for forming proper names. Yorùbá is an SVO language with rigid word order. As Northern Iroquoian, it clearly distinguishes between verbs and nouns. Basic verbal roots have the phonological structure CV, while basic nominal roots have an additional initial vowel (VCV). In addition, some property-denoting roots have their own form, some others have verbal properties, while a third type follows a nominal pattern (the data are all from Rowlands 1969). Property-denoting roots like *ga* 'be lofty' and *kéré* 'be small' behave like verbs in predicate function (*ó ga* (3.SG lofty) 'it is lofty', *ó kéré* (3.SG small) 'it is small') and take their own form in modificational function (*gíga* 'lofty', *kékeré* 'small').[26] Another type of property-denoting expressions is formed with the verb *ní* 'have' followed by a noun as in the combination of *ní* 'have' plus *agbára* 'force, power [N]', which yields *lágbára* 'have power, be powerful' after the application of some phonological rules. For expressing modification, the whole construction of [*ní* + N] is treated like a relative clause, an option which is also available for property-denoting roots with verbal properties.

As the above sketch shows, categorization basically takes place at the root level. In spite of this, there is one context in which even full clauses take the function of nouns without any additional marking—and this is the case with proper names (Ẹkundayọ 1977). This is amply illustrated by Babalọla & Alaba's (2003) dictionary of proper names with some 20,000 entries. In the following examples, we find a simple sentence in (21) and a yes–no question in (22):

(21) Yoruba (Ẹkundayọ 1977: 57; see also Babalọla & Alaba 2003: 740)
 ọmọ parí ọlá
 child complete honour/wealth
 'Ọmọparíọlá' [= 'a child epitomizes wealth']

(22) Yoruba (Ẹkundayọ 1977: 57, 66; see also Babalọla & Alaba 2003: 38)
 adé kàn mí bí
 crown reach 1.SG:O Q
 'Adekanmbi' [= 'Is it my turn to reign?']

---

[25] Notice that the use of bare nouns in verbal function is ungrammatical (see Chapter 30, section 30.5 in this volume).
[26] The modificational forms are mostly derived by reduplication. Monosyllabic property-denoting roots reduplicate the first consonant, which is followed by the vowel /i/ with high tone (CV > CíCV; see *gíga* 'lofty'). The other roots are characterized by partial reduplications. The details are lexical.

The cultural and grammatical restrictions on the productivity of creating clause-based proper names are excellently described in Ẹkundayọ's (1977) paper.

3.5.3 Type VIII: root:rig/stem:rig and word:rig, the case of Turkish

This section presents a short sketch of Turkish based on Haig (2006). Another language of this type is Yimas, in which action-denoting roots and object-denoting roots clearly differ in terms of behavioural potential (for more, see Foley 1991 and Chapter 6 in this volume).[27] The Iroquoian languages and Yorùbá can also be largely subsumed under this type but they show flexibility to a certain extent at the level of the word or the clause (see section 3.5.2 on type VII).

In Turkish, the basic distinction is between verbs (action-denoting roots) and non-verbs (object-/property-denoting roots), which can be further subclassified into nominal and adjectival roots at a lower level.[28] A first difference is related to the morphosyntactic status of non-verbal roots and verbal roots. While non-verbal roots commonly occur as free forms, verbal roots are free only in the imperative of the 2nd person singular (*bak!* 'look!', *sus!* 'be quiet!'). Verbal roots differ from non-verbal roots by being able to directly occur with the negation suffix *-me*, markers of tense–aspect–mood–evidentiality (TAME) and the corresponding set of person/number suffixes as shown in example (23). Moreover, verbal roots can be directly combined with valency-related markers (reflexive, reciprocal, passive, and causative) without any additional word-class-marking affixes (24). Non-verbal roots must first be verbalized by a derivational affix for being compatible with these markers. In example (25), the nominal root *osman* 'Ottoman' is adjectivized by the suffix *-li*, which is in turn followed by the suffix *-leş*, which predominantly generates verbal stems with inchoative meaning:

(23) *gör-me-yecek-siniz.*
see-NEG-FUT-2.PL
'You [PL] will not see.'

(24) *gör-üş-tür-ül-me-yecek-siniz.*
see-RECIP-CAUS-PASS-NEG-FUT-2.PL
'You will not be made to see/meet each other.'

(25) *osman-lı-laş-tır-ıl-ma-yacak-sınız.*
Ottoman-ADJZ-VBLZ.INCH-CAUS-PASS-NEG-FUT-2.PL
'You will not be converted into Ottomans.'

---

[27] But there is an asymmetry in word-class changing morphology, i.e. there is no morphology for verbalizing object-denoting roots, while there is an impressive number of nominalization markers for action-denoting roots (see Chapter 6).

[28] I follow Haig's (2006: 14) analysis, which starts out from verbs and describes nouns and adjectives as non-verbs in terms of 'an elsewhere or default category in morphology'.

In contrast, markers of grammatical categories like case, plural (*-ler/-lar*), indefiniteness (*bir* 'one, a'), and possessive suffixes can only be directly linked to object-denoting roots, but they are also found to a certain extent with property-denoting roots (Göksel & Kerslake 2005: 49). In (26), the plural marker (26a), the indefiniteness marker (26b), and the possessive suffix *-im* for 1st person singular (26c) are used with an object-denoting root. If the same markers occur with a property-denoting root, it gets nominal interpretation (27):

(26) a. *ev-ler*   b. *bir   ev*   c. *ev-im*
       house-PL   one   house   house-1.SG
       'houses'   'a house'   'my house'

(27) a. *genç-ler*   b. *bir   hasta*   c. *güzel-im*
       young   one   ill   beautiful-1.SG
       'the young'   'a sick man'   'my beauty' [affectionate address][29]

Verbal roots can only take these markers if they are nominalized. Turkish adjectival roots can be clearly distinguished from nominal roots and other minor word classes by their ability to take comparative (*daha* 'more') and superlative (*en* 'most') marking.

As for derivation, the derivational suffix *-leş* as introduced in (25) and various other markers can only be combined with non-verbal bases (e.g. *serin* 'cool' > *serin-leş-* 'to become cool'; *mektup* 'letter' > *mektup-laş-* 'to correspond', *bir* 'one' > *bir-leş-* 'to become united'; Lewis 1967: 228–229).

Nominalization is marked by suffixes like *-im* (e.g. *öl-üm* (die-NMLZ) 'death', *iç-im* (drink/smoke-NMLZ) 'a gulp/swallow, a draught') and *-lik* for forming abstract nouns (e.g. *iyi-lik* (good-NMLZ) 'goodness, good action'). The suffix *-li* is quite frequently used as an adjectivizer (e.g. *bulut-lu* (cloud-ADJZ) 'cloudy'; *paha-lı* (price-ADJZ) 'expensive', *aç-göz-lü* (hungry-eye-ADJZ) 'avaricious'). Some of these markers can occur with various types of non-verbal roots (28) but never with verbal roots:

(28) Turkish (Haig 2006: 15)
     gibi-lik [like/POSTP-NMLZ] 'likeness', *ben-lik* [PRON.1SG-NMLZ] 'egoism, individuality', *iki-li* [two-ADJZ] 'dual', etc.

To conclude this section, it is important to mention that there is a very limited number of flexible roots in Turkish which equally occur in verbal and in non-verbal function (Lewis 1967: 227; Haig 2006). Haig (2006: 12), who talks about 'precategorial roots', lists 11 examples, among them *ağrı* 'pain, ache [–V], hurt, ache [+V]', *don* 'frost [–V], freeze [+V]', *eski* 'old [–V], become old [+V]', and *göç* 'migration [–V], migrate [+V]'. A more general description of Turkic languages is found in Doerfer (1982).[30]

---

[29] Examples (27a) and (27b) are from Lewis (1967: 53), example (27c) is from Göksel & Kerslake (2005: 49).
[30] I owe this reference to Lars Johanson.

3.6 COMBINATIONS OF TYPES: MANDE AND ENGLISH

In this section, some Mande languages and English are presented as languages which mix different types of word-class systems in considerable parts of their lexicon.

Mande languages with their cross-linguistic variation as described by Creissels (Chapter 25 in this volume) take interesting positions somewhere between Classical Chinese (type III) and types IV and VIII. In general, the languages belonging to this family are characterized by their limited morphology, by the obligatoriness of the overt expression of arguments, and by their very rigid word order, which is [Subject–Predicate Marker–Object–Verb–Adjuncts]. With these properties, word class can always be clearly distinguished through syntax. In spite of this, Mande languages differ from Classical Chinese inasmuch as only action-denoting roots can be flexible to different degrees of lexical consistency, depending on the language. If they are thoroughly flexible as in Jalonke (Lüpke 2005) or Soso (Touré 1994), action-denoting roots can generally be used in the nominal position of intransitive (but not transitive) verbal predication for expressing 'pure reification' (see section 25.3.2 in this volume). But even in these types of languages, nominalizations of other types (e.g. event, results, instruments, manner of action) are subject to lexical restrictions. Creissels mentions the Mandinka example of *búsà*, whose verbal meaning is 'hit', while its nominal meaning in terms of instrument is 'whip'. In the other type of languages as, e.g. in Soninke, action nominalization is productively expressed by derivation and there is 'a non-negligible proportion of event nouns with the same form as the corresponding verb' (Creissels mentions *sónqò* 'dispute [N & V]' and *téxù* 'cough [N & V]'—see section 25.3.3 in this volume). In contrast to action-denoting lexemes, object-denoting lexemes cannot occur in the position of intransitive verbs.

With these properties, object-denoting roots and stems are generally rigid in all Mande languages, while action-denoting roots are flexible in languages like Jalonke and Soso in the function of intransitive verbs. In the type of Soninke, roots and stems are rigid (type VIII). In both types of languages, a certain number of action-denoting roots have lexicalized functions if they occur with no additional marking in a nominal position.

As for English, the examples in (3) are all characterized by the symmetric pattern of rigid root and a rigid stem (e.g. $brain_N$ > $brain\text{-}less_A$, $false_A$ > $fals\text{-}ify_V$, $operate_V$ > $operat\text{-}ion_N$). Looking at the values in Table 3.1, which are 0.62 for roots and 0.77 for stems, this cannot be the whole story. There must be other patterns characterized by flexibility.

An obvious and frequently discussed phenomenon in this context is conversion as it is found in the many lexemes which can occur in nominal and in verbal function (e.g. *bottle, shock, cash, hammer, water, head*). Due to problems with categorial neutrality in LFR (Aronoff 1994), many theories treat conversion as an instance of zero derivation. An important argument for such analyses is the observation that there is a parallelism between the function of the zero form and a specific derivational marker. If one takes *cash* in its nominal function as the input form, the zero-derived verbal form expresses a caused inchoative meaning (CAUSE-BECOME) in the sense of 'to convert into cash'. A similar change in meaning is expressed by the suffix *-ize* in examples like *atom-ize* with its meaning of 'to convert into atoms' (Haig 2006: 33). This observation was generalized by Sanders (1988; see also Aronoff 1994: 15) through the overt analogue criterion[31]—a principle which works well with parallelisms like $cash_N > cash_V$ and $atom_N > atom\text{-}ize_V$. One problem with this analysis is that derivational morphemes like *-ize*, *-ify*, *-ate* and conversion each are semantically inconsistent in their own way (Plag 1999; Plag & Winther Balling 2020). Another problem is that there are many semantic relations between pairs of conversion for which there is no morphological analogue. In fact, many conversion pairs simply show idiosyncratic semantic shifts. In addition to this lexicosemantic side of conversion, there is also the pragmatic side with what is called 'contextuals' by Clark & Clark (1979). Based on their Innovative Denominal Verb Convention the two authors show how *porch* in *The boy porched the newspaper* gets the interpretation of 'The boy did something to cause it to come about that [the newspaper was on a porch]' (Clark & Clark 1979: 788).

There are several options to deal with this situation. Evans & Osada (2005: 365) call English a 'rampant zero conversion language' because conversion extensively violates their Compositionality Criterion. Distributive Morphology is based on the assumption that all roots are flexible/acategorial and need specification by functional heads like $\emptyset_N$ or $\emptyset_V$ (see the discussion in sections 3.7.2 and 3.7.3). From another perspective, one may see conversion as a gradient phenomenon which also allows for flexible roots (Haig 2006). Given the multiple factors needed for modelling conversion in English, the present chapter offers no decision and takes conversion as a phenomenon *sui generis* for the time being.

In addition to the pattern of root:rig/stem:rig and conversion, there is still evidence for other types in English. One of them is root:flex/stem:rig (type V). To illustrate this, let's look at the following examples of derivation quoted from Don (Chapter 13 in this volume), in which the roots of *form*, *sort*, and *coast* are combined with the adjectivizing affixes *-al* and *-able*. Even though both suffixes produce adjectives, *-al* generally takes nominal roots, while *-able* takes verbal roots. From the perspective of the UBH (Aronoff 1976), it is argued that the root bases of *form-al*, *sort-al*, and *coast-al* are nominal, while the same roots are verbal in *form-able*, *sort-able*, and *coast-able*. Such an analysis needs zero derivation in both cases, in which $form_N$ takes the affix *-al* and $form_V$ is marked by *-able*. In an alternative analysis, the three roots are interpreted as flexible and get their word-class membership from the properties of the derivational affix, which needs either nominal (*-al*) or verbal (*-able*) input. With this analysis, the above derivations are instances of type V.[32]

If there is root:flex/stem:rig, one may wonder if there is also root:rig/stem:flex (type VI). And in fact, there are some derivational suffixes whose output is associated with more than one word class (e.g. Lowenstamm 2015, as discussed in Don, Chapter 13 in this volume, from whom I take the examples). The suffix *-ian* derives nouns (*librar-ian*) and adjectives (*reptil-ian*), similarly to the suffix *-ant* in $defend\text{-}ant_N$ and $defi\text{-}ant_A$. What is remarkable about these suffixes is that they do not create derived forms which are flexible at the token level. Thus,

---

[31] 'One word can be derived from another word of the same form in a language (only) if there is a precise analogue in the language where the same derivational function is marked in the derived word by an overt (nonzero) form' (Sanders 1988: 160–161).

[32] It is quite remarkable that root:flex/stem:rig is a very strong pattern in Latin (sections 3.2 and 3.4.3), from which *-al* and *-able* made their way into English via Romance. Even if this may no longer be of synchronic relevance, it is an interesting diachronic observation which may explain the distributional properties of these markers.

the derived form of a concrete lexical input is lexically restricted to a single category, depending on the individual root/stem. While this type of derivation may not be very frequent in English, it is clearly more common in Khmer morphology (section 3.5.1).

Summarizing the above discussion of English, word class is marked in a rather inconsistent way, irrespective of the frequency of lexical items that can be associated with the individual patterns. There are instances of (i) root:rig/stem:rig (VIII), (ii) root:flex/stem:rig (V), (iii) root:rig/stem:flex (VI), and (iv) conversion.

3.7 Discussion from the perspective of different linguistic models

3.7.1 Functional views: Hengeveld and Croft

Up to this point, the focus of this chapter has been on functional approaches which explicitly address the internal morphological structure of words. As it turned out, Haig (2006) and Lehmann's (2008, 2013) generalizations still hold if one looks at those types which are strong enough to extend over vast proportions of the lexicon of a language. In this section, we look at how more general functional typological approaches fare if one compares them to the eight morphological types of word-class systems.

There are two functional typological approaches to word class which stand out in particular. One is based on Hengeveld (1992b, 2013) and his perspective of Functional Discourse Grammar (Hengeveld & Mackenzie 2008; see also Chapter 10 in this volume); the other one is developed by Croft (1991, 2000, 2001) in his framework of Radical Construction Grammar (Croft 2001: ch. 11). Even though there are differences between these two approaches, there are considerable similarities in their methodology of cross-linguistic comparison from the perspective of this chapter. Both define word class by combining a set of functional domains with differences in markedness. Hengeveld (1992b, 2013) starts out from a four-slot space formed by the combination of two parameters with two values each. One parameter involves the opposition between predication (predicate phrase) and reference (referential phrase), the other between heads and modifiers. Each slot is associated with a particular word class. Thus, the slot combining predicate and head is a verb; the other slots are associated with nouns (head of referential phrase), adjectives (modifier of referential phrase), and manner adverbs (modifier of predicate phrase). Individual word-class systems are defined depending on the degree of flexibility or rigidity with which a lexical item can occur in one or more slots without additional coding or 'further measures being taken' (1992: 58).

Croft (2001, 2005, 2010b; Croft & van Lier 2012) criticizes Hengeveld (1992b) for not considering the semantics of the lexical items involved (see also section 3.7.3) and for randomly picking out a set of language-specific constructions in his four-slot model. To avoid this problem, he starts out from three lexical items belonging to the semantic classes of objects, properties and actions which are filled into three constructions which express the three universal propositional acts of predication, reference, and modification. The combination of the three propositional-act constructions with the three semantic classes creates a conceptual space for parts of speech with nine cells for identifying cross-linguistic universals in terms of markedness. Each cell is associated with a given construction which will have its specific markedness properties in individual languages. Within this space, there are three prototypically unmarked combinations which can be called nouns (reference to an object), adjectives (modification by a property), and verbs (predication of an action).

Comparing the constructions selected by the two approaches, it turns out that they are not that different. If the object reference construction is the relevant construction for prototypical nouns in terms of Croft, this construction basically corresponds to a construction whose head is a referring expression in terms of Hengeveld. Similarly, if the action predication construction is associated with verbs in Croft's theory, this construction is basically identical to Hengeveld's definition in terms of the head of a predicate phrase. Finally, both approaches are based on modification, with the difference that Croft only discusses adjectives, while Hengeveld looks at adjectives and (manner) adverbs. On the form side, both are based on markedness. While Hengeveld is relatively unspecific, Croft makes a further distinction between structural coding and behavioural potential (Croft 2001: 88–91). Structural coding is concerned with the markedness that is needed for a given morphological unit to be compatible with a given word class. It is thus strongly associated with stem formation. In contrast, behavioural potential is concerned with the number of contexts in which a linguistic item can occur, whereby the marked member has 'a smaller range of morphosyntactic behaviour than the unmarked member' (Croft 1991: 59). In the unmarked case, verbs typically are marked for categories like TAME, while the unmarked contexts for nouns are case, number, gender, definiteness/indefiniteness, and possession. To the extent that the relevant markers are morphological rather than syntactic items, they are associated with the level of the word in this chapter.

Given their similarities, both approaches face similar challenges. The first one comes from Classical Nahuatl (type I) and Tagalog (type II). Both approaches take the existence of two separate constructions for predication and reference for granted. One unmarked construction comes with object-denoting lexemes and is expressed by equational constructions; the other one is used with action-denoting lexemes and is realized as a predicate construction. The question is: what happens if a language only has one construction for both types of lexemes, either following the pattern of equation with copulas or the pattern that is associated with verbal predication? Depending on the language, we would end up with an omnipredicative type-I language like Classical Nahuatl or with a nominalistic/equational type-II language in the case of Tagalog. While both types of word class do not fit into Croft's model, Hengeveld's approach can only account for the omnipredicative type. According to his Parts-of-Speech Hierarchy (Hengeveld 1992b),[33] abbreviated here as V > N > Adj > Adv, there are three types of rigid word-class systems characterized by a reduced number of word classes which are rigidly determined. The first one has three lexeme classes (V, N, Adj) and lacks only Adv, the second one consists of two lexeme classes (V, N) with no Adj and Adv, while the third type consists of only one lexeme class (V) with no N, Adj, and Adv. What the Parts-of-Speech Hierarchy excludes is type II, which consists only of N. If the analyses of Classical Nahuatl and Tagalog in section 3.3 are correct, the distinctions between head of predicate phrase and head of referential phrase (Hengeveld 1992b) and object predication and action predication (Croft 1991, 2000, 2001) are not universal but rather theoretical stipulations.

---

[33] For a revised hierarchy, see Hengeveld & van Lier (2010b).

In addition to the above problems with types I and II, other challenges come with types III, IV, and VII. If there are type-III languages like Classical Chinese, one has to ask why the language did not strengthen its derivational morphology as it can actually be reconstructed for Old Chinese (see Chapter 28 in this volume for more detail) for keeping up word-class distinction rather than leaving it to a probabilistic calculus based on the meaning of a given root in combination with pragmatic inference.

In type-IV languages, there are morphological markers which clearly entail important changes in meaning without concomitant effects on word class (see the suffix *-Canga* in Tongan (section 3.4.2) or the infix *-n-* in Kharia (19)). The fact that there is additional morphological marking without concomitant change in word class contradicts Hengeveld's (1992b) approach which predicts 'additional measures' in such a situation, and it should be excluded by Croft's implicational universal of structural coding.[34] If an action-denoting lexeme like Tongan *pule* 'govern' in (14) takes derivational morphology for producing the object-denoting lexeme *puleʻanga* 'government', that more marked form should not be able to occur again in the predicative function as a verb.

In type-VII languages, there is the paradoxical situation that fully inflected forms generally associated with a particular word class are used in the syntactic position of another word class. In Northern Iroquoian, fully inflected verb forms can still occur in referential function. Such cases are hard to model in Hengeveld's (1992b) approach and they contradict Croft's (2001: 91) behavioural distinction of inflectional markers associated with nouns or verbs. Even if the case of Northern Iroquoian is ultimately a matter of the lexicon, one would need an explanation for capturing the diachronic dynamics that led speakers to use such words as nouns and for modelling the different degrees of transparency associated with individual nouns of that type (section 3.5.2). A similar point can be made for using sentences as proper names in Yorùbá.

3.7.2 Formal syntactic approaches: DM

Distributed Morphology (Halle & Marantz 1993, 1994; Marantz 1997) is based on the assumption that roots are generally categorially neutral or acategorial elements which get their category after spell-out by morphological rules on the way to their phonological realization (see Chapter 13 in this volume). This makes syntax less complex because the concrete phonological form of a lexical entry is developed outside of it, depending on the syntactic environment in which it occurs. If the nearest c-commanding element of a root like $\sqrt{REFUSE}$[35] is a determiner, it is a noun or a nominalization, realized as *refusal* in *the refusal of the offer*. If its nearest c-commanding element is an aspect or tense marker, it is a verb realized as *refuse*.

At the level of syntax, roots are merged with functional or categorial heads like n or v for getting their lexical category. In the case of *refusal*, we get the syntactic structure in (29).

---

[34] 'If a language codes a typologically unmarked member of a grammatical category by n morphemes ($n \geq 0$), then it codes a typologically marked member of that category by at least n morphemes' (Croft 2001: 90).

[35] In this section, I follow Pesetsky's (1995) convention of representing roots.

Since the verb *refuse* is transitive, the root is embedded into a more complex syntactic structure as in (30):

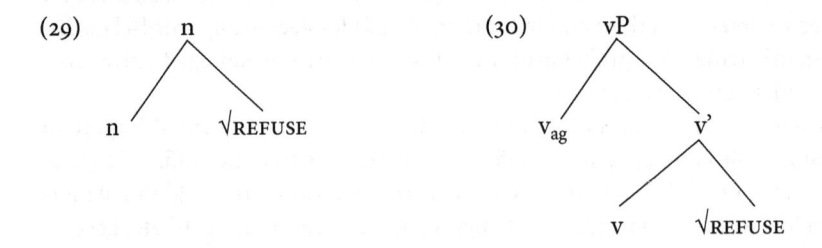

(29)
```
        n
       / \
      n   √REFUSE
```

(30)
```
         vP
        /  \
      v_ag  v'
           /  \
          v   √REFUSE
```

Phonological realization takes place separately and is determined by specific morphological rules, which are often dependent on the individual roots. Thus, √REFUSE is realized as *refusal* (similar to *proposal, disposal, recital*, etc.), while other roots like √DERIVE are formed by *-(at)ion* as in *derivation* (similar to *assertion, interpretation, protection*, etc.).

This approach clearly has its advantages from the perspective of reducing the complexity of syntax by relegating morphological idiosyncrasies to rules that apply after spell-out. It also shows the need to clarify what type of linguistic units actually form the basis of a syntactic representation. What remains less clear is to what extent DM really contributes to the understanding of word classes/lexical categories at a deeper level. As was pointed out by Baker & Croft (2017: 187), '[n]ow one needs a theory of what ns, vs and as are, rather than a theory of what nouns, verbs and adjectives are'. In addition to this general problem, there are some additional questions which are related to the eight types presented in this chapter.

If the analysis of Classical Chinese as a type-III language with probabilistic assignment of roots to the lexical categories of noun and verb is correct (section 3.4.1), assigning categorial heads like v or n to an individual root depending on its syntactic environment would only postpone the deeper analysis of the phenomenon to another level of grammar. What is missing is a theory that models the interaction of the semantics of roots with their pragmatic interpretation and syntax for merging them with zero n or zero v.

Type-VIII languages like Turkish with their rigid assignment of lexical categories at the root level (section 3.5.3) contradict the general hypothesis of the categorial neutrality of roots. Merging the roots of such languages with an additional set of categorial heads like v and n is redundant and adds to the complexity of syntax in such languages. The same problem arises in Northern Iroquoian languages and Yorùbá (section 3.5.2 on type VII) and partly also in Mande, whose object-denoting lexemes are rigidly determined as nouns at the root level (section 3.6).

Type-V languages of the Semitic type are often taken as prototypical empirical evidence for the existence of categorially neutral roots. Even though non-concatenative roots can still be taken as categorially neutral at the level of form, one would need a model for deriving the meaning of the output as it is derived from the semantics of the input word rather than from the root itself (section 3.4.3 on Glanville 2018).

The existence of flexible derivational affixes in a type-VI language like Khmer (section 3.5.1) or even flexible derivational suffixes like *-ian* and *-ant* in English (section 3.6) are not only against the Principle of Successively Increasing Categorization in (5) but they also contradict the assumption that derivational affixes are the realizations of categorial heads like n, v, or a. The categorial flexibility of some English derivational suffixes led Lowenstamm (2015) to model affixes as roots (Chapter 13 in this volume). While such a solution resolves the problem of flexible derivational affixes, it immediately raises the question of what determines lexical category. In Lowenstamm's (2015) analysis, this is still the task of the categorial heads which always remain zero in English.

The problem of zero-derivational morphemes ($-\emptyset_N$ and $-\emptyset_V$) as discussed in the context of the UBH (section 3.4.3 on Latin, section 3.6 on English) for avoiding flexible stems is even exacerbated in the context of unrealized categorial heads. One problem is concerned with categorial heads which are never phonologically realized because one would need independent evidence for stipulating them. This problem is not only intrinsic to Lowenstamm's (2015) model; it would also arise in a type-III language like Classical Chinese if one does not want to leave the assignment of zero for categories like n and v to a probabilistic calculus based on pragmatics. In the case of languages with rigid roots (type-VIII (Turkish) and Northern Iroquoian, Yorùbá, Mande), claiming the existence of zero categories of the type n and v would be redundant. Northern Iroquoian languages (type-VII) are potentially even more problematic because one would have to merge fully inflected words with a categorial head n.

3.7.3 Form meets function: The case of flexibility

DM starts out from the hypothesis that all roots are flexible and acquire their categoriality by being merged with functional or categorial heads like n or v. Functional typological approaches define flexibility in terms of markedness and the extent to which a given linguistic item can be assigned to more than one word class. As seen in section 3.2, the typological definition of flexibility is discussed in the light of more exact criteria for deciding whether a language has flexible word classes. Don & van Lier (2013) propose a solution to problems concerning the partial violation of the Exhaustiveness Criterion and the Compositionality Criterion in a language (Evans & Osada 2005) by combing linguistic typology with DM.

Don & van Lier (2013: 58) start out from the basic idea that 'meaning and function are two separate dimensions' and assume (i) that roots have inherent basic meaning, e.g. a basic action-meaning or a basic object-meaning, and (ii) that there are no strict implications concerning their categorial function, i.e. even differentiated (rigid) languages have uncategorized lexical roots (see above on the general categorial neutrality of roots in Halle & Marantz 1993, 1994; Marantz 1997). While roots like √KISS in a rigid language like English undergo a zero-derivational process which either yields a verb if the zero-element is v or a noun if the zero-element is n (if all roots are rigid in English—see the discussion of conversion in section 3.6), there are two different processes that apply in flexible languages. The first one has only a semantic effect but no syntactic categorial effect on the base root and shows unpredictable meaning shifts. This process is similar to zero derivation in rigid languages as in the case of √KISS, with the difference that it has no impact on the syntactic function of the root as a noun or a verb. A good example are cases like the following from Samoan, which is closely related to Tongan (section 3.4.2):

(31) Samoan (Don & van Lier 2013: 79)
    a. Actions or instruments with which these actions are performed:
       fana 'gun' or 'shoot'
       lama 'torch' or 'fish by torch light'

    b. Actions or the results of these actions:
       tusi 'write' or 'letter, book'

In this example, the flexible input forms are action-denoting and the flexible output forms are object-denoting in a way which cannot be predicted from the meaning of the base. Taking the example of *tusi* 'write; letter, book', there are 'two flexible, phonologically identical roots', i.e. $\sqrt{\text{TUSI}}_1$ and $\sqrt{\text{TUSI}}_2$. The first one corresponds to the underived action-denoting form, while the second one is zero-derived at the semantic level (not at the syntactic level) from $\sqrt{\text{TUSI}}_1$. The zero-derived meaning of $\sqrt{\text{TUSI}}_2$ is unpredictable, i.e. it is 'letter, book' rather than 'writer' or 'pen'. In spite of this, $\sqrt{\text{TUSI}}_2$ is still uncategorized. Thus, $\sqrt{\text{TUSI}}_2$ can still undergo the second type of process, which operates at the level of phrase structure. In this process, $\sqrt{\text{TUSI}}_2$ is combined with a particular categorial head. If that head is combined with a determiner (article), it will be interpreted as a noun meaning 'letter, book'; if it is merged with a clause-initial tense–aspect–mood marker, it will be analysed as a verb with the meaning of 'be a letter/book' (for the overall verb-initial clause structure, see example (13) from Tongan). While the first process yields semantically unpredictable outputs, the outputs produced by this second phrase structure-based process are predictable, i.e. they follow the Compositionality Criterion (Evans & Osada 2005). Like Tongan, Samoan also has overt derivational markers which are flexible (see *-Canga* in (14)). The derived semantics of these forms are object-denoting with unpredictable meaning, but they can still merge with verb-specific grammatical markers to be interpreted as verbs whose meaning can be derived regularly (section 3.4.2).

This new approach clearly has its advantages for modelling type-IV languages (Tongan, Samoan, Wakashan, Kharia), in particular with regard to the fact that unpredictable cases which contradict the Compositionality Principle are not incompatible with overall flexibility, as one can see from Tongan and Samoan as well as from a type-III language like Classical Chinese, in which there are productive compositional rules as well as lexicon-based specific interpretations (Chapter 28 in this volume). What remains are the problems of the assumption that roots are generally uncategorized (see above on type-VIII languages like Turkish and other languages with an important percentage of lexical items belonging to this type like Northern Iroquoian, Yorùbá, and Mande) and the overall lack of a theory on the status of n, v, and a. What also remains to be done is the modelling of the flexibility of the Khmer-type derivational morphology in type VI (section 3.5.1) and the flexibility of fully fledged words in type VII (section 3.5.2).

3.8 Conclusion

There are only very few systematic studies on the interaction of word class with the morphological units of root, stem, and word. This chapter adopts Haig's (2006) and Lehmann's

(2008, 2013) input–output-based approach in terms of word-class flexibility/rigidity but goes beyond it by integrating more cross-linguistic variation and more criteria. It explicitly includes a set of languages which are seen as linguistic challenges in the typological literature (e.g. Classical Nahuatl, Tagalog, Classical Chinese, Tongan) and it establishes eight types of word-class systems based on the criteria of (i) flexibility/rigidity at the levels of root, stem, and word, (ii) the use of a probabilistic calculus for directly assigning roots to word class at the level of syntax, and (iii) the question of whether a language only has a single word class (see Figure 3.1; section 3.2).

The results show that Haig's and Lehmann's generalization of a decrease in flexibility from root > stem > word still holds in the sense that it is followed by those types which can (almost) exhaustively dominate in an individual language. In addition, the chapter pointed out several challenges for LFR and for theoretical approaches like Functional Discourse Grammar, Radical Construction Grammar, and DM.

The systematic integration of roots, stems, and words into the typology of word class is still in its infancy. The observation on Haig's and Lehmann's generalization and the question of the proportion taken by a given word-class type across different languages points into a direction which seriously integrates statistical data in addition to checking for a priori criteria for assigning individual languages to individual types (Evans & Osada 2005). This begs for a cross-linguistic look at the frequencies with which different types can be distributed in individual languages on the basis of a balanced set of semantic root concepts. But this is a long way to go because we basically lack the relevant data (with the exception of Lehmann 2008).

CHAPTER 4

LEXICAL VS GRAMMATICAL WORDS

KASPER BOYE

4.1 INTRODUCTION

A distinction between what is referred to here as lexical and grammatical words seems to be applicable to most, if not all human languages, including sign languages (e.g. Smith 1990), and there is a long tradition for making such a distinction. In Western linguistics, it can be traced back at least to Aristotle and his translator Boethius, who made a distinction between *significativa* and *consignificativa*, and to Priscian, who introduced a distinction between *categoremata* and *syncategoremata*, which played a considerable role in medieval logic and language philosophy (e.g. Lyons 1968: 273; Klima 2005; Kirchhoff 2008: ch. 2; Spruyt 2011). In Chinese linguistics and philology, the contemporary distinction between content words, *shici*, and function words, *xuci*, derives from an (initially more vague) distinction between *shi* and *xu* that dates back to the Song Dynasty (960–1279 AD) (Harbsmeier 1979: 159–162; He 1998). In modern linguistics, the distinction between lexical and grammatical words coexists with a number of related, but not entirely coextensive distinctions, including: content vs function (or form) words, major vs minor parts of speech, and open-class vs closed-class words.

This chapter provides an introduction to these distinctions, focusing on the one highlighted in the title. Section 4.2 goes through a number of characteristic features that distinguish lexical and grammatical words. Section 4.3 discusses differences between the lexical–grammatical distinction and distinctions between open and closed word classes, and between content and function words. Section 4.4 discusses to which extent word classes are homogeneous with respect to the lexical–grammatical distinction. Section 4.5 deals with different definitions of the lexical–grammatical distinction. Section 4.6 looks at the distinction in light of a third type of words, holophrases; it discusses similarities between the lexical–grammatical distinction and word class distinctions in terms of the notions of structured complexity and division of labour. Section 4.7 is a brief summary.

4.2 CHARACTERISTIC FEATURES OF LEXICAL VS GRAMMATICAL WORDS

It is generally assumed that grammatical words are diachronically related to lexical words: grammatical words have developed from lexical ones through what is called grammaticalization, and they may develop further into bound grammatical morphemes, i.e. clitics and affixes.[1] This means that a number of the features that are typical of grammatical words are best appreciated when grammatical words are considered in relation to lexical ones. It also means that the literature on grammaticalization (e.g. Traugott & Heine 1991; Hopper & Traugott 2003; Lehmann 2015; Kuteva et al. 2019) is a good place to look for discussions of these features. In what follows, I first go through what can be called structural characteristics, i.e. characteristics pertaining to phonology, morphosyntax, and semantics (section 4.2.1). Subsequently, I give a brief overview of features associated with language use, processing, and acquisition (section 4.2.2). The overviews are not intended to be exhaustive, but to represent the most salient or frequently mentioned features.

4.2.1 Structural characteristics

By structural characteristics I refer to phonological, semantic, and morphosyntactic characteristics, which can be considered as associated with language as a set of conventions. Some of the structural features that characterize lexical and grammatical words respectively can be summarized in terms of the notion of '(non)reduction'. Lexical words are in some respects 'nonreduced' compared to grammatical words while grammatical words are in a similar way 'reduced' compared to lexical ones (see Lehmann 2015 on grammaticalization and reduction of structural 'autonomy').[2]

This holds above all for the phonological characteristics. Grammatical words are often phonologically reduced relative to their lexical sources (see Lehmann 2015 on 'phonological integrity'). They may possess fewer phonological segments (i.e. require fewer articulatory gestures) or be phonologically less prominent in terms of stress. As discussed by Bybee, Perkins, & Pagliuca (1994), for instance, the English auxiliary *gonna* is phonologically reduced relative to its lexical source *going to*: 'Thus the first vowel of *gonna* is a schwa reduced from a full [ow], and the medial consonant, a nasalized flap, is the coarticulated remnant of the nasal consonant of the progressive participle and the [t] of *to*' (Bybee, Perkins, & Pagliuca 1994: 6).

The characterization of grammatical and lexical words as respectively reduced and nonreduced may also hold to some extent when we consider semantics. Grammatical items

---

[1] Demonstratives are sometimes considered an exception, as lexical sources cannot be identified and there is thus no evidence for grammaticalization (e.g. Diessel 2006: 474–475). However, Boye & Harder (2012: 19–20) argue that demonstratives are in fact lexical themselves.

[2] Under reduction of structural 'autonomy', Lehmann (2015) subsumes six parameters of grammaticalization: integrity, structural scope, paradigmaticity, bondedness, paradigmatic variability, and syntagmatic variability.

are often said to be semantically reduced or bleached (e.g. Bybee, Perkins, & Pagliuca 1994: 6; see Lehmann 2015 on 'semantic integrity') relative to their lexical source. Consider again the auxiliary *gonna*: it can be said to be semantically reduced or bleached relative to lexical *go* in the sense that its meaning 'being on a course towards an endpoint in the future' can be analysed as a result of reducing or abstracting away the motion meaning of *go* (Bybee, Perkins, & Pagliuca 1994: 5).

Another semantic difference between lexical and grammatical words is less easy to understand in terms of (non)reduction. It has often been noticed or implied that while the range of concepts or functions covered by lexical items is enormous and may indeed be infinite, grammatical items cover a limited range. For instance, Slobin (1997) and Croft (2003: 225) talk about a limited set of grammaticalizable concepts. Of course, a limited set is reduced in comparison to an infinite set, but the set of grammaticalizable concepts is not the result of a reduction of the set of concepts that can be expressed lexically. Rather, the two sets are distinct, but overlapping. Some concepts can be expressed only lexically (e.g. the concept of 'engine'), others only grammatically (e.g. person and number agreement), but still others can be expressed both lexically and grammatically (e.g. Talmy 2007: 268–269; Boye & Harder 2012: 5–6). For instance, the concept of possession can be expressed both by lexical verbs (e.g. *have, own, possess*) and by grammatical morphemes (e.g. the English clitic *-s*) (Boye & Harder 2012: 5–6). Similarly, it is well documented that concepts such as 'information source' and 'degree of certainty' can be expressed both by lexical and grammatical items (e.g. Boye 2012).

Also some of the morphosyntactic differences between lexical and grammatical words can be thought of in terms of (non)reduction. One such difference has to do with dependency (see Lehmann 2015 on bondedness). Some lexical expressions require combination with other expressions, of course. This is the case with transitive verbs, which require an object. However, many lexical words can constitute a phrase, clause, or even an utterance on their own. In the right contexts, the following words would work: *Go! Red? Car!* In contrast, grammatical words always depend on combination with a host expression (e.g. Bybee, Perkins, & Pagliuca 1994: 6–7; Boye & Harder 2012). Auxiliaries and articles, for instance, cannot be uttered in isolation: **The!* **Gonna!*, at least not outside metalinguistic or corrective contexts.[3] This difference in terms of dependency is nicely captured by the ancient distinction between *significativa* and *consignificativa*, mentioned in section 4.1.

Similarly, grammatical words are sometimes morphologically reduced relative to their lexical sources. Thus, *gonna* has lost the inflectional options associated with *go*. Grammatical words may also have reduced syntactic properties (see Lehmann 2015 on 'syntagmatic variability' and 'structural scope'). The grammatical variant of the Danish type noun *slags* 'kind of' is losing its capacity for controlling the gender of an associated article (Müller, Boye, & Agerbo 2020): the noun is common gender, but when used with a bleached meaning as a hedge, in construction with an indefinite article and a neuter gender noun, the article is frequently controlled by the neuter gender noun (*et slags job* 'a kind of job'). More generally, grammatical words differ from lexical words in resisting focalization and modification (outside metalinguistic and corrective contexts), whether by morphosyntactic or prosodic

---

[3] Accordingly, Boye & Bastiaanse (2018) classify Dutch modal verb variants as lexical if they do not co-occur with another verb.

means (Boye & Harder 2012: 13–18; Messerschmidt et al. 2018). Finally, whereas lexical words are often found in open classes, grammatical words often belong to classes that are reduced in the sense of being closed (see Lehmann 2015 on paradigmaticity) and which possibly represent obligatory choices (see Lehmann 2015 on paradigmatic variability). I will return to the relationship between grammatical status and closed classes in sections 4.3 and 4.4.

4.2.2 Non-structural characteristics

A number of characteristics are non-structural in the sense that they are not directly associated with language as a system of conventions, but pertain to language use, processing, and acquisition.

As for language use, lexical words are typically much less frequently used than grammatical words. Grammatical words like *the*, *a*, *and*, and *to* are consistently found in lists of the most frequent words in English, and in prominent places in these lists. It is therefore natural to assume that frequency plays a role in grammaticalization (e.g. Bybee 2006).

Frequency of use is also a conditioning factor for the order in which different words appear in first-language acquisition. At a first glance it might therefore be surprising that the first grammatical words only appear (as independent words) after the first lexical words have appeared: in the literature, a so-called telegraphic acquisition stage is often identified, in which children tend to produce lexical words only (see Hyams & Orfitelli 2015). On closer inspection, however, the delayed appearance of the first grammatical words looks natural enough: as discussed above, grammatical words cannot be produced in isolation, but depend on combination with a host word. Grammatical words, then, can only appear after lexical words have appeared.

As for language perception, there is strong evidence that grammatical words attract less attention than lexical ones. In eye-tracking studies, for instance, grammatical words are associated with fewer eye fixations and shorter fixation times (e.g. Just & Carpenter 1987; Krejtz, Szarkowska, & Łogińska 2016), and in letter detection studies, they are associated with higher error rates (see Klein & Saint-Aubin 2016 for a review). Moreover, in a change-blindness study, where test persons had to detect changes pertaining to lexical and grammatical words, fewer changes were detected in the grammatical condition (Christensen et al. 2020). These differences may be partly due to the fact mentioned above that grammatical words tend to be more frequent than lexical ones: more frequent items tend to be more predictable, and fewer attention resources need to be allocated to more predictable items. However, the differences pertaining to attention cannot be accounted for only as a result of frequency differences (e.g. Koriat & Greenberg 1991; Christensen et al. 2020), but point to an understanding in terms of 'discourse prominence' (see section 4.5).

The research on production differences between lexical and grammatical words is considerably more limited than that on perception differences. In particular, only a few studies exist in which lexical and grammatical words are contrasted in the production of multi-word utterances. Recent experiments with multi-word utterance production found that grammatical words are associated with longer response times or higher error rates (Michel Lange et al. 2017; Ishkhanyan, Boye, & Mogensen 2019). Both findings can perhaps be accounted for with reference to the claim mentioned above that grammatical words are always dependent, whereas many lexical words are not. This claim entails that, all else being equal, the production of grammatical words is associated with a higher processing cost as they come with a demand for combination with a host expression. Moreover, it entails that grammatical words can only be planned when lexical host words have been planned; in other words, grammatical words are planned later.

In aphasiology, finally, the distinction between lexical and grammatical words plays an important role in differential diagnosis of aphasia types. In particular, grammatical words are often (depending on the degree of aphasia severity) left out or substituted in the type of non-fluent aphasia known as agrammatic aphasia. In contrast, grammatical word production is often less impaired than lexical word production in fluent aphasias (e.g. Boye & Bastiaanse 2018; see Bastiaanse & Thompson 2012 for an overview of research on agrammatic aphasia).

4.3 Related distinctions

As mentioned in section 4.1, the distinction between lexical and grammatical words goes under a number of different and not entirely coextensive names. In what follows, I will focus on what seems to be the three most common distinctions: content vs function words, open- vs closed-class words, and lexical vs grammatical words.

The distinction between content and function (or form) words invokes an opposition between two types of meaning. Lyons traces this opposition back to the Aristotelian opposition of matter and form:

> Only the major 'parts of speech' ... were meaningful in the proper sense of the term: they 'signified' the objects of thought which constituted the 'matter' of discourse. The other 'parts of speech' ... did not 'signify' anything of themselves, but merely contributed to the total meaning of sentences by imposing on them a certain 'form', or organization.
>
> (1968: 273)

This idea forms the basis for the denotational and truth-conditional approaches to linguistics, which dominated semantics up until the mid-20th century (Harder 1996). In Relevance Theory (which assumes a truth-conditional semantics), for instance, lexical expressions are often claimed to have conceptual meaning and grammatical expressions to have procedural meaning (Blakemore 1987; Nicolle 1998). This idea is incompatible with later cognitive and functional approaches, where it is argued that all meaning is basically procedural (see Harder 1996 and Evans 2009 on meanings as instructions or prompts). Moreover, there are empirical problems concerning the distinction between content and function words: proper names are standardly taken to be content words (e.g. McDonald 1993; Kaljurand & Kuhn 2013), but arguably have no conceptual content at all; they simply refer (see Langendonck 2008: 7). The terms 'content' word and 'function word' can still be used as convenient labels, of course, but in the absence of a solid theoretical anchor for the distinction, it becomes hard to use the terms as more than labels. As discussed in Boye & Bastiaanse (2018), the distinction between content and function words is too ill-defined to be translated into precise definitions or criteria.

The distinction between open- and closed-class words is an empirical one. Open word classes have lots of members, and readily accept new ones, whereas closed word classes have relatively few members. This distinction is often assumed to be coextensive with distinctions between lexical and grammatical words and between content and function words. For instance, Martinet (1960: §4.19), Bybee et al. (1994), Segalowitz & Lane (2000), and Harley (2006: 118) use it to define the inherently ill-defined distinction between content and function words, whereas Lyons (1968: 435–436) takes it to be the 'most satisfactory' criterion for the distinction between lexical and grammatical items. It has occasionally been argued, however, that the open- vs closed-class distinction and the other distinctions are not in fact coextensive. According to Bisang (2010: 291): '[t]he distinction between content words and function words is not identical to the distinction between open and closed word classes. The opposition of open vs closed merely concerns the question of whether class membership is limited or not'. In support of Bisang's claim, closed classes are found, which comprise words that seem to be clearly lexical. Bisang mentions that some languages have closed classes of adjectives (see Schachter & Shopen 2007 for a more thorough discussion). Another case in point is Classical Latin praenomina. As mentioned, proper names are standardly taken to be content or lexical words. However, Classical Latin praenomina form a closed class comprising limited numbers of female and masculine proper names (note that the class has a clear distributional definition: the praenomina take the first of three slots in the Latin person name construction). Moreover, the closed classes of pronouns and adpositions may comprise content or lexical words in quite a few languages (e.g. Carnie 2011: 47; see section 4.4 in this chapter).

The distinction between lexical and grammatical words differs from the two distinctions discussed above in that it does not embody any specific empirical (open vs closed classes) or theoretical (content vs function) claims regarding the two classes of words contrasted. However, in ascribing some words to the lexicon and others to the grammar, the distinction presupposes a theory of the more general opposition between these two notions. In addition, it entails a complication of such a theory. The opposition of lexicon and grammar is often understood as basically an opposition between an inventory of items on the one hand and a set of rules for combining the items into complex wholes on the other. The idea of grammatical words then represents a complication of this understanding: it entails that grammar is not only rules but also has an item aspect. Thus, lexical words are in opposition not only to grammatical rules, but also to grammatical words.

This complication has been handled in different ways. One strategy is to claim that grammatical items (including words) differ from lexical ones in being integrated with grammar. This claim preserves the basic understanding of grammar as having to do with rules, and thus also an understanding of the grammar–lexicon opposition as an opposition between essentially different phenomena. For instance, Chomsky (2014: 48) takes the lexicon to include both 'lexical' and 'functional' items, but proposes that the presence or absence of the latter 'is determined by principles of UG, with some parameterization', assuming that they are 'inserted in the course of derivation, unless some general condition on D-structure requires their presence' (see also, e.g., Harley 2006: 118). A completely different strategy is associated with construction grammars. Construction grammars abandon the strict distinction between grammar and lexicon and reanalyse rules as schemata for item combination. This means that lexical items, grammatical items, and rules (or rather, schemata) can be handled by an inventory of items: a 'construction', which comprises substantive constructions side by side with fully or partially schematic ones (see Croft 2001 for a radical version of this approach).

4.4 THE GRAMMATICAL–LEXICAL DISTINCTION AND WORD CLASSES

There is a long tradition for seeing word classes as homogeneous with respect to the lexical–grammatical distinction: membership of a 'major word' class entails lexical status, whereas membership of a 'minor word' class entails grammatical status (see Lyons 1968: 273). There is also some consensus as to which word classes count as major and lexical, and which count as minor and grammatical. Nouns, verbs, adjectives, and often adverbs are often considered lexical classes, whereas, for instance, adpositions, articles, conjunctions, auxiliaries, classifiers, particles, and pronouns are often considered grammatical (e.g. Cazden 1968; Segalowitz & Lane 2000; Hopper & Traugott 2003: 4; Shi, Werker, & Cutler 2006; Chomsky 2014: 48). Interjections are sometimes considered grammatical too, but there are good arguments for considering them neither lexical nor grammatical (see section 4.6).

This homogeneity view can to some extent be seen as based in the tradition, discussed in section 4.3, of equating lexical (or content) words with open-class words, and grammatical (or function) words with closed-class words: word classes identified as major are typically open; word classes identified as minor typically closed. As discussed in section 4.3, there are good reasons to question these equations. Moreover, consensus about the relationship between word classes and the lexical–grammatical opposition is not absolute. For instance, some (e.g. Chomsky 2014) do not include adverbs among the major or lexical word classes. In particular, the status of pronouns and adpositions has been under debate. Some linguists consider these word classes grammatical because they form closed classes (e.g. Chomsky 1981: 48; Harley 2006: 77). However, the two word classes share properties with words that typically form open classes. For instance, adpositions take complements and may assign case, and the distribution of pronouns overlaps with that of nouns. For this reason, some linguists assume that adpositions and pronouns are lexical (see Jackendoff 1973 and Leikin 2002 on adpositions, and Carnie 2011: 47 on pronouns). Others see adpositions as grammatical-lexical hybrids (Bordet & Jamet 2010; Mardale 2011). Still others consider the classes of adpositions to potentially comprise both lexical and grammatical members (e.g. Kean 1979; Rauh 1993; Littlefield 2005; Boye & Harder 2012).

There is psycholinguistic and neurolinguistic evidence for the latter position. In a French letter detection experiment, Foucambert & Zuniga (2011) contrasted a number of words assumed to be lexical (nouns, adjectives, verbs, and adverbs) and a number of words assumed to be grammatical (determiners, conjunctions, relativizers, and prepositions). They found that in general, the participants detected more letters in the words classified as lexical than in the words classified as grammatical, presumably because they paid more attention to the former words (in line with the expected findings; see section 4.2.2). There was one exception, however. Letters in prepositions were detected at a level in between that of letters in lexical words and that of letters in grammatical words. The authors therefore conducted an additional analysis in which they contrasted 'full' (roughly, contentful or lexical) and 'empty' (i.e. functional or grammatical) prepositions. The result of this analysis was that more letters were detected in the former than in the latter group of prepositions.

Some neurolinguistics studies point in the same direction. For instance, Bennis, Prins, & Vermeulen (1983) made a distinction in Dutch between 'syntactic' (i.e. grammatical), 'lexical', and 'subcategorized' prepositions (the latter of which can be considered a distinct subtype of lexical prepositions), and looked at the production of the three groups of prepositions in Broca's aphasia, which is associated with grammatical deficits, as well as in Wernicke's aphasia, which is associated with lexical deficits. They found that in Broca's aphasia, the production of the grammatical prepositions was more impaired than the production of the two groups of lexical prepositions, whereas in Wernicke's aphasia, the grammatical prepositions tended to be less impaired (see also, e.g., Bastiaanse & Bennis 2018, but compare Branchereau & Nespoulous 1989). Similar results were found in studies of pronouns and of other word classes. Ishkhanyan et al. (2017) made a distinction between lexical and grammatical pronouns in French based on Boye & Harder (2012), and found that the production of the latter was more severely impaired in autobiographic agrammatic speech. Nielsen et al. (2019) made a distinction between lexical and grammatical determiners (i.e. numerals and indefinite articles) in Danish and showed that speakers with agrammatic aphasia have problems producing the grammatical ones, but not the lexical ones. Finally, Boye & Bastiaanse (2018) contrasted lexical and grammatical variants of Dutch verb forms (including modal verbs) and found that agrammatic speakers have more problems with the latter than with the former.

These studies suggest that word classes may be heterogeneous with respect to the lexical–grammatical opposition in the sense that they contain both lexical and grammatical members. At least as far as open word classes are concerned, this should come as no surprise when grammaticalization is taken into account, and in the case of verbs, it is standard practice to treat grammaticalized variants as a distinct class: auxiliaries. There is no similar practice for other word classes, however (but see Emonds 1985: 162–164 on grammatical 'subclasses' of nouns, verbs, adjectives, and prepositions). Nouns, for instance, may undergo grammaticalization for some time and still be considered nouns. A case in point is the Danish type noun *slags* 'kind of', mentioned in section 4.2.1, which has developed a semantically bleached variant that unlike other nouns cannot control gender (Müller, Boye, & Agerbo 2020). There is simply no class or label available for this variant, except possibly the rather vague 'particle'.

The studies mentioned above also suggest that languages may differ considerably in terms of how lexical and grammatical words are distributed across word classes. According to Boye & Harder (2012), for instance, English 3rd person pronouns include a contrast between lexical *that* and grammatical *it*, but nothing like this is found in, for instance, Danish. Cross-linguistic variation is limited conceptually, however, as highlighted by the notion of grammaticalizable concepts discussed in section 4.2.1, and the notion of grammaticalization paths (e.g. Kuteva et al. 2019).

4.5 Definitions of lexical and grammatical words

The distinction between lexical and grammatical words is rather undertheorized (Boye & Harder 2012: 1), perhaps because it is in certain respects found in a theoretical no man's land: on the one hand, major formal approaches to grammar such as Generative Grammar focus on grammar in the sense of rules (see section 4.3) and thus pay relatively little attention to the word opposition (but see, e.g., Emonds 1985; Corver & Van Riemsdijk 2001). On the other hand, major functional and cognitive linguistic approaches such as construction grammars downplay the opposition, perhaps in reaction to the strict distinction made in Generative Grammar between grammar and lexicon.

For a number of purposes it is convenient or even compulsory to have at least a rough idea about the distinction. In particular, it is a prerequisite for any study of grammaticalization of lexical words into grammatical ones. For this reason, a number of attempts to understand or at least define the distinction exist, especially in grammaticalization research. Below, I will briefly discuss some of these attempts (see Boye & Harder 2012: 3–6).

Most definitions are empirically anchored in the sense that they point to one or more characteristic structural features of lexical and grammatical words such as those mentioned in section 4.2.1. The most widely used definition of this kind is the definition of lexical words as open-class words and grammatical words as closed-class. As discussed in sections 4.3 and 4.4, this definition is problematic in several respects. First, the definition is hard to anchor in a general theory of the lexicon–grammar distinction. Second, uncontroversially lexical words such as adjectives and proper names may form closed classes. Third, psycholinguistic and neurolinguistic evidence suggests that word classes need not be homogeneous with respect to the lexical–grammatical opposition.

Other definitions give a privileged role to other features. In her definition of 'grammatical evidentiality' as opposed to lexical ways of expressing 'source of information', Aikhenvald (2007) combines closed- vs open-class membership with 'obligatoriness' (see Lehmann 2015: 148–152 for a thorough discussion of the latter notion): 'In the same way as tense refers to closed grammatical systems, "grammatical evidentiality" refers to a closed set of obligatory choices of marking information source' (Aikhenvald 2007: 221).[4] Haspelmath's (2004: 26) definition of grammaticalization as 'a diachronic change by which the parts of a constructional schema come to have stronger internal dependencies' entails an understanding of lexical and grammatical items as differing in terms of 'strength of dependencies', thus alluding to the fact mentioned in section 4.2.1 that grammatical items depend on combination with a host item, while some lexical items may constitute a phrase or clause on their own.

Defining grammatical or lexical items in terms of characteristic structural features poses two problems. The first one is that the features that are typical of grammatical items may be found also with lexical items, and vice versa (see Campbell 2011 on grammaticalization). For instance, while phonological reduction is characteristic of grammatical items, lexical items are sometimes reduced phonologically too, relative to a source item, as in the case of the name of the Danish capital: *København* < *Køpmannæhafn* 'merchants' harbour'. Dealing with a related problem in defining grammaticalization, Lehmann's (2015: 174) solution is to require of normal grammaticalization that it involves changes along all of the six parameters in terms of which he defines grammaticalization (see n. 2). Aikhenvald's definition above may be seen as employing a similar type of strategy: grammatical evidentiality is defined both in terms of closed classes and in terms of obligatoriness.

---

[4] Aikhenvald's definition applies most obviously to inflectional paradigms, but obligatoriness can also be thought of as applying to particles, for instance.

The second problem is that the features in terms of which grammatical items are defined are characteristic features, but not necessarily omnipresent (see Fischer 2007: 119–120 on grammaticalization). For example, the Danish auxiliary *have* 'have' is (at least in certain constructions) not phonologically reduced relative to its lexical source *have* (Michel Lange et al. 2017), and some evidential items dealt with by Aikhenvald under grammatical evidentiality are not obligatory (Boye 2018). This second problem is obviously not solved by Lehmann's and Aikhenvald's solutions to the first problem.

Avoiding the problems associated with definitions of the lexical–grammatical opposition in terms of characteristic structural features, some linguists turn to definitions in terms of a more abstract feature. As a generalization over his six structural grammaticalization parameters, Lehmann (2015) proposes that grammatical items are less autonomous than lexical ones (see section 4.2.1). However, from a functional–cognitive perspective (and for most linguists who take an interest in the issue), it is clear that the opposition must be basically functional–cognitive. Many functional or cognitive linguists therefore take meaning to be the distinguishing feature and define the opposition in terms of distinctions between different types of meaning. Often, the opposition is simply defined in terms of a distinction between lexical and grammatical meaning. Occasionally, however, an effort is made to be more precise about how lexical and grammatical meaning differ. Diewald (2010) assumes that grammatical meanings are 'weakly deictic', and as mentioned in section 4.3, Blakemore (1987) and Nicolle (1998) take lexical meaning to be conceptual and grammatical meaning to be procedural, thus relating the lexical–grammatical distinction to a distinction between truth-conditional and non-truth-conditional items.

A number of problems in such definitions in terms of inherent–semantic differences are discussed in Boye & Harder (2012) (see also section 4.3 for some already noted problems). A major problem was mentioned in section 4.2.1: approximately the same meaning can sometimes be expressed both lexically and grammatically (e.g. Talmy 2007: 268–269; Boye & Harder 2012: 5–6). Illocutionary meanings are one set of examples of this not previously mentioned. The illocutionary meanings of assertion, question, and directivity (or 'command') can be expressed lexically by means of performative verbs (as in: *I claim that they left*; *I ask you whether they left*; *I order you to leave*). Alternatively, they can be expressed grammatically by means of sentence type markers; for instance, word order (as in: *They did in fact forget it* vs *Did they in fact forget it?*), affixes, particles, and clitics (as in the Crow clitic distinction between *-k* 'declarative', *-?* 'interrogative', and *-h* 'imperative'; Graczyk 2007: 391–392). Thus, in the words of Lyons (1968: 438), 'there seems to be no essential difference between the "kind of meaning" associated with lexical items and the "kind of meaning" associated with grammatical items'.

Boye & Harder (2012) therefore suggest another direction for a functional–cognitive understanding of the lexical–grammatical opposition. They understand the opposition as having to do with conventionalized (i.e. coded) discourse prominence (see section 4.2.2): lexical items (whether morphemes, words, or schematic constructions) are defined as potentially discursively primary; grammatical items, in contrast, are by convention discursively secondary. In other words, lexical items have the potential to express foreground meaning (whether they do so or not depends on context and speaker intentions), while grammatical items can only express their meaning as background information (outside metalinguistic and corrective contexts where conventions may be overridden).

These definitions entail a set of criteria for distinguishing between grammatical and lexical items: it follows from the difference in terms of conventionalized discourse prominence that only lexical items can be independently focalized, addressed, and modified, as long as convention are not overridden in metalinguistic contexts (on the latter criterion, see Messerschmidt et al. 2018).[5] These criteria are language and word-class general, but obviously depend on language and word-class specific means for focalizing, addressing, and modifying.

While the definitions thus distinguish grammatical and lexical items from each other, they simultaneously highlight a link between the two, which makes it possible to think of them as poles in a continuum: grammatical items (background) have one of the two possible discourse prominence statuses of lexical items (background or foreground). A number of recent psycholinguistics and neurolinguistics studies support this understanding of the distinction between lexical and grammatical items: the theory in Boye & Harder (2012) makes correct predictions about the language perception and production of both non-brain-damaged individuals and individuals with grammatical impairment (e.g. Michel Lange et. al. 2017; Christensen et al. 2020; Ishkhanyan et al. 2017; Nielsen et al. 2019).

4.6 Similarities between the lexical–grammatical distinction and word class distinctions: Structured complexity and division of labour

It is worthwhile considering at a more abstract level to what extent the distinction between lexical and grammatical words is similar to word class distinctions between nouns, verbs, adjectives, etc. There are obvious differences between the two kinds of distinctions. Word classes are to some extent homogeneous both structurally and functionally. In fact, word classes like noun, verb, and adjective are often defined structurally and functionally. For instance, nouns can in some languages be defined structurally as words that can take subject position, and functionally as words that designate a (more or less abstract) entity. In contrast, neither the class of lexical words nor the class of grammatical words is structurally or functionally homogeneous. The latter class comprises a number of distributionally distinct words (such as articles and auxiliaries), which have a number of distinct functions (such as definiteness, illocution, and aspect).

However, at a more abstract level there are also similarities between the two kinds of distinctions. As for structural similarities, both presuppose a context of 'structured complexity' (Harder 2010: 240–241) in the sense that both pertain to words that are part of a more complex structure. To be sure, some word classes have members that can potentially constitute a clause or utterance on their own, as in the case of *Go! Red? Car!* (see section 4.2.1). As mentioned above, however, what defines them structurally is their distribution; that is, the slot(s) they can fill as parts of a more complex whole. If there were no structured

---

[5] Some of these criteria are mentioned also in earlier literature. For instance, both Bybee, Perkins, & Pagliuca (1994: 7) and Keizer (2007: 40) discuss the focusability and modifiability criteria. The theory in Boye & Harder (2012) provides these criteria with a common theoretical anchor.

complexity—that is, if word classes only occurred in isolation—they could be distinguished only on functional grounds. The same thing goes for the distinction between lexical and grammatical words: it does not make sense to draw the distinction outside a context of structured complexity. In particular, grammatical words cannot be used in isolation (see section 4.2.1). They depend on and require combination with a host expression. Both word class distinctions and the distinction between lexical and grammatical words therefore strictly speaking exclude holophrases. Holophrases—for instance, interjections like *hello*— do not presuppose complexity. Rather, the notion entails simplicity. Holophrases represent a more simple language state than both nouns, verbs, and adjectives on the one hand, and lexical and grammatical words on the other. Accordingly, they are the first type of words to appear both ontogenetically (e.g. Tomasello 2003: 36–40) and, most likely, phylogenetically (Hurford 2012: 585). In light of this, it seems wrong to classify interjections as grammatical words, as is sometimes done. Holophrases are neither lexical nor grammatical words, but a distinct third class of words (Boye & Harder 2020).

Also functionally, there are similarities between the two kinds of distinctions. Both can be seen as representing a division of labour. Word classes can be seen as dedicated to one or a few of the several functions holophrases may have (see Hurford 2012: 596–605). When toddlers want to direct their mothers to hold them, they can do so by uttering a holophrase like *Up!* In a complex clause which would serve the same purpose, the many functions of the holophrase are divided into different words from different, functionally specialized word classes. In a clause like *Mum, take me up!* for instance, the overall labour of the clause is divided into: designation of a relation by means of the verb *take*; designation of two entities by means of the nominals *mum* and *me*; designation of a direction by means of the adverb *up*; and specification that the illocution is directive by means of the imperative construction. Likewise, lexical and grammatical words can be understood as dividing the labour of the complex whole of which they are part. In the account of Boye & Harder (2012), for instance, they represent a prioritization of the many bits of information in a complex message: lexical words are specialized for potential foreground information bits, while grammatical words are specialized for background bits.

Thus, both word class distinctions and the distinction between lexical and grammatical words presuppose structured complexity as a way of dividing labour. In fact, word class differences are arguably a consequence of structured complexity: with complex linguistic signs (i.e. messages composed of more than one sign) arises the need for structure, and with structure emerges a differentiation of sign types. The same does not seem to apply to the contrast between lexical and grammatical words, however. A language with only lexical words can in principle be imagined, and it is perfectly natural to find languages such as those in the Mekong-Mamberamo area that are characterized by a 'low grammatical-morpheme density' (Gil 2015: 319). According to the theory in Boye & Harder (2012), the contrast between lexical and grammatical items rather provides a solution to the issue of information prioritization that inevitably accompanies complex linguistic messages.

4.7 Summary

The distinction between lexical and grammatical words to some extent remains pretheoretical: lexical and grammatical words tend to be distinguished based on criteria such as open- vs closed-class membership that are neither theoretically anchored nor fully accurate. A likely reason for this is that the distinction is outside the focus of dominant linguistic theories. On the one hand, Generative Grammar to some extent ignores it because it is occupied with the idea of grammar as a set of rules rather than as a set of items. On the other hand, some functional and cognitive linguistic models downplay the distinction, perhaps in response to the central role the more general distinction between grammar and lexicon plays in Generative Grammar.

However, the distinction is crucial for understanding a number of phenomena ranging from first-language acquisition to agrammatic aphasia. The distinction thus ought to be taken seriously by all theories of grammar, whether they consider it a strict distinction between different kinds of linguistic phenomena (rules vs items) or a gradual distinction between poles in a continuum. In one respect, the distinction between lexical and grammatical words is crucial to understanding what lexicon and grammar are: since it applies to words only (and not to both rules and words), it represents the place where lexicon and grammar can most easily be compared. In order to arrive at a full understanding, the two kinds of words must be compared also with a third kind: holophrases, which are distinct in not being parts of more complex wholes.

Acknowledgements

Thanks are due to Andrej Malchukov and an anonymous reviewer for valuable comments on a first version of this chapter.

CHAPTER 5

TRANSCATEGORIAL OPERATIONS

ANDREJ L. MALCHUKOV

5.1 TRANSCATEGORIAL OPERATIONS AS DECATEGORIZATION AND RECATEGORIZATION

AMONG transcategorial operations the most studied is nominalization (see, in particular, the typological studies by Comrie & Thompson 1985; Noonan 1985; Lehmann 1988; Koptjevskaja-Tamm 1993; see also Shibatani 2019 for a different take on this subject).[1] Although it is a traditional view that nominalization involves both acquisition of nominal properties and the loss of verbal properties, it has been only recently acknowledged that transcategorial operations such as nominalizations involve both decategorization and recategorization (Malchukov 2004). The term decategorization was introduced by Hopper & Thompson (1984) who showed that verbs or nouns when used not in their primary function tend to lose some of the morphosyntactic properties associated with their primary function of reporting events and referring to terms, respectively. For example, when a noun is incorporated it usually loses the ability to distinguish number and to take case markers and definite articles. Equally important is another facet of transcategorial processes, which was aptly termed by D. N. S. Bhat (1994) recategorization, i.e. when an item used in an extended function acquires some of the properties of those categories to which this function properly belongs. Thus, a verb used as a referring expression, apart from losing some of its verbal trappings, usually also acquires some of the nominal properties such as case or determiners. Hence, as argued in Malchukov (2004),

---

[1] In a series of recent publications on the typology of nominalizations, Shibatani (2019) suggests that in a number of languages (including Japanese) relative clauses headed by participles are actually nominalizations (argument nominalizations in the attributive function). This approach is interesting and original, yet it is less useful for addressing the question of constraints on category mixing, central to our study, since it focuses on similarities between lexical categories (basic or derived) rather than on differences in their categorial potential.

traditional terms like 'nominalization' actually conflate two properties: deverbalization and substantivization (acquisition of noun properties).[2]

The most straightforward way to demonstrate the (relative) independence of the processes of decategorization and recategorization is to regard cases where only one process is at work. Some arguments for their independence have been already discussed in the literature. As demonstrated by Hopper & Thompson (1984), decategorization need not entail recategorization: there are examples of incorporation/compounding, which involve decategorization without recategorization. It is important to stress, however, that recategorization does not need entail (total) decategorization either (Bhat 1994; Malchukov 2004). Thus, as noted in Malchukov (2004: 6–8), with regard to nominalizations there are four theoretically possible options (D and R symbols stand for decategorization and recategorization, respectively).

[−D/−R] sentential complements (*I know that he comes*)
[+D/−R] infinitives (*I want him to come early*)
[−D/+R] 'clausal nominalizations' (*I disapprove of his driving the car so carelessly*)
[+D/+R] deverbal nouns (*arrival*, etc.)

In the first case, involving neither decategorization nor recategorization, we are dealing with a sentential complement. Although it occurs in an NP (Object) position, it retains the structure of a sentence, hardly acquiring any nominal features (e.g. *that*-clauses generally do not combine with prepositions). In the second case we are dealing with 'infinitives', which may be viewed as a verb form involving decategorization (deverbalization) without recategorization (substantivization).[3] In particular, although the infinitive retains VP-internal syntax (e.g. the possibility of taking a direct object) and inflects for aspect and voice, it cannot take tense/mood and agreement markers or combine with the subject in the sentential (nominative case) form. The third case involving recategorization without (total) decategorization is illustrated here with the gerund in English. Note that the (verbal) gerund combines certain verbal and nominal features; in particular, it is capable of taking the accusative object while the subject is expressed as possessor in an NP. Finally, in the last case involving both decategorization and recategorization, the verb is completely morphosyntactically assimilated to the (nonderived) nouns, taking all the nominal inflection and retaining hardly any verbal characteristics. The case of clausal ([−D/+R]) nominalizations is most interesting for the purposes of our study since it addresses the question of which combinations of nominal and verbal properties are permitted for nominalizations.

Starting from the assumption that transcategorial operations subsume both decategorization and recategorization, I outline a model for constraining sets of grammatical categories

---

[2] Note also the two types of 'asymmetry' of finite and non-finite (adverbial) clauses, distinguished by Bisang (2000). The asymmetry can be achieved either by leaving out categories (tense, declarative marker, person) in the subordinate form that are compulsory in the main clause (minus-asymmetry), or by adding markers to the subordinate form (subordination marker, case, switch-reference) that is not necessary in the main clause (plus-asymmetry).

[3] Another case of deverbalization not accompanied by recategorization is found in clause-chaining structures of the 'co-subordinate' type, which involve sharing of tense/mood operators (Foley & Van Valin 1984). Such cases are not considered here since they do not pertain to the domain of complementation/nominalization.

revealed by 'mixed categories' such as nominalization. This model, called Generalized Scale Model (GSM) in (Malchukov 2004), will be applied to nominalization and, more briefly, to verbalization. In section 5.2, I briefly summarize theoretical and typological proposals to mixed categories, leading to postulations of deverbalization and substantivization hierarchies (in section 5.3). Section 5.4 presents the data for deverbalization and substantivization clines drawing on the sample used in Malchukov (2004). The following two sections discuss further interfering factors (section 5.5), as well as presenting GSM (section 5.6). Section 5.7 applies the same model to verbalization, which can be similarly constrained through verbalization and denominalization hierarchies. While the sections above draw on my previous work (Malchukov 2004), section 5.8 discusses some follow-up studies making use of GSM, including my own more recent work. Section 5.9 discusses formalization of the GSM, in particular its reconstruction in Optimality Theory (OT) (as already done in Malchukov 2006), but also relates the model to some other theoretical approaches. Section 5.10 presents a brief conclusion.

5.2 Theoretical and typological approaches to nominalizations

Given that the processes of decategorization and recategorization are both independent of each other and gradual (for example, a nominalized verb may lose some of its properties, e.g. tense, while retaining some other property, e.g. voice), the outcome of nominalization processes may be quite diverse. In the light of this observation, the central question we may ask is whether there is any ordering of the features that are acquired and lost during nominalization. Although this question has not been answered fully until recently in the literature, there do exist a number of proposals that have been presented in the typological studies (see, in particular, Comrie & Thompson 1985; Noonan 1985; Mackenzie 1987; Lehmann 1988; Givón 1990; Croft 1991; Koptjevskaja-Tamm 1993; Dik 1997; Cristofaro 2003; Koptjevskaja-Tamm 2003; see also a more recent study by Nikolaeva 2013 relevant for the issue at hand). Thus, Comrie & Thompson (1985) note that aspect and voice may be retained in lexical nominalizations, tense rarely so, and mood and verbal agreement virtually never. Another generalization, originally due to Comrie (1976), concerns the syntactic typology of nominalizations. It was noted that among verbal arguments, the subject is the first candidate to receive possessive (genitive) encoding. That is, both S (subject/agent) and O (object/patient) may retain sentential encoding, or both may be genitivized, but if only one argument is genitivized, it will be S, while O may retain its sentential marking. Consider the much-discussed case of the gerund form in English: note that the 'verbal gerund' in (1a) takes the object in the sentential and the subject in the possessive form (POSS-ACC type of nominalizations, in terms of Koptjevskaja-Tamm 1993), while the 'nominal gerund' in (1b) takes both arguments in the possessive form (POSS-POSS, or DBL-POSS type of nominalizations, in terms of Koptjevskaja-Tamm 1993):

(1) a. *My horse's winning the race was no surprise*
    b. *My horse's winning of the race was no surprise*

Importantly in the present context, there are concomitant morphosyntactic differences between the verbal and nominal gerund constructions: in particular, while the verbal gerund allows for aspectual distinctions and adverbial modification as a finite verb (cf. *My horse's having won the race quickly was no surprise*), the nominal gerund allows for neither (for further discussion of the English gerund constructions see, e.g., Pullum 1991).

Many issues raised by Comrie & Thompson (1985) have been elaborated on in subsequent literature (see Malchukov 2004: 9–13 for further discussion and references). Comrie's syntactic typology of nominalizations has been refined and extensively documented by Koptjevskaja-Tamm (1993). Lehmann (1988) and Mackenzie (1987) are two representative accounts pertaining to deverbalization and substantivization aspect of nominalizations, respectively:

Lehmann's (1988) 'Desentialization Scale' (> represents a 'prior to' relation).

Constraints on/loss of illocutionary elements > constraints on/loss of mood/modal elements > constraints on/loss of tense and aspect > dispensability of complements > loss of personal conjugation/conversion of subject into oblique > no polarity > conversion of verbal into nominal government > dispensability of subject/constraints on complements

Mackenzie's (1987) nominalization hierarchy (> represents entailment relation):

acquisition of noun features (number/gender, combinability with adjectives) > encoding arguments as genitives/obliques > case marking of nominalization > conversion to non-finite form

Although functional–typological research has yielded a number of important inductive generalizations, no principled account has been suggested that would allow us to predict the order in which verbal features are lost and nominal categories acquired. Drawing on my previous work (Malchukov 2004; 2006), I demonstrate below that such predictions can be based on hierarchies of verbal and nominal categories as suggested in the functional typological literature. This is reminiscent of certain proposals in generative literature that derive distribution of nominal and verbal properties in nominalizations from the fact that nominalization can apply on different phrasal levels (see, among others, Abney 1987; Pullum 1991; Borsley & Kornfilt 2000; Kornfilt & Whitman 2011). The next sections, drawing on Malchukov 2004, apply this approach to nominalization (sections 5.3–5.6) and, more briefly, to verbalization (section 5.7). Some extensions of this approach in more recent work (including my own work) will be discussed in section 5.8.

5.3 Deverbalization and Substantivization Hierarchies

In this section I demonstrate that deverbalization processes are constrained by the semantically based hierarchies of verbal and nominal categories. Such hierarchies have figured prominently in the functional–typological literature (see Malchukov 2004: 13–25 for further discussion and references). For example, different versions of the hierarchy of verbal (relative to clausal) categories have been proposed by Foley & Van Valin (1984), Bybee (1985), Dik (1989), Hengeveld (1992b), and Van Valin & LaPolla (1997). The ranking of features in the hierarchies is determined by the relative scope of particular categories, as in the Functional

Grammar (FG) and Role and Reference Grammar (RRG) traditions, or by a more general principle of the semantic 'relevance' of a given category to the (verbal) stem, as suggested by Bybee (1985). For example, tense is taken to be ranked higher than aspect in the verbal hierarchy since tense operators scope over aspect (locating an aspectually profiled predication within one of the temporal planes) and are considered to be less 'relevant' than aspect (i.e. tense affects the meaning of the verb stem less directly than aspect does).

Following the earlier suggestions in the functional–typological tradition, I assume the following hierarchy of verbal (and/or clausal) categories given in Figure 5.1.

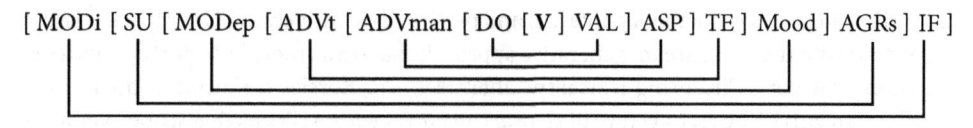

[MODi [SU [MODep [ADVt [ADVman [DO [V] VAL] ASP] TE] Mood] AGRs] IF]

FIGURE 5.1 Hierarchy of verbal categories

On the one hand, I assume, along with FG and RRG grammarians, a matching relation between grammatical categories ('operators') and their syntactic correspondents ('satellites'). The 'horizontal bracketing' in the representation above indicates a matching relation between operators and satellites within a certain layer in a manner familiar from FG literature (Rijkhoff 2002: 216–224; cf. Dik 1989; Hengeveld 1992b). For example, adverbial satellites of manner and frequency are taken to refine distinctions that in some languages are expressed by corresponding aspectual operators. On the other hand, I assume, with Bybee, an 'extended' version of the hierarchy by including agreement and valency/voice categories. The innermost layer hosts valency and voice operators, as well as direct object and object agreement markers. The next layer hosts aspectual operators and adverbial satellites expressing aspectual values (e.g. manner adverbs). The next two layers introduce tense and (epistemic) mood operators with corresponding adverbial satellites (tense and modal adverbs). The two outermost layers introduce subject agreement (AGRs) matched with the clausal subject and illocutionary force (IF) markers pertaining to speech act distinctions.

Further, in the line of Rijkhoff (2002) and Van Valin & LaPolla (1997) (cf. Lehmann & Moravcsik 2000), I assume the hierarchy of nominal categories given in Figure 5.2.

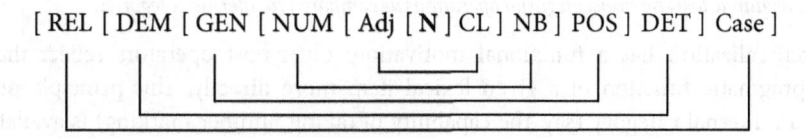

[REL [DEM [GEN [NUM [Adj [N] CL] NB] POS] DET] Case]

FIGURE 5.2 Hierarchy of nominal categories

The innermost layer, called Quality Layer by Rijkhoff (2002), hosts qualitative operators ('nominal aspect' markers) pertaining to individuation such as singulative/collective markers or noun classifiers, as found in a number of languages. The nominal class (gender) markers may also be assigned to that layer, as long as they are expressed by overt markers on the head (as in Bantu languages) and have semantic import rather than being assigned purely on formal grounds. Adjectives are satellites within the quality layer. Rijkhoff's Quantity Layer hosts number markers (operators) and numerals (satellites). The next two layers, roughly corresponding to Rijkhoff's Location and Discourse Layers, introduce possessive agreement markers (matched with genitive satellites) and determiners, which may be fully grammaticalized operators (articles) or not completely grammaticalized demonstratives, etc. Finally, I propose to expand the nominal hierarchy by the Relational Layer hosting case operators (which may be rendered by adverbial relators or coverbs in languages lacking the case category). Again, as in the case of the verb feature hierarchy, internal categories in the noun hierarchy (e.g. noun class) are (more) relevant to the meaning of the stem, while external categories (e.g. case, determiners) are (more) relevant to syntax and discourse.

It should be emphasized that the idea of hierarchical structure of verbal (clausal) and nominal (NP) categories is not theory-internal and pertinent exclusively to FG[4] or RRG. It is also consistent with the mainstream generative approach that treats morphological categories as functional categories 'licensing' lexical specifiers (see, e.g., Borsley & Kornfilt 2000; Kornfilt & Whitman 2011). The architecture of clausal categories with AGRs having scope over tense is accepted in some versions of generative grammar (see Chomsky 1995; Cinque 1999). In a similar way, the proposed hierarchy of nominal categories is similar to the hierarchy of functional projections within the determiner phrase as suggested by Abney (1987) and much subsequent generative literature.[5] Thus, the proposed hierarchies are motivated both theoretically and empirically. In particular, Bybee (1985) validated the verbal hierarchy by looking at affix ordering preferences in a sample of languages, and Malchukov (2004) provided a similar confirmation for both verbal and nominal hierarchies on the basis of a 50-language (convenience) sample.

Clearly, much more needs to be said about how cross-linguistic variation in the verbal and nominal domains can be accounted through the proposed hierarchies, given cross-linguistic variation in this domain. The cross-linguistic variation cannot be discussed here in any detail (but see Malchukov 2004: 38–42, 53–56 for discussion). The basic question to be addressed, however, is how these hierarchies, once adopted, can be used to predict and constrain category mixing processes across languages. Now, Malchukov's (2004, 2006) central proposal, which has a direct bearing on the issue of constraints on transcategorial operations such as nominalization, is the following:

> Hierarchy constraints on transcategorial operations:
>
> *Categories belonging to the external layers of the respective hierarchies are more readily affected (i.e. acquired/lost) by transcategorial operations as compared to internal categories.*

This generalization has a functional motivation: outermost operators reflect the syntactic/pragmatic function of a given lexical item more directly. This principle predicts that if an internal category (say, the capability of taking number marking) is available for nominalizations, external categories (such as case/adposition marking and combinability with determiners) should be available as well. Similarly, if an internal category (such as valency/voice and the capability of taking direct objects) is lost, the capability of tense–aspect–mood (TAM) marking or subject agreement should be lost as well. This principle thus imposes constraints on possible combinations of verbal and nominal categories in mixed

---

[4] Van Lier (2009) discusses how this architecture of nominal and verbal hierarchies relates to more recent work of Functional (Discourse) Grammar, as developed by Kees Hengeveld, Lachlan Mackenzie, and their associates (see, in particular, Hengeveld & Mackenzie 2008).

[5] See, e.g., contributions to Alexiadou & Wilder (1998) which assume or argue for the (subparts) of the following architecture of nominal functional projections: [DetP[PosP[NumP[KindP[NP]]]]].

categories, which can also be conceptualized as constraint hierarchies in OT (see Malchukov 2006 and section 5.9 below).

5.4 THE CLINES OF DEVERBALIZATION AND SUBSTANTIVIZATION

As noted above, the constraints on transcategorial operations such as nominalizations can be derived from verbal and nominal hierarchies. On this account, the two processes—deverbalization and substantivization—proceed basically independent of each other. Of course, this is a simplification, and below we will see how the two hierarchies can be combined in one model (called GSM), and what sort of complications arise from that (Blocking effects). Before we proceed, I illustrate briefly deverbalization and substantivization clines below, drawing on the 50-language convenience sample used in my earlier study (see appendix in Malchukov 2004: 133–134 for the language sample).

The cline of deverbalization as predicted by my model is represented in Figure 5.3. Here I concentrate on morphological categories of verbs, disregarding for the moment possible discrepancies between operators and satellites (see section 5.5). The line indicates the range of the verbal categories retained. Note that the cited examples are intended to represent the cut-off points on the hierarchies; they are less committed to the availability of other categories (which may be lacking in a language altogether).

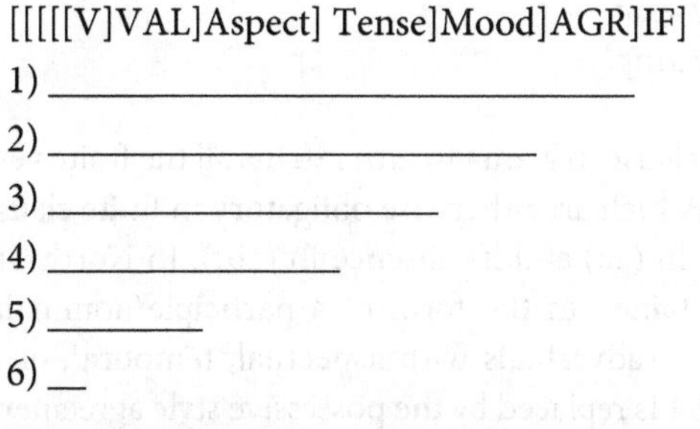

[[[[[V]VAL]Aspect] Tense]Mood]AGR]IF]
1) _____
2) _____
3) _____
4) _____
5) _____
6) __

FIGURE 5.3 The cline of deverbalization

In what follows, I will illustrate the effects of deverbalization and substantivization clines drawing on the sample of languages in Malchukov (2004). The following examples illustrate gradual loss of verbal categories starting from outermost layers in a selection of languages (used in Malchukov's 2004 sample).

(2) Nama (Hagman 1973: 235)
 a. *Tiíta ke //nãatí kè ≠'aj hãa 'ií*
    I DC this.way PST think PST.PFV
    'I had thought this way.'

 b. *Tiíta //nãatí kè ≠ aj hãa 'ií-s*
    I this.way PST think PST.PFV-NZR
    'My thinking/that I had thought that way.'

(3) Even (Malchukov 2002)
  Hin eme-nne-ve-s   dolda-ri-v
  your arrive-NEC.PART-ACC-2SG.POS hear-PAST-1SG
  'I heard that you should come.'

(4) Korean (Sohn 1994: 55)
  Na-nun apeci-ka o-si-ess-um-ul   al-ass-ta
  I-TOP father-NOM come-SH-PST-NZR-ACC know-PST-DC
  'I knew that father came.'

(5) Eskimo (West Greenlandic) (Fortescue 1984: 45)
  Umiarsu-up qassi-nut   tikin-ni-ssa-a   nalunngil-ara
  ship-REL how.many-ALL arrive-NZR-NOM.FUT-its know-IND.1S->3
  'I know when the ship arrives.'

(6) Abkhaz (Hewitt 1979: 84)
  A-ç-š-rà   ø-yə-taxə-wpʼ
  the-self-kill-NZR it-he-want-STAT
  'He wants to kill himself.'

(7) Ket (Werner 1997: 249)
  Isʼ   qasʼ-ku-tnʼ
  eat.INF want/-2S-/want
  'You want to eat/eating.'

Thus, the complement clause in Nama in (2b) retains all the finite verbal marker, apart from illocutionary markers, which are otherwise obligatory in finite clauses (see the presence of the declarative marker in (2a) and its absence in (2b)). In North-Tungusic Even (see (3)), TAM categories are retained in the form of a participle/nominalization along with the corresponding satellites (adverbials with aspectual, temporal, or modal functions), but the finite verb agreement is replaced by the possessive style agreement found on nouns. This pattern is typical of the POS-ACC type of nominalizations in terms of Koptjevskaja-Tamm (1993), although is manifested here in agreement (head marking) rather than case marking (dependent marking). The pattern with Mood lost but tense/aspect retained is illustrated by one of the nominalization patterns from Korean illustrated in (4) (see Malchukov 2004: 33–37 for more discussion of Korean nominalizations). In (West Greenlandic) Eskimo (derivational) aspects are lost, while tense is represented in a nominal fashion. In Abkhaz, TAM categories as well as AGR are lost on 'masdar' nominalizations, but some voice/valency markers are retained (see reflexive marker in (6)). Finally, in Ket, nominalizations/infinitives, as illustrated in (7), do not feature any of the verbal categories (Werner 1997: 175), in stark contrast to verbs, which show a heavy polysynthetic structure. Of course, examples of strongly nominalized deverbal nouns lacking all verbal characteristics can be cited from many other languages.

In a similar way, it can be shown that acquisition of nominal properties proceeds stepwise in accordance with the hierarchy of nominal features (as in Figure 5.3, the line in Figure 5.4 indicates the range of nominal categories available).

[[[[[N]CL]NB]POS]DET]CASE]
1) ____
2) _____
3) _____
4) _____
5) _____

FIGURE 5.4 The cline of substantivization

The following examples (from the sample languages used in Malchukov's 2004 study) illustrate the gradual acquisition of nominal categories in substantivization:

(8) Ngiyambaa (Donaldson 1980: 303)
     Ŋadhu dhi:rba-nha ngana-gal guruŋa-nha-ba
     I.NOM know-PRES   that.ABS-PL swim-PRES-SUB
     'I know that they are swimming.'

(9) Mangarayi (Merlan 1982: 21)
     Ya-ø-yaŋ-gu-wana   wa-ŋa-ṇaya-wu
     SUB-3SG-go-INT-ABL IRR-1SG->3SG-cook-INT
     'After he goes I want to cook it.'

(10) Diegueño (Miller 2001: 219)
     [Me-xap]-pu   nya'wach ny-uuwiw
     2-enter-DEM   we.SUBJ 1,2-see.PL
     'We saw (that) you come in.'

(11) Fijian (Dixon 1988: 131)
     au tadra-a   [a   o-mu   aa/na   la'o mai]
     1SG dream-TR ART CLASS-your PAST/FUT come here
     'I dreamt that you had/will come.'

(12) Fula (Arnott 1970: 372)
     duudu-ki bel-ki   ki'i
     pipe-INF sweet.CL CL.the
     'this sweet piping'

In Ngiyambaa, none of the nominal categories are present in the complement clause, as illustrated in (8). In Mangarayi, another Australian language, the complement clauses (as in (9)) take case but not the other nominal categories. In Diegueño, nominalizations (as illustrated in (10)), case, and determiners are acquired but not the other nominal categories. For Fijian, which lacks the morphological number marking, it is explicitly stated that nominalizations (as in (11)) do not combine with numerals (in the quantifying '*e*+number construction'), although they are able to take possessors, articles, and case markers (Dixon 1988: 132, 143). The same pattern is true for many other nominalizations of the POSS-ACC type, as illustrated in (3) for Even. And in Fula, verbal nouns (as in (12)) feature all the nominal categories including number and class marking, this displaying full recategorization. Many other languages, which lack an overt noun class system or numeral classifiers, have 'strong nominalizations' that reveal all properties of nonderived nouns.

The current model, which bases its predictions on the functionally based hierarchy constraints, correctly captures many generalizations that have been proposed in the literature. Thus, the different susceptibility of tense, aspect, and mood categories to deverbalization, as originally suggested by Comrie & Thompson (1985) and Lehmann (1988), and confirmed in more recent studies by Cristofaro (2003) and Malchukov (2004), is reflected by their different ranking on the deverbalization cline. Another well-known generalization to the effect that S-arguments genitivize prior to O-arguments (Comrie 1976; cf. Koptjevskaja-Tamm 1993) is also predicted by the model. As noted above, subjects (linked to subject agreement) rank higher on the hierarchy of verbal categories than objects, and are therefore 'affected' (converted to possessor or lost) by transcategorial operations before objects (pertaining to the voice/valency layer) can be 'affected'. Before we address the question as to how the two hierarchies can be combined in order to constrain the outcome of transcategorial operations, we need to consider interfering factors, which may run counter to the predictions of the hierarchies above.

5.5 COMPLICATIONS AND INTERFERING FACTORS

The data presented in the previous sections lend support to the hypothesis concerning the role of hierarchies in nominalization processes. However, the presented model needs to be qualified in several respects. First, the model should be qualified to allow for a potential asymmetry between operators and satellites in transcategorial processes. In its most general form, the Operator–satellite asymmetry principle (OSAP) can be stated as in Malchukov (2004: 37):

> *If an operator is available for a certain category, expression of a concomitant satellite should also be available. However, availability of a satellite does not entail availability of an operator.*

The OSAP is trivially true for isolating languages where the semantics of (verbal) morphological categories is rendered by lexical means. Furthermore, the OSAP has special bearing on the issue of transcategorial operations, including nominalizations. As predicted by the OSAP, an operator may be lost in nominalization, while a corresponding satellite may be maintained. This is illustrated by data from Basque, where we see a loss of verbal agreement (subject and object agreement), but the sentential marking of arguments (subjects and objects) is retained:

(13) Basque (Saltarelli 1988: 258)
Su-k   ni-ri   gezurra   esa-te-ak
you-ERG me-DAT lie-SG.ABS tell-NZR-SG.ERG
harri-tzen n-a-u
surprise-HAB 1SG.A-PRES-AUX(-3SG.ERG)
'That you tell me a lie surprises me.'

Note, in particular, that the nominalization with the suffix *-te* in (13) loses all verbal inflectional TAM and agreement morphology (expressed on the auxiliary in (13)), but this does not affect the syntax of the nominalized clause, i.e. its ergative-style case marking. This means that operators are generally better predictors with regard to retention of (verbal) characteristics as compared to satellites. If an operator is available, retention of both lower operators and satellites is predicted. If a satellite is retained, predictions hold only for the (lower) satellites.

Second, the outcome of transcategorial operations cannot be predicted solely on the basis of the function of a particular category; one should also take into account how this category is expressed. Consider the case of nominalizations in Limbu (a Kiranti language), where the nominalization with the *-ba* suffix (also used as a participle) loses Mood and Aspect markers but retains Tense distinctions. The loss of Mood prior to Tense is consistent with the proposed hierarchy, but the relation between Tense and Aspect is puzzling. Note that in contrast to the finite verb (as in (14)), the nominalization in (15) lacks the outermost aspect marker:

(14) Limbu (Van Driem 1987: 90)
Kɛ-ips-ɛ-tchi-ba-i̧
2-sleep-PRET-du.ABS-IPF-Q
'Have you been sleeping?'

(15) Limbu (Van Driem 1987: 198)
Kheŋ hopt-ɛ-ba   nis-ɛ-tch-u-waŋ
that not.be-PRET-NZR see-PRET-du.A-3P-GER
'seeing that it was not there'

As argued in (Malchukov 2004; 2006), 'early' loss of aspect (i.e. prior to the loss of the tense morphology) in Limbu nominalizations can be attributed to structural factors. The outermost affixes are less morphologically integrated, hence tend to be lost early in decategorization. Of course, the effect of this factor is not detectable, if the ordering of affixes follows functional principle of scope (or 'relevance', in terms of Bybee 1985), yet, if the linear order is not iconic, structural factors may interfere with the clines of deverbalization (or substantivization).

This principle of structural dependency for the outcome of transcategorial operations is dubbed the Isomorphism Principle in Malchukov (2004: 108): features encoded similarly will show similar behaviour in transcategorial operations. Apart from linearity, another complication captured by the Isomorphism Principle relates to cumulative expression of categories. If the respective categories rank differently on deverbalization or substantivization hierarchies, this leads to conflicting predictions concerning their retention (or acquisition). For example, in Nenets and (Modern) Greek voice distinctions (active/middle) are expressed cumulatively with agreement. In Nenets, non-finite forms (participles/gerunds/infinitives) lose agreement and by the same stroke voice distinctions are lost as well. In (Modern) Greek, the middle voice agreement morphology, as found on finite verbs, is lost on non-finite forms (gerunds and participles), but voice distinction is retained in a modified form (through the use of special medial forms of gerunds and participles). Thus, for Nenets the Isomorphism Principle wins in competition with functional constraints, while in Greek, functional constraints gain the upper hand. We will return to the issues of the interaction of functional and structural constraints when addressing the formalization of the proposed approach in OT (section 5.9).

5.6 Generalized scale model

Now the question is: how are the two hierarchies (presented in Figures 5.1 and 5.2) related to each other? Let us assume as a null hypothesis (to be revised later) that there are no constraints on possible 'mappings' between these two hierarchies. This will yield the model in Figure 5.5, which I call the GSM.

[[[[[N]CL]NB]POS]DET] CASE

⟵────────────────────────

nominalization

[[[[[[V]VAL]ASP]Tense]Mood]AGR]IF]

⟵────────────────────────

deverbalization

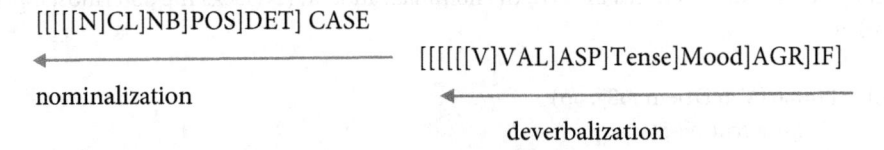

FIGURE 5.5 Generalized scale model for nominalizations

The GSM is intended to constrain the possible resultant sets of (nominal and verbal) categories exhibited by nominalized forms by disallowing discontinuous strings on the scale. Note, however, that the GSM does not predict availability of certain grammatical categories in particular languages, but rather pertains to their expression in nominalization—if a category is grammaticalized. If certain morphological categories are not grammaticalized at all, such gaps on the scales for nominalized forms are expected and do not qualify as contiguity violations. Note also that the position of the nominalizer on the scale is on the dividing line between the hierarchies. Here it is not represented independently since the nominalizer often cumulates with one of the verbal categories retained or one of the nominal categories acquired.

Below I 'map' some of the nominalizations from the languages discussed above onto the GSM. Thus, clausal nominalizations in Mangarayi, as illustrated in (9), when mapped onto the GSM, yield the following Generalized Scale Representation (GSR) (categories available to nominalization are indicated in **boldface**):

<<GSR-1: Mangarayi>>
N-CL-NB-POS-DET-**CASE**//**V-VAL-Voi**-ASP-TE-Mood-AGR-IF

GSR-1 reflects that nominalizations in Mangarayi take case markers but otherwise retain all sentential/verbal characteristics.

The pattern of nominalizations in Even, exemplified in (3), is represented by GSR-2:

<<GSR-2: Even>>

N-CL-NB-**POS**-(DET)-**CASE**//**V**-**VAL**-**Voi**-**ASP**-**TE**-Mood-AGR-IF

As is clear from GSR-2, nominalizations in Even lose (sentential) subject agreement, but retain tense/aspect categories. As for nominal categories, the availability of case markers, as well as of possessive marking (in particular possessive style agreement), has been illustrated in (3) (there are no grammaticalized determiners in Even).

Finally, the mapping of the verbal nouns in Fula (as in (12)) onto the GSM yields GSR-3:

<<GSR-3: Fula>>

N-**CL**-**NB**-**POS**-**DET**-**CASE**//**V**-(**VAL**)-ASP-TE-Mood-AGR-IF

GSR-3 shows that verbal nouns acquire all nominal categories (including the overt class/number marker), while losing all verbal categories (except for derivational valency markers).

There are, of course, various complicating factors, which can determine the outcome of nominalizations; thus, interference of structural factors considered above may lead to 'ill-formed' GSR representations (see Malchukov 2004: 42, 58 for discussion and exemplification). More important for the model, however, are additional constraints on mapping the two hierarchies on each other. Indeed, it can be shown that for certain categories the choice of a nominal encoding for a certain category blocks (excludes) its coding in a clausal fashion. In particular, Malchukov (2004: 59–69) distinguishes between 'Argument Blocking' related to the expression of verbal arguments and 'Modifier Blocking' related to the expression of modifiers in a nominal (adjectives) or sentential (adverbs) fashion (cf. *His quick returning* and *His returning quickly*). For argument blocking, it is important to distinguish between Subject Blocking and Object Blocking, since they have very different effects on the retention of verbal categories. In Subject Blocking, the subject is expressed in a nominal fashion (converts to a possessor). Subject Blocking excludes sentential expression of the subject and (finite) subject agreement (as well as illocutionary force), but allows for expression of internal categories such as TAM and valency/voice, as well as expression of modifiers and objects in clausal form. Object Blocking involving expression of the object in the possessive form has a more far-reaching effect, as the object is associated with the innermost valency/voice layer; in this case, expression of all verbal categories and corresponding sentential satellites (e.g. adverbs) is excluded in one stroke. The effects of Modifier Blocking are broadly comparable to that of Object Blocking (see Malchukov 2004 for further discussion and qualification).

The effects of Subject Blocking and Object Blocking are illustrated in Figures 5.6 and 5.7, respectively (see Malchukov 2004: 67–68). Note that in the representations below the bold-faced categories are predicted to be retained in nominalizations, the categories indicated through strikethrough are predicted to be lost, while the model is noncommittal as to availability of other categories (not highlighted in the representations).

[[[[[N]~~CL]NB~~] **POS**]DET]Case]
 ←─────────────── [[[[[V]**VAL**]ASP]TE]Mood]~~AGR]IF~~]
    nominalization   ←───────────────
                                deverbalization

FIGURE 5.6 Subject Blocking

[[[[[N]**CL**]NB]**POS**]DET]Case]
 ←─────────────── [[[[[V]~~VAL]ASP]TE]Mood~~]AGR]~~IF~~]
    nominalization   ←───────────────
                                deverbalization

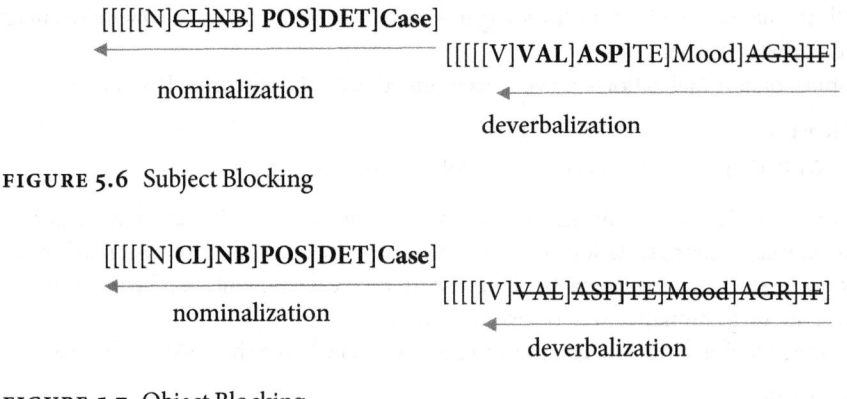

FIGURE 5.7 Object Blocking

The predictions of this model have been evaluated against a convenience sample of 50 languages and have been generally confirmed (Malchukov 2004). The effects of the Subject and Object Blocking can be illustrated by the much-discussed case of nominal and verbal gerunds in English, as illustrated in (1a) and (1b). For the verbal gerund, which takes the subject (rather than the object) as a possessor, the model predicts correctly that verbal characteristics may be retained; in particular, it may distinguish aspect and voice and combine with adverbs (cf. *his having driven the car so dangerously*). By contrast, the nominal gerund is predicted to undergo strong recategorization by virtue of Object Blocking. Indeed, the nominal gerund combines with adjectives and not adverbs and loses verbal aspectual and voice distinctions (cf. **his having driven of the car*). Thus, the morphosyntactic characteristics of the English *ing*-form largely follow the predictions of my model (Malchukov 2004: 65; see also Malchukov 2019 for further discussion).[6]

Thus, blocking imposes further constraints on the unification of verbal and nominal categories from the respective hierarchies. The major types of nominalizations which arise from imposing blocking constraints on the GSM are: (i) weak nominalizations when no Blocking applies (which at most acquire case marking and determiners); (ii) mixed category nominalizations resulting from subject blocking; and (iii) strong nominalizations when object and/or modifier blocking applies.[7]

5.7 VERBALIZATION

The GSM as proposed above is not intended to apply exclusively to nominalization. In this section I show the applicability of the GSM to verbalization (see Malchukov

---

[6] The only exception is that the verbal gerund cannot combine with the article, although it can take a possessor and combine with prepositions; yet its use with other determiners is not excluded (Quirk et al. 1985: 1064).

[7] The effects of modifier blocking and object blocking also differ subtly (Malchukov 2004: 67–69). It may be noted in this context that the four types of nominalizations arising through object blocking, modifier blocking, subject blocking, and no-blocking correspond roughly to the distinction between VP nominalization, vP nominalization, TP nominalization, and CP nominalization in Kornfilt & Whitman (2011).

2004: 85–107). It should be noted, though, that the mechanism of verbalization has been controversially discussed in the literature. Thus, Hopper & Thompson (1984) argue that while nominalizations (events conceptualized as objects) show morphosyntactic features of both nouns and verbs, when objects are conceptualized as events, they acquire all the verbal features appropriate for that function and should therefore count as denominal verbs. By contrast, Bhat (1994) holds a different view claiming that—just like in the case of nominalization—when nouns are used as verbs they can both be decategorized and recategorized.

I follow Bhat (1994) rather than Hopper & Thompson (1984) assuming that, as long as decategorization and recategorization involved in transcategorial operations are functionally motivated, they should equally apply to nominalizations and verbalizations. Furthermore, just as in the case of nominalization, these processes can be shown to be gradual and relatively independent of each other. At one pole one finds 'predicate complements', which hardly show any signs of decategorization or recategorization (cf. *John is/remains my best friend*): the predicate nominals retain their nominal status while the predicative function is performed by the auxiliary (copula) verb. At the opposite pole one finds denominal verbs, involving both (full) decategorization and recategorization (cf. *John hammered on the door*). However, just as in the case of nominalizations, intermediate cases are found as well. Thus, if a nominal predicate is decategorized, but does not acquire any verbal categories, the feature combination [+D−R] yields 'bare' nominal predicates, as in *John is chairman* (Hopper & Thompson 1984; cf. Hengeveld 1992b). If, on the other hand, a nominal predicate retains (to some extent) nominal categories but acquires verbal features, the feature combination [−D + R] yields 'verbalizations proper'. This latter option can be illustrated with verbalizations ('inactive verbalizations') in West Greenlandic Eskimo, which lose their possessive and number marking, as found on nominals, but retain combinability with adnominal attributes (Fortescue 1984: 70, 301):

(16) Eskimo (West Greenlandic) (Fortescue 1984: 70)
Illuqarvi-u-vuq angisuuq
town-be-IND.3SG big.ABS.SG
'It's a big town.'

In what follows I focus on cases of verbalization proper, showing the feature combination [−D + R], since they are most instructive with regard to the question of which combinations of nominal and verbal features are available in verbalizations. Clearly, such cases demonstrating that verbalization does not necessarily lead to denominalization are more in line with Bhat (1994) rather than with Hopper & Thompson's (1984) approach.[8] On the other hand, my data show that there is indeed a difference between the two processes: verbalization tends to be indeed more 'abrupt', as already anticipated by Hopper & Thompson (1984). Below we shall see how my model can account for both similarities and differences between the processes of verbalization and nominalization.

---

[8] Also Mel'čuk (1998: 271) draws a sharp distinction between the predicative conjugation of nouns as a nominal inflectional category (as found, e.g., in Turkish) and 'identificative' verbalizers, deriving verbs from nouns (as found, e.g., in Eskimo). As is clear from the above, the distinction is not clear-cut, though. For example, (inactive) verbalizations in Eskimo are not totally devoid of nominal properties.

The generalized scale for verbalization, which is the mirror image of the scale for nominalization, can be represented as in Figure 5.8.

[[[[[V]VAL]**ASP**]TE]Mood]AGR]IF]
⟵ verbalization   [[[[[N]CL]NB]POS]DET]Case
                                  ⟵ denominalization

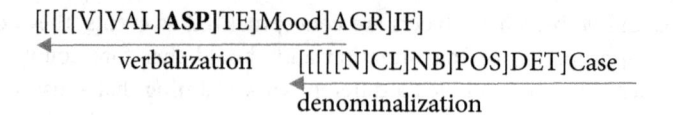

FIGURE 5.8 Generalized scale model for verbalization

As in the case of nominalizations, the generalized scale for verbalization is constrained by the contiguity requirement imposed by the feature hierarchies. That is, if the internal category is acquired (or lost), the external one will be affected as well. This contiguity requirement will be illustrated below making use of the data from the sample languages used in (Malchukov 2004). Consider Ket, as in (17), where locative predicates appear in the verbalized form. Note that the verbalized noun acquires (subject) agreement, but retains case, possessive, and plural marking (Werner 1997: 305):

(17) Ket   (Werner 1997: 305)
     Na-ang-n-bes'-n-nangta-ru
     her-female-PL-hare-PL-ADESS-3M
     'He is/was by her female hares.'

The mapping of the weak verbalization in Ket (as in (17)) on the GSM for verbalization yields the following GSR (again, categories available for the verbalized noun are boldfaced):

<<GSR-5: Ket>>

V-VAL-ASP-Te-Mood-**AGR-IF**//**N-CL-NB-POSDET-Case**

GSR-5 shows that the verbalized nominal in Ket retains all nominal categories including case while AGR (and, sometimes, IF) are the only verbal categories acquired.

Fijian shows a more complex (even) mixture of verbal and nominal categories in verbalizations. According to Dixon (1988: 66), Fijian disallows the (common) article on nominal predicates but allows for the retention of other nominal categories (e.g. number), as well as NP modifiers including possessors, numerals, and adjectives. The use of adjectival modifiers within the predicative NP is illustrated in (18):

(18) Fijian   (Dixon 1988: 66)
     Sa   [marama sava.savaa] gaa   [o   Aneta]
     NONFUT lady   clean   MODIF [ART Aneta]
     'Aneta is a very clean lady.'

The GSR for Fijian verbalizations (as in (18)) shows that they allow for retention of all categories except the determiner (the common article) and case markers while acquiring tense as well as higher categories.

<<GSR-6: Fijian>>

V-VAL-**ASP-Te-Mood-AGR-IF**//**N-CL-NB-POS**-DET-Case

Finally, let us consider 'active' verbalizations in Eskimo (West Greenlandic) as an example of 'strong verbalizations'. Eskimo features two different types of verbalization, dubbed 'inactive' and 'active' in Fortescue (1984). In contrast to 'inactive verbalizations', illustrated in (17), 'active verbalizations' (derived by suffixes such as *-qar-* 'have', *-si-* 'get', *-liur-* 'make') are recategorized more strongly: in particular, they take a modifier in the adverbial (marked by the instrumental case), rather than attributive form (Fortescue 1984: 83). Additionally, active verbalizations may express all the aspectual and modal distinctions of non-derived verbs. As regards valency, the majority of 'active' verbalizations is morphologically intransitive (they take the intransitive AGR), but some (e.g. *-gi-* 'have as', as illustrated in (19)) are transitively conjugated, taking cumulative subject/object agreement.

(19) Eskimo (West Greenlandic) (Fortescue 1984: 71)
Anaana-ga-ara
mother-'have as'-IND.1->3
'She is my mother.' (lit. 'I have her as my mother')

GSR-7 provides a representation of the 'active verbalizations' in Eskimo (as in (19)), which reveal full recategorization: all verbal categories (with the possible exception of the valency/voice layer) are acquired, while all the nominal categories are lost.

<<GSR-7: Eskimo>>

V-VAL-**ASP-Te-Mood-AGR-IF**//N-CL-NB-POS-DET-Case

As is clear from the above, the contiguity requirements are generally corroborated by my data (some counterexamples conditioned by structural factors are discussed in Malchukov 2004: 104–107).

Let us consider next how Blocking applies to the generalized verbalization scale. Argument Blocking has restricted force when applied to verbalizations insofar as the possessor may be encoded (construed) as an object (see (19)), but cannot be construed as a subject. Object Blocking entails acquisition of all the verbal categories, since the valency layer to which the object belongs is the innermost layer of the verbal hierarchy. As for Modifier Blocking, it has a more radical impact on verbalizations than on nominalizations. In accordance with the model, as soon as a nominal predicate acquires aspectual distinctions and manner adverbs, adjectives and class markers involved in Modifier Blocking are excluded. Since the innermost layer, hosting adjectives/class markers, is eliminated, all the other nominal categories that are external to this layer will be lost as well. The pattern resulting from Modifier Blocking, which involves acquisition of the aspectual/adverbial layer, is represented in Figure 5.9 (as before, categories predicted to be available are boldfaced, categories predicted to be absent are marked with strikethrough).

[[[[[V]VAL]**ASP**]Te]Mood]AGR]IF]
⟵ verbalization   [[[[[N]~~CL~~]NB]~~POS~~]~~DET~~]~~Case~~
                        ⟵ denominalization

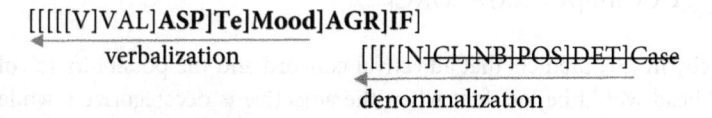

FIGURE 5.9 Modifier Blocking in verbalization

Thus, the abrupt loss of nominal categories once the aspectual/adverbial layer is acquired finds a natural explanation within the model: the 'breakdown' of nominal categories is due to Modifier Blocking. As predicted by the model, two major verbalization patterns are available cross-linguistically: (i) 'weak' verbalizations prior to the acquisition of the aspectual/adverbial layer, which show a mixture of verbal and nominal characteristics; and (ii) 'strong' verbalizations, which are totally devoid—due to Modifier Blocking—of nominal features and may be viewed as denominal verbs.

5.8 Extensions of the model

As also noted in Malchukov (2004: 131), the advocated GSM is in principle applicable to any transcategorial operations (beyond nominalization and verbalization), but the model presupposes the existence of functional hierarchies for individual lexical categories. For some lexical categories such as adverbs the functional structure is minimally developed, so the issue of recategorization of verbs and nouns as adverbs largely boils down to the discussion of decategorization of nouns and verbs (but see Bisang 2000 on 'plus-asymmetry' patterns observed for converbs).

More interesting are transcategorial operations involving adjectives, which have not been explicitly addressed in my earlier work, but have been taken up in some follow-up studies. Talamo (2017) is a recent study of nominal uses of property concepts in Italian. Talamo, adopting the general approach of Malchukov (2004), proposes a 'Hierarchy of de-adjectivalization', where the loss of the Relational Layer (called 'valency' by Talamo) precedes the loss of Gradation Layer (hosting degree modifiers). Talamo (2017: 103) cites the example (20) where the property concept retains gradation, but is otherwise assimilated to the morphosyntax of nouns.

(20) Italian (Talamo 2017:103)
　　　La　　　　*troppa*　　　　　*bell-ezza*
　　　the.DEF　too.much.AUGM　beautiful-NMLZ.(F).SG
　　　'the excessive beauty'

To bring the 'Hierarchy of de-adjectivalization' more in line with the architecture of the verbal and nominal hierarchies above, the hierarchy for adjectives can be represented as in (21), where the Relational Layer (Talamo's 'valency') hosts adjectival concord as well as providing for a possibility of taking nominal heads-satellites, while Gradation Layer hosts degree operators and corresponding satellites (in the form of degree adverbs and/or objects of comparison).

(21)　$[N_{head}[OCOMP[A]GRAD]CONC]$

The hierarchy in (21) predicts that adjectival concord and the possibility to combine with a nominal head would be lost first when the adjective is decategorized, while the use of comparative forms/and or combinability with corresponding satellites (e.g. object of comparison) may be retained. This is, generally, confirmed by Talamo's study through a close inspection of the Italian corpus data (large-scale cross-linguistic confirmation is left for future research). Correspondingly, one would expect that under the verb-to-adjective transposition the relational concord layer would be acquired first. This is obviously true for participles, which show the inflectional/syntactic behaviour of adjectives, but rarely the possibility of occurring in a comparative construction—unless lexicalized.

A recent study of the mixed categories by Nikolaeva & Spencer (2019) provides new insights into Noun-to-Adjectives recategorizations (transposition). Such 'noun-adjective hybrids' can be illustrated by the Even constructions like *hoja oro-lkan-du bei-du* [many reindeer-PROPR-DAT man-DAT] 'to the man with many reindeer', where the proprietive modifier *orolkan* 'with reindeer' agrees with the head in case (like an adjective), while retaining a possibility to take modifiers (like a noun); see discussion of similar examples by Nikolaeva & Spencer (2019: 344ff). for another Tungusic language Evenki. The focus of Nikolaeva & Spencer's study is more theoretical rather than typological (i.e. sample-based), and is further framed in a lexicalist framework, rather than in the model espoused here. That said, the puzzling behaviour of 'noun-adjective hybrids', which retain the possibility of attributive modification, while simultaneously acquiring adjectival inflection, is fully compatible with predictions of GSM. On the approach adopted here 'noun-adjective hybrids' retain the innermost Class Layer (hosting adjectival attributes) on the nominal hierarchy, while simultaneously acquiring the outermost Relational layer (Talamo's 'valency') on the adjectival hierarchy (as in (21)).

While the study by Talamo concerns categorial mixture in cases of Adjective-to-Noun recategorization and Nikolaeva & Spencer's study deals with Noun-to-Adjective recategorization, the typological studies by van Lier (2009) and Shagal (2019) address Verb-to-Adjective recategorization. The study by van Lier is broader and is mostly concerned with (mis)matches between lexical categorization at the basic level and at the level of derived forms, including categorial (mis)matches between nouns and nominalizations, but also adjectives and participles. As far as these (mis)matches are manifested morphosyntactically, van Lier makes use of GSM for purposes of typological comparison (see van Lier's 'two-step typology of Dependent Clauses'). A follow-up study by Shagal (2019) addresses more specifically participles, again paying more attention to deverbalization aspect.[9] Both typological studies generally confirm the validity of hierarchy constraints as proposed in Malchukov (2004) (as well as in related work by Cristofaro 2003 and Nikolaeva 2013), but also show a possibility of extensions of the GSM to other types of transcategorial operations beyond nominalization (and verbalization).

Still another extension, partially addressed in Malchukov (2004), and followed up by Malchukov (2019), is the applicability of the model to more complex scenarios. As already mentioned in Malchukov (2004: 55), the case of a verbal gerund in English is a case in point. Indeed, while from a synchronic perspective the verbal gerund is a result of nominalization, diachronically we are dealing here with a more complex scenario where a deverbal noun increased its verbal properties (see Tabor & Traugott 1998; see also Van der Pol 2019 and

---

[9] Shagal (2019) also provides an interesting discussion of the expression of some other verbal categories in participles, in particular, the expression of negation. Negation has also been used for probing into verbal and nominal features in some earlier studies of nominalizations (in particular, by Comrie & Thompson 1985 and Koptjevskaja-Tamm 1993), but not in Malchukov (2004), because negation may take different scopes over other categories and therefore cannot be unambiguously located on the hierarchies.

Fonteyn 2019 for more discussion of the diachrony of the English gerund). Thus, diachronically, the nominal gerund represents a conservative pattern, while the verbal gerund an innovating pattern. While histories of individual constructions are complex and may involve multiple shifts, the resultant patterns generally comply with the GSM (see Malchukov 2019 for discussion of this point in relation to English gerunds).[10] In other words, since the hierarchy constraints as well as Blocking mechanisms are general well-formedness constraints on category mixing residing in general functional factors, they have a panchronic status, relatively independent of the complex histories of individual constructions. This does not mean, however, that diachronic sources are irrelevant; at the very least they perspire in the forms of structural constraints which can condition violations of GSM constraints. Recall the case of 'early' loss of aspect in Limbu in (15), which, viewed diachronically, is rather conditioned by a 'late' grammaticalization of aspectual auxiliaries.

5.9 Formalization

As is clear from the discussion above, the presented model relying on deverbalization and substantivization hierarchies in interaction with other factors is basically a kind of competing motivation approach, grounded in functional factors. For this reason, it lends itself naturally to Optimality-Theoretic formalization. Malchukov (2006) provided an Optimality-Theoretic reconstruction of the GSM. OT is particularly successful at modelling interaction between different kinds of constraints, both functional and structural. Moreover, an OT approach predicts that possible reranking of constraints (factorial typology) would produce typological variation.

In my earlier work (Malchukov 2004, 2006), I followed Croft (1991) in assuming two main motivations for parts of speech differentiation: the pragmatic function of a lexical item and the semantic class of a lexical root. On Croft's view (1991: 50–53; see also Chapter 11 in this volume), the unmarked combination of the lexical class and pragmatic function (action words in the predicative function for verbs, and objects used in the argument function, in case of nouns) gives rise to lexical differentiation between prototypical nouns and verbs. Most importantly in the present context, Croft's theory also predicts that morphosyntactic trappings of nouns and verbs would show up (if available in a particular language) on the prototypical items displaying a harmonic combination of lexical class and discourse function, while the marked combinations will be impoverished with respect to these features.

---

[10] Some other 'mixed categories' that evolved through multiple categorial shifts may be more challenging for GSM, as well as for hierarchy-based approaches, in general. One such challenging case has been described by Nikitina (2007) for Wan (a Mande language) under the name of 'embedded clauses with nominal internal structure'. It should be noted, though, that such constructions are not nominalizations syntactically (as is also clear from their structural representation as a verbal projection), but rather function as infinitives. Overall, this challenging construction in Wan is most reminiscent of nominalization-turned-infinitive patterns with partial retention of nominal morphosyntax. Malchukov (2004: 118, fn. 75) mentions similar cases in Hixkaryana, Ket, and Abkhaz where nominalizations have extended their function to the infinitive use but retain in the latter function certain nominal properties (e.g. possessive agreement used to cross-reference the object).

Within the framework of OT (Prince and Smolensky 2004), these two factors contributing to lexical categorization can be considered as two constraints (or rather two families of constraints, as we will see below) on the morphosyntactic marking of lexical categories:

FuncFaith: *Assign (morphological) categories to a lexical item in accordance with its discourse function;*

LexFaith: *Assign (morphological) categories to a lexical item in accordance with the semantic class of a lexical root.*

While in the case of the unmarked (harmonic) combinations of the discourse function and the semantic class of a lexical item both constraints are (vacuously) satisfied, in the case of a mismatch between the two as in case of nominalization, these constraints are in conflict. The outcome of the conflict will depend on the ranking of the two constraints: FuncFaith >> LexFaith or LexFaith >> FuncFaith. With regard to nominalization, the former ranking will result in 'strong' nominalizations, which show all the nominal properties and are devoid of verbal properties. The latter ranking yields weakly nominalized sentential complements hardly showing any nominal properties.

Note that in case of a mismatch between a lexical class and pragmatic function one cannot fully satisfy both constraints since they are in conflict and lead to conflicting outcomes. For example, with regard to deverbalization, FuncFaith predicts that a nominalized verb will not show any verbal categories since it is no longer used as a predicate, while LexFaith predicts that the verbal categories will be retained in accordance with the semantic class of the root. However, given that there is a large set of nominal and verbal categories, it is perfectly possible that some of the verbal categories will be lost due to FuncFaith, while some other will be retained due to LexFaith. In Malchukov's (2006) approach FuncFaith constraints are seen as driving decategorization processes, and correspondingly LexFaith constraints are conceived as a hedging device. If a FuncFaith constraint (e.g. *Mood) outranks a corresponding LexFaith constraint (*– Mood) the category in question will be lost, otherwise it will be retained. The set of verbal categories retained depends on the point at which LexFaith constraints are interpolated in the FuncFaith hierarchy. The Deverbalization Hierarchy (as in Figure 5.3) is recast in (22) as a constraint hierarchy, which compels all verbal categories to be lost as long as the (nominalized) verb is not used as a (finite) predicate, and where higher (external) categories incur more serious violation than lower (internal) categories:

(22)   * IF >> *AGRs >> *Mood >> *Tense >> *Aspect >> *Voice >> *Valency

For the sake of concreteness, consider the following constraint hierarchy (in (23), representing the pattern where mood is lost, but tense is retained (cf. example (4) from Korean):

(23)   *IF >> *AGRs >> *Mood >> LexFaith >> *Tense >> *Aspect
       >>*Voice>>*Valency

The Substantivization Hierarchy is similarly derived by the interaction of conflicting FuncFaith and LexFaith constraint hierarchies. The FuncFaith hierarchy for substantivization is represented in (24) (see the Substantivization Cline in Figure 5.4):

(24)   *–Case >> *–Det >> *–Pos >> *–Nb >> *–CL

The hierarchy in (22) reflects the fact that FuncFaith compels the marking of nominalization—in accordance with its argument function—for all nominal categories available, and it does this to a greater degree the more external (function-related) the categories in question are. Again, by way of illustration, the following hierarchy in (25) captures the pattern of nominalization with a cut-off point between determiners (acquired) and possessors (cf. example (10) from Diegueño):

(25)   *–Case >> *–Det >> LexFaith >>*–Pos >> *–Nb >> *–CL

While the hierarchy constraints can capture different degrees of decategorization/recategorization along the hierarchies, they are not sufficient for capturing Blocking Effects. To achieve the latter an extra constraint, which can be dubbed LexFaith Dependency Principle, is needed:[11]

> LexFaith Dependency Principle: For any pair of the Blocking Categories x:
>
> If FuncFaith/x outranks LexFaith/x on a nominal hierarchy, then FuncFaith/x should outrank LexFaith/x on a verbal hierarchy as well.

For example, if possessive encoding for an argument is acquired (as reflected in the ranking *–Pos >> LexFaith) then (finite) agreement and sentential subject encoding should be lost (as reflected in the ranking *AGRs >> LexFaith on the verbal constraint hierarchy).

Finally, to capture effects of (interfering) structural factors, due to the Isomorphism Principle discussed in section 5.5, additional constraints are needed. In Malchukov (2006) structural constraints are conceived as constraints on Output–Output Correspondences (OOCs) (Prince & Smolensky 2004), which is a conventional way of capturing analogical effects in OT, or as constraints derived from OOCs. These OOC constraints are intended to capture the well-known typological observation[12] that nominalizations rarely have grammatical categories peculiar to themselves; rather they draw from the available resources in a particular language, combining categories, as found on prototypical (finite) verbs and prototypical (nonderived) nouns. In addition, Malchukov (2006) introduces Linearity Constraints (related to morphological integration) to account for hierarchy violation resulting from affix ordering:

- *ExtAff: *Affixes in outer(most) slots are lost in Transcategorial Operations*
- IntAff: *Affixes in inner(most) slots are retained in Transcategorial Operations*

Recall the case of nominalizations in Limbu (illustrated in (15)), where the outermost aspect is lost—in violation of the hierarchy constraints—prior to tense. This pattern is derived under constraint ranking, as in (26), with OOC constraints (requiring identical expression/linearity in basic and derived verbal forms) and *ExtAff constraint dominating the functional hierarchy constraints:[13]

(26)   … *ExtAff >> LexFaith >> … * Tense >> *Aspect …

---

[11] LexFaith Dependency Principle was not explicitly introduced in Malchukov (2006).

[12] Thus, Koptjevskaja-Tamm refers to the fact that nominalizations (action nominal constructions (ANC)) are usually modelled on either finite clauses or non-derived NPs as the 'ANC-parasite universal' (Koptjevskaja-Tamm 2003: 747).

[13] See table 1 in Malchukov (2006: 995) for an explicit representation and Malchukov (2006: 992–997) for more discussion of the structural factors from the OT perspective.

As is clear from the above, OT is able to capture the interaction of different factors (both functional and structural) determining the outcome of transcategorial processes. Admittedly, the advocated approach bears certain similarities to other approaches to nominalizations. This is perhaps to be expected since (as also acknowledged in Malchukov 2004: 25) his approach was informed by various strands of research, including empirical typological work and the Amsterdam school of Functional Grammar, but also by certain strands of generative grammar. Within generative approach, it is closest to minimalist approaches where constraints are derived from sequences of functional projections (such as Borsley & Kornfilt 2000; Kornfilt & Whitman 2011). Thus, under specific assumptions,[14] verbalization and substantivization hierarchies may be reconstructed in versions of Minimalism. Blocking, however, is more in line with unification-based approaches than with derivational approaches. Unification-based approaches produced interesting analyses of category-mixing (see Bresnan 1997 in LFG; Malouf 2000 in Head-driven Phrase Structure Grammar (HPSG)), but as they stand, these models remain fairly unrestricted; that is, they need additional mechanisms for capturing hierarchy constraints, possibly in the form of Feature Specification Defaults (Malouf 2000: 129), or through use of OT in the context of LFG.[15] Indeed, the most interesting consequence of Blocking is not exclusion relation (unification failure) between a pair of blocking categories, but rather interaction of Blocking with the hierarchies (Blocking Effects). Overall, OT proved to be the most flexible modelling tool, as it allows one to combine hierarchy constraints with unification-based constraints, as well as with structural constraints modelling the effects of analogy. It is also important to stress that the constraints employed are all functionally 'grounded' (motivated) and in this sense universal; indeed, all of them are adopted from the typological literature rather than introduced ad hoc for particular purposes of category mixing. Even though it is possible to reconstruct some aspects of this approach in other frameworks, this work remains to be done in these other traditions—at this typological scale.

5.10 Conclusion

Based on my previous work (Malchukov 2004; 2006), I outlined a model for constraining typology of transcategorial operations and applied this model to nominalization and verbalization. In particular, I showed how functional and structural features conspire in determining the outcome of transcategorial operations (i.e. the resultant sets of nominal and verbal categories). The crucial concepts of the proposed GSM, as outlined above, are:

- functionally based hierarchies of verbal and nominal categories, which determine their susceptibility for loss/retention in transcategorial operations (see section 5.4);

---

[14] At the very least, these assumptions will include semantic/scope-based functional sequence, as well as strict functional matching between functional heads and specifiers (this would be compatible with a version of generative grammar, where subject agreement rather than, say, tense is responsible for case assignment to subjects).

[15] See also Nikolaeva & Spencer (2019: ch. 4) for an in-depth discussion and critique of different current analyses of mixed categories.

- structural features, pertaining to the way categories are expressed morphologically, which interfere with the hierarchy constraints (see section 5.5);
- Generalized Scale formation as a result of integrating the hierarchies of verbal and nominal categories (see section 5.6);
- Blocking Effects imposing additional constrains on the GSM (see section 5.6).

In this chapter I presented a competing motivations approach to the typology of transcategorial operations (see also MacWhinney, Malchukov, & Moravcsik 2014 for a collection of linguistics and psycholinguistics studies showing the power of the competing motivations approach). The hierarchy constraints have been argued to be iconically motivated under the assumption that the hierarchies themselves are determined by the functional principles of semantic scope/relevance. Blocking Effects imposing additional constraints on the outcome of transcategorial processes can also ultimately be derived from the hierarchy constraints as they pertain to the functional equivalence of the 'rival' categories (Blocking categories) from the verbal and nominal hierarchies. The manifestations of the hierarchy constraints are complicated by the fact that decategorization and recategorization can proceed relatively independently on the morphological and syntactic levels. It has been shown that the range of mismatches between morphology and syntax in transcategorial processes is constrained by the OSAP (see section 5.5). On the other hand, it has been demonstrated that structural factors such as affix order and category cumulation can interfere with the iconically motivated hierarchy constraints. These factors have been subsumed under the Isomorphism Principle which requires that categories encoded similarly (by the same cumulative marker or through the same affix slot) show similar behaviour in transcategorial processes.

In principle, the GSM is not restricted to any particular lexical categories (such as nouns or verbs), although it presupposes the existence of feature hierarchies for particular lexical categories. In my earlier study (Malchukov 2004), as summarized here, GSM was applied to nominalization (see sections 5.3–5.6), and, more briefly, to verbalization (see section 5.7). Subsequent work (reviewed in section 5.8) has shown that GSM can be extended to other categories (e.g. adjectives) as well as applied to more complex situations of multiple shifts (see also Malchukov 2019). Furthermore, GSM allows for formalization, as discussed in section 5.9. As already shown in Malchukov (2006), most naturally GSM can be reconstructed in OT, which can incorporate constraints of different types, but some of the features of the model resonate with other theoretical analyses as well. To conclude: GSM provides a fully fledged typologically grounded model of transcategorial operations, which can be profitably applied both in cross-linguistic work and in language-descriptive studies.[16]

---

[16] See, for example, Rojas-Berscia (2019) for a recent application of GSM-style analysis to Shawi/Chayahuita (an Amazonian language).

CHAPTER 6

WORD-CLASS SYSTEMS AND OTHER GRAMMATICAL PROPERTIES

WILLIAM A. FOLEY

6.1 THE IMPORTANCE OF VARIATION

THE central task of linguistics is to determine through detailed cross-linguistic investigation just what are the limits of linguistic variation, and not assume at the outset what a set of universal categories must be, and then proceed to develop theories based on those assumptions. For example, assuming that all languages share the same basic lexical categories of nouns and verbs, and then searching for evidence for such in obscure corners of an uncooperative language and putting to the side all contrary evidence, will ultimately not aid much in tracing the contours of possible variation in human language, the real goal of linguistic science. The more interesting question is not 'does this language have distinct classes of nouns and verbs?', but, rather, 'how and in what degree does this language have distinct classes of nouns and verbs?'. In other words, 'how is the grammar structured and what role(s), if any, do these categories play in that structuring?' (see Chapter 2 in this volume).

On a first pass we will quickly discover the role they play across languages is highly variable, as the contrast between Yimas (Foley 1991), Southern Wakashan (Jacobsen 1979; Davidson 2002), and Northern Iroquoian (Mithun 2000; 2019; see also Chapter 30 in this volume) will exemplify. Only when such questions are answered in detail and for many languages of diverse types and genetic stocks will the outlines of an answer to what are the limits of a possible human language emerge: what is favoured in the construction of a possible language and what disfavoured, and what are the implications of favoured or disfavoured, but not impossible, options for the patterns of grammatical structure. This chapter is offered as a very preliminary first step towards this goal.

The issue of variation in word-class typologies and its interaction with other grammatical properties is vast, and a short chapter such as this can only be introductory, and its span limited. To that end, I will draw evidence mainly, though not exclusively, from morphological patterns for typological generalizations about variation in word classes and grammatical properties (though this limitation is also in part a function of the choice of morphologically rich languages for exemplification). For a typological discussion of word classes and their interaction with syntactic structures I refer the reader to Hengeveld (2013) and Skalička (1979), as well as Creissels (Chapter 25 in this volume) on Mande, and Bisang (Chapter 28 in this volume) on Sinitic, which treat mainly isolating morphologically depauperate languages.

6.2 THE BASIS OF THE NOUN–VERB DISTINCTION

Let me start with the most widespread and fundamental claim in the area of word classes: that all languages have distinct classes of nouns and verbs (Croft 2000; Beck 2002; Baker 2003; Dixon 2010; Baker & Croft 2017). My purpose here is not to refute this claim, though I believe it to be far more problematic than it is often regarded, but rather to demonstrate just how deeply different languages can be in their morphosyntactic treatment of words which correspond to nouns and verbs in classical languages like Latin and Ancient Greek from which our grammatical descriptive tradition has derived. Since antiquity, early grammarians, for example Dionysius Thrax, defined word classes not just on semantic criteria, but on formal ones as well. Semantics may inform word classes, but does not determine them. Nouns may in the main denote objects, but they need not; *meeting, battle, riot, party, stunt*, and even *event* all denote events, the typical denotation of verbs. Adjectives may denote properties, but the property of being hungry can be expressed by a noun as in *my hunger* or a verb *to hunger*, in addition to the derived adjective *hungr-y*. Because modern theories of grammar are fundamentally lexical, where morphosyntactic structures are viewed as endocentrically projected from lexical specifications of heads (though for an intriguing alternative exocentric view, see the work of Borer (2003; 2005a; 2005b; 2013), word classes like nouns and verbs are typically viewed as lexical categories (Baker 2003), so that any noun or verb is first and foremost a lexeme. But, as Lyons (1977) points out, the notion of a lexeme is itself anything but simple. He argues that any lexeme can have up to four levels of distinct types of information, represented in Figure 6.1 (Lyons 1977: 512).

stem (e.g. phonological representation)

inflectional class

syntactic properties

semantic specifications

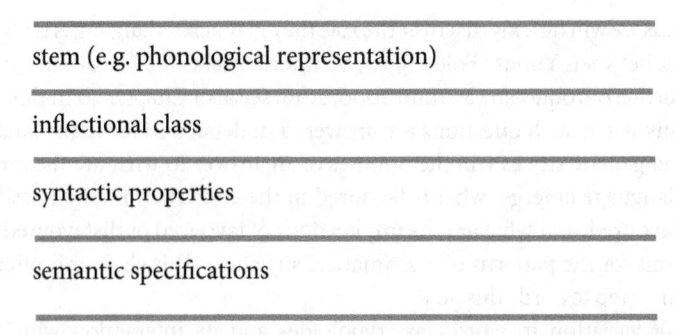

FIGURE 6.1 Schematic representation of a lexeme

The traditional division of word classes in a language draws heavily from implicit assumptions about lexical organization made explicit in Figure 6.1 (see also Chapter 28 in this

WORD-CLASS SYSTEMS AND OTHER GRAMMATICAL PROPERTIES 111

volume). The reason, for instance, that the noun–verb distinction was so salient for Ancient Greek and Latin grammarians is the sharp differentiation in morphological behaviour between them in these two languages. Not only do Ancient Greek and Latin have distinct morphological behaviour for nouns and verbs due to their syntactic properties (level (iii)), for instance, case for nouns and tense for verbs, but in addition different noun and verb lexemes belong to distinct inflectional patterns (level (ii)), declensions for nouns and conjugations for verbs. There is overkill for the distinctiveness of these two classes in these classical languages, so grammarians could not fail to notice it. Figure 6.2 schematizes the basic distinction between nouns and verbs in Latin along the lines of Figure 6.1 (see also Chapter 27 in this volume).

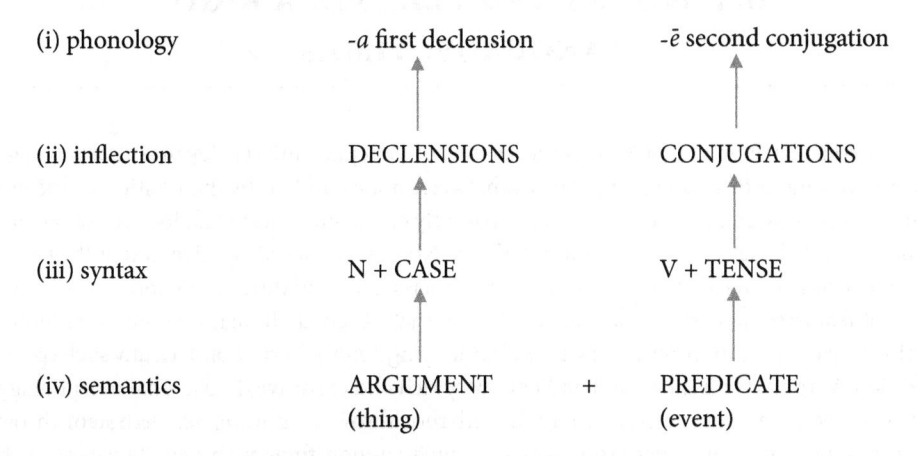

(i) phonology	-*a* first declension	-*ē* second conjugation
(ii) inflection	DECLENSIONS	CONJUGATIONS
(iii) syntax	N + CASE	V + TENSE
(iv) semantics	ARGUMENT (thing) +	PREDICATE (event)

FIGURE 6.2 Schema of noun–verb alignment in Latin

As Figure 6.2 makes clear, there is one class of words that functions as arguments, i.e. participants in a clause, takes case marking to indicate role as participants, and inflects in different ways for different lexemes to signal that case (declensions), and one of these different ways to mark case is marked by the vowel -*a*; this class is dubbed nouns. And a second class functions as predicates, i.e. expressing the event the argument participants are involved in, takes tense marking to indicate the time of that event, and inflects in different ways for different lexemes to signal that tense (conjugations), and one of these different ways to mark tense is a paradigm marked by the vowel -*ē*; this class is called verbs. At every level of Figure 6.2 the contrast between nouns and verbs is sharply drawn. Latin is an example of a synthetic inflectional language with a sharp noun–verb distinction in its lexemes, a structural type very familiar from the Indo-European languages. Lexemes of course can be morphologically complex, so level (i) stems can be derived from roots plus derivational affixes before any inflection. Lehmann (2008) argues that while the noun–verb contrast is indeed sharp for Latin at the level of stems and all other levels in Figure 6.2, this is not true for the level of roots from which stems are derived. In his view Latin has many uncategorized roots which must be derived, a process which establishes these stems lexically as nouns or verbs before they can be inflected. In this analysis, the stem vowels of classical Indo-European languages, the markers of declensions or conjugations like -*a* for first declension and -*ē* for second conjugation in Latin, are word class-deriving suffixes added to acategorial roots which then permit the stems to inflect according to the lexical class, noun, or verb, they now belong to, i.e. take the proper allomorphs of case or tense. Thus, the root *tim-* is derived via the suffix *-or* and then inflected in genitive case in the third declension as *tim-or-is* 'of dread' or derived via the suffix *-ē* and then inflected in first person singular future tense in the second conjugation as *tim-ē-bo* 'I will dread'. Much depends on the details of the analysis and how widespread such a conversion phenomenon is in the grammar of Latin (it appears not more than 15% of roots are convertible like this), but it does illustrate one of the possible parameters of variation in word-class systems cross-linguistically.

6.3 NOUNS AND VERBS IN A RIGID LANGUAGE: YIMAS

Yimas, a Papuan language of New Guinea of the Lower Sepik family (Foley 1991), is a language of an even more thoroughgoing contrast between nouns and verbs than Latin or Ancient Greek. But as we shall see, in spite of its apparently exotic morphosyntax, its basic organization of word classes is broadly similar to theirs. Noun roots are distinctive in that they bear inherent class, being assigned to one of ten noun classes on a mixture of semantic and phonological features: *apak* 'sister' belongs to class II, that of female humans, while *tanm* 'bone' belongs to class VII for roots ending in *-m* (underlying /-mp/). Verb roots lack any such specification. Verb roots on the other hand have very rich and exclusive derivational morphology by which verb stems are derived: *wampaki-* verb root 'throw' > *ira-wampaki-* verb stem 'throw towards someone', *ampa-* verb root 'weave' > *ampa-ru-* non-finite verb stem 'to weave'. Such derivations in this polysynthetic language can result in very complex verb stems: *mampi-pay-ma-takat-cu-* again-first-inside-touch-NFN 'to touch (it) inside first again'.

Nouns lack derivational morphology; for example, while there is an extensive inventory of derivational nominalization suffixes, converting verbs to nouns, *ampa-r-mprum* weave-NFN-II.DL 'two (female) weavers', there is no derivational verbalizing morphology. Noun roots and noun stems must be identical, but verb roots and verb stems can be very different. So while Latin may have some roots which are unspecified for the category of noun or verb, this is impossible in Yimas: all roots must be explicitly marked in the lexicon as either noun or verb and all derivation or inflection is determined by that.

Turning to level (ii) of Figure 6.1, nouns and verbs are again very distinctive. Verbs have no inflectional classes, all can take the same set of inflections, and although, for example, there are inflectional differences between intransitive and transitive verbs, any intransitive verb roots can end up inflecting like a transitive or even ditransitive verb, given the extensive derivational options of valency increasing. Nouns fall into ten inflectional classes depending on class; they are inflected with suffixes for number, singular, dual, and plural, with multiple allomorphs for number determined by noun class, the plural marking being much more diverse than that for dual. That is almost the sum total of inflection for nouns. Though verbs lack inflectional classes, they can carry very extensive inflection. Tense is the only obligatory inflection, always marked by suffixes. In addition, verbs can be inflected for aspect and mood, and they typically have class and number agreement marking for their core arguments, maximally subject, object, and indirect object. Core arguments in the unmarked case are indicated by prefixes. So, class and number marking for nouns is always suffixal, but mainly prefixal for verbs, a sharp difference.

Yimas is a polysynthetic head-marking language (Nichols 1986), and the roles of the core arguments of a verb are signalled by sets of pronominal agreement affixes, not by nominal case marking; the only nominal case marking in the language is an oblique suffix -*n* ~ -*nan* for non-core non-subcategorized arguments, typically locatives (Roman numerals indicate noun class):

(1) pŋkmp-n   yaw-n   muraŋ
    guts.VII.SG-OBL path.IX.SG-OBL oar.VI.SG
    k-n-kaw-kaca-kia-ntuk-nakn
    VI.SG.NOM-3SG.ERG-straight-swing-NIGHT-RM.PAST-3SG.DAT
    'he swung his oar straight down its esophagus' (of a crocodile)

Yimas like many polysynthetic languages has little in the way of phrase structure, but even here the sharp contrast between noun and verb manifests itself. The language is non-configurational (Hale 1983) so there are no phrasal projections of verbs to VPs. Clausal word order is quite free. Nouns, on the other hand, do project NPs, but these are minimal, consisting at most of two elements, a possessor or adjective plus a head noun and in that fixed order: *kpa nam* big house 'a big house'. Only nouns can fulfil this role of head in projecting NPs; verbs are entirely prohibited from this role: **yua wampaki* 'a good throw' is impossible, though perfectly fine in English.

Finally turning to level (iv) of Figure 6.1, the logico-semantic structure of clauses as expressions of propositions through the functions of predicate and its associated arguments, we find again that Yimas transparently links this to the contrast between nouns and verbs. Only NPs, normally just a bare noun, can function as arguments. If a verb is to function as an argument it must be nominalized, and in keeping with the tenor of the language, it must be assigned to a noun class and bear a noun class-marking suffix (-*mpwi* is the noun class marker of the nominalization in example (2) and *pia-* the corresponding verbal cross-referencing prefix for this class marker):

(2) patn   wayk-r-mpwi   pia-ka-i-c-mpun
    betelnut.V.SG buy-NFN-TALK   TALK.NOM-1SG.ERG-tell-PERF-3PL.DAT
    'I told them to buy betelnut.'

The role of nouns and verbs in predication in Yimas brings up the complexity of this notion. There are two notions of predication currently used in linguistics (Rothstein 2006), both adapted from logic. One, the more modern one due to Frege that I have employed thus far, is that of a function over variables, i.e. PRED (x,y,z), where the variables are the arguments. The other goes back to Aristotle in *On Interpretation*, where a predicate is defined as something 'which asserts or denies something of something'. This, of course, is the familiar analysis of a proposition as made up of Subject + Predicate, where the subject refers to something and the predicate expresses a property ascribed to that entity.

Clauses do not neatly bifurcate in most languages and certainly not in Yimas into subject and predicate, though the notion has some appeal in English and some other languages. Consider the English clauses in (3), which are all given the same analysis of Subject + Predicate:

(3)   Subject   +   Predicate   Predicate asserts:

   (a) the tall man   is reading   an event

   (b) the tall man   has a book   possession

   (c) the book   is red   a property

   (d) the book   is on the table   a location

   (e) the tall man   is the reader   identification

Such a bifurcation is of course the source of the structural analysis of English clauses as NP + VP. There is some justification for this analysis in English, as all predications in English must contain an overt tense-bearing verb, and, when what is actually predicated belongs to the classes of adjectives (3c) or nouns (3e), a supporting copulative verb *be* must be used.

English clauses on the whole seem rather cooperative with analyses along the lines of Subject + Predicate, but polysynthetic nonconfigurational Yimas is anything but, and its lack of conformity is closely aligned to the different word classes of nouns and verbs. Only verbs can straightforwardly predicate in Yimas, either in Aristotle's sense of 'assert something of something' or as a function over some variable(s). Predicating Verbs agree in number and class with their core arguments and take the full range of tense–aspect–mood marking, as in (4):

(4) *kaŋ   k-ka-ŋa-r-mpun*
    shell.VI.SG   VI.SG.NOM-1SG.ERG-give-PERF-3PL.DAT
    'I gave the shell to them.'

The language avoids casting nouns (and adjectives which are a subclass of nouns) as predicates, using grammatical structures to express the meanings of (3b–e) which reframe erstwhile predicating nouns actually as arguments, their proper function. Consider how the assertion of possession is expressed in (5):

(5) a. *impan   arm   kantk-nmprum   aympak*
       3DL   liquid   with-II.PL   COP.3DL
       'those two (females) have kerosene' (literally 'those two are with kerosene')

    b. *arm   ima-n-na-taŋ-taw-n?*
       liquid   LIQUID.NOM-2SG.ERG-PRES-COM-sit-PRES
       'do you have kerosene?' (literally 'are you sitting with kerosene?')

In these examples, both the possessor and possessed are treated as arguments, subject for the possessor and either object of a postposition (5a) or object of the derived transitive verb (5b) for the possessed. A similar pattern is found with assertion of locations, as in (6):

(6) *panmal   nam-n   wampuŋn   na-na-taw-n*
    man.I.SG   house-OBL   inside   3.SG.NOM-PRES-sit-PRES
    'the man is inside the house'

Only in the assertion of a property or identification do nouns function like predicates as in English, but even here there are major differences related to the preferred restriction of nouns to arguments. Consider examples (7a) and (b):

(7)   a. identification
       k-n   akrŋ   akk
       VI.SG-FR.DIST   frog.VI.SG   COP.VI.SG.INVIS
       'that's a frog (overheard croaking in the reeds)'

   b. property ascription
       m-n   kpa-n   anak
       NR.DIST-1SG   big-1SG   COP.1S
       'He's big.' (literally 'he's a big one')

Other than its use in possessive constructions like (5a), the copula can only be used to connect two noun phrases. While *kpa-* 'big' is one of the three true adjectives in the language, when suffixed with a noun class and number marker it becomes a noun like any other; a non-nominalized adjective can never function predicatively, only attributively, in marked contrast to the situation in English. Note the class and number concord across all three constituents in the examples in (7). By default the subject and the predicate noun must agree in these features, but most notably so must the copula; in other words an apparently predicating noun functions like any other core argument in the language, by being caseless and by being cross-referenced for class and number on its governing verb, the salient diagnostics of argument function in Yimas. Such nouns may be functioning semantically as predicates, but their formal realization is that of any other core argument. Hence again the thoroughgoing sharp split of nouns versus verbs in Yimas is demonstrated: nouns are arguments and verbs are predicates. Yimas demonstrates perhaps even better than Latin or Ancient Greek the type of organization of the word classes noun and verb formulated by the grammarians of antiquity and bequeathed to Western linguistic theory.

6.4 THE PROBLEMATIC NATURE OF THE NOUN–VERB DISTINCTION IN SOUTHERN WAKASHAN

The situation in Southern Wakashan (Jacobsen 1979; Davidson 2002), spoken along the west coast of Vancouver Island and in the extreme north-west corner of Washington State, could hardly be more different. Southern Wakashan is a subfamily of three very closely related languages, Nuu-chah-nulth, Dididaht, and Makah, and here I will draw on data from both Nuu-chah-nulth and Makah. The status of nouns and verbs as distinct basic lexical categories has long been controversial in Southern Wakashan, along with other language families of the region such as Northern Wakashan, Salish (see Chapter 29 in this volume), and Chimakuan. It is not my intention here to stake a position on this controversy (see Sapir 1921; Sapir & Swadesh 1939; Swadesh 1939; Jacobsen 1979; Nakayama 2001; Wojdak 2001; Davidson 2002; Braithwaite 2015), except to say that I find the issue far from closed, and, as we shall see, the strongest argument that has been advanced for the distinction of noun and verb in Southern Wakashan is in fact empirically questionable. Rather my point here is simply to demonstrate the enormous variation in how the purported basic distinction between noun and verb lexical classes can be realized cross-linguistically by contrasting Southern Wakashan with Yimas and drawing out some generalizations of what the basis of such variation could be. Because the status of nouns and verbs is so controversial in Southern Wakashan, I will avoid using such terms, opting instead for object-denoting roots versus event-denoting.

Unlike Yimas where nouns are arguments and verbs predicates, both object-denoting roots and event-denoting roots can function freely as predicates in Southern Wakashan, with no morphological differences (Nuu-chah-nulth data from Wojdak 2001), as shown in (8).

(8)   a.   *mamuuk=ʔiš*   *čaku=ʔii*
            work=3SG.IND   man=D
            'the man is working'

       b.   *čaku=ʔiš*   *mamuuk=ʔii*
            man=3SG.IND   work=D
            'the working one is a man'

       c.   *hiixwatḥi=ʔiš*   *mamuuk=ʔi*
            cranky=3SG.IND   work=D
            'the working one is cranky'

       d.   *čakup=ʔiš*   *hiixwatḥi=ʔii*
            man=3SG.IND   cranky=D
            'the cranky one is a man'

Predicates in Southern Wakashan languages are clause initial and take a set of agreement clitics, here marking subject and mood (see Nakayama (2001: 30–38) and Stoneham (2004: 66–84) for lists and a discussion of the paradigms for subject–mood marking in Nuu-chah-nulth). Note that event-denoting (8a), object-denoting (8b,d), and property-denoting (8c) roots all function identically as predicates in sharp contrast to Yimas. These subject–mood predicating clitics always attach to the first element of a complex predicate, indicating that these are not actually syntactic phrasal constituents; Southern Wakashan languages, like Yimas, seem to disfavour phrasal structures (again data from Nuu-chah-nulth from Nakayama (2001)):

(9)   a.   *ʔiiḥw-'ači(λ)='iim*   *čaʔak*
            big-PERF=2SG.IMP.FUT river
            'you should become a big river'

       b.   *ʔiiḥw=waaʔiš*   *taʔił*
            big=3SG.QUOT   sick
            'he is reportedly very sick'

The predicate in (9a) is 'big river', but the subject–mood clitic occurs on 'big', the first element, separating the modifier from its apparent head; the predicate is a unit in expression, but apparently not syntactically. The preference for first position is a general feature of clitics in these languages.

When we turn to the other major clausal function, argumenthood, the crux of the issue of word classes in these languages, comes into view. Jacobsen (1979) argued that there is a crucial syntactic asymmetry between object-denoting roots and event-denoting roots. Roots of both types can function as predicates and arguments. When predicates, roots of all types behave alike, as in (8), but when functioning as arguments, there is a crucial difference. Object-denoting roots can function as arguments while morphologically bare, but event-denoting roots can only do so when they bear the determiner clitic -ʔii in Nuu-chah-nulth or the cognate -ʔiq in its sister language Makah, as these examples from Makah illustrate (Jacobsen 1979):

(10) a. *huudii=waad*   *čitʼapuk*
    drift.ashore=3SG.QUOT whale
    'a whale has reportedly drifted ashore'

  b. **hixwaa=ʔal*   *čiλiičʼiiy* *haʔub*
    work.hard=3SG.TEMP.IMPERF cut.RED   food
    'the cutter of food is working hard'

Jacobsen (1979) uses this asymmetry to claim that roots that behave like *čitʼapuk* 'whale' are nouns, while roots like *čʼiλi* 'cut' are verbs. Supposedly, verbs need to be nominalized by being complements of the determiner clitic before functioning as arguments. Nouns can function as arguments either as NPs or DPs, but verbs only as DPs. This is in keeping, it seems, with the less favoured association of verbs with argument function, coded by this need for overt marking (Croft 1991; 2000; 2001), a marking nouns can dispense with by virtue of their inherent link to argumenthood. The correlation between this behaviour, optional DP and obligatory DP, and their semantics, object-denoting and event-denoting respectively, reinforce the plausibility of the claim that this is rooted in the contrast between nouns and verbs.

But there are some serious doubts about the strength of the evidence for this claim, first empirically and then in terms of the wider patterns of the language. It is simply not true that event-denoting roots must take a determiner in all cases to function as arguments. Even in Jacobsen's (1979) paper there are problematic examples that seem to have been ignored. For instance, there is a predicate *ʔuxuu* in Makah which allows an argument functioning as subject to be focused, as in (11):

(11) a. *ʔuxuu-al*   *tʼuucabuub=iq*
    FOC-3SG.TEMP.IMPERF give.haircut=D
    'he's the barber'

  b. *ʔuxuu=ʔ*   *su*
    FOC-3SG.IMPERF hold
    'he's the holder'

The crucial point is that *t'uucabuub-iq* in (11a) 'the one who cuts hair, the barber' contains an event-denoting stem, a verb in Jacobsen's terms, and, consequently, as expected, is encliticized with the determiner *-iq*. But consider (11b), which is exactly parallel in structure to (11a), but in which the event-denoting stem *su* is not encliticized with-*iq*. No explanation has been forthcoming for this difference. Clearly, the potential presence or absence of the determiner cannot be used to define a difference between nouns and verbs in Southern Wakashan. Its distribution is not determined syntactically, but pragmatically, like determiners in most languages. Its usage in Southern Wakashan languages is poorly understood (but see Inman 2018; Davidson 2002: 136–142), yet what is most striking about it is its diachronic source in a mood morpheme, the essential predicating marker in these languages. Compare the forms across the three Southern Wakashan languages, in Table 6.1.

Table 6.1 Determiner clitics across three Southern Wakashan languages

	Nuu-chah-nulth	Ditidaht	Makah
D	=ʔii	=ʔaq	=ʔiq
3SG.IND	=ʔiš	=ʔa	=ʔi

These comparative data leave no doubt that the determiner clitic is derived historically from the indicative mood suffix for third singular. This is powerful evidence that at base all roots and stems are predicative (as claimed by Swadesh 1939, Davidson 2002, and Inman 2018), even when used as heads of arguments. They are first and foremost predications, saying something is something, hence the origin of the determiner clitic in the third singular mood suffix. Nor is this only a diachronic fact. The close relationship is apparent synchronically. Note that the determiner clitic in Makah cannot be added directly to the independent forms of object-denoting roots; they must be in their predicative stem forms (the glottal stop of *-ʔi* causes morphophonemic changes to final consonants and the vowel is deleted word finally), to which the determiner is then encliticized (Jacobsen 1979):

(12) Independent   Predicating 3SG.IND   DP with -iq
     q'idiiƛ 'dog'   q'idiil 'it's a dog'   q'idiil=iq 'the dog'
     ɬaaxuk 'man'   ɬaaxuu 'it's a man'   ɬaaxuw=iq 'the man'

Further, the determiner clitic is absolutely excluded from co-occurring with an overt mood clitic, and this argues that they are paradigmatically related (Makah from Davidson 2002):

(13) *huxxtak-saaq-tiʔi=ʔiq=(*ʔi)*   Bill
     know.how-CAUS.PERF-AGT=D=(3SG.IND)   PN
     'Bill is the teacher.'

Even more striking, the determiner clitic can be replaced by the conditional mood clitic, if an argument is indefinite; in other words an object-denoting root can be marked with an overt predicating morpheme, even if it is functioning as an argument (Makah from Jacobsen 1979):

(14) ʔu-suba=s   p'atqsac=qey
      ROOT-need=1SG.IND   suitcase=3SG.COND
      'I need a suitcase [what could be a suitcase]'

It is quite clear that these data are in accord with the views of Swadesh (1939), Davidson (2002), and Inman (2018) that all roots and stems in Southern Wakashan languages are inherently predicative. Event-denoting roots perhaps most transparently so, but object-denoting ones are too, and, even when they function as arguments, their predicative basis is still apparent (12). The determiner clitic is simply a relativizer: *mamuuk = ʔii* 'he who works', *čakup = ʔii* 'he who mans'. But note the determiner clitic is not necessary to do this: *čakup* 'he who mans', *su* 'he who holds'.

Derivational and inflectional morphology in Southern Wakashan is extremely complex, with hundreds of distinct suffixes plus reduplication and vowel changes, so I cannot fully explore the possibilities of the higher levels of (i)–(iii) of Figure 6.1 in this short chapter. The vast majority of suffixes and morphological changes apply indiscriminately to roots and stems of both object-denoting and event-denoting roots. There may be some specialized suffixes that derive an object-denoting or event-denoting stem (Davidson 2002: 186–195), but this is definitely not the general pattern. I will illustrate this morphological promiscuity with plural marking, a prototypical feature for nouns, and tense–aspect marking, a characteristic of verbs, in languages like Yimas with clear noun–verb distinctions. Plural marking in Southern Wakashan is complex and highly irregular, involving suffixation, infixation and reduplication, and vowel lengthening, but the crucial point is that there is no general restriction of one type of plural marking to object-denoting roots and another to event-denoting roots, but the same types of pluralization applies to roots of both types (Nuu-chah-nulth data from Davidson 2002):

(15) a. suffixation of -ṁinḥ
         ʔap-iis-ṁinḥ   aama-ṁinḥ
         carry.on.shoulders-carry-PL   loon-PL
         'carry them on shoulders'   'loons'

      b. suffixation of -iih
         huquuɫ 'wear a mask'   huquuh < huquuh + -iih 'several wear masks'
         čakup 'man'   čakup-iih 'men'

      c. suffixation of -yu plus reduplication or vowel lengthening
         ciq 'speak'   ciciq-yu 'several speaking'
         č'iḥ 'ghost'   č'iiḥ-yu 'ghosts'

      d. infixation of -ýV-
         t'iqwiɫ 'sit in the house'   t'iýaqwiɫ 'several sit in the house'
         čapac 'canoe'   čaýapac 'canoes'

e. reduplication
   m̉awa 'deliver'   *m̉am̉awa* 'several deliver'
   quuʔas 'person'   *quqwaas* 'people'

f. reduplication plus vowel lengthening
   saḥas 'pick cedar bark'   *sasaaḥas* 'several pick cedar bark'
   ṅuw̉iiqsu 'father'   *ṅuṅuuw̉iqsu* 'fathers'

Aspect is a pervasive inflectional category in Southern Wakashan, indicated by a range of formal devices, suffixation, reduplication, vowel change, etc., and expressing a fundamental division into perfective and imperfective aspects (imperfective aspect has a number of subtypes; I will illustrate here with durative). Both object-denoting and event-denoting roots can be inflected with either perfective or imperfective aspect, as shown in (16).

(16) Nuu-chah-nulth (Davidson 2002)
Perfective aspect (-*šiƛ*):
λ'iλq-šiƛ   łuč-šiƛ
explode-PERF   woman-PERF
'exploded'   'give a woman' (in ransom)

Durative aspect (-*akw* ~ -*uk*):
ʔih-akw   nayaq-akw
cry-DUR   child-DUR
'be crying'   'child'

Tense is much more marginal in Southern Wakashan, there being two optional clitics, one for past tense and another for future, but again they may both occur on object-denoting and event-denoting roots; see (17):

(17) Nuu-chah-nulth (Davidson 2002)
past tense: =(*m*)*it*
ʔačyaa=mit   miʔaa=it
gather.wood=PAST   sockeye.salmon-PAST
'had gathered wood'   'the former sockeye salmon (now cut up)'

future tense: =*ʔaaqƛ*
qaḥ-šiƛ=ʔaaqƛ   kaaʔuuc-šiƛ=ʔaaqƛ
dead-PERF=FUT   grandchild-PERF=FUT
'will die'   'future grandchild'

Clearly, inflectional categories like number, aspect, or tense are not restricted to roots of particular semantic or lexical types in Southern Wakashan, as they are in Yimas or Latin, but are available to all roots as befits their basic predicating function; these inflectional categories simply delimit the domain of predication.

6.5 PARAMETERS OF VARIATION IN DETERMINING NOUN AND VERB CLASSES

Davidson (2002: 325) claims that 'the essential difference between Southern Wakashan and a language like Latin (and by extension Yimas, WAF) is one of degree, not of kind'. I beg to differ. To claim that the difference between Southern Wakashan and Yimas is one of degree, and not kind, diminishes any rigorous typology of language variation; just what difference would count as a difference in kind if not these? Southern Wakashan languages fundamentally do not divide their lexemes, their roots and stems, into classes specialized for predication and argumenthood, a division Yimas wholeheartedly embraces. Is there a link to wider grammatical patterns in the two languages that correlates with this? I believe there is, and crucially it is tied to level (ii) of Figure 6.1, inflectional class. Southern Wakashan languages have no inflectional classes, no breakdown of their roots and stems into groupings determined by gender, noun class, declension class, transitivity, aspectual class, or conjugation class. Their roots and stems carry no subcategorizing features that determine that some stems are inflected in one way and others in another; all are potentially inflected the same.

Latin, as Figure 6.2 illustrates, definitely does subcategorize its stems this way, some belonging to declensions and others to conjugations, clearly bifurcating them into distinct classes of nouns and verbs. Yimas, as we have seen, lacks inflectional classes for its event-denoting words, but it does have these for its object-denoting words, dividing them into ten classes which determine the allomorphy of number marking. The opposition of the roots bearing class inflections to those that lack them defines the sharp contrast between nouns and verbs in this language. The language builds in certain features for those words which function as arguments, nouns, to a certain extent on the basis of properties of the real-world referents of those words, such as gender and number, and defines the other class, verbs, against this.

The contrast, though, can be drawn on the opposite pole as well. Consider Aghu, another Papuan language, this time of the Awyu–Dumut family (Drabbe 1957; Wester 2014; see also Chapter 36 in this volume on another group of Papuan languages). Nouns and verbs are also formally sharply contrastive in this language. But Aghu nouns have no inflection whatsoever, not even case. This again is a head-marking language, and the role of arguments is signalled by verbal agreement or left to context. Verb stems, on the other hand, are inflected for tense, aspect, and person–number of the subject. In addition, verbs stems fall into two inflectional classes, one for realis events and the other for irrealis, expressed by distinct stem forms, as shown in Table 6.2.

Table 6.2 Inflectional Verb classes in Aghu

Realis	Irrealis	Root meaning
mi-	ami-	'drink'
kū-	akume-	'die'
da-	ade-	'hear'
kū-	kume-	'put in'

(continued)

Table 6.2 Continued

Realis	Irrealis	Root meaning
ad-	adfe-	'bind'
da-	dafi-	'come'

The proper verb stems then determine compatible tense marking, for example today's past for realis and future for irrealis: *da-ak-i* hear.R-FR.PAST-2/3SG.SUBJ 'you/he/she/it heard', *ade-n-ɛ* hear.IRR-2/3SG.SUBJ-FUT 'you/he/she/it will hear'. In Aghu it is the inflectional classes for verbs which sharply define the noun–verb distinction, as the Nouns lack any such distinguishing features.

We propose, then, that inflectional classes, i.e. elaboration at level (ii) of Figure 6.1, are correlated with a sharp noun–verb distinction. The converse, i.e. lack of inflectional classes, is correlated with a weak noun–verb distinction; however, this does not seem to hold universally. While it does account for Southern Wakashan languages and some others that I will mention shortly, there are certainly languages with a clear noun–verb distinction which lack inflectional classes, such as Turkish and Japanese, as well as the more obvious cases of extreme isolating languages like Hmong that lack inflection altogether. It may that in the latter case syntactic constraints such as word order play the major role in imposing a stricter word-class categorization (Hengeveld 2013).

The language Bauplan illustrated by Southern Wakashan is not that rare. Besides the language families adjoining it along the North-West Pacific coast, Salish (see Chapter 29 in this volume) and Chimakuan, it is found in Austronesian, particularly Polynesian and Philippine–Formosan languages (Chapter 35 in this volume), Mayan languages (Lois & Vapnarsky 2006; Lois et al. 2017; Chapter 32 in this volume), and the Bolivian isolate Movima (Haude 2009). What is common to all of these languages is predicate initial word order, with the predicate typically overtly marked by a tense–aspect–mood affix or clitic. Arguments are usually overtly marked as well, by a case marker or a determiner or a marker that combines the features of both, as in Tagalog. Strictly speaking it is not necessary to explicitly mark both the predicate and arguments overtly and, for example, Movima does not: predicates are clause initial but bear no overt inflection for tense–aspect–mood, while arguments take determiners. Hence the clause structure in Figure 6.3 seems predisposed to categorical neutrality, although it is neither a necessary nor a sufficient condition, as there are languages like the Austroasiatic Munda language Kharia (Peterson 2010) with verb final clausal word order and an elusive noun–verb distinction (K is for case markers).

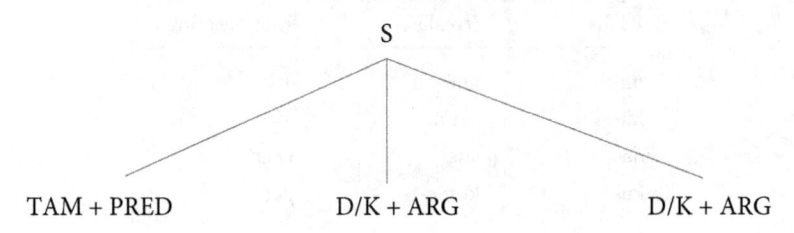

```
                    S
         _____|_____
        /           |           \
   TAM + PRED   D/K + ARG    D/K + ARG
```

FIGURE 6.3 Clausal structure predisposed to categorial neutrality

But even with adherence to this Bauplan there can be interesting twists. Tagalog conforms quite closely to Figure 6.3, but whereas in Southern Wakashan all roots and stems are inherently predicative, i.e. preset for the predicate function, Tagalog roots are exactly the opposite, preselected for an argument function. This is the source of the often mentioned 'nouniness' of Philippine languages (Kaufman 2009). Both object-denoting roots and event-denoting roots can freely function as arguments without derivation, usually simply by being complements of a case-marked D head, *ang* for nominative case, *ng* for genitive case (used for all non-subject core arguments), and *sa* for obliques: *ang aso* 'the dog', *sa tindahan* 'at the store', though this is not always necessary. But when functioning as arguments, the roots that are event denoting actually denote objects, prototypical meanings of nouns (Himmelmann 2008; Kaufman 2009): *bigay* 'give', *ang bigay* 'the gift'; *patay* 'die', *ang patay* 'the corpse'; *kita* 'see', *ang kita* 'the thing seen'; *sunog* 'burn', *ang sunog* 'the fire'; *bili* 'buy/sell', *ang bili* 'the price'; *kuha* 'take', *ang kuha* 'the thing taken'; *sabi* 'say', *ang sabi* 'statement'; *sira* 'destroy', *ang sira* 'the destroyed part'. The argument function is thus built, so to speak, into Tagalog roots, as the predicative function is into Southern Wakashan ones. Tagalog then has a rich array of morphemes, particularly voice affixes, that put roots into predicative function and these again apply to object-denoting and event-denoting roots equally: object-denoting roots: *aso* 'dog', *mag-aso* 'take care of dogs'; *asawa* 'spouse', *mag-asawa* 'get married'; *tubig* 'water' *mag-tubig* 'add water to something'; *bola* 'ball', *mag-bola* 'play with a ball'; *sopas* 'soup', *mag-sopas* 'cook soup'; event-denoting roots: *bigay* 'give' *mag-bigay* 'give something to someone'; *langoy* 'swim', *mag-langoy* 'swim'; *hugas* 'wash', *mag-hugas* 'wash something'; *bukas* 'open' *mag-bukas* 'open something'; *salin* 'pour', *mag-salin* 'pour something'. See Kaufman (2009) and Mosel (Chapter 35 in this volume) for more discussion of this topic in Austronesian languages.

6.6 Categoriality or its lack in Northern Iroquoian

I mentioned earlier that according to Lehmann (2008), Figure 6.2 does not tell the whole story about Latin. His claim is that while Latin stems and words are clearly divided into noun and verb classes, and Latin roots are not, but remain uncategorized. Whatever turns out to be true of Latin, it does point out that categoriality can be established or fail at different grammatical levels, roots, stems, full words, phrases, etc. The Northern Iroquoian languages, as described by Mithun (2000; 2019; see also Chapter 30 in this volume), provide an interesting contrast to Southern Wakashan. This is a group of closely related languages of about the same degree of divergence as Southern Wakashan, and like them also of a polysynthetic structural type. However, unlike them, noun roots carry inherent gender, and when nouns are used independently, their gender is overtly indicated by a prefix, and they also take a suffix indicating their status as nouns (Northern Iroquoian languages have complex morphophonemics, so examples are presented in their underlying forms; the examples in (18) are from Cayuga (Mithun 2000) and N indicates neuter gender):

(18) a. *o-hn-aʔ*   b. *o-hnǫhs-aʔ*
  N-fat-NOUN.SUF   N-squash-NOUN.SUF
  'grease, lard, fat'   'squash, melon, cucumber'

Verbs are much more complex as befitting these polysynthetic languages, but their only required inflection is a prefix indicating the person and number, and if third person, the gender of their core argument(s), just subject for intransitive verbs but both subject and object for transitive verbs, and a final suffix indicating aspect, perfective, imperfective/habitual, or stative (Oneida data in (19) from Mithun 2000):

(19) a. *ka-hnanyu-heʔ*
      N.AGT-bark-IMPERF
      'it's barking'

b. *yo-itaʔ-s*
   N.PAT-sleep-IMPERF
   'it's sleeping'

While nouns and minimally inflected verbs may at first look similar, this is deceiving. The gender-marking prefixes for nouns and verbs are almost always distinct (Mithun 2000), though diachronically they are clearly related:

(20) neuter prefixes in Oneida

Verbs	Nouns	
Set 1 (AGTS)	Set 1	
w-	—	before *a, e, ʌ*
y-	—	before *o, u*
ka-	ka-	before consonants, *i*
Set 2 (PATS)	Set 2	
yaw-	aw-	before *e, ʌ*
ya-	—	before *o, i*
yo-	o-	before consonants, *a, i*

Nor does the final noun suffix look like any of the final aspectual suffixes; for example, the stative suffix, the most likely candidate to correlate to the noun suffix *-aʔ*, has a number of allomorphs in Cayuga (Mithun 2000), but none of them match *-aʔ*.

It is clear then on inflectional data that Northern Iroquoian languages have distinct classes of noun and verb roots. Not only are they distinct, they are exclusive: only nouns roots can appear in the morphological array of (18) and only verb roots take the inflections of (19), a complete contrast with the situation in Southern Wakashan. Furthermore, noun roots stripped of the gender marker and noun suffix can incorporate into verbs, and it is verbs and only verbs which license such incorporation (Mohawk examples from Mithun 2019):

(21) a. *wa-hshako-hkwenni-a-hr-a kw-ʔ*
FACT-M.SG>3PL-clothing-LINK-be.on-LINK-REV-PERF
'he removed their harness'

b. *waʔ-t-ka-nienʔkw-atase-hon-ʔ*
FACT-DV-N.AGT-snow-go.around-DISTR-PERF
'it snowed'

This noun–verb contrast in roots carries forward into stems as well, for it is possible to incorporate a verb stem into another verb, but only when it has been formally nominalized, i.e. the verb stem becomes a noun stem (Cayuga example (22) from Mithun 2000):

(22) *w-[ate-khw-a-ha-hsr]-owan-ɛ*
N-REFL-food-EPEN-set-NOMZ-be.big-STAT
'the table is big'

The verb stem *ate-khw-a-ha-* REFL-food-EPEN-set 'food is set' is a verb with its own incorporated noun *khw-* 'food' which had been nominalized and hence converted into a noun stem (note no gender prefix or noun suffix, so not a full noun word) and then incorporated with *owan-* 'be big'.

But at the level of fully inflected words, Northern Iroquoian begins more to resemble Southern Wakashan. Because unlike Yimas, where verbs can only be predicates, and when used as arguments must be formally nominalized, Northern Iroquoian is much less restrictive. Many object-denoting words in Northern Iroquoian are formally verbs and can be used as arguments without any overt nominalizations. Here are some examples from Mohawk (Mithun 2019) of formal verbs with object denotations:

(23) a. *te-io-nhonskw-a-ront*
DV-N.PAT-jowl-LINK-be.attached
'it protrudes double jowls' = 'cow'

b. *ka-wisto-ht-haʔ*
N.AGT-cold-CAUS-HAB
'it makes (things) cold' = 'refrigerator'

c. *ie-raʔwist-ohtshi-a-ʔt-haʔ*
INDEF.AGT-peeling-remove-LINK-INSTR.APPL-HAB
'one removes peels with it' = 'potato peeler'

Of course, these words only have object denotations when they function as nouns prototypically do, i.e. as arguments, core or oblique, etc., but crucially when doing so, they have no overt markers of noun status, no gender prefixes or noun suffixes, but look for all the world as verbs still. This can be seen in (24)–(26):

(24) Cayuga (Mithun 2000)
 ka-rǫt-a-nehkwi hni? t-ka-kǫ:t
 N.AGT-log-EPEN-haul.IMPERF too CLOC-N.AGT-necessary.STAT
 ɛ-yakwa-nǫte-ho:-ʔ
 FUT-1EX.PL-feed-DISTR-PERF
 'we have to feed the horses (literally "it hauls logs") too'

(25) Mohawk (Mithun 2019)
 iah thaʔ-te-t-iaw-e-n-on
 NEG CONTR-DV-CLOC-M.PAT-go-DIR.APPL-STAT
 ki:ken ne te-io-nhonskw-a-ront
 this the DV-N.PAT-jowl-LINK-be.attached'
 'the cow (literally "it protrudes double jowls") didn't return home'

(26) Cayuga (Mithun 2000)
 ka-nǫhs-es=ke
 N.AGT-house-be.long.STAT=LOC
 'at the longhouse'

While describing Classical Nahuatl, Launey (1994) coined the term 'omnipredicative' to denote languages like Southern Wakashan that permit words of different classes, such as nouns and verbs, to function identically as the basis of predications. Northern Iroquoian is not like that. Nouns and verbs are very different in predicative function; for example, nouns require a particle to function as predicates, verbs do not, but predicate directly. Unlike Southern Wakashan languages or Launey's Nahuatl, nouns can never function predicatively on their own in Northern Iroquoian, only verbs can; they are not omnipredicative languages. Northern Iroquoian exemplifies the opposite type: at the level of full words they are 'omniargumentive'. Fully inflected nouns and fully inflected verbs can equally function as arguments, with no derivational morphology to indicate a change in class; their grammatical properties determined solely by their syntactic status as arguments. While the categorial flexibility in Southern Wakashan is apparent at the root and stem levels and illustrated by their omnipredicativity, this is not the case for the Northern Iroquoian, where it only appears at the full word level, and there through the languages' omniargumentivity. For more discussion of word classes in Northern Iroquoian languages, see Michelson (Chapter 30 in this volume).

6.7 THE QUESTION OF ADJECTIVES

Given constraints of space, I will treat the other two major lexical categories, adjectives and adpositions, more schematically, adjectives here and adpositions in the next section.

Adjectives are those words which attribute properties, and attribution is their core function (see Chapter 18 in this volume). In a language like Watam, a Papuan language of the Lower Ramu family, they can both attribute and predicate properties: *endau imbrot an* house small D 'the small house' versus *endau an imbrot* house D small 'the house is small'. But other languages restrict adjectives to their core function of attribution only. In Yimas, adjectives in attributive function can form an NP with a noun head, *kpa kay* big canoe 'a big canoe', but in predicative function they must be derived into nouns via a noun class marker: **kay kpa ayk* canoe.VIII.SG big COP.VIII.sg must be *kay kpa-y ayk* canoe.VIII.SG big-VIII.SG COP.VIII.SG 'the canoe is a big (one)'. Both Baker (2003) and Dixon (2010) claim that a class of adjectives, along with nouns and verbs, is universal, found in every language, but I regard this claim as still unsettled, and in any case not my main concern here. Rather I again wish to explore the variation in the formal expression of roots for property concepts across languages. In a classic paper, Dixon (1977) demonstrated that the class of adjectives across languages can vary enormously, in his sample from a low of eight in Igbo to hundreds in a language like English. But Igbo is not the lower limit; Yimas has only three true adjectives, *kpa* 'big', *yua* 'good', and *ma* 'other'. If only three, why not none? Could the lower limit be zero? And as I will argue, there are indeed strong cases for languages without a distinct word class of adjectives, although, of course, all languages have lexemes that denote properties.

To see how this could be the case, it is best to start with a language with a minimal class of adjectives, in this case Yimas. Yimas adjectives can be defined by a number of properties, most obviously that they can form a depauperate two-term NP with a noun head, in the fixed order ADJ + N, and in such phrases the adjectives carry no concord suffix for class and number: *yua kumpwi* good boy.I.PL 'good boys'. And adjectives cannot be directly derived into inchoative verbs; that requires them to be nominalized by a noun class suffix and incorporated with the support verb *t-* 'become, do, make, feel', as in (27).

(27) kumpwi   i-ɲa-yua-t-n
     boy.I.PL I.PL.NOM-PRES-good-become-PRES
     'the boys are growing up well'

But the three adjectives exhaust this class; other property-denoting words are apportioned into the classes of verbs and nouns. Colour words, for example, along with many others of Dixon's (1977) semantic subclasses of property-denoting words, fall into the class of verbs. The root of the word for 'black, dark', *urkpwica-* actually has an inchoative meaning, 'to become black, dark', and, unlike the true adjective *kpa* 'big', can be used directly in a clause in this meaning:

(28) narm   p-na-urkpwica-n
     skin.VII.SG VII.SG.NOM-PRES-darken-PRES
     'the skin is darkening'

But unlike an adjective, this root cannot form an NP with a head noun directly: **urkpwica narm* darken skin 'dark skin'. In order to attribute the property to a modified noun, the verb must be nominalized with a noun class suffix agreeing in class and number with the noun modified. It must also carry the irrealis tense suffix *-k* indicating an event unbound in time, hence a state. And further, although the order is rather free, the modifier commonly follows its head noun, rather than preceding it, as true adjectives must:

(29) *narm*   *urkpwica-k-m*
     skin.VII.SG   darken-IRR-VII.SG
     'dark skin'

Attributing verbs like this need not even be adjacent to the nouns they modify:

(30) *parwa-n*   *kanta kamta-k-wa*   *ta-pu-tay-kiak-rm*   *kay*
     dock.IX.SG-OBL   but   empty-IRR-IX.SG   NEG-3-see-IRR-3DL.NOM   canoe.VIII.SG
     'but they both didn't see a canoe at the empty dock'

Other property-denoting words belong to the class of nouns and like all nouns bear inherent noun class. Words denoting human propensity typically are nouns, such as *tamana* 'sickness', assigned to noun class IX, as it terminates in an underlying /aw/. Because words like *tamana* 'sickness' are nouns, attribution with them is treated like possession (compare (5a)):

(31) *ama*   *tamana*   *kantk-n*   *amayak*
     1SG   sickness   with-SG   COP.1SG
     'I am with sickness.'

But more strikingly, because these are nouns, they can function directly as core arguments, and such uses are more commonly the most colloquial way to express attribution with them:

(32) *tamana*   *wa-ŋa-tal*
     sickness.IX.SG   IX.SG.NOM-1SG.ACC-hold
     'sickness is grabbing me'

The division of labour of property-denoting words in Yimas points the way to the possible two types of languages that may lack them altogether: allocate them totally to the class of nouns or completely to the class of verbs. Dixon (2010) has noted that languages of the first type tend to be dependent marking, while those of the second either are neutral or head marking (Nichols 1986). The Australian language Ngiyambaa (Donaldson 1980; see Chapter 26 in this volume) treats property-denoting words as nouns, and a similar claim has been made for Quechua (Lefebvre & Muysken 1988; see Chapter 34 in this volume). Ngiyambaa is a dependent-marking language, and its nouns lack gender or noun class: the only inflection they take is case. Both object-denoting and property-denoting words take case; verbs do not. Furthermore, property-denoting words on their own can refer to either the property or an object characterized by that property: *gi:djan* 'green' or 'the green one'. There is one formal difference, however, that could be seized upon to distinguish them: object-denoting words do not generally reduplicate, but property-denoting ones can, to mean 'more or less'. But note that this seems a purely semantic characterization and hence not definable for a structural lexical class. It makes no sense to say *miri-miri*, 'dog' reduplicated, because something is either a dog or not, while *bubay-bubay*, 'short' reduplicated, is and should be fine on semantic grounds. And when reduplication of an object-denoting word does make sense semantically, it is possible, *ŋimbi* 'bone', *ŋimbi-ŋimbi* 'on the bony side, somewhat bony', demonstrating that the distribution of reduplication is a purely semantic fact and not a diagnostic of a distinct class of adjectives in this language. The most straightforward conclusion here is that property-denoting words simply are nouns in Ngiyambaa.

Languages in which property-denoting words are allocated to the class of verbs may be more common cross-linguistically, given the similar semantics of properties and states. Claims that adjectives are simply stative verbs have been advanced for Mandarin Chinese (Li & Thompson 1981 Thai (Prasithrathsint 2000), and Lao (Enfield 2004), all neutral languages, i.e. languages which are neither dependent nor head marking, though this has been disputed for Mandarin (Paul 2015). Many head-marking languages, such as some in the Oceanic subgroup of Austronesian (see Chapter 35 in this volume) or Northern Iroquoian (see Chapter 30 in this volume), also arguably classify all property-denoting words as stative verbs. Here I will illustrate with Seneca, another Northern Iroquoian language, drawing on an article by Chafe (2012), in which this claim is demonstrated with great care and closely reasoned arguments. As was discussed above, all verbs in Northern Iroquoian must consist minimally of a pronominal prefix, a verb root, and an aspectual suffix, in that order, and so must a property-denoting word: *yo-ste-ʔ* N.PAT-be.heavy-STAT 'it's heavy'. And as we saw, verb roots incorporate nouns, and so do property-denoting roots: *yo-skohr-a-ste-ʔ* N.PAT-branch-LINK-be.heavy-STAT 'it's a heavy branch'. A particularly interesting argument that Chafe (2012) advances for treating property-denoting words in Seneca as stative verbs concerns the cislocative prefix, which normally means towards the speaker, but with stative verb roots means 'the most':

(33) a. *t-ha-nǫhwe-ʔs*
CLOC-M.SG.AGT-like-HAB
'he likes it the best'

b. *t-ke-swahǫ-hs*
CLOC-1SG.AGT-hate-HAB
'I hate it the most'

Exactly the same prefix is used with property-denoting roots to mean the superlative degree (note also the etymology of *superlative* in 'beyond + 'carried', sourced also in a motion metaphor):

(34) a. *t-h-ǫkwʔt-iyo-:h*
CLOC-M.SG.AGT-person-good-STAT
'(he's) the nicest man'

b. *t-ka-khw-ahetkę-ʔ*
CLOC-N.SG-food-bad-STAT
'(it's) the worst food'

The evidence in Seneca therefore supports the conclusion that property-denoting roots are verb roots; more precisely, stative verb roots restricted to occurring only with the stative aspect suffix.

6.8 Adpositions

Adpositions (see Chapter 20 in this volume) are head words that take NPs or DPs as their complements and signal the role of that NP or DP within the clause, most commonly in oblique or peripheral argument functions. They are called prepositions or postpositions whether they occur before their complement or after respectively, and it has been known since Greenberg (1963a) that there is a correlation between the order of the direct object and its governing verb and whether the language is prepositional or postpositional: VO languages favour prepositions (English) while OV languages favour postpositions (Japanese), though the correlation is far from perfect. As with adjectives, languages vary enormously as to whether they have a large inventory of adpositions (English, German) or very few (Yabem) or perhaps even none (Au, Mam). Of course, the primary function of adpositions, to signal the role of oblique or peripheral constituents, must be carried out in all languages, but again like adjectives, this task can be allocated to other word classes or even inflections. The function of adpositions is very much like case markers, and in some languages case suffixes have usurped that function. The North Caucasian language Lak (Daniel & Lander 2011) has about three dozen case suffixes, and most of these correspond directly in meaning to prepositions in English:

(35) (a) *qˤat-lu-w*
house-OBL-in
'in the house'

(b) *qˤat-lu-x*
house-OBL-behind
'behind the house'

(c) *qˤat-lu-wu-n*
house-OBL-in-towards
'into the house'

(d) *qˤat-lu-j-n*
house-OBL-on-towards
'onto the house'

(e) *qˤat-lu-x-n*
house-OBL-behind-towards
'to the back of the house'

(f) *qˤat-lu-w-a*
house-OBL-in-from
'from inside the house'

Interestingly no language, to the best of my knowledge, presents such an extensive array of case prefixes. It seems that postpositions rather easily grammaticalize to case suffixes, but prepositions do not do so to case prefixes. In fact, cross-linguistically case prefixes are limited (for example, Dryer 2013a in his typological survey lists 575 languages in which case is signalled by suffixes or postpositions, but only 55 in which it is marked by prefixes or prepositions, a 10:1 ratio), and in languages which do have case prefixes the inventory is always much smaller than the elaborations exemplified by Lak (though the prepositives of Takelma (Sapir 1922: 253–258) pose an interesting question as to their status: are they prefixes or prepositions?). Why this is so remains to be determined, but I suspect it has to do with processing constraints (Hawkins 1994; 2004).

The solution that languages employ to deal with a restricted or null set of adpositions are much the same as with adjectives: assign the function to one or the other of the two major classes, nouns, or verbs. The assignment to verbs is probably more common cross-linguistically, given that adpositions are complement selecting just as transitive verbs are.

This assignment seems particularly common in VO languages in which the function of prepositions is met by verbs in serial verb constructions, leading of course diachronically in some cases to the reanalysis of such verbs in series into prepositions (Lord 1993), or to situations in some East Asian languages like Chinese or Vietnamese, where there has been ongoing debate as the synchronic word-class status of the forms in question; are they still verbs or now prepositions? (Clark 1978; see Chapter 3 in this volume).

In the two languages to be considered here, there is no doubt as to their status as verbs. Consider the Oceanic Austronesian language of New Guinea, Yabem (Dempwolff 1939; Zahn 1940; Bradshaw 1983; 1993; Bisang 1986; Ross 2002). Verbs are a distinctly obvious word class in Yabem. They require agreement for person and number of their subjects, and, if the number is singular, they inflect for mood, realis versus irrealis; no other word class exhibits such behaviour. Yabem has a small set of three adpostions, two prepositions *nga* 'with' and *angga* 'from' and a postpositional clitic = *nga* 'to, for, at', but the vast majority of adpositional-type meanings are expressed by verbs in serial verb constructions:

(36) a. *ka-sing   I   ga-wing   teocac*
      1SG.R-catch fish 1SG.R-accompany my.elder.brother
      'I caught fish with my elder brother'

   b. *eng kê-pê   moc   kê-kô   ondoc*
      3SG 3SG.R-shoot bird   3SG.R-stand where
      'where did he shoot birds?'

   c. *aê   ka-kêng   bing   gê-ja   malac*
      1SG 1SG.R-give   talk   3SG.R-go.to village
      'I brought a message to the village'

   d. *ja-mu   ja-mêng   malac   ê-ndêng   ocsalô*
      1SG.IRR-return 1SG.IRR-come.   village 3SG.IRR-reach forenoon
      'I'll come back to the village before noon'

A limiting case seems to be Au, a language of the Torricelli family also in New Guinea, which according to the grammar sketch by Scorza (1985) appears to completely lack adpositions, and solely uses verbs in their functions. All verbs inflect for person, number, and gender of their subjects with prefixes, but in addition some transitive verbs have suffixes (occasionally infixes) for person, number, and gender of their objects. Lexemes expressing adpositional-type meanings occur in serial verb constructions and inflect identically:

(37) a. *k-enkwewɨ   k-eit   witeik*
      3SG.M.SUBJ-fall.down 3.SG.M.SUBJ-at village
      'he fell down at the village'

   b. *n-ewis-ɨm   m-au   si*
      3PL.M.SUBJ-put-3PL.N.OBJ   3PL.N.SUBJ-on   fire
      m-e   wɨtaan
      3PL.N.SUBJ-of   night
      'they put it on the fire during the night'

c. *tipir   k-irɨr   k-eriwe-r-ek*
   spirit   3SG.M.SUBJ-flee   3SG.M.SUBJ-with-LINK-3SG.N.OBJ
   'the spirit fled with it'

Languages which employ nouns in the function of adpositions are a particular feature of languages of Mesoamerica, where they are referred to as relator nouns in grammatical descriptions of these languages. Mam (England 1983), a language belonging to the Mayan family and spoken in Guatemala, exemplifies this well. Like Au, it appears to lack adpositions, using relator nouns in all their functions. Nouns are marked by prefixes to mark their possessors (homophonous with the ergative prefixes on verbs), which are obligatory for inalienably possessed nouns; relator nouns belong to the class of inalienably possessed nouns. As in many Mesoamerican languages, relator nouns, particularly those for locational notions, often are metaphorical uses of body part terms (all relator nouns here are prefixed with the third singular possessor prefix *t-* 'his, hers, its'):

(38)
noun root	relator noun
witz- 'face'	*t-witz* 'on'
wiʔ- 'head'	*t-wiʔ* 'above'
txaʔn 'nose'	*t-tzaʔn* 'at the edge'
tziiʔ- 'mouth'	*t- tziiʔ* 'at the entrance'

In (39) are some examples of the use of these relator nouns in Mam:

(39) a. *jaw-lee-t   jun   xaq   kyeeʔyax   t-jaq'   yooxh*
        go.up-CAUS-PASS   one   rock   precious   3SG.POSS-below   red
        tx'otx'   t-kub
        earth   3SG.ERG-go.down
        'a precious stone appeared below the red earth'

   b. *juun   y-xileen   t-iʔj   axiʔn   ojtxa*
      one   3SG.POSS-explanation   3SG.POSS-about   corn   before
      'an explanation about corn in the old days'

   c. *aq'naa-n   kyeel   t-uʔn   asdoon*
      work-ANTIPASS   miguel   3SG.POSS-with   hoe
      'Miguel worked with a hoe'

   d. *k-tzaaja-l   asta   maax   t-wiʔ   witz*
      3SG.ABS-come-POT   up.to   to.there   3SG.POSS-above   hill
      'it has to come from there above the hill'

6.9 Conclusion

As I mentioned in the introduction, the goal of this chapter was not to answer the question 'do all languages have distinct basic lexical classes of nouns and verbs, as well as adjectives or adpositions?' Ultimately, I regard such a question as ill formulated and ill posed. Rather what was of concern here is how and to what degree do languages have lexical classes of nouns, verbs, adjectives, and adpositions and what are the parameters of variation in their expression? For the two minor classes, adjectives and adpositions, the answer is more straightforward: languages can vary from very large lexical inventories in these classes to very small or even null ones, and these classes can have unique morphosyntactic properties or be subsumed morphosyntactically into one or the other of the two major classes of nouns and verbs. Which of these two options is adopted often seems to be related to wider morphosyntactic typological properties of the languages, head versus dependent marking, VO versus OV constituent order, etc. The two major word classes, nouns and verbs, present much greater complexities.

Cross-linguistically, each of these seems to be specialized for a different linguistic function: argumenthood for nouns and predication for verbs. But the answer to the question how and to what degree languages have lexical classes of nouns and verbs revolves around how built into the structure of a language is a prior specialization of two distinct lexical classes—one class, nouns, for argument function, and another, verbs, for predication function. The greater the degree of specialization that is lexically built in, the stricter a noun–verb distinction holds for a language. Yimas is the limiting case here: noun roots can only serve as arguments and verb roots only as predicates; overlapping is not possible. This is a language with a very sharp noun–verb distinction. Southern Wakashan and Philippine languages represent the opposite pole. Roots are not divided lexically into two classes: one specialized for argumenthood and one for predication; roots are undifferentiated along these lines. But this similarity hides a deep contrast. In Southern Wakashan languages, all roots have the predication function built into them; argument function requires derivation. Yet in Tagalog and other Philippine languages, all roots are preselected for the argument function; there they need to be derived to function freely as predicates. To treat nouns and verbs in Southern Wakashan and Philippine languages as the same types of grammatical categories would eclipse such fundamental and typologically revealing differences between these two families of languages.

Our theoretical models need to be both rigorous and flexible enough to describe the lexical categories of Yimas, Nuu-chah-nulth, Tagalog, and Cayuga without erasing their differences in the pursuit of some elusive and probably illusory Universal Grammar of such categories. In my view Universal Grammar will ultimately not turn out to be a set of universal categories found in every language but rather a set of constraints of variable weighting that languages select from, such as the communicative need to say something (predication) about something(s) (argumenthood). What the languages discussed here reveal is just some of the constrained variation we find cross-linguistically in the expression of that communicative need. I am sure that detailed study of further languages will uncover many more surprises.

PART II
THEORETICAL APPROACHES

CHAPTER 7

WORD CLASSES IN FORMAL SEMANTICS

YOAD WINTER

FORMAL semantics of natural language grew out of works that assume a strong relationship between syntactic categories and semantic types (Lewis 1970; Montague 1973). In its strictest formulation, this assumption entails that any two words of the same category must have the same type of meaning. Thus, by learning the morphosyntactic category of a word, you learn some of its most important semantic aspects. This idea is theoretically appealing, but it comes with a heavy toll. A too restrictive matching between syntactic categories and semantic types is descriptively untenable. In many languages, one and the same word class may systematically correspond to more than one semantic type, or contribute to sentence meaning in ways that are not easy to describe using types alone. Much of the progress in formal semantics since the 1970s has been achieved by articulating a richer palette of semantic objects suitable for describing meanings of the major word classes in Germanic and Romance languages. This has been accompanied by a principled relaxation of the matching between categories and types. Starting from the mid-1990s, much research in formal semantics has been devoted to less well-studied languages (Von Fintel & Matthewson 2008), with a more recent keen interest in the cross-linguistic analysis of categories in formal semantics (Francez & Koontz-Garboden 2017).

One of the assets of formal semantics is its explicitness regarding processes of nominal quantification and anaphora. This has led to a focus on the semantics of nouns and its extensions to other categories. The semantic connections between nouns and other word classes are also the main topic of this chapter. To review this state of the art, section 7.1 starts out by introducing the classical notion of types in formal semantics, which describe function argument relations like those that appear between verbs and their arguments, or between determiners and nouns. We illustrate this 'extrinsic' use of types in analyses of English and of Warlpiri, whose word order is freer and case system is richer than most European languages. Extrinsic typing does not distinguish nouns from verbs, adjectives, and prepositions. These word classes are distinguished by their phrase-internal semantic arguments, which play a central role in modification. This is the topic of section 7.2. The analysis of phrasal modifiers allows us to characterize category-specific arguments for meanings of verbs (states and events), gradable adjectives (degrees), and locative prepositions (spatial objects). Unlike these other word classes, nouns are assumed not to have intrinsic semantic arguments, and their extrinsic entity argument is directly targeted by phrase-internal modifiers. Section 7.3 addresses another property that distinguishes nouns from other categories: their ability to restrict the domain of quantification. This property of *N-conservative* quantification, together with phrase-internal modification, is illustrated by analysing the semantic disambiguation of N/V-like words in Hebrew. Section 7.4 addresses another characteristic of nouns: their ability to introduce identity criteria, as proposed in the philosophical work of Geach (1962). We discuss challenges for linguistic works that rely on Geach's proposal, and review part of the controversy surrounding ongoing attempts to adapt Geach's ideas to formal semantic frameworks. Section 7.5 addresses some major issues in the semantics of nouns in relation to their ability to refer to *kinds* and *mass* substances. Adding another dimension to classifications of semantic restrictions on word classes, this discussion also shows the intimate relation between mass terms and property expressions, which affects the choices that languages make when manifesting certain property meaning as nominal or adjectival.

7.1 Extrinsic types of words and function–argument relationships

Different word classes contribute differently to sentential meaning. Formal semantics encodes this fact using different *types* that are associated with different word classes. This section concentrates on standard semantic types that describe a word class's contribution to relations between functions and arguments in a sentence's meaning. To distinguish them from other aspects of word meaning in formal semantics, we refer to these types as *extrinsic*. After describing some elements of the theory of extrinsic types, we illustrate their application to configurational and non-configurational analyses of English and Warlpiri.

7.1.1 Extrinsic types and function application

All languages have ways of referring to entities and propositions, whose types are denoted using the labels 'e' and 't', respectively. Proper names and definite noun phrases refer to (concrete or abstract) entities, whereas declarative sentences refer to propositions. The notation 't' for the propositional type reflects the analysis of propositions as having *truth values* relative to given situations (Frege 1892).

In principle, any mathematical function that operates on entities and propositions is a legitimate candidate for being the meaning of linguistic expressions. Accordingly, types of different word classes are described using the basic types e and t and their combinations. One-place predicates are viewed as functions from entities to propositions, whose type is denoted $\langle e,t \rangle$. Such meanings are assigned to intransitive verbs (V), common nouns (N), and adjectives (A). Transitive verbs, as well as most prepositions and relational nouns (*brother of*) and adjectives (*fond of*), are viewed as functions from *pairs* of entities to truth values. The type

⟨e·e,t⟩ is used for describing such *two-place predicates*.[1] Functional categories like articles, demonstratives, conjunctions, determiners, and comparatives are assigned more complex types, which are nonetheless mathematically straightforward. Let us exemplify this using the English definite article. In the noun phrase *the flutist*, the article combines with a noun of type ⟨e,t⟩ to yield an entity. Accordingly, English articles and demonstratives receive the following type:

⟨⟨e,t⟩,e⟩ functions from one-place predicates to entities

By assigning types like ⟨e,t⟩, ⟨e·e,t⟩ or ⟨⟨e,t⟩,e⟩ to an expression, we describe its 'extrinsic' semantic interactions with other expressions in terms of function–argument relations. Some conventional assignments of extrinsic types to categories are summarized in Table 7.1.

Table 7.1 Different categories with their extrinsic types and intrinsic arguments

PN	proper name	e	—		
N	noun	⟨e,t⟩	—		
V	verb (in.)	⟨e,t⟩	E	event	for eventive and stative verbs
	(tr.)	⟨e·e,t⟩	E		
A	adjective	⟨e,t⟩	d	degree	for gradable adjectives for
P	preposition	⟨e·e,t⟩	r	region	locative prepositions
ADV	adverb	⟨e,t⟩	d	degree	for manner and degree adverbs
ART	article	⟨⟨e,t⟩,e⟩	—		

Extrinsic types help to explain how words from different word classes support the assignment of meaning to complex expressions, including full sentences. A central mode of meaning composition is *Function Application* (FA). This rule describes situations where an expression of a function type combines with its argument. For instance, when the function denoted by the intransitive verb *runs* combines with the entity meaning of the name *Ben*, the result is the propositional meaning of the sentence *Ben runs*, of type t. We describe this FA as follows:

$$\langle e,t \rangle + e \xrightarrow{FA} t$$

FA is treated as a commutative operation. Thus, when writing '⟨e,t⟩+e' we refer to both VS and SV constructions. Another example for the operation of FA is the meaning composition between determiners and nouns. For example, the noun phrase *the flutist* involves the following composition rule, from the typed meanings of the article and the noun to the entity denotation of the noun phrase:

$$\langle\langle e,t\rangle,e\rangle + \langle e,t\rangle \xrightarrow{FA} e$$

---

[1] An equivalent way of treating two-place predicates is as functions from entities to one-place predicates, whose type is ⟨e,⟨e,t⟩⟩. This 'Curried' type is often useful in compositional semantic analysis (Winter 2016: 52–59).

As we saw, the $\langle\langle e,t\rangle,e\rangle$ predicates to entities. When this meaning is combined using FA to the one-place predicate denoted by the noun *flutist*, the result is an entity-denoting noun phrase of type e.

A two-place predicate like the transitive verb *see* combines with an entity argument to form a one-place predicate like the verb phrase *see Ben*. This is described using the following rule:

$$\langle e{\bullet}e,t\rangle + e \xrightarrow{\text{FA}} \langle e,t\rangle$$

7.1.2 Extrinsic types in configurational and non-configurational analysis

Assigning types to categories as in Table 7.1 is suitable for analysing meaning in different languages, and does not depend on a specific syntactic theory. Rather, it applies type theory to generalize insights which are common in the typological literature (Croft 1991; Hengeveld 1992), and is applicable to languages whose word order is freer and whose case system is richer than English and other European languages. Here we illustrate this point by comparing the semantic analysis of simple sentences in English and Warlpiri.[2]

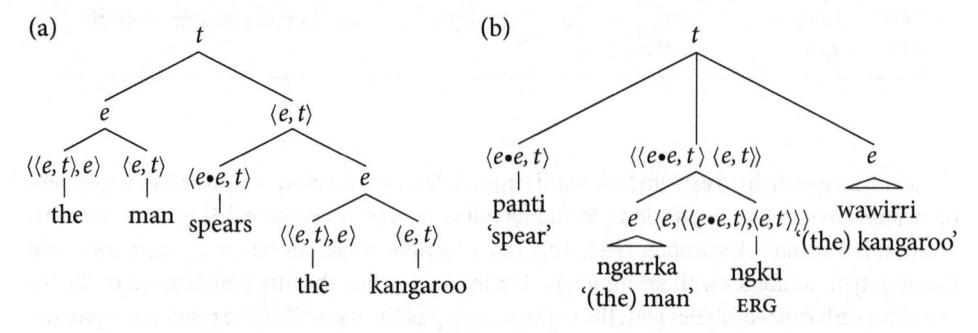

FIGURE 7.1 English vs Warlpiri. Arguments are identified in English using a configurational analysis; in Warlpiri this is achieved by case marking with Hale's non-configurational analysis and Keenan's semantics. For presentational reasons, Figure 7.1b suppresses the non-past suffix *rni* and the auxiliary *ka* in (1). The one-place predicate denotations of the bare nouns *ngarrka* ('man') and *wawirri* ('kangaroo') are assumed to be mapped to single entities using a morphologically covert definite article (sections 7.1.2 and 7.5.1).

In Figure 7.1a, the three cases of FA that are illustrated above are applied to a configurational analysis of a simple English sentence. In this analysis, the expression that combines first with the transitive verb *spear* is the patient *the kangaroo*. When describing the semantics of this composition, the two-place predicate that is denoted by the verb *spear* is assumed to have the patient as its first argument. This is described as follows:

> *spear* = the 2-place predicate holding of the pairs $\langle x, y\rangle$ where x is the patient and y is the agent ('y spears x')

[2] For further details on case in formal semantics, see the review in De Hoop & Zwarts (2008).

Thus, we obtain the following one-place predicate as the meaning of the verb phrase:

spear the kangaroo = the 1-place predicate holding of the entities *y* such that
⟨*the_kangaroo,y*⟩ is a pair in the 2-place predicate *spear*

This semantic analysis is suitable for configurational accounts of SVO languages like English, but it is also suitable for languages where configurational assumptions have been contended. To consider one such case, let us look at the following Warlpiri example from Hale (1983):

(1) panti-rni ka ngarrka-ngku wawirri
 spear-NONPAST AUX man-ERG kangaroo
 'The man is spearing the kangaroo.'

Word order in Warlpiri is famous for being much more permissive than in English. The semantic role of Warlpiri arguments is identified using case markers and not necessarily by their position in the sentence. Hale (1983) and others propose to deal with that using a 'non-configurational' analysis, where a transitive verb, subject, and object (essentially) form a trinary sentential structure. To interpret such structures, we must analyse the semantic contribution of case markers. For instance, without a semantic interpretation of the marker *ngku*, we would have no way to identify the noun *ngarrka* ('man') as the agent of the action in (1), for the same case-marked noun may appear in different positions while retaining its agentive meaning.[3] Such a move is not necessary for 'configurational' languages like English, where case markers are less operational.

In Keenan (1989), case markers like *ngku* in (1) are analysed as 'arity reducers': functions that map an *n*-ary predicate to an (*n-1*)-predicate by specifying one of its *n* arguments as a target for reduction. In our present terms, the ergative case marker *ngku* in (1) is assigned the following type:

⟨*e*,⟨⟨*e·e,t*⟩,⟨*e,t*⟩⟩⟩

The noun *ngarrka* is analysed as denoting an entity ('the man') using an implicit process interpreting it as a definite.[4] This entity combines with the meaning of the case marker *ngku* by FA. Consequently, the noun phrase *ngarrka-ngku* ('the man'-erg) gets the type ⟨⟨*e·e,t*⟩,⟨*e,t*⟩⟩: an arity-reducing function from two-place predicates to one-place predicates. Keenan assumes that the marker *ngku* has a 'nominative' meaning, which leads to the following analysis of the noun phrase:

ngarrka-ngku = the function mapping any 2-place predicate *P* to the 1-place predicate
holding of the entities *x* such that ⟨*x,the_man*⟩ is in *P*

This semantic analysis of the case marker makes sure that the noun *ngarrka* ('man') in (1) is identified as the verb's agent. It allows us to identify the nominative argument semantically in a flat structure like Hale's. In Keenan's analysis, unlike the configurational analysis of

---

[3] Hale mentions that the orders *ngarrka-ngku ka wawirri panti-rni* and *wawirri ka panti-rni ngarrka-ngku* are also possible, among others.

[4] The introduction of silent definite articles as in Figure 7.1b is not special to the semantic analysis of Warlpiri, and is used for many other languages with bare nominal arguments (see section 7.5.1).

the English phrase *spear the kangaroo*, it is the meaning of the overt case marker (rather than syntactic adjacency) that determines the meaning composition.[5] This analysis of sentence (1) is summarized in Figure 7.1b, ignoring the auxiliary and the tense suffix. Note that unlike the English sentence, analysing the Warlpiri example does not require assumptions about binary configurations, and not even common categories. The key to the semantic analysis of Warlpiri in Figure 7.1b is the type and meaning assumed for the case marker, and the process of FA.

7.2 Intrinsic meanings of different word classes: Intersective modification

The extrinsic types that were introduced above account for function–argument relations, which are relevant for all word classes in all phrases and expressions. However, extrinsic types do not cover more specialized aspects of meaning that characterize specific word classes. For instance, intransitive nouns, verbs, and adjectives are all assigned the extrinsic type $\langle e,t \rangle$, with no regard to more specific aspects of word meaning that distinguish these classe.

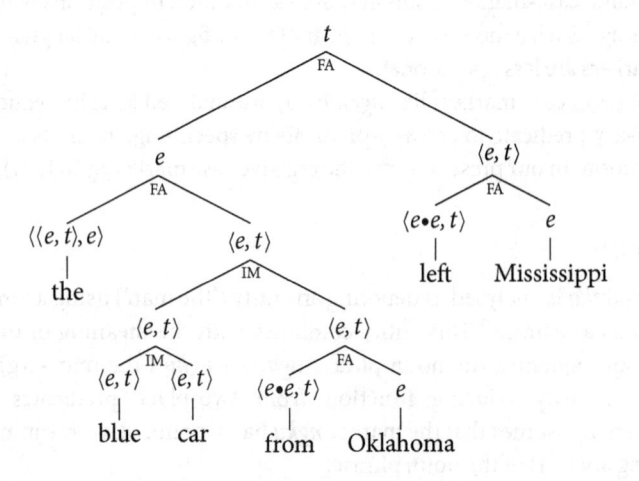

FIGURE 7.2 Intersective modification of nominals. In nominals, standard intersective modifiers (here 'blue' and 'from Oklahoma') are predicates of type $\langle e,t \rangle$ that target the e argument of the noun.

Some of these aspects can be observed by looking at modification constructions with different categories. In this section we consider nominal modification and its differences

---

[5] Warlpiri case has further functions. Croft (2001: 186) mentions that the ergative case can establish a connection between a noun and an attributive adjective at a distance. This does not rule out Keenan's analysis, but it requires a more careful formulation than what is given here.

from modification with verbs, adjectives, and prepositions, and show how these differences are reflected in the formal semantic analysis.

Modification of nouns by adjectives often has a conjunctive meaning, for example:

(2) *x* is a *blue car* = *x* is a car <u>and</u> *x* is blue

In this paraphrase, both the noun and the adjective act as predicates that apply directly to the entity *x*, and the two propositions that this gives rise to are conjoined. We refer to this analysis as *intersective* modification (IM).[6] It is accounted for by introducing another way of combining types on top of FA.[7] Specifically, IM with $\langle e,t \rangle$ predicates is described using the following rule:

$$\langle e,t \rangle + \langle e,t \rangle \xrightarrow{\text{IM}} \langle e,t \rangle$$

This rule applies in many other cases of nominal modification besides adjectives, which is illustrated in Figure 7.2.

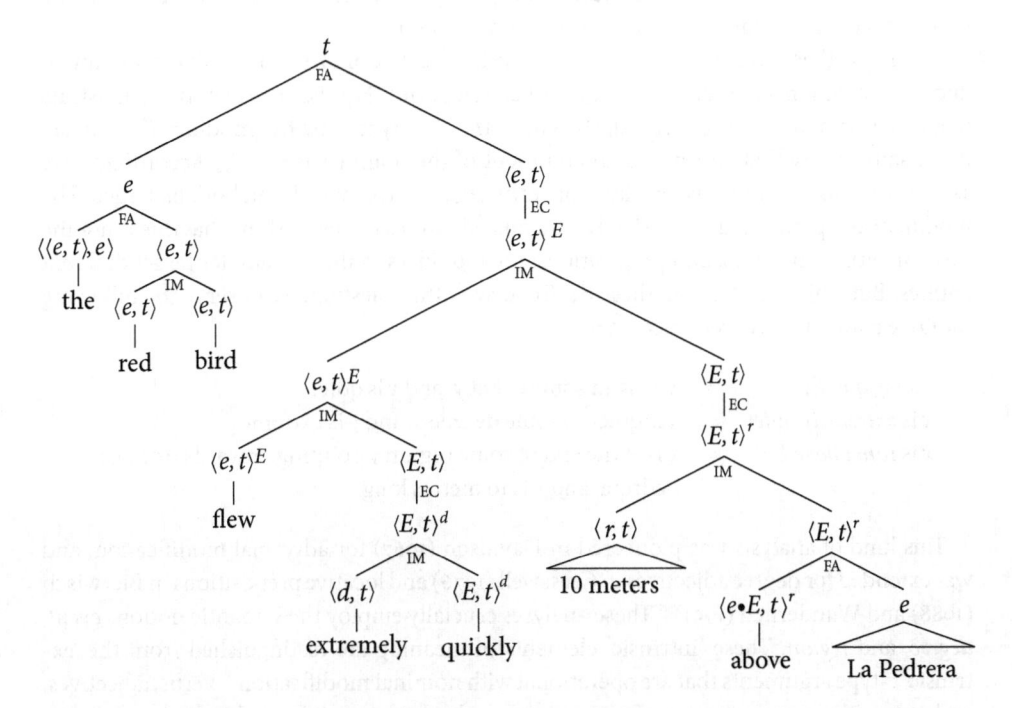

FIGURE 7.3 Intersective modification and extrinsic/intrinsic arguments

---

[6] This analysis is not applicable to adjectives like *skilful*, whose predicative meaning may shift depending on the nominal they modify. For instance, *a skilful driver* is skilful *at driving*, and it would be underinformative to describe her as being 'skilful'. Other adjectives (e.g. *main*) do not even appear in predicative positions. See Siegel (1976) and Partee (2010) for a non-intersective analysis of such adjectives, and Baker (2003: 205–211) for relevant discussion.

[7] Another way to achieve IM is to assign a function of type $\langle \langle e,t \rangle, \langle e,t \rangle \rangle$ to the modifier. Such meanings allow us to do the intersection as part of the modifier's semantics using only FA.

Our analysis of IM with nominals is inadequate when it comes to modelling modification with other categories. Consider for instance the following sentences:

(3) a. Karl *sang quietly*.
 b. Eileen is *extremely quick*.
 c. Jonathan flew *10 metres above La Pedrera*.

When analysing the modified phrases in these examples, we should pay attention to the following semantic differences:

x sang quietly	≠	*x* sang and *x* is quiet
x is extremely quick	≠	*x* is quick and *x* is extreme
x is 10 metres above La Pedrera	≠	*x* is above La Pedrera and *x* is 10 metres (high?)

In contrast with nominal modification, we see that modifiers of verbs, degree adjectives, and locative prepositions are not readily analysed as intersective. Someone who sang quietly is not necessarily a quiet person; an extremely quick person is not necessarily extreme; being 10 metres above La Pedrera does not mean 'being 10 metres'.

To analyse these constructions we retain the intersective analysis of modifiers, but introduce a distinction between nouns and other categories. Equivalences as in (2) illustrate that as far as nouns are concerned, the entity that is targeted by the modifier ('*x* is blue') is the same entity that appears as an argument of the noun ('*x* is a car'). Accordingly, we assume that nouns only have one kind of entity argument(s), which can both be targeted by modifiers and predicated extrinsically. The non-identities in (3a–c) show that this is not the case for verbs, adjectives, and prepositions: the modifiers in these examples target different entities. But which entities can these be? To answer this question, we observe the following intuitive paraphrases of sentences (3a–c):

x sang quietly	=	*x* sang in some **event** *y*, <u>and</u> *y* is quiet
x is extremely quiet	=	*x* is quiet to some **degree** *y*, <u>and</u> *y* is extreme
x is 10m above L.P.	=	*x* is at the end of some **region** *y* pointing upwards from La Pedrera, <u>and</u> *y* is 10 metres long

This kind of analysis was pioneered in Davidson (1967) for adverbial modification, and was extended for degree adjectives in Cresswell (1976) and locative prepositions in Bierwisch (1988) and Wunderlich (1991).[8] These analyses crucially employ the semantic notions *event*, *degree*, and *region*. These 'intrinsic' elements of meaning are distinguished from the 'extrinsic' e-type arguments that are operational with nominal modification.[9] Verbs, adjectives, and prepositions, in contrast to nouns, are assumed to have two different kinds of arguments. The entity argument(s) that is described by the extrinsic type of Vs, As, and Ps is the entity that they apply to as predicates. For instance, the e in the $\langle e,t \rangle$ type of the intransitive verb *run* refers to the entity that acts as a subject argument in the sentence *Ben runs*. By contrast,

---

[8] Davidson's proposal was revised in Parsons (1990) and Kratzer (1996); for a review, see Maienborn (2011). On degree modification, see the book-length overview (Morzycki 2016). On vectors in spatial semantics, see Zwarts (1997, 2020).

[9] The terms 'intrinsic' and 'extrinsic' are semantic, and should be distinguished from the syntactic terms *internal/external argument*.

modification with Vs, As, and Ps targets a different entity in their meaning: event (e) with Vs, degree (d) with As, and region (r) with Ps, as illustrated in the analyses above. We refer to these specialized entity arguments as *intrinsic*.

Modification of manner adverbs (ADV) is analysed similarly to degree adjectives. Many adverbs are derived from degree adjectives, and we assume that they inherit their intrinsic degree argument. This is in view of examples like the following:

Sue ran *extremely fast* = Sue ran in some event z, <u>and</u> z was fast to some **degree** y, <u>and</u> y was extreme

With some notable exceptions (see below), intrinsic arguments are not accessible to extrinsic operation of FA. Thus, events, degrees, and regions do not as a rule appear as subjects or objects predicated in the sentence. Conversely, the extrinsic arguments of Vs, As, Ps, and ADVs are not a natural target for modification. This is one way in which the category N is distinguished from other categories: it is the only lexical category that systematically supports IM of its extrinsic argument. This leads us to a general principle about categories in formal semantics:

Principle 1—IM:
IM targets the extrinsic argument of Ns, but the intrinsic argument of Vs, As and Ps.

One exception to this principle is *noun incorporation*. Mithun (1984: 863) defines this phenomenon as an 'N stem [that] is incorporated to narrow the scope of the V', where 'the compound stem can be accompanied by a more specific external NP which identifies the argument'. For instance, consider the following Chamorro example from Chung & Ladusaw, (2003: 109):

(4) si   Carmen   gäi-ga'   i   ga'lagu
     UNM[10]   Carmen   AGR.*have-pet*   the   dog
     'Carmen has the dog as pet.'

Chung and Ladusaw analyse the incorporated noun *ga'* ('pet') as a modifier that targets the object argument of the verb *gäi* ('have'). The modified verb applies to the extrinsic argument *i ga'lagu* ('the dog'). This analysis is informally stated as:

x *gäi-ga'* y = x has-pet y = x has y <u>and</u> y is a pet

The noun 'pet' in this analysis modifies an extrinsic argument (y) of the verb, in contrast to Principle 1. Cross-linguistically, however, such cases of N incorporation involve special morphological processes, and do not have the default status of common adverbials that target the intrinsic event argument.[11]

Another exceptional semantic process concerns sentences like *Laura laughed a loud laugh* (Mittwoch 1998). In such cases, the 'cognate' indefinite syntactically acts like a complement of the verb. Semantically, however, it modifies the event argument, and similarly to adjuncts

---

[10] UNM = unmarked morphological case.
[11] For more on noun incorporation in Catalan, Spanish, and other languages, see Espinal & McNally (2011) and references therein.

it licenses further adverbial modification. Thus, it does not 'saturate' or 'reduce' an argument of the verb like ordinary, 'extrinsic', objects do. This modificational behaviour is illustrated in the following Hebrew example:

(5)   ha-matos   naxat nexitat xerum   be-sade natuS
      the-aircraft landed landing emergency in-field deserted
      'the aircraft made an emergency landing in a deserted field'
      = 'there is an event x with the aircraft as agent, where x is an emergency landing
          and x occurred in a deserted field'

This behaviour is perfectly in line with Principle 1, but it highlights the semantic nature of this principle: the intrinsic event argument in (5) is semantically modified (rather than saturated), although its modifier is syntactically realized without a preposition as if it were an object 'argument' of the intransitive verb.[12]

Summing up, Figure 7.3 showcases the formal analysis of the English categories we have discussed so far. In this analysis, FA only targets extrinsic arguments, whereas IM targets intrinsic or extrinsic arguments according to Principle 1. Thus, with the noun *bird* in Figure 7.3, IM targets the extrinsic entity (e) argument, while with other categories IM targets the intrinsic argument: event (E) with Vs, degree (d) with As and ADVs, and region (r) with Ps. For example, the $\langle E,t \rangle$ meaning of *extremely quickly* modifies the intrinsic event argument of the verb *flew* without affecting the verb's extrinsic argument (e). The analysis is similar with the degree modifier *extremely* within the adverbial phrase, and the region modifier *10 metres* in the prepositional phrase. At the phrase level, the intrinsic $E/d/r$ argument is 'erased' using an Existential Closure (EC) operator ('there is an event/degree/region such that ... '). Thus, while the verb *flew* has the meaning of a relation between entities and events (type $\langle e,t \rangle^E$), the verb phrase headed by *flew* ends up having the standard meaning of one-place predicate over entities (type $\langle e,t \rangle$).

7.3 NOUNS AS RESTRICTORS OF QUANTIFICATIONAL DOMAINS

Principle 1 above is a formal semantic criterion that distinguishes nouns from other lexical categories in terms of their combination with intersective modifiers. Typological studies also distinguish nouns from other categories in terms of their intuitive semantic function for identifying individuals (Croft 1991: 63; Hengeveld 1992: ch. 4). As we will see in section 7.4, such intuitive criteria are not easy to state in the precise terms of formal semantic theories. Before entering this controversial territory, however, we examine a related but more

---

[12] Hebrew does not mark bare nouns for case, but Mittwoch remarks that in Ancient Greek, Standard Arabic, and other languages, cognate objects are usually marked with the accusative. Russian and Hebrew also allow cognate objects with instrumental case/preposition.

consensual formal semantic characteristic of nouns: their ability to act as restrictors of quantificational domains. Let us consider the following sentences:

(6) a. Every cat ate.
    b. Some cat ate.
    c. Most cats ate.

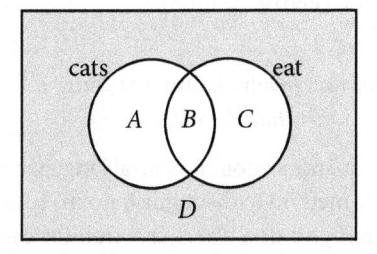

Sentence:	*True* if and only if:
every cat ate	A is empty
some cat ate	B is not empty
most cats ate	B includes more elements than A

FIGURE 7.4 N-conservativity. In the sentences on the right (=6a–c), it is only elements of the N-set (i.e. members of A and B) that determine whether the sentence is true or false. Elements of the V-set that are outside the N-set (i.e. members of C), and entities that are outside both the N-set and the V-set (i.e. members of D) are semantically irrelevant.

To determine whether simple sentences like (6a–c) are true or false in a given situation we need to consider the set of cats and the set of entities that ate, as well as the relation between them. That relation is expressed by the determiners *every*, *some*, and *most*. In (6a) the required relation between the two sets is *inclusion*: for every cat to be eating we need to have the set of cats included in the set of eaters. In (6b) the required relation is *having a non-empty intersection*: for some cat to be eating there must be some element(s) in the intersection of the cats and the eaters. In (6c) the relation is that *the intersection set of the cats and the eaters has a majority of cats*.

We see that the truth conditions of sentences as in (6a–c) are determined by different relations involving the N-set (e.g. the cats) and the V-set (the eaters). However, there are important limitations on these relations. As it turns out, in (6a–c) we do not need to consider entities that are neither cats nor eaters. Furthermore, we also do not need to consider all the eaters: only *cats* that ate are relevant for determining whether these sentences are true or false. In Figure 7.4, this is observed by considering that only the sets A (the cats that didn't eat) and B (the cats that ate) are relevant for determining the truth or falsity of (6a–c). The sets C (the eaters that are not cats) and D (the non-eaters that are not cats) can be safely ignored.

This observation shows an important asymmetry between Ns and Vs. It is the N-set that 'sets the stage' for the quantificational process by determining which elements within the V-set are relevant for the sentence's truth or falsity. We say that the noun *restricts the domain of quantification*, or, in more technical terms, that quantification in (6a–c) is *N-conservative*.

This property is quite general, and holds for a variety of quantificational expressions, including the following English expressions (Keenan 1996):

(7) *every, each, some, no, several, neither, both, most, ten, a dozen, a few, many, few, between five and ten, exactly/approximately/more than/fewer than/at most ten, too many, a few too many, (not) enough*

The prevalence of N-conservativity among determiners has led formal semanticists to propose the following hypothesis (Barwise & Cooper 1981; Glanzberg 2006):

Principle 2—N-conservativity:
Across languages, in all quantificational constructions that involve nouns and verbs, it is the noun that restricts the quantificational domain, rather than the verb.

Principle 2 is a robust semantic generalization about quantification in natural language.[13] Together with Principle 1, it provides us with a semantic method to distinguish nouns from verbs in situations where morphology and syntax do not give us a direct criterion for categorization. Although this point is implicit in many semantic discussions, it has not been emphasized enough in the semantic literature. The analysis below of genericity in Modern Hebrew, which appears to be new, demonstrates the implications of this point.

7.3.1 Example: Semantic disambiguation of noun–verb flexibility in Hebrew

The fact that Principles 1 and 2 hold for nouns but not for other categories gives a semantic twist to the search for definitional criteria of lexical categories. As semantic criteria, these principles are applicable to words that are morphosyntactically underspecified between N and V (Rijkhoff & van Lier 2013). According to Principles 1 and 2, a language may still give us a semantic indication of categorical differences with such words by: (1) allowing modification of entity arguments with noun-like elements, as opposed to other word classes; (2) restricting quantificational processes on nominal-like items, but not on verb-like elements. We illustrate these general points using profession nouns/verbs in Modern Hebrew.

Hebrew has a large class of participle forms, which function both as the present tense of verbs and as nominal modifiers (Doron 2013). Additionally, many Hebrew participles are also nouns, as illustrated by the following profession terms in three morphological templates:

(8) V/N participles in Hebrew (singular masculine forms):
  (i) *oved* 'work/worker', *yoec* 'advise/adviser', *xoker* 'research/researcher'
  (ii) *metaxnet* 'program/programmer', *me'amen* 'coach', *mefaked* 'command/commander'
  (iii) *mamci* 'invent/inventor', *malxin* 'compose/composer', *mafik* 'produce/producer'

---

[13] A potential counterexample is the word *only*. In *only cats ate*, the sentence's truth or falsity depends on whether *non-cats* ate. Thus, *only* may be viewed as giving rise to quantification that is not N-conservative. However, the consensus has been that *only* should be treated as a special case of focus-sensitive adverbials, which are exempt from Principle 2 (Glanzberg 2006 and references therein).

Unlike the other verbal tenses in Hebrew, participles are not inflected for person. The result is that inflections of present tense verbs are the same as nominal inflections. Consequently, the profession terms in (8) can form sentences without any formal difference between N and V. For instance, let us consider the bare singular sentence *metaxnet metaxnet* ('a programmer programs'), where the subject and the predicate are phonologically identical. Any assignment of categories to such occurrences of N/V words must rely on indirect considerations like the semantic Principles 1 and 2.

Let us first illustrate it using Principle 1, in relation to the participle *oved* ('work/worker') and the adjective/adverb *naki* ('clean/ly'). When the verb 'work' appears in the past tense it is inflected for person and has no nominal reading. Accordingly, *naki* is disambiguated as an adverb ('cleanly'):

(9) Hebrew
    tal avad   naki
    Tal worked-3.MASC.SG cleanly
    Unambiguous: 'Tal worked cleanly'

Sentence (9) refers to Tal's manner of work, and does not imply anything about his being a clean person. To put sentence (9) in the present tense we have to use the verb in its participle form, which leads to the following ambiguity:[14]

(10) *tal oved   naki*
    Tal works/worker clean/ly
    Ambiguous: 'Tal worked cleanly' or 'Tal is a worker and is clean'

Sentence (10) is ambiguous between a present tense version of (9), and another reading that refers to Tal's clean habits. Principle 1 directly expects this variation under the assumption that *oved* is ambiguous between N and V. In sentence (9), with a non-ambiguous verb in the past tense, Principle 1 expects event-oriented modification, which make the interpretation refer to Tal's manner of work. With the V-analysis of the participle in (10), the adverbial modification works the same. By contrast, under the N-analysis of the participle in (10), Principle 1 expects reference to Tal as being a 'clean entity'. This is in agreement with the sentence's other meaning where *oved* is interpreted as 'worker'.[15]

Principle 2 about N-conservativity also has implications for categorical identification, specifically in quantificational sentences with bare nominal arguments. Hebrew has bare nominals both in the singular and in the plural. The quantificational processes with Hebrew bare nominals are morphologically silent, and similarly to English bare plurals (Krifka et al. 1995), they support generic readings as well as existential readings. For instance, in the following examples the bare singular *kelev* ('dog') leads to two different interpretations:

---

[14] A related kind of ambiguity appears in English, with some adjectives and *-er* nouns that are fully specified categorically, as in *Olga is a beautiful dancer*. For discussion and analysis of such cases, see Larson (1998); Winter & Zwarts (2012); Alexeyenko (2015); Maienborn (2021).

[15] The predicative N-reading of *oved* ('worker') in (10) appears without a copula, which is not obligatory with predicative nominals in Hebrew (Doron 1983).

(11) Hebrew
    a. *kelev nove'ax kshe-margizim oto*
       dog barks when-annoy-1PL it
       'a dog barks when annoyed' (generic)

    b. *kelev navax kshe-nixnasnu*
       dog barked when-entered-1PL
       'a dog barked when we entered' (existential)

An independent fact about Hebrew is that subjects may often appear in postverbal positions. This is illustrated by the following examples with the verb *nigmar* 'ended':[16]

(12) *ha-mamtakim nigmeru li   / nigmeru li   ha-mamtakim*
     the-sweets   ended to-me / ended to-me the-sweets
     'I ran out of all sweets'

Taken together, these facts give us an opportunity to look at the effects of N-conservativity on categorial identification. Let us consider the following sentence:

(13) *eclenu ba-xevra   oved   metaxnet*
     at-us in-the-company work/er program/er
    (i) 'in our company, a worker programs'
       ≈ 'most workers program'   (generic)
    (ii) 'in our company, some programmer is employed'
       ≈ 'some programmer works'   (existential)

As the gloss indicates, example (13) is ambiguous. Without analysing this ambiguity there is no way to disambiguate the category of the words *oved* ('work/er') and *metaxnet* ('program/er') in (13). This is so because in syntactic contexts like (13), occurrences of these words might give rise to either an SV order or a VS order. This is seen in similar sentences with an adjacent <u>un</u>ambiguous word:

(14) a. *eclenu ba-xevra   oved fisikai*
       at-us in-the-company work physicist(N)   *oved* is V-like
       'in our company, some physicist is employed'

    b. *eclenu ba-xevra   oved mita'mec*
       at-us in-the-company worker labour(V)   *oved* is N-like
       'in our company, a worker labours'

    c. *eclenu ba-xevra   mistovev metaxnet*
       at-us in-the-company hang(V) programmer   *metaxnet* is N-like
       'in our company, some programmer hangs around'

---

[16] Although the discussion below does not hinge on this fact, it should be noted that this verb is unaccusative. Non-unaccusatives do not so easily support postverbal subjects (Costa & Friedmann 2012; Kastner 2020).

d. *eclenu ba-xevra   fisikai metaxnet*
   at-us in-the-company physicist(N) program   *metaxnet* is V-like
   'in our company, a physicist programs'

We conclude that from a morphosyntactic point of view, the string *oved metaxnet* in sentence (13) can be analysed either as an N–V sequence or as a V–N sequence. However, the sentence's interpretation reveals a curious asymmetry: the only generic reading of (13) is 'most workers program' and there is no reading like 'most programmers work'. This asymmetry follows from Principle 2 if N–V is the only category assignment that supports the generic reading. An N–V order can be responsible for the attested reading 'most workers program' since such a generic reading is N-conservative when *oved* is assumed to be a noun ('worker'). By contrast, a reading like 'most programmers work' (or similarly, 'most people who program are workers') is ruled out for the N–V category assignment. According to Principle 2, assigning the category sequence N–V to *oved metaxnet* ('worker program') means that we are not allowed to consider entities outside of the N-set for *oved* ('worker') when assessing the sentence's truth value. For the hypothetical reading 'most people who program are workers' to be true, the set of workers who program should constitute a majority among the people who program. Such a procedure would require us to consider programmers who are not workers. Since these entities are outside the N-set of *oved* ('worker'), the process would not be N-conservative, thus violating Principle 2.

We have seen that Principle 2 predicts a possible categorical origin for the asymmetric availability of generic readings for (13). There is independent evidence for this account, which is well known across languages. In situations where V/N categories are lexically or morphologically specified, Hebrew—similarly to other languages—has severe restrictions on generic readings of postverbal indefinites. This is illustrated by the following sentences (cf. (12)):

(15)   Hebrew
   a. *mamtakim te'imim nigmarim li   maher*
      sweet-PL tasty-PL end-PL to-me quickly
      'I run out of tasty sweets quickly'—generic

   b. *?nigmarim li   maher mamtakim te'imim*
      end-PL   to-me quickly sweet-PL tasty-PL

In (15), the words *mamtakim* ('sweets') and *nigmarim* ('end') are categorically specified: as a noun and a verb, respectively. The generic sentence (15a) has the noun preceding the verb, and it is perfectly acceptable. By contrast, inverting the verb and the subject as in (15b) leads to an unacceptable sentence.[17] Similar semantic effects are well known in other languages, under the heading of the *Mapping Hypothesis* (Diesing 1992). For example, let us consider the following examples from German (Diesing) and Italian (Longobardi 2000):

---

[17] Sentence (15b) is marked as questionable and not as downright unacceptable, since with a very specific intonation (heavy stress on *maher* and a clear break afterward) it might become acceptable. This is similar to the effect that Longobardi (2000) describes for the Italian example in (17), though in the Hebrew example (15) the effect is somewhat clearer due to the lack of an existential reading.

(16) German
 a. ... *weil Kinder ja doch auf der Straße spielen*
   ... since children indeed in the street play
   '... since (typically) children play in the street'—generic
 b. ... *weil ja doch Kinder auf der Straße spielen*
   ... since indeed children in the street play
   '... since there are children playing in the street'—existential

(17) Italian
 vengono chiamati spesso medici del reparto di pronto intervento
 are called up often doctors of department of early intervention
 (i) with an intonational break between V *chiamati* and N *medici*:
   'typically, doctors of the first aid department are called up often'—generic
 (ii) without an intonational break between V *chiamati* and N *medici*:
   'some doctors of the first aid department are often called up'—existential

To summarize, we have seen that Hebrew profession terms give rise to sentences like (13), which morphosyntactically are underspecified in terms of their N/V categorization. However, the semantic Principle 2 on N-conservativity leads us to deduce that the only available generic reading, 'most workers program', must be derived from a specified N–V structure. This prediction is supported by the fact that with morphosyntactically specified nouns and verbs, Hebrew does not allow generic readings for postverbal indefinites, similarly to German and Italian.

7.4 NOUNS AS INDIVIDUATORS

As mentioned above, some typological works distinguish nouns from other categories in terms of their intuitive referential properties (Croft 1991; Hengeveld 1992). In a bold attempt to transcend informal classifications, Baker (2003) set out to provide a cross-linguistic semantic criterion that explicitly *defines* what characterizes noun meanings. Baker builds on the semantic intuitions of Geach (1962: 39, 54) and Gupta (1980), who address specialized aspects of noun meanings using the philosophical notion of *identity criteria*. Informally, such criteria are taken to be 'a component of meaning that makes it legitimate to ask whether some X is the same (whatever) as Y' (Baker 2003: 96). This property of nouns is assumed to be responsible for the fact that we can refer to *the same giant* but not to *the same huge, or to *the same bride* but not to the *the same marry. According to Baker, such contrasts are syntactic effects that point to a 'deeper truth': noun meanings involve identity criteria whereas meanings of other categories do not. Baker proposes that identity criteria are what allows nouns to support referential expressions, which, according to the conventions of Government and Binding theory, he annotates using referential indices.

There is no reason to deny the intuitive appeal of identity criteria as a basis for the semantics of nouns, or to contend their usefulness for descriptive studies (see e.g. Abner et al. 2019).

However, incorporating identity criteria into the exact theoretical machinery of formal semantics is a harder enterprise than what Baker assumes. Indeed, most current works in formal semantics adopt the simple extrinsic typing reviewed in section 7.1, which does not distinguish nouns from other predicative categories. As we saw, intransitive nouns, verbs, and adjectives are all treated using the extrinsic type $\langle e,t \rangle$. Adapting Geach's approach to conform with the massive literature that emerged from type theory is a major task, and there is little agreement on the motivation for such an enterprise. Two major stumbling blocks are discussed below.

7.4.1 The elusiveness of sameness 1: Co-predication

One and the same noun may intuitively refer to very different kinds of objects. For example, a *newspaper* may be a physical object, an informational object, or an institution:

(18)   a. My cat sat on the newspaper.
     b. The newspaper contains a lot of fake news.
     c. The newspaper fired the editor.

Similar multifunctionality is observed with *book, lunch, sonata,* and many other nouns (Pustejovsky 1995). This on its own is not necessarily problematic for Geach's approach: we might adopt the inelegant assumption that such nouns are ambiguous between different readings. Each of those readings might involve different identity criteria and surface with predicates of different selectional restrictions. Thus, while in (18a) the 'physical reading' is manifest, the informational and institutional readings are absent: it is hard to 'sit on' an institution or an abstract piece of information. However, the problem has other aspects that cannot be simply analysed by the ambiguity approach. To see that, let us consider the following scenario (Chomsky 2000: 16):

(19)   In the municipal library there are two copies of *The Man without Qualities*: one copy with a red cover and another with a blue cover. Samantha borrowed the red copy and Annabel borrowed the blue copy.

Now let us consider the following sentences:

(20)   Samantha and Annabel borrowed the same book.
(21)   a. Samantha borrowed a well-written book with a red cover.
     b. The book that Annabel borrowed is well written and has a blue cover.

Sentence (20) is judged as true when we consider *book* as referring to an informational unit, but false if *book* refers to physical copies. This may again be attributed to a putative ambiguity of *book*, and to two different sets of identity criteria. However, these criteria cannot work separately from one another, as the sentences in (21) show. In these sentences, the same occurrence of the noun *book* is used with an 'informational' predicate and a 'physical' predicate simultaneously. This so-called *co-predication* requires a much more complex semantic analysis than ambiguity of nouns. In one way or another, we need to allow nouns to refer to abstract objects with both 'physical' and 'informational' aspects. In some cases, these aspects are invoked separately from one another, as witnessed by the ambiguity of (20); in other cases, they are invoked simultaneously (21). A general analysis of such contrasts is required before the 'deeper truth' about the semantics of nouns can be fathomed. For some proposals see Gotham (2017) and the references therein.

7.4.2 The elusiveness of sameness 2: Stage-referring nouns

Gupta (1980: 23) pointed out the following example:

(22) National Airlines served at least two million passengers in 1975.

Sentence (22) can be true although the number of different *people* taking National Airlines flights was fewer than two million. In semantic jargon, we say that in (22), different *stages* of the same individual may be counted separately (Carlson 1977). Gupta proposes to account for this fact by assuming different identity criteria for the nouns *passenger* and *person*.

This proposal is problematic for at least two reasons. First, as Krifka (1990) points out, the kind of reading that Gupta illustrates using the 'stage noun' *passenger* also appears with nouns that typically refer to individuals. Krifka's example is:

(23) Four thousand ships passed through the lock last year.

Sentence (23) may describe a situation with fewer than four thousand individual ships. Its most prominent reading counts stages of ships: snapshots of ships as they were passing through the lock. Barker (2010) illustrates the same point for the noun *people*:

(24) Newton has a new, state-of-the-art, award-winning library which served 602,951 people in 1993.

As Barker points out, the prominent reading of (24) counts stages of book borrowers rather than individual people. The accepted conclusion is that stage readings may appear with any noun, including nouns like *ship* and *people* that intuitively refer to 'temporally rigid' entities. Conversely, Barker discusses examples like the following (see also Gotham 2021):

(25) How many of National Airlines's passengers live in your house?

Barker considers a situation where your household only has three people, each of them flew National Airlines twice. He points out that in such a situation it would be odd to give the answer 'six' to the question in (25). Thus, in (25), the noun *passenger*, which intuitively refers to stages of people, may be used for counting individuals. Thus, we cannot lexically encode the intuitive 'individual' reading of *person* and 'stage' reading of *passenger* in their identity criteria. The same point applies to many other nouns. This is an obstacle for using Geach's idea as a semantic criterion that distinguishes nouns from other predicates, as suggested by Gupta, Baker, and more recent work (see Chatzikyriakidis & Luo 2020 and references therein). Against proposals along these lines, we find alternative semantic proposals, as described by Barker (2010: p.15):

> criteria of identity are not exclusively part of lexical meaning, but depend also on compositional or pragmatic variability [...] variability in tolerance for degrees of similarity, is a pervasive, systematic feature of language use, and should not be encoded in information associated with specific lexical items. Rather, this variability is a matter of semantic interpretation (e.g., Nunberg 1984) or pragmatics (e.g., Lasersohn 2000).

Given this ongoing controversy, at this point it is too early to judge if Geach's approach to nouns can be adapted to conform with the bulk of work in formal semantics. Without denying its intuitive appeal and potential usefulness, the semantic properties of 'sameness' that Baker relies on are not currently understood well enough to serve as a definition of the category 'noun' in a cross-linguistic formal semantics.

7.5 Mass meanings cross-linguistically

So far we have discussed standard syntactic categories, with little attention to more finegrained semantic distinctions within each such word class. Distinctions within traditional word classes are critical for natural language semantics: think of telic vs atelic verbs, gradable vs non-gradable adjectives, spatial vs temporal prepositions, or definite vs indefinite determiners. In relation to nouns, one of the central semantic distinctions is between mass nouns and count nouns. This section reviews two important contributions to the cross-linguistic semantics of mass terms and its connection to the distinction between the nominal and adjectival categories. Chierchia (1998) proposes a cross-linguistic generalization which aims to describe major classes of languages in terms of their treatment of bare nouns and the count–mass distinction. Francez and Koontz-Garboden (2017) introduce a related cross-linguistic generalization about the N–A distinction and the common use of mass nouns across languages ('Dan has wisdom') for conveying 'adjectival' meanings ('Dan is wise').

7.5.1 Chierchia (1998): Bare nouns and the mass–count distinction

Many languages allow nouns to appear without articles or determiners in argument positions. The conditions under which such *bare nouns* are licensed vary dramatically between languages: from languages like French with strong prohibitions against bare nouns (26), to languages like Mandarin Chinese where bare nouns are widespread (27):

(26) French (Le Bruyn et al. 2017)
J'ai acheté (un/le/*ϕ) livre / (des/les/*ϕ)   livres /
I-have bought (a/the/*ϕ) book / (INDEF.PL/the/*ϕ) books /
(du/le/*ϕ)   lait
(INDEF.MASS/the/*ϕ) milk
'I have bought a book/the book/books/the books/milk/the milk.'

(27) Mandarin Chinese (Rullmann & You 2006)
zuotian wo mai le *shu*
yesterday I buy ASP book
'Yesterday, I bought one or more books.'

gou jintian tebie tinghua
dog today very obedient
'The dog/s was/were very obedient today.'

In between these two extremes there lie many other options. English shows a rather liberal use of bare plural and mass nouns, but with a general prohibition against bare singular count nouns. Italian uses bare nouns more restrictively than English, but not as restrictively as French (Longobardi 1994).

Chierchia's proposal makes a cross-linguistic connection between the licensing of bare nouns and the count–mass distinction. In many languages, numeric expressions can only combine with nouns by adding a classifier expression, without an obvious mass–count distinction. For instance, in (28) from Mandarin Chinese, both nouns *niu* ('cow') and *tang* ('soup') require a classifier for counting:

(28) Mandarin Chinese (Cheng & Sybesma 1999)
ba   tou/*ϕ niu   san wan/*ϕ tang
eight cl-head/*ϕ cow   three cl-bowl/*ϕ soup
'eight cows'   'three bowls of soup'

According to Chierchia, the apparent similarity between count nouns and mass nouns in Chinese is related to the licensing of bare nouns. Languages like Chinese, which generally allow bare nouns, are assumed not to have $\langle e,t \rangle$ nouns to begin with. Chierchia proposes that in Chinese and other languages without a clear mass–count distinction, nouns are lexically of type e, and refer to *kinds* of entities (Carlson 1977). According to Chierchia, Chinese nouns like *niu* ('cow') and *tang* ('soup') refer to 'kind entities' that describe general semantic properties of the noun: being a domestic animal for *cow*, being liquid for *soup*, etc. By contrast, the $\langle e,t \rangle$ meanings of *cow* and *soup* in English describe individual cows or quantities of soup, not the general kind.

On top of this cross-linguistic distinction between the types and the meanings of nouns, Chierchia adopts some fairly standard formal semantic assumptions on mass terms and plurality. From these assumptions, two prototypical types of languages are deduced:

Languages with argumental (A) nouns: languages like Chinese, where the e type of nouns allows them to appear as bare arguments. Chierchia's semantics deals with all e-type nouns as kinds of mass entities, hence such nouns are expected not to have plural marking, and to require classifiers for counting.

Languages with predicative (P) nouns: languages like French, where the $\langle e,t \rangle$ type of nouns disallows them to appear as bare arguments. Nouns of type $\langle e,t \rangle$ may have countable or non-countable meanings. Countable meanings support plural marking and counting without classifiers, whereas non-countable meanings support a mass term behaviour.

These deductive considerations about two extreme 'prototypical' kinds of languages leave room for some variation. English and other Germanic languages are classified as *A/P* languages. These are languages where nouns may be of either type *e* or type ⟨*e,t*⟩, hence they are (correctly) expected to show a mixed behaviour: a count–mass distinction together with licensing of bare nouns.[18] Italian, as well as other Romance languages, is classified as a *P*-language, but with a complex set of additional syntactic assumptions regulating a postulated empty determiner position (Longobardi 1994; Chierchia 1998: 383–394). This theoretical picture is summarized in Table 7.2.

Chierchia's assumptions about the possible types of noun meanings across languages have been hotly debated in recent work. It is widely agreed that only a small part of the massive cross-linguistic data on bare nouns, classifiers, plural marking, and the mass–count distinction is formally derived as resulting from the cross-linguistic parameter that Chierchia postulated. Notwithstanding, Chierchia's approach marked an important step in formal semantics by showing how the type system reviewed in section 7.1 can be used for addressing major cross-linguistic puzzles about the meaning and distribution of nouns. Accordingly, elements of Chierchia's proposal are adopted in many recent works on cross-linguistic semantics. For some of these developments, see Doron 2003; Dayal 2004; Rothstein 2017; Dayal & Sağ 2020; Dayal 2021, and the references therein.

Table 7.2 Chierchia's cross-linguistic classification of noun meanings

Parameter	N-type	bare nouns?	classifiers?	plural marking?	example
A	*e* (mass)	+	general	–	Chinese
P	⟨*e,t*⟩ (mass/count)	– (w. empty D)	only mass	+	Romance
A/P	*e* or *e,t*	+ (restricted)	only mass	+	Germanic

Table 7.3 Languages with a productive possessive strategy (FKG 2017: 25–32)

Hausa	*àkawai su da kyâu!* exists 3PL with beauty	lit. 'there is them with beauty' = 'they're really beautiful!'
Huitoto	*rozilli naimé-re-de* pineapple sweet-have-3SG	lit. 'the pineapple has sweetness' = 'the pineapple is sweet'
Bisa	*a gwilli ta-w* 3SG weight exists-in	lit. 'there is its weight' = 'it is heavy'
Ulwa	*yâka û-ka yâka yûh-ka* that house-3SG.POSS that long-3SG.POSS	lit. 'that house has length' = 'that house is long'

---

[18] Germanic languages do not have bare singulars, which Chierchia tries to account for on general considerations (but see Doron 2003; Dayal, 2004, 2021 for problems and further considerations).

7.5.2 Francez & Koontz-Garboden (2017): Mass terms and predicates, nouns, and adjectives

Francez and Koontz-Garboden (FKG) address a major cross-linguistic variation in the way an entity's properties are expressed. In English, as in many other languages, the most natural way of saying that an entity has a certain property is to use predication as in 'he is hungry'. Other languages prefer possessive constructions like 'he has hunger', which are only occasionally used in European languages (e.g. French *il a faim*). Some of FKG's examples for languages that extensively use the possessive construction are reproduced in Table 7.3.

FKG's semantic study aims to account for the cross-linguistic aspects that regulate the relations between predication/possession constructions and the use of an adjectival/nominal category. FKG analyse meanings of nouns like *wisdom* and *beauty* on a par with 'concrete' mass terms like *milk* and *sugar* (see Moltmann 2009). They point out the linguistic similarity between such mass terms in terms of disjointness (milk is disjoint from sugar, wisdom is disjoint from beauty, etc.) and *ordering*: two people can be compared in terms of their wisdom or beauty, whereas two cakes can be compared in terms of the milk or sugar that they contain. Meanings of 'abstract' mass terms like *wisdom* and *beauty* are referred to as *qualities*, and FKG propose the following generalization:

(29) *A/N property meanings*: cross-linguistically, *adjectives* can only refer to properties of entities by denoting predicates, but they never denote qualities. By contrast, *nouns* can refer to properties using either predicates or qualities.

Generalization (29) is proposed as a language universal on the matching between property meanings and categories. It describes both European languages, where the adjectival–predicative strategy is widespread, and languages like Hausa, which prefer using qualities in the nominal–possessive strategy (Table 7.3). Importantly, (29) also describes the uncommon strategy where nouns express properties not using qualities, but using predicative meanings, similarly to adjectives. FKG rely on an early version of work by Jenks et al. (2018), who study 'adjectival nouns' in Basaá. These are Basaá items that generally behave like other nominals, but appear in predicative constructions like adjectives (Hyman et al. 2013). Jenks et al. observe that adjectival nouns are licensed in predicative constructions like (30a), which are also characteristic of adjectives and locatives in Basaá. This is contrasted with other predicate nominals that describe properties, which ascribe these properties to entities in possessive constructions as in (30b):

(30) Basaá
    a. *hí-nuní híí   hí   yé li-múgê*
       19-bird 19.that 19.SUB be 5-quiet
       'that bird is quiet'

    b. *a   gweé ma-sódá*
       1.AGR have 6-luck
       lit. 'he/she has luck' = 'he/she is lucky'

FKG account for such differences between nouns by letting the noun in (30a) denote a property of entities (similarly to the English adjective 'quiet'), while the noun in (30b) denotes a quality (similarly to the English noun 'luck'). Further, FKG point out that adjectival nominals behave like count nouns. Thus, the noun in (30a) describes 'quiet entities'. By contrast, quality nominals as in (30b) behave like uncountable mass terms that describe quantities (of 'luck'). This distinction corresponds to Chierchia's distinction between predicative count nouns of type $\langle e,t \rangle$ and kind-denoting mass terms of type e. In this way, FKG's principle (29) describes the cross-linguistically flexible kind/predicate meaning of nouns, as opposed to a rigid predicative analysis of adjectives.

7.6 Conclusions

This chapter has reviewed basic principles and recent proposals in formal semantics that bear on the relationships between word classes and meaning. The core assumption is that expressions have *extrinsic types*, which describe the function–argument relations that words give rise to. Intersective meaning composition regulates the semantics of *modification* across categories, with a major distinction between nouns and other word classes. While nominal modifiers predominantly target the extrinsic entity argument of the noun, modification with other categories involves intrinsic aspects of the category's meaning. One of the main contributions of nouns to sentential meaning is their support of *conservative quantification*, which restricts the way quantificational determiners interact with the rest of the sentence. Other important aspects of nominal meaning concern their ability to individuate entities, their specification of mass and count properties, and the division of labour between nominal meanings and adjectival meanings in different languages. Ongoing research in formal semantics aims to give precise shape to our understanding of the connections between categorical identity of words and their contribution to sentential meaning. At the same time, these developments are reshaping formal semantics itself, including its relationships with research in language typology, historical linguistics, philosophy of language, and psycholinguistics.

Acknowledgements

Work on this chapter was partially funded by the European Research Council (ERC) under the European Union's Horizon 2020 research and innovation programme (grant agreement no. 742204). For their help, I'm grateful to Bert Le Bruyn, Veneeta Dayal, Martin Everaert, Itamar Francez, Naama Friedmann, Matthew Gotham, Itamar Kastner, Ed Keenan, Giada Palmieri, Denis Paperno, Dana Seggev, Yael Seggev, Shalom Zuckerman, Joost Zwarts, and an anonymous reviewer. All errors are mine.

CHAPTER 8

WORD CLASSES IN COGNITIVE GRAMMAR

CRISTIANO BROCCIAS

8.1 INTRODUCTION

COGNITIVE Grammar (Langacker 1987b; 1990; 1991; 1999; 2008a; 2009; Taylor 2002) (CG) aims to provide a conceptual characterization of word classes valid for all languages which is anchored in well-established findings from Cognitive Science, although some of the proposed analyses still require empirical testing. It is thus very different from typical contemporary accounts, which rely on distributional evidence and do not necessarily answer the question as to why we observe the word classes that we do, although a notable exception is, for example, Croft's typological research within his Radical Construction Grammar framework (Croft 2001; see also Chapter 11 in this volume), which has many similarities with CG. In this chapter, the language used for illustration will be English, but this does not detract from the assumed universality of the cognitive abilities and models which are taken to underpin word classes. Section 8.2 introduces some basic concepts and terminology and illustrates how words and word classes fit into the overall 'architecture' of CG. Section 8.3 discusses the prototypical and schematic characterizations of nouns and verbs, but also illustrate how adjectives, adverbs and prepositions are understood in CG. Particular attention is given to the notions of sequential and summary scanning as they play a crucial role in the identification of the various classes. Section 8.4 addresses the issue of distributional evidence in relation to the schematic description offered in the previous sections. Finally, section 8.5 briefly tackles determiners and modals, which are traditionally regarded as two function word classes.

8.2 WORDS AND WORD CLASSES

Before delving into the CG treatment of word classes, it is necessary to clarify what is meant by 'word' and, hence, 'word class' in CG. CG contends that all linguistic expressions can be described as assemblies of symbolic structures or pairings of a semantic pole and a phonological pole of varying degrees of specificity and complexity. For example, the lexeme *sea* is analysed as having a meaning represented as [SEA] and a form represented as [sea], although a phonological transcription such as [siː] is sometimes also used. The two poles are linked by a symbolizing relation and thus, together, constitute the linguistic expression [[SEA]/[sea]]. Both the semantic pole and the phonological poles should be understood more broadly than the adjectives 'semantic' and 'phonological' suggest. The semantic pole also includes information that is traditionally regarded as encyclopaedic. This is information that is not strictly speaking necessary for making sense of an expression's denotatum, such as the fact that many people enjoy swimming in the sea or that certain stretches of the sea may be infested with sharks. Similarly, the phonological pole is not restricted to segmental and suprasegmental information but may also involve gesture (as in sign languages), including facial expressions. The proximal demonstrative *this*, for instance, is often used in conjunction with a gesture on the speaker's part pointing at an item which is close to the speaker, and this would also be included in the semantic pole of the expression.

Symbolic structures may differ in terms of their complexity, ranging from single items such as *sea* to progressively more elaborate expressions as illustrated in the hierarchy *sea > blue sea > beautiful blue sea > beautiful blue sea in front of my house*. Also, symbolic structures can range from less specific to more specific, as in *thing > body of water > sea > ocean*. Nor do assemblies of symbolic structures need to be completely 'filled'. Out of the commonality of expressions such as *Alice slapped/kicked/punched Bob*, we may extract, metaphorically speaking, the more schematic expression (effectively, a cognitive routine) *Alice V$_b$ed Bob*, where V$_b$ed is the past tense of a verb of impact involving a body part such as Alice's hands (*slap, punch*) or legs (*kick*). Examples such as these are endless and illustrate the nature of CG as a usage-based or bottom-up model in that cognitive routines or high-level schemas are extracted out of the commonalities observed across specific examples.

Also, CG does not treat expressions such as *What's your name?, How are you?, Where are you from?* any differently from non-transparent ones such as *by and large*. The former are so entrenched in the English language that they probably do not require much constructive effort on the speaker's part but are likely to be stored as units or routines in the speaker's mind.[1] Still, as will be highlighted below, the fact that they are complex expressions means that they are not treated as 'words' or prototypical lexical items in CG.

In sum, all linguistic expressions receive the same treatment in CG, by virtue of being analysed as assemblies of symbolic structures. The crucial theoretical consequence is that lexicon and grammar cannot be separated sharply but form a continuum. Although CG retains traditional labels like morphology, lexicon, and syntax, it recognizes no sharp boundaries between them because they can all be reduced to assemblies of symbolic structures. This also means that grammar is meaningful. Even 'abstract' elements like 'grammatical word' (e.g. prepositions, auxiliaries, determiners) and grammatical constructions (e.g. the ditransitive construction, as exemplified by *Alice sent Bob a present*) are meaningful since they involve a semantic pole by definition. A useful visualization of linguistic

---

[1] Langacker points out that pervasive in contemporary linguistics is the building block metaphor, which stipulates that words have clear-cut meanings and that words can be combined into more complex expressions in compositional fashion. Apparently similar expressions such as *mosquito net* and *butterfly net* clearly dispel such a view. A mosquito net is a net used to keep mosquitoes away while a butterfly net is a tool for capturing butterflies. Accordingly, CG views words as stepping stones for the creation of complex meaning rather than building blocks, insisting that meaning creation is flexible and negotiable.

expressions is given in Figure 8.1, which arranges linguistic expressions in terms of the two dimensions 'symbolic complexity' and 'schematicity'. Prototypical lexical items (*cat*) tend to be characterized by a low degree of symbolic complexity, i.e. they tend to be what are usually described as single words, and to be fairly specific semantically (it is easy to describe what a cat is). Symbolically more complex items such as *What's your name?* are also part of the lexicon since they are fairly specific semantically (as well as phonologically). Grammar, by contrast, is a useful label for schematic symbolic assemblies or constructional schemas (Langacker 2008a: 167). Partly specific structures such as *on a X day*, where *X* stands for an open-ended set of elements such as *bright, windy, hot*, cannot be assigned exclusively to either the lexicon or grammar since they are neither fully specific nor fully schematic and thus illustrate the continuous nature of lexicon and grammar. 'Grammatical' markers like auxiliaries, agreement markers, and derivational affixes, which are all specific phonologically, have a schematic semantic pole, which therefore may be difficult to describe. Grammatical classes ('class descriptions' in Figure 8.1), which we will be concerned with here, differ from grammatical markers in that they are also schematic phonologically. As we will see below, the noun class, for example, can be abbreviated as [[THING]/[...]]. In other words, its semantic pole describes a thing (a technical term in CG—see section 8.3.1) and its phonological pole is maximally schematic (but see section 8.4).

The discussion so far should have alerted the reader to the fact that, as is well known (see e.g. Taylor 2002: ch. 9), it is difficult to define what a word is. The reason is quite simply that much in language is a matter of degree. Here, however, we will understand a 'word' as a linguistic expression that is relatively low in schematicity and symbolic complexity.[2] By 'word class', we will mean a linguistic expression that is low in symbolic complexity but relatively high in schematicity.

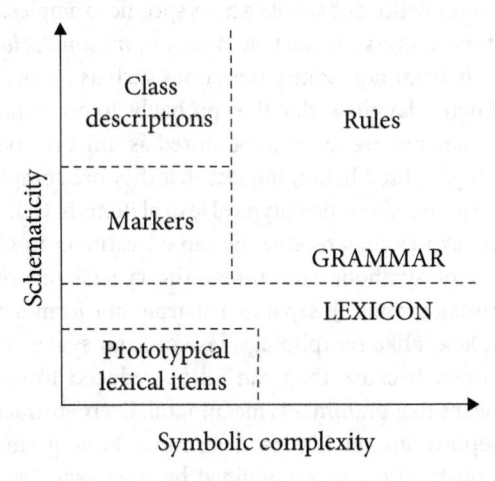

FIGURE 8.1 The grammar–lexicon continuum

---

[2] Taylor (2002: 173–175) highlights that it is also possible, at least to some extent, to provide a phonological characterization of what a word is. He classifies as words those linguistic expressions that are (relatively) stable, have phonological integrity, and are phonologically promiscuous. The word *light*, in *light blue*, can be realized as [laɪt] or [laɪpˀ] but not as [dɑːk]; that is to say, words are relatively stable despite allophonic variation. Also, words usually cannot be interrupted, so that *She really admires the poetry of TS Eliot* cannot be rendered as **She ad-really-mires the poetry of TS Eliot*. Still, German 'separable verbs' are problematic in this respect. The verb *ankommen* 'to arrive' is separated in *Sie kommen (an)* 'They arrive'. Expletive insertion in English, as in *im-bloody-possible*, is another problematic case. Finally, unlike bound morphemes, which only combine with certain bases (e.g. *-ful* requires a nominal base, as in *beautiful*), words can be adjacent to virtually any other word.

8.3 FROM PROTOTYPES TO SCHEMAS: A CONCEPTUAL CHARACTERIZATION OF WORD CLASSES

In most of modern linguistics, word classes are identified by relying on distributional (i.e. morphosyntactic) evidence. CG, instead, strives to provide a conceptual characterization based on cognitive abilities and models. In addition, CG proposes that at least the word classes 'noun' and 'verb' are universal and that it is possible to distinguish between a prototypical and a schematic description for them.

Before introducing the schematic characterization of nouns and verbs as well as other major classes such as adjectives, adverbs, and prepositions, it is useful to illustrate how the verb and noun prototypes are understood in CG. Langacker claims that they are grounded in two basic cognitive archetypes, that of a physical object for nouns and that of an energetic or 'force-dynamic' event (see Talmy 1988) for verbs. Both archetypes are part of what Langacker calls the billiard-ball model:

> We think of our world as being populated by discrete physical objects. These objects are capable of moving about through space and making contact with one another. Motion is driven by energy, which some objects draw from internal resources and others receive from the exterior. When motion results in forceful physical contact, energy is transmitted from the mover to the impacted object, which may thereby be set in motion to participate in further interactions.
>
> (1991: 13)

In terms of this model, the noun and verb prototypes are maximally distinct, as the following properties, reproduced with slight modifications from Langacker (2008a: 104), show:

1. A physical object is material.
2. A physical object resides primarily in space, where it is bounded.
3. A physical object does not have a particular location in time.
4. A physical object is conceptually autonomous, because it can be conceptualized independently of its participation in any event.

1. An energetic event is not material.
2. An energetic event resides primarily in time, where it is bounded.
3. An energetic event has a location in space that depends on the locations of its participants.
4. An energetic event is conceptually dependent, because it can only be conceptualized with reference to its participants.

Thus, in *Alice kicked Bob*, it is clear that Alice and Bob are prototypical nouns and *kick* is a prototypical verb.

While the prototypes are grounded in the billiard-ball model, the schematic characterizations of nouns and verbs, as well as other word classes, involve basic cognitive abilities, namely our capacity for grouping, for reification, for apprehending relations, and for tracking relations through time.

At a schematic level, the CG description of word classes is best discussed with reference to Figure 8.2, after Langacker (1987b: 249, fig. 7.5), which shows how basic categories of predications are related to one another and which should be kept in mind for the rest of the chapter. The categories will be explicated in the following sections. For now, it is enough to point out that the shaded boxes correspond to the semantic poles of word classes. For example, the all-encompassing category [ENTITY] does not correspond to the semantic pole of any specific word class but expresses the commonality between [THING] and [RELATION], the former of which corresponds to the semantic pole of a word class (namely, the noun class) while the latter, like [ENTITY], does not.

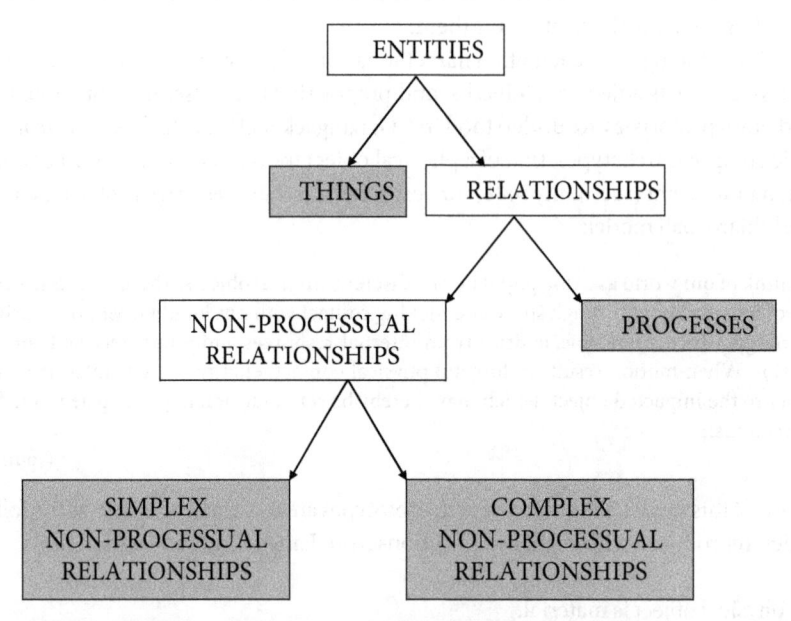

FIGURE 8.2 The Cognitive Grammar analysis of grammatical classes

8.3.1 Nouns

THING,[3] a technical term in CG, corresponds to the semantic pole of nouns. Originally, Langacker defined a THING as a region in some domain, where a region is to be understood as a set of interconnected entities (Langacker 1987b: 198). More recently, Langacker has characterized a THING as the product of the two basic cognitive abilities called **grouping** and **reification** (see Langacker 2008a: 105) in order to avoid the spatial metaphor implied by the use of the term 'region' (see Langacker 2008a: 105, n. 11).

Our capacity for grouping and reification can be illustrated using Figure 8.3 (after Langacker 2008a: 105, fig. 4.5b). Grouping relies on various factors, such as similarity and contiguity. Based on similarity of colour, the black dots and the white dots in Figure 8.3 form two groups and, at a higher level of organization, we may group the black dots into two groups of three on the basis of spatial contiguity. At even higher levels of organization, a group can also be manipulated as or reified into a unitary entity. In Figure 8.3, the two groups

---

[3] From now on, I will refrain from bracketing semantic poles for the sake of simplicity.

of three dots may be reified into two lines that are parallel. This is what happens with nouns as well. Consider, for instance, the noun *team* in a sports context. This noun does not describe each single player. Rather, it profiles a set of players (grouping), who are treated as a unit (reification) by virtue of being engaged in a common purpose such as winning a match.

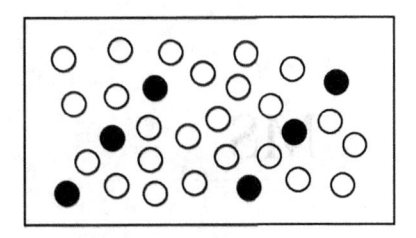

FIGURE 8.3 Grouping

Langacker contends that his characterization is abstract enough to encompass any type of noun, from those depicting physical objects to abstract ones.

Nouns can be divided into two major types, count nouns (e.g. *cup*) and mass nouns (e.g. *water*). Count nouns, unlike mass nouns, involve bounding within the immediate scope in the domain of instantiation (Langacker 2008a: 132); see Figure 8.4.

(a) Count Noun   (b) Mass Noun

MS   MS

IS   IS

Domain of Instantiation   Domain of Instantiation

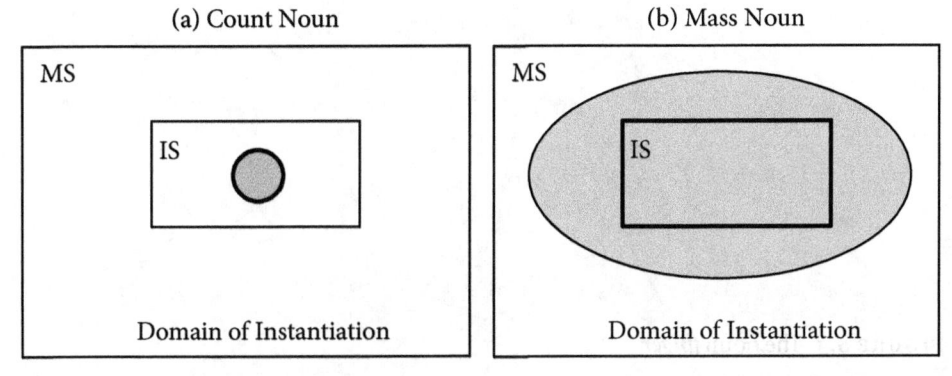

FIGURE 8.4 Count and mass nouns

Let us try to make sense of this characterization by considering the count noun *finger*; see Figure 8.5. This lexical item evokes the conception (or domain) of the human body as its maximal scope (MS) (the full extent of awareness), MS in Figure 8.4a and Figure 8.5, but is understood against a specific subpart of the body, namely the hand, which thus constitutes the expression's immediate scope (IS in Figure 8.4a and Figure 8.5), which is also referred to (metaphorically) as the 'onstage region' or, alternatively, base; see also Figure 8.14. Within that base, *finger* refers to or, in CG parlance, profiles a specific substructure, which is the focus of attention, shown as the circle shaded in grey in Figure 8.4a and the stylized finger highlighted in grey in Figure 8.5. Although the boundary of a finger is not clear, a finger is clearly bounded within the immediate scope in the body domain as it is conceptualized as a subpart of the hand.[4] The body

---

[4] There are various bases for bounding. Langacker (2008a: 136–139) mentions contrast with surroundings, which is relevant for example to the noun *beep* (a noise surrounded by silence on either end), internal configuration, which is relevant for example to the noun *bicycle*, and function, which is relevant for example to the noun *handle*.

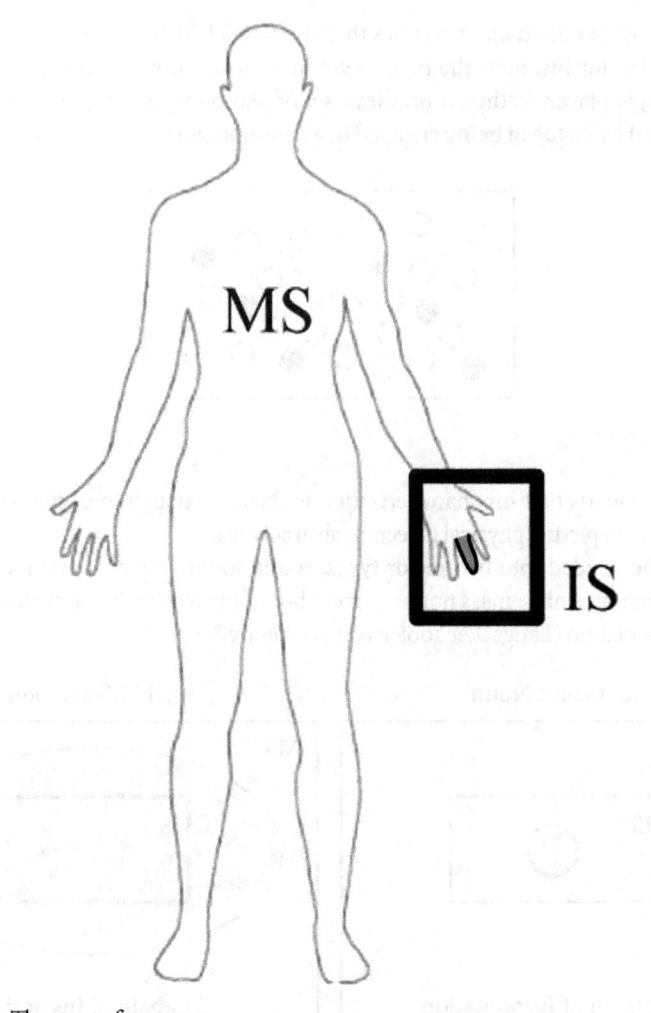

FIGURE 8.5 The noun *finger*

domain, or perhaps the more general domain 'space', is its domain of instantiation. Langacker (2008a: 134) explains that a noun profiles a type of thing and specifies the properties that instances of this type must have. The domain within which the instances are taken to reside is what Langacker calls the domain of instantiation. Thus, if we consider the noun *skin*, for which the body or, more generally, space also counts as the domain of instantiation, then we observe that *skin* does not profile a bounded entity within the immediate scope of awareness (see Figure 8.4b) because when we focus on any part of the body (the immediate scope), the skin is not limited to that part but also surrounds the immediate scope. Thus, *skin* would correspond to the ellipse 'overflowing' the immediate scope in Figure 8.4b. Obviously, domains of instantiation do not only involve space but also time (as in the case of temporal expressions such as *hour*, *minute*, *time*, and event nouns such as *explosion*, *beep*) and colour (as with *blue*), just to mention a couple.

As the count–mass distinction is conceptual, it is to be expected that alternative construals or different ways of portraying the same conceptual content are possible. Although certain nouns are typically used as either count (e.g. *cat*) or mass (e.g. *wine*), it is not difficult to trigger a shift from count to mass or vice versa. Well-known examples, usually treated as instances of metonymy, are given in (1), where (1a) shows count-to-mass conversion and (1b) mass-to-count conversion, as signalled, respectively, by the absence vs presence of the indefinite article:

(1) a. After a cat got in the way of our SUV, there was *cat* all over the driveway.
    b. I'd like to have *a dry wine*, please.

Bounding is intimately connected with other factors that bear on the distinction between count and mass nouns, namely homogeneity, contractibility, and replicability. Mass nouns are construed as being homogeneous. This is self-evident in cases such as *water* but homogeneity, being a matter of construal, is also relevant to mass nouns such as *sand*, *grass*, and even *furniture*, where the constituent parts (grains of sand, blades of grass, items of furniture) are not afforded any particular salience. Contractibility refers to the fact that a subpart of a certain mass still counts as a valid instance of that mass, so that a portion of *water* is still *water* but a portion of a *lake*, a count noun, is not a *lake*. Similarly, a mass is expansible or not replicable: adding more water to water still constitutes a single instance of *water*.

8.3.2 Verbs and scanning modes

While interconnections are not profiled in nominals, they are in relation(ship)s. Thus, while *Alice* and *cake* profile two things, in the CG sense of the word, the verb *ate* in *Alice ate the cake* profiles the relation or, in more detail, the process (see below on the difference between relations and processes) obtaining between two participants, Alice and the cake. This also means that Alice and the cake are conceptually autonomous because they can be conceptualized independently of their participation in any relationship, while a relationship such as *eat* is conceptually dependent as it can only be conceptualized with reference to two participants, namely an eater, e.g. Alice, and something which is consumed, e.g. a cake. Of these two participants, Alice is somehow more prominent than the cake because it is the 'energy source' or entity from which the process departs, while the cake is the target or 'energy sink' of the profiled process. The former kind of participant is called a 'trajector' (technically, the primary focal relational element) while the latter type is called 'landmark' (technically, the secondary focal relational element).[5] Another crucial point is that *eat* is a relation that the conceptualizer follows or tracks stage by stage through processing time: this relation involves Alice putting a piece of cake into her mouth, masticating it and ingesting it.

Accessing sequentially these constitutive parts of the process profiled by *eat* is called 'sequential scanning' in CG and the process is said to have a 'positive temporal profile', which is represented by means of a bold temporal line in Figure 8.6, which offers a diagrammatic representation of the process at hand ('e' = eat, 'tr' = trajector, 'lm' = landmark, 't' = time). Similarly, in its concrete sense, the verb *enter* (see Figure 8.7) describes a

---

[5] Processes can also involve more than one landmark, as in the case of *give* and *rob*, e.g. *Alice gave a flower to Bob* and *Alice robbed Bob of his money*. In such instances, the focal entity that corresponds to the direct object is identified as the primary landmark and the other object is described as a secondary landmark.

spatial relation between a mover, which counts as the trajector, and (the inside of) a location, which represents the target of movement and constitutes the landmark. The conceptualizer accesses the positions occupied by the mover in sequential fashion; hence, the emboldened temporal line in Figure 8.7 as well.

The idea that the conceptualizer tracks a relation sequentially is crucial in CG because it has repercussions for word classification. The point is that, in CG, not all relations involve sequential scanning or, to put it differently, not all relations have a positive temporal profile. Instead, relations come in two flavours, processual and atemporal (see Figure 8.2). Processual relations or processes such as *eat* and *enter* have a positive temporal profile and constitute the semantic pole of verbs.[6] Atemporal or non-processual relations, instead, are relevant to a motley collection of word classes, including prepositions and adjectives. In fact, nouns, despite not being relational, are also atemporal in nature. The key distinguishing feature between verbs and the other classes, whether relational (such as adjectives and prepositions) or non-relational (i.e. nouns), resides in the fact these other classes have a null temporal profile. In order to appreciate this point, it is easier to contrast again verbs/processes vs nouns/things rather than verbs vs non-processual relations and go back to non-processual relations later (see section 8.3.3).

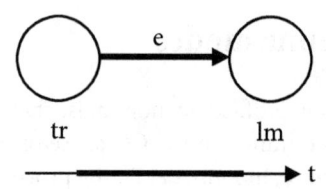

FIGURE 8.6 The process *eat*

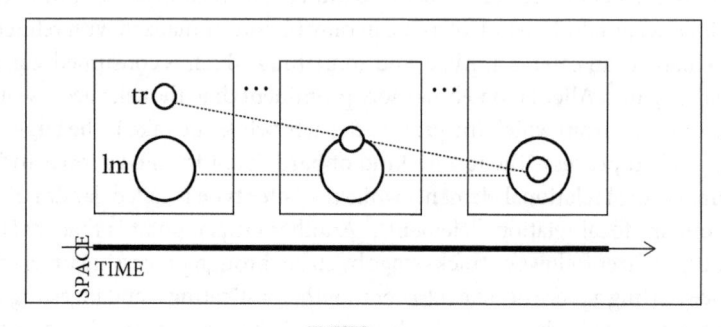

FIGURE 8.7 The verb *enter* (after Langacker 1987b: 245)

Obviously, nouns such as *Alice* and *cake* do not have a temporal profile in the sense that we conceptualize them as being located primarily in space rather than time (see also the discussion of the billiard-ball model above). Thus, it is clear why CG contends that they have a null

---

[6] This is a simplification because non-finite verbal forms such as the participles (*eating*, *eaten*) are in fact analysed as non-processual in CG. Strictly speaking, the characterization above only applies to base (i.e. *to*-less) forms and tensed forms. For reasons of expository convenience, I have glossed over these details, which are, however, very important in CG.

temporal profile. A complication arises, however, in connection with nouns such as *fall* and *path* because, intuitively, they do require a temporal characterization, e.g. we may talk of *a short fall* or *a long path*, where the adjectives *short* and *long* provide information concerning the temporal extension of the processes of falling and walking along a path. This is where, in CG, another scanning mode, called 'summary scanning', comes into play. Let us consider the downward motion of a ball as an illustrative example.

We can describe the motion of the ball by either focusing on the position occupied by the ball at each fleeting instant of time (this is sequential scanning; see Figure 8.8a) or in terms of its overall path, i.e. a downward linear path in Figure 8.8b, which illustrates summary scanning. This path is obtained by keeping active and superimposing the various positions occupied by the ball in processing time (see the build-up phase in Figure 8.5b), which coalesce into a gestalt or holistic conception, akin to a multiple-exposure photo. In CG parlance, a conception scanned summarily is also said to have a null temporal profile. Thus, a null temporal profile is not incompatible with motion. It just means that the constitutive parts of a process are accessed cumulatively rather than sequentially.

As in the example just given, the difference between the two scanning modes should be quite clear when contrasting the trajectory followed by an object with the actual position of the object through space instant by instant. This is reflected linguistically in the difference between the noun *fall* (and more generally the noun *path*) and the verb *fall*. The former involves summary scanning while the latter involves sequential scanning. The contrast between sequential and summary scanning is, however, not limited to verbs and nouns involving objects moving through space. A nominal such as *the murder of the president* would also be analysed as involving summary scanning while the tensed clause *The president was murdered* would be taken to involve the sequential scanning of the killing event. Nor, as was pointed out above, is scanning only relevant to the distinction between nouns and verbs but it also allows for the distinction between verbs/processes and other relational classes, namely the so-called atemporal ones. Crucially and to reiterate, while a process involves sequential scanning and corresponds to the semantic pole of a verb, atemporal relations do not involve sequential scanning, but may involve summary scanning. This will be picked up in the next section.

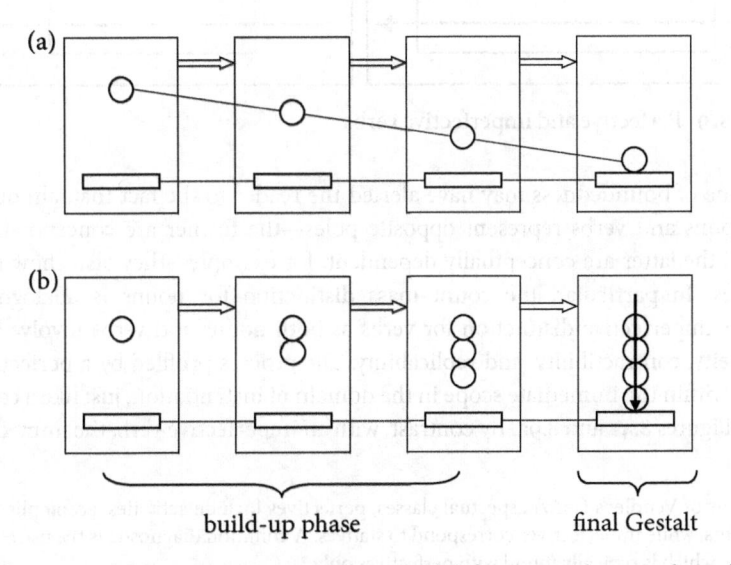

FIGURE 8.8 Sequential (a) vs summary scanning (b) (after Langacker 1987 b: 144)

Before doing so, it is worth commenting briefly on the appropriateness of the term 'relation(ship)' as a cover term for various types of processes. As in ordinary language the term 'relation(ship)' evokes the conception of two entities, it may be asked whether the relational characterization of verbs can truly be extended to so-called intransitive verbs, such as the activity verb *sleep* (*Bob was sleeping when Alice came back home*) or the change-of-state verb *grow* (*Bob is growing up*). Taylor (2002: 215) explains that in both cases the relation obtains between 'the tr[ajector] and an activity or change-of-state in which the tr[ajector] participates'. Admittedly, this description is not very clear because an activity or a change of state is not conceptually autonomous but necessarily involves a participant already. An alternative solution would be to view activities and change of states as relations between a trajector and a state (e.g. *Bob was asleep*) but this issue deserves further scrutiny.

We noted above that nouns can be divided into count and mass. Verbs can also be assigned to two types, namely perfective and imperfective, although the distinction, as usual, is often a matter of construal. Perfectives (e.g. *learn*), unlike imperfectives (e.g. *know*), are bounded within the immediate scope in the domain of instantiation, which is time. The difference between a perfective relationship and an imperfective relationship is shown in Figure 8.9.[7] With a perfective verb, the profiled relationship is construed as temporary within the stretch of time considered (technically, the temporal immediate scope), while, with an imperfective verb, the profiled relationship is construed as stable within the immediate scope. This is a matter of construal and the progressive, for example, can be used to render a perfective process imperfective, as in *I am learning German*, where the initial and final endpoints of the learning process are 'offstage' (cf. instead *I learned German in six months*).

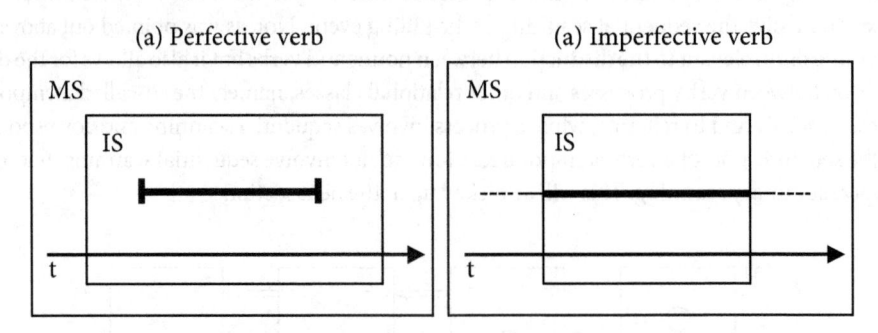

FIGURE 8.9 Perfective and imperfective verbs

The issue of boundedness may have alerted the reader to the fact that, although prototypical nouns and verbs represent opposite poles—the former are conceptually autonomous and the latter are conceptually dependent, for example—they also show interesting similarities. In particular, the count–mass distinction for nouns is analogous to the perfective–imperfective distinction for verbs as both nouns and verbs involve bounding, homogeneity, contractibility, and replicability. The process profiled by a perfective verb is bounded within the immediate scope in the domain of instantiation, just like a count noun; compare Figures 8.4a and 8.9a. By contrast, with an imperfective verb, the immediate scope

---

[7] In terms of Vendler's (1967) aspectual classes, perfectives include activities, accomplishments, and achievements, while imperfectives correspond to statives. A common diagnostic is the use of the present progressive, which is typically found with perfectives only.

only includes a portion of the process, as with a mass noun; compare Figures 8.4b and 8.9b. Further, the constitutive states of an imperfective process are construed as being identical, unlike those of a perfective process. As an imperfective process is made up of identical states, it is contractible: if I knew a poem the whole of last month, it is also true that I knew it in the second half of the month. But if I learned the poem last month, it is not necessarily true that I learned it in the second half of the month; I may have learned it only during the first half of the month. Finally, an imperfective process is non-replicable or expansible in the sense that two instances of an imperfective process constitute a larger instance of the same process. If I knew the poem in January and I knew the poem in February, then I knew the poem over the whole two-month period, but if I learned the poem in January and then in February, then I must have learned it twice.

8.3.3 Adjectives, adverbs, and prepositions

Processes do not just profile relations; they also have a positive temporal profile: its constitutive states are accessed sequentially through processing time. Lack of a positive temporal profile is constitutive of atemporal relations. The traditional labels 'adjective', 'adverb', 'preposition' all refer to words that profile atemporal relations and are illustrated in Figure 8.10. (For the time being, I am ignoring the difference between 'stative' prepositions like *in* and 'dynamic' prepositions like *into*.)

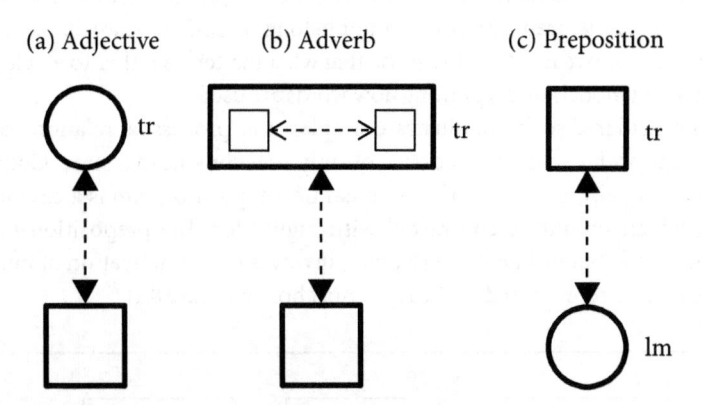

FIGURE 8.10 Adjectives, adverbs, and prepositions

Note first of all that, in a significant departure from earlier work, Langacker (2008a) claims that adjectives and adverbs, unlike prepositions, have a single focal participant, hence a trajector, but no landmark; see Figures 8.10a and 8.10b, which lack the label 'lm' for landmark, vs Figure 8.10c, where the label 'lm' is present. Langacker (2008a: 113–114) explains that:

> an adjective like *pretty*, *tall*, or *stupid* situates its trajectory [e.g. *child*, as in *a pretty/tall/stupid child*] vis-à-vis a scale representing the degree to which it exhibits a certain property. There is just one focal participant because the adjective itself specifies both the property and the scalar position. Neither is construed as an independently existing entity requiring separate identification.

Previously, both adjectives and adverbs were analysed as having a landmark, albeit an 'incorporated' rather than an 'overt' one; see for example Taylor (2002: 221, fig. 11.10).

The difference between adjectives and adverbs resides in the nature of the entity that has trajector status: a thing in the case of adjectives (e.g. *child* in *tall child*) and a relation in the case of an adverb (e.g. *fix* in *She fixed her car quickly*). In Figure 8.10a, the circle, as is customary in CG, stands for a 'thing' (e.g. *child*) and the bottom square identifies a region along a height scale (not represented in the diagram) corresponding to above-average height. In Figure 8.10b, the rectangle stands for an entity that corresponds to a relation, shown within it as the two squares connected by a double-headed arrow. The bottom square again identifies a region along a speed scale (not represented in the diagram) corresponding to above-average speed.

Prepositions, unlike adjectives and adverbs, involve both a trajector and a landmark but their trajector can be a thing or a relation. In the 'adjectival' use of *on* as in *the pillow on the couch*, the trajector is the nominal *the pillow* and the landmark is the nominal *the couch*. In the 'adverbial' use of *till* as in *Alice waited till December*, the trajector is the process *Alice waited* and the landmark is the noun *December*. The fact that the trajector can be a thing or a relation is represented, as usual, by a square in Figure 8.10c, while the thing-like nature of the landmark is shown by means of a circle in Figure 8.10c. Nevertheless, certain prepositions (*till*, *after*, etc.) can also be used as what are traditionally called 'subordinating conjunctions' (*Alice waited till Bob came back*). This happens when the landmark is a relation (*Bob came back*) rather than a thing. Nowadays, grammarians tend to classify expressions such as *till* as prepositions in either case. For instance, Huddleston & Pullum (2002) and Aarts (2011) do so, although Aarts for example distinguishes between the subclass of 'regular' prepositions, which take an NP complement, and that of 'conjunctive' prepositions, which take a clausal complement. Thus, the preposition *till* would belong to both subclasses. Such an issue is, however, not substantive in CG in the sense that what matters is rather to elucidate the cognitive abilities and models underpinning how words are used.

The cases considered so far all illustrate simplex non-processual relations, as they have a null temporal profile and are made up of only one constitutive state. Complex atemporal relations are also possible and the 'dynamic' preposition *into* is a case in point; see Figure 8.11, which should be contrasted with Figure 8.7. The preposition *into*, like the nouns *fall* and *path*, but unlike the verb *enter*, involves the co-activation of multiple states into a single gestalt, represented as the rightmost box in Figure 8.11.[8]

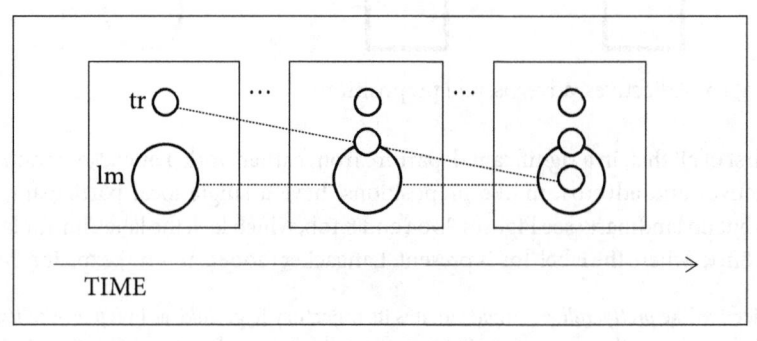

FIGURE 8.11 The dynamic preposition *into*

[8] Langacker claims that -*ing* forms also portray complex atemporal relations; see for example Langacker (2008a: 117–122).

It should by now be clear that the categorization of words in CG depends in a fundamental way on the difference between sequential and summary scanning. Still, the relevance of the distinction between the two to the characterization of word classes has been questioned by Broccias & Hollmann (2007). It is not necessary to go through their arguments here, but it is worth asking, as they do, whether the difference between summary and sequential scanning can be dispensed with for example in the case of *enter* vs *into*. As Langacker himself observes in his response to Broccias and Hollmann's paper:

> both involve the trajector occupying a temporally ordered series of locations [...] It would seem that the difference can only reside in the degree of prominence accorded to the temporal basis of the ordering—whether the profiled relationship is viewed *primarily* as developing through time, or whether its temporal evolution remains in the background.
>
> (2008b: 581, emphasis in the original)

More generally, while Langacker (2008b) seems to concede that the difference between the two scanning modes may be a matter of degree and summary scanning may be the result of sequential scanning receding into the background, he still emphasizes that the difference between the two scanning modes is crucial in separating out *enter* and *into*. Although this is an issue that can only be settled experimentally, it is important to stress, as Broccias and Hollmann try to do, that *enter* and *into* could in principle be differentiated independently of the scanning modes in such a way that is consistent with the tenets of CG.

In the spirit of Broccias and Hollmann, it must be highlighted that Langacker's analysis does not rely on distributional facts, in particular (although this is not how Broccias and Hollmann account for the contrast between *enter* and *into*) the fact that *enter* can be inflected for tense while *into* cannot. In CG terminology, the process profiled by *enter* can be grounded (see also section 8.5) : it can be related to the ground (the interlocutors and their spatiotemporal setting) by specifying its temporal orientation vis-à-vis the temporal setting of the speech event, as in *Alice entered the room at 5 o'clock*, which places the profiled event in the past relative to the time of speaking. This trivial distributional fact may account for the difference between *enter* and *into* without the need for invoking the two scanning modes: verbs can be grounded while prepositions cannot. Importantly, grounding is not a 'formal' notion but has the status of a cognitive operation and thus invoking it is consistent with the spirit of a CG conceptual approach to word categorization.

Of course, this does not mean that the two scanning modes cannot be relevant to word classes more generally. The relevance of the two modes to the distinction between nouns and verbs is undoubtedly more convincing, as the contrast between the noun *path* and the verb *fall* mentioned above shows. The crucial point is whether this distinction bears on the difference between, for example, verbs and 'dynamic' prepositions. To reiterate, it could be claimed that both verbs and dynamic prepositions profile relations scanned sequentially, but while the former can be grounded, the latter cannot.[9]

---

[9] Grounding can be covert, as in Chinese, where verbs are not inflected for tense (on covert grounding, see also Langacker 2008a: 265, n. 6).

8.4. Beyond a purely conceptual characterization?

The schematic characterization of word classes is conceptual in Langacker's work. Nevertheless, Taylor (2002: 180–185) and Hollmann (2012; 2013), who refines Taylor's analysis, point out that verbs and nouns can also be characterized, at least prototypically or at a lower level with respect to their schematic description, in phonological terms (see also n. 2 on the definition of 'word'). Here, for reasons of space, I will only consider verbs. Hollmann (2013) proposes the verb network in Figure 8.12 for English verbs (see also Taylor's 2002: 184, fig. 9.2), which is based on the results of a production experiment. Each box represents a prototype for the verb class, although these prototypes are not necessarily entrenched to the same degree. Length, understood as the number of syllables, appears to be the strongest determinant for verbhood in that verbs tend to be monosyllabic, as indicated by the single symbol σ. Hence, monosyllabicity is given a heavier profile in Figure 8.12, unlike the other prototypes. These have to do with the absence of nasal consonants, the presence of a stressed front vowel, and the presence of a final voiced obstruent.[10] Thus, *subdue, deceive, leave, (to) house* are all instances that accord with this characterization, *leave* being the one exhibiting all four features. By contrast, *conquer* and *abolish* have features clashing with these prototypes because both *conquer* and *abolish* are more than one syllable long, have a stressed back vowel, do not end in a voiced obstruent, and *conquer* also contains a nasal.

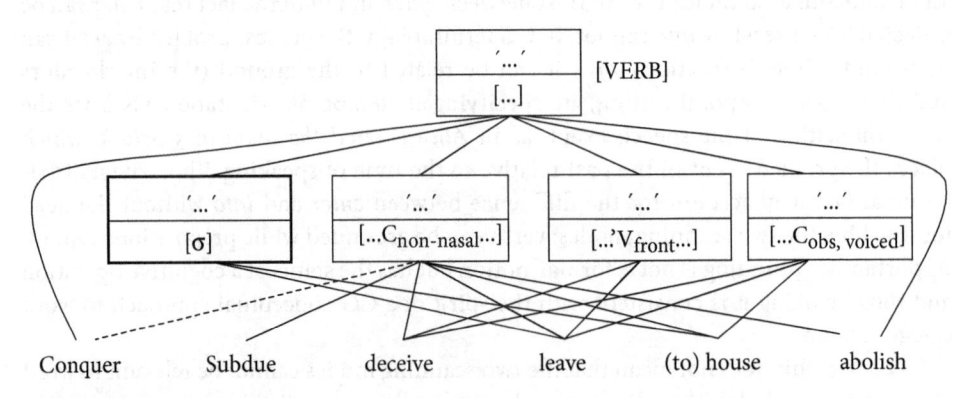

FIGURE 8.12 Hollmann's (2013) verb network

Hollmann speculates that sub-schemas along the lines of those in Figure 8.12 may be more salient than the schematic characterizations 'proposed by Langacker, which in fact (some) speakers may not extract at all' (Hollmann 2013: 304). Nevertheless, this point is based on the view of super-schemas as being detached from sub-schemas. Instead, Langacker (2008a: 56) points out that '[a] schema should [...] be seen as immanent in its varied instantiations, not as separate and distinct (even if shown individually for analytical purposes)'. Thus,

---

[10] As final, 'voiced' obstruents are in fact (at least to some extent) devoiced—see Roach (2009)—it would be more accurate to describe such obstruents as lenis.

Hollmann's criticism does not, strictly speaking, impinge on Langacker's analysis. Also, while distributional evidence allows us to identify classes, it does not answer the question as to why we observe the classes that we do. By contrast, the aim of CG is that of providing cognitive justification for the emergence of the observed classes by invoking cognitive abilities and models.

8.5 GROUNDING ELEMENTS

Traditionally, nouns and verbs, as well as adjectives and adverbs, are described as content words, unlike determiners and auxiliaries, which are classified as function words. In CG, determiners and modal auxiliaries are analysed as grounding elements because they specify the status of a nominal or the process profiled by a clause in relation to the ground, which is made up of the speech event, its participants, their interaction, and their spatiotemporal location.[11] More technically, grounding is a semantic function that transforms a 'type conception' into an 'instance conception' at the discourse level, where an instance 'is thought to have a particular location in the domain of instantiation' (Langacker 2008a: 268). For example, the noun *cat* can be grounded by using the proximal demonstrative *this*, obtaining the nominal *this cat*, which singles out a specific instance of the type *cat* in the spatial domain (the domain of instantiation) relative to the ground; see Figure 8.13 ('G' = ground).

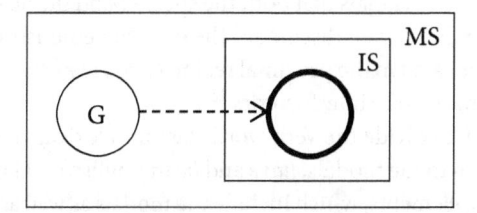

FIGURE 8.13 The determiner *this* as a grounding element

The process of conceptualization in relation to the ground can be represented as in Figure 8.14, which identifies an 'offstage' region including the ground (comprising the speaker, S, and the hearer, H) and an 'onstage' region including what is viewed as the focus of attention, represented as a generic entity by means of the emboldened square in Figure 8.14. The conceptualizer (S and/or H) is the subject of conception while what is put onstage for focused viewing is the object of conception. Clearly, the conceptualizer can also be put on stage, as when the pronouns *I* and *you* are used. It is important to stress that grounding elements do not profile either the ground or the connection with the ground. Although they set up an epistemic relation between the ground and the profiled entity, they profile the thing or process which is put onstage.

---

[11] Non-modal auxiliaries, i.e. *be* and *have*, are not grounding elements. Instead, they have to do with how a given process is viewed (see, e.g., Langacker 2008a: 299).

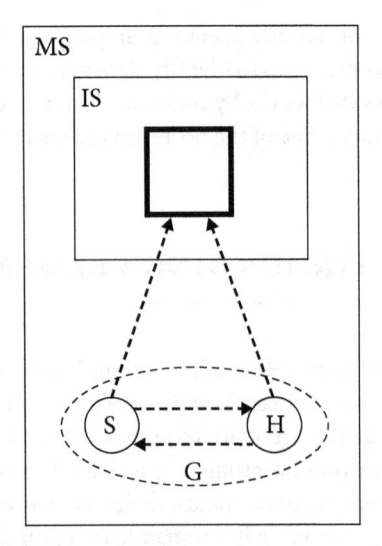

FIGURE 8.14 The baseline viewing arrangement

Nominal grounding makes use of the articles (*the*, *a*), demonstratives (*this*, *that*, and their plural forms), and certain quantifiers (*all*, *most*, *some*, *no*, *every*, *each*, *any*). All single out a referent out of a pool of candidates. The articles and demonstratives do so in a way where the role of the interlocutors is most evident. Choosing the definite article (*I saw the cat*) over the indefinite article (*I saw a cat*) signals that both the speaker and the hearer are able to identify the instance uniquely in the current discourse. The use of a demonstrative indicates whether the profiled nominal is located in the proximal region (*I don't like this cat*) or the distal region (*I like that cat*) with respect to the interlocutors.[12]

While it is customary to divide the verb word class into lexical verbs and auxiliary verbs (the latter corresponding to the modals, *have* and *be* in English), CG draws a distinction between verbal grounding elements, which include the modals as well as tense (obviously not a word category), and all other verbs (see Langacker 1991: §5.1). With root or deontic modals, the ground is involved in trying to control what happens or to 'effect' the grounded process. For example, in *You may leave now*, it is the speaker, an element of the ground, that permits the event of the hearer's leaving to take place, i.e. to be 'effected'.[13] With epistemic modals, the speaker aims at 'epistemic control' of the grounded process by assessing its likelihood, as in *Alice may have left by now*, where the speaker is engaged in establishing the likelihood of the occurrence of Alice's having left. Crucially, both types of modal are related to a cognitive

---

[12] Grounding quantifiers differ from non-grounding quantifiers (numerals, *many*, *several*, *few*, etc.) because the former specify magnitude in relative terms. Given a certain type, the reference entity is called 'reference mass' or 'maximal extension' of the type. By contrast, non-grounding quantifiers specify magnitude in absolute terms by invoking a range rather than a reference mass (see, e.g., Langacker 2008a: 273–280).

[13] Technically, we say that the 'source of potency' resides in the speaker. Note, however, that this may be the prototypical case in the example quoted in the text but need not be so, as in *You may leave now—Mother says so*, where the ultimate source of potency is Mother, not the speaker (see Langacker 2008a: 165).

'control' model, thus illustrating the relevance and importance of a cognitive analysis to word classification.

8.6 Conclusion

CG stands out against other contemporary linguistic theories because it takes to heart the task of trying to offer a conceptual characterization of words classes valid for all instances, not just prototypical ones. This characterization is grounded in well-established findings from cognitive science and is instrumental in motivating why we observe the word classes that we do based on distributional evidence. Also, it shows indirectly that word classes need not be universal because only certain languages may have dedicated forms for specific conceptual configurations. For example, the fact that 'nouns' can be used as modifiers in English, such as the noun *evening* in *an evening course*, while other languages have dedicated forms as in Italian *un corso serale*, lit. 'a course evening', where *serale* is an adjective derived from the noun *sera*, 'evening', does not detract from the observation that the cognitive operations involved are the same: what we identify as word classes are just dedicated assemblies of symbolic structures. Still, CG contends that at least two classes, nouns and verbs, are probably universal in the sense that all languages have specific forms for things and processes. Admittedly, some issues such as the notion of relationship in the case of intransitive verbs and the distinction between sequential and summary scanning deserve further investigation, especially of an experimental nature, but CG remains quite unique among current linguistic theories in its efforts to go beyond a formal description of language.

CHAPTER 9

WORD CLASSES AND GRADIENCE

EVELIEN KEIZER

9.1 INTRODUCTION

THE approach to defining and distinguishing word classes outlined in this chapter has its origin not in any particular theoretical theory or model, but rather in two major developments in the second half of the 20th century. The first was the development of a scientifically based alternative to the classical view of categorization. Inspired by insights and findings from various disciplines (philosophy, psychology, linguistics, anthropology, biology, neuroscience), a new approach emerged, where categorization on the basis of similarity to a central case (or prototype) replaced the Aristotelian emphasis on necessary and sufficient features and strict boundaries. The result was an approach to categorization that allowed for gradience within categories and fuzzy boundaries between categories (see e.g., Aarts et al. 2004).

The second important development took place within linguistics, where a growing number of researchers (mostly from functional and cognitive backgrounds) felt that, rather than being ignored, as had been done previously, this categorial gradience should be awarded a place in grammatical theory. The two passages below clearly illustrate the two positions. The first is from Bouchard and argues for a grammar without gradience; the second is from Langacker, who accepts that non-discreteness should form an integral part of any theory of language:

> fuzziness is of interest, but since it has no effects relevant to the behavior of grammatical entities such as words, it is not of concern to the linguist, but rather to the psychologist.
> (Bouchard 1995: 31)

> Eventually the predilections of the analyst [for discrete linguistic entities] must give way to the actual complexity of the empirical data. Non-discrete aspects of language structure must be accommodated organically in the basic design of an adequate linguistic theory.
> (Langacker 1987b: 14)

In what follows, we first take a more detailed look at the background against which the gradience approach to word classes emerged (section 9.2). Section 9.3 then presents a number of examples which clearly demonstrate that word classes cannot be treated as classical categories, first providing synchronic evidence of categorial gradience (sections 9.3.1 and 9.3.2), and subsequently describing the diachronic processes that have contributed to its existence (section 9.3.3). Section 9.4 discusses some of the ways in which gradience in word classes has been modelled and accounted for in linguistic theory. Section 9.5 provides a short conclusion.

9.2 Gradience in cognition and grammar

9.2.1 The classical view of categorization

For many centuries, the prevailing view of categorization was the classical (or Aristotelian) view, according to which boundaries were strict and category membership an all-or-nothing affair, determined on the basis of necessary and sufficient features (e.g. Aristotle's *Metaphysics* IV/4: 1589). Despite numerous dissenting voices, this view held sway until well into the 20th century, being propagated, for instance, in the work of philosophers like Frege ([1903] 1997) and Russell (e.g. 1923), and adopted in both logical positivism and structuralism (see e.g., Aarts 2004a).

Although attractive in that it allows for the kind of 'categorical statements and strong predictability' that are 'highly valued in science' (Langacker 2008a: 13), the classical view is in many ways problematic; Taylor (2003: 35) even states that 'the supposed advantages of the classical theory turn out to be largely illusory'. One serious problem is epistemological in nature: if determining category membership consists in checking necessary and sufficient features, then categorization brings no cognitive benefit, no new knowledge (Taylor 2003: 35). Another problem is the danger of infinite regress: since the necessary and sufficient features of a category themselves also constitute categories, their features will also need to be checked (Taylor 2003: 36). The only way to avoid such infinite regress is to postulate a set of primitives—but what would these look like? Taylor (2003: 38) does not deny that classical categories exist (in bureaucratic, legal, or scientific language), but concludes that most categories in everyday experience cannot be precisely and exhaustively defined.

9.2.2 Gradience in cognition

Meanwhile, evidence from a variety of sources had come to support the idea that categorization is not an all-or-nothing affair (for an overview, see Lakoff 1987: ch. 2). In philosophy, Wittgenstein used the example of the German word *Spiel* 'game' to show that members of a category need not share any properties, but may be related through 'a complicated network of similarities overlapping and criss-crossing' (1953: § 66). Wittgenstein characterized these similarities as 'family resemblances', and concluded that some concepts cannot be defined precisely and have blurred boundaries (1953: § 71).

In linguistics, Labov (1973) contributed to the discussion of the nature of categorization with an experimental study requiring groups of subjects to name a variety of cup-like objects. The results showed that, although subjects agree on the clear cases, there is no clear cut-off point between, for instance, a cup and a bowl; instead there is a 'fringe area' where the object in question can with equal truth be called a cup or a bowl. Moreover, it turns out that the position of this fringe area may shift with a change in context; in a food-related context, for instance, objects at or near the fringe area are more likely to be classified as bowls. Labov concludes, first of all, that in many cases categorization takes place on the basis of relative distance from an optimal value, rather than on the basis of necessary and sufficient features. This leads to the further conclusion that there are different types of categories: those that are bounded and non-graded (classical type); those that are bounded but do allow for internal gradience; and those that are both graded and non-bounded (fuzzy).

Meanwhile, in anthropology, colour research conducted in the 1960s and 1970s provided further evidence for the existence of internally graded, non-bounded categories. Cross-linguistic research into colour terms showed that whereas the boundaries between colour ranges differ (rather arbitrarily) from language to language, speakers agree on what constitutes the best example of a colour term (the focal or basic colour; Berlin & Kay 1969). In other words, colour categories are characterized by internal gradience as well as by a lack of strict boundaries.

Around the same time, the possibility of non-discrete boundaries also came to be recognized in logic, with Zadeh's (1965) introduction of 'fuzzy set theory'. Unlike in classical set theory, where an entity is either in a set (membership value 1) or outside a set (membership value 0), Zadeh accepted the existence of peripheral members, with in-between values. Such members could be found in the intersection between two sets, sharing features with each set.

It was the psychologist Eleanor Rosch, however, who developed a theory that could accommodate all these different findings (e.g. Rosch 1973; 1975; 1978). On the basis of a large number of experiments she concluded that 'to increase the distinctiveness and flexibility of categories, categories tend to become defined in terms of prototypes or prototypical instances' (Rosch 1978: 30), where prototypes are to be understood as 'the clearest cases of category membership defined operationally by people's judgments on goodness of membership in the category' (Rosch 1978: 36). Rosch thus rejected categorization on the basis of necessary and sufficient properties, choosing instead 'to achieve separateness and clarity of actually continuous categories [...] by conceiving of each category in terms of its clear cases rather than its boundaries' (Rosch 1978: 36–37).

According to Rosch, the existence of such clear cases, or prototypes, follows from the acceptance of two general principles. The first is the principle of 'cognitive economy', according to which 'the task of category systems is to provide maximum information with the least cognitive effort' (Rosch 1978: 28–29). Here the notion of 'cue validity' plays an important role: features that are frequently associated with a particular category, but not with any other category, serve as better predictors of category membership (have higher cue validity) than features that are more frequently associated with other categories. For example, barking, as a highly distinctive property of dogs, has higher cue validity for membership of the category 'dog' than having four legs. The second general principle is that of 'perceived world structure' (Rosch 1978: 29), which states that humans do not perceive the world as an unstructured set of arbitrary and unpredictable attributes; instead, some attributes (including functional ones) tend to be perceived as coming in clusters (wings tend to co-occur with feathers; having a seat co-occurs with the notion of sitting).

Finally, it is important to note that the only direct evidence for the existence of prototypes comes in the form of (observable, superficial) prototype effects, i.e. judgements of degrees of prototypicality. As Rosch (1978: 40) emphasizes, these cannot be taken as direct evidence of how categories are structured or represented in the mind (a warning not always heeded by everyone working with the notion of prototype; see also Lakoff [1987] 1999: 391–392).[1]

9.2.3 Gradience in grammar

During the 1970s and 1980s, more and more linguists moved away from a purely formal approach, preferring analyses and theories that assigned a prominent role to semantics. Langacker, for instance, states that for him '[t]he most fundamental issue in linguistic theory is the nature of meaning and how to deal with it' (1987b: 5), whereby meaning (captured in the form of symbolic associations between a semantic and a phonological structure) came to be deployed for lexical and grammatical structures alike (1987b: 58; see also Chapter 8 in this volume). Moreover, Langacker (1987b: 5) regarded meaning as a cognitive phenomenon, a view shared by Jackendoff, for whom 'to study semantics of a natural language *is* to study cognitive psychology' (1983: 3, original emphasis).

One consequence of this shift in perspective was that the insistence on strict categories came to be abandoned. Unlike structuralist linguists (e.g. Joos 1950: 702; Hockett 1955: 17; Jakobson 1959), and later also generativist linguists (Bouchard 1995; Newmeyer 2000), semantically oriented linguists like McCawley (e.g. 1976; 1995), Jackendoff (e.g. 1983; 1990), Langacker (e.g. 1987b; 2002), and Lakoff (e.g. 1987; [1987] 1999) accepted gradience and fuzziness. For them, gradience was no longer just a matter of cognition, but also of linguistic theory, and prototype theory was regarded as having 'considerable linguistic and cognitive plausibility' (Langacker 1987b: 17; cf. Jackendoff 1983: 125–128; for further discussion, see Aarts 2006).

In the decades to follow, the notion of gradience came to be implemented in various cognitive and functional approaches, including Construction Grammar (e.g. Goldberg 2006), Word Grammar (e.g. Hudson 2006; 2010), Jackendoff's Parallel Architecture (2002; 2010), emergent grammar and interactional linguistics (e.g. Hopper 1987; 2012; Thompson 2002), and usage-based approaches (e.g. Bybee 2010). Moreover, the idea of gradience fitted in perfectly with the increasing interest in historical linguistics in the role of grammaticalization and lexicalization processes in language change (e.g. Heine et al. 1991; Hopper & Traugott 1993; Brinton & Traugott 2005; Traugott & Trousdale 2013).

And where originally prototype theory was predominantly applied to the study of word meaning and polysemy in cognitive semantics (e.g. Geeraerts 1988; 1989; 1997; 2008; Taylor

---

[1] For the role of prototype structure in the acquisition of word classes, see also Ibbotson & Tomasello (2009) and Ibbotson (Chapter 43 in this volume). At the same time, it needs to be mentioned that, also within psycholinguistics research, the notion of prototypes and their role in categorization is not undisputed (see, e.g., Nosofsky 1992; Nosofsky et al. 2020).

1996a), it soon came to be applied also to grammatical elements, including case and past tense (Tyler & Evans 2001; Taylor 2003) and classifiers (Lakoff 1987), as well as grammatical constructions, such as noun phrases (Ross 1973), *there*-constructions (Lakoff 1987), transitive constructions (Hopper & Thompson 1980), subject–auxiliary inversion (Goldberg 2006: 170–181), possessive constructions (e.g. Taylor 1994; 1996b; 2015), and the distinction between complements and modifiers (e.g. Aarts 2007: 186; Keizer 2004). In the next section, we will see how this new perspective on categorization has also influenced linguists' thinking on word classes.

9.3 Evidence for gradience in word classes

The literature describes many instances where the classical approach to word classes is not tenable and some kind of gradience needs to be accepted.[2] These instances come in two kinds: 'subsective gradience', where gradience can be observed within a class, and 'intersective gradience', where gradience can be observed between classes (terms introduced by Aarts 2004b; 2007). Since the latter type of gradience presupposes the former, we will start with the former type.

9.3.1 Subsective gradience

Subsective gradience (differing degrees in class membership) can be found in all the major word classes (nouns, verbs, adjectives, and prepositions). Here we will look at examples demonstrating gradience within the categories noun and adjective.

9.3.1.1 Subsective gradience in nouns

Crystal (1967) was one of the first to systematically address the problems involved in finding the right set of criteria to distinguish between the major word classes in English. Arguing that previous attempts were typically characterized by overspecification (setting up as many classes as there are words of different behaviour; Crystal 1967: 27–28) or underspecification (using only major binary distinctions, such as full vs empty, or open vs closed; Crystal 1967: 30–41), Crystal (1967: 45) proposes the use of a limited number of morphosyntactic criteria, ranked for relevance. By way of illustration, Crystal selects just four criteria to

---

[2] Most of the literature on the topic of gradience in word classes is concerned with specific languages (in particular English) and specific cases (i.e. with specific items illustrating gradience between specific word classes); this is reflected in the choice of examples discussed in this chapter. Gradience phenomena have, however, also been investigated in other European languages (e.g. deverbal nominalization in Hartmann 2014 for German; see Demske 2019 for a comparison between English and German; Bekaert & Enghels 2019 for Spanish).

categorize items as belonging to the class of nouns (Crystal 1967: 45–47): (i) the ability to act as a subject;[3] (ii) the ability to inflect for number/case; (iii) the ability to co-occur with a definite article; and (iv) the presence of a (derivational) morphological affix. By applying these criteria (represented in Figure 9.1 by means of four circles) to the nouns *news, information, hardship, peroration, boy, girl,* and *phonetics*, Crystal shows that five subgroups can be distinguished exhibiting different degrees of nounhood. With a 100% score, *hardship* and *peroration* represent the central subgroup, while *phonetics*, which only fulfils the first criterion, belongs to the most peripheral subgroup. The five subgroups and their respective scores are represented in Figure 9.1 (from Crystal 1967: 46).

+1
−2 e.g.
+3 'news'
+4

+1
−2 e.g.
+3 'information'
+4

central class
+1
+2 e.g. 'hardship'
+3 'peroration'
+4

1. May act as subject
2. Inflect for number
3. Co-occur with article
4. Morphological indication

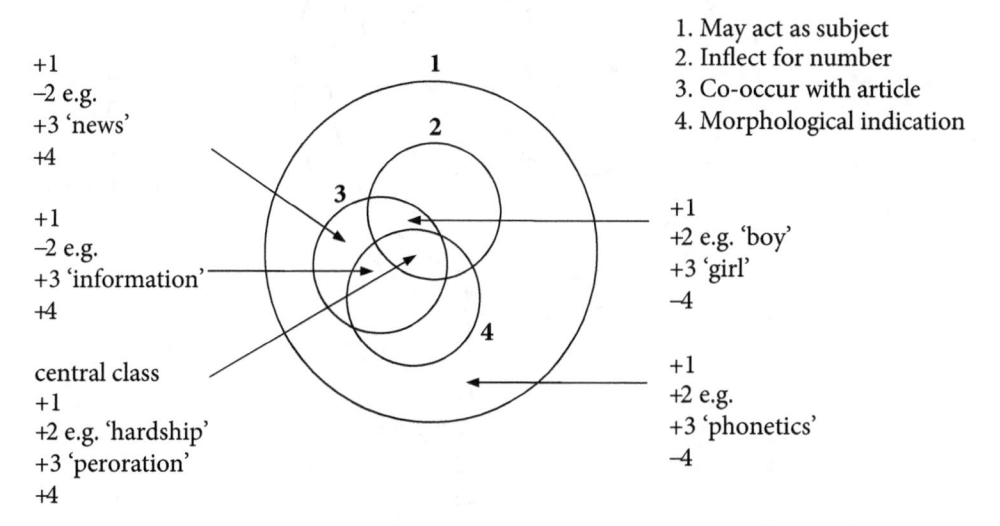

+1
+2 e.g. 'boy'
+3 'girl'
−4

+1
+2 e.g.
+3 'phonetics'
−4

FIGURE 9.1 Crystal's representation of nominal subclasses

As pointed out by Aarts (2007: 102), however, there is an implicational relationship between criteria 2 and 3 that is not captured in Figure 9.1, since every noun that can inflect for number can also co-occur with a definite article (though not the other way around). Another improvement suggested by Aarts concerns the classification of the noun *phonetics*, which, contrary to its classification in Figure 9.1, does fulfil the third criterion (as in *the phonetics of English*), and as such belongs to the same subgroup as *news*. This leaves us with no nouns in subgroup 1 (i.e. no nouns fulfilling only the first criterion); as an example of such a noun, Aarts suggests (existential) *there* (as in *There is cheese in the fridge*, where *there* can be claimed to act as the subject, given its position and the fact that it inverts with the finite verb in questions). In that case we still have five subgroups, representing four different degrees of class membership, but now organized as in Figure 9.2 (from Aarts 2007: 105).

---

[3] As pointed out by Aarts (2007: 102fn.), in constituency-based grammars, this would have to be interpreted as 'the ability to head a phrase which functions as subject'.

184   EVELIEN KEIZER

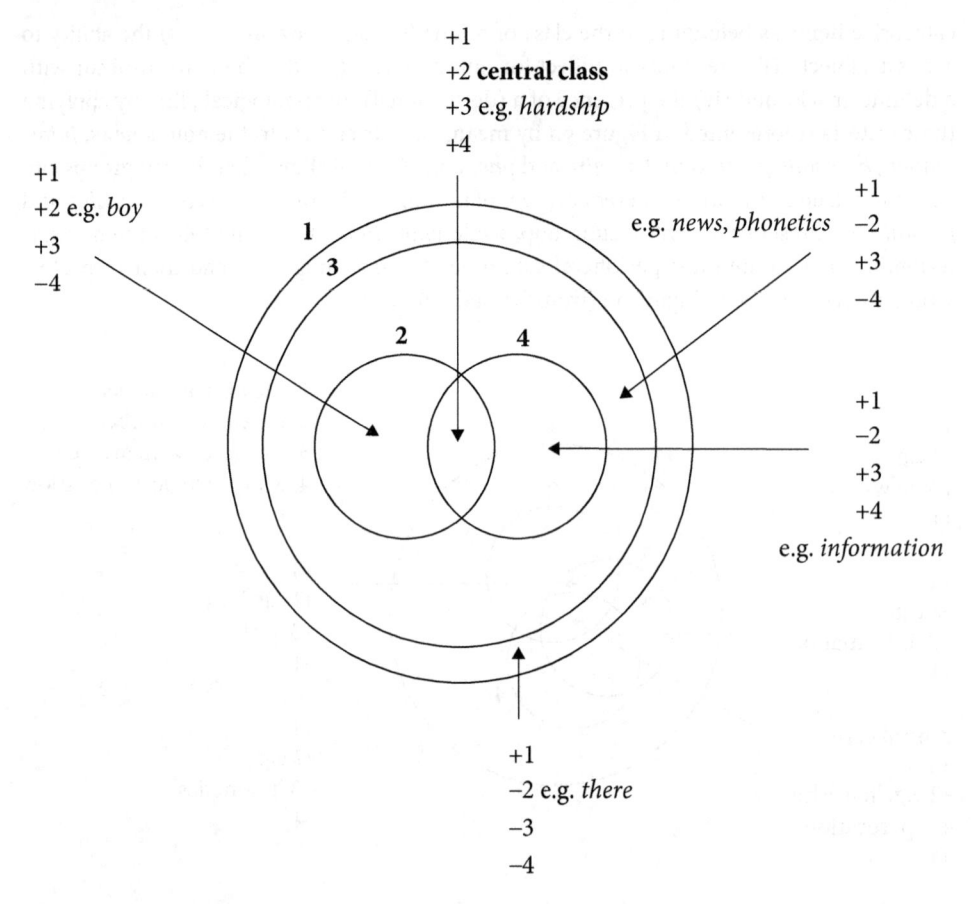

+1
+2 **central class**
+3 e.g. *hardship*
+4

+1
+2 e.g. *boy*
+3
−4

e.g. *news, phonetics*
+1
−2
+3
−4

+1
−2
+3
+4
e.g. *information*

+1
−2 e.g. *there*
−3
−4

FIGURE 9.2   Aarts's revised version of Figure 9.1

9.3.1.2 *Subsective gradience in adjectives*

A similar approach can be taken to the categorization of adjectives. Aarts (2007: 105–107), for instance, recognizes different degrees of class membership for different (subsets of) adjectives on the basis of a number of generally accepted morphosyntactic criteria (see also Quirk et al. 1985: 403–404):

(1) a. adjectives can occur in attributive position (*a happy woman*)
    b. adjectives can occur in predicative position (*she is happy*)
    c. adjectives allow for intensification (*very happy*)
    d. adjectives can be graded (*happy/happier/happiest*)
    e. adjectives allow for *un*-prefixation (*unhappy*)[4]

Aarts subsequently applies these criteria to four adjectives: *happy, thin, alive, utter*. What we find is, again, a prototype effect, in the sense that some of these adjectives are more adjectival than others. Thus, as shown in (1), *happy* fulfils all criteria; *happy*, in other words, is a central

---

[4] Note that this criterion is applied differently here than in Crystal (1967): what counts here is the possibility of adding the prefix, not its presence.

member of the class of adjectives. This is not the case, however, for the other adjectives, which exhibit different degrees of class membership. Aarts (2007: 107) thus proposes the following gradient, listing the adjectives from more to less adjectival:

(2) *happy > thin > alive > utter*

Although the presence of gradience is again clearly demonstrated, exact classification, of course, depends on the selection of the criteria.[5] Taylor (2002: 211), for instance, includes another criterion, namely that the modified noun can be replaced by *one*. This criterion is clearly in an implication relationship with the first criterion, since it applies only to adjectives that can be used attributively (though not to all of these adjectives). Applying this criterion would not change the gradient in (2) (since only *alive* and *utter* cannot be followed by *one*). Nevertheless, inclusion of this criterion might lead to another subclass for a word like *former*, which would end up between *thin* and *alive*. Crystal (1967: 51) applies the same criteria as Aarts, except that he does not mention *un*-prefixation, but includes, as his first criterion, 'ability to form adverb by adding *-ly*'. Applying this criterion would lead to yet another subclass for adjectives like *old* and *big*, which would end up between *thin* and *former*. Moreover, applying these criteria to yet other items (e.g. *inside*, *downstairs*) would seem to add another degree of class membership.

An overview of the various criteria and their application to the selected adjectives is given in Table 9.1, which clearly shows that, although all items listed have something in common with the prototype, there is not a single feature shared by all members (note also that *alive* and *utter* do not have any features in common), a situation best described in terms of Wittgenstein's family resemblances (see Jackendoff's 2002: 352–356 notion of 'cluster concepts', Quirk's 1965 'serial relationships', and Taylor's 2003: 113–118 'meaning chains').

Table 9.1 Gradience in the class of adjectives

	attr	adj + *one*	pred	*very*	*-ly*	comp/sup	*un-*
happy	+	+	+	+	+	+	+
thin	+	+	+	+	+	+	−
old	+	+	+	+	−	+	−
former	+	+	−	−	+	−	−
downstairs	+	+	+	−	−	−	−
alive	−	−	+	+	−	?	−
utter	+	−	−	−	+	−	−

Moreover, as pointed out by Taylor (2015: 569), most of these criteria are not strong diagnostics by themselves (have low cue validity), since they do not apply to adjectives alone. Thus, nouns can also occur in attributive and predicative position (*a silk tie*, *this tie is silk*), *one* can also be preceded by demonstratives and ordinals (*that one*; *the first one*), *very* can also precede adverbs (*very quickly*), quantifiers (*very many/much*; *very few/little*) and nouns

---

[5] Other criteria may also play a role, such as different degrees of bleaching and metaphorical use; to discuss these would go beyond the scope of this chapter.

(*the very person*), and *un-* can also quite productively attach to verbs (*undo, undress*),[6] etc. The only unique diagnostic for adjectival status is the use of the comparative and superlative form—a feature that is not, however, shared by all adjectives.

This brings us to the next question: that of whether we are dealing only with degrees of class membership or perhaps also with fuzzy boundaries. With regard to Table 9.1, for instance, lexical items like *downstairs* are typically regarded as adverbs. Crystal (1967: 50–52) therefore concludes that, for words like *downstairs, asleep*, and *old*, 'it seems better to take [them] as constituting a peripheral area between the two classes, with an as yet undetermined number of sub-classes' (Crystal 1967: 52; see also Aarts 2007: 136–138), i.e. as cases of intersective gradience.

9.3.2 Intersective gradience

Gradience between classes has been argued to exist not only between most of the major word classes, but also between major and minor word classes (e.g. adjectives and determiners, adverbs and determiners, prepositions and conjunctions; see, e.g., Aarts 2007: ch. 6; see also Denison 2010; 2013; see also Chapter 4 in this volume). In this section, we will look at two cases of intersective gradience between major word classes: between noun and verb, and between preposition and adjective.

9.3.2.1 Intersective gradience between nouns and verbs

A much-quoted example of intersective gradience between nouns and verbs is the English *-ing* form. Quirk et al. (1985: 1291) use the following examples to show that there is no natural cut-off point between the two categories, but that we are dealing with a continuum from purely nominal to purely verbal cases (see also Anderson 1997: 83–91; Huddleston 2002: 1220–1222; Aarts 2007: 142–144).[7]

(3) a. *some paintings of Brown's*
b. *Brown's paintings of his daughters*
c. *The painting of Brown* is as skilful as that of Gainsborough.
d. *Brown's deft painting of his daughter* is a delight to watch.
e. *Brown's deftly painting his daughter* is a delight to watch.
f. I dislike *Brown's painting his daughter*.
g. I dislike *Brown painting his daughter*.
h. I watched *Brown painting his daughter*.
i. *Brown deftly painting his daughter* is a delight to watch.
j. *Painting his daughter*, Brown noticed that his hand was shaking.
k. *Brown painting his daughter that day*, I decided to go for a walk.

---

[6] According to Maling (1983: 272), '[e]vidence from derivational morphology is notoriously unreliable as evidence for category assignment'.

[7] For an in-depth discussion of the problems involved in categorizing English *ing*-forms, see De Smet (2010); for discussions of the differences between nominal and verbal gerunds, see e.g. Heyvaert et al. (2019) and Maekelberghe (2019).

l. *The man painting the girl* is Brown.
m. *The silently painting man* is Brown.
n. Brown *is painting* his daughter.

In examples (3a) and (3b) we are dealing with purely nominal uses of *painting* ('deverbal nouns'): they occur in the plural, are preceded by a determiner (quantifier, genitival NP), and take an *of*-PP as their complement. Moreover, as pointed out by Quirk et al. (1985: 1291), they can be replaced by the basic nouns *picture* and *photo*. Examples (3c) and (3d) are also clearly nominal (note the presence of the premodifying adjective *deft* in (3d)), but cannot be replaced by *picture* or *photo*; Quirk et al. (1985: 1291) classify these instances as 'verbal nouns'. Examples (3j) to (3n), on the other hand, are all clearly verbal: in all these cases *painting* clearly functions as a present participle, as evidenced by the presence of an object NP or the presence of an adverb. Moreover, in none of these cases does *painting* display any nominal features.

The peripheral instances are given in (3e) to (3i); these examples (traditionally referred to as gerunds) combine nominal and verbal characteristics: on the one hand, they all head phrases functioning as subject or object (a nominal property), while at the same time they all take an object NP (a verbal property). Further differences can be observed within this group: (3e) and (3f) still contain a genitival NP (making them more nominal); (3e) and (3i) contain the adverb *deftly* (a verbal property). Given the gradience involved, Quirk et al. (1985: 1292) see no reason to use a separate term for cases like (3e) to (3i); instead, they avoid a clear-cut distinction between gerund and participle, using the term participle for all the examples in (3e)–(3n) (see also Anderson 1997: 90; Huddleston 2002: 1222).

9.3.2.2 *Intersective gradience between prepositions and adjectives*

Another interesting item, first discussed in Ross (1972: 317–319), is *near*, which has been shown to display virtually all characteristic features of both prepositions and adjectives. The examples in (4) seem to support categorization of *near* as a preposition:[8]

(4)   a. I met him near the museum.
      b. right near the museum
      c. the museum near which I met him
      d. *I became near the museum.
      e. *unnear

As shown in (4a), *near* can take an NP complement and head a non-predicative clause adjunct. Example (4b) shows that *near* can be modified by *right*, while in (4c), the phrase headed by *near* is relativized. None of these criteria apply to adjectives (**big the museum*; **I met him very tall*; **right big*; **big which*). Conversely, *near the museum* cannot follow the verb *become* (which is possible for APs) and does not accept *un*-prefixation. In all these respects *near* behaves like a preposition.

---

[8] The criteria applied here are a combination of those mentioned in previous publications on the topic (Ross 1972: 317–319; Maling 1983; Anderson 1997: 73–82; Pullum & Huddleston 2002: 609; Aarts 2007: 156–158, 216–217).

In other contexts, however, *near* exhibits adjectival behaviour. Thus, it can be modified by degree adverbs like *very* and *too* and can take a PP-complement (example (5a)); it can be used attributively and can be inflected for comparative and superlative (example (5b)); it can be used 'intransitively' in post-copular position (example (5c)); it can be postmodified, but not premodified, by *enough* (example (5d)); and it takes the adverbial *-ly* ending (example (5e)).

(5) a. I live very near to the museum.
     b. I invited only my near(est) relatives.
     c. The museum is near.
     d. The museum is near enough (?our house)[9] / *The museum is enough near our house
     e. We are nearly there.

What makes *near* even more special is that it can display prepositional and adjectival properties simultaneously, as shown in (6), where *near* appears in the comparative form while at the same time taking an NP-complement.

(6) I met him *nearer the museum* than the townhall.

So how do we go about categorizing *near*? Here linguists disagree. First there are those that do not accept fuzziness. Maling (1983: 270–272), for instance, categorizes *near* as a transitive adjective on the basis of its many adjectival properties; however, she only really looks at the adjectival properties, and ignores the prepositional features *near* displays. Aarts (2007: 215–218), using a more evenly distributed set of adjectival and prepositional features, concludes that *near* behaves like a preposition in some (actually most) cases, and as an adjective in others. Finally, both Newmeyer (2000: 243) and Pullum & Huddleston (2002: 609) argue for dual membership, with *near* being a full member of both classes; this, however, fails to account for the combination of prepositional and adjectival features in (6).

Another way of dealing with the messy data is, of course, to accept that the boundary between the two classes is fuzzy. Ross (1972: 319), for instance, places *near* right in the middle of a cline (or 'squish') from adjective to preposition (*proud > opposite > near > like > in*). Anderson (1997: 75, 79), like Maling (1983), concludes that *near* is an adjective behaving like a preposition when used as a (non-predicative) adjunct; he does, however, suggest that there is gradience between adjectives and prepositions, with *near* appearing more towards the adjectival end of the cline (Anderson 1997: 79). Yet another approach to fuzziness of this kind is to accept dual (or multiple) inheritance. On such an approach, *near* would inherit its features from two sources: it would be an adjective and preposition at the same time, a member of a 'mixed category' (e.g. Hudson 2006: 168–171; 2010: 259; see also Chapter 15 in this volume; cf. Chapter 5 in this volume). In that case, none of the examples given above would be problematic, provided that the relation between mixed category and its source categories can be both explained and constrained.[10]

---

[9] Acceptability judgement as given in Anderson (1997: 78).
[10] On the concept of mixed categories, see also, e.g., Malouf (2000a,b), Bresnan & Mugane (2006), and Nikolaeva & Spencer (2020: 126–170) Dalrymple and Toivonen Chapter 15 in this volume.

9.3.3 Gradience and language change

So far, we have only considered synchronic evidence for the existence of gradience in and between word classes. However, another important source for such evidence is research on changes in syntactic category over time (e.g. Denison 2001; 2010; 2013; 2017a; 2017b). Such changes come again in two kinds: those that only result in a shift in category and those that also involve structural change (e.g. Denison 2010). The latter typically result from a process of decategorization, as part of a process of grammaticalization or lexicalization; examples would be the gradual change from full noun to part of a quantifying expression (e.g. *lot > a lot of*; Langacker 2009: 59–80; Traugott & Trousdale 2013: 23–29), from full noun to part of a discourse marker (e.g. *sort/kind > sort of/kind of*; Brems & Davidse 2010; Denison 2017a: 310–311); or from full noun to part of a complex preposition (e.g. *spite > in spite of*; *search > in search of*; Quirk et al. 1985: 671–672; Hoffmann 2005; Denison 2010: 118–122).

In what follows we will consider the first type of category change, whereby a shift in word class is not accompanied by structural change. Such shifts may be abrupt, as in the case of conversion, which results in dual membership of the item in question and does not involve any fuzziness (a lexical item like *natural* behaves either as an adjective or as a noun). In other cases, however, changes take place gradually, in a stepwise fashion (see Denison 2001; 2013; 2017a; 2017b), without any clear cut-off point between the two categories. This will be illustrated here with the word *fun*,[11] which has been shown to have undergone a gradual shift (in both British and American English) from (mass) noun to adjective (e.g. Bolinger 1963; Denison 2001; 2013; De Smet 2012: 621–625; see also Kiparsky 2014: 66–67). Thus, in (7), we have two unequivocal nominal uses of *fun*: in (7a) it heads an NP that is the complement of a preposition, in (7b) it is premodified by an adjective.

(7) a. We did it just *for fun*.
    b. It was *great fun*.

In (7b) *fun* appears in predicative position, which is also available for adjectives. In its bare form, *fun* in this position is therefore indistinguishable from an adjective; and this is where the reanalysis of *fun* as an adjective begins (De Smet 2013: 622, 625). Thus, in the following examples *fun* in predicative position is modified by the degree adverb *rather*, a property of adjectives:

(8) a. It would be *rather fun* to see his odd ways. (1827, OED Online)
    b. it was *rather fun* playing at being the bachelor again (1935, COHA; De Smet 2012: 622)

---

[11] For a similar discussion of the noun *key*, see De Smet (2012) and Denison (2013); for the noun *rubbish*, see Denison (2010). Moreover, note that, as pointed out in numerous studies, gradual change can also be observed between major word classes, e.g. between noun and verb (for English, see e.g. De Smet 2008; Fonteyn 2019; for German, see Hartmann 2014; for a comparison between English and German, see Demske 2019; for Spanish, see Bekaert & Enghels 2019).

In this example, *fun* could still be regarded as a noun which adopted a single adjectival feature. Next, however, *fun* also starts to occur in prenominal position, as a modifier of the following noun, another feature typically associated with adjectives.[12]

(9)   a. I was remembering Marianne and the *fun times* we have had. (1968, OED Online; Denison 2001: 127)
       b. and then slowly he began to realize the *fun meaning* of the thing. (1944, COHA; De Smet 2012: 622)

Then, gradually, *fun* starts to become more and more adjectival. In (10a), for instance, it is coordinated with an adjectival phrase, in (10b) it appears as a postmodifier of an indefinite pronoun, in (10c) it is premodified by *so*:

(10)   a. She's so completely *lovely and fun and joyful*. (ICE-GB; Denison 2001: 127)
       b. We have the Osborns, the Beals, the Hartungs, the Falmers, and us. Now let's think of *someone fun*. (1971, OED; Denison 2001: 127)
       c. It was *so fun*. (1991, COCA; see also Bolinger 1963)

Finally, in the examples in (11) *fun* occurs in the superlative and comparative form:

(11)   a. Skiing's the *funnest* thing I've ever done and probably the *funnest* thing I'll ever do. (1972, OED Online)
       b. Besides skiing, it's the *funnest* thing I do ... (1983, COHA)
       c. Walking and looking is boring. Touching is *funner*. (1990, COCA; Denison 2017a: 308)

For Denison (2013: 173), such a stepwise progression from noun to adjective 'demonstrates genuine gradience between N and Adj, and [...] strongly supports the idea that word classes are prototype-based rather than Aristotelian'.

An interesting feature of this category shift is that, although *fun* gradually changes into an adjective, it continues to be used as a noun as well; we are, in other words, dealing with a case of layering. Moreover, individual speakers are likely to differ in their judgements about which of the more adjectival uses of *fun* are acceptable (see Denison 2013: 171; 2017a: 308). Thus, in a sentence like (12):

(12)   Skiing is fun.

a more conservative speaker will only accept *fun* as a noun, a more advanced speaker may accept some adjectival properties (e.g. *rather fun*), but not others (e.g. *funnest*), while an even more advanced speaker will simply have *fun* as a noun and an adjective. For this last group of speakers *fun* in example (12) is underspecified: it could be a noun or an adjective. Any choice between the two categories would in fact be arbitrary (Denison

---

[12] This position can, of course, also be filled by nouns functioning as classifiers (e.g. *a jade figure*). However, in the examples provided *fun* has a descriptive function, not a classifying one.

2013: 172), and '[t]o insist on a unique category [...] would be to practise an artificial pseudo-rigour imposed by certain linguistic theories and not by the facts of the language' (Denison 2010: 114).

9.4 DEALING WITH GRADIENCE IN WORD CLASSES

On the basis of such evidence as provided in the previous section, many linguists have come to accept that gradience not only exists, but should be dealt with in the grammar. In itself, however, such an approach does not provide any indication of how word classes are defined, i.e. of what it means to be a noun, verb, or adjective; nor does it tell us what it means for a particular item to be a better example of a word class than another, i.e. where the gradience comes from and what it represents.

So far, evidence of gradience has been given in terms of the morphosyntactic behaviour of linguistic elements. This, of course, makes sense, given that this is the only hard evidence available to the analyst. For this reason, some linguists choose to rely on structural properties only. A prime example of this approach is Aarts (2004b; 2007), who uses sets of relevant morphosyntactic properties of each word class to determine class membership of an item on a particular use. Aarts concludes that whereas subsective gradience is a widespread feature of languages, there is no evidence for the existence of fuzzy boundaries: although categories may (and often do) converge, 'languages have a tendency to avoid true hybridity', a likely reason being that 'cases where the categorial scales are perfectly balanced are presumably hard to process, and hence disfavoured by language users' (Aarts 2007: 233; see also 2004b: 3).

We already saw an example of this in the discussion of *near* in section 9.4: on the basis of a set of relevant prepositional and adjectival properties, Aarts (2007: 215–218) argues that in each of its uses, *near* is either an adjective (converging on the class of prepositions) or a preposition (converging on the class of adjectives). Applying the same method to the *-ing* forms given in example (3), Aarts concludes that here, too, we are dealing with a case of convergence, rather than true hybridity, as a boundary can still be drawn between examples (3a)–(3d), where *painting* is a noun, and (3e)–(3n), where it functions as a verb.[13] In both cases, however, subsective gradience can be observed, with varying degrees of membership on each side of the divide (Aarts 2007: 228–233). The relation between the major word classes can thus be represented as in Figure 9.3 (from Aarts 2007: 236).

---

[13] As Aarts (2007: 225–228) himself concedes, such a model is not without its problems. After all, how can we be sure that we have identified all the relevant properties, and that these properties are independent of each other? How do we know that all properties are equally important? How can we be sure that certain properties uniquely characterize a particular word class? These are all legitimate questions that do indeed need to be addressed in any comprehensive approach to gradience in word classes that relies on structural properties. For a critical, typologically inspired, reply to Aarts (2007), see Croft (2007).

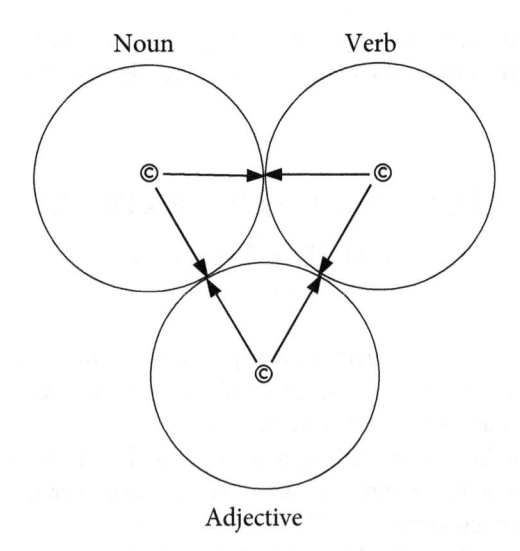

FIGURE 9.3 Gradience within and between the categories of noun, verb, and adjective

In Figure 9.3, © represents the core (or prototype) of a category (in this case only three categories are included, represented by three contiguous circles).[14] Non-prototypical members are positioned within the category at varying distances from the core. In those cases where a non-prototypical member takes on properties of another category, it converges on that category (as indicated by the arrows). In each case, however, there is a boundary: an item still belongs to only one class at a time.

What such a purely structuralist account does not tell us, however, is what gradience stands for—what is it that a speaker communicates by using non-prototypical expressions, how are the prototype effects observed to be interpreted? One way of answering these questions is to resort to the traditional definitions of word classes in semantic terms. This approach received severe criticism from both structuralists and generativists in the course of the 20th century, as being unreliable and circular (see Hollmann 2020). According to Lyons (1968: 317–319), however, such criticism is unjustified: we can use a notional (semantic, ontological) definition A to name a word class, while using formal features to establish membership of a syntactic category B. As long as there is considerable overlap between the notional and formal classes, we can accept A as a definition (label) of B. In other words, we can define the class of nouns in notional terms as lexical items denoting persons, places, and things, since 'a distinguished subclass' of the total class of nouns does indeed match this description. Any lexical items that do not share this denotation (e.g. *truth* or *beauty*), but which belong to the same syntactic category as such items, will also be called nouns. Those nouns that do fit the notional definitions are simply more focal (prototypical) than those that do not (Lyons 1977: 440).

Givón (1984: 51–52) also provides a purely semantic characterization of the major word classes in terms of time-stability. Thus, nouns typically denote 'experiences which stay **stable over time**'; prototypical examples are '**concrete, physical, compact** entities made out of durable,

---

[14] As further categories are added to the constellation in Figure 9.3, it becomes clear that not all categories are contiguous; prepositions, for instance, converge on verbs and adjectives, but not on nouns or adverbs (see Aarts 2007: 236–237).

solid matter, such as "rock", "tree", "dog", "person", etc.' (Givón 1984: 51, original emphases). Verbs, on the other hand, are lexicalizations of 'experiential clusters denoting **rapid changes** in the state of the universe. These are prototypically events or actions' (Givón 1984: 51, original emphases). These prototypical examples form two poles of a scale, with less prototypical cases (as well as adjectives) in between the two extremes. Givón (2001: 49-50), however, defines word-class membership by 'three baskets of criteria': semantic, morphological, and syntactic. This again results in gradience, but only of the subsective kind—the existence of boundaries is still assumed (cf. Givón 1984: 49; see also Givón 1986; 1995):

> [in] using a prototype-clustering approach to the membership of lexical categories, rather than rigid Platonic definitions, one merely acknowledges that lexical categories [...] may include members that display less than 100% of the criterial properties. That is, some members are more prototypical, while others are less prototypical but still members.
>
> (Givón 2001: 49)

A more sophisticated semantics-based characterization of word classes has been proposed by Langacker within the framework of Cognitive Grammar (e.g. Langacker 1987b; 2002; 2008a; 2009; see also Chapter 8 in this volume). Langacker accepts that prototypical nouns denote physical objects, and prototypical verbs overt physical actions (e.g. 2002: 60; 2008a: 95), but in addition, assumes the existence of higher-level schemas which are instantiated by all members of a word class (Langacker 1987: 190; 2002: 60). These schematic realizations are universal in nature, and are formed on the basis of a number of basic cognitive abilities: grouping and reification in the case of the noun schema; apprehending relationships and tracking relationships through time in the case of the verb schema (e.g. Langacker 2008a: 105, 108). Word classes are thus defined at two levels, distinguishing their universal characterization from their (prototypical or non-prototypical) manifestation (see Figure 9.4). At the level of the (universal) schema, classes are provided with a semantic definition: a noun designates a THING, i.e. a region in some domain, and a verb designates a PROCESS, i.e. a temporal relation. At the next level, we find the (local) prototype (central instance or basic value) along with its extension (or extended value, included on the basis of perceived similarity with the basic value) (Langacker 2002: 271).

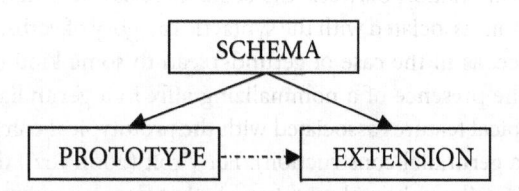

```
              SCHEMA
              /     \
             /       \
      PROTOTYPE ----▶ EXTENSION
```

FIGURE 9.4 Langacker's two-level network of categorization

Word classes are thus given a purely semantic characterization; the grammatical behaviour of a word class 'is best regarded as SYMPTOMATIC of its schematic value, not the sole or final basis for a critical definition' (Langacker 2002: 60, original emphasis).[15] Note finally

---

[15] Note that Langacker does not deny that other than semantic factors may play a role in the definition of word classes. Taylor (2002: 180–185), accepting Langacker's semantic characterization, suggests that since nouns and verbs are associated (statistically, not predictably) with different phonological content, this information should also be part of the noun and verb schemas (as subschemas). Similarly, Hollmann (2012; 2013) argues, on the basis of a range of psycholinguistics experiments, that distributional (in this case, phonological) cues must not be ignored.

that Langacker's approach to word classes appears to allow for subsective gradience, but not for fuzziness between the classes, as lexical items instantiate only one schema at a time.

Another way of explaining gradience is provided by Hopper & Thompson (1984). Although they do not deny that nouns and verbs have different denotations, they believe that such semantic features are secondary to the roles lexical items play in discourse. Thus, according to Hopper & Thompson (1984: 703), 'the basic categories N and V are to be viewed as universal lexicalizations of the prototypical discourse functions of "discourse-manipulable participant" and "reported event", respectively', with the cross-linguistic morphosyntactic behaviour associated with nouns and verbs correlating with the degree to which the forms in questions are performing their respective prototypical discourse functions (Hopper & Thompson 1984: 711). A prototypical noun, for instance, is used to introduce a discourse-manipulable participant into the discourse; such nouns display all the formal characteristics associated with the class of nouns; lower degrees of manipulability are reflected in the absence of one of more of these markings. Hopper & Thompson (1984: 747) conclude that '[c]ategoriality—the realization of a form as either N or V—is imposed on the form by discourse'. A form may have a propensity to appear as a noun or a verb, but this may always be overruled; in the end, forms only manifest themselves as noun or verb when the discourse requires it.

A final example of how to approach the problems involved in defining the major word classes can be found in Croft (1991; 2002; 2007; see also Chapter 11 in this volume), who uses a combination of semantic definitions and pragmatic functions to define (universal) prototypes for what are traditionally referred to as nouns, verbs, and adjectives. Thus, Croft distinguishes three semantic classes, OBJECTS, PROPERTIES, and ACTIONS; these he regards as the TYPOLOGICAL PROTOTYPES for the pragmatic functions (or propositional acts) of reference, modification, and predication, respectively (Croft 2001: 87). For Croft, the terms noun, adjective, and verb are thus merely traditional labels for the prototypical correlations between semantic class and pragmatic function. There is, for instance, an unmarked (prototypical) relation between the semantic class of object and the pragmatic function of reference, which is structurally coded by means of what is traditionally referred to as a noun. Similarly, there is a prototypical relation between the semantic class of actions and the pragmatic function of predication, associated with the syntactic category of verbs. Marked correlations (e.g. action–reference, as in the case of gerunds) lead to some kind of overt morphosyntactic coding (e.g. the presence of a nominalizing affix in a gerundial construction) and/or the absence of typical features associated with the prototypical combination (e.g. lack of tense indication in a gerundial construction). For Croft (2001: 102), the terms noun, verb, and adjective thus describe universal prototypes rather than language-particular grammatical categories. These prototypes describe only the core of a category; they tell us nothing about their boundaries, which are provided by the grammar of a particular language (e.g. Croft 2001: 103).

9.5 CONCLUSION

This chapter has described an approach to word classes that accepts that categorization is characterized by gradience, and that category membership is determined not on the basis of a clearly definable set of necessary and sufficient features, but rather on the basis of perceived similarity to a central case (prototype). The evidence provided in section 9.3 also makes it clear that gradience does affect linguistic form and, as such, needs to be part of any grammatical theory, and dealt with in as consistent a manner as possible.

We have also seen, however, that different linguists deal with gradience in different ways. Some accept both intracategorial (subsective) and intercategorial (intersective) gradience, others only the former. Some stop at modelling gradience on the basis of morphosyntactic features, while others also look for explanations in terms of denotation of the word (semantics) or discourse function (pragmatics). Due to these different ways of handling the non-discrete nature of word classes, and the different degrees in accepting fuzzy boundaries, the notion of linguistic gradience has turned out to be compatible with a large number of theoretical frameworks. However, as the brief overview in section 9.4 suggests, its strongest advocates can be found among linguists working with the various cognitive and functional theories developed in the second half of the 20th century, as well as among historical linguists describing processes of grammaticalization and lexicalization.

Acknowledgements

I am grateful to David Denison and Lachlan Mackenzie, as well as to the internal reviewer, Walter Bisang, and the anonymous external reviewer for their valuable comments on earlier versions of this chapter. Any remaining errors are, of course, entirely my own.

CHAPTER 10

LEXEME CLASSES AND WORD CLASSES IN FUNCTIONAL DISCOURSE GRAMMAR

J. LACHLAN MACKENZIE

10.1 INTRODUCTION

FUNCTIONAL Discourse Grammar (FDG) (Hengeveld & Mackenzie 2008) draws a distinction between lexeme classes and word classes. Lexeme classes belong to the lexicon, where each lexeme is classified according to its functional properties, for example Verb as the head of an independent Ascriptive Subact, while word classes pertain to morphosyntax, where each word is classified according to its morphological and/ or syntactic properties, for example 'Noun word' as the head of a Noun phrase. FDG assumes the set of lexeme classes {V, N, Adj, Adv} to be universal, in the sense that the lexicon of each language makes a principled choice from that set. The set of word classes is language-specific, and can include classes that align more or less well with a language's lexeme classes, namely Verbal, Nominal, Adjectival, and Adverbial Words {Vw, Nw, Adjw, Advw}, but also, depending on the language, such classes as Auxiliary, Complementizer, and or Discourse marker. A language will recognize at least as many word classes as lexeme classes: for example, one that does not distinguish the lexeme classes Adj and Adv may nevertheless distinguish adjectival and adverbial words in morphosyntax.

It is against this backdrop that this chapter will begin by presenting FDG as the successor theory to Dik's (1978; 1989; 1997) Functional Grammar (FG) (section 10.2), progressing in section 10.3 to an exposition of Hengeveld's (1992b) proposals for lexeme classes. Section 10.4 discusses the integration of these proposals into FDG and the formalization of lexeme classes and word classes. Section 10.5 turns to the three-way distinction among flexible, differentiated, and rigid language systems in FDG, and the research results that have flowed from it. Section 10.6 considers the impact of FDG work on language typology, and section 10.7 concludes the chapter.

10.2 The Origins and Basic Principles of FDG

FDG arose in the first two decades of the 21st century as the successor theory to FG as developed by Simon C. Dik (1940-1995). FG had established itself in the 1980s and 1990s as one of the major European approaches to the grammatical organization of human languages; it was *functional* in positing that language is first and foremost an instrument of communication between human beings, and it was a *grammar* in being concerned with describing and explaining the formal properties of language structure. Linguistic phenomena were elucidated in terms of their instrumentality, i.e. the contribution they make to language users' attempts to influence each other by using language.

Dik's FG, although in programmatic statements oriented to the 'linguistic expression' in general (Dik 1997: 3), in practice took the clause to be the largest unit of structure and assumed that each clause encodes a meaning that can be represented in a precise formalism. This formalism combined various sorts of information into a single representation that indicated the major lexemes in the sentence (known as *predicates*); the valency requirements of those predicates (the *semantic functions* of the *terms* that are their *arguments*); the speaker's perspective on the clause (*syntactic functions*); the speaker's expectations regarding the addressee's awareness of various segments of the information imparted (*pragmatic functions*); and ways, grammatical and lexical respectively, in which the speaker can specify various additional components of the meaning (*operators* and *satellites*). Even in the earliest versions of FG, this led to rather complex underlying representations. (1), in Dik's (1978) model, was analysed as in (2):

(1) The attractive boy was kissed by the girl.
(2) Past kiss$_V$
  (d1x$_i$: girl$_N$ (x$_i$))$_{AgFoc}$[1]
  (d1x$_j$: boy$_N$ (x$_j$): attractive$_A$ (x$_j$))$_{GoSubjTop}$

where *kiss*$_V$, *girl*$_N$, *boy*$_N$, and *attractive*$_A$ are predicates, the variables (x$_i$) and (x$_j$), with their semantic functions Agent and Goal (in the sense of 'Patient'), represent the argument structure of the predicate *kiss*$_V$, Subj(ect) is a syntactic function, Foc(us) and Top(ic) are pragmatic functions, and Past, d(efinite), and 1 are operators.

Later work brought further complexity to the meaning representation, as linguists found more and more meanings that needed to be incorporated into the structure. The most far-reaching innovation was Hengeveld's (1989) proposal to replace Dik's monostratal representation with a *layered* structure. This was supported, for example, by the observation that satellites apply to different sections of a representation. Thus *passionately* in *The attractive boy was kissed passionately by the girl* applies only to the verb *kiss*$_V$, whereas *in the library* in

---

[1] The formalism is akin to that of predicate logic: this representation is to be read as 'definite singular x$_i$, such that the second occurrence of (x$_i$) has the property "girl", classified as a N(oun)'. To clarify matters, the two arguments have been placed on separate lines. Since this is not standard practice in FG or FDG, this will not be done in later examples, with the exception of (13).

The attractive boy was kissed in the library by the girl applies to the entire representation in (2). Other satellites, such as *allegedly*, do not apply to the event represented in (2) but to the proposition entertained by the speaker: there must therefore be a higher layer of analysis to which such satellites can apply. Finally, satellites such as *To tell you a secret* apply neither to the event nor to the proposition, but to an even higher layer, that of the speech act. The conclusion, which was shown to be relevant to many other phenomena, was that the underlying representation should consist of four nested layers. The result was a single complex structure showing each sentence as a *speech act*, incorporating a *proposition*, which contained a *predication*, the nucleus of which was a *predicate*; each layer had its own set of operators and satellite positions. The resultant edifice was incorporated wholesale into the final statement of FG in Dik (1989; 1997).

The complexity of the single layered representation was tackled by Hengeveld (2004a), who proposed an FDG in which the *formulation* of meaning was divided over two levels, an

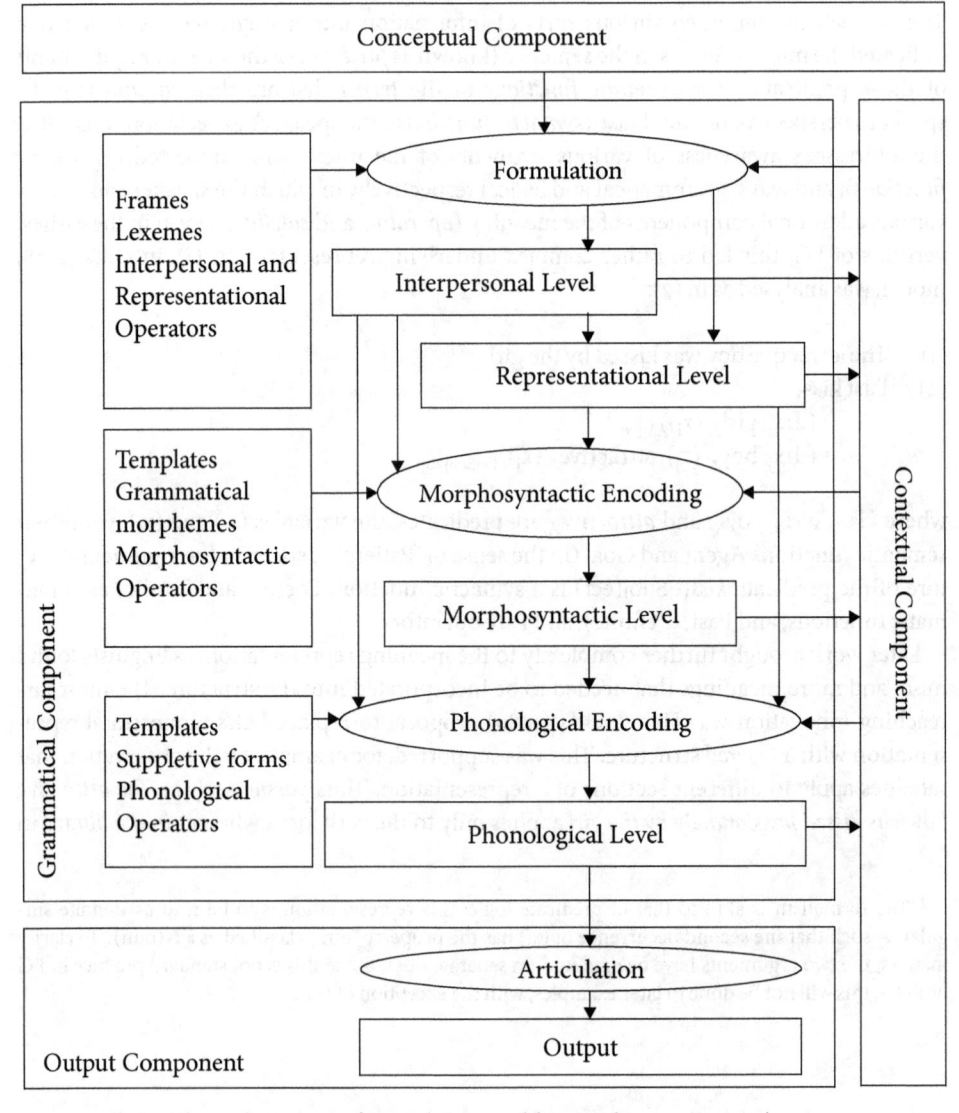

FIGURE 10.1 The architecture of FDG (Hengeveld & Mackenzie 2008: 13)

interpersonal level (IL) that accounts for the discursive and pragmatic aspects of a linguistic unit, and a *representational level* (RL), which covers the strictly semantic aspects; both of these levels are characterized by the kind of layering that had been introduced by Dik and Hengeveld into FG. The grammar (as enshrined in the *locus classicus* for FDG, Hengeveld & Mackenzie 2008) also encompasses another operation, *encoding*, which yields the morphosyntactic and phonological levels (ML and PL), which are also internally layered. The overall architecture of the model is displayed in Figure 10.1, in which it is additionally shown that the *grammatical component*, the FDG proper, is one of four components of the overall model of verbal interaction, which also includes a *conceptual component*, a *contextual component*, and an *output component*.

FDG preserves the overall functionalist goals of FG and retains, *mutatis mutandis*, several of its core concepts, such as pragmatic, semantic, and syntactic functions, as well as operators and satellites (the latter now reanalysed as *modifiers*). Nevertheless, it differs in four crucial respects. First, while FG took individual predicates and built up a structure around them, FDG has a *top-down organization*, starting with the speaker's communicative intention and working its way down to the articulation of the linguistic expression. Second, FDG takes an actional view on communication, identifying the *discourse act* rather than the clause as the basic unit of analysis; as such it accommodates in both theory and practice linguistic expressions that are larger or smaller than the clause focused on by FG. A third difference, one that is particularly important for this chapter, concerns the organization of lexemes. While FG recognized a 'lexicon' and saw it as a collection of predicates, each of which is marked for its lexeme class and is associated with a *predicate frame*, FDG distinguishes sharply between the *fund* (Hengeveld & Mackenzie 2021: 19), which covers the totality of primitives shown in boxes in Figure 6.1 and contains a *lexicon*, a list of simple and derived *lexemes*, and the *frameset*, as a list of grammatical frames with various quantitative and qualitative valencies. Formulation in FDG involves first the selection of one of the frames from the frameset and then the selection of a lexeme that is compatible with that frame (Hengeveld & Mackenzie 2016). Finally, FDG differs from FG in not assuming meaning definitions: the meaning of a lexeme is seen as not being capable of formal specification but rather as a matter of a speaker's personal experience of its use.

Each lexeme in FDG is associated with the symbol '$', as first proposed by Smit & Van Staden (2007); the symbol applies to both simple and derived lexemes. Thus the lexeme 'porch' is listed as in (3):

(3) $\$_{1032}$ | /pɔːtʃ/
where '1032' is the (arbitrary) number or 'address' of the lexeme

As proposed by Hengeveld & Mackenzie (2016: 1145), this lexeme will be marked in the fund as available for association at RL with the frame in (4), which is the frame for Locations; the lozenge symbol ♦ indicates the position to be taken by the lexeme, while (f_1) here symbolizes a lexical property and (l_1) a location:

(4) $(l_1: (f_1: ♦_N (f_1)) (l_1)_U)$

The result of associating the lexeme with the frame is shown in (5), to be read as 'one location, such that it has (i.e. is the U[ndergoer] of) the property "porch"':

(5) $(1l_i: (f_1: \$_{1032} | /pɔːtʃ/_N (f_1)) (l_1)_U)$

Now, (5) can be inserted through the above-mentioned process of formulation into the RL analysis of a Discourse Act such as (6):

(6) We swept the porch.

Consider now an example like (7), showing a 'creative' use of *porch* (Clark & Clark 1979: 787; García Velasco 2016: 924-925):

(7) The attractive boy porched the newspaper.

Here the language user chooses to associate the lexeme shown in (3) with the following frame from the frameset, i.e. a *configurational property* (f_1) which consists of a lexical property (f_2) with two arguments, both of them Individuals ((x_n), i.e. first order entities), with the semantic functions A[ctor] and U[ndergoer]:

(8) (f_1: [(f_2: ◆$_V$ (f_2)) (x_1)$_A$ (x_2)$_U$] (f_1))

to give (9):

(9) (f_1: [(f_2: \$$_{1032}$ | /pɔːtʃ/$_V$ (f_2)) (x_1)$_A$ (x_2)$_U$] (f_1))

These examples, where we see the same lexeme functioning as Noun (in (6)) and as Verb (in (7)), are designed to show the FDG formalism at work and also to provide the basis for understanding FDG's functional approach to lexeme classes. As we shall see in the following section, the essence of this approach was already present in Dik's (1989) and Hengeveld's (1992b) definitions of Noun, Verb, and Adjective.

10.3 Dik's functional definitions and Hengeveld's elaboration thereof

As mentioned, Dik (1989: 54) says that lexemes are analysed as predicates. He distinguishes three main categories: V(erbal), N(ominal), and A(djectival) predicates. He rejects semantic and structural definitions, believing that 'it is profitable to take a functional view of the categories, and define them in terms of the prototypical functions they fulfil in the construction of predications' (1989: 194). The definitions he proposes are as in (10):

(10) a. A Verbal predicate (V) is a predicate which is primarily used in predicative function.
b. A Nominal predicate (N) is a predicate which is primarily used as head of a term.
c. An Adjectival predicate (A) is a predicate which is primarily used in attributive function.

An advantage of these statements is that the defining functions are assumed to be universally valid across languages: by *predicative function* is meant 'appearing as the main predicate of a predication', like $kiss_V$ in (2), repeated below for convenience; by *head of a term* is meant 'the first (or only) predicate in a referring expression', like 'girl' or 'boy' in (2); by *attributive function* is meant 'the second (or later) predicate in a referring expression', like 'attractive' in (2):

(2)   Past $kiss_V$ ($d1x_i$: $girl_N$ (x_i))$_{AgFoc}$ ($d1x_j$: boy_N (x_j): $attractive_A$ (x_j))$_{GoSubjTop}$
      'The attractive boy was kissed by the girl.'

Dik stresses his use of the hedge 'primarily': it is possible for any type of predicate to be put to secondary use, with or without a change of form (e.g. a nominalizing affix) and with or without a supportive morpheme (e.g. a copula). This is summarized in Table 10.1.

Table 10.1 Primary and secondary uses of Verbs, Nouns, and Adjectives in FG

	Predicative function	Head of a term	Attributive function
V	*Primary use*	Deverbal nominalization or conversion	Relativization/participialization
N	Copula support	*Primary use*	Compounding/adjectivalization
A	Copula support	Deadjectival nominalization or conversion	*Primary use*

Dik also emphasizes (1989: 195) that not all languages will necessarily distinguish all three categories. If there is a language in which no category is primarily used in attributive function, the category A will be indistinguishable from V, and Dik speculates that Bahasa Indonesia may be such a language; if there is a language in which no primary use of predicates can be discerned, then it would have no categories of predicate at all, and the suggestion is made that Salish languages may come close to this. The three pillars of Dik's view, in summary, are that predicates should be categorized in terms of their primary function, secondary functions are possible, and languages differ in how many of the three categories they display.

Dik's approach to lexical categories was developed by Hengeveld, still within the framework of FG. Building on Dik's analysis of terms as involving the *variable* (x), Hengeveld (1992b: 51-55) proposes to provide each predicate with its own variable, (f) (cf. (4)-(5) and (8)-(9) in section 10.2). This is justified by the fact that a predicate can serve as an antecedent for anaphoric reference, as in (11) and (12), where *which* and *so* refer back to the predicates *intelligent* and *fall*, respectively:

(11)   John is intelligent, which you are not.
(12)   John fell, and so did I.

Under this proposal, (2) would now appear as (13):

(13)　(Past e_i:
　　　　　　$[(f_i: kiss_V (f_i))$
　　　　　　　　$(d1x_i: (f_j: girl_N (f_j)) (x_i))_{AgFoc}$
　　　　　　　　$(d1x_j: (f_k: boy_N (f_k)) (x_j):$
　　　　　　　　　　$(f_l: attractive_A (f_l))$
　　　　　　　　$(x_j))_{GoSubjTop}$
　　　(e_i))

Note that—in the spirit of the above-mentioned layering (Hengeveld 1989)—the entire predication also has its own variable (e).

Among a number of advantages of this proposal is that Hengeveld was able to treat the relation between adverbs (of a certain type) and verbs in parallel with the relation between adjectives and nouns, i.e. seeing both as modifier–head relations. His specific proposal (1992b: 55) is shown in (14), where α = variable over different variables, including (x) and (e):

(14)　　　　Head　　　　　　　　　Modifier
　　　　$(f_1:$　verb　　　　　　$(f_1):$　$(f_2: adverb (f_2))$　$(f_1))$
　　　　$(\alpha_1:$　$(f_3: noun (f_3)))$　$(\alpha_1):$　$(f_4: adjective (f_4))$　$(\alpha_1))$

This allows him to propose a four-way categorization of predicates (1992b: 58):

(15)　a.　A *verbal* predicate is a predicate which, without further measures being taken, has a predicative use *only*.
　　　b.　A *nominal* predicate is a predicate which, without further measures being taken, can be used as the head of a term.
　　　c.　An *adjectival* predicate is a predicate which, without further measures being taken, can be used as a modifier of a nominal head.
　　　d.　An *adverbial* predicate is a predicate which, without further measures being taken, can be used as a modifier of a non-nominal head.

The expression 'without further measures being taken' refers to the various processes already alluded to in Table 10.1, such as the formation of a relative clause: in *the attractive boy*, *attractive* is an Adjective that modifies the nominal head *boy*; in *the boy who was attractive*, the modifier in bold print results from the 'further measure' of introducing the relative pronoun; in addition, the adjective *attractive* here occurs in predicative use, which calls for another 'further measure', the introduction of the copula (*was*). Notice, too, that the definitions accord a special status to verbs: whereas all four categories in (14) are explicitly shown as predicates, the characteristic feature of verbs is that they—again without further measures being taken—can only be predicates. The main novelties of Hengeveld's (1992b) approach, then, are the generalization of the structure Dik (1989) proposed for terms to all types of lexical predicate, the expansion of the theory to include adverbs, and the aforementioned special status of the verb.

10.4 LEXEME CLASSES AND WORD CLASSES IN FDG

Many of the proposals in Hengeveld (1992b) have been adopted, *mutatis mutandis,* into FDG (Hengeveld & Mackenzie 2008). Notably, the structural template shown in (16) is applied throughout the grammar, at the Interpersonal, Representational, Morphosyntactic, and Phonological Levels respectively (IL, RL, ML, and PL):[2]

(16) $(\pi \alpha_n: h (\alpha_n): \sigma (\alpha_n))$, where α = some variable, h = head, σ = modifier, π = operator

Operators (π) were already present in FG, cf. 'Past' in (2), but in FDG they are generalized to all layers of the IL, RL, and PL. Operators are abstract elements that have consequences at later stages in the dynamic implementation of the model: operators at IL and RL, for example, trigger elements at ML and PL.

As for parts of speech, FDG draws a distinction, as mentioned in the introduction, between lexeme classes and word classes (Hengeveld & Mackenzie 2008: 217). The *lexeme classes* correspond to FG's four-way categorization of predicates in (15), i.e. V, N, Adj, and Adv.[3] These now apply, indicated as a subscript, to lexemes, so that the lexeme shown in (3), when classified as a Noun, will appear as follows:

(17) $\$_{1032}$ | /pɔːtʃ/$_N$

The class of a lexeme is determined functionally, in the sense that it correlates, in ways to be explained below, with its positioning at IL and RL.

As mentioned, FDG is a grammar of the Discourse Act, and it is at the Interpersonal Level that the Discourse Act is represented. A core component of the Discourse Act is its Communicated Content, which in turn consists of a number of Subacts. FDG recognizes two types of Subact: the Subact of Reference (R_1), realized in encoding as a referential expression, and the Subact of Ascription (T_1), which is the Speaker's attempt to evoke a property. The definitions of the four lexeme classes are then as follows (Hengeveld & Mackenzie 2008: 219), where an f-unit is any segment of an RL representation that has the variable (f):

(18) a. Verb: head of an f-unit that is used as an independent Ascriptive Subact
 b. Noun: head of an f-unit that is the head of a representational unit that is used as a Referential Subact
 c. Adjective: head of an f-unit that is a modifier of an f-unit that is the head of a representational unit that is used as a Referential Subact
 d. Adverb: head of an f-unit that is a modifier of an f-unit that is used as an independent Ascriptive Subact

---

[2] However, in the current development of the theory no need has been established for operators at ML or for modifiers at ML and PL.

[3] Hengeveld & Mackenzie (2008: 224–225) later add a further lexeme class Adposition, but this class plays no part in the FDG typology of lexeme class systems and will not be further examined here; see Mackenzie (2013) for discussion.

These very precise but cumbersome definitions can be reduced to the following shorthand:

(19) a. Verb: head within an independent Ascriptive Subact
b. Noun: head within a Referential Subact
c. Adjective: modifier within a Referential Subact
d. Adverb: modifier within an independent Ascriptive Subact[4]

These definitions can be seen at work in (20):

(20) a. The tall girl sings well. (Hengeveld & Mackenzie 2008: 219-220)
b. IL: $(C_I: [\quad (T_I) \quad (+id\ R_I)] \quad (C_I))$
RL: $(Pres\ e_i: (f_i: [(f_j: sing_V\ (f_j): (f_k: well_{Adv}\ (f_k))\ (f_j))\ (1x_i: (f_l: girl_N\ (f_l))\ (x_i): (f_m: tall_{Adj}\ (f_m))\ (x_i))_{Ag}]\ (f_i))\ (e_i))$

What we see in (20b) is that *sing* is head of the f-unit (f_j) and that it corresponds to an independent Subact of Ascription (T_I) (i.e. one that is not part of a higher Subact) and thus qualifies as a Verb; *girl*, as head of the f-unit (f_l) that itself is head of the x-unit (x_i) and corresponds to a Subact of Reference (R_I), qualifies as a Noun; *tall* is head of the f-unit (f_m) and modifies a lexical property (f_l) whose head is a Noun and thus qualifies as an Adjective; and *well* is head of the f-unit (f_k) and modifies a lexical property (f_j) whose head is a Verb and thus qualifies as an Adverb.

Example (20a) shows default correspondences, equivalent to the 'primary uses' shown in Table 10.1. Where a lexeme Noun enters into a non-default correspondence with what is functionally a Subact of Ascription, as with *girl* in *The captain of the team is a girl*, this non-default line-up is what, in English and other languages, triggers the insertion of the copula *be* at the Morphosyntactic Level. Where a Verb corresponds to a Subact of Reference, the 'problem' is rectified through a nominalization of the verb at the Representational Level, as in *The tall girl is a good singer*, which restores the default correspondence of Noun (*singer*) and Subact of Reference; and so on for other non-default correspondences.

Here is where languages can differ, however. If in some language one and the same item can occur without any morphosyntactic repercussions as the head of a Referential Subact, as a modifier within a Referential Subact and as a modifier within an Ascriptive Subact, then that language lacks any distinction between Noun, Adjective, and Adverb. Such a language is Warao (Romero-Figueroa 1997: 21, 50, 119; Hengeveld & Mackenzie 2008: 225-228), in which the word *yakera* can best be classified as, lexically, a Non-Verb:

(21) a. *Ka-asiraha   hebere-mioroi   yakera   oko   nona-te.*
1PL.POSS-evil   get.rid.of-in.order.to   goodness   1PL   do-NONPST
'We should do goodness in order to get rid of our evil.'

b. *Hiaka   yakera   auka   saba   tai   nisa-n-a-e.*
garment   goodness   daughter   for   3SG.F   buy-SG-PUNCT-PST
'She bought a beautiful dress for her daughter.'

---

[4] Please note that Adverb is here used in the sense of manner adverb.

c. *Oko   kuana   yaota-te   arone   yakera   nahoro-te, ...*
   1PL   hardness   work-NONPST   although   goodness   eat-NONPST
   'Although we work hard and eat well, ...'

We shall return to this matter in section 10.5, but let us now briefly return to *word classes*. In FDG, word classes (as opposed to lexeme classes) pertain at the Morphosyntactic Level and are determined morphosyntactically rather than functionally. Consider the case of Adjectives and Adverbs in Dutch: in the fund, they are not distinguished, since one and the same set of lexemes (e.g. *goed* 'good, well') can be used to modify Verbs or Nouns:

(22) a. *Het   lang-e   meisje   zing-t   goed.*
        DEF.NEUT   long-ATTR   girl   sing-3SG   good
        'The tall girl sings well.'

    b. *Het   goed-e   meisje   zing-t   lang.*
       DEF.NEUT   good-ATTR   girl   sing-3SG   > long
       'The good girl sings for a long time.'

Note, however, that the attributive, Noun-modifying (i.e. Adjectival) use—with the exception of neuter nouns used in indefinite Subacts—is marked by the suffix *-e* and by its syntactic position. Morphosyntactically, then, Dutch makes a distinction between the word classes Adjective word (Adjw) and Adverb word (Advw) but lexically it does not distinguish between the lexeme classes Adjective and Adverb and is accordingly analysed as having the lexeme classes Noun, Verb, and Modifier.[5] Similarly, in Warao (see ex. (21)) there is a syntactic distinction of word classes, each with its own positional characteristics, with *yakera* appearing as a Noun word (Nw) in (21a), as an Adjw in (21b), and as an Advw in (21c).

It should further be noted that just as languages can differ in their lexeme classes, so they also have different sets of word classes. Such word classes as 'complementizer', 'auxiliary verb', 'negator', 'coordinator', 'particle' are > language-specific. They come about as a result of morphosyntactic operations that are triggered by non-lexical features of the Interpersonal and Representational Levels such as functions and operators or by non-default correspondences between the levels of the type discussed above. Whereas lexeme classes are a feature of the fund that feeds formulation, word classes are found among the primitives that feed morphosyntactic encoding (Genee, Keizer, & García Velasco 2016). To use one of the authors' examples (2016: 888), among these primitives in a grammar of English there will be a word class Determiner (Detw) which has specific positional characteristics within the Noun phrase and whose members express different groupings of operators at IL and RL; this contrasts with the word class Nw (= Noun word), which corresponds to the lexeme class N(oun), but differs in being inflectable:

---

[5] Note that in a functional approach to parts of speech it is acceptable to have a lexeme class that names its function.

(23) (*I like*) *these bananas*
   IL (+id R$_I$)
   RL (prox m x$_i$: [(f$_i$: banana$_N$ (f$_i$))] (x$_i$))$_U$
   ML (Np$_i$: [Detw$_i$: this-PL (Detw$_i$)) (Nw$_i$: /bəˈnænə/-PL (Nw$_i$))] (Np$_i$))$_{Obj}$
   PL (PP$_i$: [(pw$_i$: /ði:z/ (pw$_i$)) (pw$_j$: /bəˈnænəz/ (pw$_j$))] (PP$_i$))

10.5 Typology of languages as differentiated, flexible, or rigid

A language in which all four lexeme classes are distinguished is described in FDG as *differentiated*. English is arguably such a language, as exemplified in (20). However, not all languages are differentiated in this sense. Languages are accordingly typologized in FDG for how many lexeme classes they distinguish. We saw above that Dutch distinguishes Verb, Noun, and Modifier and that Warao only distinguishes two lexeme classes, Verb and Non-Verb, with Non-Verbs appearing as Nw, Adjw, or Advw in morphosyntax; such languages are said to be *flexible*, with the most extreme flexibility occurring in languages that do not distinguish lexeme classes at all and where all lexemes are simply Contentives.[6] There is another type of language which lacks lexeme classes with certain functions, e.g. a language that has no class of Adverb lexemes associated with the function 'modifier within an independent Ascriptive Subact'. In such languages, the manner in which an action is executed can only be indicated by means of a circumlocution such as *in an* Adj *manner*. Languages that lack one or more lexeme classes associated with a function are said to be *rigid*. On this basis, it is possible to categorize languages into seven types, as shown in Table 10.2.

Table 10.2 Lexeme class systems

Lexeme class systems	Type	Head within Ascriptive Subact	Head within Referential Subact	Modifier within Referential Subact	Modifier within Ascriptive Subact
1		Contentive			
2	FLEXIBLE	Verb	Non-Verb		
3		Verb	Noun	Modifier	
4	DIFFERENTIATED	Verb	Noun	Adjective	Adverb
5		Verb	Noun	Adjective	
6	RIGID	Verb	Noun		
7		Verb			

Source: Hengeveld & Mackenzie (2008: 228).

---

[6] Note that Contentive, Non-verb, and Modifier are proposed as new lexeme classes whose properties cannot be reduced to any of the traditional classes.

An example of a system-6 rigid language is the Tibeto-Karen language Garo (Burling 1961: 27; Hengeveld & Mackenzie 2008: 226), which has neither Adverbs nor Adjectives. Modification within a Referential Act therefore has to be expressed by means of a relative clause, as in (24):

(24) da'r-gipa   man.de
     be.big-REL   man
     'the man who "bigs", the big man'

In FDG, languages that have only one lexeme class are thus not lumped together but represent two maximally distinct systems, 1 and 7. In system 1, each lexeme can, without any further measures being taken, play any role, as Head or Modifier in either a Referential or an Ascriptive Subact, while in system 7, there are only Verbs, and to take on a function other than Head within an Ascriptive Subact they require special marking; analogous considerations allow the typology to distinguish between systems 2 and 6, and systems 3 and 5. Finally, note that Table 10.2 yields an implicational hierarchy that applies across the division into flexible, differentiated, and rigid languages: the further to the left a function stands, the more likely it is for a language to have a separate class of lexemes realizing that function:

(25) Head within Ascriptive Subact < Head within Referential Subact < Modifier within Referential Subact < Modifier within Ascriptive Subact

The systematization presented in Table 10.2 represents seven 'ideal types'. In practice, many languages do not fully conform, and the approach therefore recognizes intermediate systems, which show characteristics of two contiguous systems. For example, although English was initially classified above as differentiated on the basis of the data in (20), it is better seen as belonging to intermediate system 3/4, since the great majority of manner adverbs are formed by suffixation of *-ly*; *well* is unusual in being lexically classified as an Adverb. Hengeveld et al. (2004) observe that Mundari is a system-1 language for its basic lexemes but also has derived lexemes that are non-verbs and therefore treat it as 1/2; and they classify Pipil, which lacks native manner adverbs but has borrowed some from Spanish, as 4/5.

The value of the FDG systematization of lexeme classes is that it serves as a basic typological determinant (Hengeveld 2013). This has, above all, implications for flexible languages, where the language must ensure that the hearer can identify the function of each lexeme in a clause. Let us now consider various predictions that flow from the classification of languages as flexible, differentiated, or rigid.

10.5.1 Word order and morphological marking

Given the need to ensure identifiable functions, it is to be expected that flexible languages will prefer a fixed word order, i.e. flexibility in the fund will be compensated by rigidity in syntax. In rigid languages, by contrast, where identifiability of parts of speech is not an issue, word order is expected to be freer. This hypothesis was tested by Hengeveld, Rijkhoff, &

Siewierska (2004), with the specific prediction that highly flexible languages will use word order to safeguard the identifiability of the main predicate, avoiding clause-medial placement and preferring the more salient initial or final position; indeed, no language of systems 1 to 2/3 was found in the sample that used medial position for the predicate. Where flexible languages allow variation in word order, special morphological markers are inserted to indicate the deviation. Rigid languages were, as expected, found to display greater word order freedom, with a tendency not to mark non-basic word orders morphologically. For the functions of Modifier within the Referential Subact and Modifier within the Ascriptive Subact, the tendency towards fixed word order among flexible languages was even stronger.

10.5.2 Morphological types

In flexible languages, one and the same lexeme is used in more than one of the functions identified in Table 10.2. It may be expected, then, that such lexemes will resist such operations as morphologically conditioned stem alternation, which decrease its applicability across different functions. What is meant here is a change to the phonological form of a stem that is conditioned by non-phonological factors, as in English ablaut in *see* vs *saw* or cases of stem suppletion, for example where the stem varies according to the inflectional category that has to be expressed, e.g. French *all-er* 'go-INF' vs *ir-ai* 'go-1.SG.FUT'. Hengeveld (2007) tests this hypothesis against a sample of languages ranging across all seven systems and finds it to be corroborated; the conclusion is that verbs are 'the most likely candidates for stem alternation, followed by nouns, adjectives, and, trivially, manner adverbs' (2007: 46).

Connectedly, the need for flexible languages to have identifiable stems predisposes them to resist fusional morphology and to favour either the isolating or the agglutinative type, in which the stem never changes. Another corollary is that highly flexible languages will lack conjugation and declension classes, i.e. lexical sets of stems that intrinsically require different expression of inflections, since these would undermine the freedom of the stem to take on different functions. Hengeveld & Valstar (2010) examined this in a sample of languages ranging across all seven systems and found that intrinsic conjugation classes are absent from languages with systems 1 or 1/2 and that intrinsic declination classes are not found in languages with systems 1 to 3. As yet unexplained is their additional finding that both intrinsic conjugation and declination classes are only found in differentiated languages.

10.5.3 Dependent clauses

Hengeveld & van Lier (2010a) examine possible correlations between the typology of lexeme class systems and the range of dependent clauses available in a language. They draw a direct parallel between the four functions of lexemes and four types of dependent clause; see Table 10.3.

Table 10.3 Typology of dependent clauses

Function	Type of dependent clause	Example (segment in bold)
1. Head within Ascriptive Subact	Predicate clause	To hesitate is **to lose**.
2. Head within Referential Subact	Complement clause	The man regrets **that the boy is ill**.
3. Modifier within Referential Subact	Relative clause	the man **who saw the boy**
4. Modifier within Ascriptive Subact	Adverbial manner clause	The man walked out **stamping his feet**.

Source: Hengeveld & van Lier (2010a).

A dependent clause (or the strategy for forming it) will show flexibility if one and the same form can fulfil more than one of the functions in Table 10.3. Thus, in Turkish, a clause formed with the suffix -AcAK can be used as a complement clause or a relative clause (i.e. functions 2–3). Hengeveld & van Lier hypothesize that three types of flexibility will be found: 2–3–4, 2–3, 3–4, and three types of rigidity: 2, 3, and 4. The hypothesis they examine is that a language will use the same strategies for expressing functions with dependent clauses as they do with lexemes. This hypothesis, specifically that flexible languages allow (rather than require) flexible dependent clauses and that rigid languages allow rigid dependent clauses, is reasonably well borne out in the sample of 23 languages. Those rigid languages that do have flexible dependent clauses are shown to distinguish their functions through other means, morphological marking or word order.

10.5.4 Towards greater typological adequacy: A two-dimensional hierarchy

During the testing of the seven lexeme class systems distinguished in Table 10.2 (which had their origin in Hengeveld 1992b) and the additional six intermediate systems it became apparent that certain flexible languages showed types of multifunctionality that were at odds with the hypothesis. Languages like Hungarian have 'nominals', a class of lexemes that can be used (only) as the Head or Modifier of a Referential Subact, while languages like Kayardild have 'predicatives', a class of lexemes that can be used (only) as the Head or Modifier of an Ascriptive Subact (although only in combination with non-verbs). In addition, languages like Garo have a rigid system without Adjectives but with Adverbs. These exceptions to the systematization are accounted for by Hengeveld & van Lier (2010b) by replacing the single implicational hierarchy mentioned in section 10.5 with a pair of functionally justified implicational hierarchies:

(26) a. Predication < Reference (i.e. Ascriptive Subact < Referential Subact)
      b. Head < Modifier

(26a) is justified by the fact that Reference presupposes Predication/Ascription (since you cannot refer to an entity without naming properties) and (26b) by the fact that Heads are obligatory while Modifiers are optional. Separating hierarchy (25) out into two, as in (26), has the advantage that the exceptions evaporate and that a new 10-system constellation emerges, as shown in Table 10.4. Note that differentiated systems are now reanalysed as rigid (since they lack any flexibility).[7]

Table 10.4 Revised overview of lexeme class systems

Lexeme class systems	Type	Head within Ascriptive Subact	Head within Referential Subact	Modifier within Referential Subact	Modifier within Ascriptive Subact	Example languages
1	FLEXIBLE	Contentive				Samoan, Kambera, Santali, Kharia, Tagalog
2		Verb	Non-Verb			Quechua, Turkish
3		Verb	Noun	Modifier		Lango, Abun, Dutch, German
4		Predicative	Non-Verb		Predicative	Kayardild
5		Verb	Nominal		Adverb	Ma'di, Hungarian
6	RIGID	Verb	Noun	Adjective	Adverb	Basque, Abkhaz, Georgian
7		Verb	Noun	Adjective		Mandarin, Pipil
8		Verb	Noun		Adverb	Garo
9		Verb	Noun			Krongo
10		Verb				Tuscarora, Hupa

10.5.5 Summary

Summarizing the preceding sections, it may be concluded that flexible language systems (see Rijkhoff & van Lier 2013 for further details and refinements) tend to (i) be predicate-initial or predicate-final; (ii) be either agglutinative or isolating; (iii) have lexemes that are not inherently specified for conjugation or declination class; and (iv) be flexible across all layers of morphosyntactic analysis. Generalizations over rigid language systems are less systematic.

---

[7] In response to Hengeveld & van Lier (2010b), Mauri (2010) suggests that, additionally, 'a flexible class may only occur in ... functions which are contiguous', a suggestion to which the authors respond favourably.

10.6 Impact on language typology

In terms of the familiar contrast between 'splitters' and 'lumpers', the FDG approach to the categorization of lexeme classes clearly falls into the latter category. The focus is on the 'big picture' and the insights it can deliver. Croft (2000: 67), himself generally a defender of 'splitting' within functional approaches, finds Hengeveld's (1992b) analysis, which grew into the FDG view, to be 'perhaps the most sophisticated "lumping" approach' as well as the 'most detailed and systematic'; Bisang (2015: 560), in his survey of the field, finds Croft's and Hengeveld's approaches to be 'the most thorough accounts of parts of speech from a universal perspective'. A more critical view is taken by Evans (2000: 728-729), who takes issue with three aspects of the Hengeveld approach: (i) the questionable empirical justification for some of the language-specific analyses that underlie the systematization; (ii) the insecure theoretical justification for the pride of place given to Verb, in the light of languages with highly restricted classes of verb; (iii) the danger of brushing over the distinctions between different types of highly rigid language (system 10 in Table 10.4), e.g. Tagalog as more nominal and Straits Salish as more verbal.[8]

The Hengeveld/FDG view sparked off a flurry of articles in the journal *Linguistic Typology* and elsewhere, specifically with regard to Mundari, classified as a system-1, i.e. maximally flexible, language. Evans & Osada (2005: 357) claim that Mundari 'makes wide use of zero conversion' and that such conversion adds unpredictable meaning elements that justify assuming separate input and output lexemes that belong to different classes. Hengeveld & Rijkhoff (2005) retort that the flexible lexemes have a single, vague sense, different aspects of which are highlighted or downplayed in each syntactic context.

Don & van Lier (2013) take a third position, arguing that the semantic shifts undergone by flexible lexemes in Mundari are in fact fully compositional. Their central claim aligns with the FDG distinction between lexemes (as units of formulation) and words (as units of encoding), arguing that in flexible languages derivational relationships do not involve categorization into lexeme classes: 'syntactic categorization occurs only at the phrase-structural level' (2013: 57), i.e. at the Morphosyntactic Level of FDG. In differentiated and rigid languages, things are quite different: here derivations are lexical and carry over from formulation into encoding.

10.7 Conclusion

The FDG approach to parts of speech, with its distinction between lexeme classes and word classes, reflects its commitment to relating function to form. The class of a lexeme follows from its interpersonal and representational functions while the class of a word follows from

---

[8] Note, however, that FDG sees Tagalog as maximally flexible (system 1 in Table 10.4), and thus does not disregard how its structure differs from maximally rigid languages.

its morphosyntactic properties. In recent years this architecture has stimulated interest in the interfaces among the various levels of the grammar, distinguishing default correspondences and mismatches. Future years will likely witness further work on the 'special measures' taken by rigid languages to signal the presence of mismatches (see García Velasco & Contreras García 2021).

Acknowledgements

My sincere thanks go to Evelien Keizer, Kees Hengeveld, and Eva van Lier, as well as to two anonymous reviewers, for their invaluable comments on earlier drafts of this chapter.

CHAPTER 11

WORD CLASSES IN RADICAL CONSTRUCTION GRAMMAR

WILLIAM CROFT

11.1 INTRODUCTION

RADICAL Construction Grammar (Croft 2001; 2005a; 2013) is a construction-based theory of grammar that allows for the representation of both cross-linguistic and language-internal grammatical diversity. Radical Construction Grammar analyses conform to the following three basic principles:

(1) Word classes and other syntactic structures are language-specific and construction-specific. What is universal (see section 11.5) is patterns of variation in the verbalization of experience, represented for example in conceptual space.
(2) The internal structure of the morphosyntactic form of constructions consists solely of the part–whole relation between construction roles ('slots') and the whole construction. The complexity of constructions rests in the symbolic relations between the roles and their meanings/functions, and the rich semantic/functional structure expressed by the construction and its parts.
(3) The morphosyntactic forms of constructions are language-specific; that is, there is potentially gradient variation of constructional form across and within languages.

Radical Construction Grammar (Croft 2001) and *Morphosyntax: Constructions of the World's Languages* (Croft 2022a) propose many specific analyses of constructions and universals of constructional variation. Apart from those analyses, any analysis that conforms to the principles in (1)–(3) can be considered a Radical Construction Grammar analysis. Many if not most analyses of grammatical phenomena in the functional–typological approach conform to the principles of Radical Construction Grammar (although they are not always presented that way).

These three principles result from the observation of the great diversity of morphosyntactic form used to verbalize experiences within and across languages. They also result from a critique of methods of syntactic argumentation used in contemporary grammatical analyses that have their roots in the structuralist and generative traditions (for general overviews, see Croft 2009a; 2010a; for critiques of specific analyses, see those references and Croft 2005b; 2007a; 2010b; Croft & van Lier 2012).

These assumptions involve deeply held—often unconsciously held—theoretical principles that clash with the empirical fact of diversity of grammatical form. Word classes are a classic illustration of this problem, and constitute the focus of this chapter as well as many of the publications cited above. Word classes play a quite different role in Radical Construction Grammar than they do in other grammatical theories. For this reason, after an initial discussion of word classes in Radical Construction Grammar in sections 11.2–11.3, I will discuss the role of word classes in other grammatical theories in sections 11.4–11.7, and the theoretical assumptions they serve: methodological opportunism, the skeleton model of language universals, the building block model of grammars, and the essentialist theory of categories. In sections 11.7–11.9, I describe the role of word classes in a theory like Radical Construction Grammar that does not make these theoretical assumptions.

11.2 WORD CLASSES AND DISTRIBUTIONAL ANALYSIS

Word classes are identified by distributional analysis. For example, English Adjectives[1] such as *tall* are defined by:

(i) their occurrence as modifiers of nouns: *a **tall** tree*
(ii) their occurrence as the complement of a copula *be* in predication: *That tree **is tall***
(iii) the fact that they inflect in a certain way (a morphological construction): *tall-er, tall-est*
(iv) the fact that they can in turn be modified by certain degree expressions: ***very** tall, **a little** tall*).

In contrast, English Verbs such as *jump* are defined by:

(i) their inflection for Tense and (in the Present) person in predication: *The deer **jumped***
(ii) their occurrence in a relative clause as modifiers of nouns: *the deer **that** jumped*
(iii) the fact that they can occur in the Progressive or the Pluperfect: *the deer **is** jumping; the deer **had** jumped*
(iv) the fact that they can in turn be modified by certain other degree expressions: *the deer was jumping **a lot**.*

At least as important is distributional absence. English Adjectives do not inflect for Tense and Person (*That tree talls), nor can they directly occur in the Progressive or Pluperfect (**That tree had talled*). English Verbs do not inflect for degree with *-er/-est* (**jump-er,* *jump-est), nor can they be modified by *very* (**The deer very jumped*). English Verbs cannot

---

[1] In this chapter, names of word classes in specific languages are capitalized; see section 11.8.

occur in their inflected or root form as modifiers of nouns (*The jumped deer was a doe). These distributional facts, occurrence and non-occurrence, distinguish English Adjectives from English Verbs.

This type of argumentation, DISTRIBUTIONAL ANALYSIS, is universally used in syntactic argumentation for word classes, and for other morphosyntactic units, in structuralist, generative, functional, and 'theory-neutral' analysis of a language. In the American structuralist tradition, distributional analysis was based purely on linguistic form. In other traditions, including generative grammar and typology, meaning or function may also play a role in defining constructions used in distributional analysis. The distribution of English Adjectives above makes reference to degree expressions, a category partly defined by meaning, and the *be* of predication, as opposed to other functions of *be*.

Distributional analysis is essentially OCCURRENCE IN A PARTICULAR ROLE IN A PARTICULAR CONSTRUCTION. For example, the distribution of English Adjectives described above can be defined as the occurrence of a word in the English Adjective word class in the underlined role in the following constructions:

(i) Noun Modification (Attributive): [Art __ Noun]
(ii) Copula Predication: [Sbj *be* __]
(iii) Comparative Degree, Superlative Degree: [__-*er*], [__-*est*]
(iv) Degree Modification: [*very/a little* __]

'Construction' is defined as in contemporary construction grammar (Fillmore, Kay, & O'Connor 1988; Goldberg 1995; Croft & Cruse 2004): any morphosyntactic structure, complex or atomic (like a single word), syntactic or morphological (occurrence with an affix or other morphological operation), with elements of the construction being either substantive morphemes (like *be*, *-er*, or *a little*) or schematic elements (like Art, Noun, Sbj).

The definition given above acknowledges the role of constructions in distributional analysis—something which is not generally done. The constructions used to define word classes are called many different things instead of constructions: 'criteria' (Givón 2001: 49; Dixon 2010b: 38), 'tests' (McCawley 1998; Carnie 2013: 47, 98–100), 'evidence', 'phenomena', 'operation', and 'process' (Mulder 1994: 114). The words in a word class are said to have a particular grammatical or syntactic 'distribution' (Harris 1951: 5; Carnie 2013: 47), 'behaviour' (McCawley 1998: 186), 'properties' (McCawley 1998: 18; Evans & Osada 2005: 452; Schachter & Shopen 2007: 2), 'features' (Amha 2001: 89), 'use' (Jagersma 2010: 268), or 'function' (Palmer 2009: 94), instead of simply saying that they occur in certain roles in certain constructions and not in others. As a result, an important point is often overlooked: DISTRIBUTIONAL ANALYSIS PRESUPPOSES THE PRIOR IDENTIFICATION OF THE CONSTRUCTIONS USED IN DISTRIBUTIONAL ANALYSIS.

One consequence of the use of distributional analysis to identify word classes (and other grammatical categories and structures) is that DISTRIBUTIONALLY DEFINED WORD CLASSES ARE LANGUAGE-SPECIFIC. The simple reason for this is that such word classes are defined by their occurrence in a particular role in a particular construction (or set of constructions), and those constructions are language-specific. English Adjectives do not occur in German constructions, and German Adjectives do not occur in English constructions. Although this property of word classes appears to be self-evident, it is in fact a highly contentious issue, because it is incompatible with certain assumptions about language universals and individual language grammars. This issue will be discussed in sections 11.3–11.5.

Distributional analysis usually involves occurrence of forms in roles in multiple different constructions. In fact, it is usually considered a stronger argument for a particular theoretical analysis if one can argue for the same distribution in multiple constructions. However, a fundamental empirical fact of languages is that DIFFERENT CONSTRUCTIONS DEFINE DIFFERENT DISTRIBUTIONS. That is, the class of words defined by occurrence in a certain role in one construction is almost always different from the class of words defined by occurrence in a certain role in another construction (Croft 2001: 34–36). For example, the four constructions used to define English Adjectives above define slightly different classes, as can be seen in the problematic cases below:

(4) *Modification of a referent:*
 a. This insect is alive.
 b. * an alive insect

(5) *Predication with a copula:*
 a. An entire chapter is devoted to this problem.
 b. * This chapter is entire.

(6) *Degree inflections:*
 a. tall-er, tall-est
 b. * intelligent-er, *intelligent-est

(7) *Degree modifiers:*
 a. a very tall tree
 b. *a very even number

In other words, the different constructions in (4)–(7) do not define a single word class of English Adjectives. Instead, they define a set of distinct but overlapping word classes.

These empirical observations were made by the American structuralists, who provide the most explicit and careful methodological discussion of distributional analysis. For example, Bloomfield writes, 'Form-classes are not mutually exclusive, but cross each other and overlap and are included one within the other, and so on' (1933: 269). And Harris writes, 'If we seek to form classes of morphemes such that all the morphemes in a particular class will have identical distributions, we will frequently achieve little success' (1951: 244). In a very large grammar of French containing 600 rules covering 12,000 lexical items, no two lexical items had exactly the same distribution, and no two rules (that is, constructions) had exactly the same domain of application (Gross 1979: 859–860).

Hence, a consequence of the careful application of distributional analysis to word classes within a single language is that WORD CLASSES ARE ALSO CONSTRUCTION-SPECIFIC. This conclusion is at least as contentious as the conclusion that word classes are language-specific, because it is incompatible with other deeply or unconsciously held assumptions about the nature of individual language grammars. This issue will be discussed in greater detail in sections 11.6–11.7.

11.3 WORD CLASSES AND COMPARATIVE CONCEPTS

If word classes are language-specific, then they cannot play the role in Radical Construction Grammar that word classes play in other grammatical theories. In other grammatical theories, word classes form the basis for a significant set of language universals. For those theories, word classes must be comparable across languages: that is, one should be able to treat English Adjectives and Lango Adjectives as instances of a cross-linguistic category of 'adjective', which has certain universal properties associated with it.

In such an approach, it makes sense to ask the question: does a particular language have adjectives or not? But this approach—word classes as cross-linguistic categories—is incompatible with distributionally defined word classes. In a strictly distributional definition of word classes, this question makes no sense. Word classes are defined by their occurrence in a particular role in a particular construction in a particular language. Hence a word class must be language-specific, as noted in section 11.2. English Numerals are defined by their occurrence in the relevant slot in the English Numeral Modification Construction [__ N(-PL)]. Lahu Numerals do not occur in the English Numeral Modification Construction. Conversely, English Numerals do not occur in the Lahu Numeral Modification Construction.

For this reason, Radical Construction Grammar, in concert with a number of typologists (most recently, Dryer 1997a and Haspelmath 2010, but also many earlier typologists including Greenberg, as will be seen below), posits a different type of theoretical entity, which Haspelmath (2010) has christened a COMPARATIVE CONCEPT. A comparative concept, unlike a distributionally defined word class, is defined on a cross-linguistically valid basis.

The simplest type of comparative concept is a semantic or pragmatic concept; here we will call it a FUNCTIONAL COMPARATIVE CONCEPT. For example, a property, in the sense of a unary valency, stable, inherent, gradable category, such as age, dimension, and value (Dixon 1977), is a functional comparative concept. Words denoting property concepts can be identified in any language, and compared across languages. Functional comparative concepts were introduced into typology by Greenberg in his seminal paper on word order typology (1966: 74).

Comparative concepts that are more interesting for typologists are those that combine both function and grammatical form (Haspelmath 2010). These can be called HYBRID COMPARATIVE CONCEPTS (Croft 2016a). Hybrid comparative concepts are possible because there are certain formal traits that can be cross-linguistically defined, i.e. not with respect to distributional occurrence in a role in a language-specific construction. For example, the order of elements, such as Adjective–Noun order in English vs Noun–Adjective order in Zuni, is a cross-linguistically defined formal property. Another cross-linguistically defined formal property is zero vs overt coding of a semantic category, such as zero coding of singular number in English vs overt coding of singular number in Lithuanian. It is worth noting that cross-linguistically valid formal traits in morphosyntax always involve a functional category in their definition (Croft 2009: 161–162). For example, the order of elements requires a functional definition of the elements that occur in that order, in our example the Adjective and Noun categories; and zero vs overt coding is always coding of some semantic category.

Two types of hybrid comparative concepts are widely used in typology. The first is a CONSTRUCTION (Croft 2014; 2016a). A construction is a pairing of form and meaning/function, as in Construction Grammar (see section 11.2). A construction as a comparative concept in typology is generally a construction that expresses a particular function. For example, a study of the typology of the 'passive construction' (Siewierska 1985) or the typology of 'intransitive predication constructions' (Stassen 1997) covers any morphosyntactic form that encodes the relevant function. A construction contrasts with a functional comparative concept, which is just the function, although the function serves as the basis for identifying form–function pairings that are instances of the construction.

The second widely used type of comparative concept in typology is a STRATEGY (Croft 2014; 2016a; the term is used early in modern typology; cf. Keenan & Comrie 1977; Givón 1979). A strategy is a construction that expresses a particular function with a particular cross-linguistically valid formal trait. For example, property modification can be expressed with a prenominal strategy (Adjective–Noun) or a postnominal strategy (Noun–Adjective).

Of course, constructions and strategies are broad categories subsuming many hybrid comparative concepts, just as there are many different functional comparative concepts. More specific comparative concepts, such as 'numeral modification construction' or 'prenominal modifier strategy', have been defined by typologists. Haspelmath (2010) suggests that comparative concepts are created by typologists for their 'usefulness'. But their 'usefulness' is ultimately founded on an empirical basis, namely the existence of language universals that require the relevant comparative concepts to be formulated, such as Greenberg's Universal 18: 'When the descriptive adjective precedes the noun, the demonstrative and the numeral, with overwhelmingly more than chance frequency, do likewise' (Greenberg 1966: 86; see also Croft 2019).

11.4 Cross-linguistic word classes and methodological opportunism

Comparative concepts are not word classes—that is, they are not distributionally defined in terms of roles in language-specific constructions. However, word classes play an important role in other grammatical theories. Specifically, word classes such as 'noun', 'verb', and 'adjective' are considered to be cross-linguistic categories as well as language-specific categories in other grammatical theories. How do word classes serve as cross-linguistic categories as well as language-specific categories in those theories? (See also Baker & Croft 2017.)

One approach is to define cross-linguistic categories in essentially semantic terms. The most consistent approach in this respect is that of Cognitive Grammar (Langacker 1987a; 1987b; 2008a). Langacker offers conceptual definitions of 'noun', 'verb', and all other categories that play a role in his general theory of language. In the two closely related functional theories Role and Reference Grammar (Van Valin & LaPolla 1997) and Functional Grammar (Dik 1997), the basic theoretical categories are predicates and arguments/terms, which are functional categories; they are subdivided into semantically defined subclasses. Functionally defined categories are analogous to functional comparative concepts. But their relationship to distributionally defined language-specific word classes is unclear.

A second approach is to posit abstract formal categories that represent word classes, and to argue that the abstract formal categories are—or, sometimes, are not—manifested directly in word classes in specific languages. These abstract formal categories are defined in terms of their role in the abstract formal structures posited in the grammatical theory. The most consistent approach in this respect is generative grammar, particularly Baker (2003). One could also include here the less theoretically oriented practice of many typologists and field linguists who assume that 'noun', 'verb', and 'adjective' are cross-linguistic categories, and then ask whether a particular language has 'adjectives' or not. Abstract formal categories are not comparative concepts in the sense defined in section 11.3. But their relationship to distributionally defined language-specific word classes is unclear as well.

Radical Construction Grammar argues that the only way that traditional word classes could be identified as cross-linguistic categories is through an inconsistent and selective use of distributional analysis which is called their METHODOLOGICAL OPPORTUNISM (Croft 2001: ch. 1). A simple example of two closely related languages, English and German, illustrates the point (Croft 2007a: 411–412, 416–417). German Adjectives are defined distributionally by the fact that they index (agree with) the Number and Case values of the German Noun that they modify. English Adjectives do not index the English Nouns that they modify; the main distributional definition is their occurrence in the relevant role in the English Noun Phrase.

Now, 'English Adjective' and 'German Adjective' are language-specific categories. They are defined in terms of certain English and German constructions respectively. Hence, at one level, it is completely arbitrary that they are both called 'Adjective'. But they are considered to be instantiations of the same word-class 'Adjective' for the purposes of cross-linguistic comparison in many theoretical approaches, including generative grammar. From the point of view of distributional analysis, the equating of German Adjectives and English Adjectives is opportunistic. Not only do English Adjectives not occur in German and German Adjectives not occur in English, but the constructions used in distributional analysis are totally different.

One could use the 'same' constructions for distributional analysis across the two languages. The only way to do that is by comparative concepts, in particular of indexation of particular semantic categories such as cardinality (number) and participant role (case) in modification. But the only modifiers in English that index any feature of the head are the English Demonstratives *this/these* and *that/those*. So this approach would equate German Adjectives with English Demonstratives (only approximately, since English Demonstratives index Number but not Case). It is obvious that the reason English Adjectives and German Adjectives are called 'Adjective' is functional: the two word classes both include words that correspond to property concepts, and the words are also used as modifiers in referring expressions. The use of distributional analysis is inconsistent and selective, designed to identify two word classes as the 'same' across languages for other reasons—based on function in this case, but based on abstract theoretical reasons in other theories. Or they are based on a preconception regarding whether the language has Adjectives at all.

11.5 CROSS-LINGUISTIC WORD CLASSES AND THE SKELETON MODEL OF LANGUAGE UNIVERSALS

Dryer (1997a) poses the problem of cross-linguistic categories with respect to grammatical relations, but notes parallels with phonemes and parts of speech; that is, the word classes discussed here. He suggests four things that grammatical theories might propose that exist (Dryer 1997a: 116–117, as adapted in Croft 2001: 32):

a. categories and relations in particular languages
b. similarities among these language-particular categories and relations across languages
c. functional, cognitive, and semantic explanations for these similarities
d. categories and relations in a cross-linguistic sense

The assumption of (d), the existence of cross-linguistic categories and relations, reflects a hidden assumption about the nature of language universals, which can be called the SKELETON MODEL of language universals. The skeleton model presupposes that language universals are of the form 'All languages have X', where 'X' is a particular grammatical category or structure; 'X' constitutes the 'bones' of the skeletal model. Another way to describe the skeleton model is the widely held assumption that a language universal is only something 'which is found in all languages', as described by an anonymous reviewer. Some theories describe the set of language universals in this sense as 'Universal Grammar'.

In fact, most adherents to the skeleton model allow that not everything that is a language universal in this sense may be found in a language. For example, for many linguists, including typologists who adhere to the skeleton model, 'adjectives' do not need always to be present. (This has been called the 'cafeteria' model: a language can pick and choose its categories from Universal Grammar.) But enough of the skeleton has to be instantiated in a particular language grammar, and language universals in the skeleton sense must be instantiated in enough languages, to be considered 'universal'.

A consequence of the skeleton model is the assumption that the theoretical entities that are language universals in this sense are of the same type as the entities in particular language grammars—e.g. word classes. In the skeleton model, language universals are a subset of what is found in particular language grammars. Particular language grammars also have many arbitrary patterns that 'flesh out' the skeleton of structure provided by language universals. But particular language grammars always include instantiations of the language universals (the 'bones'). For example, for many linguists, the skeleton includes 'noun' and 'verb': all languages are assumed to have nouns and verbs in the skeleton sense.

In contrast to the skeleton model, Dryer argues that in a theory of cross-linguistic universals, one does not need (d); one only needs (c) (Dryer 1997a: 139). In fact, trying to establish (d) impedes the explanation of cross-linguistic patterns (Dryer 1997a: 140).

Radical Construction Grammar, and much of modern typology, follows Dryer and does not adopt the skeleton model. In Greenbergian typology, the vast majority of language universals, and certainly most of the interesting language universals, are universals of patterns of cross-linguistic variation. In Greenbergian typology, a language universal is a proposition that is true of all languages. The proposition need not be of the form 'All languages have X'. In particular, Greenberg proposed implicational universals of the form 'If a language has Y, then it also has X'. Universal 18, presented in section 11.3, is an implicational universal. Universal 18 is not the description of a particular grammatical structure that may or may not be found in a language, but it is true of all languages. Hence there is no need in Radical Construction Grammar, or in typology, for cross-linguistic categories such as 'noun' or 'adjective'. Language universals are empirical generalizations that reflect 'functional, cognitive and semantic explanations' for word-class variation—Dryer's (c).[2] But language universals in the typological sense are based on patterns of word-class variation that are systematically, not opportunistically, defined. The role of word classes in uncovering these types of universals and their explanation will be discussed in sections 11.7–11.9.

In Radical Construction Grammar, universal patterns of variation—that is, similarities and differences among language-particular categories, Dryer's (b)—in the realm of parts of speech are explained in terms of certain combinations of semantic concept categories and information-packaging functions, such as modification by property concepts. These are comparative concepts, not word classes. These universal patterns of variation do not require positing a cross-linguistic category of 'adjective'. Universal patterns of variation in the occurrence of indexation in modification constructions, for example, can be characterized in terms of implicational universals defined over semantic categories, e.g. 'If a property concept modifier indexes the referent, then the deictic concept modifier does as well'.

11.6 LANGUAGE-SPECIFIC WORD CLASSES AND THE BUILDING BLOCK MODEL OF GRAMMAR

The preceding sections show that a major difference between Radical Construction Grammar and other theories is the nature of language universals. In particular, word classes are not doing the work of providing a skeleton for language universals. But the role of word classes in the analysis of the grammars in specific languages in Radical Construction Grammar also differs from other theories. In the debates over the relationship between language universals and language-specific word classes, there are hidden assumptions about specific language grammars as well.

It is generally assumed that there is a small number of word classes in a language. The major word classes are Noun, Verb, and (in some cases) Adjective; in addition a larger but not enormous set of minor word classes is posited. It is also generally assumed that the word classes are mutually exclusive and form an exhaustive partition of the words in a language, although most grammatical descriptions allow for some polycategoriality or polysemy; that is, membership in more than one word class. In particular, word classes are GLOBAL in the sense of being shared across grammatical constructions of the language (Croft 2001: 45).

Many reference grammars include chapters on word classes near the beginning of the grammar. Some reference grammars are entirely organized around word classes. With this

---

[2] In fact, universals such as Universal 18 are typically not exceptionless. However, even when they are not, they may still manifest the underlying functional, cognitive, and semantic explanation that does apply to all languages (see Dryer 1997b).

assumption, it seems more plausible to consider the small number of word classes to be universal in the sense of being shared across languages, and hence part of the skeleton model of language universals.

Radical Construction Grammar argues that this is not what is found in the grammars of specific languages. As noted in section 11.2, the word class defined by occurrence in a role in one construction will not in general be the same as the word class defined by occurrence in a role in another construction in the same language. A consistent, strictly distributional analysis will lead to a very large number of word classes. Moreover, the word classes will overlap everywhere and will therefore not form a partition of the words in the language. In other words, word classes are not global; they are specific to the construction that defines them.

How is the result of consistent, strict distributional analysis reconciled with the assumption of a small number of (largely) mutually exclusive word classes that partition the words of a language? Again, Radical Construction Grammar argues that the only way that word classes can be rendered global is through an inconsistent and selective use of distributional analysis, namely methodological opportunism. One selects just one construction and ignores the other constructions, or a handful of constructions with strongly overlapping distribution and ignores the differences in distributions of the individual constructions (and any other constructions that are not used). For example, the differences in distribution of English Adjectives in (4)–(7) in section 11.2 are ignored in positing a construction-independent, global word class of Adjective in English.

There is a hidden assumption here as well. The motivation for seeking a small set of word classes that is shared across grammatical constructions of a language is the BUILDING BLOCK MODEL of grammar. In the building block model, word categories are atomic, primitive units of grammatical analysis and structure. Constructions are built out of word categories. For example, a simplified characterization of the English Noun Phrase construction is [Dem Num Adj N], or [Dem [Num [Adj N]]]. There are of course other modifiers in the English Noun Phrase, but including them would simply show that there are more building blocks necessary to define the English Noun Phrase construction.

Radical Construction Grammar rejects the building block model along with its prerequisite, global word classes. There is a circularity of argumentation in the building block model of word classes. Word classes are defined by their occurrence in constructions (see section 11.2). But once they are defined by constructions, word classes are assumed to be atomic primitive units, and constructions are defined as being built out of combinations of word classes (Croft 2001: 34–37). In other words, identification of constructions is presupposed in order to define word classes, but then constructions are defined in terms of word classes.

The way out of this circular reasoning that is taken by other grammatical theories is an a priori assumption that word classes as building blocks are 'already there', and distributional analysis is merely a way of 'discovering' their existence (Croft 2001: 10–11). But, as with the assumption of cross-linguistic word classes, linguists do not agree on what the building blocks are. So they opportunistically select just the distributional facts that support their a priori assumptions. When two linguists disagree, there is no way one can resolve the disagreement because both linguists are being methodologically opportunistic: both are right for the distributions they present in their arguments, and both are wrong due to the distributions they ignore or dismiss. These a priori language-specific word classes are also the a priori cross-linguistic word classes we observed in the preceding sections.

Instead, Radical Construction Grammar follows the consequence of consistent, strict distributional analysis and recognizes that constructions, not word classes, are the primitive units of grammatical analysis. Word classes are defined in terms of roles in constructions. They are not the building blocks out of which constructions are made. There is a many-to-many mapping of the words of a language to roles in the constructions of the language. Overlapping word classes are the starting point of grammatical analysis of particular languages. This approach is illustrated in sections 11.8–11.9, but first we turn to another hidden assumption about word classes and their role in grammatical theory.

11.7 LANGUAGE-SPECIFIC WORD CLASSES AS POPULATIONS RATHER THAN ESSENTIALIST CATEGORIES

In Radical Construction Grammar, distributionally defined language-particular word classes are completely different from the comparative concepts with which language universals are described. Comparative concepts are essentialist categories, while language-particular word classes are populations in the sense of the neo-Darwinian synthesis of evolutionary biology.

Of these two, the nature of comparative concepts is the more familiar. Comparative concepts like humanness (the semantics of animacy), cardinality (the semantics of number and numerals), or linear order (a cross-linguistically definable temporal property of morphosyntactic form) are defined by essential properties. These essential properties allow us to identify a linguistic construction (form–meaning pairing) as instantiating—or not instantiating—the comparative concept, in any language. This is, of course, the 'classical' definition of a category as a kind: a grouping of individuals by virtue of a set of properties that all and only the individuals possess. This type of grouping of individuals goes under many names; for example, Dahl (2016: 428) calls it 'Universal'. Here we use the term 'essentialist', which describes the defining feature of this type of category and is also the term used in evolutionary biology (Mayr 1982: 256; Hull 1976; 1988: 215–216).

Individuals, by contrast, are spatiotemporally bounded, historical entities: they exist only in a particular space and time. The individuality of a quartz crystal is its unique spatiotemporal existence: it was formed at a point in time, it exists in some location for some period of time, and it will pass out of existence when it is destroyed. In other words, individuals are historical entities. A spatiotemporally bounded set of historical entities (individuals) is also a historical entity (an individual): this is a POPULATION in the biological sense (Ghiselin 1974; Hull 1976; Mayr 1982: 272–275).

Population thinking emerged with the neo-Darwinian synthesis in evolutionary biology (see Mayr 1982: ch. 6 for a brief history). Population thinking resolved serious problems with the essentialist theory of a biological species by abandoning the essentialist theory. Biological species cannot be defined in terms of a set of essential properties. There are species that share seemingly essential structural traits, yet do not interbreed (Hull 1988: 104). Above all, the 'essential' traits of species evolve over time and may disappear. The 'essential' traits of species therefore cannot define the species.

Instead, species are defined as a reproductively isolated population of organisms. As such, a species is a historical, spatiotemporally bounded individual: 'Just as the name "Gargantua" denotes a particular organism from conception to death, "*Gorilla gorilla*" denotes a particular segment of the phylogenetic tree' (Hull 1988: 215). Populations may be a grouping of individual entities, but they are a very different type of grouping from an essentialist category. Since a species is itself an individual, a species name is a proper name, not the name of a type (Ghiselin 1974), and the relation between the constituent organisms and the population is not a type–instance (token) relation, but more like a part–whole relation (Hull 1976).[3]

What sort of 'category' is a distributionally defined language-particular word class? Dahl suggests that single values of a language-particular category such as the Future Tense 'tend to be Individual-like', but questions this conclusion for language-particular, distributionally defined word classes such as Adjective (Dahl 2016: 429).

In Radical Construction Grammar, distributionally defined language-particular word classes are populations. Radical Construction Grammar is a component of the evolutionary framework for understanding language presented in Croft (2000). In the evolutionary framework, speech communities are populations, and so are the linguistic entities dependent on them: languages, utterances, and the structural parts of utterances. A speech community is a population of (relatively) communicatively isolated speakers (Croft 2000: 17–19); it is a spatiotemporally bounded, historical entity. A language is the population of the actual utterances produced by the speech community (Croft 2000: 26)—hence Radical Construction Grammar is a completely usage-based theory of language. All of the familiar 'problems' of defining languages are found in defining species, and can be addressed in the population theory of a language (Croft 2000: 13–20; the 'problems' are mostly due to the gradual process of speciation/language birth, and the incompleteness of reproductive/communicative isolation).

The population of utterances that constitutes a language forms a population not only by virtue of being produced by members of a speech community. Single-word utterances are replications of the words that make them up. That is, words are replicated from prior uses of that word. Multiword utterances are the result of the recombination of linguistic units replicated from prior uses of those units. The linguistic units that are replicated and recombined are the constructions and the words that fill the roles in the constructions. The replication process is of course mediated by speakers, who replicate and recombine words and constructions and other linguistic units in language use, based on their knowledge about their language—the utterances they have been exposed to, and have used themselves. A speaker's grammar is also a spatiotemporally bounded individual—the speaker's lifetime knowledge about her language—and so is the collection of the grammatical knowledge about their language of all the members of the speech community.

In contrast, structuralist and generative theories of language and language structure are essentialist. Words and constructions exist as abstract entities, not bound to time or space; the same applies to the rules that govern their combination (not RECombination, which implies replication and thus historical existence). Grammars in either the sense of

---

[3] The population theory of species is still contested in evolutionary biology (Mayr 1982: 276, 279; Hull 1988: 213, fn. 2). Dahl proposes using a modified essentialist theory for language-specific categories, adopted from biologists who do not accept the population theory of species (Dahl 2016: 435–436; Dahl does not discuss the population theory).

an idealized speaker-hearer's knowledge or in the sense of an abstract description of grammatical structures and rules are also essentialist. It is likely that the widespread essentialist representation of a grammar, the sentences generated or sanctioned by the grammar, and the parts of those sentences including word classes, underlies arguments that language-specific word classes are the same kind of thing as comparative concepts, which are defined in essentialist terms (see above).

The Radical Construction Grammar definition of a word class is an example of the population definition of linguistic units, including words, phrases, and constructions. In order to explain the population definition of word classes, we will start with the definition of a single word, such as English *heart*. In an essentialist theory, English *heart* is a single individual abstract unit with a particular form and meaning, possibly multiple meanings, as in a dictionary entry. In the essentialist view, the word has as an essential property its word class, as asserted in introductory linguistics and syntax textbooks in various approaches, generative and otherwise (e.g. O'Grady et al. 1997: 164; Fabb 2005: 11; Finegan 2007: 35; Carnie 2013: 44).

In the population view, English *heart* is a population of uses of the word, replicated through the lifetimes of speakers of English and, thanks to the overlap of generations of speakers, through the history of the language. Thus, a word as a population has a historical (temporal) as well as a spatial dimension. Of course, for a single speaker, the most relevant uses are those in that speaker's direct experience. But the uses that speaker is exposed to are replications of prior uses outside the speaker's immediate spatiotemporal experience, and those prior uses influenced the uses that the speaker experiences. The uses of *heart* in the English speech community form a LINEAGE, or rather a set of intertwining lineages of replications of prior uses. These lineage structures may not seem very relevant to the analysis of a common word such as *heart*. However, the lineage of uses is more obviously central to the understanding of a linguistic term such as *adjective* or *universal*, and is reflected in citations in the linguistic literature referring to prior uses of the term, tracing the lineage of its use and the evolution of its meaning.

The same is true of constructions. A construction such as the English Progressive construction, described in essentialist terms as [SBJ *be* VERB-*ing* ...], is a population of its uses. The population is defined by the replication of the construction by speakers of the English speech community. Unlike a simple word, a construction also involves recombination: recombination of the construction, forms of *be*, the morpheme -*ing*, and the fillers of the roles: the English Passive Verbs that have occurred in the construction and the English Passive Subject phrases that have occurred in the construction—and the latter in turn are recombinations of the elements of the Subject phrase. Since the English Progressive construction involves recombination, an utterance replicating the Progressive construction constitutes multiple intertwining lineages.

Now we may provide a Radical Construction Grammar definition of word classes as populations. Word classes are distributionally defined. They are therefore language-specific and construction-specific. As such, a word class is a population: the population of elements that have filled, and will fill, a particular role in the replications of a particular construction (i.e. in specific utterances), which also forms a population. The names for word classes, like other language-specific linguistic entities, are proper names. Hence the convention adopted in typology and in Radical Construction Grammar to capitalize the names of language-specific word classes (and constructions) accurately captures their nature as populations.

As a population, a word class is completely different from a comparative concept, which is a kind, defined by the essential traits of the kind. Word classes are 'made up of' particular linguistic entities—individuals in a language. Comparative concepts are also 'made up of' particular linguistic entities—individuals within and across languages. But the relation between a population and its constituent entities, and the relation between a kind and its instantiations, are totally different. The first is a relation between a spatiotemporally bounded individual and its component parts (the replications); the second is a relation between a universal kind and instances that share the essential traits of the kind (Hull 1976).[4]

11.8 THE ROLE OF WORD CLASSES IN RADICAL CONSTRUCTION GRAMMAR: LANGUAGE-INTERNAL AND CROSS-LINGUISTIC VARIATION

Sections 11.3–11.7 focused largely on what word classes in Radical Construction Grammar are not, because what they are not is linked to deeply or unconsciously held assumptions about the nature of words, grammar, and language universals by advocates of other linguistic theories. Word classes are not essentialist categories; they are populations defined by occurrence—and recurrence—in a particular role in a particular construction. Word classes are not building blocks for grammatical structure; they are the product of recombination in the replication of the constructions that define them. Finally, word classes as spatiotemporally bounded populations cannot be used to provide a skeleton of grammatical categories for Universal Grammar; language universals must be built on comparative concepts, which are kinds; that is, essentialist categories.

Radical Construction Grammar, and typology in general, proceeds by the inductive analysis of empirical linguistic data. Empirical linguistic research forms generalizations over samples of the populations of words, constructions, and utterances produced by speakers of the language, and seeks to explain those generalizations. Freed from requiring word classes to be essentialist kinds, building blocks of grammars, and the skeleton for language universals, Radical Construction Grammar uses patterns of distribution of words to uncover language universals.

Radical Construction Grammar is based on distributional analysis. In section 11.2, it was observed that, empirically, word classes defined by distributional analysis are construction-specific and language-specific. In the grammatical description of a single language, distributional analysis produces a many-to-many mapping between words and constructions, or

---

[4] Dahl (2016) and Gil (2016) suggest that different dialects, varieties, and even languages may have the 'same' category, e.g. the Perfect in different English dialects or the Relative Case in Eskimo–Aleut languages (Dahl 2016: 430). Gil extends this idea to code mixing and borrowing. What these categories have in common is a shared lineage (language contact can lead to category lineages 'jumping' languages). Lineages are historical entities, so they are not comparative concepts of the type discussed in section 11.3. Language-specific categories are single branches of shared lineages, though there are complex issues in deciding whether there is sufficient communicative isolation to define a separate language lineage, as noted above.

more precisely, between words and a particular role in a construction. This many-to-many mapping does not 'clump' words into a small number of global (construction-independent) word classes.

Taking this view means taking a less restrictive perspective on the representation of word classes. Word classes are not mutually exclusive. However, in most grammatical theories, overlap is generally restricted to a taxonomic hierarchy (a tree), or a set of shared features, which leads to a lattice. A lattice quickly becomes unreadable when every construction determines a different distribution. More significantly, it does not easily capture generalizations linking overlapping distributions. In order to capture these generalizations, we must also find a basis for cross-linguistic comparison of word classes.

Constructions are defined in terms of both form and function. Typically this is done informally, not least because distribution is commonly not described as occurrence in constructions (section 11.2). In construction grammar, distributional analysis is defined explicitly in terms of words occurring in roles in complex constructions. Words and complex constructions are both pairings of form and function. The function of words and (complex) constructions provides a basis for cross-linguistic comparison, because functions are comparative concepts. Thus, words can be compared in terms of translation equivalents for the relevant word sense, and constructions can be compared in terms of equivalent functions, such as predication and modification. Methodological opportunism is avoided by comparing distributions across languages of semantically equivalent words in functionally equivalent constructions. Finally, hybrid comparative concepts allow for the comparison of formal morphosyntactic properties of constructions.

In other words, language-particular distributional facts can be viewed not just as parts of language populations, but also as instantiations of essentialist comparative concepts, defined by function and also form. Typology uncovers language universals manifested by language-particular distributional facts. Functional, cognitive, and semantic explanations for language universals (see section 11.5) account for significant facts of languages as historical entities (see section 11.7): constraints on distributional patterns, and constraints on paths of evolution of words and constructions.

For example, English uses different constructions with different strategies for predication of action concepts, property concepts, and object concepts:

(8) a. Donna sings.
b. Donna is tall.
c. Donna is an Alabaman.

These constructions share the same function, predication, and so they can be compared. One can also compare predication constructions across languages—'predication construction' is a comparative concept. We can then examine distribution patterns for words expressing action concepts, property concepts, and object concepts across languages as well as within languages.

In this case, there is an implicational universal across languages with respect to the strategies used for predication, specifically the use of a separate morpheme (overt coding) vs absence of such a morpheme (zero coding) for predication of action, property, and/or object concepts: a predication construction for any semantic type on the hierarchy Action < Property < Object uses at least as many morphemes as predication of any semantic type to the left on the hierarchy (Croft 1991: 130; Stassen 1997: 127; Pustet 2003). In English, overt coding is found in property and object predication; see (8b–c). In Mandarin, overt coding is found in object predication only (Li & Thompson 1981; but see below). In Makah, no overt coding is used for action, property, or object predication (Jacobsen 1979).

The language-particular word classes defined by the zero coded and overtly coded predication constructions are different. Based on the predication constructions in each language, one might say that English 'distinguishes Predicated Adjective and Predicated Verb word classes', Mandarin 'has a single Predicated Non-Nominal word class', and Makah 'has a single Predicate word class'. But Mandarin, Makah, and English all instantiate the language universal given at the beginning of this paragraph. Specifically, this universal and other universals of predication, modification, and reference constructions indicate that action concepts are prototypically predications, and that property concepts are prototypically modifiers and object concepts are prototypically referring expressions (Croft 1991; 2001).

Yet this hierarchy is already manifested in English alone. English has both overt coding and zero coding strategies for its predication construction. Most object predication constructions involve two morphemes, *be* and *a*, whereas property predication involves just one morpheme, *be*. In fact, most typological universals involve comparison of patterns of distribution—variation in use—of multiple constructions in a language, and equivalents of those same constructions across languages. In other words, 'grammatical variation within a language and grammatical variation across languages are governed by the same universal patterns and principles' (Croft 2001: 107).

If we drill deeper into language use in a single language, this principle continues to hold. In some languages, for example Lango, constructions exhibiting different strategies for modification—zero, the Attributive Particle, or the combination of Attributive Particle and Relative Pronoun—are used in both property and action modification. Hence there is no difference in the distribution of the different modification constructions in categorical terms. However, the more overtly coded Attributive + Relative combination, using two morphemes instead of one, is less normal for property concepts but preferred for action concepts (Croft 2001: 78–80, from Noonan 1992 and personal communication), as expected from the universal that property concepts are prototypically modifiers. In Mandarin (and Cantonese; Li & Thompson 1981: 143; Matthews & Yip 1994: 158; Croft 2020: Lecture 3 and references cited therein), the degree modifier for property concepts is frequently used in predication without denoting intensification; that is, it is grammaticalizing into overt coding for property predication.

11.9 WORD CLASSES, THE SEMANTIC MAP MODEL, AND EXEMPLAR SEMANTICS

In Radical Construction Grammar, construction-specific word classes can be compared within and across languages using the meanings of words and the functions of constructions. This comparison reveals universal patterns of variation in distribution. The preceding section gives simple cases where implicational hierarchies familiar from typology capture the universals.

Other universal patterns of distribution are more complex, and different methods are used to capture the patterns. The basic method is the SEMANTIC MAP MODEL, also with a long lineage in typology (for overviews, see Croft 2003: 133–139; Haspelmath 2003). In the semantic map model, word meanings occurring in distributionally defined word classes are mapped in a conceptual space structured according to variation in distribution within and across languages. For example, one can organize word meanings in a conceptual space according to their distribution in different predication constructions, as is done by Stassen (1997). The classic semantic map model uses a graph (network) structure for the conceptual space: word meanings that occur in the same construction(s) are nodes joined by edges (links) in the graph (for an algorithm for constructing the graph, see Regier et al. 2013; for fitness statistics for the algorithm, see Croft 2022b).

For even more complex patterns of distribution, multidimensional scaling (MDS) can be used (Croft & Poole 2008; Croft 2010c; 2022b; for an implementation for use in linguistics, see Timm 2020). MDS uses a Euclidean spatial model: word meanings that occur in the same construction(s) are spatially near each other. Otherwise it is constructed in the same way as the traditional graph structure model: organize meanings in a conceptual space such that meanings of words that occur in the same overlapping construction-specific distributions are 'closer' to each other, either in terms of paths through the graph or in terms of Euclidean distance. For example, Rogers (2016) uses the distribution of 49 object, property, and action concept words in reference, modification, and predication constructions in 11 languages to reveal universal patterns of variation in so-called parts of speech.

Semantic map model research using the graph-based or MDS methods has used progressively more fine-grained meanings. For example, Rogers's MDS analysis of property concepts confirms that different subclasses of property concepts form a scale from 'more nouny' to 'more verby' 'adjectives' (terms are in scare quotes because these are not word classes as building blocks, but a way to convey the scalar quality of the language universal; see also Dixon 1977; Wetzer 1992: 245; Stassen 1997: 168–169; Croft 2001: 96–97; Ye 2021).

The logical conclusion to this process is to use nonlinguistic stimuli, such as the Bowerman–Pedersen spatial relations pictures (found in Levinson & Wilkins 2006: 570–575) that cover the spatial dimensions roughly covered by English *at*, *in*, and *on*. Empirical research in eliciting words using nonlinguistic stimuli, such as the adpositions used to express these spatial relations in nine languages by Levinson et al. (2003), reveals even finer-grained variation in distribution across languages than was previously realized. Distributional variation should not be thought of as being organized into a network of discrete concepts but rather as multiple continuous dimensions of meaning or function (Croft 2010c). The dimensions of meaning/function in conceptual space underlie typological language universals (see section 11.5); language-specific word classes 'cut' these dimensions into constructionally defined categories constrained by the conceptual dimensions.

Even this research does not fully capture the nature of variation in distributional patterns. This research assumes that any particular meaning/function, even a very finely defined specific function, is expressed by one word or construction in a language. The reality of course is that speakers vary in their choice of word or construction for a particular experience, even including the spatial situations represented in the Bowerman–Pedersen stimuli (the Levinson et al. study abstracts away from within-language speaker variation). This is a truism: different speakers, and even the same speaker at different times, verbalize an experience in different ways. Variation in verbalization of scenes in the Pear Film (Chafe 1980), for example, is ubiquitous (Croft 2010d).

In order to integrate variation in verbalization to the theory of word classes, one must shift from an essentialist view of word classes, in which a word is a possible filler of a constructional role, to the population view of word classes described in section 11.7, in which actual frequencies of occurrence are what matters. And one must look at the distribution of word plus construction across the situations mapped in conceptual space.

This is a far more complex task than simply recording occurrences of words in constructions. But preliminary studies suggest it is a fruitful approach. A study of the 20 verbalizations of scenes in the Pear Film found in Chafe (1980) shows that variation in verbalization is the source of grammatical, lexical, and constructional change found in language histories and across languages (Croft 2010d). A follow-up study of the same data showed that the frequency distribution of words and constructions varied according to well-known semantic dimensions (Croft 2020: Lecture 9). For example, animacy and alienability governs preference for definite article vs 3rd singular possessive for recurrent reference, degree of control over an event governs preference for subject vs oblique realization of the experiencer in unintended human events, and direct manipulation and individuated theme vs indirect causation and less individuated theme governs preferences in the choice of verb in the application ('putting') argument structure construction.

The conclusion that can be drawn from these studies is that VARIATION IN LANGUAGE USE (VERBALIZATION) AS WELL AS GRAMMATICAL VARIATION WITHIN A LANGUAGE AND GRAMMATICAL VARIATION ACROSS LANGUAGES ARE ALL GOVERNED BY THE SAME UNIVERSAL PATTERNS AND PRINCIPLES (Croft 2010d; 2020). Distributional patterns of words and constructions are best thought of as probability distributions of use over conceptual space (Croft 2020: 271). These probability distributions are directly manifested in language use; that is, the verbalization of experience. These patterns of variation get conventionalized in grammatical patterns of the speech community. Conventions change over time, and as speech communities split, the patterns of variation in language use come to be reflected in typological universals of cross-linguistic variation (Croft 2016b).

CHAPTER 12

WORD CLASSES IN MINIMALIST SYNTAX

HEDDE ZEIJLSTRA

12.1 INTRODUCTION

WHEN investigating the notion of (lexical and functional) categories, contemporary (minimalist) generative grammar approaches put most emphasis on what exactly constitutes such categories. Within minimalism, categories are not taken to be grammatical primitives. Rather, grammatical objects that belong to a particular category are taken to do so because they contain particular morphosyntactic features. And it is these morphosyntactic features, and possibly acategorial roots as well, that grammatical rules target.

In such an approach, the question of which categories are present in a particular language thus boils down to the question as to which morphosyntactic features there may be, and what other kinds of elements can be targeted by the morphosyntactic component(s) in grammar. Within contemporary formal (generative) theoretical frameworks, mostly within minimalism, several types of morphosyntactic features are distinguished. Examples are, for instance, lexical features such as [V] or [N], and formal features, like *Wh-*, tense, person–number–gender-features (generally referred to as φ-features) and case features (see Adger 2003; Adger & Svenonius 2010). Such formal features are often taken to come about in interpretable and uninterpretable features (or, more recently, into valued and unvalued features). On top of that, minimalist frameworks, most notably Distributed Morphology (DM) (see Chapter 13 in this volume), also make reference to acategorial, featureless roots.

In this chapter, I first briefly outline why contemporary minimalism does not make reference to words or categories, but rather to formal features (section 12.2). In section 12.3, I discuss what the consequences of such a perspective is for the analysis of lexical categories and whether the underlying features are lexical features or rather functional features that combine with categoryless roots. Section 12.4 discusses more general properties of those formal features that underlie grammatical categories, and I assess how these features can be arranged in structural hierarchies or feature geometries, and what their current status is within minimalist grammatical theory. Section 12.5 briefly concludes.

12.2 From words to categories, from categories to features

There are many reasons to assume that grammar does not make reference to words as such. For one, the grammaticality of sentences is not sensitive to individual words. Take the following two examples:

(1)   a. Cats love dogs
      b. Children drink milk

Even though the two sentences in (1) contain different words, the reasons why both are grammatical are the same. There is no reason to assume that syntax would, for instance, treat *cats* differently from *children*. A natural step would then be that the rules of grammars are sensitive to the categories that words belong to. Since *children* and *cats* belong to the same category, that of (plural count) nouns, they are grammatically treated in the same way. Consequently, *cats* and *children* are always fully interchangeable in grammatical sentences.

At the same time, a new question arises, one that is at the heart of formal generative grammar approaches, such as minimalism: what constitutes grammatical categories? Within the minimalist programme, categories are not grammatical primitives. Grammatical objects that belong to a particular category do so because they contain particular morphosyntactic features. And it is these morphosyntactic features that form the building blocks of grammar. Hence, even though prima facie grammatical rules appear to target elements belonging to particular categories, in fact they target elements containing to particular categories morphosyntactic features, a perspective introduced by Chomsky (1970) and widely adopted ever since.

There are at least three arguments that have been provided to explain why instead of categories morphosyntactic features should be taken to be the primitive units of syntax.

The first argument concerns the fact that categories do not behave in a uniform way. Clearly all forms *eat, eats, ate, eaten, to eat*, and *eating* belong to the category of verbs. At the same time, they are all treated differently by the grammar as witnessed by contrasts like *I eat* vs **I eaten*. Such contrasts do not follow directly from the differences in morphological shape. For instance, the past and perfect forms of *(to) sleep* are both *slept*, but *slept* in *I slept* is grammatically different from *slept* in *I have slept*. Apparently, more abstract properties must determine the grammatical differences between elements that belong to the same category. But that means that whatever constitutes a grammatical category must be reduced to these more abstract properties as well (see Koeneman & Zeijlstra 2017: ch. 1 for more discussion and overview).

As a second argument, such abstract properties cannot reduce to other properties of words, such as their phonological or semantic properties. There is nothing in the pronunciation of the word *table* that makes it a noun. Other nouns have completely different pronunciations. Even if in some language certain particular categorial properties correspond to certain particular phonological properties, this does not hold across languages and is rather epiphenomenal in nature. Alternatively, one could hypothesize that the meaning of a word reveals its category. It is a well-known fact that most nouns denote individuals or entities, whereas most verbs denote events, processes, or states. Nevertheless, there are nouns that actually denote events (*war, dance*) and verbs that do not denote events, processes, or states (this is the case, for instance, for most verbal auxiliaries). Even though nouns and verbs quite often show semantic (i.e. meaningful) differences, there is no clear-cut semantic difference between the two (see again Koeneman & Zeijlstra 2017: ch. 1 for more discussion and overview).

What distinguishes different categories in the grammar is thus independent of their form and meaning. Belonging to a particular category can only be distributionally determined (for instance, every common noun can be preceded by a definite article, or every verb may have finite forms), given that categorical identity between different elements guarantees full substitutionability. The consequence of this is that every lexical item must have three types of properties: phonological, semantic, and abstract morphosyntactic properties. The question is indeed what such abstract syntactic properties amount to.

This brings us to the third argument. It may be natural to assume that these abstract syntactic properties could be categorial properties themselves. Then, every verb must have the syntactic property of belonging to the category of verbs. The difference between different forms of verbs could then be cast in terms of subcategories: there is a subcategory of finite and a subcategory of non-finite verbs. The former could be further split up into two sub-subcategories, present finite verb and past finite verbs. Similar sub-subcategorizations could apply to non-finite verbs. A problem for such an approach is that if categorial behaviour is indeed defined in terms of syntactic distribution, this behaviour is not restricted to words. Take the following minimal examples:

(2) a. Wine tastes good
 b. Red wine tastes good
 c. Wine from Italy tastes good
 d. Red wine from Italy tastes good

In the examples in (2) the subjects are fully interchangeable. This does not only apply to these sentences. Every grammatical sentence containing the noun *wine* remains grammatical if *wine* is replaced by *red wine, wine from Italy*, or *red wine from* Italy. Categorial properties are not restricted to particular words but can also apply to phrases that consist of such words. Categorial properties can thus not be taken to be restricted to particular word classes (see Grimshaw 1991; Van Riemsdijk 1998; Adger 2003 for overviews and discussion of this notion of syntactic endocentricity).

Instead, such syntactic properties can be very well defined in term of *morphosyntactic features* (sometimes also referred to as *formal features*). Nouns carry a formal feature [N] that can project through entire phrases and the same holds for verbs that carry a feature [V]. Furthermore, there is no restriction to there being one feature per word or lexical element. *Took*, for instance, carries formal features [V], [finite], and [past]. With this in mind, we can now explore what types of features there are, what their grammatical behaviour amounts to, and how they are furthermore constrained.

12.3 LEXICAL FEATURES AND FEATURELESS ROOTS

We focus here on the features underlying the main lexical categories: nouns, verbs, and adjectives. Given the reasoning above, under a minimalist perspective the underlying features of categories should be features [N], [V], and [A]. But the question arises as to whether these different features should just be postulated as such, or whether these features can be further reduced to more basic grammatical features or properties. Also, is an element that belongs to a particular lexical category stored in the lexicon with its corresponding feature, or does the lexicon contain categoryless roots that become nominal, verbal, and adjectival in the course of the derivation? A final question, both related to whether noun and verbs are lexically stored or not, and whether noun and verbs share a common core or not: does every language in the world distinguish nouns from verbs? These three questions will be addressed in the next three sections.

12.3.1 Reducing lexical features

The first attempt to categorize the formal features underlying lexical categories is by Chomsky (1970), who defines the categories of nouns, verbs, and adjectives in terms of binary features. For Chomsky, lexical categories contain both a feature [±V] and a feature [±N]. Nouns then are underlyingly [+N, −V], verbs [−N, +V], and adjectives [+N, +V].

One of the advantages of such a binary feature system is that it can account for the somewhat hybrid nature of adjectives. Whereas the syntactic behaviour of nouns and verbs is complementary, adjectives can sometimes behave both nominally and verbally (as observed by Ross 1972). For instance, the verbal participle *destroyed* in (3a) is used adjectively in (3b).

(3) a. Caesar destroyed the city
    b. The destroyed city

Another advantage of such a system is that it makes predictions about the number of lexical categories. A binary system like the one sketched above also allows a fourth category of the type [−N, −V]. Jackendoff (1977) took elements carrying [−N, −V] to be adpositions. This has led to a dominant view in generative grammar that the four lexical categories are nouns, verbs, adjectives, and adpositions to the exclusion of adverbs, an aspect in which generative grammar differs from most functional paradigms.

Naturally, the question arises as to whether features [±V] and [±N] are lexical primitives or whether they can be reduced to some more fundamental properties. One attempt to do the latter was pursued by Stowell (1981) who argued that nominality and verbality can be defined in terms of the (in)ability to license case. Déchaine (1993), by contrast, has argued that the noun–verb distinction reduces to the interplay of [nominal] and [referential] features. For her, nouns carry a feature [referential] and a feature [nominal], while adjectives only carry [nominal] and verbs only [referential].

The most advanced grammatical theory that aims at explaining the differences between verbs, nouns, and adjectives is Baker (2003). For Baker, verbs are the only lexical category that always project a specifier, a 'subject'. By contrast, nouns carry referential indexes. Adjectives, finally, are negatively defined as the lexical category that lacks referential indexes and cannot project a specifier either. One of the core tenets of Baker's work is that he clearly takes lexical items to carry particular formal features. That is, being a noun, verb, or adjective is a property already encoded in the lexicon.

12.3.2 Roots in syntax

Such a perspective runs against more recent ideas by Halle & Marantz (1993), Marantz (1997), and Harley & Noyer (1998), who argue that the grammatical properties that lexical categories like verbs, nouns, and adjectives exhibit are not lexically encoded but result from the functional structure above category-less roots. In terms of Marantz (1997) such roots become 'nouns' and 'verbs' as a result of where they are inserted in the syntactic structure (see also Chapter 13 in this volume). *Destruction* and *destroy* are not different lexical elements but different syntactic structures that share the same categoryless, and thus featureless, root √DESTROY. In *destruction*, √DESTROY is the head of a nominal extended projection; in *destroy*, the head of a verbal one. As pointed out by Acquaviva (2008), the notion of a morphological root is ultimately based on the intuition that complete words may share a minimal 'core', which remains invariant when all other morphological formatives have been abstracted away. Within DM, consensus has emerged that roots correspond to this non-grammatically definable part of a word (Marantz 1997). This leads to the hypothesis that all lexical categories are made up of categoryless roots combined with category-assigning heads (Marantz 2001; Embick & Marantz 2008; Embick & Noyer 2007). For example, nouns and verbs are not syntactic atoms, but are derived from a structure [n + √] and [v + √], respectively, where n and v are syntactic functional heads carrying nominal/verbal features. The noun *cat*, for instance, has [$_n$ n √CAT] as its underlying structure.

An advantage of dismissing lexical categories/features in narrow syntax lies in the fact that roots differ from other functional elements in at least two respects (Halle & Marantz 1993; Harley & Noyer 1999; Embick 2000; Alexiadou 2001; Borer 2005a; 2005b; 2013; De Belder & van Craenenbroek 2014). First, following the examples in De Belder & van Craenenbroeck, who base themselves on Borer (2005a), open class lexical items can generally be modified both nominally and verbally. As they show, a lexical item such as English *stone* can be used in a wide variety of ways, some nominal (4a–b), some verbal (4c), or adjectival (4d):

(4) a. I've got a stone in my hand.
    b. There's too much stone and metal in this room.
    c. They want to stone this man.
    d. Billy-Bob should lay off the weed; he's always stoned.

Second, as De Belder & van Craenenbroeck point out, many properties, traditionally assigned to verbs or nouns in (for instance, agreement or case assignment), are nowadays performed by functional heads (see Marantz 1997; Borer 2005a; 2005b; Adger 2011). What roots do is add conceptual meanings to the structures built by syntax, but for this it does not need to have a specific syntactic category.

Borer (2014) even takes a further step and dismisses categorial features like [n] and [v] altogether. The reason for her is that this removes redundancy from the grammatical architecture. If it already follows that elements that merge with a determiner must be nominal (as determiners only select nominal elements) and that elements that merge with complementizers must be verbal (as complementizers only select verbal elements), it also follows that the complements of D/T are nominal/verbal and there is no need to reduplicate that in the grammatical architecture.

Despite the great conceptual advantages of assuming that morphemes become categorial in the context of a syntactic structure, the assumption that, therefore, roots are categoryless—and thus also featureless—is problematic in one important respect: it substantially complicates the notion of what constitutes the set of syntactic objects. If roots are categoryless and lack any morphosyntactic features, then the question arises what all syntactic objects, roots and morphosyntactic features alike, have in common. For instance, the structure-building operation Merge should now be said to apply to both elements carrying morphosyntactic features and to featureless roots instead of elements carrying morphosyntactic features only. Of course, one can try to motivate why Merge can apply to two different types of objects, as is standardly done in approaches like DM, or even provide arguments why the lowest element in a derivational domain must be featureless (see Fortuny 2008; Zwart 2009; 2011; De Belder & van Craenenbroeck 2014; Biberauer 2017 for notable attempts). However, the question is whether such additional steps are actually necessary. The crucial argument in approaches that take roots to be categoryless is that problems emerge once it is assumed that roots must be either nominal or verbal. The crucial underlying assumption is thus that roots must be underspecified with respect to being nominal or verbal; they cannot just be lexical categories nouns or verbs. But, as argued for by Zeijlstra (2020b), taking roots to be acategorial is not the only way to explain this underspecification. Assuming that there is a supercategory—superfeature above nouns and verbs (and, arguably, predicatively used adjectives as well) exactly derives that as well. All conceptual arguments outlined above in favour of roots being featureless/acategorial are also compatible with roots carrying a formal superfeature, which could be dubbed [PRED(ICATE)] or [CONTENTIVE] that can get valued for being either verbal, nominal, or (predicatively) adjectival.

12.3.3 The universality of nominal and verbal lexical categories

The question whether such a supercategory above nouns and verb, and thus a superfeature above nominal and verbal features, exists is closely related to the question whether every language in the world exhibits a noun–verb distinction or whether there are languages that exhibit a single supercategory above nouns and verb. In the latter case, this supercategory and its underlying superfeature would grammatically reveal themselves.

Traditionally, it has been assumed that languages minimally distinguish nouns and verbs (see, e.g., Greenberg 1963a; Pinker & Bloom 1990; Halle & Marantz 1993; Whaley 1997; Baker 2003; 2008; Borer 2003; Croft 2003; 2005b; 2009b). For some of these scholars (e.g. Baker), this universal noun–verb distinction is directly given by Universal Grammar (UG). However, there are a number of languages that display a behaviour that may make one cast doubt on this assumption as such languages do not show any morphosyntactic noun–verb distinction at all.

For instance, in Samoan, all content words can systematically be used both verbally and nominally. Samoan *alu* in (5) may either mean 'to go' or '(the) going', depending on the grammatical context: combined with a tense marker it obtains a verbal reading 'to go'; combined with an article, it yields a nominal reading '(the) going' (see Mosel & Hovdhaugen 1992; Don & van Lier 2013), as is illustrated below.

(5) Samoan (Don & van Lier 2013: 77)
   a. E   alu   le   pasi   i   Apia.
      PRES go   the   bus   to   Apia
      'The bus goes to Apia.'

   b. Le   alu   o   le   pasi   i   Apia
      The   go   of   the   bus   to   Apia
      'The going of the bus to Apia.'

Similar claims have been made for Mundari (Hengeveld & Rijkhoff 2005), Kharia (Peterson 2006), and Riau Indonesian (Gil 2013b; 2013c). In Mundari and Kharia, just as in Samoan, content words can be used both nominally and verbally. For instance, in Mundari nominally used *buru* means 'mountain' and verbally used *buru* means 'to heap up' (6); in Kharia nominally used *lebu* means 'man' and verbally used *lebu* 'to become a man' (7).

(6)   Mundari (Evans & Osada 2005: 354, 355)
   a. *Buru=ko*   *bai-ke-d-a*
      Mountain=3PL.S make-COMPL-TR-IND
      'They made the mountain.'

   b. *Saan=ko*   *buru-ke-d-a*
      Firewood=3PL.S mountain-COMPL-TR-IND
      'They heaped up the firewood.'

(7)   Kharia (Peterson 2006: 60)
   a. *Lebu del=ki*
      Man came.MV.PST
      'The man came.'

   b. *Baghwan lebu=ki*
      God   man.MV.PST
      'God became a man.'

And for Riau Indonesian, Gil (2013a; 2013b) has claimed that the syntactic distribution of any thing-denoting or action-denoting word is the same. For example, both *abang* ('(elder) brother') and *kencing* ('to pee') can be modified by a demonstrative (as shown in (8)), and may also appear in existential constructions, form the complements of adpositions, or combine with topic markers.

(8) Riau Indonesian (Gil 2013a)
    a. *Abang*   *in-i*
        Elder.brother   DEM-PROX
        'that brother/man'

    b. *Ter-kencing*   *in-i*
        NON_AG.pee   DEM-PROX
        'to pee'

The question is thus whether the examples in Mundari, Kharia, Samoan, and Riau Indonesian (and other languages that exhibit the same pattern) form counterexamples to the claimed universal noun–verb distinction, or whether these languages nevertheless underlyingly exhibit distinct nouns and verbs.

Within the functional paradigm, Hengeveld (1992a; 2005) and Hengeveld & Rijkhof (2005) have argued that languages that lack a morphosyntactic noun–verb distinction exhibit a supercategory dubbed *contentives*. The same conclusion has been reached by Mosel & Hovdhaugen (1992), who have also argued that languages such as Samoan lack distinct nouns and verbs, and exhibit a single lexical supercategory instead. By contrast, Croft (2005b), among others, has argued that in this type of language such nouns and verbs are actually homophonous: in (5) there are two instances of *alu*, a noun *alu* '(the) going' and a verb *alu* 'to go'. The central argument for postulating a noun–verb distinction in languages where there are no visible morphosyntactic differences between nouns and verbs, and thus for denying the existence of contentives, is that the meanings of the verbal and nominal usages of such alleged contentives do not follow compositionally. For instance, Samoan *tusi* means 'to write', 'letter', and 'book'. Similarly, Samoan *fana* means 'to shoot' and 'gun', *gaoi* 'to steal' and 'thief', and *eklaesia* 'to go to church' and 'church member'. It would be very hard to come up with a fully compositional analysis purely on the basis of the linguistic environment that can derive these meanings, and these meanings only, from a single semantic core. Evans & Osafa (2005) for this and other reasons assume that languages that seem to exhibit contentives (Mundari is their example) actually involve zero-derivation and do not exhibit a lexical supercategory 'contentives'. In order to address these problems, Hengeveld & Rijkhoff (2005) have argued that in such flexible languages, interpretation does not have to proceed in a strictly compositional fashion. For them, the underlying semantics is vague, so that both readings can come about, even though it is not predictable which meanings must be yielded. Contentives only have some flexible core, and the more specific meaning has to come about contextually.

Within minimalism, there are different ways to approach this question, depending on whether the categorial status of nominals, verbals, and adjectivals is lexically encoded or not. For Baker (2003), such lexical categories are indeed universally available and for him there exists no supercategory above them. To strengthen his case, he presents data as well from other languages that are generally taken to lack a noun–verb distinction, such as Makah. In Makah, what both look like verbs and nouns can function as an argument when followed by a determiner. But Baker points out that closer scrutiny still reveals differences between real verbs and nouns. For instance, real nouns can also be used as bare arguments (i.e. without the determiner), but real verbs and adjectives cannot, suggesting that in these cases obligatory nominalization is going on.

For non-lexical approaches, there is no such thing as a noun–verb distinction as what look like nouns and verbs are roots that are embedded in different syntactic structures. Hence, the question here boils down to whether roots can universally be embedded by both functional heads of an extended nominal and an extended verbal projection, and whether every root must first merge with a feature [n] or [v].

12.4 THE NATURE OF FORMAL FEATURES

As outlined above, the grammatical behaviour of lexical categories follows from the underlying features they carry. In that sense, lexical categories do not behave fundamentally different from functional categories, such as tense and agreement markers, determiners and complementizers. That a present tense marker like English *-s* in one way or the other realizes a present tense feature and a 3rd person singular feature is a well-established fact (see the discussion below for specific references). But if the grammatical behaviour of grammatical categories, lexical and functional categories alike, reduces to their underlying formal features, at least two questions immediately arise: what constitutes the set of potential formal features—is it universal or not? And what types of formal features can be distinguished—does every tense or verbal feature always display the same behaviour? These two questions will be addressed below.

12.4.1 Universal vs emergentist views on formal features

Over the past two decades, several proposals have been formulated that aim at accounting for the set of potential formal features in natural language grammars. For one, it has been argued that UG provides this set of formal features, and that every language has the same set of formal features at its disposal—a view much in line with the so-called cartographic approach, which, in its most radical version, assigns a universal syntactic structure to all natural language clauses with variation lying solely in the way that (parts of) this structure are phonologically realized (Pollock 1989; Beghelli & Stowell 1997; Rizzi 1997; 2004; Cinque 1999; 2002; 2006; Starke 2001; 2004; Caha 2009; Miyagawa 2009; Baunaz et al. 2018).

More recently, an alternative view arose which states that the set of formal features is as minimal as possible in every language. Under this view, sometimes referred to as *emergentist* or *WYSIWYG (What You See Is What You Get)* approaches, formal features and, consequently, their corresponding categories should only be assumed to be present if there is overt evidence for it (Iatridou 1990; Grimshaw 1997; Bobaljik & Thráinsson 1998; Koeneman 2000; Nilsen 2003; Zeijlstra 2008; 2014; Biberauer & Roberts 2015).

The main difference between these building-block grammar–WYSIWYG approaches and the cartographic approach (in its most radical sense) is that the visible presence of a particular formal feature in a particular language (for instance, if it projects some functional category) does not, under the former approach, imply its presence in all languages, whereas this is the basic line of reasoning under the latter approach (Cinque 1999; Kayne 2000; Starke 2004; Miyagawa 2009). This reduces the question as to what constitutes the set of formal features to a question about the nature of UG. Is UG a rich body of knowledge that contains the set of all formal features that a language may be sensitive to, or is UG, as has been proposed in more recent minimalist views (see Chomsky 2005), much poorer in nature, and are the relevant formal features to be acquired in the course of first-language acquisition?

The question whether the set of formal features is determined by UG naturally has strong repercussions for the nature of categories. If this is indeed part of UG, then, no specific account needs to be provided as to what categories a language may have. But if this set does not follow from UG then this begs the question as to what determines which categories can be present in a particular language and why they often appear to be very similar across languages (*pace* Haspelmath 2020).

Two types of arguments have been provided why the set of formal features should be part of UG. The first one comes from observed structural featural hierarchies and feature geometries. The starting point for cartography is Cinque (1999), who famously showed that the relative order between adverbials is uniform across languages. For instance, under neutral intonation speaker-oriented adverbs like *allegedly* must always be in a structurally higher position than aspectual adverbs such as *completely*, and the same holds for epistemic modal adverbs like *probably* and temporal adverbs like *always*, as illustrated for English below:

(9) a. Allegedly, Mary completely finished her painting.
    b. * Completely, Mary allegedly finished her painting.

(10) a. Suzanne probably always went to her classes.
     b. * Suzanne always probably went to her classes.

Cinque observed that adverbials in all languages in the world appear to be subject to the following structural hierarchy.

(11) [*frankly* Mood$_{speech\,act}$ [*fortunately* Mood$_{evaluative}$ [*allegedly* Mood$_{evidential}$ [*probably* Mod$_{epistemic}$ [*once* T(Past) [*then* T(Future) [*perhaps* Mood$_{irrealis}$ [*necessarily* Mod$_{necessity}$ [*possibly* Mod$_{possibility}$ [*usually* Asp$_{habitual}$ [*again* Asp$_{repetitive(I)}$ [*often* Asp$_{frequentative(I)}$ [*intentionally* Mod$_{volitional}$ [*quickly* Asp$_{celerative(I)}$ [*already* T(Anterior) [*no longer* Asp$_{terminative}$ [*still* Asp$_{continuative}$ [*always* Asp$_{perfect(?)}$ [*just* Asp$_{retrospective}$ [*soon* Asp$_{proximative}$ [*briefly* Asp$_{durative}$ [*characteristically*(?) Asp$_{generic/progressive}$ [*almost* Asp$_{prospective}$ [*completely* Asp$_{SgCompletive(I)}$ [*tutto* Asp$_{PlCompletive}$ [*well* Voice [*fast/early* Asp$_{celerative(II)}$ [*again* Asp$_{repetitive(II)}$ [*often* Asp$_{frequentative(II)}$ [*completely* Asp$_{SgCompletive(II)}$

For Cinque, each of these adverbial categories involves a formal feature of their own. For him, these features head different phrases that must stand in this particular hierarchical order.

Cinque's hierarchy is not the only one of its kind. Rizzi (1997) made similar observations about the relative order between structural positions in the left periphery (involving formal features like topic and focus) and Ramchand (1997) has argued that within verbal phrases similar hierarchical relations can be observed.

Whereas Cinque essentially proposes a syntactic hierarchy, his proposal boils down to the existence of a hierarchy between different formal features in combination with the conjecture that each of these features heads a phrase of its own. Such featural hierarchies have also been proposed in other domains, albeit without such syntactic ramifications, for instance when it comes to the various formal (φ-)features that constitutes pronominal paradigms. Harley & Ritter (2002) propose that these features stand in a feature-geometric relation as depicted in Figure 12.1.

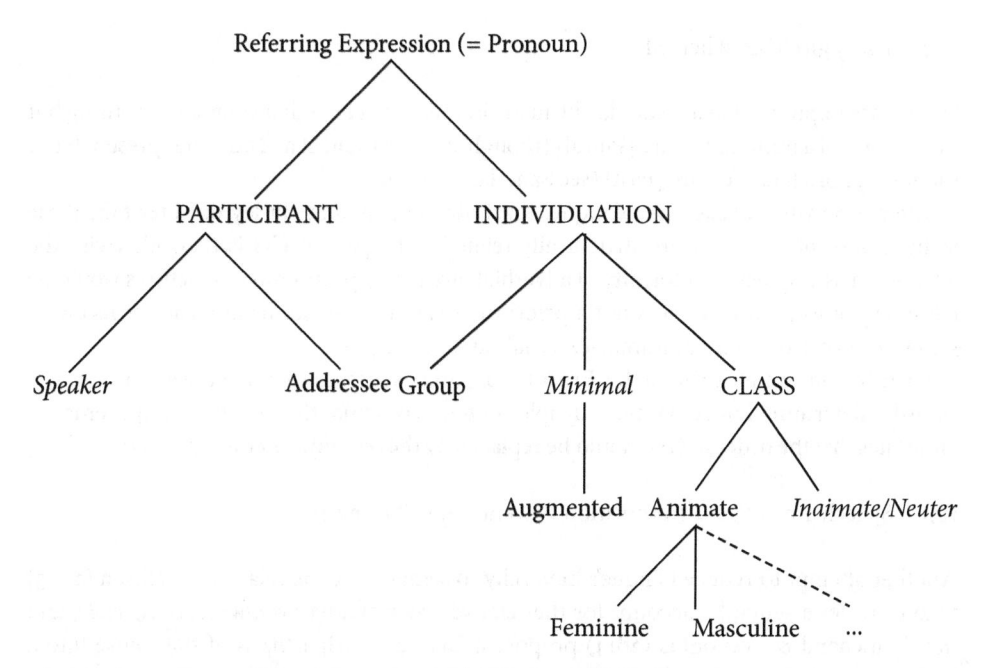

FIGURE 12.1 Feature hierarchy proposed by Harley & Ritter (2002)

Such feature-geometries do not only determine which formal features constitute pronominal paradigms, but also which features are dependent on others. For instance, the features [Feminine] and [Masculine] can only be grammatically active in a particular language if its grammar also exploits a feature [Animate]. Harley & Ritter (2002) claim that such feature hierarchies must also be acquisitionally reflected. The acquisition of [Feminine] and [Masculine] can only take place if [Animate] has been acquired before.

An important aspect of this featural hierarchy is that it can also account for markedness effects. It is often observed that certain features are more marked, i.e. morphologically or semantically more complex than others. For instance, the feature underlying the 2nd person, [Addressee], is generally considered more marked than the feature underlying the 1st person. And 3rd person is considered the most unmarked form. Outside pronominal domains, past tense morphology is considered more marked than present tense morphology. Rather than just postulating that certain features happen to be more marked, within a feature hierarchy like (12), markedness can be seen as a reflection of the distance to the highest node. A third person, then, reflects the absence of a feature [Speaker] or [Addressee]; it simply lacks specific person features (see Forschheimer 1953; Benveniste 1971; Heim 2008; Sauerland 2008; Kratzer 2009; Zeijlstra 2015). Unmarkedness follows from featural underspecification.

Supporting evidence for the view that certain pronouns, like 3rd person pronouns, are featurally underspecified comes from the fact that 3rd person subjects like *he* or *she* are known to be able to make reference to a speaker or hearer too. As Heim (2008) has shown, a sentence like (13) cannot only be used to talk about a set of girls that does not include the speaker or hearer. Example (13) can also be uttered by, or addressed to, a member of the same set of the girls that are being talked about. This is evidenced by the fact that adding a continuation to (12) like 'including me (and you)' is felicitous.

(12) Every girl invited herself.

Similar assumptions that are standardly made in this respect are that singular is nothing but the absence of a number feature [Plural] (though see Sauerland et al. 2005) and present tense the absence of a tense feature [Past] (see Sauerland 2002).

The reason why scholars like Cinque, Rizzi, Ramchand, and Harley & Ritter take these features and the way they are structurally related to be part of UG is that otherwise the attested cross-linguistic uniformity of adverbial orders and pronominal structures would be left unexplained. However, it is not a priori the case that this uniformity cannot receive a syntax-external, or even a grammar-external explanation.

Focusing on Cinque's Hierarchy, Ernst (2002) argues instead that that adverb ordering is (mostly) determined by semantic principles in terms of semantic selectional requirements. He argues that the order in (11) should be replaced by the semantic hierarchy in (13).

(13) Speech-Act > Fact > Proposition > Event > Specified event

Another attempt to reduce Cinque's hierarchy to semantic scope relations is Nilsen (2003) who provides a semantic account for the relative order of adverbs *always*, *completely*, and *not*. Ramchand & Svenonius (2014) propose a UG-based tripartition of the clause into a V-domain, a T-domain, and a C-domain, which for them reflects a conceptual hierarchy Proposition > Situation > Event. Further articulation within these domains can then be language-specific (see also Wiltschko 2014 for a similar proposal). Also, featural hierarchies like the one proposed by Harley & Ritter have received semantic explanations (see, e.g., Heim 2008; Sauerland 2008; Kratzer 2009).

A second type of argument in favour of a universal pool of formal features comes from so-called *ABA effects. As Caha & Vanden Wyngaerd (2017: 2) put it:

> Morphological paradigms can be ordered so as to observe the *ABA restriction, i.e. such that only contiguous cells in a paradigm are syncretic. Syncretisms thus reveal a hierarchy in paradigms, which is in turn accounted for in terms of a hierarchy of underlying features. Consequently, syncretisms can be used as a tool for the diagnosis of feature structures.

Foundational discussions of *ABA patterns are found in Caha (2009) in case markers and Bobaljik (2012) on suppletion in comparative and superlative forms of adjectives. Concerning the latter, as Table 12.1 shows, positive, comparative, and superlative adjectives may have one shared base or employ two or even three different bases. However, what is impossible is that the positive and the superlative form of an adjective employ the same base to the exclusion of the comparative.

Table 12.1 Suppletion for comparative vs superlative adjective forms

	Pattern	Positive	Comparative	Superlative	Language
a.	AAA	small	small-er	small-est	English
b.	ABB	good	bett-er	be-st	English
c.	ABC	bon-us	mel-ior	opt-imus	Latin
d.	*ABA	good	bett-er	good-est	English'

*ABA patterns have been used to motivate proposals that paradigmatic orderings reflect structural containment hierarchies. For example, Bobaljik (2012) argues that the structure of the superlative contains the structure of the comparative, which in turn contains that of the positive. The restrictions on possible syncretisms are then derived from the workings of spell-out, whereby (underspecified) vocabulary items expone contiguous regions or spans of featural hierarchies. If such *ABA effects hold universally, as is claimed by Bobaljik (2012), these featural hierarchies should be universal as well.

By contrast, others have argued against a universal set of formal features. For instance, Iatridou (1990) provides several arguments that the formal features that are active in the inflectional domain vary from one language to another and should not be taken to be universally present. Zeijlstra (2004) has argued that negation is a formal feature only in some, but crucially not all languages. These authors argue that formal features are not universal but rather language-specific.

Such emergentist/WYSIWYG views of grammar assume that a language-learning child presupposes the existence of certain syntactic features only if there is overt morphosyntactic evidence for them in the language input. In other words, only those syntactic features of which there is a grammatical reflex—for instance, different categories, involvement in agreement relations, triggers of movement—can be considered part of the formal feature inventory of the target language. Other potential syntactic features must be taken to be absent, irrespective of whether they are active in other languages.

Even though the latter view should be taken to be the default hypothesis (given that one should only postulate grammatical knowledge to be part of UG if the presence of that knowledge cannot otherwise be accounted for), its correctness can only be evaluated against a concrete proposal of how these formal features can be acquired in the first place. Not many proposals for this have been developed, though (see Zeijlstra 2014; Biberauer & Roberts 2015 for some examples), so it remains to be seen what such an emergentist perspective should really amount to.

12.4.2 Types of formal features

Irrespective of the question of whether formal features are part of UG or not, the question arises to what exact properties formal features have. The central question in this respect concerns the relation between formal and semantic features. This is again fundamental for understanding the nature of categories, as it is very hard, if not impossible, to define lexical and functional categories in purely semantic terms (see section 12.2).

For Chomsky (1995), the set of formal features, i.e. the set of features that may participate in syntactic operations, is one that intersects with the set of semantic features (the architecture of grammatical features is depicted in Figure 12.2). Consequently, formal features come about in two kinds: interpretable and uninterpretable formal features. Interpretable formal features ([iF]s) are features that are part of the intersection of the sets of formal and semantic features; therefore, both participate in syntactic operations and receive an interpretation. Uninterpretable features, by contrast, are features that are only formal, and not semantic in nature, and therefore cannot receive a semantic interpretation.

Phonological features   Formal features   Semantic features

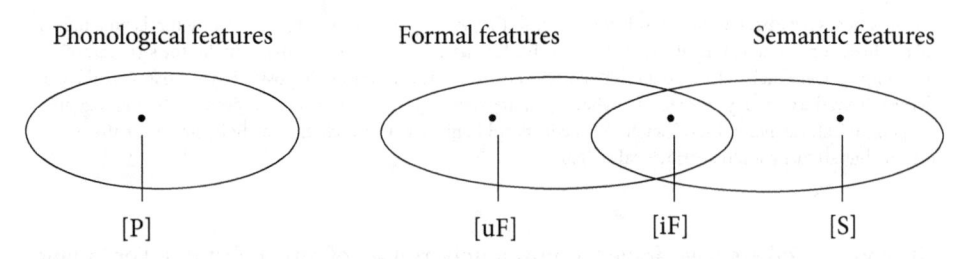

[P]   [uF]   [iF]   [S]

FIGURE 12.2 Feature sets based on Chomsky (1995)

Examples of interpretable features are for instance φ-features on nominals. The 1st person plural feature on *we* is what gives rise to its reference to a plurality including the speaker. By contrast, φ-features on finite verbs are void of semantics. There is nothing in the meaning of a finite verb like *sleeps* that makes reference to a 3rd person singular.

Chomsky (1995; 2001) furthermore argues that every feature that reaches the semantic and phonological interfaces must be interpretable, something he refers to as the Principle of Full Interpretation:

(14) Full Interpretation (FI): Every element of an output representation should provide a meaningful input to the relevant other parts of the cognitive system.

To satisfy Full Interpretation, all uninterpretable formal features must be deleted in the course of a syntactic derivation, as those, by definition, do not provide any meaningful input. For Chomsky (1995; 2001), Agree is the only available operation that is capable of deleting uninterpretable formal features: If a matching interpretable and an uninterpretable formal feature stand in a particular (c-command) configuration, the uninterpretable feature can be checked off against the interpretable one and, as a consequence, be deleted. Once every uninterpretable feature has been deleted, the derivation can be fully interpreted at the interfaces; after the deletion of those features that are only formal in nature, all features left are either phonological or semantic features, which are interpretable at the relevant interfaces.

The core motivation behind (14) is that it reduces two ununderstood issues in grammar to one, namely the existence of semantically redundant material and the triggering of movement operations. If movement takes place to check off uninterpretable formal features, it remains an open question why there would be uninterpretable features in the first place.

At the same time, the idea that semantic redundancy triggers movement is problematic in at least one sense. Since it can only be determined within the semantic component of grammar whether a particular feature is interpretable, the (un)interpretability of a feature is not visible in narrow syntax (which precedes semantic interpretation). Hence, deletion of uninterpretable features as such cannot be a trigger for syntactic operations, since it would yield a *look ahead problem*, as pointed out by Epstein et al. (1998) and Epstein & Seely (2002). For this reason, in later work, Chomsky argues that deletion of uninterpretable features is not the trigger of syntactic operations, but that, rather, feature valuation is.

Chomsky (2001) proposes enriching the feature taxonomy by including a second parameter, feature (un)valuedness. For him, all formal features that are interpretable are already valued within the lexicon, and formal features that are uninterpretable are also lexically unvalued. In other words, for him, interpretability and valuedness always go hand in hand, and the number of different types of formal features remains identical (interpretable valued formal features and uninterpretable unvalued formal features). The 1st person plural feature on *we* is thus not only semantically active, but also already part of the lexical representation of *we*. A φ-feature on a finite verb is then, apart from being meaningless, a feature whose φ-values are determined by the grammatical context (i.e. they come from the subject). This architecture is shown in Figure 12.3, where '___' means *unvalued* and 'val' means *valued*.

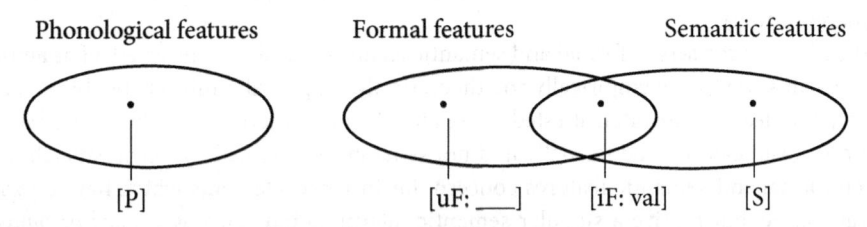

FIGURE 12.3 Feature sets based on Chomsky (2002)

Now, Chomsky postulates that, during syntax, all lexically unvalued features must be valued under Agree and subsequently deleted before reaching the semantics interface. Since every uninterpretable feature is taken to be lexically unvalued, only those formal features that are interpretable will thus feed semantics.

Note that it is by pure stipulation, though, that (un)valuedness and (un)interpretability should always coincide. If that stipulation is given up, formal features should actually come about in four kinds: (i) interpretable and unvalued features; (ii) interpretable and valued features; (iii) uninterpretable and unvalued features; and (iv) uninterpretable and valued features. This is exactly what has been proposed by Pesetsky & Torrego (2007), who argue that valuedness and interpretability are disentangled notions. Then, both types of interpretable features form a subset of the set of semantic features, and both types of uninterpretable features do not do so. Pesetsky & Torrego's (2007) taxonomy thus looks as in Figure 12.4.

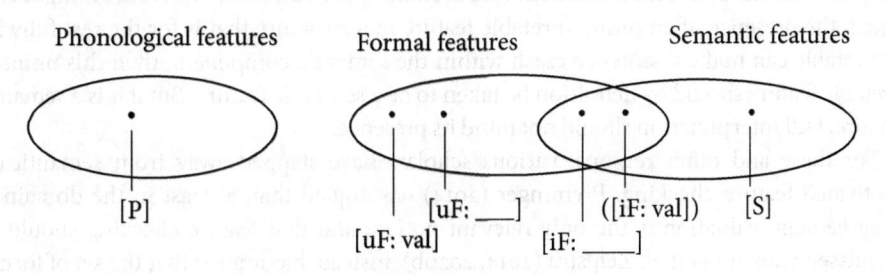

FIGURE 12.4 Feature sets based on Pesetsky & Torrego (2007)

Again, lexically unvalued uninterpretable formal features are for instance φ-features on finite verbs, just as φ-features on nominals are valued interpretable formal features. An example of lexically valued but uninterpretable formal features would be tense features on finite verbs. Even though tense is only marked on a finite verb (and must therefore enter a syntactic derivation from the lexicon with its tense value already present), tense is not interpreted on the verb itself but higher up in the structure. A sentence like *Mary studied syntax* means that in the past a study event took place of which Mary is the agent and syntax the theme. Tense thus takes scope over the entire VP (i.e. the predicate and its argument) and does not just apply to the verb. Consequently, the tense value on the finite verb must be uninterpretable but values a higher tense operator (see Ogihara 1995; Abusch 1997; Kratzer 2009). Finally, an example of lexically unvalued but interpretable formal features may be the φ-features on an anaphor (like *herself*). Since anaphors must have exactly the same set of φ-features as their antecedents, one could argue that anaphors enter the sentence unvalued and only receive their φ-features from their antecedents; at the same time, being a nominal, such φ-features on an anaphor must still be interpretable (see, e.g., Kratzer 2009; Tucker 2011; Sundaresan 2012).

The idea that the sets of formal and semantic features overlap has received a fair amount of criticism as well, both empirically and theoretically. Empirically, mismatches between the two types of features are often attested, as we already saw in section 12.2 where it was shown that categories can only be formally and not semantically defined. Other mismatches between formal and semantic features concern, for instance, elements which have a formal plural feature, but receive a singular semantic interpretation, such as *scissors* or *pants* in English. Examples in the other direction can also be attested; *furniture, family* are semantically plural, but syntactically singular. Likewise, certain nouns can be formally neutral but semantically feminine, such as German *Mädchen* ('girl'). Similar mismatches can also be attested in the verbal domain. Deponent verbs, like Latin *loqui* ('talk'), are formally passive but semantically active.

Theoretically, the evidence against the model in (18)/(19) faces certain problems as well. The central idea behind this model is, as said, Chomsky's Principle of Full Interpretation. For Chomsky, any uninterpretable feature must be deleted/erased in syntax. However, it is unclear why particular formal features should be able to disappear from the structure just by appearing in particular configuration with a matching interpretable feature. Moreover, one may even wonder why features need to be deleted in order for the derivation to survive semantically. Why could the zero meaning contribution of an uninterpretable feature not simply be ignored by semantics? In fact, as noted in Zeijlstra (2014) not ignoring the vacuous meaning contribution of an uninterpretable feature even yields a logical contradiction. Semantic features are defined as features that can constitute a distinction between two different semantic representations (see Svenonius 2006b). Now, if, all other things being equal, the presence of an uninterpretable feature in a structure that is for the rest fully interpretable can make a sentence crash within the semantic component, then this uninterpretable feature should by definition be taken to be a semantic feature. But if it is a semantic feature, Full Interpretation should not mind its presence.

For these and other reasons, various scholars have stepped away from semantically motivated feature checking. Preminger (2014) has argued that, at least in the domain of φ-agreement, valuation is the only relevant notion, and that feature checking should be dismissed with altogether. Zeijlstra (2014; 2020b), instead, has argued that the set of formal features should be fully disentangled from the set of semantic features (see also Smith 2015). Other scholars (e.g. Richards 2010; 2016) have argued that formal features should not be alluded to in the first place to account for particular syntactic operations, such as movement. All these approaches disentangle formal features from semantic features, and thus grammatical categories from different types of semantic objects. This paves the way for a fully distributional, morphosyntactic approach to the nature of categories.

12.5 BY MEANS OF CONCLUSION

The discussion on grammatical categories in this chapter is based on the observation that morphosyntactic rules are not sensitive to word classes or categories, but rather to the lexical and formal morphosyntactic features that underlie them, potentially augmented with roots. Consequently, understanding the nature, distribution, and hierarchical ordering of such categories reduces to understanding the nature, distribution, and hierarchical ordering of these underlying features. In this chapter I have addressed what I think are the most important approaches in this respect. Needless to say, what I have captured is only a small selection of what has been discussed and described in the literature on formal features. Such a selection is always subjective and other authors most likely would have made different choices. Nevertheless, I hope that this selection has provided readers with a representative impression of what has been and what can be said about the morphosyntactic features underlying both lexical and functional categories.

CHAPTER 13

LEXICAL CATEGORIES IN DISTRIBUTED MORPHOLOGY

JAN DON

13.1 INTRODUCTION

THERE is a long tradition in linguistics that considers content words (as opposed to function words) such as *house*, *work*, or *red* to be a member of the lexical categories noun, verb, and adjective respectively. These categorial labels, or word classes, by and large determine the syntactic distribution of the elements carrying the given label. In earlier versions of generative theory, the lexicon contained items including their category among other things, such as their subcategorization, meaning, and phonological properties (see e.g. Lieber 1981 for such a view). So, in a lexical framework, *house*, *work*, and *red* would be lexical elements, more or less represented as in (1a–c).

(1) a. [/haʊs/, N, 'HOUSE']   b. [/wɜːk/, V, 'WORK']   c. [/rɛd/, A, 'RED']

Such lexical elements could not only be inserted in the syntax, but would also function as potential targets for word-formation rules that operate 'in the lexicon' in lexical theories of morphology. Distributed Morphology (DM) stands in radical opposition to such lexical theories of morphology (Halle & Marantz 1993; Marantz 1997). The view that individual lexical items are stored as objects containing syntactic, semantic, and phonological information is abandoned, and DM deconstructs these lexical items, strictly separating the syntactic from the phonological and the semantic information (as was originally proposed in Anderson 1992 and Beard 1995). Furthermore, rather than having word-formation rules in the lexicon, words are derived in the syntax. Consequently, the categorial information is no longer a fixed property of an item (as in (1)), but results from the merger of a particular root with a functional head that determines the category of the resulting complex as in (2). Categories no longer originate in the lexicon, but are syntactic.

(2) (a) n / (n, √HOUSE)   (b) v / (v, √WORK)   (c) a / (a, √RED)

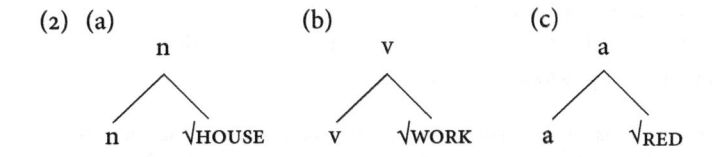

Consequently, lexical categories are no longer different from functional categories, but join the realm of categories such as D, Tense, Comp.

In this chapter, I first discuss the basic motivation for this non-lexical approach to lexical categories which requires a small excursus to the classic paper 'Remarks on Nominalization' (Chomsky 1970) in section 13.2. There, I also offer some new evidence for the existence of roots. I continue in section 13.3 by focusing on the question what factor is responsible for the categorization of words; if the roots are not the elements containing the categorial information, where does it come from? Here, I also briefly go into some interesting alternatives for some of the assumptions within DM[1] as offered by Lowenstamm (2015) and Borer (2014). In section 13.4, this theoretical perspective is confronted with the observation that word classes may sometimes be linked with phonological requirements, and the consequences of this state of affairs for the theory is discussed. Finally, in section 13.5, I will briefly conclude.

13.2 Why do we need uncategorized roots?

Chomsky (1970) first proposed that lexical items are unspecified for categorial information. He discusses a particular type of nominalization, aiming to find empirical evidence (Marantz 1997) that could decide between different analytical options that the theory offered at that time. The nominalizations in question are known as derived nominals which are characterized by less than full productivity, and different semantic relations between the nominal and the base from which it is supposedly derived. Furthermore, they head noun phrases, rather than verb phrases, as in the case of so-called gerunds. Below we have given some examples of this type of nominalization (the (c) examples), including the presumed base (the (a) examples) and the so-called gerund (the (b) examples):

(3) a. John refuses the offer
     b. John's refusing the offer
     c. John's refusal of the offer

(4) a. John criticizes the book
     b. John's criticizing the book
     c. John's criticism of the book

(5) a. John is eager to win
     b. John's being eager to win
     c. John's eagerness to win

---

[1] See Borer (2015) for an overview of some of the theoretical issues involving the precise nature of the root.

One of the analytical options is to make the rules of syntax more complex so that the difference between the gerunds and the derived nominals would fall out of these rules. The other option is described by Chomsky as follows:

> We can enter *refuse* in the lexicon as an item with certain fixed selectional and strict subcategorization features, <u>which is free with respect to the categorial features [noun] and [verb]</u>. Fairly idiosyncratic morphological rules will determine the phonological form of *refuse*, *destroy*, etc. when these items appear in the noun position. The fact that *refuse* takes a noun phrase complement, either as a noun or as a verb, is expressed by the feature structure of the 'neutral' lexical entry, as are selectional properties.
>
> (1970: 190, emphasis supplied in underlined text)

As one can see, Chomsky proposes category-neutral elements in the lexicon, i.e. a precursor of the notion root as it later developed within the theory of DM (Marantz 1997).

Chomsky finds empirical evidence for this position (vis-à-vis making the syntactic component more complex) in examples such as (6)–(8). It would be difficult to explain the difference between the (c) examples and the (b) examples if they were both (syntactically) derived from the bases in the (a) examples. We would have to complicate the syntactic component in such a way that the derived nominals somehow would not be allowed to have sentential complements (as in (6)), or nominal objects (as in (7) and (8)), while the gerunds (the (c) examples) do allow for such complements.

(6) a. John is certain to win the prize
     b. * John's certainty to win the prize
     c. John's being certain to win the prize

(7) a. Eric amused the children
     b. * Eric's amusement of the children
     c. Eric's amusing the children

(8) a. John grows tomatoes
     b. * John's growth of tomatoes
     c. John's/the growing of tomatoes

However, once we admit categoryless items to the theory, the ungrammaticality of the (b) examples can be easily explained. To see how this works, let us focus on the example in (8). Similar reasoning applies to the other examples. The verb *to grow* has two readings: it can be either inchoative (*tomatoes grow*) in which case there is no agent involved, or it can be causative (8a) implying some agent. Note that the ungrammaticality of (8b) tells us that the causative reading is not available in the case of the derived nominal *growth*, while this is a possible reading of the gerund (8c).

Suppose we have an item that does not carry any categorial information, i.e. the root √GROW. This removes the necessity of having to derive both the gerund and the derived nominal from the same verb. We can propose instead that the derived nominal is directly derived from the root (plus some nominalizing head), whereas the gerund is derived from a structure, involving the root, and a verbal head.

More specifically, the inchoative reading of the verb *to grow* derives from a structure in which this root is merged with a verbal head (9a). The 'derived nominal' *growth* no longer derives from the verb, but is built from the same root, merged with a nominal head (9b). The causative reading involves the more complex structure (9c), including a causative verbal head. Furthermore, we may observe that the causative reading is present in the gerund (*John's growing of tomatoes*) (9d), showing that the gerund can be made from the complex causative verb.

Crucially, the agent-taking property of the causative verb *grow* is not located in its underived core, which it shares with the noun *growth*, but is a property of the verbal functional element that turns the root into a verb. Since the noun *growth* is not derived from this verb, but from the verb's root, it does not have this causative reading.

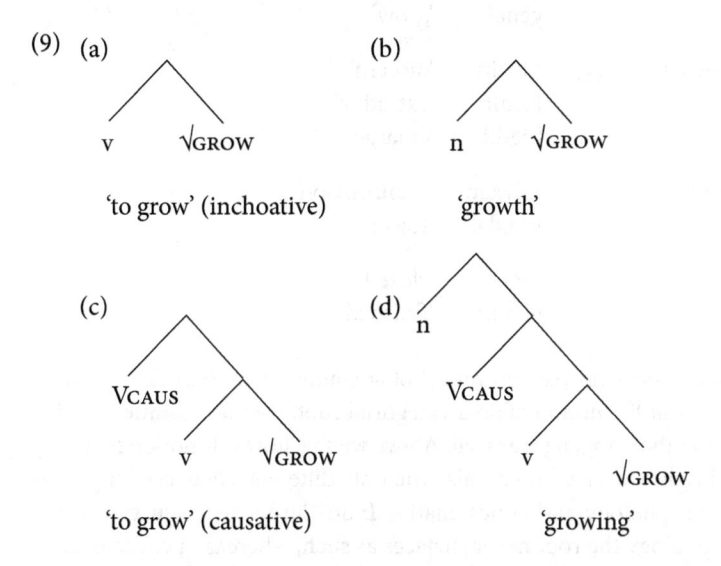

(9) (a) [v √GROW] 'to grow' (inchoative)

(b) [n √GROW] 'growth'

(c) [v_CAUS [v √GROW]] 'to grow' (causative)

(d) [n [v_CAUS [v √GROW]]] 'growing'

Next to this motivation for the existence of roots, which may strike some readers as rather theory-internal, additional evidence comes from Semitic languages that show so-called root-and-template morphology. In such a non-concatenative system, words are typically built from a root consisting of a series of consonants that are separated by a pattern of vowels marking some morphological category. In (10) we have given some examples from Hebrew. The root is linked to the consonants (capital Cs in (10)) of the patterns (data from Arad 2003: 743; Ravid 2016: 129).[2]

(10) Roots: /ʔmd/, /sgr/, /gdl/;
    pattern: CaCaC   pattern: hi-CCiC
  a. ʔamad 'be standing'   b. hi-ʔemid 'make stand up'
     sagar   'close'   hi-sgir   'extradite'
     gadal   'grow'   hi-gdil   'enlarge'

From such data we can conclude that the core meaning ('stand up', 'close', 'grow') correlates with the appearance of the consonantal root, which itself is an element that cannot be

---

[2] There are several morphophonological operations that may alter the root consonants in particular environments. We do not go into these details. The identity of the roots should be clear from these examples.

used without the morphology realized by the vowel pattern.[3] These roots should always go together with some other element that minimally categorizes the word as either verbal, nominal, or adjectival. In (11) we have given some examples of the same root occurring in different lexical categories (Arad 2003: 743; Ravid & Schiff 2006: 790):

(11) Root: /bxn/,[4] /sgr/, /gdl/, /gmr/

a. CaCaC (v) baxan   'test, examine'
              sagar   'close'
              gadal   'grow'

b. hiCCiC (v) hivxin 'discern'
              hisgir 'extradite'
              higdil 'enlarge'

c. miCCaC (n) mivxan 'examination'
              migdal 'tower'

d. CaCuC (a) sagur   'closed'
              gamur   'finished'

If this system, often called root-and-pattern morphology, attested in Semitic languages cannot be understood without the notion of an a-categorial root, we may assume that this same notion plays a role in other languages as well. Above we saw how this notion may play a role in the analysis of English 'derived nominals'. The only difference between languages using root-and-pattern morphology and concatenative Indo-European languages is that in root-and-pattern morphology the root never surfaces as such, whereas in concatenative systems it does. The appearance is different, but not the underlying system.

A third argument that, as far as I know, has not previously been put forward comes from the observation that there are phonological idiosyncrasies that need to be located in an element that is smaller than a categorized word. Let us consider the following data from Dutch:

(12)
verb (stem)		'gloss'	noun		'gloss'
baad	[bat]	'to bathe'	bad	[bɑt]	'bath'
daag	[dax]	'to dawn'	dag	[dɑx]	'day'
daal	[dal]	'to descend'	dal	[dɑl]	'valley'
(ver-af-)good	[xot]	'divinize'	god	[xɔt]	'god'
loot	[lot]	'to draw'	lot	[lɔt]	'destiny'
speel	[spel]	'to play'	spel	[spɛl]	'play'

Note that the paired words share a semantic core, even though the relation between the two meanings is not systematic. In this respect, the situation is not unlike the examples from Hebrew.

If we compare the phonological forms of the verbs in (12) with those of the corresponding nouns, we observe that the stem of the verb (which is identical to the first person singular,

---

[3] These patterns may be compared with English patterns that we find in words based on Latinate roots. One may think of examples such as *trans-mit, re-mit, e-mit*, and *miss-ion, miss-ive, miss-ile*.
[4] Note that the initial *b* of the root shows up as *v* after a vowel (in examples (9b–c)).

present tense, in Dutch) contains a tense vowel, while the corresponding vowel in the stem of the noun (identical to the singular noun) is a lax variant of that vowel. The same tense vowel that is present in the verb also shows up in the plural of the noun, as can be seen from the data in (13):

(13) a.
sing.[5]   pl.   b. sing.   pl.
bad [bɑt] ba.d-en [badən] 'bath'   tak [tɑk]   takk-en [takən] 'branch'
dag [dɑx] da.g-en [daxən] 'day'   kat [kɑt]   katt-en [katən] 'cat'
dal [dɑl] da.l-en [dalən] 'valley'   kwal [kwɑl] kwall-en [kwalən] 'jellyfish'
god [xɔt] go.d-en [godən] 'god'   stop [stɔp] stopp-en [stɔpən] 'stop'
lot [lɔt] lo.t-en [lotən] 'destiny'   krot [krɔt] krott-en [krɔtən] 'shack'
spel [spel] spe.l-en [spelən] 'play'   bel [bel]   bell-en [belən] 'bell'

The phonological alternation in the vowels of the singular and plural nouns in (11a) is commonly referred to as Open Syllable Lengthening (OSL) (Zonneveld 1978). In syllables not closed by a consonantal coda, the vowel is lengthened (i.e. tensed). Since the nominal plural suffix (-ən) begins with a vowel, resyllabification of the final stem consonant removes the closure of the prefinal syllable, which creates the environment for OSL. Crucially, OSL is not an automatic phonological rule in Dutch, as can be seen from the data in (11b). Here, we find a lax vowel in both the singular and the plural, with an ambisyllabic consonant.

The pattern in (13a) only occurs in a handful of nouns that have to be learned by the native speaker. Therefore, the information that they undergo OSL should somehow be stored. It seems logical to store this information in the lexical entry of the noun. However, the surprise is that all the corresponding verbs also have tensed vowels in their stem. Put differently, we may set up the following generalization about the Dutch examples (14):

(14) OSL generalization[6] (Dutch)
No nouns showing OSL have corresponding verbs with a lax vowel.

Therefore, storage of the idiosyncratic OSL information in the noun would leave this generalization unexplained. Similar to what we saw in the English derived nominals, the generalization in (14) is immediately explained if there is an element underlying both the verbs and the nouns that is the location of this phonological idiosyncrasy. Once we acknowledge the fact that nouns are complex, and consist of a root plus a categorizing head, the root is the obvious place for the storage of the idiosyncratic information, explaining the non-existence of corresponding verbs with a lax vowel.

Summarizing: the different types of English nominalizations can be easily dealt with once we assume that at the heart of verbs, nouns, and adjectives lie elements without categorial information which are the locus of the lexical semantics and the phonological core of these

---

[5] The final obstruent in these examples is voiceless due to the regular rule of *Auslautverhaertung*. The doubly spelled consonants in the plural examples are just an oddity of the Dutch spelling convention to indicate the lax vowel before the consonant.

[6] We know of one exception to this generalization; the verb *statten* 'to city' which means something like to go to the city and do shopping. The plural of *stad* 'city' is *sted-en* and showing OSL. Apparently, in this particular case, it is the noun [n [√STAD]] that is used as a verb, rather than the root.

verbs and nouns.[7] Exactly the same type of element is needed to explain so-called root-and-pattern morphology that we encounter in Semitic languages. Furthermore, the idea of roots without category is further supported by a generalization from Dutch which shows that the root is the locus for idiosyncratic phonological information, explaining a generalization that is unexpected if we would have to store this information separately in verbs and nouns. All in all, there seems to be sufficient evidence for the existence of a class of morphemes that is not categorized, and that forms the core of content words.

13.3 WHAT ARE THE CATEGORIZERS?

Above we have seen why roots need to be severed from categorial information. The immediate question that this position raises is where the categorial information comes from if it is not in the root. We will see that this question is answered differently by different proponents of the root-plus-category view on morphology. The difference in view may have consequences for the analysis of derivational affixes, which traditionally have been taken as elements that determine or change the category of complex words. Before I get to this, a few more general remarks about DM are in order, which will form the context of the discussion.[8]

Words, like sentences, are built by merging feature bundles which yields structures that are interpreted semantically and phonologically at a later stage in the derivation. DM is 'piece-based' in the sense that it does not allow for other spell-out operations than the insertion of phonologically specified items (so-called vocabulary items). In this respect the theory differs from one of the earliest proposals of a realizational theory of morphology, i.e. Anderson (1992) (see also Stump 2019). Let me illustrate the idea of a piece-based realizational morphology with the example already discussed in section 13.1. The word *growth* consists in the merger of a root, and a categorial head 'n'. So, after syntax, and, depending on the structure we are dealing with, after the application of one or more postsyntactic operations,[9] structures such as (10b) result, here repeated as (15):

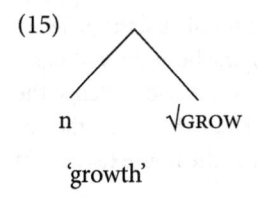

(15)

      n   √GROW

'growth'

---

[7] Note that there are different views concerning the question whether the root has a phonological characterization. Here we assume it has. See Harley et al. (2017) for discussion and a different view.

[8] I refrain from introducing DM in general, however, since that would go far beyond the limits of this chapter. The reader is referred to Embick (2015) for an elaborate introduction to the theory.

[9] DM allows for some other postsyntactic operations, such as head movement, fusion, fission, and lowering, that we leave aside here (see Halle & Marantz 1994; Embick & Noyer 2001). These operations are not relevant for the main discussion and would therefore only complicate matters in an unnecessary way.

This structure is sent to Phonological Form where spell-out takes place, and Logical Form where semantic interpretation takes place. There are different views what this means for the root. In its original conception it is argued that individual differences between roots (i.e. the difference between, e.g. *dog* and *cat*) are not relevant to syntax. This difference only becomes relevant at spell-out and semantic interpretation. Consequently, insertion of roots can also be postponed until after syntax. However, Harley (2014) shows that there are languages showing true cases of root suppletion which makes this view untenable. She argues (following Pfau 2000 and Acquaviva 2008) that what is inserted in syntax is just a unique identifier (one may think of it as an integer) that allows the retrieval of the phonological representation and semantic information linked to this particular root.

For the categorial head 'n', there may be spell-out rules that determine its phonological form. These rules may be context-sensitive in the sense that, dependent on the (realization of the) root, the categorial head may receive one or the other spell-out. So, the rule that may realize the n-head as the suffix *-th* could have the form (14a), whereas the same head may be realized differently (e.g. as zero) in the context of another root (such as $\sqrt{\text{WALK}}$) (16b).

(16) a. n → -th / ____ {$\sqrt{\text{GROW}}$, $\sqrt{\text{STRONG}}$, ...}
     b. n → -∅ / ____ {$\sqrt{\text{LIE}}$, $\sqrt{\text{WALK}}$, ...}

On this view, categorization comes from separate categorial heads that may be spelled out by what traditionally has been called derivational affixes. This view has been proposed by, e.g., Marantz (2001; 2007), Marvin (2002), and Embick & Marantz (2008). More generally, it has been proposed that what has been referred to as inflectional affixes are the realizations of syntactic–semantic feature bundles, whereas derivational affixes are the realization of categorial heads (Harley & Noyer 1999). However, it is not the only view that has been proposed in the literature. Others have answered the question as to what the categorizers are in different ways. Below, I discuss two such proposals. Each of these involves a different perspective on the notion 'derivational affix'.

First, Lowenstamm (2015) argues for a view in which categorial heads (at least in English) are not realized by derivational affixes, but are always zero. The reason is that according to Lowenstamm the view that derivational affixes are functional categorizers stands in the way of an explanation of stress shift.[10] Without wanting to go into too much technical detail here, consider the reasoning. Under fairly standard assumptions about the way spell-out is organized, in a configuration [z [y [x [root]]], where x, y, and z are categorial heads, either x triggers the spell-out of the root, or y triggers the spell-out of the complement of x, i.e. the root. This implies that z cannot be a stress-shifting affix since an affix in this structural position is never able to influence the spell-out of the root. However, in words such as *atomicity* and *originality*, the stress-shifting affix *-ity* is in the structural position of z, and does influence the spell-out of the root. Consequently, either the assumptions about spell-out, or the assumption that derivational affixes realize categorial heads, needs changing.

Furthermore, Lowenstamm also notes that many affixes in English display categorial flexibility, i.e. the same affix can be found in more than one category. Similar observations

---

[10] See Embick (2014) for a different view.

have been made by De Belder (2011) for Dutch. Some English examples are given in (17) (from Lowenstamm 2015: 234):

(17)   Noun   Adjective

-an   librarian   reptilian
-ant   defendant   defiant
-ary   functionary legendary
-ive   incentive   auditive
-ish   rubbish   foppish

This empirical observation does not sit well with the view that affixes are the realization of functional categorizers. It would force us to doubly list these affixes in the lexicon. For each category they may realize, we would need a separate entry. Lowenstamm, therefore, proposes that affixes are roots. This immediately explains their categorial flexibility, and it removes the blockage for an explanation of stress shift, since words such as *atomicity* should be analysed as involving a structure consisting of different roots (*atom*, *-ic* and *-ity*) with only a single nominal categorizer at the top, thereby creating a single domain for spell-out. Now, again this raises the question, if it is not the roots, and it is not the derivational affixes, then what are the categorizing elements? Lowenstamm submits that categorial heads are never realized (in English, at least). There is simply no spell-out of these heads, which therefore remain 'silent'.

As a second alternative, Borer (2014; 2015) submits that there is no need for separate categorial heads in the theory. She points out that one of the drawbacks of the DM system is that it leads to the assumption of numerous categorial heads that are never spelled out (i.e. so-called zero affixes). As we have seen, the same objection holds a fortiori against Lowenstamm's proposal. Borer observes that *-al* derived words, such as *formal*, *sortal*, *coastal*, are all related in form and meaning to the nouns *form*, *sort*, and *coast*, etc. whereas *-able* derived words, such as *formable*, *sortable*, and *coastable*, are all related to the verbs *form*, *sort*, and *coast*. Apparently, affixes such as *-able* and *-al* require a categorized (in these cases nominal and verbal, respectively) base, i.e. they have subcategorization properties. However, there is nothing in the phonology of these forms that distinguishes the verb from the noun. Therefore, within DM we are led to assume that both the verb and the noun *form* contain a 'zero' categorial head that turns the root without category (√FORM) into a verb and a noun, respectively (18):

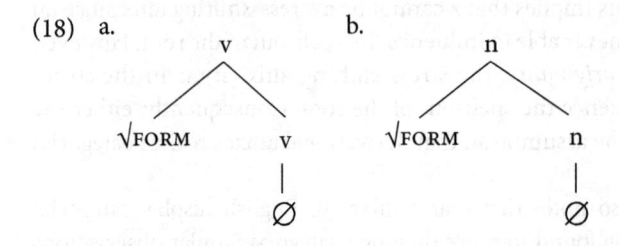

(18)   a.   b.
              v   n
            /   \   /   \
         √FORM   v   √FORM   n
                 | |
                 ∅   ∅

It is hard to find independent evidence for such empty heads, which renders the proposal completely ad hoc. Therefore, Borer proposes an interesting alternative that will also help us explain the observations that we make in the following section regarding phonological restrictions on word classes.[11]

Rather than assuming empty categorial heads responsible for the categorization of roots, Borer proposes that it is the syntactic environment itself that forces the categorization of the root. Since the root does not contain any categorial information, it can be moulded into different categorial 'shapes', depending on the requirements of the environment. The logic Borer proposes is that the syntactic environment (typically, the head) sets requirements on the category of the element it merges with (typically, the complement). Take for example the context of a determiner head as in (19):

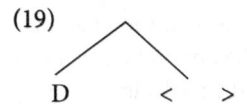

(19)

```
      /\
     /  \
    D   < >
```

The element D requires that its complement is a noun, or should be noun-equivalent, which means that it has the properties needed to fill the slot of a noun. Now apply this same logic to the -al cases, discussed above. Since a root (such as *form*) is noun-equivalent (which we may read as: a root does not have any features that preclude it from being categorized as a noun) it fulfils the categorial requirement of the head, and it may appear in this particular context, where it will be interpreted as a noun. However, by the same logic, a root is also 'verb-equivalent', which entails that it may also occur in the complement of a tense operator. This reasoning obviates the need for the zero elements in (16). We can now say that the derivational affix -al is a head that requires a noun-equivalent complement. This implies that in the word *formal*, the part *form* is interpreted as a noun. The affix -able on the other hand is a derivational affix that takes a verb-equivalent complement forcing the verbal interpretation of *form* in *formable*.

To sum up: different answers have been given to the question what the categorizers are in a theory that separates roots from their categorial information. Some have argued that derivational affixes are the spell-out of categorial heads, whereas others have argued for root status of derivational affixes. In Borer's theory, categorial heads force a categorial interpretation of the material in their complement. This view does away with numerous zero affixes that are a consequence of the idea that derivational affixes are merely categorial heads.

13.4 PHONOLOGICAL CONSTRAINTS ON CATEGORIES

Above I have sketched how word classes are treated in DM, also pointing out a few issues that have led to alternative viewpoints and discussion. In this section, I want to address an

---

[11] Note that Lowenstamm (2015) takes a different position with respect to so-called *Class-1 affixes*. He assumes that in a word such as *atomicity* there is no 'intermediate' categorization of both *atom* and *atomic* (*-ic* being a class-1 affix). Support for this position comes from the observation that there is no compositional interpretation of *atomicity*. In Lowenstamm's view, *atomicity* does not contain the adjective *atomic*, but just the complex root. In the same way *atomic* only contains the root *atom* rather than the noun *atom*.

observation indicating that the phonological make-up of a root may put limits on its categorization. We may wonder that if there are such phonological restrictions whether we should stick to the idea of strictly separating phonological information from the root. If not just any root can merge with any categorial head, then we may want to include the information about the identity of the root in the syntactic computation.

Albright (2008) notes that phonological rules or patterns may be specific for a particular word class, or a subclass of a major word class. Such patterns are normally handled by relativizing the responsible phonological rule or constraint to the word class in question. Here, however, the pattern is a little bit different in the sense that there is no rule or constraint that can be relativized since it is the segmental (or syllabic) make-up of the item itself that gives native speakers some information as to their categorization (see also Smith 2011; Lohmann 2017). As far as I know, the DM literature has not addressed this issue. However, this type of observation might form a challenge for the root-plus-category theory. In the following, I make a suggestion as to how such restrictions may be expressed in the current theory.

Trommelen (1989) observes that in Dutch the possibilities for the phonological make-up of underived stems differ per category. Verbs and adjectives are far more restricted in their syllable structure than nouns. For concreteness's sake, let us have a look at the restrictions on verbs that Trommelen finds by investigating the complete set of monomorphemic verbs in Dutch (20):

(20) Phonological restrictions on verbs in Dutch:[12]
– verbs are monosyllabic;[13]
– verbs do not end in a monophthongal vowel (including schwa);[14]
– rhymes larger than three elements do not occur in verbs (apart from *peins* 'to consider', and *veins* 'to pretend' both with the diphthong [eɪ]);
– verbs ending in schwa followed by [n] or [r] and [l] do occur, but verbs ending in schwa followed by [m] do not occur.

Nouns in Dutch do not conform to the restrictions in (18). Nouns may be polysyllabic (*spinazie* 'spinach', *pagina* 'page', etc.), may end in a monophthong (*zee* 'sea', *pa* 'dad', *knie* 'knee' etc.), may have larger rhymes (*feest* [fest] 'party', *oogst* [oxst] 'harvest', *herfst* [hɛrfst] 'autumn', etc.), and may end in syllables containing a schwa plus [m] (*bezem* [bezəm] 'broom', *totem* [totəm] 'totem').

First of all, we may ask ourselves to what extent such restrictions are really part of the knowledge that native speakers have of their language. In this regard, it is noteworthy that there is experimental evidence supporting this idea. Native speakers have been shown to be far more inclined to categorize nonce words as verbal once these words meet the criteria

---

[12] This is my translation of Trommelen's Dutch text, cited from Don & Erkelens (2008).

[13] A note is in order with respect to the notion 'monosyllabic' in (18), which is a little more complex than one might expect. Apart from words with a single full vowel, this notion in Trommelen's use also includes stems containing a full vowel syllable, and a final syllable with a schwa as the nuclear vowel (such as *lepel* [lepəl] 'spoon', *bezem* [bezəm] ' broom'). The reason is that there are sound arguments to consider these words as underlyingly monosyllabic (see for extensive motivation Kager & Zonneveld 1986).

[14] There are a few exceptions to this statement: *doe* ('to do'), *ga* ('to go'), and *sta* ('to stand').

in (18) than when they somehow override these criteria (Don & Erkelens 2008; De Belder 2019). Furthermore, there is some more evidence for the existence of these restrictions from the language itself.

Dutch hosts a class of complex verbs, consisting of an unstressed prefix, and a nominal (or adjectival) stem as their right-hand element. Interestingly, we can only find nouns (and adjectives) in this position that conform to the restrictions in (20). In (21) we have given some illustrative examples with the verbal prefixes *om-* 'around' and *onder-* 'under'.

(21) om-arm   'embrace'   onder-lijn   'underline'
      om-cirkel   'encircle'   onder-mijn   'undermine'
      om-gord   'gird'   onder-streep   'underline'
      om-singel   'surround'   onder-tunnel   'tunnel'
      om-wikkel   'wrap around'   onder-titel   'undertitle'

For the reasons given above, I believe that the phonological restrictions on word classes should be included in the grammar. Note, however, that some care should be taken. Clearly, it is not the case that all verbs in Dutch comply with the restrictions in (20). The restrictions only apply to underived verbs, as Trommelen carefully points out. There are a lot of verbs in Dutch that result from conversion of nouns (or adjectives) which are not bound by these restrictions. Some illustrative examples are given in (22):

(22) badminton   'to play badminton'
      kaart   'to play cards'
      olie   'to oil'
      ruzie   'to argue'

So, on the one hand, it seems necessary to include the constraints on the phonological form of verbs in the grammar of Dutch; on the other hand, we should allow conversions of the type in (20) to escape these constraints.

We are, therefore, forced to link the morpheme structure constraint to underived verbal items. However, given that verbs are complex objects in DM, always minimally consisting of a categorizing head and a root, there is no obvious anchor point in the grammar to which we can link such restrictions.

A solution might be possible when adopting Borer's position, albeit with a twist. Recall that Borer (2014; 2015) proposes doing away with categorial heads. Instead, she proposes that functional elements are operators that not only determine the category of the output, but also determine the category of their complement/argument. Affixes belonging to this functional vocabulary operate in the same way: *-al* in *formal* determines that its complement is a noun, whereas *-able* determines *form* to be a verb in *formable*. Viewing it a little more abstractly, we may say that the affixes determine the form that their complement may take. Under such a view, we can formulate the morpheme-structure constraint not as some separate statement in the grammar generalizing over underived verbs, but as a restriction that an affix puts on its complements. To make it more concrete again, we can assume that the prefixes in (21) (*om-*, and *onder-*), as functors, force their complements to be verbal, and restrict the material in their complements to the limitations formulated in (20).

This fares well as long as we have a functor that is the location of the phonological requirement (i.e. an affix). Apparently, the extended projections of V (T, Agr, etc.) in Dutch do not host such a restriction, since 'conversions' can easily escape the restrictions in (20). But now a new problem arises, since it becomes unclear how Dutch native speakers are able to recognize underived verbs. From the experiments referred to above we concluded that Dutch native speakers have knowledge of the notion 'underived verb', but there does not seem to be a clear counterpart in Borer's theory of such a notion, since there is no difference between a converted noun (such as (22)) and an underived verb (such as *brei* 'to knit', or *loop* 'to walk').

Put differently, what does it mean in Borer's theory to be an underived verb? One might think that what comes closest to this notion is a root directly merged under T. But this functional node does not put any phonological restrictions on its complement (in Dutch at least), since it is very well possible to have all sorts of 'nouns' that are converted. Think of the examples in (22) that, as verbs, in Borer's view, are simply roots that are merged with T. So, if there is a notion 'underived verb' that native speakers of Dutch recognize, this cannot be the whole story. I therefore propose that Dutch hosts a zero affix that derives verbs from roots. The zero affix forces the phonological restrictions in (20) upon the material in its complement, in the same way that the prefixes *om-* and *onder-* do. This gives us a distinction between the verbs having the structure in (21a), and those having the structure in (23b):

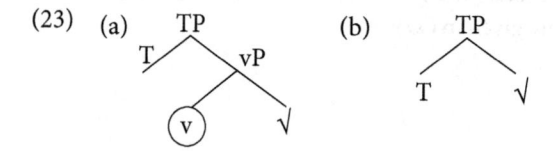

(23) (a) TP   (b) TP
     T vP   T √
     v √

The encircled 'little v' in (23a) is the location of the phonological requirements in (20). In some cases, this head is spelled-out as a prefix (such as *om-*, *onder-*, or any other of the unstressed prefixes in Dutch) (as in the examples in (21)); in some other cases it has no overt realization. Native speakers of Dutch know the difference between (23a) and (23b), which becomes apparent once they are asked to categorize a nonce word. Roots of which the phonological make-up overrides the restrictions in (21) are only compatible with the structure in (23b).

13.5 Conclusion and Outlook

DM claims that native speakers' knowledge about the word classes of their language derives from categorially underspecified roots that get categorized in a particular syntactic context. The core message DM brings us is that knowledge of word classes is context-dependent. Speakers cannot say about a particular form in isolation whether it is a noun, a verb, or an adjective; they can only do so in the context of some other linguistic elements that determine the class of the form under consideration. Conversion is the process which eminently fits this view, because it shows that one and the same lexical element (i.e. a root) may be used in different syntactic contexts, forcing a different interpretation (verbal, nominal, adjectival) of the root in question. At first sight this purely contextual view on categorization is at odds with an observation about Dutch word classes. Native speakers of this language do seem to be able to judge whether a particular form in isolation is a verb or a noun. We have shown that this type of observation can be incorporated in the theory once we adopt Borer's proposal in which affixes are functors determining the category of their complements. This theory allows us to locate the phonological restrictions on verb classification in the affixal heads.

Although many questions as to the exact status of the root remain, the analysis of words in terms of a root plus a categorial functional head is by now a well-established theory. Detailed analyses embracing this theoretical stance exist of languages as different as English (Borer 2014; Embick 2015; Lowenstamm 2015; Adamson 2018), Amharic (Kramer 2016), Catalan (Oltra-Massuet 2013), Dutch (De Belder 2011; Creemers et al. 2018), French (Don et al. 2015), Greek (Alexiadou 2009), Hebrew (Arad 2003; Borer 2013; 2014), Hiaki (Harley 2014), Japanese (Volpe 2005), Latin (Embick 2000), Kuikuro (Franchetto 2006), and many more. The success of the theory will be further determined by the power it has to raise new questions and direct research into new avenues.

CHAPTER 14

WORD CLASSES IN HEAD-DRIVEN PHRASE STRUCTURE GRAMMAR

FRANK VAN EYNDE

14.1 INTRODUCTION

HEAD-DRIVEN Phrase Structure Grammar (HPSG) is a branch of generative grammar that is characterized by its surface-oriented nature and its lexicalist approach. It originated in the 1980s, when a number of alternatives emerged for the then prevailing transformational approach. The alternatives included Lexical Functional Grammar, Categorial Grammar, and Generalized Phrase Structure Grammar (GPSG) (Gazdar et al. 1985). Attempts to use the GPSG framework for computational applications, especially parsing, led to a number of modifications, resulting in HPSG (Pollard & Sag 1987). While matters of formalization and computation were given most attention in the first decade, the focus has shifted to theoretical and descriptive issues in more recent times, starting with Pollard & Sag (1994). A recent comprehensive presentation is Mueller et al. (2021) Didactic surveys are provided in Sag et al. (2003) and Levine (2017).

Turning to the topic of this volume, HPSG adopts the age-old distinction between verbs, nouns, and other parts of speech. Its role in the grammar is relativized, though, by the fact that it is only one of the many distinctions in terms of which word classes are defined. To spell out what this means in practice, we first discuss the role of the part-of-speech distinction in the definition of syntactic word classes (section 14.2). Then we also discuss its role in the definition of semantic word classes (section 14.3) and morphological word classes (section 14.4). Examples will be taken from a range of Germanic and Romance languages and modern Greek. The restriction to Indo-European languages reflects the author's limitations, not the framework's. HPSG treatments of the part-of-speech inventories of non-Indo-European languages are presented among others in Malouf (2000) and Koenig & Michelson (2014).

14.2 Syntactic word classes

The part-of-speech distinction plays a central role in the definition of syntactic word classes. To show this we discuss its role in the modelling of phrase formation, first informally (section 14.2.1) and then in terms of the Typed Feature Structure notation of HPSG (section 14.2.2). Evidence will be provided for a differentiation between five parts of speech: verb, noun, adjective, adverb, and adposition. This is considerably less than what is proposed in most other generative frameworks. Transformational Grammar and its offspring, for instance, employs a large set of functional categories, ranging from D(eterminer) and Q(uantifier) over C(omplementizer) and T(ense) to DEG(ree), AGR(eement), ASP(ect), and beyond—see Chapter 12 in this volume. Some of these also crop up in the HPSG literature. Pollard and Sag (1987), for instance, add *determiner* to the list of five and remarks that 'this list ... does not pretend to be exhaustive or definitive' (1987: 59). In fact, it is changed in Pollard & Sag (1994: 396), who make a distinction between substantive parts of speech (*noun, verb, adjective, preposition, relativizer*) and functional parts of speech (*determiner, marker*).[1] The inventory is changed again in Ginzburg & Sag (2000: 360), who add *complementizer* and *gerund*, while dropping *marker*. In sum, while the part-of-speech inventory of HPSG has a relatively stable core, it also has a more volatile fringe. It is that fringe that we focus on in the sections on functional categories (section 14.2.3) and minor categories (section 14.2.4).

14.2.1 Phrase formation

In Pollard & Sag (1987: 53–67) the need to differentiate between parts of speech is motivated by the fact that it captures constraints on the combination of a verb and its complements. The transitive *devour*, for instance, selects an NP complement, and the fact that it is not compatible with a PP, VP, or AP complement provides evidence for differentiating NPs from other XPs.

(1)   a.   Kim [devoured the three-day-old bagel].
       b.   * Kim [devoured on the three-day-old bagel]
       c.   * Kim [devoured leave on the next train]
       d.   * Kim [devoured melancholy]

In the same vein, the verb *depend* selects a PP complement, and the fact that it is not compatible with an NP, VP, or AP complement provides evidence for differentiating PPs from other XPs.

(2)   a.   Kim [depended on her eccentric uncle].
       b.   * Kim [depended her eccentric uncle]
       c.   * Kim [depended leave on the next train]

---

[1] The part-of-speech *relativizer* was assigned to a phonetically empty element that got employed in the analysis of relative clauses. It was dispensed with in Sag (1997), who provides an analysis of relative clauses without empty elements.

       d.   * Kim [depended melancholy]

The same holds *mutatis mutandis* for verbs which select a VP complement, such as *must*, and verbs which select an AP complement, such as the inchoative *wax*.

(3) a. Chris [must leave on the next train].
    b. * Chris [must the three-day-old bagel]
    c. * Chris [must on her eccentric uncle]
    d. * Chris [must melancholy]

(4) a. Kim [waxed melancholy].
    b. * Kim [waxed the three-day-old bagel]
    c. * Kim [waxed on her eccentric uncle]
    d. * Kim [waxed leave on the next train]

In combination with the assumption that phrases of category XP are headed by a word of category X, this provides evidence for a distinction between nouns, prepositions, verbs, and adjectives.

The need to differentiate between parts of speech is further motivated by the fact that it captures constraints on the addition of adjuncts. Adjectival adjuncts, for instance, combine with nouns, but not with verbs or adjectives.

(5) a. They are selling [old cars].
    b. * He [old smiled]
    c. * This car is [old fast]

This provides further evidence for differentiating nouns from verbs and adjectives. At the same time, it also suggests the relevance of a distinction between adjectives and adverbs, since adverbs do combine with verbs and adjectives, as in *he never smiled* and *this car is very fast*. Confirming evidence for treating adverbs as members of a separate part of speech is provided by the fact that they are occasionally used as complements of verbs, as in *behave badly* and *word the message carefully*. The fact that these cannot be replaced by adjectives, as in **behave bad* and **word the message careful*, shows that adverbial complements must be differentiated from adjectival complements.

While the part-of-speech distinction plays a central role in the formulation of co-occurrence restrictions on complementation and adjunction, there are other finer-grained distinctions that are equally relevant for that purpose. The NP complement of a transitive verb, for instance, is required to be accusative in English; a nominative NP is not admissible.

(6) Kim devoured him/*he.

Similar restrictions hold for PP and VP complements. The PP complement of *depend*, for instance, must be introduced by *on*, and that of *wait* by *for*.

(7) a. Kim depended on/*of/*for her eccentric uncle.
    b. George is waiting for/*of the bus.

In the same vein, the VP complement of *will* must be in the base form, while that of the progressive *be* must be a present participle and that of the perfect *have* a past participle.

(8)   a. They will leave/*leaving/*left tomorrow.
       b. Cindy is leaving/*leave/*left tomorrow.
       c. Cindy has left/*leaving/*leave.

Interestingly, these finer-grained distinctions provide additional evidence for the part-of-speech distinction, since many of them are part-of-speech specific. The case distinction, for instance, is relevant for nouns, but not for verbs or prepositions, and the distinction between present and past participles is relevant for verbs but not for nouns or prepositions.

At this stage now, we have evidence for differentiating between five parts of speech (V, N, P, Adj, Adv), some of which are differentiated in terms of finer-grained distinctions. In the next section, we show how this is modelled in the Typed Feature Structure notation of HPSG.

14.2.2 Modelling

The basic notion of linguistic analysis in HPSG is that of the sign, defined as a pair of phonological properties, on the one hand, and syntactic and semantic properties, on the other hand.

(9)   *sign:* $\begin{bmatrix} \text{PHONOLOGY} & \textit{list (phoneme)} \\ \text{SYNSEM} & \textit{synsem} \end{bmatrix}$

The representation in (9) is a feature declaration, to be read as: objects of type *sign* have a PHONOLOGY feature, whose value is a list of phonemes, and a SYN(TAX-)SEM(ANTICS) feature, whose value is an object of type *synsem*. This is reminiscent of the Saussurean definition of the sign as a unit of form (*signifiant*) and meaning (*signifié*). In contrast to Saussure (1916), though, where the sign is meant to be a lexical sign, the HPSG notion of sign subsumes both lexical and phrasal signs. Moreover, the objects of type *synsem* not only concern the meaning of a sign, but also its syntactic properties. Technically, objects of type *synsem* are declared to have a CATEGORY feature and a CONTENT feature.

(10)   *synsem:* $\begin{bmatrix} \text{CATEGORY} & \textit{category} \\ \text{CONTENT} & \textit{semantic object} \end{bmatrix}$

Objects of type *category* are in turn declared to have a HEAD feature, the valence features SUBJ(ECT) and COMP(LEMENT)S, and a MARKING feature.

(11)   *category:* $\begin{bmatrix} \text{HEAD} & \textit{part-of-speech} \\ \text{SUBJ} & \textit{list (synsem)} \\ \text{COMPS} & \textit{list (synsem)} \\ \text{MARK} & \textit{marking} \end{bmatrix}$

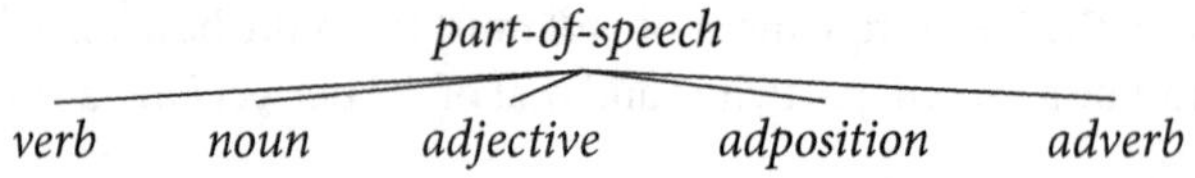

```
                        part-of-speech
         ┌───────────┬────────┴────┬──────────┬─────────┐
       verb        noun       adjective    adposition   adverb
```

FIGURE 14.1 The part-of-speech inventory

Of particular relevance in this context is the HEAD feature, since its value is declared to be a part of speech, such as *verb* or *noun*. Technically, these are subtypes of *part of speech*; see Figure 14.1. Being types, the part-of-speech values may be declared to have extra features. Nouns, for instance, are declared to have a CASE feature, verbs a VFORM feature and adpositions a PFORM feature.

(12) a. *noun*: [CASE   *case*]
     b. *verb*: [VFORM   *vform*]
     c. *adposition*: [PFORM   *pform*]

The inventory of values is language specific. English, for instance, has two CASE values (nominative and accusative), German has four (adding genitive and dative), and Latin six (adding vocative and ablative). Similarly, the VFORM inventory for English includes separate values for present and past participles, but there are also languages with a larger inventory, such as Latin and Lithuanian, which also have a future participle. The language specificity is especially clear for PFORM, whose inventory includes such types as *of*, *in*, and *on* for English, *de*, *à*, and *par* for French, etc.

The defining property of the HEAD values is that they are shared between a word and its phrasal projection. A nominative noun, for instance, projects a nominative NP, a finite verb projects a finite VP, the adposition *on* projects a PP[*on*], and so on. This is captured by the Head Feature Principle. Technically, it is an implicational constraint on objects of type headed-phrase.[2]

(13)   Head Feature Principle
        headed-phrase ⇒ [SYNSEM | CATEGORY | HEAD [1] *part-of-speech*]
                        [HEAD-DTR | SYNSEM | CATEGORY | HEAD [1]   ]

What this says is that the HEAD value of a headed phrase is identical to that of its head daughter. The boxed number represents the sharing of information.

For the definition of syntactic word classes, the distinctions which are captured by the HEAD values play a central role, but, as stated in the introduction, there are other distinctions at play as well. Some of those are captured by the valence features, SUBJ and COMPS. In contrast to the HEAD feature which models inherent properties of a lexical item and its phrasal projection, the valence features model the properties which a sign requires its dependents to have. The verb *devour*, for instance, requires an NP as its subject and another NP as its complement. This is modelled by the values of SUBJ and

---

[2] Not all phrases are headed. Coordinate phrases, such as *Gilbert and George*, are treated as non-headed in HPSG.

COMPS. In both cases, this is a list containing a bundle of syntactic and semantic features, abbreviated as NP, see (14).

(14) $\begin{bmatrix} \text{HEAD} & verb \\ \text{SUBJ} & \langle NP \rangle \\ \text{COMPS} & \langle NP \rangle \end{bmatrix}$

Words which select more than one complement, such as the ditransitive *give*, have a COMPS value, whose members are separated by commas, as in (15), and words which do not select any complement, such as the intransitive *disappear*, have the empty list (<>) as their COMPS value, as in (16).

(15) $\begin{bmatrix} \text{HEAD} & verb \\ \text{SUBJ} & \langle NP \rangle \\ \text{COMPS} & \langle NP,NP \rangle \end{bmatrix}$

(16) $\begin{bmatrix} \text{HEAD} & verb \\ \text{SUBJ} & \langle NP \rangle \\ \text{COMPS} & \langle \rangle \end{bmatrix}$

There are two reasons for keeping the valence features distinct from the HEAD feature. One is that the part-of-speech distinction is orthogonal to the valence distinctions. It is, for instance, not only verbs that can select a PP complement, but also adjectives, nouns, and adpositions. The other reason is that the values of HEAD are treated differently from the values of the valence features in the modelling of phrase formation: while the HEAD value is shared between a word and the phrase which it projects, the values of the valence features are not. In *devour the bagel*, for instance, the HEAD value is shared between the verb and its projection (VP), but the COMPS value is not, since the VP no longer requires an NP complement. This is made explicit by assigning it the empty list as its COMPS value, as in Figure 14.2, which is a partial representation of *devour the bagel* in tree format. Also here, the boxed numbers are used to represent the sharing of information. The verb shares its HEAD value with the VP because of the Head Feature Principle ([1]), and the NP shares its syntactic and semantic properties with those that are in the COMPS list of the verb ([2]). It is this sharing requirement that blocks combinations in which the valence restrictions of the head are not matched by the syntactic and semantic properties of its dependent. *devour*, for instance, is compatible with an NP, but not with a PP, AP, or VP complement.

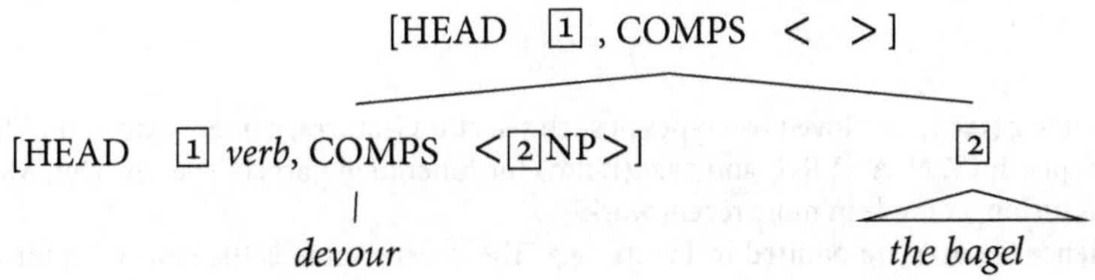

[HEAD [1], COMPS < >]

[HEAD [1] verb, COMPS <[2]NP>]   [2]
           |
        devour   the bagel

FIGURE 14.2 Complementation

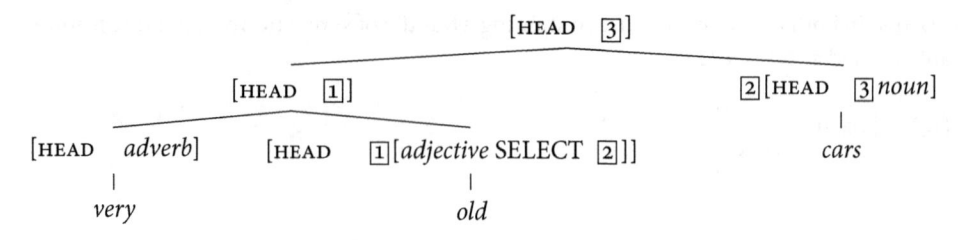

```
                              [HEAD  3]
        ┌─────────────────────────┴──────────────────────────┐
               [HEAD  1]                           2[HEAD  3noun]
        ┌──────────┴──────────┐                            │
   [HEAD  adverb]   [HEAD  1[adjective SELECT 2]]          cars
        │                     │
       very                  old
```

FIGURE 14.3 Adjunction

While valence features model the requirements which a sign imposes on it dependents, there are also requirements which a dependent may impose on its head sister. Adjectival adjuncts, for instance, require their head sister to be nominal, rather than adjectival or verbal, as illustrated in (5). To model this, HPSG uses a feature that is assigned to objects of type *part of speech*.[3]

(17) *part-of-speech*: [SELECT *synsem* ∨ *none*]

In contrast to CASE, VFORM, and PFORM, which are declared for specific parts of speech, SELECT is declared for all parts of speech. This is motivated by the fact that an adjunct can belong to any part of speech. Examples of adjectival and adverbial adjuncts were given in section 14.2.1. Examples of adpositional, verbal, and nominal adjuncts are given in (18), (19), and (20) respectively.

(18) a. The [man with the telescope] is my nephew.
     b. They [danced on the roof].

(19) a. The [wine produced in this region] is of exceptional quality.
     b. They [left the building yelling and screaming].

(20) a. The [girl next door] is also on the soccer team.
     b. I [did it my way].

The SELECT value models the constraints which an adjunct imposes on its head sister. Technically, its value is an object of type *synsem*, which is shared with the *synsem* value of the selected head sister. Since SELECT is declared for objects of type *part-of-speech*, it is part of the HEAD value, which implies that it is subsumed by the Head Feature Principle. Phrases, hence, share the SELECT value of their head daughter. The SELECT value of the adjective *old*, for instance, is shared with that of the AP *very old*, as shown in Figure 14.3.[4] In this example, the

---

[3] Pollard & Sag (1994) employed two types of such selection features, namely MOD(IFIED) for substantive parts of speech (V, N, A, P, Rel) and SPEC(IFIED) for functional parts of speech (Det, Marker). This distinction is no longer made in more recent work.

[4] The valence features are omitted in Figure 14.3. The COMPS value is the empty list for each of the categories, since neither *cars* nor *old* nor *very* select a complement.

SELECT value of the adjective contains the information that its head sister must be nominal, rather than verbal or adjectival. This value is shared with the AP ([2]) and matched with the selected head sister. The latter shares its HEAD value with the top node ([3]).

Signs which do not select their head sister are assigned the alternative value *none*. Predicative adjectives, for instance, are complements and are, hence, selected by their head sister, rather than the other way round. Notice that the alternation between *none* and *synsem* provides the means to capture one of the parameters of syntactic variation for adjectives. Those which are only used predicatively, such as *awake* and *ablaze*, have the value *none* in the lexicon and are, hence, not licensed in attributive positions. By contrast, those which are only used attributively, such as *mere* and *former*, have a SELECT value of type *synsem* in the lexicon and are, hence, not licensed in predicative positions. And adjectives that can be used either way, such as *old*, have the disjunctive value in the lexicon. When used in context, this is resolved to *none* or to some specific type of *synsem*.

Summing up, we have discussed evidence for the postulation of five parts of speech (Figure 14.1). Since many frameworks employ a (much) larger inventory, the question is whether 'the big five' are sufficient. We will argue that they are, showing how the distinctive characteristics of the members of the so-called functional categories can be captured without adding them as separate values to the part-of-speech inventory. This will first be done for pronouns, determiners, degree markers, and complementizers (section 14.2.3) and then for articles and coordinate conjunctions (section 14.2.4).[5]

14.2.3 Functional categories

So far, we have defined syntactic word classes in terms of HEAD and valence features. To capture the distinctive characteristics of functional categories we add a third ingredient, namely the MARKING feature. It was introduced in Pollard & Sag (1994: 44–46) for a treatment of complementizers and certain adpositions and was given a broader range in Allegranza (1998) and Van Eynde (1998), who both used it to model any kind of sign. This generalized version is also adopted in Sign-Based Construction Grammar (Sag 2012).

14.2.3.1 Determiners

Nominals may contain any number of adjuncts and those adjuncts can belong to any part of speech, as shown in (21).

(21) a. They are selling those [cheap old cars].
b. The [man with the telescope in the corner] is my nephew.
c. The [wine produced in this region] is of exceptional quality.
d. The [girl next door] is also on the soccer team.

---

[5] It may be worth adding that these sections are largely based on work of the author. Much but not all of it is adopted by the HPSG community at large.

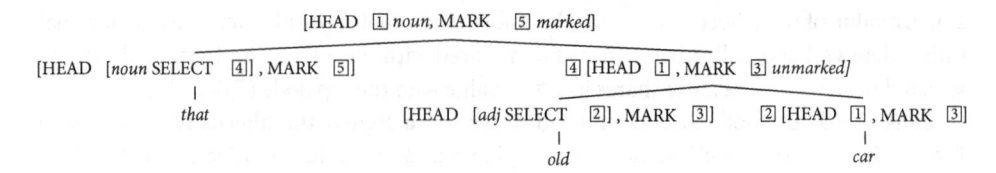

```
                          [HEAD [1] noun, MARK [5] marked]
                          ─────────────────────────────────────────────
[HEAD [noun SELECT [4]], MARK [5]]              [4] [HEAD [1], MARK [3] unmarked]
         │                                      ────────────────────────────────
        that                    [HEAD [adj SELECT [2]], MARK [3]]   [2] [HEAD [1], MARK [3]]
                                         │                                 │
                                        old                               car
```

FIGURE 14.4 A noun phrase

Determiners also combine with nominals, but in contrast to the adjuncts they cannot be stacked: *the (*that) car* and *those (*our) riots*. To capture this difference, we employ the MARK(ING) feature. Its value is of type *marking*, and its two subtypes, *marked* and *unmarked*, model the distinction between nominals with and without determiner. In combination with the SELECT value, the MARKING value provides the means to differentiate stackable from non-stackable dependents. This is illustrated by the analysis of the nominal projection in Figure 14.4.[6] The noun *car* is the HEAD of the NP and, hence, shares its HEAD value with both *old car* and *that old car* ([1]). The adjective *old* selects an unmarked nominal ([2]) and shares its MARKING value with that nominal ([3]). Moreover, it also shares its MARKING value with the resulting phrase (*old car*). This follows from the Marking Principle, which stipulates that in a headed phrase the MARKING value is shared with the non-head daughter, if the latter is an adjunct or a specifier.[7] The demonstrative *that* also selects an unmarked nominal ([4]), but its own MARKING value is of type *marked* and it is this value that is shared with the NP ([5]). Once marked, a nominal is no longer compatible with another determiner, since determiners require an unmarked nominal as their sister. This accounts for the ill-formedness of **the that car* and **those our riots*.

In this treatment determiners are exhaustively defined as marked selectors of an unmarked nominal. There is no need for a separate part of speech to capture their properties. On the contrary, the use of a separate part of speech for determiners stands in the way of capturing relevant generalizations. To illustrate this let us take some Italian data. In that language, adjectives show inflectional variation for number and grammatical gender, and when they modify a noun, as in (22), they must show agreement with the noun's number and gender.

(22) a. *libro   nuovo/*nuova/*nuovi/*nuove*
        book.SG.M new.SG.M/*new.SG.F/*new.PL.M/*new.PL.F
        'new book'

   b. *scatola   nuova/*nuovo/*nuovi/*nuove*
      box.SG.F new.SG.F/*new.SG.M/*new.PL.M/*new.PL.F
      'new box'

   c. *libri   nuovi/*nuovo/*nuova/*nuove*
      book.PL.M new.PL.M/*new.SG.M/*new.SG.F/*new.PL.F
      'new books'

---

[6] The valence features are omitted. Their value is the empty list for each of the categories.
[7] If the non-head daughter is a complement or a subject, the MARKING value is shared with the head daughter, in the same way as the HEAD value.

d. *scatole nuove/*nuovo/*nuova/*nuovi*
   box.PL.F new.PL.F/*new.SG.M/*new.SG.F/*new.PL.M
   'new boxes'

The same is true for many of the Italian determiners. The demonstrative *questo* 'this', for instance, shows the same inflectional variation and agreement with the noun as *nuovo* 'new', see (23).

(23) a. *questo/*questa/*questi/*queste   libro*
        this.SG.M/*this.SG.F/*this.PL.M/*this.PL.F book.SG.M
        'this book'

   b. *questa/*questo/*questi/*queste   scatola*
      this.SG.F/*this.SG.M/*this.PL.M/*this.pl.f box.SG.F
      'this box'

   c. *questi/*questo/*questa/*queste   libri*
      this.PL.M/*this.SG.F/*this.SG.F/*this.PL.F book.PL.M
      'these books'

   d. *queste/*questo/*questa/*questi   scatole*
      this.PL.F/*this.SG.M/*this.SG.F/*this.PL.M box.PL.F
      'these boxes'

Treating *questo* as belonging to a part of speech other than *nuovo* is hence counterproductive. Moreover, it is unnecessary, since the difference between them is already captured by the MARKING value, as made clear in (24)–(25).

(24) $\begin{bmatrix} \text{HEAD} \begin{bmatrix} adjective \\ \text{SELECT} \begin{bmatrix} \text{CATEGORY} \begin{bmatrix} \text{HEAD} & noun \\ \text{MARK} & unmarked \end{bmatrix} \end{bmatrix} \end{bmatrix} \\ \text{MARK} \ marked \end{bmatrix}$

(25) $\begin{bmatrix} \text{HEAD} \begin{bmatrix} adjective \\ \text{SELECT} \begin{bmatrix} \text{CATEGORY} \begin{bmatrix} \text{HEAD} & noun \\ \text{MARK} & unmarked \end{bmatrix} \end{bmatrix} \end{bmatrix} \\ \text{MARK} \ unmarked \end{bmatrix}$

A further consequence is that determiners can belong to any part of speech. This possibility is in fact explored in some detail in Van Eynde (2006: 143–150), who shows that the Dutch determiners include both adjectives and pronouns. In the same vein, Abeillé et al. (2004) argue that some of the French determiners are adverbs. Moreover, we will see in section 14.2.4 that French also has an adpositional determiner. In sum, determiners are singled out by their SELECT and MARKING values, and can belong to any part of speech, ranging from *adjective* over *noun* and *adverb* to *preposition*.

Independent evidence for the relevance of the MARKING distinction is provided by the fact that it plays a role in co-occurrence restrictions on complementation. The French prepositions *au* and *du*, for instance, require their nominal complement to be unmarked: *au (*le) marché* 'on.the market' and *du (*le) vin* 'of.the wine'.

It is worth stressing that the distinction which the MARKING value captures is a syntactic distinction, rather than a semantic one. Possessive determiners, for instance, have the value *marked* in languages where they cannot be preceded by another determiner, as in English ((**the) my dog*) and French ((**le) mon chien*), but they have the value *unmarked* in languages like Italian, where they are canonically preceded by an article, as in *il mio cane* 'the my dog'. Similarly, demonstrative determiners are marked in English, Italian, and French, but not in modern Greek, where they are canonically preceded by the definite article.

14.2.3.2 Pronouns

Descriptive grammars often treat pronouns as belonging to a separate part of speech, distinct from nouns, because they form a relatively small and nearly closed class. HPSG, by contrast, treats nouns and pronouns as members of the same part of speech (Pollard & Sag 1987: 59). This is motivated among others by the fact that they are not distinguishable in co-occurrence restrictions on complementation: verbs which take an NP complement, such as *devour*, do not care whether that NP is headed by a noun or a pronoun. In fact, there are no verbs that require a pronominal NP complement as opposed to a nominal NP complement, or vice versa. Further evidence for assigning the same part of speech is provided by the fact that the features which are declared for nouns, such as CASE, are also relevant for pronouns. The assignment of the same part of speech does not imply that they belong to the same syntactic word class. A relevant difference, for instance, is that common nouns routinely combine with a determiner (*this car*), while pronouns do not ((**this) he*). This difference is already captured by the MARKING value, as shown by the CATEGORY values of *car* and *he* in (26), and does not need to be duplicated by the HEAD value.

(26) $\begin{bmatrix} \text{HEAD} & noun \\ \text{MARK} & unmarked \end{bmatrix}$ $\begin{bmatrix} \text{HEAD} & noun \\ \text{MARK} & marked \end{bmatrix}$

Since determiners select an unmarked nominal, it follows that *this car* is licensed, while *this he is not. Syntactic differences between nouns and pronouns can thus be captured without extending the part-of-speech inventory.

The factorial nature of this analysis paves the way for a more uniform treatment of the English demonstratives. As is well known, they are routinely used in both nominal and adnominal positions, as in (27) and (28) respectively.

(27) a. I do not like that.
     b. Let us have these.

(28) a. I do not like that dog.
     b. Let us have these vegetables.

The difference is often captured in terms of a part-of-speech distinction (N vs Det), but this is not necessary in the treatment presented so far, since the SELECT value is sufficient for that purpose: while nominal demonstratives do not select anything, as spelled out in (29), their adnominal counterparts select an unmarked nominal, as spelled out in (30).

$$(29) \begin{bmatrix} \text{HEAD} & \begin{bmatrix} noun \\ \text{SELECT} & none \end{bmatrix} \\ \text{MARK} & marked \end{bmatrix}$$

$$(30) \begin{bmatrix} \text{HEAD} & \begin{bmatrix} noun \\ \text{SELECT} & \begin{bmatrix} \text{CATEGORY} & \begin{bmatrix} \text{HEAD} & noun \\ \text{MARK} & unmarked \end{bmatrix} \end{bmatrix} \end{bmatrix} \\ \text{MARK} & marked \end{bmatrix}$$

The values of the other features are identical. In both uses the demonstrative is a noun and has a MARKING value of type *marked*. This simultaneously accounts for the fact that the demonstratives do not take a determiner when they are used in nominal position (*I like (*the) that*), and that they cannot be preceded by another determiner when they are used in adnominal position ((**the) that dog*).

14.2.3.3 Degree markers

The interaction of SELECT and MARKING values is also useful for the analysis of degree markers. They are selectors of an unmarked adjectival projection and can themselves either be unmarked or marked. For English, the unmarked ones include *very* and *rather*; when combined with an adjective, as in *very fast* and *rather close*, the result is an unmarked AP, and since the combination of an unmarked AP with a nominal yields an unmarked nominal, it is possible to combine the latter with a determiner, as in *that very fast horse* and *a rather close encounter*. The marked ones include *this*, *that*, *so*, *as*, and *how*; when combined with a prenominal adjective, as in *so fast* and *that close*, the result is a marked AP, and since the combination of a marked AP with a nominal yields a marked nominal, it is not possible to combine the latter with a determiner, as in **the so fast horse* and **a that close encounter*. Instead, the marked AP has to precede the determiner, as in *so fast a horse* and *that close an encounter*, but this is only possible if the nominal is introduced by the indefinite article. A proposal on how to model this combination, widely known as the Big Mess Construction, is presented in Van Eynde (2018).

Orthogonal to the distinction between marked and unmarked degree words is the part-of-speech distinction. In English, most of the degree words are adverbs (*very*, *rather*, *as*, *how* ...), but *this* and *that* can more plausibly be treated as pronouns, just like the homophonous demonstratives in (27)–(28). What differentiates them from the latter is captured by their select value, as shown in (31).

$$(31) \begin{bmatrix} \text{HEAD} & \begin{bmatrix} noun \\ \text{SELECT} & \begin{bmatrix} \text{CATEGORY} & \begin{bmatrix} \text{HEAD} & adjective \\ \text{MARK} & unmarked \end{bmatrix} \end{bmatrix} \end{bmatrix} \\ \text{MARK} & marked \end{bmatrix}$$

14.2.3.4 Complementizers

Comparable to the role of determiners in nominal projections and the role of degree markers in adjectival projections is the role of complementizers in verbal projections: they select an unmarked saturated verbal projection and have a MARKING value of type *marked*. The English *that*, for instance, has the CATEGORY value in (32).

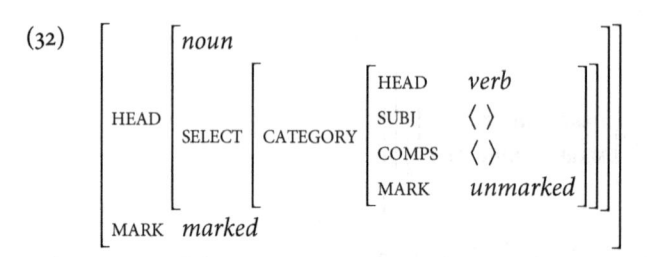

$$(32) \begin{bmatrix} \text{HEAD} & \begin{bmatrix} noun \\ \text{SELECT} & \begin{bmatrix} \text{CATEGORY} & \begin{bmatrix} \text{HEAD} & verb \\ \text{SUBJ} & \langle\,\rangle \\ \text{COMPS} & \langle\,\rangle \\ \text{MARK} & unmarked \end{bmatrix} \end{bmatrix} \end{bmatrix} \\ \text{MARK} & marked \end{bmatrix}$$

Since the complementizer shares its MARKING value with the dominating node, the latter is marked, and hence, no longer compatible with another complementizer; see Figure 14.5. Notice, once again, that the HEAD value can belong to any part of speech. In this case, it is *noun*, capturing the intuition, already expressed by Jespersen, that there is a link between the demonstrative pronoun *that* and the homophonous complementizer. In fact, what differentiates the pronoun *that*, the determiner *that*, the degree marking *that*, and the complementizer *that* is not their part of speech, or their MARKING value, but their SELECT value. Predictably, there are also complementizers that belong to other parts of speech, such as the adverb *if* and the adposition *for*. Distinctive of the complementizers is not their part of speech, but the combination of their SELECT and MARKING values.

[HEAD [1] *verb*, SUBJ < >, COMPS < >, MARK [2] *marked*]
——————————————————————————————————
[HEAD [*noun* SELECT [3]], MARK [2]]   [3] [HEAD [1], SUBJ < >, COMPS < >, MARK *unmarked*]
           | |
          that   the earth is round

FIGURE 14.5 A marked clause

14.2.4 Minor categories

Having argued that the factorial nature of the definition of syntactic word classes in HPSG makes it unnecessary and indeed counterproductive to introduce separate parts of speech for determiners, pronouns, degree markers, and complementizers, we now turn to a treatment of the so-called small words, such as articles and coordinating conjunctions. To model their syntactic properties, we introduce the distinction between major and minor categories, as defined in among others Van Eynde (1999).

14.2.4.1 Major vs minor pronouns

Most words can take dependents and head a branching XP, but there are some that cannot.[8] To illustrate this, we take the Dutch pronouns. Many of them come in two guises: one with a

---

[8] A branching XP is a phrase that is headed by a member of X and that has at least one other daughter.

diphthong as nucleus, as in *wij* 'we', and one with the schwa as nucleus, as in *we*.[9] As shown by the contrasts in (33), the pronouns with the diphthong can take dependents and head a branching NP, while the pronouns with the schwa cannot.

```
                    category
                   ╱        ╲
               major       minor
```

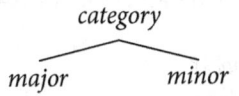

FIGURE 14.6 The major vs minor distinction

(33) a. *[Alleen zij/*ze die het verdienen] worden beloond.*
     [only they who it deserve] get rewarded
     'Only those who deserve it get a reward.'

   b. *[Wij/*we allen] hebben daar belang bij.*
     [we all] have there import with
     'We all have a stake in that.'

A correlated difference is that the pronouns of the first type can be conjoined, while those of the second type cannot.

(34) *Ze kan niet kiezen tussen [jou/*je en mij/*me].*
     she can not choose between [you and me]
     'She cannot choose between you and me.'

Given that both types are pronouns and, hence, marked members of N, it follows that the property which differentiates them is orthogonal to both the part-of-speech distinction and the MARKING distinction. To capture it we add a distinction between two subtypes of CATEGORY values, called *major* and *minor*, as spelled out in Figure 14.6 (Van Eynde 1999).[10] In terms of this distinction the pronouns with a diphthong as nucleus have a CATEGORY value of type *major*, while those with the schwa have a one of type *minor*, as illustrated in (35).

(35) $\begin{bmatrix} major \\ \text{HEAD} \quad noun \\ \text{MARK} \quad marked \end{bmatrix}$ $\begin{bmatrix} minor \\ \text{HEAD} \quad noun \\ \text{MARK} \quad marked \end{bmatrix}$

That the minor pronouns cannot take dependents or be conjoined is captured by constraints on the relevant phrase types. Head daughters, for instance, are declared to have a CATEGORY value of type *major*, and so are conjunct daughters. Complements, adjuncts, and subjects, by contrast, are not constrained in this way.

---

[9] The distinction also applies to *mij/me* 'me', *zij/ze* 'they/she', *jij/je* 'you.nom', and *jou/je* 'you.acc' (Van Eynde 1999).
[10] The distinction is deliberately reminiscent of the GPSG notion of minor categories as categories that 'fall outside the X-bar system' (Gazdar et al. 1985: 25).

14.2.4.2 Articles

Articles differ from the other determiners in the same way as minor pronouns differ from the major ones. The Dutch demonstrative *dat* 'that', for instance, can be conjoined, but its phonologically reduced counterpart, the article *het* 'the', cannot.

(36) Wil je [dit of dat/*het] boek?
 want you [this or that/*the] book
 'do you want this or that/*the book?'

The demonstrative determiner is, hence, a major pronoun, while the article is a minor pronoun. What differentiates *het* from *dat* is not its part of speech, or its SELECT or MARKING value, but the subtype of its *category*, as spelled out in (37).

(37) $\begin{bmatrix} & \text{minor} \\ \text{HEAD} & \begin{bmatrix} \text{noun} \\ \text{SELECT} & \begin{bmatrix} \text{CATEGORY} & \begin{bmatrix} \text{HEAD} & \text{noun} \\ \text{MARK} & \text{unmarked} \end{bmatrix} \end{bmatrix} \end{bmatrix} \\ \text{MARK} & \text{marked} \end{bmatrix}$

In this analysis, articles are minor marked selectors of an unmarked nominal and can belong to any part of speech, just like their major counterparts. This cannot only be N, but also A or P. The Spanish indefinite article, for instance, shows the same inflectional variation and agreement with the noun as the adnominal adjectives, as shown in (38).

(38) a. *un/*una/*unos/*unas momento*
 a.SG.M/*a.SG.F/*a.PL.M/*a.PL.F moment.SG.M
 'a moment'

 b. *una/*uno/*unos/*unas escuela*
 a.SG.F/*a.SG.M/*a.PL.M/*a.PL.F school.SG.F
 'a school'

 c. *unos/*un/*una/*unas detalles*
 a.PL.M/*a.SG.M/*a.SG.F detail.PL.M
 'some details'

 d. *unas/*un/*una/*unos casas*
 a.PL.F/*a.SG.M/*a.SG.F/*a.PL.M house.PL.F
 'some houses'

The most straightforward treatment is, hence, as a minor marked adjective that selects an unmarked nominal with matching number and gender values. An example of P is the French *de*. This word is not only used as the complement-selecting head of a PP, as in (39), but also as the 'article partitif', as in (40).

(39) Elle vient de Lyon.
 she comes from Lyon
 'She is from Lyon.'

(40) *Je n'ai   plus   de monnaie.*
    I NEG.have no.more of money
    'I don't have any money left.'

The difference between these uses is captured by their COMPS value, which is <NP> for the former and the empty list for the latter, as well as by the major–minor distinction. A welcome corollary of this treatment is that languages without articles, such as Latin and Russian, do not have to be claimed to lack a part of speech. All they lack is minor counterparts for their determiners.

14.2.4.3 Coordinate conjunctions

The notion of minor category is also useful for the treatment of coordinate conjunctions, such as *and*, *or*, and *but*. In the HPSG treatment, these words do not project a phrase: *the man and his dog*, for instance, is not treated as a ConjP, but rather as an NP whose daughters are the first NP, the conjunction and the second NP. The conjunctions, hence, lack the possibility to head a branching XP, which implies that they are minor. Confirming evidence is provided by the fact that they cannot be conjoined themselves (**and or but*). Being minor, though, does not say anything about their part of speech. Just like the articles, they may belong to any part of speech, and in order to find out what the most plausible candidate is, it is instructive to look at uses other than the coordinating ones.

The English *but*, for instance, is used as a coordinating conjunction in *a small but comfortable room*, but not in *all but five of the participants*, where its role is more similar to that of *except*. Since the difference is captured by the values of the CONTENT feature and the CATEGORY feature (minor vs major), it is not necessary to add a part-of-speech distinction on top of that. Instead, given that the non-coordinating *but* is adverbial, it is reasonable to treat the coordinating *but* as an adverb too, more specifically as a minor adverb.

Similar remarks apply to the Dutch *of*. It is used a coordinating conjunction in *Tom of Jerry* 'Tom or Jerry', and in that use it corresponds to the English *or*, but this is not the case in *vragen of hij komt* 'ask whether he is coming', where it is a subordinate conjunction, and in *een stuk of twintig pagina's* 'around twenty pages', where it is part of an approximativity marker. Also here, the differences can be captured in terms of independently needed distinctions and need not be made by different parts of speech. In fact, given the adverbial nature of its use in the approximativity marker, it makes sense to treat the homophonous coordinate conjunction as an adverb too, more specifically as a minor adverb.

14.2.5 Summing up

At the beginning of the section we made a distinction between a stable core of the speech part inventory and a more volatile fringe. The core was argued to consist of 'the big five', i.e. verb, noun, adjective, adverb, and adposition (section 14.2.1). It was shown to play a central role in the definition of syntactic word classes in HPSG, but it was also made clear that other factors play a role as well, such as the distinctions that are captured by the valence features (COMPS and SUBJ), the SELECT feature, and the MARKING feature (section 14.2.2). In the resulting factorial analysis, it was argued to be unnecessary and indeed unmotivated to introduce separate parts of speech for functional categories, such as determiners, pronouns, degree markers, and complementizers (section 14.2.3). In the last section, it was shown that also minor categories, such as articles and coordinate conjunctions, can be accommodated by adding a cross-categorial distinction between two types of CATEGORY values (section 14.2.4). The net result is that there is no need for the volatile fringe.

14.3 SEMANTIC WORD CLASSES

While the part-of-speech distinction plays a central role in the definition of syntactic word classes, its role in the definition of semantic word classes is marginal and indirect. This is due to the fact that semantic representations in HPSG are not defined in terms of syntactic categories, but in terms of model-theoretic notions, such as *state of affairs, proposition, relation*, and *index*; see Ginzburg & Sag (2000: 386). For this purpose, HPSG draws inspiration from Situation Theory, a branch of logic with a relatively rich ontology of semantic types (Barwise & Perry 1983; see Chapter 7 in this volume). Technically, the semantic representations in HPSG are values of the CONTENT feature, and the distinctions that are captured by its values are orthogonal to those that are captured by the CATEGORY values. Words that denote a relation, for instance, can belong to any part of speech, which shows that the relation between semantic types and syntactic categories is one-to-many. Conversely, sentences can denote propositions, as well as questions or exclamations, which shows that the relation between syntactic categories and semantic types is one-to-many too. This does not imply that there is no relation between syntactic word classes and semantic word classes (see among others Chaves 2013). It only shows that the relation is not one-to-one, and— more importantly in this context—that semantic considerations are irrelevant for the definition of syntactic word classes in general and the part-of-speech distinction in particular.

14.4 MORPHOLOGICAL WORD CLASSES

For the sake of completeness, we also briefly discuss the role of the part-of-speech distinction in the definition of morphological word classes, or more generally, its role in the modelling of word formation. Crucial for that purpose is the distinction between words and lexemes: while words are the stuff that phrases are made of, lexemes are more abstract signs. The lexeme *RUN*, for instance, stands for a family of words, including *run, runs, running*, and *ran*. The main purpose of the lexemes is to capture properties of signs that are common to their various inflected forms. It is, for instance, at the level of the lexeme *RUN* that one defines the properties of being intransitive and of denoting a type of locomotion. Likewise, it is at the level of the lexeme that one defines the properties which the Italian words *nuovo, nuova, nuovi*, and *nuove* 'new' have in common, such as the fact of being an adjective and of denoting the property of novelty. Lexemes are organized in a multidimensional type hierarchy and get most of their properties by multiple inheritance (Koenig 1999). They are related to words by means of lexical rules; (41), for instance, relates verbal lexemes to their past tense form.[11]

---

[11] This is an inflectional lexical rule. There are also derivational lexical rules, relating lexemes to other lexemes (Riehemann 1998).

(41) $\begin{bmatrix} \text{lexeme} \\ \text{PHONOLOGY } \boxed{1} \\ \text{SYNSEM} \begin{bmatrix} \text{CAT | HEAD } \textit{verb} \\ \text{CONTENT } \boxed{2} \end{bmatrix} \end{bmatrix} \Rightarrow LR \begin{bmatrix} \text{word} \\ \text{PHONOLOGY } F_{past}(\boxed{1}) \\ \text{SYNSEM} \begin{bmatrix} \text{CATEGORY} \begin{bmatrix} \text{HEAD | VFORM } \textit{finite} \\ \text{SUBJECT } \langle \text{NP [CASE } \textit{nom}]\rangle \end{bmatrix} \\ \text{CONTENT } \boxed{2} \oplus ... \end{bmatrix} \end{bmatrix}$

In (41), $\boxed{1}$ stands for a verbal stem, such as *RUN*, and the morphophonological function F_{past} relates this to the corresponding past tense form. For regular verbs, this involves the addition of the *-ed* affix; for other verbs it usually involves stem alternation, as in the case of *ran*. The CATEGORY value of the input contains the constraint that the lexeme must be a verb, and that of the output adds more specific information about VFORM and about the properties of the subject which the sign selects, namely that it must be nominative. The CONTENT value of the input is of type *state of affairs* and so is that of the output ($\boxed{2}$), but the latter also includes a constraint which captures the semantic contribution of the past tense, namely that the denoted state of affairs temporally precedes the time of utterance. For reasons of brevity it is designated by three dots in (41).

As this example makes clear, lexemes and words are both signs and the rules which relate them may involve any combination of their phonological, syntactic, and semantic properties. The role of the part-of-speech distinction in that mixture may differ from rule to rule. In (41), for instance, it plays a pivotal role, since the rule applies to all lexemes whose HEAD value is *verb*, but there are also rules in which the constraints on the input lexeme are of a semantic nature and for which it is, hence, more appropriate to express them in terms of the CONTENT value. Koenig & Michelson (2014), for instance, argue that this is the case for the word formation rules of Oneida, an Amer-Indian language. For a detailed recent treatment of morphology in HPSG, see Crysmann & Bonami (2016).

14.5 Conclusion

HPSG employs the age-old distinction between verbs, nouns, and other parts of speech. The distinction, in fact, plays a central role in the definition of syntactic word classes, but since there are other distinctions which play a role as well, it is not necessary or desirable to treat all syntactically relevant distinctions as part-of-speech distinctions. In fact, we have seen that a differentiation between five parts of speech suffices, if it is combined with distinctions that are captured in terms of other syntactic features. The net result is a part-of-speech inventory that is more parsimonious than that of most other frameworks. Interestingly, this brings it in line with the widespread practice in typological work of keeping the inventory of parts of speech rather limited. Hengeveld (1992), for instance, argues for a universal inventory of four parts of speech, i.e. verb, noun, adjective, and adverb. For the sake of completeness, we also briefly discussed the role of part-of-speech distinction in the definition of semantic word classes and in the definition of morphological word classes.

Acknowledgements

For their comments on earlier versions of the text of this chapter, I wish to thank Jean-Pierre Koenig, Eva van Lier, Bram Bulté, and two anonymous reviewers.

CHAPTER 15

WORD CLASSES IN LEXICAL FUNCTIONAL GRAMMAR

MARY DALRYMPLE AND IDA TOIVONEN

LEXICAL Functional Grammar (Kaplan & Bresnan 1982; Bresnan et al. 2016; Dalrymple et al. 2019) assumes that word order and phrasal constituency is modelled at a syntactic level called *constituent structure*, represented as a phrase structure tree.[1] A separate syntactic level, *functional structure*, represents grammatical functions such as subject and object as well as features such as person and tense. Word class[2] is relevant at constituent structure but is not represented at functional structure. We discuss word class, its place in the LFG architecture, and the inventory of word classes that most LFG analyses assume, including the distinction between projecting and nonprojecting categories. Some LFG literature proposes that word classes can be decomposed into sets of more primitive features which reflect basic aspects of their syntactic behaviour. We also review some LFG literature addressing challenges to simple assumptions about diagnostics for word-class membership. Finally, we discuss the principle of lexical integrity and the LFG view of the structure of the lexicon.

15.1 ARCHITECTURE OF LFG

LFG is a nontransformational linguistic theory which assumes separate linguistic levels, with distinct representations, for different aspects of linguistic structure. Constituent structure (c-structure) encodes word order and phrasal constituency, and is represented as a phrase structure tree conforming to a modified version of X-bar theory (Toivonen 2003; Bresnan et al. 2016; Lovestrand & Lowe 2017; Dalrymple et al. 2019; Lowe & Lovestrand 2020), as depicted on the left-hand side of example (1). Functional structure (f-structure) encodes

---

[1] The authors are listed alphabetically and they contributed equally to this chapter.
[2] In the LFG literature, word classes are often referred to as *lexical categories* or *parts of speech*, and sometimes by the use of the more general term *syntactic category*. We use the terms *lexical category/word class/part of speech* interchangeably, in contrast with *phrasal category*: that is, the set of syntactic categories of a language consists of its lexical categories/parts of speech together with its phrasal categories.

abstract grammatical relations and features, and is represented as an attribute–value structure, as depicted on the right-hand side of example (1). Other aspects of linguistic structure, including semantic structure, prosodic structure, information structure, and argument structure, are related by functional correspondence to c-structure and f-structure; we do not discuss details of the representation of these levels or their relation to the syntactic levels of c-structure and f-structure which are our main focus.

(1) The syntactic structures of LFG: constituent structure and functional structure

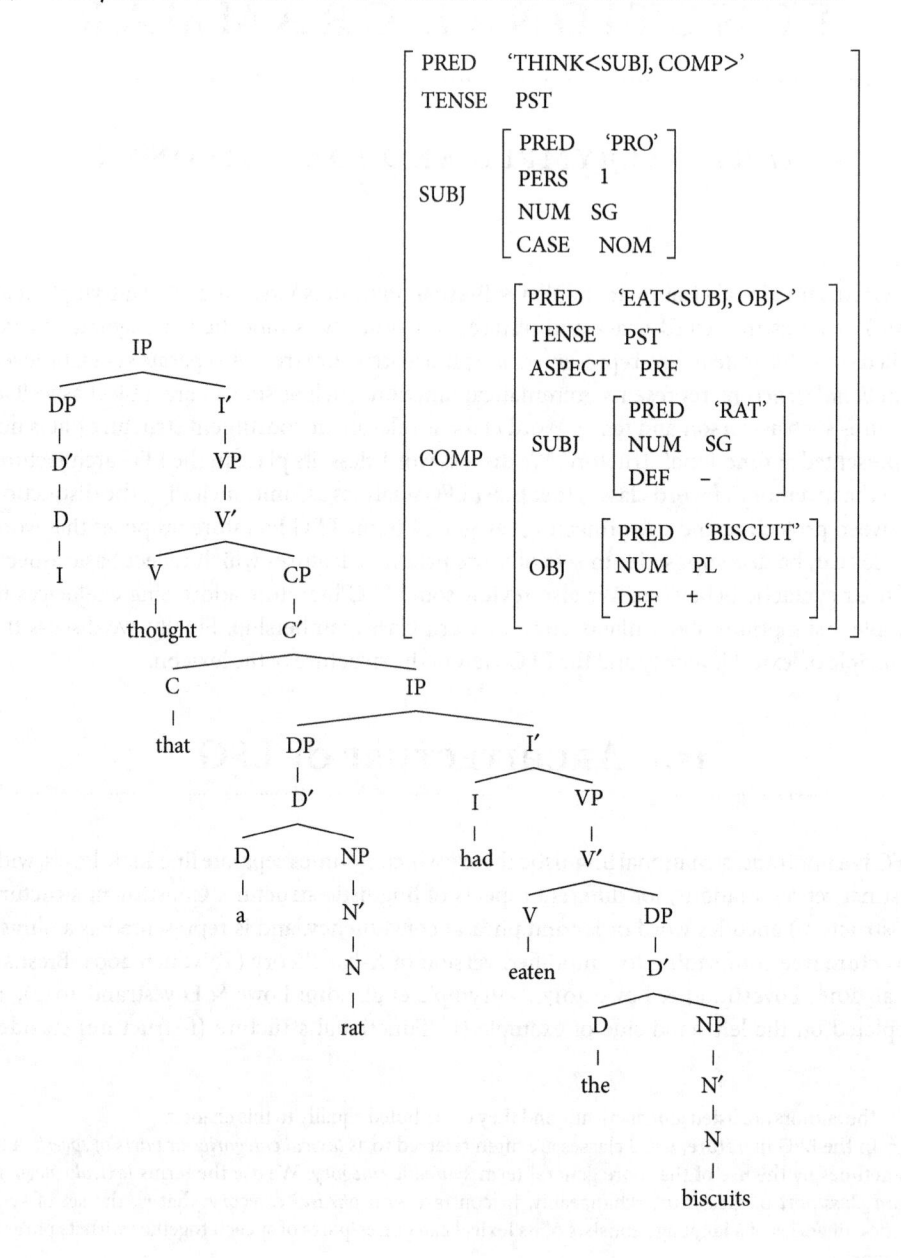

$$\begin{bmatrix} \text{PRED} & \text{'THINK<SUBJ, COMP>'} \\ \text{TENSE} & \text{PST} \\ \text{SUBJ} & \begin{bmatrix} \text{PRED} & \text{'PRO'} \\ \text{PERS} & 1 \\ \text{NUM} & \text{SG} \\ \text{CASE} & \text{NOM} \end{bmatrix} \\ \text{COMP} & \begin{bmatrix} \text{PRED} & \text{'EAT<SUBJ, OBJ>'} \\ \text{TENSE} & \text{PST} \\ \text{ASPECT} & \text{PRF} \\ \text{SUBJ} & \begin{bmatrix} \text{PRED} & \text{'RAT'} \\ \text{NUM} & \text{SG} \\ \text{DEF} & - \end{bmatrix} \\ \text{OBJ} & \begin{bmatrix} \text{PRED} & \text{'BISCUIT'} \\ \text{NUM} & \text{PL} \\ \text{DEF} & + \end{bmatrix} \end{bmatrix} \end{bmatrix}$$

Nodes of the constituent structure tree are labelled with category labels such as N, V′, and IP, and preterminal node labels like D, V, and N are zero-level category labels reflecting word classes. Such category labels are often treated as abbreviations for complex feature structures encoding word–class distinctions, bar level, and the distinction between functional and lexical categories, as we discuss in section 15.5. Following standard practice in LFG, the representation of functional structure features in (1) has been simplified: only a representative set of features appears, and simple values are provided for features like NUM, TENSE, and ASPECT rather than the complex values motivated by feature resolution and underspecification.

As (1) shows, differences of word class are relevant at constituent structure but not at functional structure. In fact, words of different classes can contribute functional structure that is very similar. For example, deverbal nominalizations can share argument structure with the verbs from which they are derived; gerunds like *working* can take an object, just like the corresponding verb *work*, as we discuss in section 15.6.4. Syntactic similarities involving unrelated words can also be manifested at functional structure: for example, predicative nouns and adjectives can be analysed as requiring a subject, giving rise to similar functional syntactic structures for examples like *He is scholarly* and *He is a scholar*, though the word classes of *scholarly* and *scholar* are different. Differences in morphosyntactic realization at constituent structure can also be neutralized at functional structure: a bound morpheme, a nonprojecting word (section 15.4), or a fully projecting word can provide the same information to functional structure.

The various facets of the structure and meaning of words are represented in the lexicon, and correlations involving word class and meaning are a part of the theory of the structure of the lexicon. The modular nature of LFG theory requires that meaning be represented at semantic structure, not constituent structure or functional structure; constituent structure encodes only word class and phrasal category, not meaning or functional syntactic information.

15.2 CATEGORY INVENTORY

LFG assumes an inventory of lexical categories (or word classes: as noted above, we use the terms interchangeably in this text) that is potentially relevant for all languages; grammars of languages vary as to which distinctions between categories are relevant. Some languages make use of more distinctions than others do, which means that the inventory of lexical and phrasal categories can vary from language to language even though they are drawn from the same universal inventory: for example, Bresnan (1982a) observes that Warlpiri does not have words of the category adjective, and that Warlpiri nouns play a role in noun modification similar to the role played by adjectives in a language like English.

LFG assumes that the lexical categories N(oun), V(erb), Adj(ective), Adv(erb), and P(reposition) are part of the universal inventory of categories. Lexical entries are specified for category, as illustrated in the following lexical entry for the noun *rat* (using simplified, nonstandard notation to represent functional structure features and their values: for an explanation of the full standard notation, see Bresnan et al. 2016 and Dalrymple et al. 2019):

(2) *rat*: N; PRED = 'RAT'
            NUM = SG

This lexical entry encodes both the word-class N of the noun *rat* (allowing this word to appear as the daughter of a preterminal node labelled N at constituent structure) and the functional features PRED and NUM and their values (requiring these features to appear at functional structure). In this simplified lexical entry, we do not include features relevant to non-syntactic aspects of linguistic structure, such as semantic structure, information structure, or prosodic structure.

There is a separate lexical entry for the corresponding plural noun, with the same word-class (N) but a different value for the NUM feature:

(3) *rats*: N; PRED = 'RAT'
             NUM = PL

The internal morphological structure of words is not represented at constituent structure: on Lexical Integrity, see section 15.7.

Functional categories do not play a major role in LFG's c-structure. LFG makes use of phrase structure rules to govern word order, and many core syntactic phenomena (e.g. agreement) are analysed at f-structure. For these reasons, only a select few functional categories, C(omplementizer), I(nflection), and D(eterminer), are standardly adopted in LFG. The motivations for adopting these categories are not LFG-specific: they date back to work by Stowell (1981), Brame (1982), and Abney (1987). CP and IP, the phrases that host C and I, are considered extended projections of the VP (in the sense of Grimshaw 1991, 2005): CPs, IPs, and VPs all contain verbal featural information (see section 15.5). Similarly, DPs are nominal, and extended projections of NPs.[3] Besides C, I, and D, a few other functional categories have been argued for within the LFG literature, though not all LFG researchers agree on the need for these categories: for example, CONJ (for conjunctions; see, e.g., Kaplan & Maxwell 1988), NEG (for negation; see, e.g., Sells 2000; Alsharif & Sadler 2009), K (for case; see, e.g., Butt & King 2004), and Q (for quantifier; see, e.g., Guo et al. 2007).

It is important to note that these functional categories are lexically specified categories rather than positions hosting movement. To illustrate, let us consider French finite verbs as an example. French finite verbs are assumed to appear in I in regular declarative sentences, unlike some other languages, for example English, where finite and non-finite lexical verbs consistently appear in V. The traditional arguments for this difference between French and English finite verbs are based on the placement of negation and adverbs (see Pollock 1989

---

[3] Grimshaw (2005: 2) writes: 'Extended Projection involves an extended notion of an X-bar theoretic *projection*, in which noun-headed constituents and verb-headed constituents form (extended) projections, which include both the projection of their lexical heads and the functional shell which surrounds the lexical projection.'

and references given there for the history of this idea). In an LFG analysis that adopts this classical generative proposal, French finite verbs appear higher in the phrase structure than French non-finite verbs (and all English verbs) because they belong to a different word class, and not because of a movement transformation: French finite verbs are of category I, and non-finite verbs are of category V. The lexical entries for a non-finite form (the regular infinitive) and a finite form (the first person plural present tense form) of the verb *rire* 'to laugh' are given in (4) and (5):

(4) *rire*: V;   PRED = 'LAUGH'
               VERBTYPE = INF

(5) *rions*: I; PRED = 'LAUGH'
               VERBTYPE = FIN
               TENSE = PRS
               SUBJ NUM = PL
               SUBJ PERS = 1

These appear in the phrase structure position appropriate for their category:[4]

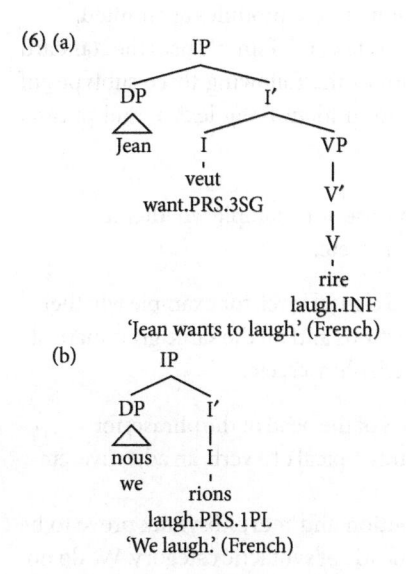

(6) (a)
```
              IP
            /    \
          DP      I'
          △     /   \
         Jean  I     VP
               |     |
              veut   V'
          want.PRS.3SG |
                       V
                       |
                      rire
                    laugh.INF
```
'Jean wants to laugh.' (French)

(b)
```
              IP
            /    \
          DP      I'
          △      |
         nous    I
          we     |
                rions
             laugh.PRS.1PL
```
'We laugh.' (French)

Again, the categories of the verbs directly determine their phrase structural positions, and there is no V-to-I movement. The French tensed verb *rions* has the functional category

---

[4] Glosses follow the Leipzig Glossing Rules (Bickel et al. 2015). We have simplified some of the glosses in our examples to restrict focus to the issues under discussion.

I, even though it is a content word and not a function word. Functional categories are not the same as function words: a word that is of a functional category is not necessarily a function word.

15.3 IDENTIFYING CATEGORIES

Both traditional grammars and theoretical analyses rely on distinctions in word classes, though the criteria for defining them are not always made explicit. The question of how to distinguish among word classes has been discussed by Kornfilt & Whitman (2011), Denison (2013), Lowe (2019), and the contributors in Heny & Richards (1983). These authors generally agree that defining and representing word–class distinctions is useful, despite the existence of some tricky cases, some of which we discuss in section 15.6.

It is generally assumed that criteria for distinguishing between categories broadly divide into semantic and syntactic ones. In LFG, word classes are native to constituent structure, and the majority of work on identification of word class within LFG therefore appeals to syntactic criteria. Non-syntactic criteria for word-class membership, including lexical semantics, have not been a primary focus of study in an LFG setting. Given LFG's strong commitment to modularity, this is expected: constituent structure is a separate module of grammar with its own internal structure, and interactions across modules are limited.

There are no LFG-specific criteria for identifying word class: LFG simply uses the standard syntactic criteria for identification. Lowe (2019) identifies the following three subtypes of syntactic characteristics that are frequently appealed to in identifying lexical and phrasal syntactic categories:

(7) a. Internal syntax: the internal structure of the phrase, for example whether it contains determiners, adjectives, objects, adverbs, etc.

b. Distribution: the distribution of the phrase at a clausal level, for example whether a phrase can appear in the same structural positions and fill the same grammatical functions as unambiguous noun phrases or verb phrases, etc.

c. Morphosyntax: the morphosyntactic properties of the head of the phrase, for example whether it shows the agreement features typical of a verb, an adjective, etc.

Lowe (2019) argues that of these criteria, both distribution and morphosyntax prove to be problematic, and only internal syntax is a reliable diagnostic of syntactic category. We do not take a stand here on which criteria are most useful: rather, we simply note that multiple kinds of syntactic and morphosyntactic criteria are frequently appealed to in the literature both within and outside LFG. When considering the criteria in (7a–b), it is important to keep in mind the flexibility of heads assumed in LFG. Diagnostics for identifying phrasal categories provide evidence for the word class of their heads, under the standard X-bar theoretic assumption that the category of a phrase is determined by the category of its lexical head. However, in LFG the picture is more complicated: optionality of phrase structure positions and the existence of extended projections mean that phrases can appear without an internal head, as illustrated in (8) for the French VP, which need not contain a V head; as discussed in section 15.2, French finite verbs are of category I, not V.

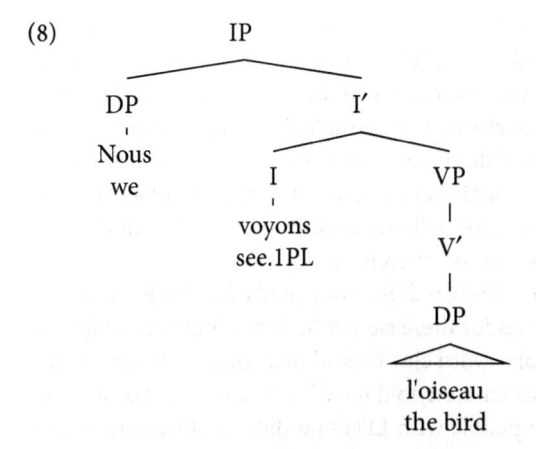

(8)
```
          IP
         /  \
       DP    I'
        |   /  \
      Nous I    VP
       we  |    |
        voyons  V'
        see.1PL |
                DP
                /\
             l'oiseau
             the bird
```

'We see the bird.' (French)

Since the structure in (8) includes a VP that does not have a V head, the test in (7a) is not useful for identifying the final phrase as a VP in this particular example, or for detecting the presence of a word of category V.

15.4 Projecting and nonprojecting categories

In addition to the categories listed above, researchers working in the LFG framework (and indeed researchers from other frameworks as well) sometimes label words in the c-structure as belonging to minor categories such as clitic (Cl) or particle (Prt) (see, e.g., Schwarze 2001 for clitics and Forst et al. 2010 for particles). This is exemplified in (9), with the French clitic pronoun *le* in (9a) and the English verbal particle *out* in (9b):

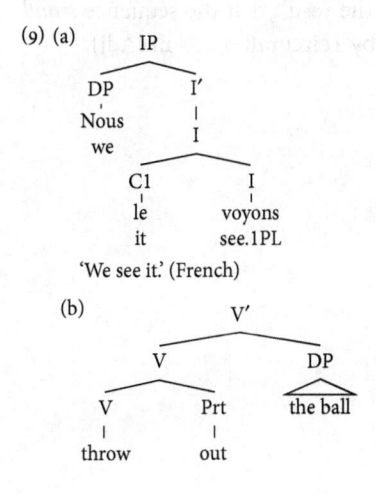

(9) (a)
```
        IP
       /  \
     DP    I'
      |    |
    Nous   I
     we   / \
         Cl  I
         |   |
         le voyons
         it see.1PL
```
'We see it.' (French)

(b)
```
          V'
         /  \
        V    DP
       / \   /\
      V  Prt the ball
      |   |
    throw out
```

The use of the labels Cl and Prt in the constituent structure implies that clitics and particles are word classes on a par with verbs and adjectives. The motivation for positing categories such as particles and clitics in addition to more standard word classes is, of course, that these entities display some distinguishing characteristics. For example, French clitics such as *le* in (9a) cannot be stressed, and their word order differs from that of stressed pronouns and non-pronominal nouns. English particles such as *out* in (9b) can appear before the object (unlike other modifiers), and they typically form an especially tight meaningful unit with the verb (see for example Dehé et al. 2002 for discussion and references).

An alternative view, adopted by a number of researchers within and outside LFG, does not involve proposing special syntactic categories for these elements. According to this alternative view, these words are drawn from regular word classes, and their special characteristics are due to other factors (Jackendoff 1973; Sadler & Arnold 1994; Toivonen 2003; Lowe 2016a; Barbu & Toivonen 2018). This view is compatible with LFG's modular architecture, which assumes that the grammar consists of multiple independent levels of representation, with possible mismatches between the levels. For example, generalizations concerning stress for both particles and clitics are accounted for at the independent level of prosodic structure, not on the basis of word class. Semantically, the interpretations of verb–particle combinations like *blow up* and *pass out* are not directly predictable from the combination of the individual words, but these facts do not affect constituent structure and are not represented there. They are instead handled in the lexicon, functional structure, and semantic structure. In addition, particles can alter the argument structure of verbs. For example, *wait* does not take a direct object, but *wait out* does (e.g. *wait out the storm*, Larsen 2014: ch. 3). Regular argument structure alternations are captured at argument structure, and idiosyncratic argument structures are listed in the lexicon. At constituent structure, these structures are represented no differently than fully regular, compositional verb–particle combinations.

LFG's theory of constituent structure allows for *nonprojecting words*; that is, syntactically independent words (words that are not morphologically bound) that do not project full phrases. Nonprojecting words have been proposed in the analysis of prenominal adjectives in English (Sadler & Arnold 1994), certain adverbs and negation markers in Korean (Sells 1994), verbal particles in Swedish (Toivonen 2003), and serial verbs in Barayin (Lovestrand 2018). According to Sadler & Arnold's analysis, illustrated in (10), English nonprojecting prenominal adjectives are adjoined at the N level, with the result that the sequence *small mouse* is of category N. Nonprojecting words are marked by a circumflex accent ($\widehat{\text{Adj}}$).

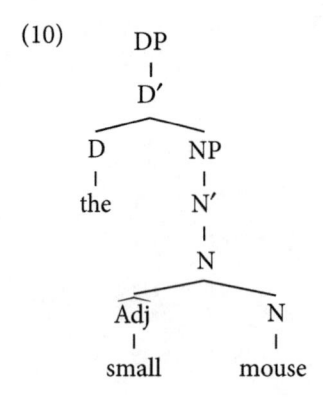

(10)
```
        DP
        |
        D'
       / \
      D   NP
      |   |
     the  N'
          |
          N
         / \
        Adj  N
        |    |
       small mouse
```

Similarly, the adverb *very* is a nonprojecting modifier of adjectives, so the sequence *very small* is a nonprojecting sequence of category Adj, and *very small mouse* is also of category N:

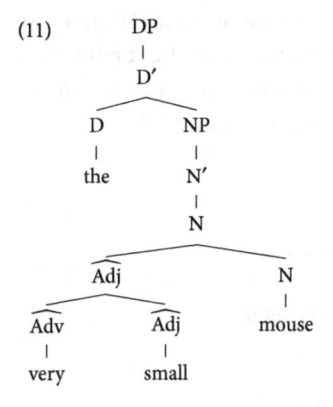

(11)
```
            DP
            |
            D'
           / \
          D   NP
          |   |
         the  N'
              |
              N
             / \
           Adj   N
           / \    |
         Adv  Adj mouse
          |    |
        very small
```

On this view, words drawn from any of the regular word classes can but need not project full phrases. Importantly, the projecting–nonprojecting distinction is orthogonal to the prosodic status of a word: nonprojecting words can be prosodically either weak or strong. French clitics are examples of nonprojecting, prosodically weak pronouns (presumably of the category D; Somesfalean 2007 and references therein). Swedish verbal particles are nonprojecting, prosodically strong words drawn from various word classes: they are typically prepositions, but can also be adjectives, nouns, and arguably even verbs (Toivonen 2003: ch. 2).[5]

According to this view, differences in constituent structure projections and prosody need not be explained in terms of word class distinctions. It is thus possible to understand and define elements that behave unusually with respect to word order and stress without positing novel word classes. However, there are no constraints in the formal LFG architecture that would in principle prohibit unconventional categories like Cl or Prt. Both alternatives that have been described in this section have been explored within the general LFG framework, and it is up to future theoretical and empirical studies to decide between the two approaches.

15.5 FEATURAL DECOMPOSITION OF CATEGORY LABELS

Word classes are not necessarily primitive categories. It is often assumed that word classes are composed of more primitive features that allow generalizations across classes. Such features also make it possible to state explicit constraints on how lexical and functional categories interact.

---

[5] The analysis of English verbal particles is controversial; see Larsen (2014: ch. 2) for a thorough review of the literature. Larsen assumes that particles are nonprojecting words that can adjoin to heads.

Proposals to treat word-class labels such as N and V as abbreviations for complex feature structures originate with Chomsky (1970) and Jackendoff (1977), who defined the major word-class categories in terms of sets of primitive features. Jackendoff (1977) proposes features such as ± SUBJ and ± OBJ, where the categories V and N are classified as + SUBJ, and V and P are + OBJ.

Bresnan (1982a) proposed the integration of a similar set of features into LFG, on the basis of the features 'predicative' (for forms taking a subject) and 'transitive' (for forms which can take an object). 'A' in (12) is a cover term for the categories of adjective and adverb.

(12) Categorial features (Bresnan 1982a)

	'predicative'	'transitive'	
V	+	+	verbal
P	±	+	pre- or postpositional
N	±	−	nominal
A	+	−	adjectival

Bresnan observes that these features are definable in terms of the functional structure primitive relations of subject and object, thus allowing the elimination of primitive features in defining word classes.[6] Note that according to Bresnan's (1982a) classification, V and A are + predicative, while N and P can be either positively or negatively specified for that feature. As with Jackendoff's classification, V and P are + transitive, while N and A are −transitive.

In subsequent work, P and N are generally assumed to be −predicative: Bresnan et al. (2016: 126) define predicative categories as 'those which cannot stand alone as arguments but require an external subject of predication'. On this view, word-class categories can be unambiguously identified by their features:

(13) Categorial features (Bresnan 2001)

	'predicative'	'transitive'
V	+	+
P	−	+
N	−	−
A	+	−

Even though the classification in (13) is perhaps overly simplistic, it has proven a useful starting point and has been adopted in much recent work, including Toivonen (2003) and Bresnan et al. (2016).

Besides these categorial features, we have seen that words can be classified according to whether they realize a functional or a lexical category. Following Grimshaw (1998), Bresnan et al. (2016) posit additional privative features F_1 and F_2, associated with functional but not lexical categories. Bresnan et al. (2016) propose that the categories N and D are nominal categories (−predicative, −transitive), but D is additionally specified with the functional feature F_1; I, C, and V are all verbal categories (+predicative, +transitive), but I and C are

---

[6] We do not include the sentential S feature proposed by Bresnan (1982a) for clausal categories: the subsequent development of the theory of functional categories has caused a rethinking and reorganization of the treatment of clausal structure.

marked with different functional features F1 and F2, as shown in (14), where ØF indicates the absence of a functional feature.

(14) V: [+predicative, +transitive, ØF]
      I: [+predicative, +transitive, F1]
      C: [+predicative, +transitive, F2]
      N: [−predicative, −transitive, ØF]
      D: [−predicative, −transitive, F1]

The features are numbered (F1 and F2) to distinguish the categories from each other and to indicate how far they are removed from the lexical category (the IP is embedded in the CP and not vice versa.). Note that there is only one level of nominal functional projection in (14). Bresnan et al. (2016) suggest that English does not have an F2 category for nominal projections, but Grimshaw (1998) treats PP as F2 for nouns (above DP, which is F1).

Marcotte (2014) and Lowe & Lovestrand (2020) propose additional features to distinguish zero-level X-bar-theoretic categories from X' and XP, providing a principled means of determining the features of a phrasal category on the basis of the features of its head. Their theories differ in how nonterminal/phrasal nodes of the tree are treated, whether nonbranching chains are allowed, and how the different levels of X-bar theory are distinguished.[7]

15.6 CHALLENGING PATTERNS

Several challenges to simple assumptions about word-class membership have been examined in an LFG setting. Some mismatches involve conflicting morphological, phrase structural, or functional criteria: the word class of some forms is unexpected in light of their morphological or syntactic properties. In section 15.6.1 we examine cases in which the morphological marking on a word is unexpected for its word class; for example, nouns bearing tense or aspect marking. In section 15.6.2 we examine cases in which a phrase fills a syntactic role that is unexpected for its phrasal category; for example, prepositional or clausal subjects. A single word may also appear to fill two different positions in the phrase structure; such cases are analysed as instances of lexical sharing, as we discuss in section 15.6.3. Finally, a word may head a phrase that has syntactic features of more than one word class: the English gerund is a typical example of these mixed categories, as we discuss in section 15.6.4.

---

[7] Although we are not concerned here with differences among non-zero-level phrasal categories, we observe that these features also enable a treatment of the difference between projecting and nonprojecting categories introduced in section 15.4. Marcotte (2014) proposes two features, terminal and maximal, and proposes that nonprojecting words have both of these features: they are terminal nodes which are maximal, and do not project a larger phrase. Lowe & Lovestrand (2020) identify some difficulties with Marcotte's analysis, and propose two features, level and projection, each with values 0/1/2. Projecting words have a projection feature and can project additional structure, while nonprojecting words do not have a projection feature and cannot project.

15.6.1 Unexpected morphology for word class

Some morphological properties are naturally associated with particular word classes. For example, nouns tend to carry information about number, gender, and case, and verbs tend to carry information about tense and aspect. However, there are exceptions to these natural matches between morphology and word classes, and we revisit LFG analyses of some such exceptions here.

Tense, aspect, and mood (TAM) marking is typically associated with verbs. However, TAM marking is also found on nominal elements in some languages. Nordlinger & Sadler (2004a) provide a cross-linguistic survey of nominal tense morphology, showing that there are two types of nominal tense. One type pertains solely to the interpretation of the tense-marked nominal itself: this type is similar (but not identical) to morphemes such as English *ex*, as in *ex-president*. The other type of nominal tense contributes to the interpretation of the entire proposition. This latter type is thus the same as regular verbal tense marking, but the tense morphology surfaces on a nominal rather than a verb. An example from the Pama-Nyungan language Pitta Pitta is given in (15), from Nordlinger & Sadler (2004b: 611) (originally from Blake 1987):[8]

(15) *Ngamari-ngu   ngunytyi ngali-ku*
     mother-FUT.NOM give   we.DU-FUT.ACC
     mangarni-marru-nga-ku   kathi-ku.
     bone-having-GEN-FUT.ACC   meat-FUT.ACC
     'Mother will give us the doctor's meat.'

In (15), the future tense information is provided on the nominative and accusative case markers, rather than as tense morphology on the verb.

Nordlinger & Sadler (2004b) provide an LFG analysis of propositional TAM marking on nominals in which TAM information that appears on a noun in the constituent structure tree can be passed up to the functional structure of the clause. This is accomplished formally through the use of 'inside-out' expressions referring to syntactic domains containing the TAM marking. Nordlinger & Sadler (2004b: 611) propose a lexical entry for the Pitta Pitta accusative case marker *-ku* that results in the following f-structure:

(16) *-ku*: $\begin{bmatrix} \text{OBJ} \begin{bmatrix} \text{CASE} & \text{ACC} \end{bmatrix} \\ \text{TENSE} \quad \text{FUT} \end{bmatrix}$

The lexical entry for *-ku* specifies accusative case for the nominal to which it attaches; crucially for our purposes, it also specifies that the outer (clausal) f-structure has the TENSE feature with the value FUTURE.

Arka (2013) builds on Nordlinger & Sadler's analysis in his account of TAM marking in Marori; he focuses on the specific perfective aspect marker *-on* in Marori, but he remarks that Marori also has other TAM markers that are realized on nouns. Arka (2013: 46) concludes: 'There is increasing evidence from under-described languages that TAM is not

---

[8] According to Blake (1987), 'doctor' in Pitta Pitta is 'death-bone-having one'.

exclusively associated with the verbal domain. While it is true that the verb remains the native domain of rich and complex TAM coding, the semantics of non-verbal TAM is arguably equally complex.'

Let us now turn to case marking, which prototypically appears on nouns. However, case-marked adjectives also occur, as exemplified in the Finnish sentence in (17):

(17) *Sanna asuu   tässä   pienessä   talossa.*
      Sanna live.3SG this.INESSIVE little.INESSIVE house.INESSIVE
      'Sanna lives in this little house.'

Example (17) is an instance of case concord: the adjective *pienessä* ('little', *pieni* in nominative case) agrees with the noun, as does the demonstrative *tässä* ('this', the nominative form is *tämä*).

Examples similar to Finnish (17) are not uncommon across languages and language families. Latin, for example, also displays agreement between attributive adjectives and nouns. Haug & Nikitina (2016) provide an analysis of Latin agreement alongside a thorough evaluation of different theories of agreement. Sadler (2019) further builds on Haug & Nikitina (2016) in her LFG analysis of agreement in Modern Standard Arabic (MSA). In MSA adjective–noun concord, the adjective carries multiple features that typically appear on nominals: in addition to case, an adjective agrees with the noun it modifies in number, gender, and definiteness. This is illustrated in example (18):

(18) Modern Standard Arabic (Sadler 2019)
      qiṣṣat-un   ṭawīl-at-un
      story.FSG-NOM.INDEF long-FSG-NOM.INDEF
      'a long story'

The agreement features in (18) reflect typical nominal characteristics. Sadler (2019) analyses the morphological realization of these features on adjectives as a case of concord agreement, making use of the distinction between INDEX and CONCORD agreement features argued for by Wechsler & Zlatić (2000), Haug & Nikitina (2016), and Sadler (2016). Agreement between heads and dependents (that is, not concord-style agreement) is discussed later in this section.

Case marking on adjectives is not limited to concord: adjectives can also display case marking according to their function in the clause. For example, Finnish adjectives that denote a change take translative case marking (19), and the default case for Hungarian secondary predicates is dative (Rákosi 2006: 84); see example (20) from Szűcs (2018):

(19) Finnish
      Ilma   muuttui   kylmäksi.
      weather.NOM change-PST.3SG cold.TRANSLATIVE
      'The weather turned cold.'

(20) Hungarian
      Kati boldog-nak   tűnik.
      Kate happy-DATIVE seems
      'Kate seems happy.'

Together, the examples in (17)–(20) illustrate that case morphology appears on various types of adjectives, even though morphological case is most prototypically associated with nouns.

Case marking also appears on verbal elements in some languages, for example Finnish, Latin (Blake 1999), and many Australian languages (Blake 1999; Nordlinger 2002; Evans & Nordlinger 2004). In none of these languages does the main finite verb in a sentence take case marking. Instead, case marking can be found on subordinate verbs and non-finite forms. These forms are often analysed as nominalizations (see, e.g., Blake 1999). Nordlinger (2002) and Evans & Nordlinger (2004) argue that the so-called nominalized deverbal forms with case marking in some Australian languages are not nouns, but adjectives or adverbs. Tamm (2011) discusses case marking on non-finite verb (or deverbal) forms in Finnish and Estonian, remarking that there is disagreement in the literature about whether case-marked infinitives are verbs or not. The question is of course rendered more complex by the fact that case marking itself is considered 'a marker of the nominal category' (Tamm 2011: 839).

The fact that word classes other than nouns can take case marking in many languages is not problematic in LFG. There is no particular mechanism in LFG that prevents case morphology from appearing on categories other than nouns. The fact that case marking most prototypically appears in the nominal domain instead follows from the fact that the main function of case is to mark the role of the dependents of a head, and dependents of clausal predicates tend to be nominal phrases.

Agreement marking is unlike case marking and tense marking in that it is not as clearly associated with a particular word class. In the prototypical of INDEX agreement marking case, a head agrees with one or more of its dependents; for example, a verb may agree with its subject, or a noun may agree with its possessor. However, some languages display agreement marking that diverges from the typical pattern. For example, complementizers agree with the embedded subject in some dialects of German and Dutch and with the matrix subject in some Bantu languages (Van Koppen 2017).

The Nakh–Dagestanian language Archi is an example of a language that displays highly unusual agreement patterns, as described and analysed in the LFG framework by Sadler (2016). The absolutive argument controls clausal agreement in Archi, and the agreement features are number and gender (the four genders are glossed with Roman numerals, I–IV). The predicate agrees with the absolutive argument, but there is also agreement between the absolutive argument and various other dependents, including certain first person pronominal forms and some adjuncts. In the Archi example (21) (Sadler's example (50)), agreement with the absolutive argument appears not only on the predicate, but also on the adverb *horo:keijbu* 'a long time ago':

(21) *godo-b   maèla   gudu-m-mi*
    that-III.SG house(III)[SG.ABS] that-I.SG-SG.ERG
    horo:keij<b>u   a<b>uli   e<b>di
    long.time.ago<III.SG> <III.SG>make.pfv-cvb <III.SG>be.PST
    'He built that house a very long time ago.'

Sadler (2016) provides a lexicalist analysis of Archi where the lexical elements that display agreement are associated with constraints requiring that they agree with the absolutive argument.

We conclude that agreement marking often appears on verbs and nouns, as those often have direct dependents to agree with. However, there are also more unusual cases of agreement, as illustrated by the Archi data, where different dependents agree with each other. More generally, the data in this section illustrate that there are exceptions to typical matches between morphology and word classes. Criterion (7c) for how to identify word classes should therefore be taken more as a rule of thumb than an absolute principle (as argued by Lowe 2019).

15.6.2 Unexpected syntactic role for phrasal type

There are certain canonical correspondences between constituent structure category and functional structure role: for example, the main predicate of a clause is typically provided by a verb, and subjects and objects are typically headed by nouns. However, these are tendencies and not universal requirements.

For example, prototypical subjects are NPs. However, PPs in locative inversion (22) share a lot in common with regular NP subjects (Bresnan 1994), and some predicates can also take clausal (CP) subjects ((23); Bresnan 2001; Bresnan et al. 2016):

(22) [Into the bar] walked an angry man.

(23) [That Philippa was annoyed] was highly likely.

In these cases, the PP and CP share some characteristics in common with NP subjects; for example, they can undergo raising-to-subject, and they thus pass one of the standard subjecthood tests for English. However, they also differ in some respects from NP subjects. For example, in locative inversion, the verb agrees with the inverted theme and not with the 'subject' PP (Bresnan 1994). Additionally, subject–aux inversion is most natural with regular NP subjects, and is dispreferred or ungrammatical when the subject is headed by something other than a noun:

(24) * Did [into the bar] walk an angry man?

(25) * Was [that Philippa was annoyed] highly likely?

Bresnan (1994), Bresnan (2001), and Bresnan et al. (2016) propose that the PP and CP subjects in the examples above play two grammatical roles: they are both TOPIC and SUBJ. TOPIC is one of the grammaticalized discourse functions, and as such, it needs to be linked to another grammatical function, in this case the SUBJ function. At c-structure, the topic is adjoined to IP, which is the default position for topicalized and focused elements in English, as illustrated in (26).[9]

---

[9] The c-structure and f-structure for locative inversion examples such as (22) would look the same as (26) in relevant respects, but with a PP instead of a CP adjoined to the IP.

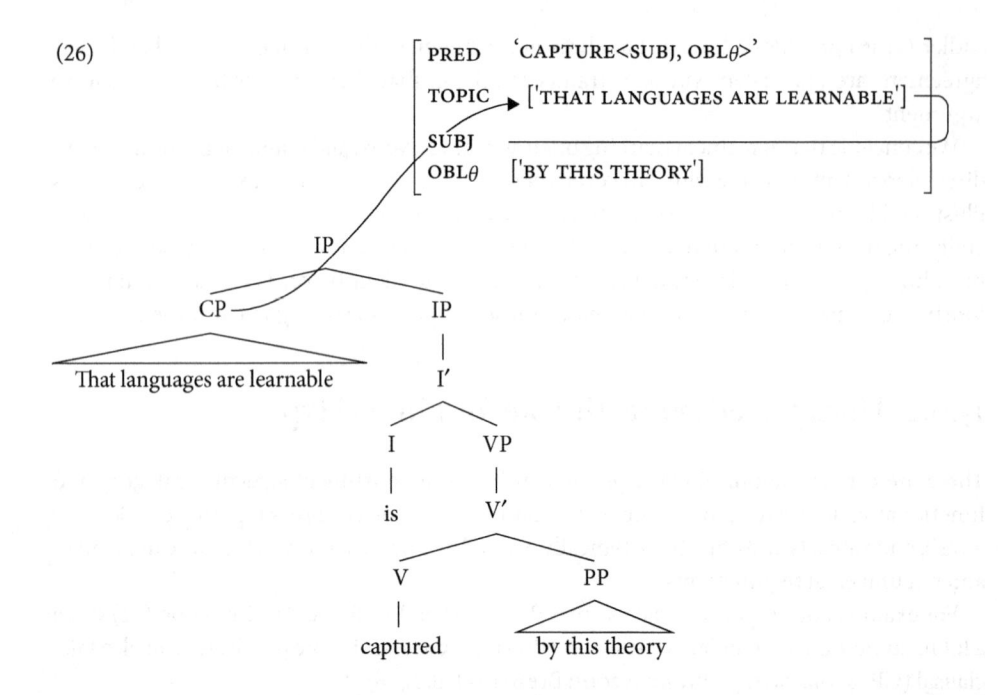

(26)
$$\begin{bmatrix} \text{PRED} & \text{`CAPTURE}\langle\text{SUBJ, OBL}_\theta\rangle\text{'} \\ \text{TOPIC} & [\text{'THAT LANGUAGES ARE LEARNABLE'}] \\ \text{SUBJ} \\ \text{OBL}_\theta & [\text{'BY THIS THEORY'}] \end{bmatrix}$$

```
              IP
         ╱         ╲
       CP           IP
   ⌢⌢⌢⌢⌢⌢⌢⌢         │
That languages       I'
  are learnable     ╱  ╲
                   I    VP
                   │    │
                   is   V'
                       ╱  ╲
                      V    PP
                      │   ⌢⌢⌢
                  captured by this theory
```

The CP (or PP) is thus a topic *and* a subj at f-structure, and appears in an adjoined position at c-structure instead of in the [Spec, IP] position which typically hosts regular subjects. The IP specifier position is reserved for nominal categories, according to the LFG theory of the mapping between c-structure and f-structure.

Other examples of unusual mappings between c-structure and f-structure can be found in various languages. For example, Lødrup (2012) discusses the grammatical function COMP, which typically corresponds to a clausal complement of category CP, IP, or S (the exocentric category S is discussed in Bresnan et al. 2016: §6.3.1 and Dalrymple et al. 2019: §4.2.6). However, Lødrup (2012) provides evidence that certain verbs take a nominal COMP in Norwegian.

Maling (1983) provides a thorough discussion of prototypical mappings between syntactic categories, grammatical functions, and semantic roles. She points out that mismatches are rare, but they do occur. She also discusses the fact that words sometimes have subcategorization frames that are unexpected for their word class. For example, she shows that the word *near* in English can take an NP complement even though it is an adjective, as in *near the meadow*. Recall from section 15.5 that adjectives are classified as [−transitive] and would therefore not be expected to take NP complements. Other examples of transitive adjectives are provided by Mittendorf & Sadler (2008) for Welsh and Lowe (2017) for early Indo-Aryan.

15.6.3 Lexical sharing

The French portmanteau word *au* has been analysed as an obligatory contraction of the preposition *à* and the masculine singular determiner *le*:

(27)　au　　garçon / *à le　　garcon
　　　to.the boy　　to the.M boy
　　　'to the boy'

There is no corresponding feminine contracted form, and the expected two-word sequence *à la* is found instead:

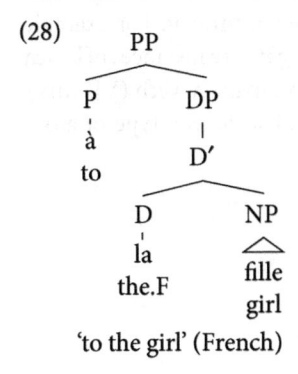

(28)
```
           PP
          /  \
         P    DP
         |    |
         à    D'
         to  /  \
            D    NP
            |    △
            la   fille
          the.F  girl
```
'to the girl' (French)

Wescoat (2002) argues that these portmanteau words should not be analysed simply in terms of phonological contraction of two syntactic words into a single phonological word; instead, they should be treated as morphologically derived single syntactic words. He proposes to treat them as exemplifying what he calls *lexical sharing*, where a single syntactic word can contribute to more than one preterminal node in the phrase structure tree. Wescoat proposes the rule in (29a) for portmanteau forms such as *au*, which licenses the tree in (29b):

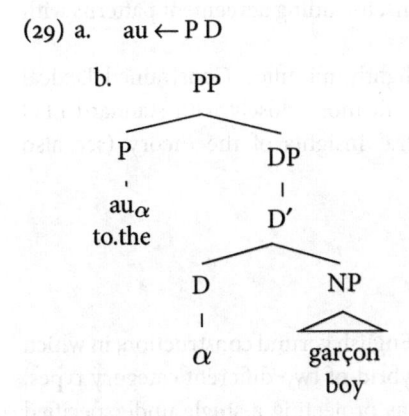

(29) a.　au ← P D

　　 b.
```
              PP
             /  \
            P    DP
            |    |
           au_α  D'
          to.the /  \
                D    NP
                |    △
                α    garçon
                     boy
```

The alpha (α) co-indexation in the tree indicates that the same form *au* is related to two preterminal nodes, one labelled P and one labelled D. In this way, the form *au* is a member of two word classes simultaneously: it is both a preposition and a determiner, and fills both positions in the constituent structure tree. An important aspect of Wescoat's lexical-sharing analysis is what he calls *homomorphic lexical integrity*: the two preterminals involved in lexical sharing must be adjacent, and no material can intervene between them. In (29b), for example, nothing can appear in the specifier of DP, since any material appearing there would intervene between the P and D nodes dominating *au*, and this is disallowed.

A prediction of this analysis is what Wescoat calls 'schizocategorization': a portmanteau word has no single word class, and can exhibit characteristics of multiple word classes simultaneously. In particular, Wescoat notes what he calls the 'Janus effect', where a single form satisfies different requirements for its leftward and rightward environment. For example, Wescoat proposes that English contracted forms like *wanna* or *oughta* are instances of lexical sharing, and are associated with a sequence consisting of a non-auxiliary verb (V[−AUX]) followed by an auxiliary verb (V[+AUX]); Wescoat treats infinitival *to* as a type of auxiliary verb):

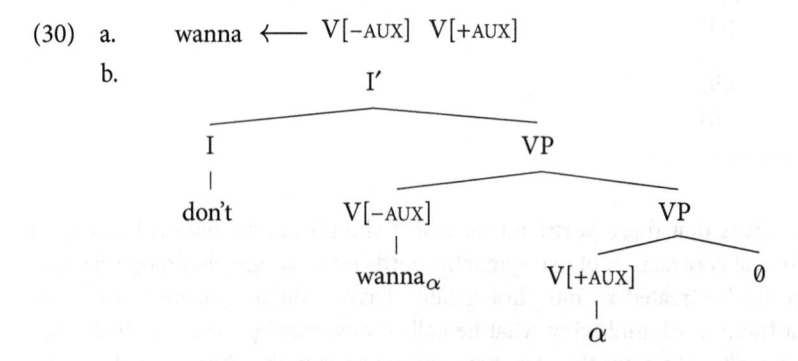

(30) a.   wanna ⟵ V[−AUX] V[+AUX]
    b.

$$\begin{array}{c} I' \\ \diagup \quad \diagdown \\ I \qquad\qquad VP \\ | \qquad\qquad \diagup \quad \diagdown \\ don't \quad V[-AUX] \qquad VP \\ \qquad\quad | \qquad\qquad \diagup \; \diagdown \\ \qquad wanna_\alpha \quad V[+AUX] \quad \emptyset \\ \qquad\qquad\qquad | \\ \qquad\qquad\qquad \alpha \end{array}$$

As Wescoat notes, the environment to the left of *wanna* is what we would expect to the left of a non-auxiliary verb which requires *do*-support and cannot host negation; to the right of *wanna*, ellipsis is allowed, as expected for an auxiliary verb. Wescoat provides additional evidence of schizocategorization in other constructions, including agreement patterns with Upper Sorbian possessive adjectives.

In subsequent work, Lowe (2016b) proposes a slightly modified Constrained Lexical Sharing approach, which adapts Wescoat's theory to fit more closely with standard LFG architectural assumptions while retaining the central insights of the theory (see also Lowe 2015).

15.6.4 Mixed categories

Bresnan (1997) discusses *mixed categories* such as the English gerund construction, in which 'a single word heads a phrase which is a syntactic hybrid of two different category types'. She argues against analyses which treat the gerund as projecting a single underspecified category, noting that such analyses fail to predict that such examples are *phrasally coherent*, and can be partitioned into distinct inner and outer subtrees each of which exhibits the full expected phrasal structure of one of the categories. She proposes that such cases are best treated in terms of *head sharing*, where the two phrasal structures share the same head at functional structure.

Following Bresnan (2001), Bresnan et al. (2016) propose the analysis in (31) for the gerundive nominal *Mary's frequently visiting Fred*, where the VP and the DP dominating the gerundive nominal correspond to the same functional structure, and the possessor *Mary's* is treated as both a possessor (POSS) and the subject (SUBJ) of the gerund *visiting*:

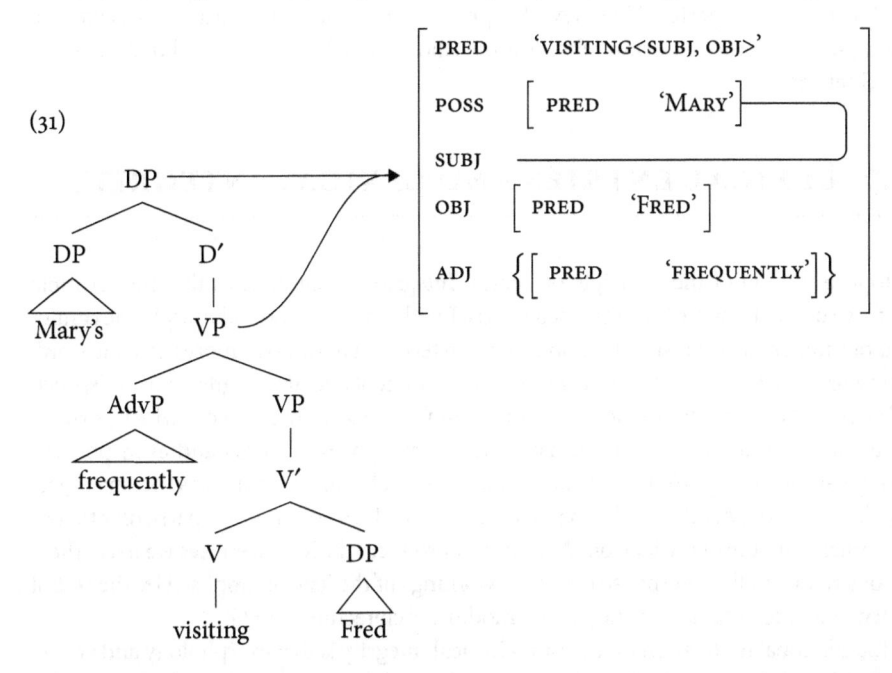

(31)

$$\begin{bmatrix} \text{PRED} & \text{'VISITING<SUBJ, OBJ>'} \\ \text{POSS} & \begin{bmatrix} \text{PRED} & \text{'MARY'} \end{bmatrix} \\ \text{SUBJ} \\ \text{OBJ} & \begin{bmatrix} \text{PRED} & \text{'FRED'} \end{bmatrix} \\ \text{ADJ} & \left\{ \begin{bmatrix} \text{PRED} & \text{'FREQUENTLY'} \end{bmatrix} \right\} \end{bmatrix}$$

According to this mixed-category analysis, the verbal characteristics of this construction are explained as a result of the internal phrasal syntax of the VP, and the nominal characteristics are explained by the DP structure which contains the gerundive VP. At functional structure, the DP and the VP share a common head, the gerund *visiting*, with the result that the DP and the VP nodes both correspond to the same functional structure. Notice that the head-sharing analysis of mixed categories is unlike the lexical-sharing analysis described in the previous section, in that the gerund head is not assumed to be dominated by more than one preterminal node of the tree. According to the head-sharing analysis, both the DP and the VP correspond to a functional structure whose head is the gerund, but the gerund is of category V and appears within the VP. One consequence of this difference is that, unlike the situation with lexical sharing, the heads of the two phrases in a head-sharing construction need not be adjacent (or indeed present: there is no D in (31)). A lexical-sharing analysis of *Mary's frequently visiting Fred* would entail that *visiting* is dominated by both D and V, incorrectly predicting that the adverb *frequently* could not appear, since it is an adverb adjoined to VP and would therefore necessarily intervene between V node and the D head of a DP containing the VP.

Bresnan's theory of mixed categories has been adopted by a number of other authors. Bresnan & Mugane (2006) provide a mixed-category analysis of agentive nominalizations in Gĩkũyũ, which have both nominal and verbal characteristics. Nikitina (2008) presents an extensive study of mixed categories, with particular reference to Italian nominalized infinitives and Wan nominalizations, and Nikitina & Haug (2016) present a mixed-category analysis of the Latin 'dominant participle' construction, which has the syntactic distribution of a noun phrase but the meaning of a clause. Börjars et al. (2015) discuss Arabic deverbal 'masdar' forms, claiming that they are in fact not mixed categories, but can be analysed in terms of a purely nominal structure; Lowe (2019) provides a thorough discussion of Arabic masdars, English gerunds, and Sanskrit attributive participles, arguing that they are all best analysed as mixed categories. Nikolaeva & Spencer (2019) provide a critical overview of these analyses and some important observations about mixed categories and their analysis in an LFG setting.

15.7 Lexical entries and Lexical Integrity

LFG adopts a version of the principle of Lexical Integrity which dictates that the terminal nodes of c-structure trees are fully inflected words. In other words, a bound morpheme cannot appear alone under its own c-structure node, and no terminal node hosts more than one word. Syntactic words are formed in the morphological component and are assigned parts of speech there. The morphological component is assumed to form part of the lexicon, which is richly structured and includes detailed information about morphemes, words and even phrases. Lexical regularities are captured with lexical redundancy rules and/or templates (Bresnan 1978; Dalrymple et al. 2004; Asudeh et al. 2013). However, LFG does not impose a particular theory of the internal structure of the lexicon. As long as it produces the lexical entries we need, there are no constraints on the internal structure or workings of the lexicon imposed by the rest of the theory. This is consistent with the general modular architecture of LFG.

One foundational motivation for adopting Lexical Integrity is that morphology and syntax are governed by different ordering principles, as discussed by Bresnan & Mchombo (1995), Sells (1995), and Cho & Sells (1995). However, the Lexical Integrity principle has been and continues to be controversial (Bruening 2018; Müller 2018). In considering the debate on Lexical Integrity, it is important to note that the LFG version of the principle specifically refers to c-structure and not f-structure. Terminal c-structure nodes are assumed to dominate fully inflected nodes, but there is no assumption that an f-structure or an f-structure function must correspond exactly to a morphological word (Bresnan & Mchombo 1995). For example, information about the subject of a clause can come from the subject DP and also from inflectional morphology on the verb. In particular, in the English sentence *Martha laughs*, the verb provides information about the subject (it is third person singular) and the clause (the head is 'laugh', the tense is present). However, *laughs* nevertheless has the c-structure category V; the fact that the *-s* inflection on the verb provides information about the subject does not mean that *laughs* is a noun or that the ending *-s* is a noun. Moreover, the subject information is distributed across words, as it comes from both *Martha* and the inflection on the verb. This simple example illustrates that there is not (necessarily) a one-to-one mapping between individual words and f-structures, even though words are assumed to form 'leaves' of the c-structure trees, in accordance with the standard LFG interpretation of Lexical Integrity.

Mismatches between morphologically complete words and f-structure functions have been carefully explored in the LFG literature. Bresnan & Mchombo (1995), Van Egmond (2008), Baker et al. (2010), and many others explore how morphologically rich individual words may contain information that distributes to different parts of the f-structure of a sentence. More recent work also investigates different kinds of multi-word expressions within the

LFG framework; see, for example, Asudeh et al. (2013), Biswas (2017), and Findlay (2019). Recall also that under Wescoat's (2002) lexical-sharing approach, portmanteau words can correspond to more than one preterminal c-structure node, on the condition that the two preterminal nodes are adjacent. He refers to this as 'homomorphic lexical integrity'. We conclude that Lexical Integrity is a key principle in LFG: fully inflected words are nodes of the c-structure tree. However, the mappings between the lexicon, c-structure, and f-structure allow individual morphemes to contribute syntactic information in a transparent way.

15.8 Conclusion

LFG's inventory of word classes is very similar to what is found in traditional descriptive grammars. The basic lexical categories assumed, supported by much typological work, are nouns, verbs, adjectives, adverbs, and prepositions. LFG also adopts a limited set of functional categories that have been argued for in the general generative tradition.

The word classes are modelled at the grammatical level of c-structure. Much of the data that leads researchers working within other syntactic frameworks to assume a more fine-grained inventory of word classes or a larger number of functional categories is explained in an LFG setting at other grammatical levels, in particular using the grammatical features of LFG's functional structure.

Acknowledgements

For helpful comments, we are grateful to Roxana Barbu, Jamie Findlay, Joey Lovestrand, Tanya Nikitina, Raj Singh, Andy Spencer, Frank van Eynde, Nigel Vincent, and an anonymous reviewer.

PART III
SPECIFIC WORD CLASSES

CHAPTER 16

VERBS

ALEXANDER LETUCHIY

16.1 Definition

VERBS are highly different across languages. Thus, no single feature or aspect of behaviour can be used as a base for a definition. However, several properties that are typical for verbs can be listed.

(i) If the verb has a non-derived form or a series of non-derived forms this form or series of forms by default occupies the rhematic (focus) position and is or belongs to the main piece of information expressed by the utterance.

In other words, according to Haspelmath (1993), Navarro & González (2017), and others, the configuration *The girl is running* is more expected to contain a non-derived verb form than *The running girl*. In the first example, *is running* carries the main piece of information and belongs to the focus part, while in the second example, the participle *running* belongs to the topic part, while the focus part should contain another verb form.

(ii) Verbs have NP arguments. Of these arguments, some are syntactically higher than others. In some languages, this leads to a clear opposition of subject vs direct object vs other objects (see Keenan 1976; Keenan & Comrie 1977; Kittila 2002; Næss 2007 about possible approaches to argument hierarchy).

By contrast, configurations where non-finite/nonverbal heads have arguments are often avoided in the world's languages. This is especially the case when an argument is clausal itself (see, e.g., Grimshaw 1990, Alexiadou 2004 on the argument structure of nominalizations, Haspelmath & König 1995 on properties of converbs, and Haspelmath 1993b on the behaviour of passive and active participles). Kholodilova (2015) and Letuchiy (2015) argue that even infinitives differ from finite verb forms in the distribution of NP vs CC (complement clause) argument types: mainly finite verbs have embedded clauses in argument positions.

Although some other parts of speech are also compatible with NP arguments, their occurrence is restricted. For instance, adverbials almost never inherit valency from adjectives of the same stem (see *proud of his son* and **proudly of his son*, Russian *gordyj svoim synom* 'proud of his son' and **gordo svoim synom* 'proudly of his son'). Nouns formed via nominalization sometimes retain verbal complements but sometimes lose them, as in *it is important that he came—*importance that he came*. Finally, adjectives also take arguments restrictedly and more rarely than verbal forms (participles): compare *ustavšij ot raboty* 'tired of work' with an adjective *ustalyj* which tends to have no arguments expressed (?*ustalyj ot raboty* 'tired of work'). Only prepositions and conjunctions/subordinators tend to have obligatory dependent elements; the former host NP arguments, the latter infinitive constructions and finite embedded clauses.

(iii) Verbs have predicative categories (expressed morphologically or in another way), such as modality, tense, aspect.

Although there are constructions that do not contain an explicit verb, they often have reduced or non-obligatory tense, aspect, and modality marking. According to Arutjunova & Shirjaev (1983) and Letuchiy (2021: 133–134), in Russian and Kabardian conditional constructions, the TAM marking of the main clause can be left unexpressed with initially nominal heads:

Kuban Kabardian
(1) ʔjejə   mə   pojezd-əm   wə-qe-č'eraxʷə-nə-r.
     bad   this   train-OBL   2SG.ABS-DIR-be.late-POT-ABS
     'It will be bad if we don't catch this train.'

(1') ʔjejə-ne   mə   pojezd-əm   wə-qe-č'eraxʷə-nə-r.
     bad-FUT   this   train-OBL   2SG.ABS-DIR-be.late-POT-ABS
     'It will be bad if we don't catch this train.'

(2) pšedje   thamexʷe=maxʷe-te-me   de   də-lež'e-ne-te-qəmi.
     tomorrow   Sunday=day-IPF-COND   we   1PL.ABS-work-FUT-IPF-NEG
     'If tomorrow had been Sunday we wouldn't work.' (Arkadiev 2016: 1)

(2') *pšedje   thamexʷe=maxʷe-te-me   de   də-lež'e.
     tomorrow   Sunday=day-IPF-COND   we   1PL.ABS-work
     Intended: 'If tomorrow had been Sunday we would work.'
     (author's field data, 2016, Letuchiy 2021: 134)

At the same time, there are word categories very close to verbs in (1) and (2), but not in (3). For instance, Slavic 'predicatives' (predicative adverbs) are mainly found in the predicate position. Some of them are almost impossible in the verb modifier position, as in (4), from Russian (author's native-speaker intuition):

(3) a. *Mne   bojazno.*
        I.DAT   cosy.PRAEDIC
        'I am afraid.'

b. *Polin-e   skučno.*
   Polina-SG.DAT   dull.PRAEDIC
   'Polina feels dull.'

(4) **Polin-a   bojazno   vzgljanu-l-a.*
    Polina-SG.DAT   cosy.PRAEDIC   look-PST-SG.F
    'Polina looked at me, as if she was afraid / so that I got afraid.'

However, all of these constructions can be regarded as structures without an explicit verb, since in other tenses the forms of verb *byt* 'be' should be added to the construction.

(iv) Verbs typically (but not obligatorily) express dynamic actions (causation of change, spontaneous change of state of the participant(s), change of location, and so on).

In languages with poor morphology, such as Chinese and languages like Tsez, where a subset of verbs are invariable (Polinsky & Comrie 2009: 47; Polinsky 2015), the notion of verb is more problematic than in languages with rich morphology. In other words, in these languages the decision to regard a word as a verb is partially taken because the meaning of dynamic actions is normally expressed with verbs or because the word bears some syntactic verb features—however, morphological features do not always prove this claim to be right. For instance, in Tsez, according to Polinsky & Comrie (2009: 47), only a subset of verbs agrees with their arguments. For these kinds of cases, the semantic property (iv) is crucial for verb definition.

This means that if a subgroup of the lexicon expresses only states like 'lie' and 'be' and occurs in the rhematic (focus) position but shows no other verbal features, they should not be regarded as verbs. Some semantic fields, such as physical properties and evaluation, are primarily served by nonverbal predicates.

16.2 VERB DERIVATION

Verbs can often be derived from various parts of speech, such as nouns and adjectives, and many languages possess a large set of derivational mechanisms. However, most frequent are verbs derived from nouns and adjectives. Deadjectival verbs often mean a spontaneous or externally caused acquirement of the property described by the base adjective (cf. French *noircir* 'become black; make black' from *noir* 'black'). At the same time, some other semantic types occur, such as 'act as if having the property described by the base adjective, cf. Russian *glupit'* 'act as someone who is stupid' from *glup(yj)* 'stupid'. Denominal verbs have more semantic types: for instance, apart from the meaning of caused and spontaneous change of state, they can mean 'act with the base noun referent as an instrument' (*encolar* 'glue' (verb) from *cola* 'glue (noun)' in Spanish), 'do something related to the base noun referent to another object' (*bone* (verb) 'remove the bones from something' from *bone* (noun) in English), 'behave like a base noun' (*durit'* 'behave stupidly (verb)' from *durak* 'fool (noun)' in Russian) and so on. According to Hale & Keyser (2002: 105–158), this difference results from fundamental differences between the syntactic structure of adjectives and nouns.

Derived verbs are often unmarked for transitivity: for instance, in Bulgarian *nadebeljava* (become/make fat.PRS.3SG 'fatten', from *debel* 'big, fat') can be transitive or intransitive, as well as French, *blanchir* 'become/make white' (from *blanc* 'white'), By contrast, many non-derived verbs, such as Bulgarian *stoplja* 'become warm', are strictly transitive or strictly intransitive.

Along with morphological verb formation, analytic situation expression with light verbs or copulas are widespread. For instance, in Circassian (see Rogava & Kerasheva 1966; Smeets 1984), the verbs *χwən* 'become' and *ṣ̂ən* 'do, make' can be used as 'analytic verbalizers', the former for intransitive, and the latter for transitive verb formation:

Adyghe (Circassian, Adyghea Republic, Russia)
(5) jəzə   χwə-n
    full   become-MSD
    'fill (become full)'

(6) jəzə   ṣ̂ə-n
    full   make-MSD
    'fill (make full)' (Rogava & Keraševa 1966)

A special type of verbalization are equipollent valency pairs, as they are described by Haspelmath (1993a: 91–92). Sometimes, pairs of transitive and intransitive verbs like 'learn/teach', where one of the members is normally derived from the other one, become derivational. There is no base verbal stem; both verbs are derived from a stem that does not exist as a verb or a noun:

Khakas (Turkic, Russian, author's field data)
(7) ügre-n-   'learn'
    ügre-t-   'teach'

Khakas does not have a base verb *ügre-*. The causative/non-causative relation is represented by two derived verbs. This makes the causative/non-causative pair similar to transitivity marking.

Verbalization is more widespread than adjectivization and organized in a way other than nominalization. Adjectivization is restricted due to the fact that not all names of objects and situations can be naturally transposed to names of features. Moreover, when names of physical objects are adjectivized, the resulting adjective usually denotes a 'relative', not autonomous type of features that simply means 'related to an object X'. Nominalization usually derives abstract nouns that conceptualize features or situations as non-physical objects. By contrast, derived verbs can denote any type of action. Verbal derivational markers are closely related to inflectional paradigms. In those cases, derivational markers are just intermediate elements that are not necessary for the meaning composition; rather, they are needed for an inflectional marker to be attached to the verbal form. Thus, no special semantic type is linked to the class of derived verbs. The derived nature of the verb does not necessarily mean that the verb expresses a meaning that is non-prototypical for a verb or related to some more basic object it is derived from. Sometimes a verb bears a suffix, but no 'more basic' verb is present in the language system, thus, no derivational meaning can be defined. For instance, the verb *celovat'* 'kiss' in Russian is formally derived: it contains not only a root, but also the suffix *-ova-*. However, it cannot be regarded as a semantically non-prototypical verb, and its derived nature has a historical reason, rather than being a synchronic grammatical requirement. Synchronically, it is not derived from any basic lexeme.

At the same time, verbs often serve as a base for further derivation. Given that verbs are the part of speech that tend to have arguments, deverbal nominalization is productive and often switches the verb meaning to the meaning of one of the arguments.

Some grammatical forms occupy an intermediate position between derivation and inflection. These include forms generated by valency change mechanisms. For example, passivization can be regarded as an inflectional form because it does not change the semantics of the situation nor the number and semantic roles of the participants. By contrast, causative and anticausative are intermediate cases. On the one hand, causative increases and anticausative reduces the number of participants and adds a subevent ('causation') to the initial meaning. On the other hand, causative and anticausative are often productive: the semantic effect and syntactic change they bear are predictable and regular. This makes them closer to inflectional mechanisms.

16.2.1 Inflection classes and/or derivation

As mentioned, contrary to nouns, most verbs in morphologically rich languages are derived, or, more precisely, they bear an additional suffix between the root and the marker of personal forms, tenses, or infinitive. Very often they have a suffix that correlates with inflectional classes. For instance, the French infinitival marker *-r* (in the written form), requires a vowel before it. The choice of the immediately preceding infinitival marker correlates with the inflection type:

(8) *grandir* 'become big'—PRS.1SG *je grandis*
     embracer 'kiss'—PRS.1SG *j(e)'embrace*
     venir 'come'—PRS.1SG *je viens*
     fondre 'melt'—PRS.1SG *je fonds*

Not only do verbs in (8) have different infinitive forms (*-ir* vs *-er* vs *-re*), but the inflection type in the present tense is also different. However, the stem in the present tense does not necessary literally coincide with the infinitive marker, because the final *e* is not pronounced in *j'embrace*, and the verb *venir* 'come' does not have the *i*-variant of the present ending. Thus, synchronically it is impossible to say that *-e-* in *embracer* or *-i-* in *venir* is a derivational marker—or, at least, it is not retained in all inflectional forms.

The treatment of these oppositions faces the problem of distinguishing inflection from derivation. Classes like those in (8) can either be analysed as derivational classes or as types of verbal paradigms (i.e. inflectional classes). The precise solution depends on the paradigmatic properties of verbs in a particular language. For instance, Russian verbs mostly belong to one of two inflectional types in present tense paradigm ('i' type vs 'e' type) but bear one of several markers before the infinitive suffix *-t*.

(9) ljub-i-t'   ljub-i-l 'he loved'   ljub-it '(s)he loves' (*i* type)
     plak-a-t'   plak-a-l 'he cried'   plač-et '(s)he cries' (*e* type)
     terp-e-t'   terp-e-l 'he suffered, tolerated'   terp-it '(s)he suffers, tolerates' (*i* type)
     vy-nu-t'   vy-nu-l 'he took (it) out'   vyn-et '(s)he will take (it) out' (*e* type)

In this sense, Russian inflection type markers in (9) are derivational, though they influence the choice of inflectional markers. However, they are not canonical derivational markers, because they are not retained in the present, but retained in the past tense (the infinitive thematic vowel does not correspond to the vowel of the present tense). By contrast, many French verb classes are compatible with phonologically zero inflectional markers in present:

(10)   *ouvrir*   *ouvr-e* [*uvr*] '(s)he opens'
       fermer   *ferm-e* [*ferm*] '(s)he closes'

Perhaps, in French, where inflection class markers in the infinitive are not numerous and are sometimes manifested only in infinitives, they should be regarded as variants of infinitive inflectional markers. The personal forms of different verb classes are sometimes indistinguishable from each other, and vowels in the inflectional suffixes are not always identical to vowels in the infinitive. By contrast, Russian verb types like *-i-t'* or *-ova-t'* contain suffixes that reappear in other paradigms (though not all, mainly derived from the past tense stem). This is why they can be considered to represent a part of the (infinitive/past) verbal stem; the present tense stem being different.

Importantly, some inflection types/derivation patterns are reserved for derived verbs and are never or rarely used as a mechanism of infinitive formation. In Russian, verbs in *-et'* (*tolstet'* 'become fat'), *-it'* (*belit'* 'paint white, make white'), *-ovat'* (*adresovat'* 'address, direct') are often derived. By contrast, *at'*-verbs (*plakat'* 'cry') or *-et'*-verbs in *i*-inflection (*terpet'* 'suffer') are usually not derived compositionally. Although the base stem can be present in the lexicon (e.g. *plač* 'cry, crying'), the semantic category that the inflection suffix marks is not easy to describe.

16.2.2 Incorporation

Verbs are the most plausible candidates to participate in incorporation (see Muravjeva 2004; Olthof 2020 for a typological study), i.e. to include in their form a root or stem that has originally been an autonomous noun. The incorporation domain includes two different subfields: incorporation in the proper sense and compounding. The boundary between the two phenomena is not always clear. To distinguish them, the following features can be used (mainly adopted from incorporation parameters proposed by Muravjeva (2004) and compared to compounding):

(i) Incorporation (which is not widespread in Standard Average European, but is found in some other groups, including Chukotko-Kamchatkan and West Caucasian languages) is applicable to verb forms without nominalization.

Consider for instance:

Yucatec (Mayan) (based on Mithun 1984: 857)
(11)   *čak- če'-n-ah-en* (true incorporation)
       chop-tree-ANTIPASS-PERF-I (ABS)
       'I wood-chopped' = 'I chopped wood.'

By contrast, compounding, which is found in Europe, as well as many other areas, is often applied to nominalized forms or is subject to parallel compounding: for instance, in German, one of the European languages with the most productive compounding, the noun *Hausbau/ Hausbauen* 'building of a house', lit. 'house' + 'building' has no verbal parallel like *hausbauen* 'house' + 'build'—only a free combination *Haus bauen* 'to build a house' is possible.

Incorporation, but not compounding, can be absolutely productive and is not always restricted by words or word classes, while compounding is usually lexically restricted.

(ii) In compounding, but not usually in incorporation, special markers of compounding are used (interfixes like Bulgarian *-a-* in *paraxod* 'steam train').

At the same time, the two phenomena show a common feature. They both tend to add a non-specific noun to the verb stem, but both sometimes involve specific participants: Kantarovich (2020: 256) cites several examples from Chukchi, such as *qejʔatʔəg-jələ-tku-lʔ- ən ŋeekkeqej* 'the girl who gives a puppy', and *qlawəl Ø-kejŋə-nmə-gʔe* 'the man killed a bear' (see Muravjeva 2004; Olthof 2020 for additional examples). Similarly, the Russian word *otceubijca* 'a person who killed (his own) father' shows a specific stem *otc-* 'father', included in the nominalized verbal stem, though normally, in nouns like *korablestroitel'* 'builder of ships', the first (embedded) noun stem *korabl'-* 'ship' is non-specific.

16.3 VERB PARADIGMS

16.3.1 Verb subparadigms

Verbs often have distinct formal organization in different subparadigms. In other words, in different parts of the paradigm (e.g. different tenses or different aspects) the entire organization of the verb inflection marking (person, number, gender, and so on) is also different.

This distinguishes verbs from other word classes (nominals, adverbials, adjectives). These either do not have an inflectional paradigm or have a poorer paradigm, compared to the verbal one. This is why the relevant distinctions in adverbial, adjectival, and nominal domains are often realized lexically, not inside the paradigm. For instance, adverbials and adjectives fall into two or several classes which, as Cinque (2014: 20–27) shows, correspond to structurally 'high' vs 'low' adverbials and adjectives. Low adverbials and adjectives express special types of the situation (e.g. *go fast, play chess very well, spicy soup*), while high adverbials and adjectives express the evaluation of the situation or its place in the world as real vs irreal (e.g. *suddenly fall, expectedly lose, a surprising result*) (see also Chapter 19 in this volume). Another feature that opposes adjectives to each other is the state-level vs individual-level distinction. In the noun class, semantic class-based distinctions oppose mass nouns, unique nouns, and nouns that are neutral with respect to number. Another type of opposition is related to taxonomic classes, such as gender, animacy, human vs non-human distinction, classes based on form, size, and other physical properties (see Chapter 17 in this volume).

By contrast, verb classes are often rather uniform morphologically, though some exceptions like English modal verbs lacking many morphological forms (e.g. *can—*is canning*) also exist. The main distinction type lies in the verbal paradigm where past vs non-past, embedded vs main, finite vs non-finite features strongly oppose forms to each other. The reason is that verbs are specialized for the predicate position, and special formal changes are required to derive a form with the properties of a nominal, adverbial or modifier. Limbu (Tibeto-Burman, van Driem 1997a: 158) is an example of language with different subparadigms: the form of negation marking is different according to the person and number of the subject:

		Affirm	Neg		Affirm	Neg
(12)	1sg Npast	R-ʔɛ	mɛ-R-ʔɛn	1sg Past	R-aŋ	mɛ-R-aŋnɛn
	1du.inc	a-R-si	an-R-sin			
	3sg	R	mɛ-R-nɛn			

In Latin (Kennedy 1871), the person marking is different in different tense forms: for instance, the perfect series is different from the present one:

(13) Present tense personal markers   Perfect tense personal markers

1SG	-o	1PL	-mus	1SG	-i	1PL	-imus
2SG	-s	2PL	-tis	2SG	-isti	2PL	-istis
3SG	-t	3PL	-nt	3SG	-it	3PL	-erunt

The uniformity of morphological markers across the paradigm is supposed to be characteristic of agglutinating languages. Morphological variance, including the existence of different series for different subparadigms, is frequent across flective languages. The difference between subparadigms often goes back to diachronic change of the paradigm status. For example, the presence of number and the lack of person marking in Slavic past tense results from their previous participial status.

The non-uniformity of the verbal paradigm is pervasive in Classical Arabic (see Aoun et al. 2009 for details). In this language, the past (perfective) and the nonpast (imperfective) paradigms not only bear different agreement markers, but also different morphological techniques: past forms employ suffixation, while in nonpast forms, complex morphemes (transfixes) are used.

(14)   *katab-at* 'she wrote' (write.PST-3SG.F)   *t-aktub-u* 'she writes 3F-write.PRS-INDIC.SG'

16.3.2 Verb agreement and its relation to pronominal expression

Verbs, more than words of any other class, often agree with their arguments. Agreement abilities vary from the total absence of agreement in dependent-marking and isolating languages to multipersonal agreement, especially in polysynthetic languages (e.g. Chukotko-Kamchatkan, West Caucasian, Salish).

Agreement is to be distinguished from pronominal marking, and this problem includes two aspects:

(i) opposition of non-morphologized agreement markers and free pronouns. Free elements can behave as non-obligatory anaphoric means (in this case they are

supposed to be anaphoric pronouns) or be regularly and obligatorily used with verbs of particular argument structure type (thus, they are classified as agreement markers situated outside the head word); and
(ii) oppositions of morphological agreement markers and morphologized pronouns that are parts of the verbal word but behave like pronouns in some respects. Although morphological markers are usually obligatory and tend to mark (obligatory) syntactic agreement, rather than refer to a phrase, as pronouns, some exceptions exist.

According to Baker (1996: 360), the second distinction is especially problematic for polysynthetic languages, such as Adyghe (West Caucasian, Russia) or Mohawk (Iroquoian, USA and Canada), where a verb form can constitute an utterance by itself. In these languages, agreement markers are the main device of argument expression, while NP expression is syntactically similar to modifiers or adjuncts; see for instance (15) from Mohawk (Iroquoian):

(15) y-a-hi-háh-ra'-t-e'
TRANS-FACT-1SG.S/M.SG.O-ROAD-Ø-reach-CAUS-PUNCT
'I led him to the right road.' (Baker 1996: 360)

Verb agreement in some languages differs in many respects from noun–adjective agreement inside the NP. In general, adjective agreement tends to be grammatically motivated, while verbal agreement often has many variants and is either grammatically or semantically motivated. For instance, in some languages, numeral phrases require a plural form of the adjective, but are compatible with singular forms of verbs, because numerals are not morphologically plural. Consider for instance the following corpus data from Polish:

(16) Wcześniej na świat przysz-ł-o pięć sióstr.
Before to world.ACC come-PST-SG.N five.NOM SISTER.GEN.PL
'Before this, five sisters and three brothers were born.' (singular agreement).

(17) #to pięciu/pięć ludz-i
this.N.SG.NOM five people-NOM.PL
Only in the meaning 'that is five people', but not 'these five people'.

Corpus data and native-speaker surveys show that examples like (16), with a singular verbal agreement with the numeral *pięć* 'five' are acceptable. However, no examples like (17), with singular adjective/pronominal agreement with the same numeral, are found.

16.3.3 Paradigm deficiencies

In many languages, deficient verbs lacking some morphological forms exist. Deficiency can be observed in various grammatical categories including the following ones:

- Tense/aspect
- Person
- Infinite forms (converbs, participles)

For instance, English modal verbs lack a third person singular form with the suffix -s (can—*cans), aspectual forms, except Present Simple and Past Simple (*is canning), and conjunctive mood (*would can). This fact results from the high degree of grammaticalization of modal verbs.

By contrast, some other deficiencies are explicable from the phonological complexity of the respective forms or the complexity of their formation because of stem alternations: this is why the Russian verbs *pisat'*, *bežat'* 'run', *gnit'* 'rot' *gnut'* 'bend', and some others lack present tense converbs: the forms *gnija* 'rotting' or *gnja* 'bending' would be non-canonical from the phonological point of view, while the forms *piša* 'writing' and *beža* 'running' are avoided due to the fact that the verb stem of *pisat'* includes a consonant alternating between s and š, and the stem of *bežat'* a consonant alternating between z and ž. Note that verbs with similar semantics but of different inflection types, such as *zapisyvat'* 'write down', *vybegat'* 'run out', *sgibat'* 'bend', are not deficient and have normal present tense converb forms: *zapisyvaja* 'writing down', *vybegaja* 'running out' and *sgibaja* 'bending'.

16.3.4 Some additional remarks on person

Some verb forms are incompatible with non-third persons because of their meaning, such as the lexeme *rassvetat'* 'dawn' in Russian. Sometimes these restrictions are purely semantic, while in other cases, the semantic oddness creates morphological problems in building first and second person verb forms.

More interesting are special verb features that are closer to tendencies than to strict rules. For instance, though normally the third person is unmarked and more frequent than other person values, some verbs are used in the first person more than in the third person. Consider for example emotional predicates ('be afraid', 'worry') and cognitive activities ('suppose', 'think', 'have opinion').

This fact correlates with another one, more pragmatic than syntactic: some types of speech acts are associated with only one person. For instance, sometimes the speaker's opinion about the addressee should be marked as a question, although the speaker knows the answer exactly. Consider the Russian example (18):

(18) Vy,   vidimo   Ivanov-Ø?
      You.NOM   presumably   Ivanov-SG.NOM
      'Presumably, you are Ivanov?'

Person values are not symmetrical for syntax, which is manifested in various syntactic tests. For instance, in Russian, if subjects of different persons are coordinated, the agreement choice obeys the hierarchy 1 > 2 > 3:

(19) Ja   I   mam-a   / mam-a   i   ja
      I.NOM   AND   mother-SG.NOM   mother-SG.NOM   and   I.NOM
      pojd-em / *pojd-ut   v   kino.
      go-PRS.1PL/go-PRS.3PL   to   cinema.SG.ACC
      'My mother and me, we will go to the cinema.'

16.4 Verbal categories

In this section, I briefly discuss verbal categories. Among verbal categories, a subset called 'predicative categories' or 'utterance categories' is particularly important. They characterize not only the situation the speaker wants to describe, but, simultaneously, the relation between the situation and the speech act conditions:

- absolute tense (temporal relation between the speech act and the described events);
- mood and modality (relation between the world of event and the real world where the sentence is uttered); and
- evidentiality (source of information about the described events).

Predicative categories are important because they show the degree of finiteness of the form. Verbs are special in word-class systems in that they often possess a large set of forms that differ in their syntactic features. For instance, converbs occur in the position of adjunct; participles are used in the NP modifier position; nominalizations and (mostly) infinitives occur in the argument position.

Some languages also possess grammatical markers that allow syntactic transposition of nouns or adjectives to the predicate position or their predicative use without explicit markers (for instance, Abkhaz-Adyghe languages allow marking nouns with verbal/predicate markers to be inserted in the predicate position in constructions like 'He is a teacher'). However, these markers are by far less frequent than verbal transposition markers. This fact results both from syntactic and semantic factors.

Syntactically, as we noticed, verbs bear markers of their head position (finite markers, markers of predicate categories, and so on). According to formal structural theories, verbs also have the richest structure of functional projections, including CP, which is responsible for complementizers and independent predicate position, and TP, which hosts tense marking and allows the verb to have its own canonical subject. This means that the non-canonical position of the verb (not as the head of the sentence, but as an argument or adjunct of another predicate) should be specially marked, for instance, to distinguish between the main and the embedded predicate.

Semantically, situations seem to be less stable in time and, sometimes, less perceivable than objects and their physical properties. Situations often coincide or overlap in time with each other, one being highly important, other ones backgrounded. Derived forms serve to describe a particular situation when it is not the main semantic component of the given utterance:

(20) a. *Bill goes to school.*
(the property of Bill, which is the main one for the current discourse)
b. *Bill noticed a bird when going to school.*
(a background situation)

The larger the difference in the occurrence of the given category in the finite vs non-finite verb form, the more probable it is that it belongs to the list of predicative categories. This means that verb grammar fulfils the function of main predication marking, together with what is called 'main clause phenomena' by Paducheva (1996) and Lobke, Haegeman, & Nye (2012). The meaning of main clause phenomena often includes subjective components, related to the speaker's feelings, cognitive activity, and evaluation of events (e.g. constructions like Russian *Nu i dom!* 'What a house!), the speaker's relations with the addressee (see Basque special allocutive inflection marking addressee's characteristics in the verb form, described by Miyagava 2012), and so on. However, Haegeman (2012) shows that some grammatical phenomena, such as argument fronting in English, are also restricted or absent in subordinate clauses.

16.4.1 Inheritance of the set of categories

Often, the set of categories that a verb form has is not explicable from its synchronic semantics. More illustrative is the function that the form used to have before. This is the case for Russian subjunctive and past tense. Both of them are marked for gender and unmarked for person, contrary to the present tense that is marked for person and unmarked for gender, because the Slavic past *l*-forms have previously been *l*-participles, and person marking is not characteristic of non-finite verb forms.

Below I will briefly describe some of typical predicative verb categories.

16.4.2 Tense

Verbs are special in that they can be marked for tense. Tense includes in fact several values related to each other:

- tense in the proper sense (absolute tense anchored to the moment of speech);
- relative tense (tense anchored to the tense of another event, usually of the event in the main clause); and
- temporal distance (category marked whether the distance between the event and the speech act is small or large).

The general tendency related to the absolute vs relative tense in languages where both types of marking is available is formulated in (21):

(21) The more tightly two events are integrated, the more probable is relative marking in one of the clauses. For instance, as Slavic data shows, relative tense marking is more probable for complement clauses than for sentential adjuncts, and complement clauses are tighter connected with the main event.

However, another tendency conflicting with (21) is often also relevant:

(22) In some cases when the two events are integrated very tightly, they repeat each other's marking, and the marking looks like absolute tense but may in fact be identity marking.

This latter tendency is applicable the case of phasal verbs and in some other cases, as can be seen in Russian:

(23) Sluči-l-o-s'   tak   čto
     happen-PST-SG.N-REFL   so   that
     on   popa-l-Ø   na   Zemlj-u.
     he.NOM   get-PST-SG.M to   earth-SG.ACC
     'It happened that he got to the Earth.'

The past tense in the form *popal* in (23) is interpreted absolutely. The reason is that in this case, the matrix and the embedded verb denote, roughly speaking, one situation (the embedded verb marks the lexical content of the situation, while the matrix one introduces its evaluation, phase, and so on). This is why iconicity in terms of Givón (1980; 1990) makes the identical marking rather probable.

16.4.3 Mood: Imperative

Mood denotes several meaning types related to the reality status of the situation (see van der Auwera & Plungjan 1998; Boye 2012 for details). In particular, it can describe the reality status itself (e.g. in conditional constructions of many languages, the choice of mood is different depending on whether the condition can be realized) or the speaker's relation to the situation (e.g. the fact that the speaker wants the situation to be realized or has to participate in it is often described by subjunctive embedded clauses). Below I will briefly discuss the specific status of imperative in the verbal system.

Imperative is special in being often shorter and less grammatically marked than indicative forms. This makes the description of imperative in terms of finiteness problematic: though imperative, according to Gusev (2013), often lacks many predicative categories, it is used only or almost only as the main predicate. Thus, the morphological criterion of finiteness (predicative categories) contradicts the syntactic one (independent or main predicate position). Imperative, according to works by Kasevich, Levitskiy, and Asatiani in Birjulin & Khrakovskij (1990), is used as a 'direct speech causative': the speaker seeks to cause the addressee or a group of people to do something s/he wants.

The shortness of imperative forms mirrors the fact that commands tend to be short and pronounced quickly because of their functional properties. The same fact results in some special features of imperative constructions:

- In imperative constructions of many languages (see Gusev 2005: 164–171), the addressee is often omitted/not mentioned. To mention the addressee explicitly is pragmatically marked, for instance, to place extra emphasis on the addressee.
- In imperative constructions, direct and indirect objects are often left implicit.
- In imperative constructions, the embedded clause also tends to be shorter and less explicit (Letuchiy 2022). For instance, the subject of the embedded clause is often omitted, and the overall length is shorter than for indicative constructions.
- As (24) and (25) from Russian show, the embedded clauses of imperative constructions are more likely to lack an explicit verb, the same type of construction being often ungrammatical if repeated in indicative sentences.

Russian

(24) *Smotri   kak-aja   babočk-a.*
    look.IMV   which-F.SG.NOM   butterfly-SG.NOM
    'Look which butterfly is here!'

(25) **On   smotr-it   / posmotre-l-Ø   kak-aja   (by-l-a)*
    he.NOM   look-PRS.3SG   look-PST-SG.M   which-F.SG.NOM   be-PST-SG.F
    babočk-a.
    butterfly-SG.NOM
    Intended: 'He looks/looked which butterfly was there.'

16.4.4 Aspectual categories

Aspectual categories show significant variation across languages. The general rule concerning non-finite forms is formulated in (26):

(26) Lexical aspectual values are better retained in non-finite forms than grammatical aspectual values (see Tatevosov 2002; Comrie 1976; Smith 1991 for special features of aspect expression).

At the same time, in many languages no aspectual values are ascribed to verbs lexically. Often these languages possess a richer system of aspectually marked grammatical forms, such as French complex past and simple past, English present perfect, past simple, and past continuous (see Smith 1991). For these forms, the rule in (26) is also valid: for instance, English does not have a special participle for Past Simple, Past Continuous, and Present Continuous.

As Tatevosov (2002) shows, lexical aspectual properties are tightly connected with grammatical aspectual forms. Specifically, he demonstrates that defining the actional/aspectual lexical class of a verb is only possible if its concrete aspectual meaning in different aspectual forms of verbs is described.

16.4.5 Voice categories

Voice categories are compatible with finite verb forms, while non-finite forms vary in their ability to express voice. The general rule is as in (27):

(27) The closer the verb form is to word formation, the greater is the probability of voice category loss.

In Standard Average European, participles and converbs usually retain voice categories (e.g. the opposition of caused change described by the base transitive verb and passive/anticausative denoted by a verb with the reflexive marker), but nominalizations often lose them. In French, the deverbal nominal *ouverture* 'opening' may refer to a spontaneous opening (28) or to the situation when someone opens something (29):

(28) *Philharmonie sera desservie, au moment de son ouverture, par tous les modes de [...] transports.*
'The philharmonic society will be served at the moment of its opening by all types of transport.'

(29) *La guerre de 1914–1918, l'ouverture de l'Amérique du Sud aux capitaux nord-américains accroissent encore l'attention intéressée des Yankees.*
'The war of 1914–1918, the discovery of South America to the North American capitals made Yankees' interest even greater.'

At the same time, some exceptions exist: for instance, in Czech, the opposition of transitive and reflexive/passive verbs is retained under nominalization: *namalování* 'painting (something)' vs *namalování se* 'painting of oneself' (see Hron 2005; Kettnerová & Lopatkova 2019 for details).

16.4.6 Topic–focus distinctions

Finite verb forms have special communicative properties: in the default case, the verb is a topic, rather than a focus, while the subject is a topic in the unmarked case. At the same time, 'narrow focus' constructions that focus only the verb are often linearly undistinguishable from 'wide focus' on the whole VP. Compare the Russian examples in (30) focus on the part [*xuligany pobili*] and (31) only the verbs *pocarapal* and *pokusal* are focused.:

(30) Čto   s   nim   sluči-l-o-s'?
 what.NOM to   3SG.INS   happen-PST-SG.N-REFL
 Ego   xuligan-y   pobi-l-i.
 3SG.ACC   bully-PL.NOM beat-PST-PL
 'What happened to him? Some bullies beat him.'

(31) Vasj-u   tigr-Ø   pocarapa-l-Ø,
 Vasja-SG.ACC   tiger-SG.NOM   scratch-PST-SG.M
 a   Polin-u   pokusa-l-Ø.
 and   Polina-SG.ACC   bite-PST-SG.M
 'The tiger scratched Vasja, while Polina, he bit.'

In the embedded clause, verbal constituents are cross-linguistically less prone to topicalization than NPs, this tendency being relevant even for non-finite verbal forms (infinitives). Consider the following Russian pairs where an NP argument has more chance to become a topic than a complement clause of the same matrix verb: the second position in Russian is a typical non-contrasted topic position. The infinitive *plavat'* '(to) swim' has less chance to occur in this position than the nominalization *plavanie* 'swimming', the meaning being basically identical (see the detailed description of the opposition in Letuchij 2021). This is why (33) is worse than (32).

(32) S   kak-ix   èto   por-Ø   plavani-e
     from   which-PL.GEN   PART   time-PL.GEN   swimming-SG.NOM
     tebe   tak   nrav-it-sja?
     you.DAT   so   like-PRS.3SG-REFL
     'Since when do you like swimming so much?'

(33) ?S   kakix   èto   por-Ø   plava-t'
     from   which-PL.GEN   PART   time-PL.GEN   swimming-SG.NOM
     tebe   tak   nrav-it-sja?
     you.DAT   so   like-PRS.3SG-REFL
     Intended: '= (32).'

In some other languages, a number of linear positions characterized by the topical status are simply incompatible with nonnominal arguments: see restrictions on the second position existing in English (Davies & Dubinsky 2009):

(34) *Does this strange animal annoy you?*
(35) Intended: Does that I left early annoy you?

16.4.7 Distribution of nominal and verbal strategies

In many cases, several subordination strategies are possible, one of them with a finite or non-finite verb form, the other one with a participle or a nominalization. Although semantic difference is not always obvious, some tendencies can be remarked (see Boye 2012).

First, finite verbs often emphasize the process phase of the situation, while nominalizations mark its result or stative phase. For example, Grimshaw (1990) shows that nominalizations of some process and stative verbs acquire result reading. While Bulgarian *dokazvam* 'prove' denotes a concrete process event, *dokazatelstvo* 'proof' very often has a result/physical object meaning: 'a formulaic sequence showing the process/ the way of proving something', which is written as a result of the proving process. The same focus on the result phase is often observed for some non-finite verb forms such as participles.

This leads to the development of some secondary meanings of participial constructions that are related to the emphasis on the result phase. For instance, Henkin (1992; 2021) and Isaksson (2000) claim that in Arabic dialects, participles in embedded clauses have an evidential flavour, as in (36) from Negev Arabic. This results from the fact that they mainly mark the result of the action, and evidentiality is closely related to resultative meanings.

(36) u   ba'ad   ǧa   hal-habar bašširō-h   gālaw   inn
     and   then   come.PRF   DEF-news   good.news-3SG.M   tell.PRF.3P.M COMP
     Āl Dufīr   ćāsb-īn   u   lā   'alē-ham
     Al-Dafir   win.PART-PL   and   NEG   on-3PL.M
     'And then good news came; they said that Al-Dafir won (evidentially), not lost.'
     (Isaksson 2000: 392)

In (36), the participle *ćāsbīn* 'winners, winning' is used instead of some of finite forms of the *ćāsaba* 'win' (e.g. *ćāsabū* 'they won') in order to mark the embedded clause as evidential. Only the result ('the Al-Dafir are winners') is directly known to the speaker, while the preceding process remains unknown to them. The same is true for Lithuanian, where, according to Aikhenvald (2004) and others, constructions with participles (and without a finite verb form) express evidential meanings.

Second, nominalizations are more commonly used with factive verbs like 'know', 'annoy', and verbs with subjective modal meaning, such as 'want' or 'insist'. By contrast, with epistemic verbs like 'suppose', 'consider', 'think', clausal strategies are more common than nominalizations. In Abaza (West Caucasian, author's field data), Bulgarian, Russian (examples (37)–(40)) and other Slavic languages, English, French, and many others, verbs of knowledge take nominalizations, while verbs of opinion do not. Although (38) is possible, *dumat'* can only mean here the process of thinking, but not an opinion.

(37) Ja   ne   zna-l-Ø   ob   ego   uxod-e.
     I.NOM   NEG   know-PST-SG.M   about   his   leaving-SG.LOC
     'I did not know about the fact that he had left.'

(38) Ja   ne   zna-l-Ø   čto   on   uše-l-Ø.
     I.NOM   NEG   know-PST-SG.M   COMP   he.NOM   leave-PST-SG.M
     I did not know that he had left.'

(39) #Ja   duma-l-Ø   ob   ego   uxod-e.
     I.NOM   think-PST-SG.M   about   his   leaving-SG.LOC
     'I was thinking about the situation of his leaving'; #'I thought that he had left.'

(40) Ja   duma-l-Ø   čto   on   uše-l-Ø.
     I.NOM   think-PST-SG.M   COMP   he.NOM   leave-PST-SG.M
     'I thought that he had left.'

16.5 VERBAL CONSTRUCTIONS AND ARGUMENT STRUCTURE

In this section, some special features of verb argument structure will be described. I do not aim to cover the entire set of structures, language elements, and marking types—the purpose is rather to mention relevant features and to show that some of them are only compatible with verbs or behave in a special way with verbs.

16.5.1 Differential object and subject marking

In many languages of the world, differential object or subject marking is observed: this means that an argument with the same syntactic status can acquire different case or adpositional markers depending on its specificity, animacy, free/possessed status, and so on (see Bossong 1991 on differential object marking, and Arkadiev 2009, as well as other studies in the volume edited by de Hoop & de Swart 2009 for differential subject marking).

Khakas (author's field data):

(41) suy   / suy-dy   is-če
      water / water-ACC   drink-PRS
      'The girl drinks water.'

This pattern is mainly observed in the nominative subject and accusative object position, and this is why it has no analogue in nominalizations, if a language has deverbal nominalizations.

16.5.2 Argument raising and nominalization

Raising (see Culicover & Jackendoff 2005; Polinsky 2013) is defined as a structure where an element, which gets a semantic role in the embedded clause and is a participant of the embedded event, is raised to the main clause, where it gets a syntactic position (mainly of subject or direct object) and case (if any). Raising is observed almost exclusively with verbal heads. As shown by Chomsky (1970) and Lieber (2016), examples like (42) are expected to be ungrammatical, because the English raising construction has no parallel in nominalizations:

(42) *Fenster's appearance to be smart (Lieber 2016: 32)

At the same time, some Russian structures with deverbal nouns are similar to raising. For instance, in (43), the dative NP *jaxte* 'yacht-DAT' is not an inherent argument of the word *trebovanie* (this nominalization cannot host objects, except prepositional ones). It is rather raised from the embedded clause 'that the yacht leave the surf zone':

(43) trebovani-e   jaxt-e   vyj-ti   iz   pribojn-oj   zon-y
      request-SG.NOM   yacht-SG.DAT   go.out-INF   from surf-F.SG.GEN   zone-SG.GEN
      'the request for the yacht to leave the surf zone'

16.5.3 Change of verbal syntactic pattern under nominalization

Even when the pattern is possible either in both verbal and nonverbal structures, it sometimes undergoes changes when the verb is nominalized. This is the case of Russian, where the transitive (S and DO) pattern does not always correspond to the genitive/instrumental pattern of nominalizations:

(44) a. On   ljub-it   drug-a.
        he.NOM   love-PRS.3SG   friend-SG.ACC
        'He loves his friend.'

   b. ljubov'-Ø   k   drug-u   /   #ljubov'-Ø   drug-a
      love-SG.NOM   to   friend-SG.DAT   love-SG.NOM   friend-SG.GEN
      'His love to his friend.'

The transitive pattern of the verb *ljubit'* 'love' does not yield a nominalization taking a genitive object. The nominalization *ljubov'* can only take an object marked with the preposition *k* + dative, while the genitive argument can only have the subject reading.

At the same time, some languages have special nominalization strategies that retain main 'verbal' features: this is the case of English *-ing*-gerund and Caucasian masdars. Arabic masdar, according to Tayalati and Van de Velde (2014), is a mixed category: it has both a 'verbal' pattern with an accusative object and a 'nominal' pattern with a genitive object. To compare (45) and (46) from Modern Standard Arabic: (45) shows a standard nominal pattern, with a genitive object and a subject marked in the same way as an agent of passives; (46) illustrates the 'verbal' pattern, where the object is in the accusative, and the initial subject in genitive.

(45) qaṣf-u   l-madīnat-i   min   ṭaraf-i   l-'aduww-i
     bombing.NOM   DEF-city-GEN   from   side   DEF-enemy-GEN
     'the bombing of the city by the enemy'

(46) qaṣf-u   l-'aduww-i   l-madīnat-a
     bombing.NOM   DEF-enemy-GEN   DEF-city-ACC
     'the enemy('s) bombing (of) the city'

16.5.4 Special features of verb argument structure

Some syntactic features and mechanisms of verbs have no parallels in nouns or other parts of speech, even formed through nominalizations. In some more complicated cases, features expressed with verbs have some parallels but with significant changes. I list some of these features below.

16.5.4.1 *Reflexive and reciprocal*

Some reflexive and reciprocal pronouns are mainly compatible with verbs. When the verb is nominalized, these markers are sometimes used restrictedly. For instance, in Russian, argument reflexives with verbs are often converted to possessive adjectival reflexives under nominalizations. While with most transitive verbs, such as *znat'* 'know', *oskorbljat'* 'offend', the reciprocal pronouns *drug druga* 'each other' are possible, they are often dubious with nominalizations (see the volume by Nedjalkov et al. 2007 for details), as shown in (47)–(48):

(47) Oni   znaj-ut   drug drug-a.
     they.NOM   know-PRS.3PL   each other-ACC
     'They know each other.'

(48) ?znani-e   drug   drug-a
     knowledge-SG.NOM   each   other-GEN
     'knowledge of each other'

16.5.4.2 Anaphoric pronouns

Anaphoric, interrogative, relative, and some other pronouns are often restricted in their compatibility with verbs and verb phrases. Although some languages, such as Alutor (Kibrik et al. 2000), have special devices for pronominal reference to verbs and VPs (e.g. the stem *tatə-* 'what do, to do what'), most others either prohibit non-nominal antecedents of pronouns or employ devices originally serving for NPs. No special 'pronominal verbs' are used for anaphoric purposes.

For instance, Abkhaz-Adyghe (West Caucasian) languages (see Rogava & Kerasheva 1966; Smeets 1984) employ the same anaphoric pronouns for sentential anaphora as for NP anaphora, such as *ar* '(s)he, it, that', *mər* 'this one'.

Adyghe (West Caucasian, author's field data)

(49) Ahmad   qe-ḵʷa-ʁ.   A-r   s-jə-ʁe-gʷəbžə-ʁ
     Ahmad   DIR-go-PST   this-ABS   1SG.ABS-3SG.ERG-CAUS-be.angry-PST
     'Ahmad came. This made me angry.'

In Russian, the set of anaphoric pronouns *on* 'he', *ona* 'she', *ono* 'it', *oni* 'they' are inappropriate for sentential anaphora. To refer to the situation expressed with a clause, the demonstrative pronoun *èto* 'this' is employed, not only in the deictic/indexical function, but also as a pronominal.

(50) Polin-a   opozda-l-a,
     Polina-SG.NOM   be.late-PST-SG.F
     i   èt-o   vs-ex   rasstroi-l-o.
     and   this-SG.NOM   everyone-PL.ACC   upset-PST-SG.N
     'Polina was late, and this upset everyone.'

In French, however, demonstrative pronouns like *ce, cela* 'this' are mainly used for sentential anaphora, but the regular anaphoric pronoun *il* 'he, it' is also possible:

French:
(51) S'il est possible, je veux avoir une idée sur le test des infirmières
     'If it is possible, I would like to have information about the test for nurses.'

16.6 Finiteness and clausality

Normally, we suppose that each finite verbs heads one clause, and vice versa. However, the very notion of finiteness is problematic (see, for instance, Noonan 2007). In this section, I will discuss some possible criteria of finiteness and problems related to the use of grammatical categories in non-finite or not fully finite forms.

16.6.1 Embedded forms and non-finite forms

An important opposition in many verbal systems is between finite and non-finite forms. Although the notion is intuitively clear (the opposition between fully-fledged verb forms that serve as predicates in independent clauses vs verb forms that are distinct from them), in fact, the opposition cannot be reduced to one feature. There are at least two groups of features that compose the feature of finiteness:

(i) Syntactic: possible contexts where the form can occur (e.g. embedded clause; matrix clause; all types of clause).
(ii) Morphological: whether the verb in the given form has the whole range of predicative and other grammatical categories.

Moreover, a third group of features can be added to these two: namely, syntax of dependent elements—which arguments and adjuncts can and which cannot be expressed with the given form.

The difference between the notions 'embedded form' and 'non-finite form' shows that syntax and morphology of verbal forms do not always match. On the one hand, finiteness is understood in one type of approaches as related to the main/embedded clause position. On the other hand, as Noonan (1985; 2007) shows, the finite vs non-finite form opposition is valid in embedded clauses in many languages. Finite forms are opposed to non-finite ones as expressing the full set of predicate meanings, while non-finite forms express only a subset of these categories or do not express them at all.

However, it is not true that all non-finite forms have no predicative categories. Thus, there is no clear-cut boundary between finite forms with all possible categories and non-finite verbs with no predicative categories: very often, non-finite forms have some of the relevant categories, in other words, a form can be 'more finite' and 'less finite'. One possibility is to regard finiteness as a multifactor opposition, related to whether the form is morphologically identical to the one used in the independent clause and if not, which differences it shows. However, the problem is that the same categories and grammatical values can be expressed with different markers in embedded clauses. The most adequate is to describe finiteness as the degree of similarity of the grammatical category set and their values between independent (finite) and dependent (non-finite) verb forms, including (i) similarity of categories themselves, (ii) similarity of values, and (iii) similarity of markers.

In this manner, it is possible to measure the finiteness of the infinitive and subjunctive in Russian, compared to the independent past and present forms as fully finite forms. Subjunctives and infinitives are marked for aspect, voice in the same way as finite forms. Tense and person are unmarked. The categories that make subjunctives more finite are number and gender. This fact corresponds well to the criterion of dependent elements: subjunctive, but not infinitive forms can have their own subject, which controls the gender and number agreement. However, both infinitive and subjunctive can be main clause predicates, thus, the first criterion does not differentiate them.

The notion of finiteness is problematic for typological comparison. In one languages, finite forms have many categories, such as mood, tense, aspect, argument agreement/cross-reference, while non-finite forms are unmarked for these categories (see Arabic masdar, Slavic subjunctive and/or infinitive). By contrast, in other languages, even finite verbs lack these predicative categories. Finally, in Latin even infinitives have the category of tense, and subjunctives the categories of tense and person. Thus, the notion of finiteness can be used in typology only as a relative concept: non-finite forms tend to have less morphological predicate categories than finite ones.

16.6.2 Lack of categories and dependent categories

The main criterion of non-finiteness is the lack of predicate categories. However, even if a form has a grammatical category value, its type may point to the embedded status. Some forms have dependent category interpretation as opposed to independent interpretation, typical for main clause verb forms. Dependent interpretation is characteristic of tense, aspect, and modality (see the dependent uses of perfective aspect in Russian in (52) and indicative mood in (53)), but similar phenomena are observed in the voice domain.

(52) On   zaxodi-l-Ø   k   nam
     he.NOM   come-PST-SG.M   to   we.DAT
     pered   tem   kak   uexa-t'.
     before   that.INS   COMP   leave-INF
     'He tended to visit us before leaving.'

(53) Menja   besi-l-o   by   čto   polovin-a   mo-ego
     I.ACC   drive.crazy-PST-SG.   IRR   COMP   half-SG.NOM   my-M.SG.GEN
     zarabotk-a   uxod-it   na   bezdel'nik-ov.
     salary-SG.GEN   go.out-PRS.3SG   on   slacker-PL.ACC
     'It would drive me crazy that a half of my salary is spent on slackers.'

The use of perfective in (52) in the embedded clause, in the meaning of a repeated situation, can be explained by the fact that the aspect value is interpreted relatively, as corresponding one-to-one to the instances of the main event 'He visited us'. Similarly, in (53), the whole situation is irreal, but no irreal mood is used in the main clause—the indicative form *uxodit* 'goes out, is spent' is interpreted relatively to the main event *besilo by* 'would drive crazy', which is already marked for irrealis.

In the domain of voice and valency change, dependent uses are those which copy the value of the other verb. In Russian, this type of construction is also sometimes observed for the verb *načat'* 'begin' used as a matrix predicate, where the reflexive passive marking can be occasionally used twice: on the phasal verb and on the embedded verb, as in (54) (though this type of construction is highly colloquial):

(54) Cerkov'-Ø   nača-l-a-s'   stroi-t'-sja,   no   oni
     church-SG.NOM begin-PST-SG.F-REFL build-INF-REFL but they.NOM
     sožg-l-i   ee.
     burn-PST-PL she.ACC
     'The building of the church has started, but they burnt it.'

In Adyghe, the dependent use of causative is possible: the embedded verb in a construction with *ježen* 'begin' can inherit the causative marking from the matrix verb:

Adyghe (author's field data)
(55) č'elejeʁaže-m   te   txəλ   tə-r-jə-ʁe-že-n-ər
     teacher-OBL   we   book   1PL.ABS-3SG.IO-OBL-CAUS-read-POT-ABS
     tə-r-jə-ʁe-ʁe-ža-ʁ.
     1PL.IO-LOC-3SG.A-CAUS-CAUS-BEGIN-PST
     'The teacher began to make us read books.' (lit. 'The teacher made us begin [he makes us read books]')

The causative meaning semantically combines only with the main predicate ('made us begin')—the beginning of the situation is forced by the teacher. However, due to the semantic and syntactic affinity between the two predicates, the causative meaning is expressed twice: on the phasal and the embedded verb. The resulting structure is syntactically peculiar because the 'beginner' participant ('we') does not correspond to the subject of the embedded verb ('the teacher').

16.6.3 'Label use' of infinitives

Infinitive has a mixed function in the language system: semantically, it refers to situations that have not (and perhaps will not) become true. Syntactically, they are used in various configurations where a main clause argument coincides (in a sense) with the embedded clause argument: raising, control, and intermediate structures.

At the same time, infinitives tend to have 'absolute' uses where they do not mark coreference. Rather, they describe a situation as such, with any possible participant and in any possible time and space. In this type of use the covert subject of the infinitive can hardly be identified with anything in the main clause, as in (56):

(56)   *To live is to suffer.*

Constructions with infinitives headed by a nonverbal matrix predicate are intermediate between argument and independent reflexives. For instance, coreference restrictions are weaker for infinitives with a nonverbal predicate, as in Russian:

(57) Tut   ujutno   side-t'.
      here   cosy.PRAEDIC   sit-INF
      'It is cosy to sit here.'

In this type of uses, an infinitive is not restricted by the matrix verb argument structure. Its properties can be different and vary from 'more nominal' to 'more verbal'. For instance, in German (see Russ 2013), infinitives can behave as nouns of neutral gender. They control agreement and are used with a neuter article:

(58) Das Essen wird gekocht 'The food is being cooked.' (Russ 2013: 51)

In Russian, the 'nominal' use of infinitives is highly restricted. Infinitives behave as nouns only in contexts where they refers to things used for some purpose, most often eating and drinking:

(59) Ja   tebe   poes-t' / popi-t'   / počita-t' prines.
      I.NOM   YOU.DAT eat-INF   drink-INF   read-INF   bring.PST.SG.M
      'I brought you (something) to eat.'

However, even in this use, a coordinate structure with two infinitive conjuncts is unable to control plural agreement:

(60) *Na stol-e   leža-l-i   poes-t'   i   popi-t'.
       on   table-SG.LOC   lie-PST-PL   eat-INF   and drink-INF
       Intended: 'There were (something) to eat and (something) to drink on the table.'

16.6.4 Verb forms and clausality

Typically, as mentioned before, the number of verb forms corresponds to the number of clauses (Givón 1980; 1990; Noonan 2007). A clause is a constituent that may belong to different syntactic types (finite/non-finite, CP, TP, or VP) but denotes a separate event and is formally similar in some respects to an independent sentence. The link between verb and clause is bidirectional: on the one hand, the verb serves as a criterion of clausality and shows that the constituent is regarded as expressing a separate situation. For instance, the expression 'Peter made Jerry sit' regards each event as more autonomous than in 'Peter sat Jerry down'. On the other hand, the degree of autonomy that each part of the sentence has, calls for empirical testing, those tests being also dependent on the semantic status of the situation.

At the same time, there are configurations where the iconicity between (syntactic) number of verbs and (semantic) number of situations does not hold. Sometimes one verb denotes more than one situation (and, perhaps, introduces more than one clause), while in other cases several verbs denote only one event.

Cases in which the number of verbs is fewer than the number of situations include (i) causative constructions, (ii) constructions with causative-like verbs like 'invite', and (iii) morphological complementation constructions. This type of configuration is manifested in various diagnostics, including for example the possibility of several adverbials of the same type, non-canonical reference of agent-based units (such as purpose markers), PRO control, and some others. For instance, some Russian verbs like *priglasit'* 'invite' behave as if they head a two-clause structure. This is why they are compatible with future time adverbials like *zavtra* 'tomorrow' when used in past: the adverbial describes the embedded event time, e.g. in (61), *zavtra* means the time of the caused event: 'he is invited to come tomorrow'.

(61) *Imperator-Ø   don-Ø   Pedro   priglaš-en-Ø   zavtra*
     emperor-SG.NOM   don-SG.NOM   Pedro.SG.NOM   invite-PART.PASS.PST-SG.M
     tomorrow
     k   imperatorsk-omu   zavtrak-u.
     to   Emperor's-M.SG.DAT   breakfast-SG.DAT
     'The emperor Don Pedro is invited tomorrow to participate in the emperor's breakfast.'

Some special configurations occur with other categories, such as threat construction (Russian) or evidentiality (Matses, Panoan, see Fleck 2007). In Matses, evidential verb forms allow two tense markers, which shows that the evidence and the situation the speaker makes an inference about are regarded as two separate events:

Matses (Panoan)
(62) *aid   nid-ak-ondaid   ne-e-k.*
     that.one   go-REC.PAST.INF-DIST.PAST.EXP.NMLZ   be-NPAST-INDIC
     'This is the one who (evidently) left (more than a month ago).' (Fleck 2007: 590)

In (62), the recent past morpheme *-ak-* refers to the time the speaker perceives the evidence, and the distal past suffix *-ondaid* to the time the event evidently took part.

In Russian, the threat construction behaves as a complex clause in reflexive binding, though it is morphologically simple and contains only one verb form:

(63) *Ja   emu   poizdevaj-u-s'   nad   svo-imi   roditelj-ami.*
     I.NOM   he.DAT   mock-PRS.1SG-REFL   above   own-PL.INS   parent-PL.INS
     'I will show him how to mock his parents.'

This is why the possessive reflexive *svoj* can refer to the addressee *emu* 'he.DAT' which is an indirect object of the main clause but a subject in the omitted embedded clause expressed only by the verb form *poizdevajus'* 'I will mock (him)'.

Let us now turn to constructions in which the number of verb forms/verb stems is larger than the number of situations: complex verb forms, serial verbs, and phasal verb constructions.

In complex verb forms, an auxiliary can denote modal, temporal, or aspectual meanings. Sometimes, auxiliaries also bear some other functions: for instance, in English, the use of auxiliaries is related to negation and questions. Auxiliaries have special features that set them apart from lexical verbs, such as tense deficiency (English *be* does not take progressive) and paradigm exclusiveness (the present tense of Russian *byt'* is *est'* in all persons and numbers of present tense).

Auxiliaries are problematic for the verb vs nonverb demarcation. In complex verb forms, often only the auxiliary behaves as a finite verb, while the lexical verb form is non-finite and does not have many (or any) verbal categories. Thus, the boundary between nonverbal predicates like Russian *ujutno* 'cosy' requiring a copula and forms of lexical verbs in non-finite forms, such as a passive participle *ubit* 'killed' is far from clear. Moreover, the same construction can be regarded as a periphrastic verb form and a copular construction in different uses.

Passive with an auxiliary *byt'*:

(64) On   by-l-Ø   ubi-t-Ø   na   vojn-e.
     he.NOM   be-PST-SG.M   KILL-PART.PASS.PST-SG.M   on   war-SG.LOC
     'He was killed in the war.'

(65) V èt-o   vremj-a   dver' Ø   uže   by-l-a
     at this-N.SG.ACC time-SG.ACC   door-SG.NOM   already be-PST-SG.F
     otkry-t-a.
     open-PART.PASS.PST-SG.F
     'At this time, the door has already been opened.'

Copula construction with *byt'*:

(66) Odežd-a   dolžn-a   by-t'   velikolepn-oj.
     clothes-SG.NOM   must-SG.F   be-INF   excellent-F.SG.INS
     'The clothes must be excellent.'

Periphrastic forms often result from the grammaticalization of copula and multiverb construction. This grammaticalization combines three processes: (i) decrease of autonomy of the parts (copula/auxiliary and the lexical verb); (ii) change of semantic (for example, aspectual) properties; (iii) fixation of one variant of the form (e.g. the short form in Russian).

For instance, on the one hand, the auxiliary uses of *byt'* in (64)–(65) are less semantically restricted than the copula uses in (66). In the copula use, the whole clause can only behave as imperfective (which is natural for the lexical verb 'be'), while the construction with the auxiliary can be either imperfective (65) or perfective (64). On the other hand, semantically, the lexical meaning of state is more obvious in the copula construction than in the auxiliary one.

In many languages, a subtype of 'semi-auxiliaries' is found which is not described as auxiliaries due to their autonomous status but behave similarly to auxiliaries. For example, the Russian *stat'* that does not take modifiers concerning 'exact location' in time and resultative markers like *uže* 'already':

(67) Ty   uže   nača-l-Ø   / *sta-l-Ø   pisa-t' knig-u?
     you.NOM   already   begin-PST-SG.M   begin-PST-SG.M   write-INF book-SG.ACC
     'Have you begun to write a book?'

Some languages have special strategies for cases when the matrix and the embedded verbs are syntactically and semantically one situation. For instance, Arabic employs a strategy with two finite verbs and without a complementizer for phasal and causative verbs (see Melnik et al. 2017 on Arabic subordination strategies). Abaza allows a strategy where the embedded verb does not have a personal prefix when the matrix verb is in imperative:

    Modern standard Arabic
(68) *Bada'-a*   *y-ughni:*
       begin.PST-3SG.M 3SG.M-sing.PRS
       'He began to sing.'

    Abaza (author's field data)
(69) *Wara* *wə-dwə́-χa-ṭ*   *tdzə* *rgə́l-wa*   /
       you   2M.ABS-big-JAM-DCL house build-IPF
       wa-rgə́l-wa   *w-ə́-laga!*
       2M.ERG-build-IPF   2M.ABS-3SG.IO-begin-IMV
       'You are already an adult, begin to build a house.'

The semantic and syntactic affinity finds its expression even if no special strategy is used. For instance, according to Letuchiy and Viklova (2020), Russian phasal verbs lack some properties characteristic of complex clauses (Polinsky 2013 regards the phasal class as raising verbs): the matrix verb is not passivized and the embedded clause cannot be referred to by the anaphoric pronoun *to*, the main device of clause pronominalization:

(70) *Ja   *nača-l-a*   *rybači-t',* *i*   *moj-Ø*   *otec-Ø*
       I.NOM begin-PST-SG.F fish-INF   and my-M.SG.NOM father-SG.NOM
       tože *éto*   *nača-l-Ø*.
       also   this-N.SG.ACC begin-PST-SG.M
       Intended: 'I began fishing, and my father also began it.'

(71) *By-l-o   *nača-t-o*   *bega-t'*.
       be-PST-SG.N begin-PART.PASS.PST-SG.N run-INF
       'it was begun to run'

Turning to serial verbs, they are the type of verbal sequences where the link between the stems is looser than in complex verb forms but tighter than in structures with finite complementation. According to Dixon & Aikhenvald (2006) and Haspelmath (2016), this term applies to series of verb forms where only the last one is marked for the full set of tense–aspect–mood categories and other values dealing with finiteness. At the same time, the whole chain of forms denotes one situation, each of the forms being used to characterize a different aspect of the situation, as in (72)–(73). This differs from the situation with complex verb forms where the two elements build a complex form together, and it is not true that each element expresses its own semantic aspect.

Edo (Benue-Congo; Hagemeijer & Ogie 2011: 47)
(72) Òzó sàán rrá ógbà.
Ozo jump cross fence
'Ozo jumped across the fence.' (Lit. 'Ozo jumped (he) crossed the fence')

Hoan (Tuu, Botswana; Collins 2002: 4)
(73) Ma ǀoe na ka hoam-hoam tca.
1SG still AUX SUB jog come
'while I was still coming jogging'

Some languages have embedding devices close to serialization but lacking some core properties of serialization. For instance, Russian double verbs, in terms of Weiss (1993), are also chained without any embedding marking. However, both forms are marked for the full set of finite categories:

(74) Sid-it chita-et.
sit-PRS.3SG read-PRS.3SG
'He is sitting and reading.'

Also, though the forms denote simultaneous situations, they are not used to mark various aspects of one situation.

A special strategy is syntactic doubling (see Letuchiy 2021 for details): in principle, it is similar to serial verbs in that the two verbs denote one situation, but the two verbs have identical forms e.g., imperative, in (75).

Russian
(75) Načn-i-te s t-ogo čto pozvon-i-te načal'nik-u.
begin-IMV-PL with that-N.SG.GEN COMP call-IMV-PL boss-SG.DAT
'Begin with calling your boss.'

16.7 SOME PARAMETERS OF VERBAL SYSTEMS

In this section, I will consider some parameters that characterize verbal systems. Some of them, such as pro-drop or the number of arguments, characterize the verb argument structure; others, such as the domain covered by verbal lexemes, are lexical, rather than grammatical features.

16.7.1 Variation in the word/affix status of grammatical markers

It is often the case that some verbal categories are expressed morphologically (inside the verb form), while others are expressed with separate words. The set of values expressed morphologically varies across languages.

In Russian, for instance, negation is written as a separate word, while the reflexive marker is an affix (*On ne breet-sja* [he.NOM NEG shave-REFL] 'He does not shave himself').

In Czech, by contrast, the negation marker is an affix, and the reflexive is a separate word (Hron 2005) (*On se neholí* [he.NOM REFL NEG-shave] 'He does not shave himself'). The difference is not just in the spelling. For instance, the Czech reflexive marker is sometimes postposed and sometimes preposed to the verb, while in Russian, the reflexive marker is always a suffix.

At the same time, the precise grammatical status of markers is sometimes hard to test. For instance, the Russian *ne* behaves as a prefix in many respects, though it is written separately. When attached to a verb, *ne* cannot modify the entire phrase:

(76) On   sil'no   pj-et.
      he.NOM   strongly   drink-PRS.3SG
      'He drinks much.' (lit. 'He drinks strongly')

(77) #On   ne   sil'no   pj-et.
      he.NOM   NEG   strongly drink-PRS.3SG
      'He does not drink much.' (lit. 'He does not drink strongly')

Example (77) is grammatically correct but *ne* can only be interpreted as a term negation that scopes only over the adverbial *sil'no*. Thus, the sentence means 'He drinks, but not much/strongly', and normally cannot be interpreted as a phrasal negation like 'It is not true that he drinks much' (and, perhaps, he does not drink at all). This means that there are some grammatical markers with intermediate status between a verbal affix and a separate word, and that the status of verbal markers varies across languages.

16.7.2 Difference in the domain covered by the verbal lexicon

The domain covered by the verbal lexicon is different in different languages. Some semantic fields are served by verbs in some languages and by nonverbal predicates in others. Some of them are listed below:

- predicates of logical relations ('be equal', 'be more')
- evaluation predicates ('be good', 'be interesting')
- emotional predicates ('be angry with')
- physical senses ('hurt')

Languages can be located along a 'verbality' scale showing how strong the tendency to express meanings through verbs is. For instance, Germanic languages are more verbal than Russian; some meanings expressed with predicative adverbials in Russian are translated into Germanic as verbs.

(78)

meaning	Russian	English	German
'pleasant'	*prijatno* (ADV), *rad* (ADJ)	*(it is) pleasant* (ADJ) *happy* (ADJ)	*(sein) froh* (ADJ) *freuen sich* (V)
'afraid'	*bojat'sja* (V), *strašno* (ADV)	*be afraid* (V) *fear* (V)	*haben angst* (V + N)
'hurt'	*bol'no* (ADV), *bolit* (V)	*hurt* (V)	*tun weh* (V)
	xolodno	*be cold* (V + ADJ)	*frieren* (V) *(sein) kalt* (ADJ)

16.7.3 Valency number

Languages are different in one more syntactic respect, namely, the number of syntactic arguments that a non-derived verb allows. Although semantically, a great number of semantic participants are allowed, in some languages, their expression is restricted. For instance, in English, the multivalent verb *rent* is not restricted in the argument expression:

(79) Sue rented a car from Wilson until Tuesday for 50 dollars.

The verb *rent* has at least four valency slots: Agent, Possessor/Source, Theme, Price, and the date of return. All of them can be expressed in the same sentence.

By contrast, some languages restrict the number of arguments a verb can have without valency increase marking. For instance, Abkhaz-Adyghe languages (see Rogava & Kerasheva 1966; Smeets 1984 for details) have a restriction saying that no verb can have more than two lexical (i.e. not introduced by a valency change) syntactic arguments. In these languages, each argument is cross-referenced in the verb form, thus, verbal dependents that do not control cross-reference cannot be regarded as arguments. Given this restriction, verbs like 'give', 'buy', 'speak about/discuss' are not trivalent. For example, the Adyghe verb *jetən* 'give' is bivalent (with an Agent and a Theme), the Recipient being introduced by a default applicative marker *je-*. A tendency can be formulated saying the following:

"In many languages where arguments are formally distinct from adjuncts - e.g., they control cross-reference markers - a base verb usually cannot have many arguments".

16.7.4 Personal vs impersonal verbs

Another scale shows the degree to which personal vs impersonal verbs are used (impersonal constructions are thoroughly described in the volume edited by Malchukov & Siewierska 2011 and Kor Chahine & Guiraud-Weber 2013 for Slavic) and the role of impersonal verbs in the lexicon. Some languages, such as French, English, and others only allow verbs with a subject. Others, such as German, have a small class of impersonal verbs:

(80) Mich   dürste-t.
     I.ACC   be.thirsty-PRS.3SG
     'I am thirsty.'

Russian and many other languages allow impersonal verbs not as a marginal phenomenon, but as one of the core classes. In such languages, impersonality can also be the endpoint of valency change (see the impersonal reflexive passive in (81), or the inagentive unmarked construction in (82)):

    Bulgarian
(81) a. *Ne   mi   se   spi.*
          NEG I.DAT REFL sleep.PRS.3SG
          'I cannot sleep.'

      b. *Ne   mu   se   vliza-še   vătre*
          NEG I.DAT REFL enter-IPF.3SG inside
          'He did not want to come in.' (Ivanova 2007: 10)

    Russian
(82) *Lodk-u   unes-l-o   ot   bereg-a.*
     boat-SG.ACC carry.out-PST-SG.N from bank-SG.GEN
     'The boat was carried out of the bank (e.g. by the river or by the wind.)'

16.7.5 Pro-drop

The pro-drop parameter (see Prasad 2000; Butt 2001 for details) refers to the (in)ability of the language to use subject personal pronouns. Languages which normally or frequently omit the pronominal subject are pro-drop languages. The pro-drop parameter may correlate with the personal/impersonal one, but they are not strictly linked to each other. In principle, languages without impersonal verbs, such as English (83) or French (84), usually do not have pro-drop, while languages with impersonal verbs may have or lack it:

(83) **Is going/went to the library.*

(84) **Marchait dans la rue.*
     Intended: '(He) was going along the street.'

Russian (85), Bulgarian (86)–(87) and Arabic have both frequent pro-drop and impersonal verbs, including derived impersonal passives (87):

(85) *Id-u   včera   po   ulic-e.*
     go-PRS.1SG yesterday along street-SG.DAT
     'I was going along the street yesterday (lit. 'I am going along the street yesterday').'

(86) *Vǎrvja-še   iz   ulica-ta.*
     go-IPF.3SG along street-DEF.3F
     'He/she was going along the street.'

(87) *Ne   mi   se   spi.*
     NEG I.DAT REFL sleep.PRS.3SG
     'I cannot sleep.'

In other words, the presence vs absence of pro-drop and impersonal verbs reflect the same general parameter: the degree of strictness of the constraint on filling the subject slot, though the referential status is different, because pro-drop constructions normally presuppose a specific subject, while impersonal verbs usually do not semantically contain any type of subject participant or point to a non-specific subject.

16.8. VERBAL AND NONVERBAL PREDICATES

Although, as I have shown, a canonical utterance includes a verb form, some finite clauses contain no verb form. This class includes several construction types that differ in the type of event (static/dynamic), lexical semantics, and combinational properties. Example (88) illustrates a copular construction in Modern Standard Arabic:

(88) *Muḥammad-un muhandis-un.*
Muhammad.SG-NOM engineer.SG-NOM
'Muhammad is an engineer.'

Examples (89) and (90) show a Russian construction without a verb but with the meaning of dynamic situation:

Russian
(89) *Ty na vokzal-Ø?*
you.NOM on railway.station-SG.ACC
'Are you (going) to the railway station?'

(90) *A žen-a ego skovorodk-oj.*
and wife-SG.NOM he.ACC pan-SG.INS
'And his wife (hit) him with a pan.'

Contrary to copular constructions, dynamic constructions like (89) or (90) do not alternate with explicit stative forms like *byl /byla / bylo / byli* 'was, were'. This is why they are regarded as dynamic, rather than stative.

In some languages, constructions without an explicit verb form get a quotative reading. For instance, *so* in English and *takoj* 'such' in Russian often mean 'he says, utters like this'. The pronoun is not linked to any verb, but is interpreted based on the embedded clause (the speech description).

Predicate constituents containing no explicit predicate are treated differently in linguistic studies (see the survey of possible points of view in Testelets 2008 and Roy 2013), e.g. as similar to usual VPs, as cases of reduced VP or as cases of juxtaposition. Irrespective of the account we choose, the structures without verbs have intermediate properties between verbal and nonverbal ones. On the one hand, they allow adverbial modification. On the other hand, the patterns of negation (and negative concord) and some modifiers set them apart from verbal analogues. Consider the Russian examples (91) and (92):

Russian

(91) Ja   segodnja   cel-yj   den'-Ø   v   institut-e.
      I.NOM   today   whole-M.SG.ACC   day-SG.ACC   in   institute-SG.LOC
      'I am in the institute the whole day today.'

(92) a. *Nikto   ne   durak-Ø   ili   dur-a.
        nobody   NEG   fool-SG.NOM   or   fool.woman-SG.NOM
        'Nobody is a fool (m.) or a fool woman.'

     b. Nikto   ne   by-l-Ø   durak-om   ili   dur-oj.
        nobody NEG   be-PST-SG.M   fool-SG.INS   or   fool.woman-SG.INS
        'Nobody was a fool (m.) or a fool woman.'

Example (92a) shows that no negation of coordinate NPs are possible in structures with a zero copula. The same is possible if the copula is expressed, for example, in past (92b).

Arabic, according to Aoun et al. (2013), has another restriction on structures without a lexical verb. These structures are ungrammatical or bad in the embedded clause and have to be supplemented with the pronoun *huwa / hiya / hum* 'he / she / they' serving in those cases as a type of copula:

Modern Standard Arabic

(93) Fahim-tu   ʔanna   Muhammad-an   *(huwa)   ka:tib-un.
      understand-PST.1SG COMP   Muhammad-NOM   he.NOM   writer.SG-NOM
      'I understood that Muhammad is (lit. "he") a writer.'

16.9 CONCLUSIONS

In this chapter, verbs were defined as words with typical syntactic head function and the rhema / focus position that have the maximal set of predicative utterance categories. Semantically, verbs express situations. Further, categories related to finiteness are addressed (grammatical category expression, autonomous tense reference, voice marking, and so on) and are opposed to those related to argument structure (impersonality, pro-drop, valency restrictions). I have also shown that verbs are opposed to adverbs and adjectives in that major distinctions are observed inside the verbal paradigm (between finite and non-finite, predicate and argument forms), while for adverbs and adjectives, the main distinctions are observed between word classes (for instance, between 'high' and 'low' adverbs and adjectives, names of state-level vs individual level properties, and so on). This is why the very notion of verb paradigm is problematic because what is a non-finite form in one language (e.g. unmarked for tense, mood, and/or aspect) is a finite form in another.

The fact that verbs denote situations is grammaticalized in some purely syntactic features. For instance, verbs often have arguments, while this is not characteristic of nouns and adjectives and very rare for adverbs. Another fact that correlates with verbhood is clausality: not only are verbs most frequently the head of a clause, but also structures without verbs (nominal predications, copula structures) often have a reduced set of clause and VP characteristics. Thus, purely syntactic properties are not autonomous from morphological and word-class characteristics and directly correlate with the presence of explicit verb forms.

The richness of verbal categories makes it problematic to distinguish finite verbs from non-finite verbs and derivational markers from inflectional ones (e.g. in the case of vowels marking inflection types). This distinguishes verbs from other word classes and renders systems with multilevel word formation, where infinitive stems; stems in different tense paradigms; non-finite forms; and deverbal nouns can be related to each other in complicated and irregular ways.

CHAPTER 17

NOUNS

JAN RIJKHOFF

17.1 INTRODUCTION

THE prototypical noun is a basic, underived content word, which serves as the head of a noun phrase that is typically used to refer to one or more concrete, physical objects like cups, cats, or cars ('first order entities'; Lyons 1977: 442). However, nouns are also employed to talk about masses (*water*$_N$), places (*valley*$_N$), collectives (*crowd*$_N$) and emotions (*love*$_N$, *fear*$_N$), as well as events ('second order entities') like *wedding*$_N$ or *meeting*$_N$, propositions or possible facts ('third order entities') like *belief*$_N$ or *opinion*$_N$, and speech acts ('fourth order entities') like *question*$_N$ or *comment*$_N$. For reasons explained below (see in particular section 17.3), the current chapter is mostly concerned with basic, unmarked nouns that are used to refer to a concrete object in the physical world.

This chapter offers an overview of members of the word-class Noun from a typologically informed, cross-linguistic perspective (see Part II of this volume for other approaches to word classes). It is sometimes assumed that a distinct lexical category Noun is attested in every natural human language (Sapir 1921: 119; Whaley 1997: 32; Croft 2003: 183; Chung 2012), but this appears not to be the case. It has been argued, for example, that nouns cannot be distinguished syntactically from other major word classes like verbs or adjectives in the Polynesian languages Samoan and Tongan (Mosel & Hovdhaugen 1992: 73; Broschart 1997; see also, e.g., Himmelmann 2005a: 128). Furthermore, it has been noted that reference to a concrete object in Oneida and other indigenous North American languages commonly involves the use of verbal forms or constructions (Michelson 1990: 76; Mithun 1999: 60–61, 82; Abbott 2000: 48).

The remainder of this chapter proceeds as follows. Section 17.2 is concerned with the status of the word-class Noun as a cross-linguistic lexical category. Section 17.3 presents a cross-linguistic classification of the nominal lexemes that are central in this chapter: nouns that are used to talk about a spatial object in the external world, also known as 'concrete nouns' or 'first order nouns'. Section 17.4 is concerned with lexemes that do not fit easily in the classification of nominal subcategories presented in section 17.3. Section 17.5 offers a brief overview of certain (other) semantic, morphological, phonological, or cognitive properties of nouns. The chapter ends with a conclusion (section 17.6).

17.2 Nouns as a cross-linguistic lexical category

It is important to note at the outset that the problem of identifying members of the cross-linguistic word-class Noun is not so much trying to identify words in the various languages whose grammatical properties are completely identical (no two linguistic forms or constructions are exactly the same grammatically, not even in a single language; Gross 1979), but rather making sure that the units are similar enough to allow for a responsible cross-linguistic comparison (Rijkhoff 2016: 333).

In the European linguistic tradition, nouns are often defined in terms of certain formal, morphosyntactic features, but form-based characterizations of members of linguistic categories are too language-specific to be useful for an overall, cross-linguistic comparison. For example, one of the most conspicuous properties of (count) nouns in European languages is the fact that they can be inflected for plural number (cat_N vs $cat\text{-}s_N$). From a cross-linguistic perspective, however, this is not a suitable criterion, because number marking is absent or at best optional (but see section 17.3.2.3) in many, possibly even most of the world's languages (Rijkhoff 2004: 110–111, 146–152). Besides, even languages with compulsory number marking have a significant number of nouns that do not inflect for plural number, such as mass nouns (*gold-s) and abstract nouns (*courage-s).

Semantic criteria have also turned out to be unhelpful (Rijkhoff 2007: 711). As mentioned, prototypical nouns are associated with concrete, spatial objects, but many nouns are used to talk about non-spatial entities such as events ($meeting_N$), feelings ($love_N$), and other abstract entities ($linguistics_N$). Furthermore, a pre-linguistic notion that is lexicalized as a noun in one language may be expressed in another language as a verb (Evans 2000; Urban 2012: 152–168) or an adjective (Wierzbicka 1986: 354–355; Rijkhoff 2015: 645).[1] As noted by Lehmann (1990: 181), 'the choice of one lexical categorization instead of another has far-reaching consequences for the whole linguistic system' (see also Hengeveld 2013; Chapter 6 in this volume).

In sum, whereas word classes that are defined in terms of morphosyntactic properties (such as the ability to be inflected for number, definiteness, or case) are too narrow in that they do not cover all the relevant words in languages across the globe, semantically defined lexical categories are typically too wide, because they include words that belong to different parts of speech in the various languages (Rijkhoff 2009, 2016).

In this chapter, I will use Hengeveld's (1992b, 2013) approach to word classes as the point of departure, one of the main reasons being that his classification of parts-of-speech systems is based on descriptions of word classes in a representative sample of 50 languages (see also

---

[1] The fact that across languages the same notion may be lexicalized as a member of a different word class has been discussed in various publications, notably Lehmann (2010: 166–171; see also, e.g., Croft 1993). See, for example, Ross (1998a: 90) and Devos (2008: 136) on the way adjectival notions like English $pretty_A$ or $silent_A$ are expressed as relative clauses headed by a stative verb like $tikiraoi_V$ 'be_pretty' in Kiribati (an Oceanic language) or as genitival noun phrases headed by an abstract noun like $\text{-}búúli_N$ 'silence' in Makwe (a Bantu language), respectively (see also, e.g., Dixon 1982).

Chapter 10 in this volume).[2] Notice furthermore that Hengeveld's classification is included in Bisang's (2015: 553) comparison of the two most comprehensive typological approaches to word-class categorization (the other approach was proposed in Croft 2000; see also Chapter 11 in this volume).

The observation that nouns and other major lexical word classes appear to be language-particular categories regarding their formal or semantic properties does not mean they cannot be matched across languages. Members of the cross-linguistic word-class Noun may be compared on functional and structural grounds in terms of likeness (Rijkhoff 2016; McGregor 2019a: 208), as in Hengeveld's (here: slightly reformulated) definition of nouns as part of his classification of parts-of-speech systems (Hengeveld 1992b: 68): A DEDICATED NOUN IS A CONTENT WORD THAT CAN BE IMMEDIATELY USED AS THE HEAD OF A NOUN PHRASE.[3] Thus, English words like *think*$_V$ (a verb), *tall*$_A$ (an adjective) or *today*$_{Adv}$ (an adverb) can only serve as the head of a noun phrase when they appear as derived nouns (such as *think-er*$_N$ or *tall-ness*$_N$).

This definition leaves open two possibilities, both of which are attested in natural human languages. First, it allows for the possibility that there are languages without a separate, dedicated class of nouns (see section 17.1): (a) languages with a flexible word class like Samoan (see Chapter 35 in this volume), where—syntactically speaking—a separate category of nouns is absent, and (b) languages such as Oneida, whose speakers generally use verbs or verb-based expressions to talk about concrete, physical objects. Second, the definition also permits nouns not to appear as the head of a noun phrase, but by themselves when they serve as a non-verbal clausal predicate (see n. 3), as in the case of Dutch professional names like *leraar*$_N$ 'teacher' or *loodgieter*$_N$ 'plumber', regardless of the number of the subject noun phrase (NP).

Dutch (Germanic): the non-verbal predicate *loodgieter*$_N$ is just a noun (any form of inflection or modification would turn the bare noun into the head of a noun phrase):

(1) Ben en Peter zijn *loodgieter*$_N$
    Ben and Peter be:PL.PRES plumber
    'Ben and Peter are plumbers'.

It is also possible to have a full noun phrase instead of just a bare noun as the non-verbal predicate here, as in (2).

Dutch: the inflected noun *loodgieters*$_N$ is the head of a noun phrase:

(2) Ben en Peter zijn [(twee ervaren) *loodgieter-s*]$_{NP}$
    Ben and Peter be:PL.PRES (two experienced) plumber-PL
    'Ben and Peter are (two experienced) plumbers'.

The difference between having just a nominal lexeme (N) or a phrasal construction (NP) as the non-verbal clausal predicate is reflected in a subtle semantic difference, where the

---

[2] See Majid & Levinson (2010) and Dahl (2015) on the influence of languages spoken in Western, Educated, Industrialized, Rich, and Democratic (WEIRD) societies in linguistic studies.

[3] Non-verbal lexemes like nouns, adjectives and adverbs may also be used in predicative function, i.e. as the head of the clause, as in *Marianne is professor*$_N$/*happy*$_A$/*here*$_{Adv}$ (see Hengeveld 1992 for further details).

predicate noun seems to appear as a semantically stripped version of the lexicalized meaning of the noun, affecting the way the nominal property is represented in the spatial dimension (see section 17.3.1 on the 'mode of being' or *Seinsart* of a noun). The difference has been described in terms of individuation in that the bare (number-neutral or transnumeral) predicate noun is said to 'not to individuate' (Geerts et al. 1984: 145). The same seems to hold true for incorporated nouns, such as 'book' in *book-shop*$_N$ (Rijkhoff 2004: 56–57; on this topic, see also Wackernagel 1920: 84; Hundt 2016; Görgülü 2018; see Mithun 1984 for a discussion of various types of incorporation).[4]

17.3 A Cross-linguistic classification of nouns

It was mentioned in section 17.2 that the objects in a cross-linguistic comparison must be sufficiently similar to warrant a responsible investigation. So as to be able to do a more focused comparison between members of the cross-linguistic category Noun, another criterion has been added to the general definition of nouns provided earlier, ensuring even better that nouns in different languages are studied against each other in terms of the same properties (Song 2001: 11). On the assumption that there are concrete objects in the physical world ('common sense metaphysics'), these objects are used as external reference points (TERTIA COMPARATIONIS) to make certain that the nouns in our cross-linguistic comparison are sufficiently similar in function, meaning and form (Rijkhoff 2008: 732; cf. Ursini & Acquaviva 2019). In other words, even though nouns can be used to talk about many different kinds of entities (section 17.1), ranging from concrete physical objects (*cup, car*) to very abstract entities (*objection, trapezium, courage*) and anything in between (*game, wedding*), the current chapter will mostly focus on nouns with the widest cross-linguistic distribution: underived nouns that are used to refer to concrete objects in the external, physical world. The fact that abstract nouns are rare or generally absent in certain languages is mentioned in, for example, Dixon (1980: 272) and Corbett (2000: 87).

Due to this restriction, nouns denoting abstract and higher-order entities, like *fear, game,* or *opinion*, remain undiscussed here, as well as derived and other morphologically complex nominal forms like compounds and nominalizations (Koptjevskaja-Tamm 1993; Malchukov 2006; Bauer 2017). This also includes cases where a language employs a complex noun where another language would use a non-complex noun for the same object in the physical world. A case in point is the Papuan language Kalam, which 'has a fair supply of nominal morphemes', but lacks a simple nominal lexeme for *child* and certain other 'conceptual categories which one might expect to be universal' (Pawley 1993: 99f.; see also e.g. Goddard 2001: 1194; Lucy 2010: 268; Urban 2012).

---

[4] The bare predicate noun and the incorporated noun discussed in this chapter should not be confused with the category of 'bare nouns' in formal semantics or syntax, where 'bare nouns' also include nouns inflected for e.g. plural number (Delfitto 2006). In the formalist tradition, the term 'bare noun' (or 'bare noun phrase') is commonly used in the context of the Determiner Phrase (DP) analysis of noun phrases and basically refers to a noun or noun phrase without a quantifier or determiner (see de Swart & Zwarts 2009).

Furthermore, I will ignore special cases such as light nouns, i.e. nouns which under certain conditions lose some of their referential potential (Simone & Masini 2014), generic nouns (Dixon 1980: 272–273; Vittrant 2005), numerative nouns (Nurmio & Willis 2016) as well as PLURALIA TANTUM like *scissors*$_N$ or *pajamas*$_N$, which have no singular form (Wisniewski 2010: 181–184; Corbett 2019), and SINGULARIA TANTUM such as *jewellery*$_N$ or *furniture*$_N$, which have no plural form.[5] The reason that a noun like *furniture*$_N$ has no singular–plural opposition is that things of different kinds cannot be counted together (Frege 1950: 62; Mithun 1999: 92–93; Wierzbicka 1985: 320–321). Other types of nouns that have been regarded as SINGULARIA TANTUM include verbal nouns/infinitives (Dutch *het verkopen van ...* lit. 'the selling of ...'), abstract nouns (*thirst*$_N$, *love*$_N$, *linguistics*$_N$, *politics*$_N$), proper names (*Mark*$_N$, *Lisa*$_N$; see Van Langendonck 2007; Pina-Cabral 2015; Hough 2016; Mackenzie 2018), and names for chemical elements (*helium*$_N$).

Although mass nouns are normally not used to talk about concrete objects in the external world (and would therefore strictly speaking fall outside the scope of this chapter), they are discussed in this chapter for reasons that will become clear later (sections 17.3.3.3 and 17.3.3.4).

Finally, even though this chapter focuses on basic, unmarked nouns that are used to refer to concrete objects in the physical world, it is interesting to note that derived and higher-order nouns have a strong tendency to model themselves grammatically after the underived first order nouns in the same language. For example, the noun *arrival*$_N$ is derived from the verb *arrive*$_V$ and behaves just like a basic count noun (compare *one arrival—many arrivals* and *one umbrella—many umbrellas*), whereas the noun derived from the verb *sleep*$_V$ behaves like a mass noun (*much sleep*$_N$, *much water*$_N$). This is captured by the Principles of Formal and Semantic Adjustment (Dik 1997, Part 2: 20, 158–164); other manifestations of this principle are discussed in Lehmann (1990), who also refers to Benveniste (1957).

17.3.1 Classifying nouns: Introducing the semantic features Shape and Homogeneity

Concrete objects in the physical world, like cats or umbrellas, are typically characterized by a perceptual spatial boundary (i.e. they have a shape) and consist of connected parts (i.e. they have an internal structure) that stay together when the object is moved (Acquaviva 2008: 99–101; Levin & Rappaport Hovav 2011). By contrast, liquids and other masses lack a definite spatial outline and are homogeneous entities, i.e. they typically consist of non-individuated units or portions (rather than connected parts) that are all of the same kind, e.g. drops of a liquid or slices of a substance. It turns out that the properties SHAPE and HOMOGENEITY (or 'Likepartedness') can be felicitously exploited to characterize nouns that are employed in languages across the globe to talk about spatial entities (Rijkhoff 2004: 28–59; Rijkhoff 2008).

---

[5] SINGULARIA TANTUM such as *furniture* or *jewellery* are sometimes called 'collective mass nouns', 'object mass nouns', 'fake mass nouns', 'collective aggregates', or simply 'collectives', but they should not be confused with the collective nouns like English 'crew' or 'swarm' (which can all be pluralized) or the genuine mass nouns discussed in sections 17.3.2.2 and 17.3.3.3.

It is important to emphasize that the features SHAPE and HOMOGENEITY are here used for a linguistic classification of nouns rather than for an ontological classification of physical objects, so there need not be a direct relationship between noun type and (real world) entity type. In other words, we use ontological features of spatial entities for a linguistic classification of nouns, which may or may have lexicalized these features. This is, of course, precisely the reason that different kinds of nouns in languages across the globe can be used to talk about the same physical object (or *Sein*-correlate) in the external world (Rijkhoff 2004: 55–56). As noted by Levin & Rappaport Hovav (2011: 1): 'since any entity in the world is constituted of many attributes of which a noun lexicalizes only some, two nouns may refer to the same entity, but in lexicalizing different attributes, they may construe it as an entity in different ways'. The fact that the same real-world object (such as an umbrella) can be referred to by using different kinds of nouns may even reflect 'differences in the ontological beliefs the speakers of these languages hold about the referents of nouns' (Foley 1997: 231; more on the topic of linguistic relativity in section 17.3.3). The classification of nominal subcategories in Figure 17.1 shows that the six nominal subtypes have different values for the features Shape and Homogeneity: positive (+), negative (−) or neutral (no value).

As only entities with a definite outline can be counted directly, one may assume that an English noun like *umbrella*$_N$, which can be in a direct construction with a numeral ('two umbrellas'), has a positive value for the feature Shape (+Shape). In this case, a positive value for the semantic feature Shape matches a conspicuous ontological property of an umbrella in the real world.

The same English word (*umbrella*$_N$) is characterized by a negative value for the semantic feature Homogeneity. Liquids like water and other homogeneous entities do not come in distinct, individuated units but consist of portions of the same kind. In English, these portions can be referred to by the same name as the whole. For example, when we pour some water from a pitcher in a glass, both the liquid in the glass and the remaining liquid in the pitcher are still referred to as 'water'. But since we do not speak of two umbrellas when we break one in two pieces, we may infer that the English noun *umbrella* is characterized by a negative value for the semantic feature Homogeneity (−Homogeneity; notice that children up to age 4 count parts as wholes; Shipley & Shepperson 1990), in this case, too, the value of the semantic feature corresponds to an ontological property of umbrellas in the real world.

If we now compare the English noun *umbrella* (which is classified as a SINGULAR OBJECT NOUN below) with its translational equivalent in Thai *rôm*$_N$ 'umbrella(s)', we find that Thai *rôm*$_N$ is a number-neutral or transnumeral noun that cannot enter into a direct construction with a cardinal numeral.[6] This is because Thai nouns, like other languages with true numeral (or 'sortal') classifiers (see n. 13), are deemed to 'purely denote concepts and, for this reason, are incompatible with direct quantification' (Hundius & Kölver 1983: 166), which suggests that the Thai noun *rôm*$_N$ 'umbrella(s)' is characterized by a negative value for the feature Shape (−Shape). This does not mean that speakers of Thai do not know that an umbrella in the physical world is a discrete object, but rather that this particular piece of encyclopaedic knowledge is not part of the lexicalized meaning of *rôm*$_N$ 'umbrella(s)' (Rijkhoff 2008: 747; for a similar point see e.g. Unterbeck 1993).

---

[6] Notice that the term 'general number' is sometimes used in connection with different kinds of transnumeral nouns (including, e.g. set nouns and sort nouns, discussed in sections 17.2.3.2 and 17.3.3.1), when 'the meaning of the noun can be expressed without reference to number' (Corbett 2000: 10).

Before *rôm*$_N$ and other first order Thai nouns like *mánaaw*$_N$ 'lemon(s)' can be counted, they must be provided with a numeral or sortal classifier (CLF), which serves to individualize the property denoted by such nouns (Lyons 1977: 462), as in:

Thai (Austro-Tai) (Hundius & Kölver 1983: 172, 167)
(3) rôm   sǎam   khan
     umbrella(s)   three   CLF:LONG, HANDLED OBJECT
     'three umbrellas'

(4) mánaaw   sǎam   lûuk
     lemon(s)   three   CLF:FRUIT
     'three lemons'

The sortal classifier is required, because the lexicalized meaning of nouns like *rôm*$_N$ and *mánaaw*$_N$, which are categorized as SORT NOUNS in Figure 17.1, does not seem to include the notion of spatial boundedness or discreteness (Hundius & Kölver 1983; Bisang 1999; Vittrant 2005: 135). The employment of sortal classifiers can allow speakers to emphasize different aspects of an entity (Adams 1989: 3). This is shown in (5) from Mandarin Chinese, where the classifier *duo*$_{CLF}$ indicates that the noun phrase is used to refer to the bud of a plant or flower, while *zhu*$_{CLF}$ makes clear that the noun phrase with the same head noun (*hua*$_N$) is used to refer to the plant itself. In either case, the classifier coerces the noun to have a certain reading, depending on the information 'entailed' in the classifier (on coercion, see also e.g. Audring & Booij 2016):[7]

Mandarin Chinese (Sino-Tibetan) (Huang & Ahrens 2003: 361)
(5) a. yi   duo   hua   b. yi   zhu   hua
        one   CLF   flower(s)/plant(s)   one   CLF   flower(s)/plant(s)
        'one flower'   'one plant'

Seen from a European perspective, one could say that sort nouns such as Mandarin *hua*$_N$ 'flower(s)/plant(s)' are semantically vague or underspecified and have a wider meaning than a singular object noun like English *plant*$_N$, which can be said to have a narrow meaning in comparison. Nevertheless, it is important to emphasize that singular object nouns and sort nouns are equally good exemplars of first order nouns and the same holds true for members of other nominal subcategories that are used to talk about spatial objects in the real world (Rijkhoff 2008: 738), such as set nouns and general nouns, which are discussed below.

---

[7] Sometimes we also find variable classification in languages with a genuine gender or noun class system, in which nouns normally always belong to the same gender or noun class (Dixon 1986). For example, the Danish noun *studie*$_N$ occurs with common and neuter gender, but there is a difference in meaning: *en studie*, with common gender, means 'a branch of learning' (e.g. architecture or mathematics), whereas *et studie*, with neuter gender, means 'a thesis'. The Danish noun *hamster*$_N$ 'hamster' can also be used with common or neuter gender (*en hamster* or *et hamster*), but in this case there is no semantic difference. Here gender shift is due to the speaker's individual preference or incomplete language change (Trap-Jensen 2007; Skafte-Jensen 2011; see Visser 2011 on historical gender change in West Frisian). Since the lexicalized meaning is not vague or ambiguous in these Danish examples, they are not cases of semantic under-specification. On the special case of polarity, the reversal of gender between the singular and the plural of nouns, see, e.g., Reh (1985) and Nilsson (2016); also Rijkhoff 2004: 85–86).

Sort nouns like Thai *mánaaw*$_N$ 'lemon(s)', which combine with a sortal classifier, should not be confused with mass nouns like *water*$_N$ or *oil*$_N$ (section 17.3.3.3), which occur in combination with a measure word or a mensural classifier as in *a litre/bucket/bottle/cup (of water)*; on grammatical and other differences between sortal and mensural classifiers, see e.g. Seifart (2010: 722).

In sum, it appears that a positive, negative, or neutral value for the semantic features Shape and Homogeneity can be used to characterize first order nouns in languages across the globe (Rijkhoff 2004: 28–59; Rijkhoff 2008; the reader is referred to Part II of this volume for overviews of various theoretical approaches to word classes). A classification of nouns based on these features is shown in Figure 17.1, in which each nominal subtype is lexically specified for a different *Seinsart* (literally 'mode of being', the nominal counterpart of the established German term *Aktionsart* 'mode of action' in verb semantics; see Rijkhoff 2004: ch. 2, for details).

	–HOMOGENEITY	+HOMOGENEITY
+SHAPE	Singular Object Noun	Collective Noun
	Set Noun	
–SHAPE	Sort Noun	Mass Noun
	General Noun	

FIGURE 17.1 Nominal subcategories ('*Seinsarten*'; based on Rijkhoff 2004: 54)

Each of the nominal subtypes in Figure 17.1 is discussed below, including mass nouns, even though they are not normally used to talk about concrete objects in the physical world (but see sections 17.4.2–17.4.3). Section 17.3.2 is concerned with nouns that have a positive value for the feature Shape as part of their lexicalized meaning, which makes it possible for these nouns to be counted directly (hence: count nouns): singular object nouns, collective nouns, and set nouns. Section 17.3.3 discusses nouns that have a negative value for the feature Shape, which is the reason they cannot be counted directly: sort nouns, general nouns, and mass nouns. Notice that several nominal subtypes in Figure 17.1 may co-occur in the same language. For example, in languages that have singular object nouns (section 17.3.2.1), they may co-occur with collective nouns (section 17.3.2.2), set nouns (section 17.3.2.3), or mass nouns (section 17.3.3.3).

If we temporarily ignore collective nouns and mass nouns, i.e. nouns with a positive value for the feature Homogeneity (+Homogeneity), it appears that across languages four kinds of nouns are used to talk about the same single object in the real world (like a banana or an umbrella): singular object nouns, set nouns, sort nouns and general nouns.

It is important to underscore, once again (see the quotation above from Levin & Rappaport Hovav 2011), that Shape and Homogeneity in Figure 17.1 do not refer to properties of real-world objects or substances, but rather specify coded values for semantic features in the lexicalized meaning of a first order noun. It should also be stressed that the nominal subcategories in Figure 17.1 are idealizations, as boundaries between linguistic categories are not always clear cut (see also section 17.4).[8] One of the reasons for this is that categorization is sometimes a matter of (inadequate) perception (Russell 1923). Thus 'hair' is a mass noun in 'long hair' and a singular object noun in 'a long hair'. Language change is another reason that

---

[8] On gradience and continuity in grammar, see, e.g., Bolinger 1961; Sasse 1993; Aarts 2007; Aarts et al. 2004; Sorace & Keller 2005; Langacker 2006: 116.

nouns may not always fit neatly into one of the categories of Figure 17.1. Linguistic categories (just like languages themselves) are dynamic entities and since processes of language change do not happen overnight, this means we may also encounter nouns whose membership of a specific subcategory is (currently) not quite clear (sections 17.3.3.1 and 17.4.1).

It is not obvious why the feature Shape (relevant for all six nominal subcategories in Figure 17.1) would be more basic or significant than the feature Homogeneity in noun semantics or in grammar generally. Still, the classification in Figure 17.1 confirms Friedrich's (1970: 380) observation that 'the category of shape appears to be a typological universal in grammar […] and of not inconsiderable significance for a theory of semantics in grammar' (see Wierzbicka 2006, Rijkhoff 2008; see also section 17.3.4). Friedrich (1979: 256) further demonstrated the widespread influence of Shape in different areas of grammar in languages across the globe, suggesting that 'shape ranks with time, aspect and the like as one of the fundamental ideas in grammar and, by implication, in the mind of the speakers of natural language' (see also e.g. Mithun 1999: 104–117).

One reason why the feature Shape takes precedence over the feature Homogeneity may be due to the idea that spatial orientation is primary in human cognition, which links up well with observations about the fundamental role of spatial notions in various grammatical domains, including lexical semantics (see e.g. Gentner 2001; Goddard 2001; Casasanto & Boroditsky 2008; Majid et al. 2013), sometimes discussed under the heading 'localism' (Lyons 1977: 718–724; Fortis 2018). The role of shape in grammar and cognition has often been investigated by comparing languages using different types of nouns for the same object in the real world; more on this topic in section 17.3.4.

Notice, finally, that since the classification in Figure 17.1 concerns nouns in their basic, unmarked form, plural nouns do not constitute a nominal category by themselves in the current approach, as opposed to certain logical treatments of nouns, where plural nouns are often discussed together with collective or mass nouns (Lasersohn 2011).

17.3.2 Nouns that can be in a direct construction with a cardinal numeral (count nouns)

Figure 17.1 shows that there are three types of noun whose meaning includes a positive value for the feature Shape, which means that they can be counted directly. The three + Shape nominal subcategories can be characterized as follows:

- SINGULAR OBJECT NOUNS (+Shape, −Homogeneity) like English *chair* or *cat* designate a non-agglomerative, spatially bounded property of a single object;
- COLLECTIVE NOUNS (+Shape, +Homogeneity) like English *crew* or *swarm* designate an agglomerative, spatially bounded property that applies to all the members of what is regarded as a group;
- SET NOUNS (+Shape) like Lango *gúlú* 'pot(s)' or Turkish *çocuk* 'child(ren)' designate a spatially bounded property of one or more objects.

The fact that nouns with a positive value for the feature Shape are counted directly (hence the label 'count nouns') does not necessarily mean that they can be marked for plural number (Allan 1980; Acquaviva 2008). This is only true in the case of singular object nouns (cat_N—cat-s_N) and collective nouns ($swarm_N$—$swarm$-s_N), both with and without a modifying numeral (on the various kinds of plurals, see Corbett 2000).[9] This is shown in examples (6) and (7) from Dutch (under certain circumstances a plural marked form can have a number-neutral interpretation; Sauerland et al. 2005). An example of a set noun, which is transnumeral, is given in (8); set nouns are discussed in more detail in section 17.3.2.3. In each case (singular object noun, collective noun, set noun), the noun can be directly modified by a cardinal numeral; hence they are assumed to be lexically coded for the feature + Shape. Notice that Lango nouns (or rather: noun phrases) are usually not marked as definite or indefinite (Noonan 1992: 161).

Dutch: SINGULAR OBJECT NOUN
(6) a. *een boek*   b. *boek-en*   c. *twee boek-en*
       a   book   book-PL   two   book-PL
       'a book'   'books'   'two books'

Dutch: COLLECTIVE NOUN
(7) a. *een kudde*   b. *kudde-s*   c. *twee kudde-s*
       a   herd   herd-PL   two   herd-PL
       'a herd'   'herds'   'two herds'

Lango (Nilotic) (Noonan 1992: 167): SET NOUN (a set noun is transnumeral)
(8) a. *gúlú*   b. *gúlú àryô*
       pot(s)   pot(s) two
       'a/the pot(s)'   '(the) two pots'

In some languages, nouns are always overtly marked for number, possibly also for e.g. gender or case (see Armoskaite 2019 on Lithuanian, where no bare roots are allowed). Below are some examples from Sesotho, a representative of the large Bantu family. In Bantu languages, the singular–plural opposition is expressed through the noun class system by (presumably) derivational affixes (on the derivational nature of noun class markers, see e.g. Schadeberg 2001 and references in Cobbinah & Lüpke 2014: 206). Generally speaking, countable nouns are members of two noun classes, one singular and one plural (the number before the Sesotho noun indicates noun class, e.g. *thọ* 'person(s)' belongs to Noun Class 1 in the singular and Noun Class 2 in the plural).

Sesotho (Bantu): singular–plural opposition in some noun class pairings (Demuth et al. 1986: 455)

(9)
CLASS	SINGULAR		CLASS	PLURAL	
1	mọ-thọ	'person'	2	ba-thọ	'persons'
3	mọ-sẹ́	'dress'	4	mẹ-sẹ́	'dresses'
5	lẹ-tsatsí	'day'	6	ma-tsatsí	'days'
7	sẹ-liba	'spring/well'	8	li-liba	'springs/wells'
9	Ø-ntjá	'dog'	10	li-ntjá	'dogs'

---

[9] Recall that the classification in Figure 17.1 concerns nouns in their basic, unmarked form, which means that plural nouns do not constitute a nominal category in their own right here (section 17.3.1).

Apparently, some languages from the Atlantic branch of Niger–Congo, such as Banyun or Baïnounk, distinguish between two kinds of plural: the 'limited/count plural' and the 'unlimited/collective plural' (see Greenberg 1972: 20, fn.23, quoting Sauvageot 1967). Further details on the so-called unlimited plural in three Baïnounk languages can be found in Cobbinah & Lüpke (2014) and in Corbett (2000: 30–35, 238), who discusses it under the heading 'greater plural' or 'plural of abundance'.

In Zuni (a language isolate spoken in New Mexico) nouns are also overtly marked as singular or plural, according to Newman (1965: 56; as quoted in Mithun 1999: 79).

Zuni (Language Isolate): inflectional number on Zuni nouns
(10)   a. *ča-ʔleʔ*   b. *ča-weʔ*
          'child'   'children'

Presumably languages like Sesotho and Zuni have transnumeral nominal roots, but since nouns do not appear in their unmarked form, it is difficult to determine what kind of nominal subcategory they belong to. Therefore, such 'bound nouns' are ignored in the current chapter (see also Mithun 1999: 57 on the relation between bound morphology and lexical categories). In languages with a case system, the nominative singular is typically used as the reference form of the noun, as this is usually regarded as the unmarked case. A related problem determining nominal subcategories concerns languages in which number marking is expressed outside the noun phrase proper, commonly as an optional phrase-final clitic which is clearly related to the third person pronoun or as an optional appositional element that is mutually exclusive with a numeral. This is the case in, for example, Alamblak, Bambara, and Nama Hottentot (Rijkhoff 2004: 31–32). The optional character of these markers suggests that the nouns are transnumeral set nouns (section 17.3.2.3), but since sufficient data are not available, such cases will also remain undiscussed here. Below is an example from Guaraní, where the (so-called) plural marker appears after all postnominal modifiers and is mutually exclusive with numerals (Gregores & Suárez 1967: 144, 150, 155).

Guaraní (Gregores & Suárez 1976: 150)
(11)   upé   la   ʔógo   itá   nte   gwigwà   kwéra
       that   the   house(s)   just   stone of   PL
       'just those houses of stone'

17.3.2.1 Singular object nouns

As shown in (6), a singular object noun denotes a property of single object (person, animal, plant, thing) and is marked for plural number if reference is made to more than one object, both with and without a modifying cardinal numeral higher than 'one':

Dutch: SINGULAR OBJECT NOUN
(12)   a. *(een)   tafel*   b. *tafel-s*   c. *twee   tafel-s*
          (a)   table   table-PL   two   table-PL
          '(a single) table'   '(multiple) tables'   'two tables'

In Dutch, the plural suffix is normally realized as *-en* or *-s*, but some nouns have an irregular plural. For example, the plural form of *kind* 'child' is *kinderen* 'children', which is an instance of metanalysis (or 'rebracketing'): when at some point in the history of Dutch the original plural suffix -*er* on *kind* 'child' was no longer recognized as a pluralizing morpheme, the plural suffix -*en* was added to the erstwhile plural form *kinder*, yielding *kinderen* 'children' (see Harris 2017 for a comprehensive treatment of MULTIPLE EXPONENCE, the occurrence of multiple realizations of a single morphosemantic feature). Diachronic developments also explain why English has so-called invariant plurals, which seem mostly restricted to animal-denoting nouns such as (*one/two/many*) *deer, fish*, or *sheep*. Irregular plural forms of English nouns can also be the result of a vowel shift (*Umlaut*), as in singular *foot* vs plural *feet*.

When the plural form involves a different root or stem, we speak of total suppletion. In Lango, for example, only some nouns have a plural form (mainly those denoting humans and animals), but since there is no regular plural formation 'each singular/plural pair must be individually lexicalised' (Noonan 1992: 167), as in *dákô* 'woman' vs *món* 'women'. Most Lango nouns, however, are transnumeral set nouns (section 17.3.2.3). Apparently lexical plurals are typically attested in languages with 'limited plural marking' (Mithun 1999: 83). In addition to suppletion, Ngiti (a Nilo-Saharan language) has two other strategies of plural marking: the use of Bantu-like prefixes *mU-* and *pba-*, and tone (Kutsch Lojenga 1994: 133f.).

Plural number (if it is that) can also be expressed through partial or full reduplication, a morphological process that has many functions, including marking distributivity or collectivity (Moravcsik 1978a; Rubino 2005). In addition to the plural, languages may have what has been referred to as 'minor number categories', such as the dual, the trial or the paucal (see Universal 34 in Greenberg 1966: 94; Corbett 2000; Harbour 2020).

Notice finally that in a few languages the same so-called number marker can have different values (see Tiersma 1982 on local markedness). This is attested in languages of the North American Kiowa–Tanoan family, which have only the suffix -*sh* to mark the unexpected or inverse number (Mithun 1999: 81; see also Grimm (2012) on Dagaare, a Gur language of the Niger–Congo family). For example, the unmarked number of animate nouns is singular, so on these nouns -*sh* marks dual or plural number, but in the case of inanimate nouns, which tend to be used in connection with less individuated or multiple entities, plural is the expected number, so here -*sh* marks singular or dual number.

17.3.2.2 *Collective nouns*

A collective noun denotes a property of objects (persons, animals, plants, things) which are conceived of as a unit and which is marked for plural number if reference is made to more than one collective entity, both with and without a modifying cardinal numeral higher than *one*. The fact that these nouns can be counted directly suggests they have a positive value for the feature Shape, just like singular object nouns (section 17.3.2.1) and set nouns (section 17.3.2.3).

English (Germanic): COLLECTIVE NOUN

(13) a. (*a*) *crew* b. *crew-s* c. two *crew-s*
(a) crew crew-PL two crew-PL
'(a single) crew' '(multiple) crews' 'two crews'

Greenberg (1972: 25) already observed that the term COLLECTIVE NOUN has been given various interpretations, which has led to confusing analyses (see also Gil 1996; Nurmio

2017: 66). For example, Wiese (2012: 55) does not regard group nouns like *family* or indeed *group* as collective nouns. Here we will confine ourselves to collective nouns in the strict sense of the word: nouns which can be counted directly, which can be pluralized and which in their basic, unmarked form are used to refer to a group of people, animals, or objects like English *herd*, *team* or *family* (see Kuhn 1982; de Vries 2021).

Collective nouns (like mass nouns) have a positive value for the feature Homogeneity, because they are cumulative (or agglomerative) and dissective (or divisive) entities (Goodman 1966; Rijkhoff 2008: 734–735; Doetjes 2012: 2561). When someone in a family dies, the others are still family, and when we take one flower out of a bunch, the remaining flowers are still part of a bunch—up to a point (Quine 1960: 91). Since the property of dissectiveness or divisibility has a lower limit (do two flowers together constitute a bunch?), it is more attractive to say that homogeneous entities are agglomerative or cumulative in that they can be expanded with more members or portions without affecting the grammatical number. By adding members to a collective we do not get more collectives, as it will only increase the size of a collective, and by adding portions to a mass, we only increase the size, weight, or volume of that mass entity. In other words, collective nouns and mass nouns can be said to have 'cumulative reference' (but strictly speaking it is noun phrases rather than nouns that have referential potential). For instance, when a child is born into the family, this does not result in more families; it only affects the number of individuals that make up that family. Notice that the number of individuals in certain collectives, such as soccer teams, is fixed by the rules of the game.

There is considerable variability within and across varieties of English regarding agreement patterns involving subject noun phrases headed by a collective noun (Depraetere 2003; Hundt 2009). In British English, the focus can be on the group or on the members in that group, hence we find singular as well as plural verb agreement, whereas in American English collective nouns usually trigger singular verb agreement (Corbett 2006: 206–213). Collective nouns often denote groups of animals (e.g. *clowder*$_N$ *of cats*), and the same is true for (British) English, where many such nouns are used in connection with hunting events (for an early list, see Berners [1486] 1881; cf. Biber et al. (1999) on 'quantifying collectives'), like *pride*$_N$ (*of lions*), *gaggle*$_N$ (*of geese*), or *parliament*$_N$ (*of owls*).

In addition to these lexical collectives, some languages have what are sometimes called morphological collectives. Like lexical collectives, they are used to refer to units containing multiple members, but they can be affixed with a singulative marker to denote a single object. Compare, for example, Breton *gwez* 'trees, forest' (collective) and *gwez-enn* 'a (single) tree'. In its turn, *gwez-enn* can be inflected with a regular plural suffix: *gwezenn-où* '(multiple individual) trees'. Whereas the so-called lexical collectives in Welsh, another Brittonic language, often denote human groups, members of the relatively small group of morphological collectives are typically used to talk about non-human collectives, like groups of animals, insects, fruits, or vegetables; compare the Welsh collective *moch* 'pigs' and *moch-yn* 'a (single) pig' (Stolz 2001; Nurmio 2015 and 2017).[10] There are, however, good reasons to assume that the singulative in, for example, Breton is a derivational rather than an inflectional suffix,

---

[10] The discussion of lexical and morphological collectives in Brittonic languages has a complicated history, with various conflicting analyses. It should also be added here that in Welsh, for example, the so-called lexical collective or corporate noun (Corbett 2000: 188) does not appear to have the same properties as English collective nouns like *swarm*$_N$ or *crew*$_N$. For a detailed discussion of the two kinds of 'collectives' in Welsh, see Nurmio (2017).

since it also serves as a nominalizing morpheme on verbal and adjectival bases (Greenberg 1972: 20; Acquaviva 2008: 246). Derivation is also used to turn mass nouns such as Dutch *bier* 'beer' into words denoting a single countable unit, as in *een bier-tje* (a beer-DIM) 'a glass of beer' (Jurafsky 1996).

As shown in section 17.3.2.3, set nouns can also appear with a singulative marker (which is presumably inflectional rather than derivational), but there is an important difference: whereas an unmarked morphological collective noun always denotes a group of multiple objects (like Breton *gwez* 'trees, forest'), an unmarked set noun is transnumeral, which means it can also be used to talk about a single object.

In numeral classifier languages like Thai (examples (3) and (4); see also section 17.3.3.1), expressions that are used to talk about collective entities contain what is sometimes called a (quantitative) collective classifier, as in this example from Burmese (Okell 1969: 211): *pyà hnǎ ouñ* (bee(s) two swarm$_{CLF}$) 'two swarms of bees'. Collective classifiers (as well as collective aspect markers, section 17.3.2.3) constitute one of the historical sources from which plural markers may develop (Rijkhoff 2004: 116–117). Collective nouns are assigned their own noun class (often noun class 14) in Bantu languages (section 17.3.2). For an account of the way speakers talk about collective entities like a choir or a boat crew in Samoan, a language that is claimed not to distinguish syntactically between major lexical word classes, see Mosel & Hovdhaugen (1992: 89–93).

17.3.2.3 Set nouns

The third nominal subcategory whose members can be directly modified by a cardinal numeral concerns the number-neutral or transnumeral SET NOUNS, so-called because they designate a set entity, rather than an individual object or a collective. A set may contain any number of individuals, including 'one' (in which case we talk about a singleton set). Set nouns are attested in many languages, where they often occur alongside members of another nominal subcategory, such as singular object nouns (section 17.3.2.1; see also sections 17.3.1 and 17.4.1 on set nouns co-occurring with sort nouns). In such cases, the singular object nouns tend to be used to talk about humans or higher animals, whereas the set nouns usually denote lower animals or inanimate entities (Rijkhoff 2004: 30).

Since set nouns have only recently been recognized as a distinct nominal subcategory, they will receive some extra attention here. Set nouns are sometimes called general number nouns (Corbett 2000: 9–18, 73), together with sort nouns (section 17.3.3.1), but there are important differences (n. 6); for example, set nouns—unlike sort nouns—do not require a numeral classifier when modified by a cardinal numeral. Confusingly, set nouns are sometimes regarded as collective nouns or mass nouns (e.g. Ojeda 1998: 249; Corbett 2000: 5, 13; Wiese 2012).

17.3.2.3.1 Set nouns and numerals

When a set noun is modified by a numeral, it remains in its unmarked, transnumeral form, as shown in these examples from Oromo and Turkish (see Lewis 1967: 25–26; see Schroeder 1999 for a detailed study of Turkish nouns and noun phrases):

Oromo (Cushitic) (Stroomer 1987: 107)
(14) a. *gaala*   b. *gaala   lamaani*
       camel(s)   camel(s)   two
       'camel' or 'camels'   'two camels'

Turkish (Altaic) (Görgülü 2012: 69; Bamyacı et al. 2014: 25)
(15) a. *çocuk*   b. *beş   çocuk*
         child(ren)   five   child(ren)
         'child' or 'children'   'five children'

This suggests that a cardinal numeral which modifies a set noun serves a different function than a numeral that modifies a member of the other two + Shape noun types. Whereas in the case of a singular object noun or a collective noun the modifying numeral seems to multiply the number of singular objects or collectives (hence the plural -s suffix in *two umbrella-s* and *two crew-s*), in the case of a set noun the numeral seems to specify the number of members that make up the set. In other words, when a cardinal numeral modifies a set noun, we do not get multiple sets; instead the numeral seems to indicate the size of the (single) set.

In some languages, a noun phrase headed by a numerated set noun triggers singular number agreement on the verb. This has been labelled 'number discord', which appears to be a misnomer because number agreement is with the set, which is always a singular entity, whether it contains one or more individuals. Below is an example from Oromo, but the same phenomenon is attested in other languages with subject–verb agreement in which the subject noun phrase is headed by a set noun, such as the Caucasian (Kartvelian) language Georgian (Harris 1981: 22) and Lango (Noonan 1992: 168).

Oromo (Stroomer 1987: 59, 107)
(16) *gaala   lamaani   sookoo   d'ak'-e*
       camel(s)   two   market   go-3SG.M.PAST
       'Two camels went to the market.'

17.3.2.3.2 Set nouns and nominal aspect marking

In some languages, set nouns can optionally appear with what superficially looks like a plural number marker (although this element is normally absent when the set noun is modified by a cardinal numeral) or even a so-called singulative number marker (see e.g. Stroomer 1987: 74–88). However, due to the distinctive semantic and formal properties of these so-called number markers, it has been argued that they are better analysed as members of another grammatical category: NOMINAL ASPECT MARKERS (the nominal counterparts of verbal aspect markers; Rijkhoff 2004: 101–121). Whereas number markers are concerned with quantitative properties of the referent, nominal aspect markers specify a QUALITATIVE property of the referent, viz. the KIND of set the speaker is referring to: a set with just one member (singleton set) or a set that has multiple members (collective or distributive set). Confusingly, the term 'singulative marker' is also used in connection with morphological collectives (section 17.3.2.2), but whereas this element seems to derive a singular object noun from a morphological collective noun (and collectives always involve multiple individuals), a singulative marker on a transnumeral set noun has a specifying (disambiguating) function.

Notice that genuine number marking would be logically or semantically incompatible with the transnumeral character of set nouns: the 'singular' or 'plural' of a number-neutral noun leads to nonsensical analyses (see also section 17.3.3.1 on the absence of number marking on sort nouns, another transnumeral subtype). Rather than indicating the number of individual objects or collectives (sections 17.3.2.1 and 17.3.2.2), nominal aspect markers specify whether the speaker refers to a singleton set (with just one member) or to a collective or distributive set (with multiple members). For example, in Oromo the collective marker is used on set nouns to refer to a group of individuals or objects (Stroomer 1987: 76). Nouns in several North American indigenous languages may occur with a distributive marker, which indicates the spread of individuals or objects of a group over various locations ('here and there') or over various sorts (Boas 1911a: 37–38; Mathiot 1967; Ojeda 1998: 248f.; Mithun 1999: 88–93; Corbett 2000: 111–120). For example, Mohawk *onén:ia'* means 'rock(s)' and *onenia'-shòn:'a* 'various rocks' (of assorted types, usually consisting of different shapes, sizes, and colours). In many languages, there is a historical connection between collective or distributive markers and plural markers. For example, a diachronic development from collective or distributive to plural has been observed in languages of Native North America (Boas 1911b: 444; Mithun 1999: 91) as well as languages from the Kartvelian, Mesoamerican, and Semitic families (Rijkhoff 2004: 116–117, fn. 22). Such a diachronic change also implies a shift from set noun to singular object noun (section 17.4.1).

It should be noted, finally, that our understanding of expressions of nominal collectivity and distributivity in languages across the globe is still rather inadequate, which is at least partly due the fact that the notions collectivity and distributivity, both of which presuppose multiplicity, have been defined and applied in rather different ways (Gill 1996; Corbett 2000: 111, 117). Notice also that in some languages a collective or distributive marker can (optionally) co-occur with a (true or apparent) plural marker, which is why, for example, Corbett (2000: 120) prefers to regard these markers as members of categories that are 'distinct from but related to number'.

17.3.3 Nouns that cannot be in a direct construction with a cardinal numeral

Three nominal subtypes have a negative value for the feature Shape (−Shape):

- SORT NOUNS (−Shape, −Homogeneity) like Thai *rôm*$_N$ 'umbrella(s) or *mánaaw*$_N$ 'lemon(s)' designate a non-agglomerative, spatially unbounded property of one or more objects;
- GENERAL NOUNS (−Shape) like Yucatec Mayan *há'as* (see (19) for examples) designate a property that is only characterized as not having a definite spatial outline;
- MASS NOUNS (−Shape, +Homogeneity) like English *water* or *butter* designate an agglomerative property that is characterized as not having a definite spatial outline.

Members of these nominal subtypes cannot be in a direct construction with a cardinal numeral; modification by a numeral typically requires the employment of an individualizing element such as a sortal or mensural classifier (languages in which nouns that are used to talk about masses can combine directly with a numeral are discussed in section 17.4.3).

The role of shape in grammar and cognition has often been investigated by comparing languages using −Shape nouns (notably 'classifier languages') with languages using + Shape nouns (Foley 1997: 239–245; also e.g. Lucy 1992 and Evans 2010). For example, Perniss et al. (2012) is concerned with the role of shape in Bora (a classifier language spoken in the

Amazonian regions of Columbia and Peru) and they found that its speakers systematically encode shape, more so than speakers of English and Spanish. Lucy (1992) is a comparative study of relations between language and cognition in English and Yucatec Maya, another classifier language (see section 17.3.3.2). Native speakers of both languages were first shown a single object and then two different objects. Subsequently they had to say which of the two different objects they believed resembled the first object most. It turned out that native speakers of English usually choose the object on the basis of its shape (e.g. box-shaped). Yucatec speakers, on the other hand, commonly focused on the kind of material the object was made of (e.g. cardboard), suggesting that the shape of the object played a far less important role (see Bowerman & Choi 2003 and Bowerman (2018: 134) on the role of first language acquisition in spatial categorization). Imai & Gentner (1993; 1997) reported similar results when they compared speakers of English and Japanese, another language that is deemed to use −Shape nouns for concrete objects (section 17.3.3.1). Li et al. (2009) is an attempt to account for these facts (which seem to confirm the idea of linguistic relativity, also known as the 'weak Whorfian hypothesis') in non-relativistic terms.[11]

The three −Shape subtypes (sort nouns, general nouns, mass nouns) are discussed in turn below.

17.3.3.1 Sort nouns

Members of the nominal subcategory SORT NOUN are used to refer to one or more concrete objects in the real world, even though these nouns do not seem to include the notion of spatial boundedness or discreteness as part of their lexical meaning (Lyons 1977: 460–466; Hundius & Kölver 1983; Bisang 1999).[12] As mentioned earlier, sort nouns as attested in, for example, languages spoken in East and mainland South East Asia are not marked for number and generally need individualizing elements, called sortal classifiers (a.k.a. numeral or count classifiers), when they are modified by a cardinal numeral.[13]

---

[11] On linguistic relativity, see, e.g., Grace 1987; Gumperz & Levinson 1996; Boroditsky 2003; Levinson 2003b; LaPolla 2020.

[12] In logical approaches to noun semantics, sort nouns have been analysed as members of various traditional, European nominal subcategories, such as collective nouns (Wiese 2012: 55) or mass nouns (Chierchia 1998b).

[13] Confusingly, the term 'classifier' has been used for a variety of elements; see, for example, Schroeder's (1999: ch. 4) discussion of 'the "so-called classifier" *tane*' in Turkish. The sortal (numeral, count) classifiers discussed in this section are typically attested in languages of East and mainland South-East Asia and must appear when sort nouns are counted. Elsewhere, in particular in e.g. Mesoamerica (e.g. Jacaltec) and in the Amazon region (e.g. Tariana or Yagua), elements that have also been called numeral classifiers are typically morphologically bound forms which also have inflectional or derivational properties (Payne 1987; Derbyshire & Payne 1990). Furthermore, these forms are often all part of a larger system of classificatory elements in the noun phrase, in which a single, complex system of 'multiple classifiers' seems to be composed of various subtypes (Craig 1986; Aikhenvald 2000; Seifart 2010: 722, 724). Systems with multiple or mixed classifiers are ignored here, because they tend to become 'increasingly heterogeneous and typological predictions associated with them (e.g. type-specific semantics or grammaticalization patterns) are weakened' (Seifart 2010: 724). As noted below, in some languages (erstwhile) numeral classifiers have also assumed non-individualizing functions due to grammaticalization (Bisang 2008c).

Thai (Hundius & Kölver 1983: 167)
(17)   lûuk   sǎam   khon
       child(ren)   three   CLF:PERSON
       'three children'

The wide meaning of sort nouns is often counterbalanced through coercion (Huang & Ahrens 2003) or by pragmatic factors (see Bisang 2009 and 2014 on hidden complexity). It is perhaps good to recall (section 17.3.1) that sort nouns as well as members of the other nominal subcategories discussed here are equally good exemplars of the lexical category Noun from a cross-linguistic perspective (Rijkhoff 2008: 738–739). The ambiguous or vague semantics of nouns with a 'wide meaning' (set nouns, sort nouns and general nouns) may be difficult to handle for grammatical theories that do not take contextual factors into account, but it makes them rather versatile ('flexible') for referential purposes (see also section 17.4.3 on the role of context).

As an illustration of the communicative or pragmatic versatility of sort nouns, consider these well-known examples from Burmese (Sino-Tibetan), which has various classifiers for *myiʔ* 'river(s)'. According to Becker (1975: 113; see also Hle Pe 1965; Vittrant 2005), it is possible to refer to a river in at least eight contexts:

Burmese (Sino-Tibetan) (Becker 1975: 113)
(18)   *myiʔ tə yaʔ*   'river one place' (e.g. destination for a picnic)
       myiʔ tə tan   'river one line' (e.g. on a map)
       myiʔ tə hmwa   'river one section' (e.g. a fishing area)
       myiʔ tə ʻsin   'river one distant arc' (e.g. a path to the sea)
       myiʔ tə θwɛ   'river one connection' (e.g. tying two villages)
       myiʔ tə ʻpa   'river one sacred object' (e.g., in mythology)
       myiʔ tə khu'   'river one conceptual unit' (e.g. in a discussion of rivers in general)
       myiʔ tə myiʔ   'river one river' (the unmarked case)

The number of sortal classifiers differs from language to language. If a language employs a large set of numeral classifiers, the way they are used depends on the speaker's social status and competence (Adams 1989). For a more detailed discussion of numeral classifiers, sometimes in the larger context of 'nominal classification' or 'noun categorization devices', see e.g. Aikhenvald 2000, Grinevald 2000 and 2007; Rijkhoff 2004: 115–117, 162–166; Seifart 2010; Bisang & Wu 2017.

It has been known for some time that sortal classifiers and plural markers appear to be mutually exclusive (Greenberg 1972; Sanches & Slobin 1973; it was stated in section 17.3.2.3 that genuine number markers are semantically incompatible with transnumeral nouns). Recently it has been suggested that there may be exceptions to this claim and that the so-called Greenberg–Sanches–Slobin generalization is a statistically highly significant correlation rather than an absolute universal (Doetjes 2012; Tang & Her 2019; see Bisang 2012 and other chapters in Xu 2012 for critical discussion). It should be noted, however, that at least some of the (apparent) counterexamples involve an optional collective aspect marker on a set noun (section 17.3.2.3) rather than a true, compulsory plural marker on a singular object noun. For example, the so-called plural suffix *-men* in Mandarin Chinese is optional, incompatible with counting and restricted to human nouns, as in *háizi-men* '(a certain group of) children' (Norman 1988: 159). Iljic (2001: 95; see also Iljic 2005) calls *-men* a 'personal collective' which 'differs radically from the Indo-European plural endings' (Iljic 2001: 74) and argues that *-men* is probably the result of the grammaticalization of the Mandarin translational equivalent of 'clan'. This could indicate that certain nouns in Mandarin Chinese are in the process of changing (or already have changed) from sort noun to set noun.

It is important to note that due to language change, (erstwhile) numeral classifiers can assume non-individualizing functions in combination with e.g. demonstratives or adjectives (or rather stative verbs, which are typically used to express adjectival notions in South East Asian languages), where their appearance is often optional rather than compulsory (McGregor & Wichmann 2018). For example, Bisang (2008c) shows that Thai and other languages of East and mainland South East Asia also have highly grammaticalized classifiers, which no longer serve as individualizers of sort nouns, but have preserved their original phonological shape (i.e. grammaticalization without coevolution of form and meaning).

17.3.3.2 General nouns

There are also languages with transnumeral nouns that are used to talk about both objects and masses, called 'general nouns' (Rijkhoff 2004: 49f.). There do not seem to be many languages employing such general nouns, but Yucatec Maya appears to be one of them. According to Lucy (1992: 76, 83), this language does not make a fundamental distinction between sortal classifiers (section 17.3.3.1) and mensural classifiers (section 17.3.3.3) in the case of certain nouns (which may be few in number): hence we have labelled these elements 'general classifiers'. Here are some examples of general classifiers which all involve the general noun *háas* and which, as shown below, are rather difficult to translate into English.

Yucatec Maya (Mayan) (Lucy 1992: 74)

(19) a. 'un-ɛ'íit   háas   'one/a 1-dimensional banana (i.e. the fruit)'
     b. 'un-wáal   háas   'one/a 2-dimensional banana (i.e. the leaf)'
     c. 'un-p'éel háas   'one/a 3-dimensional banana (i.e. the fruit)'
     d. 'un-kúul   háas   'one/a planted banana (i.e. the plant/tree)'
     e. 'un-kúuch háas   'one/a load banana (i.e. the bunch)'
     f. 'um-p'íit háas   'a_little_bit_of/some banana'
        a/one-CLF banana(s)

17.3.3.3 Mass nouns

Just like 'collective noun', the label 'mass noun' is sometimes applied in rather unusual ways. For example, in certain logical approaches to word classes (e.g. Borer 2005a: 108), it has been suggested that at some abstract, underlying level of representation all nouns start out as mass nouns. By contrast, this section is concerned with mass nouns as an overt nominal subcategory, i.e. nouns whose lexicalized meanings have a negative value for the feature Shape (−Shape) and a positive value for the feature Homogeneity (+Homogeneity). As indicated in section 17.3.1, this does not necessarily mean that there is a direct relationship between the denotation of a mass noun and what counts as a mass from a physical or ontological standpoint. This is shown by the fact that the same physical entity can be referred to by using a count noun in one language and by a mass noun in another language, as in the case of English *onion*~CountN~ and its Russian translational counterpart *luk*~MassN~ (Wierzbicka 1985: 314): the difference between mass nouns and count nouns rests in the coded features of the nouns rather than properties of physical entities in the external world.

The current chapter does not explore possible cognitive or cultural reasons why, within or across languages, speakers are not consistent in discriminating between objects and masses (Koptjevskaja-Tamm 2006). Thus, any motivations behind the choice between mass noun vs count noun in cases like 'foliage'~Mass~ vs 'leave(s)'~Count~, 'gravel'~Mass~ vs 'pebble(s)'~Count~ or 'mail~Mass~ vs letter(s)'~Count~ remain undiscussed here (Wierzbicka 1985; Middleton et al. 2004; Wisniewski 2010: 168; see Levin & Rappaport Hovav 2011 on such mass–count doublets). Instead this section aims to give a brief overview of the way mass nouns are distinguished from other nominal subcategories across languages, using as the key diagnostic feature the compulsory employment of a measure construction when a numerically unmarked noun is modified by a cardinal numeral (see Greenberg 1972: 16). The requirement that the noun must occur in its unmarked form excludes plural count nouns like 'books' or 'flowers' in expressions like *two boxes of books* or *two bunches of flowers*, where 'box' and the collective noun 'bunch' might also be interpreted as measure terms. The same requirement also means that pluralized mass nouns like 'wines' are excluded in, for example, *We tasted three or four wines*, because here 'wines' refers to different, countable types of the mass entity (see Dik (1997: 14) on 'subcategorial conversion'; see also Doetjes 2012 and 2017). Languages that are deemed to lack a separate category of mass nouns are discussed in sections 17.4.2 and 17.4.3.

The actual form of the measure construction can vary from language to language. For example, whereas English uses a measure term with a preposition, like 'cup of' in *two cups of tea*, the preposition is absent in Dutch *twee koppen thee*, lit. 'two cups tea'. Mass nouns in classifier languages also require a measure construction, which in these languages involves the use of a mensural rather than a sortal classifier (Cheng & Sybesma 1998; Cheng 2012). Differences between measure terms and mensural classifiers are discussed in e.g. Allan 1977, Grinevald 2005, and Doetjes 2012.

Thai (Hundius & Kölver 1983: 170)
(20) náamtaan   sǎam   thûaj
      sugar   three   cup
      'three cups of sugar'

Across languages there are various ways to express the portions of a linguistic mass entity (see Koptjevskaja-Tamm 2001 for an overview), in addition to (a) the construction that involves the use of an adposition as exemplified by the English *two cups of tea*, (b) the 'zero-strategy' exemplified by Dutch *twee koppen thee* (lit. 'two cups tea'), and (c) the variant that involves a mensural classifier (as in the Thai example (20)), there are also languages that use case marking, as in:

Russian (Slavic) (Koptjevskaja-Tamm 2001: 524)
(21) čaška   čaja/čaju
      cup:NOM   tea:GEN/tea:PRTV
      'a cup of tea'

It has been argued that measure terms like Italian *manciata* 'fistful' in *una manciata di riso* ('a fistful of rice') or *bottiglia* 'bottle' in *una bottiglia di whisky* ('a bottle of whisky') belong to the category of so-called light nouns (Simone & Masini 2014), i.e. the nouns that are less than fully referential in certain syntactic contexts, in particular when they occur as part of a binominal construction as in the two examples above (on binominal NPs, see e.g. Foolen 2004 or Kim & Sells 2014). In such constructions, it is sometimes not clear which noun is the semantic head (Brems 2003; Doetjes 2017). Notice, finally, that classifiers have also been analysed as more or less grammaticalized elements, with sortal classifiers perhaps more at the more grammatical end of the continuum than mensural classifiers (Craig 1992).

17.3.4 The role of Shape and the place of nouns in an implicational hierarchy of word classes

It was shown above that nouns with a positive or a negative value for the feature Shape appear to correlate with various grammatical properties. Here we briefly mention yet another area where the feature Shape appears to play a significant role, namely the parts-of-speech hierarchy proposed in Hengeveld (1992b: 68):

(22)   Verb > Noun > Adjective > (manner) Adverb

This hierarchy states, for example, that languages with a distinct class of adjectives must also have distinct classes of nouns and verbs and, importantly, that it may or may not have a dedicated class of manner adverbs. Thus, the implication only works one way: having a distinct class of nouns implies the language also has a distinct class of verbs, but it does not necessarily mean that the same language also has distinct classes of adjectives and manner adverbs.

An important question is: what determines whether a language can have the next word class in the hierarchy shown in (22)? Restricting ourselves momentarily to nouns and adjectives, data from a representative sample of the world's languages indicate that all languages with a distinct class of adjectives also employ nouns which can be counted directly, i.e. +Shape nouns (Figure 17.1). In other words, it seems that the implication 'if a language has adjectives, then it has nouns', can now be reformulated more precisely as follows: 'if a language has adjectives, then it has +Shape nouns' (Rijkhoff 1999). The reverse is not true, i.e. languages with + Shape nouns do not necessarily have a distinct class of adjectives. For example, both Dutch and Lango have + Shape nouns (examples (6)–(8)), but whereas Dutch has distinct classes of verbs, nouns, and adjectives, Lango only has distinct classes of verbs and nouns and lacks a dedicated class of adjectives (Noonan 1992: 103). Speakers of Thai use –Shape nouns when they talk about objects like umbrellas and lemons, therefore nouns in this language lack the necessary positive value for the feature Shape (+Shape) that would allow for the next lexical category in the hierarchy: a distinct class of adjectives.

Cross-linguistic data suggest that the role of the feature Shape is part of a larger picture, involving the coding of prototypical features of entities in the lexical meaning of verbs, nouns, and adjectives (Rijkhoff 2003 and 2008). Apparently, languages can only have these major word classes, if the basic meaning of the content words encodes prototypical properties of temporal or spatial entities (events and things). A prototypical event is a transitive activity involving an agent and a patient; a prototypical thing is a concrete, physical object. Thus, a language can only have major, distinct classes of verbs, nouns and adjectives, if the lexicon contains (a) lexemes that designate a dynamic relationship between an agent and a patient (i.e. transitive verbs), and (b) lexemes that designate a property that is specified as having a boundary in the spatial dimension (i.e. +Shape nouns). A modified version of the hierarchy that includes the necessary (but not: sufficient) semantic features looks as follows (see Rijkhoff 1999 and 2003 for details, with examples of languages occupying different positions in the hierarchy):

(23)   Verb   > Noun   > Adjective   >manner Adverb
   CONDITION: $V_{+Transitive}$ N_{+Shape} $?A_{+Gradable}$

The question mark under manner Adverb indicates that more cross-linguistic research is needed to determine if it is the feature + Gradable in the lexical meaning of adjectives that is required to allow for the occurrence of next distinct word class: manner Adverbs (see Wierzbicka 1986: 374–377; Beck 2011; Constantinescu 2015).

17.4 OTHER PART-OF-SPEECH SYSTEMS AND LANGUAGE CHANGE

In addition to the nouns that belong to the six nominal subcategories discussed in sections 17.3.2 and 17.3.3, there are lexemes denoting properties of spatial entities that do not quite fit the six-way classification presented in Figure 17.1. On closer inspection, such lexemes belong to at least three different groups:

(a) true nouns that are in the process of changing nominal subcategory (section 17.4.1);
(b) words which, properly speaking, are not dedicated nouns but lexemes that belong to a flexible word class (section 17.4.2).
(c) true nouns that are underspecified for the count vs mass distinction (section 17.4.3). Since these 'count–mass' nouns can be characterized in terms of Shape and Homogeneity, they could be added to the classification of nominal subcategories in Figure 17.1.

Interestingly, measure constructions (section 17.3.3.3) seem to be absent in languages with lexemes of types (b) and (c); on this topic see, e.g., Greenberg 1972: 17).

17.4.1 Nominal subcategories and language change

The role of language change can be illustrated with examples from Mandarin Chinese and Hmong Njua (see also n. 8 on gradience and continuity between linguistic categories). Both languages have what some have called plural markers and thus seem to contradict the idea that numeral classifiers (which appear with sort nouns) and plural markers (which appear on singular object and collective nouns) are mutually exclusive (see Xu 2012 for more discussion on this topic). It was already proposed in section 17.3.3.1 that human nouns in Mandarin are changing (or have changed) from sort noun to set noun and that the optional 'plural' suffix -*men* is better analysed as a collective aspect marker. Similar things can be said about Hmong Njua (Rijkhoff 1999: 241–242), which has sortal classifiers and where the collective classifier *cov* is said to be in the process of replacing all other classifiers to express 'plurality' (Harriehausen 1990: 115–117). According to Ratliff (1991), however, *cov* has a collective meaning and most probably derives from *cɔy*^{51} 'bunches or clusters of fruit' (superscript 51 indicates tone marks). In this case, too, one might argue that the nouns in question are changing membership from transnumeral sort noun to transnumeral set noun. Ultimately, these set nouns may turn into singular object nouns, as elements marking collectivity are a well-known diachronic source of plural markers (section 17.3.2.2; Rijkhoff 2004: 116–117).

17.4.2 The absence of the so-called count–mass distinction in languages with 'nominals' (a flexible word class of Australian languages)

In quite a few languages, problems in assigning lexemes to one of the six nominal subtypes in Figure 17.1 may be attributed to the fact that these languages lack a distinct class of nouns (recall that this chapter is only concerned with languages in which nouns constitute a separate word class), but instead have lexemes that belong to a so-called flexible word class (Rijkhoff & van Lier 2013). Languages with a flexible word class not only include languages with a single class of lexemes (called 'contentives' in Hengeveld 1992b, 2013) like Samoan or Tongan (see section 17.1), in which there is no clear distinction between verbs, nouns and members of other lexical categories, but also languages with a word class that Hengeveld coined 'non-verbs'. These languages have two major lexical word classes: (a) a distinct class of verbs and (b) a flexible class of non-verbs whose members translate in other languages as a noun or as an adjective (or even as a manner adverb). Such flexible lexemes are attested, for example, in Australian languages, many of which have a word class called 'nominals', which translate as nouns or adjectives in English (Dixon 1980: 271; Donaldson 1980: 70–71; McGregor 2013: 222; McGregor 2019b). The evidence suggests that members of the flexible class of non-verbs are not lexically coded to specifically denote a mass or a collective. Perhaps this should not be surprising: if a language has no dedicated class of nouns, nominal subcategories can at best be a marginal phenomenon.

17.4.3 The absence of a count–mass distinction in languages in languages with a separate class of nouns

There are quite a few languages in which notional count and mass nouns essentially share the same 'mini-grammar' (Wiltschko 2012; Lima 2018). Whereas members of the Australian class of 'nominals' are strictly speaking flexible lexemes rather than dedicated nouns (section 17.4.2), many native North American languages have count–mass words that appear to be true nouns. These languages also lack a separate class of adjectives (just like many Australian languages), but here adjectival notions ('qualities') are expressed through verbs or nouns (Mithun 1999: 56). Another conspicuous difference between 'non-verbs' or 'nominals' in Australian languages and count–mass nouns in native North American languages concerns plural marking. In some North American Indian languages with a category of count–mass nouns, all members can appear with a plural marker. For example, in Ojibwe, where the count vs mass distinction is absent, all nouns can be pluralized (Rhodes 1990: 153–154; as reported in Corbett 2000: 87; for similar cases, see e.g. Mithun 1999: 80).

> In Ojibwa, there is no grammatical distinction like the mass/count distinction of Indo-European. Thus, *mkwam* can equally mean 'ice' or 'a piece of ice'. *Nbiish* can mean 'water' or 'an amount of water'.
>
> Nouns which might be expected not to have a plural do in fact form plurals freely, interestingly with the unit reading and not with the sort reading. Thus *mkwam* 'ice' or 'piece of ice', *mkwamiig* (plural) 'pieces of ice'. Rhodes is unable to find a noun that cannot be pluralized in Ojibway.

The absence of a count–mass distinction in nouns was also noted in Greenberg (1972: 16–17, referring to Whorf 1941: 80), who wrote that Hopi and many other native American Indian languages have no formally distinct category of mass nouns, as shown by the fact that, for example, numerals can directly modify nouns used to talk about masses and nouns used for countable objects: 'One says [in Hopi] not "a glass of water" but *kəˈyí* "a water" [...] not "a piece of meat" but *sikwí* "a meat"'. The fact that it is possible to say something like 'I brought them two water' (i.e. without a mensural construction) in languages with a category of count–mass nouns could be accounted for by assuming that the cultural or physical context would give sufficient clues about the appropriate container for the occasion. This is explicitly stated to be the case in, for example, the Brazilian language Yudja.

(24) Yudja (Tupi) (Lima 2018: 7, 13–14)
   Una   txabïu   apeta   izaku
   1S   three   blood   see
   'I saw three units of blood' (the unit—drops, puddles, or containers—is identified by the context; in this case the speaker was referring to drops)

(25) Una   txabïu   awïla   wãẽ   he   izaku
   1S   three   honey   pan   in   see
   'I saw three pans of honey' or 'I saw portions of honey in a pan' (with a container like 'pan' the sentence may interpret both as referring to the units of counting (e.g. 'I saw three pans that contained honey') or as the location of these units)

This is probably not very different from wat happens when a speaker of Dutch orders coffee in a café or restaurant, as in: '*Mag ik één/twee/drie/... koffie?*' (lit. 'May I one/two/three/... coffee?') 'I'd like to order one/two/three/... cups of coffee' where the Dutch mass noun *koffie* 'coffee' is directly modified by a numeral, i.e. without the usual measure construction, which requires a measure term like 'cup' as in *two cups of coffee*. Such a request is perfectly acceptable in restricted contexts ('pragmatic coercion') and it is clear that the unexpressed measure here is 'cup' (Greenberg 1972: 16; Lyons 1977: 463; see LaPolla 2020 for an overview on the role of context in linguistics in the last two centuries; also Malinowski 1923).

As mentioned earlier, one could assume that in languages like Ojibwa the count–mass lexemes constitute a underspecified nominal subcategory in their own right with neutral values for the features Shape and Homogeneity, which would suggest that these count–mass nouns are simply characterized as designating properties of spatial entities, including spatial entities with or without a perceptual distinct spatial contour (±Shape) as well as entities with or without an internal structure (±Homogeneity).

17.5. OTHER PROPERTIES OF LANGUAGES WITH A DEDICATED CLASS OF NOUNS

The previous sections offered a predominantly lexically meaning-based classification of nouns with some attention for certain associated formal properties (such as the employment of number markers, nominal aspect markers or numeral classifiers) to the extent that they reflect semantic features of the various nominal subcategories. This section briefly mentions some other general properties of nouns, and how some of these properties are interconnected, beginning with genders and noun classes.

Systems of nominal categorization occupy an important place in the literature on nouns, as only true nouns can be assigned to a grammatical gender or noun class (Rijkhoff 2008: 730). If a language has genders or some other system of noun categorization, it must have a distinct class of nouns. However, the reverse does not hold, as there are many languages with nouns but without nominal genders or noun classes, including English. Another important generalization concerning gender or noun class was proposed by Greenberg (1966: 95): '*Universal 36*. If a language has a category of gender, it always has the category of number'. Nouns can also be classified in terms of parameters like Animacy, Incorporability (Woodbury 1975) or Possession (e.g. alienably vs inalienably possessed nouns; Chappell & McGregor 1996). Due to space limitations, such cases are not discussed here; instead the reader is referred to the large number of detailed publications on gender and other systems of nominal classification.[14]

Greenberg (1966: 93) also put forward a universal about the ordering of derivation and inflectional affixes on nouns and other lexemes. Universal 29 reads as follows: 'If both the derivation and inflection follow the root, or both precede the root, the derivation is always between the root and the inflection'. Morphological and other properties of the noun are also discussed in Lehmann & Moravcsik (2000); general, cross-linguistic overviews of the way new (derived) nouns are formed (including locational nouns) can be found in Bauer (2007, 2013) and Lieber (2017), in some languages, nouns are classified on the basis

---

[14] See, for example, Fodor 1959; Greenberg 1978; Craig 1986; Corbett 1991; Aikhenvald 2000 and 2006; Unterbeck et al. 2000; Seifart 2010; Corbett 2014; McGregor & Wichmann 2018. A comprehensive bibliography on this topic by Alexandra Aikhenvald (2011) can be found under the heading 'Classifiers' in *Oxford Bibliographies Online* (http://www.oxfordbibliographies.com).

of morphophonological criteria that determine the form of the appropriate plural marker (Rijkhoff 2004: 79–80; Terrill 2003: 105, 112–125). Furthermore, in Vinmavis and some other Oceanic languages 'the majority of nouns have initial *n*-, which is historically not part of the root' (Crowley 1985: 165). This is due to grammaticalization of an erstwhile determiner that gradually became an integral part of the noun (on this topic, see also Greenberg 1981 and 1991; Hoskison 1983: 24). It also appears that nouns and verbs can display distinct phonological behaviour. More specifically, in certain languages nouns appear to show more phonological contrasts than verbs. For example, Spanish nouns, but not verbs, have contrastive stress location (Smith 1997, 2011).

There has also been a considerable amount of neuroscientific research on the way verbs and nouns are processed in the brain; for a recent overview see Vigliocco et al. 2011 (also Chapter 44 in this volume). In the area of first language acquisition, it has been argued that there is a (possibly language specific) noun bias, in that children seem to produce more nouns than verbs in the early stages of first language acquisition (see Childers 2014). Another difference between nouns and verbs is reported in a study by Seifart et al. (2012), who found that 'there is a robust cross-linguistic tendency for slower speech before nouns compared with verbs, both in terms of slower articulation and more pauses'. They argue that this slowdown effect is due to the increased amount of planning that nouns require compared with verbs.

17.6 CONCLUSION

This chapter has offered a cross-linguistic classification of basic (underived, unmarked) nouns that are used to talk about spatial objects, and which is based on the lexical features Shape and Homogeneity (section 17.3.1). It may be worth emphasizing once again that this concerns a linguistic classification of nouns and not a classification of physical objects in the real world. Four nominal subcategories are characterized by a combination of positive or negative values for the lexical features Shape and Homogeneity ('Likepartedness'): singular object nouns (+Shape, −Homogeneity), collective nouns (+Shape, +Homogeneity), sort nouns, (−Shape, −Homogeneity), and mass nouns (−Shape, +Homogeneity). Nouns characterized by the feature + Shape designate a property with a spatial outline, which means they can be counted directly; nouns that have a negative value for the feature Shape (−Shape) require an extra, individualizing element (e.g. a sortal or mensural classifier) when they are modified by a cardinal numeral. Two nominal subcategories in this classification have a neutral value the feature Homogeneity: set nouns (+Shape) and general nouns (−Shape). Some languages appear to have an undifferentiated nominal subcategory, whose members can be used to talk about objects as well as masses (section 17.4.3). This seems to indicate that these mass–count nouns have neutral values for both Shape and Homogeneity.

CHAPTER 18

ADJECTIVES

DAVID BECK

OF the 'big three' parts of speech—nouns, verbs, and adjectives—adjectives are in many ways the best suited for the typological study of parts-of-speech systems. Unlike nouns and verbs, which are regarded by most researchers as universal (or, at least, categorizations applicable to all but a very few languages—Croft 1991; Evans & Osada 2005), most researchers accept that there are languages with no, or few, words that we would want to call 'adjectives'. Like nouns and verbs, adjectival classes have a fairly strong association with a particular semantic domain, that of property concepts (Thompson 1988); however, unlike meanings most typical of the other two classes, individual property concepts are frequently lexicalized as adjectives in one language but belong to different parts of speech in others (e.g. 'hard': Eng. *hard*$_{ADJ}$, Lushootseed *x̌tadis*$_V$, Hauta *t'auṛi*$_N$). For this reason, determining the most desirable classification of property concept words in specific languages can be difficult. In Otomí, for example, one group of words expressing property concepts serves in the syntactic role we expect of adjectives, adnominal modifier, in contexts such as that shown in (1):

Otomí (Otomanguean, Mexico) (Palancar 2006: 331)
(1) da='<ñ>ế't'-Ø-a[=nŏ=r   bojó   Ø   Ø=dǒtá]
     3FUT=<NPS>place.volume-3OBJ-B[=DEF.SG=SG iron   REL   3PRES=be.big $_{NP}$]
     'They'd set up the big iron (i.e., the crane).'

Here we find a word, *dǒtá* 'big', which both modifies a noun and expresses a property concept, and this might naturally incline us to place *dǒtá* in the class of adjectives. However, as is apparent from the gloss, Palancar (2006), analyses this word and others of its kind as a verb, and treats the modification construction in (1) as a relative clause. Part of the evidence for this is seen in (2), where the same lexical item appears as the syntactic predicate of a sentence, bearing overt aspectual inflection:

(2) ma   ngǔ   mí=dǒtá
     1POSS   house   3IMP=be.big
     'My house was big.'

(Palancar 2006: 333)

Evidence for Palancar's assertion that the structure in (1) is a relative clause comes from the examination of additional examples of words in this group:

(3) dá=hŏx-'-a[='na=r   t'ó   nŏ   xi=mě]
    1PST=bring-2DAT.OBJ-B[=INDEF.SG=SG stick REL.SG 3PFV=be.hard _{NP}]
    'I brought you a hard stick.'

(Palancar 2006: 331)

(4) nú=nú=r   ză   xi=mě
    DEF=DEM.II.SG=SG   wood   3PFV=be.hard
    'That stick is hard.'

(Palancar 2006: 333)

Unlike (1), where dŏtá is analysed as bearing a zero TAM/person clitic, mě 'hard' in (3) has an overt perfective aspect marker attached to it, the same clitic that expresses the perfective when mě acts as the predicate of a simple clause in (4). In addition, the relative clause in (3) is introduced by a relative pronoun, nŏ.[1] As Palancar (2006) demonstrates, the full range of morphosytactic behaviours of words like dŏtá and mě, both in modifying and predicative roles, is identical to that of verbs (or, more specifically, monovalent verbs expressing states), leading Palancar to conclude that such words in Otomí are better classified as verbs than as adjectives.

It is because the syntactic distribution of words expressing property concepts is so variable, and their morphosyntax so language-specific, that their cross-linguistic study forces us to confront some of the most fundamental issues in the analysis of typological variation in parts of speech, not least of which is what is meant by the term 'part of speech' itself. The range of proposals found in the literature run the full gamut from claims that parts of speech are structural categorizations reflecting innate formal features of a universal grammar (e.g. Baker 2003) to positions where parts of speech are purely language specific groupings that provide little, or no, basis for cross-linguistic comparison (e.g. Haspelmath 2012a). For the purposes of this chapter, I have adopted an essentially lexicographic, semasiological approach somewhere in the middle, whereby parts of speech are treated as categorizations imposed by linguists on groups of words based on commonalities of syntactic behaviour and meaning, many of which are commonly shared across languages. Parts of speech are considered, as they have been traditionally, to be high-level taxonomic distinctions among lexemes—as opposed to roots or inflected word forms—defined by their distribution with respect to generalized syntactic roles/functions and by the semantic class of the meanings expressed by most or all of their members, as shown in Table 18.1. The term 'adjective' will be used to describe a lexical–syntactic class of word that contains primarily expressions of property concepts and whose syntactic distribution can be distinguished from that of other word classes in that it shows a specialization for adnominal modification. While this is a common approach to the issue, it is by no means universal, and in what follows I will take care to highlight some of the different conclusions that have been reached by analysts with

---

[1] According to Palancar (2009: 121), the relative pronoun is optional in relative clauses, hence its absence from (1).

alternate points of view. A comparative approach to both linguistic data and theory seems most likely to shed light on adjective classes across languages, and to highlight some of the current methodological issues in the typological study of parts-of-speech systems.

Table 18.1 Semantic class and syntactic function

	Syntactic argument	Clausal predicate	Adnominal modifier
Object	Noun		
Action		Verb	
Property concept			Adjective

This chapter begins with an examination of the core semantic domain expressed by words typically described as adjectives, that of property concepts (section 18.1), followed by a discussion of the core syntactic function associated with the adjectival class, modification (section 18.2). The issue of typological variation in adjectives will be discussed in section 18.3, which presents case studies of languages where the distinction between adjectives and verbs (section 18.3.1) and adjectives and nouns (section 18.3.2) is claimed to be absent, as well as examples of languages where adjectives show overlap in syntactic function with one (section 18.3.3) or more (section 18.3.4) lexical classes. The implications that the cross-linguistic diversity and variation observed in this chapter have for typology and for debates about language specificity and universalism will be considered in the conclusion (section 18.4).

18.1 PROPERTY CONCEPTS

Perhaps the only aspect of words classified as adjectives on which there is widespread consensus is that cross-linguistically their meanings cluster around the semantic domain of 'property concepts' (Thompson 1988). Property concepts are generally characterized as meanings that fall into one of the following seven categories identified by Dixon (1982):

(5) Categories of property concepts
 DIMENSION — 'big', 'small', 'long', 'wide' ...
 AGE — 'new', 'young', 'old' ...
 VALUE — 'good', 'bad', 'pure', 'delicious' ...
 COLOUR — 'red', 'black', 'white' ...
 PHYSICAL PROPERTIES — 'hard', 'heavy', 'smooth' ...
 HUMAN PROPENSITY — 'jealous', 'happy', 'clever', 'generous', 'proud' ...
 SPEED — 'fast', 'slow', 'quick' ...

In addition to these seven, a few other categories have been identified as being commonly lexicalized as adjectives. Dixon (2004) lists, inter alia, DIFFICULTY ('easy', 'hard', 'simple'), SIMILARITY ('like', 'unlike', 'similar'), and POSITION ('high', 'low', 'near'). Another category that has been proposed is that of HUMAN CHARACTERISTICS ('elder', 'youthful', 'mute'), which frequently constitutes a distinctive subclass of property concept words, particularly with respect to being able to function flexibly as both nouns and adjectives (Beck 1999a, 2002).

In languages with small adjective classes, Dixon (1982) observes that the members of this class tend to belong to the first four semantic domains, DIMENSION, AGE, VALUE, and COLOUR. In the Bantu language Venda, for example, there are 20 adjectives, shown in Table 18.2. Seven are expressions of DIMENSION, two of AGE, two of VALUE, and seven of COLOUR, while the remaining three belong in other categories. Languages like Venda are often said to have a 'closed' class of adjectives, the analogy here being to parts of speech like adpositions and determiners, which are numerically small and only infrequently change their membership through neologism or derivation. How well this analogy holds with adjectives is somewhat unclear. Closed classes tend to be highly grammaticized and express fairly abstract meanings, whereas adjectives express concepts that are traditionally thought of as being 'lexical' as opposed to grammatical. Claims that adjectival classes are closed are rarely backed up with historical evidence that their membership is not subject to frequent change, nor is it clear how infrequent that change needs to be to declare a class to be closed. Dixon (2004) suggests that the relevant criterion for a closed class is that it does not allow the addition of new members via borrowing; however, some languages that have been characterized as having a closed class of adjectives include borrowed lexical items in that class (e.g. Hausa—Newman 2000; Manange—Gennetti & Hildebrandt 2004). The fact that the frequency and type of lexical borrowing depends crucially on the type and intensity of language contact (Thomason & Kaufman 1988) suggests that by this criterion a closed class in a particular language would be as much a sociological artefact as a grammatical/typological one.

Table 18.2 Adjectives in Venda (Dixon 1982: 4–5)

hulu 'big'	*swa* 'young, new'	*rema* 'black'
ṭuku 'small'	*lala* 'old'	*tshena* 'white'
vhi 'bad'	*tete* 'soft'	*tswu* 'black'
lapfu 'long'	*khwivhilu* 'red'	*hulwane* 'important'
denya 'thick'	*sekene* 'thin'	*ṋu* 'wet'
vhisi 'raw, green'	*pfufhi* 'short'	*seṱha* 'yellow'
vhuya 'good-natured'	*tswuku* 'red'	

Whether or not it is meaningful to apply the term 'closed' to the adjectival class in any particular language, it is still true that there are many languages that are described as having adjectival classes with fewer than a dozen members. Such descriptions, of course, raise the question of how property concepts that are not expressed as adjectives are lexicalized in these languages. Dixon (1982) observes that:

1. DIMENSION, AGE, VALUE, and COLOUR terms, if not lexicalized as adjectives, tend to be lexicalized as verbs;
2. HUMAN PROPENSITY terms, if not lexicalized as adjectives, tend to be lexicalized as nouns;

3. PHYSICAL PROPERTIES, if not lexicalized as adjectives, tend to be lexicalized as verbs;
4. SPEED terms, if not lexicalized as adjectives, tend to be lexicalized as adverbs.

While more recent work on specific languages has suggested that there might be somewhat more variation than what Dixon initially encountered four decades ago, these observations still seem quite robust today and reflect genuine cross-linguistic preferences for lexical classification.

18.2 MODIFICATION

The consideration of languages with small adjectival classes also shows us that it is not possible to simply equate words expressing property concepts to the part-of-speech 'adjective': a language like Venda with 20 adjectives will certainly have many more lexical items expressing notions from this semantic domain that analysts have chosen to classify as other parts of speech. In general, the basis for this choice is functional or syntactic, with the term 'adjective' being reserved for words that serve as adnominal modifiers. A rationale for this approach is provided by Croft (1991), who observes that words that typically serve one of three principal 'pragmatic functions' have a tendency to express a particular class of meanings, as shown in Table 18.3. According to Croft, prototypical adjectives are words that express properties (or, in our terms, property concepts) and are used in modification. Not all words in a given language that express property concepts are necessarily adjectives, nor are words expressing meanings in one of the other broad semantic domains, object or action, necessarily excluded from the pragmatic function of modification, though it is predicted that these latter cases will typically be marked in some language-specific way in the grammar.

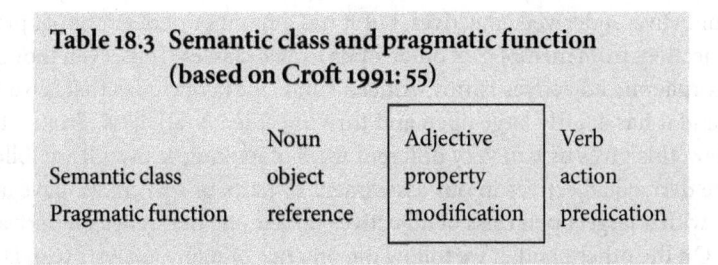

Table 18.3 Semantic class and pragmatic function (based on Croft 1991: 55)

	Noun	Adjective	Verb
Semantic class	object	property	action
Pragmatic function	reference	modification	predication

The link between the functional/syntactic role of modification and adjectives is also made by Hengeveld (1992a, 1992b), who defines an adjective as a lexical item that can be used as the modifier of a noun without recourse to any 'additional function-indicating morphosyntactic devices' (Rijkhoff & van Lier 2013: 8). Hengeveld (1992a: 58) illustrates such devices with the following set of English attributive constructions:

(6) a. the *intelligent* detective
    b. the *singing* detective
    c. the detective *who is singing*

For Hengeveld, only *intelligent* qualifies as an adjective, while *sing* does not. Whereas *intelligent* is simply juxtaposed to *detective* in order to serve as a modifier, the verb *sing* either requires the participial suffix *-ing* (6b) or it must be embedded in a relative clause (6c). Both of these measures, the suffix and the relative construction, qualify as function-indicating morphosyntactic devices.

The major practical objection to Hengeveld's approach is that it is often difficult to distinguish what types of morphosyntactic 'devices' are relevant for lexical classification, which devices are simply features of the modification construction, and which are subparts of the lexical item that we are trying to classify. Many languages, for instance, require adjectives to agree with the noun they modify (e.g. Sp. *el sombrero rojo* 'the red hat' vs *las rosas rojas* 'the red roses'), yet it would clearly not be desirable (or Hengeveld's intent) to use agreement to disqualify modifying words in such languages as adjectives, even if agreement is arguably a function-indicating morphosyntactic device. It is also unclear what role derivational morphology would play here. On the one hand, one might argue that a derived adjective like *hairy* in *the hairy detective* bears a function-indicating morpheme, *-y*, but it seems a mistake to conclude that *hairy* is not an adjective. A partial solution to this problem would be to treat part-of-speech classification as a taxonomy of lexemes. This takes most inflectional morphology like agreement out of the picture (inflected word forms belong to the same lexeme), and ensures that the item being classified is the lexeme *hairy* and not its derivational base, *hair*, given that they are distinct in meaning, form, and distribution.[2]

Whether or not derived forms are taken into account is of great importance to the question of whether or not a language is characterized as having a closed class of adjectives, as many languages with small classes of underived adjectives have adjective-forming derivational processes. Papantla Totonac, for example, has around 125 underived adjectives (Levy 1992), but, like other Totonacan languages, has a variety of means of deriving adnominal modifiers from verbs, adverbs, and (to a more limited extent) nouns (Levy 2004). An even more extreme example is Ewe (Ameka 1991). Ewe has traditionally been described as having only five underived adjectives, but it has a number of derivational processes for forming adjectives from members of other, open lexical classes. Thus, even though the class of monomorphemic adjectives is tiny, Ameka (1991: 108) concludes that 'Ewe is strongly adjectival and it has a fairly large open and thriving adjectiv(al) class'. From a typological point of view, this gives us two very different ways of looking at Ewe. If we follow Ameka and include derived adjectives in our assessment of parts of speech, we have a picture of a language with a large, open class of adjectives (albeit one that relies on derivation to fill this class). On the other hand, if we follow the practice of many analysts (e.g. Dixon 2004; Haspelmath 2012a) and exclude derived forms from consideration, Ewe appears to (almost) lack adjectives and to lexicalize property concepts for the most part as verbs. Which of the two views of Ewe, or other languages with 'open' closed classes, is preferred depends entirely on the goals of the analysis, in particular whether the focus is on how particular types of meanings are lexicalized (specifically, what meanings are lexicalized as adjectives?), on the organization of the lexicon (what parts of speech do we need to describe a particular language?), or on the existence or non-existence of adnominal modification in the syntax.

---

[2] This does not, however, account for the participial suffix *-ing*, which most analysts treat as inflectional, although it might be argued that its nature as a formative used to allow verbs to be extended to adnominal modification makes it a special case.

The question of whether (many) adjectives in a given language are derived or not is of more relevance to the first question, while the existence of processes to create adjectives is of more relevance to the latter two.

Nevertheless, many researchers deliberately steer clear of derived forms when investigating parts-of-speech inventories, in part because of the perceived challenges of distinguishing between word formation and other types of processes on purely structural grounds (e.g. Haspelmath 2010). This lack of attention to word formation and meaning highlights the second problem with a purely structure-based approach to lexical classification like Hengeveld's, which is the inability to distinguish formally identical lexical items that have different meanings in different contexts. This situation arises most commonly in two situations. The first, perhaps less relevant to adjectives than it is to the distinction between nouns and verbs (Vonen 2000; Evans & Osada 2005; Beck 2013), occurs in the context of *categorial conversion*, a morphological process that creates homophonous but distinct lexemes, each of which has a particular meaning associated with a particular syntactic role or roles (Mel'čuk 2006). Thus, for example, in Quechua we find the adjective *uchilla* 'small' used as an adnominal modifier, and the noun *uchilla* 'child' used as a syntactic argument (Floyd 2011). From a lexicographical or semasiological point of view, these would count as separate lexemes, in spite of their superficial formal identity, and so—if we take meaning into account—they would not count as evidence of overlapping distribution between adjectives and nouns.

A similar but more pervasive problem arises from constructions in which words that we might otherwise classify as nouns appear in attributive roles inside noun phrases, as in *straw hat*, *kitchen table*, and *winter jacket*. The presence of such constructions has been used to argue that certain languages do not distinguish adjectives from nouns based on the structural parallelism to phrases such as *stylish hat*, *low table*, and *green jacket*. The difficulty here is that the former constructions involve a non-compositional semantic relationship between the two words such that their combined meaning must be either learned by rote, be based on inference of a plausible semantic relation between the words, or be gleaned from context. In some cases, the meaning of the combination is transparent (i.e. intuitively plausible—*straw hat* 'hat MADE OF straw'), but the meanings of many combinations are not, and even nouns that are used in a transparent way may have different meanings in different contexts (*alligator shoes* 'shoes made from alligator hide', 'shoes made for alligators', 'shoes shaped like alligators', etc.—Mithun 1984). Ultimately such expressions—even if transparent or semi-arbitrary (not random, but not predictable)—are non-compositional (not the strict sum of their component meanings): either the dependent noun in a noun + noun combination like *straw hat* must be considered to have undergone a semantic shift, or the combination as a whole needs to be treated as a non-free lexicalized expression (a *phraseme*—Mel'čuk 1995). Bhat (1994) proposes that such uses of nouns indicate partial recategorization as adjectives and thus should not be used as a basis on which to claim that nouns and adjectives share a common distribution (i.e. the 'modifying' noun isn't exactly a noun anymore); Beck (1999a, 2002) goes a step further and argues that the presence of the understood semantic predicate ('hat MADE OF straw', 'table TYPICAL OF kitchens', 'jacket WORN DURING winter') means that such constructions are not genuine modification constructions at all, and therefore are not directly comparable to adjective–noun phrases such as *stylish hat*. The degree to which researchers attend to the meaning of lexical items has been at the heart of a great deal of discussion about lexical classification, and has led analysts to very different conclusions about the lexical inventories that languages have and which parts of speech are useful for descriptions of particular languages. We will return to this issue in section 18.3.2.

Thinking of adjectives in terms of modification rather than as simply 'words expressing property concepts' also allows us to recognize certain types of languages that may altogether lack a class of words dedicated to adnominal modification that we would want to call 'adjectives'. Languages that lack a part of speech able to fulfil a particular syntactic role are classified as 'rigid' languages by Hengeveld (1992a, 1992b). The most common pattern of rigidity with respect to adnominal modification is one where property concept words are largely categorized as verbs and adnominal modification is carried out by means of relative clauses (e.g. Lushootseed—Beck 1999a, 2002; Otomí—Palancar 2006; Wolof—McLaughlin 2004). Another type of rigid language would be one that lacks the syntactic function of adnominal modification altogether. This seems to be the case of Seneca, where the functional equivalent of adnominal modification is carried out by the incorporation of a noun to a property-concept verb, forming what is essentially a free or headless relative construction:

Seneca (Northern Iroquoian, Eastern North America) (Chafe 2012: 19–20, 24)
(7) *högwé'di:yo:h*
     h–ökwe't–iyo–:h
     MASC.SG.AGT–person–good–STA
     'nice man'

(8) *gakwáetgë'*
     ka–khw–ahetkë–'
     NEU.SG.AGT–food–bad–STA
     'bad food'

(9) *gajísdöje'*
     ka–tsist–ötye–'
     NEU.SG.AGT–ember–be.flying–STA
     'a flying ember'

The first two examples here are compounds formed by the incorporation of a noun (*-ökwe't-* 'person' in (7) and *-khw-* 'food' in (8)) to a verb stem (*-iyo-* 'be good' and *-ahetkë-* 'be bad', respectively), where the incorporated noun corresponds to the modified noun in the English gloss. These parallel exactly the structure in (9), where the noun *-tsist-* 'ember' is incorporated to the verb *-ötye-* 'be flying'; the resulting construction can, as shown here, be glossed as an English NP—specifically, a noun modified by the participial form of the verb *fly*.

Although (7)–(9) are glossed as noun phrases, in Seneca they are inflected verb forms, their nominal use reflecting the facility with which Iroquoian languages form complex substantival expressions from clauses (Sasse 1993; Mithun 2000). Such expressions are, out of context, potentially ambiguous between 'nominal' and 'clausal' readings, as Chafe (2012: 22) illustrates with the following examples:

Seneca (Northern Iroquoian, Eastern North America)

(10) *osde'*
      yo-ste-'
      NEU.SG.PAT-be.heavy-STA
      'it's heavy'
      'that which is heavy'

(11) *osgóäsde'*
      yo-skohr-a-ste-'
      NEU.SG.PAT-branch-LK-be.heavy-STA
      'it's a heavy branch' (lit. 'it is heavy in the manner of a branch')
      'a heavy branch' (lit. 'that which is heavy in the manner of a branch')

Each of the constructions here has two potential glosses, one as a clause and one as a free or headless relative construction. Clauses with the second interpretation are used in Seneca in substantival roles (i.e. as syntactic arguments). Structures with an incorporated noun such as that in (11) are the functional equivalent of adjective–noun constructions in English and other languages that have the syntactic role of adnominal modification necessary to identify a class of adjectives. An approach to adjectives based purely on semantics might, for Seneca, be able to classify a number of verbal roots like *-ste-* 'be heavy' as adjectives based on the fact that they express property concepts; however, as Chafe (2012) demonstrates, a class identified in this way shows no coherent set of morphosyntactic properties that would differentiate it consistently from other verbs, making the distinction of little utility for grammatical or lexicographical description.

18.3 ABSENCE AND FLEXIBILITY

Since Dixon (1982), typological work on variation in adjective classes has typically begun with identifying those words in a language that express property concepts and then sorting these according to their syntactic distribution. Property concept words that are found to function as adnominal modifiers are then classified as adjectives. One of the key findings of such investigations has been that in many languages the 'adjectival' class identified in this way is not wholly distinguishable in distribution from some other class(es) of word associated with other semantic domains. In such cases, the part-of-speech distinction between adjectives and some other lexical class X may be said to be *absent* (i.e. not descriptively relevant to the language), provided the following two conditions are met:

A. Adjectives are freely able to fill the syntactic role(s) taken by words belonging to class X;
B. Words belonging to class X are freely able to fill the role of adnominal modifier.

This sort of functional overlap is known in the literature as *flexibility* and lexical classes that serve more than one of the principal syntactic functions (argument, predicate, modifier) are referred to as being *flexible* (Hengeveld 1992a, 1992b; Rijkhoff & van Lier 2013).

In order for a part-of-speech distinction to be genuinely absent, flexibility must be *bidirectional* (Evans & Osada 2005)—that is, both the conditions in (A) and (B) must be met. As it turns out, bidirectional flexibility of adjectives with verbs (section 18.3.1) appears to be a reasonably well-attested pattern, whereas bidirectional flexibility between adjectives and nouns is somewhat more problematic (section 18.3.2). Another pattern commonly found across languages is that adjectives show flexibility with respect to the syntactic function of some other lexical class, but that flexibility is not reciprocated (i.e. condition A holds but B does not). This type of flexibility is *unidirectional* (Beck 2013) and under such circumstances the part-of-speech distinction can be maintained. Two such scenarios are considered in sections 18.3.3 and 18.3.4.

18.3.1 Bidirectional flexibility with verbs

There is general agreement among researchers that there are languages where the distinction between adjectives and verbs is absent.[3] As noted above, this claim requires an analyst to show that (a) property concept words are, on the whole, able to act as syntactic predicates (that is, they are able to fill the primary syntactic role of verbs), and (b) verbs are able to act as adnominal modifiers of nouns (that is, verbs are capable of filling the role of adjectives). In such languages, words expressing property concepts are classified by most analysts as verbs (as opposed to classifying what most people would consider to be verbs as adjectives).

One language that follows this pattern is Semelai, described in Nicole Kruspe's (2004) contribution to Dixon & Aikhenvald (2004).[4] In Semelai, property concepts appear freely as intransitive syntactic predicates, (12) and (13), and are structurally parallel to other intransitive verbs (14):

Semelai (Southern Aslian, Malaysia) (Kruspe 2004: 288, 298, 286)
(12) ləpɔc   deh   səlәh
     stomach 3PL   be.hungry
     'They were hungry.' (lit. 'Their stomachs were hungry.')

(13) dehn   lʊc   dədɛs
     3PLS   already   be.near
     'They (were) already near.'

(14) kənɔn   cʊh   təɲah   tərɔŋ
     offspring be.born   middle   path
     'The baby was born on the way.'

Words expressing property concepts like *səlәh* in (12) and *dədɛs* in (13) are distinguishable from words like *cʊh* in (14) only on the basis of a handful of morphological properties, most

---

[3] A notable exception is Dixon (2004), who (contra Dixon 1982) takes the position that all languages accord special treatment to at least a subset of property concept words.

[4] See also the discussion of Lao (Enfield 2004) in the same volume.

of them having to do with derivational potential and none of them having to do with syntactic distribution. Thus, while it is possible to find some criteria that single out a core group of property concepts, it is not clear that these are relevant for part-of-speech classification, or that other morphological tests could not be used to single out another subgroup of verbs which might then lay claim to its own part of speech.

In terms of adnominal modification, property concept words and intransitive verbs also pattern together:

Semelai (Southern Aslian, Malaysia) (Kruspe 2004: 296, 297)
(15) dɔs kəloc   bəri   deh, bəri   **jəruh**
     reach inside jungle 3PL   jungle be.deep
     'They reached the jungle, the deep jungle.'

(16) nəl–cəl   **ləmbut**
     NR–pronounce   be.weak
     'weak pronunciation'

(17) səmaʔ   **pər**
     people fly
     'flying people'

(18) rɛɲɛs, rɔh   dalɔŋ **kʰəbas**
     twig   branch tree   die
     'twigs (are) dead tree branches'

Property concepts words like *jəruh* (15) and *ləmbut* (16) and event/action words like *pər* (17) and *kʰəbas* (18) modify nouns through simple juxtaposition, predicating a property or state of the noun that precedes it. There is thus no distributional/functional distinction to be drawn between property concept words and intransitive verbs, leaving no basis on which to claim that they constitute separate parts of speech.

The situation with transitive verbs is, understandably, more complicated given that there are two semantic arguments (event participants) that could potentially correspond to the modified noun. According to Kruspe, if the noun modified by a transitive verb corresponds to the A (transitive subject), the verb must be inflected for imperfective aspect, and if the modified noun corresponds to the O (transitive object), the verb is required either to be in the middle voice or the irrealis mood. One infers from Kruspe's reference to such constructions as 'modification of the verb' (p. 297) and as 'derived forms' (p. 302, table 7) that she considers them not to be what we would call 'free' uses of transitive verbs as adnominal modifiers. This gives us the choice of either drawing a part-of-speech distinction between transitive verbs and a novel lexical class combining adjectives and monovalent stems expressing event/actions, or of classifying all three types of word as verbs. In the latter case, the difference in behaviour between transitive and monovalent stems used as modifiers would be treated as a valency-driven distinction within a single part of speech.[5]

---

[5] A similar situation is reported for the Salishan language Nuxalk in Beck (1999a, 2002).

18.3.2 Bidirectional flexibility with nouns

The other pattern often alluded to in the literature is one where property concept words pattern syntactically with nouns. This is a claim commonly made for the Quechuan family of languages (Schachter 1985; Schachter & Shopen 2007; Hengeveld & van Lier 2010a; Hengeveld & Valstar 2010), although this has been disputed (Beck 1999a, 2002; Floyd 2011). The difference of opinion, naturally, hangs on some of the theoretical issues discussed above, in particular the way in which the analyst wishes to treat noun–noun 'modification'. An examination of the Quechuan data presented in Floyd (2011) thus provides a good illustration of how different approaches to lexical classification lead to different assessments of the same data.

The first hurdle in establishing that nouns and adjectives belong to a single part of speech is demonstrating that property concept words are, like nouns, used freely as the syntactic arguments of verbs. At first blush, this seems to be relatively straightforward in Quechuan, given the following sentences from Floyd (2011), which are based on those in Schachter (1985: 17):

Ecuadorian Highland Quechua (Quechuan, Ecuador) (Floyd 2011: 33)
(19) Rika-ška: **hatun-(kuna)-ta**
see–PTCP.1SG big–(PL)–ACC
'I saw (the/a) big one(s).'

(20) Rika-ška: **alkalde-(kuna)-ta**
see–PTCP.1SG mayor–(PL)–ACC
'I saw (the) mayor(s).'

In (19), the property concept word *hatun* 'big' occupies argument position—specifically, it serves as the direct object of a verb and takes both a plural suffix and a suffix marking accusative case. In this it appears to be an exact parallel to the noun *alkalde* 'mayor' in (20). It is important to note, however, that the meaning expressed by *hatun* in (19) is not that of a property concept: instead, *hatun* functions as an anaphoric expression, referring back to an antecedent that is identified by a particular property (i.e. it means 'one that is big'), rather than expressing the property itself ('large size/bigness'). As Floyd (2011: 45) notes, a Quechua property concept word like *hatun* only 'heads noun phrases when an elliptical modified noun is available anaphorically'. In this regard, the use of *hatun* in such constructions plays out in the same way that it would in more familiar languages such as Spanish (e.g. *Quiero el rojo* 'I want the red (one)'), where it is not uncommon to see adjectives as the apparent heads of noun phrases in contexts where there is an understood referent to which the property they express can be applied.

How one responds to this data depends entirely on one's inclinations as an analyst. Those inclined to draw trees would likely posit an elided nominal head, removing the property concept word itself from argument position and making it de facto a modifier of the elided noun. An alternative solution would be to consider such uses the result of a general process of categorial conversion, creating what are essentially pronouns that use the property concept expressed by the adjective to identify an antecedent in discourse or the context of the speech act in the same way that a pronoun uses person, number, or gender, or a demonstrative acting as a third person pronoun uses deixis. Still others might choose to ignore the semantic shift and treat examples like (19) as free uses of adjectives as syntactic arguments. Floyd (2011: 45–46) notes that there are certain property concept words that do not function like this, but the pattern may be general enough to interpret this as a type of (unidirectional) flexibility if we choose to overlook the change in meaning and simply look at form; however, this would require the concession that parallel anaphoric uses of adjectives in other languages be interpreted as evidence that those languages have a flexible class of adjectives as well.

The second requirement for claiming that adjectives and nouns form a single part of speech is to show that nouns function freely in the role of adnominal modifier. This claim is also made by Schachter (1985), who gives the following examples:

Ecuadorian Highland Quechua (Quechuan, Ecuador) (Schachter 1985: 17)
(21) chay hatun runa
     that big   man
     'that big man'

(22) chay alkalde runa
     that mayor   man
     'that man who is mayor'

The example in (21) shows the property concept word *hatun* 'big' modifying *runa* 'man', whereas (22) shows *runa* juxtaposed in the same way with another noun, *alkalde* 'mayor'. As noted in section 18.2, whether an expression like *alkalde runa* is directly comparable to *hatun runa* depends how one understands the notion of 'modification', and whether or not the formal parallelism between (21) and (22) is given more weight than the fact that *alkalde runa* 'man WHO IS mayor' is not strictly compositional and might be better treated as a compound rather than as modification.

The position that Quechua N-N constructions are compounds is taken by Floyd (2011), who points out that such constructions express a range of non-compositional semantic relationships between their members, running from the highly transparent to the completely opaque. Consider, for example, the use of the nouns *aki* 'hand', *kaspi* 'wood/stick', and *fierro* 'metal' in (23):

Ecuadorian Highland Quechua (Quechuan, Ecuador) (Floyd 2011: 36)
(23) aki   telar-pi   awa-n   ka-rka-nchi,   kaspi   telar   ka-shka-pi,
     hand loom-LOC   weave-INF   be-PST-1PL   wood/stick loom   be-PTCP-LOC

     solamente fabrika-kuna-lla-mi   chari-n   ka-riya-n,
     only   factory-PL-LIM-EV.AFF   have-INF   be-REFL-3SG

     kay   fierro telar-ta-ka.
     DM.PROX   metal   loom-ACC-FOC
     'We had to weave on hand looms, as they were wood looms; only just the factories have them, these metal looms.'

In (23) we see all three nouns in juxtaposition to *telar* 'loom'. In each case, the meaning of the combination, although transparent, is non-compositional and construction-specific: the combination of *fierro* 'metal' and *telar* 'loom' yields *fierro telar* 'loom MADE OUT OF metal', whereas *aki* 'hand' and *telar* 'loom' yields *aki telar* 'loom OPERATED BY hand'.

Floyd observes that even though there are a few classes of nouns (like nouns expressing materials) that combine with others in fairly predictable ways, there are far more that take on idiosyncratic meanings, such as *urku* 'mountain' in (24):

Ecuadorian Highland Quechua (Quechuan, Ecuador) (Floyd 2011: 38)
(24) Pay-ka   **urku**   taruka ni-shka, kunu, **urku**   kunu   ni-shka.
     3SG-FOC mountain deer   say-PTCP rabbit mountain rabbit say-PTCP
     'That's called a (wild) "mountain" deer, rabbit, called a (wild) "mountain" rabbit.'

The use of *urku* to mean 'wild' is specific to its use with the names of fauna, and thus must be treated as a conventionalized, idiomatic use of *urku* rather than as an example of the noun 'mountain' used in modification. Other examples offered by Floyd (2011: 36–37) are even more opaque, and would have to be memorized by speakers and listed in the lexicon as multi-word lexical expressions. In general, it seems that Quechua nouns take on non-compositional and semi-arbitrary, context-specific meanings when used in noun-noun constructions, and as such can only be treated as free or unmarked modifiers if we turn a blind eye to what they mean. Likewise, we saw above that property concept words used as arguments undergo significant shifts in both meaning and function. Beck (1999a, 2002) observes that both difficulties seem to plague other putative cases of bidirectional noun-adjective flexibility, and that these problems seem to follow from the nature of the meanings that nouns and adjectives typically express, which rules out genuine absence of the distinction between adjectives and nouns for analysts that prioritize meaning over form.

18.3.3 Unidirectional flexibility

In order for a part-of-speech distinction to declared absent from a language, members of the putative classes being examined must be shown to be bidirectionally flexible—that is, members of class X must be able to fill the role typical of members of class Y, and members of class Y must be able to fill the role of class X (Evans & Osada 2005). However, there are also cases where class X is flexible in the sense that it can fill the role of Y, whereas Y may not fill the role of X—that is, rather than being bidirectional, the flexibility shown by X would be unidirectional (Beck 2013). Unlike bidirectional flexibility, unidirectional flexibility still allows us to maintain a lexical class distinction between X and Y.

A case where adjectives show unidirectional flexibility with adverbs is found in Upper Necaxa Totonac. In Upper Necaxa, adjectives like *há'lha'* 'big' are flexible in that they function equally well in both adnominal (25) and adverbal (26) modifier position:

Upper Necaxa Totonac (Totonacan, Mexico) (Braulio Cevedeo, 'The flying serpent', line 71)
(25) pus   tza'má chichí'-n mat ta-min   tza'má la'h–*há'lha'* chichí'-n
     INTJ that   dog-PL   QTV 3PL.SUB–come   that   APL-big   dog-PL
     'Well then, the dogs, it's said, two big dogs came.'

(26) tza'má kunéju la'h-**há'lha'** ta-ha'lhí: i'x-a'hax'ólh-ka'n
　　 that rabbit APL-big   3PL.SUB-have 3PO-ear-PL.POSS
　　 'Rabbits, they have their ears long.'

(Porfirio Sampayo, author's fieldnotes)

In (25), *há'lha'* 'big' forms part of a noun phrase and optionally agrees in number with its head, *chichí'n* 'dogs'; in (26), *há'lha'*—also showing number agreement—appears in the preverbal slot typical of adverbs in the language, although it clearly still bears semantically on the noun *a'hax'ólh* 'ear', the direct object of the clause.

Words that fall into the adverb class, however, do not show the same flexibility:

　　 Upper Necaxa Totonac (Totonacan, Mexico) (Louisa Cabrera, author's fieldnotes)
(27) **tze'h**   chi'pá i'x-tumí:n
　　 hidden   hold   3POSS-money
　　 'He's got his money hidden.'

(28) **tze'h tumí:n*
　　 intended: 'hidden money'

In these examples, we see that the word *tze'h* 'hidden' can be used as an adverbal modifier (27) but not as an adnominal modifier (28), this in spite of the fact that the meaning 'hidden' seems to be, if not a canonical property concept, certainly a descriptive property of the noun *tumí:n* 'money'. Indeed, a great many Upper Necaxa words that show the distributional pattern of *tze'h* express meanings that are expressed by adjectives in languages like English, and many of these come in synonymous pairs like that illustrated in (29)–(32):

　　 Upper Necaxa Totonac (Totonacan, Mexico) (Longino Barragán, author's fieldnotes)
(29) ka:ná: **wilé'hlh** sta'k-li'   kí'wi'
　　 truly   twisted   grow-PFV tree
　　 'The tree grew very twisted.'

(30) ** ka:ná: **wilé'hlh** kí'wi'*
　　 intended: 'very twisted tree'

(31) ka:ná: **wilé'hlh-wa'** sta'k-li' kí'wi'
　　 truly   twisted-SEM   grow-PFV tree
　　 'The tree grew very twisted.'

(32) ka:ná: **wilé'hlh-wa'** kí'wi'
　　 truly   twisted-SEM   tree
　　 'very twisted tree'

Here we see the adverb/adjective pair *wilé'hlh/wilé'hlhwa'* 'twisted'. Like *tze'h*, *wilé'hlh* can serve as modifier adverbally (29) but not adnominally (30); its adjectival derivative *wilé'hlhwa'*, on the other hand, is acceptable in both syntactic roles, as seen in (31) and (32). Pairs such as these are quite numerous and include words expressing meanings in semantic domains such as COLOUR (*pu'tzé'nhs/pu'tzé'nhe'* 'black'), PHYSICAL PROPERTIES (*chaláj/ chalájwa'* 'brittle'), CONFIGURATION (*nuks/nukswa'* 'tightly spaced'), SHAPE (*moj/mójwa'* 'round and bulky', *lhto'jó'h/lhto'jó'hlu'* 'baggy, sack-like'), and a variety of others typically thought of as property concepts. This is clear evidence that the adjectival class in Upper Necaxa is not demarcated by meaning (property concept ≠ adjective), but does constitute a part of speech associated with the particular role of adnominal modification.

Unlike bidirectional flexibility, unidirectional flexibility allows us to maintain a part-of-speech distinction, even if one class of word can fulfil the syntactic role of the other. This becomes apparent in Table 18.4, which compares the distribution of the *tze'h* and the *há'lha'* class of words in the examples in (25)–(28). Upper Necaxa has two classes that take on the syntactic function of what we would normally call 'adverbs', but only one of these classes, the *há'lha* class, can take the role expected of adjectives. Barring the use of bespoke terminology, which hardly seems justifiable here, the best option is to designate the *tze'h* class 'adverb' and treat the *há'lha'* class, which contains the majority of 'core' property concept words, as a distinct but flexible class of adjectives that can also fill the syntactic role of adverbal modification.

Table 18.4 Unidirectional flexibility of modifying words in Upper Necaxa Totonac

	adverbal	adnominal	
tze'h-class	✓	✗	(= adverbs)
há'lha'-class	✓	✓	(= adjectives)

18.3.4 Multilateral flexibility

It is also possible for adjectives (or other parts of speech) to be unidirectionally flexible with more than one other word class. This seems to be the case of Tukang Besi, as described in Donohue (2008).[6] Tukang Besi has a class of words, which Donohue refers to as 'adjectives', that can function freely in all three of the syntactic roles of predicate (31), adnominal modifier (34), and argument (35):

Tukang Besi (Mayo-Polynesian, Sulawesi) (Donohue 2008: 596–597)
(33) No–*toʻoge*   na   woleke   iso.
      3R–big   NOM   rat   yon
      'That rat is big.'

(34) Te   woleke   toʻoge
      CORE   rat   big
      'the big rat'

---

[6] See also the discussion of Sri Lanka Malay in Nordhoff (2013).

(35) Te   to'oge
     CORE big
     'the bigness/the big one'[7]

Donohue shows that words like *to'oge* 'big' with the flexible distribution seen above contrast both with a class of words, verbs, that can appear freely in the context shown in (33) but not those shown in (34) and (35), and with a class of words, nouns, that can appear freely in the context shown in (35) but not in (33) or (34). This gives us the pattern in Table 18.5. As with unidirectional flexibility, the multilateral flexibility shown by the adjective class in Tukang Besi clearly allows us to distinguish adjectives on distributional grounds. Although adjectives also meet the criteria for nouns and verbs, they are unique in being able to fill the role of adnominal modifier. That, and the fact that their meanings appear to fall into the domain of property concepts, makes them comparable to what we call adjectives in other languages, the significant difference being that they show an unusual degree of flexibility in their distribution.

Table 18.5 Multilateral flexibility of adjectives in Tukang Besi

	Syntactic predicate	Adnominal modifier	Syntactic argument
Noun	✗	✗	✓
Adjective	✓	✓	✓
Verb	✓	✗	✗

18.4 Conclusions

What are called adjectives in many languages present a diverse profile, differing widely in their grammatical properties and the meanings of words that belong to that class: there is such diversity, in fact, that some researchers have called into question the utility of terms like 'adjective' as a basis for cross-linguistic comparison in the first place. Haspelmath (2010: 110), for example, asserts that 'word-classes cannot be compared directly across languages because of their language-particular nature', and goes on to attribute efforts make such comparisons to a 'categorialist universalist position' that 'starts out with the assumption that [all languages] will basically have the same categories' (p. 111). It should be apparent

---

[7] More than a little hangs on the glossing here. My own interpretation is that this expression is ambiguous between two different structures, one with an understood nominal antecedent ('the big one') and the other ('the bigness') which represents a genuine use of a property concept word as a syntactic argument without a significant change in meaning.

from the discussion above, however, that this is a bit of an overreaction: the starting point of the cross-linguistic comparisons made here is the recognition that a word class we could call 'adjectives' may not always be part of the grammar of a language, and that when it is, there may be significant differences in the distribution and behaviour of the words it encompasses. Any 'universalist' positions taken have been only the premises that all languages have lexical expressions of property concepts, and that the relevant syntactic function, adnominal modification, is generalizable across languages (though not universal, as we saw in our discussion of Seneca). Cross-linguistic comparison simply rests on the claim that when these two things intersect in a language, they can be used to define word classes that an analyst can usefully call 'adjective', in the same way that the intersection of the corresponding semantic domains and syntactic functional roles associated with nouns and verbs can be used to identify these classes, as shown in Table 18.1. Taking this approach avoids the categorial universalist position criticized by Haspelmath in that it changes the research question from 'does language L have adjectives?' to 'does L have a class of words that we would want to label "adjectives"?' It is a subtle difference, but it makes it clear that part-of-speech terms like 'adjective' belong to the descriptive metalanguage, and are not universalist entities claimed to be part of a speaker's internal grammar. Diversity and variation in part-of-speech systems thus becomes expected, rather than problematic, and debate over it is an opportunity to sharpen our terminological tools. Differences of analysis like those discussed above can be seen to fall out as much from the differing interests and goals of researchers, and from the underlying questions they are really asking of the data, as they do from the fundamental organization of the lexica of different languages.

CHAPTER 19

ADVERBS

KEES HENGEVELD

19.1 INTRODUCTION

THE word class of adverbs has often been used as a residual category, covering everything not covered by other well-established word classes such as verbs, nouns, adjectives, and adpositions. Considerable attention will therefore be given, in section 19.2 of this chapter, to the definition of adverbs. The definition arrived at covers a wide range of subtypes of adverbs, which differ from each other in terms of their scope and their semantic domain. These subtypes are discussed in section 19.3. Section 19.4 then moves on to show from a typological perspective that the scopal subclasses show different behaviour, as regards their morphological encoding, their syntactic ordering, and their very existence. The chapter is rounded off in section 19.5.

19.2 ADVERBS AS A WORD CLASS

19.2.1 Introduction

This section focuses on the definition and general characterization of the word class of adverbs. After providing a detailed definition in section 19.2.2, the delimitation of adverbs from other word classes is discussed in section 19.2.3. Adverbs frequently show some degree of overlap with other word classes. This issue is addressed in section 19.2.4. Finally, section 19.2.5 presents some frequent diachronic sources for adverbs.

19.2.2 The definition of adverbs

The definition of adverbs that I will use in this chapter (see also Schachter & Shopen 2007: 20; Hengeveld 1997: 121) is given in (1):

(1)   An adverb is a lexical word that may be used as a modifier of a non-nominal head.

Several aspects of this definition require further explanation. First of all, the fact that an adverb is a *modifier* means that it is an optional element, depending on a head that is obligatory. Thus, in (2) the adverb *quickly* can be left out without affecting the grammaticality of the sentence, while its head *run* cannot:

(2) a He runs *quickly*.
 b He runs.
 c * He *quickly*.

Second, an adverb is defined as a *word* here, given the focus of the current volume on word classes. This means that not only bare adverbs such as *often* but also morphologically derived ones such as *quickly* are included in the definition. Of course, one could also define adverbs as constituting a stem class, in which case *quick-* in *quickly* would not be classified as a true adverb, since it can be used as an adjectival stem as well.

Third, an adverb is a *lexical* element, which means that it is neither syntactically compositional nor grammatical. As for syntactic compositionality, consider the following examples:[1]

Hausa (Chadic) (Newman 2000: 44)
(3) dà gaggāwā
 with haste
 'quickly' (litt. 'with haste')

Garo (Brahmaputran) (Burling 2004: 263)
(4) jakrak-e
 be.quick-ADV.SUB
 'quickly' (litt. 'being quick')

In Hausa, adverbial expressions regularly take the form of prepositional phrases, as in (3). In Garo, the adverbial subordinating suffix *-e* creates converbs, used as predicates of adverbial clauses, as in (4). In both cases the modifier is not lexical, and hence does not count as an adverb.

As for the distinction between lexical and grammatical modification, consider the following example:

Hupa (Athabaskan–Eyak–Tlingit) (Golla 1970: 135)
(5) Yeh-ʔɪ.ʔɪ-n-yaW.1.
 INTO.THE.HOUSE-HAB-2.SG-move
 'You always go in.'

Hupa has a large set of adverbial prefixes, many of which express directional meanings. This is illustrated in (5) with the prefix *yeh-* 'INTO.THE.HOUSE'. In other languages this meaning might be expressed by an adverb, but in order to express this meaning in Hupa, grammatical means have to be used.

---

[1] Languages are classified as belonging to the (sub)phylum that triggered their inclusion in the sample, which is described in section 19.4.1. The classification used is Glottolog 4.2.1 (Hammarström et al. 2020).

Fourth, an adverb *may* be used as a modifier of a non-nominal head, but it may have other functions as well. In (6) an adverb is used as an argument of the verb *behave*, which requires the presence of a manner expression in its subcategorization frame; in (7) an adverb is used as a non-verbal predicate, accompanied by a copula.

(6)   He behaves *well*.
(7)   He is *abroad*.

The presence or absence of these uses may vary from language to language, and is therefore not a defining use of adverbs: their use as modifiers of non-nominal heads is what distinguishes them from other word classes.

The fifth aspect of the definition that requires further explanation concerns the types of head that adverbs modify. The fact that adverbs modify *non-nominal heads* sets them apart from adjectives, which modify nominal heads. Many types of heads qualify as being non-nominal. First of all, lexical heads of all classes but the nominal one may be modified by adverbs:

(8)   walk *quickly* (verbal head)
(9)   *extremely* rich (adjectival head)
(10)   *surprisingly* quickly (adverbial head)
(11)   *exactly* behind the building (adpositional head)
(12)   *instantly* after he left us (conjunctional head)
(13)   *almost* three (numeral head)

But heads may be compositional as well. In (14) and (15) the adverbs may be said to modify the sentence as a whole.

(14)   *Apparently* Sheila has left.
(15)   *Honestly*, you are a crook.

In section 19.3 the various types of non-nominal heads, both lexical and compositional, will be the point of departure for a fine-grained classification of adverbs.

It has sometimes been argued (e.g. Ramat & Ricca 1998) that adverbs may also modify nominal heads, as in the case of focus particles, illustrated in the following examples:

(16)   *Even* the members of his own party protested against him.
(17)   He arrived at *just* the right time.

Note, however, that in this case it is not the nominal head but the noun phrase as a whole that is being modified, as is clear from the fact that *even* and *just* precede the article in (16) and (17).

19.2.3 Delimitation with other word classes

Adverbs may be distinguished from neighbouring word classes quite straightforwardly on the basis of the different properties that show up in the definition given in the previous section.

Adjectives share with adverbs the property that they are modifiers, it is just the class of heads that is being modified that is different.

(18) a. *Quick* steps crossed the street.
b. He crossed the street *quickly*.
c. *Quickly*, he crossed the street.

In (18a) *quick* modifies the noun *steps*, in (18b) *quickly* (meaning 'in a quick manner') modifies the verb *cross*, and in (18c) *quickly* (meaning 'after a short interval of time') modifies the sentence. In English the distinction between adjectives and adverbs is in most cases clearly marked morphologically, exceptions being words like *fast, hard, right*, and *wrong*.

Particles may express meanings similar to adverbs, are free words like adverbs, and may modify non-nominal heads like adverbs do, but they differ from adverbs in being grammatical rather than lexical in nature. The two classes can be distinguished by the fact that adverbs, being lexical in nature and therefore heads themselves, can be modified, while particles cannot. Thus, in Goemai elements such as *kàt* 'maybe' and *mé* 'really' are particles, as they cannot be modified by any type of modifier (Hellwig 2011: 296), whereas true adverbs can be. Similar examples for English are given in (19):

(19) a. Quite *possibly* she will arrive by train.
b. * Quite *maybe* she will arrive by train.

Though expressing roughly the same type of meaning, *possibly* and *maybe* behave quite differently, in the sense that *maybe* cannot be modified, whereas *possibly* can (Haumann 2007: 363; Keizer 2018: 365). Thus *possibly* is an adverb, but *maybe* is a particle. Along the same lines, it can easily be established that *even* and *just*, illustrated in (16)–(17), are grammatical rather than lexical elements. On a language-specific basis other criteria may be useful to distinguish between the two classes. Thus in Ngiti, adverbs (or rather flexible modifiers, see below) can be nominalized, whereas particles cannot (Kutsch Lojenga 1994: 335).

Adpositions and *conjunctions* differ from adverbs in that they are relators rather than modifiers. Compare in this respect the following examples:

(20) He moved to Brazil *after* the war.
(21) She went on a holiday *before* anyone else had been.
(22) She will come back *soon*.

In (20) the preposition *after* establishes a temporal relation between two events: one being the move to Brazil and the other one being the war. In (21), similarly, two events are temporally related to one another, now by means of the conjunction *before*. The adverb *soon* in (22), however, does not establish such a relationship, but just specifies a temporal property of a single event.

19.2.4 Overlap with other word classes

In many languages adverbs show overlap in form with other word classes.

Overlap with *nouns* is frequently found in the case of locative and temporal adverbs, which may have to do with the deictic nature of these adverbs. An example is the word *ganji* in Koyra Chiini, illustrated in (23). In (23a) it is used nominally, where it is the head of a noun phrase contained in a postpositional phrase. In (23b) it is used in its bare form as a directional adverb.

Koyra Chiini (Songhay) (Heath 1999: 441, 123)
(23) a. *I-i   boyrey   ganji   di   ra.*
         3.PL.S-IMPF converse wilderness   DEF   LOC
         'They were conversing in the bush.'

   b. *Ni   fatta   ganji.*
      2.SG.S exit   wilderness
      'You emerged from the wilderness.'

One could argue that *ganji* in (23b) is actually a noun phrase, just as in (23a), the difference being that the postposition is being suppressed. An argument in favour of such an analysis is that the verb in (23b) already expresses directionality, and that in many languages locative adpositions are suppressed when accompanying verbs of movement or location. An argument against this analysis is the absence of the definite article in (23b). I take the latter feature to be decisive here, and analyse *ganji* in (23b) as an adverb.

Overlap with *adjectives* is especially frequent in the case of adverbs of manner and degree. In Hengeveld (1992a, 1992b, 2013, see also Chapter 10 in this volume), I show that this follows quite naturally from the fact that adjectives (A) and adverbs of manner and degree (MAdv) are neighbouring categories in a parts of speech hierarchy of the following form:

(24) V $\supset$ N $\supset$ A $\supset$ MAdv

In languages with a flexible parts-of-speech system, the functions of the parts of speech on this hierarchy may be combined in a single word class, starting from the right. So there are languages where the functions of MAdv and A are combined in a single class of *modifiers*, languages where the functions of MAdv, A, and N are combined in a single class of *non-verbs*, and languages where all four functions are combined in a single class of *contentives*. In all these cases, the manner adverb does not occur as a separate class in the language, and in all cases it overlaps with adjectives.

Ingush has a class of modifiers, as shown in (25):

Ingush (Nakh–Dagestanian) (Nichols 2011: 217)
(25) a. *dika sag*
        good person
        'good person'

   b. *dika ealar*
      well say.PST.WITN
      'said (it) well'

The following examples are from Turkish, which has a class of non-verbs:

Turkish (Turkic) (Göksel & Kerslake 2005: 49)
(26) a. *güzel-im*
        beauty-1.POSS
        'my beauty'

b. *güzel bir köpek*
   beauty INDEF dog
   'a beautiful dog'

c. *Güzel konuş-tu-Ø*
   beauty speak-PST-3.SG
   'S/he spoke well.'

Overlap in form with *adpositions and conjunctions* is again frequently found for locative and temporal adverbs. The following examples illustrate this for English:

(27) a. I met him *outside* the office.
     b. I will wait for you *outside*.

(28) a. I saw him *before* he left the office.
     b. I have met him *before*.

The non-relational uses of *outside* in (27b) and *before* in (28b) are probably related to their relational uses, as a default contextual interpretation is imposed on these non-relational uses: *outside* in (27b) is interpreted with respect to the location of either the speaker or the addressee, and (28b) is interpreted with respect to the moment of speaking.

19.2.5 Sources for adverbs

As suggested by the hierarchy in (24), adverbs are the least likely to occur as a separate word class among the parts of speech represented in that hierarchy. It is therefore not uncommon to find languages with no adverbs at all. An example is Lao, a language for which Enfield (2007: 239) states that '[a]dverbs are not a distinct word class, but are simply verbs used in certain slots.' Similarly, Peterson (2010: 129) remarks that '[i]n principle there is no need to discuss "adverbials" separately in Kharia as they do not differ from other types of Case-syntagmas'. In languages that do have adverbs, these sometimes form large classes of basic lexical items. This is for instance the case in Bardi, for which Bowern (2012: 561) reports the existence of 352 adverbs, 'comprising 7.3% of the total number of headwords in the dictionary'. In many languages, however, adverbs form a small closed word class, and in many cases there is evidence that these words were recruited from elsewhere. I will briefly consider their sources here, some of which are located within the language system itself, and some outside it.

Within the language system a frequent source for adverbs is derivation through affixation (Ramat 2011: 506–508), as with *-ly* in English or *-mente* in Spanish. These affixes themselves go back to independent words, such as the ablative form of Latin *mēns* 'mind' in the case of Spanish *-mente*. A few examples from Spanish are given in (29):

Spanish (Italic)
(29) *natural-mente ilegal-mente real-mente evidente-mente*
     natural-ADVR   illegal-ADVR real-ADVR   evident-ADVR
     'naturally'   'illegally'   'really'   'evidently'

Another frequent source is derivation through reduplication of verbal stems, as illustrated for Garo in (30):

Garo (Brahmaputran) (Burling 2003: 31, 38, 111, 211)
(30) bra~bra   chap~chap   jrip~jrip   srang~srang
     pour.into~ADVR   attach~ADVR   be.silent~ADVR   be.clear~ADVR
     'in large numbers'   'side by side'   'silently'   'clearly, fluently'

Adpositional phrases and case marked phrases can be used as adjuncts, but may become frozen and then turn into unanalysable adverbs (Ramat 2011: 505). In Udihe, for instance, nouns may be inflected for a whole series of locative cases, but some occur in one case form only, which may be reduced as well, such that the resulting frozen form may be considered an adverb, as shown in (31). A parallel case in Dutch is given in (32).

Udihe (Tungusic) (Nikolaeva 2001: 370)
(31) *zugdu* 'at home' < *zugdi-du* 'house-DAT' 'in the house'

Dutch (Germanic)
(32) *thuis* 'at home' < *te huis* 'in house'

Similarly, Hill (2005: 245) speculates that in Cupeño, the adverb *wiyika* 'around' may contain the directional suffix *-(y)ka*.

In several languages, serial verbs fulfil functions similar to adverbs, in that one of the verbs semantically modifies the other. Modifying serial verbs may develop into adverbs over time. The contrastive examples in (33) from Moskona illustrate this:

Moskona (East Bird's Head) (Gravelle 2010: 142)
(33) a. *Dif   di-ecira   di-okog.*
        I   1.SG-walk   1SG-precede
        'I walked [and] preceded (them).'

     b. *Dif   di-ecira   kog.*
        I   1.SG-walk   ahead
        'I walked ahead.'

The adverb *kog* 'ahead' in (33b) is an uninflected and reduced form of the serial verb *okog* 'precede' in (33a).

Sources outside the language system itself may also be exploited, which leads to the incorporation of new material in the language system. Gómez Rendón (2008) gives the following examples of Spanish adverbs borrowed into Otomí:

Otomí (Otomanguean) (Gómez Rendón 2008: 333, 334, 411)
(34) *mälmente* 'wrongly'   < Sp. malamente
     pobremente'na 'poorly'   < Sp. pobremente
     prinsipalmente 'mainly'   < Sp. principalmente
     lwego 'afterwards'   < Sp. luego

Ideophones have their source outside the language system too. These are 'marked words that depict sensory imagery' (Dingemanse 2012: 654, see also Chapter 22), and are often used in the creation of manner adverbs. To mention just one language, Sohn (1994: 88) states for Korean that '[t]housands of ideophones (sound symbolic or onomatopoeic expressions) [...] are manner adverbs'. A few examples are given in (35):

Korean (Koreanic) (Sohn 1994: 88)
(35) ttalkak-ttalkak   sol-sol   mikkun-mikkun
'rattling'   'gently, smoothly'   'smoothly, sleekly, oily'

Once borrowings or ideophones have been adopted by the speech community, they do become an integral part of the language system into which they have been incorporated.

19.3 CLASSES OF ADVERBS

19.3.1 Introduction

In this section I will present a detailed classification of adverbs. The classification is based on two parameters. The first concerns the semantic–pragmatic *scope* of adverbs. This parameter follows from the idea that utterances can be analysed as hierarchically organized layered structures, where layers correspond to pragmatic or semantic categories that are in scopal relationships. This parameter is introduced in section 19.3.2. The second parameter concerns the semantic *domain* to which adverbs pertain. Domains are introduced in section 19.3.3. The cross-classification following from the two parameters is presented in section 19.3.4.

19.3.2 The scope of adverbs

In many grammatical theories, the notion of hierarchy plays an important role. Underlying representations are assumed to contain multiple branches or layers that are in scopal relationships. One way in which these layers become visible at the surface is in ordering phenomena, such as the ones illustrated in (36) and (37).

(36) a. He left *quickly recently*.
     b. * He left *recently quickly*.

(37) a. *Reportedly* he *probably* left the building.
     b. **Probably* he *reportedly* left the building.

The temporal adverb *recently* has to occupy a more peripheral position than the manner adverb *quickly* when expressed at the same side of the verb, as in (36). Likewise, in (37) the evidential adverb *reportedly* has to occupy a more peripheral position than the modal adverb *probably*. In the approaches mentioned above, this is the reflection of a higher position in the hierarchy of *recently* and *reportedly* respectively. The hierarchical approach has been applied to both grammatical modification, in the classification of categories of tense, mood, aspect, evidentiality, and polarity, and to lexical modification, in the classification of classes of adverbs.

Within the group of hierarchical approaches, some define layers in syntactic terms, while others define them in pragmatic and semantic terms. An example of the former is the Cartographic Approach within Generative Syntax (see e.g. Cinque & Rizzi 2010). In Cinque (1999) this approach is applied to the parallel classification of tense–mood–aspect (TMA) systems and adverbs. An example of the latter approach is Functional Discourse Grammar (FDG) (see, e.g., Hengeveld & Mackenzie 2008; Keizer 2015; see also Chapter 10 in this volume). This is the approach that I will take in the present chapter.

The layers distinguished in FDG belong to different levels of grammatical organization: the Interpersonal (pragmatic) Level, the Representational (semantic) Level, the Morphosyntactic Level, and the Phonological Level. These are related in a top-down manner, as indicated in Figure 19.1. As this figure indicates, pragmatics governs semantics, pragmatics and semantics govern morphosyntax, and the three together govern phonology. For the classification of adverbs this means that in FDG the pragmatic and semantic aspects of adverbs are considered to determine their formal behaviour.

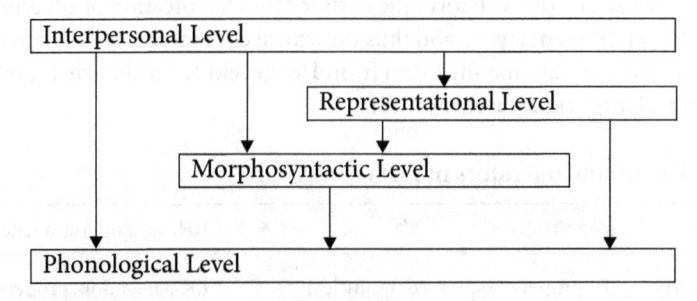

FIGURE 19.1 Levels in FDG

Every level is internally organized in terms of hierarchies of layers, the nature of which corresponds to the level to which they pertain. For the purposes of this chapter, only the internal structure of the first two levels is relevant. These are given in Figure 19.2, which also shows the hierarchical relations between them. Scopal domination is indicated by means of the symbols '>' and 'V'. Only layers relevant to this chapter are listed.

Every layer may be modified by (grammatical) operators or (lexical) modifiers,

Interpersonal Level	Discourse Act > Illocution > Communicated Content
Representational Level	Propositional Content > Episode > State-of-Affairs > Configurational Property > Lexical Property

FIGURE 19.2 Scope relations at the Interpersonal and Representational Levels in FDG

represented as π and σ respectively in a formula like the following, where both are given as modifying a Propositional Content (p):

(38) $(\pi\, p_1\colon [\text{------------------}]\,(p_1)\colon \sigma\,(p_1))$

For instance, a Propositional Content may be modified by an inferential operator or by an inferential modifier, as shown in (39):

(39) a. She *must* be the happiest woman in the world.
(infer p_1: [–she is the happiest woman in the world–] (p_1))

b. She is *presumably* the happiest woman in the world.
(p_1: [–she is the happiest woman in the world–] (p_1): presumably (p_1))

In (39a) the auxiliary *must* is a grammatical expression of inference represented as an operator 'infer' preceding the propositional content, while *presumably* in (39b) is a lexical expression of inference represented in its lexical form as a restrictor following the propositional content. Similar examples could be given for every layer.

In Table 19.1 all layers from Figure 19.2 are listed, a definition is provided, and the operators relevant at each layer as detected in earlier research, summarized in Hengeveld & Fischer (2018), are given. This will form the basis for the classification of adverbs, which are lexical modifiers at different layers, and thus the lexical counterparts of the operators listed in Table 19.1. Definitions are mainly taken from Hengeveld & Mackenzie (2008), operator categories from Hengeveld & Fischer (2018).

Table 19.1 Layers and operators in FDG

Layer	Definition	Relevant operator categories
Lexical Property	the property expressed by any lexical predicate	local negation, property quantification, directionality
Configurational Property	the combination of a predicate and its arguments that characterizes a set of States-of-Affairs	participant-oriented modality, failure, qualitative aspect, participant-oriented quantification
State of Affairs	events or states, i.e. entities that can be located in relative time and can be evaluated in terms of their reality status	event-oriented modality, non-occurrence, event perception, relative tense, event quantification, event location
Episode	one or more States-of-Affairs that are thematically coherent, in the sense that they show unity or continuity of time, location, and participants	objective epistemic modality, subjective deontic modality, co-negation, deduction, absolute tense
Propositional Content	a mental construct that does not exist in space or time but rather exists in the mind of the one entertaining it	subjective epistemic modality, disagreement, inference
Communicated Content	the totality of what the Speaker wishes to evoke in his/her communication with the Addressee	denial, reportative, mirative
Illocution	the lexical and formal properties of a Discourse Act that can be attributed to its conventionalized interpersonal use in achieving a communicative intention	illocutionary modification
Discourse Act	the smallest identifiable unit of communicative behaviour	irony, reinforcement, mitigation, rejection, quotative

In order to determine to what layer a certain class of adverbs belongs, a number of criteria will be applied below.

The first criterion involves co-occurrence restrictions that hold between adverbs and operators. Where such co-occurrence restrictions hold, the adverb must be of the same layer as the operator. Take for instance the following examples:

(40) She will arrive *shortly/*recently*.
(41) She arrived *recently/*shortly*.

These examples show that *shortly* and *recently* show co-occurrence restrictions with operators of absolute tense, which are operators at the Episode layer. *Shortly* and *recently* must therefore apply at the Episode layer as well.

The second criterion concerns co-occurrence restrictions obtaining between adverbs and lexical properties of the layer at which they apply. This criterion only applies at the layers of the Lexical and Configurational Properties, which together provide the basic lexical specification of a Discourse Act. An adverb applies at the layer of the Lexical Property when its application is lexically restricted. This is illustrated in (42) (Allerton 2002: 139):

(42) a. to *deeply* disappoint/*to *deeply* injure
b. * to *severely* disappoint/to *severely* injure

Degree adverbs such as *deeply* and *severely* show co-occurrence restrictions that depend directly on the lexical item they modify. They therefore must apply at the layer of the Lexical Property.

An adverb applies at the layer of the Configurational Property when it exhibits participant-oriented co-occurrence restrictions or *Aktionsart* restrictions. These are illustrated in (43) and (44):

(43) They/*he organized the conference *jointly*.
(44) She reached the summit *completely.

Jointly in (43) cannot occur with a singular subject. Since participants are introduced in the underlying representation at the layer of the Configurational Property, this means that *jointly* is an adverb at that layer. In (44) *completely* cannot be used, as it cannot combine with a momentaneous *Aktionsart*. This shows that *completely* is a modifier of the Configurational Property, as *Aktionsart* is a property of the combination of a lexical predicate with its arguments.

A third criterion concerns semantic and/or pragmatic scopal relationships, as illustrated in (45)–(46):

(45) They *completely* emptied their rooms *simultaneously*.
(46) *Recently* they emptied their rooms *simultaneously*.

Example (45) expresses that the complete emptying of the rooms was simultaneous, not that the simultaneous emptying of the rooms was complete. Thus *simultaneously* has scope over *completely*. Conversely, (46) expresses that the simultaneous emptying of the rooms was recent, not that the recent emptying of the rooms was simultaneous. Thus *recently* has scope over *simultaneously*. By applying the transitivity principle (Cinque 1999: 6), it can now also be concluded that *recently* has scope over *completely*. An important application of the scope criterion is the following. Since it is possible to establish by means of the previous criteria that *recently* modifies the Episode layer, as shown in (40)–(41), and *completely* the layer of the Configurational Property, as shown in (44), one can safely conclude that *simultaneously* applies at the layer of the State-of-Affairs, as this is the only intervening layer between Episode and Configurational Property. This is also consistent with the fact that the State of Affairs layer hosts relative tense operators.

The last criterion does not help to identify at which layer a certain adverb applies, but it does help to establish that adverbs do not belong to the same group. If two or more adverbs from the same domain can co-occur in a single sentence, this demonstrates that they apply at different layers, provided that they are not coordinated. Thus, (46) illustrates that *recently* and *simultaneously*, both from the temporal domain, cannot pertain to the same layer.

19.3.3 The domains of adverbs

The domains to which adverbs belong concern the types of meaning and the types of function adverbs express. This translates into general domains such as manner, modality, and location. Domains are generally identified on the basis of descriptive convenience, and this chapter will not be an exception to this general approach. The domains that I identify are the following: Degree, Manner, Participation, Quantification, Location, Time, Modality, Perspective, Evidentiality, Speaker Evaluation, and Textual organization. Note that this list is not exhaustive, as further subdivisions would be possible within several domains. The precise meanings and functions expressed within each of these domains depend on the layer at which the adverbs are applied, which is why they will be presented in more detail in the next section, which provides a cross-classification of the two parameters.

19.3.4 The classification of adverbs

By combining the two parameters *scope of adverb* and *domain of adverb*, a detailed classification may be arrived at. The possible combinations are listed in Table 19.2, which is partly inspired by Wanders (1993), Ramat and Ricca (1998), and Cinque (1999). The remainder of this section will motivate this classification using the criteria outlined in section 19.3.2. All classes will be discussed below and exemplified by English *-ly* adverbs, which can be used for all the relevant combinations of the two parameters. In section 19.4, I will turn to other languages.

Note that many adverbs that will be shown below to operate at higher layers of semantic organization can also occur within noun phrases. Compare the following examples:

(47) a. He *probably* left early.
b. a *probably* expensive car

(48) a. He is *definitely* not very healthy.
b. a *definitely* weird idea.

The exact treatment of the b-examples, in which the adverb modifies a modifier within a noun phrase would require a separate study and will not be addressed below, but see van de Velde (2010) and Keizer (2019) for discussion.

Table 19.2 Cross-classification of adverbs

	Lexical Property	Configurational Property	State-of-Affairs	Episode	Propositional Content	Communicated Content	Illocution	Discourse Act
Degree	Degree *extremely*							
Manner	Predicate-oriented *beautifully*	Subject-oriented *angrily*						
Participation		Additional participant *manually*						
Quantification		Event-internal *briefly*	Event-external *frequently*					
Location		Direction *diagonally*	Relative location *internally*	Absolute location *nationally*				
Time		Aspect *completely*	Relative Time *simultaneously*	Absolute Time *recently*				
Modality		Participant Oriented *easily*	Event-oriented *mandatorily*	Objective epistemic *really*	Subjective epistemic *probably*			
Perspective					Perspective *technically*			
Evidentiality			Event perception *visibly*	Deductive *seemingly*	Inferential *presumably*	Reportative *reportedly*		
Intensification						Intensification *definitely*		
Speaker evaluation					Sp. eval. of Prop.Cont. *foolishly*	Sp. eval. of Comm.Cont. *fortunately*	Sp. eval. of Illocution *frankly*	Sp.eval. of Discourse Act *sadly*
Textual organization								Situating the Discourse Act *finally*

19.3.4.1 Degree

Degree adverbs specify the degree to which the property or relation expressed by a lexical item applies. Degree adverbs may modify all kinds of lexical items:

(49) *severely* injure (verb)   Degree—Lexical Property
(50) *excessively* rich (adjective)   Degree—Lexical Property
(51) *remarkably* quickly (adverb)   Degree—Lexical Property
(52) *exactly* behind the building (adposition)   Degree—Lexical Property
(53) *instantly* after he left us (conjunction)   Degree—Lexical Property
(54) *nearly* five hundred (numeral)   Degree—Lexical Property

Degree adverbs modify the Lexical Property. This is evident from the fact that they may impose collocational restrictions on the lexical item with which they combine, as illustrated for verbal heads above in (42), repeated here as (55) (Allerton 2002: 139):

(55) a. *deeply* disappoint/*deeply injure
     b. *severely disappoint/*severely* injure

An example of a collocational restriction involving adjectival heads from Dutch is given in (56). Klein (2001: 234-235) observes that some degree modifiers in this language are limited to adjectival heads with a negative content, such as *lastig* 'difficult' in (56a).

Dutch (Germanic)
(56) a. *knap lastig*
       quite difficult
       'quite difficult'

     b. *knap gemakkelijk
       quite easy
       'quite easy'

19.3.4.2 Manner

Manner adverbs may apply at two different layers, that of the Lexical Property and that of the Configurational Property. These different uses are illustrated in (57) and (58):

(57) She danced *beautifully*.   Predicate-oriented Manner—Lexical Property
(58) She left the room *angrily*.   Subject-oriented Manner—Configurational Property

There are several differences between the adverbs in (57) and (58). First of all, in (57) only the dancing is beautiful, the subject *she* not necessarily is, while in (58) the *angriness* includes the subject. This is why, in the latter case, the Configurational Property is being modified, as this represents the predicate with its arguments, while in the former case it is just the Lexical Property that is modified (Hengeveld & Mackenzie 2008: 208-209).

Another difference between the two classes is that manner adverbs modifying a Lexical Property may impose very specific collocational restrictions as to the kind of predicate with which they may combine (García Velasco 1996: 154), as shown in (59) (Matthews 1981: 137):

(59) a. They build *shoddily*.
　　 b. * They cook *shoddily*.

Such restrictions do not hold for manner adverbs modifying a Configurational Property:

(60) a. She *angrily* left the room.
　　 b. He *angrily* slept on the sofa.
　　 c. They were listening *angrily*.

The fact that there are two types of manner adverbs operating at different layers is also evident from the fact that the two may be combined in a single sentence:

(61) 　She *angrily* danced *beautifully*.

Similar at first sight are adverbs such as *stupidly* in (56) (Hengeveld & Mackenzie 2008: 209):

(62) 　John *stupidly* answered the question.

Here the subject *John* may well have given an intelligent answer to the question, but the current speaker considers it stupid of John to have given an answer at all. This type of adverb will be treated as an adverb of speaker evaluation below, following Keizer (2020), among others.

19.3.4.3 *Participation*

Adverbs of participation introduce additional participants or specify relations between participants, and therefore modify the Configurational Property, as this is the layer at which the predicate and its arguments are combined. Examples are:

(63) 　She laminated the dough *manually*.　　Instrument—Configurational Property
(64) 　They *mutually* support each other.　　Reciprocal—Configurational Property
(65) 　They organized the conference *jointly*.　　Company—Configurational Property

The fact that these adverbs modify the Configurational Property is reflected in the restrictions that apply to their application. Other than degree adverbs and adverbs of manner modifying the Lexical Property, which show collocational restrictions that have to do with just the lexical item that they modify, participation adverbs are sensitive to properties of arguments. Thus, both *manually* and *mutually* can only apply to Configurational Properties involving an Actor, and *mutually* and *jointly* only to Configurational Properties with a plural first argument.

19.3.4.4 Quantification

Adverbs of quantification are of two types: event-internal ones, such as *briefly* in (66), which specify the internal duration of a State-of-Affairs, and event-external ones, such as *frequently* in (67), which quantify over States-of-Affairs.

(66) She frowned *briefly*.   Event-internal Quantification—Configurational Property
(67) She visited her friends *frequently*.   Event-external Quantification—State-of-Affairs

The first type operates at the layer of the Configurational Property, the latter at the layer of the State-of-Affairs. This is reflected in the fact that there are collocational restrictions on the former type as regards its interaction with *Aktionsart*, a category pertaining to the Configurational Property. Thus, *briefly* cannot combine with Configurational Properties with a momentaneous *Aktionsart*, while *frequently* can, as shown in (68).

(68) She reached the summit *briefly/*frequently*.

The fact that these two types of quantification occupy different layers is also evident from the fact that the two may be combined in a single sentence.

(69) She *frequently* frowned *briefly*.

19.3.4.5 Location

Within this domain there are three subclasses: direction at the layer of the Configurational Property (70), relative location at the layer of the State-of-Affairs (71), and absolute location at the layer of the Episode (72).

(70) He crossed the square *diagonally*.   Direction—Configurational Property
(71) The bank was reorganized *internally*.   Relative Location—State-of-Affairs
(72) The policy was implemented *nationally*.   Absolute Location—Episode

A directional adverb such as *diagonally* in (70) has scope over adverbs modifying the Lexical Property, as illustrated in (73), in which it has the degree adverb *badly* in its scope:

(73) The car sways *badly diagonally*.

On the other hand, it falls within the scope of State of Affairs modifiers such as *internally*, to be discussed below, as in (74):

(74) The metal pipes run *diagonally internally*.

Together these facts indicate that *diagonally* modifies the Configurational Property.

In (71), *internally* expresses relative location, as it needs a reference point with respect to which an interior area can be defined. *Nationally* in (72) does not require such a reference point. The fact that these adverbs belong to different classes is also evident from the fact that they may co-occur in one and the same sentence. In (75) all three classes of adverbs are combined.

(75) *Probably*, in their installations the metal pipes run *diagonally internally nationally*.[2]
 (i.e. 'Probably, nationwide the metal pipes run diagonally in the internal part of their installations.')

This sentence is admittedly overloaded with *-ly* adverbs, but can certainly be interpreted. The example also shows that *diagonally* is in the scope of *internally*, which in turn is in the scope of *nationally*. All three are in the scope of *probably*, which is shown below to belong to the Propositional Content layer. Thus *nationally* must be at the Episode layer, *internally* at the layer of the State-of-Affairs, and *diagonally* at the layer of the Configurational Property.

19.3.4.6 Time

The class of adverbs of time comprises adverbs expressing aspect, relative time, and absolute time. These are illustrated in (76)–(78):

(76) He emptied the room *completely*.   Aspect—Configurational Property
(77) The shops opened *simultaneously*.   Relative Time—State-of-Affairs
(78) She met her friends *recently*.   Absolute Time—Episode

The layers at which these adverbs apply become evident from their collocational restrictions. *Completely* cannot be used with Configurational Properties with a momentaneous *Aktionsart*, while the other two adverbs can, as shown in (79):

(79) They reached the summit **completely/simultaneously/recently*.

Simultaneously cannot be combined with non-simultaneous relative tenses, which operate at the layer of the State-of-Affairs.

(80) Having emptied the room *completely/*simultaneously*, he treated himself to an espresso.

Recently cannot combine with non-past absolute tenses, which operate at the layer of the Episode.

(81) The shops will open *completely/simultaneously/*recently*.

The fact that these adverbs belong to different classes is also evident from the possibility of their occurring in one and the same sentence. In (82), all three classes of adverbs are combined.

(82) *Recently* they *completely* emptied their rooms *simultaneously*.

---

[2] Adapted from https://eurosafeuk.org/thieves-break-though-wall-to-attack-safe/, consulted 14 July 2020.

19.3.4.7 Modality

Modal expressions belong to four different classes (Hengeveld 2004b; Hattnher & Hengeveld 2016; Keizer 2018). Participant-oriented modality, illustrated in (83), 'describes a relation between a participant in a state-of-affairs, and the potential realization of that state-of-affairs' (Hattnher & Hengeveld 2016: 2). Event-oriented modalities, illustrated in (84), 'characterize a state-of-affairs in terms of its feasibility or desirability' (Hattnher & Hengeveld 2016: 3). Episode-oriented modality, illustrated in (85), 'characterizes episodes in terms of the (im)possibility of their occurrence in view of what is known about the world' (Hattnher & Hengeveld 2016: 3). Finally, proposition-oriented modality, illustrated in (86), 'expresses the speaker's commitment with respect to the truth value of a propositional content' (Hattnher & Hengeveld 2016: 4).

(83) She climbed the tree *competently*. Modality—Configurational Property
(84) One *mandatorily* takes off one's shoes here. Modality—State-of-Affairs
(85) She will *really* lose her temper. Modality—Episode
(86) She is *probably* ill. Modality—Propositional Content

Participant-oriented modalities apply at the layer of the Configurational Property, which shows up in the fact that they require the presence of an Actor argument. If such an argument is not available, the use of an adverb expressing this modality is ungrammatical, as shown in (87).

(87) The fire extinguisher is **competently/mandatorily/really/probably* full.

Event-oriented modal adverbs apply at the layer of the State-of-Affairs, which explains why they cannot combine with a modal operator pertaining to that layer that expresses an opposite value, such as permissive *may* in (88).

(88) One may **mandatorily/really/probably* take off one's shoes here.

Both *really*[3] and *probably* express epistemic modality, but the former is located at the Episode layer and expresses objective epistemic modality, while the latter is located at the Propositional Content layer and expresses subjective epistemic modality. They have in common that they may have absolute temporal modifiers, which pertain to the Episode layer, in their scope:

(89) He *really/probably* went to Paris and had his hair done yesterday.

But they differ in that *really* but not *probably* may appear in questions:

(90) Did he *really*/*probably go to Paris and have his hair done yesterday?

---

[3] *Really* has many different uses (see, e.g., Keizer 2018); the one that is relevant here can be paraphrased as 'in reality' or 'it is the reality that'.

Questions contain a Propositional Content with an operator specifying an indeterminate propositional attitude, which is incompatible with a lexical expression, such as *probably*, that does express a propositional attitude at that same layer. *Really* expresses the objective existence of reality at the Episode layer, and therefore does not clash with the propositional operator.

Modal adverbs of the different subclasses can combine in a single sentence, though the result is awkward due to the stacking of four -*ly* adverbs:

(91)   *Probably* people *really* have to *mandatorily* be able to swim *competently* in order to enter the swimming pool. (i.e. 'Probably it is the reality that one has to be able to swim in order to enter the swimming pool.')

Pairwise combinations of hierarchically continuous adverbs are certainly more natural:

(92)   Your behaviour will *probably really* lead to your dismissal.
(93)   He *really* had to stay away *mandatorily* from the office after his dismissal.
(94)   One *mandatorily* has to swim *competently* in a country with lots of water.

19.3.4.8 Perspective

The class of adverbs of perspective has only one subclass, which is illustrated in (95):

(95)   *Technically*, they won the war, but *morally*, they did not.
                                                    Perspective—Propositional Content

These adverbs specify the perspective from which the truth of the Propositional Content with which they combine has to be evaluated (Wanders 1993: 48). Adverbs of perspective can be shown to be lower in scope than adverbs operating at the layer of the Communicated Content such as *reportedly*, to be discussed below:

(96)   *Reportedly* they *technically* won the war.

On the other hand, as shown in (95), these adverbs have absolute temporal reference in their scope, which shows that they operate at a layer higher than the Episode layer. Thus, they must be situated at the layer of the Propositional Content.

19.3.4.9 Evidentiality

Evidential adverbs come in four different classes (Hengeveld & Hattnher 2015; Kemp 2018), illustrated in (97)–(100):

(97)   She *visibly* winced.   Evidentiality—State-of-Affairs
(98)   She has *seemingly* left the building.   Evidentiality—Episode
(99)   She is *presumably* ill.   Evidentiality—Propositional Content
(100) She is *reportedly* on holiday.   Evidentiality—Communicated Content

Visibly in (97) expresses event perception, which 'indicates whether or not a speaker witnessed the event described in his or her utterance directly' (Hengeveld & Hattnher 2015: 487). In (98), *seemingly* expresses deduction, which indicates 'that the information the speaker presents is deduced on the basis of perceptual evidence' (Hengeveld & Hattnher 2015: 486). *Presumably* in (99) expresses inference, which indicates that the speaker 'infers a certain piece of information on the basis of his/her own existing knowledge' (Hengeveld & Hattnher 2015: 485). Finally, *reportedly* in (100) expresses reportativity, which indicates 'that the source of the information that the speaker is passing on is another speaker' (Hengeveld & Hattnher 2015: 484).

Visibly differs from the other three in that in the intended reading it cannot take negation, which is an operator at the Episode layer in English (Hengeveld & Mackenzie 2018), in its scope.

(101)   She **visibly/seemingly/presumably/reportedly* didn't wince.

The other way around, *visibly*, but not the other three adverbs, can be in the scope of negation:

(102)   She didn't *visibly/*seemingly/*presumably/*reportedly* wince.

Seemingly differs from *presumably* and *reportedly* in that it imposes restrictions on the absolute tenses with which it can combine, as deduction requires perception first. Since absolute tenses apply at the Episode layer, this restriction shows that *seemingly* applies at the Episode layer as well.

(103)   She will **seemingly/presumably/reportedly* leave the building by eight o'clock.

Presumably differs from *reportedly* in that the latter can take a propositional adverb such as *certainly* in its scope, while the former cannot co-occur with it. This shows that *presumably* operates at the layer of the Propositional Content, while *reportedly* (on the intended reading 'according to reports') is situated at a higher layer.

(104)   *Reportedly/*presumably* she *certainly* left the building.

Finally, *reportedly* can be shown to apply at the layer of the Communicated Content, as it can be within the scope of illocutionary adverbs, which, as shown below, apply at the layer of the Illocution.

(105)   *Honestly* she *reportedly* left the building at eight o'clock.

Pairwise combinations of adverbs from contiguous layers, in (106)–(108), further show that the different types of adverbs may be combined, and hence must belong to different classes.

(106)   *Reportedly* she *presumably* left the building.
(107)   *Presumably* she had *seemingly* left the building, which may be why he did not knock on her door.
(108)   *Seemingly* she *visibly* winced, as she turned away her face so that I wouldn't notice.

19.3.4.10 Intensification

Adverbs of intensification place particular stress on the message that is being transmitted. An example is given in (109):

(109)   I am *definitely* going to vote in the next elections.

These adverbs can be shown to operate at the layer of the Communicated Content, which captures the message transmitted in a Discourse Act. They can take adverbs operating at the layer of the Propositional Content in their scope, as shown in (110) which contains a subjective epistemic modal adverb:

(110)   He is *definitely probably* going to run for president.

On the other hand, intensifying adverbs are within the scope of illocutionary adverbs, as shown in (111):

(111)   It is quite *frankly definitely* not the best day to go to the beach!

These combined facts show that the intensifying adverb can only be at the layer of the Communicated Content.

19.3.4.11 Speaker evaluation

This is another large class of adverbs, and also one of which the status may be rather controversial. Examples of adverbs from this class at the various layers are given in (112)–(115):

(112)   She *foolishly* slept the whole day.   Speaker Evaluation—Propositional Content
(113)   *Fortunately*, she came alone.   Speaker Evaluation—Communicated Content
(114)   *Frankly*, she doesn't seem interested.   Speaker Evaluation—Illocution
(115)   *Sadly*, your mother has died.   Speaker Evaluation—Discourse Act

All these adverbs can be paraphrased in a way that brings out the fact that they express an evaluation by the speaker:

(116)   I think it was foolish of her to sleep the whole day.
(117)   I think it was fortunate that she came alone.
(118)   I am saying frankly that she doesn't seem interested.
(119)   I am sad that I have to tell you that your mother has died.

What all these adverbs have in common, is that they are non-truth conditional. This shows up in the fact that they cannot be denied in pairs like the following:

(120)   A: She *foolishly* slept the whole day.
        B1: That's not true. (She did not sleep the whole day.)
        B2: * That's not true. (That isn't foolish.)

(121) A: *Fortunately*, she came alone.
       B1: That's not true. (She did not come alone.)
       B2: * That's not true. (That is not fortunate.)

(122) A: *Frankly*, she doesn't seem interested.
       B1: That's not true. (She does seem interested.)
       B2: * That's not true. (You are not being frank.)

(123) A: *Sadly*, your mother has died.
       B1: That's not true. (She hasn't died.)
       B2: * That's not true. (You are not sad.)

Note that in general only adverbs applying at the Interpersonal Level are non-truth-conditional, but with this class of adverbs even those that can be shown to apply at the Representational Level (Keizer 2020) have this property. This is the case of *foolishly* in (112), which modifies the Propositional Content layer. Adverbs of speaker evaluation at the layer of the Propositional Content are in a way two-faceted: on the one hand, a speaker attitude is being expressed, which gives these adverbs an interpersonal flavour; on the other hand, the layer that is being evaluated is propositional in nature. For this reason, Keizer (2020) treats these adverbs as separate Propositional Contents, within which the adverbs predicate a property of a certain representational layer. Thus, in (108), *foolishly* predicates a property of the State-of-Affairs *she slept the whole day*, which functions as its argument, but this Propositional Content as a whole provides further information about the main Propositional Content, which it modifies. This analysis explains why the adverbs of this class show a behaviour different from that of the other adverbs discussed here. I will not go into the technical details here, but treat this subclass of adverbs as modifiers of the Propositional Content.

Foolishly in (112) is analysed as a modifier of the Propositional Content, since it can occur preceding and following other propositional modifiers, such as *probably*, as in the following examples, taken from Keizer (2019: 13):

(124) They *probably foolishly* believed the American Defense Department Big Lie that radiation does not hurt you. (*NOW, US*)

(125) Last year in MUT I *foolishly probably* spent between $750–$1000. (https://answers.ea.com/t5/FIFA-15/Packs/td-p/4556769)

The fact that the adverbs in (124)–(125) may occur in both orders means that they must be operating at the same layer.

Furthermore, adverbs of speaker evaluation at the Propositional Content layer can be shown to have scope over absolute tense, an Episode operator, as shown in (126), again taken from Keizer (2019: 13):

(126) Former Enron president *wisely* left firm in 1996, uncomfortable with 'asset light' strategy. (COCA, magazine)

In (126), the leaving the firm in 1996, so including the temporal interval, is considered wise by the speaker, as not long after this moment Enron collapsed.

Fortunately in (113) is analysed as a modifier of the Communicated Content. It indicates the speaker's positive attitude with respect to the message he or she is transmitting. This adverb can scope over an adverb modifying the Propositional Content, as shown in (127).

(127) *Fortunately*, she *wisely* slept the whole day yesterday.

At the same time, *fortunately* can be shown to be within the scope of illocutionary adverbs, discussed below, which apply at a layer one step higher than the Communicated Content.

(128) *Frankly*, she *fortunately* slept the whole day yesterday.

From these facts it may be deduced that *fortunately* indeed operates at the layer of the Communicated Content.

Frankly in (114) modifies the Illocution. This shows up in the fact that there are co-occurrence restrictions on the use of illocutionary adverbs in combination with certain illocutions. Thus, Han (2000: 166) notes that *frankly* is less felicitous with commands, a restriction that does not apply to *honestly*:

(129) ?*Frankly/honestly*, go home!

Furthermore, combining one and the same adverb with different illocutions may lead to a shift in perspective (Woods 2014: 211):

(130) a. *Seriously*, Andy can play rugby.
       b. *Seriously*, can Andy play rugby?

In (130a) the speaker is presenting himself or herself as being serious, in (130b) it is the addressee who is requested to be serious in providing an answer.

Furthermore, as shown in (128), illocutionary adverbs scope over adverbs of speaker evaluation at the layer of the Communicated Content. The following example shows they are within the scope of adverbs of textual organization operating at the layer of the Discourse Act, to be discussed below.

(131) *Finally*, I *frankly* did not like the way you acted today.

Taken together, these facts establish that illocutionary adverbs apply at the layer of the Illocution.

Sadly in (115) modifies the Discourse Act. In (132) it scopes over an illocutionary adverb, showing it is at a layer higher than the Illocution:

(132) *Sadly*, I *honestly* think you have made a big mistake.

19.3.4.12 *Textual organization*

The last class of adverbs consists of those fulfilling a role in textual organization, such as *briefly, finally,* and *importantly,* as illustrated in (133)–(135):

(133)   *Finally*, this was my last lecture.   Textual Organization—Discourse Act
(134)   *Importantly*, the students should be involved.   Textual Organization—Discourse Act
(135)   *Briefly*, the bill seeks more justice for tenants.   Textual Organization—Discourse Act

The fact that these operate at the highest layer shows up in the possibility of their occurring in all kinds of speech acts, as illustrated for *finally* in (133) above and (136)–(137):

(136)   *Finally*, do not forget to close the door.
(137)   *Finally*, do you like it or not?

19.4 Formal and behavioural correlates cross-linguistically

19.4.1 Introduction

In the previous section, I provided a detailed classification of adverbs in terms of the parameters of *scope* and *domain*. As mentioned earlier, the latter parameter is motivated primarily by descriptive convenience, grouping together adverbs that share a certain overall meaning or function, as shown in the rows in Table 19.2. The former parameter groups adverbs together in a different way, across the specific domains, based on their shared scope. These groupings are visible in the columns in Table 19.2. The grouping in terms of scope is the one that is reflected in the form and behaviour of classes of adverbs across languages, as will be shown in this section. I will focus on three aspects: the existence of adverbs (section 19.4.2), the morphological marking of adverbs (section 19.4.3), and the order of adverbs (section 19.4.4).

All observations in this section are based on the inspection of a 60-language sample, given in Table 19.3. The sample was created applying the method proposed in Rijkhoff et al. (1993) to the Glottolog 4.2.1 classification (Hammarström et al. 2020). In Table 19.3 the names of the phyla and subphyla, the names of the languages, and the published sources used to collect information about the languages are specified. It is important to note that in the following sections I can only indicate tendencies in the data, as most grammars provide relatively little information on the word class in question, and do not apply a classification as detailed as the one that was presented in section 19.3. Also, grammars often do not contain explicit statements about the (non-)existence of adverbs, nor do they study their ordering explicitly. Therefore, I present the observations below with caution, and as generalizations that may invite further testing in specific languages.

For the languages marked with an asterisk in Table 19.3, insufficient data were available to include them in the generalizations below.

Table 19.3 The sample

Phylum	Subphylum	Sub-subphylum	Language	Source
A'ingae			A'ingae	Fischer & Hengeveld (2023)
Indo-European	Albanian		Albanian	Newmark, Hubbard, & Prifti (1982)
Arawakan			Apurinã	Facundes (2000)
Nyulnyulan			Bardi	Bowern (2012)
Sko			Barupu	Corris (2006)
Basque			Basque	Hualde & Ortiz de Urbina (2003)
Dravidian			Betta Kurumba	Coelho (2003)
Gunwinyguan			Bininj Gun-wok	Evans (2003)
Burushaski			Burushaski*	Berger (1998)
Eskimo–Aleut			Central Alaskan Yupik	Miyaoka (2012)
Muskogean			Choctaw	Broadwell (2006)
Chukotko-Kamchatkan			Chukchi	Dunn (1999)
Uto-Aztecan			Cupeño	Hill (2005)
Atlantic–Congo	Volta–Congo		Gã	Campbell (2017)
Gaagudju			Gaagudju	Harvey (2002)
Sino-Tibetan	Brahmaputran		Garo	Burling (2003)
Afro-Asiatic	Chadic		Goemai	Hellwig (2011)
Uralic			Hungarian	Kenesei, Vago & and Fenyvesi (1998)
Athabaskan–Eyak–Tlingit			Hupa	Golla (1970)
Nakh–Daghestanian			Ingush	Nichols (2011)

(continued)

Table 19.3 Continued

Phylum	Subphylum	Sub-subphylum	Language	Source
Mande			Jalkunan	Heath (2017)
Ket			Ket*	Georg (2007)
Austroasiatic			Kharia	Peterson (2010)
Afro-Asiatic	Cushitic		Konso*	Ongaye (2013)
Koreanic			Korean	Sohn (1994)
Songhay			Koyra Chiini*	Heath (1999)
Nilotic			Lango	Noonan (1992)
Tai-Kadai			Lao	Enfield (2007)
Kartvelian			Laz	Lacroix (2009)
Narrow Talodi			Lumun	Smits (2017)
Sino-Tibetan	Sinitic		Mandarin	Li & Thompson (1981)
Atlantic-Congo	Mei		Mani	Childs (2011)
Araucanian			Mapudungun	Smeets (2008)
Pano-Tacanan			Matsés	Fleck (2003)
Nuclear Trans New Guinea	Madang		Mauwake*	Berghäll (2015)
Sepik			Mehek	Hatfield (2016)
Nuclear Trans New Guinea	Asmat Awyu Ok		Mian	Fedden (2011)
East Bird's Head			Moskona	Gravelle (2010)
Movima			Movima*	Haude (2006)
Austronesian	Malayo-Polynesian	Malayo-Sumbawan	Mualang*	Tjia (2007)
Salishan			Musqueam	Suttles (2004)
Central Sudanic			Ngiti	Kutsch Lojenga (1994)
Nivkh			Nivkh	Nedjalkov & Otaina (2013)

Atlantic-Congo	North-Central Atlantic		Noon*	Wane (2017)
Austronesian	Paiwan		Paiwan	Chang (2006)
Indo-European	Indo-Iranian		Palula	Liljegren (2016)
Pidgins and Creoles			Pichi	Yakpo (2019)
Austronesian	Puyuma		Puyuma*	Teng (2008)
Quechuan			Quechua*	Weber (1989)
Austronesian	Malayo-Polynesian	Central Eastern Malayo-Polynesian	Rapanui	Kievit (2017)
Pomoan			Southern Pomo*	Walker (2013)
Sumerian			Sumerian*	Jagersma (2010)
Afro-Asiatic	Berber		Tamashek*	Heath (2005)
North Halmahera			Tidore	Staden (2000)
Khoe-Kwadi			Ts'ixa*	Fehn (2014)
Turkic			Turkish	Lewis (1967)
Warao			Warao	Romero-Figeroa (1997)
Pama-Nyungan			Warrongo	Tsunoda (2011)
Hmong-Mien			Xong	Sposato (2015)
Nuclear Torricelli			Yeri	Wilson (2017)

19.4.2 The existence of adverbs

Languages differ in the extent to which they have specific classes of adverbs in their lexical inventory if at all. As mentioned above, Lao (Enfield 2007: 239) and Kharia (Peterson 2010: 129) are claimed to have no adverbs at all, while other languages, such as Bardi (Bowern 2012), are particularly rich in adverbs. The languages in between these two extremes have varying quantities and subtypes of adverbs, and the variation observed in this respect does not seem to be random. More specifically, it seems that the presence of subclasses of adverbs can be described in terms of the following hierarchy, which coincides with the layered hierarchical structure of FDG:

(138) Lexical Property ⊃ Configurational Property ⊃ State-of-Affairs ⊃ Episode ⊃ Propositional Content ⊃ Communicated Content ⊃ Illocution ⊃ Discourse Act

That is to say, when a language has a certain scopal subclass of adverbs on this hierarchy, it will also have the scopal subclasses to the left on the hierarchy. And when it does not have a certain scopal subclass of adverbs on this hierarchy, neither will it have the scopal subclasses to the right on the hierarchy. If a language has, for example, a class of adverbs operating at the layer of the Propositional Content, it will have adverbs operating at the layers of the Episode, State-of-Affairs, Configurational Property, and Lexical Property as well. And if a language does not have a class of adverbs operating at the layer of the Communicated Content, then neither will it have adverbs operating at the layers of the Illocution and the Discourse Act.

In Table 19.4, the languages exhibiting the different types predicted by the hierarchy in (138) are listed. This table is entirely based on adverbs reported on in the grammars, classified in terms of the subclasses in Table 19.2, and not on explicit metastatements that other adverbs do not exist. It is furthermore important to note that only true adverbs, as defined in section 19.2, are listed in Table 19.4, and not other types of adverbial expressions. Yeri, for instance, uses true adverbs at the layers of the Lexical Property and Configurational Property, nominal phrases at the layers of the State of Affairs and Episode, and particles at the layer of the Propositional Content. Similarly, Basque uses true adverbs up to the layer of the Episode, and at higher layers it uses adpositional phrases and particles.

The results shown in Table 19.4 are quite remarkable, as the generalization seems to hold across the sample. I should emphasize, however, that the presence of a subclass of adverbs in Table 19.4 may be based on the existence of just one type of adverb relevant to a certain layer. For example, at the layer of the Configurational Property I have above identified adverbs in six different domains: subject-oriented manner, additional participants, event-internal quantification, direction, aspect, and participant-oriented modality. The presence of just one of these would lead to a positive value in the relevant cell in Table 19.4. This does suggest, however, that the scope of an adverb is a more important predictor of its existence than its domain.

Another remarkable result is that there is only one language in the whole sample, Turkish, for which adverbs at the highest two layers have been identified. This may be a result of the fact that grammars generally do not discuss these adverbs as separate classes, an impression that is reinforced by the fact that the adverbs concerned were only identified after consulting an extensive dictionary of the language (Avery 1983). For most of the other sample languages such an additional source is not available.

Table 19.5 illustrates the overall findings presented in Table 19.4. For one language of each group, examples are given of adverbs pertaining to the different layers for which adverbs

Table 19.4 The existence of adverbs

Languages	#Languages	Lexical Property	Configurational Property	State-of-Affairs	Episode	Propositional Content	Communicated Content	Illocution	Discourse Act
Apurinã, Lao, Choctaw, Kharia	4								
Paiwan	1	+							
Warao, Xong, Yeri	3	+	+						
Barupu, Cupeño, Garo, Mian, Moskona	5	+	+	+					
Basque, Betta Kurumba, Bininj Gun-Wok, Central Alaskan Yupik, Goemai, Laz, Mani, Matses, Mehek, Ngiti, Nivkh, Jalkunan, Warrongo	13	+	+	+	+				
Alingae, Chukchi, Gaguudju, Lango, Lumun, Mandarin, Mapudungun, Musqueam, Palula, Rapanui, Tidore	11	+	+	+	+	+			
Albanian, Bardi, Gã, Hungarian, Hupa, Ingush, Korean, Pichi	8	+	+	+	+	+	+		
Turkish	1	+	+	+	+	+	+	+	+

Table 19.5 The existence of adverbs—illustrations

Language	Lexical Property	Configurational Property	State-of-Affairs	Episode	Propositional Content	Communicated Content	Illocution	Discourse Act
Paiwan	*aravac* 'very'							
Xong	*fut~fut* 'quickly'	*bos~bos* 'loudly'						
Barupu	*tororo* 'badly'	*rokorapo* 'expertly'	*āri* 'inside'					
Mani	*kèkè* 'quickly'	*icèntèni* 'loudly'	*pè* 'again'	*gbɛ̀n* 'tomorrow'				
A'ingae	*jùnde* 'quickly'	*tuyi* 'involuntarily'	*khase* 'again'	*vaeyi* 'recently'	*nane* 'surely'			
Albanian	*mirë* 'well'	*furishëm* 'furiously'	*shpesh* 'often'	*motit* 'long ago'	*sigurisht* 'certainly'	*fatmirës'isht* 'fortunately'		
Turkish	*iyi* 'well'	*heyecanlı* 'excitedly'	*içeri* 'inside'	*şimdi* 'now'	*kültüren* 'culturally'	*maalesef* 'unfortunately'	*sahiden* 'honestly'	*kısaca* 'briefly'

are available in the language. The sources for the examples in this table are: Paiwan (Chang 2006: 108), Xong (Sposato 2015: 528, 521), Barupu (Corris 2005: 124, 123), Mani (Childs 2011: 96, 55), A'ingae (Fischer & Hengeveld 2023: 22), Albanian (Newmark et al. 1982: 213, 217, 223, 317, 226), Turkish (Lewis 1967: 193, 198, 203, 196; Avery 1983: 1075, 466, 116).

A phenomenon accompanying the absence of adverbs at the higher layers is that periphrastic constructions are more often used at these layers to express the relevant adverbial notions. Even in languages that do have adverbs available for these layers, there may be a preference for additional marking of these adverbs. In English, one finds *strangely enough* (speaker evaluation—propositional content) versus *strangely* (manner—lexical property), *frankly speaking* (speaker evaluation—illocution) versus *frankly* (manner—lexical property), etc. (see Ramat & Ricca 1998 for further discussion).

19.4.3 The morphological marking of adverbs

A study of the morphological marking of adverbs reveals a number of further phenomena that additionally provide partial support for the hierarchy in (138). These concern:

(i) the use of reduplication as an expression strategy at certain layers;
(ii) the use of flexible modifiers (adjectives/adverbs) at certain layers;

19.4.3.1 Reduplication

An interesting generalization that shows up in the data is that languages use reduplication as an adverb-creating strategy at the lowest layers only. Here part of the hierarchy in (138) seems to be relevant too. In some languages one finds reduplication as an adverb-forming strategy at the layer of the Lexical Property only. This is for instance the case in Basque, where reduplicated adjectives are used as manner adverbs at this layer and are subject to restrictions of a lexical nature, in the sense that they 'form a collocation with specific verbs, and sound strange with other predicates' (Hualde & Ortiz de Urbina 2003: 194):

Basque (Basque) (Hualde & Ortiz de Urbina 2003: 194)
(139) arin~arin   labur~labu   Manner—Lexical Property
       fast~ADVR   short~ADVR
       'quickly'   'briefly'

In other languages adverbs derived by reduplication apply at the layers of the Lexical Property and the Configurational Property, as in Warrongo:

Warrongo (Pama-Nyungan) (Tsunoda 2011: 239, 240)
(140) ngarrban~ngarrban   Manner—Lexical Property
       quick~ADVR
       'rapidly'

(141) mori~mori   Manner—Configurational Property
       IDEO~ADVR
       'greedily'

In Garo, finally, one finds reduplication as an adverb-forming strategy at these two layers as well as at the layer of the State-of-Affairs:

Garo (Brahmaputran) (Burling 2003: 16, 106, 107)
(142)   bak~bak   Manner—Lexical Property
        chop~ADVR
        'quickly'

(143)   bing~bang   Manner—Configurational Property
        IDEO~ADVR
        'carelessly'

(144)   jem·~jem   Quantification—State of Affairs
        repeat~ADVR
        'repeatedly'

Table 19.6 shows how these systems map onto the hierarchy in (138).

19.4.3.2 *Flexible modifiers*

A further tendency that shows up clearly in the data is that languages with flexible modifiers use these adverbially at the lower layers only. At higher layers there are dedicated adverbs. Again, part of the hierarchy in (138) seems relevant to understanding the distribution of these adverbial uses.

In Lango, flexible modifiers may only be used at the layer of the Lexical Property: *à beber* 'good, well' in (145) can be used both adjectivally and adverbially. Modifiers of the Configurational Property are specialized adverbs: *nî lwájé* 'clumsily' in (146) cannot be used adjectivally.

        Lango (Nilotic) (Noonan 1992: 181)
(145)   à   bèbèr   Manner—Lexical Property
        ATTR   good
        'good, well'

(146)   nî   lwájé   Manner—Configurational Property
        ADVR   clumsy
        'clumsily'

In Ingush, flexible modifiers are allowed at the two lowest layers, but not at the layer of the State-of-Affairs. *Sixa* 'rapid' in (147) and *xaarc* 'false, falsely' in (148) can be used both adjectivally and adverbially, while e.g. *hwaalxagh* in (149) can only be used adverbially:

        Ingush (Nakh–Daghestanian) (Nichols 2011: 377, 252, 381)
(147)   sixa 'rapid, rapidly'   Manner—Lexical Property
(148)   xaarc 'false, falsely'   Manner—Configurational Property
(149)   hwaalxagh 'previously'   Relative Time—State of Affairs

Table 19.6 Reduplication as an adverb-forming strategy in the language sample

Languages	#Languages	Lexical Property	Configurational Property	State-of-Affairs	Episode	Propositional Content	Communicated Content	Illocution	Discourse Act
Basque, Gã	2	+							
Korean, Lango, Mandarin, Turkish, Warrongo, Xong	6	+	+						
Garo	1	+	+	+					

Table 19.7 Flexible modifiers in the language sample

Languages	#Languages	Lexical Property	Configurational Property	State-of-Affairs	Episode	Propositional Content	Communicated Content	Illocution	Discourse Act
Albanian, Cupeño, Gã, Lango	4	+							
Ingush, Warao, Xong	3	+	+						
Mapudungun	1	+	+	+					
Mian, Ngiti, Rapanui	3	+	+	+	+				

Mapudungun does allow flexible modifiers at the lowest three layers, as illustrated in (150)–(152). Modifiers at the layer of the Episode, however, can be used adverbially only. This is the case of *chumül* 'recently' in (153).

Mapudungun (Araucanian) (Smeets 2007: 71, 72)
(150) *küme* 'good, well' — Manner—Lexical Property
(151) *rüf* 'truthful, truthfully' — Manner—Configurational Property
(152) *we* 'new, just' — Relative Time—State-of-Affairs
(153) *chumül* 'recently' — Absolute Time—Episode

In Mian flexible modifiers can be used adverbially up to the layer of the Episode, as illustrated in (154)–(157). At higher layers neither flexible modifiers nor dedicated adverbs are found.

Mian (Nuclear Trans New Guinea) (Fedden 2011: 116, 117), 117)
(154) *ayam* 'good, well' — Manner—Lexical Property
(155) *gaang* 'wise, wisely' — Manner—Configurational Property
(156) *mikik* 'new, firstly' — Relative Time—State-of-Affairs
(157) *dam* 'true, truly' — Modality—Episode

Table 19.7 shows how these systems map onto the hierarchy in (138).

19.4.4 The order of adverbs

A last generalization, one that was established already by Cinque (1999) and that is confirmed in the data, is that the higher the layer at which an adverb applies, the more peripheral its position.[4] The most peripheral positions are the clause-initial and clause-final ones, while moving inward from both sides one arrives at ever less peripheral positions. The many English examples with multiple adverbs given in section 19.3 confirm this generalization. Example (158) serves as another illustration.

(158) *Finally*, she *honestly reportedly probably* left the building at eight o'clock.

The adverb highest in scope here is *finally* which modifies the highest layer of the Discourse Act and is in the most peripheral position; the adverb one step lower in scope is *honestly*, which modifies the Illocution and occupies the next position in line. *Reportedly* modifies the Communicated Content, the next layer in the hierarchy, and occupies the next position. And *probably*, which modifies the next lower layer, the Propositional Content, follows.

In some cases adverbs start in positions at both ends of the sentence, in which the predicted order holds for the two subsets of adverbs. This is illustrated in (159):

(159) *Fortunately*, he *apparently* has been playing soccer more *frequently lately*.

---

[4] Note that in some cases focus assignment may overrule this ordering principle.

In the initial field, *fortunately*, a modifier of the Communicated Content, is in a more peripheral position than *apparently*, which modifies the Propositional Content. In the final field, *lately*, a modifier of the Episode, is more peripheral than *frequently*, which modifies the State of Affairs.

Some assorted examples from sample languages further illustrate the phenomenon that scope determines order. In Mandarin Chinese, adverbs at higher layers, from the Episode onwards, expressing e.g. absolute time (160) and inference (161), may occur in sentence-initial position. All other adverbs, including those of manner (162) and quantification (163), have to occur after the sentence initial subject or topic.

Mandarin Chinese (Sinitic) (Li & Thompson 1981: 321, 323, 329)
(160)   Jīntiān wǒ   bu   shūfu.
        today   1.SG   NEG   comfortable
        'Today I don't feel well.'

(161)   Xiǎnrán   Zhāngsān   bu   gāoxing.
        obviously Zhangsan   NEG   happy
        'Obviously, Zhangsan is not happy.'

(162)   Tā   kuài.kuài.de   zǒu.
        3.SG quickly   walk
        'He/she walked quickly.'

(163)   Tā   yòu   chī   le.
        3SG   again   eat   PERF
        'She is eating again.'

In Korean, the position of an adverb correlates with its interpretation, as the following examples show:

Korean (Koreanic) (Sohn 1994: 87)
(164)   Hwaksilhi   Minca-nun   ka-n-ta
        surely   Minca-CONTR.TOP   go-IND-DECL
        'Surely Minca is going.'

(165)   Minca-nun   ku   kes-ul   hwaksilhi   a-n-ta
        Minca-CONTR.TOP   DEF   thing-ACC   surely   knows-IND-DECL
        'Minca knows it for sure.'

Hwaksilhi can be used as a subjective epistemic modal adverb at the layer of the Propositional Content, as in (164), or as a manner adverb at the layer of the Lexical Property, as in (165). The position of the adverb leads to disambiguation, with the higher epistemic adverb occupying the peripheral position, and the lower manner adverb occupying an internal position.

In Pichi, adverbs of relative location and absolute location may, as expected, co-occur in a sentence:

Pichi (Creole) (Yakpo 2019: 267)
(166) Bɔt ín sidɔ́n dɔ́n dɔ́n dɔ́n yandá.
but 3SG.INDP stay down REP REP yonder
'But he stays far down over there.'

In this example *yandá* 'yonder' expresses absolute location and takes the more peripheral final position, while *dɔ́n* 'down' expresses relative location and occupies an internal position, following the verb.

19.5 CONCLUSION

In this chapter, I have first defined adverbs as lexical words that can be used as modifiers of non-nominal heads, and considered the implications of this definition for the proper identification of adverbs. I then classified adverbs along two parameters: the semantic/pragmatic domain to which they belong and their semantic/pragmatic scope, where scope is defined in terms of the hierarchical layered framework of FDG. Finally, I showed that the classification in terms of semantic/pragmatic scope provides the basis for a series of generalizations concerning the existence, the form, and the ordering of classes of adverbs defined in hierarchical terms. Thus, the application of a hierarchical approach to linguistic structure to adverbs not only served to provide a comprehensive classification of this word class, but also provided further support for this approach itself.

ACKNOWLEDGEMENTS

I am indebted to Guglielmo Cinque, Evelien Keizer, Lois Kemp, Lachlan Mackenzie, and an anonymous reviewer for their generous and helpful comments on an earlier version of this chapter.

CHAPTER 20

ADPOSITIONS

BORJA HERCE

20.1 INTRODUCTION

ADPOSITIONS have traditionally been defined (e.g. Hagège 2010; Bakker 2013) as a class of words (i.e. not bound formatives like case markers, but rather independent words) that take a noun or noun phrase as their complement and specify its grammatical or semantic relation to another element, typically a verb (e.g. providing information about the time or location of the event) but also a noun (e.g. in possessive constructions) in the same clause.

As is customary in our discipline, however, not everyone agrees with (everything in) this definition. Certain adpositions, for example, seem to be used intransitively in certain contexts (e.g. *come in!*), and some words seem to be completely unspecified for (in)transitivity (see (9)). The problem that this represents is complex because sometimes the meaning of a transitively and an intransitively used adposition may differ substantially. When a word has intransitive uses (exclusively), it is often called a 'particle' or an adverb, and may not be considered adpositional in nature, see Broekhuis 2013: 35). Even when an adposition does occur with a noun, there may be disagreements with regard to their respective syntactic roles in the phrase. It is sometimes argued, for example, that (some) adpositions may not be the head of their respective phrases. This would be the case of so-called minor (Van Eynde 2004) or 'grammatical' (Mackenzie 2013) adpositions.

These disagreements notwithstanding, research on adpositions has classified them in various types on the basis of their more concrete properties. According to their position with respect to their accompanying noun (phrase), adpositions can be classified as either prepositions (if they precede it), postpositions (if they follow it), circumpositions (if they appear at both ends simultaneously, Van Riemsdijk 1990), ambipositions (if they can be either pre- or postposed, Libert 2006), or inpositions (if they occur inside the phrase, Dryer 2013b). Adpositions can also be classified by their morphological or syntactic complexity (simple adpositions, complex adpositions, adpositional locutions, Lehmann 1998), by their semantic content (spatial, temporal, others), their syntactic use (complementive, supplementive, adverbial, argumental, attributive, Broekhuis 2013), etc.

Although they have been less studied than other word classes like verbs and nouns, research on and around adpositions is still extensive and has led to many findings. The word order of adpositions (i.e. the presence of pre- or postpositions in a language), for example, has been famously found to correlate with the order of a noun and its possessor, a verb and its object etc. (Greenberg 1963a; Tsunoda et al. 1995; Dryer 2013b).

An adposition class is not universal (see e.g. the case of Klamath in DeLancey 2005) but is very widespread in the languages of the world. According to Bakker's (2013) counts, 315 out of 378 languages (83%) have adpositions and their absence is only common in North America and Australia. When a language has adpositions, their number can vary dramatically: from only a handful of them to several dozens, as in the better-known Standard Average European languages. In the latter, e.g. in English or German, it can even be argued to be an open class of words, as new adpositions are continuously being added. Mackenzie (2013) argues that it is 'lexical' adpositions (rather than the aforementioned 'grammatical' adpositions) that would be the most numerous subclass and constitute syntactic heads.

As the above paragraphs have suggested, therefore, individual adpositions, both within and across languages, may show very acute differences indeed with regard to both their semantic specificity and in their grammatical behaviour. Contrast, for example, the English adposition *ago* (postposed, stressed, devoted to denoting past) with *in* (preposed, unstressed, with various spatiotemporal uses).

Most of the literature on adpositions (e.g. Hagège 2010; Libert 2013; Mackenzie 2013) has emphasized their location at the intersection between lexicon and grammar, and between other word classes (e.g. verbs, nouns, and adverbs) both at the synchronic and the diachronic levels. This makes it difficult to draw the boundaries between adpositions and other elements like relational nouns, serial verbs, or case markers. In the context of a handbook on word classes, these may be quite 'convenient' properties if they mean, as argued by Hagège (2010: 332), that research on adpositions can 'make a significant contribution to a theory of the category in linguistics'. With that end in mind, this chapter will first explore in section 20.2 the traditional definition of adpositions and its borders with other classes. Next, in section 20.3, the synchronic properties of adpositions will be explored in three genetically unrelated languages. Section 20.4 moves on to diachronic changes as an explanation of the synchronic profile of adpositions, and of their links to other word classes. Section 20.5 summarizes the main findings and claims of the chapter.

20.2 DELIMITING THE WORD CLASS

The traditional definition of adposition which was advanced in section 20.1, it may be noticed, makes reference not only to their semantic contribution or to their functional role, but also to morphological notions (wordhood), to other word classes (nouns), and to abstract grammatical relations (complement). Once we recognize that structural categories are language-particular (see e.g. Haspelmath 2007) this can be considered a problem. However, an exclusively notional/semantic definition of adposition (for example based on its perceived functional core of conveying spatial and temporal information) is hardly a viable solution. It would constitute a clean break with previous uses of the term and most importantly, it would fail to distinguish a set of elements that would belong together grammatically in any evident way.[1] Because of this, the traditional definition will be provisionally adopted here.

---

[1] Of course, one may wonder whether the traditional definition of adpositions does define a class of elements that belong together in any deeper sense. As mentioned by Bickel (2010), we would ideally want our terms to correspond to sets of elements that somehow cluster together by virtue of their grammatical properties. This chapter explores whether this is the case.

One of the reasons why structural properties have traditionally been part of the definition of adposition is therefore that, if we failed to adopt them, we would not be allowed to exclude from the ranks of adpositions many phenomena, both grammatical and lexical, which seem to be completely heterogeneous. Some of the functional roles of adpositions, for example, can also be performed by purely lexical items:

(1) (a) He went **into** the house (b) He **entered** the house

(2) (a) He went **with** John (b) He **accompanied** John

The illative or comitative semantics of the prepositions *into* and *with*, respectively, is already part of the lexical semantics of English verbs like *enter* and *accompany*. The (a) and (b) sentences are, therefore, functional equivalents but we most certainly would not want to say that the (b) sentences include an adposition.

Some other more grammatical and systematic phenomena can also perform similar functions but still look very different from traditional adpositions in other respects. Consider, for example, the 'locative–directive stems' of Klamath:

(3) Klamath (DeLancey 2005: 192)
g-**awl**-**apga**-**bli**   lac'as-dat
go-on.top-back-again   house-LOC
'(He) climbed back up on the house.'

(4) Klamath (DeLancey 2005: 192)
sqel   g-**oLii**   limaas-am   ciis-dat
Marten   go-into   limaas-GEN   dwelling-LOC
'Marten went into the Limaas' house.'

The formatives in bold in the above sentences belong to a class of 120–150 such elements which carry out functions very similar to those of adpositional systems in European languages. As mentioned by DeLancey (2005: 195), the two categories 'are in many ways quite comparable, in terms of semantic function and range, numbers, and degree of openness of the class'.[2] The fundamental difference why we generally would not want to call these formatives adpositions is that they attach to the verb rather than forming a constituent with the noun phrase (i.e. the nouns for 'house' in the examples above).

According to the most traditional definition of adposition, however, this grammatical property is not sufficient either. Consider the following forms:

(5) Russian
Ja slomal dver'   bol'š-im   krasn-ym   molotk-**om**
I   broke   door   big-INS.SG red-INS.SG hammer-INS.SG
'I broke the door with a/the big red hammer.'

---

[2] It must be acknowledged, however, that the Klamath system appears to be still somewhat lexicalized. DeLancey (2005: 194) mentions that not all logically possible combinations are allowed and that idiomatic meanings are common.

(6) Basque
Mailu gorri handi bat-ez apurtu nuen atea
hammer red big one-INS open AUX door
'I broke the door with a big red hammer.'

In these examples, the formatives in bold (usually considered case markers) do indeed belong structurally together with the noun (phrase). In terms of their semantics, it is widely agreed that '[e]verything you can do with adpositions you can do with case inflections and vice versa' (Zwicky 1992: 370). The reason why a categorial distinction is sometimes drawn[3] has to do with the degree of integration between those formatives and the noun phrase itself. According to the traditional definition advanced in the introductory section, adpositions have to be independent grammatical words. It is usually agreed that the forms above are bound, which is why they are often (e.g. Bakker 2013) not considered adpositions.

The difficulties in determining wordhood cross-linguistically are well known (Haspelmath 2011) and even in individual languages, different criteria (phonological, morphological, syntactic) do not necessarily converge on the same domains (Schiering et al. 2010; Bickel & Zúñiga 2017). Because of this, disagreements abound, particularly on how elements like Basque *-ez* in (6) should be classified. While the Russian instrumental marker *-om* has to attach necessarily to the noun (which suggests it is a property or inflectional category of the noun itself), the Basque instrumental marker is syntactically 'promiscuous' and attaches simply (and exclusively) to the last word in the noun phrase. Although both forms are, thus, phonologically dependent, their syntactic status appears to be different, which is the reason why so-called 'adpositional clitics' (Hagège 2010) or 'clitic case markers' (Dryer 2013b) like the Basque one in (6) are often classified as adpositions.

The jury is still out, therefore, on where exactly the boundary should be drawn between these two categories and on the nature (sharp vs gradient) of the distinction. Thus, although some mention that 'between adpositions and [...] case affixes there are many differences in all domains' (Hagège 2010: 6), most of the research mentions only general tendencies as distinguishing the former from the latter. It is said, for example, that adpositions tend not to cumulate with other feature values, tend not to be repeated within the same noun phrase, tend not to show allomorphy, etc. Case affixes, in turn, usually cannot be conjoined, usually cannot appear without a noun, usually cannot be separated from it, etc.

Another area where definition of the adposition class sometimes becomes difficult is in relation to other word classes. Consider the following example:

(7) Chinese (Li & Thompson 1974: 266)
Tā **yòng** kuàizi chī-fàn
he use chopsticks eat-food
'He eats with chopsticks.'

Sometimes (e.g. in serial verb constructions), quite verb-like elements can be used in ways very similar to adpositions. In (7), *yòng* 'use' takes a noun phrase complement and informs

---
[3] Some other times, a distinction is purposefully avoided, and terms have been coined to refer to both adpositions and case markers together (see e.g. Schachter & Shopen's 2007: 34–37 'role marker' and Haspelmath's 2019 'flag').

us about its semantic (instrumental) role with respect to the verb 'eat'. However, *yòng* can be also used as the main verb in a sentence, and in a sentence like (7) can denote an event of its own (i.e. the sentence could also be paraphrased as 'he uses chopsticks to eat', or 'he uses chopsticks and eats' ...) and can combine with the aspectual suffix *le*. Because it has properties very close to run-of-the-mill verbs in the language, thus, it might be problematic to classify expressions like these as adpositional. Something similar happens in the case of constructions like (8).

(8) Lezgian (Haspelmath 1993a: 221)
Čarx-ari-n **arada** xür kutu-nwa
rock-PL-GEN between village found-PRF
'A village has been founded between the rocks.'

The word *arada* is used to specify the (intrative) role of the noun 'rocks' with respect to the verb 'found'. The expression, however, looks like the inessive singular (= oblique) form of a noun *ara* which means 'space in between'. The noun *ara* can be used referentially (e.g. in 'I saw the space in between'), can occur in other grammatical cases (e.g. the elative *aradaj*, the dative *aradiz*, etc.) to express other spatial relations (i.e. 'from between', 'to between') etc. Because they have properties very close to run-of-the-mill nouns, thus, many linguists have been reluctant to grant adpositional status to such 'relator' nouns (also sometimes called 'axial parts', see Svenonius 2006a).

Another source of uncertainty in distinguishing adpositions from other word classes is related to transitivity. According to their traditional definition (see section 20.1), adpositions must be transitive and should thus co-occur with a noun (phrase) complement. A problem arises, then, when (what appears to be) a single form has both transitive and intransitive uses:

(9) (a) Today he came early **in** the office   (b) Please come **in**!

(10) (a) I found him **inside** the house   (b) I found him **inside**

The forms in bold are used transitively in the (a) sentences but intransitively in their (b) counterparts. Because, as I say, adpositions should be transitive by definition, many linguists would say that the forms in (a) are adpositions and the forms b) are something else (e.g. adverbs) despite their identical semantic content.[4] Different words, however, may also have more constrained or more flexible syntactic properties. Thus, the intransitive uses of *in* are much more limited in general than those of *inside* (cf. *I found him in), which may lead us to think of *in* as somewhat 'more adpositional' than *inside*. It should be pointed out, however, that because of their functional similarity, unified treatments of adverbs and adpositions have also been proposed (see Mackenzie's 2001 'Ad' class).

Although the traditional definition of adposition advanced in section 20.1 did not make explicit reference to the grammatical properties of other classes, these have also played a big

---

[4] Note, however, that practices differ in other word classes. Because transitivity has usually not been considered a definitional characteristic of verbs, intransitive uses of otherwise transitive verbs (e.g. *I like how you eat*, *You need to stop*, etc.) are not generally analysed as involving conversion into another word class.

role in practice when determining what counts or does not count as an adposition. Thus, for example, in order not to classify elements like the ones in (7), (8), and (10) as adpositional, Bakker (2013) mentioned that he would only classify a word as an adposition if it 'displays morphosyntactic behaviour distinct from more clearcut verbal, nominal or adverbial elements in that language'. This is an executive decision that could be understandable in a certain context. It is, however, just one possibility among many.

When faced with the variability and richness of empirical data, different linguists may have different tendencies or personal biases. Different goals will also sometimes require different approaches. There is basically, as Croft (2000) calls them, the 'lumper' and the 'splitter' approaches.[5] The former may be happy to say that many or all of the forms in bold in examples (1)–(10) are 'the same thing' at some level of abstraction. The latter will say that they are all different and, furthermore, that there is much more variation involved, and categories that have been left unaddressed here (e.g. various classes of adpositions). Regardless of our individual likings, however, the question of whether there is a class of adpositions or many in a particular language, and what its members and borders are like could in principle be framed and answered empirically. Section 20.3 explores the adpositional systems of various genetically unrelated languages in search of answers.

20.3 A QUANTITATIVE APPROACH TO ADPOSITIONS IN THREE GENETICALLY UNRELATED LANGUAGES

20.3.1 Hungarian

The domain of adpositions and their closest neighbours in Hungarian constitutes an ideal object of study to gain insight into the synchronic organization of these words in the grammar. This is so because of the comparatively large number of adpositions of different general profiles (e.g. from more relator–noun-like expressions to more case-like bound formatives), and because of the applicability in the language of many grammatical properties and tests that can potentially be used to classify these expressions into different types.

As expected from a predominantly head-final language, Hungarian adpositions and adposition-like forms are overwhelmingly placed after their complement noun phrases. Only some can be optionally preposed for emphasis, as in (11b):

(11) (a) *mellett János   (b) együtt János-sal
    next.to János.NOM   together János-INS
    'next to János'   'together with János' (Asbury 2008: 38)

Another property that distinguishes different postpositions, as the phrases in (11) show, is that some occur together with the unmarked (= nominative) form of the noun, while others

---

[5] Somewhat more opaquely, these two types of linguists have also been called the 'hedgehogs' and the 'foxes' by Aronoff (2016).

govern other (marked) cases such as the superessive, instrumental, adessive, allative, etc. Adposition-like elements can differ in other ways too:

(12) (a) *en-nél a ház-nál*
 this-at the house-at
 'at this house'

(b) *az **alatt** a fa alatt*
 that under the tree.NOM under
 'under that tree'

(c) *az-zal a fiú-val **együtt***
 that-INS the boy-INS together
 'together with that boy'

(Asbury 2008: 56)

In noun phrases containing a demonstrative and a noun, some adpositions (see (12a) and (12b) vs (12c)) have to appear not only at the end of the noun phrase but also after the demonstrative. Different forms may also differ on whether or not they are subject to allomorphy triggered by vowel harmony (see (12a) vs (12b) and (12c)).

Adpositions (or adposition-like formatives) can also differ on whether or not they inflect for person (see (13)), and whether or not they can inflect for different local cases (see (14)):

(13) (a) *mögött-em*
 behind-1SG
 'behind me'

(b) *vel-em szemben / * szemben-em*
 INS-1SG opposite opposite-1SG
 'opposite me' (Asbury 2008: 56)

(14) (a) *a ház-on **túl-ról***
 the house-SUB beyond-DEL
 'from beyond the house'

(b) *?a ház **mögött-ről***
 the house.NOM behind-DEL
 'from behind the house'

(Kenesei et al. 1998: 87)

Other properties that may distinguish some adpositions from others are (i) the ability to stand without a complement (15), or (ii) the ability to introduce a subordinate clause as in (16):

(15) *Föl-néz-t-él az ég-re? **Föl.***
 up-look-PST-2SG the sky-DAT up
 'Were you looking up at the sky? Yes.' (Dávid Győrfi, p.c.)

(16) *Az-**után**, hogy Péter meg-érkezett...*
 it-after that Peter PFV-arrived...
 'After Peter had arrived...' (Kenesei et al. 2002: 89)

All the grammatical properties described so far constitute logically independent variables, so it is a matter for empirical discovery to find out whether they actually map onto different sets of adpositions or not. In addition, there is no reason to believe aprioristically that one (or a subset) of these properties can be used as necessary and sufficient conditions for membership into a particular class while others can be swept freely under the rug. Measuring all the relevant variation and incorporating all its richness into linguistic analysis (see Multivariate Typology, Bickel 2010) is surely the best way to proceed from an empirical perspective. With that conviction and with the goal of acquiring the finest-grained knowledge possible about the structure of the Hungarian adpositional domain, 52 words/formatives of the language have been independently classified according to their capacity to exhibit these different grammatical properties and to participate in particular constructions.

The first finding to emerge from this (see Figure 20.1 and the full list of grammatical properties A–J in the Appendix) is that no two properties are coextensive in the adposition lexicon, i.e. no two properties can be identified which classify the 52 elements[6] in my sample in the same way. According to their grammatical behaviour, a total of 22 different classes of adpositions have been identified in the sample, half of which are singleton. This may well

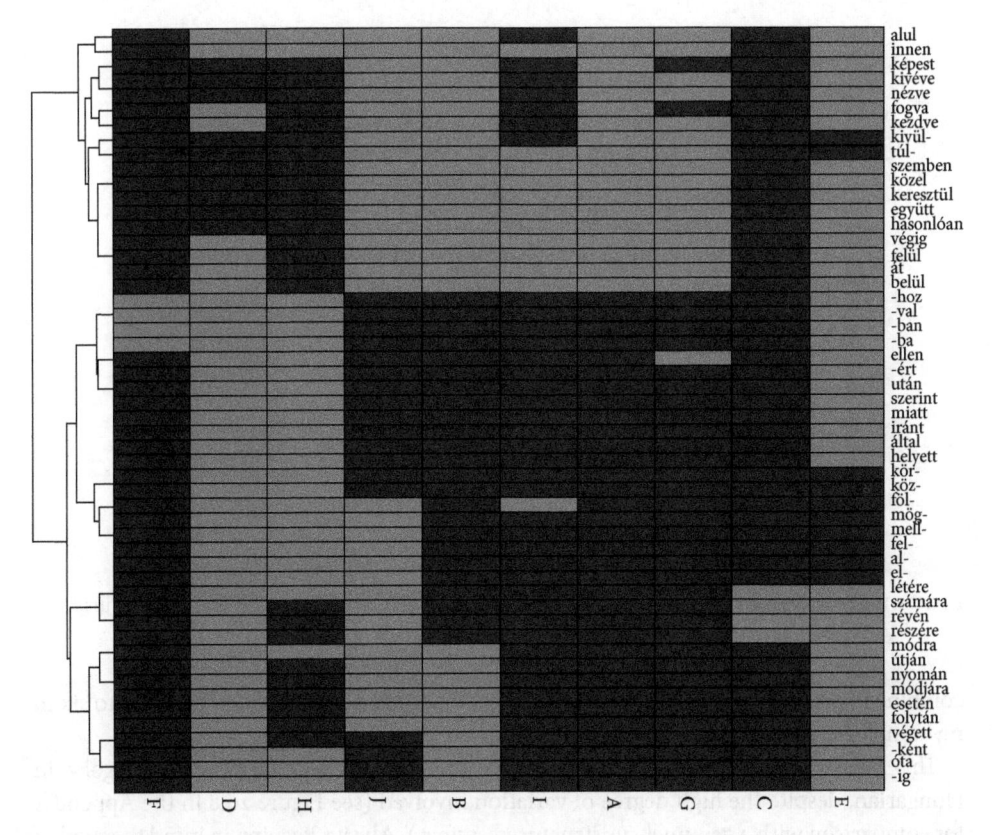

FIGURE 20.1 Classification of the 52 adpositions for 10 grammatical properties (dark grey = has property, light grey = lacks property)

---

[6] These 52 items and 10 grammatical properties of Hungarian have been obtained from the cited sources on the language but have, of course, no claim to exhaustivity. Many other (adposition-like) items and grammatical variables could be analysed, in addition to, or instead of, the ones that have been chosen here, which should thus be understood only as a representative subset. The same thing applies to the items and grammatical properties analysed for Basque (Figure 20.3), German (Figure 20.4), and Spanish (Figure 20.7).

lead one to wonder whether variation is completely unconstrained. If this were the case we would have little reason to even talk about a class of adpositions, which could be seen rather as a residue of heterogenous elements not fitting in the other, bigger classes. Consider the Hungarian data in Figure 20.1 (from Kenesei et al. 2002, Asbury 2008, and Dávid Győrfi, p.c.).

Figure 20.1 reveals that, as advanced before, the surveyed grammatical properties all behave differently. Despite the large amount of grammatical variation and idiosyncrasies involved, however, one can still observe a great amount of structure. Thus, one property can often be used to predict another.[7] Notice, for example, how −A implies −B (that is, if an adposition lacks property A it will also lack property B), +D implies −A and −B, +E implies + B or + D etc. Thus, although these four logically independent grammatical features could

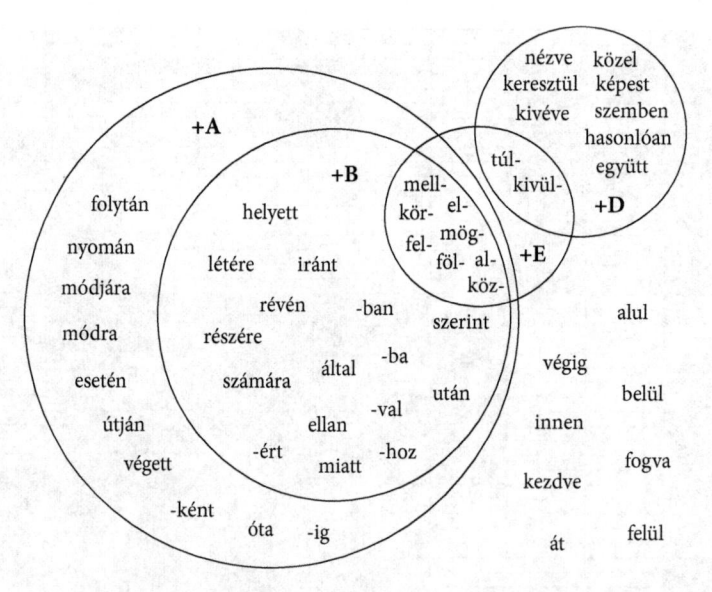

FIGURE 20.2 Some Hungarian adpositions according to four grammatical properties

combine to produce up to $2^4=16$ different classes of adpositions, they only give rise to six in my sample (Figure 20.2).

This speaks to the high degree of structuredness of the adpositional category in Hungarian, despite the high degree of variation involved (see Figure 20.8 in the Appendix for comparison with a genuinely unstructured system). Always keeping in mind the total of 22 classes found in Figure 20.1, a clustering analysis can group them into a smaller number of them by merging those classes of adpositions that are progressively closest in terms of

---

[7] Predictability relations have always had a central role in morphology, where linguists have long been aware that 'one inflection tends to predict another' (Matthews 1991: 97). By contrast, the predictability of more abstract grammatical properties from each other has received much less attention. I can think of no reason, however, why predictability should not be a powerful force in the organization of these grammatical traits too.

their grammatical properties (consider, e.g. the first two adpositions *alul* 'below' and *innen* 'on this side of', which only differ in property I). If we do that, it is very revealing (see the y-axis in Figure 20.1) that the last two macroclasses of adpositions are comparatively far from each other in Hungarian. In other words, recognizing two separate parts of speech may be justified.

They would correspond very closely to the division between what the literature (e.g. Asbury 2008) has called non-inflecting postpositions on the one hand, and inflecting postpositions and case markers on the other. This lends support to some previous qualitative analyses like that of Kiss (2002), who claimed that both case suffixes and inflecting postpositions are manifestations of case, unlike uninflecting postpositions (which would actually constitute adverbs under her analysis). Figure 20.1 also shows that property A (whether a formative governs the unmarked = nominative form in its noun complement or not) is coextensive with this macro-division and suggests itself as the most important grammatical property in the structuring of the adposition category in Hungarian (see Kenesei et al. 2002: 337–339).

There is no quantitative empirical support, on the contrary, for other claims and hypotheses in the literature such as a primary division between 'case suffixes' and postpositions (see e.g. Marácz 1989, who claimed that the category of Hungarian postpositions was composed of inflecting and uninflecting postpositions to the exclusion of [orthographically] bound case forms). The present quantitative evidence also appears to argue against a three-way division between 'case suffixes', inflecting postpositions, and uninflecting postpositions.

20.3.2 Basque

Although Basque is a completely unrelated language, its adpositional system shows quite a few parallels to Hungarian. We see many of the same issues that were problematic in the latter language in determining adpositional status: some postpositions in the case-marker spectrum vs. some others in the relator–noun spectrum, some that occur with the unmarked form of the noun (=absolutive) vs others which govern other cases (genitive, dative, instrumental, etc.), some that have allomorphic variants while others do not, etc.

Examples (17a) and (17b) show how some adpositions/relator nouns can inflect for different spatial cases. In addition, some of these expressions, but not all, can also be used referentially as prototypical nouns (e.g. *barrua* 'the inside', *ingurua* 'the surroundings', but *artea 'the space in between' cf. ex. (8)). Example (18) shows that, as in many other languages, different adpositions demand different cases on their complement: the unmarked absolutive (e.g. *gabe*), the genitive (-*kin*), the dative (*buruz*), etc:

(17) (a) *Kajoi* **barru-an** *ipini zuen* (b) *Kajoi* **barru-tik** *hartu zuen*
 drawer inside-LOC put PAST.3SG>3SG   drawer inside-ABL grab PAST.3SG>3SG
 '(S)he put it inside the drawer.'   '(S)he grabbed it from inside the drawer.'

(18) *Zu-re-kin,* edo zu **gabe,** zu-ri **buruz** hitz egin-go dute
 you-GEN-COM or you without you-DAT about word do-FUT 3PL>3SG
 'With you, or without you, they will talk about you.'

Examples (19a) and (19b) show that different postpositions also have different levels of phonological dependency of their hosts. In standard Basque, stress is not contrastive and is assigned at the phrase level (see Hualde & Ortiz de Urbina 2003), so it is complicated (or impossible) to draw distinctions based on it. However, other properties can distinguish them, such as the possibility of omitting the notional object (i.e. *bila joan zen* vs **tzat erosi zuen*). Example (19) and Table 20.1 also show that all these forms (even those which signal core grammatical roles like absolutive or ergative) are always phrase-final clitics/adpositions in Basque and not a property or inflectional form of nouns.

(19) (a) *Neskato berria-ren **bila** joan zen* (b) *Neskato berria-ren-**tzat** erosi zuen*
 girlfriend new-GEN search go PAST.3SG   girlfriend new-GEN-BEN buy PAST.3SG>3SG
 'He went to look for his new girlfriend.' 'He bought it for his new girlfriend.'

Table 20.1 Definite forms of the phrase 'black valley' (*haran* = valley) for six different cases

	SG	PL
ABS	Haran beltz-a	Haran beltz-ak
ERG	Haran beltz-ak	Haran beltz-ek
DAT	Haran beltz-ari	Haran beltz-ei
GEN	Haran beltz-aren	Haran beltz-en
LOC	Haran beltz-ean	Haran beltz-etan
ALL	Haran beltz-era	Haran beltz-etara

Table 20.1 shows, in addition, that adpositional clitics are often fused with definiteness and number-marking morphology in the language in ways that are hard to predict morphophonologically. The ergative, for example, might lead one to identify -*k* as the ergative clitic/postposition and the forms -*a* and -*e* as number and definiteness-related. A look at the dative forms, however, does not reveal the same regularity, as the form -*r*- unexpectedly appears in one number value but not in the other. A look at the locative or allative postpositions reveals something different once again: a segment -*e*- in the singular and -*et*- in the plural. One cannot recast this allomorphy as phonologically derived, as there is nothing wrong phonotactically with hypothetical forms like **beltzai, *beltzeri, *beltzan, *beltzatan*. Some of these forms actually appear in other dialects.

Although some grammatical properties are relevant in many languages and are thus often mentioned in descriptions (e.g. case-government, word order, morphological integration with host), the properties which determine adposition variation differ from one language to another. In Basque, for example, postposition is compulsory and thus no adposition (with the possible exception of *duela* 'ago') can ever be placed before its complement, unlike in Hungarian (see (11b)). Similarly, a notional pronominal object is never expressed with person inflection on the adposition (see (13a)). It is no secret, then, that 'word classes must be recognized for each language on grammatical criteria internal to that language' (Dixon 2010: 102). Based on some of the grammatical properties relevant to Basque, then, Figure 20.3 shows how adpositional elements classify in the language.

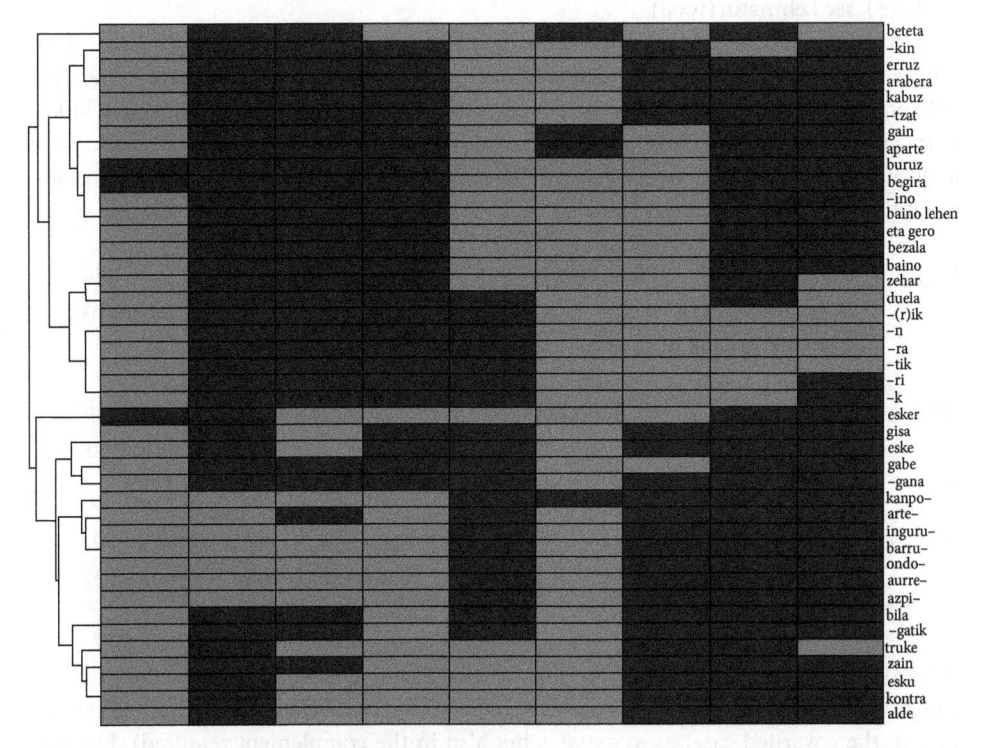

FIGURE 20.3 Grammatical properties of 42 Basque adpositions (Hualde 2002, personal knowledge; Hualde & Ortiz de Urbina 2003)

As Figure 20.3 shows, like in Hungarian, all the grammatical properties identified map onto different sets of adpositions. As a result, the 42 adpositions (or adposition-like elements) in my sample classify into 21 different classes, 11 of which are singleton. Like in Hungarian, however, implicational relations are not difficult to find: –E implies + C, –C implies + D and –B, +D implies + I etc. In addition, some properties (e.g. A, B, and C; H and I) classify postpositions very similarly. This is all evidence for structuredness within the class.

20.3.3 German

In the interest of maximizing variation, a genetically unrelated language like German, which unlike Basque and Hungarian is predominantly prepositional, would be an interesting addition to the present synchronic exploration. German adpositions, like Hungarian and Basque ones, can also govern different cases. They also vary strongly in their degree of grammaticalization (from the most compact and desemanticized like *zu* 'to' to the most complex and synchronically analysable as denominal (e.g. *aufgrund* 'because of' < *auf Grund*, lit. on reason) or deverbal (e.g. *ausgenommen* 'except for' < participle of *ausnehmen* 'exclude'), see Lehmann (1998).

German adpositions, like Hungarian ones, also show some degree of word order flexibility with respect to their complement, although in this case it is not a productive operation with pragmatic nuances but rather a property of individual adpositions, and it is often linked to specific heterogeneous constructions. Like in Basque, some of the more grammaticalized adpositions can also fuse or contract with the definite article. Observe some of these grammatical properties in the examples below:

(20) (a) *Ich laufe den Fluss entlang*
I walk the.ACC river along
'I walk along the river.'

(b) *Ich laufe entlang des Flusses*
I walk along the.GEN river
'I walk along the river.'

(21) (a) *Ich habe das fürs Auto gekauft*
I have this for.the car bought
'I have bought this for the car.'

(b) **Ich bin jetzt ohnes Gepäck*
I am now without.the luggage
'I am now without the luggage.'

(22) (a) *Da-für habe ich das gekauft*
that-for have I that bought
'I have bought it for that.'

(b) **Dar-ohne will ich nicht sein*
that-without want I not be
'I don't want to be without it.'

As (20) shows, some adpositions like *entlang* 'along' can be used both before or after their complement. A difference in word order, however, can correlate with other differences (e.g. in the governed case, as in *entlang*, but also in the complement required). Example (21) shows that some prepositions can fuse with the definite article (*für* + *das* = *fürs*) while others cannot do so. Example (22) shows yet another grammatical property of some German adpositions, which, when they take a neuter object pronoun, they do so by hosting a prefix *da-* (*dar-* before a vowel) instead of taking the regularly expected form **für das/es*. On the basis of these and other grammatical properties (see appendix), observe the overall (sub) classifications within the German adpositional system in Figure 20.4.

Not very differently from our observations for the previous languages, every single grammatical property surveyed maps onto a different set of adpositions. According to these, the 47 adpositions in my sample classify into 26 different classes. Although somewhat less structured than adpositions in the previous languages (because there are more classes even with less grammatical properties surveyed), there are still clear predictive relations in place: −H implies −F and −D, −F implies +C, etc.

It is hardly contentious to point out that different languages are characterized by different overall typological and grammatical profiles. Throughout this section I have shown that this applies as well, of course, to the domain of adpositions. All the properties that are not part of the linguist's definition of the category (e.g. case government, word order, person inflection, fusion with articles) might be relevant to describe the grammatical behaviour of (some) adpositions in some languages but not in others.

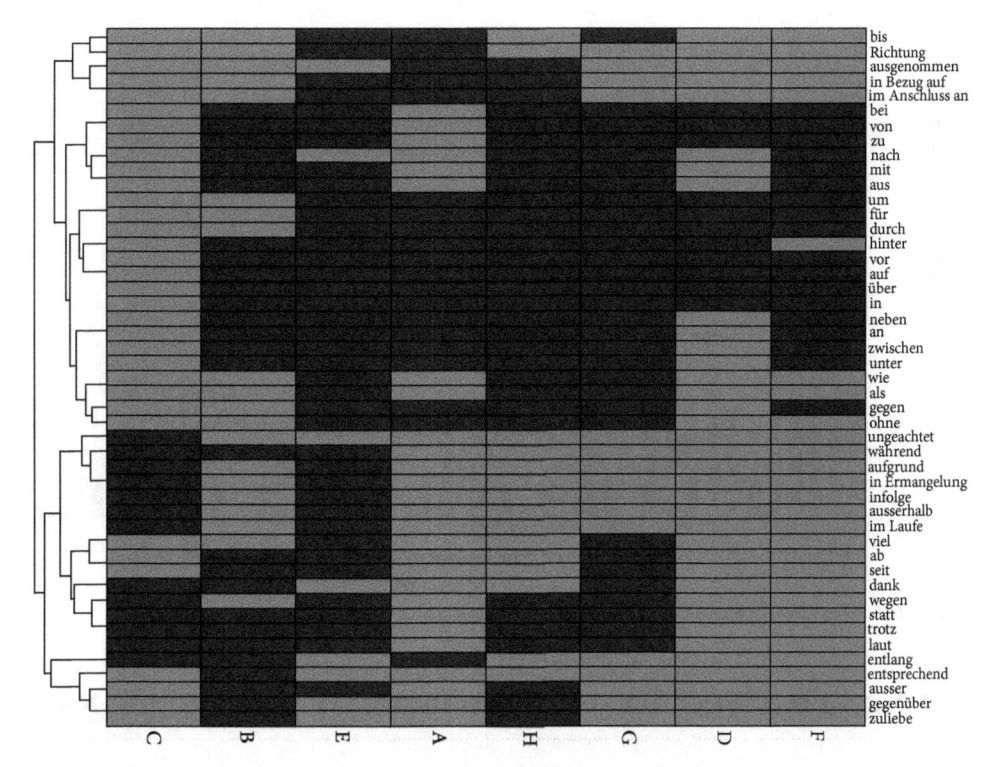

FIGURE 20.4 Classification of 47 German adpositions for 8 grammatical properties

I have also shown how even in genetically unrelated languages, the adpositional domain is characterized by a considerable degree of both internal diversity and structuredness. Regarding the latter, individual grammatical properties are not completely independent of each other, so structure and constraints of some kind are obvious. At the same time, however, and considering all properties, many adpositions exhibit idiosyncratic and unparalleled grammatical behaviour. This deserves some explanation.

Frequency of use is one of the most powerful sources of explanation in language. The graph above shows the proportion of adpositions among the 4000 most frequent words in the English language (in the corpus COCA, Davies 2008). It shows that, among the 100 most frequent words (first column from the left), there are 13 adpositions.[8] That group of words is the one with the highest proportion of adpositions, as the next 100 (second column from the left) includes only 7 adpositions, the next (third column) 5, etc. The overall downward trend is clear and far-reaching, with the 1000 most frequent English words including 51 adpositions, the next 1,000 14, the next 12, and the next 7. As Figure 20.5 shows, thus, there is a pronounced tendency for adpositions to be characterized by a very high frequency of use. This is one of the most prominent traits of adpositions overall and one of the main sources of explanation for the synchronic grammatical variability that we have discussed here. The other obvious force to shape adpositions, diachrony, will be discussed in the next section.

---

[8] This refers to one-word adpositions only. Words with both adpositional and adverbial uses were counted as different words (e.g. *inside1* [preposition, see (10a)] vs *inside2* [adverb, see (10b)]).

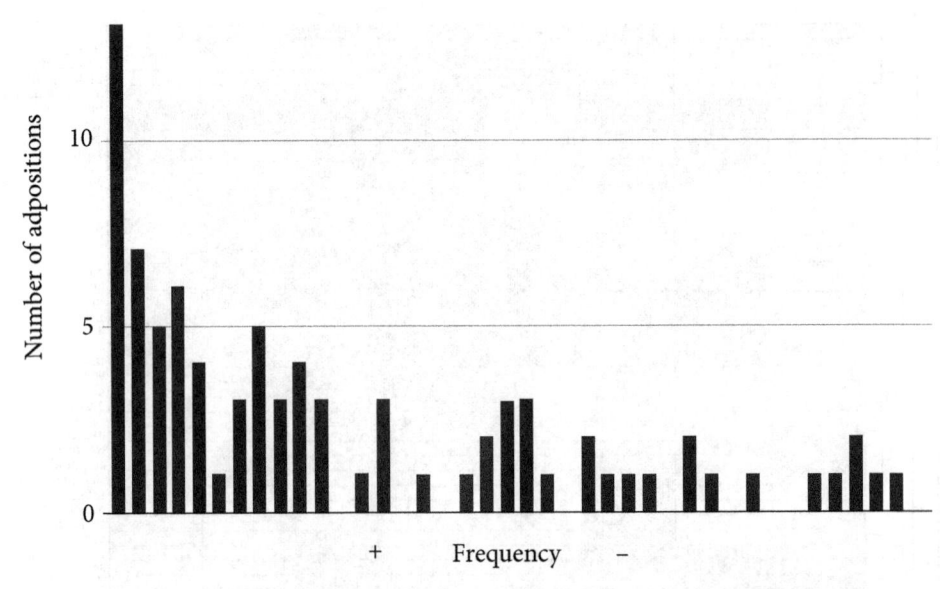

FIGURE 20.5 Number of adpositions in different token frequency ranges (COCA)

20.4 THE DIACHRONIC PROFILE OF ADPOSITIONS

Adpositions have been characterized in the literature as a word class trapped between the lexicon and the grammar (Hagège 2010: 332). Lexical adpositions (Mackenzie 2013) have also been described as a category that is located at the crossroads between the other large lexical classes, thus often sharing properties with nouns, verbs, and adverbs (see section 20.2). These properties, as well as the ones that were discussed in the synchronic section 20.3 (e.g. the high token frequency of adpositions, and the idiosyncratic grammatical behaviour of many of them), derive at least partially from diachrony. Adpositions are both targets and sources of various frequent grammaticalization processes and are also at the mercy of language contact and borrowing from other languages.

Regarding the latter, adpositions have usually been considered comparatively difficult to borrow. Matras (2007) proposes the following borrowability hierarchy:

> nouns, conjunctions > verbs > discourse markers > adjectives > interjections > adverbs > **adpositions** > numerals > pronouns > derivational affixes > inflectional affixes

According to it, adpositions would be less frequently borrowed than words from the major word classes (i.e. nouns, verbs, adjectives, adverbs). When adpositions do cross language boundaries they do not always retain their original grammatical behaviour. The Basque adposition *kontra*, for example, was borrowed from Spanish *contra* and, in the process, adopted some of the grammatical properties typical of Basque adpositions.

(23) Spanish   Basque
   (a) *Lo puse   contra   la pared*   (b) *horma-ren **kontra** jarri nuen*
       it put.1SG against the wall   wall-GEN   against   put   AUX.1SG
       'I put it against the wall.'   'I put it against the wall.'

Unlike its Spanish equivalent and predecessor, Basque *kontra* appears postposed to its complement, which is declined in the genitive, a pattern found in many native adpositions (see (19)). This does not mean that borrowed adpositions will always be assimilated to the properties of inherited ones. Quite on the contrary, preservation of word order appears to be more common, even when borrowing takes place, as in (23), between languages with different overall word order profiles (see Grossman 2017).

(24) Spanish   Caviñena (Guillaume 2008: 77)
    (a) ***hasta aquí***   (b) ***hasta rejeka***
       until   here   until   here
       'Up to here.'   'Up to here.'

The Spanish preposition *hasta*, for example, has preserved its original word order when borrowed into Caviñena, where it now constitutes the only preposition in an otherwise exclusively postpositional language.

Concerning the language-internal origins of adpositions, it is well known that verbs are a very common source for them (see, e.g., Kortmann & König 1992; Haspelmath 1998: 330). The change may occur in a wide variety of contexts, among others in finite verbs in serial verb constructions (see the Chinese example (7)), and in nonfinite forms of verbs in subordinate clauses (e.g. English *concerning, following, given, provided*, etc.). Similarly, it is well known that nouns can also give rise to adpositions (see e.g. Lehmann 1985; De Lancey 1997). This may happen out of relator nouns that become conventionalized to express certain spatiotemporal relations with respect to their possessor (cf. English *on top of, in front of*, etc. and see also the Lezgian example in (8)). It is also not uncommon for adpositions to arise out of adverbs (see (10)) or adjectives (e.g. English *near*).

Words from any large, open, lexical class, therefore, can grammaticalize into adpositions in the right environment. Adpositions, however, can also grammaticalize in turn into other entities like case markers, infinitive markers (cf. English *to*), complementizers (see Heine & Kuteva 2002: 152), etc. Because of the mentioned diachronic links between lexical classes and adpositions (see also Kahr 1975), and between adpositions and case markers, the boundaries between these classes also tend to be synchronically problematic (see ex. (5)–(8)), as they are blurry and not discrete.

Language change is sneaky. This means that when they are transitioning from one class to another, words cannot change (all of) their grammatical properties overnight. Thus, for example, German *anstatt* and English *instead* (from *an/in* 'in' + *stat/stede* 'place') have been shedding their nominal characteristics, but only progressively. For example, possessive constructions (i.e. *an seiner Statt* or *in my stead*) have been slowly losing ground (to *anstatt ihm* or *instead of me*) during the last two centuries but are still not impossible.

Because of this and because of the high token frequency that characterizes many adpositions (see Figure 20.6), it is only to be expected that there will be many idiosyncratic uses and different grammatical properties among them, particularly among the most peripheral (i.e. more nouny or more verby) and the newest members of the category.

Consider, for example, the case of Spanish. The list of adpositions that Spanish children learn in school consists of the following 19 items: *a, ante, bajo, con, contra, de, desde, en, entre, hacia, hasta, para, por, según, sin, sobre, tras, durante,* and *mediante*. The last two, as their non-alphabetical order reflects, were added later to the 'official' list and are clearly deverbal (Castro Zapata 2010). Be that as it may, although some grammatical differences between the

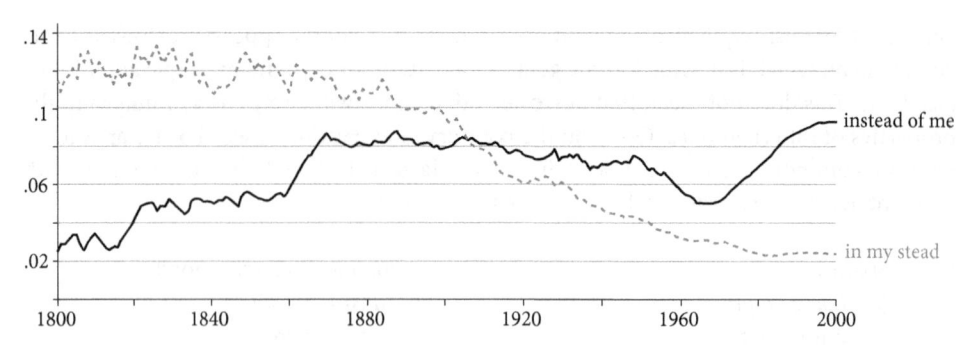

FIGURE 20.6 Frequency (tokens per million words) over time of *instead of me* vs *in my stead* (Google Books Ngram Viewer: http://books.google.com/ngrams)

traditional, core set of prepositions can also be found (see (25)), their grammatical properties are still relatively homogeneous in comparison with more peripheral members of the class (see Figure 20.7):

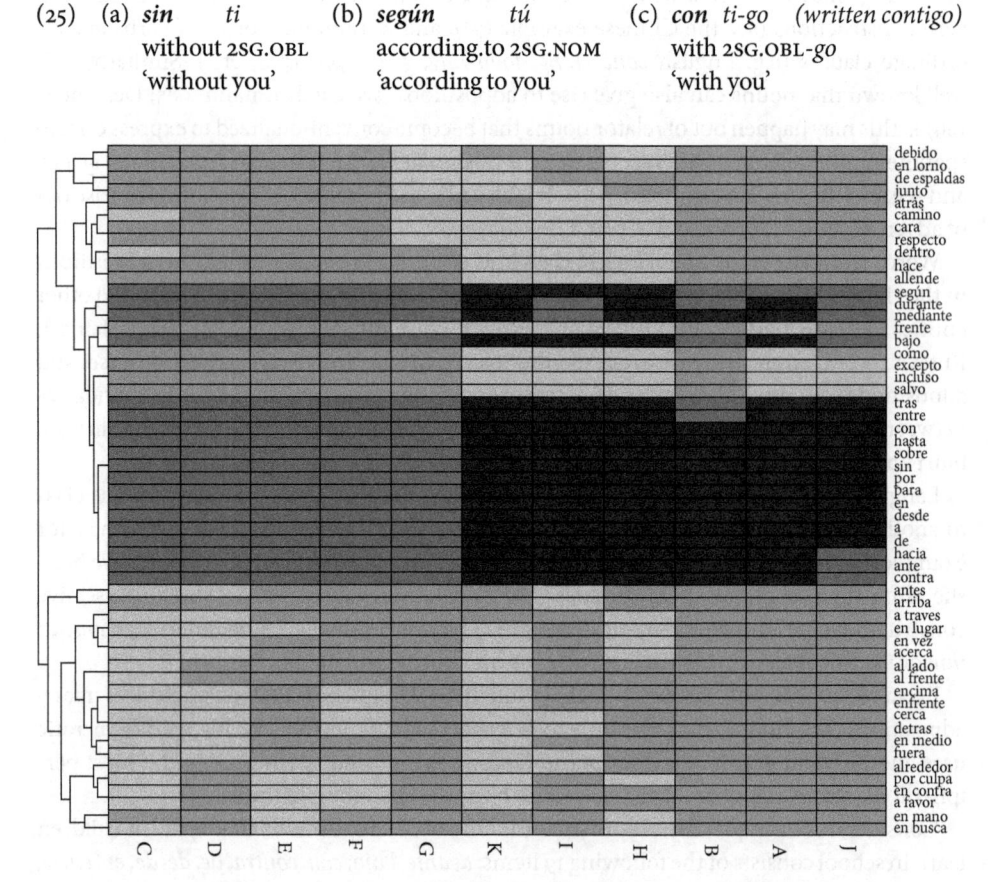

(25) (a) **sin   ti**   (b) **según   tú**   (c) **con ti-go**   (written *contigo*)
       without 2SG.OBL   according.to 2SG.NOM   with 2SG.OBL-*go*
       'without you'   'according to you'   'with you'

FIGURE 20.7 Properties of 55 Spanish adpositions, with the 19 traditional prepositions darker

Whereas most of the core prepositions of Spanish govern the oblique form of pronouns (see (25a)), some others do not and have inherited other requirements as a result of their history. This is the case, for example, of *según* (from Latin *secundus*), which occurs with nominative pronouns (cf. (25b)), or *con*, which occurs with *go*-final pronouns (from an earlier postpositional word order i.e. *tē cum* > *tigo* > *con tigo*, see Rini 1990) (cf. (25c)).

Despite these quirks, as I mentioned before, the grammatical properties of the oldest and most frequent Spanish prepositions (i.e. *de, en, a*) appear to cluster together very tightly. The y-axis in Figure 20.7 shows how they are grouped in larger classes than the others and occupy a central position by virtue of the grammatical properties they have in common.

Thus, although the 11 grammatical properties that have been surveyed in Spanish (see appendix) all characterize once again different sets of adpositions and group them into a total of 31 different classes, most of the variation is found in the periphery of the category, where different expressions (e.g. more verby ones like *hace* 'makes' (see below), more nouny ones like *camino* 'way' (see (26a)), more adverby ones like *fuera* 'outside', etc.) evolve slowly and in their own specific ways towards a more grammatical and adpositional status.

The specific path followed by different expressions will depend, thus, on their original categorial membership and properties, as well as on the particular construction where they take on an adpositional/relational role. Broad tendencies (subsumed under the cover-term 'grammaticalization') will be common to many of these transcategorizations: an increase in frequency of use, word order fixation, loss of grammatical properties characteristic of their previous word-class membership, etc.

Spanish *hace* 'make.3SG.PRES', for example, has been shown (see Herce 2017a) to have moved towards an adpositional status with the same (past time) meaning as English *ago*. On its way there, it increased its token frequency tenfold, it became compulsorily preposed to its complement, and it lost many of its most typically verbal properties like negation, time adjunction, tense, and person morphology. The cross-linguistic recurrence of some diachronic sources for certain adpositions and meanings (e.g. verbal sources for 'ago'-type adpositions, see Herce 2017b) is also likely to have a very significant impact on the crosslinguistic properties of these expressions.

Something similar happens to denominal adpositions. First of all, a concrete noun (e.g. *camino* 'way') may become conventionalized for the expression of a particular meaning (see (26a)). When the choice of competing forms is no longer possible (see (26b)), this leads to an increase of its token frequency. The repeated use of the expression with an ancillary, discursively secondary role (see Boye & Harder 2012) brings about a loss of the properties typical of its previous categorial membership. Thus, the 'noun' *camino*, when it is used in this allative/toward construction has lost its ability to be inflected or modified (see (27)).

(26) (a) Voy   camino de Madrid   (b) *Voy   carretera de Madrid
        go.1SG way   of Madrid   go.1SG road   of Madrid
        'I'm on my way to Madrid.'   'I'm on my road to Madrid.'

(27) (a) *Voy   camino-s de Madrid   (b) *Voy   ancho camino de Madrid
        go.1SG way-PL   of Madrid   go.1SG wide road   of Madrid
        'I'm on my ways to Madrid.'   'I'm on my wide way to Madrid.'

However, because, as was mentioned before, grammatical properties are hardly ever lost in one fell swoop, let alone by all adpositions at the same pace, variation is unavoidable, particularly among these expressions that are, as it were, between word classes. Consider, for example, the expression of possession (see also Figure 20.6) among some common denominal adpositional expressions in Spanish:

(28) (a) en mi lugar (b) *en lugar mío (c) *en lugar de mi
      in my place(M)   in place mine.M   in place of me
      'Instead of me.'

(29) (a) por mi culpa (b) por culpa mía/*mío (c) *por culpa de mi
      for my fault(F)   for fault mine.F/mine.M   for fault of me
      'Because of me.'

(30) (a) a mi lado (b) al lado mío/*mía (c) *al lado de mi
      to my side(M)   to.the side mine.M/mine.F   to.the side of me
      'By my side'.

(31) (a) *en mi cima (b) encima mío/*mía (c) encima de mi
      on my top(F)   on.top mine.M/mine.F   on.top of me
      'On top of me.'

(32) (a) *a mi través (b) ?a través mío (c) a través de mi
      to my bend(M)   to bend mine.M   to bend of me
      'Through me.'

All of the adpositional expressions above require a complement headed by *de* (i.e. the construction in (c) when they take nouns or noun phrases as their complement. When the notional complement is a pronoun, however, the strategy can vary, and possessive pronouns are sometimes used instead (see (28)–(31)). These can be attributive and preposed like *mi*, or predicative and postposed like *mío/mía*. The agreement, where required (i.e. in 1PL, 2PL, and predicative possessive pronouns), can be sometimes with the (original) gender of the noun (i.e. *culpa* in (29) is feminine, while *lado* in (30) is masculine), but can also be fixed by default in the masculine form (i.e. *cima* in (31) is [or was] feminine but no longer triggers feminine agreement here). The presence or absence of the article (where this would be grammatically possible, i.e. not with the preposed possessives) is also a trait that is present in some of these adpositions but not others (compare (30) and (31)).

The above expressions can be placed, thus, on a scale between more noun-like ones (see (28), where *lugar* 'place' has the same grammatical properties as other nouns in the language) and more typically prepositional ones (see (32), which behaves exactly like prototypical Spanish adpositions concerning these grammatical properties). It is these grammaticalization pathways that have sometimes led linguists to describe the class as a 'functional attractor, which draws unwary verbs or nouns into its orbit' (DeLancey 2005: 192).

These frequently travelled diachronic routes towards adpositionhood constitute, therefore, one of the main shaping forces of the category. Together with high token frequency (see Figure 20.5), they explain the grammatical diversity of adpositions and the structure of the word class, which is characterized, most clearly in Spanish (see Figure 20.7), by blurry boundaries to other classes, and by a fuzzy periphery. This contrasts with a comparatively orderly core occupied by the oldest and most grammaticalized adpositions which have lost most of the properties characteristic of their former word-class membership.

20.5 CONCLUSION

This chapter has explored (section 20.2) the ways in which the class of adpositions has been defined traditionally. Only with formal and functional qualifications, and relying on notions like 'word', 'noun phrase', and 'complement', can one distinguish adpositions from other classes, grammatical cases, and from other heterogeneous grammatical and lexical phenomena.

Section 20.3 presented the synchronic profile (i.e. the grammatical properties) of adpositions in three genetically unrelated languages: Hungarian, Basque, and German. Besides the obvious observation that the grammatical properties of adpositions differ from one language to another, the main conclusion is that we never find necessary and sufficient conditions for membership. No two grammatical properties seem to ever agree, and there appears to be no grounded way to trust some traits over others.

This cross-classification of grammatical properties gives rise to a large number of different (sub)classes of adpositions in the surveyed languages, many of which are singleton classes, i.e. adpositions whose overall grammatical profile is unique. Such a significant degree of variation is possible because of the high frequency of use of most adpositions, which are robustly present in the input and thus have the potential to retain many idiosyncratic traits. Despite these facts, the grammatical properties of adpositions are of course not utterly random but structured in such a way that one can often predict one property from another.

Diachronically, as section 20.4 has shown, adpositions are found at a crossroads between the lexicon and the grammar, and between the major word classes: nouns, verbs, and adverbs. Due to grammaticalization, words from these large lexical classes can become more adposition-like in specific constructions (notably in serial and subordinate verb uses, and in relator noun uses). In these particular contexts or others, a word sometimes becomes conventionalized for the expression of some concrete semantic relation. As a result, it will increase its scope and usage frequency, and will start to lose some of its former grammatical properties (e.g. inflection, word order variability).

Diachronic trends also reveal that core adpositions often behave as an attractor to more peripheral and grammatically idiosyncratic relational expressions, which progressively become more integrated into the category. The periphery of the adposition class and its borders to other classes are, in any case, messy and blurry, which facilitates, in turn, the slow integration of new members.

The present findings notwithstanding, much more work remains to be done to increase our understanding of the synchrony and diachrony of adpositions. Most urgent, in my opinion, is the adoption of typologically and empirically responsible approaches (e.g. Multivariate Typology, see Bickel 2010) to the description of syntactic variation. A detailed quantitative description of grammatical properties must logically precede all efforts to propose generalizations, types, and other higher-order abstractions. Despite the phonological, morphological and syntactic complexity that this chapter has exposed, adpositions continue to be an under-researched topic and will continue to occupy a relatively short section in typical reference grammars until their full complexity is known and appreciated.

APPENDIX

Figure 20.8 shows the (lack of) structure that would be expected from 10 binary grammatical properties randomly distributed across 50 different adpositions.

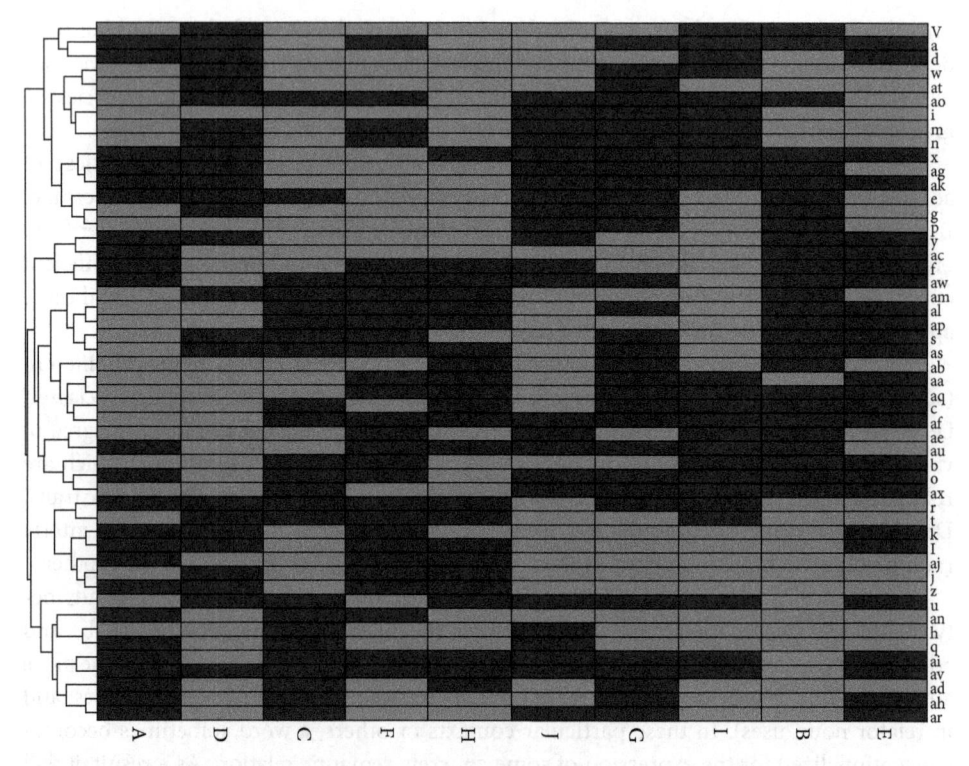

FIGURE 20.8 Adpositions and grammatical properties, randomly generated

Observe how, if variation were random, 50 adpositions would end up grouping into a much greater number of classes (49 in this case) than we saw in natural languages. Similarly, under the hypothesis of random variation, none of the variables can be used to predict other values. Comparison of this hypothetical system to what we actually find across languages (see Figures 20.1, 20.3, 20.4, and 20.7) shows very clearly that adpositional systems are, despite their large variability, highly constrained. Below is a list of the adpositions/forms and grammatical properties that were surveyed in this chapter.

Hungarian

-ba 'into', *-ban* 'in', *-ért* 'for', *-hoz* 'to', *-ig* 'up to', *-ként* 'as', *-val* 'with', *al-* 'under', *által* 'by', *alul* 'below', *át* 'through', *belül* 'inside of', *együtt* 'together', *el-* 'in front of', *ellen* 'against', *esetén* 'in

case of', *fel-* 'towards', *felül* 'over', *fogva* 'as a result of', *föl-* 'above', *folytán* 'as a consequence of', *hasonlóan* 'similarly to', *helyett* 'instead of', *innen* 'on this side of', *iránt* 'towards', *képest* 'compared to', *keresztül* 'through', *kezdve* 'beginning from', *kivéve* 'except for', *kívül-* 'outside', *kör-* 'around', *köz-* 'between', *közel* 'close to', *létére* 'despite being', *mell-* 'near', *miatt* 'because of', *módjára* 'in the manner of', *módra* 'in the mode of', *mög-* 'behind', *nézve* 'regarding', *nyomán* 'based on', *óta* 'since', *részére* 'for', *révén* 'through', *számára* 'for', *szemben* 'opposite', *szerint* 'according to', *túl-* 'beyond', *után* 'after', *útján* 'by way of', *végett* 'with the aim of', *végig* 'to the end of'

> Property A: Governs the nominative/unmarked form of the noun
> Property B: Can be inflected for person
> Property C: Can be uninflected for person
> Property D: Can take a pronominal complement
> Property E: Can be inflected for a spatial case
> Property F: Does not have vowel harmony allomorphy
> Property G: Is obligatorily postposed
> Property H: Is not repeated when it takes a demonstrative + noun complement
> Property I: Must take an overt complement and cannot stand alone.
> Property J: Can take a finite clause as complement: *a(z)*-postpostition

Basque

-(r)ik 'of', *-gana* 'to Xs place', *-gatik* 'because of', *-ino* 'until', *-k* ERG, *-kin* 'with', *-n* 'in', *-ra* 'to', *-ri* 'to', *-tik* 'from', *-tzat* 'for', *alde* 'in favour of', *aparte* 'apart from', *arabera* 'according to', *arte-* 'between', *aurre-* 'front of', *azpi-* 'under', *baino* 'apart from', *baino lehen* 'before', *barru-* 'inside', *begira* 'looking at', *beteta* 'full of', *bezala* 'like', *bila* 'looking for', *buruz* 'about', *duela* 'ago', *erruz* 'Xs fault', *eske* 'asking for', *esker* 'thanks to', *esku* 'in Xs hand', *eta gero* 'after', *gabe* 'without', *gain* 'apart from', *gisa* 'like', *inguru-* 'around', *kabuz* 'on Xs own', *kanpo-* 'outside', *kontra* 'against', *ondo-* 'near', *truke* 'in exchange for', *zain* 'waiting for', *zehar* 'through'

> Property A: Does not have referential uses
> Property B: Cannot stand without an object, e.g. predicatively
> Property C: Cannot itself inflect (e.g. with spatial case endings)
> Property D: Can govern genitive case
> Property E: Can govern absolutive case
> Property F: Can govern dative case
> Property G: Can govern instrumental case
> Property H: Does not have allomorphy dependent on its host
> Property I: Can take a pronominal complement

German

ab 'from', *als* 'as', *an* 'on', *auf* 'up', *aufgrund* 'because of', *aus* 'out', *auserhalb* 'apart from', *ausgenommen* 'except for', *ausser* 'except for', *bei* 'at X's place', *bis* 'until', *durch* 'through', *entlang* 'along', *entsprechend* 'including', *für* 'for', *gegen* 'against', *gegenüber* 'opposite', *hinter* 'beyond', *im Anschluss an* 'concerning', *im Laufe* 'during', *in* 'in', *in Bezug auf* 'with respect to', *in Ermangelung* 'in the absence of', *infolge* 'as a consequence', *laut* 'according to', *mit* 'with', *nach* 'to', *neben* 'near', *ohne* 'without', *Richtung* 'towards', *seit* 'since', *statt* 'instead of', *trotz* 'despite', *über* 'about', *um* 'around', *ungeachtet* 'despite', *unter* 'under', *viel* 'a lot of', *von* 'from', *vor* 'in front of', *während* 'during', *wegen* 'because of', *wie* 'as', *zu* 'to', *zuliebe* 'for Xs sake', *zwischen* 'between'

    Property A: Can govern accusative case
    Property B: Can govern dative case
    Property C: Can govern genitive case
    Property D: Can fuse with the definite article
    Property E: Compulsorily precedes complement
    Property F: Is prefixed with *da(r)*- when it takes a pronominal complement
    Property G: Is morphologically simple
    Property H: Can take a 1st or 2nd person complement

Spanish

a 'to', *a favor* 'in favour of', *a través* 'through', *abajo* 'down', *acerca* 'about', *adentro* 'inside', *al frente* 'to the front', *al lado* 'beside', *allende* 'beyond', *alrededor* 'around', *ante* 'before', *antes* 'before', *arriba* 'up', *atrás* 'back', *bajo* 'under', *camino* 'way', *cara* 'face', *cerca* 'near', *como* 'like', *con* 'with', *contra* 'against', *de* 'of', *de espaldas* 'behind', *debido* 'due to', *dentro* 'inside', *desde* 'since', *detrás* 'behind', *durante* 'during', *en* 'in', *en busca* 'in search for', *en contra* 'against', *en lugar* 'instead of', *en mano* 'depending on', *en medio* 'in between', *en torno* 'around', *en vez* 'instead of', *encima* 'on top of', *enfrente* 'in front of', *entre* 'between', *excepto* 'except for', *frente* 'front of', *fuera* 'outside', *hace* 'ago', *hacia* 'towards', *hasta* 'until', *incluso* 'even', *junto* 'next to', *mediante* 'by means of', *para* 'for', *por* 'by', *por culpa* 'because of', *respecto* 'with respect to', *salvo* 'except for', *según* 'according to', *sin* 'without', *sobre* 'on', *tras* 'behind'

    Property A: Is phonetically unstressed
    Property B: Can govern the oblique form of pronouns (e.g. *mi, ti*)
    Property C: Can govern a complement phrase headed by the preposition *de*
    Property D: With pronouns, it can govern the preposition 'de' (e.g. *de mi, de ti*)
    Property E: Can take a preposed possessive pronoun (e.g. *mi* X, *tu* X)
    Property F: Can take a postposed possessive pronoun (e.g. X *mío/a*, X *tuyo/a*)
    Property G: Can govern a complement phrase headed by the preposition *a*
    Property H: Must take a complement
    Property I: Is morphologically simple
    Property J: Can take an infinitival clause as complement
    Property K: Must precede its complement

CHAPTER 21

DEMONSTRATIVES

HOLGER DIESSEL

21.1 INTRODUCTION

THE term demonstrative refers to a particular class of function words that are (primarily) defined by their communicative function and meaning. In their basic use, demonstratives serve to coordinate interlocutors' joint focus of attention and to indicate the location of a referent relative to the deictic centre (Diessel 2006, 2014). In addition, demonstratives are often characterized as members of particular word-class categories. Traditionally, they are categorized as pronouns and adjectives (e.g. Bloomfield 1933: 203). However, recent research in typology has argued that demonstratives can also function as adverbs of space, manner, and degree, determiners, nonverbal predicates, presentatives, and verbs (Himmelmann 1997; Diessel 1999; Dixon 2003; König 2012; Guérin 2015; Breunesse 2019).

This chapter provides an overview of grammatical word-class categories of demonstratives from a cross-linguistic perspective. The chapter builds on data and analyses from current research in typology and presents some new statistical information on the cross-linguistic distribution of demonstrative word classes from a large and balanced language sample. The sample consists of 150 languages distributed across 128 genera and six large geographical areas, which are commonly distinguished in typology (Dryer 1992), i.e. Eurasia (N = 36), Africa (N = 26), South East Asia and Oceanic (N = 17), Australia and New Guinea (N = 30), North America (N = 21), and South America (N = 20). Although the sampling method has not been fully systematic, the sample is arguably sufficient to provide estimates regarding the cross-linguistic distribution of demonstrative word classes.[1]

21.2 DEFINITION OF KEY TERMS

In the older literature, demonstratives are commonly defined with reference to particular word-class categories. Karl Brugmann (1904), for example, defined demonstratives

[1] A list of languages included in the sample is given in the Appendix.

as a particular class of pronouns. However, since the morphosyntactic properties of demonstratives are cross-linguistically diverse, the current definition of demonstratives does not include any grammatical categories such as the traditional world classes; rather demonstratives are defined by two non-structural criteria in this chapter.

First, demonstratives are deictic expressions that are usually interpreted within an egocentric, body-oriented frame of reference (Diessel 2014). In this use, demonstratives refer to entities, events or locations that are perceptually accessible to the speech participants (e.g. *This is my bike* [speaker is pointing to the bike]). There are other uses of demonstratives in which they refer to linguistic elements in discourse or abstract concepts that are not immediately accessible to perception (Bühler 1934; Fillmore 1997). However, following Bühler (1934: 202), it is widely assumed that the basic use of demonstratives involves a 'coordinate system' grounded by the 'origo', which is the centre of a 'deictic frame of reference' that is usually determined by the speaker's body, gesture, and location.[2]

The second feature that defines demonstratives as a particular class of function words concerns their communicative function. Recent research in conversational analysis and psycholinguistics has emphasized that demonstratives are not just used for spatial reference, but also to coordinate interlocutors' social interaction (Laury 1997; Piwek et al. 2008; Stukenbrock 2015), or more precisely, demonstratives 'serve to establish joint attention' (Diessel 2006: 463). Joint attention is a key concept of social cognition providing a prerequisite for communication and for what psychologists call 'theory-of-mind' (Tomasello 1999). In order to communicate, the speech participants must be focused on the same referent and must be able to understand that the communicative partner looks at the shared referent from a different perspective. While there are many strategies to create and manipulate joint attention, it has been argued that demonstratives provide the quintessential linguistic device to accomplish this important task (Diessel 2006; see also Clark 1996: 168).

Given the particular communicative function of demonstratives to establish joint attention, it does not come as a surprise that demonstratives have a particular status in language (see Diessel and Coventry 2020). In contrast to most other function words (e.g. adpositions, auxiliaries), demonstratives are not derived from content words by grammaticalization (Himmelmann 1997: 20) and are likely to be universal (Diessel 2006: 472–474). Recent research in typology has argued that language universals are rare and difficult to find (Evans and Levinson 2009). Yet, experts agree that demonstratives may exist in all languages (Himmelmann 1997; Dixon 2003; Breunesse 2019; see also Levinson 2018).

However, while demonstratives are likely to be universal, they exhibit a great deal of cross-linguistic variation in their morphological structure and syntactic use, making it difficult, or even impossible, to subsume demonstratives under a particular set of universal word classes. Following Croft (2001), I assume that word-class categories are language- and construction-particular (see Diessel 2019: 142–171). Nevertheless, while demonstratives cannot be universally assigned to particular word-class categories, they tend to share certain structural properties across languages, which has led typologists to divide them into a few basic types that can be seen as prototypes of demonstrative word classes (e.g. Himmelmann 1997; Diessel 1999; Dixon 2003; Guérin 2015).

---

[2] Not all researchers share Bühler's view of deixis. Levinson (2003a: 71), for instance, argued that the traditional notion of a 'deictic frame of reference' is 'conceptual nonsense'; but see Diessel (2014) for a critique of this view (see also Diessel and Coventry 2020).

In Diessel (1999), I have proposed a syntactic typology of demonstratives with four word-class categories: (i) demonstrative pronouns, which serve as arguments of verbs and adpositions, (ii) demonstrative determiners, which specify a co-occurring noun or noun phrase, (iii) demonstrative adverbs, which modify a verb or adjective, and (iv) demonstrative identifiers, which accompany the predicate nominal of a nonverbal or copular clause. However, in the meantime, a number of studies have argued that demonstratives can also function as verbs as evidenced by the occurrence of verbal categories such as tense, aspect, and mood (Dixon 2003; Guérin 2015; Breunesse 2019).

Adopting this analysis, the current chapter outlines a typology of demonstrative word classes with five basic categories and several sub-categories. The typology rests on two basic criteria: (i) a distributional criterion, which concerns the occurrence of demonstratives in particular structural positions of constructions, and (ii) a morphological criterion, which concerns the morphological forms of demonstratives, i.e. the forms of their stems and their inflectional features.

Crucially, the two criteria do not always coincide. As we will see, many languages use the same morphological forms of demonstratives in different structural positions across several constructions (e.g. *this house* [DET] vs *I like this* [PRO]). If the demonstratives of different structural positions are morphologically distinct from one another, they are readily assigned to distinct word classes (e.g. French *celui-ci/là* [PRO] vs *ce-N-ci/là* [DET]). However, if the demonstratives of different structural positions have the same forms, their categorical status is often difficult to determine (see the discussion of *this* and *that* in Diessel 1999: 62–71).

In order to distinguish the two cases, I will restrict the above proposed categories to demonstratives in different structural positions that are formally distinct from one another, and I will use the terms 'pronominal', 'adnominal', 'adverbial', 'identificational', and 'verbal' for demonstratives in particular structural positions irrespective of their morphological forms or any other structural properties that may or may not distinguish them (see Table 21.1).

Table 21.1 Word-class typology of demonstratives

CATEGORY	DISTRIBUTION
demonstrative pronoun	pronominal demonstrative
demonstrative determiner	adnominal demonstrative
demonstrative adverb	adverbial demonstrative
demonstrative identifier	identificational demonstrative
demonstrative verb	verbal demonstrative

21.3 DEMONSTRATIVE PRONOUNS

Demonstrative pronouns are paradigmatically related to other types of pronouns and lexical NPs. They typically function as arguments of verbs and adpositions and tend to occur with the same inflectional categories as nouns; that is, demonstrative pronouns are often inflected for number, gender, and/or case. Most frequent is the occurrence of number marking. In my sample, 102 languages have demonstratives marked for number, 56 languages have demonstratives inflected for gender or noun class, and 45 languages have case-marked demonstratives. Needless to say, these features often cooccur in one form. In German, for instance, demonstratives pronouns are inflected for gender, number, and case.

Overall, there are 112 languages in the data in which pronominal demonstratives share at least some inflectional properties with other nominal expressions, notably with nouns. In the remaining 38 languages, pronominal demonstratives are uninflected, as for instance in Hdi, in which demonstrative pronouns are formed from simple forms (used in other contexts) by reduplication (see (1)).

(1) Hdi (Frajzyngier 2002: 85)
    bà-f-b-í   tá   ná-ná
    build-UP-build-1SG   OBJ   DEM.PROX-DEM.PROX
    'I built this.'

Note that the case role of the demonstrative is marked by a free morpheme in this example, but number is not overtly marked in the Hdi demonstrative pronouns (Frajzyngier 2002: 85). In most of the languages in which demonstratives do not occur with inflectional affixes, nouns are also uninflected, but in Hdi plural nouns are commonly marked by a number suffix (e.g. tàm-xà 'onion-PL'; see Frajzyngier 2002: 46).

Since adnominal demonstratives are not reduplicated in Hdi, there is a clear formal contrast between demonstrative pronouns and demonstrative determiners. Yet, in other languages where pronominal demonstratives are uninflected, the same deictic forms are also often used as adnominal and/or adverbial demonstratives, which can make it difficult to determine their categorical status (see Diessel 1999: 89–90). We will come back to this in section 21.5.

A related problem concerns the analysis of pronominal demonstratives in locative case. Consider, for instance, the following examples from Tauya and Finnish.

(2) Tauya (MacDonald 1990: 101)
    apu   me-i   mene-i-ʔa
    now   DEM.PROX-LOC   stay-3PL-IND
    'Now they stay here.'

(3) Finnish (Laury 1997: 133)
    sit   leipä   viskataan   tonne
    then   bread   throw.PASS   DEM.DIST.LOC
    'Then the bread gets thrown over there.'

As can be seen, the demonstratives in these examples correspond semantically to English *here* and *there* (as indicated by the translation). However, unlike English *here* and *there*, Tauya *mei* and Finnish *tonne* include a locative case marker. Since the same deictic roots are also used in demonstratives with other case roles functioning as subject or object pronouns, one could analyse the forms in (2) and (3) as demonstrative pronouns in locative case rather than spatial demonstrative adverbs. On this account, pronominal and adnominal demonstratives are expressed by members of the same word-class category in Tauya and Finnish (Diessel 1999: 75–78).

However, while this analysis may be appropriate for locational demonstratives in Tauya, the situation is more complex in Finnish. According to Laury (1997), Finnish has several series of locational demonstratives marked by locative case suffixes (e.g. adessive, allative, inessive). All of these forms are morphologically transparent, but some of them have syntactic and semantic properties that are not compatible with their analysis as pronouns. Considering these properties, Laury (1997: 138) argues that the Finnish demonstratives constitute a category continuum ranging from forms that are best analysed as pronouns to forms that are syntactically and semantically similar to adverbs.

Finally, there are several languages in my sample, in which demonstratives cannot be used as free pronouns. Korean, for example, has three demonstrative roots, *i* 'this (near speaker)', *ku* 'that (near hearer)', and *ce* 'that (distal, i.e. away from both speaker and hearer)', that can function as determiners (see (4)).

(4) Korean (Sohn 1994: 251)
 [*ku*   *cha*]
 that (near H)   car
 'that car'

Unlike English *this* and *that*, Korean *i*, *ku*, and *ce* cannot be used without a cooccurring nominal; that is, there are no simple demonstrative pronouns in Korean. However, the determiners are commonly combined with 'defective nouns' (e.g. *il* 'thing/fact', *i* 'person') to form demonstrative NPs that are semantically equivalent to demonstrative pronouns in other languages (see (5)) (Sohn 1994: 294).

(5) Korean (Sohn 1994: 295)
 [*ce*   *il-ul*]   *nwu-ka*   *mak-keyss-ni?!*
 that (DIST) thing-ACC who-NM block-will-Q
 'Who would be able to block that (mess that I have just mentioned).'

Apart from Korean, there are several other languages in the data in which the pronominal use of demonstratives typically involves an NP (e.g. Ainu, Lao, Taba, Vietnamese, Kotiria, Pichi, Zapotec). In Ainu, for example, pronominal demonstratives involve a 'dependent noun' (see (6)) (Tamura 2000: 91), which Refsing (1986: 93) calls a 'nominalizer', and in Zapotec they include a 'classifier' (see (7)) (Sonnenschein 2004) functioning as nominal head of a noun phrase.

(6) Ainu (Tamura 2000: 61)
 [*tan*   *pe*]$_{NP}$ *en-kore*   *hawe?*
 this   thing   1SG.ACC-give   EVD
 'Will (you) give this to me?'

(7) Zapotec (Sonnenschein 2004: 267)
 bi   *dx-een=da'*   [*be=nga*]$_{NP}$ *dx-een=da'*   [*be=na'*]$_{NP}$
 NEG CONT-want=1SG.EXP CLF=DEM.MED CONT-want=1SG.EXP CLF=DEM.DIST
 'I don't want this one, I want that one.'

Note that English *this* and *that* are often combined with the impersonal pronoun *one*, forming NPs similar to those in the above examples. However, while the English demonstratives are frequently accompanied by *one*, *this* and *that* are also used as free pronouns. Yet, the occurrence of these forms is restricted to particular pragmatic contexts and constructions: If *this* and *that* refer to an event or proposition, they are usually used alone as pronouns (e.g. *I know this*); but if they refer to a concrete object chosen from a set of alternatives, they are usually accompanied by *one* (see *I will take this one, not that one*). In addition, *this* and *that* are used as subject pronouns in copular clauses (see *This is my friend*); but, as we will see below (section 21.6), the demonstratives of copular constructions are often formally distinct from pronominal demonstratives in other contexts.

There are two different ways of analysing expressions such as English *this one* or Korean *i il* 'this thing'. Either the demonstrative is analysed as a determiner of a noun phrase, or the whole NP is interpreted as a complex pronoun. The latter analysis is suggested by the fact that demonstrative NPs are often reduced to simple pronouns in the process of language change. There are several languages in my data in which demonstrative pronouns are historically based on a demonstrative and a third person pronoun or classifier that have been fused into one form, as, for instance, French *celui*, which includes the pronoun *lui* 'him' (Harris 1978).

21.4 DEMONSTRATIVE DETERMINERS

Demonstrative determiners occur in a particular structural position of a definite NP. There is general consensus in the literature that adnominal demonstratives modify, or specify, a co-occurring noun semantically, but their syntactic function has been subject to debate (see Diessel 1999: 62–71). As we will see, not all adnominal demonstratives qualify as determiners.

In many languages, adnominal demonstratives have the same forms as demonstrative pronouns, but in about 30% of the world's languages, adnominal and pronominal demonstratives are formally distinguished (Diessel 2005). In the current sample, there are 47 languages with a particular series of demonstrative determiners distinct from demonstrative pronouns. The distinction concerns different aspects of linguistic structure. To begin with, there are 14 languages in which the stems of demonstrative determiners differ from those of demonstrative pronouns, as for instance in French (see *ce* [DET] vs *celui* [PRO]) and Awa Pit (see Table 21.2).

Table 21.2 Demonstratives in Awa Pit (Curnow 1997: 87)

	PRONOUN	DETERMINER
PROXIMAL	*ana*	*an*
DISTAL	*suna*	*sun*

Second, adnominal demonstratives are frequently reduced to clitics. In my sample, there are eleven languages in which adnominal demonstratives may cliticize to an adjacent noun (or attribute), whereas the corresponding pronouns are expressed by free forms (e.g. Anywa,

Ik, Lango, Meithei, Nihali, Pohnpeian, Tidore, Ubykh). One of these languages is Ubykh, where adnominal demonstratives are both phonetically reduced and bound to a subsequent noun (see Table 21.3).

Table 21.3 Demonstratives in Ubykh (Fenwick 2011: 79)

	PRONOUN		DETERMINER	
	SG	PL	SG	PL
PROXIMAL	jinɜ́	jiɬɜ́	ji=N	jiɬɜ=N
DISTAL	wɜnɜ́	wɜɬɜ́	wɜ=N	wɜɬɜ=N

Third, in some languages, adnominal demonstratives are restricted in their inflectional behaviour compared to the inflection of demonstrative pronouns (e.g. Kambaata, Lezgian, Menya, Trumai, Turkish, Wolaytta, Kolyma Yukaghir). In Kambaata, for example, demonstrative pronouns indicate number and gender and occur with nine different cases, whereas adnominal demonstratives are only marked for gender and confined to three cases (Treis 2019). Similarly, in Evenki, demonstrative pronouns are always inflected for case and gender, whereas adnominal demonstratives 'usually do not agree in case with the head', though they are always inflected for number (Nedjalkov 1997: 83). In the extreme case, adnominal demonstratives do not have any of the inflectional properties of demonstrative pronouns. In Lezgian, for example, demonstrative pronouns occur with case and number suffixes, whereas the demonstrative determiners are uninflected particles that precede an inflected noun (see Table 21.4) (see also Turkish).

Table 21.4 Demonstratives in Lezgian (Haspelmath 1993a: 190)

	PRONOUN				DETERMINER		
	PROX	MED	DIST		PROX	MED	DIST
SG ABS	i-m	a-m	at'a-m	SG/PL	i	a	at'a
SG ERG	i-da	a-da	at'a-da				
SG GEN	i-dan	a-dan	at'a-dan				
PL ABS	i-bur	a-bur	at'a-bur				

Finally, demonstrative pronouns may contain an extra morpheme that does not occur in the (corresponding) determiners. For example, above, we have seen that demonstrative pronouns in French include a third person pronoun that has merged with a preceding demonstrative. Similar types of demonstrative pronouns occur in several other languages of the sample, as, for instance, in Ambulas (8a)–(8b) (see also Nivkh, Tidore, and Toqabaqita).

(8) Ambulas (Wilson 1980: 56, 154)
 a. *dé-wan*
   3SG.M-DEM.DIST
   'that one'

b. *wani*   *baalé*
   DEM.DIST   pig
   'that pig'

There are also demonstrative determiners that include an extra morpheme (compared to demonstrative pronouns), but this seems to be a rare phenomenon. There are only two languages of this type in my data: Pangasinan, in which demonstrative determiners are composed of a demonstrative root, the article prefix *sá-*, and a (neutral) number suffix (see *sá-ta-y* 'ART-this-SG/PL'; Benton 1971: 51–52), and Mapudungun, in which demonstrative determiners consist of a demonstrative base and an 'adjectivizer' (see *tüfa-chi* 'this-ADJZ'; Smeets 1989: 105).

If adnominal demonstratives are formally distinct from demonstrative pronouns, it is reasonable to analyse them as determiners. However, when adnominal demonstratives are expressed by the same forms as demonstrative pronouns, one has to consider their syntactic properties in order to determine their word-class status. To simplify, adnominal demonstratives occur in two different types of constructions.

In some languages, adnominal demonstratives are tied to a particular determiner position in a hierarchically structured NP. English provides a case in point. The English noun phrase is a tightly organized construction with a particular slot for a small class of semantically related expressions including definite and indefinite articles, possessive pronouns, and genitive nouns.

Since the English demonstratives occur in a particular structural position hosting a closed class of related expressions, we may analyse them as determiners (see Diessel to appear). On this account, *this* and *that* are polyfunctional expressions that pertain to two distinct word-class categories: (i) they are pronouns when they appear in argument position of a verb (or adposition), and (ii) they are determiners when they occur in the initial slot of a noun phrase.

Crucially, while demonstratives are commonly used to modify a noun semantically, some languages lack a particular class of demonstrative determiners (Diessel 1999: 68–70). Hixkaryana, for example, has three demonstratives that are either used as free pronouns in argument position of a verb or in conjunction with a noun. Yet, the adnominal demonstratives are only loosely adjoined to the co-occurring noun. In contrast to the English NP, the Hixkaryana NP does not include a particular determiner slot: Bare nouns can serve as full NPs; i.e. they do not need a determiner. If a noun is accompanied by a demonstrative, constituent order is variable; i.e. the demonstrative may follow or precede the associated noun (9a)–(9b). Moreover, in adpositional phrases, both constituents, i.e. noun and demonstrative, are usually marked by the same postposition and the two PPs may be separated by a pause (9c).

(9) Hixkaryana (Derbyshire 1985: 53, 1979: 68, 40, adapted from Krasnoukhova 2012: 49)
  a. [*ow-otɨ*   *mosonɨ*]$_{NP}$ *Ø-ar-ko*   *ha*
     2-meat.food   DEM.PROX.AN   3-take-IMP   INTENS
     'Take this meat for you.'
  b. *kaywana*   *y-omsɨ-r*   *y-oknɨ*   [*mokro*   *kaykusu*]$_{NP}$
     Kaywana   LK-daughter-POSSD   LK-pet.POSSD   DEM.MED.AN   dog
     'That dog is Kaywana's daughter's pet.'

c. k-omok-no   [[moson   y-akoro]_PP ... [ro-he-tx   y-akoro]_PP]
   1-come-PST   DEM.PROX.AN   LK-COM   ... 1-wife-POSSD   LK-COM
   'I have come with this one, with my wife.'

Considering these data, Derbyshire (1979: 131) argued that Hixkaryana does not have a grammatical class of demonstrative determiners, but uses instead free demonstrative pronouns in conjunction with a noun.[3] Similar types of constructions occur in several other languages of the sample, including Imonda, Nunggubuyu, Oneida, Tümpisa Shoshone, Wardaman, and West Greenlandic.

Let me emphasize, however, that the proposed distinction between demonstrative determiners and adnominal demonstrative pronouns constitutes a continuum rather than a clear-cut opposition. As it turns out, in many languages adnominal demonstratives have properties of both pronouns and determiners (Diessel to appear). In Hungarian, for example, demonstratives precede all other modifiers of the noun, suggesting that the Hungarian NP includes a particular slot for adnominal demonstratives, similar to English. However, in contrast to English *this* and *that*, the Hungarian demonstratives are not paradigmatically related to other noun modifiers. In fact, adnominal demonstratives have to be combined with a definite article in Hungarian and may co-occur with possessive pronouns and other noun modifiers that are mutually exclusive in English (see (10)). Considering these properties, Moravcsik (1997) argued that the Hungarian demonstratives share properties with both pronouns and determiners.

(10) Hungarian (Moravcsik 1997: 307)
      ez   a   te   két   szép   nagy ... kerted,   melyet   eladtál
      this   the   your   two   nice   big   ... our.yard   which   you.sold
      'These two nice big yards of yours which you sold.'

21.5 DEMONSTRATIVE ADVERBS

Adverbial demonstratives modify a verb or adjective (Diessel 1999: 74-8). The typological literature has been mainly concerned with demonstrative adverbs of space such as English *here* and *there*. Since these expressions are commonly used to specify the location of an action or event denoted by a verb (e.g. *She went there*), they are categorized as adverbs. Note, however, that the same expressions are also often used to reinforce demonstrative pronouns and determiners, as for instance in German (see *der hier* 'DEM here' vs *der da* 'DEM there') and French (see *celui-ci* 'DEM here' and *celui-là* 'DEM there').

In the vast majority of languages, spatial deixis involves a particular set of demonstrative adverbs, formally distinct from demonstrative pronouns and determiners; that is, there are only a few languages in the sample in which adverbial demonstratives of space have the same

---

[3] More precisely, Derbyshire (1979: 131–132) characterized the adnominal demonstratives in Hixkaryana as pronouns of 'equative sentences' that are often embedded in larger structures and functionally equivalent to a demonstrative noun phrase.

forms as pronominal and/or adnominal demonstratives (e.g. Abui, Acehnese, Dom, Tukang Besi). Abui, for example, has a set of invariable demonstratives that can function as pronouns, noun modifies, and spatial adverbs (11a)–(11c). While the various uses of demonstratives are recognizable from their appearance in particular constructions, Kratochvíl (2007) does not divide them into distinct word classes. Since the Abui demonstratives are NOT paradigmatically related to other types of expressions, they are perhaps best analysed as deictic particles that can serve a variety of semantic and syntactic functions.

(11)   Abui (Kratochvíl 2007: 128, 162, 269)
   a. *it   do   nala?*
      lie.CPL   PROX   what
      'What is this (lying here)?'

   b. ***do***   *fala*
      PROX   house
      'this house (located by me)'

   c. *a   do   mi-a   maiye, ama   e-l   feng   kang*
      2SG   PROX   be.in-DUR   when   person 2SG.LOC-give injure be.good
      'If you stay here, people can harm you.'

While spatial demonstrative adverbs are usually distinct from demonstrative pronouns and determiners, they typically include the same deictic roots as demonstratives in other contexts. Overall, there are only ten languages in the entire database for which I was not able to determine a formal or diachronic connection between demonstrative adverbs of space and demonstrative pronouns/determiners (e.g. Apurinã, Oneida, Supyire, Ubykh).

Unlike demonstrative pronouns, demonstrative adverbs tend to be uninflected. In particular, gender and number are hardly ever encoded by demonstrative adverbs. Nevertheless, as pointed out above, some languages have demonstrative pronouns in locative case that are similar to English *here* and *there* (e.g. Tauya and Finnish). In my sample, there are 35 languages of this type (e.g. Kxoe, Mangarrayi, Nunggubuyu).

Another strategy to form adverbial demonstratives of space is to combine adnominal demonstratives with a generic noun or classifier denoting a place or location. Two examples from Hdi and ǂHòã are given in (12) and (13).

(12)   Hdi (Frajzyngier 2002: 228)
   lá-m-là   dífà-úgh-tà   xàdì   yá,   mà   tùghwázàk…
   go-IN-go   hide-SO-REF   place   DEM   P   hibiscus
   'Go hide yourself here, in the hibiscus, …'

(13)   ǂHòã (Collins and Gruber 2014: 124)
   'àm   ču   šú   kyŏa   kì   'a   'ám
   1SG.GEN   father   place   that   EMPH   PROG   eat
   'My father is eating there.'

Like demonstratives in locative case, these forms are often frozen or lexicalized. In fact, there are several languages in the data in which demonstrative NPs including a noun meaning 'place' have developed into (monomorphemic) adverbs. Korean, for example, has three locational demonstratives, i.e. *yeki* 'here (near speaker)', *keki* 'there (near hearer)', and *ceki* 'there (distal)', that are historically derived from a demonstrative determiner and the base *eki* meaning 'place' (14).[4]

(14) Korean (Sohn 1994: 296)
  i-eki   'this place (near S)'   >   *yeki*   'here (near S)'
  ku-eki 'that place (near H)'   >   *keki*   'there (near H)'
  ce-eki 'that place (distal)'   >   *ceki*   'there (distal)'

All languages have spatial demonstrative adverbs that may indicate the relative distance between the deictic centre and a more distant location. Yet, apart from distance, spatial demonstratives may encode various other semantic features (Diessel 1999: 35–55). Imonda, for example, has two deictic roots, *ōh* 'PROX' and *ed* 'DIST', that occur in various structural positions. Adverbial demonstratives denoting a location are often marked by the locative suffix *-ia*; but in addition to *ōh-ia* 'here' and *ed-ia* 'there', Imonda has three other pairs of spatial demonstrative adverbs indicating direction and elevation as shown in Table 21.5.

Table 21.5 Spatial demonstrative adverbs in Imonda (Seiler 1985: 43–46)

	PROXIMAL	DISTAL
LOCATION	*ōh-ia* 'here'	*ed-ia* 'there'
DIRECTION	*ōsm* 'hither'	*esm* 'thither'
ELEVATION [UP]	*ōh-puhō* 'up here'	*ed-puhō* 'up there'
ELEVATION [DOWN]	*ōh-gō* 'down here'	*ed-gō* 'down there'

Semantically similar demonstratives occur in Belhare, Dyirbal, Tauya, Tidore, and Yakkha (as well as in several other languages of the sample), but note that while these features are particularly common with demonstrative adverbs, they also appear with demonstrative pronouns and demonstrative determiners (see Schapper 2014 for examples; see also Forker 2020).

In addition to spatial concepts, adverbial demonstratives may express non-spatial concepts such as manner and degree. Manner demonstratives have long been neglected, but a number of recent studies have been specifically concerned with this important class (König 2012, 2017; König & Umbach 2018; Treis 2019). Like all other types of demonstratives, manner demonstratives can be used exophorically with reference to elements in the outside world. However, in contrast to demonstrative pronouns and spatial demonstrative adverbs, manner demonstratives do not refer to entities, events or places, but focus interlocutors' attention onto the way an action is carried out (for an in-depth semantic analysis of manner

---

[4] Incidentally, contrary to what Heine and Kuteva (2007: 84–86) claim, there is little evidence in my data that demonstrative pronouns and determiners are commonly derived from demonstrative adverbs (though this is certainly possible). On the contrary, the data suggest that spatial demonstrative adverbs are often derived from demonstrative pronouns by the addition of locative case markers, postpositions or nouns meaning 'place'.

demonstratives, see König & Umbach 2018). Consider, for instance, the following example from German, including the manner demonstrative *so*.

(15) German
 Einen guten Eindruck macht man so! [pointing gesture]
 a good impression make one like.this
 'This is how you make a good impression.'

According to König & Umbach (2018), manner demonstratives indicate similarity between the manner of the event referred to by the demonstrative and some other event, or generic concept of an event, that is currently activated. In (15), for example, *so* refers to the manner of an action in the interlocutors' visual focus of attention, which is compared to the general concept of 'to make a good impression' referred to in the initial phrase.

Although manner demonstratives are often ignored in reference grammars, I have found evidence for a particular (morphological) class of manner demonstrative adverbs in 67 languages. A few examples are given in Table 21.6.

Table 21.6 Demonstratives pronouns and demonstrative adverbs of space and manner in Lezgian (Haspelmath 1993a), Japanese (König 2012), Croatian (Brala-Vukanović 2015), and Korean (Sohn 1994)

		DEM PRO	DEM ADV OF SPACE	MANNER DEM
Lezgian	PROX	*i*-INFL	*ina*	*ik'*
	DISTAL	*a*-INFL	*am*	*ak'(a)*
Japanese	NEAR S	*kore*	*koko*	*koo*
	NEAR H	*sore*	*soko*	*soo*
	DISTAL	*are*	*asoko*	*aa*
Croatian	PROX	*ovaj*	*ovdje*	*ovako*
	MEDIAL	*taj*	*tu*	*tako*
	DISTAL	*onaj*	*ondje*	*onako*
Korean	NEAR H	*i* N	*yeki*	*i-le-key*
	NEAR S	*ku* N	*keki*	*ku-le-key*
	DISTAL	*ce* N	*ceki*	*ce-le-key*

As can be seen, in all four languages shown in this table, manner demonstratives are lexemes that are formally distinct from demonstrative pronouns and spatial demonstrative adverbs. However, manner demonstratives are also expressed by multi-word expressions, or phrases, consisting of a demonstrative pronoun and a similative marker (such as Engl. *like*) or an adnominal demonstrative and a noun meaning 'manner', as illustrated by the following examples from Awa Pit (16) and Semelai (17).

(16) Awa Pit (Curnow 1997: 144)
 an=kana 'this=like' [*kana* = 'like']
 sun=kana 'that=like'

(17) Semelai (Kruspe 1999: 311)
      deŋ nɔʔ 'manner this'   [deŋ = 'manner']
      deŋ ke 'manner that'

Like spatial demonstrative adverbs, manner demonstratives are not (usually) inflected, though they may occur with case markers (e.g. in Kambaata). However, in contrast to spatial demonstrative adverbs, manner demonstratives are not always deictically contrastive. There are several languages in the sample in which manner demonstratives are distance-neutral, like German *so*, French *ainsi*, Italian *così* 'so/thus', and Kambaata *hittíta* 'like this'.

What is more, while manner demonstratives may refer to actions or events in the outside world, they are very often used with reference to linguistic elements in discourse. In fact, English *so* and *thus* (which are related to (exophoric) manner demonstratives in other Germanic languages) are almost exclusively used in this way (18).

(18) Peter is sick. **So/thus** he will not be able to attend the meeting.

Since manner demonstratives are frequently used with reference to propositions, they often develop into clause linkers. Across languages, manner demonstratives provide a frequent source for the grammaticalization of conjunctive adverbs and markers of direct speech (Güldemann 2008; König 2012; Diessel & Breunesse 2020). In particular, the development of manner demonstratives into quotative markers is cross-linguistically very common (Güldemann 2008). Usan, for example, has two manner demonstratives, *ete* and *ende* (which both include the proximal root *e* 'this/here') that are commonly used as quote markers. Interestingly, while *ete* 'thus/so' serves to announce an upcoming quotation, *ende* 'thus/so' refers to a preceding quote (19).

(19) Usan (Reesink 1987: 184)
      munon   eng   ete   yo-nob   qâm-ar: 'mâni   âib   ne-teib-âm,'
      man   the   thus   me-with   say-3SG.PST   food   big   you-give.SG.FUT-1SG
      ende   qâm-arei
      thus   say-3SG.PST
      'The man said thus to me: "I will give you a lot of food", thus he said.'

Semantically related to demonstratives of manner are demonstratives of degree (König 2012, 2017). They also indicate a comparison, but are usually related to adjectives rather than to verbs. In this use, degree demonstratives indicate the degree or quantity of a property relative to some standard measure. Two examples from German and Lezgian are given in (20) and (21).

(20) German
      Die   Schlange   war   **so**   lang.
      the   queue   was   that   long
      'The queue was that long.'

(21) Lezgian (Haspelmath 1993a: 312)
      kün   wučiz   **iq'wan**   pašman   ja?
      you.all.ABS   why   so.much   sad   COP
      'Why are you-all so sad?'

Note that German uses the demonstrative *so* to indicate both the manner of an action and the degree of a property. However, in Lezgian, the degree demonstratives *iq'wan* 'so much' and *aq'wan* 'so much' are formally distinct from the manner demonstrative *ik'* 'this way' and *ak'(a)* 'that way'.[5]

21.6 DEMONSTRATIVE IDENTIFIERS

Demonstratives are very frequent in copular and nonverbal clauses (e.g. *This/there is my friend*). Usually, the demonstratives of copular and nonverbal clauses are regarded as pronouns; but in many languages, they are formally distinct from demonstratives in other contexts. In particular, the demonstratives of nonverbal clauses often have special properties. Consider, for instance, the demonstratives in Table 21.7 from Pohnpeian (Table 21.7 and (22a)–(22c)).

Table 21.7 Demonstratives in Pohnpeian (Rehg 1981: 150–153)

	PRONOUN		ADVERB	IDENTIFIER	
	SG	PL		SG	PL
NEAR S	*me(t)*	*metakan*	*me(t)*	*ie(t)*	*ietaka*
NEAR H	*men*	*menakan*	*men*	*ien*	*ienakan*
DISTAL	*mwo*	*mwohkan*	*mwo*	*io*	*iohkan*

(22) Pohnpeian (Rehg 1981: 143, 152, 150)
  a. **met** pahn mengila
     this will wither
     'This will wither.'
  b. e wahdo **met**
     he brought here
     'He brought it here.'
  c. **ien** noumw pinselen
     there your pencil
     'There is your pencil.'

The demonstrative in (22a) functions as subject pronoun of an intransitive verb. As can be seen (in Table 21.11), demonstrative pronouns are inflected for number, but the singular forms are also used as spatial demonstrative adverbs (see (22b)). In addition to

---

[5] Another semantically related type of demonstrative indicates the 'quality' of an object (e.g. *such a fool*). Quality demonstratives can have the same forms as degree and/or manner demonstratives (König 2012), but they are usually used to modify (or specify) a co-occurring noun rather than a verb or adjective.

demonstrative pronouns and demonstrative adverbs, Pohnpeian has a special series of demonstratives that are exclusively used in nonverbal equational constructions (see (22c)) (or in one-word utterances, e.g. *Iet!* 'Here it is!'). Rehg (1981: 150) refers to the demonstratives in these constructions as 'pointing demonstratives', suggesting that they are frequently accompanied by a pointing gesture.

Traditionally, the demonstratives of nonverbal clauses are analysed as subject pronouns, which seems to be appropriate as long as the demonstratives of nonverbal clauses have the same forms as demonstrative pronouns in verbal clauses. However, if the demonstratives of nonverbal clauses are formally distinct from demonstrative pronouns in other constructions (as in Pohnpeian), we may analyse them as a separate grammatical class, which I call 'demonstrative identifiers' (Diessel 1999: 78–88).

Demonstrative identifiers are similar to deictic presentatives such as French *voici* and *voilà* or Russian *vot* and *von*. Both types of expressions serve to focus interlocutors' attention onto a referent in the surrounding situation and are frequently accompanied by a pointing gesture. However, in contrast to identifiers, presentatives are not associated with a particular construction. Identifiers are defined by their occurrence in nonverbal or copular clauses, whereas presentatives are typically used alone or in loose combination with a co-occurring clause or phrase. Nevertheless, there is no clear-cut distinction between deictic presentatives and demonstrative identifiers: When presentatives are used together with a noun, they are often strikingly similar to demonstrative identifiers in nonverbal clauses (e.g. *Voici ton train* 'Here comes your train').

Like Pohnpeian, Uduk has a particular morphosyntactic class of demonstrative identifiers (Killian 2015: 149–166). The demonstrative system is very complex in Uduk. Table 21.8 shows only a subset of the available forms. Since demonstrative identifiers occur in verbless clauses (see (23)), Killian characterizes them as 'verb-like' elements. They are accompanied by the 'identificational particle' *ā* but do not conjugate like ordinary verbs for tense and aspect.

Table 21.8 Demonstratives in Uduk (Killian 2015: 152–162)

	PRONOUN		ADVERB	IDENTIFIER	
	SG	PL		SG	PL
PROXIMAL	yá-nhān	gwǎ-nhān	má-nhān	ā 'dán	ā nán
MEDIAL	jǎ-'dān	gwǎ-'dān	má-'dān	ā cî'dān	ā nî'dān
REMOTE	jǎ-tāān	gwǎ-tāān	má-tāān	ā cíttān	ā níttān
DISTAL	jà-ttáán	gwà-ttáán	má-ttāān	ā cīttáán	ā nīttáán

(23) Uduk (Killian 2015: 163)
 à rìs ḵá'bāl ā **nán**
 CL2 many sheep IDENT DEM.PL.MED
 'There are a lot of sheep.'

In Pohnpeian and Uduk, demonstrative identifiers have particular stems that distinguish them from demonstratives in verbal clauses (see also Maori, Musqueam, Pangasinen,

Supyire). In other languages, demonstrative identifiers differ from demonstrative pronouns and adverbs in terms of their inflectional properties, as, for example, in Tümpisa Shoshone (see (24a)–(24b)).

(24)   Tümpisa Shoshone (Dayley 1989: 76, 145)
    a. *s-a-tü*　　　　　*to'ehi*
       OBV-that-SBJ.SG　emerge.hither
       'That (one) is coming out.'
    b. *a-sü*　　　　　*hipikkahni*
       that-IDENT　bar
       'That is a bar.'

Example (24a) includes a demonstrative pronoun functioning as subject of the verb meaning *to'ehi* 'emerge' or 'come out'. The demonstrative consists of three morphemes: the deictic root *a* 'that', the prefix *s-*, which Dayley (1989: 136) calls an 'obviative marker', and a number-case suffix. Example (24b) shows a demonstrative identifier that includes the same deictic root as the demonstrative pronoun in (24a), but in contrast to the latter, the demonstrative identifier is not inflected for case and number and does not include the obviative marker. Instead, demonstrative identifiers are marked by the suffix *-sü(n)* (Dayley 1989: 144, 372). Both types of demonstratives occur with several deictic roots, but Table 21.9 shows only the distal forms.

Table 21.9 Distal demonstratives in Tümpisa Shoshone (Dayley 1989: 137–145)

	PRONOUN			IDENTIFIER
	SINGULAR	DUAL	PLURAL	
SUBJECT	(s-)a-tü	(s-)a-tungku	(s-)a-tümmü	a-sü(n)
OBJECT	(s-)a-kka	(s-)a-tuhi	(s-)a-tümmi	
POSSESSIVE	(s-)a-kkan	(s-)a-tuhin	(s-)a-tümmin	

Like demonstratives in Tümpisa Shoshone, the demonstrative identifiers of several other languages are deprived of their inflectional properties. In German and Russian, for example, demonstrative pronouns are inflected for gender, number, and case, but the demonstratives of identificational constructions are invariable (and thus do not agree with the predicate nominal; see (25) and (26)). The only forms that are permissible in these constructions are the neuter-singular demonstratives *das* and *3mo* 'this/that/it'.

(25)   German
    Das　　　　　　　　sind　meine　Sachen.
    DEM.N.SG.NOM　are　my.PL　thing.F.PL
    'These are my things.'

(26) Russian (Sergei Monakhov p.c.)
 Это моя сестра.
 DEM.N.SG.NOM my.F.SG.NOM sister(.F).SG.NOM
 'That's my sister.'

Another example of a language in which demonstrative identifiers lack any inflectional properties is Inuktitut. As can be seen in Table 21.10, demonstrative pronouns are composed of a deictic root, a nominalizer and a case suffix in Inuktitut; but demonstrative identifiers, which Denny (1982: 365) characterizes as 'predicate particles', are invariable.

Table 21.10 Demonstrative pronouns and identifiers in Inuktitut (Denny 1982: 364–365)

	PRONOUN		IDENTIFIER	
PROXIMAL	*uv-sum-ing* PROX-NML-ACC	'this (one)'	*uvva*	'here (is)'
DISTAL	*ik-sum-ing* DIST-NML-ACC	'that (one)'	*ikka*	'there (is)'

Finally, there are several languages in my data in which demonstrative pronouns are accompanied by a classifier (or pronoun) that does not occur with the demonstratives in copular or nonverbal clauses. For instance, as can be seen in (27a), demonstrative pronouns are preceded by a classifier in Vietnamese, whereas the demonstratives of copular clauses occur alone, i.e. without a classifier (see (27b)).[6]

(27) Vietnamese (Khanh Linh Hoang p.c.)
 a. *tôi lấy cái này*
  I take CLF.INAN this
  'I take this one.'

 b. *đây là nhà tôi*
  this COP house I
  'This is my house.'

Note that the demonstratives of nonverbal clauses are reminiscent of copulas if they resume a preceding noun or noun phrase. Consider, for instance, the following examples from Wappo.

(28) Wappo (Thompson et al. 2006: 101, 101)
 a. *ce k'ew ceʔeʔ i nokh*
  that man DEM/COP 1SG friend
  'That man is my friend.'

---

[6] Note that if a copula is followed by a predicative adjective in Vietnamese, the demonstrative is accompanied by a classifier like a demonstrative pronoun in argument position of a full verb.

b. *ceʔeʔ*   *k'ešu*
   DEM/COP deer
   'That's a deer.'

Wappo has two demonstrative pronouns, *he* 'this' and *ce* 'that', that are included in the morphemes *heʔeʔ* and *ceʔeʔ*, which Thompson et al. (2006: 100–103) analyse as nonverbal copulas when they follow a topicalized NP, as in example (28a). However, since *heʔeʔ* and *ceʔeʔ* can also occur without a topicalized referent (see (28b)), one could regard them as demonstrative identifiers rather than copulas. Nevertheless, there is plenty of evidence that nonverbal copulas are often historically derived from demonstratives in nonverbal clauses that resume a preceding topic (Li and Thompson 1977; Diessel 1999: 143–150).

21.7 DEMONSTRATIVE VERBS

Demonstrative verbs include the same deictic roots as demonstrative pronouns, determiners, adverbs, and identifiers, but serve as predicates and share inflectional categories with verbs. Demonstrative verbs have been described in three recent typological studies by Dixon (2003), Guérin (2015), and Breunesse (2019). In accordance with these studies, my data show that demonstrative verbs are cross-linguistically infrequent. Overall, there are only eleven languages in the entire database in which some demonstratives share some inflectional properties with verbs: Dyirbal (Dixon 2003: 101–103), Epena Pedee (Harms 1994: 63, 176), Kambaata (Treis 2019: 12–13), Mapudungun (Smeets 1989: 424), Mauwake (Berghäll 2015: 172), Musqueam (Suttles 2004: 351), Nivkh (Guérin 2015: 159), Ngalakan (Merlan 1983: 62), Quechua (Shimelman 2017: 207), Kolyma Yukaghir (Maslova 2003: 242), and Yuracaré (Van Gijn 2006: 130).

Demonstrative verbs constitute a heterogeneous class of expressions that vary along several parameters.

- First, demonstrative verbs are either derived from other demonstratives by a verbalizing morpheme or they are inherently verbal (see Guérin 2015).
- Second, demonstrative verbs either refer to entities or places or, more frequently, to the manner an action is carried out (or to a proposition) (see Breunesse 2019).
- And finally, demonstrative verbs vary on a scale of verbhood, ranging from expressions that appear with the full range of verbal morphemes available in a particular language to expressions that share only some morphological properties with verbs.

In what follows, we will consider these parameters based on a few selected examples.

Mauwake has two 'locational verbs' derived from the demonstrative adverbs *fan* 'here' and *nan* 'there' (see Table 21.11). Since the verbal use of *fan* and *nan* does not involve a verbalizing morpheme, Berghäll (2015: 134, 172) argues that demonstrative verbs are formed by 'zero derivation' in Mauwake. Examples show *fan* and *nan* with tense and person marking (see (29)), but note that tense inflection is restricted to the past tense suffix *-e*, which, according to Berghäll, has lost its past tense meaning when combined with a demonstrative.

Table 21.11 Demonstratives in Mauwake (Berghäll 2015: 116, 121, 172)

	PRONOUN	ADVERB	VERB
PROXIMAL	*fain*	*fan*	*fan-e-agr*
DISTAL	*nain*	*nan*	*nan-e-agr*

(29) Mauwake (Berghäll 2015: 172)
aa,   o   koora   fan-e-k   a
INTJ   3SG   house   here-(PST)-3SG INTJ
'Ah, this house is here.'

Quechua has a series of demonstrative verbs that are derived by the verbalizing suffix *-na*. They include the same deictic roots as demonstrative pronouns and adverbs but occur with tense and evidential markers rather than with case and number affixes (see (30a)–(30b)). Note that while demonstrative verbs are built on the same deictic roots as demonstrative pronouns and adverbs, they refer to the manner of an action rather than an entity or location.

(30) Quechua (Shimelman 2017: 207, 40)
 a. *mana   hampi-chi-pti-ki-pa   chay-na-nqa-m*
    no   cure-CAUS-SUB.DS-2-TOP   DEM.DIST-VRBZ-3FUT-EVD
    'If you don't have her cured, it's going to be like that.'

 b. *kanan   chay-kuna-kta   wañu-chi-shaq*
    now   DEM.DIST-PL-ACC   die-CAUS-1.FUT
    'Now I'll kill those.'

With few exceptions (e.g. Mauwake), the demonstrative verbs included in my data are semantically similar to manner demonstratives: They evoke a comparison and refer to an event or proposition. Here are two more examples from Mapudungun (31) and Kolyma Yukaghir (32).

(31) Mapudungun (Smeets 1989: 426)
kawellu   fe-m-nge-y
horse   become.like.that-CAUS-PASS-IND-(3)
'It looks like a horse.'

(32) Kolyma Yukaghir (Maslova 2003: 242)
alhudō-l   lebie   unuŋ-pe-gi   čumut   tāt-mie-l'el-ŋi
low-ANR   earth   river-PL-POSS   all   that-QLT-INFR-3PL.INTR
'All rivers on the Lower Earth are reported to be like that.'

In Mapudungun, demonstrative verbs are based on the roots *fa-* 'become like this' and *fe-* 'become like that'. The same roots appear in demonstrative pronouns and adverbs (e.g. *tüfá* 'this', *tüfey/fey* 'that', *tüfá-mew* 'here-P', *fey-mew* 'there-P'), but in contrast to the latter, demonstrative verbs are inflected for aspect, mood, voice, and person.

In Kolyma Yukaghir, demonstrative verbs are derived by the suffix -*mie*, which serves to form 'qualitative verbs' (Maslova 2003: 92ff.). The demonstrative verbs occur with the full paradigm of verb inflection, except that they do not have converb forms (Maslova 2003: 67).

Like manner demonstrative adverbs, demonstrative verbs are often used with reference to direct speech, as in example (33) from Epena Pedee. Note that while demonstratives may be accompanied by a speech verb when referring to a quote, there is no verb apart from the demonstrative in the clause introducing the quotation in this example.

(33) Epena Pedee (Harms 1994: 176)
 ma-ga-hí,   'pʰáta   kʰo-páde   a-hí'
 that-like-PST 'plantain   eat-IMP   say-PST
 'That is: "Eat your plantains".'

Concluding this section, let us take a short look at ǂHòã, a Kx'a language of Botswana, in which the semantic equivalent of a demonstrative pronoun has the structure of a 'minimal relative clause' (Collins & Gruber 2014: 118). There are two demonstrative determiners in ǂHòã, *ha* 'this/these' and *kyŏa* 'that/those', that can modify a preceding noun but cannot be used alone as pronouns. In order to use *ha* and *kyŏa* as pronouns (i.e. without a cooccurring noun), they have to be combined with two other morphemes: the 'relative pronoun' *ǁna* and the 'perfective relative marker' *m̀*, as in (34b).

(34) ǂHòã (Collins & Gruber 2014: 108, 118)
 a. *O'ú*   [*ǁna*   *m̀*   *ăm-'a*   *ǀqhŭi-qà*]
    duiker which   REL.PERF   eat-PERF   grass-PL
    'the duiker that ate grass'
 b. [*ǁna*   *m̀*   *ha*]   *kì*   *nǀna'a*
    which   REL.PERF   this   EMPH   ugly
    'This one is ugly.' (said of a person)

Both examples in (34) include a relative clause marked by *ǁna* and *m̀*. However, where the relative clause in (34a) occurs with the verb *ăm* 'eat', the relative clause in (34b) occurs with the demonstrative *ha* 'this', suggesting that the demonstrative in (34b) serves as predicate of the relative clause. Similar types of demonstratives occur in other Kx'a languages and have been analysed as verbs (see Lionnet 2014). Note, however, that while the demonstratives in ǂHòã appear in the verb slot of a relative clause, they do not carry verbal inflection affixes such as tense, aspect, or mood (see Collins & Gruber 2014).

21.8 SUMMARY

In conclusion, all languages have demonstratives, but their morphosyntactic properties are cross-linguistically diverse. In traditional grammar, demonstratives are commonly categorized as pronouns and/or adjectives, but if we look at demonstratives from a cross-linguistic perspective, we find a great deal of variation, making it very difficult to divide demonstratives into a universal set of word classes. Nevertheless, there are some cross-linguistic tendencies in the morphological encoding and syntactic behaviour of demonstratives that can be interpreted as prototypes of certain (demonstrative) word classes.

Drawing on data from a sample of 150 languages, this chapter has outlined a word-class typology of demonstratives with five basic categories: (i) demonstrative pronouns, (ii) demonstrative determiners, (ii) demonstrative adverbs, (iv) demonstrative identifiers, and (v) demonstrative verbs. Each type is defined by two basic criteria: (i) a distributional criterion, which describes the use of demonstratives in a particular construction (or syntactic context), and (ii) a morphological criterion, which specifies the morphological forms of demonstratives, notably the forms of their stems and their inflectional properties.

Since the two criteria do not always coincide, one has to distinguish between the syntactic use of a demonstrative and its categorical status. As it turns out, many languages use the same demonstratives in multiple constructions. For instance, as we have seen, it is very common for demonstratives functioning as free pronouns to also serve as semantic modifiers of a cooccurring noun. If the demonstratives of different constructions are formally distinct from one another, they can be immediately categorized as members of separate word classes. However, if a language uses the same demonstratives in several constructions, we have to consider other aspects of their syntactic use in order to determine their word-class status. For instance, as we have seen, in English, adnominal demonstratives are paradigmatically related to articles and other noun modifiers that can be grouped together into a class of syntactic determiners. Yet, in other languages, adnominal demonstratives are only loosely associated with the noun they modify, suggesting that these forms are best analysed as free pronouns in apposition to a noun (rather than determiners).

In general, there is an enormous amount of cross-linguistic variation in the structure and syntactic use of demonstratives, making it impossible to divide demonstratives into a universal set of word-class categories. Grammatical word classes are language- and construction-particular (Croft 2001). However, given the communicative function of demonstratives to create and to manipulate joint attention, it does not come as a surprise that demonstratives tend to occur in similar constructions (across languages) where they often acquire similar structural properties (through grammaticalization) that are characteristic of certain word classes.

Appendix: Language sample[7]

AFRICA: Aghem (Niger-Congo, Bantoid), Anywa (Eastern Sudanic, Nilotic), Arabic [Egyptian] (Afro-Asiatic, Semitic), Dagik (Narrow Talodi, Buram-Saraf), Dime (Afro-Asiatic, South Omotic), Ewondo (Niger-Congo, Bantoid), Goemai (Afro-Asiatic, West Chadic), Gumuz (Isolate), Hausa (Afro-Asiatic, West Chadic), Hdi (Afro-Asiatic, Biu-Mandara), ǂHõã [=|Hoan] (Kx'a), Ik (Eastern Sudanic, Kuliak), Jamsay (Dogon), Kambaata (Afro-Asiatic,

---

[7] The genetic classification of languages has been adopted from *The World Atlas of Language Structures* (Dryer & Haspelmath 2013), supplemented by information from *Glottolog* (Hammarström et al. 2020) when *The World Atlas of Language Structures* did not provide (sufficient) information. Alternative language names (or alternative spellings of language names) are indicated in square brackets.

Cushitic), Koyra Chiini (Songhay), Kxoe [Khwe] (Khoe-Kwadi), Lango (Eastern Sudanic, Nilotic), Masalit (Maban), Mende (Mande, Western Mande), Pichi (Creole), Sandawe (Isolate), Shabo [Chabu] (Isolate), Supyire (Niger-Congo, Senufo), Tamashek (Afro-Asiatic, Berber), Uduk (Koman, Central Koman), Wolaytta (Afro-Asiatic, North Omotic)

NORTH AND CENTRAL AMERICA: Chimariko (Hokan, Chimariko), Choctaw (Muskogean), Inuktitut (Eskimo–Aleut, Eskimo), Jamul Tiipay (Hokan, Yuman), Keresan (Isolate), Kiowa (Kiowa-Tanoan), Lealao Chinantec (Oto-Manguean, Chinantecan), Passamaquoddy-Maliseet (Algic, Algonquian), Molala (Penutian), Montagnais (Algic, Algonquian), Musqueam (Salishan, Central Salish), Oneida (Iroquoian, Northern Iroquoian), Quileute (Chimakuan), Slave (Na-Dene, Athapaskan), Stoney [Assiniboine] (Siouan, Core Siouan), Tümpisa Shoshone (Uto-Aztecan, Numic), Tzeltal (Mayan), Tzutujil (Mayan), Wappo (Wappo-Yukian, Wappo), West Greenlandic (Eskimo–Aleut, Eskimo), Zapotec (Oto-Manguean, Zapotecan)

SOUTH AMERICA: Apurinã (Arawakan, Purus), Awa Pit (Barbacoan), Bora (Huitotoan, Boran), Epena Pedee (Choco), Hixkaryana (Cariban, Parukotoan), Hup (Nadahup), Kamaiurá (Tupian, Tupi-Guaraní), Kotiria (Tucanoan), Kwaza (Isolate), Macushi (Cariban), Mapudungun [Mapuche] (Araucanian), Matsés (Pano-Tacanan, Panoan), Mosetén (Isolate), Pilagá (Guaicuruan), Quechua (Quechuan), Trumai (Isolate), Warao (Isolate), Wari' (Chapacura-Wanham), Yagua (Peba-Yaguan), Yuracaré (Isolate)

EURASIA: Ainu (Isolate), Bao'an Tu (Altaic, Mongolic), Basque (Isolate), Belhare (Sino-Tibetan, Mahakiranti), Burushaski (Isolate), Cantonese (Sino-Tibetan, Chinese), Chukchi (Chukotko-Kamchatkan, Northern Chukotko-Kamchatkan), Croatian (Indo-European, Slavic), English (Indo-European, Germanic), Evenki (Altaic, Tungusic), Finnish (Uralic, Finnic), French (Indo-European, Romance), Georgian (Kartvelian), German (Indo-European, Germanic), Hinuq (Nakh-Daghestanian, Avar-Andic-Tsezic), Hungarian (Uralic, Ugric), Italian (Indo-European, Romance), Japanese (Japanese), Ket (Yeniseian), Kolyma Yukaghir (Yukaghir), Korean (Korean), Lezgian (Nakh-Daghestanian, Lezgic), Marathi (Indo-European, Indic), Meithei (Sino-Tibetan, Kuki-Chin), Nihali (Isolate), Nivkh (Isolate), Persian (Indo-European, Iranian), Qiang (Sino-Tibetan, Qiangic), Russian (Indo-European, Slavic), Saami (Uralic, Saami), Spanish (Indo-European, Romance), Swedish (Indo-European, Germanic), Tamil (Dravidian, Southern Dravidian), Turkish (Altaic, Turkic), Ubykh (North-West Caucasian), Yakkha (Sino-Tibetan, Kiranti)

SOUTH EAST ASIA AND OCEANIA: Acehnese (Austronesian, Malayo-Sumbawan), Bajau (Austronesian, Sama-Bajaw), Begak-Ida'an (Austronesian, North Borneo), Chamorro (Austronesian, Chamorro), Jahai (Austro-Asiatic, Aslian), Khamti (Tai-Kadai, Kam-Tai), Khasi (Austro-Asiatic, Khasian), Lao (Tai-Kadai, Kam-Tai), Malay (Austronesian, Malayo-Sumbawan), Maori (Austronesian, Oceanic), Pangasinan (Austronesian, Northern Luzon), Pohnpeian (Austronesian, Oceanic), Semelai (Austro-Asiatic, Aslian), Taba [East Makian] (Austronesian, Eastern Malayo-Polynesian), Toqabaqita (Austronesian, Oceanic), Tukang Besi (Austronesian, Celebic), Vietnamese (Austro-Asiatic, Viet-Muong)

AUSTRALIA AND NEW GUINEA: Abui (Timor-Alor-Pantar, Greater Alor), Alamblak (Sepik, Sepik-Hill), Ambulas (Sepik, Ndu), Bilua (Solomons East Papuan, Bilua), Dom (Trans-New Guinea, Chimbu-Wahgi), Duna (Trans-New Guinea, Duna), Dyirbal (Pama–Nyungan, Northern Pama–Nyungan), Hatam (West Papuan, Hatam), Imonda (Border), Komnzo

[Anta-Komnzo-Wára-Wérè-Kémä] (Yam, Morehead-Maro), Lavukaleve (Solomons East Papuan), Mangarrayi (Mangarrayi-Maran), Martuthunira (Pama–Nyungan, Western Pama–Nyungan), Mauwake (Trans-New Guinea, Madang), Menya (Trans-New Guinea, Angan), Mian (Trans-New Guinea, Ok), Mparntwe Arrernte (Pama–Nyungan, Central Pama–Nyungan), Nankina (Trans-New Guinea, Finisterre-Huon), Ngalakan (Gunwinyguan, Ngalakan), Nunggubuyu (Gunwinyguan, Nunggubuyu), Tauya (Trans-New Guinea, Madang), Tidore (West Papuan, North Halmaheran), Urim (Torricelli, Urim), Usan (Trans-New Guinea, Madang), Wambaya (Mirndi, Wambayan), Wardaman (Yangmanic), Yagaria (Trans-New Guinea, Eastern Highlands), Yawuru (Nyulnyulan), Yelî Dnye (Yele), Yimas (Lower Sepik-Ramu, Lower Sepik)

CHAPTER 22

IDEOPHONES

MARK DINGEMANSE

22.1 INTRODUCTION

AT least since the 1850s linguists have recognized that many languages have a sizable lexical class of words that depict sensory scenes. A commonly accepted cross-linguistic term for these words today is IDEOPHONES, though 'mimetics' and 'expressives' are also used in the prolific fields of Japanese and South East Asian linguistics (Voeltz & Kilian-Hatz 2001; Akita & Pardeshi 2019). Ideophones have long been studied for their striking phonological features, their iconic associations between form and meaning, and their rhetorical uses. Here I survey the topic from the point of view of word classes. How can we characterize ideophones as a cross-linguistic category? What is the morphosyntactic behaviour of ideophones across languages? And how do ideophones relate to other word classes such as adjectives, adverbs, and verbs?

For comparative purposes, we can define ideophones as an open lexical class of marked words that depict sensory imagery (Dingemanse 2019). The definition has five elements. First, ideophones form an OPEN LEXICAL CLASS, i.e. a group of words open to new additions. Second, ideophones are MARKED: their structural make-up is distinctive relative to other classes of words, especially in terms of phonology and prosody. Third, ideophones are WORDS, or more precisely lexical items with conventional meanings. Fourth, ideophones DEPICT: they use a mode of signification that highlights iconic associations between aspects of form and meaning. Fifth, their meanings lie in the domain of SENSORY IMAGERY, evoking rich sensory scenes in colourful ways. Each of these elements has been the target of much research. Here I will highlight only those most relevant for an understanding of ideophones in the context of word classes across languages.

Defining ideophones as an open lexical class means that we can recognize them as a widespread linguistic phenomenon independently from their morphosyntactic status in particular languages. Seeing them as words with a depictive mode of signification helps us distinguish them from interjections and helps explain remarkable crosslinguistic commonalities, as we will see below. And observing that they evoke sensory imagery draws attention to their colourful meanings and indicates that in many languages they go far beyond onomatopoeia, the minor subclass of sound imitatives that has historically been seen as the main example of lexicalized depictions in spoken languages.

22.2 DISTINGUISHING IDEOPHONES AND INTERJECTIONS

Although we will come to the relation between ideophones and other word classes, there is one matter we need to address up front: the difference between ideophones and interjections (Poggi 2009; Meinard 2015). These are formally and functionally distinct classes in any language for which we have good descriptions, but somehow they are easily conflated or even confused (Dialo 1985; Landar 1985; Hofstede 1999; Haiman 2018). There are indeed some superficial similarities between the two. Both ideophones and interjections seem quite expressive. Both are said to be able to make up stand-alone utterances. And both are often described as having anomalous phonology and phonotactics. However, on closer inspection, the differences outweigh the similarities on all counts.

MODE OF SIGNIFICATION. Both ideophones and interjections may seem to be broadly about sensory and emotional experiences. But they differ in the nature of this aboutness. Ideophones are typically depictions *of* events, while interjections are typically responses *to* them. Perhaps a slap in the face will help the reader to appreciate the difference. The *sound* of the slap is the main business of an ideophone to depict; your *outcry* in response to it is an interjection. The semiotic difference is parallel to that between icon and index, and is also seen in the associated lexical items: 'slap' bears an iconic similarity to the sound of a strike with the open hand; whereas 'ow!' harkens back to an instinctive pain vocalization that provides indexical evidence of your feeling but is not itself iconic of that feeling. Each of them is non-arbitrary in its own way.

MORPHOSYNTAX. Both ideophones and interjections are aloof from sentential syntax, but in different ways and for different reasons. Interjections are by definition one-word utterances. Ideophones tend to appear at utterance edge, but rarely on their own. One source of confusion may be the cross-linguistically common use of ideophones use in quotative-like constructions (as in 'The car went *vroom*'). If we peel down such constructions, it seems the kernel is a one-word utterance 'Vroom' that is similar to the one-word utterances we call interjections (compare: 'The reader went *ow!*'). As the car goes *vroom*, so the reader goes *ow!*, and we may feel there is a deeper kinship. However, this would be a category mistake. Quotations can incorporate just about any sensory scene we may wish to depict (Clark & Gerrig 1990; Keevallik 2010), including someone producing an interjection, as here. This does not imply that the depicted material is alike. Likewise, the fact that an interjection like *ow!* can be used to mimic being in pain does not warrant the conclusion that it is therefore of one kind with the lexicalized depictions we call ideophones.

MARKEDNESS. Ideophones tend to use the phonological system to the fullest, rearranging and extending it in creative yet systematic ways. If they stray outside of the existing inventory, they do so by stretching or contracting it, filling gaps, adding secondary articulations, or playing with tonal melodies (Diffloth 1979; Mithun 1982; Nuckolls et al. 2016). Interjections, in contrast, under-use the larger phonological inventory and at the same time easily recruit elements that bear no systematic relation to the larger system, like the click in the disapproving *tsk* and the bilabial trill in the transition display *brrr* (Goffman 1978; Gil 2013b; Pillion et al. 2019). Ideophones and interjections are each structurally distinct from other word classes in their own way. If we think of the phonology of ordinary words as providing the harmonic backbone to a jazz piece, ideophones are the solos soaring above it, and interjections the percussive elements that build the tight groove holding it all together.

A century ago, 'interjections' formed the catch-all bin for anything with a complicated relation to sentential syntax, including the lexicalized depictions we now call 'ideophones'. Today however we have ample theoretical and empirical reasons to recognize interjections and ideophones as meaningfully different. Distinguishing them matters in theoretical debates. When Evans & Levinson (2009) drew attention to ideophones as a major word class that had flown under the radar of mainstream linguistics, one of the replies cited 'response cries such as *yum, splat, hubba-hubba, pow!*' (Pinker & Jackendoff 2009) as evidence that English had something similar. The cited words form a motley crew of exclamations (*yum, hubba-hubba*) and sound imitatives (*splat, pow*), and the notion that the latter would be 'response cries' evokes visions of wide-eyed English speakers uttering *splat!* anytime something hits the ground and going *pow!* at every unexpected blast. The effect of this kind of oversimplification is to obscure meaningful distinctions between word classes, and to contribute to the marginalization of ideophones as a major word class. More generally, distinguishing ideophones and interjections matters for our ability to understand and explain language structure. If we lump them together, we lose the ability to explain how and why they differ in terms of markedness, morphosyntax, and mode of signification.

22.3 AN OPEN LEXICAL CLASS THAT HAS ELUDED WORD-CLASS DEBATES

In one sense, the class of ideophones is quite similar to other open word classes: it often consists of a large set of items that fit core definitional properties rather well, and fuzzy edges where it shades into other word classes (Childs 1994; Ibarretxe-Antuñano 2017). Yet there is a telling difference. Traditional word classes like nouns, verbs, and adjectives periodically elicit high-stakes theoretical debates focusing on the nature of parts of speech, their crosslinguistic distribution, and the possibility of recognizing language-specific stem classes as instantiating putative universal categories (Dixon 1977; Kinkade 1983; Wetzer 1996; Croft 2001; Croft & van Lier 2012). In contrast, ideophones tend to be approached from the other side, as it were: they stand out as speech heard in a special way even before one has started to consider their grammatical status.

Mundari, an Austroasiatic language of India, offers a useful example. The fluidity of its word-class system has been a site of considerable debate ever since an early grammar claimed that its lexical items could function flexibly as nouns, verbs, adjectives, and so on (Hoffmann 1903). Contributions to the debate rely on subtle distributional facts and intricate theoretical arguments to argue for or against recognizing distinct noun-like and verb-like word classes in the language (Evans & Osada 2005; Peterson 2005; Croft 2005b; Hengeveld & Rijkhoff 2005). Amid the theoretical skirmishes it is easy to overlook that one large class of content words in the language comes off scot-free: ideophones, or to use the regionally appropriate term of trade, expressives. Like most Austroasiatic languages, Mundari has long been described as having a distinct class of these words (Osada 1992). Nor is this a minor class: a dedicated dictionary documents at least 1500 unique lemmas (Badenoch & Osada 2019) and they are 'found in most all arenas of language use' (Badenoch et al. 2019: 4). And yet the status of this considerable lexical stratum in the language has not featured in any word-class debates.

How does a major class elude any mention in theoretical debates focused on the fundamentals of word classes in a language? One reason for this touches directly on the nature of ideophones. In the words of Felix Ameka, 'ideophones are first and foremost a type of words' (Ameka 2001: 26). This statement, which may seem a bit tautological at first, is appropriate in talking about ideophones because they are structurally and semiotically recognizable as special. Mundari ideophones for instance are primarily identified by their reduplicative forms and highly detailed semantics (Osada et al. 2020). The recognizability of ideophones as a lexical class means that it is often possible to identify them by ostension ('words like this') and to forego careful description of their morphosyntactic profile. Paradoxically then, the fact that Mundari ideophones stand out as a distinct lexical class has enabled us to stop short of learning about their proper place in the larger system of word classes in the language.[1]

Getting this right is not merely a matter of language-specific description; it also affects our typological generalizations. Take typological work on adjectives, which classifies languages in terms of the kinds of adjective classes they exhibit (Dixon 1977; Dixon & Aikhenvald 2004). Ideophones have generally been kept out of the relevant comparisons, despite the fact that in many languages they share semantic and grammatical features with word classes identified as adjectival. The surprising result is that languages like Igbo or Ewe are in a kind of quantum superposition with regard to their place in the larger typology of adjectives: they may count as having either a tiny closed class or an enormous open class of adjectives, depending on whether ideophones have been observed or not (Ameka 2001). Something similar holds for typological work on adverbs: ideophones are sometimes noted for their semantic and structural overlap with adverbs, but more often they are excluded due to scope limitations (Hallonsten Halling 2018). Such extreme observer dependence does not bode well for the generalizability of typological classifications. At the very least, this means we must improve our grasp of the morphosyntactic profile of ideophones within and across languages.

22.4 CASE STUDY: EXPRESSIVE ADVERBIALS IN JAMSAY

Jamsay, a Dogon language spoken in Mali, provides an instructive case study of how the apparent tension between cross-linguistic commonalities and language-specific realizations

---

[1] Descriptions of Mundari expressives typically focus on word-level structural and semantic characteristics. Individual examples show predicative as well as loose appositional uses (Badenoch & Osada 2019), but their morphosyntactic profile awaits systematic description.

can play out (Heath 2019). Besides the usual major stem classes of noun, adjective, and verb, Dogon languages have an open stem class for which Heath proposes the descriptive term 'expressive adverbials'. The items in this class form a distinct lexical stratum, are 'uninflectable' and 'grammatically marginal', and do not enter into regular processes of tonosyntax. As Heath concludes, many of them 'fit current definitions of ideophones (marked forms, sensory imagery)' (2019: 18).[2] Some are illustrated in (1).

(1) Jamsay (Dogon) (Heath 2019: 5–6).
    a. *dém→*   'straight (object, road, trajectory)'
    b. *gǔjⁿ→*   'jutting out'
    c. *pép*   'chock-full, full to the brim'
    d. *kák*   'stopping/arriving abruptly (noisily)'
    d. *bέɲέ-bέɲέ*   'flickering, glimmering'
    e. *járálálá*   'moving (light, child's toy kite)'
    f. *táw-táw*   '(very) fast'

Structurally, Jamsay expressive adverbials are characterized by final lengthening (marked with '→'), by CVC shapes with final obstruents that are otherwise disallowed in the language (1c), and by several forms of full and partial reduplication (1d)–(1f). Both lengthening and reduplication can be varied for rhetorical purposes. These features are in line with what we know from ideophones across languages, and receive a straightforward explanation if we think of them as originating in the depictive use of linguistic material. Here as elsewhere, ideophones freely exploit the expressive resources of phonology and prosody for depictive purposes.

At the same time, and as with all word classes, there are important language-specific intricacies to Jamsay expressive adverbials. At first sight, they are quite similar to adjectives like *bán* 'red', as shown by the fact that both can be used as stative predicates using a copula-like auxiliary *kɔ̀* (2a)–(2b). However, their paths diverge under negation: whereas the predicative colour adjective is negated using a negative clitic *=lá* (3a), predicative expressive adverbials require the negative form of the locational–existential quasi-verb (3b).[3] Moreover, to use them as adnominal modifiers, expressive adverbial predicates like (2b) need to be embedded into a relative clause with a participial 'be' quasi-verb (3c). From this and other evidence, Heath concludes that Jamsay expressive adverbials like *gǔjⁿ→* and kin are not adjectival, but rather form one-word adverbial phrases.

---

[2] While the cross-linguistic similarities stand out, Heath stops short of identifying Jamsay expressive adverbials as 'ideophones' and stresses the importance of 'delving into individual grammars, only loosely guided by crosslinguistic categories' (Heath 2019: 4).

[3] Incidentally, the evidence from negation here allows us to nuance the view that ideophones are categorically 'not subject to negation' (Kilian-Hatz 2006). As with many properties of culturally evolving linguistic systems, it is more useful to speak in terms of tendencies rather than absolutes, and to explain regularities rather than expect exceptionless rules. For instance, the fact that ideophones are unlikely to be negated in everyday language use can be straightforwardly explained by their nature as depictions (just as direct quotation is used more often to report what someone said rather than what they did not say). But this functionally motivated generalization does not preclude the occasional negative use (again, just as in rare cases, it may be important to stress what someone did *not* say).

(2) Jamsay (Dogon) (Heath 2019: 7–9)[4]
   a. *bán kɔ̀*
      red be.NONH
      'It is red.'

   b. *gŭjⁿ→ kɔ̀*
      jutting.EA be.NONH
      'It is jutting out.'

(3) a. *bán=lá-ɸ*
      red=STAT.NEG-3SG.SJB
      'He/she/it is not red.'

   b. *gŭjⁿ→ kɔ̀:-rɔ́*
      jutting.EA be.NONH-NEG
      'It is not jutting out.'

   c. *kòmò^L gŭjⁿ→ kɔ̀:-ɸ*
      back^L jutting.EA be.NONH.PPL-NONH
      '(a/the) back that is jutting out'

One further wrinkle can serve to display the intricate mixture of language-specific and cross-linguistically convergent features we find in any ideophone system. In the tonosyntax of Jamsay Dogon, adjectives control tone-dropping of the preceding noun. Expressive adverbials do not in general have the same effect, which is another reason to distinguish them from adjectives. However, sometimes expressive adverbials do have tonal effects on their immediate environment. For instance, in the example below, the expressive adverbial *dém-dém*, an expressively modified form of *dém→* 'straight', seems to cause the preceding noun *tègú* 'speech' to tone-drop to *tègù* (4a):

(4) Jamsay (Dogon) (Heath 2019: 13–14)
   a. *[á tègù] [dém-dém kɔ̀:-rɔ́]*
      2SG.POSS speech straight.EA be.NONH-NEG
      'Your talk is not straight (candid).'

   b. *[á tègú] ↓ dém-dém ...*

Is this evidence that expressive adverbials like *dém→* may be similar to adjectives after all, or is something else going on? In Heath's analysis (shown in (4b)), the effect is not tonosyntactic at all: it is 'an intonationally motivated and phonetically variable pitch-lowering, whose effect is to make the following [expressive adverbial] more salient acoustically' (Heath 2019: 14). Without this lowering, the final high tone of *tègú* would distract from the following expressive adverbial; with it, the expressive adverbial stands out more clearly from the surrounding material.

While this may seem to be a notable quirk of Jamsay (and a testimony to the acuity of the observer), it happens to be perfectly in line with cross-linguistic generalizations about the prosody of ideophones in relation to their depictive nature. Recent work recognizes

---

[4] Glosses as in the original, with the only difference that I have marked expressive adverbials with '.EA'.

three depiction marking strategies often found in combination with ideophones (Akita 2020): ideophones may be marked as depictions by framing (e.g. with quotative markers), by foregrounding (e.g. exaggerated prosody on the ideophone), or by backgrounding (e.g. by deemphasizing the non-ideophonic part to draw out the ideophone more clearly). The process described for Jamsay expressive adverbials by Heath appears to be a clear example of the backgrounding strategy.

The overall picture that emerges is a combination of recurrent features that make ideophones recognizable as a comparative concept (Dingemanse 2019), and morphosyntactic intricacies that show their integration into local linguistic systems. In Childs's apt formulation, this is how ideophones 'reconcile the twin dicta of "be different" and "be recognizably language"' (2014:341). Even if ideophones are structurally marked and recognizable as lexicalized depictions, they are not insulated from other aspects of the language. Nothing in language is. The mere fact of being built from recognizably linguistic material opens up ideophones to being co-opted by morphosyntactic processes, undergoing semantic change, and eroded by frequent usage. This also means that ideophone inventories, as open lexical classes, can be as much in flux as other word classes: they are open to new additions but may also undergo attrition.

22.5 UNITY AND DIVERSITY IN GRAMMATICAL FUNCTIONS

There is an old and widespread idea that ideophones have no syntax worth speaking of, or even that they 'cannot be generated by the grammar' (Voorhoeve 1964). This is not in line with current understandings of the morphosyntax of ideophones. Although ideophones definitely take some syntactic liberties (Diffloth 1972; Childs 1994), they rarely show up all on their own, and indeed the ways they 'burrow into the grammar' (Heath 2019) are worthy of careful description. But how can we reconcile the tension between the notions that ideophones are prototypically aloof yet also linguistically integrated?

The answer is that the diversity is not endless, and a large part of it can be captured in terms of a single generalization: the morphosyntax of ideophones within and across languages owes much to the nature and origin of ideophones as depictive words. There are two parts to this generalization. First, the most prototypical ideophone constructions show strong convergence across languages because ideophones are fundamentally depictive words. Second, the grammatical realization of ideophones within languages can be understood as a consequence of what happens when depictive material gets in the grip of grammar. Let's discuss each of these in turn.

The prototypical relation between descriptive utterances and depictive words like ideophones is much like that between a text and its accompanying illustrations. The illustrations need a degree of freedom to be recognized as images: they need to be framed or set apart from the text in some way. But they also need a degree of proximity to the text to be recognized as accompaniments. The result is that text and image are clearly distinct, yet support each other's interpretations. This is, at base, how ideophones work (Kunene 1965; Nuckolls 1996; Güldemann 2008). They use speech in a special way, inviting listeners to see structural similarities—iconic associations—between their spoken forms and the sensory scenes they depict. In order to be recognizable as depictions, ideophones need some degree of freedom. In order to support and be supported by the surrounding descriptive material, they tend to co-occur with some speech. Some key cross-linguistic similarities in ideophone morphosyntax fall out from this: their common appearance in quotative-like constructions; their frequent loose appositional relation to sentential syntax; and their antipathy to morphological operations like inflection and negation.

At the same time, there is room for considerable language-specificity in terms of morphosyntactic functions and word-class status. In some languages like Zulu, Semai, or Japanese, ideophones may be recognized as a distinct part of speech—indeed it was this distinctive status that moved Doke (1935) to introduce 'ideophone' as a novel grammatical category in the description of Bantu languages. In others like Jamsay, Gbaya, or Upper Necaxa Totonac, their use as predicate qualifiers motivates treating them as part of a larger adverbial class (Roulon-Doko 2001; Beck 2008). In yet others like Hausa and Tera, there are ideophonic subclasses of verbs, adverbs, and adjectives (Newman 1968). There are also languages like Ewe and Basque in which ideophones show evidence of multicategoriality, allowing predicative and attributive uses while remaining mostly free of inflectional or derivational morphology (Ameka 2001; Ibarretxe-Antuñano 2017).

Although the diversity in grammatical functions may seem bewildering at first, there is method to the madness, and again the depictive nature of ideophones can help us understand it. The key observation is that not all kinds of meanings are equally easy to express by means of vocal depiction. It is hard to depict an object in speech, but much easier to evoke aspects of its sound, the irregularity of its shape, the roughness of its surface, or the wobbling way in which it moves. Speech can do all these things because it offers a rich bundle of acoustic features, articulatory gestures, and phonological contrasts that can ground cross-modal iconic associations (Bühler 1934; Jakobson & Waugh 1979; Ahlner & Zlatev 2010). It follows that ideophones, as lexicalized vocal depictions, lend themselves well to expressing properties and actions, and serving functions of predication and modification.

We can overlay this observation about the semiotics of depiction in speech onto a widely used conceptual framework for grammatical categories (Croft 1990), usefully extended by Hallonsten Halling to make room for adverbs (2018: 38). If the meanings of ideophones tend to evoke properties and actions, not objects—and if their discourse functions are more likely to involve modification and predication than reference—then those areas are the ones where we should expect to see them turn up. And sure enough, for each of the structural coding categories found in the union of these areas (Table 22.1) it is easy to find examples of ideophones being connected to, or realizable as, that category: adjectives in Ewe (Ameka 2001), adverbs in Gbaya (Roulon-Doko 2001), predicate adjectives in Japanese (Akita 2009), verbs in Shona (Fortune 1971), converbs in Wolaitta (Amha 2010), and relative clauses in Jamsay (Heath 2019). In short, the kinship of ideophones to adjectives, adverbs, and verbs emerges as a consequence of the affordances for depicting sensory imagery in speech.

Table 22.1 Semantic classes and discourse functions (Hallonsten Halling—Croft model)

	Reference	Modification		Predication
		of reference	of predication	
Objects	NOUNS	genitive, adjectivizations, PPs on nouns	PPs on verbs	predicate nominals, copulas
Properties	deadjectival nouns	ADJECTIVES	ADVERBS	predicate adjectives, copulas
Actions	action nominals, complements, infinitives, gerunds	participles, relative clauses	converbs	VERBS

Given the semiotic affordances of depiction in speech, ideophones are most likely to show up in areas shown in black.

One way to think about this table is as visualizing likely landing grounds for lexicalized vocal depictions. As vocal depictions, ideophones originate on a different plane, where sound and sense are intertwined. Strong evidence for this is that ideophone inventories typically form a separate stratum of original root material that shows no clear relations to existing vocabulary. But as linguistic signs, they inevitably intersect at some point with the more prosaic plane of grammatical systems that structure and canalize linguistic resources. Note that the point is not that ideophones must necessarily be realized as one of the linguistic categories mentioned here; these are just some of the nooks and crannies that ideophones may come to inhabit when they become enmeshed with morphosyntax. In languages like Ewe, Basque, or Semelai, a separate word class of ideophones can flexibly fulfil roles of modification and predication in ways that partially supplant categories like adverbs and adjectives.

Scope limitations prevent cashing out the full implications of these observations, but this is an area that is sure to yield important generalizations in terms of typological distributions, semantic maps, and pathways for language change. We can already begin to sketch some of them. It may be that the typological profile of a language influences likely landing places for ideophones. For instance, in languages that typically separate the lexical expression of manner from motion, ideophones may be more likely to occur adverbially (Schaefer 2001). From the perspective of language change, the table may help us understand and predict pathways for deideophonization. Bantu languages are generally described as featuring an open lexical class of ideophones that must be recognized as a distinct part of speech (Doke 1935). Certain Bantu languages show evidence of a process of deideophonization in which some ideophonic roots become more like verbs. For instance, in Tsonga a subset of ideophones appears with agreement morphology typical of verbs (Marivate 1983; Msimang & Poulos 2001), while others tend to appear in a quotative frame more typical of ideophones in Bantu. The two realizations exist in parallel, indicating a degree of flexibility or perhaps an ongoing process of deideophonization (Dingemanse & Akita 2017).

Halfway around the world, Aslian languages of the Malay Peninsula provide a picture of a possible outcome of such a process of deideophonization. Semai (Central Aslian) and

Semelai (Southern Aslian) are in many ways prototypical ideophone languages, with large class of ideophones (called 'expressives' in this part of the world) that are maximally free and behave in every respect as expected of prototypical ideophones (Diffloth 1976; Kruspe 2004; Tufvesson 2011). However, two Northern Aslian languages, Jahai and Maniq, show no synchronic evidence of an open lexical class of this kind (Burenhult & Majid 2011; Wnuk 2016). Instead, these languages have a minor class of stative verbs that covers some of the same semantic domains. The clinching evidence is that we find cognate forms that function as expressives in one language but function as stative verbs in another (e.g. Semai *pɲũs* '(expr) of mould; wet fur' versus Jahai *pʔus* '(v) mouldy or musty odour'). Given that most present-day Aslian languages have an open class of expressives, this may well be the ancestral state, with historical change bringing about their assimilation to the verb class in Jahai and Maniq.

22.6 IN CLOSING: LESSONS FOR THE TYPOLOGY OF WORD CLASSES

Even if ideophones often come in great numbers, they have rarely been considered one of the major word classes, which appears to be an honour reserved for the traditional Latinate categories of noun, verb, and adjective. This is mostly a matter of historical accident: an example of the 'ethnocentrism' (Haspelmath 2012b) that has often haunted the study of word-class universals. Had typology started from the point of view of Austroasiatic or Bantu, it is likely that ideophones would have been among the classes recognized as major, and scholars would have tied themselves into knots over questions like productive reduplication in Aslian expressives, the verb–ideophone distinction in Southern Bantu, and the dearth of depictive vocabulary in Indo-European.

The solution is not to elevate ideophones to the pantheon of major word classes and call it a day. Instead, ideophones are best seen as an enduring reminder of the path-dependence of typological inquiry and the need to take linguistic diversity seriously. This path-dependence surfaces in at least two ways. First, starting points shape routes and destinations: if a particular set of concepts is handed down from earlier work, or happens to have proven useful for the first bunch of languages looked at, it is likely to become entrenched, making later-discovered phenomena seem more exotic or exceptional. Ideophones help us shake off this effect to some degree because even if we can make do with noun, verb, and adjective in Standard Average European languages, classes of lexicalized vocal depictions are simply too large to be treated as marginal in, say, Bantu or Austroasiatic.

Second, terminological choices have a tendency to become reified and turn from attention-guiding hypotheses into attention-narrowing assumptions (Croft 2001). Research questions can easily devolve from exploring and explaining diversity into box-ticking exercises like 'does this language have category X?'. Work on ideophones has largely been spared this kind of exercise, in part because it has always shown a healthy resistance to pigeon-holing (Newman 1968; Dingemanse 2019; Heath 2019). Another factor is that the prolific research traditions of Japanese and South East Asian linguistics maintain their own terms 'mimetics' (Iwasaki et al. 2017) and 'expressives' (Diffloth 2020). Terminological diversity can be confusing, but in this case it is also a sign of the robustness of the phenomenon: we know there is something here precisely because several research traditions have independently identified, in unrelated phyla, an open lexical class of marked words depictive of sensory imagery. Amid the diversity, there is enough convergence in structural and morphosyntactic properties to warrant a common term like 'ideophones', if only to draw attention to typological explanations and generalizations (Akita & Pardeshi 2019; Dingemanse 2019). Typology always has to walk the fine line between charting linguistic diversity and achieving comparability, and ideophones provide us with exactly the right amount of recalcitrance to keep us on our toes.

Recent years have seen a number of wide-ranging reviews and comparative studies. For a more complete picture of ideophones, the reader is referred to work on the semantic typology of ideophones (McLean 2020; Nuckolls 2019); on the typology and morphosyntax of depiction marking (Güldemann 2008; Akita 2020); and on the notion of 'ideophone' as a comparative concept that can inform typological work without losing sight of diversity (Ibarretxe-Antuñano 2017; Dingemanse 2019). Rather than rehash findings from this work, here I have made an effort to highlight matters that have received less attention and are most relevant to the treatment of ideophones in the context of word classes: the distinction between ideophones and interjections, the delicate balance between cross-linguistic commonalities and language-specific peculiarities, and the place of ideophones among other word classes.

Overlooking the themes highlighted here, one thing is abundantly clear: we need more high-quality descriptions of the form, meaning and use of ideophones in a wide array of languages. Their treatment in grammar-writing is still erratic and too often confined to some pages lumping together 'minor' word classes. A model of grammar that devotes more pages to comparatives and superlatives than to ideophones and interjections perpetuates a most peculiar view of language structure. Fortunately the last decades have seen an increase in work that treats ideophones in considerable detail, both in individual studies (Beck 2008; Ibarretxe-Antuñano 2017; Lahaussois 2018; Heath 2019; Nuckolls 2019) and in grammatical descriptions (Newman 2000; Nikolaeva & Tolskaya 2001; Kruspe 2004; Veikho 2019; Yliniemi 2019; Rüsch 2020). Equipped with a sketch of the morphosyntactic terrain in which ideophones find their place, and with a clearer view of the central roles played by depictive vocabulary in modification and predication, we are now in a position to appreciate new horizons in grammar writing, typology, and theoretical linguistics. Or to give the last word to a Siwu ideophone, the future is bright, *wǎj*→

Acknowledgements

Some small parts of this chapter incorporate material from the author's unpublished PhD dissertation but the whole has been so thoroughly revised and reimagined that few traces remain. I dedicate it to Bill Samarin (1926–2020) and Tucker Childs (1948–2021), whose work has meant so much for the study of ideophones in African languages and beyond. Thank you to Calle Börstell and an anonymous reviewer for ever so helpful feedback, and to Eva van Lier for just the right mix of reassuring patience and gentle pressure in unprecedented times.

CHAPTER 23

INTERJECTIONS

MARK DINGEMANSE

23.1 INTRODUCTION

INTERJECTIONS rank among the most frequently used words in interaction, include some of the earliest elements to emerge in language development, and have the best claim to universal occurrence across widely varied languages. They are also, in Ameka's memorable formulation, 'the universal yet neglected part of speech' (Ameka 1992a: 101)—a three-decades-old verdict that still holds for too many grammars (Lahaussois 2016). However, even if grammar writing may be slow to adapt, the ground is shifting under our feet as general linguistics comes to terms with the importance of interjections in everyday language use. This chapter surveys interjections in terms of three sets of themes. It shows that an understanding of interjections requires close attention to both form and function. It argues that interjections offer insights that can help linguistics extend its reach from isolated sentences to interactional sequences. And it shows that with functional and sequential aspects of interjections in mind, we can better understand patterns of unity and diversity.

First, some terminological housekeeping. The most widely used definitions of interjections converge on at least the following two formal characteristics: prototypical interjections are (i) monolexemic lexical items that (ii) typically make up an utterance (Jespersen 1922; Ameka 1992a; Wilkins 1992; Nübling 2004; Elffers 2007; Poggi 2009). The first condition restricts the scope to uninflected, conventionalized linguistic items. The second condition sets apart prototypical interjections from utterance fragments that arise from ellipsis, from discourse particles that typically attach to larger wholes, and from lexicalized depictions like onomatopoeia and ideophones (Ameka & Wilkins 2006; Poggi 2009; Meinard 2015). Many words can be uttered alone given the right context, but only few are typically uttered alone.

A number of auxiliary provisions are sometimes added to these core characteristics. A common structural distinction is between primary and secondary interjections (Bloomfield 1914). Primary interjections are items that are most likely to occur in stand-alone utterances (think *Mmhm* or *Huh?*); secondary interjections recruit material that also regularly occurs in larger structures (think *Thanks!* or *Pardon?* along with other formulaic expressions). The broader class of inserts—non-clausal single-word units (Biber et al. 1999: 1082–1095)—unites primary and secondary interjections and also contains such items as greetings, pragmatic markers, delay markers and expletives, many of which can also appear in or around larger structures. The two conditions above privilege the primary subset, which suits our focus on interjections as a lexical class.

Some accounts include semantic criteria linking interjections to the expression of feelings or mental states (Goffman 1978; Wierzbicka 1992; Wharton 2009). While this does capture a folk understanding of interjections as public emissions of private emotions, it risks prematurely excluding classes of one-word utterances less clearly in the business of expressing affect. When we talk about interjections in the context of word classes, the two formal characteristics of monolexemicity and conventional utterancehood are probably sufficient to achieve a degree of typological comparability, while alerting us to the possibility of considerable diversity in terms of form and function.

23.2 FORM AND FUNCTION

For the longest time, interjections have been primarily seen in terms of what they are not. Going back to Latin grammar, the term 'interjection' has invited linguists to accord these items at most an *ad interim* status and to use the notion as a catch-all bin containing everything that finds no easy home within the sentence. The result is a category that seems to host a bewildering variety of items. One could almost call this a pretheoretical notion of interjections, were it not for the fact that it actually reveals a fairly explicit theoretical stance: namely, that what matters in linguistics is complex sentences and their structure, and that the things thrown in between them—*inter iectio*—are a sideshow at best. A moment's thought reveals this stance to be incoherent. The linguist selectively disregarding items that happen to typically occur on their own is rather like the chemist who discounts helium and neon just because they seldom combine with other elements. A linguistics without interjections is like a periodic table without the noble gases.

As a group, primary interjections appear to deviate from other words in terms of structure (Karcevski 1941; Ehlich 1986). To be precise, they tend to be composed of a set of elements that is (i) smaller than and (ii) only partly overlapping with the larger phonological system of a language. This makes them one of the prime places where we can find evidence for multiple coexistent phonemic systems within a language (Fries & Pike 1949). While some degree of phonological or phonotactic deviance is common, it is not definitional of interjections. The vowelless acknowledgement token *mm* is not more or less of an interjection than the change of state token *oh*.

Another striking feature of some common interjections is that relative to most other words, their forms appear to be more fluid and subject to prosodic modification: they are like verbal gestures (Bolinger 1968; Eastman 1992; Ward 2006; Grenoble 2014). Intimately related to this is their frequently multimodal nature, with nods for instance accompanying and sometimes replacing interjections like *mmhm*. Sometimes this has led to interjections being described as 'non-lexical', a term avoided here because it detracts from the systematic, conventionalized nature of these items. Interjections could be said to form a distinct lexical stratum subject to its own selective pressures and with its own semiotic properties. This should not surprise us: if natural languages feature sets of monolexemic items whose main business is at levels that transcend clause structure, it is to be expected that such items will adapt to this ecology.

The earliest formal characterizations of interjections often went hand in hand with a narrow functional description: interjections were seen as words expressing the speakers' emotions. Even scholars whose frameworks provided room for recognizing a larger range of functions of language (Bühler 1934; Jakobson 1960) typically reduced interjections to this kind of emotive or expressive role (Foolen 1997; Elffers 2008). However, a look at actual usage shows that this is too limited a conception: some of the most frequently used interjections are not of the emotive kind, and even those that appear primarily emotive often serve other discursive purposes (Kockelman 2003).

Ehlich's monumental (1986) work on German—possibly the most in-depth study of interjections in any one language so far—marked a change in the study of interjections because of its empirical focus and broad theoretical scope, taking inspiration from general linguistics, pragmatics, and the philosophy of language. Starting from a formally defined category of freestanding monosyllabic V and CV forms, this work catalogued the interactional and interpersonal functions of a range of German interjections. Its strict empirical grounding in corpus data meant that rather than featuring stereotypical examples like expressions of sudden pain or surprise (as most treatments of interjections did and still do), the account focused on the highly frequent yet often overlooked *hm* and kin, and their primarily interactional functions of signalling recipiency.

Other corpus studies have since borne out the relative rarity of purely emotive interjections. For instance, in one corpus of spoken Dutch (Huls 1982), the great majority of interjection tokens was found to have interactional and interpersonal functions, and only about 7% (29 out of 412) was expressive of the speaker's mental or affective state (Hofstede 1999). Likewise, a corpus-based study of interjections in Swedish Sign Language showed that the most frequent lexical signs categorized as interjections have backchannelling and affirmative functions, and account for over 80% of corpus tokens (Mesch 2016). Based on this, we can say that the idea of interjections as primarily emotive words, though understandable from a historical perspective, is untenable and provides only a partial view of the word class as a whole.

If interjections are not merely and not even mainly emotive words, how can we better characterize their communicative uses? A useful framework is provided by Ameka (1992a; and see Ameka & Wilkins 2006). Adopting a set of distinctions made by Jakobson (1960), Ameka observes that most interjections can be characterized in terms of three broad sets of communicative functions. EXPRESSIVE interjections are primarily symptoms of a producer's cognitive or emotive state; CONATIVE interjections primarily invite an action or response from another party in the interaction; and PHATIC interjections are primarily used to establish and maintain communicative contact.

Though examples could be given of interjections that occupy focal points within these categories (e.g. expressive *wow*, conative *sh!*, phatic *mmhm*), the functions are not mutually exclusive. A repair initiating interjection like *huh?* is both conative (in that it invites a repetition from the other) and phatic (in that it is tasked with preventing communicative breakdown). And a continuer like *mmhm* can be seen as both expressive (in that it indicates a state of attention) and phatic (in that it is used to maintain communicative contact). The main utility of this framework is that it provides an effective way to characterize and understand the diversity of items grouped under the term 'interjections'.

23.3 FROM SENTENCE TO SEQUENCE

Since interjections typically make up an utterance of their own, it is tempting to think we can understand them in the same way: as items that can be picked up and inspected in isolation. But to do so would be to miss the opportunity to see them as part of an organization that transcends the sentence and that provides its own sets of constraints and structuring principles. The true home of interjections is in conversational sequences, and this is where we should study them. The need for such a SEQUENTIAL perspective (Evans 1992) is perhaps clearest in the case of interjections that serve social–interactional communicative functions, so that is where we will start.

23.3.1 Phatic interjections

One of the most common functions served by interjections in interaction is to display an understanding that an extended unit of talk is underway (Schegloff 1982). Interjections with this function are known as continuers, backchannels, acknowledgement tokens, reactive tokens, or pragmatic markers (Yngve 1970; Allwood et al. 1990; O'Keeffe & Adolphs 2008; Norrick 2009), the variety in terms reflecting the fact that they have historically been approached from many different disciplinary directions. Items with this kind of function occur at the boundaries of turn-constructional units, where they 'demonstrate both that one unit has been received and that another is now awaited' (Goodwin 1986: 206).

The following transcript is from a conversation in Siwu (a Kwa language of Ghana) in which Foster and Beatrice talk about housebuilding and discuss why there might be several unfinished compound houses in their hometown in eastern Ghana. The excerpt starts with Foster providing his own take on the situation, in response to which Beatrice produces a continuer m̀:hm (line 53). Continuing his account, Foster gives one example of an unfinished house in the neighbourhood. He quickly follows up with another example (line 56), a turn that ends up fully overlapping a further continuer m̀:hm by Beatrice that targeted his first example (line 57). After a two-second silence, Beatrice produces a short >mm<. (line 59), just as Foster reaches the conclusion of his telling. The closing is marked by Beatrice's appreciative ↑m꞉m꞉ at line 62.[1]

---

[1] Transcription follows conversation analytic standards (Jefferson 2004), including the following conventions: (0.5) silence in seconds, - self-repaired item, [overlapping speech,: lengthening, >< shortening, . final intonation, m relative prominence, ↑ higher pitch. Siwu orthography is fairly close to IPA with tone marked à-a-á Low-Mid-High. Interlinear glosses use Leipzig conventions.

Extract 1. Siwu (Kwa, Ghana) (Maize3_1013516)

51 F àlà kɔ̃rɔ̃ ɔmagɛ̀ amɛ néè-
      because now town inside TP
      Because currently in town,
52   màturi sɛ́ mafɔ mìkã maḍé màtéré ɔ́só nɛ̀
      people HAB 3PL.collect PL.money 3PL.eat 3PL.run reason nɛ
      people have been collecting advances, consuming them and running off, that's why.
53 B m̀:hm
54   (0.5)
55 F nyɔ álé kɔ̃rɔ̃ nyɔ, nyɔ fóò Kofi ayo   gɔ́ ákãmu àɣéè
      look like now look look brother PSN A.houses how A.rooms AGR.stand
      Look even now look, look at bro Kofi's houses, how the rooms stand.
56   kà [wɔ̀èkpɔ́ Ká]bèlè ayo akãmu aɣéè ḿmɔ̀.
      now you.see PSN A.houses A.rooms AGR.stand there
      Or check out Kabɛlɛ's compound rooms just standing there.
57 B [m̀:hm   ]
58   (2.1)
59   >m[m.<
60 F   [nɔso kà ɔturi- sí ɔ́túri ɔba ɔtã́ íɣó, ɔto ɔnígã́
       now   imm person- if person 3SG.have 3SG.give house 3SG.PROG 3SG.fear
       So now person-if a person has a house to build, they fear!
61   (0.9)
62 B ↑m:m̀:
63 F hɛ̃̀:ɛ̃̀:

A stretch of conversation like this affords unparalleled analytical purchase on interjections because we see them in their own habitat, produced and interpreted by people in the flow of social interaction (Schegloff 1982; Bavelas et al. 2000). The established fields of conversation analysis and interactional linguistics provide us with the technical and conceptual tools to describe the construction of turns and the sequential relations between them—a prerequisite for the sequential analysis of interjections and other minimal particles (Clift 2016; Couper-Kuhlen & Selting 2017).

A first thing to note is that the placement of the items in focus is highly precise and matters for participants (Goodwin 1986). Beatrice's m̀:hm's occur exactly when and where they are due, namely following complete turn-constructional units in anticipation of further material (lines 53, 57). It so happens that Beatrice's m̀:hm at line 57 is produced just as Foster is one syllable into his second example, showing it to be addressed to the first (line 55), which was indeed audibly complete. As Foster's increment is completed, another space where a continuer would be relevant opens up. The silence that follows at this point (line 58) is 'owned' by both participants (Hoey 2020a). By withholding a response, Beatrice provides room for further expansion, which, however, does not follow. By not continuing to speak now, Foster creates a noticeable absence, showing that this is indeed a place where some kind of response would be due. The silence grows to 2.1 seconds—decidedly long in the context of the rapid-fire turn-taking that characterizes everyday language use (Stivers et al. 2009)—and is then broken near-simultaneously as Beatrice delivers a brisk continuer >mm.< and Foster delivers the punchline to his telling. Beatrice's final ↑m:m̀: responds to this ending and is followed by a sequence-closing third (Schegloff 2007).

The sum of Beatrice's contributions in this excerpt is a series of *mm*-like tokens, which brings home one important function of this kind of item: acknowledging the other's turn while passing the opportunity to take the floor (Schegloff 1982). But the forms are not all the same: they come in multiple variants and appear to be finely adjusted to their sequential environment (Goodwin 1986). We find *m̀:hm* [ʔm̩m̩m̩ː], equivalent in function to English *Uh-huh* and with a disyllabic form that seems well-fitted to its two-headed sequential nature, part retrospective acknowledging the prior turn, part prospective anticipating the next. We also have a brief >*mm*.< [m̩] that appears addressed to the urgency created by the turn-taking scuffle. And finally we have a longer ↑*m:m:* [m̩ːm̩ː] whose high–low prosodic delivery can be heard as indicating involvement and appreciation (Wilkinson & Kitzinger 2006), fitting the sequential environment of story completion. Its prosodic delivery is replicated at lower pitch in Foster's final *hẽːẽ̀ː*, closing the conversational sequence.

The diversity in surface forms makes items like this pliable tools for showing various degrees of recipiency, alignment, and involvement (Müller 1996; Wilkinson & Kitzinger 2006; Williams et al. 2020). But below this lies a deeper commonality that is likely functionally motivated: as vowelless nasals produced with labial closure, continuers are among the most minimal tokens of recipiency available to users of spoken language (Gardner 2001). As we saw earlier, acknowledgement tokens account for 80% of interjections attested in a corpus of Swedish Sign Language (Mesch 2016). Likewise, in the CallHome corpora of American English, Arabic, German, Mandarin Chinese, and Japanese, these items occur in up to one in five turns, making continuers likely the most frequent type of interjection within and across languages.

Another common type of phatic interjection is bound up with the organization of repair (Schegloff et al. 1977). In the following example from Norwegian Sign Language, Abe and Carl discuss the amount to be paid for some shared presents at a Christmas party. The transcript shows gaze, interlinear glosses corresponding to lexical signs, and a free translation in English. At line 1, Abe presents a tentative understanding of the monetary arrangements. While this would ordinarily invite confirmation or disconfirmation, Carl instead produces a freeze-look (a marked lack of mobility often responded to as a repair initiation (Manrique & Enfield 2015)) and after that a non-manual assemblage that is functionally equivalent to an articulatorily minimal 'Huh?' (line 3). This prompts a redoing by Abe of the original turn (line 4).

Extract 2. Norwegian Sign Language (Skedsmo 2020: 9–11)

1. Abe   Gaze : Forward–Carl- - - - - - - - - - - - -
            Sign : MEAN MEAN I MY WOMAN SUM 400
            Trns : So, for me and my girlfriend, the sum is 400?
2. Carl   Gaze : Abe - - - - - - - - - - -
   →A   Sign : (Freeze-look 0.6)
3.   Gaze : Abe -
   →B   Sign : (Leans forward, raises upper lip and lowers eyebrows)
            Trns : **Huh?**
4. Abe   Gaze : Carl -
            Sign : MEAN WOMAN MY WITH MEAN I TRA[NSFER 4] 00
            Trns : So, if my girlfriend is coming I transfer four hundred.
5. Carl   Gaze : Abe -
            Sign : [NO NO–NO]   NO–NO
            Trns : No, no, no,   no, no.

It may be tempting to see a repair expression like this simply as an instinctive expression of surprise, not even worthy of linguistic status. However, typological work shows that across languages, these items are calibrated to local linguistic systems and are an integral part of a larger paradigm of formats for repair initiation (Enfield et al. 2013). For instance, in the example from Norwegian Sign Language above, the non-manual composition of the repair-initiating turn at line 3 taps into the prosodic system of the language, in which eyebrow actions are used to mark questions. Moreover, the sequential follow-up—a redoing of the prior turn—makes clear that these items are treated as initiating repair, not as expressing an emotion like surprise.

The short excerpts of conversation shown here represent the primary ecology of language as a social phenomenon. This is where language thrives, where it is learned and where it adapts to our communicative needs and cognitive capacities. Even without going into detail about the larger system of continuers in Siwu or repair initiation formats in Norwegian Sign Language, it is clear that phatic interjections serve important communicative functions, are deployed in systematic ways, and are finely adapted to their sequential environments.

Since the sequential perspective is not one that has been historically prominent in language description and typology, Table 23.1 provides a nonexhaustive list of three basic interactional practices and sequential positions that should be available for inspection in even the shortest stretches of conversation in any language (Schegloff 1982; Heritage 1984; Jefferson 1972). Given the metacommunicative importance of these practices, it is to be expected that every natural language will have at least some means to realize them; and given their sequential contexts of occurrence, it is likely that interjections will be prominent among them. Note that the practices are characterized in terms of function and sequential position rather than by form. Such language-agnostic technical characterizations enable comparative research (Zimmerman 1999) in a way that is quite similar to the use of semantic-functional characterizations rather than language-specific categories in linguistic typology. The examples are from Siwu, but cross-linguistic similarities may crop up, a matter discussed below.

Table 23.1 Three frequent interactional functions covered by interjections, with examples from Siwu and English translations

Practice	Sequential context	Examples (Siwu)
Continuer	between turns during a telling-in-progress	$\grave{m}$:hm 'mm-hm'
Repair initiator	following any turn and inviting a redoing in next turn	$\tilde{a}$? 'huh?'
News receipt	following an informing turn (closing-implicative)	a: 'oh'

As the most frequent and dependable little words shaping our linguistic lives, phatic interjections deserve pride of place in our accounts of the word class of interjections. Yet somehow they are the least likely to occur in grammatical descriptions and comparative studies. One reason for the neglect of phatic interjections is that the sheer degree to which we depend on these items may have blinded us to their significance. Just as glasses or shoes sink below our awareness as they seamlessly augment our perceptual and motor systems, so phatic interjections have become so wound up with the very machinery of social interaction that we no longer see them for what they are: highly adaptive tools that streamline our language use at every turn. A more mundane reason for the neglect of these items is that at least until recently, most grammars were written based on elicitation and predominantly monological text corpora. Fortunately, documentary linguistics is enriching its data and methods, and there is a growing number of grammars that do orient to interactional data (Ameka 1991; Biber et al. 1999; Enfield 2007; Mihas 2017; Rüsch 2020; Sicoli 2020).

23.3.2 Conative interjections

While the main orientation of phatic interjections is at the flow of social interaction, conative interjections are primarily directed at others. Sequentially they are mostly bound up with securing attention and recruiting others to do something. A common case are summonses for calling people across a distance, as in the following example from Ewe, in which the call *ú:ru* is repeated by the other to indicate receipt and open the interaction (Ameka 1992b). From a sequential perspective, such repetition is another piece of evidence that the interjection is treated not as a mere private expression but as a move in interaction that creates the conditions for a specific type of next move. Many languages have summonses like this; as Ameka notes, Australian English *cooee!* (Wierzbicka 1991) is functionally similar. Commonly mentioned under this rubric are also calls for silence like *sh!* (in English), which do not so much demand that the other does something but rather refrains from doing something.

Extract 3. Ewe (Kwa, Ghana) (Ameka 1992b: 12)

```
1    A  ú:ru
2    B  ú:ru
3    A  me-ɖu    ŋgɔ ló ló
        1SG-eat  front  FP.ADV
        'I'm taking the lead!'
4       yoo m'-a-va!      fífíá!
        OK  1SG-IRR-come  now
        'OK, I'll come soon.'
```

A subset of conative interjections in need of broader description is animal-oriented calls. People have interacted with animals since time immemorial, and especially domestic animals are regular targets for directives. While it is certainly possible to talk to animals using complex language (and some pet owners will go to great lengths in interpreting a fairly limited set of responsive behaviours), the most effective directives appear to be monolexemic calls that can function as standalone utterances; in other words, interjections. Two broad classes of animal-oriented interjections are those that aim to make animals move off and those that call animals to come. Table 23.2 shows animal-oriented interjections in Lao corresponding to these two categories. While the 'go' forms appear as single units, the 'come' forms 'are usually repeated, over and over (e.g. as *cuuj1-cuuj1-cuuj1-cuuj1-cuuj1* for calling pigs to come)'. Two of them also feature falsetto phonation.

Table 23.2 Animal-oriented interjections in Lao (Enfield 2007: 315)

Animal	'Go'	'Come'
Cattle	*huj1* or *huj5* or alveolar click	*heeq2* or *qaawq5*
Chicken	*soo4* or rounded [ʃːˑ]	*kuk2* (falsetto)
Pig	(not attested)	*cuuj1* (falsetto)
Dog	*sêêq2*	*qèèq5* or *qèèk5*
Cat	*mèèw5* (breathy)	*mòng1*

Studies of such directives are relatively rare (Bynon 1976; Ameka 1992b; Amha 2013) and few grammars consider them worthy of mention (rare exceptions are Enfield 2007 on Lao; Orkaydo 2013 on Konso; Visser 2020 on Kalamang). Within the class of interjections, however, they do present an instructive case of how human language can adapt to radical asymmetries in agency and action–perception systems (Dingemanse 2020). The most important functional pressure on these words is that they have to serve as a stimulus that reliably results in the desired response. What counts as an effective stimulus may differ across species, and so we may find clicks used with cattle and sibilants with chickens. At the same time, these items do adapt to the larger linguistic system to some extent, as seen for instance in the fact that many of the Lao forms conform to the phonotactics of the language.

23.3.3 Expressive interjections

So far we have seen the importance of a sequential perspective for understanding interjections that take up phatic and conative work in social interaction. But a sequential perspective can also enrich our understanding of expressive interjections. A first inkling of this is provided in Goffman's study of English response cries. As he showed, even expressive interjections often crucially depend on the larger context of situation and manage expectations about the next move in the sequence. For instance, while it is possible to think of the strain grunt as merely a symptom of physical exertion, in fact it often has an interactional function, alerting others or serving in the temporal coordination of joint efforts. In stylized form, a strain grunt can serve as a marker of a transition from a joint activity to an assessment of that activity, as Pehkonen (2020) showed for Finnish [ʰuhʷʰuhʷ] following the physical exertion of a climb with others. It is worth noting that this is another case that is not easily observed in monologic textual materials: Pehkonen observed it in video recordings of forest hikes for berry foraging.

Similarly, a moan might be seen as no more than an outcry of suffering; but to stop there would be to overlook the fact that most often, when we encounter 'moans' or other indexes of suffering in interaction, they are transformed and ritualized versions that are multiple steps removed from the putative original crisis, recruited to do subtle interactional work. For instance, empirical work on playful 'moans' in the context of board game interaction shows that they signal suffering as well as a willingness to continue play (Hofstetter 2020). This use relies on one of the affordances of an expressive interjection, namely that it does not directly appeal to the audience for a response. Goffman's example is of an 'ouch' when presented with the plumber's bill: 'To the plumber, we are precisely NOT saying: "Does the bill have to be that high?"—such a statement would require a reply, to the possible embarrassment of all' (1978: 807).

23.3.4 From liminal signs to interjections

The sequential perspective on interjections brings into view a neighbouring phenomenon that I have elsewhere described using the notion of LIMINAL SIGNS: 'signs that derive interactional utility from being ambiguous with respect to conventionality, intentionality, and accountability' (Dingemanse 2020b:191). These are items like sighs, sniffs, and other bodily conduct that neither users nor analysts of language have been inclined to count as linguistic or even communicative, but that on closer look turn out to benefit precisely from being in the borderland between language and non-language. In English, for instance, a sniff placed before or during a turn can serve to delay the progression of that turn, signalling delicacy (Hoey 2020b); and a central alveolar click [!] is sometimes observed in the service of signalling a disapproving stance without explicitly saying anything (Ogden 2020).

A sketch of the lay of the land here will help us to better understand the relation between liminal signs and interjections. Crucially, while sequential analysis makes visible how people skilfully use liminal signs in interaction, they are not treated as 'on the record' or accountable in the same way as more conventionalized linguistics items are, in part because they often repurpose bodily conduct that is going on anyway. After all, a sniff might be 'just' an inhalatory action and a click 'just' the percussive sound made as the articulators separate in preparation to speak. This liminality is precisely what makes such items useful for transitory interactional work and for things that are better left unsaid.

In comparison, interjections play much more explicit, on-record roles in language and interaction. They tend to have clearly conventionalized forms and functions. Even if they can exhibit nonstandard phonology, they also recruit elements from the larger phonemic system of the language. And the fact that there are dedicated sequential environments in which they reliably occur, invite certain responses, or can be noticeably absent (as we saw for continuers, repair interjections, and distance calls) shows that they are treated as conventionalized and accountable interactional resources, distinct from liminal signs.

Though we can draw distinctions based on conventionality and accountability, liminal signs and interjections are best seen as designating regions in a space gradiently inhabited by a range of interactional practices. For instance, one account of the standalone central alveolar click [!] in English conversation shows it to be used as a device to deliver an unspoken comment without being taken to respond (Ogden 2020): a prime example of the in-betweenness exploited by liminal signs. On the other hand, Laal and a number of other languages in Chad have recruited a series of clicks to form a paradigm of interjections with interactional and interpersonal functions, which speakers recognize as conventionalized and treat as accountable actions (Lionnet 2020). This makes visible one source path for interjections: bodily conduct may be recruited in liminal signs, which in turn may develop into full-blown interjections as they become increasingly conventionalized and on-record.

A related kind of gradience can be found for items with ostensibly similar functions. An interjection like *yes* is widely recognized as a conventional, on-record response (Enfield & Sidnell 2015), but not far removed from it we find gesturally modified variants like *yep* (Bolinger 1946), which shade into closed-mouth affirmative continuers like *uh-huh* and *mm-hm* and, ultimately, head nods. We seem to move from clear affirmation to mere passive recipiency along a cline of increasing informality and decreasing on-recordness. One piece of evidence for this cline is that an outright *yes*, but not an *uh-huh* or a head nod, counts as confirmation in court (Ward 2006). The origins of interjections, and the ways in which people flexibly use semiotic resources to navigate conventionality, intentionality and accountability represent key areas for future research.

We have seen how a sequential perspective can help to untangle variation in the form and function of interjections, and can provide the working linguist with a methodological framework to guide the study of interjections. As we develop a more comprehensive understanding of the forms, functions, and sequential positions of interjections, we will also be in a better position to understand their relations to other linguistic items and systems.

Even though we have focused here on items that typically function as stand-alone utterances, they are not insulated from other turns and can sometimes attach to larger wholes (Ameka & Wilkins 2006; Rühlemann 2020). For instance, response particles like *oh* or *mm* can also function as turn prefaces, where they serve as pivot points allowing participants to fine-tune the orientation of the current turn to its prior. This brings us full circle to one of our starting observations: it is incoherent to exclude interjections from linguistic inquiry. We see now that this is not just 'because they're there' (to paraphrase what a mountaineer said about Everest), but also because they provide new vantage points from which to explore the larger landscape of linguistic resources.

23.4 Unity and diversity

The notion of interjections has long been a mirror reflecting theoretical assumptions and preoccupations (Elffers 2007). Nowhere is this seen more clearly than in how we deal with the themes of unity and diversity. To scholars for whom interjections are barely more than instinctive grunts, they are universally available response cries with at most a little bit of language-specific varnish (Whitney 1874; Jackendoff 2002). To scholars for whom interjections represent an area of cultural expression, they show a veritable flowering of forms and functions (Karcevski 1941; Wierzbicka 1991). To resolve this tension, we need neither pick one of the extremes nor settle for a boring middle ground. The solution is to recognize that it is only an apparent tension that results from treating interjections as a monolithic group. The inventory of one-word utterances is rich enough, and their communicative functions diverse enough, to allow and indeed expect diversity in some places and unity in others.

Let us start with the theme of diversity. There are many interjections with highly specific meanings (Wierzbicka 2003). For instance, Ewe has an interjection *babaà* expressing commiseration. It is sometimes translated as 'sorry' and can indeed also be used in apologies, but its primary meaning foregrounds an element of compassion and excludes the personal responsibility associated with 'sorry' in English (Ameka 1991: 582–585). Konso, a Cushitic language of south-west Ethiopia, has an interjection *eʃ* 'I am disgusted by what you said and I want you to stop talking about this' (Orkaydo 2013: 256), a highly specific conventional meaning that combines expressive, phatic and conative elements. Kalamang of West Papua has an interjection to call a cassowary *luːaluːaluːaluːaluːa* (Visser 2020: 114), while Zargulla (Omotic, Ethiopia) has a paradigm of interjections directed at oxen, including *horó* 'directive to resume movement after stopping for a while' (Amha 2013: 238). Clearly, there is room for a great deal of diversity in form and function.

Further, even interjections with similar functions need not have the same form, as seen in forms used in communication over distance like Ewe *uːrú*, Australian English *cooeee*, Polish *hop, hop*, and Russian *au* (Wierzbicka 1992; Ameka 1992b). And vice versa, interjections similar in form often turn out, on closer inspection, to feature significant functional differences. For instance, Polish *pst* can be used to warn someone else to be silent, while Russian *pst* is more like an expression of disapproval (Wierzbicka 2003: 295–296). Even a fundamental interactional practice like backchannelling may show important differences in form and frequency across languages (Dingemanse & Liesenfeld 2022).

In short, in the realm of interjections there is ample room for linguistic and cultural diversity, as documented by semantic and lexicographical work (Ameka & Wilkins 2006; Jensen et al. 2019). Seen in this light, it is no surprise that Anna Wierzbicka has staked out the position that 'far from being universal and "natural" signs that don't have to be learnt, interjections are often among the most characteristic peculiarities of individual cultures' (Wierzbicka 2003: 258).

23.4.1 Sources of commonality

Alongside room for diversity we can recognize sources of commonality. To do this—for interjections as for any linguistic resource—we need to consider the relevant causal–temporal frames (Enfield 2014). Most relevant in the context of interjections are the frames of *phylogeny* (the biological evolution of language), *diachrony* (the cultural evolution of language, or language change) and *enchrony* (the moment-by-moment unfolding of language in interaction). These frames raise two questions, whose answers may differ for each subtype of interjections: first, where do interjections come from? And, second, what selective pressures shape them?

Phylogeny tells us that some interjections can be linked to ancestral vocalizations or bodily responses. Pain interjections provide an instructive example. Most spoken languages appear to make available a pain interjection that has as its nucleus and prosodic peak an open central unrounded vowel. It is hard to escape the conclusion that such forms harken back to a common mammalian pain vocalization (Darwin 1872; Ehlich 1985). Some disgust interjections may be similarly motivated by bodily motions of revulsion. Of course, even having probable phylogenetic precursors does not stop particular languages from imposing a degree of conventionalization and diversification, as we see in interjections of pain and disgust (Byington 1942; Wierzbicka 1991).

While direct ancestral precursors may be plausible for some expressive interjections, the story is likely to be more subtle for most other interjections. Above we saw how the bodily conduct recruited in liminal signs offers another possible source for interjections. The flexible harnessing of semiotic resources for communicative purposes brings us into the cultural realm, where processes of semiosis and convention formation conspire at the enchronic and diachronic timescales to arrive at adaptive solutions. Here the possibilities are virtually endless—hence the attested diversity—but to the extent that there are interactional needs shared by embodied participants everywhere, we may also expect similar solutions to emerge.

A well-known example is the repair interjection, which in spoken languages tends to sound a lot like 'a?', or more precisely, a monosyllable with a low-front central vowel and questioning intonation (as first reported in Dingemanse et al. 2013 for 31 languages). The deep commonality cannot be separated from the fact that all languages share the same high-stakes sequential environment, where misunderstanding is always possible and time is in short supply. This enchronic environment calls for a form that is maximally easy to plan and produce, yet still recognizably interrogative. Given enough diachronic time, the selective pressures exerted by this environment are likely to result in convergence towards what we might call the simplest possible question word—a reasonable gloss for *a?* and kin in spoken languages (with language-specific tuning as expected). Known sign language equivalents appear to conform to the same logic, formulating a minimal question using non-manual prosody (Manrique 2016 for Argentine Sign Language; Skedsmo 2020 for Norwegian Sign Language).

Continuers have not been subjected to the same kind of systematic comparison yet, but they seem to present a similar case. In the Siwu example we saw how *m:hm* helps shape the delivery of stories by displaying alignment with the storytelling activity. Many spoken languages appear to make a similar nasal vocalization available for the same interactional work, as seen in *m-hm* in English (Gardner 2001), *mm* in Danish (Steensig & Sørensen 2019), *'m̩m̩* in Wa'ikhana (Williams et al. 2020), and *m/ŋ* in Cantonese (Liesenfeld 2019). Such forms are well adapted to serve as continuers because they signify ongoing attention with minimal articulatory effort and provide the perfect canvas to overlay with prosodic contours for stance marking (as Gardner 2001 argues for English). Again, known sign language equivalents similarly seem to recruit articulatorily minimal, prosodically flexible expressions that are well-adapted to the functional requirements of continuers (Mesch 2016), suggesting that common interactional ecologies can result in convergent cultural evolution across modalities.

Conative interjections represent further pressures towards cross-linguistic commonalities. Calls that need to bridge long distances, occluded environments, or other obstructions to joint attention need to be conspicuous enough to do so. This helps explain some structural aspects of distance calls in spoken languages but also the nature of attention-getting signs in sign languages, which frequently employ visually salient movements and sometimes even touch (Haviland 2015). These signs are shaped not so much by the exigencies of turn-taking and timing as by the challenges of achieving perceptual access and attracting attention.

In explaining cross-linguistic and cross-modal commonalities in interjections, we reap the fruits of a sequential perspective. This allows us to see how a particular conversational ecology can exert its own set of selective pressures (of timing, turn-taking, effort, salience, unobtrusiveness, and more) and so, over time, squeeze frequently used interactional resources into optimally adaptive shapes. This process is particularly relevant for interjections found in high-stakes sequential environments. Indeed, we can formulate this in terms of a weak statistical universal: *Human languages are likely to make available similar semiotic resources for interactional functions that are both (i) sequentially comparable and (ii) highly frequent.* This is a statistical universal in that it expresses a probability, not a universal law; and a weak one in that it predicts such resources to be available without excluding the use of other, more divergent, or more functionally heterogeneous resources.

The limiting case is formed by animal-oriented interjections. These items are adapted to near-incommensurable asymmetries in agency, perception, and action. We see here a rare corner of language that is close to putting behaviour under direct stimulus control (Skinner 1957)—an extreme narrowing of the justly celebrated flexibility of human language (Chomsky 1959). Here, constraints on the receiving end form direct pressures towards convergent cultural evolution, which explains why, for instance, words for shooing away birds overwhelmingly feature sibilant sounds across unrelated languages, as in English *shoo*, Siwu *shuɛ* and Lao *soo4* or [ʃːː] (Dingemanse 2020a). The most effective animal-oriented interjections appear to harness instinctive responses on the part of the animals: a case of mimicry in culturally transmitted signalling behaviour. Still, even here we find room for conventionalization, as we see in the English, Siwu and Lao shooing words. And so, even in the unlikely area of cross-species communication, we encounter interjections as fundamentally linguistic signs.

23.5 IN CLOSING

A central insight of the mathematical classic *Flatland* (Abbott [1884] 1991) is that we can learn to see dimensions beyond the ones we regularly inhabit. When a Sphere sets out to visit protagonist Square in the two-dimensional world of Flatland, the only way Sphere can manifest itself is in terms of planar intersections. And just like the sphere's intersections at some point compel Square to contemplate a three-dimensional outlook, so interjections compel us to look at dimensions beyond the sentence. In the land of sentences, interjections are mere points without relations to other items; but in the higher dimensions of conversational sequences, they turn out to have lives of their own that are richly rewarding of study.

We have surveyed interjections from the perspectives of communicative functions, conversational sequences, and comparative linguistics. The picture that emerges is one of constrained diversity. Interjections, as conventionalized linguistic signs, can express culturally diverse meanings and can be put to a wide range of communicative purposes. But their diversity is constrained by phylogenetic origins, functional requirements, interactional ecologies, articulatory affordances, and perceptual factors. When we look beyond the handful of stereotypical examples that have come to be associated with interjections, a complex mosaic of forms and functions comes into view. Charting these forms and functions requires methods and theories that can deal with the interactional and sequential aspects of language. This means enriching general linguistics and grammar-writing with insights from pragmatics, interactional linguistics, and conversation analysis.

As word classes go, interjections likely will always be the odd one out: relatively small, internally diverse, and serving functions that seem foreign to the flatland of the sentence. Considered in isolation, as they so long have been, interjections may seem to exhibit bewildering variation. But when they come alive in conversational sequences, the variation turns out to be regimented by interactional ecologies that are the true home of interjections, and indeed of language.

Acknowledgements

Thank you to Florian Lionnet, Felix Ameka, Andreas Liesenfeld, Christoph Rühlemann, Michael Erard, and Elsa Oréal for their critical and constructive readings of this work. In memory of Pieter Muysken (1950–2021), with deep gratitude for his ever-cheerful encouragement to venture into parts unknown.

PART IV
WORD CLASSES IN GENETIC AND AREAL LANGUAGE GROUPS

PART IV

CHAPTER 24

WORD CLASSES IN EGYPTIAN, SEMITIC, AND CUSHITIC (AFROASIATIC)

ELSA ORÉAL AND MARTINE VANHOVE

24.1 INTRODUCTION

TODAY, the exact number of living Afroasiatic languages is still disputed, with upwards of 375 languages, though the actual number may be fewer (for a discussion, see Frajzyngier & Shay (2012: 1). The number of speakers is probably around 300,000,000. The languages are spoken in Northern and Central Africa, the Horn of Africa, the Arabian Peninsula, the Near and Middle East, and Central Asia (Arabic only).

Afroasiatic (AA) is the phylum with the longest written record: over five millennia. Thus, it provides linguists with a wealth of documentation that, among other things, shows the fluidity of some word categories on a long-term scale. Nevertheless, this exceptional time depth only applies to three of the six Afroasiatic families. Egyptian has been attested since approximately 3,000 BC, over a period covering more than four and a half millennia, from ancient Egyptian to Coptic. The latter ceased to be spoken in the 15th century AD, but still survives as a liturgical language. For Semitic (98 languages), the first documents date back to the third millennium BC, and were written in Akkadian, a language that used to be spoken in Mesopotamia during the earliest Antiquity between the third and first millennium BC. In North Africa, where Berber (27 languages) is spoken, an old writing system on funerary steles is poorly understood. Its exact relationship with Berber is still difficult to figure out (Galand 2010: 16–17). Documentation increased in the Middle Ages for what is traditionally called 'Old Berber', whose affiliation to contemporary Berber is clear (Galand 2010: 18). The three other families, Chadic (202 languages), Cushitic (46 languages), and Omotic (24 languages) have no written tradition, and only started to be significantly described by scholars and missionaries during the 19th century, an undertaking which went along with European colonization and Christianization of Africa. A handful of these languages started to be written in the 20th century. Somali (Cushitic) is a partial exception. An adapted Arabic script was in use as early as the 13th century for writing Arabic with some Somali words in varied proportions (Lewis 1958: 136). The literature also reports thus far undeciphered ancient scripts (Rigby 1877: 447).

Within the Afroasiatic phylum languages of the same period belonging to different groups show strong divergences (Cohen 1988b: 4), whereas across millennia languages belonging to the same group remain strikingly similar. Such a situation led Diakonoff (1988) to push very far back in time a Proto-Afroasiatic stage that he evaluated at 8,000 years BP. This explains why the hypothesis of an Afroasiatic linguistic unit was gradually built up and why its internal organization is still debated. The main discussions concerned the integration of Chadic within AA, whether or not Beja (North-Cushitic) constituted a separate branch (Hetzron 1980; Tosco 2003). Recently, the status of Omotic has given rise to many discussions. It was initially separated from Cushitic (Fleming 1969; Lamberti 1991), and some linguists (e.g. Theil 2012; Güldemann 2018) consider it as an independent phylum until further proven, without yet convincing most specialists of Omotic. The Glottologue catalogue (Hammarström et al. 2020) preferred a temporary careful exclusion, while the Ethnologue catalogue (Eberhard et al. 2022) still includes Omotic within AA, as does Azeb (2012).

In two branches of Afroasiatic, Semitic, and Berber, the word, for a large part of the vocabulary, consists of a discontinuous sequence of phoneme called the 'root', most often composed of two or three consonants, to which a small number of templates (e.g. approx. 200 in Arabic and Akkadian is applied—see e.g. Cohen 1988c: 16–18; Gragg & Hoberman 2012: 166–167).

Templates add root vowels, consonants, reduplication, gemination, affixes, which convey particular semantic values, very abstract at times, as well as grammatical functions and categories. This non-concatenative structure differs between nouns and verbs. Nominal templates with affixes often select dedicated thematic bases that do not exist independently (e.g. in Arabic *maḥmil* 'belt', from the root *ḥ.m.l*, whereas **hmil* is not an independent word), while derived verbs with affixes may be directly built on a verbal templatic base (e.g. ʕ*allama* 'teach' > *taʕallama* 'to learn') (Cohen 1988c: 17). The non-concatenative system is rather rigid in Semitic, Berber and Egyptian, but to various degrees depending on the language and the period in its history. It only survives marginally or not at all in the other families, Chadic, a large part of Cushitic, and Omotic. In all families, derivative transcategorial and intracategorial morphemes are limited to a series of phonemes, at least partly represented in each branch, the most common ones being *ʔ, h, s, ʃ, t, n, w, j, a, u* and *i* (Cohen 1988c: 20).

In this chapter, we focus on three families within the domains of our expertise: Ancient Egyptian, Semitic, and Cushitic, in this order. They allow us to illustrate different scenarios in the make-up and evolution of word categories, benefiting from the unique time depth provided by two of these families. As required by the format of this part of the volume we discuss only the three main word classes: verbs, nouns, and adjectives. Other categories that played an important role in the grammaticalization of verbs will be mentioned when need be.

24.2 ANCIENT EGYPTIAN

Ancient Egyptian is usually considered as an isolated family of the Afroasiatic phylum. Its specific position within the Afroasiatic phylum remains a much discussed topic and is still in need of further investigation, as well as, more generally, the relevance of the tree model for the Afroasiatic case. The oldest attested stage, Old Egyptian (3000–2000 BC) indeed presents some common features with Semitic and Berber, but also important differences.

The language has verbs, nouns, adjectives, pronouns, prepositions, and particles. The extent to which the root-and-pattern system known from Semitic languages is attested in Ancient Egyptian remains a matter of discussion. Biconsonantal and triconsonantal roots are mostly present but roots with one or four consonants are also attested. It is more difficult to observe specific templates since the writing system does not indicate vowels. Vocalic patterns cannot be reconstructed with certainty for Earlier Egyptian (3000–1300 BC). However, evidence from Coptic, the last stage in the history of the language written in the Greek alphabet, together with information brought by the transcription of Egyptian words in other ancient languages, still allows a partial reconstruction of some vocalic patterns. As far as word classes are concerned, the writing system of Earlier Egyptian offers some additional information that is worth taking into account. Graphemic classifiers regularly appear at the end of words, thus showing that scribes conceptualized at least some words as a kind of unit (Selz et al. 2017). Moreover, these signs are often related to the semantics of the lexeme, albeit not always in a clear manner. For example, the classifier of motion verbs is often a sign showing a pair of moving legs. These classifiers are not straightforwardly related to word classes. However, some of them appear to be relevant in the perspective of word classification inasmuch as they allow to disambiguate potentially homographic forms. A seated man used as a classifier at the end of a verb root may, for example, indicate that the root functions as an agent noun, thus differentiating the meanings and functions of the same root and its different graphical forms. Consequently, a number of noun categories may be graphically distinguished.

The distinction between nouns and verbs prompted a heavy debate in Egyptian linguistics (Vernus 1997; reply by Satzinger & Shisha-Halevy 1999). Polotsky (1944) discovered the function of a verbal paradigm dedicated to utterances with marked information structure, where a circumstantial adjunct is in focus, while the rest of the informational content is presented as shared knowledge. These findings first pertained to Coptic forms but were later extended to other, previous, stages of the language. These forms called 'second tenses', 'emphatic', or 'nominal' forms syntactically share many features with substantives, while related 'relative forms' appear to function as attributes. In some versions of this analysis, all verb forms are considered as better characterized according to their syntactic function in the sentence, as a nominal, an attribute, or even an adverb when the form is used as a circumstantial converb. This general line of structural analysis has been contested (Collier 1992; Winand 2007). Opponents to this theory highlight the verbal features of the forms. Without entering into too much detail here, one may state that a better understanding of the questions raised by these paradigms may be reached by assuming a diachronic perspective (Oréal 2014, 2017). It remains difficult to define the criteria which can be used to decide exactly when a form in a given construction no longer may be analysed as nominalization in a periphrastic construction and has become a 'true' verb form. Further research is still needed in Egyptian linguistics for a better understanding of this evolution.

24.2.1 From nouns to verbs: Transcategorial change and grammaticalization paths

Morphologically, Earlier Egyptian shows a number of verbal prefixes that also appear in other families of the Afroasiatic phylum, including *n-* for reflexive verbs or causative s-. However, there are strong differences between this language and the other branches, in accordance with the fact that the whole verbal system of Earlier Egyptian results from a diachronic process of renewal involving nominalizations in various constructions. Only one of these grams has a potential cognate in other branches of the Afroasiatic family, namely the Old Perfect. It is based on a periphrastic construction similar to the source construction of the West-Semitic Perfect or the Akkadian Stative (see section 24.3.2). However, one cannot simply infer from this analogy that these forms represent a common inheritance from a previous stage in the history of those languages. From a typological point of view, the source construction 'past participle + zero copula + NP or pronoun' is too common to exclude a similar independent development. Moreover, if the forms are similar, their function is distinct. The Egyptian Old Perfect is originally ambitransitive; the choice between an active and a passive reading depending on the presence of a second participant in the construction when possible, as illustrated in examples[1] (1)–(4).

(1) jri-k   sw
    do\PTCP.PFV-1SG 3SG.M
    'I made him.'

(2) jri-k   jn   ḥr
    do\PTCP.PFV-1SG by   Horus
    'I was made by Horus.'

(3) jri   wj   ḥr
    do\PTCP.PFV   1SG   Horus
    'Horus made me.'

(4) pri   ḥr
    go\PTCP.PFV   Horus
    'Horus is gone.'

The Egyptian Old Perfect cannot be formed from a substantive, as is the case in Akkadian. Thus, common features between both forms could boil down to the person endings. Pronominal morphology is indeed the most salient argument to ascertain membership within the Afroasiatic phylum.

The rest of the Earlier Egyptian conjugation system shows forms with other pronominal suffixes that are also used after prepositions or to encode the possessor after a noun. No trace of a prefix paradigm appears in this language, which is a crucial difference with Semitic (see section 24.4.1). While the Egyptian Old Perfect belongs to the category of 'be-perfects' with a zero copula as auxiliary, its functional successor as an anterior gram has some common features with a 'have-perfect' resulting from a possessive construction (Werning 2008).

(5) X   n=f
    X   to=3SG.M
    'He has X.' (lit. X is to him)

---

[1] Unless otherwise stated, examples are extracted from grammar books.

In historical sources, one can observe the final replacement of the Old Perfect as a main verbal predicate by the form known as *sḏm-n* (+ NP or suffix pronoun). The latter thus results from the grammaticalization of a periphrastic construction based on the Old Perfect with an indefinite agent, encoded by a zero, as shown in Table 24.1.

Table 24.1 The morphogenesis of the 'have-perfect'

sḏm	Ø	P
hear\PTCP.PFV	3SG.M	P
'(He/one) has heard P.'		
>		
sḏm	P	n=f
hear\PTCP.PFV	P	to=3SG.M
'P was heard to him.'		
>		
sḏm-n=f	P	
hear-ANT=3SG.M	P	
'He has heard P.'		

In the non-past domain, the traditionally called *sḏm(=f)* verb forms show a base *sḏm* followed by a subject encoded like a possessor if pronominal. Such an encoding, along with its syntactic distribution, strongly argues for a nominal origin. Moreover, the basic form can be shown to have been subject to grammaticalization within various constructions whose syntactic and semantic features explain the emergence of distinct conventionalized tense–aspect–mood (TAM) readings (Oréal 2017). From a typological point of view, it is interesting to note that some former nominal morphological features have been reinterpreted as verbal morphology within given constructions. Thus, the suffix <-w>, graphically marked with some morphological classes of verbs, identifies class membership or indefiniteness on nominalizations (agent nouns but also action nouns). A modal form often designated as the *sḏm-w-f* prospective form, showing the same ending, emerged from source constructions with a zero copula, as a complement of a perception verb, a manipulative verb, or with the stative negation *ni*.

(6) sḏm-w Ø A/P
    hear\NMLZ-INDF COP A/P
    'It is a (case of) hearing A/P.' > 'A should hear' or 'one should hear P.'

(7) wḏ-n=k ḥmsi-w ppy pn jr-gs=k
    order-ANT=2SG.M sit\NMLZ-INDF Pepy this at-side=2SG.M
    'You ordered that this Pepy may sit at your side.' (*Pyramid texts* 1480cP)

(8) ni sḏm-w A/P
    NEG.EX hear\NMLZ-INDF A/P
    'There is no hearing A/P.' > 'A should not hear' or 'one should not hear P.'

Negation in Earlier Egyptian was renewed according to a diachronic process known as the negative existential cycle, where the standard negation emerges as the existential negation combined with a nominalization of the verb (Veselinova 2014; Oréal 2022). This change might have contributed to triggering the general renewal process of the verbal system by way of grammaticalizing nominalizations within various source constructions. Its precise role in this respect remains to be explored further.

In Earlier Egyptian, subordinating conjunctions mainly derive from the use of prepositions with former nominalizations reanalysed as verbal forms.

(9) ḥr   nfr=f
     on   be_good\NMLZ=3SG.M
     'Because he is good (lit. on his being good).'

24.2.2 Nouns

Gender (masculine and feminine) and number (singular, plural, and recessive dual) marking are characteristic of the category of nouns (including adjectives). Case marking in Proto-Egyptian remains purely hypothetical, based on postulated analogy with Semitic languages, as there are no traces in daughter languages. Egyptian nominal morphology includes suffixes (feminine -t, plural -w) and possibly internal changes (Loprieno 1995: 58). Various semantic templates have been hypothesized as characteristic of a number of nominals in Ancient Egyptian. For the older phase of the language, they remain partly speculative, and it is difficult to assess the extension of vocalic patterns. A prefix m- is attested for instrumental, place and agent nouns, without being as productive as in other Afroasiatic languages. Endings that appear graphically as the semi-vowels -w and -j also play a prominent role in nominal morphology. It can be shown that a marker -w, distinct from the plural ending, emerged as a semantic class membership marker that could be used to encode indefiniteness as well as a predicative function. In Earlier Egyptian, agent and patient nouns show a nominal template that may or may not have been distinct.

(10) jri-w
     do\PTCP-INDF
     'A doer (lit. one who does).'

(11) mri-w
     love\PTCP-INDF
     'Beloved (lit. a loved one).'

The -j ending is used to form a stative participle with passive or resultative readings.

(12) jrij-j
     do\PTCP.PFV-ADJ
     'Done.'

(13) mrij-j
     love\PTCP.PFV-ADJ
     'Loved.'

Specialized templates for semantic categories may be partially reconstructed. One observes a tendency to replace inflectional morphemes by analytic constructions over the long term. In Demotic, a later stage of the written language that is attested from about 650 BC to 450 AD, a construction is attested for some verbs, replacing the former agent noun with *rmṯ jw = f +* infinitive 'a person who does' + V-*ing*. This gave rise to the Coptic prefix *ref-*. It is relevant for the understanding of how the Egyptians themselves perceived the notion of word classes, that a preserved student's text contains a list of such compounds (Hess 1897: 147). The same pattern is well attested for names of professions. However, *rmṯ* 'person' is also used directly followed by another noun, and is sometimes joined by the genitive marker *n*, as is the case of *rmṯ nj Kmt* 'man of Egypt, Egyptian'. Such a formation gave rise to the Coptic prefix *rm(n)-* which forms names of professions. Thus, Earlier Egyptian *b3k* 'servant' has a functional successor *rmṯ b3k*, lit. 'person of work', 'labourer'. This form is emergent in Demotic, and is later found in Coptic *rmbeke* 'salaried worker' (Johnson 2017: 168).

Action nouns in Earlier Egyptian may also show various endings, including -*w* and -*t*. In Later Egyptian (1300 BC–1300 AD), while such nouns may survive, new forms emerge according to a compounding pattern. Thus, Demotic *gy* 'manner' is used in compounds as a prefix producing action nouns (Johnson 2017: 167): *gy n wnm* 'manner of eating > eating', *gy n pnᶜ* 'manner of changing > changing'.

In Earlier Egyptian, composition is also attested as a means to form a noun, generally with abstract semantics, based on an adjective, following a noun like *bw* or *st*, both meaning 'place':

(14) *nfr* *bw-nfr*
     good place-good
     'Goodness.'

(15) *wᶜ* *bw-wᶜ*
     one place-one
     'Unity.'

(16) *wšb*   *st-wšb*
     answer place-answer
     'Answer.'

In Later Egyptian, such a process takes place with the noun *md.t* 'affair', which developed into the Coptic abstract prefix *mnt-*, as for example with the noun meaning 'truth, justice'. In Earlier Egyptian, it was *m3ᶜt* 'truth'. In Demotic, it lost its ending -*t* like other feminine words and combined with the former *md.t*: *mt(.t) m3ᶜ(.t)* > Coptic *mntme*.

24.2.3 Adjectives

The distinction between nouns and adjectives in Ancient Egyptian is not straightforward. There is no clear-cut morphological distinction between the two word classes. However, the adjectives word class may be syntactically defined by the fact that gender is not an inherent part of an attributive adjective but dependent on the agreement with the head noun. From a syntactic point of view, any adjective, included participial forms, can be used as a substantive. The only primary adjective is the quantifier *nb* 'every'. Other adjectives may be analysed as derived forms based on a noun or a preposition (most of which are grammaticalized from nouns) (i), or as participles of property-denoting verbs (ii).

(i) The ending *-j* used to derive adjectives in Semitic (the so-called *nisba*, see also section 24.3.4) is attested in Ancient Egyptian as well. However, its functional and semantic extension is different, for it can be suffixed not only to a nominal base, as is the case in Arabic, but also to a preposition.

(17) njwt   >   njwt-j
     City   >   'of the city.'

(18) ḥr   >   ḥr-j
     On   >   'the one who is above.'

(ii) Property-denoting verbs are generally used with various types of predication to express a state or quality. A perfect gram can be used; this is a typologically common strategy.

(19) jw=f   nfr-w
     AUX=3SG.M   be_perfect\PTCP.RESUL-PRED
     'He is well.'

The nominal predication involving independent pronouns for the first two persons or a construction with a copula is also possible. It encodes property as class membership.

(20) jnk   nfr
     1SG   be_perfect\PTCP.PFV
     'I am a good one.'

(21) nfr   pw
     be_perfect\PTCP.PFV   COP
     'It is a good one.'

However, one predication type appears to be dedicated to the expression of a property with an adjectival predicate. The word order is predicate-subject, and the subject, if pronominal, is dependent.

(22) nfr   ṯw
     be_perfect\PTCP.PFV   2SG.M
     'You are well.'

Both nominal and adjectival predications are unmarked for tense and may have a past or a non-past reading, depending on the context.

Forms with -*j*- also appear as predicates in the same kind of construction.

(23) *n-j   tw   šrt*
     of-ADJ 2SG.M   nostril
     'You belong to the nostril.' (Pyramid text, § *1901e)

24.3 SEMITIC

Semitic languages extend throughout North Africa to the Near and Middle East.

Semitic is the AA branch where non-concatenative morphology is best represented. Arabic and Modern South Arabian (MSA) languages are the languages where such a system is the most robust. Usually, words are based on triconsonantal roots and various templates, including a vocalic alternation in the stem. For the evolution of word categories, we can rely on Cohen (1984), who thoroughly studied the role of syntax, namely verbless sentences and auxiliaries, in the evolution of the verbal system.

Semitic languages, at any stage of their known history, make a clear categorical distinction between nouns and verbs. The distinction is based on morphological features and distributional properties, not only functional or syntactic ones, since in many Semitic languages the predicative function is not restricted to verbs. Nouns can be used as predicates without any overt predicative element. Linear order and intonation may be the only cues that signal subject and predicative functions, as opposed to noun phrases. Compare (24a) and (24b) from Geʿez, a South Semitic language of the Ethiopic branch:

(24) Geʿez (Cohen 1984: 19)
     a. *ʾab   ḍaḥāy*
        father   sun
        'The Father is the sun.'
     b. *ḍaḥāy   ʾab*
        sun   father
        'The sun is the Father.'

In Geʿez there are often morphemes that mark the functions of juxtaposed nouns, e.g. agreement in gender and number on the nominal predicate and copulas (Cohen 1984: 158).

Even if the verb–noun distinction is not up for debate, the fluidity between the two categories—from nouns to verbs—has prevailed throughout the history of Semitic languages, as in Egyptian.

24.3.1 Verbs

a. There are at least two verb paradigms based on an aspectual opposition between a perfective and an imperfective. Only the imperfective with prefixes can be reconstructed to the proto-stage. The paradigms consist in a theme (i.e. a root and a template) and inflectional morphemes (prefixes or suffixes), which vary for person, number, and gender. The perfective suffixes can be traced back to verbless clauses composed of a verbal–nominal form and a personal pronoun (Cohen 1988c: 24). In this respect, the origin of the Akkadian (an ancient language of Mesopotamia) stative form is quite transparent: it is built on a specific theme derived from the verb root, CaCiC- (CaCC- before a vowel), for tri-consonantal roots, and subject personal pronouns. Examples (25)–(27) show the parallel constructions of a verbless sentence with a personal pronoun functioning as a subject suffix on a noun (25), an adjective (26), and a stative form based on the verbal–nominal template (27).

Akkadian

(25) ʃarraːq-aː-ku
thief-DET-1SG
'I am a thief.' (Cohen 1988d: 46)

(26) ʃurrux-aː-ku
magnificent-DET-1SG
'I am magnificent.' (Cohen 1984: 247)

(27) gaʃr-aː-ku
being.powerful-DET-1SG
'I am powerful.' (Cohen 1984: 245)

Since a third person subject can be either a pronoun or a noun, the stative third person is the bare verbal–nominal form: *gaʃir* 'he is powerful'.

b. Whereas the Akkadian stative form never became fully integrated in the verbal system (Cohen 1984: 247), it is admitted that a similar construction is the source of the perfective aspect in Arabic and Geʿez. The correspondence between personal indices and personal pronouns is not always straightforward, since analogical reformation and phonetic reductions took place differently in the two languages on the basis of independent or suffix pronouns. Third persons retained their gender and number nominal morphemes (e.g. *-at* for F.SG.). Table 24.2 displays the two sets of pronouns in Classical Arabic, and Table 24.3 the perfective paradigm.

Table 24.2 Classical Arabic independent and suffix pronouns

	Independent pronouns			Suffix pronouns		
	sg.	dual	pl.	sg.	dual	pl.
1	ʔanaː		naħnu	-iː / -niː		-naː
2m	ʔanta	ʔantumaː	ʔantum	-ka	-kumaː	-kum
2f	ʔanti		ʔantunna	-ki		-kunna
3m	huwa	humaː	hum	-hu	-humaː	-hum
3f	hija		hunna	-haː		-hunna

Table 24.3 Classical Arabic perfective paradigm of *katab* 'write'

	sg.	dual	pl.
1	katab-tu		katab-na:
2m	katab-ta	katab-tuma:	katab-tum
2f	katab-ti		katab-tunna
3m	katab-a	katab-a:	katab-u:
3f	katab-at	katab-ta:	katab-na

Table 24.4 shows the parallelism between the Akkadian stative paradigm, the perfect in Geʿez, and the perfective in Arabic.

Table 24.4 Paradigms of Akkadian stative, Geʿez perfect, and Classical Arabic perfective

		Stative	Perfect	Perfective
		Akkadian	Geʿez	Arabic
sg.	1	parsa:ku	gabarku	labistu
	2m	parsa:ta	gabarka	labista
	2f	parsa:ti	gabarki	labisti
	3m	paris	gabra	labisa
	3f	parsat	gabrat	labisat
pl.	1	parsa:nu	gabarna	labisna:
	2m	parsa:tunu	gabarkəmu	labistum
	2f	parsa:tina	gabarkən	labistunna
	3m	parsu:	gabru	labisu:
	3f	parsa:	gabra:	labisna

Source: Cohen (1984: 109–110)

c. In Neo-Syriac, an endangered language of the Middle East, the verbal system was renewed by means of old participial forms, active and passive, and the infinitive. For the imperfective, reduced forms of independent personal pronouns were affixed to the active participle, and for the preterit a directional preposition and the suffix pronouns were added to the passive participle (Cohen 1988f: 100; 1984: 510–513). Table 24.5 presents the imperfective, the preterit, and their reconstructions.

d. A large part of today's Arabic dialects (in particular the so-called sedentary dialects), and Modern Hebrew have undergone an expansion process of their TAM paradigms partly similar to that of Neo-Syriac. In the Arabic varieties, one of the new paradigms was grammaticalized from the active participle templates (including gender and

Table 24.5 Imperfective and preterit in Neo-Syriac

	IPFV	origin	PRF	origin
1sg.m	garʃ-ən	*gaːriʃ ʔana	grif-li	*griʃ l-i
1sg.f	garʃ-an	*garʃaː ʔana		
2sg.m	garʃ-ət	*gaːriʃ at	grif-lox	*griʃ l-ox
2sg.f	garʃ-at	*gaːrʃaː at(i)	grif-lax	*griʃ l-ax
3sg.m	gaːriʃ	*gaːriʃ	grif-le	*griʃ l-e
3sg.f	garʃ-a	*garʃaː	grif-la	*griʃ l-a
1pl	garʃ-ax	*garʃiː axnan	grif-lan	*griʃ l-an
2pl	garʃ-iːtun	*garʃiː atun	grif-loːxu	*griʃ l-oːxu
3pl	garʃ-i	*garʃiː	grif-lon	*griʃ l-on

Source: adapted from Cohen (1984: 512–513).

number nominal markers, but without agglutinated pronouns). Most often, they are limited to motion and posture verbs, and to mark the progressive aspect. In Modern Hebrew, active participle templates have expanded to all semantic types of verbs to mark present tense.

Moroccan Arabic is one of the dialects that developed a more complex system. The former active participle expresses different TAM values depending on semantic classes. Below is a simplified version of Caubet's (1993: 223–237) analysis of the Fez variety.

Verb class 1 (V1) comprises motion verbs and verbs indicating body and intellectual activities: the former active participle is either an *actual*, a *progressive* or a *prospective*.

Verb class 2 (V2), the most numerous one, cannot be characterized semantically (but contains no V1 or V3): the active participle is either the sole *perfect*, a particular type of *perfect* and a *prospective*, or a particular type of *perfect* and *actual*. Some verbs have all three values.

Verb class 3 (V3) contains inchoative and middle verbs. They have not incorporated the active participle in their system.

Moroccan Arabic
(28) ṛaː-ni   naːzl-a   mən   əṣ-ṣṭaħ
      here.is-1SG   descend\PTCP.ACT-SG.F   from   ART-terrace
      'Here I am, going down from the terrace.' (V1, progressive; Caubet 1993: 224)

(29) yədda   aːna   ṭaːlʕ-a   l-<la ville>
      tomorrow   1SG   go_up\PTCP.ACT-SG.F   ART-the town
      'Tomorrow, I am going up to town.' (V1, prospective; Caubet 1993: 226)

(30) ṣaːfi   ħaːʒəm   l-u
      enough   bleed\PTCP.ACT.SG.M   to-3SG
      'That's it! He has bled him.' (V2, perfect; Caubet 1993: 232)

(31) ħna   zaːr-iːn   yədda
      1PL   sow\PTCP.ACT-PL   tomorrow
      'We are sowing tomorrow.' (V2 prospective; Caubet 1993: 233)

(32) ṛaː-ni   faːhm-a   ʃnu   ka-t-guːl   daːba
      here.is-1SG understand\PTCP.ACT-SG.F what   IPFV-2SG-say now
      'But I understand what you are saying!' (V2 actual; Caubet 1993: 234)

e. Semitic languages also have series of derived non-finite forms with dedicated templates, whose number and functions vary depending on the language. They mark various voices and semantic values, such as middle, passive, reciprocal, reflexive, or intensive. They may have a more abstract function such as that of transitivizer or denominative.

In dialectal varieties of Arabic, verbal templates are still productive. Only in a few varieties that have undergone extended contact with European languages do they tend to collapse. The system is now largely frozen in Maltese (Vanhove 1993: 26), in contact with Sicilian, Italian and more recently English, and in Cypriote Arabic (Roth 1975: 91), in contact with Greek.

24.3.2 Nouns

The nominal category can be divided into several subcategories on morphological grounds, marking more or less abstract semantic categories.

a. In Ancient Semitic languages (Akkadian, Amorite, Ugaritic, old stages of Geʽez), nouns are marked for case. This system is still present in Classical Arabic, today's written Arabic, and MSA (e.g. Mehri, Soqotri) spoken in Yemen and Oman. Case is maximally differentiated in the singular, marked by vocalic suffixes, and is identical in all languages: -*u* marks subjects, -*a* direct objects, -*i* indirect objects. A nasal consonant -*m* or -*n* is added to these suffixes under various conditions. In Classical Arabic, -*n* occurs with indefinite nouns. In Biblical Hebrew, Biblical Aramaic, and in today's spoken varieties of Arabic, the case system collapsed, as in most other contemporary Semitic languages, with the exception of MSA and Amharic (spoken in Ethiopia). In the latter, only an accusative marker -*n* survives with definite nouns (Meyer 2011: 1192).
b. Most often, a root has both verbal and nominal templates that clearly differ from each other. A few are only nominal, e.g. *kalb-* 'dog'. Some templates are intermediary between nouns and verbs in their syntactic behaviour, such as in the case for *masdars* (a kind of infinitive), and for active and passive participles.

Classical Arabic has no fewer than 44 masdar templates for verbs in the base form (Blachère & Gaudefroy-Demombynes 1975: 78), e.g. CuCuːC- for motion and posture verbs with the CaCaC- perfective template: *daxal-a* 'he entered', *duxuːl-* 'the fact of entering'; CaCaːC-at- for verbs denoting properties with the template CaCuC-a: *saʕud-a* 'he was happy', *saʕaːd-at-* 'being happy'.

Some templates correlate with precise semantic fields: CiCa:C-at- indicates a profession or a function: *tadʒar-a* 'he traded', *tidʒa:r-at-* 'trader'. CaCCa:C- has either an intensive meaning (*ʔakkal-* 'glutton', *ʔakal-a* 'he ate'), or denotes nouns of artisans (*xabba:z-* 'baker', *xubz-* 'bread'). CiCC-at- is a template for nouns of manner (*kitb-at-* 'way of writing'), or of parts (*firq-at-* 'sect, party', *faraq-a* 'he broke'). ma-CCaC- and ma-CCiC- indicate place names (*ma-dʒlis-* 'audience room'). mi-CCa(:)C- is a template for instrument nouns (*mi-fta:ħ-* 'key').

In dialectal varieties of Arabic, nominal templates are still robust. This is far less the case for Maltese and Cypriot Arabic.

c   In Semitic, nominal number is overtly marked for plural, either by dedicated suffixes (often *-Vm* or *-Vn* in the masculine), or more frequently by specific templates. The proportion between the two strategies is the reverse in some modern languages, e.g. Amharic.

Classical Arabic has at least 30 plural templates which are not predictable on the basis of the singular: *kita:b* 'book', pl. *kutub*, *kalb* 'dog', pl. *kila:b*. As those examples show, the same template may be plural for one word and singular for another.

Dual is marked by a suffix in Old Semitic (Akkadian, Biblical Hebrew, Biblical Aramaic, Ugaritic, Ancient South Arabian, Classical Arabic, but not Geʽez). It is lost or unproductive in modern languages, except MSA.

d. Feminine is marked on nouns by a suffix (usually *-(a)(t)*), a morpheme which is actually attested in all branches of AA, except Omotic), while masculine is unmarked: Geʽez *bəʔesi* 'man', *bəʔesi-t* 'woman'. A few feminine nouns are not overtly marked: Classical Arabic *da:r-* 'house', *bi:r-* 'well', *ʃams-* 'sun'. Amharic has lost the morpheme on the noun, but it shows up in the singular as agreement marking on determiners and verbs (Kapeliuk 1988: 151):

(33) a. *dəmät-wa*   b. *dəmät-u*
cat-DEF:F   cat-DEF(:M)
'The (female) cat.'   'The (male) cat.' (Meyer 2011: 1191)

24.3.3 Adjectives

Although the distinction between noun and adjective categories is often not straightforward, there are a few differences and particularities that we want to discuss here.

a. In many languages, only the morphosyntactic context can help decide whether a template has a nominal or an adjectival reading. For instance, in Amharic there is no clear-cut boundary between the two (Meyer 2011: 1187–1189).

(34) Amharic (Meyer 2011: 1189)
kä-dähna   täwäläd   wäym kä-dähna   tạ̈täga! (*common noun*)
from-good be_born:IMP:2SG.M or   with-good   be_near:IMP:2SG.M
'Be born into a well-to-do [family] or be a protégé of one!'

(35) dähna   säw (adjective)
      good   person
      'Good, honest, polite person.'

However, Amharic shows morphological differences, at least for part of the lexicon. In contrast to common nouns whose plural is formed with the suffix -*očč*, adjectives 'can form their plural by reduplication of a consonant with or without the insertion of the vowel *a*: *addis* > *adaddis* "new/PL", *təlləq* > *təlalləq* "big/PL' " (Meyer 2011: 1190).

b. In Ugaritic, syntax is a relevant criteria: Some nominal forms only appear in attributive position after a noun: *ḥrb mlḥt* 'good sabre' (lit. sabre good) (Cohen 1988e: 62).
c. In Arabic, most adjectives share a good number of templates with nouns. However, adjectives of colour and physical deformities have a dedicated template, ʔa-CCaC- : *ʔa-ḥmar-* 'red', *ʔa-ʕwar-* 'one-eyed', as well as the so-called elative forms that mark comparative and superlative of adjectives, differentiating number and gender: M ʔaCCaC- (*ʔakbar-*), F CuCCa: (*kubraː*), M.PL ʔaCaʔCiC- (*ʔakaːbir-*), F.PL CuCCajaːt (*kubrajaːt-*) 'bigger, biggest', from *kabiːr-* 'big'.
d. MSA have a series of dedicated adjectival templates. In Mehri, the most common ones are C(a)CiːC and CiːCaC. The active and passive participles also function as adjectives (as in many Semitic languages and Egyptian). Adjectives can be derived from nouns with the template CVCC (Watson 2012: 104).
e. Most Semitic languages also have a dedicated suffix, traditionally called *nisba*, (see section 24.2.3), to derive adjectives from ethnic and place names, names of substance, and a few other semantic domains. This device tends to extend in modern varieties. The suffix is -*ijj* in Arabic, -*iː* or -*aj*, in Mehri: *mahr-aj* 'relating to Mahra as a clan or an area', *xarf* 'monsoon period', *xarf-iː* 'relating to/from the monsoon period' (Watson 2012: 55, 104).
f. Some Semitic languages have developed different, but functionally limited, strategies. The Neo-Aramaic variety of Ma'lula in Syria, for instance, reanalysed the absence of a former definite article to an adjective marker in predicative function (Cohen 1988f: 97).

24.4 CUSHITIC

Most Cushitic languages are spoken in the Horn of Africa (Ethiopia, Eritrea, Somalia, Djibouti), and a few outliers are found in Eastern Sudan (Beja) and in the African Great Lakes region (Tanzania, Kenya: South Cushitic, e.g. Iraqw, Alagwa). The internal classification of Cushitic is still debated (for a recent overview, see Mous 2012: 347).

Since Cushitic languages are only recently attested, the focus will be less on historical aspects of word classes than that of the previous sections.

If vocalic alternation in the stem as a non-concatenative morphological device is highly marginal or inexistent in the vast majority of the Cushitic languages (with the exception of Beja, and more marginally Somali and Afar-Saho), the structural consonantal root is often still visible in many of the languages for both nouns and verbs. Unlike Semitic, biconsonantal verbal roots predominate triconsonantal roots in many languages such as Sidamo (69.9% vs

20.3%) or Afar (53.4% vs 35.6%), but it is the reverse in a few others such as Beja (39.3% vs 52.8%), or the proportion is balanced between the two as in Kemantney, a language of the Agaw branch (Cohen 1988g: 256).

All Cushitic languages make a clear morphological distinction between nouns and verbs, be it concatenative or not. The existence of an adjective category is not always attested or straightforward, and may fall within the nominal or verbal domain.

24.4.1 Verbs

a. Verbs are characterized by their morphological make-up in all Cushitic languages, which show a variety of paradigms. In spite of the differences, person marking is remarkably stable across the family, as Table 24.6 shows.

Table 24.6 Personal indices in Cushitic languages

		SG	PL
Prefixes			
	1	(ʔ-) / Ø	n-
	2	t-	t- … -Vn
	3m	j- / Ø	j- / Ø- … -Vn
	3f	t-	
Suffixes			
	1	-(ʔ-) / -Ø-	-n-
	2	-t-	-t- … -Vn
	3	-(j-) / -Ø-	-(j-) / -Ø- … -Vn

Source: Cohen (1988g: 257).

b. In all languages, the basic verbal inflection is marked by several sets of suffixes, which agglutinate, or more rarely fuse, person, TAM, gender, and number distinctions. For some languages (e.g. Beja, Afar), these constructions can be partly traced back to light verb constructions with a 'be' or 'say' verb conjugated with prefixes (Cohen 1973) (see Table 24.7).

A few languages also preserved an ancient verb class whose basic aspectual distinction is marked by prefixes both in the perfective and imperfective. This class represents the majority (57%) in Beja (Vanhove 2017: 66), over one-third in Afar-Saho, but only five verbs in Southern Agaw and Somali (Cohen 1988g: 256).

c. Non-concatenative morphology with vocalic alternation for TAM is limited to a handful of languages. In Somali, ablaut in the stem is restricted to aspectual

Table 24.7 Comparison of paradigm of *di* 'say' and verb class 2 inflectional morphemes in Beja

	'say' PFV	V2 IPFV
1sg	a-ni	-ani
2sg.m	ti-ni-ja	-tnija
2sg.f	ti-niː	-tiniː
3sg.m	i-ni	-iːni
3sg.f	ti-ni	-tini
1pl	ni-di	-nej/-naj
2pl	ti-diː-na	-teːn(a)
3pl	eː-n(a)	-eːn(a)

Source: Vanhove (2020: 666).

oppositions for the few prefixed verbs (*ja-qaːn* 'he knows' vs *ji-qiːn* 'he knew'). In Afar, ablaut only occurs on the inflectional morpheme (*ab-te* 'you/she did' vs *ab-taː* 'you/she do(es)'). In Beja, change of vowel length in the stem is the rule for the prefix verb class (*a-dif* 'I went', vs *an-diːf* 'I go', where the *-n-* element goes back to the root *n* 'say').

d. Many languages have proclitic elements on the verb that usually mark a pragmatic value of focus:

(36) Oromo (Stroomer 1995: 73)
ammoː inniː   hijiː hin=hoj-at-e
but   3SG.NOM work   FOC=work-MID-3SG.M.PAST
'But he did work!'

e. East-Cushitic languages show reduced paradigms in dependent and relative clauses, often without a person index.
f. All Cushitic languages also have a converb category, more or less finite depending on the language (Azeb and Dimmendaal 2006). For instance, in Kambaata, converbs still 'have a reduced number of aspect[s] (...) and person values' (Treis 2012: 219), while in Beja, the four converbs used in deranked subordinate clauses are strictly finite. Only the manner converb shows gender agreement, marked by a nominal morpheme (Vanhove 2016: 94).

Converbs sometimes have been reused to form new paradigms. That is the case for the Beja manner converb, which, together with the nominal copula and indefinite articles, has become a finite verb form marking the perfect aspect (Vanhove 2016). Compare (37) with a deranked clause and (38) with the perfect in an interrogative utterance.

Beja (Vanhove 2017: 98, 138)

(37) kʷibs-a   kalla:f-i:na
     hide-CVB.MNR   feed-AOR.3PL
     'They were feeding him on the sly.'

(38) kak   jʔ-aː=b=wa?
     how   come-CVB.MNR=INDF.M.ACC=COP.2SG.M
     'How have you come?'

g. All Cushitic languages allow derivation from the base form to express various voice and semantic values. The most common ones are total or partial reduplication for pluractionality, an affix *s* for causative, *t* for middle, and *(a)m* for passive and/or reciprocal, the latter three also found in Semitic languages. Derivational markers can combine with each other. Beja has no fewer than 11 of these combinations, sometimes piling up three morphemes, such as reciprocal, middle, and pluractional markers.

(39) Beja (Vanhove 2017: 93)
     uː=din=wa   ani=wwa
     DEF.SG.M.NOM=Odin=COORD   1SG.NOM=COORD
     ni-m-takʷ~kʷaːkʷ
     1PL-RECP-repare\MID~PLAC.PFV
     'Odin and I, we difficultly came to an agreement.'

Beja is the sole Cushitic language that shows ablaut in the stem for several derived forms of the verb class with prefixed indicative paradigms (Vanhove 2017: 71).

Other than the values mentioned so far, some are sporadically found, e.g. in Dullay the doubling of the last consonant expresses a singular event: ʕuk 'to drink', ʕukk 'to take one drink' (Cohen 1988g: 260).

24.4.2 Nouns

Morphologically, nouns differ from non-finite verbs by the absence of TAM marking and person, and from finite and non-finite verbs, in that they are marked for case.

a. The number of cases and their morphophonological make-up vary from one language to another, and case encoding strategies may include affixes, accent patterns or tone. In a few languages, cases have been lost, e.g. Dahalo, a minority moribund language spoken in Kenya, for which Tosco (1991) does not report anything about case marking. In other languages, e.g. Beja, most cases are not marked on the noun itself, but on determiners. The East-Cushitic languages Alaaba (Schneider-Blum 2007), Kambaata (Treis 2008), and Harar Oromo (Owens 1985) have between six to eight cases, e.g. Alaaba has nominative, absolutive, genitive, dative, ablative, locative, instrumental and similative. In comparison, Beja (Vanhove 2017) has four cases, nominative, accusative, genitive, and vocative; Somali (Af Tunni variety, Tosco 1997) also has four, nominative, absolutive, genitive and vocative; Dhaasanac Tosco 2001) has three, nominative, absolutive, and genitive.

The Southern Cushitic languages (e.g. Burunge, Iraqw) are a typological rarity in that they mark case on the verb, not on the nominal arguments, by means of clitics (Kießling's 2000: 86).

In spite of this variation, a -(t)i suffix is common to several Cushitic languages either for the expression of a focused subject and/or the genitive as shown in Table 24.8.

Table 24.8 Common case markers in Cushitic

	Beja	Agaw	Afar	Somali	Oromo	Sidamo
Focused subject			-i	-i	-i/-y	-i/(-u)
Genitive	-i	-i/-u	-i/-ti	-ti	-ti	-u/-i

Source: Cohen (1988g: 266).

b. A gender distinction between feminine and masculine exists in all Cushitic languages, sometimes just as traces, by means of tone (Somali), stress (Afar), and, more often, affixes or clitics (e.g. Afar, Beja, Kambaata, Somali, Xamtanga). Gender is not necessarily marked on the noun itself, and may surface only (or also) as agreement markers on the predicate or modifier, as in Alagwa where gender is a morphological agreement phenomenon on the head noun within an NP or on the predicate (Mous 2016:102).

There is a debate between specialists of Cushitic (Mous 2012: 364ff), who consider number as a gender feature on the basis of the agreement system on verbs, and typologists (Corbett 1991: 210) who consider that this is a marginal feature better explained in terms of syncretism. In a number of Cushitic languages (east and south), plural is actually analysed as one of a three-term gender system, in addition to feminine and masculine (for a discussion see Mous 2008), e.g. in Alagwa (Mous 2016: 44–45). This echoes the agreement system with numerals in Semitic from three onwards where the numeral bears the feminine marker with masculine nouns but not with feminine ones. For a historical explanation of the phenomena, see Cuny & Feghali (1924).

While masculine is usually covert (Dhaasanac and Arbore are exceptions), feminine is overtly expressed with a *t* marker in most Cushitic languages, sometimes only as a trace, as in Xamtanga (Darmon 2017: 66), or in Dhaasanac where feminine is often synchronically expressed with a final vowel -*i*, and masculine with -*u* (Tosco 2001: 71). In Kambaata *t* is generalized to almost all nouns as a suffix (Treis 2008: 126): *am-á-t-* 'mother', *hix-í-t-* 'grass'. In other languages, feminine only surfaces under specific morphosyntactic conditions, e.g. as article clitics in Beja: *deː = t* 'a mother', *toː = ndi* 'the mother (acc.)' *hamoː = t* 'a hair', *t = hami* 'the hair', and on demonstratives. The category of gender is dying out in endangered Dahalo (Tosco 1991: 20).

c. Number on nouns is marked in several ways. Various suffixes are found, some shared by two languages or more, e.g. -*a* in Beja and Afar, -*oːta* in Sidamo and Oromo. Gemination of the final root consonant is quite common (with various additional vowels or suffixes) as attested in Alagwa, Afar, Saho, Somali, Xamtanga, but rarely in Sidamo, and unattested in e.g. Beja. Ablaut in the stem is more marginal and concerns a limited number of nouns in Beja (*meːk*, 'donkey', pl. *mak*), Afar or Xamtanga, the latter also using consonantal alternations (*giziŋ* 'dog', pl. *gisʼiŋ*). In the plural of some languages, e.g. Afar and Xamtanga, the final vowel of a noun which ends in a vowel is deleted.

Beja is particular in also having a nominal non-concatenative system, similar, but not identical, to that of Arabic (Vanhove 2012: 321–323; 2017: 24–27; 2020).

24.4.3 Adjectives

The status and morphological make-up of adjectives vary a lot from one language to the next and, in some of them, in particular East-Cushitic languages (Banti 1986), their existence is even disputed. In fact, property concepts are often related to either the verbal or nominal category; Afar, with its dedicated verbal paradigm (in addition to a few primary adjectives) is a good example of the former case.

   a. Once again, Beja is unusual in having dedicated non-concatenative templates for adjective formation, precisely eight, two of which are shared with nouns: *dawil* 'close' < *diwil* 'to be close'. Beja has the suffix *-i*, also found in Egyptian and Semitic.
   b. In Dahalo (Tosco 1991: 18), nouns are marked only for number, whereas adjectives are marked for number and gender; in Somali (Af Tunni, Tosco 1997: 49) adjectives are derived from nouns via the suffix *-san*: *geesi* 'hero' *geesi-san* 'heroic'. In Bayso, '[a]n adjective may contain up to three distinct elements: an associative particle, an adjectival stem, and a gender suffix' (Hayward 1979: 113). Sidaama (Kawachi 2007: 134) only has seven underived adjectives, but has many adjectives derived from verbs or nouns by means of suffixes (*-ado, -allo, -aššo, -aaleessa* for verbs, *-iweelo, -čČo, -aame* for nouns). Similarly, Xamtanga has only three primary adjectives (i.e. morphologically different from nouns, and not relativized verbs), but property-denoting lexemes mostly behave as relativized verbs, or as nouns (Darmon 2017: 40–41). On the other hand, languages such as Saho have no adjective category but use stative verbs instead (Banti & Vergari 2005: 106).

24.5 CONCLUSION

In this overview, we have discussed the most salient properties of the three major word classes: nouns, verbs, and adjectives, in three branches of Afroasiatic, Egyptian, Semitic, and Cushitic. They can be summarized as follows:

- There is a distinction between nouns and verbs in all three branches.
- However, in the long term grammaticalization processes show that verbal systems are often replaced on the basis of nominal constructions.

- The adjective category is less easily defined and characterized and, depending on the family and the language, is more (but not exclusively) akin to nouns (Semitic), or verbs (Cushitic), or to both nouns and verbs (Egyptian).
- Non-concatenative morphology is pervasive in most Semitic languages, less so in Egyptian, and only limited to a handful of languages in Cushitic.

CHAPTER 25

WORD CLASSES IN MANDE LANGUAGES

DENIS CREISSELS

25.1 THE MANDE LANGUAGE FAMILY

THE Mande language family includes about 70 languages with a total of more than 50 million speakers. Mande languages are spoken in 12 West African countries, from Senegal to Nigeria. The languages of the Manding group (Bambara, Maninka, Jula, Mandinka, etc.) are by far the most widely spoken and best-documented Mande languages.

The genetic depth of the Mande family is estimated at about five millennia. The Mande language family was recognized very early in the history of African linguistics, essentially because of its remarkable typological homogeneity and the clear-cut typological contrasts between Mande languages and their neighbours in many respects. There is no doubt about the validity of the Mande language family as a genetic unit. What is, however, controversial is the inclusion of the Mande language family within the Niger–Congo phylum (Dimmendaal 2011).

As regards the internal structure of the Mande language family, as discussed by Vydrin (2009, 2016), there is a relative consensus about the recognition of 11 lower-level groupings: Manding, Mokole, Vai-Kono, Jogo-Jeri, Soso-Jalonke, Southwestern, Soninke-Bozo, Samogho, Bobo, Southern, and Eastern. Most specialists agree on the hypothesis that the first split was between two branches, one of them constituted by the Southern and Eastern groups, the other one (designated as West Mande) constituted by the other nine groups. By contrast, there is no consensus about the intermediary stages of classification, especially within the West Mande branch. In Table 25.1, the only intermediary grouping that has been retained is Central Mande (consisting of Manding, Mokole, Vai-Kono, and Jogo-Jeri), on which there is a relative consensus.

25.2 THE TYPOLOGICAL PROFILE OF MANDE LANGUAGES

25.2.1 Some general characteristics of Mande languages

Mande languages are tonal languages, with as many as five contrasting tone heights in some Dan varieties. In general, they have rather unremarkable consonant and vowel inventories,

Table 25.1 The Mande language family

South & East Mande	South Mande	Dan, Guro, Mano, Beng, Gban, Mwan, Wan, Tura, Yaure
	East Mande	Bisa, San, Busa, Boko, Bokobaru, Kyenga, Shanga
West Mande	Soninke-Bozo	Soninke, Jenaama, Soroko, Kelinga, Tigemaxo
	Bobo	Bobo
	Samogho	Dzuun, Duun, Banka, Jo, Kpan, Kpeen, Seenku
	Central Manding	Bambara, Jula, Maninka, Mandinka
	Mokole	Kakabe, Koranko, Lele, Mogofin
	Vai-Kono	Vai, Kono
	Jogo-Jeri	Jogo, Jeri, Ligbi, Jalkunan
	Soso-Jalonke	Soso, Jalonke
	Southwestern	Mende, Kpelle, Looma, Bandi, Loko

but exceptions to this generalization can be found among the languages of the Southern branch. Mande languages typically have complex systems of tonal alternations involving sandhi phenomena, tonal alternations triggered by syntactic structure, and tonal marking of inflectional categories.

Mande languages have rich systems of affixal derivation (mainly suffixal) and very productive systems of nominal compounding. By contrast, most of them have very reduced inflectional morphology, and with very few exceptions, the inflectional morphology found in individual Mande languages seems to be the result of grammaticalization processes that occurred in a relatively recent past rather than the reflex of an inflectional system that could be traced back to their common ancestor.

In most Mande languages, valency-changing morphology is limited to a causative marker (either a suffix or a preverb). Detransitivizing markers (with either an antipassive or mediopassive function) are rarely found in Mande languages, and applicative markers are not attested at all. 'Deobliquative' derivation making it possible to omit otherwise obligatory oblique arguments constitutes an interesting particularity of some Southern and Eastern Mande languages (Idiatov 2008).

Mande languages have neither gender–noun class systems nor classifier systems,[1] and show no compelling evidence that the situation on this point might have been different in their common ancestor.

A striking characteristic of Mande languages is the extreme degree of rigidity of word order.

25.2.2 The basics of Mande morphosyntax: Clause structure

25.2.2.1 *Transitive–intransitive alignment and grammatical relations*

As regards the coding characteristics of core arguments, ergative–absolutive alignment is not totally unknown in Mande (see Vydrin (2011) on TAM-based split ergativity in

---

[1] Note, however, that the adnominal possession construction of Kpelle as described for example by Konoshenko (2017: 299) can be analysed as involving a rudimentary system of possessive classifiers.

Southwestern Mande), but the neutral and nominative–accusative types of alignment are strongly predominant.

The Mande languages for which the relevant information is available have systems of grammatical relations in which the sole argument of intransitive clauses and the A term of transitive clauses share a number of behavioural properties that distinguish them from the P term of transitive clauses. This justifies using the traditional labels 'subject' for NPs showing the coding properties shared by the sole core argument of intransitive clauses and the A term of transitive predication, and 'object' for the P term of transitive predication. For detailed analysis of the grammatical relation system of a Mande language, see Creissels (2019) on Mandinka.

25.2.2.2 Transitive and intransitive predicative constructions

The verbal clauses of Mande languages are characterized by a particularly rigid (and typologically unusual) constituent order, with the object invariably in immediate preverbal position and the obliques in postverbal position. Transitive verbal clauses can be schematized as S O V X*, and intransitive verbal clauses as S V X*.[2] A so-called predicative marker (a kind of auxiliary) is often found immediately after the subject NP. Example (1) illustrates the S O V X order in some Mande languages. In all the sentences given in this example, any change in the linear order of constituents would automatically result in ungrammaticality.

(1) a. Sékù   bé   Mǎdù   kálán   tùbàbùkân   ná.
       Sékou ICPL   Madou   teach   French.language POSTP[3]
       S   pm   O   V   X
       'Sékou is teaching French to Madou.' (Bambara, pers. doc.)[4]

   b. Yúgò-n   dà   dòròkê-n   qóbó   yàxàré-n   dà.
      man-D   CPL.TR   dress-D   buy   woman-D   for
      S   pm   O   V   X
      'The man bought a dress for the woman.' (Soninke, pers. doc.)

   c. Ń   nìngée   fíi-mà   í   má.
      1SG   cow   five-FUT   2SG   POSTP
      S   O   V   X
      'I will give you a cow.' (Soso, pers. doc.)

---

[2] In this schematization, S, O, and X are 'subject', 'object' and 'oblique', respectively. The asterisk is the Kleene star: X* representing a string of an arbitrary number of obliques, including the empty string.

[3] The generic gloss POSTP is used throughout the chapter for postpositions whose range of possible meanings is difficult if not impossible to analyse in terms of extensions of some core meaning. Such postpositions are widely used in Mande languages to flag oblique arguments (i.e. semantic arguments of the verb that are not encoded as subject or object NPs).

[4] The abbreviation 'pers. doc.' (personal documentation) refers either to data I directly collected in field work with native speakers, or to data taken from a variety of sources other than language descriptions and subsequently checked with native speakers.

d. *Kpanâ   gbɔ́ɔ   lé-ni   bí   má?*
   Kpana   what   say-CPL   2SG   to
   S   O   V   X
   'What did Kpana say to you?' (Mende, Innes 1971: 137)

Example (2) illustrates intransitive predication. Note that, in Mande languages, a significant proportion of semantically bivalent verbs do not select the transitive construction as their coding frame, and occur in an extended intransitive construction with one of their two arguments encoded as an oblique.

(2) a. *Sékù   búká   láfí   í   là   kódòo   lá*
     Sékou   ICPL.NEG   want   2SG   GEN   money.D   POSTP
     S   pm   V   X
     'Sékou doesn't want your money.' (Mandinka, pers. doc.)

  b. *Ń   mùŋgú   dò   léminè-n   tòxó-n   ŋà.*
     1SG   forget   with   child-D   name-D   POSTP
     S   V   X
     'I forgot the child's name.' (Soninke, pers. doc.)

  c. *Sukúlu   lopoí   jísia   tíi   li-má   sukúlií   hu   hâ.*
     school   child   DEM.PL   3PL.ICPL.NEG   go-PROG   school.D   in   today
     S   pm   V   X   X
     'These school children are not going to school today.' (Mende, Innes 1971: 91)

  d. *E   nɔ̄ɲī   kālē   gó.*
     3SG   get.lost.PST   forest   in
     S   V   X
     'He got lost in the forest.' (Wan, Nikitina 2018: 110)

25.2.2.3 Ditransitive constructions

In contrast to most language families of sub-Saharan Africa, Mande languages do not have double-object constructions.[5] One of the arguments of semantically trivalent verbs must obligatorily be encoded as an oblique in postverbal position. In ditransitive constructions, both indirective and secundative alignments are common.

25.2.2.4 TAM and polarity

In Mande languages, grammaticalized TAM distinctions can be expressed by verbal suffixes (such as *mà* in (1c)), predicative markers immediately following the subject NP (and

---

[5] The only exception I am aware of is Gban (Fedotov 2017: 981), and it has a simple historical explanation. The point is that the S O₁ O₂ V X construction of Gban is only possible with the causative form of transitive verbs, and consequently can be traced back to a source construction in which what has become a causative suffix still was a causation verb taking a nominalized transitive clause as its object, something like 'X caused [Y's V-ing Z]' for 'X made Y V Z'.

consequently separated from the verb by the object NP, such as *bé* in (1a)), or a combination of both. The division of labour between predicative markers and TAM suffixes of verbs varies from one language to another.

In Mande languages, polarity distinctions are commonly expressed by pairs of predicative markers, often with no formal resemblance at all between the negative member of the pair and its positive counterpart, as in (3). Pure negative markers, either in post-subjectal or clause-final position, are less common.

(3) Mandinka (pers. doc.)
    a. *Fàatú   yè   Fántà   máakóyì   kódòo   tó.*
       Fatou CPL.TR   Fanta   help   money.D LOC
       'Fatou helped Fanta financially.'

    b. *Fàatú   mâŋ   Fántà   máakóyì   kódòo   tó.*
       Fatou CPL.NEG Fanta   help   money.D LOC
       'Fatou did not help Fanta financially.'

25.2.2.5 Transitivity marking

Predicative markers may be sensitive to transitivity distinctions, especially those expressing completive aspect. For a historical analysis of this phenomenon and a discussion of proposals previously made by other authors (including Creissels 1997), see Idiatov (2020).

For example, in Mandinka, as illustrated in example (4), to be compared with (3), negative intransitive clauses in the completive aspect are marked by the same predicative marker *mâŋ* as the corresponding transitive clauses, but in positive clauses, the suffix *-ta* expressing the completive aspect in intransitive clauses is in complementary distribution with the predicative marker *yè* expressing the same TAM value in transitive clauses.

(4) Mandinka (pers. doc.)
    a. *Fàatú   táa-tá   fàrôo   tó.*
       Fatou go-CPL.INTR rice.field.D LOC
       'Fatou went to the rice field.'

    b. *Fàatú   mâŋ   táa fàrôo   tó.*
       Fatou CPL.NEG go   rice.field.D LOC
       'Fatou did not go to the rice field.'

25.2.2.6 Flagging and indexation

As can be seen from the examples above, in Mande clauses, the general rule is that subjects and objects are not flagged. The only case of core argument flagging I am aware of in a Mande language is the system of differential subject flagging found in Soninke, with a special suffix used exclusively to flag focalized NPs and interrogatives in subject function—Creissels (2018a: 772–773).

As a rule, in Mande clauses, obliques are flagged by adpositions, although obliques flagged by prepositions and/or unflagged obliques can also be found, depending on language-specific rules. Example (2b) illustrates a case of oblique flagging involving both a preposition and a postposition. Note that, given the rigidity of the S O V X constituent order, in Mande languages, unflagged obliques cannot be confused with objects. On the special status of obliques (including oblique arguments) in Mande syntax, see Nikitina (2009a, 2011).

Indexation is absent from most West Mande languages, but in Southwestern Mande languages and in the majority of South and East Mande languages, the cliticization of subject pronouns has resulted in subject indexation mechanisms.[6] In all cases, subject indexes attach to the predicative marker (with which they tend to fuse), not to the verb. Some of the languages in question have subject indexes in complementary distribution with free pronouns in subject function, whereas others have obligatory subject indexes and optional subject NPs, as illustrated in (5) for Kpelle.

(5) Kpelle (Konoshenko 2017: 304, 327)
    a. Ŋǎă pá.   /1SG.RES/come/   'I have come.'
       Yǎă pá.   /2SG.RES/come/   'You (sg.) have come.'
       Ǎă pá.   /3SG.RES/come/   'He/she has come.'
       Gwǎă pá.   /1PL.INCL.RES/come/   'We (incl.) have come.'
       Kwǎă pá.   /1PL.EXCL.RES/come/   'We (excl.) have come.'
       Kǎă pá.   /2PL.RES/come/   'You (pl.) have come.'
       Dǎă pá.   /3PL.RES/come/   'They have come.'

    b. Pépèè   ǎă   pá.
       Pepe   3SG.RES   come
       'Pepe has come.'

    c. Nààkɔi   dà   Pépèè   dǎă   pá.
       Niakwei   3.and   Pepe   3SG.RES   come
       'Niakwei and Pepe have come.'

    d. Ŋǎă   wúlú   ɓélá.
       1SG.RES   tree   saw
       'I sawed the tree.'

    e. (Zààwòlò)   ǎă   ɓá   mèě.
       Zawolo   3SG.RES   rice   eat
       'Zawolo/he has eaten the rice.'

In Southwestern Mande languages, cliticization also affects object pronouns, resulting in paradigms of object indexes attached to transitive verbs. The object indexes are always in complementary distribution with object NPs. Their interaction with the initial consonant of the verb may result in total fusion, as in (6b), where the initial z of the verb form results from the fusion of its initial consonant with a 1st person singular index whose underlying form can be analysed as ŋ- (Konoshenko 2017: 330).

---

[6] The discussion of indexation is limited here to indexation mechanisms operating within the limits of the clause, but person–number agreement on clause-linking markers is also found in a limited number of Mande languages (see Idiatov 2010).

(6) Kpelle (Konoshenko 2017: 303)
   a. Ŋàă   é-háyá.
      1SG.RES 2SG-hurt
      'I have hurt you.'

   b. Ŋàă   záyá.
      1SG.RES 1SG.hurt
      'I have hurted myself.'

25.2.2.7 Unspecified core arguments

A salient feature of Mande clause structure is that in almost all Mande languages, there is a total ban on unexpressed subjects or objects, be it with a non-specific or anaphoric reading (see Creissels (2015) for a detailed discussion of this aspect of Mandinka syntax). In particular, it is generally impossible to refer to an unspecified participant normally encoded as the object of a transitive construction by simply deleting the object NP. However, as illustrated in (5), the strategies used to leave the object argument of transitive verbs unspecified vary from one language to another: antipassive derivation (Soninke), antipassive periphrases (Manding languages), or generic nouns in object function (Wan).

(7) Soninke (pers. doc.)
   a. Sámáqqè-n   qíñí-ndì
      snake-D   bite-ANTIP
      'The snake bit (someone).'

   Mandinka (pers. doc.)
   b. Fàatú   yè   ñìnìŋkàarôo   ké.
      Fatou   CPL.TR asking.D   do
      'Fatou asked (someone).'

   Wan (Nikitina 2018: 108)
   c. Dèlɔ̀tɔ́ á   pɔ̄   lɔ́   lé
      Deloto COP thing eat <PROG
      'Deloto is eating.'

25.2.2.8 Lability

As a rule, Mande languages have very limited classes of A-labile verbs (i.e. verbs used transitively or intransitively with the same semantic role assigned to their subject), whereas P-lability, illustrated in (8), is pervasive.

(8) Wan (Nikitina 2018: 108)
   a. Dèlɔ̀tɔ́ séŋgè klā   tābālī é tā.
      Deloto knife put.PST table   D on
      'Deloto put a knife on the table.'

b. *Yrēé klā à tā.*
    tree put.PST 3SG on
    'A tree fell on him.'

Moreover, in Mande languages, P-lability is not limited to the cross-linguistically common causal–noncausal type illustrated in (8). Cobbinah & Lüpke (2009) rightly observe that particularly clear cases of languages with morphologically unmarked passive constructions can be found among Mande languages. Example (9) illustrates active–passive lability in Guro.[7]

(9) Guro (Kuznetsova & Kuznetsova 2017: 786)
    a. *Tālá vàṵ kīlḭ̄.*
       Tra shirt sew.CPL
       'Tra sewed the shirt.'

    b. *Vàṵ kīlḭ̄ (Tālá pḛ̀ì yā).*
       shirt sew.CPL Tra track with
       'The shirt was sewn (by/because of Tra).'

Manding languages are an extreme case of languages with systematic active–passive lability, since in Manding languages, all the verbs that can be used in a transitive construction can also be freely used without any specific marking in an intransitive construction in which their subject is assigned the same semantic role as the object in the transitive construction, as in (10). Note that, with the Bambara verb *dún* 'eat' (and this constitutes the general rule in Bambara), there is no possible ambiguity on the semantic role of the subject, since a periphrasis with the light verb *kɛ́* 'do' (10c) is the only way to avoid specifying the patient.

(10) Bambara (pers. doc.)
    a. *Wùlû má sògô dún.*
       dog.D CPL.NEG meat.D eat
       'The dog didn't eat the meat.'

    b. *Sògô má dún (wùlú fɛ̀).*
       meat.D CPL.NEG eat dog.D by
       'The meat was not eaten (by the dog).'

    c. *Wùlû má dúmúní kɛ́.*
       dog.D CPL.NEG eating do
       'The dog didn't eat.'

---

[7] In most cases, in the passive construction of the verbs having this kind of lability, either the expression of the demoted agent as an oblique is not possible, or the oblique phrase that can be interpreted as expressing the demoted agent has other possible readings, as in the Guro example (9).

25.2.3 The basics of Mande morphosyntax: NP structure

Mande languages do not have gender–noun classes. The structure of Mande noun phrases can be schematized as follows, with two possible positions for demonstratives and other determiners:[8]

(AdPoss) (Det₁) N (Attr) (Quant) (Det₂)

(11) Mandinka (pers. doc.)

í	lá	ñìŋ	dímmúsú	màlùbálí	sàbôo
2SG	GEN	DEM	daughter	cheeky	three.D
AdPoss		Det₁	N	Attr	Quant.Det₂

'These three cheeky daughters of yours.'

The noun modifiers occupying the Det₁ position may be proclitics, and those occupying the Det₂ position may be enclitics. The phonological interaction between clitic determiners and their host may go as far as complete fusion, as in example (10), where the enclitic determiner ò fuses with the last vowel of sàbá 'three'.

Many Mande languages have a clitic determiner (glossed D) that can be characterized semantically as a definite article with a very wide range of uses, or as a default determiner (i.e. a determiner which in most contexts carries no particular semantic specification, and must simply be present if the speaker does not consider useful to select a determiner with a more specific meaning). In most Manding varieties, the default determiner (Mandinka ò) is reduced to a floating tone.

Most Mande languages express number on nouns by means of a single plural marker (with just phonologically conditioned variants) occupying the Det₂ position. However, more complex systems of number marking are found in Soninke and Bobo.

Mande languages may have a single adnominal possession construction (this is for example the case in Soninke), but most of them have two possible constructions for adnominal possessors distinguished by the presence vs absence of a postposition (glossed GEN) following the adnominal possessor, depending on the semantic nature of the relationship between adnominal possessors and their head, as in Mandinka *Músáa díŋòlú* 'Moussa's children' vs *Músáa lá nìnsôolú* 'Moussa's cows'—on this question, see section 25.5.

In some other languages (for example, Kpelle), adnominal possessors are obligatorily indexed, either directly on their head, or on a possessive pronoun that precedes their head, depending on the semantic nature of the relationship between adnominal possessors and their head, as in Kpelle *(Hèhèe) ǹáŋ* /Hehe/3SG.father/ 'Hehe's father / his father' vs *(Hèhèe) ŋɔ́ ɓéláá* /Hehe/3SG.POSS/sheep/ 'Hehe's sheep / his sheep' (Konoshenko 2017: 299).

In some languages, adnominal possessors trigger the use of a tonally marked 'construct form' of their head (as in Soninke *kìtáabè* 'book' vs *Múusá kìtàabê* 'Moussa's book').

---

[8] AdPoss = adnominal possessor, Det = determiner, N = noun, Attr = attributive modifier, Quant = quantitative modifier (including numerals).

Mande languages may have postnominal relative clauses occupying the rightmost position in the noun phrase, but in many of them, the commonest relativization strategy is a correlative strategy, illustrated in (12), displaying the following characteristics:

- the relative clause precedes the matrix clause;
- whatever the relativized position may be, the constituent order within the relative clause is invariably the same as in the corresponding independent clause;
- the semantic head of the relative clause occupies the relativized position;
- the semantic head of the relative clause is marked by a relativizer, and resumed in the matrix clause by a demonstrative or personal pronoun.

(12) Mandinka (pers. doc.)
Sùŋôo   yè   mùsôo$_i$ mîŋ   ná   kódóo   tǎa,
thief.D   CPL.TR   woman.D   REL   GEN   money.D   take
ŋ́   níŋ   wǒo$_i$ běn-tà.
man.D   with   DEM   meet-CPL.INTR
'I met the woman whose money was taken by the thief.'
lit. something like 'The thief took which woman's money, I met that one.'

25.3 NOUNS AND VERBS

25.3.1 Introductory remarks

Given the rigidity of word order patterns in Mande languages, there is no difficulty in identifying verbs and common nouns on the basis of the following definitions: in Mande languages, verbs have the ability to act as the nucleus (V) of the S O V X* predicative construction in association with a paradigm of TAM-polarity markers that follow either S or V, and common nouns have the ability to act as the nucleus of noun phrases having the structure described in section 25.2.3. In fact, not all descriptions of Mande languages operate with an explicit definition of the verb vs noun distinction, but the way they manipulate the labels 'noun' and 'verb' is always consistent with the definitions formulated above.

V–N polycategoriality can be broadly defined as the use of identical forms with related meanings both as verbal stems and as nominal stems, as in (13) and (14).

(13) Mandinka (pers. doc.)
a. Kèê   **kúmà**-tá   à   ñíŋ-ò   kótò.
   man.D   speak-CPL.INTR   3SG   tooth-PL   under
   S   V   X
   'The man mumbled.' lit. 'The man spoke under his teeth.'

b. Kèê   yè   wǒo   **kúmá**   kílíŋ-ò   lè   sèyìŋkâŋ.
   man.D   CPL.TR   DEM   word   one-D   FOC   repeat
   S   pm   O   V
   'The man repeated the same words.'

(14) Mandinka (pers. doc.)
    a. *Músáa*   *năa-tà*   *ńtè*   *dóróŋ*   *nè*   *yé*   *jăŋ*.
        Moussa   come-CPL.INTR   1SG   only   FOC   for   here
        S   V   X   X
        'It is only for me that Moussa came here.'

    b. *Músáa*   *lá*   *nàâ*   *mâŋ*   *kúydá*   *ŋ́*   *ñè*.
        Moussa   GEN   coming.D   CPL.NEG   be.unpleasant   1SG   for
        S   pm   V   X
        'Moussa's coming does not bother me.'

This phenomenon is widespread across Mande languages, and is particularly prominent within three particular subgroups of Western Mande languages, viz. Central Mande, Soso-Jalonke, and Southwestern Mande.[9]

The first question that should be clarified is how general V–N polycategoriality is in the lexicon of Mande languages. The second question is whether it involves semantic regularities making it possible to analyse it in terms of general conversion rules, either from V to N or from N to V.

In the literature, the question of the recognition of 'parts of speech' in Mande languages has been much discussed, especially with reference to the languages of the Manding group, due to the imbalance between the documentation available on Manding languages and on the Mande languages belonging to other groups. Recall that Manding languages are among those in which V–N polycategoriality is particularly prominent, to the point that a superficial observation of the categorial flexibility of lexemes in Manding languages may suggest the absence of any distinction between nouns and verbs at lexical level, as was argued by Tomčina (1978) for Guinean Maninka.

Vydrine 1999 provides an overview of the positions taken by different authors on this matter.

The views expressed by Maurice Houis in several publications (see among others Houis 1981) have been particularly influential. Houis rightly observed that, in the description of many sub-Saharan languages (including Manding and other Mande languages), approaches that do not posit lexical categories as logically secondary in relation to the notions of noun phrase and verbal predicate are problematic because of the categorial flexibility of many lexemes. Expressed in terms less idiosyncratic than the ones Houis used, the idea was that verbal clauses should be defined as constructions with a given structure, and noun phrases should be defined with reference to their internal structure and contribution to the construction of the clause, without presupposing the existence of classes of lexemes specialized in the role of nuclei of either clauses or NPs. Houis further elaborated a theory according to which sub-Saharan languages have two major lexical categories he designated as 'nominal lexemes' and 'verbo-nominal lexemes'. According to Houis's definitions:

– 'nominal' lexemes in their underived form can be used as nuclei of NPs, but not of verbal clauses;

---

[9] Idiatov (2018) puts forward a historical explanation for the fact that the Mande languages characterized by a particular prominence of V–N polycategoriality are also those in which P-lability is particularly prominent.

- 'verbo-nominal' lexemes can be used in both functions without necessitating the intervention of derivational morphology.

For example, according to Houis's definitions, *kúmà* in example (13) and *nǎa* in example (14) are equally verbo-nominal lexemes.

The position I defended in an article devoted to the verb vs noun distinction in Mandinka (Creissels 2017), similar to that defended for Bambara by Dumestre (2003), is that the dichotomy proposed by Houis results in an oversimplified view of the categorial flexibility of Mandinka lexemes, because it leads to grouping together lexemes that are equally productive in the function of verbal predicate but greatly differ in the way they can be used as nuclei of NPs, both formally and semantically. In Creissels (2017), I argued that three major classes of lexemes must be distinguished in Mandinka, 'verbal', 'verbo-nominal', and 'nominal', and I proposed to define the contrast between verbal and verbo-nominal lexemes as follows:

- a verbal lexeme can be used in its non-derived form as the verbal nucleus of predicative constructions, and its only possible meaning as the nucleus of noun phrases is that of action nominalization; this is the case of *nǎa* 'come' illustrated in example (14);
- a verbo-nominal lexeme, in addition to its use as the verbal nucleus of predicative constructions, can be used as the head of noun phrases with meanings that, although semantically related to the meaning it conveys in its verbal use, are not limited to action nominalization; this is the case of *kúmà* 'speak / word' illustrated in example (13), and also for example of *kèlé* 'fight / war', *búsà* 'hit / whip'.

25.3.2 The flexibility of the noun vs verb distinction in Mande languages

An accurate assessment of the flexibility of the noun vs verb distinction in Mande languages must take into account the distinction between the various possible types of semantic relationships between the verbal and nominal uses of the stems that lend themselves to both types of uses without any change in their form.

A first important observation is that no documented Mande language allows prototypical nominal lexemes (i.e. lexemes referring to concrete entities) to act as nuclei of intransitive verbal predication with the meaning of 'be/become an X'. In other words, the flexibility of the noun vs verb distinction in Mande languages is very different from omnipredicativity as defined by Launey (1994).

A second important observation is that many Mande languages have a general conversion rule according to which any stem that can be used as the nucleus of the verbal predication construction can also be used nominally, without any change in its form, as an action nominalization (i.e. the pure reification of the action denoted by the verb). This is in particular the situation found in Mandinka, as illustrated by example (14).[10]

---

[10] Cross-linguistically, morphologically unmarked action nominalization may be limited to some specific constructions, or involve restrictions in the combination of the verb used nominally with nominal modifiers, which may affect its 'visibility'. In this respect, Mandinka is among the languages in which morphologically unmarked action nominalization is particularly visible.

By contrast, for the other possible semantic types of nominal uses of stems also used verbally (event, result, instrument, manner of action, etc.), no similar generalization can be made in any of the Mande languages for which the relevant information is available, and the ability to be used nominally and verbally with related meanings must be considered as a lexical property of individual lexemes, which may be relatively widespread but is nevertheless not predictable.

For example, in Mandinka, *búsà* is used as a noun with the meaning 'whip', and as a transitive verb with the meaning 'hit'. However, in contrast to the type of N–V polycategoriality illustrated by *nǎa* 'come / coming', there is no general rule allowing nouns typically used as instruments to be used as verbs with the meaning 'do what one typically does with the help of X', and there is no general rule allowing verbs referring to actions typically performed with an instrument to be used as nouns with an instrumental meaning either. In Mandinka, instrument nominalization is regularly marked by the suffix *ráŋ* (as in *sìi-ráŋ* 'seat' < *sǐi* 'sit'), and the possibility of using *búsà* nominally with the meaning 'whip' and verbally with the meaning 'hit' must be viewed as an unpredictable lexical property of this individual lexeme.

Similarly, in Dan, unmarked action nominalizations can be produced for all verbs, but according to Vydrin (2017), only 7% of the verbs have formally identical nouns of other semantic types.

However, some very limited generalizations may be possible about stems that lend themselves to nominal and verbal uses without any formal marking and cannot be characterized as action nominalizations in their nominal use. For example, in Manding languages, nouns referring to things typically offered as gifts can also be used as transitive verbs with the meaning 'offer s.o. X as a gift', as in (15).

(15) Mandinka (pers. doc.)
    a. *Músáa   yè   kùdée   nàatí   ŋ̀   ñé.*
       Moussa CPL.TR meat.portion.D bring 1PL for
       S   pm   O   V   X
       'Moussa brought a portion of meat for us.'

    b. *Músáa   yè   ŋ̀   kùdêe.*
       Moussa CPL.TR 1PL give.a.meat.portion
       S   pm   O   V
       'Moussa gave us a portion of meat.'

25.3.3 Unmarked action nominalization in Mande languages

It is difficult to evaluate the cross-linguistic variation in the proportion of the lexicon showing the type of N–V polycategoriality illustrated above by Mandinka *búsà* 'hit / whip'. It seems to be present, at least sporadically, in all Mande languages, but it is never fully productive. By contrast, at least for the languages for which relatively precise descriptions are available, it is possible to establish a distinction between Mande languages in which no type of relationship between nominal and verbal meanings gives rise to systematic N–V polycategoriality (and in which suffixation is the regular way of forming action nominalizations), and others in which a general conversion rule allows verbs to be used as action nominalizations without any change in their form.

Soninke illustrates the first type of situation, which is basically similar to that observed in French or English. There is in Soninke (as in French or in English) a non-negligible proportion of event nouns with the same form as the corresponding verb (for example *sónqò* 'dispute (N & V)' or *téxù* 'cough (N & V)'), but the only productive way of forming action nominalizations is the addition of a derivational suffix to verb stems (as *dàgá* 'go, leave' > *dàgá-yè* 'going, departure').

Suffixation as the regular way of forming action nominalizations is also found in Wan (Nikitina 2009b).

By contrast, Soso (Touré 1994) and Jalonke (Lüpke 2005: 129–130) are uncontroversial cases of languages in which morphologically unmarked action nominalization is the rule.

Example (16) illustrates morphologically unmarked action nominalization in Jalonke. In this example, *dɔ̌ɔ* 'pull out' does not undergo any derivational operation, but the fact that it combines with the definite article *-na* and that the phrase it projects (*láŋgée kwĭi dɔ̌ɔná*) is the complement of the postposition *yí* provides clear evidence of nominalization.

(16) Jalonke (Lüpke 2005)
 Ɲ̀ bìrà láŋgée kwĭi dɔ̌ɔn'ɛ́ɛ.
 ɲ̀ bìrá láŋgé-ná kwĭi dɔ̌ɔ-ná yí
 1SG fall garden-D in pull.out-D POSTP
 'I started weeding in the garden.'
 lit. 'I fell in the pull(ing) out in the garden.'

25.3.4 Marked vs unmarked action nominalization in Manding

As regards the possibility of unmarked action nominalization, Manding languages present some complications that are interesting to examine, since they suggest a possible origin of action nominalization markers that has not been discussed so far in the general grammaticalization literature.

As already mentioned, Mandinka is basically a language in which all verbs lend themselves to unmarked action nominalization. However, with transitive verbs (and only with transitive verbs!), a suffix *-ri* (with phonologically conditioned allomorphs *-li* and *-diri*) is required IF AND ONLY IF THE PATIENTIVE ARGUMENT OF THE TRANSITIVE VERB IS NOT MENTIONED IN THE CONSTRUCTION. This suffix is not a typical antipassive marker, since with just one exception (*dómó-rì* < *dómò* 'eat'),[11] the *ri*-form of Mandinka verbs can be used as the nucleus of noun phrases, but not of intransitive clauses. However, the suffix *-ri* is involved not only in the nominal use of verbal lexemes, but also in a number of derivational processes operating on verbs in which it regulates semantic role assignment, and in all cases, the way it does this job fully meets the definition of antipassivization.[12]

---

[11] A possible historical explanation of this anomaly, suggested by Grégoire's (1990) etymological analysis of the Manding verbs for 'eat', is that *dómò* might be a back-formation from a verb root (originally a compound) whose direct reflex would be *dómórì*.

[12] As discussed in (Creissels forth.), the hypothesis that *ri*-forms were originally verbal forms that have only subsisted in their use as event nouns is supported by the fact that Soninke has a perfectly canonical antipassive marker *ndí ~ -ndì* which constitutes a plausible cognate of *-ri*.

As illustrated by examples (17) and (18), the suffix -*ri* does not occur if the P argument is expressed as a modifier of the nominalized verb, forms a compound with it, or can be identified with the referent of a noun phrase included in the same construction:

- In (17a), the role that *sòosôo* 'contradict' assigns to its object in the transitive construction is assigned to the genitival modifier of *sòosôo* used nominally, and the agentive argument of *sòosôo* is interpreted as non-specific.
- In (17b), *Músáa* cannot be identified with the agentive argument of *sòosôo*, since this would leave the role of patientive argument of *sòosôo* unassigned, hence the passive interpretation.
- In (17c), the presence of -*ri* blocks the assignment of the semantic role of patientive argument of *sòosôo*, and *Músáa* can be identified to the agentive argument of *sòosôo*.

(17) Mandinka (pers. doc.)
    a. *Kèebâa-lú   sòosôo   mâŋ   díyâa   Músáa yè.*
       elder.D-PL   contradict.D CPL.NEG be.pleasant Moussa for
       'Moussa doesn't like to contradict elders.'
       lit. 'Contradicting elders is not pleasant for Moussa

    b. *Sòosôo   mâŋ   díyâa   Músáa yè.*
      contradict.D CPL.NEG be.pleasant Moussa for
      'Moussa doesn't like to be contradicted.'
      lit. 'Contradicting is not pleasant for Moussa.'

    c. *Sòosòo-rôo   mâŋ   díyâa   Músáa yè.*
      contradict-ANTIP.D CPL.NEG be.pleasant Moussa for
      'Moussa doesn't like to contradict.'
      lit. 'Contradicting.ANTIP is not pleasant for Moussa.'

- In (18a), *màaní* 'rice' saturates the P valency of *tǔu* 'pound', and consequently the subject of the copula can only be identified with the unexpressed A argument.
- In (18b), none of the arguments of *tǔu* 'pound' is expressed within the phrase projected by *tǔu*, and in the absence of -*ri*, the subject of the copula is identified with the unexpressed P argument.
- In (18c), none of the arguments of *tǔu* 'pound' is expressed within the phrase projected by *tǔu*, but -*ri* saturates the P valency of *tǔu* 'pound', so that the subject of the copula is identified to the unexpressed A argument. Note that *mùsôo bé tùwôo lá* could only be interpreted as 'the woman is being pounded'.

(18) Mandinka (pers. doc.)
    a. *Mùsôo   bé   màanì-túwòo   lá.*
      woman.D LCOP rice-pound.D POSTP
      'The woman is pounding rice.'
      lit. 'The woman is at the rice-pounding.'

    b. *Màanôo   bé   tùwôo   lá.*
      rice.D LCOP pound.D POSTP
      'The rice is being pounded.'
      lit. 'he rice is at the pounding.'

c. *Mùsôo   bé   tùu-rôo   lá.*
   woman.D   LCOP   pound-ANTIP.D   POSTP
   'The woman is pounding.'
   lit. 'The woman is at the pounding.ANTIP.'

To summarize, when a transitive verb is used nominally, in the absence of *-ri*, the semantic role assigned by the verb to its object in the transitive construction has priority over that of the subject of the transitive construction. By contrast, in the presence of *-ri*, the only semantic role available is that of the subject of the transitive construction, and the patientive argument of the transitive verb must be interpreted as non-specific.

The suffix *-ri* is involved, in exactly the same conditions and with exactly the same consequences on semantic role assignment, in several types of morphological operations (for example, the derivation of agent or instrument nouns, as for example in *màanì-tùu-láa* 'person who pounds rice' vs *tùu-rì-láa* 'person who pounds', where *-láa* is the suffix used to derive agent nouns from verbs, or in *màanì-tùu-ráŋ* 'rice-pestle' vs *tùu-rì-láŋ* 'pestle', where *ráŋ ~ láŋ* is the suffix used to derive nouns of instruments from verbs—for a detailed discussion, see Creissels & Sambou 2013: 63–65, 119–120). When followed by other suffixes, *-ri* cannot be analysed as marking nominalization, since the suffixes that follow it select verbal stems. When *-ri* is not followed by another suffix, it is true that its presence implies nominalization. Nevertheless, rather than a true nominalization marker, *-ri* must rather be analysed as regulating semantic role assignment for verbs used as action nominalizations, since all verbs have the ability to be used as action nominalizations without any morphological marking.

A suffix *-li* cognate with Mandinka *-ri* and also involved in action nominalization can be found in Bambara, but the details of its distribution are very different. Crucially, in the conditions that trigger the use of *-ri* in Mandinka, *-li* is obligatory in Bambara too, but *-li* is also widely used in conditions in which the use of *-ri* in Mandinka would be rejected by speakers as incorrect (Dumestre 2003: 74–75). In other words, the distribution of *-li* is not strictly bound to the conditions on valency and semantic role expression described above for Mandinka.

A first crucial observation is that, contrary to Mandinka *-ri*, Bambara *-li* can attach to intransitive verbs used nominally. Forms like *sìgì-lí* < *sìgí* 'settle' or *nà-lí* < *nǎ* 'come' are perfectly correct (and usual) in Bambara, whereas in Mandinka, intransitive verbs like *sìi* 'settle' or *nǎa* 'come' simply cannot combine with the suffix *-ri*.

The second crucial observation is that, in Bambara, contrary to Mandinka, *-li* does not block the expression of the patientive argument of transitive verbs. In the nominalization of transitive verbs, Bambara and Mandinka make the same distinction between direct genitives (simply juxtaposed to their head) referring to the patientive argument of the transitive verb, and indirect genitives (marked by *ká* (Bambara) or *lá* (Mandinka)) referring to the agentive argument. However, in Mandinka, this distinction strictly correlates with the absence vs presence of the *-ri* suffix, whereas there is no such correlation in Bambara, as illustrated by examples (19) and (20).

(19) Bambara (pers. doc.)
   a. *jàrá   fàgà-lí*
      lion.D   kill-LI.D
      'the fact that the lion was killed'

b. *járâ ká fàgà-lî*
   lion.D GEN kill-LI.D
   'the fact that the lion killed (someone)'

(20) Mandinka (pers. doc.)
   a. *jàtóo fàâ*
      lion.D kill.D
      'the fact that the lion was killed'

   b. **jàtóo fàa-rôo*
      lion.D kill-RI.D

   c. *jàtôo lá fàa-rôo*
      lion.D GEN kill-RI.D
      'the fact that the lion killed (someone)'

Consequently, contrary to Mandinka *-ri*, there would be no justification for analysing Bambara *-li* as an atypical kind of antipassive marker. Bambara *-li* can only be analysed as an action nominalization marker whose use is obligatory in the conditions in which Mandinka speakers use the antipassive marker *-ri*, and optional in the conditions in which the use of *-ri* would be incorrect in Mandinka.

Moreover, as observed by Dumestre (2003: 75), the extensive use of *-li* is not typical of traditional texts, in which the use of *-li* tends to be restricted to the contexts in which *-ri* is used in Mandinka, whereas the tendency to generalize the use of *-li* is particularly strong in educational material produced by various non-governmental organizations or in the context of official literacy programmes, that is, in the kind of written texts in which calques from French abound. This suggests that Bambara *-li* had formerly the same distribution as Mandinka *-ri*, but the conditions that limited its use have been relaxed, resulting in the reanalysis of an atypical antipassive marker as a plain action nominalization marker.

25.4 SUBCLASSES OF VERBS

In Mande languages, verbs can be divided into valency classes (see among others Lüpke (2005) on Jalonke, and Creissels (2015) on Mandinka), but regardless of the possible complexity of the classification of verbs according to their valency properties, most Mande languages have a single inflectional class of verbs, in the sense that all verbs combine with the same set of predicative markers and TAM suffixes, the only possible complication being that some TAM-polarity values may be expressed differently in transitive and intransitive clauses. However, a more complex situation is found in most of the languages belonging to the Central sub-branch of the West Mande branch, including Manding languages (Mandinka being an exception), and in Soninke. In the languages in question, the lexemes identifiable as verbs in the sense that they can be analysed as occupying the V slot in the S O V X* pattern divide into two classes associated to two distinct sets of predicative markers

(Creissels 1985, 2018b; Dumestre 2003: 169–178; Vydrine 1990, 1999). In such situations, one of the two inflectional classes of verbs has the following characteristics:

- it includes a relatively limited number of lexemes (about few tens);
- all the verbs belonging to this class are intransitive;
- the verbs belonging to this class have no suffixal inflection, and are compatible with a single pair of predicative markers, one positive and the other negative.

An important property of such verbs is that they cannot express the aspectual and modal distinctions that the other verbs express via suffixal inflection and/or combination with a variety of predicative markers. They can only refer to states, hence the label 'stative verbs' I proposed in my 1985 article.[13] In the languages that have a class of stative verbs, the verbs combining with a set of predicative markers and/or suffixes expressing aspectual distinctions can conveniently be termed 'dynamic verbs'.

In the languages in which an inflectional class of stative verbs can be recognized, it typically includes verbs with meanings commonly considered as typically adjectival, such as 'be big', 'be small', 'be young', 'be old', 'be short', 'be long', 'be hot', 'be cold', 'be easy', 'be difficult'.

Note that, in the Mande languages that do not have an inflectional class of stative verbs (and also in the languages that have a class of stative verbs, for the meanings that are not lexified as stative verbs), states are commonly expressed by means of the completive form of dynamic verbs. Reference to states by means of a completive form of change-of-state verbs also interpretable with a dynamic meaning is a very common strategy throughout sub-Saharan Africa, and Mande languages are no exception. For example, in Bambara (a language with an inflectional class of stative verbs), 'be far, distant' is expressed by the stative verb *jǎn*, and 'move away' by the dynamic verb *jànfá*, but in Mandinka (a language with a single inflectional class of verbs), 'is far' is expressed by a form of the verb *jàmfá* 'move away' also interpretable as 'has moved away', depending on the context.

(21) Bambara (pers. doc.)
    a. *Yàn   ní   Bàmàkɔ́   ká   jàn.*
       here   and   Bamako   ST   be.distant
       'Bamako is far from here.'

    b. *Móbílí   jànfà-rá   dùgû   lá.*
       car.D   move.away-CPL.INTR   village.D   POSTP
       'The car moved away from the village.'

(22) Mandinka (pers. doc.)
    a. *ŋ́   ná   sàatêe   jàmfá-tà.*
       1PL   GEN   village.D   move.away-CPL.INTR
       'Our village is far (from here).'

---

[13] Terms such as 'predicative adjectives' or 'qualifying verbs' are also found in the literature as labels for this particular class of verbs.

b. *Wòtóo   jàmfá-tá   sàatêe   lá.*
   car.D   move.away-CPL.INTR   village.D   POSTP
   'The car moved away from the village.'

25.5 Subclasses of nouns

25.5.1 Locative nouns

A very common phenomenon in the languages of sub-Saharan Africa, also found in Mande languages, is that proper names of places can be used in oblique syntactic role with the semantic role of ground in a spatial relationship without necessitating the flagging otherwise required for obliques in the semantic role of ground, and this property may be shared by a limited number of common nouns among those typically used in the semantic role of ground, as illustrated in (23).

(23) Mandinka (pers. doc.)
   a. *Músáa   táa-tà   kúnkòo   tó.*
      Moussa   go-CPL.INTR   field.D   LOC
      'Moussa went to the field.'

   b. *Músáa   táa-tá   Sěejò.*
      Moussa   go-CPL.INTR   Sédhiou
      'Moussa went to Sédhiou.'

   c. *Músáa   táa-tà   súu.*
      Moussa   go-CPL.INTR   house
      'Moussa went home.'

In Mandinka, the behaviour of *súu* 'house' in (23c) is quite exceptional among common nouns,[14] and can be accounted for as an isolated and unpredictable case of N > Adv conversion, especially as the use of *súu* illustrated in (23c) is only possible in the absence of any modifier. In some other Mande languages, such as Gban (Fedotov 2017: 914), the ability of being used without any flagging as obliques fulfilling the semantic role of ground extends to a large set of nouns for which the semantic role of ground in spatial relationships can be viewed prototypical, hence the proposal of distinguishing a subclass of locative nouns in such languages. Note that, in the languages that have a large class of locative nouns, many of them result from the fusion of a regular noun with a postposition.

---

[14] Among the common nouns that do not inherently refer to spatial relationships, *súu* 'house', *wúlà* 'bush' and *túŋáa* 'foreign countries' are the only uncontroversial cases I am aware of. The other cases I came across in texts or in elicitation sessions (for example *lòpìtáanì* '(at the) hospital') are not accepted by all speakers.

25.5.2 Free vs relative nouns

As mentioned in section 25.2.3, many Mande languages have two possible constructions for adnominal possessors distinguished either by flagging vs lack of flagging of adnominal possessors, or by the presence vs absence of a possessive pronoun preceding the possessee, depending on the semantic nature of their relationship with their head (as in Mandinka *Músáa díŋòlú* 'Moussa's children' vs *Músáa lá nìnsôolú* 'Moussa's cows').

In descriptions of Mande languages that have a contrast between two variants of the adnominal possession construction, this contrast is commonly analysed as the manifestation of a division of nouns into two subclasses reflecting their degree of semantic autonomy. According to this analysis, 'free' nouns (sometimes called 'autosemantic') denote entities that are conceived independently of any possessor, and combine with flagged adnominal possessors (or are obligatorily preceded by a possessive pronoun on which the possessor is indexed), whereas 'relative' nouns have a valency for a possessor, and combine with unflagged adnominal possessors (or do not require the presence of a possessive pronoun, the adnominal possessor being directly indexed on its head).

I am not in a position to say whether there are really Mande languages for which this analysis of the contrast between two variants of the adnominal possession construction is correct, since discussing this point would require much more data than those provided by the available descriptions. I am sure, however, that at least for Mandinka and the other languages of the Central Mande group on which I have detailed first-hand data, the analysis of the two variants of the adnominal possession construction as straightforwardly conditioned by a division of nouns into two subclasses of 'free/autosemantic' and 'relative' nouns does not stand up to scrutiny. In Central Mande languages, nouns that can combine with unflagged adnominal possessors only, or with flagged possessors only, are the exception rather than the rule, and whether the possessor is flagged or not depends both on the semantics of the possessed noun and on that of the possessor. To take just a few examples among many others, in Mandinka:

- a semantically 'relative' noun such as *pérésídáŋ* 'president' combines with an unflagged adnominal possessor in *Sènèkáalì pérésídáŋò* lit. 'the president of Senegal', but with a flagged adnominal possessor in *Sènèkàaliŋkôolú là pérésídáŋò* lit. 'the president of the Senegalese people';
- with a semantically 'relative' noun such as *díŋkée* 'son', the presence of a demonstrative determiner triggers the use of a flagged adnominal possessor, as in *Músáa díŋkèe* 'Moussa's son' vs *Músáa lá ñìŋ díŋkèe* 'this son of Moussa's';
- a semantically 'free' noun such as *kódì* 'money' takes a flagged adnominal possessor in *Músáa là kódòo* 'Moussa's money', but an unflagged adnominal possessor in *wòtôo kódòo* 'the money of the car', whatever the semantic relationship between 'car' and 'money' (the money necessary to buy the car, or to take the car, or the money from the sale of the car, etc.). Similarly, *nìnsí* 'cow' takes a flagged adnominal possessor in *Músáa lá nìnsôolú* 'Moussa's cows', but an unflagged adnominal possessor in *ñìŋ sàatée nìnsôolú* 'the cows of this village'.

The contrast between flagged and unflagged adnominal possessors in Mandinka and other Central Mande languages has clear semantic correlates that are very interesting to investigate, but it is impossible to achieve an adequate description by trying to reduce it to the manifestation of a division of nouns into two subclasses on the basis of their ability to combine with flagged or unflagged adnominal possessors. For a detailed description of the choice between flagged and unflagged adnominal possessors in a Central Mande language, see Creissels & Sambou (2013: 241–252) on Mandinka.

25.6 Adjectives

In Mande languages, common nouns and verbs are the only word classes that can be defined with reference to their ability to act as the nucleus of a given type of construction. However, a possible starting point for defining a word-class 'adjective' in Mande languages is the recognition of a construction that can be designated as the attributive construction.

The internal structure of noun phrases in Mande languages (see section 25.2.3) makes it possible to define the attributive construction as a *noun–modifier* construction in which the noun and its modifier are obligatorily adjacent to each other (i.e. cannot be separated by the insertion of an additional modifier). It may even happen that attributive modifiers form morphological compounds with their head. In Soninke, this concerns all subtypes of attributive modifiers, whereas in Manding languages, the fact that attributive modifiers form compounds with their head or not depends on their morphological structure (see for example Creissels & Sambou 2013: 230–237).

Adjectives can be defined as words acting as modifiers in the attributive construction. However, the words meeting this definition are very heterogeneous with respect to their possible formal relationships with semantically related nouns and/or verbs.

As a rule, Mande languages have relatively few 'primary' adjectives in the sense of words that meet the definition of adjectives formulated above, do not have the same form as a semantically related noun or verb, and are not derived from a noun or a verb either. For example, according to Creissels & Sambou (2013: 230–231), Mandinka has about 30 primary adjectives, and the number of primary adjectives is considerably lower in the other Manding languages, in which many of the words corresponding to the primary adjectives of Mandinka belong the class of stative verbs.

In Mande languages, the words for 'man' and 'woman' are typically found among the nouns that also have uses in which they meet the definition of 'adjective', with the meanings 'male' and 'female', respectively. The case of verbs also used as adjectives without any formal modification is illustrated in (24) by Mandinka *kóyì* 'be/become white'.

(24) Mandinka (pers. doc.)
    a. Ñìŋ   nìnsí   fùlôo   kóyì-tá   lè.
       DEM   cow   two.D   be/become.white-CPL.INTR   FOC
       'These two cows are white.' (*kóyì* as a verb)

    b. ŋ́   ŋá   nìnsì-kóyí   fùlá   săŋ.
       1SG   CPL.TR   cow-white   move.away.CPL.INTR   FOC
       'I bought two white cows.' (*kóyì* as an adjective)

However, there is no possibility of predicting which nouns or verbs lend themselves to an adjectival use without any formal modification, and which ones can only give rise to adjectives via morphological derivation.

Example (25) illustrates the possibility of V–Adj polycategoriality for ordinals derived from numerals: in Mandinka, ordinals (formed via the addition of the suffix *ñjáŋ* to numerals) can be used not only as adjectives, but also as intransitive verbs with the meaning 'occur for the nth time' and as transitive verbs with the meaning 'do something for the nth time'.

(25) Mandinka (pers. doc.)
    a. *ŋ   dímmúsú-sábá-ñján-ò   fútùu-tá   lè.*
       1SG daughter-three-ORD-D get.married-CPL.INTR FOC
       'My third daughter got married.' (*sàbà-ñjáŋ* as an adjective)

    b. *Níŋ ñǐŋ sàbà-ñjâŋ-tá,   ŋ   bé   í   báyì-lá   lè.*
       if   DEM three-ORD-CPL.INTR 1SG LCOP 2SG chase-INF FOC
       'If this happens a third time, I will chase you.' (*sàbà-ñjáŋ* as an intransitive verb)

    c. *Í   kánáa ñǐŋ   sàbà-ñjâŋ!*
       2SG PROH   DEM three-ORD
       'Don't do this a third time!' (*sàbà-ñjáŋ* as a transitive verb)

In Mande languages, adjectives do not have forms fully similar to the comparative and superlative forms found in many European languages, but they may have a 'selective' form whose meaning is that, among the potential referents of their head that are present in a given situation, the NP in which the adjective is included refers either to the only one that has the quality expressed by the adjective, or to the one that outranks the others with respect to the quality in question (see for example Creissels & Sambou 2013: 235–236 on the selective form of Mandinka adjectives).

25.7 Adverbs

Three particularities of Mande adverbs are worth mentioning here.

First, Mande languages have words that can be labelled adverbs according to the criteria commonly used to classify words as adverbs, but as a rule, the derivation of adverbs from other categories is very limited, or totally inexistent.

Second, the Mande equivalents of many words whose classification as adverbs in other languages is uncontroversial have a syntactic behaviour which might suggest classifying them rather as a subtype of nominals, alongside pronouns and proper names. For example, at least in Manding languages, the equivalent of 'today' is quite commonly found in sentences such as those quoted in (26) and (27), in which it fulfils the role of subject of transitive clauses.

(26) Mandinka (pers. doc.)
Bĭi mâŋ dúníyáa dáa, bĭi fánáŋ té dúníyáa bǎn-nà.
today CPL.NEG world create today also COP.NEG world finish-INF
lit. 'Today did not create the world, today will not finish the world either.'
> 'The world was not created today, it will not finish today either.'

(27) Bambara (pers. doc.)
Bì má Sékù nà.
today CPL.NEG Sékou come
lit. 'Today did not make Sékou come.' > 'Sékou arrived long ago.'

Third, as usual in sub-Saharan languages, Mande languages have large inventories of ideophonic adverbs whose most obvious syntactic characteristic is that each of them combines with a very limited set of verbs or adjectives (often just one).

25.8 ADPOSITIONS

In comparison with most other language families of sub-Saharan Africa, Mande languages have relatively rich inventories of adpositions, mainly postpositions. Postpositions are preceded by their complement NP in the same way as nouns by adnominal possessors. What distinguishes them is that nouns as nuclei of noun phrases are compatible with a variety of modifiers, whereas postpositional phrases cannot include additional elements.

Grammaticalization of body part names is a particularly common source of postpositions in Mande languages ('back' > 'behind', 'eye' > 'before', 'belly' > 'in', etc.), and N–Postp polycategoriality is common, as for example Mandinka *búlù* 'hand/in the sphere of'.

(28) Mandinka (pers. doc.)
  a. *Á   búlú-kénśeŋ-ò   lè   nǎa-tà.*
     2SG hand-empty-D   FOC   come-CPL.INTR
     'He came empty-handed.' (*búlù* as a noun)

  b. *Kódì   té   ń   búlù.*
     money COP.NEG   1SG in.the.sphere.of
     'I don't have money.' lit. 'Money is not in my sphere.' (*búlù* as a postposition)

In the Southern Mande languages that have a category of locative nouns (see section 25.5.1), many postpositions can be analysed as relational locative nouns, but at the same time, the languages of question always have at least one or two 'true' postpositions that do not lend themselves to such an analysis, most commonly those translatable as 'with' or 'for / as' (Dmitry Idiatov, pers.com.).

25.9 COPULAS

Some Mande languages (for example, Soso and Jalonke) make a productive use of non-verbal predicative constructions involving mere juxtaposition of noun phrases and postpositional phrases, but this is not very common. Most Mande languages have an equative copula and a locational copula with suppletive negative forms, and very often, the equative copula and the locational copula share the same negative counterpart.

Syntactically, the copulas found in Mande languages can be viewed as defective/irregular verbs, since as illustrated in (29), they combine with an unflagged NP and a postpositional phrase into a construction that can be viewed as an instance of the S V X pattern, without, however, being able to combine with the predicative markers and/or TAM suffixes normally found in intransitive verbal predication.

(29) Soninke (pers. doc.)
   a. *Dénbà wá kónpè-n dí.*
      Demba LCOP room-D in
      'Demba is in the room.'

   b. *Dénbà ntá kónpè-n dí.*
      Demba LCOP.NEG room-D in
      'Demba is not in the room.'

   c. *Dénbà ní sòxáanà-n ñà yí*
      Demba ECOP farmer-D FOC POSTP
      'Demba is a farmer.'

   d. *Dénbà hètí sòxáanà yí*
      Demba ECOP.NEG farmer POSTP
      'Demba is not a farmer.'

In Mande syntax, copulas have a special relationship with intransitive verbs acting as copulative verbs, in the sense that copulative verbs substitute copulas to express TAM values that cannot be expressed in clauses whose nucleus is a copula, due to their incompatibility with predicative markers and TAM suffixes. For example, in Mandinka, the locational copula *bé* can be substituted by *tàrá* '(tr.) find, (intr.) be found', and the equative copula *mú* can be substituted by *ké* '(tr.) do, transform, (intr.) occur, become'. In examples (30b) and (30d), what motivates the replacement of a non-verbal copula by a copulative verb is the expression of habitual aspect, usually encoded in Mandinka by means of the incompletive predicative marker *kà*.

(30) Mandinka (pers. doc.)
   a. *Fàatú bé fàrôo to.*
      Fatou LCOP rice.field.D LOC
      'Fatou is at the rice field.'

   b. *Fàatú ká tàrá fàrôo to.*
      Fatou ICPL be rice.field.D LOC
      'Fatou is at the rice field all the time.'

   c. *Ñiŋ mòô-lú mú Sùrùwâa-lú lè tí.*
      DEM person.D-PL ECOP Wolof.D-PL FOC POSTP
      'Those people are Wolof people.'

d. *Ñíŋ   mòô-lú   kà   ké Sùrùwâa-lú   lè   tí.*
   DEM   person.D-PL   ICPL   be Wolof.D-PL   FOC   POSTP
   'In general, those people are Wolof people.'

25.10 THE QUOTATIVE

In Manding languages, reported discourse is introduced by a word *kó*, distinct from the transitive verb *fɔ́* 'say', and a similar situation is found in the other Mande languages. This word, whose use is illustrated in (31), is designated here as the quotative. It has no negative counterpart and cannot combine with negative markers either.

(31) Mandinka (pers. doc.)
   Kèê   kó   díndíŋ-ò   yé: 'Táa   í   báamáa   yǎa!'
   man.D   QUOT   child-D   to   go   2SG   mother   home
   'The man said to the child: "Go to your mother's place!"'

Generally speaking, the status of quotatives in parts-of-speech systems is a complex issue. In Mande languages, a possible analysis is that the quotative belongs to the same class of defective/irregular verbs as the copulas, with, however, the additional property of requiring a complement representing the reported utterance (usually, but not necessarily, a sentence). The point is that the combination of the quotative with the NPs referring to the reporting speaker and the addressee can be viewed as an instance of the S V X pattern (S and X referring to the reporting speaker and the addressee, respectively), without, however, the predicative markers and/or TAM suffixes normally found in intransitive verbal predication.

For a more detailed discussion of quotatives, see Idiatov (2010, 2011).

25.11 PREDICATIVE MARKERS

Predicative markers (see section 25.2.2) are a class of grammatical words (or clitics) that play a central role in the syntax of the clause in most Mande languages. Their characteristic properties are their fixed position immediately after the subject NP and their interaction with the TAM suffixes of verbs. As a rule, the mere deletion of predicative markers either results in ungrammaticality, or changes the TAM-polarity value of the clause.

A very common polycategoriality pattern in Mande languages is the use of the same words as locational copulas in non-verbal predication and as predicative markers expressing the aspectual value 'incompletive' in verbal predication.

(32) Soninke (pers. doc.)
   a. *Dénbà   wá   kónpè-n   dí.*
      Demba   LCOP   room-D   in
      'Demba is in the room.'

b. *Dénbà   wá   yìllê-n   típpí.*
   Demba   ICPL   millet-D   SOW.GER
   'Demba is sowing millet.'

As already mentioned in section 25.2.2, in Mande languages, the division of labor between predicative markers in immediate postverbal position and verbal inflectional suffixes varies from one language to another. Some languages (Soso for example) make little use of predicative markers and have a relatively developed suffixal inflexion of verbs, whereas in others, almost all the values that constitute the TAM paradigm require the use of predicative markers.

Predicative markers typically express TAM and polarity distinctions, but they may also be sensitive to information structure. For example, in Soninke, in intransitive clauses in the incompletive aspect, if one of the terms of the clause is focalized, the position of the predicative marker must be left empty.

(33)   Soninke (pers. doc.)
   a. *Dénbà   wá   sálli-ní.*
      Demba   ICPL   pray-GER
      'Demba is praying.'

   b. *Dénbà   Ø   sálli-ní   yà.*
      Demba   pray-GER   FOC
      'Demba is PRAYING.'

In Southwestern Mande languages and in most Southern and Eastern Mande languages, subject indexes attach to predicative markers, and sometimes fuse with them. In some of the languages in question, subjects are obligatorily indexed, even in the presence of a co-referent NP, and subject NPs are syntactically optional, as illustrated in (5) for Kpelle.

Finally, as mentioned in section 25.2.2.5, predicative markers may also be sensitive to transitivity. In some cases, the same TAM-polarity value is marked by distinct predicative markers in transitive and intransitive clauses. For example, in Soninke, the subjunctive positive is marked by the predicative marker *nàn* in intransitive clauses, *nà* in transitive clauses.

(34)   Soninke (pers. doc.)
   a. *Dénbà   wá   à   mùndá   án   **nàn**   dàgá.*
      Demba   ICPL   3SG   want   2SG   SBJV.INTR   go
      'Demba wants you to leave.'

   b. *Dénbà   wá   à   mùndá   án   **nà**   búurù-n   qóbó.*
      Demba   ICPL   3SG   want   2SG   SBJV.TR   bread-D   buy
      'Demba wants you to buy bread.'

It may also happen that a predicative marker used exclusively in transitive clauses is in complementary distribution with a verbal suffix expressing the same value in intransitive clauses, as in (35).

(35) Kita Maninka (pers. doc.)
   a. *Mùsû   dí   sùbú   sàn.*
      woman.D CPL.TR   meat.D   buy
      'The woman bought meat.'

   b. *Mùsû   wá-dá   súgù   dò.*
      woman.D go-CPL.INTR   market.D   LOC
      'The woman went to the market.'

Finally, it may happen that a given TAM-polarity value marked by a predicative marker in transitive clauses is not overtly marked in intransitive clauses, as in (36).

(36) Soninke (pers. doc.)
   a. *Dénbà   dà   máarò-n   qóbó.*
      Demba   CPL.TR   3rice-D   buy
      'Demba bought rice.'

   b. *Dénbà   Ø   múxú   tàgáyè-n   pàllé.*
      Demba   hide   wall-D   behind
      'Demba hid behind the wall.'

25.12 OTHERS

The following word classes are commonly distinguished in descriptions of Mande languages, in addition to those discussed in the previous sections:

- numerals
- determiners
- pronouns
- proper names
- conjunctions
- discourse particles
- interjections

However, they do not display special properties that would merit discussion here.[15]

25.13 CONCLUSION

In this chapter, I have discussed the most salient properties of the word-class systems of Mande languages. The main points are as follows:

---

[15] For a detailed presentation of the numeral systems of Mande languages, readers are referred to Perekhvalskaya & Vydrin (2019). Blecke (1996) provides a detailed discussion of the lexical categories of a Bozo language (Tigemaxo).

- In most Mande languages, morphological criteria are of little use for the delimitation of word classes; by contrast, the extreme rigidity of word order patterns greatly facilitates the delimitation of word classes on the basis of distributional criteria.
- As a rule, lexical polycategoriality, although very common in Mande languages, can only be dealt with as an unpredictable property of individual lexemes, with, however, an important exception: in many Mande languages, morphologically unmarked action nominalization is a general property of verbs.
- In comparison with the word-class systems commonly found in the world's languages, the main specificity of Mande languages is the central role played in verbal predicative constructions by a special class of grammatical words designated as 'predicative markers' in descriptions of Mande languages.

CHAPTER 26

WORD CLASSES IN AUSTRALIAN LANGUAGES

DANA LOUAGIE

26.1 INTRODUCTION

At the time of European settlement in the 18th century, approximately 250 distinct indigenous languages or 700 to 800 language varieties were spoken in Australia (Dixon 2002: 5–7; Koch & Nordlinger 2014). Today, only 12 traditional languages are still being learned by children (Commonwealth of Australia 2020) and another 100 or so are being spoken by the elderly generation (Koch & Nordlinger 2014: 4). Documentation of these languages varies considerably, going from wordlists compiled in the early days of colonization to detailed grammatical descriptions and more extensive text collections. The degree of documentation is partly related to historical factors: languages from the south and south-east are for instance less well documented, as these areas were first affected by colonization (see Koch & Nordlinger 2014 for an overview).

Australian languages belong to roughly 25 language families. The largest family is Pama–Nyungan (PN), which includes roughly two-thirds of all Australian languages and covers about 90% of the continent (Bowern & Atkinson 2012: 817). Internally, there is no consensus on higher-level subgroups, but many lower-level groups are well supported; see Bowern & Atkinson (2012) for a recent account. The other 24 families and isolates, found in the north and north-east of the continent, are sometimes collectively labelled 'non-Pama–Nyungan' but are not related to each other (at least as far as evidence can tell us). These families are much smaller: the biggest is probably Gunwinyguan, with about a dozen languages, while there are also several isolates, like Tiwi and Limilngan. See Evans (2003b) for the most recent classification; note that Anindilyakwa has since been reclassified as Gunwinyguan (Van Egmond 2012). See Koch (2014) for a recent overview of issues related to genetic classification in Australian languages.

The typical part-of-speech system of Australian languages includes, according to Dixon's (2002: 66) survey of these languages, two major sets of word classes, viz. nominal and verbal ones, and a residue set of smaller classes. These sets of word classes include the following:

- Nominal classes: proper names, common nouns, adjectives, time words, locational words, demonstratives, pronouns.

- Verbal classes: simple verbs (in all languages), coverbs (in many languages), adverbals (in some languages).
- Other classes: particles, ideophones, interjections and (in some languages only) conjunctions.

(Dixon 2002: 66)

The sets are grouped together mostly based on morphological criteria: all nominal parts of speech have the same or similar case marking at least for peripheral roles, while verbal parts of speech take inflections for tense, aspect or mood; coverbs are usually uninflected, however (Dixon 2002: 67–71) (hence the alternative label 'uninflecting verbs' (UVs)). Particles and other classes do not inflect at all (Dixon 2002: 66). The word classes within each set are argued to be morphologically distinct from each other as well.

There are a few issues with Dixon's description. First, the morphological criteria discussed in the previous paragraph are not watertight, as a nominal word may occur with verbal affixes and vice versa (e.g. McGregor 2004: 102–103, on languages spoken in the Kimberley area). For instance, in Gooniyandi the word *yoowooloo* 'man' usually occurs with case markers, but may also occur with a verbal classifier as in *yoowooloo-windi* 'he became a man'; the word *ward-* 'go' usually occurs with verbal affixes but may also occur with a case marker (McGregor 2004: 102; see also McGregor 1990: 560–563). The morphological criteria do work with some refinement, however: nominal words occur with nominal morphology most of the time and can only take a small subset of verbal morphology, and the other way around (McGregor 2004: 102). This is further discussed in section 26.2.

Second, the list above includes separate word classes for nouns and adjectives, but at the same time, Dixon also argues that nouns and adjectives 'generally show the same morphological and syntactic possibilities, so that it can be difficult to give criteria for recognizing them as distinct classes' (2002: 67). In fact, much of the Australianist literature agrees with the latter position, and argues that Australian languages typically lack a clearly distinct word class of adjectives and instead have a single, flexible class of elements which can be used both referentially and attributively, usually labelled 'nominals'[1] (e.g. Hale 1983: 33–36; McGregor 2004: 102; Nordlinger 2014: 237–238). However, a more recent study has shown that, while a substantial number of languages indeed has such a single flexible class, many languages also have distinct (sub)classes of nouns and adjectives based on morphological and/or distributional criteria (Louagie 2020: 66–83). This issue is taken up in section 26.3.

Third, inflecting verbs (IVs) and uninflecting verbs (UVs) are included as distinct verbal parts of speech, but it is not clear how they relate to the function of predication. Schultze-Berndt (2017) argues that IVs are the only elements that can be used for both independent and dependent predication while UVs are restricted to dependent predication (defined by Schultze-Berndt to include use as part of a complex predicate). Moreover, McGregor (2002: 252–266) argues that in many languages an IV, when used in combination with an UV, does not in fact function as a predicate but rather as a marker of verb classification. In this way, IVs are problematic for

---

[1] The label 'nominal' is thus used in two senses in the Australianist literature: in a narrow sense for a flexible class of elements that can be used both referentially and attributively (similar though not entirely equal to Hengeveld's 1992a, 1992b use of the term), and in a broader sense as cover term for a set of word classes that regularly take case marking (including word classes such as nominals in the narrow sense, demonstratives, pronouns etc.). I will use 'nominals' for the narrow sense, and the full 'nominal word classes/parts of speech' for the broader sense in the rest of this chapter.

part-of-speech typologies where verbs are defined as being used for predication *only* (Hengeveld 1992a, 1992b). In addition, it is clear that the word class of simple or IVs is different in languages that also have a class of UVs compared to languages that do not (e.g. in terms of the concepts that are covered or the open/closed character). Note also that Dixon's classification of (manner) adverbials as one of the verbal parts of speech is only relevant for a small number of languages; in many, it seems that manner adverbials are a separate class of non-inflecting elements, or are more like nominals in that they may show case marking (e.g. Dench & Evans 1988: 14–16; Dixon 2002: 181–183). These issues are further discussed in sections 26.4 and 26.5.

Finally, Dixon's (2002: 66–71) discussion of parts of speech does not really refer to distribution over syntactic functions like predication or head of a referential phrase, while this is an important parameter for many theories of word classes (e.g. Hengeveld 1992a, 1992b; Croft 2000). Syntactic and functional distribution is especially interesting where the first set of word classes, viz. the nominal ones, are concerned: the mapping of elements to functional roles like entity, qualifier, classifier and determiner is relatively flexible in a number of Australian languages (e.g. McGregor 1990; Wilkins 2000; Louagie & Verstraete 2016; Louagie 2017), and this may play a role in the characterization of word classes.

The rest of this chapter further surveys how lexemes are generally organized in word classes in Australian languages, specifically focusing on the issues mentioned in the previous paragraphs. The discussion centres around lexical elements that may be used as heads of referential phrases (referential use), as modifiers within referential phrases (attributive use), as predicates, and as modifiers of predicates (manner adverbial use), since these are also the main focus of this handbook. I will largely ignore functional word classes, but give some references where interested readers can find good overviews of what these classes typically look like in Australian languages. I will also not further discuss particles, ideophones, or interjections. Section 26.2 discusses the distinction of nominal from verbal parts of speech (specifically nouns from verbs) and how they may show rather minimal morphological and/or distributional overlap. Sections 26.3 and 26.4 then discuss each of these sets of word classes in more detail. Section 26.3 focuses on the different nominal parts of speech as listed by Dixon (2002), discussing whether Australian languages have a separate word class of adjectives or not (section 26.3.1) and whether a separate word class of classifiers or one of determiners can be distinguished (section 26.3.2). Section 26.4 turns to verbal parts of speech, specifically focusing on the distinction between IVs and UVs. Manner adverbials are briefly commented on in section 26.5. Section 26.6, finally, concludes the chapter with a general overview of the main parts of speech and issues discussed in this chapter. Not each part of speech is discussed equally thoroughly, for reasons of space. Most attention is devoted to the question whether Australian languages have distinct noun and adjective parts of speech, because this is a frequently discussed issue in individual descriptions and in continent-wide surveys, and because there are some misconceptions (or at least overgeneralizations) in the wider typological literature. I am also personally more familiar with nominal parts of speech than with verbal ones.

26.2 Distinguishing verbal from nominal parts of speech

Dixon (2002: 66) distinguishes two major sets of word classes in Australian languages, nominal and verbal ones, following earlier suggestions in the literature (e.g. Hale 1982 on

Warlpiri). In this section, I summarize the motivations for distinguishing these sets, and for ease of discussion focus only on the distinction between the two main word classes of each set, viz. verbs on the one hand and nominals on the other hand (or nouns, depending on the language; see section 26.3.1).

In terms of syntactic distribution, nominals are mostly used for functions related to reference (e.g. as head or modifier within a referential phrase, see section 26.3.1), while verbs are used for predication. This is not a sharp division of labour, as nominals[2] can generally also be used for predication (see e.g. McGregor 2005, 2013; Simpson 2005; Schultze-Berndt 2006; Nordlinger 2014: 239–240). The predicative use of nominals is illustrated in (1a) and use as secondary predicate in (1b). The same flexibility is not found the other way around, i.e. verbs cannot be used referentially, unless they undergo derivation. There are a few examples where verbs do seem to serve a referential function, as in (1c); these are analysed in grammars as embedded clauses which may or may not take nominal inflections (e.g. Evans 2003a: 122–124 on Bininj Kunwok; Dench 1994: 198 on Martuthunira).[3] Note that verbs may have yet other functions in some languages; see section 26.4.

(1) Martuthunira (Ngayarta, PN) (Dench 1994: 205, 182, 198; example b cited in Himmelmann & Schultze-Berndt 2005: 13)
a. *Nhiyu yartapalyu-rru / **Maral.ya-ngara.***
This other(PL)-NOW Maral.ya-PL
'This other mob, now, are the Maral.ya.'

b. *nhulaa miyu mungka-rnuru wajupi-i **wanka-a=l***
DEM.NOM cat eat-PRS grasshopper-ACC alive-ACC=THEN
'That cat eats grasshoppers alive.'

c. *Thanuwa-ngara-marta nyina-layi wangkarnu-marra-rru nhartu-ngara-a*
food-PL-PROP sit-FUT talk-COLL+CTEMP-NOW thing-PL-ACC

*manku-lha-nguru wuruma-l.yarra **nyina-marri-lha-ngara-a**.*
get-PST-ABL do.for-CTEMP stay-COLL-PST-ABL-ACC
'With all the food they then sit down and talk together, having got the things for [the ones who] stayed (behind) together.'

Verbs and nominals can be distinguished morphologically as well, although there is some overlap. Thus, only verbs can inflect for TAM and/or person (see section 26.4 on UVs), while nominals normally cannot. In some languages, however, nominals which are used predicatively may show some verbal inflection, like pronominal affixes or TAM marking. They are still morphologically distinct from the word class of verbs because they cannot take all types of verbal inflectional marking. In Bininj Kunwok, for example, a nominal used predicatively can take the

---

[2] Perhaps it would be more accurate to say that noun phrases may be used for predication. Note also that in the rest of this chapter, I use the term 'noun phrase' quite loosely for any one or more elements functioning together in a nominal expression, whether showing signs of phrasality or not (i.e. being syntactically integrated or not). See Nordlinger (2014: 227–232, 237–241), Louagie & Verstraete (2016), and Louagie (2022) for discussion of this issue in Australian languages.

[3] In some cases, such phrases have lexicalized. Some examples are found in Bininj Kunwok (Evans 2003a: 123–124): e.g. *garri-mikme* (12A-avoid.NPST) used as predicate means 'we practise avoidance' but in lexicalized nominal use means 'our (inclusive) mother-in-law language, avoidance language'.

past imperfective suffix -*ni* (2a), or pronominal prefixes (2b), but not the past perfective suffix; in addition, the form of the third person pronoun prefix is different when attached to a nominal or to a verb. See section 26.3.1 for examples of inchoative suffixes on nominals, deriving them into verbs.

(2) Bininj Kunwok (Gunwinyguan) (Evans 2003a: 121)
    a. *Gorrogo   al-wanjdjuk   bininj-ni.*
       before   II-emu   person-PST
       'Long ago emu was a person.'
    b. *Nga-ngordo.   Bene-ngordo.*
       1MIN-leper   3UA-leper
       'I am a leper.'   'They two are lepers.'

Conversely, nominals in many languages regularly inflect for case,[4] while verbs normally do not. However, verbs can also take nominal case marking in some languages, but only in contexts of subordination and insubordination (e.g. Dench & Evans 1988; Blake 1999; Evans 2007). Thus, case may appear on the verb and/or other elements of a subordinate clause (depending on the language), to specify the relation between the subordinate and the main clause. This function is labelled 'complementising' in Dench & Evans (1988). A straightforward example is given in (3a), where the dative case on the (non-finite) verb *dupay-* 'sit' marks a purposive relation; compare with (3b) where a dative on a nominal also indicates purpose.[5,6,7]

(3) Wagiman (Wardaman/Wagiman) (Cook 1987: 261, 132; cited in Blake 1999: 302)
    a. *Nga-di-nya   dupay-gu*
       1SG-come-PST   sit-DAT
       'I came to sit down.'

    b. *Bolomin   bakpak   nga-ra-ng   guda-gu*
       bolomin   break   1SG-move-PST   fire-DAT
       'I broke up bolomin for fire(wood).'

---

[4] A number of non-Pama–Nyungan languages do not have case marking for core cases, and most of these are also limited in non-core case marking; for an overview, see Louagie & Verstraete (2016: 70–71).

[5] Some languages require the subordinate clause to be nominalized first, e.g. through a nominalizing affix (Dench & Evans 1988: 19), in which case there is obviously no immediate morphological overlap between verbs and nominals. Some languages have (e.g. purposive) markers which originate from a nominalizing element + case marker but are synchronically no longer analysable as such (Blake 1999: 302–309; also Blake 1993).

[6] Switch-reference inflections on the verb (indicting whether the subjects of the subordinate and main clauses are the same or not) are often also formally related to case markers (Austin 1981); they are historically related to complementizing uses of case (Dench & Evans 1988: 29–30).

[7] The use of case markers on verbs in instances of insubordination may ultimately lead to the reanalysis of erstwhile case markers as tense markers or encoders of modal meaning (e.g. Kennedy 1984; Blake 1993, 1999; Dench & Evans 1988: 23–26; McGregor 2003; Evans 2007: 405–409).

In fact, Dench & Evans (1988) distinguish two specific functions of complementizing case, which they label 't-complementiser' and 'c-complementiser'. T-complementizer functions mark temporal, spatial or logical relations between subordinate and main clauses, as with the purposive in (3a). Another example is found in (4a) where the locative marks a simultaneous temporal relation between the subordinate and the main clause. C-complementizer functions link a subordinate clause to its antecedent in the main clause through case agreement, thus marking coreference. This is illustrated in (4b), where each element of the subordinate clause, including the verb, is marked for ergative case in agreement with the antecedent 'man' (it is the man who intends to cook the wallaby). Nordlinger (2014: 244) hypothesizes that c-complementizer functions are only found in Australia.

(4) Yukulta (Tangkic) (Keen 1983; cited in Dench & Evans 1988: 21, 28)
 a. *lairri-ja=ngarri,   murruku-ya   mirrala-lh-i*
    see-IND=I:PRS   woomera-LOC   make-VB-LOC
    'I'm watching him making a woomera.'

 b. *tangka-ya=karri   ngit-a   karna-ja   makurrarra-wurlu-ya,   karna-j-urlu-ya*
    man-ERG=3A:3O:PRS   wood-ACC   light-IND   wallaby-PROP-ERG   light-VB-PROP-ERG
    'The man lit a fire in order to cook the wallaby.'

One Australian language that presents a well-known and rather far-reaching case of morphological overlap between verbs and nominals is Kayardild (Evans 1995: 89–91). In Kayardild, nouns can inflect for 'verbal case': these verbalizing suffixes turn a word into a morphological verb that agrees in tense, mood, and polarity with the main verb, but at the same time they function as oblique cases, in the sense that they are attached to every word of the NP and code case-like meanings like beneficiary or purpose. This is illustrated in (5a), where a verbal dative *-maru* is attached to each word of the noun phrase to express a role of beneficiary. Because this is a verbalizing suffix, each word is also inflected for potential mood, in agreement with the main verb. Note that the reverse situation also occurs: verbs can be nominalized and then take nominal case, while still functioning as verbs syntactically, as illustrated in (5b). What is interesting here is that both verbal case and 'ongoing nominalization' operate at phrase level and thus are inflectional rather than derivational.

(5) Kayardild (Tangkic) (Evans 1995: 90)
 a. *ngada   waa-ju   wangarr-u   [ngijin-maru-thu   thabuju-maru-thu]$_{NP}$*
    1SG.NOM   sing-POT   song-MPROP   my-VD-POT   elder.brother-VD-POT
    'I will sing a song for my elder brother.'

 b. *nyingka   kurri-n-da   warra-n-da   wirdi-n-d*
    2SG.NOM   see-NMLZ-NOM   go-NMLZ-NOM   stay-NMLZ-NOM
    'You're going around to see (people) a lot.'

Finally, some languages have a small word class whose elements show features associated with nominal word classes and features associated with verbal ones. It concerns a class of predicate nominals or adjectives, which often have (some) nominal morphology but function predicatively only. This word class often only has a smallish number of members, expressing states like 'know', 'be ignorant', 'be jealous', 'asleep', or 'pregnant'. For example,

Kuuk Thaayorre has a category of predicate adjectives, which are like elements from nominal word classes in the sense that they cannot take TAM inflections and can function as complements for copula constructions, but like verbs in the sense that they cannot take case inflections, can only function predicatively, and take one or two arguments, as illustrated in (6) (Gaby 2017: 87–88, 377–379). The class only has two members which are used commonly: *walmeerem* 'knowledgeable of' and *pamngongkom* 'ignorant of' (Gaby 2017: 87–88). Similarly, in Kayardild, predicate nominals have nominal morphology (e.g. derivational possibilities), but can only be used predicatively and can sometimes take direct or indirect objects (Evans 1995: 86, 231–232). The class has more than 30 members (listed in the dictionary in Evans 1995: 638–800). Kayardild also has a small class of 'manner nominals' which similarly have nominal morphology but can only function as secondary predicates (Evans 1995: 86, 227–229), as *kantharrk* 'alone' in (7). A similar category is found for instance in Martuthunira (Dench 1994: 53) and Yankunytjatjara ('active adjectives'; Goddard 1985: 17); see also section 26.5 on manner adverbs.

(6) Kuuk Thaayorre (Southwest Paman, PN) (Gaby 2017: 87)
    peln   nhunh   pamngongkom
    3PL(NOM)   3SG.ACC   ignorant.of
    'they didn't know about him [that he had arrived]'

(7) Kayardild (Tangkic; Evans 1995: 357)
    niya   thaldi-jarra   kurnthur-ina   kantharrk
    3SG.NOM   stand-PST   sandbank-MABL   alone.NOM
    'He stood on the sandbank alone.'

26.3 NOMINAL PARTS OF SPEECH

The previous section discussed how nominal parts of speech can generally be distinguished from verbal ones. This section focuses on nominal parts of speech, such as nouns and adjectives (if distinguished), demonstratives, personal pronouns, locationals, and temporals. These are sometimes grouped together as such (e.g. by Dixon 2002 but also in individual grammatical descriptions) because they share general inflectional possibilities such as case marking and regularly occur in referential expressions, as discussed in sections 26.1 and 26.2. Ignoring for now the question whether nouns and adjectives are separate parts of speech, the other categories listed above are usually analysed as separate (sub)classes, the argumentation for which I briefly outline in the following paragraphs.

Free[8] personal pronouns are most clearly distinct from other nominal parts of speech such as nouns. They form a closed class of deictic elements,[9] which obligatorily distinguish

---

[8] For surveys of bound pronouns, see e.g. Dixon ([1980] 2010: 362–372; 2002: 337–401); McGregor (2004: 119–125) on Kimberley languages.
[9] A small number of languages do not have third person pronouns, using demonstratives to fill the gap(s) (in nine languages out of a 75 language sample in Louagie & Verstraete 2015: 162–163; see also Dixon [1980] 2010: 276; Blake 2001; Louagie 2023).

person and number (while nouns often only optionally mark number or collectivity (e.g. Dixon [1980] 2010: 275; Louagie 2020: 91–99)). Many languages show split case alignment between pronouns and nouns, or between first/second person pronouns and third person pronouns/nouns (Dixon [1980] 2010: 285–291; Nordlinger 2014: 224–227). In a substantial number of Australian languages, third person pronouns are multifunctional: they not only occur pronominally but also adnominally (Blake 2001; Stirling & Baker 2007; Louagie & Verstraete 2015; Louagie 2017). As modifiers, they almost always occur in a determiner role, and only rarely in another role, viz. as number marker (in Djapu (Morphy 1983: 47–48; Louagie & Verstraete 2015: 177–178)) or as emphatic focus marker (in Gooniyandi (McGregor 1990: 270) and Dalabon (Cutfield 2011: 54)). Modifying pronouns sometimes show signs of grammaticalization (in all known cases with number marking or focus marking functions, and in some cases with determiner function), and could perhaps even be analysed as belonging to a different part of speech in some cases (see Louagie & Verstraete 2015: 178–183 for discussion). The examples in (8) illustrate the three different distributions for personal pronouns in Dalabon (Cutfield 2011: 54, 96–99, examples): as head of a referential expression in (8a), as determiner in (8b), and as emphatic marker in (8c). When *yibung* is used as emphatic marker, its inherent number and person values do not apply, in the sense that the form is able to modify elements with other referential values, such as a first plural pronoun in (8c) (Cutfield 2011: 54). For surveys of the make-up of personal pronoun systems, see e.g. Dixon ([1980] 2010: 275–277; 2002: 243–319) and McGregor (2004: 110–118) on Kimberley languages.

(8) Dalabon (Gunwinyguan) (Cutfield 2011: 98, 443, 54)
 a. *yibûng   yirrhyirrh   ka-h-bon-inj   biyihyirrh*
    3SG   downstream   3SG-H-go-PL   deep.down
    'he was walking downstream right down the bottom'

 b. *yibungkarn   Na-Mr. Shank*
    3SG.EMPH   M-personal.name
    'That Mr Shank.'

 c. *bah   njel   yibung   yala-h-bakah-ni-nj*
    CONJ   1PL   3SG   1PL-R/A-many-sit-PST.IPFV
    'but there were a lot of us'

Demonstratives may share morphological features with pronouns and/or nouns, or have their own, specific morphology, for example relating to case and number marking (Dixon [1980] 2010: 275–277; Louagie 2020: 91–97; Louagie 2023). In terms of distribution, Australian languages often have a set of demonstratives that can function both pronominally and adnominally (sometimes also adverbially); some have separate sets for these functions. See section 26.3.2 for some examples of adnominal demonstratives and the question whether a category of determiners can be distinguished. See Louagie (2023) for a survey of demonstratives in Australian languages; see also Dixon (2002: 335–336), and McGregor on Kimberley languages (2004: 125–126).

Locationals and temporals are two, often rather small, parts of speech including lexemes related to location and time. Although they mostly function adverbially, they are considered nominal parts of speech in many languages because they take nominal case marking and can sometimes occur as part of the nominal expression. They only take a subset of nominal cases, and sometimes have different allomorphs for the cases they do take (e.g. Dixon [1980] 2010: 282–283). Note that in some languages, temporal and locational adverbs do not inflect at all and are thus considered particles, and not nominal parts of speech (e.g. Bardi (Bowern 2012: 160)).

Having briefly introduced the parts of speech of personal pronouns, demonstratives, locationals, and temporals, I now turn to two questions which I will discuss in more detail. The first, discussed quite extensively in section 26.3.1, is whether Australian languages have separate noun and adjective parts of speech, or a single flexible part of speech whose members can function both referentially and attributively. The second, discussed more briefly in section 26.3.2, is whether separate word classes of classifiers or determiners may be distinguished among the nominal parts of speech. Both questions are specifically relevant in light of the flexibility a number of Australian languages show, especially in noun phrases but also beyond (e.g. McGregor 1990, 2013; Nordlinger 2014: 237–241; Louagie 2017, 2020).

26.3.1 Nouns and adjectives, or a flexible class of nominals?

There has been some discussion in the Australianist literature whether nouns and adjectives can be distinguished as separate parts of speech. For instance, in his first survey of Australian languages, Dixon ([1980] 2010: 274) argues that a distinct word class of adjectives may be identified, whereas in his second survey (Dixon 2002: 67), he argues there are few differences between putative nouns and adjectives so that they should be considered a single part of speech. The question is also discussed in many grammatical descriptions, using a variety of notional, morphological, syntactic, and/or functional criteria, and arriving at different conclusions based on similar criteria, or reverse, similar conclusions based on different criteria. The overall image that has found its way into the Australianist and typological literature is that Australian languages generally lack a noun–adjective distinction (e.g. Hale 1983: 83; Dixon 2002: 67; Nordlinger 2014: 237–238; Van Lier & Rijkhoff 2013: 7; see e.g. Hale 1982, 1983; McGregor 2013 for accounts of individual languages). However, a recent continent-wide survey based on a genetically diverse 100-language sample[10] has shown that the picture is not uniform across Australian languages, and a substantial number of languages in fact have separate word classes for nouns and adjectives (Louagie 2020: 66–83); the rest of this section heavily relies on this study.

The rest of this section will first discuss some of the criteria used in the typological literature and in descriptions of individual languages for (not) distinguishing nouns from adjectives, surveying notional, morphological, and distributional criteria in turn (sections 26.3.1.1–26.3.1.3). This is followed by a brief discussion of how the values for these criteria

---

[10] The sample includes 65 Pama–Nyungan languages (representing most subgroups) and 35 so-called non-Pama–Nyungan languages (representing 21 families). See Louagie (2020: 6–14) for more details and a full list of the sample.

pattern across the languages of Australia, based on the results of the survey in Louagie (2020: 66–83) (section 26.3.1.4).

26.3.1.1 *Notional criteria*

A number of grammatical descriptions broadly state that nouns in general refer to concepts and adjectives to qualities, or conversely, that a flexible class of nominals includes items of both types. If a distinction between nouns and adjectives is claimed for a particular language, it may be hard to make generalizations about which types of semantic notions are encoded as nouns or as adjectives. This is remarked on by several authors for Australian languages specifically (e.g. Harvey 2002: 130 on Gaagudju; Austin 2013: 43–44 on Diyari), but this issue has also been noted in wider cross-linguistic research (e.g. Dixon 1982: 1–62). It is clear we cannot use notional criteria as distinguishing factor for word classes alone. I will, however, briefly refer to issues pertaining to semantics at a few places in the following discussion where relevant. Note that I use the shorthand 'property-denoting' and 'entity-denoting' lexemes as general terms when I do not want to be specific about word-class status, fully realizing that this glosses over the nuances just discussed.

26.3.1.2 *Morphological criteria*

Morphological differences between putative nouns and adjectives are only found in approximately one-third of Australian languages, and have a fairly limited scope in most of these languages (Louagie 2020: 73–74; based on the 100-language sample mentioned above). The morphological criteria discussed in individual grammars, on which the previous statement is based, are quite diverse. One criterion is the need for derivation when an element is used in another syntactic function: some languages derive adjectives from nouns when they are used as modifier, or conversely, nouns from adjectives when they are used as head of a noun phrase. An example is found in Arabana/Wangkangurru, where reduplication of a noun may derive an adjective for attributive use (Hercus 1994: 96–99) as in (9a); compare with (9b) which shows the same noun as head of a noun phrase. Like many languages, Arabana/Wangkangurru also has a 'having' suffix which may be used among other things to derive adjectives from nouns (Hercus 1994: 90–92),[11] as in (9c). Nouns without any such morphological adaptation are not used as modifiers in this language, with a few specific exceptions (e.g. close apposition of a noun and proper name where the former semantically modifies, or perhaps classifies, the latter, as in (9d) (Castel 2020: 22, 25)). The use of adjectives as head of the noun phrase is not attested (based on Hercus 1994: examples). The availability of means to derive nouns from adjectives and vice versa seems good evidence for distinct classes, since a flexible class of nominals would not require any morphological adaptation for use in different functions (following e.g. Hengeveld 1992a, 1992b). This type of derivation only occurs in a small number of languages, and is always restricted to a small part of the stock of entity- and

---

[11] There is considerable debate among Australianists whether such 'having' (or proprietive) suffixes are inflectional or derivational. See e.g. Dench & Evans (1988: 10–12) for some argumentation in favour of an inflectional analysis, which still allows for specific derivational uses of these affixes.

property-denoting lexemes, which perhaps makes the evidence less strong (Louagie 2020: 75–76).

(9) Arabana/Wangkangurru (Karnic, PN) (Hercus 1994: 99, 154, 92, 297)
   a. *madla   wiRi-wiRi*
      dog   hair-hair
      'shaggy dog'

   b. *Mankarra-pula   wiRi   kuti-kuti-nta.*
      girl-DU   hair   pull-pull-REFL
      'The two girls are pulling each other's hair.'

   c. *Malyka   wayayi-rna   arluwa   irrtya-purru-ku.*
      not   like-IPFV   child   noise-having-DAT
      'I don't like noisy kids.'

   d. *Uka   thangka-rda   paku   mathapurda   Inyurla-nha,   paku   thangka-rda.*
      he   sit-PRS   unoccupied   old.man   Inyurla-NAME   unoccupied   sit-PRS
      'He is just sitting there doing nothing, old Inyurla, just sitting there.'

Other morphological criteria used in grammars relate to morphological potential. Many mention differences in derivational possibilities for either nouns or adjectives into other categories such as verbs. For example, for several languages it is mentioned that only adjectives, not nouns, can be used to form an inchoative or causative predicate, e.g. through affixation or as part of a complex verb construction. This is illustrated in (10) from Bardi, where only adjectives may occur in a complex predicate to form a stative (10a), inchoative (10b) or causative predicate; this is ungrammatical for nouns (10c)–(10d), and instead a structure with an allative case marker is needed to express a change of state, as in (10e) (Bowern 2012: 264–265). The question may be raised whether such differences are truly due to morphological restrictions, or rather an epiphenomenon of semantic differences, in which case they would not be a good argument for distinct part-of-speech status. For Bardi, alternative constructions are needed to express a change in state involving a noun or an adjective, so the morphological evidence seems solid. A similar example is found in Wambaya, where the causative suffix *-mi* can only be added to adjectives (e.g. *guriny-mi* 'make good') and not to nouns (e.g. **juwa-mi* 'make into a man'), not even when licensed by the context (e.g. in the context of Dreamtime stories) (Nordlinger 1998: 47–48). In other languages, causative derivation is possible both with entity-denoting and property-denoting lexemes, though perhaps more likely with the latter for semantic reasons (e.g. Garrwa (Mushin 2012: 170–175); Gumbaynggir (Eades 1979: 271)).

(10) Bardi (Nyulnyulan) (Bowern 2012: 264–265, 229)
    a. *boordiji   i-ni-n*
       big   3-sit-CONT
       'It's big.'

b. *boordiji   i-n-joo-n*
   big   3-TR-do/say-CONT
   'It got big.'

c. **iila*   *i-ni-n*
   dog   3-sit-CONT

d. **iila*   *i-n-joo-n*
   dog   3-TR-do/say-CONT

e. *I-ng-irr-i-ni*   *iidool-ngan.*
   3-PST-AUG-[TR]-do/say-REM.PST   pandanus.palm-ALL
   'They changed into pandanus palms (*Pandanus spiralis*).'

Other examples of morphological differences (all mentioned in Louagie 2020: 74–75) are that adjectives can derive adverbs while nouns cannot in Arabana/Wangkangurru (Hercus 1994: 60; see section 26.5 for an example), and coverbs can derive adjectives but not nouns in Bilinarra (Meakins & Nordlinger 2014: 81). Adjectives have an oblique stem in Warray, while nouns do not (Harvey 1986: 70). Finally, nouns and adjectives reduplicate to different effects in a number of languages, e.g. plurality and derivation into an adverb respectively in Kuku Yalanji (Patz 2002: 55), or plurality and intensification in Emmi (Ford 1998: 140), as illustrated in (11a)–(11b).

(11) Emmi (Western Daly) (Ford 1998: 140)
    a. *perre;   perreperre*
       'grub'   'grubs'

    b. *dukandji;   dukduk*
       'big'   'very big'

26.3.1.3 Distributional criteria

Distributional differences between nouns and adjectives are more common than morphological differences: they are found in over half of Australian languages, at least (Louagie 2020: 76–77; based on the 100-language sample mentioned earlier). Distributional criteria include both the distribution of elements with respect to the functions of reference and attribution (i.e. head or modifier in a referential phrase),[12] and more specific (morpho)syntactic differences that may exist between nouns and adjectives.

---

[12] The use of non-verbal elements as predicates is excluded from the discussion here, but see section 26.2 for some examples. It is unclear whether there is a general tendency for property-denoting words to be used for predication more easily than entity-denoting words. I came across only a few statements along those lines, e.g. for Wardaman (Merlan 1994: 58), and Warlpiri (Hale 1983; see below). Typically, both simple nominal elements and full noun phrases can be used as predicates in Australian languages. I also exclude adverbial uses from the discussion here, but see section 26.5.

Starting with the former, many grammars do not actually discuss distribution across functional roles in detail—in fact, many do not discuss functional roles at all (as one reviewer rightly pointed out). The evidence is often inconclusive and/or insufficient to draw any firm conclusions, but I will try to formulate some general tendencies and issues based on the available information. Firstly, many descriptions (often briefly) mention that property-denoting lexemes may occur as sole element of a referential expression, as in (12). Some descriptions analyse such elements as modifiers of ellipsed nouns, because these structures usually occur in contexts where the entity referred to is understood or established (e.g. Bowern 2012: 158 on Bardi). This type of analysis implies that property-denoting lexemes are not used referentially in themselves and are thus part of a distinct word class of adjectives (see also Chapter 18). Other descriptions, by contrast, analyse property-denoting lexemes in instances as (12) as head of a referential phrase (regardless of whether the referent is established). They consequently argue that both property-denoting and entity-denoting lexemes may function referentially, thus forming a single, flexible class of nominals (e.g. Eades 1979: 272 on Gumbaynggir). Their case is perhaps most convincing when any element can occur in head and modifier functions in contexts where the referent is not yet established, i.e. when there is no question of elliptical NPs (see Chapter 18). This is illustrated in (13) from Gooniyandi, where *jiginya* functions as head of the noun phrase in (13a) and as qualifying modifier in (13b); both NPs are *not* elliptical (McGregor 1990: 264).

(12) Gumbaynggir (Gumbaynggir, PN) (Eades 1979: 172)
 barway-ḍu buwa:-ŋ ḍunuy
 big-A hit-PST small.O
 'The big one hit the small one.'

(13) Gooniyandi (Bunuban) (McGregor 1990: 264, 272)
 a. *niyaji jiginya*
   this little
   'this child'

 b. *marla jiginya*
   hand little
   'little hand'

When property-denoting lexemes occur in structures such as (12) and (13a), their regular meaning is 'an X one' (e.g. 'a small one', 'a tall one') across Australian languages.[13] Sometimes the meaning may be more specific; for instance, while an element like Gooniyandi *jiginya* may be used to refer to any type of small entity, it is most frequently used in reference to children, as in (13a) (McGregor 1990: 272). Some authors even do not analyse such lexemes as inherently property-denoting. McGregor (2013) for instance argues that flexible lexemes in Gooniyandi have vague semantics: they do not have entity or property specifications. Their meaning in a phrase (or clause), he argues, is derived compositionally from their abstract coded meaning (e.g. '(the one who is) little') in combination with the grammatical

---

[13] For Gumbaynggir, Eades (1979: 270–271, 348) specifically mentions that both meanings like 'big one' and 'bigness' are available (in addition to the quality meaning 'big').

relation they are in (e.g. entity in a noun phrase in (13a)). (See Hengeveld & Rijkhoff 2005 for a slightly different approach to semantic vagueness with flexible lexemes.) Others may argue that examples such as (13a) involve conversion rather than flexibility, also in light of the fact that many nominals in Gooniyandi are actually preferred in one role, or are even restricted to a single role (see further below; see e.g. Croft 2005, Evans & Osada 2005, Don & van Lier 2013 for discussions of semantic compositionality, semantic shifts, and conversion).

Secondly, if a flexible word class of nominals is claimed, we not only expect property-denoting lexemes to be used referentially, but also entity-denoting lexemes to be used attributively (see e.g. Evans & Osada 2005 on bidirectionality). Unfortunately, very little information is available on this. For a few languages, it is mentioned that 'nouns' may function as modifiers, but most examples encountered in descriptions have only human stage-of-life terms or words for 'man' or 'woman' as modifiers. This was illustrated in (9d) from Arabana/Wangkangurru. Another example is found in (14) from Nyulnyul, where *waringkil* 'girl' is used as head in (14a) and as modifier in (14b) (McGregor 2011: 403). The limited possibilities for entity-denoting lexemes to occur as modifiers indicates that flexibility is rather limited, which implies that an analysis in terms of a single fully flexible class may be too strong in many languages (see also Evans & Osada's 2005 criterion of exhaustivity; see Chapter 18 in this volume for suggestions on unidirectional flexibility).

(14) Nyulnyul (Nyulnyulan) (McGregor 2011: 403)
    a. *bin   waringkil*
       this   girl
      'this girl'

    b. *waringkil   baab*
       girl   child
      'girl'

Third, it should be noted that even in languages for which flexibility is claimed, elements show preferences for, or even restrictions to, certain roles. For instance, in Gooniyandi, nominals can generally occur as head or attributive modifier in the noun phrase, but many individual lexemes are in fact restricted in the functions they can have. For instance, numerals (which are considered nominals for morphological and functional reasons) can only be used attributively, and conversely, several nominals referring to plant or animal species can only be used as head of the noun phrase (McGregor 2013: 236). Similarly, Hale (1983: 33–35) posits a single nominal word class for Warlpiri, but suggests a rough subclassification as presented in (15), where nominals of type (a) are most likely (or sometimes exclusively) used referentially, and nominals of type (f) predicatively, with types in the middle having an equal likelihood for either. The labels refer to 'semantic functions' (Hale 1983: 34); the label 'attributives' thus seems to indicate that elements in this group are more likely to be used attributively, although Hale does not state this explicitly.

(15) Warlpiri (Ngumpin-Yapa, PN) (Hale 1983: 34)
    a. Pronouns and determiners
    b. Names
    c. Substantives

d. Attributives and quantifiers
   e. Mental and psychological statives
   f. Locatives and directionals

Apart from distribution across the functions of reference and attribution, we find other distributional criteria, which are morphosyntactic in nature and more widely discussed in grammatical descriptions. I briefly discuss the three most commonly mentioned ones. A first morphosyntactic criterion relates to different behaviour of nouns and adjectives in nominal classification: while nouns normally belong to a single class (or gender), adjectives do not belong to any class, but agree with the noun they modify. It is sometimes argued that this is no solid evidence for separate parts of speech, since there are examples of nouns belonging to different classes as well (see e.g. Nordlinger 2014: 238; Louagie 2020: 55–59 for discussion and examples). This criterion is obviously only at play in languages that have well-established systems of nominal classification (see Louagie 2020: 26–65, 79 on the distribution of different classification systems across Australia); see also section 26.3.2.

A second morphosyntactic criterion to distinguish nouns from adjectives is when each part of speech is tied to its own position in the noun phrase, i.e. nouns and adjectives occur in a fixed linear order. This is true for about one-third of Australian languages (Louagie 2020: 78, based on the 100-language sample mentioned above); note that flexible order in itself obviously is no evidence against such a distinction. An example is found in Arrernte (Wilkins 1989: 104), where adjectives always follow nouns in noun phrases, as illustrated in (16a)–(16b). Arrernte has a few forms with both a referential and an attributive sense, like *iperte* 'hole' (N) or 'deep' (Adj).[14] It is argued that such cases do not involve a single flexible lexeme, but rather two distinct lexemes linked by conversion, one belonging to the word class of nouns and the other to the word class of adjectives. This is reflected in their distribution in the noun phrase: *iperte* 'hole' occurs in initial position, which is reserved for nouns (16a), while *iperte* 'deep' occurs in the position for adjectives (16b). When they are used together in an NP, as in (16c), speakers always identify the first element as noun and the second as adjective (Wilkins 1989: 104).[15]

(16) Arrernte (Arandic, PN) (Wilkins 1989: 421, 534, 104; corrected mistake for *atneme* in b)
   a. *Re   imerte ingkerreke itne-nhe ankertiwe-me-le   **iperte** kngerre nhenge-werne*
      3SG.A then   all   3PL-ACC   push-NPST.PFV-SS   hole   big   REMEMB-ALL
      'Then he pushed everyone towards a big hole […].'

   b. *[…] atneme   ante urtne   kweke   **iperte** renhetherrenhe*
      digging.stick and   coolomon   little   deep   3DU.ACC
      '[she collected all her things together;] her digging stick, and her two [small deep, DL] coolamons'

---

[14] There is also a reduplicated form *iperte-iperte* meaning 'rough (of roads), holey, corrugated' (Wilkins 1989: 104).

[15] One reviewer expressed their reservations about Wilkins's claim that Arrernte speakers have such clear intuitions about word-class status. However, even if there is uncertainty about examples like (16), they are rare and Arrernte only has a small number of items like *iperte*, which occur in both positions in the noun phrase and have two senses. The vast majority of lexemes only occur in one of the two positions in the noun phrase, so the evidence for distinct adjective and noun parts of speech remains strong.

c. *iperte   iperte*
   hole   deep
   'deep hole'

A third morphosyntactic criterion, which is mentioned in grammars of only a small number of languages (Louagie 2020: 79), is the different behaviour of nouns and adjectives with degree modifiers. The differences are of two types: only adjectives can be used in a construction with a particular degree modifier while nouns cannot (as illustrated in (17)), or they can occur with the same modifier but to a different semantic effect (as illustrated in (18)). The main issue with these cases is whether such differences are really syntactically determined, or rather related to semantic factors, such as the compatibility of the degree modifier with the lexical semantics of the head for (17) or the combinatorial semantics of a degree modifier with a quality-denoting item or an entity-denoting one for (18).[16]

(17) Kuuk Thaayorre (Southwest Paman, PN) (Gaby 2017: 203)
a. *waarr   ngamal*
   very   large
   'very large'

b. **waarr   nganip*
   very   father
   'very father(ly)'

(18) Arrernte (Arandic, PN) (Wilkins 1989: 105)
a. *kngerre   nthurre*
   big   INTENS
   'very big'

b. *artwe   nthurre*
   man   INTENS
   'a real man [one who has been initiated]'

26.3.1.4 Patterns across Australia

Having surveyed the main morphological and distributional criteria used in grammatical descriptions, I now discuss how these criteria pattern in and across languages of Australia. The results of the continent-wide survey based on a 100-language sample mentioned earlier (Louagie 2020: 65–83) indicate that three main types of systems can be distinguished, based on the evidence provided in grammatical descriptions. Australian languages are roughly equally divided over these three types, but it is hard to see specific areal or genetic patterns (see Louagie 2020: 83 for an overview map, which shows that each of the three types is spread across the continent and occurs both in Pama–Nyungan and non-Pama–Nyungan languages).

---

[16] For (18), one reviewer suggests the abstract semantics of the intensifier to be 'more than expected', which has a different nuance in combination with a property lexeme or entity lexeme.

In the first type of system, nouns and adjectives are clearly distinct on both morphological and distributional grounds. Almost a quarter of Australian languages have this system (Louagie 2020: 81–82). An example is found in Arrernte. In this language, nouns and adjectives are morphologically distinct in that one part of speech may derive into the other: reduplication of a noun derives an adjective (e.g. *atnerte* 'stomach' > *atnerte-atnerte* 'pregnant' Wilkins 1989: 149) but not vice versa, and some adjectives may derive a noun by other means (e.g. *kngerre* 'big' > *kngerrepenhe* 'big one; something that is big' Wilkins 1989: 105). Nouns and adjectives are also distributionally distinct, in three ways. First, whereas nouns are in principle obligatory in the noun phrase, adjectives are optional, i.e. noun phrases without a noun are the result of ellipsis (only in subsequent mentions) while noun phrases without an adjective are not (Wilkins 1989: 102–103). Second, they have their own distribution in the NP; see example (16) and discussion there. Third, both nouns and adjectives can occur in a construction with an intensifier, but to different semantic effects; note that this last criterion is less strong (see example (18) and discussion there).

In the second type of system, nouns and adjectives are distinct on distributional grounds, in that elements from each part of speech are restricted to specific distributions, but there are no morphological differences between them. Over one-third of Australian languages has this system (Louagie 2020: 82). An example is found in Yankunytjatjara (discussion based on Goddard 1985: 17; see also Bowe 1990: 8 on close variety Pitjantjatjara). Only nouns can function as the head of a noun phrase, except in the case of ellipsis, and nouns and adjectives have their own position in the noun phrase. Morphologically, nouns and adjectives are not distinct: they can take the same inflectional and derivational markers, and have similar effects in stem reduplication (viz. weakening of some sort, e.g. *pika* 'angry'—*pikapika* 'annoyed'; *ngura* 'camp'—*ngurangura* 'a sort of camp; a temporary camp' Goddard 1985: 73).

In the third type of system, there is one flexible word class of nominals, i.e. there are no morphological or distributional grounds for distinguishing nouns from adjectives (see Chapter 1 on flexible word classes in general). A bit less than one-third of Australian languages have this system (Louagie 2020: 81), although this number may turn out to be lower on further scrutiny: a language was included in this count whenever there was no clearly described distributional distinction, but as discussed in section 26.3.1.3, information on distribution across functional roles was actually often limited or inconclusive. Still, there are good candidates for this type. One is Gooniyandi (Bunuban; McGregor 1990: 141–143; 2013); see section 26.3.1.3 for discussion of the lack of distributional distinctions. Another is Martuthunira, for which Dench (1994: 51–55) proposes a single class of nominals which can occur in several functions: as head of the noun phrase, as modifier in a noun phrase, in an ascriptive clause without or with copula, and as secondary predicate. Some lexemes are restricted to the first function (e.g. *wirra* 'boomerang'), others are flexible between the first three (e.g. *ngapala* 'mud(dy)') or between all functions (e.g. *pinkarranyu* 'dry'). Distributional flexibility between head and modifier roles in the noun phrase is illustrated in (19a)–(19c), with *pinkarranyu* as head in (19a) and as modifier in (19b)–(19c), in pre-head and post-head position respectively. Although some nominals are restricted in the roles they may have, Dench (1994: 55) suggests that there is no neat classification into subclasses, and that 'these possibilities of occurrence cannot be predicted by general syntactic or semantic rule'.

(19) Martuthunira (Ngayarta, PN) (Dench 1994: 54, 268)
 a. *Nhuwana-yi pawulu-ngara parrani-Ø yilangu nyina-lu **pinkarranyu-la**.*
    2PL-VOC child-PL return-IMP here sit-PURP(SS) dry-LOC
    'You children come back here and stay in the dry.'

 b. *Nhulaa manku-Ø, **pinkarranyu** kalyaran!*
    near.you grab-IMP dry stick
    'Grab that, a dry stick!'

 c. *Manku-layi kalyaran-ku **pinkarranyu-u**.*
    grab-FUT stick-ACC dry-ACC
    'Then get a dry stick.'

For some languages for which a flexible class of nominals is proposed,[17] the internal structure of the noun phrase has been meaningfully described in terms of functional roles (capitalized) and not in terms of word classes. The functional roles have a fixed position in the noun phrase, where each role may be filled by different types of elements and elements may generally occur in more than one role. Such descriptions obviously do not only include nominals but also other parts of speech like demonstratives and personal pronouns, as well as more complex elements like embedded phrases or elements. An analysis in terms of functional roles may offer insight in noun phrase structure in languages with high levels of flexibility in particular, as it takes into account semantic and functional differences with different word orders. This type of analysis was introduced in Australianist linguistics by McGregor (1990: 253–276) for Gooniyandi, and taken up by several other authors, including Dench (1994: 189–193) for Martuthunira. The template for the Martuthunira noun phrase is given in (20); nominals may occur in at least the Entity, Classifier, and Qualifier roles, as illustrated in (19a)–(19c) respectively. Some may also occur in a Quantifier role (e.g. *kupuyu* 'little, small'; Dench 1994: 190).[18]

(20) Martuthunira (Ngayarta, PN) (Dench 1994: 189)
    NP template: (Determiner) (Quantifier) (Classifier) Entity (Qualifier(s))

It is clear from the preceding discussion that not all Australian languages have similar part-of-speech systems for elements involved in reference and attribution, despite the generalizations in some of the typological literature. About one-third of Australian languages have a single, flexible class of nominals, while the others have separate word classes for nouns and adjectives, which are distributionally, and less frequently also morphologically, distinct.

---

[17] Similar descriptions also exist for other languages, where the mapping of word class to functional roles is more direct (e.g. Umpithamu (Verstraete 2010); Tiwi (Lee 1987)).

[18] A few Australian languages seem to have noun and adjective parts of speech that are only morphologically distinct, and not distributionally (Louagie 2020: 82). However, the distributional evidence is often uncertain and/or the morphological evidence has limited significance, which invites the possibility that these languages could be reassigned to one of the other three types (pending further analysis).

26.3.2 Do classifiers and determiners form separate word classes?

Australian languages have received some attention in the typological literature for two further features which are also related to word class: their systems of nominal classification, and their lack of obligatory determiners while at the same time allowing multiple determiner-like elements in a single noun phrase. Both are interesting for the current chapter because they invite the question whether a class of classifiers and one of (non-obligatory) determiners can be distinguished, and if so, in what way. I will discuss these questions briefly, first focusing on classifiers and then on determiners.

About two-thirds of Australian languages have at least one system of nominal classification, whereby nouns/nominals are overtly classified into subclasses (Louagie 2020: 27). The two main types found in Australia are noun class systems and noun classifier systems (Dixon 1982). Noun classes are marked in agreement patterns, as in (21), where the nouns *diban* and *yibi* are marked as belonging to the fourth and second noun class respectively by the agreement shown on the adnominal demonstratives. Noun class systems are not further considered here, but see Dixon (1982), Sands (1995), Dixon (2002: 460–514), McGregor (2004: 146–150), Louagie (2020: 23–65), and Skilton (2023) for surveys. In contrast to noun classes, noun classifiers are free forms that occur in juxtaposition to the noun they classify, as in (22), where the generic nouns *mayi* and *bama* mark the specific nouns *jimirr* and *yaburu* as belonging to the categories of vegetables and persons respectively. The use of noun classifiers is optional in all Australian languages that have them (Louagie 2020: 34), and in most languages the order is fixed to generic noun-specific noun as in (22) (Louagie 2020: 29). See Dixon (1982: 159–206), Harvey & Reid (1997), Wilkins (2000), Dixon (2002: 449–460), and Louagie (2020: 23–65) for surveys and more detailed studies of noun classifiers.

(21) Dyirbal (Dyirbal, PN) (Dixon 1982: 161)
 bala diban ya-ŋgu-n yibi-ŋgu buran
 there.ABS.IV stone.ABS here-ERG-II woman-ERG look.at
 'The woman here is looking at the stone there.'

(22) Yidiny (Yimidhirr-Yalanji-Yidinic, PN) (Dixon 1982: 185)
 mayi jimirr bama-al yaburu-ŋgu julaal
 vegetable.ABS yam.ABS person-ERG girl-ERG dig.PST
 'The girl dug up the vegetable yam.'

If a language has a system of noun classifiers as illustrated in (22), the question may be raised whether there is consequently also a separate word class of classifiers. If this question asks about the presence of a (potentially closed) word class of elements which are dedicated to this classifying function, the answer is negative:[19] elements which can serve as classifiers are not dedicated to this role. This is illustrated in (23) from Arrernte: in (23a) the generic noun *kere* marks the category to which the referent of the specific noun *aherre* belongs, while

---

[19] This is one of the reasons why many Australianists are reluctant to label elements like *mayi* in (22) as noun classifiers; most prefer 'generic-specific structures' for the structure as a whole.

in (23b) the same element is used independently. It is, however, still possible to distinguish a distributional class of noun classifiers, which could be defined as the set of elements which can occur in initial position in a 'classifying construction'. The classifying role that elements like *kere* in (23a) have precisely arises from their use in the construction as a whole, and is not inherent in the individual elements (Wilkins 2000). This analysis was proposed by Wilkins (2000) for Arrernte (and preliminarily for Yankunytjatjara and Warlpiri), but has the potential to be applied more broadly in Australia (Louagie 2020: 33–35).[20]

(23) Arrernte (Arandic, PN) (Wilkins 2000: 151, 152)
   a. *Ikwere-nge   re-therre   perte-ke   anteme, kere   aherre   ikwere.*
      3SG.DAT-ABL 3DU.NOM   creep.up-PST.CONT now   game/meat kangaroo   3SG.DAT
      'After that, the two of them now crept up on the kangaroo.'

   b. *Kele   kwele artwe re   irrtyarte-rlke ikwerenhe-ø   ine-rle.lhe-ke*
      OK   QUOT   man   3SG.ERG spear-TOO   3SG.POSS-ACC   get-DO&GO-PST.CONT
      amirre-rlke   kere-ø   twe-tyeke   lhe-tyeke, tanthe-tyeke.
      woomera-TOO   game-ACC   kill-PURP   go-PURP   spear-PURP
      'So the man got his spear and womera and set off to go kill some meat, to spear it.'

Turning to determiners, Australian languages generally have no word class of articles or obligatory determiners (e.g. Blake 2001; Dixon 2002: 66–67; Stirling & Baker 2007). All languages have elements that may have determining functions, like demonstratives, but these are optional in the sense that a bare noun may for instance have a definite or indefinite interpretation. There are only a few exceptions (Louagie 2020: 182–183), such as the adnominal personal pronoun in Arrernte, which is obligatory in definite contexts, while a bare noun has indefinite reference (Wilkins 1989: 165); see examples (16) and (23) for illustration.

Nonetheless, several authors identify a determiner position in the noun phrase in which elements with determining function coalesce (e.g. McGregor 1990: 253–276 on Gooniyandi; Dench 1994: 189–193 on Martuthunira; Louagie 2017 for a continent-wide study). In other words, they identify a distributional class of determiners: those elements which may (but must not) appear in this particular slot in the noun phrase. This is very similar to the approach to classifiers as discussed in the previous paragraphs. An example is found in Harvey's analysis of Gaagudju (Harvey 2002: 316–320), who identifies a determiner slot in initial position in the noun phrase (24a). Demonstratives, pronouns, the numeral 'one', interrogative-indefinites and 'other' may all appear in this slot and may thus be argued to form a distributional category of determiners. Multiple determiners may occur at the same time, as in (24b). However, none of these elements seem to be specialized, as they may also occur in post-head position with a qualifier function. This is illustrated in (24c), where the demonstrative does not so much contextualize the phrase, but rather has a pointing function, behaving as an attribute (Harvey 2002: 317; see also McGregor 1990: 267–268 for a detailed discussion of a similar analysis in Gooniyandi). The mapping between the determiner slot and the elements which may fill it is very flexible in Gaagudju, but it may also be relatively

---

[20] A few languages allow flexible order between generic and specific nouns, where Wilkins's type of analysis works less well. For some of these, an alternative analysis is proposed, highlighting the semantic differences associated with the different word orders; see e.g. McGregor (1990: 253–276) on Gooniyandi.

fixed, as in Mawng (Forrester 2015: 45) or Umpila (Hill 2018: 126–140). Some elements may also show more flexibility than others: while adnominal pronouns are restricted to the determiner slot in almost all languages, as discussed earlier, possessive pronouns and numerals tend to show much more flexibility within and across languages; see Louagie (2017) and Louagie (2020: 164–207) for extensive discussion.

(24) Gaagudju (Gaagudju) (Harvey 2002: 316, 318, 317)
    a. (Deictic(s)) Entity (Qualifier)
    b. *njinggooduwa=ngaayu*   ø-*an-galeemarr-wa=nu*IV-3M-jealous-AUX:PST.
       woman=3F.DAT   PFV=3MIO
       magaarra   ngoondji   djirriingi
       that:I   other   man
       'He is jealous of that other man over the woman.'

    c. *gooyu   djaarli   naarri   biirda   ibárdbi   i-rree-nj-dja*
       mother   meat   I:here   tough   NEG   3I<1-FUT-eat
       'Mother, this meat here is tough. I cannot eat it.'

In sum, while Australian languages generally do not have dedicated word classes of classifiers or determiners, relevant categories may be identified distributionally, as a set of elements which may occur in a particular position in a larger structure, with a particular functional role tied to that position. Classifiers are those elements that may occur in initial position in a classifying construction; determiners are those elements that may occur in a determiner slot in the noun phrase. Such elements may be more or less strongly tied to these positions in different languages.

26.4 VERBAL PARTS OF SPEECH: INFLECTING AND UNINFLECTING VERBS

A number of northern Australian languages, mainly non-Pama–Nyungan ones but also some Pama–Nyungan ones, have two distinct word classes that may be characterized as verbs: IVs and UVs (e.g. McGregor 2002; Schultze-Berndt 2003, 2017; Bowern 2014).[21] Their most typical uses are illustrated in (25a)–(25b) from Bardi. Example (25a) shows how an IV and an UV are combined into a complex construction, which Bowern (2014: 264) characterizes as a complex predicate, in which 'the information normally associated with the head of a verbal predicate is spread over several parts of the predicate'. The UV *wajim* determines the semantic roles of the participants in the event, while the IV *inmanirr* provides information about tense, aspect, person and number, as well as the event type (Bowern 2014: 264–265).[22] Note

---

[21] IVs are sometimes labelled light verbs (when co-occurring with a UV), while UVs are also commonly called preverbs or coverbs.
[22] Note that elements from other word classes may also appear in complex predicates instead of UVs, as illustrated in (10) in section 26.3.1.2.

that the IV cannot be analysed as an auxiliary, as it also has lexical content (Schultze-Berndt 2017: 245). Example (25b) shows how an IV is used as independent verb, i.e. in a simple predicate construction.

(25) Bardi (Nyulnyulan) (Bowern 2014: 264)
    a. *wajim*   *i-n-ma-n=irr*
       wash   3-TR-'put'-CONT=3PL.O
       'He/she washes them.'

    b. *i-n-ma-n=irr*
       3-TR-'put'-CONT=3PL.O
       'He/she put them [somewhere].'

There is good morphological and distributional evidence for distinguishing IVs and UVs as separate word classes. Morphologically, IVs inflect for TAM categories, while UVs do not usually inflect (although in some languages they occasionally do, see Bowern 2014: 279–280 for examples).[23] Distributionally, IVs and UVs occupy different positions and functions in complex constructions as in (25a), and UVs cannot occur as independent predicates in simple verb constructions while IVs can. The nature of these classes is also different. IVs often form a closed class, which can consist of anything between one and hundreds of elements; in most languages IVs cannot be derived from any other lexical category (Bowern 2014: 276; Schultze-Berndt 2017: 247). UVs, by contrast, form an open class allowing borrowings, as illustrated in (25a), and can also be derived from other parts of speech such as nouns or adverbs (Bowern 2014: 274). Semantically, it appears that elements from the class of IVs typically encode more generic concepts, while UVs are semantically more specific (Schultze-Berndt 2017: 264; McGregor 2002). The class of UVs may include translational equivalents of verbs, manner adverbs and spatial adverbs in English, e.g. Jaminjung *waya* 'call', *gaabardag* 'quick(ly), *walthub* 'inside' (Schultze-Berndt 2017: 246–247).

It makes sense to analyse both IVs and UVs as verbal parts of speech, for different reasons: IVs show inflection that is cross-linguistically typically associated with verbs, such as marking for tense, aspect, and person/number of the subject and/or object, while UVs are functionally closer to verbs in other languages, in that they designate an event (McGregor 2002: 25).[24] The question is, however, how these classes are precisely related to the function of predication. In the next paragraphs, I survey the different distributions and functions elements from each class may have in languages that have both, and discuss different analyses for such constructions. I also particularly focus on issues that have repercussions for part-of-speech theories in general.

The most common use of UVs is in combination with an IV in a complex construction (also called compound verb construction), as illustrated in (25a) and (26a)–(26b). Many authors analyse such constructions as complex predicates (or compound verbs), where 'two

---

[23] In some ways, UVs show morphological similarities to nouns or nominals, which also cannot take TAM inflections. However, there is never any doubt about UVs and nouns/nominals forming clearly distinct word classes. For example, UVs can never be used as head of a referential phrase, e.g. in combination with a demonstrative or qualifying modifier.

[24] Some grammatical descriptions analyse UVs as a type of adverbs, because of their lack of inflectional possibilities (e.g. Merlan 1994 on Wardaman; cited in Bowern 2014: 274).

or more predicative constituents jointly contribute to the argument structure of the clause' (Butt 1997: 108; cited in Schultze-Berndt 2017: 252). In other words, both UVs and IVs are analysed as having a predicate function. In a number of languages, however, constructions as in (26) may be analysed as verb classifying constructions, in which the IV overtly classifies the UV, thus 'indicating the category into which the stem is assigned in a particular instance of use, and correspondingly, the category to which the referent event is considered to belong' (McGregor 2002: 44). Thus, in example (26a) the UV *jarrbard* is assigned by the IV *-k* 'carry' to a category of atelic activities where something is moved by constantly applied force to a new location, while in combination with the IV *-m* 'put', as in (26b), *jarrbard* is classified as a telic activity which induces a thing to enter a new state, condition or location (McGregor 2002: 112–114).[25] For languages where such constructions may be analysed as involving verb classification, McGregor (2002) convincingly argues that the IV in fact does *not* have a predicate function, but rather a category marking function.[26]

(26) Nyulnyul (Nyulnyulan) (McGregor 2002: 273; 2011: 729)
a. *war-in   baab   jarrbard   i-na-ng-k   kumbarr*
   one-ERG child   lift   3MIN.NOM-TR-EN-carry stone
   'One child lifted the rock.'

b. *kinyingk-kun / jarrbard i-nga-rra-m   ral /*
   DEF-ABL₂   lift   3NOM-PST-AUG-put   soon
   'After that they lifted him away.' (about a person who has just died, DL)

IVs can also occur alone, as independent predicate in main clauses, as illustrated in (25b), and as dependent predicate in finite subordinate clauses, as in (27). UVs, by contrast, cannot occur as independent predicates in main clauses, but they may occur as only predicate in a subordinate clause, as in (28a) (Schultze-Berndt 2017: 253). UVs may also function as pragmatically dependent predicates, where the verbal or nonverbal context provides the necessary contextualization and where 'the use of the UV itself is the only formal correlate of dependent status' (Schultze-Berndt 2017: 254). An example is when the UV has the illocutionary force of a command, in a so-called 'condensed directive', as in (28b); such uses are stylistically marked, for example in comparison with the use of an imperative IV (Schultze-Berndt 2017: 254).

(27) Jaminjung (Mindi) (Schultze-Berndt 2000: 110)
   *nami=biyang   yirrgbi   ba-iyaj \   [ngalanymuwa=ma   ngantha-mila] *
   2SG=NOW   talking   IMP-BE   echidna=SUB   2SG:3SG-GET/HANDLE.IPFV
   'you now, you talk, (about) when you used to catch porcupine' (handing over the microphone to another speaker)

---

[25] In many ways, verb classification of this type is similar to the nominal classifying constructions described in section 26.3.2. Note that verb classification can also occur in languages that do not have two distinct word classes for predication (see McGregor 2002).

[26] Not all theories agree with this analysis. For instance, Lexical Functional Grammar argues classification 'comes for free' in such constructions (Bowern 2014: 272; referring to a study by Wilson 1999).

(28) Jaminjung (Mindi) (Schultze-Berndt 2017: 253)
   a. *Guyug=biyang   nganji-bili=rrgu* \   [*wujuwuju*   **wirrigaja**=*wu*]
      fire(wood)=SEQ 2SG>3SG-POT:get/handle=1SG.OBL small   cook=DAT[27]
      'You should get fire(wood) for me now, for cooking the small (fish).'

   b. *Gabardag,   gad   ba-manggu,   **gad**| jarr::| gurdij* /
      quick   cut   IMP-hit   cut   put.down   stand
      'quick, cut it! cut! down! stand up!' (to a boy cutting up a kangaroo while being filmed)

The functional–distributional differences between IVs and UVs are summarized as follows by Schultze-Berndt (2017): IVs can be used for dependent and independent predication, while UVs are restricted to dependent predication. Dependency may be syntactic (as in (25a), (26), and (28a)) or pragmatic (as in (28b)). Thus, Schultze-Berndt specifically includes the use of UVs in complex constructions in the function of dependent predication, arguing that their lack of inflectional morphology is evidence for syntactic dependency.

Both as part of a complex construction and on their own, UVs may be used expressively in some languages, i.e. with performative foregrounding (Schultze-Berndt 2001: 367–368; McGregor 2002: 330–331; Schultze-Berndt 2017: 256). Such instances show expressive prosody such as interruption of rhythmic flow, lengthening, higher intensity, larger pitch range or marked voice register (Schultze-Berndt 2001: 367; McGregor 2002: 330). Expressive use is illustrated in (29) from Jaminjung and (30) from Gooniyandi. Although Schultze-Berndt (2017: 255) labels UVs in such uses in Jaminjung as mimetic predicates, arguably not all instances may be analysed as involving predication rather being syntactically independent.

(29) Jaminjung (Mindi) (Schultze-Berndt 2001: 367, 368)
   a. *ning=biji   yirri-ma   gurunyung   **barr::*** \
      break.off=ONLY   1PL.EXCL:3SG-hit.PST   head   smash
      'We only killed it, smashing its head.' (flying fox who had bitten a woman)

   b. *wardi   gad   yirra-nangga:,   'jang 'jang 'jang 'jang,   yathang=ung* \
      tree.species   cut   1PL.EXCL:3SG-chop.PST chew   all.right=COTEMP
      'We cut (bark off) the wardi tree, chew!, chew!, chew!, chew!, all right then.'
      (describing how a stick for obtaining tree honey is made from a piece of fiber by chewing it intensely)

(30) Gooniyandi (Bunuban; McGregor 2002: 330)
   *mariwa-wirri-nhi-yi,   nanggid-birrini,   **doorl**;*
   sneak:up-3PL.NOM+I-3SG.OBL-DU   miss-3PL.NOM/3SG.ACC+BINI   bang
   ***doorl**;   nanggid-birrini-yi*
   bang   miss-3PL.NOM/3SG.ACC+BINI-DU
   'They were sneaking up on him, but missed him, bang!, bang!, they missed him.'

---

[27] The dative is used for a purposive adverbial clause (see also Schultze-Berndt 2000: 111–112); see section 26.2 on complementizing case.

The word classes of IVs and UVs in Australia raise some issues that are relevant for general theories of parts of speech. First, on the basis of the Australian data, Schultze-Berndt (2017) argues that the functional basis used for cross-linguistic research on word classes should take into account both independent and dependent predication. In this sense, she argues, other languages could be analysed as having one flexible category of verbs that can serve both independent and dependent predication. Second, as pointed out by an anonymous reviewer, the use of IVs as markers of verb classification in complex constructions as in (26) and the expressive use of UVs as in (29)–(30) pose a more serious problem to theories of parts of speech like Hengeveld's (1992a, 1992b), because they show that 'verbs' may have functions other than predication (while restriction to predicational use only is crucial to such theories). Both points show that more grammatical functions need to be recognized in part-of-speech typologies if we want to capture the relevant cross-linguistic diversity. Third, Australian languages show an interesting link between UVs and ideophones: a subset of UVs in Australian languages have their origin in ideophones, and UVs and ideophones also share a number of characteristics synchronically, such as distinctive phonological and phonotactic features, sound symbolism and minimal morphological possibilities, as well as expressive uses as in (29)–(30) (McGregor 2001; Schultze-Berndt 2001; McGregor 2002: 324–339). See Chapter 22 in this volume on ideophones as a word class.

Finally, note that a number of Australian languages exhibit related phenomena, but ones that do not imply the presence of two distinct classes of verbs. They for example have compound predicates consisting of two elements which may originally have been an IV and an UV, but that are synchronically indivisible and distributionally behave as a single unit, i.e. that have grammaticalized (Schultze-Berndt 2017: 247–248; McGregor 2002: 149–152). In fact, it is argued by McGregor (2002: 28–29, 351–354) that markers of conjugation classes in many Pama–Nyungan languages too are remnants of IVs in compound verb constructions. For more discussion of compound verb constructions and the categories of IVs and UVs, see for example Nicolas (1998), Wilson (1999), Schultze-Berndt (2000; 2001; 2003; 2017), McGregor (2002; 2004: 174–186), and Bowern (2008; 2010; 2014), among many others. For discussion of inflectional categories on verbs, see for instance Dixon ([1980] 2010: 378–437; 2002: 209–236; mostly on Pama–Nyungan languages) and McGregor (2004: 159–174) on languages from the Kimberley.

26.5 Manner adverbs

Locational and temporal adverbs were discussed in the introduction to section 26.3; this section briefly touches on manner adverbs. Unfortunately, no detailed surveys are available about manner adverbs as far as I am aware (though there are some notes in Dixon [1980] 2010: 281–282; 2002: 181–183 and McGregor 2004: 104), nor have I collected data on adverbs systematically for the languages of my sample, so discussion here remains largely anecdotal. Depending on the language, manner adverbs may have more in common with nominal parts of speech, with verbal parts of speech, or with neither, which is the reason I discuss them in a separate section.

In some languages, manner adverbs show morphological similarities to nominal parts of speech such as nouns and adjectives (or nominals, if not distinguished), in that they may inflect for case marking. In some languages, manner adverbs optionally exhibit instrumental or locative marking. This is for instance the case in Nyulnyul, where a small set of manner adverbs may show instrumental marking, as in (31) (McGregor 2011: 171). In other languages, a manner adverb may agree for nominal case with one of the participants in the clause, for instance in Martuthunira as in (32) (Dench & Evans 1988: 14–16) and in Yankunytjatjara (Goddard 1985: 29–30). In such cases, adverbs behave much like depictive secondary predicates morphosyntactically, although they are semantically subtly different (see Dench & Evans 1988: 14–16 and Himmelmann & Schultze-Berndt 2005 for discussion).

(31) Nyulnyul (Nyulnyulan) (McGregor 2011: 171)
 irr-in   i-ngi-rr-barrkand   **ngarrij-ang**   wangal-in   dub   i-li-ny-an
 they-ERG 3NOM-PST-AUG-tie   hard-INS   wind-ERG   blow   3NOM-IRR-catch-IMP
 'They tied it down tightly, lest the wind blow it away.'

(32) Martuthunira (Ngayarta, PN) (Dench & Evans 1988: 14–15)
 ngunhu-ngara pawulu-ngara **jarruru-lu** wangka-yangu   ngulu   wartirra-lu.
 that.NOM-PL   child-PL   slowly-EFF   speak-PASS.PFV   that-EFF   woman-EFF
 'Those children were spoken to, slowly, by the woman.'

Despite these morphological similarities, it seems that the word class of manner adverbs is distinct from other word classes in most languages (Dixon [1980] 2010: 282). Several languages allow derivation from adjectives or nouns into adverbs (Dixon 2002: 181), usually with an adverbializing suffix, as illustrated in (33). At least one language, Kuku Yalanji, can also derive adverbs from adjectives by reduplication (Patz 2002: 110).

(33) Paakantyi (Paakantyi, PN) (Hercus 1982: 233)
 gila   bari-y-aḏu   **balīra-mala**
 not   go-GC-3SG.S   good-ADV
 'He can't walk properly.'

Flexibility of (at least some) lexemes between adjectival and adverbial functions is found for instance in Bardi (Bowern 2012: 562), Diyari (Austin 2013: 112–114; though no examples are provided) and Martuthunira (Dench 1994: 52–55).[28] An example from Martuthunira is given in (34a)–(34b), showing the element *panyu* 'good' used in adjectival and manner adverbial functions respectively.

(34) Martuthunira (Ngayarta, PN) (Dench 1994: 297, 250)
 a. *yinka-l.yarra*   ngurnu   kayarra-a   wirra-tharra-a   **panyu-tharra-a.**
    chisel-CTEMP   that.ACC   two-ACC   boomerang-DU-ACC   good-DU-ACC
    '[He] chipped out those two good boomerangs.'

---

[28] Hengeveld's (1992a, 1992b) typology predicts that languages with a flexible class of nominals (see section 26.3.1) also show flexibility of lexemes between adjectival and adverbial functions. This prediction does not seem to hold for Australian languages: it is argued that both Bardi and Diyari have distinct parts of speech for nouns and adjectives (Bowern 2012: 158, 263–265; Austin 2013: 40–41), while showing flexibility between adjectival and adverbial functions. By contrast, it is argued that Martuthunira has a single class of flexible elements which allow all three functions (see also the discussion of Martuthunira in section 26.3.1).

b. *Kartu   kangku-layi   yirnaa   pawulu-u   **panyu**   paju.*
   2SG.NOM   carry-FUT   this.ACC   child-ACC   good   REALLY
   Mir.ta   wilawila-ma-rninyji   thurla-npa-wirri-i.
   not   shake-CAUS-FUT   eye-INCH-LEST-ACC
   'You carry this child very carefully. Don't shake him or he'll wake up.'

In other languages, manner adverbs have more in common with verbal parts of speech. For instance, in at least a few languages, adverbs must agree with the verb they modify in transitivity and/or tense, aspect or mood marking (Dixon [1980] 2010: 281–282; 2002: 181–183). In Yukulta, adverbs are derived from adjectives and then take either an intransitive or a transitive suffix, in agreement with the main verb (Keen 1983: 226; cited in Dixon 2002: 183). In Gumbaynggir, manner adverbs likewise must agree with the verb in transitivity and in other inflections like tense (Eades 1979: 304–308). A final example of manner adverbs resembling verbs is found in Dyirbal (Dixon 2002: 181–182), where 'adverbs' are purely verbal in that they have inherent transitivity values and may inflect for TAM as well. They are unlike other verbs, however, in that they generally do not occur alone, but with a main verb, modifying it. Adverbs must agree with the main verb in transitivity and final verbal inflection. If an inherently transitive adverb modifies an intransitive main verb, the adverb is suffixed with a reflexive marker which basically functions as an intransitivizer, as illustrated in (35) with the adverb *gudi* 'do too much'.

(35) Dyirbal (Dyirbal, PN) (Dixon 2002: 182)
     *galga   bungi-m   **gudi-yirri-m***
     DON'T   sleep-NEG.IMP   do.too.much-REFL-NEG.IMP
     'don't sleep too much!'

Apart from languages where adverbs may resemble IVs, there are also languages where adverbs are very close to UVs, e.g. because they also do not inflect and may have similar types of denotations, although there is usually some way of distinguishing them, for instance because they are optional while UVs are not; for some discussion see for example Merlan (1994: 59) on Wardaman and Schultze-Berndt (2000: 72–73) on Jaminjung. This brings us to languages where adverbs do not resemble nominal or verbal parts of speech: they do not inflect at all. Some examples are Bardi (Bowern 2012: 160, 569–570), Dhuwal (Wilkinson 1991: 678–680), and Kuuk Thaayorre (Gaby 2017: 359–361).

26.6 CONCLUSION

This chapter discussed the major lexical parts of speech in Australian languages, both from the large Pama–Nyungan family and from the smaller families in the north and northwest of the continent. Australian languages clearly distinguish verbs from nouns (or nominals): verbs are used for predication and not for reference, at least not without formal adaptation, while nouns are used for both, though mainly for reference. There is some morphological overlap between nouns and verbs in some languages, but it is usually rather minimal and restricted to specific contexts.

Australian languages are more heterogeneous with respect to nouns and adjectives. About one quarter of the languages have morphologically and distributionally distinct word classes of nouns and adjectives; roughly one-third have nouns and adjectives that are only distributionally distinct, but not morphologically; and another third have a single flexible class of 'nominals' that can function both referentially and attributively. In relation to the latter, it was also pointed out that a number of languages more generally show flexibility between elements and functional roles in the noun phrase, for instance where demonstratives or possessive pronouns may be flexible between determiner, qualifier, and entity roles. It was argued that classes of determiners and nominal classifiers may only be identified on a distributional basis, in terms of the elements that may take up the positions in the noun phrase associated with these roles. Overall, the discussion showed the importance of teasing apart morphological and distributional characteristics of lexemes, and showed that more detailed research is needed on the relation between (types of) elements and the functional roles they can fill in a noun phrase, including entity and qualifier, but also roles such as classifier, quantifier, and determiner. This is a question that not only deserves more attention in research on Australian languages, but also outside Australia, as it can offer a more fine-grained perspective on parts of speech.

A number of Australian languages, especially in the north, have two distinct parts of speech associated with predication: IVs and UVs. The latter are, according to Schultze-Berndt (2017), used for dependent predication only, e.g. as part of a complex predicate, or as main predicate in a dependent clause or insubordinated clause. Schultze-Berndt (2017) thus also advocates using more fine-grained functional distinctions as baseline for typological research, including both independent and dependent predication, to capture relevant cross-linguistic variation. At the same time, McGregor (2002) shows that IVs may have another function than predication, viz. as markers of verb classification, thus also problematizing the restriction some part-of-speech theories place on verbs serving predicational functions *only*.

Manner adverbs, finally, are often a distinct part of speech in Australian languages that may show morphological similarities with nominals (such as case marking) or verbs (such as marking for transitivity or tense). In some languages, manner adverbs do not show any inflections. A few grammars note some flexibility of lexemes between adjectival and adverbial functions.

Acknowledgements

I would like to thank David Beck, Eva van Lier, Jean-Christophe Verstraete, and an anonymous reviewer for their valuable feedback on earlier versions of this chapter, which pushed me to discuss some issues more carefully and much helped improve the general structure and flow of the chapter. Work on this chapter was supported by a postdoctoral grant from the Research Foundation-Flanders (FWO), and carried out at the University of Leuven.

CHAPTER 27

WORD CLASSES IN INDO-EUROPEAN LANGUAGES

PAOLO RAMAT

27.1 PRELIMINARIES

IT is well known that the parts of speech (PoS) of modern Indo-European (IE) languages[1] are fundamentally based on the PoS of classical languages, as described first by the Greek grammarians ((pseud)Dionysios Thrax (170–90 BC); Apollonios Dyskolos (2nd cent. AD)) and then by the Latin grammarians (Donatus (late 4th cent.), Priscian (begin 6th cent.), among others).[2] Donatus writes in a catechistic form: '*partes orationis quot sunt? octo. quae? nomen, pronomen, uerbum, aduerbium, | participium, coniunctio, praepositio, interiectio*', 'How many are the parts of speech? Eight. And which ones? Pronoun, verb, adverb, participle, conjunction, preposition, interjection', *Ars minor*, K IV 355, 5–6. In order to have the eight parts of the Greek tradition, as established by Dionysios, Donatus adopted the term *interiectio* ('something interposed or interjected') and thus substituted the article (Gk. *árthron*) which was not present in Latin and was later developed in the Romance languages and other IE languages (but, for instance, not in the Slavonic ones; see section 27.7).

The Latin grammatical categorization was fixed by the Modistae of the Middle Ages,[3] up to the modern era. This tradition has strongly influenced the grammatical descriptions of most standard languages of Europe. It is also well known that Latin PoS are not valid for

---

[1] There is a very large literature on the IE languages, particularly on the ancient ones. The reader is referred to the classical presentations by Meillet 1922, Kuryłowicz 1968 and Watkins 1969, Adrados 1975, Georgiev 1981, Szemerényi 1989, and, more recently, Lehmann 1993, Giacalone Ramat & Ramat 1993. An easy readable introduction, also for non-linguists, is Haudry 1981. See also Villar 1991.

[2] Note that Aristotle (384–322 BC) had written (*Poet.* 20,1456f. and *Interpr.* 2,16ᵃ18–3) about the *mérē tês lékseōs* 'parts of the sentence', i.e. the structure of the sentence with its minimal elements (*stoicheîa*), syllables, conjunctions (*sýndesmoi*), noun (*ónoma*) with cases (*ptôseis*), and verb (*rhêma*). But the later grammarians shifted their attention from the sentence constituents to the word classes, called *mérē toû lógou*, 'parts of speech', whereby *lógos* means 'speech, discourse' (and *léxis* 'sentence').

[3] The Modistae (13th–14th cent.) are speculative grammarians, who based their theory on the 'modes' of meaning in language: modes of being (*modi essendi*), modes of understanding (*modi intelligendi*), and modes of signifying (*modi significandi*).

all languages of the world, although they have often been imposed on the descriptions of very 'exotic' languages as, e.g., North and South American ones and that, for instance, the distinction between Noun and Verb is not so straightforward in the Polynesian languages Samoan and Tongan (see section 27.1 in this volume; Zimmermann & Kellermeier-Rehbein 2015; Bakkerus et al. 2020).

This is not the place to tackle the long-lasting discussion about linguistic universals, and more specifically about the universal nature of verbs and nouns. I just note that linguists studying those 'exotic' languages have found it useful to speak of verbs and nouns or, in a functional approach, at least of 'verbiness' and 'nouniness', or of 'nouny' and 'verby' applied to lexemes or constructs which at the predication level play the role of verbs and nouns in languages that, like Samoan and Tongan, do not have the PoS that characterize the Standard Indo-European as well as the Standard Average European (Stassen 1997; Hengeveld & van Lier 2008, Simone & Masini 2014).[4]

From a general point of view, PoS are categorizations imposed by the linguist on groups of words that show morphosyntactic commonalities as well as functional similarities. PoS represent taxonomic distinctions among lexemes (see Chapter 18) and it is often the case that taxonomies are not able to draw sharp dividing lines between two or more PoS.

However, since the present chapter has to do with the IE word classes, the Greek and Latin PoS (*mérē toû lógou*, *partes orationis*) represent a viable, useful starting point. Clearly, for reasons of space, it will not be possible to consider the details of all PoS in all different IE languages. With reference to the PoS of the old grammarians, the category 'Adjective' (ADJ) was lacking in the classical tradition: Apollonius, following Aristotle, did not divide ADJ and Noun and spoke of *substantia cum qualitate* 'substance with quality'. The notion of ADJ as a category 'per se' was introduced only later by Thomas of Erfurt (*De modis significandi*, the standard modist textbook of the 14th cent.) and then by the famous *Grammaire de Port Royal* [1660] under the label 'accident' of the 'substance' (e.g., *soleil*$_{SUBST}$ *rouge*$_{ACCID}$ 'red sun').

At the same time, participles (PARTs) were considered as an independent *pars orationis*, though they show, like ADJs, agreement with their head nouns (Lat. *fatigantem*$_{ACC.Sg.}$ *operam*$_{ACC.Sg}$ 'a fatiguing work' vs *fatigantes*$_{ACC\ Pl}$ *operas*$_{ACC\ Pl}$ 'fatiguing works'). This contrasts with the treatment of the ADJs which, as we have seen, were included into the category of Nouns (*nomina cum qualitate*). The difference is due to the fact that the *parti-cipium* (a compound from *parte(m)*+the root of the verb *capere* 'take', thus 'take part' as a calque of the Greek term *metochê*) is a double face lexeme which 'parti-cipates' in the verbal nature, having its own argumental structure, as well as agreeing in case, number and gender with a nominal head (cp. [*ambae*$_{NOM\ Pl}$ *te*$_{ACC}$ obsecramus $_{NP}$[*aram*$_{ACC}$ *amplexantes*$_{NOM\ Pl}$]], Plaut. Rud. 694f., 'we both pray you, embracing/while we embrace the altar'), where the participle *amplexantes* agrees, like an adjective, with the subject *ambae* and at the same time has its own object (*aram*) like a verb: Palaemon (1st cent. AD) *ars gramm.* V 545,38 K: *Participia dicta sunt, quod partem capiant nominis partemque verbi. Trahunt enim a nomine casus, a verbo tempora* 'they are named *participia* because they take part of the noun and of the verb. In fact, they take their cases from the noun, their tenses from the verb'.

---

[4] On the notion of Standard Average European (SAE) see *Language Sciences* 20/3 (1988) and the 'General preface' by Ekkehard König to the nine volumes of the EUROTYP series, published by Mouton de Gruyter (1997–2006).

Moreover, a second important difference between PARTs and ADJs is that the latter are capable of gradation, namely as comparative and superlative. Ancient IE languages had synthetic forms of comparative and superlative characterized by suffixes: cf. Skr. *priya-* 'dear'→ *priyatara* 'dearer', *priyatama* 'dearest', AGk. *leukós* 'white' →*leukóteros* 'whiter', *leukótatos* 'whitest'; or—with other suffixes—*kakós* 'bad'→ *kakíōn* 'worse', *kákistos* 'worst', OPers. *tauma 'strong'→ *tauvīyā* 'stronger' (superl. not attested) and *maθištā* 'greatest' from a base *maθa-* (cf. AGk., Doric, *mákistos* 'greatest' connected with *makrós* 'great'). Comparatives and superlatives, like their base adjective and the PARTs, agreed with their head nouns. The synthetic forms of comparative were in most cases progressively substituted by analytic ones: Rum. *mai înalt* < Late Lat. *magis altu(m)* lit. 'more high', instead of Classical Lat. *altior* 'higher' from *altus* 'high'; MGk. *piò leukós* lit. 'more white' (while the comparatives introduced by a determiner (DET) acquired the status of a NP: *ho leukóteros* lit. 'the most white'). Lat. *fortis* 'strong' became It. *forte*, Span. *fuerte*, Fr. *fort*; its comparative was *fortior* 'stronger' while the Romance comparatives are, respectively, *più forte, más fuerte, plus fort* 'stronger'. In a similar way Bulgarian uses prefixes: *goliam* 'old' and *po-goliam* 'older' *naĭ-goliam* 'oldest'.

Italian, Spanish, and Portuguese kept the superlative Latin form for the so-called absolute form: *fortissimus* →It. *fortissimo, audacissimus* →Span. *audacísimo*, Port. *audacíssimo*, but French passed to a periphrastic *très fort* 'very strong', *longissimus* ~ *très long*. The 'relative superlative' as MGk. *ho leukóteros* is an NP introduced by the article: *il più forte, el más audaz, o mais audaz, le plus fort*. The same holds for the Slavonic languages: Ru. *vysokiĭ* 'high' *bolee vysokiĭ* 'higher' (lit. 'more high') *samyĭ vysokiĭ* 'highest' (lit. 'the more high'). In Germanic and Romance only a tiny minority of very frequently used ADJs kept the ancient forms: *better* and *best* (Swe. *bättre* and *bäst*), *worse* and *worst* are considered as comparative and superlative of *good* (Swe. *god*) and *bad* but actually they are autonomous, so-called suppletive lexemes ('qui relèvent plus du vocabulaire que de la morphologie' 'that pertain more to dictionary than to morphology', Ernout 1945: 125); cf. Lat. *meliorem*$_{ACC\ Sg}$ →It. *migliore*, Span. *mejor*, Port. *melhor*, Fr. *meilleur*. Rum. *mai bun* and It. *più buono* (instead of *migliore*) show the pervasiveness of the analytic form even in the most used comparatives, in spite of their high frequency. See further *pēiore(m)* 'worse' and *pessimu(s)* 'worster' →It. *peggiore*, Span. *peor*, Port. *pe(j)or*, Fr. *pire* (but Rum. *mai rău*!) and It. *pessimo*, Span. *pésimo*, Port. *péssimo* (but Rum. *foarte rău*, Fr. *très mauvais*!).

As for the article (ART), which was not included in the traditional eight PoS (*octo partes orationis*) of the Latin grammarians, it was first reintroduced in grammatical accounts by Leon Battista Alberti in his *Grammatichetta* (1438–1441). In the humanist times the knowledge of Greek was diffused among literate people: no wonder that the old *árthron* (lit. 'limb, part') came again to the fore as a descriptive category since in the Romance languages the *articolo* (a calque on *árthron*) had exactly the same function (see section 27.7).

A last remark before we start with the description of the word classes. As shown in the case of the PARTs, in many cases it is not possible to deduce the appurtenance of a lexeme to a particular word class from its morphological marking alone: we need its syntactic context, as well as the general meaning of its context: *happening* means a chance event or a show but in *what's happening?* it has a verbal value: 'What's going on?' Span. *tripulante* 'crewman', properly the PART of *tripular* 'to pilot', has become a fully fledged noun denoting the person who has to do with the action of piloting. As we shall see below, the overlapping of classes along a continuum is much more frequent than usually assumed.

27.2 NOUNS

Nouns are lexemes which syntactically may constitute the head of a noun phrase and semantically refer to concrete objects (*table, book, sphere*), abstract concepts (*justice, democracy*), and emotional states or physical sensations (*courage, fear, hunger, fever*). Forms of the verbal paradigm can act in the role of a noun (Span. *cantante* 'singer', Fr. *étudiant* 'student', properly the present PARTs of the verb *cantar* 'to sing' and *étudier* 'to study', respectively; and see also *wedding, meeting*, strictly related to the verb), up to be inflected like nouns (*los cantantes, les étudiants* and also *the weddings, the meetings*). Original participles became autonomous lexemes, no longer recognized as verbal forms: Lat. *infantem*$_{ACC}$ 'child' (→Fr. *enfant*, It., Span. *infante*)[5] meant originally 'not-speaking'. Even infinitives can be used as nouns with or without a preceding ART: see for instance the It. proverb *Tra il dire e il fare c'è di mezzo il mare* 'between saying and doing there is the sea' (Germ. transl. in the *Reverso Wörterbuch: Zwischen **dem** Sagen und **dem** Tun liegt oft das Meer*); the It. translation of the title of the famous book by John Austin, *How to Do Things with Words* was rendered *Quando dire è fare* (Fr. *Quand dire, c'est faire*: no ART before the infinitives).

To derive nouns that denote the person that accomplishes (or has to do with) a verbal action—the so-called *nomina agentis*—IE languages make use of affixes, normally suffixes, that in part go back to the IE protolanguage as Skr. *dā-tár-as*$_{NOM\ Pl}$ 'donors' = AGk. *dō-têr-es* (IE suffix with vowel 'ablaut' *-ter/-tor/-tr̥* and *-tēr/-tōr/-tr̄*): Lat. *impera-re* 'command' →*impera-tor* 'emperor' and *impera-tricem*$_{ACC\ F}$> It. *imperatrice* 'empress'; *scrib-ere* 'write' →*scriptor* 'the person who writes, writer'.

Other suffixes have specialized uses for indicating professional activities as in *writ-er* (< *to write*): cf. Germ. and Engl. *sing-er* from *sing-en* and *to sing*: Lat. *macell-arius* 'the one who has to do with the *macellum* "slaughter-house", i.e. "butcher". It would take too long to enumerate all the suffixes used in the IE languages, to form nouns from verbs as well as from other PoS (ADJs, abstract nouns, etc. as in Lat. *na-tura* "nature"). Just note that the already mentioned Germ. and Engl. *-er* that we find in *Sing-er, Schreib-er, writ-er* derives from Lat. *-arius* "who has to do with X", while Germ. *-erei*, Engl. *-ery* derive from the corresponding feminine suffix *-aria* which is continued in Fr. *-erie* as in *boulangerie* "bakery, Germ. Bäckerei" (from *boulang-er* "baker, Germ. Bäcker")'.

The *nomina agentis* are included in the larger group of deverbal nouns that includes also the action nouns (*nomina actionis* and *nomina rei actae*. The latter refer to an already accomplished action: *statutum* 'what has been stated, decree'). But action nouns (*nomina actionis*) do not have temporal reference: *destruct-ion* may refer to the past, the present and the future according the context. Action nouns denote the action expressed by the verb or the verbal root they derive from: Ru. *prepodavanie, presledovanie, starenie* from *prepodavat', staret'* 'teach', 'pursue', 'grow old', respectively. *Translation, education, transformation* are Latinate words deriving (often via French) from *translatare, educare, transformare*. In the quoted examples German has preferred to 'Germanize' in *Übersetzung, Erziehung* and

---

[5] Spanish *infanta* 'little girl' (an honorific title reserved to the king's daughters) shows how the Latin origin of this word was completely lost: Latin PARTs in *-ens*$_{NOM}$/*-entem*$_{ACC}$ did not distinguish masculine and feminine. *Infanta* is the Spanish feminine form simply derived from *infante*.

Änderung from *übersetzen, erziehen* and *ändern* (the first two verbs are semantic calques from Latin too). At any rate, the word formation strategy does not change: a suffix is added to the verbal base. Note that, as in the Sanskrit and Greek examples *dā-tăr-as* and *dō-têr-es* 'donors', we have the concatenative strategy that is typical of the IE languages, as we shall see when dealing with verbs (section 27.4): base + suffix denoting the category of the lexeme + morphological information, as Germ. *Zeit*$_{BASE}$-*ung*$_{ABSTR.NOUN}$-*en*$_{Pl}$ 'newspapers'.

A preliminary remark has to be made before speaking of compounds: compounding is a word formation process that combines two (or more) words/stems as in Germ. *Auto-bahn* 'highway', Engl. *ice-berg*; derivation is the combination of a word/stem and one or more affixes, as in *pre-podav-anie* and *Zeit-ung*. Both techniques were much used in the ancient IE languages and continue to be used in their modern heirs, so that it is worth having a closer look at the different types of compounding.

27.2.1 Nominal compounds with a nominal base

Special attention to nominal compounds has been paid since the Indian grammarians (Pāṇini, Patanjali, Śākaṭāyana, etc.)[6] who distinguished various types of compounds that may be found in the contemporary IE languages too (for reasons of space we disregard here the possible phonological adjustments such as linking vowels and morphological variants that can be found in every type):

(a) *dvaṃdva* (lit. 'pair') i.e. copulative compounds whose meaning is often more than the sum of the component parts, as Skr. *mātā-pitárau* 'mother-father' i.e. 'parents', Ru. *otec-mat'* lit. 'father-mother' i.e. 'parents' (a *dvaṃdva* that is found also in many non-IE languages, e.g. in Dravidian Malayalam), OBulg. *brátĭ-sestra* lit. 'brother-sister' i.e. 'siblings'. Copulative compounds are also called co-compounds as they denote a superordinate-level concept, such as *brátĭ-sestra* (see Wälchli 2015). Historically, we note a progressive increasing of this type of compounded nouns, up to MGk. *machairo + pērouno* 'knife-fork' i.e. 'cutlery', It. *cassa + panca* lit. 'case-bench' i.e. 'settle'. On the contrary, Germ. *Hemd + hose* 'a dress formed by shirt plus trousers', Ru. *divan-krovat'* 'sofa-bed', i.e. a piece of furniture that can be used both as sofa or as bed, are just the sum of the two coordinated members;[7] in the language of sport this holds for the colours of a team which metaphorically designate the team itself: It. *i*$_{ART\,Pl}$ *rossoblù*$_{undeclinable}$ lit. 'the red-bleus' i.e. 'the players of the Bologna soccer team' > 'the Bologna team', *i*$_{ART\,Pl}$ *bianconeri*$_{declinable:Pl.}$ lit. 'the white-blacks', i.e. 'the players of the Juventus soccer team' > 'the Juventus team (Turin)'. This type of *dvaṃdva* is found in many IE languages: see Ru. *tëmno-sinij* 'dark-blue'. In *dvaṃdva*s as Fr. *aigre-doux*, It. *agrodolce* 'sour-sweet' the members of the composition are at the same level,

---

[6] An excellent description of the Indian compounds can be found in Thumb & Hauschild 1959, 3rd part: 'Compositum und Satzbau'. The Indian names of the compound types, like 'dvandva', have been kept even in the modern handbooks (listed in n. 1). A general survey on compounds can be read in Bußmann 2002, s.v. 'compound' (with references to the previous literature).

[7] Compounds of this type may be hyphenated as in the French and Russian examples. In the other quoted words I have inserted a <+> between the two non-hyphenated members.

and it is not possible to say that one is the head while the other is its determiner: *doux-aigre* would amount to mean the same. Cf. further the three members compounds like Slov. *bę́lo-mǫ́dro-rdèč* 'white-blue-red' (said of a flag).

(b) *tatpuruṣa-* (lit. 'of this man') are determinative endocentric compounds, where one component is in the attributive relation to the other one: see *madhyāhna* = Span. *mediodia*, Engl. *midday*, MGk. *mesēméri*, Cze. *poledne* etc., Germ. *Jungfrau* lit. 'a woman who is young' > 'virgin'. The *tatpuruṣa-* are endocentric compounds, i.e. they have inner reference: in place names like Gk. *Acró + polis*, Ru. *Volgo + grad* it is clear that the second member is the head of the compound which is determined by the first one: *Volgograd* is the town that is located near the Volga river. Note that the determiner may be an ADJ (*madhya-, akro-, jung-*), or a noun as in Germ. *Eisen + bahn*, It. *ferro + via* 'railway' that are different from Fr. *chemin-de-fer* and Ru. *železnaja*$_{ADJ}$ *doroga*, as French shows a syntactic construct and Russian makes use of an agreeing ADJ. Thus, we have both possibilities: ADJ + N and N + N (as in Port. *ferrovia* and *caminho-de-ferro*): see Sb-Cr. *vèle-mājstor* 'grand master' and Germ. *Hand-schuh* 'glove' from 'hand+shoe'. Different from the *dvaṃdva*, *tatpuruṣa-* compounds have a head and its determiner.

(c) *bahuvrīhi-* (lit. '(who) has much rice') are exocentric compounds, i.e. they have external reference. The *bahuvrīhi-* can be understood as ADJs like AGk. *rhodo + dáktylos* '(who has/having) fingers like roses', Lat. *magn + animus* '(who has a) big soul' or even as Nouns (< nominalized ADJs/Nouns): *redskin*. Modern IE languages make use of the *bahuvrīhi*-type: see *snow + white*, Swe. *snö + wit*, Afr. *Schneeu + witjie*, Gael. *geal.sneachda*, It. *Bianca + neve* lit. '(who is /being) as white as snow' (Germ. *Schnee + wittchen*); *red + skin*, It. *pelle + rossa* lit. '(who has/having a) red skin', i.e. an American Indian.

However, nominal compounds on a verbal base are much more frequent (see next section). Nigel Fabb (in Spencer and Zwicky 2007: § 1.1.1) makes a point concerning the distinction between exocentric and endocentric compounds and says that sometimes it is a matter of interpretation: whether you think that *greenhouse* is endo- or exocentric depends on whether you think it is a kind of house. At any rate, there cannot be any doubt that *green* is the attributive determiner of *house*.

27.2.2 Nominal compounds with a verbal base

This is the most usual type of compounds since the oldest IE languages: cp. Skr. *madya + pa-* 'wine-drinker', OPers. *aršti + bara-* 'spear-bearer', AGk. *thēro + tróphos* 'wild beast-nourisher', Slav. *vodo + nosi* lit.'water carrier' >'water-pot', Lat. *agri + cola* lit. 'land-care-taker' > 'farmer'. The constituents' order is OV and this strategy has been kept up to modern times in many languages: cp. *baby-sitter, caretaker*, and further Germ. *Wolken + kratzer*, Du. *Wolkenkrabber*, calques of *skyscraper*, Rus. *nebo + skreb*, Cze. *mrako + drap* (both Slavonic languages are zero-suffixed), etc. This compounding technique is very productive and new compounds may also be created as *story-teller, water-stopper, wine-drinker* which may also be not registered in the dictionaries. Note the *-er* ending of the deverbal *nomina agentis*, already seen in section 27.2. According to their general trend OV →VO, Romance languages have inverted the order of these compounds and thus we get It. *grattacielo*, Fr. *gratte-ciel*, Port. *arranha-céu*, Span. *rascacielos*. Rum. *zgârie-nori*. Along with the *nomina agentis* we have the action nouns of the already mentioned *destruction*- and *prepodavanie*-type: abstract nouns which derive from verbs.

27.2.3 Nouns from/with univerbation

Univerbation is the union of two syntagmatically adjacent forms into one, as in Span. *terremoto* 'earthquake' from Lat. *terrae*$_{GEN}$ *motus*$_{NOM}$, properly 'earth's quake'(see Lehmann 2020), or in It. *acquedotto* 'aqueduct' from the Latin phrase *aquae*$_{GEN Sg}$ *ductus*. In order to be a real compound, it should be something like **acqua*$_{NOUN}$ + *dotto*, but **dotto* does not exist in Italian: consequently, we cannot say that *acquedotto* is formed by a determiner + its head. In other words, it is not a compound in the proper sense. Indeed, it is not always easy to distinguish univerbations and compounds (see Lehmann 2020: §§ 4.2.2 and 6.1.1). At any rate, univerbation also produces new nouns, as *terremoto* -and that is why a special subsection of the NOUN section is here dedicated to it. If we compare *terremoto* and *acquedotto* with *acrópolis* (see section 27.2.1) we see a main difference in their diachronic evolution: *terrae motus* and *aquae ductus* were 'syntagmata' but *acrópolis* wasn't (it should have been **akrê*$_{ADJ\ NOM F}$ *pólis*$_{NOUN\ NOM F}$ with the determiner agreeing with its head).

There are also univerbated nouns which have been dubbed 'pseudo-compounds', as the first member is not a simple stem (Wortstamm) but rather an inflected form: classical examples are *Diós*$_{GEN}$-*kouroi*, properly 'Zeus' sons' (namely Castor and Polydeuces) and the already quoted *terraemotus*. In Sanskrit, we find 'pseudo-compounds' like *divas*$_{GEN}$-*pati*- 'heaven's king'. Actually, pseudo-compounds are (stereotyped) NPs. Note, however, that -*as* was seen as compounding marker and extended also to first member nouns having different inflection (Thumb & Hauschild 1959: § 666): *ráthas-pati* 'master of the war-chariot' (the genitive of *ratha* -Av. *raθa* - is actually *rathasya*). The same holds for German where, alongside univerbated (pseudo)compounds like *Bundes*$_{GEN}$-*post* lit. 'post of the federation' and *Götter*$_{Pl}$-*blume*$_F$ lit. 'gods$_{Pl}$-flower' > 'carnation', there is also *Regierungs-chef* 'prime minister' where the -*s*- does not belong to the inflection of the -*ung*-Nouns.

As we can observe in the above examples, the PIE language was basically an OV language with the determiner (or 'modifier') preceding the determinee (or 'head'). We know lots of personal names of this type in all ancient IE languages: OPer. *Aspa* + *canah*- lit. 'horse-love', Av. *Zarə* + *θuštra* lit. 'golden-camel', AGk. *Asty* + *ánax* lit. 'town-lord', Run. *Hlewa* + *gastiR* lit. 'glory-guest', Celt. *Dumno* + *rix* lit. 'world-king', Slav. *Mirĭ* + *slava* lit. 'peace-glory' (> Serb., Bulg. etc. Miroslav), Lith. *Algi* + *mantas* lit. 'salary-wealth'.[8]

Many modern IE languages have kept this order: Engl. *sawfish* (without hyphen), Ru. *pila-ryba*, but the Romance languages have a VO order: It. *pesce-sega*, Span. *pez serra* (but Port. *serra-peixe*!) Fr. *poisson scie*, Rum. *pește-fieră*.

Finally we have to consider univerbated nouns such as *republic* (present in all modern IE languages) which was originally a phrase (a 'syntagma'): *res publica* with inflection (*rei*

---

[8] Whether such personal names are to be considered univerbations or compounds is not relevant in this presentation of the IE PoS.

publicae etc.): since *re-* no longer exists with the meaning of 'thing', the modern word *republic* has to be considered as an example of univerbation without compound: 'loss of compositionality is a process accompanying univerbation in lexicalization' (Lehmann 2020: § 5.3).

27.3 ADJECTIVES AND PARTICIPLES

ADJs and PARTs belong to the large class of nominal modifiers that also includes determiners, case constructions, relative clauses, PPs.[9] However, while relative clauses and case constructions are phrases and therefore do not represent PoS, ADJs (+ PARTs) do. ADJs, contrary to PARTs,[10] cannot have ARGs, particularly adjectives that derive from bases of other PoS such as *foolish* from *fool*_Noun or Ru. *železnyĭ*_ADJ 'ferrous' from *železo*_Noun 'iron', or are autonomous lexemes as *grey* and Port. *doce* 'sweet'. On the contrary, PARTs have always a verbal base:

(1) French
 *Ce livre*_M *bien intéressant*_M *raconte une histoire*_F *passionnante*_F
 'This very interesting book tells an exciting story.'

(2) Polish
 Znalazłem ich, chowając się w szafie.
 I.found them hiding REFL in closet
 'I found them while I was hiding in the closet.' (*chowając* agrees with the speaking subject)

(2bis) *Znalazłem ich chowających się w szafie.*
 'I found them while they were hiding in the closet.' (*chowających* is an adjectival participle from the VB *chowaj* 'hide', grammatically agreeing with the object 'them').

ADJs express property concepts which modify and define the properties of the head noun they refer to: *a/the foolish fellow* (see Chapter 18 in this volume with reference to Croft 1991). As in the case of *sweet*, ADJs can metonymically take up the role of Nouns and even of ADVs: with a determiner (DET: a_{INDEF}/the_{DEF}) *sweet* is 'a/the cake, a/the candy'; in Hittite, Sanskrit, Anc. Greek, Latin the accusative neuter could function as qualification of a Verb, i.e. as its ad-verb:[11] cf. Hitt. *mekki* 'much', Gk. *ády phōneísas* (Sappho, frgm.2), Lat. *dulce loquentem* (Catullus, *Carm*. 1, 23) 'sweetly speaking', still to be found in Petrarch (Sonetto 126) *dolce parla* while in Modern Italian one has to say *dolcemente parla*. Conversely, one finds ADJ + Noun where it would be possible to use an ad-verb specifying the 'modus' of the

---

[9] See, respectively, *Those girls, Aquae ductus, The man who has a red beard, The man with a read beard*, i.e. 'Barbarossa'. Note that the nickname of the German emperor Friedrich is a *bahuvrīhi*-compound.

[10] Recall the example in section 27.1: *aram amplexantes*. On the main differences between ADJs and PARTs, see section 27.1.

[11] Remember that Lat. *ad-verbium* is a calque of AGk. *epírrhēma* where *rhêma* means 'verb' (and not 'discours').

verb: cp., e.g., OIran. Avesta (*Yašt* 10,20) *apaši*$_{NOM Sg.F}$ (not *apaša*$_{ADV}$) *vazaiti*$_{3Sg}$ *arštiš*$_{NOM Sg F}$ (lit. '(the) backward (*apaši*) spear (*arštiš*) flies (*vazaiti*)'. English and other modern IE languages would use an adverb and not an agreeing adjective as *apaši*: 'backwards flies the spear'.

In compounded ADJs Proto-Indo-European (PIE) had normally the OV order with determiner + determinee and Germanic languages have kept this order as unmarked: cp. Engl. *barefoot(ed)*, Germ. *barfuß* properly a *bahuvrīhi*-ADJ (see section 27.2.1 (c): '(who has) bare foot'. In Russian and the other Slavonic languages, the unmarked order is the same: *vsenarodnyi* lit. 'all-popular' i.e. 'national, public', where *vse*- determines -*narodnyi*.

27.4 VERBS

The verb (VB) is the core/nucleus of the predicative sentence and has its arguments (ARGs). However, there exist non-verbal predications and VBs without ARGs (basically the meteorological verbs: MGk. *bréchei* ['vrexi], Lat. *pluit* > It. *piove*, Span. *llueve*, Fr. *il pleut* 'it rains'—with a 'dummy subject', as French, like English is a 'non-pro-drop' language, i.e. a language with an obligatory subject before the verb in non-interrogative, non-imperative sentences.

It is possible to have what is called in the frame of Functional Grammar a 'non-verbal predication', i.e. constructions containing a form of the (equivalent of the) verb *to be* as well as those containing no verb at all (see Hengeveld 1992b: 1–2), like in Russian: *Ja student* 'I am a student'.

As in many non-IE languages, the category (PoS) VB in IE languages had and has features like diathesis, tense, mood, aspect, number more or less developed.[12] In turn, features have values: diathesis may be active, passive, reflexive; tense may distinguish past, present, aorist, future and aspect can be ingressive, inchoative, etc., while mood may express indicative, subjunctive, desiderative, conditional, etc. (see Ramat 1999). It is here impossible to describe the details of the various grammars. Every IE language has developed its own verbal morphology and there are not two languages which totally overlap. For instance, the Armenian imperfect is probably a PIE optative, with a change from mood to tense. Some languages have particular morphological forms to express values that other languages express via periphrasis, as the English ingressive *I'm going to* + VB, or the French construct *être en train de* + Vb 'to be in the process of [doing] +VB'. For instance, Albanian has a particular mood, usually called 'admirative' to express surprise or disagreement. An 'avertive' mood to express non-realization, frustration of the verb situation—which can be translated in English with 'to fail to VB'—is found in Bulgarian (see Kuteva 1998: 200).

Neglecting these peculiarities, the main point concerning the IE PoS is that VB is a category firmly documented everywhere.

---

[12] For instance, among the modern IE languages only Lithuanian and Slovene keep the dual which was firmly established in the ancient languages (bar Latin). As another example of different features' development one could mention the difference between the rather simple morphological system of the English verb when compared to that of Armenian and the Slavonic languages.

27.5 Adverbs

ADVs are modifiers of a head; more precisely, of a non-nominal head (see Chapter 19): one cannot say *a strongly bottle, nor *many properly bikes. ADVs apply to VBs (see n. 11) as in *he runs quickly* which could be paraphrased as *He runs in a quick way*. Besides, an ADJ or even an ADV can be qualified by an ADV (*The picture is exceptionally fine; She walked surprisingly slowly*).

We have already seen that the accusative neuter of an ADJ was used with an adverbial function (see section 27.3) and also other cases of the nominal inflection were used adverbially in the Avesta and Sanskrit. Still today Russian and other Slavonic languages use the neuter singular (short) form of ADJs as ADV: Ru. *jarko* 'brightly', Pol. *cicho* 'quietly', etc. This is a good example of blurring and blurred boundaries between categories. But adverbs as proper category have been present in IE languages since the oldest documents: they are usually formed by a suffix attached to a nominal or adjectival base: see Hitt. MUNUS-*ili* 'as a women', properly 'women-ly', *hattili* 'in the Hatti language', Skr. *yathā-vát* 'orderly', *manu-vát* 'humanly', AGk. *-ōs* as in *phílōs* 'friendly', *tachéōs* 'rapidly', Slav. *-ĭsky* from ADJs in *-ĭsk-* as in *mǫžĭsky* 'like a man, courageously'. While the origins of *-ili, -vát, -ōs, -y* are uncertain and still debated, Romance and Germanic languages show clear univerbation of phrases with agreement ('syntagmata'): Lat. *clara*$_{ADJ.ABL.F}$ *mente*$_{Noun\ ABL.F}$ lit. 'with a clear mind'> Port. *claramente*, It. *chiaramente*, Fr. *clairement* are ADVs meaning 'clearly'. In a similar way German has formed ADVs by univerbation of an inflected ADJ + *weise* 'manner': *vorsichtiger*$_{ADJ.DAT.F}$ *weise*$_{Noun\ F}$ lit. 'in cautious manner' > *vorsichtigerweise*$_{ADV}$ 'cautiously'. Dutch followed another univerbation way: *paars*$_{GEN}$-*gewijze*$_{ADV}$ 'in pairs' (see Germ. *paarweise*, but the inflected *-gewijze* is used just for forming adverbs). English *-ly* adverbs come from univerbation of Noun + OEngl. *líće* 'form, body': *frijōnd-lika* 'having the appearance of a friend'> 'friendly'. An interesting case is represented by the Armenian adverbial suffix *-(a)pēs* lit. 'manner' (cp. Germ *-weise*) which in Iranian exists as an independent word but in Armenian is used just as adverbial suffix (like Du. *-gewijze*).

Though cases and inflection can still be recognized in the ADVs, they are uninflected lexemes—and this makes a clear difference compared to ADJs in the IE languages that have kept the adjective inflection: *clara-mente* and not *claro-mente*.

A second important difference between ADVs and ADJs is that the former are movable and may have in their scope different NPs of a sentence or even the whole sentence, with meaning changes: *I did see the cloud clearly/I did see clearly the cloud* and *Clearly, I did see the cloud*, but not *Clear, I did saw the cloud*: only *I saw the clear cloud* is correct—but it has a quite different sense (see section 27.3.4). ADVs, especially modal ADVs, may concern the event (*Smoking is strictly forbidden*) or the agent/patient of an action (*John has been severely fined*), or express the speaker's attitude to the content of the sentence as in *Clearly, I did see the cloud*.

So far, we have referred mostly to manner ADVs. But there are other ADVs, like time, space, evidentiality, quotative ADVs (see Chapter 19, sections 3, 4; Ramat & Ricca 1998): see, respectively, *yesterday, circularly, seemingly, reportedly* and the equivalent expressions in the IE modern languages

As shown by *yesterday*, not all ADVs end by *-ly* and similar univerbations like *-mente* or *-weise*: see Fr. *hier*, It. and Rum. *ieri*, Germ. *gestern*, Du. *gisteren* 'yesterday', Du. *slechts* 'only, just', *evenweel* 'similarly', *dus* 'thus'. Time ADVs can constitute a sentence by themselves when answering a question: *When did John arrive?—Yesterday.* Other ADVs may perhaps be used in the same way, but in a very informal style: *How do you make it?—Thus.*

The same holds for the so-called particles, which are often rubricated under ADVs: *perhaps, maybe: Did John already arrive?—Maybe.* However —**Quite maybe* is not a possible answer, while —*Quite possibly* is correct. Finally we have to note that some ADVs admit of reduplication as a kind of superlative: *very very nice,* Fr. *très très joli,* Germ. *sehr sehr hübsch.* It is difficult to find a general rule for this kind of adverbial reduplication: every language seems to follow its own pragmatic behaviours. Port. *logo logo* and It. *sùbito sùbito* 'immediately' do not have reference to a head and are pure ADVs, while MGk, *kontá kontá* 'very near' is originally an ACC.Pl Ntr. and It. *svelto svelto* 'very rapidly' reduplicates in adverbial sense what is properly an ADJ, whereas *slowly slowly,* sometime used in fairy tales, instead of *very slowly* is not standard English.

On the deictic ADVs, see section 27.7.

27.6 ADPOSITIONS (PRE- AND POSTPOSITIONS)

Although already Donatus distinguished *praepositio* as a PoS of its own (see section 27.1), many grammars arrange under 'Local Adverbs' lexemes that are actually adpositions (ADPs) and constitute a PP with a Noun or an NP they are related with (see Chapter 20 in this volume): *[Beyond the church]*ₚₚ *there is a cemetery.*[13] ADPs in ancient IE languages were bound to cases, as in AGk. *aná* (Preposition)/*ána* (Postposition) +GEN, DAT, or ACC according to the meaning of the adpositional phrase (or VP). Slavonic and German kept this state (e.g. *meždu* 'between'+ Instrumental, *pri* 'near'+Locative, Germ. *entlang* 'along'+ DAT), and modern Slavonic languages that keep case inflection still behave this way (e.g. Ru. *ceres* 'through'+ACC). See further Alb. *nga* 'from'+ NOM; Lith. *prie* 'near'+ GEN, etc.

Particularly with movement verbs, IE languages may alternate the use of ADP + VB with purely lexical items as in *She descended the stairs* instead of *She came* ₚₚ[*down the stairs*]. It is also possible to find both constructions in the same sentence, as in It. *scender giù dalle scale,* where *scendere* means 'per se' 'go down', so that literally we have '*ᵥₚ[[go down]* ₚₚ[*down the stairs*']]. Actually, *scendere* may be used as transitive, like *to descend: scendere le scale,* i.e. a VO construct (VB+'OBJ'), is quite correct (never the OV **le scale scendere*). The ADV + VB or VB + ADV construction goes back to the oldest stages of the IE languages. In his *Grammaire homérique* Chantraine (1953: 82) quotes as example *(Odysseús) kephalês ápo phâros héleske (Od.* 8,88) 'Ulixes took away from his head the veil' and writes of 'little words' as *ápo/apó* (with movable stress) that make clearer the intended idea (*héleske* 'took away' in the example) and are autonomous (see Adrados 1975: 844, Cuzzolin, Putzu, & Ramat 2006).

---

[13] Only monorhematic forms can be considered here, though many monorhematic ADPs derive via univerbation from polyrhematic constructions: *in stead (of) > instead (of),* It. *in vece > invece (di)* 'instead (of)' (interestingly enough, the simple Noun *vece* < Lat. *vice(m)* 'place' no longer exists in modern Italian). Consequently, *instead* will be included, but not *in stead.* Considering the standardized polyrhematic expressions as *at the foot of, in front of* etc. as well as the always possible new creations for indicating space relations as *on the eyes (of)* for 'in front (of)' would largely overrun the limits of this article.

They can be used in isolation, absolutely, or with a VB either as ADVs (Du. *het water loopt door de kanalen* 'the water flows through the channels') or preverbs (Du. *hij heft de hoge school doorlopen* 'he has finished the high school'), or even with a Noun as prepositions, as Chantraine had remarked. Modern IE languages keep remnants of postpositions as in the Engl. formula *two years ago*,[14] and (old-fashioned) Germ. *des schlechten Wetters wegen* 'because of the bad weather', *seinem Wunsch zufolge* 'according to his desire'.

The French construction which has been attested since the Middle Age (*Dont m'en porteras tu avec* (Nicolas 1157), 'Then you will take me with you') and is still found in contemporary colloquial French (*ses poupées, elle ne joue jamais avec* lit. 'her dolls, she never plays with'), raises the question of the separable VBs as Germ. *aufhören* 'to stop' vs *hör mal auf!* 'stop now!' or Engl. *upgrade* vs *he graded up to first class*. This is not a problem we can discuss in the present chapter that deals with PoS (see Cuzzolin, Putzu, & Ramat 2006): suffice to note that preposed or postposed ADPs are a steady PoS in the IE languages.

26.7 ARTICLES/DETERMINATIVES/ DEMONSTRATIVES: A HYPERCLASS INCLUDING THE NOUN'S MODIFIERS

An ART is a member of a class of dedicated words that are used with Nouns or NPs to mark the identifiability of the referents (Nouns or NPs). Articles are part of a broader category called determiners, which also include demonstratives, possessive determiners, and quantifiers (hence the title of this section).

Ancient Greek had already developed a demonstrative into a preposed article, and Albanian has a so-called isolated or adjectival ART *e/të* preposed to a (feminine) Noun in its determined or undetermined form:

(3)   *e vërteta* 'the truth', Sg/*të vërtetat*, Pl. vs *e vertëtë* 'a truth', Sg/*të vërteta*, Pl.

Armenian has a consonant element which, suffixed to a word, is roughly equivalent to a definite ART and functions as a DET with a triple deictic distinction (see below in this section): *tʻag-s* 'the/this crown', *tʻag-d* 'the/that crown', *tʻag-n* 'the/yon crown' (cp. Ajello 1998: 216).

In Romani we find a preposed definite article. On the contrary, the ART, as stated in section 27.1, was unknown to the Latin grammarians and it represents one of the most important innovations of (parts of) the later IE languages. In English, we have *the* and *a(n)* as definite and, respectively, indefinite article, which combine with a noun to form a noun phrase: *the nice girl, a nice girl, an important person*. The def. ART presupposes that the referent of the NP is known to the speech act participants (at least to the speaker). Conversely, the indef. ART refers to a person, an object or, more generally, to a state of affairs that is

---

[14] *Ago* derives from *agone* < OEngl. *āgān* 'gone by' i.e. 'past', properly a past PART. But it functions as a postposition (vs the prepositional *ago fif yer*).

undefined or unknown: *I saw a cat crossing the street*. *The* and *a(n)* are invariable, but in many languages ARTs carry additional grammatical information such as gender, number, and case: cp. Rumanian, with postposed and inflected ART:

(4) *stelele*_{ART NOM Pl}   *ostașului*_{GEN.Sg}   and   *stelelor*_{GEN Pl}   *ostașului*
    stars-the   soldier-the-of   stars-of   soldier-the-of
    'The stars of the soldier' and 'of the stars of the soldier'

Postposition of the def. ART is typical of the Scandinavian Germanic languages too: *Aftonbladet* lit. 'evening journal-the'. But there are no historical ties between the Balkan and the Scandinavian postposition. East Slavonic languages do not have ARTs, while Balkan Slavic (Macedonian, Bulgarian, Serbo-Croat) have a definite postposed ART (Bulg. *knigata* lit. 'book-the') and an indefinite ART (Bulg., Maced. *eden* 'one'). Slovene (*ta*), Czech (*ten*), Serbian-Lusatian (*tòn*) partially Polish, know definiteness markers in colloquial style (see Trovesi 2004; Bažec 2019).

As in many languages around the world, such as Finnish (Laury 1997), ARTs originate(d) from demonstratives as in the Romance and Germanic languages: see for instance (late) Lat. (still inflected) *illo(m)/illo(d)* > OIt. (or Protoromance? 9th cent.):

(5) Non   dicere   **ille**   secrita a bboce
    Not   say   DET/ART   secrets at voice
    'Don't tell **the** secrets [i.e. the secret parts of the mass] out loud.'

Later, we get It. *il/lo*, Fr. *le*, Sp. *el*, Port. *o*, Rum. *-(u)l* (postposed). Trovesi (2004: 167) states that Slovene, Czech, and Serbian-Lusatian are in a transitional phase between DEMs and ARTs in an ongoing process of grammaticalization which takes place particularly in the spoken language. Notably, a larger analysis of the languages spoken around the Mediterranean since the 3rd millennium (Ancient Egyptian, Ugaritic, etc.) has shown that the definite ART appears first in non-formal documents and derives from DEMs used as reinforcement of the deictic (emphatic) function which is typical of the spoken language (Putzu & Ramat 2001): cf. the reinforcement of Fr. *ce* > *ce-lui* > *ce-lui-ci/-là*; Germ. *der* > *der hier/der da*. Germanic languages, too, derive their ARTs from the old IE demonstrative stem **to-*. As for the indefinite ART (Engl. *a(n)*), many languages—and among them some IE languages– derive it from the inflected numeral 'one' in an unstressed position: cp. Germ. *ein*, Swe. *en*, Ukr. *odyn*, MGk. *énas*, Fr. *un*, Port. *um* etc. It was absent from Latin, Ancient Greek, and Old Church Slavonic, and it is still absent from East Slavic. The same holds for Lithuanian and Latvian.

The difference between the previously mentioned French forms *celui-ci* and *celui-là* raises the question of the deixis 'stricto sensu'. DEMs are deictic expressions referring to the speech situation ('deixis in praesentia': *this book on the table*) but also to elements, persons, concepts not present at the moment of the speech act ('deixis in absentia': *that dream I had a month ago is now coming back*). In these examples, *this* and *that* are demonstrative determiners of the co-occurring Nouns (*book* and *dream*), i.e. they are adnominal DEMs. But DEMs may also function as PRO: Fr. *J'aime celui-ci, non celui-là* 'I like this one, not that one' (see Chapter 21 in this volume). Moreover, also ADVs such as *here, there, over there* pertain to the realm of deixis—and inasmuch *yesterday, today, tomorrow* or constructs as *two months ago* indicate a time related to the speech situation, also time ADVs belong to the deixis domain.

Several IE languages have a triple distinction with reference to the speaker's position (the 'origo' in Bühler's terms): near the speaker, near the hearer, distant both from the speaker and the hearer: compare Lat. *hic ~ iste ~ ille*; Cast. *este* 'proximal' ~ *ese* 'medial' or 'neuter' ~ *aquel* ('distal'), Cat. *aquest* 'this' ~ *aqueix* 'that' ~ *aquell* 'that (over there)' with the corresponding pronominal forms: *açò ~ això ~ allò*. Languages with this triple system have a tendency to reduce the triple distinction to a dual one: this is the case of the Tuscan variety of standard Italian: *questo ~ codesto ~ quello* is progressively reduced to *questo ~ quello*. Catalan, too, shows the same trend obtaining *aquest* vs *aquell*, and *això* vs *allò* (see Ramat 2015: 585). English has just a twofold opposition between *this* and *that*.

26.8 Pronouns

The classic grammatical tradition considered the *antōnymía > pro-nomen* as the PoS having the function of substituting the Noun. Actually, its function is to refer to persons, things and, more generally, States-of-Affairs without naming them. Moreover, PROs may precise the quantity, the quality and sometime the space relations of the SoA they relate to. PROs are both anaphoric and cataphoric: the *book that I have read* and *this is my book*. In the first sentence, we have a relative PRO, in the second a demonstrative/deictic one.

PIE had three main pronominal stems: **to-* as deictic, **yo-* for relative PROs and **kʷo-* for relative and/or interrogative PROs (but no IE language has both **yo-* and **kʷo-* for relatives). These forms are well attested in the oldest languages, and they continue to the present day, though often intertwined and therefore with double or changed function: see MGk. *to*₍ART Ntr₎ (shifted from deictic to article), Alb. *kë-ta*, Ru. *to(t)*, Ice. *Það*₍Ntr₎, Lith. *tàs* 'this', etc. In It. *codesto* (see section 27.7) the reinforcement that DEMs underwent in the everyday language is particularly visible: *eccu tibi iste* lit. 'here for you this' > *codesto* 'that near to you'; but already Lat. *isto(d)*₍Ntr₎ shows a reinforcement of the deictic **to-* via the other deictic base **i(s)-* of Goth. *is* Lith. *jis* 'he' etc.

All ancient IE languages had personal PROs which have been kept in the modern languages too, without gender distinction for the 1st and 2nd person (the real personal PROs): *I, you* vs *he/she/it* (cf. Goth. *is/si/ita*). The 3rd person, which is not present in the dyad of conversation, is often a DEM endowed with gender distinction and in some cases also with inflection: see Lat. *ille*₍M₎, *illa*₍F₎, *illud*₍Ntr₎ > It. *egli, ella*, Fr. *il, elle* (no Neuter), etc. The ancient IE languages knew dual forms: see Skr. *āvām* 'we two', *juvām* 'you both', Slav. *vě/va*, etc. Latin did not have a dual, but some modern languages of the IE family as Lithuanian, Slovene have kept it (see n. 12). Possessives (*my, yours*) reflexives (*myself, yourself*), indefinites (*someone, something*) relatives (*who, which*) and interrogatives (*who?, what?*) are classified as pronouns.

The demonstratives have been dealt with in section 27.7. As a matter of fact, the same form may be used as ART in a NP (*I like this book*) as well as a PRO in absolute position (*I like this*). The relative base **yo-* is well attested in some of the oldest languages (Skr. *yás*, Av. *yō*. AGk. *hós* —but Ntr. *tó* from the DEM base); it has disappeared in the contemporary languages. On the contrary, **kʷo-* has continued up to the modern times: see the *wh-* series in English (*who, what, where*, etc.), Germ *wer* (< *hwer*), Ice. *hver*[15], Fr. *qui* (*qui*₍INT₎

---

[15] Contrary to Engl. *who* and Fr. *qui*, German and Icelandic use this form for interrogatives only, not or the demonstrative.

a dit ça? 'Who said this?' *L'homme qui*~REL~ *a dit ça* 'The guy who said this'), Lith. *kas* 'who, what', Bulg. *kojto* 'who, which, that' (again with the union of *k^wo-+*to-*). Reflexive PROs refer to the person's relationship with *himself/herself/itself/themselves: John knows himself*. In Lithuanian, it has case inflection but not gender differentiation nor NOM. It is formed on the PIE base **s(e)we* of Lat. *suus* (> It. *suo*, Span. *suyo*) and a DAT form **sebhei* (> Lat. *sibi*) which may explain the *-f* of *-self*, and of Du. *zelf* as well as the *-b-* of Germ. *selbst*. Note that *self-*, *zelf-* and *selbst-* may constitute, in adjectival position, the first member of compounds as *selfcontrol*, *zelfmoord* and *selbstmord* 'suicide'—a possibility that other PROs do not have.

Finally, the indefinite PROs represent a border case of the category: Ru. *ktoto* 'somebody', *čtoto* 'something' derived from *kto* 'who'/*čto* 'what'+indefin. *To*~DEM~ and MGk. *káp(o)jos* from *p(o)jós* 'who, which' are still created by using pronominal bases, but *some-body*, *some-one*, *some-thing*, It. *qualc-uno*, *qual-cosa*, Fr. *quelqu'un*, *quelque chose* are clearly univerbated forms that use Nouns like *body* and *thing* which properly do not belong to the PRO category. This could be also the case of Lith. *pàts*~M~, *patì*~F~ connected with PIE **potis* 'master, husband' but also 'self' and used as intensifier (on the relation between reflexives and intensifiers see König & Siemund 2000):

(6) Lith. *Mergaitė patì   iškepė pyragą*
 'The girl herself baked a cake.'

27.9 CONJUNCTIONS

CONJs serve to establish a syntactic and semantic relation between words (*red and white*), nominal word groups (NPs as *the boys and the girls*) and sentences (*she smiled, though she was really sad*). It is difficult in PIE to make a clear distinction between ADVs, ADPs, and CONJs:

(7) *hoi dè   kaì   akhnýmenoí per   ep'autôi hēdỳ   gélassan*
    they however and troubled   though at him heartily they.laughed
    'But they, though troubled, laughed heartily at him.' (Il. 2.270)

In (7) the particles *dé* and *pér* are used as CONJs marking a subordinated concessive (Lehmann 1974: 234). Later, every IE language developed its own system of CONJs, specified for different functions:

  (a) coordinating as in the copulative
   (i) *Boys and girls danced and laughed heartily;*
   (ii) disjunctive as in *You may arrive on Sunday or on Monday, either by train or by car, but neither on foot nor by boat.*
   The coordinating CONJs connect two Nouns, two NPs, or two sentences that are at the same level.

(b) Subordinating CONJs. introduce a subordinate sentence. As subordinate sentences are circumstantial modifiers, they are of very different kinds. We give here just some type of subordinating monorhematic CONJs[16]:
- (i) causal (Germ. *weil*, Fr. *puisque*, Cymr. *gan*, etc.) as in *Since/As it's going to rain, I'll take my umbrella*;
- (ii) temporal (Ru. *kogda*, Fr. *pendant*, Span. *mientras*, MGk. *ótan*, etc.) as in *John arrived, while she was drinking her tea*;
- (iii) concessive (Port. *embora*, Cze. *třebaže*, Lith. *nors*, etc.): *She hasn't called, though she said she would*;
- (iv) hypothetic/conditional (Germ. *falls*, It. *se*, Ice. *ef*, Pol. *jesli*. etc.): *If you get hungry, you can eat a banana*.

27.10 Conclusions

Although it would have been impossible to follow step by step the evolution of the PoS from PIE up to the contemporary IE languages, the aim of this chapter has been to show the (relative) continuity of the tradition of a language family, from its reconstructed origins up to modern times over a time depth of more than 4,000 years. This is why this chapter, differently from other contributions in the volume, has a diachronic slant. The more so, since the PoS of the IE tradition have served as starting point for the analysis of other linguistic traditions, as stated in section 27.1.

Further analyses, more refined particularly from the syntactic point of view, could introduce further concepts, such as 'converbs' (CONVs), defined as 'a nonfinite verb form whose main function is to mark adverbial subordination' (Haspelmath 1995: 3). Examples of converbs quoted by Haspelmath from IE languages are:

(8) Portugeuse
despenhou-se   um   avião   militar;   morr-endo   o   piloto
crashed-REFL   a   plane   military   die-CONV   the   pilot
'A military plane crashed and the pilot was killed.' (lit. '... the pilot dying')

(9) Lithuanian
saul-ei   tek-ant   pasiek-ė-m   kryžkel-e
sun-DAT   rise-CONV   reach-PAST-1 PL   cross-roads-ACC
'when the sun rose, we reached a crossroads' (lit. 'The sun rising....')

---

[16] To note that complex constructions, too, may be used as conjunctions: ***At the time of** John's arrival she was drinking her tea*, instead of ***When** John arrived*... But it would be impossible to enumerate all the constructions, which can be freshly created according to the various circumstances. However, we have to skip them as not representing a particular PoS. In what follows we give some correspondences of the English CONJs just to show how cross-linguistically different are the forms. There are not CONJs that may be derived from a common PIE origin. For the ancient IE languages see W. P. Lehmann 1974: 167-174; Kulikov & Lavidas 2013. For a general overview on subordination see Ledgeway & Roberts 2017, s.v. 'subordination', p. 727.

(10) Modern Greek
I   kopéla   tón   kítak-s-e   xamojel-óndas
the   girl   him   look-AOR-3SG   smile-CONV
'The girl looked at him smiling.'

Examples (8)–(10) strictly remember the absolute constructions of the ancient IE languages, such as Greek and Latin:

(11) opus meum omne   ut uolui   perpertraui hostibus$_{\text{ABL PL}}$ fugatis$_{\text{ABL PL}}$
     work my   all   as I.wanted   I.finished enemies   driven away
     'I finished all my work as I desired, having driven away the enemies.' (Plaut. Pseud. 1269)

(12) incredibili celeritate magno$_{\text{ABL SG}}$ spatio$_{\text{ABL Sg}}$ […] confecto$_{\text{ABL SG}}$
     incredible speed   great   distance […]   covered
     'a great distance having being covered with incredible speed' (Caes. De B.G. 3:29,2)

The use of CONVs is largely attested in Late Latin and the Middle Age:

(13) omnia loca, quae filii Israhel tetigerant eundo vel redeundo ad montem
     (Peregrin. Aetheriae [5th cent.]:5.11)
     'all the places that the sons of Israhel had visited when going or coming back to the mountain'

(14) Angeli canendo$_{\text{CONV}}$ eum deferunt in excelsum (Greg. Tur., Mart. I, 4)
     angels singing   him take   in heaven
     'singing, the angels take him to the heaven'

(15) Spanish (Crónica de Alfonso XI [14th cent.]: II, 22)
     El rrey estando en Valladolid, vinieronle cartas de Vasco Perez de Meyra
     'While the king was in V. he received letters from Vasco Perez de M.'
     (lit. 'being the king in V., came to him letters from V.P.')

Unlike the PARTs of (11) and (12), (8)–(10) and (14)–(15) do not show any agreement of the CONVs with their semantic referential head, so that it makes sense to differentiate CONVs from PARTs, whose double nature as an autonomous PoS has been discussed in section 27.1 and 27.3.

As can be seen from the examples and their English translations with -ing verbal forms, CONVs are simply forms of the verbal paradigm, traditionally also called 'gerunds' (see Da Milano & Ramat 2011), or, more properly, 'satellites' (Dik 1989: 314; Ramat 1991), i.e. 'verb forms that are specialized for the expression of adverbial subordination, but cannot form a sentence on their own, i.e. they do not occur as main predicates of independent clauses' (Bisang 1995: 141). Clearly, if we speak of 'verb forms', this has not to do with the PoS and does not introduce a new element in the PoS inventory.

The same holds for particular verb forms such as 'avertive' or 'admirative' quoted in section 27.4. They represent special moods in the verbal system of some languages (Bulgarian and Albanian, respectively) but do not form a new PoS: they strictly belong to the traditional and firmly established PoS called 'verb'. Referring to the PoS, we can say that, all in all, the IE languages have been very conservative.

Acknowledgements

Thanks are due to the editor of this volume, to the internal reviewer Alexander Letuchiy, and to an anonymous external reviewer. The final version of this chapter has profited much from their helpful comments and suggestions.

CHAPTER 28

WORD CLASSES IN CLASSICAL CHINESE

WALTER BISANG

28.1 INTRODUCTION

CLASSICAL Chinese is a cover term for the written language of philosophical and historical texts between roughly the 5th century BC and the founding of the first unified empire of the Qín in 221 BC. It is commonly associated with such prestigious and highly influential texts as the *Zuǒzhuàn*,[1] the *Lúnyǔ* 'Analects' of Confucius (*Kǒngzǐ*) as well as the works of Mencius (*Mèngzǐ*), Laozi (*Lǎozǐ*), and Zhuangzi (*Zhuāngzǐ*). Even though the language reflected in these texts shows some differences in terms of dialectal and diachronic variation, there clearly is an important core of shared lexical and grammatical properties. Classical Chinese itself represents the final stage of Old Chinese, whose earliest records go back to about 1250 BC. The sources on pre-Classical Chinese are oracular inscriptions written on bones and shells, bronze inscriptions, and the earliest Chinese classical texts like the *Shījīng* 'Book of Odes', the *Shūjīng* 'Book of Documents', and parts of the *Yìjīng* 'Book of Changes'.[2]

What is common to Chinese texts is that they are written in Chinese characters which only provide limited direct information on pronunciation. From such a perspective, it comes as no surprise that word class as it is discussed in the framework of a rich linguistic and philological tradition in China and in the West is mainly based on writing, i.e. Chinese characters. Thus, the present chapter is focused on these character-based analyses, but it also includes research on the reconstruction of the phonology and morphology of Old Chinese and its most recent results. In fact, it tries to relate the traditional character-based findings to results from the field of reconstruction by developing a tentative scenario for how the results from these two rather separate domains may be integrated.

Classical Chinese is of particular typological interest because of its word-class flexibility, which is defined as the extent to which a given word (mostly identical to a single Chinese character) can occur with more than one open word class (particularly noun and verb) without

---

[1] A comment on the chronicle of the spring and autumn periods.
[2] For more on the historical periods of Chinese, cf. Norman (1988), Baxter & Sagart (2014: 1–2).

any additional marking (section 28.2.1) and with mechanisms that allow to derive its meaning (sections 28.2.2 and 28.2.3). Before entering into a more detailed discussion, the following three examples are selected for providing the reader with some concrete data. In (1a), the object denoting lexeme 君 *jūn* 'prince, ruler' is used in the syntactic position of the verb:

(1) Classical Chinese
   a. Zuozhuan, Xuan 2:
      晉靈公不君。
      Jìn   Líng gōng bù   jūn.
      Jin.state Ling duke NEG   ruler
      'Duke Ling of Jin does not behave/act like a ruler.'
   b. Zuozhuan, Zhao 17:
      夫子將有異志, 不君君矣。
      fūzǐ   jiāng yǒu   yì   zhì,   bù   jūn   jūn   yǐ.
      master/he FUT   have different intention NEG   ruler ruler PF
      'He will have different intentions, he will not consider [our] ruler as a ruler.'

In (1a), the lexeme *jūn* is used as an intransitive verb with the meaning of 'to be a prince/ruler, to act as a prince/ruler'.[3] In (1b), it occurs twice. In its first occurrence, it takes the position of a transitive verb with the meaning of 'consider someone as the lexical item in the object position', in its second occurrence it is in the object position with its nominal meaning of 'ruler'.

In (2), the lexeme 美 *měi* 'be beautiful, beauty' is found in the position of a noun (2a), a nominal modifier (stative verb) (2b) and a transitive verb followed by the object pronoun of the 3rd person (2c):

(2) Classical Chinese
   a. Lunyu (6.14):
      宋朝之美
      Sòng Zhāo zhī   měi
      Song Zhao   POSS beauty
      'the beauty of Song Zhao'

   b. Lunyu (9.12)
      有美玉于斯
      yǒu   měi   yù   yú   sī
      there.is beautiful jade/gem   LOC   here
      'There is a beautiful gem here.'

   c. Zuozhuan, Xiang 25:
      見棠姜而美之。
      jiàn Táng Jiāng ér   měi   zhī
      see   Tang Jiang   and   beautiful 3.OBJ
      'He saw Tang Jiang and thought her to be beautiful.'

---

[3] Note that the negation *bù* 'not' negates items occurring in the verbal position. There is also the negation 非 *fēi*, which is used with lexical items in nominal function. Action-denoting lexemes can be negated by *fēi* only in specific contexts of information structure.

Finally, there is a famous example which is somewhat hard to translate from Zhuangzi (about 365–290 BC). In this example, the lexeme 止 *zhǐ* is used four times. For the sake of reader-friendliness, each of its occurrences is numbered.

(3) Zhuangzi, Deyunfu (translation slightly adapted from Sun 2020: 33)
人莫鑒於流水而鑒於止₁水, 唯止₂能止₃眾止₄。
rén	mò	jiàn	yú	liú	shuǐ	ér	jiàn	yú	*zhǐ₁*	shuǐ,
people	nobody	mirror	to	flow	water	rather	mirror	in	still	water

wéi	*zhǐ₂*	néng	*zhǐ₃*		zhòng	*zhǐ₄*.
only	stillness	can	cause.to.be.still		all.things	stillness

'People cannot use flowing water as mirror, they are reflected (lit. mirrored) on **still₁** water, only **stillness₂** (of water) can **cause₃** the **stillness₄** of all things.'

In its first occurrence as *zhǐ₁*, it is used in the modifying function of a stative verb with the translation 'be still'. This analysis is supported by the parallelism with *liú shuǐ* [flow water] 'flowing water' in the preceding text. In its second and fourth occurrence (*zhǐ₂, zhǐ₄*), the same lexeme is in the syntactic position of a noun with the meaning of 'stillness'. Finally, we also find it in the function of a causative verb with the meaning of 'cause to be still' in its third occurrence (*zhǐ₃*).[4]

Since the degree of flexibility illustrated by examples like (1)–(3) no longer exists in Modern Chinese and is not observed to the same extent and in the same way in any other period of Chinese grammar, the focus of this article clearly is on Classical Chinese.

The chapter is structured as follows: section 28.2 is on Western approaches, section 28.3 on the Chinese perspective. Section 28.2.4 is on morphological reconstruction, which is a common endeavour of both sides even if the focus of this chapter will be on Baxter & Sagart (2014a, 2014b). While current Western models rather opt for full flexibility, current Chinese approaches argue that word class is a matter of the lexicon in the sense that most lexical items only belong to one word class with a subset of words which are lexically allowed to belong to more than one class. While the degree of flexibility of Classical Chinese is still debatable to a certain extent, word-class membership is clearly lexical in modern Standard Chinese, as will be briefly discussed in the conclusion in section 28.4.

28.2 Classical Chinese in terms of flexibility

28.2.1 Flexible parts of speech

The flexibility of Classical Chinese lexical items has been observed since Wilhelm von Humboldt's (1827) letter to Abel Rémusat. Georg von der Gabelentz (1881) in his impressive grammar of Classical Chinese written in German was the first who clearly pointed out that lexical items can occur in different syntactic positions. He introduced the distinction between the semantic level characterized by words typically denoting individuals, types,

---

[4] See also section 28.3.2 for the analysis of *zhǐ* by Chen (1922).

properties, actions, states, etc. and the syntactic level which he defined by syntactic positions for nouns, adjectives and verbs (Gabelentz 1881: 112–113). In more recent times, Classical Chinese parts of speech were discussed by Kennedy ([1956] 1964), Cikoski (1970), and Nikitina (1985). Nikitina's (1985) dissertation in Russian is of particular importance because she pointed out that the meaning of a particular lexical item depends on the construction in which it occurs and on the semantic class to which it belongs (for a somewhat more extensive summary in English, see Zádrapa 2011: 59–65).

An important criterion for determining if a language has flexible lexical items is compositionality, i.e. the possibility to regularly derive the meaning of a lexical item from its syntactic position (V, N) within the relevant constructions (see Evans & Osada 2005 on compositionality and its critical discussion in section 28.2.3). The extent to which compositionality applies to Classical Chinese is controversial to a certain degree. In Zádrapa's (2011: 97–100) view, there is a distinction between shifts of meaning within the confines of propositional acts and beyond these confines. The first type is based on Croft's conceptual space for parts of speech (1991, 2000, 2001; see also Chapters 3 and 11 in this volume), consisting of the three propositional acts of reference, modification, and predication and the three semantic domains of objects, properties, and actions. The combination of types of propositional acts and types of semantic domains creates a semantic space of nine cells, each of them representing a construction which has its specific morphosyntactic representation in individual languages. If a language has flexible lexemes, these lexemes can occur in different cells without any difference in form. Thus, an object-denoting lexeme like 君 *jūn* 'ruler' in (1a) cannot only occur in the construction prototypically associated with nouns (reference to an object), it can equally occur in the construction prototypically associated with verbs (predication of an action) as in (1b) 'consider someone as a ruler'. In the case of (2), the lexeme *měi* 'beautiful' takes even three cells without any difference in marking, i.e. reference to an (abstract) object (2a), modification by a property (2b) and predication of an action (2c). The lexeme *zhǐ* 'be still, stillness, cause to be still' in (3) can be assigned to the same three cells, i.e. modification by a property ($zhǐ_1$), reference to an (abstract) object ($zhǐ_2$, $zhǐ_4$) and predication of an action ($zhǐ_3$). The meanings of these three lexemes in their different constructions can be productively derived by rules (sections 28.2.2 and 28.2.3).

The second type of semantic shift, which goes beyond propositional acts, is described basically as a process of lexicalization and polysemy by Zádrapa (2011: 100–107, 177–185). In his own words, '[t]his dramatic change is not driven by the construction, it is not a simple conventional addition of a function-specific profiling: it is a consequence of a derivational process that follows the rules of word formation and exhibits the limited regularity and predictability typical for word formation' (Zádrapa 2011: 100).

28.2.2 Meaning in Classical Chinese as a flexible parts-of-speech language

While it is quite clear that there are two types of shifts of meaning within and beyond the confines of propositional acts (Zádrapa 2011), it is not that clear to what extent the former is regular and the latter is irregular (lexical). In a more recent study, Sun (2020) showed that at least a large number of meaning shifts of the second type show regularities in terms of metaphors (Lakoff 1987a, 1993; Kövecses 2010). If this analysis is true, one would have to reckon with two mechanisms of interpretation called 'rule-based' and 'metaphorical' by Sun (2020: 154–245). Adopting this distinction, both mechanisms leading to the two different types of interpretation will be presented in this section from the perspective of object-denoting lexemes and their use in the syntactic position of V (on action-denoting lexemes in the N position, see section 28.2.3).

The relation between individual lexical items (words) is summarized in the following quotation from Harbsmeier:

> When one sees a Classical Chinese word, this creates a spectrum or field of syntactic expectations, and these expectations can be stronger or weaker as the case may be. And these fields of syntactic expectation may vary individually and subtly for each word in the lexicon, so that one may end up with a tailor-made special word class for each lexical item. The words will then be distributed in a categorial continuum of syntactic tendencies.
>
> (Harbsmeier 1998: 138)

These 'syntactic expectations' reflect very well what Lehmann (2008: 550) describes as the assignment of roots to a specific word class (syntactic positions of N and V) on the basis of a pragmatic 'probability calculus' which depends on the semantics of a root (see Chapter 3). This idea will be further developed in the remainder of this section.

The overall likelihood of assigning an object-denoting lexeme to the V position is governed by stereotypical implicatures, defined by Levinson (2000: 115) as 'connotations associated with meanings, but not part of them, which nevertheless play a role in them'. In the case of flexibility as discussed here, the underlying assumption is that lexemes denoting concrete objects are more prototypical nouns which are less likely to take the V position than abstract object-denoting lexemes. In terms of stereotypes, this means that concrete object-denoting lexemes are more stereotypically associated with the N position than abstract object-denoting lexemes—a situation that can be captured by an underlying hierarchy of the type 'concrete object > abstract object' in which '>' means 'is more strongly associated with N' (Bisang 2008a: 573). As Bisang (2008a: 573) further suggests, the stereotypical implicature may ultimately follow the animacy hierarchy in the form of '1st/2nd person > proper names > $\text{Noun}_{\text{human}}$ > $\text{Noun}_{\text{animate(non human)}}$ > $\text{Noun}_{\text{abstract}}$'.

If such a stereotype-based analysis is correct, it is to be expected that many nouns denoting concrete objects (or objects more to the left pole of the animacy hierarchy) are not attested in the V position in Classical Chinese corpora even though their use in that position cannot be excluded and would even produce predictable meanings. The reason for using such lexical items in the V position is often of a rhetorical nature, which can be explained in terms of flouting stereotypical implicatures (Grice 1975).

If an object-denoting lexeme occurs in the V position, its interpretation either depends on rules or on metaphor (Sun 2020). As Bisang (2008a, b) in his rule-based approach has shown, the meaning of a large number of object-denoting lexemes in the verbal position can be predicted by combining information on its semantic class and the construction in which it occurs, an idea that goes back to Nikitina (1985). Sun (2020: 155–187) distinguishes the following semantic classes:

(i) human roles (functions, roles played by humans in a society)
(ii) instruments
(iii) places/buildings

(iv) garments
(iv) foodstuff
(v) body parts
(vi) animals
(vii) natural events or elements
(ix) supernatural events or elements
(x) illnesses
(xi) laws/rules/regulations/codes of conduct

Given the aim of deriving the meaning of object-denoting lexemes in the syntactic position of V, the relevant construction is the argument structure construction (Goldberg 1995), which is at the same time also taken as a word-class-indicating construction in terms of Croft (2001). For the purpose of predictability, it is important to distinguish between the intransitive and the transitive argument constructions, which are defined by the following word-order rules (S stands for single argument of intransitive verb, A and U stand for ACTOR and UNDERGOER of transitive verbs, respectively. The terminology is from Van Valin 2005):

(4) Argument structure constructions of Classical Chinese
   a. Intransitive: (i) NP_S V   or:
                      (ii)   V NP_S
   b. transitive: NP_A V NP_U

For each of the above semantic classes, there are specific rules for deriving the concrete meaning of a given lexical item in the V position of an intransitive or transitive argument structure construction. In the case of person-denoting lexemes (PDLs), which correspond to the class of human roles listed above, the rules are defined as follows (the notation is inspired from *Role & Reference Grammar*, Van Valin 2005, see also Bisang 2008a, 2008b and Sun 2020: 155–187 for similar rules):

(5) Semantics of PDLs in the V-position (Bisang 2008a: 577)
   a. in intransitive argument structure constructions:
      (i) NP_S behaves like a PDL, NP_S is a PDL
      (ii) NP_S becomes a PDL

   b. in transitive argument structure constructions:
      (i) NP_A CAUSE DP_U to be/behave like a PDL
      (ii) NP_A CONSIDER DP_U to be/behave like a PDL

The rule in (5) can be illustrated by examples (1a) and (1b) on the person-denoting lexeme 君 *jūn* 'prince, ruler'. In (1a), this lexeme takes the V position of the intransitive argument structure construction. Its meaning is that of (5a.i), producing the interpretation of 'to behave/act like a ruler'. In (1b), the same lexical item in its first occurrence is in the V position of the transitive argument structure construction and is interpreted in terms of (5b.ii) as 'to consider X as a ruler'. Since the object in X is also the lexeme *jūn* 'prince, ruler', we get the overall meaning of 'to consider [our] ruler as a ruler'.

In another example concerning body-part-denoting lexemes (BDL), the rules are as follows:

(6) Semantics of BDLs in the V-position (Sun 2020: 185)
   a. In intransitive argument structure constructions:
      NP_S does what one typically does using/with BDL.
   b. In transitive argument structure constructions:
      NP_A does to NP_U what one typically does using/with BDL *or*
      NP_A applies BDL on NP_U.

The use of rule (6b) on the lexical item *bèi* 'back' in the transitive argument–structure construction in (7) produces the meaning of 'applying one's back on something/someone, turning one's back to something/someone':

(7) Classical Chinese (Sun 2020: 188)
   bèi 'back', rule-based interpretation (Guoyang, Wuyu):
   王背屏而立, 夫人向屏
   wáng **bèi** *píng   ér   lì,   fūrén xiàng píng*
   king back screen and stand wife   face   screen
   'The king turned his back towards the screen, [while] [his] wife faced the screen.'

Other examples illustrating rule (6b) are 肘 *zhǒu* 'elbow' in its verbal function with the meaning 'hit/push someone with one's elbow' and *shǒu* 'hand' with the meaning of 'hold in one's hand' (see section 28.3.2).

The second type of meaning shift is prominently based on metaphors. Starting out again from the intransitive and the transitive argument–structure construction, Sun (2020) summarizes this process as follows for a given object-denoting lexeme N:

(8) Metaphorically motivated interpretation of object-denoting lexemes (Sun 2020: 189)
   Intransitive: NP_A does the action metaphorically associated with N.
   Transitive: NP_A applies the action metaphorically associated with N to NP_U.

The definition of metaphor adopted for the above mechanism of interpretation follows general assumptions of understanding 'one domain of experience in terms of another' (Lakoff & Johnson 1980: 117). Thus, metaphor is seen as a process of mapping in which certain attributes of a given source concept are matched with certain attributes of a target concept from a different domain. According to Sun's (2020: 197) findings, the most common target concepts in Classical Chinese are body parts, animals, instruments, illnesses, places and buildings, foodstuff (including plants), natural events, social/political human notions. The most common targets are affect ('subjective conscious experience of feeling'), spatial cognition and behaviour (Sun 2020: 223–224). The actual process of mapping a source concept onto a target concept takes place from three perspectives, i.e. those of form, function and manner/way of treatment (Sun 2020: 228–231). Examples (9) and (10) are two good examples of how an object-denoting lexeme like *yì* 'wings' is metaphorically interpreted in the V position:

(9) Classical Chinese (Zhanguo Ce, Zhao Ce)
     韓魏翼而擊之

Hán	Wèi	yì	ér	jī	zhī.
Han [Kangzi]	Wei [Xuanzi]	wings	and	attack	OBJ.3

     'Han Kangzi and Wei Xuanzi divided into two groups and attacked them [from both sides].'

(10) Classical Chinese (Zuozhuan, Ai 16; from Sun 2020: 205)
     勝如卵, 余翼而長之

Shèng	rú	luǎn,	yú	yì	ér	zhǎng	zhī.
Sheng	be.like	egg	I	wing	and	bring.up	OBJ.3

     'Sheng is like an egg, I look after him and bring him up.'

In its intransitive function in (9), the source concept of *yì* 'wings' is used for describing how two armies deploy through geographic space in analogy to the way in which the wings of a bird divide into two parts when it starts flying. The body part-term in this example is seen from the perspective of form and the target function describes that form in terms of diffusion through space. A different metaphor is used in the transitive context of (10). Here, the wings are seen from the perspective of a mother bird which takes its eggs under its wings for breeding/protecting them. The action expressed by *yì* 'wing' is seen from the perspective of function (protection), targeting the domain of behaviour.

As is to be expected from metaphors, the meaning of *yì* 'wing' in the V position goes beyond the concrete semantic domain associated with that body part and cannot be accounted for within the confines of propositional acts in terms of Croft's semantic space. In contrast, rule-based interpretations remain within the semantic domain associated with a given lexeme and consequently belong to the realm of metonymy. For that reason, Sun (2020) treats rule-based interpretations as instances of metonymy, which differ from metaphors as described above. Both mechanisms of interpretation are independent from each other and can be applied independently to one and the same lexeme. This can be illustrated by the lexeme *bèi* 'back', which was shown in (7) in its rule-based interpretation of 'applying one's back on something/someone, turning one's back to something/someone'. While this example is about the concrete movement of a body part in space, the following example is focused on a different target, i.e. the target of human behaviour from the perspective of manner/way of treatment. More concretely, it is about doing an act of treachery or turning against someone:

(11) Classical Chinese: *bèi* 'back', metaphoric interpretation (Zuozhuan, Zhuanggong 13)
     宋人背北杏之會

Sòng	rén	bèi	Běixìng	zhī	huì
Song [STATE]	people	back	Beixing [PLACE]	POSS	covenant

     'The people of Song turned against the covenant of Beixing.'

28.2.3 Methodological criteria for flexibility (Evans & Osada 2005)

Evans & Osada (2005: 367–384) discuss the three methodological criteria of compositionality, exhaustiveness and bidirectionality for deciding if a language is precategorial (having no word classes in their terminology). The criterion of compositionality requires that the meaning of a lexeme must be fully derivable from its lexical semantics and the function of the position in which it occurs. While the rule-based interpretation fully meets this criterion, the metaphorical interpretation is not compositional. To what extent such a rigid interpretation of this condition adequately reflects the real situation in the lexicon of any language is questionable. After all, metaphoric inference can be productively used as well even though the meaning it creates depends on more specific factors, among them also world knowledge. Moreover, it can also promote the emergence of lexicalized meanings with specific lexical items in a specific position. Even though such instances operate against the criterion of exhaustiveness, which excludes the existence of exceptions, it is questionable if the schematic application of this criterion adequately models the overall cross-linguistic importance of lexicalization. If lexicalization is manifested in many different morphosyntactic environments, why shouldn't it also be able to generate more specific lexicalized meanings with a certain number of object-denoting lexemes in the V position of languages with a flexible parts-of-speech system? (See also Chapter 3 in this volume on using exhaustiveness too rigidly.) If there is a certain leeway for compositionality and exhaustiveness, the precategoriality of object denoting lexemes in a language is ultimately a matter of degree. The observation that their interpretation depends on stereotypical implicatures and productive rules or metaphors provide rather solid evidence for precategoriality, in particular because the selection of object-denoting lexemes for the V position can also depend on rhetorical reasons.

The last criterion of bidirectionality is based on reciprocity, i.e. if object-denoting lexemes can take the V position of argument–structure constructions, action-denoting lexemes should equally be able to occur as nouns in the N position. Sun (2020: 110–126) presents six regular meaning shifts for action-denoting lexemes in nominal positions. One of them is the function of actor of the corresponding action (actor of action). The other functions are undergoer of the action, instrument of the action (see (13)), object involved in the action, place of the action and name of the action (see also section 28.3.2).

In spite of this, bidirectionality is problematic because action-denoting and state-denoting lexemes in N positions (subject or object) are often open to various syntactic analyses when they occur alone in these positions. In the constructed example below, the stative verb *bìng* 'to be ill' is in the subject position and may be analysed as a noun (12a), a topic (nominal or verbal, (12b)), the verb of a headless relative clause (12c), the verb of a subject clause (12d) or even as the verb in a conditional clause (12e) (modified from Bisang 2008a: 580 and 2009: 44):

(12) 病不幸
 bìng bù xìng.
 be.ill NEG fortunate
 a. 'Illness is unfortunate.'
 b. 'As for illness / as for being ill, it is unfortunate.'

c. 'The one who is ill is unfortunate.'
d. 'That he is ill is unfortunate.'
e. 'If [he/someone] is ill, [this] is unfortunate.'

Only in (12a) and in the first interpretation of (12b) is it possible to analyse the state-denoting lexeme *bìng* as a noun occurring in an N position. In the other interpretations, it is in a V position. This asymmetry between object-denoting lexemes which can clearly be analysed as verbs in the V position and action-denoting and state-denoting lexemes which often can be interpreted as nouns or verbs in N positions makes the overall assessment of bidirectionality difficult (for some examples from texts, see Bisang 2008a: 580–582). In spite of this, there are many examples in which the nominal function is clear from the context. In the following example, the lexeme *qiān* 'pull [animals]' is used in a sequence of nouns in the subject position of the verb *jié* 'exhaust, be exhausted' with the meaning of 'draft animal':

(13) Classical Chinese (Zuozhuan, Xi 33; from Sun 2020: 114)
吾子淹久於敝邑，唯是脯資餼牽竭矣
wúzǐ	yān	jiǔ	yú	bì yì,	wéi	shì	fǔ
2.SG.HON	stay	long	at	my.country.MODEST	only	DEM	dried-meat

zī	xì	qiān	jié	yǐ.
fund	grains	V:pull	exhaust	PF

'You have stayed in my country for too long and only for that the dried meat, the funds, the grains and the draft animals are exhausted.'

In constructions other than the argument–structure construction, the nominal interpretation of action-denoting and state-denoting lexemes is often straightforward. One case in point is the head position of the possessive construction as the one in (2a) *Sòng Zhāo zhī měi* [Song Zhao POSS beautiful] 'the beauty of Song Zhao'. Moreover, Classical Chinese can use additional markers for overtly specifying the syntactic structure of an utterance if necessary. Thus, an important function[5] of 之 *zhī* is the marking of noun modifiers either in the context of possession (see (2a)) or in the context of relative-clause formation. In both cases, the lexical item following it is a noun (an object-denoting lexeme in a referential construction).

Looking again at (12), straightforward indicators of the conditional analysis in (12e) are the use of conditional conjunctions like 如 *rú* or 若 *ruò* 'if' in the protasis or the marker 則 *zé* 'then' in the apodosis. The possessive pronoun of the third person 其 *qí* 'his, hers, etc.' can be interpreted as an indicator of nominalization (*qí bìng* [POSS.3 be.ill] 'his illness, his being ill'). Other markers are more versatile. The marker 者 *zhě* has the function of a nominalizer either for expressing headless relative clauses or nominalized clauses (*bìng zhě* [be.ill NMLZ] 'the one who is ill, that he is ill'). In (12c) and (12d) it is used in that function. However, the same marker has further grammaticalized into a topic marker that is also used in conditional contexts. For that reason, it may also appear in (12b) and (12e). With the combination of *qí* '3rd person possessive pronoun' and the nominalizer *zhě* in the same clause, it is possible to produce a structure which particularly specifies the analysis in (12d):

---

[5] Other important functions of *zhī* are (i) object pronoun of the third person (singular and plural) and (ii) verb of movement with the meaning 'go'.

(12) d'. 其病者不幸
   qí bìng zhě bù xìng.
   POSS:3 be.ill NMLZ NEG fortunate
   'That he is ill is unfortunate.'

This necessarily short presentation offers an impression of the complexities of using grammatical markers for clearly specifying if a lexical item is in the syntactic position of N or V.[6] Zádrapa (2011: 85) is certainly right in pointing out the importance of profiting from such markers for determining parts-of-speech function (he discusses 之 zhī, 其 qí, 者 zhě and a few others) but it is also clear that their usefulness has its limitations, particularly in the case of those which are multifunctional and which are not obligatory in the sense that their use for specification depends on discourse.

28.2.4 Morphology in Old Chinese and its relation to character-based interpretations

The existence of morphology in Old Chinese is uncontroversial (Karlgren 1940; Wang 1958; Downer 1959; Mei 1989, 2008, 2012; Pulleyblank 1995; Baxter 1992; Sagart 1999; Baxter & Sagart 2014a, 2014b; Xing & Schuessler 2020), even though many of its details are subject to divergent views. For the present chapter, I will briefly report on the most important affixes as they are reconstructed by Baxter & Sagart (2014a, 2014b, henceforth B & S 2014a, 2014b)[7] for Old Chinese in the narrow sense, i.e. 'the earliest stage of Chinese that we can reconstruct from Chinese evidence', a stage which is 'not far removed' from Proto-Sinitic, the common ancestor of Sinitic languages (B & S 2014a: 2). As one can see from that volume, there was only derivational morphology but no inflectional morphology (tense, number, etc.) in Old Chinese. On closer inspection, most affixes seem to be flexible in the sense that they can be associated with different word classes, depending on the individual root with which they are combined (on Khmer morphology, see Chapter 3 on type-VI languages). Thus, the prefix $*m_1$- either produces verbs as in (14a)–(14b) or nouns as in (14c).[8] The following examples first present the relevant Chinese character with its Old Chinese reconstruction marked by an asterisk, its representation in the modern *pinyin* transcription in brackets, plus the English translation.

(14) Old Chinese morphology: the prefix $*m_1$- (from B & S 2014a: 55)
 a. nonvolitional verb > volitional verb, at times with causative overtones:
  晶 *tseŋ (jīng) 'bright, lipid' > 淨 *m1-tseŋ-s (jìng) 'cleanse [v. tr.]'
  見 *[k]ˤen-s (jiàn) 'see [v.]' > 見 *m1-[k]ˤen-s (xiàn) 'cause to appear, introduce'

---

 [6] The reader is referred to Zádrapa (2011: 84–92) and Bisang (2008a, 2008b, 2009) for more details.
 [7] Also cf. Shā Jiāěr [Laurent Sagart] & Bái Yīpíng [William H. Baxter] (2010) and Sagart & Baxter (2012).
 [8] There are two more unrelated *m-affixes: $*m_2$- occurs in many body-part terms, $*m_3$- occurs in various nouns denoting animals.

b. noun > volitional verb:
背 *pˤək-s* (bèi) 'the back' > 背 **mɪ-pˤək-s* (bèi) 'turn the back on'
倉 (cāng) **tsʰˤaŋ* 'granary' > 藏 **mɪ-tsʰˤaŋ* (cáng) 'store, v.'
朝 *t<r>aw* (zhāo) 'morning' > 朝 **mɪ-t<r>aw* (cháo) 'go to (morning) audience at court'

c. verb > agentive/instrumental noun:
拄 **t<r>oʔ* (zhǔ) 'prop up, support' > 柱 **mɪ-t<r>oʔ* (zhù) 'pillar'
判 **pʰˤan-s* (pàn) 'divide [v.]' > 畔 **mɪ-pʰˤan-s* (pàn) 'bank between fields'

The prefix **s-* occurs in two functions. In (15a) and (15b), it has the function of valency increasing (transitivization, causativization), in (15a) with action-denoting roots and in (15b) with object-denoting roots. In (15c), it derives circumstantial nouns (places, times, instruments).

(15) Old Chinese morphology: the prefix **s-*
   a. **s₁-*, valency increasing (B & S 2014a: 56):
   烝 **təŋ* (zhēng) 'to rise (of stream)' > 升 **s-təŋ* (shēng) 'to lift up to, to save, to present to'
   視 **gijʔ* (shì) 'look, see' > 示 **s-gijʔ-s* (shì) 'show'

   b. * s-, noun > verb (Baxter & Sagart 1998: 53):
   吏 **[r]əʔ-s* (lì) 'clark, minor official' > 使 **s-rəʔ* (shǐ) '(*cause to be an emissionary:), send'
   麗 (lì) 'a pair, a couple' > 灑 **Cə.s<r>ərʔ-s* (sǎ) '(*divide, bifurcate:) sprinkle, distribute'

   c. **s₂-*, derivation of circumstantial nouns (place, time, instrument', B & S 2014a: 56):
   通 **lˤoŋ* (tōng) 'penetrate' > 窗 **s-lˤ<r>oŋ* (chuāng) 'window (< where light penetrates)'
   亡 **maŋ* (wáng) 'flee, disappear; die' > 喪 **s-mˤaŋ* (sāng) 'mourning, burial (< circumstances associated with death)'

The suffix **-s* is presented by B & S (2014a: 58) as 'a very common suffix with many functions, only a few of which are well understood'. Its first function of nominalization in (16a) is 'by far the most common function of **-s*' (B & S 2014a: 58). Other functons are given in (16b)–(16d).[9]

(16) Old Chinese morphology: the suffix **-s* (from B & S 2014a: 58–59)
   a. deverbal nouns:
   磨 **mˤaj* (mó) 'rub, grind' > 磨 *mˤaj-s* (mò) 'grindstone'
   內 **nˤ[u]p* (nà) 'bring/send in' > 內 **nˤ[u]p-s* (nèi) 'inside'

---

[9] This suffix is also clearly related to the departing tone in Middle Chinese (see fn. 10 for more).

b. denominal verbs:
   王 * Gʷaŋ (wáng) 'king'   > 王 * Gʷaŋ-s (wàng) 'to be king'
   冠 *k.ʕor (guān) 'cap, n.'   > 冠 * k.ʕor-s (guàn) 'cap, v.'
   衣 *ʔ(r)əj (yī) 'garment, clothes' > 衣 *ʔ(r)əj-s (yì) 'wear (V transitive)'

c. outwardly directed (exocentric) verbs derived from inwardly directed verbs:
   買 *mˤrajʔ (mǎi) 'to buy'   > 賣 *mˤrajʔ-s (mài) 'to sell'

d. outwardly directed (exocentric) verbs derived from stative verbs:
   好 *qʰˤuʔ (hǎo) 'be good'   > 好 *qʰˤuʔ-s (hào) 'love, like'

The above reconstructions clearly show that Old Chinese at its earliest stage had derivational morphology. To what extent that morphology was productive is an open question. In B & S's (2014b) list, about one-third of its almost 5,000 items are reconstructed with morphology. This is an impressive number and there might have been more derived forms, given that we most likely no longer have access to the full range of morphological productivity today. In spite of this, the fact that each of the above affixes produces either nouns or verbs and that its specific meaning is often lexically dependent on the individual root rather points at non-productivity (see also Khmer in Chapter 3).

Understanding the relation of this reconstructed morphology to the flexibility as it is described in sections 28.2.1–28.2.3 needs a lot more research which also takes into account that Old Chinese covers a very long period of time (about 1250–221 BC) and that some of the morphology reconstructed for its earliest period may have lost at least part of its transparency and productivity at the time of Classical Chinese. The following three issues will be further discussed for presenting a tentative scenario of the relation between the results from reconstruction and the character-based flexibility described in sections 28.2.1–28.2.3:

(i) Instances of flexible non-derived roots in the reconstructed forms
(ii) Lexemes with reconstructed morphology that has lost its relevance for word–class distinction
(iii) The extent of similarity between the functions of the reconstructed morphology and the functions derived from the meaning contributed by the argument structure constructions discussed in section 28.2.2.

Each of these issues is discussed briefly with a few representative examples. In many cases of flexibility, no derivational morphology is reconstructed. Thus, the lexeme 美 *měi* 'beautiful' is reconstructed as *[m]rajʔ (B & S 2014b: 74) with no indications of differences in form for its different functions in (2a)–(2c). This also applies to 止 *zhǐ* 'still, cause to be still, stillness' in (3), which is reconstructed as *təʔ 'foot, stop' by B & S (2014a: 158; 2014b: 153). Similarly, there is only the reconstructed form of 牽 *[k]ʰˤi[n]* (qiān) 'pull, lead, drag' and no indication of any derivational process for generating the meaning of 'draft animal' in (13). If one takes these reconstructions at face value without assuming the existence of a no longer reconstructable derivational affix, they can be taken as examples of a probability-based assignment of roots to a given word class. Some other examples of this type are discussed later in section 28.3.2, among them 臣 *chén* 'minister; to be/behave like a (proper) minister' (reconstructed as *[g]i[ŋ] 'slave, subject', B & S 2014b: 12) or 手 shǒu 'hand; hold/grasp something' (reconstructed as *n̥uʔ 'hand', B & S 2014b: 101).

Given that the morphology as it is reconstructed by B & S (2014a, 2014b) aims at the earliest period of Old Chinese/Proto-Sinitic, some of it may already have lost its transparency or may have been reanalysed as part of the root towards the period of Classical Chinese. One possible example is 翼 yì 'wing' in its metaphorical verbal interpretations in examples (9) and (10), which don't seem to be reflected in the reconstructed form of *Gwrəp (yì) 'wings', whose final consonant may have been a potential suffix *-p > *-k in some dialects (B & S 2014a: 386; 2014b: 137). Another interesting case is the lexeme 肘 zhǒu 'elbow; hit/push someone with one's elbow' (section 28.3.2), which is reconstructed as *t-[k]<r>uʔ with a prefix *t- for marking inalienable objects plus the infix <r> for double or multiple objects (B & S 2014a: 32, 57; 2014b: 155). Even though these affixes are nominal they don't prevent that lexeme to be used as a verb without any additional reconstructable morphology. A particularly complex case is 君 jūn 'ruler' as presented in (1). This character is reconstructed as *C.qur 'lord; ruler' (B & S 2014a: 82, 127) with the consonant C being a potential prefix. In earlier documents, this character was often interchangeably used with 尹 yǐn, which is reconstructed with the prefix *m- as *m-qurʔ with nominal and verbal function as indicated by its translation as 'govern, governor' (B & S 2014a: 82, 127). To what extent one should take this as an indicator of a morphology that was opaque for word class in Classical Chinese remains open. Since 君 jūn with its reconstructed meaning of 'ruler' is used in (1) rather than 尹 yǐn, it seems reasonable to assume that its interpretation in terms of (1b) 'consider X a ruler' comes from the transitive argument structure construction without additional morphology.

Even though there is not that much functional overlap between the affixes reconstructed in (14)–(16) and the object-denoting lexemes used in the verbal positions of the argument structure constructions, there are interesting parallelisms with at least some affixes in combination with some roots, three of which will be shortly presented here. The first is related to the prefix *m₁- (see (14b)) and the use of 背 bèi 'back' in its rule-based interpretation of 'turn one's back to' in (7). As one can see from (14b), B & S (2014a: 55) reconstruct the nominal interpretation as pˤək-s 'the back' and the verbal function in (7) as *m1-pˤək-s 'turn the back on' with the prefix *m₁- in its volitional/causativizing function (see (6b) 'NP_A applies BDLs on NP_U')). The second example is related to the semantics of PDLs in their causative interpretation defined in (5b.i) 'NP_A CAUSE NP_U to be X'. This interpretation is comparable to the causative meaning of the prefix *s- in (15b) 使 *s-rəʔ (shǐ) 'cause to be an emissionary, send', which is based on the root 吏 *[r]əʔ-s (lì) 'clark, minor official'. Finally, the interpretations in the examples from (16b), repeated here as (17), come close either to the interpretation given in rule (5a.i) 'be a person-denoting lexeme' for (17a) 'to be king' or the interpretation of (17b, c) in terms of 'wearing X' or 'use X on something/put X on someone' for clothes (Bisang 2008):

(17) Old Chinese morphology: the suffix *-s, denominal verbs (B & S 2014a: 58–59)
    a. 王 * Gʷaŋ (wáng) 'king'   >   王 * Gʷaŋ-s (wàng) 'to be king'
    b. 冠 * k.ʕor (guān) 'cap, n.'   >   冠 * k.ʕor-s (guàn) 'cap, v.'
    c. 衣 *ʔ(r)əj (yī) 'garment, clothes' >   衣 *ʔ(r)əj-s (yì) 'wear (V transitive)'

Starting out from the above examples of morphological markers, one may explain the semantic parallelisms with rule-based and metaphorical interpretations as a result of at least partial loss of morphology. As soon as the morphology of the above type gets reduced or opaque, what remains is the constructional syntactic environment within which the relevant markers previously occurred. Thus, intransitive interpretations in terms of 'NP is X' get the syntactic form of [NP$_S$ V] in which the object denoting lexeme takes the V-position as in 'NP$_S$ is king' in (17a) (see the structure in (4a)). Analogously, transitive/causative interpretations expressed by *m-, *s- and *-s get associated with a general transitive argument structure construction of the type [NP$_A$ V NP$_U$] with the object-denoting lexeme in the V-position (see the structure in (4b)). Given that the syntactic options of combining Vs and NPs in an SVO language are limited (see the word orders in (4)), many of the more specific distinctions formerly marked by affixes can no longer be expressed and conflate into the same construction. Thus, the affixes *m-, *s- and *-s in their transitive/causative functions are all associated with [NP$_A$ V NP$_U$]. This association at the constructional level is combined with cases of flexible non-derived roots (issue (i)), with potentially opaque morphology (issue (ii)) and with the fact that most affixes alone without their hosts are no reliable indicators of word class either because they can produce nouns and verbs (see *m-, *s- and *-s in (14), (15) and (16), respectively). If morphology gets reduced over time, there will be an increasing number of lexical items whose assignment to the syntactic positions of N and V exclusively depends on their semantics, i.e. on a probabilistic strategy (see section 28.2.2 and Chapter 3).

The combination of the increasing importance of syntactic positions for N and V and the decreasing importance of morphology to the advantage of the semantics of individual lexemes for their assignment to syntax may well be seen as the two ingredients for the situation described so far, in which word-class-indicating constructions with their syntactic positions (e.g. argument structure constructions) interact with the meaning of lexical items either in terms of semantic classes plus rule-based interpretations or in terms of metaphors.

28.3 The Chinese perspective

28.3.1 Before Ma (1898)

The discussion of how to divide words into different categories goes back to the Han dynasty (206 BC to 220 AD), focusing on the individual Chinese character as the basic unit of analysis (字 zì 'word, character, syllable', representing a syllabic unit written by a specific character). Starting out from the need of interpreting the Confucian Classics since the 2nd c. BC, scholars did not only realize that individual characters may have different meanings, they also observed that some of these differences come with different pronunciation as it is manifested in different tonality and sometimes additional differences at the syllable onset. These differences can often be observed up till today in different *pinyin*-transcriptions of one and the same character as can be seen from 好 hǎo 'be good' and hào 'love, like' in (16d). A closer examination of the tonality of these examples reveals that the forms derived by *-s always result in the falling tone in Mandarin pronunciation /`/, which is ultimately the result of loss of morphology.[10] While such differences were just noted by sporadic sound-glosses in the earlier period of this research, it culminated in impressive compendia of different pronunciations, the most famous of which is Lu Deming's (陸德明, about 550–630 AD) 經典釋文 *Jīngdiǎn Shìwén* [classical interpretation] 'Classical Interpretations' (published between about 583–589).

The Chinese terms for this process are 四聲別義 *sì shēng bié yì* [four tone discriminate meaning] 'discrimination of meaning by way of four tones' or sometimes 以聲別義 *yǐ shēng bié yì* [take tone discriminate meaning] 'discrimination of meaning by tone' (Zhang 2005: 4–6, Zádrapa 2011: 19, Sun 2020: 28–29). Its result is called 破讀 *pòdú* [break/split read] 'split reading' or 讀破 *dúpò* [read break/split] 'reading split'. While word-class changes by 'split reading' are reported for quite a few instances, the majority of cases of flexible use are not associated with any change in form (or there is at least no philological evidence for it). For that reason, the traditional research on *Sì shēng bié yì* 'discrimination of meaning by way of four tones' offers invaluable insight into the earlier pronunciation of Chinese characters but it gives little insight into the regular patterns associated with word-class flexibility (see also the limited functional similarities of morphology vs rule-based and metaphorical interpretations in section 28.2.4).

Since the Song dynasty (960–1279), a new approach to word-class flexibility has been developing (for more information, see Zhang 2005: 6–9; Zádrapa 2011: 15–19, Sun 2020: 29–31). Several key terms roughly corresponding to the notions of 'noun' and 'verb' were used by different authors for dealing with the observed flexibility of Classical Chinese lexical items. Without being able to do justice to the exact use of these terms by individual authors, approaches, or networks of scholars, the following pairs of opposing concepts for roughly describing the properties of nouns and verbs should be mentioned: 死 *sǐ* 'dead' vs 活 *huó* 'live', 實 *shí* 'solid' vs 虛 *xū* 'empty' and 靜 *jìng* 'static' vs 動 *dòng* 'dynamic, moving'. These notions were combined with the component *zì* 'word, character, syllable' for creating compound terms like *sǐzì* [dead word] 'noun' vs *huózì* [live word] 'verb', *shízì* [solid word] 'noun' vs *xūzì* [empty word] 'verb'.[11] Needless to say that the above translations of 'noun' and 'verb' should be understood in terms of translational approximations. Based on this terminology, observations on the flexible use of lexical items were discussed under headings like *sǐzì huóyòng* [dead-word live-use] 'dead words used as live [words]' or *shízì xūyòng* [solid-word use empty] 'solid words used as empty [words]', etc. (see Zhang 2005: 6–7).

The Qing dynasty (1644–1911) was particulary productive and led to some more systematic analyses of flexibility. Of particular importance in this context was 袁仁林 Yuan Renlin's work 虛字說 *Xūzìshuō* 'About empty words' (1710) (see Zhang 2005: 8–9). In a passage from the chapter 虛字總說 *Xūzì zǒngshuō* 'General explanations to empty words', he adopts a view which basically describes Classical Chinese as a language with word-class flexibility. The

---

[10] The falling tone /ˋ/ corresponds to the so-called 'departing tone' (去聲 *qùshēng* [leave/depart tone]), which is due to the loss of the suffix *-s (see e.g. Downer 1959; Norman 1988).

[11] Note, that the terms *shízì* and *xūzì* are also used in a completely different context having to do with the semantic content of a lexical item. Since *shí* can also mean 'full', we get the opposition of *shízì* '[semantically] full word' vs *xūzì* '[semantically] empty word', which basically corresponds to autosemantic vs synsemantic words.

relevant passages are quoted and translated by Zádrapa (2011: 16–18, see also Sun 2020: 30). The most instructive part is quoted here in Zádrapa's translation:

> Generally speaking, when characters are extended by scholars, all full characters can be emptied, and all dead [characters] can be brought to life. There merely are situations in which they are used in that way and in which they are not. When they are, according to their nature, described from the static point of view of their substance, they function as full or dead characters. When they are, on the basis of one's intention, expressed from the dynamic point of view of their usage, then they become empty or live ones. But their empty or live use must also be recognized from the context. If they appear separately as single characters, there is no way to ascertain it.
> (Yuan 1710, translated by Zádrapa 2011: 17)[12]

The crucial statements arguing for flexibility are Yuan's (1710) statement that any *zì* 'word, character, syllable' can be used flexibly, that their interpretation is context-dependent and that a single *zì* without context remains undetermined for word class (for further observations on Yuan 1710, see Zhang 2005: 9, Zádrapa 2011: 18 and Sun 2020: 31).

28.3.2 Since Ma (1898)

The first grammar of Chinese written in Chinese was published by Ma Jianzhong (馬建忠, 1845–1900) in 1898 under the title of 馬氏文通 *Mǎ shì wéntōng* 'Ma's Grammar'. This grammar introduces many concepts from European grammatical tradition into Chinese, but it also integrates Chinese concepts. A good example is word-class terminology, which introduces traditional European word classes with their translation into Chinese and, at the same time assigns them to the traditional Chinese-type classes of *shízì* 'solid words' and *xūzì* 'empty words', which correspond to 'autosemantic' and 'synsemantic words', respectively (see fn. 11):

(18) Ma's (1898) word–class distinctions (if there is a difference between traditional characters and simplified characters, both versions are given in that order)
 a. 'Solid words' (*shízì*): 名字 *míngzì* [name word] 'noun'
   代字 *dàizì* [substitute word] 'pronoun'
   動字 / 动字 *dòngzì* [dynamic word] 'verb'
   靜字 *jìngzì* [static word] 'adjective'
   狀字 /狀字 *zhuàngzì* [state word] 'adverb'

 b. 'Empty words' (*xūzì*): 介字 *jièzì* [interposed word] 'adposition'
   連字 / 连字 *liánzì* [connecting word] 'conjunction'
   嘆字 / 叹字 *tànzì* [sigh word] 'interjection'
   助字 *zhùzì* [auxiliary word] 'auxiliaries and particles'

Since the publication of Ma's (1898) grammar, an impressive number of suggestions for word-class terminologies and some new word classes have been developed but all of them

---

[12] The Chinese original runs as follows: 凡實皆可虛, 凡死皆可活, 但有用不用之時耳。從其體之靜者隨分寫之, 則為實為死。從其用之動者, 以意遣之, 則為虛為活。用字之新奇簡煉, 此亦一法。然其虛用活用必亦由上下文知之, 若單字獨出, 則無從見矣。

are based on his example (for an extensive presentation of the word-class discussion in China until about 1970, see Kupfer 1979). What is remarkable is that Ma (1898) uses the term 字 zì in his word-class terminology, which he distinguishes from 詞 / 词 cí. While Ma (1898) is using zì in the context of word-class terminology and cí for syntactic units within the clause (e.g. subject, object or predicate), current terminology is generally using cí for the notion of 'word' in its Western sense, irrespective of whether it is a monosyllabic word written by a single character (the traditional notion of zì) or by a word consisting of more than one syllable represented by more than one character. For that reason, parts of speech terms generally end in -cí (e.g. míngcí 'noun', dòngcí 'verb'). This also applies to additional terms like 數詞/数词 shùcí 'numerals' and 量詞/量词 liàngcí or 副名詞/副名词 fùmíngcí 'numeral classifiers'. The component cí is also part of the modern term for 'word class/part of speech', which is 詞類 / 词类 cílèi [word class/type].

Ma (1898) takes up word-class flexibility in various parts of his grammar. In his view, the flexible use of words or, as he puts it, the observation of 'one word [having] several meanings',[13] is due to its ability to concurrently appear in different syntactic contexts. This means that a single lexical item can belong to more than a single word class (e.g. it can be used in a nominal and in a verbal context). Thus, not every lexical item is flexible per se but words having this property are polycategorial and have the status of 兼類 jiānlèi [hold.concurrently class] 'concurrently belonging to more than one word class' and can be further divided into two subclasses defined by the mechanisms of 辨音 biànyīn [distinguish tone] 'distinction by tone' and 假借 jiǎjiè [temporary borrow] 'borrowing for the moment'[14] (see Zhang 2005: 22–24, Zádrapa 2011: 21–24). The former mechanism basically corresponds to the notion of 'split reading' (see section 28.3.1), while the latter refers to a process by which a given word leaves its original word class and 'borrows' its new and temporary status of belonging to another word class from which it will return back to its original class in unmarked contexts.

Ma's (1898) word–class distinction was basically taken up later by Chen Chengze (陳承澤, [1922] 1957) with some changes in terminology. What he rejected was Ma's (1898) notion of jiānlèi, i.e. the existence of lexical items which 'concurrently belong to more than one word class' by appearing in more than one context. In Chen's (1922) view, lexical items only belong to a single word class, which is associated with their 'basic/original use' (本用 běnyòng [root/base-use]'). If a lexical item occurs in a syntactic position which deviates from its original use, Chen ([1922] 1957) calls that use 活用 huóyòng ([live-use] 'live use' for denoting its temporary function in a specific context without any concomitant changes in the lexicon. In his view, the 'original use' of the lexical item 止 zhǐ in example (3) is its function of an intransitive verb with the meaning of 'stop, halt', while the three functions in which it occurs in that example (stative verb/adjective, causative verb and noun) are all instances of huóyòng (Chen ([1922] 1957: 22; see also Sun 2020: 35). Chen's (1922 [1957]) analysis in terms of huóyòng has become the standard view in linguistic research of China (see e.g. Wang 1999).[15] Thus, there are basically no longer any adherents of full flexibility in the sense of Yuan (1710) among Chinese linguists.

---

[13] In Chinese: 一字數義 yí zì shù yì [one word several meaning].

[14] Note that this term is also well established in paleography for the borrowing of a Chinese character in the sense that a Chinese character is used for writing a word for which no character was available. Thus, Ma's (1898) use of this term may eventually be 'misleading' (Zádrapa 2011: 21).

[15] As Zádrapa (2011: 26–27) points out, the term is taken up in a large number of later publications. Given that it is rarely defined with much terminological rigour, it is hard presenting a history of its use between different authors since Chen (1922).

More recent comprehensive publications are no exception to the Chinese standard view (see Zhang Wenguo 张文国 2005 and Ren He 任荷 2020). The work of Zhang (2005) will be treated in some more detail in this section. He systematically evaluates data from a corpus of twelve Classical Chinese texts and a preclassical source[16] from the perspective of 词类活用 *cílèi huóyòng* [word.class *huóyòng*] '*huóyòng* of word (sub)classes'. As is specified in its title, it is concerned with the phenomenon of *míng-dòng cílèi zhuǎnbiàn* [noun–verb word-class change/transition] 'word-class transition between nouns and verbs', i.e. with nouns temporarily used as verbs or verbs temporarily used as nouns. A crucial condition for Zhang's (2005) understanding of *huóyòng* is that it does not produce new lexical items. There must be a direct semantic relation between the *huóyòng* use of a word and its original use. If such a semantic derivation is not possible, i.e. if the two meanings of a word are indirectly or even idiosyncratically related and cannot be derived regularly, the result is not an instance of *huóyòng* and is beyond the topic of Zhang's study because it belongs to the phenomenon of *jiānlèi* 'concurrently belonging to more than one word class' (Zhang 2005: 99).[17] A good example for both functions is the word 鏡 *jìng*, whose original use (i.e. *běnyòng*) is given as nominal in the sense of 'mirror'. In the verbal position, it can either mean V_1 'use something as a mirror, look into a mirror' or V_2 'use as a reference, draw lessons from' (Zhang 2005: 111, Zádrapa 2011: 36, Sun 2020: 46). Since the meaning of V_1 can be derived regularly from the nominal meaning, it is an instance of *huóyòng*, while the meaning of V_2 must be indirectly derived from the meaning of V_1 in Zhang's (2005) analysis and is not an instance of *huóyòng*.[18]

A large part of Zhang's (2005) work is about the regularities that determine *huóyòng*. For that purpose, he identifies seven semantic classes of nouns (19a) and a set of different semantic functions (19b) these nouns can have in a verbal context (Zhang 2005: 177–330, see also Zádrapa 2011: 40–41; Sun 2020: 50–52):

(19) a. Seven semantic classes of nouns
Nouns denoting (i) humans and animals, (ii) instruments, (iii) natural phenomena (wind, fire, water, rain, lightning, clouds, fogs, peaks, lakes, etc.), (iv) body parts, (v) garments and food, (vi) buildings and abstract notions (fortune, illness, norms, law).

b. Different semantic functions of a noun in a verbal context
(i) Agent, (ii) patient, (iii) instrument, (iv) phenomenon (mostly meteorological or in the context of illnesses), (v) means (for performing an action [e.g. with body parts]), (vi) result, (vii) place.

Zhang (2005: 177–330) presents extensive data on *huóyòng* for each semantic class of nouns in (19a) in both directions, from noun to verb and from verb to noun. In the case of nouns from the semantic class of humans and animals, the direction from N—> V can be illustrated by agent-like nouns such as 王 *wáng* 'king'—> *wàng* 'to be king of' (see also (16b)), 君 *jūn*

---

[16] The source is the 詩經 *Shījīng* 'Book of Odes', a compilation of poetry with texts from the 10th to the 7th c. BC.
[17] Note that Zhang (2005) does not exclude the existence of *jiānlèi*. His point is that this is a lexical property of individual words.
[18] Zádrapa (2011: 36) rightly questions the adequacy of a chain like N —> V_1 —> V_2. Sun (2020) treats the V_1-interpretation as an instance of rule-based interpretation, while the V_2-interpretation is seen in the context of metaphoric inference without any assumptions on temporal sequence or one interpretation presupposing the other (also cf. Zádrapa 2011: 129–132 on conceptual metaphors).

'prince, ruler'—> 'be a ruler, rule as a prince' (Zhang 2005: 179; see also (1a) and rule ((5a.i)). The opposite direction from a verb to an agent noun (V—> N) can be seen from examples like 諜 *dié* 'to spy'—> 'a spy', 寇 *kòu* 'invade'—> 'invader, foe', 盜 *dào* 'steal'—> 'stealer, thief' or 賊 *zéi* 'to harm, injure, hurt'—> 'someone who does harm, etc.' (Zhang 2005: 193–194). In a similar way, there are body-part terms which develop from nouns to verbs and *vice versa*. In the case of N—> V, we find nouns which function as the means of an action as in 指 *zhǐ* 'finger'—> 'point one's finger at' or 肘 *zhǒu* 'elbow'—> 'hit/push someone with one's elbow' (Zhang 2005: 263). The other direction from a verb associated with a body part to the denotation of that body part as a result of that action can be illustrated by 皮 *pí* 'to peel'—> 'skin' and 馘 *guó* 'to cut off the left ear'—> 'left ear (cut off from enemies as a trophy)' (Zhang 2005: 274).

To provide a somewhat deeper impression of Zhang's (2005) view, this section will end in briefly highlighting three central issues of his work, some of which have been subject to criticism in the West. The first point is about the exclusion of two main types of predicative use of nouns (N—> V) from the scope of *huóyòng* (Zádrapa 2011: 34–38, Sun 2020: 46–48). The first main type is concerned with the use of nouns in the function of expository predicates,[19] either for expressing the quality of the subject of the clause or for expressing its physical characteristics (Zhang 2005: 70–97). In the former case, we typically find PDLs like 君 *jūn* 'prince, ruler' (see example (1a)) or 臣 *chén* 'minister', which get the meaning of 'to be/behave like a (proper) prince/ruler' or 'to be/behave like a (proper) minister' in the predicate position.[20] The latter case is limited to specific conditions like (i) appearances/characteristics of animals or plants and (ii) conditions of humans having to do with clothes, food, accommodation and transportation.[21] Examples for (i) are 毛 *máo* 'hair'—> 'have hairs/be hairy' and 角 *jiǎo* 'horn'—> 'have horns', examples for (ii) are 麻衣 *má-yī* [hemp-garment] 'hemp garment'—> 'to wear a hemp garment' and 車 *chē* 'chariot'—> 'to be on chariot'. The second main type of predicative use has to do with the terminological use of nouns in certain historical texts like the use of 日 *rì* 'day' with the meaning of 'to record the day' or the use of 地 *dì* 'place' with the meaning of 'to record the place'. The exclusion of these two main types of the predicate use of nouns are criticized by Zádrapa 2011: 34–38) as well as by Sun (2020: 46–48) because quite a few of these cases can actually be accounted for in a more systematic way (see the distinction of rule-based and metaphoric interpretation in Sun 2020). To give only one example, the case of lexemes like 君 *jūn* 'prince, ruler' as in (1a) can be regularly accounted for in terms of (5a.i). Similarly, its meaning of 'consider as a ruler' in (1b) can be derived from (5b.ii).

The second point is about Zhang's (2005: 116–130) motivation for why not all object-denoting lexemes can appear in the verbal position. Apart from general aspects like genre, style, formal requirements (rhyme, parallelism), the most important factor which decides if an object-denoting lexeme can undergo *huóyòng* is its 特徵义 *tèzhēngyì* 'distinctive seme'. In Zhang's (2005: 122, see also Zádrapa 2011: 116) view, there is only one single distinctive seme for each word by which it is clearly distinguishable from all other words with similar

---

[19] The Chinese term is 说明谓语 *shuōmíng wèiyǔ* [explain predicate] 'expository predicate'.
[20] The Chinese term for this subcase is 性质说明谓语 *xìngzhì shuōmíng wèiyǔ* [quality explain predicate] 'qualitative expository predicate'.
[21] The Chinese term for this subcase is 状态说明谓语 *zhuàngtài shuōmíng wèiyǔ* [state explain predicate] 'static expository predicate'.

meanings. For a given word to occur in the V position its distinctive seme must belong to the category of functional[22] distinctive semes, i.e. it must denote an action.[23] To illustrate his method, Zhang (2005: 124–130) presents pairs of words from the same semantic domain of which one has a functional distinctive seme, while the other one does not have it. A good example is the pair 足 *zú* 'foot' and 手 *shǒu* 'hand' (Zhang 2005: 125–126). For checking if a lexical item does have a functional distinctive seme, Zhang (2005) consults glosses from ancient Chinese dictionaries.[24] Since the lexical item *zú* 'foot' is defined as a body part with no reference to its functionality, while *shǒu* 'hand' is defined by its function of 'holding/grasping something', only the latter can be used in the verbal position with the meaning of 'hold in one's hand'. Zhang's (2005: 116–130) explanation has been criticized for various reasons (Zádrapa 2011: 38–39, 113–124). Two important reasons are mentioned here. One of them is his uncritical use of the dictionaries which follow different glossing strategies and often provide highly specific philological explanations. The other one is that Zhang (2005) does not base his approach on a more systematic semantic basis. As Zádrapa (2011: 38) points out, 'Zhāng's attempt to substitute semantic analysis of any kind with the ancient glosses is infelicitous'.

Finally, Zhang (2005) offers extensive data on frequency, in particular on the frequency of individual object-denoting lexemes in the positions of N and V in individual sources as well as in his whole corpus. These data are very useful, but it is important to be aware of their limited significance. The overall problem is trivial and has to do with the obvious fact that Classical Chinese is a dead language, and that the corpus is limited. For that reason, it is not possible to state with any certainty if a given lexical item is incompatible with a syntactic position like N or V nor is it possible to draw conclusions based on N: V-frequency ratios (see Zádrapa 2011: 9).[25] Given this situation, it is often hard to determine the direction of change (N—> V or V—> N). Similarly, there is ultimately no way of deciding if a given lexical item should be seen as a case of *huóyòng* 'live use' or of *jiānlèi* 'concurrently belonging to more than one word class'. In this last case, there is not only the problem of limited data but also of defining an adequate threshold in terms of a N: V frequency ratio.

28.4 Conclusion: East meets West

A closer look at *huóyòng* shows that it comes in different degrees. This has been pointed out by Lü (1979: 46–47), who makes a distinction between temporal instances of *huóyòng*[26] and instances of *huóyòng* which become more frequent and ultimately end up as instances of

---

[22] Zhang (2005: 116–130) uses the term 用 *yòng* for 'functional'.
[23] In Zhang's (2005: 123) terminology, it must be a 动作行为的名词 *dòngzuòxíngwéi de míngcí* 'actional noun'.
[24] The best-known dictionary is the 說文解字 *Shuōwén jiězì*, compiled about 100 AD by 許慎 Xu Shen.
[25] See also the following quotation: 'We can never be sure whether the fact that word A is attested verbally in five cases in three ancient books and word B in only one case in one book is purely due to chance or due to their actual patterns of distribution' (Zádrapa 2011: 114).
[26] In Chinese: 临时活用 *línshí 'huóyòng'* [temporal-*huóyòng*] 'temporal *'huóyòng'*'.

'permanent word class transition' (see also Sun 2020: 40).[27] The emergence of new instances of 'permanent word-class transition' creates the situation that is characteristic of *jiānlèi* 'concurrently belonging to more than one word class' as described in section 28.3.2. Thus, a lexical item with its old word-class function gets an additional one which results from a previous process of *huóyòng* (see Sun 2020: 40). As Zádrapa (2011: 113) points out, this shows that the difference between *huóyòng* and *jiānlèi* is rather a matter of degree than a matter of two clearly distinguishable phenomena.

If one associates the *jiānlèi*-words with flexibility or precategoriality, one gets a continuum between categorially determined words, the *huóyòng*-words, and the categorially non-determined open words, the *jiānlèi*-words. These two poles show different degrees of strength in the course of the history of Chinese (Sun 2020). In the pre-classical period in which the combination of affixes with individual roots created categorially rigid words, the *huóyòng*-type seems to be comparatively dominant. The reduction of morphology and the increasing importance of word-class-indicating constructions with their syntactic positions of N and V supported the emergence of *jiānlèi*-words (see the tentative scenario in section 28.2.4) and eventually created a situation of general word-class flexibility as it is assumed in Western approaches such as Bisang (2008a, 2008b, 2013), Zádrapa (2011), and Sun (2020). If this analysis is true the probabilistic assignment of lexemes to word class in terms of Lehmann (2008) depends on word-class-indicating constructions and semantics (see Croft 2001), plus pragmatic implicatures (based on stereotypes), metonymy, metaphor and general aspects of world knowledge. Metaphors even allow the modelling of lexicalization as a process which is not excluded in a language with flexible parts of speech (see section 28.2.3, Chapter 3).

The overall analysis of Classical Chinese as a language with a flexible word-class system is based on the power of this inventory to derive the interpretation of lexical items in different syntactic positions. In this context, the statistical observation that many if not most object-denoting lexemes are not found in the V position of the available text corpus is of secondary importance. What is crucial is the possibility to derive the meaning of a lexical item in its syntactic environment. It seems that it was this type of productivity that Yuan (1710) had in mind when he wrote that the empty or live use of a word cannot be ascertained out of context (see section 28.3.1).

Later periods of Chinese are characterized by more lexical rigour. In modern Standard Chinese (Mandarin), a large number of lexical items are associated with a specific syntactic position like N or V but there is also quite a number of lexical items which can occur in both functions (e.g. 研究 *yánjiū* 'investigate (V), research (N)', 斗争 *dòuzhēng* 'to fight, fight (N)', 代表 *dàibiǎo* 'representative (N), to act as a representative/to represent (V)', etc.). From such a perspective, there is a clear distinction between *huóyòng*-words and *jiānlèi*-words and there are, of course, different parts of speech as they were introduced in section 28.3.2 (for a more comprehensive account including statistics, see Guo [2002] 2018). Moreover, Chinese has developed an impressive number of derivational morphemes with different degrees of productivity (Chao 1968: 194–257, Wiedenhof 2015: 289–322; for a new systematic approach in Chinese, see Dong 2016). In the domain of the noun, we find derivational suffixes like 性

---

[27] In Chinese: 永久性的词类转变 *yǒngjiǔxìng de cílèi zhuǎnbiàn* [permanent MOD word.class change/transition] 'permanent word-class transition'.

-xìng (> *xìng* 'inherent nature') for deriving nouns as in *zhòngyào-xìng* [important-NMLZ] 'importance'. The suffix 化 *-huà* (> *huà* 'change') is sometimes described in the context of the formation of transitive/causative verbs similar to English *-ize*. But this is only half of the story, since some of its derivations are nominal or even nominal *and* verbal as in the case of 现代化 *xiàndài-huà* [modern-SUFF] 'modernize, modernization'. Thus, the existence of derivational morphology does not necessarily exclude *jiānlèi*-words in Modern Standard Chinese.

CHAPTER 29

WORD CLASSES IN SALISH LANGUAGES

DONNA B. GERDTS AND LAUREN SCHNEIDER

29.1 INTRODUCTION

THE Salish languages of the Pacific Northwest of North America are well known for many properties that make them interesting to linguistic typologists and theorists. One topic that has been somewhat controversial is the extent to which word classes are relevant to the description and analyses of these languages. The issue has sparked a debate about the best approaches to verifying the existence of noun, verb, and other word classes. For the purpose of this chapter, we take as a starting point that most grammars of Salish languages make useful reference to the lexical categories noun, verb, and, to a lesser extent, adjective, and adverb, as well as to the syntactic categories of predicate/VP and NP. We will survey some of the empirical details in various languages that speak to the topic of word classes, drawing as well on primary research on the Halkomelem language.

There are 23 Salish languages currently or historically spoken in British Columbia, Washington, Oregon, Idaho, and Montana (Czaykowska-Higgins & Kinkade 1998; Gerdts 2013b; Davis 2020). The Salish language family is divided into five branches—Bella Coola, Central Salish (Comox-Sliammon, Pentlatch, Sechelt, Squamish, Halkomelem, Nooksack, North Straits Salish, Klallam, Lushootseed, Twana), Tillamook, Tsamosan (Lower Chehalis, Upper Chehalis, Cowlitz, Quinault), and Interior Salish (Lillooet, Shuswap, Thompson, Coeur d'Alene, Columbian, Kalispel, Okanagan).[1] Ongoing contact between neighbouring peoples has led to a wave-like distribution of grammatical features that sometimes cross-cut languages and genetic subgroupings. Lexical items tend to spread this way as well, often catching only some of the dialects of a language in their path (Gerdts 1977; Hess 1979). This has led to major dialect differences within languages. Some Salish languages on the edge of the territory also show contact phenomena with non-Salish neighbours, and the family is also part of the Northwest sprachbund, sharing interesting features with Chemakuan,

---

[1] These names used in the scholarly literature do not reflect the self-designated names used by individual dialect groups. These will sometimes also be given, depending on the usage in the source.

Wakashan, and other nearby languages, such as the use of lexical suffixes, nominal tense, and insubordination (Kinkade 1995; Beck 2000a, 2000b).[2]

Like other languages of the Pacific Northwest sprachbund, Salish languages are well known for their complex morphosyntax. The example below from Halkomelem demonstrates some key features:[3]

(1) Halkomelem
    niʔ   xʷiʔ   xʷ-məqʼʷ-aləs-nəxʷ-əs   θə   sqeʔəq-s
    DIST.AUX   MIR   LPFX-lance-eye-LCTR-3SUB   DT   younger.sibling-POS
    tᶿə   sxʼiʔx̣ʼəɬ   ʔə   tᶿə   sc̓eštəcəs.
    DT   child<DIM>   OBL   DT   branch
    'The boy accidentally poked his little sister's eye with a branch.'

The predicate occurs in clause-initial position and is headed by the distal auxiliary *niʔ*. The main verb exhibits multiple affixes, including the lexical suffix *-aləs* 'eye' (see section 29.3.3) and a transitivity suffix (*-nəxʷ* 'limited control transitive'). Salish languages can be characterized as polysynthetic, with person marking accomplished by affixes and clitics, for example, the third person subject suffix *-əs* in (1). Typically, NP arguments follow the verb complex (in this example, the word order is VOS) and are headed by determiners (e.g. *θə* and *tᶿə* above). There is no case marking on direct arguments. Some languages license non-arguments with an oblique preposition (e.g. *ʔə*); Halkomelem has one such preposition, but the Tsamosen languages have ten (Davis 2020).

Given the robust nature of inflectional and derivational morphology in Salish languages, one might suppose that words of different classes would be easily identifiable as such, and we show below that this is indeed the case (section 29.2). Nevertheless, there are some ways that word classes in Salish languages show great flexibility, for example, in their use as predicates and as bases for further derivation. Entity-denoting and event-denoting words are for the most part quite different in appearance at both the word level and the phrase level. In addition, clausal syntax relies heavily on the distinction between plain and nominalized clauses. Section 29.3 deals with word-level derivations. The debate on noun versus verb has overshadowed research on other categories, but concepts of adjective (section 29.4) and adverb (section 29.5) are also important in constructing descriptive grammars of the languages.

29.2 THE WORD-CLASS DEBATE

Historically, there has been some doubt as to whether the traditional word classes of noun, verb, adjective, and adverb apply to Salish languages. Some early researchers maintained the claim that there were only two kinds of words—predicates and particles (Kuipers 1968;

---

[2] For example, in contact with the neighbouring Wakashan languages, which lack prefixes, Comox-Sliammon has lost many of the Salish prefixes.

[3] Halkomelem is divided into three major dialect areas: Island, Downriver, and Upriver (Elmendorf & Suttles 1960; Gerdts 1977). The Halkomelem data in this chapter, unless otherwise noted, come from Hulʼqʼumiʼnumʼ, the Island dialect. If no reference information is given, the data comes from original fieldwork. See Acknowledgements at the end of the chapter.

Kinkade 1976, 1983; Thompson & Thompson 1980; Jelinek & Demers 1994; Jelinek 1995; Czaykowska & Kinkade 1998). Predicates are lexical words that form the building blocks for NPs and VPs through the process of inflection.

In contrast, particles represent minor categories, such as discourse markers, auxiliaries, temporal, spatial, or modal notions. Salish languages have many of these small, ubiquitous, non-affixal functional elements (Gerdts & Werle 2014: 247). In Halkomelem, particles are frequent enough that a sentence sounds bare without them. For example, sentence (2) consists of two verbs (one per clause), one noun, and seven particles.

(2) Halkomelem (Gerdts & Werle: 2014: 247)
 niʔ=yəxʷ=cən=p̓eʔ   xʷiʔ=ləq̓ləq̓-ət,   naʔət   ʔəw̓kʷ   tᶿə   qaʔ.
 DIST.AUX=INFR=1SG.SUB=CERT   MIR=drink-TR<IPFV>   AUX.DT   gone   DT   water
 'I must have drunk the water too fast, since it's all gone.'

Leaving aside interjections (ʔecənə 'ouch', ʔa:sa 'shucks'), fragment expressions (heʔe 'yes'), coordinators (ʔiʔ 'and'), and demonstratives (təʔinəł 'over there), particles are best treated as *clitics* (parsed with =) since they exhibit properties midway between words and affixes (Gerdts & Werle 2014). Like affixes, clitics are typically unstressed, and express mostly functional meanings. But like words, clitics can be perceived as independent elements, and can be ordered with respect to a phrase, rather than to a stem. Clitics can be further identified as enclitics (for example, the various second position clitics, such as inferential yəxʷ, first person subject cən), proclitics (e.g. mirative xʷiʔ), ambi-clitics (e.g. first-person possessive nə) that form phonological words with either a preceding or following host, and introducer clitics (e.g. auxiliary niʔ) which host other clitics to form a phonological word (as in niʔ = yəxʷ = cən = p̓eʔ).

A main distinction between the word classes that are major lexical categories discussed in this chapter and clitics is that the former regularly host clitics, while the latter do not, with the exception of the introducer clitics, which historically grammaticized from auxiliary verbs.

29.2.1. Nouns and adjectives as predicates

Salish clauses minimally consist of a predicate, which may be verbal (3a), nominal (3b), or adjectival (3c); as Salish languages are predicate initial and lack copulas, the subject NP generally follows the predicate.

(3) Halkomelem
 a. ʔimaš=ceʔ   łə   słeniʔ.
    walk=FUT   DT   woman
    'The woman will walk.'

 b. swəstanəlwət   θə   sne-s.
    Swustanulwut   DT   name-3POS
    'Her name is Swustanulwut.'

 c. ʔiyəs=ceʔ   łə-nə   mənə.
    happy=FUT   DT-1POS   child
    'My daughter will be happy.'

Predicate nominals (3b) lack determiners, and thus are easily distinguished from NPs in argument positions. It is also easy to distinguish a predicate adjective (4a) from an adjective in a complex predicate nominal with a Ø-subject (4b); compare to the predicate nominals with an overt NP (4c) or with a pronominal subject expressed as a second position subject clitic appearing on the first element of the NP (4d).

(4) Halkomelem
    a. *θi   t^θə   məstiməx^w.*
       big   DT   person
       'The person is important.'

    b. *θi   məstiməx^w.*
       big   person
       'He is an important person.'

    c. *θi   məstiməx^w   t^θəń   məńa.*
       big   person   DT.2POS   child.
       'Your child is an important person.'

    d. *θi=č   məstiməx^w.*
       big=2SG.SUB   person
       'You are an important person.'

In Salish languages, many functional categories do not appear to select for particular lexical categories (Matthewson & Demirdache 1995). This is illustrated by the Lillooet examples below, where the completive particle *toʔ* encliticizes to the main predicate whether it is a verb (5a), a noun (5b), or an adjective (5c).

(5) Lillooet: Stʼátʼimcets (Matthewson & Demirdache 1995: 3)
    a. *q^wεčéč-ø=toʔ   k^w-š   Gertie*
       leave-3ABS=COMPL   DT-N   Gertie
       'Gertie left.'

    b. *plešmən-ø=toʔ   k^w-š   Bill*
       policeman-3ABS=COMPL   DT-N   Bill
       'Bill was a policeman.'

    c. *xzom-ø=toʔ   te   š-ʕawʼp-ε*
       big-3ABS=COMPL   DT   N-meet-DT
       'The meeting was big.'

Observing that any full word or phrase may serve as the main predicate of a Salishan sentence, Kinkade (1983: 27), among others, came to question the noun–verb distinction, influenced by structuralists like Bloomfield (1933: 20), who explicitly claimed: 'some features, such as, for instance, the distinction of verb-like and noun-like words as separate parts of speech, are common to many languages but lacking in others'. Kinkade (1983: 28) posits that words such as *póxut* 'father' should be considered as a state rather than an entity. Nouns and verbs are in fact instantiations of a category-neutral concept 'predicate'. Matthewson & Demirdache (1995) note that the following NP is in fact syntactically ambiguous:

(6) Lillooet: St'át'imcets (Matthewson & Demirdache 1995: 4)
    a. *te šmółeč-ɛ*   b. *te šmółeč- -ɛ*
        DT woman-DT   DT woman-3ABS-DT
        'the woman'   'the one who is a woman'
        [DP the [NP woman]]   [DP the [IP pro is a woman]]

This is because (i) there is no copula in the language, (ii) Salish allows null arguments, and (iii) the null subject of an intransitive clause induces absolutive marking on the predicate, and third person absolutive is phonologically null (Matthewson & Demirdache 1995). The structure in (6b) is one that could be used to represent in modern terms Kinkade's proposal that nouns are essentially stative predicates. To justify such an analysis, given the propensity of languages of the world to have word classes, one would have to find convincing evidence that a distinction between nouns and verbs is unnecessary.

29.2.2 The basics of noun and verb inflection

Authors such as Van Eijk & Hess (1986), Davis & Matthewson (1999), and Davis et al. (2014) argue that there are sufficient criteria for defining at least two major classes and that these classes are similar enough to the traditional categories of 'noun' and 'verb' to profitably apply these labels in Salish. Noticeably, nouns inflect for person via possessive affixes, while verbs inflect for person via subject clitics/suffixes and object suffixes (Kroeber 1999: 13; Davis 2000, 2020; Kiyosawa & Gerdts 2010: 36). For example, Thompson marks possession as in the following paradigm:

(7) Thompson (Thompson & Thompson 1992: 60)
     1SG n-cítxʷ   'my house'
     2SG heʔ-cítxʷ   'your (SG.) house'
     3SG cítxʷ-s   'his/her/its/their house'
     1PL cítxʷ-kt   'our house'
     2PL cítxʷ-ep   'you people's house'
     3PL cítxʷ-íyxs   'their house'

Second person singular is marked for possession with the prefix *heʔ-* and for intransitive subject with the enclitic *=kʷ*.

(8) Thompson (Kroeber 1999: 54)
    mi̓lt=kʷ=ekʷu=ƛuʔ
    visit=2SG.SUB=QUOT=just
    'They say you are just visiting.'

Subject marking differs from language to language, depending on such features as person, transitivity, and clause type (Kroeber 1999; Kiyosawa & Gerdts 2010). The Central Salish languages and the Northern Interior Salish languages Lillooet and Thompson mark main clause subjects with second position clitics, which attach to the leftmost available element of the verb complex, ordered among other clitics.[4]

(9) Comox (Kroeber 1999: 54)
čaʔt=č=ʔut gəq̓-t-uɬ tə ʔimən
now=1SG.SUB=PTC open-TR-PST DT door
'I just opened the door.'

The subject is marked on the predicate by a suffix in Southern Interior languages:

(10) Columbian (Kinkade 1982: 52, 59)
ʔəm-cí-nn.
feed-TR.2SG.OBJ-1SG.SUB
'I fed you.'

Van Eijk & Hess (1986: 323) conclude that the difference between noun and verbs is easily discernible in the inflectional morphology even if this distinction is largely irrelevant for syntactic analysis in Salish languages.[5]

In examining Salish syntactic structure, however, we find obvious differences between verbs and nouns at the phrasal level. As Montler (2003) and others have noted, verbs are easily identifiable by their role as head of a verb complex (often preceded by an auxiliary verb).

(11) Klallam (Montler 2003: 114)
a. hiyá=cn ʔítt.
   go.AUX=1SUB sleep
   'I'll go to sleep.'
b. *hiyá=cn šaʔšúʔɬ.
   go.AUX=1SUB happy
   'I'll go happy.'
c. *hiyá=cn nə-ʔáʔiŋ.
   go.AUX=1SUB 1POS-house
   'I'll go my house.'

Nouns are similarly easy to recognize because of their role as head of an NP, specified by a determiner. Salish languages have large sets of determiners (more than 70 in Halkomelem), which encode a rich set of semantic concepts, varying from language to language, including gender, number, visibility/invisibility, and deixis (see Matthewson 1998; Suttles 2004; Gerdts 2013a; Gillon 2013; Huijsmans et al 2020; Reisinger et al. 2021; Huijsmans & Resinger 2022). Determiners can be divided into two types—articles, which must be followed by an NP (12a), and demonstratives, which appear with or without an NP (12b).

---

[4] For more on second position clitics, see Gerdts & Werle (2014) and Huijsmans (2015; 2023).
[5] Person marking is one of the few phenomena characterized in terms of subject in Halkomelem, according to Gerdts (1988), who shows that most syntactic generations are characterized by the distinctions ergative versus absolutive and direct NP versus oblique NP.

(12) Halkomelem (Gerdts & Hedberg 2020)
    a. *niʔ*   *wəł=nem̓*   *həyeʔ*   *θə*   *seli.*
        DIST.AUX   PRF=go.AUX   leave   DT.F   Sally
        'Sally has left.'
    b. *niʔ*   *wəł=nem̓*   *həyeʔ̓*   *θey*   (*słeniʔ*).
        DIST.AUX   PRF=go.AUX   leave   DM.F   lady
        'That (woman) has left.'

Determiners are central to the syntax of Salish languages; in most of the languages, determiners are required before NP arguments, including plural nouns, generic nouns, proper nouns (12), and possessed nouns (13):[6]

(13) Halkomelem
     niʔ=ʔə=č   *ləm-nəxʷ*   *tθə*   *nə-məṅə?*
     DIST.AUX=Q=2SUB   see-LCTR   DT   1POS-child
     'Did you see my child?'

An objection raised to using the presence of a determiner as evidence for the word category of noun is based on data from relative clauses like those in (14), in which the N head is only optionally expressed, resulting in a construction where a determiner is followed by a verbal element, not a noun (see Beck 2013).[7]

(14) Halkomelem (adapted from Gerdts 1988)
    a. *statəl-staxʷ=can*   *kʷθə*   (*swiẃləs*)   [*niʔ*   *xʷ-mə́kʷəθ-ət-axʷ*].
        know-CS=1SUB   DT.M   (boy)   DIST.AUX   LPFX-kiss-TR-2sub
        'I know the boy/the one [who you kissed].'
    b. *statəl-staxʷ=can*   *łə*   (*q̓emiʔ*)   [*niʔ*   *xʷ-məkʷəθ-ət-axʷ*].
        know-CS=1SUB   DT.F   (girl)   DIST.AUX   LPFX-kiss-TR-2SUB
        'I know the girl/the one [who you kissed].'

Such data led to a view articulated by Davis & Matthewson (1996, 1999: 53): 'The syntactic category of the determiner's complement is unspecified, leaving the possibility for a verbal complement of D ... ' (see (14b)). However, an alternative analysis of such examples posits a head noun, i.e. an 'eclipsed' head, as evidenced by gender and number agreement on the determiner (Gerdts 1988: 62), and this obviates the need of expanding the range of categories that follow a determiner. This in turn leads to the conclusion that the ability of nouns (and adjectives) to act as predicates without an overt copula can be possible even in languages, such as Salish languages, that otherwise show evidence for the usual range of categorial distinctions (Davis et al. 2014: 197).

---

[6] NPs do not require determiners when preceded by numerals or when they are non-arguments, e.g. vocatives, appositives, and increments.
[7] A survey of our Hul'q'umi'num' corpus shows that these 'determiner-headed' (or so-called headless) relatives are actually much more popular than relative clauses built on overt noun heads.

29.2.3 Nominalized clauses

Clausal nominalizations, marked by the nominalizer prefix *s-*, are found in all Salish languages, with the exception of Tillamook (Kroeber 1999: 100). Observe the differences between a main clause (15a) and a nominalized clause (15b).

(15) Halkomelem
 a. *niʔ=cən   nem̓   həyeʔ.*
    DIST.AUX=1SG.SUB go.AUX   leave.
    'I left.'

 b. *ʔəy̓   [kʷə-nə-s   nem̓   həyeʔ]$_{NP}$*
    good   DT-1POS-N go.AUX   leave
    'I'd better go.' Lit: 'My going is good.'

The clause is nominalized by prefixing *s-* at first opportunity, e.g. in the above example, it attaches to the auxiliary verb *nem̓*. In the main clause in (15a), the subject is expressed by the second position clitic *cən*, while in (15b) the first person subject is expressed by the possessive prefix *nə-* (see *kʷθə-nə snəxʷəɬ* 'my canoe').

Nominalized clauses are used as complement and adjunct clauses, and appear robustly after a variety of higher predicates expressing time, manner, modality, etc.:

(16) Halkomelem
 hiθ   kʷə-nə-s   ʔimaš.
 last.long DT-1POS-N   walk
 'I walked for a long time.'

(17) Halkomelem
 sk̓ʷey   kʷə-nə-s   t̓iləm.
 impossible DT-1POS-N   sing
 'I can't sing.'

Salish languages are also well known for the frequent use of sentential nominalizations in connected speech. In this Halkomelem example, the nominalizer *s-* appears on the left edge of the clause followed by the linker *-əw̓*, and the subject is expressed by possessive marking:[8]

(18) Halkomelem
 ləmnəm   kʷə   šes,
 seen-PAS DT   sea.lion
 'The sea lions were seen.'

  səw   'ʔa.a.aɬ-s   tθə   swaw̓ləs   ʔə   tθə   snəxʷəɬ-s.
  N-CN   embark-3POS(RL)   DT   young.man<PL>   OBL   DT   canoe-3POS
 'And then the young men got on their canoe.' (WS 15)

---

[8] Salish nominalizations are sometimes used as complete thoughts without a main clause, i.e. 'insubordination' (Evans 2007; Watanabe 2007; Gerdts 2016).

The difference between a nominalized clause (see (16) and (17)) and a sentential nominalization (see (18)) is that the latter lacks a determiner. In sum, determiners are central to all levels of syntactic structure and serve to identify nouns within NPs, NPs within clauses, and embedded nominalized clauses within sentences (Thompson 2003).

29.2.4 Inflectional processes that do not select for lexical class

An interesting property of Salish languages is that a number of inflectional processes do not appear to select for lexical class (Kinkade 1983: 31; Watanabe 2003: 69). Inflections usually associated with verbs (e.g. tense) can appear on nouns, and inflections usually associated with nouns (e.g. plural, diminutive) can appear on verbs. The indiscriminate use of inflectional morphology in Salish is considered the strongest evidence for the category-neutral analysis (Matthewson & Demirdache 1995).

29.2.4.1 *Verb inflections that do not select for lexical class*

In Salish languages, tense marking is not obligatory; for example, each language possesses optional elements which indicate past time (Davis & Matthewson 2009: 1115):

(19) Columbian: Moses-Columbia | Nxa'amxcin (Willett 2003: 320)
  wík-ł-n=aẏ   Paul
  see-TR-1SG.ERG=PST   Paul
  'I saw Paul.'

(20) North Straits Salish: Saanich | Sənčáθən (Montler 1986: 210)
  k̓ʷən-t-éln̓əṅ=ləʔ=sən
  see-TR-3OBJ-DESID=PST=1SG.SUB
  'I wanted to see it.'

Tense markers can appear on any word class. Future tense in Halkomelem, for example, is encoded by a second position clitic *ceʔ*. In the following sentence, *ceʔ* encliticizes onto an auxiliary.

(21) Halkomelem
  nem̓=ʔə=č=ceʔ   q̓ʷał-ət łə sti:č?
  go.AUX=Q=2SG.SUB=FUT   wait-TR DT bus
  'Are you going to wait for the bus?'

In this example, there are three second position clitics, which attach to the first available host in a predetermined order, in this case the auxiliary verb (see Gerdts & Werle 2014). When a future or past tense marker appears on the first available host in the clause, it has scope over the entire clause. In contrast, when a future or past tense marker appears within an NP, it only has scope over the entity referred to by the NP.

(22) Halkomelem
qel-nəxʷ-əs   kʷθə=nə šxʷəw̓weli   kʷθə=nə   staləs=ceʔ.
angry-LCTR-3SUB   DT=1POS parent<PL>   DT=1POS   spouse=FUT
'My parents are angry at my future husband.'

The future marker applies only to the DP *kʷθənə staləs* 'my spouse (out of view)'. Frequently, future will be marked on various entities and events within a sentence.

(23) Halkomelem
niʔ=ceʔ   xʷə=nə-s-tənəw̓txʷ   tə-nə   šxʷʔaq̓ʷaʔ
DIST.AUX=FUT   INCH=1POS-N-nearby.house   DT-1POS   sibling
ʔə   tə-nə   leləm̓=ceʔ   niʔ   θəy-t-əm=ceʔ.
OBL   DT-1POS   house=FUT   DIST.AUX build-TR-PAS=FUT
'My sister will become my neighbour when my house is built.'

We find a similar pattern when we look at the past tense marker, encoded with the clitic =əɬ.

(24) Halkomelem
ʔiʔ   niɬ=əɬ   ʔəw̓   ćew-əθamiš-əs=əɬ   tə   silə-s=əɬ.
CNJ   3SG.PRO=PST   CN   help-TR.1SG.OBJ-3SUB=PST   DT   grandparent-3POS=PST
'And that was how his late grandmother used to help me.'

In this example, the past tense morpheme appears three times: first, on the introducer clitic (*niɬ* signals emphatic focus), second, on the verb (√*ćew* 'help'), and third, on the subject NP (*silə-s* his grandparent). The first occurrence has scope over the main clause, the second occurrence has scope over the subordinate clause, and the third has scope over just the DP *tə silə-s* 'his grandmother', expressing a decessive meaning. Thus, tense on nouns differs from tense on verbs—when cliticized to the predicate, the tense morpheme takes scope over the entire event; when cliticized to an NP, it only has scope over that entity.

These tense markers can also appear on Halkomelem adjectives. In (25), the adjective is the first available host for the future clitic and the tense takes scope over the entire clause.

(25) Halkomelem (ST 8068)
ʔiʔ   ʔəy̓=ceʔ   ʔəw̓   nem-əs   xʷəʔaləm̓.
CNJ   good=FUT   CN   go.AUX-3SUB   return
'And it will be good when he goes back.'

In (26), past tense takes scope only over the noun phrase.

(26) Halkomelem (PM 32641)
niɬ   kʷəʔeɬ   nəw̓   šnex̌əńs   ʔəl   kʷey̓   qeqəl=əɬ   məstiməxʷ.
3FOC   thus   AUX.CN be.at.end-3POS   just   DM   bad<PL>=PST   people
'And that's as far as it goes about how it was with those evil people of the past.'

The adjective is the first available host for the clitic within the noun phrase.

29.2.4.2 Noun inflections that do not select for lexical class

Not only do Salish languages allow inflectional morphology typically associated with verbs to appear on nouns and adjectives, but inflection associated with nouns also appears on adjectives, verbs, and even adverbs. Table 29.1 provides some examples of Halkomelem nouns inflected for diminutive, plural, and plural diminutive (Gerdts 2012: 1).

Table 29.1 Inflected forms for some Halkomelem nouns

gloss	plain	plural	diminutive	plural diminutive
'man'	swəy̓qeʔ	səw̓əy̓qeʔ	swiwiʔqeʔ	swəliwiʔqeʔ
'basket'	sitən	seʔəltən	siʔstən̓	səli̓ʔstən̓
'shoe'	qʷləy̓šən	qʷəłəy̓šən	qʷiʔqʷłiʔšən̓	qʷəliʔqʷłiʔšən̓
'wood'	syał	syaʔəłł	syay̓ł	sliy̓ay̓ł

Halkomelem adjectives also inflect for diminutive, plural, and plural diminutive. Some examples are provided in Table 29.2.

Table 29.2 Halkomelem adjectives inflected for plural and diminutive (Gerdts 2012: 2)

gloss	plain	plural	diminutive	plural diminutive
'good'	ʔəy̓	ʔeliʔ	ʔeʔi:y̓	ʔe:liʔi:y̓
'bad'	qəl	qeqəl	qiqəl	qəli̓qəl
'big'	θi	θiθə	θeʔθəθi	θəleʔθəθi

The predicate adjective is plural in (27) and diminutive in (28), agreeing with the subject; adjectives in complex NPs are discussed in section 29.4.

(27) Halkomelem
θiθə   tᶿə   haleləm̓   niʔ   ʔəƛ̓   cəw̓aθən.
big<PL> DT   house<PL> DIST.AUX OBL.DT   Tsawwassen
'The houses at Tsawwassen are big.'

(28) Halkomelem
qiqəl   θən̓   sqʷiʔqʷmiʔ.
bad<DIM>   DT.2POS   dog<DIM>
'Your little dog is mean.'

Besides appearing on nouns and adjectives, plural and diminutive morphology also appears on verbs; see Table 29.3 (Gerdts 2012, Suttles 2004).[9] Verbs in the perfective aspect do not form diminutives.

Table 29.3 Halkomelem plural and diminutive verbs

		plain	plural	diminutive	plural diminutive
'sing'	PFV	tíləm	táltiləm	∅	∅
	IPFV	títələm̓	tí:ltələm̓	tətiʔtələm̓	təlitiʔtələm̓
'swim'	PFV	tícəm	tʼelʼəcəm		
	IPFV	títəcəm̓	tíctəcəm	tətiʔtəcəm	təliʔtəcəm
'fly'	PFV	ɬakʷ	ɬaləkʷ	∅	∅
	IPFV	ɬáɬəkʷ	ɬákʷɬəkʷ	ɬáɬalhəkʷ	ɬəlálhəkʷ
'tear it'	PFV	sq̓et	səq̓səq̓ət	∅	∅
	IPFV	seq̓t	seq̓səq̓t	siʔseq̓t	səliʔseq̓t
'break it' (stick)	PFV	ləkʷat	ləkʷləkʷət	∅	∅
	IPFV	həlkʷət	hələlkʷət	hiʔhəlkʷət	həliʔhəlkʷət

In the following examples, the plural verb agrees with the subject in (29) and with the object in (30).

(29) Halkomelem
ʔi   ƛ̓eʔ   wəɬ=tiltələm̓   kʷəña   q̓eləmiʔ.
PROX.AUX again   PRF=sing<IPFV.PL>   DM   girl<PL>
'The young ladies are singing again.'

(30) Halkomelem
ʔeʔət   kʷətkʷəɬ-t-əs   tθə   šləlameləʔ.
AUX.DT   pour-TR-3SUB<PL>   DT   bottle<PL>
'He is pouring out the bottles.'

The meaning conveyed by the diminutive is that the event being described is done just a little bit or that a small entity is involved, usually as the subject of an intransitive verb or the object of a transitive verb.

(31) Halkomelem
naʔəθ   wəɬ=x̌əliʔx̌ax̌əñəq̓t   θə   pəluʔps.
AUX.DT   PRF=open<IPFV.PL.DIM>   DT   cat<PL.DIM>
'The kittens are opening their eyes.'

---

[9] Munro (1988) lists Creek, Chickasaw, Lakhota, Natchez, and Maricopa as examples of other Native American languages that allow diminutive inflection on verbs.

(32) Halkomelem
ɫᶿixʷəm ʔiʔ nem=č ƛ̓iʔƛ̓əƛ̓aʔ-t θə qeq.
please CNJ go.AUX=2SG.SUB stop.cry-TR<IPFV.DIM> DT baby.
'Please go stop the baby from crying.'

Adverbs also inflect for plural and diminutive, as shown in Table 29.4.

Table 29.4 Halkomelem plural and diminutive adverbs

gloss	plain	plural	diminutive	plural diminutive
'first, in front'	yəwen̓	yələwen̓	yəy̓iwen̓	yəliy̓əwen̓
'almost'	xʷeləq	xʷəlxʷeləq	xʷiʔxʷəw̓xʷələq	xʷəliʔxʷələq
'only'	txʷay	txʷaliʔ	txʷhiʔhay̓	txʷhəliʔha:y̓
'twice'	θəme	θəmθəme	θiʔθəme	θəliʔθəme

(33) Halkomelem
yələwen̓=ceʔ tᶿə słənłeniʔ kʷs q̓ʷim-s.
first<PL>=FUT DT woman<PL> DT.N disembark-3POS
'The women will get off first.'

(34) Halkomelem (Gerdts 2017)
xʷiʔxʷəw̓xʷələq ʔiʔ hiləm tᶿə qeq ʔə tᶿə šxʷʔamət-s.
almost<DIM> CNJ fall DT baby OBL DT bed-3POS
'The baby almost fell off his bed.'

(35) Halkomelem
txʷhəliʔha:y̓=ceʔ ʔəl̓ kʷθə məmən̓ł sƛ̓əliqəł
only<PL.DIM>=FUT just DT little.one children
niʔ=ceʔ ʔamət ʔə łə leləm̓.
DIST.AUX=FUT be.home<IPFV> OBL DT house
'Only the little children will be left at the house.'

In the above examples, the plural and/or diminutive inflection on the adjective, verb, or adverb reflects a plural and/or diminutive entity playing the role of the subject or object. However, we find examples of plural verbs even when there are no plural entities.

(36) Halkomelem
niʔ ləmlameʔ-t-əs tᶿə sƛ̓iʔƛ̓qəł tᶿə sqeʔəq-s.
DIST.AUX kick-TR-3SUB<PL> DT child DT younger.sibling-3POS
'The boy kicked his younger brother many times.'

(37) Halkomelem
  niʔ q̓eləkʷ-θamš-əs   tθə sqʷəmeẏ.
  DIST.AUX bite-TR:1OBJ-3SUB<PL> DT dog
  'The dog bit me in several places.'

The term 'pluractional' is used to describe verb forms whose function is to indicate plurality of action or event (Newman 1980; Lasersohn 1995; Corbett 2000; Matthewson 2000). Pluractionality, found in hundreds of languages of the world, is used for verb actions that indicate a multiplicity of some kind, either the plurality of entities involved in a single event, or the plurality of the event. Pluractionality is distinct from plural agreement, but one could easily see how the same morphology that is used to signal plural participants could also be used to signal that the event is repeated or distributed in some way.[10]

Similarly, there are many examples where there are no small (or dear) entities involved and yet the verb is diminutive.

(38) Halkomelem
  ʔeʔət x̌ʷi:ṅceṅəṁ   tθə stiqiw.
  AUX.DT run<IPFV.DIM> DT horse
  'The horse is trotting.'

(39) Halkomelem
  ʔi   cən   ċeʔċiʔ-ət   kʷθə swəẏqeʔ
  PROX.AUX 1SG.SUB show.appreciation-TR<IPFV.DIM> DT man
  niʔ   wəƛ̓əċ.
  DIST.AUX fall
  'I am showing a little sympathy to the man that fell.'

(40) Halkomelem
  niʔ   ċaċeʔċəwə-θamš-əs   kʷθə-nə men.
  DIST.AUX help-TR:1OBJ-3SUB<IPFV.DIM> DT-1POS father
  'My father is helping me out a little bit.'

The meaning conveyed by the diminutive is that the event being described is done just a little bit or in a subdued or restrained manner. Audring et al. (2021) survey diminutivized verbs in 248 languages and give a typology of the range of meanings they convey.

Parallel to what we saw with verb inflection (tense) on nouns in the previous section, plural and diminutive inflection do occur on categories other than nouns, though they do not necessarily convey the same meanings. Given that pluractionality and verbal diminution are found in a wide variety of languages of the world, we are led to the conclusion that they can exist in languages that otherwise show evidence for the usual range of word classes, and therefore their presence in Salish languages does not constitute evidence for a lack of categorial distinctions.

---

[10] Mellesmoen & Huijsmans (2019) and Huijsmans & Mellesmoen (2021) discuss two types of plural marking on verbs in ʔayʔajuθəm (Comox-Sliammon), and posit that one marks event-external pluractionality, while the other marks plural agreement. In contrast, Donna Gerdts has found no correlation between meaning of plurals and plural marking.

29.3 DERIVATIONAL MORPHOLOGY

Additional evidence for word classes in Salish is the existence of category-shifting morphological processes that change nouns into verbs and vice versa, which would be unnecessary if all lexical words were acategorical. Based on our research on Halkomelem, we know of no words that can function both as a noun and a verb without some sort of modification, i.e. no words that behave like English *walk, stop, drink, work*. Rather, each base (i.e. root or stem) is categorized as a noun or verb, and is used and inflected accordingly, and only with additional derivational morphology can it shift functions; you cannot simply substitute a noun (*qaʔ* 'water') for a verb (*qaʔqaʔ* 'drink').

(41) Halkomelem
 niʔ=cən   qaʔqaʔ/*qaʔ   ʔə   tᶿə   qaʔ/*qaʔqaʔ.
 AUX=1SG.SUB   drink/ water   OBL   DT   water/drink
 'I drank the water.'

However, we again find that Salish languages exhibit an unusual property in that most derivational morphology is quite flexible with respect to the lexical class of the base that it attaches to, even though the lexical class of the word that is formed is stipulated.

29.3.1 Deriving nouns

29.3.1.1 *The nominalizing prefix s-*

Salish languages, with the exception of Comox[11] (Kroeber: 1999: 11), have a nominalizer prefix *s-*, which among other functions, derives a noun expressing the cognate object of the action of the verb root (or often from a stem formed from the verb root and the middle suffix -*m*):

(42) Salish verbs nominalized with *s-*
  a. Halkomelem (Hukari & Peter 1995)
     ya:ys   'work (v)'   s-ya:ys   'work (n)'
     qʷal   'speak, talk'   s-qʷal   'word, speech, language'
     tiləm   'sing'   s-tiləm   'song'

  b. Squamish (Kuipers 1967: 66; Kroeber 1999)
     táqʷ   'drink'   s-táqʷ   'water'
     łəṅt   'weave it'   s-łəṅ   'mat, woven fabric'

  c. Lillooet (Van Eijk 1997)
     qaʔ   'eat'   s-qaʔ   'food'
     q̓ʷlawəm   'pick berries'   s-q̓ʷlawəm   'picked berries'

---

[11] Comox-Sliammon does use the nominalizing prefix *s-* for nominalizing clauses (Watanabe 2003: 72).

d. Sechelt (Beaumont 1985, 2011)
   haqʷ   'smell (v)'   s-haqʷ   'smell (n)'
   čə̓ɬ   'rain' (v)   s-čə̓ɬ   'rain' (n)
   qʷumay   'snow' (v)   s-qʷumay   'snow, years old (n)'

One way that we have investigated the productivity of this prefix in Halkomelem is to take verb roots, prefix them with *s-*, and then ask speakers if they form meaningful words. To verify the word's status as a noun, we construct examples in which the noun takes nominal inflection (a possessive affix) and a preceding determiner, and furthermore we disallow an auxiliary verb nor any aspectual marking (imperfective or stative resultative) that would attest to its status as a clausal nominalization (or relative clause). So for example, the verb *čakʷx̌* 'fry' (43a) forms the noun *sčakʷx̌* 'fried food' in (43b).

(43) Halkomelem
   a. *nem̓*   *čakʷx̌*   *ʔə*   *kʷθə*   *sce:ɬtən.*
       go.AUX   fry   OBL   DT   salmon
       'Go fry some salmon.'

   b. *nem̓=č*   *lem-ət*   *kʷθənə*   *s-čakʷx̌.*
       go.AUX=2SG.SUB   look-TR   DT.1POS   N-fry
       'You go look after my fried food.'

Similarly, the verb *ɬakʷ* 'fly' forms the noun *sɬakʷ* 'airborne objects'. Some verb roots, e.g. √*caxʷ* are not words without modification, as in *cxʷat* 'blow on it', but can nevertheless form nouns.

(44) a. Halkomelem
      cxʷat   *tθən̓*   *celaš.*
      blow.TR   DT.2POS   hand
      'Blow on your hands.'

   b. *ʔi*   *can*   *ɬeɬaw̓*   *ʔə*   *tθə*   *s-caxʷ-s*   *tθə*   *q̓alɬanəməcən.*
       PROX.AUX   1SG.SUB   flee<IPFV>   OBL   DT   N-blow-3POS   DT   orca
       'I'm running away from the orca's spray.'

We tested 488 verb roots (or stems with the middle suffix) denoting events that were easily associated with an entity and found that 237 (48.5%) of them formed nouns with the prefix *s-*, but that 251 (51.5%) roots did not. Here are some examples of rejected forms.

(45) ɬəmc̓ 'pick (berries)   rejected: *sɬəmc̓ (expected meaning: something that is picked)
      kʷan 'be born'   rejected: *skʷan (expected meaning: something that is born)
      celəm̓ 'hear'   rejected: *sceləm (expected meaning: something that is heard)

We got a very different result when we approached the *s-* prefix from the direction of a list of nouns. Using a database of the 1,798 nouns in the Hul'q'umi'num' dictionary (Hukari & Peter 1995), we found that 529 nouns had the prefix *s-*, but of these only 214 were monomorphemic roots (or bases with *-əm*), and the other words contained other morphemes. Of these 214 words formed with s-, only 34 had corresponding verb roots. Here is a sample:

(46) Halkomelem (Hukari & Peter 1995)
    sləmáxʷ 'rain (n)' cf. ləmáxʷ 'rain (v)'; sx̌tek̓ʷ 'totem pole, carving' cf. x̌tek̓ʷ 'carve'; stey 'canoe race' cf. tey 'race canoes'; spák̓ʷ 'flour' cf. pák̓ʷ '(dust) to spread'; stᶿú:m 'berry' cf. ƛᶿu:m 'pick perries'; sθímaʔ 'ice' cf. θímaʔ 'freeze, frozen'; sq̓ʷəl 'barbecued meat, cooked bread' cf. q̓ʷəl 'barbecue, bake'; sx̌əɬ 'sickness' cf. x̌əɬ 'ache, be sick'; stᶿem 'outgoing tide' cf. ƛᶿem '(tide) to go out'; sq̓aʔ 'companion, mate, spouse' cf. q̓aʔ 'be added'

This is a very small result given that speakers were able to produce 237 nouns working from a list of verbs. However, the dictionary forms represent high frequency words, and many of the noun forms elicited from the verb list were not high frequency and also not very useful, in that their meanings are predictable from the verbal semantics. Perhaps a good parallel to make is with English lexicography and the decision of what nouns formed with -ing to put in a dictionary.

Another interesting result of our search through the dictionary is that, of the 214 words formed with s- and no other morphology, 180 had no corresponding verb root. Here are some examples.[12]

(47) Halkomelem (Hukari & Peter 1995)
    sɬéniʔ 'woman', swə́yqeʔ 'man', sqeʔəq 'younger sibling', stíwən 'niece/nephew', sx̌əńə 'foot, leg', sx̌əyəs 'head', scápxʷəń 'wart', stíwən 'niece/nephew', sqʷəmə́y̓ 'dog', stqé:yeʔ 'wolf', stᶿáqʷiʔ 'spring salmon', sqáléw 'beaver', stíqiw 'horse', skʷíƛᶿəc 'blue jay (Steller's jay)', scíyə 'strawberry', staləẃ 'river', sɬéwən 'bulrush mat'

Our analysis of the roots of these words, given there is no corresponding verb form, is that they are most likely nouns, and therefore the s- prefix appears not only on nouns nominalized from verbs but also root nouns as well. The use of s- is thus a marker of noun-hood, not nominalization per se. Some other languages that have a morpheme whose sole function seems to be to identify the word as a noun are the Northern Iroquoian languages (see Chapter 30)—for example the suffix aʔ on the word oyú·kwaʔ 'tobacco' in Mohawk—and the Uto-Aztecan languages—see the absolute suffix -tl which appears on non-possessed nouns like ā-tl 'water' in Nahuatl (Karttunen 1992: 14).

Furthermore, we also discovered that there were 272 (of 486) nouns in the dictionary that do not have a nominalizing prefix and cannot be further parsed into component morphemes (see Montler 2003: 105 on Klallam, Van Eijk 1997: 48–49 on Lillooet).

(48) Halkomelem (Hukari & Peter 1995)
    ten 'mother', sílə 'grandparent', ʔíməθ 'grandchild', celáš 'hand', yənəs 'tooth', metsúń 'testicles', k̓ʷəláw̓ 'skin, hide', qeyəx̌ 'mink (as trickster in stories)', qʷənəs 'whale', təmás 'sea otter', k̓ʷáləxʷ 'dog salmon', qʷəní 'seagull', ɬə́q̓əs 'seaweed', méqeʔ 'snow (n.)', liláʔ 'salmonberry', kʷəmləxʷ 'root', təməɬ 'ochre', x̌acaʔ 'lake', sítən 'basket', népəs 'woven cedar cape'

---

[12] That the s- is a prefix can be shown by various related words, for example the plural sɬánɬeníʔ 'women' formed with CVC reduplication of the root; compare this to the plural of sílə 'grandparent', sə́lsilə 'grandparents', where CVC reduplication shows that the initial s- is not a prefix.

Again, there is no reason to assume that these forms are anything other than nouns.

Of the 486 nouns studied, only 44% were formed with the prefix *s-*, and only 7% of the total sample were formed by prefixing *s-* to a verb root. The noun roots with the prefix *s-* (180) and without (272) total 452 noun roots, exemplified in the lists in (47) and (48). What these nouns have in common is that they refer to entities in day-to-day pre-contact life, including words for kin terms, body parts, fauna, flora, words referring to the natural environment, basic materials, and implements. Comparing the list of presumed nouns to our list of 680 verb roots is very revealing, in that verb roots are overwhelmingly monosyllabic, with the most common shapes being CVC, CCV, CVCC, CCVC, while noun roots are overwhelmingly bisyllabic, with the most common root shapes being CVCV, CVCVC, and CVCCVC (see Suttles 2004: 200–203).

We conclude that it is useful to posit a noun–verb distinction that is manifested—at the root level as well as at the word level—by differences in phonology and semantics. The prefix *s-* functions as both a nominalizer converting verbs to nouns and as an inflectional prefix. Perhaps future research on the range of the prefix *s-* in the lexicon of Salish languages will uncover generalizations about the noun roots that bear this prefix and also the verb roots that do not.

29.3.1.2 *Other nominalizing morphology*

Salish languages have dozens of prefixes and suffixes that are used derivationally to create nouns with specific meanings. Some, e.g. the Halkomelem prefix *čł-* and suffix *-min*, appear on both N and V bases, while others, e.g. *xʷs-* and *-tən* appear exclusively on V bases. Table 29.5 gives a few examples.

Table 29.5 Some Halkomelem nominalizing morphemes

affix	gloss	base	gloss	derived N	gloss
čł-	'fellow, co-'	xʷəlməxʷ (n)	'First Nations person'	čłxʷəlməxʷ	'fellow-FN person'
		xiẋələẋ (v)	'going to war'	čłxiẋələẋ	'fellow-warrior'
		ẋe:m̓ (v)	'crying'	čłẋe:m̓	'mourners'
-min	residue, leavings	ʔipəls (n)	'apple' < English	ʔəpəlsmin	'apple juice'
		qʷə́ls (v)	'boil'	qʷə́lsmən	'broth'
		qeləč̓ (v)	'spin (wool)'	qeləč̓mən	'bits left over from spinning wool'
xʷs-	habitual actor, professional	t̓iləm (v)	'sing'	xʷst̓iləm	'singer'
		łəłétʰt (v)	'make fun of him/her'	xʷsłəłétʰ	'jokester, bully'
		teti? (v)	'racing (canoes)'	xʷsteti?	'canoe puller'
-tən	instrument	ləẋʷət (v)	'cover it'	ləẋʷtən	'blanket'
		ʔiẋət (v)	'scrape it'	ʔəxtən	'scraper, knife'

29.3.2 Deriving verbs

The overall number of verb roots in each Salish language is not large (e.g. 680 verb roots in Halkomelem), but the total number of words formed from a root is quite large due to dozens of affixes and non-concatenative processes (reduplication, ablaut, etc.) to form bases that then undergo further derivation and inflection. We can illustrate this in Table 29.6 with some of the many verbs formed from the root √pqʷa '(substance) to break apart', which is also metaphorically used to mean 'to go broke, run out of money'.

Table 29.6 Verbs derived from the root √pqwa

root	pəqʷ	√pqʷa	'break (substance)'
	pəpəqʷ	√pqʷa<IPFV>	'breaking (substance)'
transitive	pqʷat	√pqwa-t	'break (substance) it'
	paqʷt	√pqwa-t<IPFV	'breaking (substance) it'
	pəqʷpəqʷət	√pqwa-t<PL>	'break (substance) them'
	piʔpaqʷt	√pqʷa-t<IPFV.DIM>	'breaking (little substance) it'
	pəliʔpaqʷt	√pqʷa-t<IPFV.PL.DIM>	'breaking (little substances)'
non-control	pəqʷnexʷ	√pqʷa-nexʷ	'manage to break (substance) it'
	paqʷnəxʷ	√pqʷa-nexʷ<IPFV>	'accidentally breaking it'
	pəqʷnamət	√pqʷa-namət	'finished going broke'
reflexive	pqʷaθət	√pqʷa-θat	'go for broke, go broke'
middle	pqʷeʔəm	√pqʷa-m	'break (substance) some off'
benefactive	pqʷəɬcəm	√pqʷa-ɬc-m	'break (substance) up for me'
	pqʷəɬcət	√pqwa-ɬc-t	'break (substance) up for him'
desiderative	pəqʷəlmən	√pqʷa-əlmən	'start to go broke'
stative	spəpiqʷ	ST-√pqʷa<RES>	'broken (substance), out of money'
	spələpiqʷ	ST-√pqʷa<RES.PL>	'(substance) broken into many bits'

While there were dozens of verbs based on √pqʷa, our search revealed only two nouns formed from √pqwa: spəqʷ 'broken off piece' with the nominalizing prefix s- and pqʷacan 'sand' with the lexical suffix -əcən meaning 'surface'.

For any given suffix, we find hundreds of verb roots (or stems) that combine with it (see Gerdts & Hukari 2005). Below is a list of verbs with the reflexive suffix -θət.

(49) Halkomelem (Hukari & Peter 1995)
  ċq̓ʷəθət   'pierce oneself'
  həliθət   'save oneself, come to life'
  kʷay̓əθət 'step away, move oneself away'
  laməθət   'look at oneself, look after oneself'
  ɬaq̓əθət   'lie oneself down'

But also, we find that many of the erstwhile verbal suffixes can occasionally attach to noun (and adjective) bases with the effect of converting the noun to a verb, often with a specialized meaning.

29.3.2.1 Intransitivizing and transitivizing suffixes

Salish languages make heavy use of valence-changing suffixes. For example, they have a ubiquitous middle suffix -əm that appears on many intransitive verbs, such as Halkomelem ƛiləm 'sing', nəqəm 'dive', q̓ewəm 'kneel', p̓iləm 'overflow'. In addition, the middle suffix can be added to a handful of nouns (both native and borrowed) to derive intransitive verbs.

(50) Halkomelem (Gerdts & Hukari 1998: 2)
stekən   'stocking' < English   təkenəm   'put on one's socks'
kəpu   'coat' < French   kəpu:m   'put on one's coat'
wekən   'wagon' < English   wəkenəm   'go by wagon'
q̓əwət   'drum (n.)'   q̓əwətəm   'drum (v.)'
patən   'sail, rag (n.)'   patenəm   'sail (v.)'
q̓łan   'bow of boat'   q̓łanəm   'go to the bow'
/get in front seat of car'

As seen in the first example in the list stekən, from English 'stocking', the s- noun prefix is deleted from verbs derived from nouns.

Other verbal morphology, such as the general transitive suffix -t (see q̓aʔ 'get added, q̓aʔt 'add it in') and the causative suffix -stəxʷ (ʔiməš 'walk', ʔiməšstəxʷ 'take him/her for a walk') can also suffix to nouns (51) and adjectives (52), converting them to verbs.[13]

(51) Halkomelem (Hukari & Peter 1995)
kəpu   'coat' < French   kəpu:t   'put coat on him/her'
stekən   'stocking, sock' < English   təkent   'put socks on him/her'
słeniʔ   'woman'   łeniʔstəxʷ 'turn it into a woman'

(52) Halkomelem (Hukari & Peter 1995)
θi   'big'   θistəxʷ   'find, keep it big'
ƛ̓iʔ   'dear, expensive' ƛ̓iʔstəxʷ   'like it/ find it expensive'
ʔəy̓   'good'   ʔəy̓stəx   'like it/ find it good'
qəl   'bad'   qəlstəxʷ   'dislike it, find it bad'

These valence-changing affixes most often occur on verbs and are attested on only a few nouns. When they occur on nouns, their function is to turn them into verbs.

29.3.2.2 Denominal verbs

Salish languages have a variety of affixes that are added to nouns to create verbs of particular meaning (Gerdts & Hukari 2008). This is shown in Table 29.7.

---

[13] Lillooet (Van Eijk 1988: 108) gives examples of nouns such as s-k̓ʷuk̓ʷmit being suffixed with transitiviser -s and the reflexive suffix -cút 'oneself' to derive verbs such as k̓ʷuk̓ʷmit-s-cút 'act like a child'.

Table 29.7 Halkomelem denominal morphology

affix	gloss	base	gloss	derivative	gloss
-a:ɬ	'travel by'	t̪θikt̪θik	'buggy'	t̪θikt̪θik-a:ɬ	'go by buggy'
c-	'have, get, make, do'	kʷəmləxʷ	'root'	c-kʷəmləxʷ	'get roots'
ɬ-	'ingest, partake'	səplil	'bread'	ɬ-səplil	'eat bread'
txʷ-	'buy'	leləṁ	'house'	txʷ-leləṁ	'buy a house'
ƛ-	'go to'	tawən	'town'	ƛ-tawən	'go to town'

The denominal verb prefixes, which appear productively on native and borrowed words, have been attested for languages in at least three branches of the Salish family (Gerdts & Hukari 2008). If the noun has an *s-* prefix (e.g. *s-nəxʷəɬ*), the prefix does not appear in the denominal form. The noun base can be plural or diminutive, as shown in Table 29.8.

Table 29.8 Halkomelem plural and diminutive noun bases (Gerdts & Hukari 2008)

	noun		verb	
plain	s-nəxʷəɬ	'canoe'	c-nəxʷəɬ	'make, have a canoe'
plural	s-ənixʷəɬ	'canoes'	c-ənixʷəɬ	'make, have canoes'
DIM.	s-niṅxʷəɬ	'little canoe'	c-niṅxʷəɬ	'have a little car'
PL.DIM	s-nəṅəxʷəɬ	'little canoes'	c-nəṅəxʷəɬ	'have little cars'
plain	sitən	'basket'	c-sitən	'make, have a basket'
plural	seʔəltən	'basket'	c-seʔəltən	'make, have baskets'
DIM	siʔstəṅ	'little basket'	c-siʔstəṅ	'have a little basket'
PL.DIM	səliʔstəṅ	'little baskets'	c-səliʔstəṅ	'have little baskets'

These denominal verbs can appear in the imperfective aspect typical of verbs, as seen by the forms in the third column of Table 29.9 (Gerdts & Hukari 2008: 491).

As expected of the verb word class, denominal verbs can also take verbal derivational (e.g. reflexive and causative) and inflectional suffixes (e.g. object marking).

(53) Halkomelem
  a. ʔəwə k̓ʷənəs   c-yays-namət.
     NEG   DT.1POS.N VBL-work-LC.REFL
     'I couldn't manage to find a job.'
  b. neṁ   c-ləpat-staṁš   ʔə   k̓ʷ   θe:qən!
     go.AUX VBL-cup-CS.1OBJ OBL DT   big-container
     'Go get me a big cup!'

Table 29.9 Halkomelem imperfective denominal verbs (Gerdts & Hukari 2008)

noun		verb		IPFV	
put	'boat'	c-put	'make a boat'	c-pupət	'making a boat'
p̓əwiʔ	'flounder'	c-p̓əwiʔ	'catch flounder'	c-p̓əp̓əwiʔ	'catching flounder'
s-nəxʷəɬ	'canoe'	c-nəxʷəɬ	'have/make a canoe'	c-hənxʷəɬ	'making a canoe'
s-ce:ɬtən	'salmon'	ɬ-ce:ɬtən	'eat salmon'	ɬ-cecələɬtəṅ	'eating salmon'

Finally, denominal verbs can be (re-)nominalized by prefixes such as $x^w s$-:

(54) Halkomelem
    s-p̓aƛ̓əm   'tobacco, smoke (n)'
    ɬ-p̓aƛ̓əm   'tobacco, smoke (n)'
    xʷs-ɬ-p̓aƛ̓əm 'a smoker'

In this section, we have illustrated a variety of derivational affixes that are attached to nouns to derive verbs. Some affixes, like causative and reflexive, are primarily used on verbs and only infrequently used on nouns. Other morphology, like the denominal verb prefixes, almost exclusively occur on nouns to convert them to verbs.

29.3.3 Lexical suffixes and categoriality

Salish languages, and other languages in the Pacific Northwest, have lexical suffixes, which are bound morphemes with the semantic content of a noun (Gerdts & Hinkson 1996; Hinkson 1999; Czaykowska & Kinkade 1998; Gerdts 2000, 2003). Most languages in the family have approximately one hundred lexical suffixes and some of them have well over 200 (e.g. Kinkade 1991: 342–364 lists 298 suffixes for Upper Chehalis). Typical meanings for lexical suffixes are body parts (*hand, foot, heart, nose*), basic physical/environmental concepts (*earth, fire, water, wind, tree, rock*), cultural items (*canoe, net, house, clothing*), and human/relational terms (*people, spouse, child*). The suffixes (especially ones denoting body parts) have a range of extended means to express shape, location, and relational meanings (Hinkson 1999) and some lexical suffixes are grammaticalized into morphemes functioning as desideratives, applicatives, etc. (Gerdts & Hinkson 1996; Kiyosawa & Gerdts 2010).

In some cases, lexical suffixes appear to be a truncated version of a noun, suggesting compounding as a historical origin:

(55) Halkomelem (Gerdts 2010: 189)

noun		suffix		example	
məqsən	'nose'	-əqsən	'nose, point'	tənəqsən	'duck (mallard)'
θəθən	'mouth'	-(a)θən	'mouth, edge'	laʔθən	'plate, tray, dish'
təpsəm	'nape of neck'	-əpsəm	'neck'	təmələpsəm	'woodpecker'
təməxʷ	'earth, ground'	-məxʷ	'earth, people, breast'	məstiməxʷ	'person, people'

In most cases though, lexical suffixes bear little or no phonological resemblance to free-standing nouns of similar meaning, leading to the speculation that lexical suffixes might be archaic nouns that lost their status as independent words as other words with similar meanings were created.

(56) Halkomelem (Gerdts 2000: 337)
sxǝẏǝs   'head'   -aʔqʷ   'head, sphere'
lǝwǝx̌   'rib'   -wił   'rib, vessel'
leləm̓   'house'   -ew̓txʷ   'building, room'
qeq   'baby'   -ǝyəł   'baby, child'

Lexical suffixes are added to words from all lexical classes: nouns (57a), verbs (57b), and adjectives (57c) to form nouns.

(57) Halkomelem (Gerdts 2000: 337)
  a. N + N > N
    təmələpsəm   'woodpecker' (təmał 'ochre' + -əpsəm 'neck')
    qʷłeẏšən   'shoe' (qʷłeẏ 'log' + šən 'foot')
    x̌peẏcəs   'cedar branch' (x̌peẏ 'red cedar' + -cəs 'hand')

  b. V + N > N
    łiwiʔəłew̓txʷ 'church' (łiwiʔəł 'pray' + -ew̓txʷ 'building')
    ʔitətəlwət   'pajamas' (ʔitət 'sleep' + -əlwət 'blanket, clothing')
    laʔθən   'plate' (leʔ- 'set aside, store' + -aθən 'mouth')

  c. ADJ + N > N
    θe:w̓txʷ   'longhouse' (θi 'big' + -ew̓txʷ 'building')
    xʷƛ̓əqtnəc   'cougar' (xʷ prefix + ƛ̓əlqt 'long' + -nec 'bottom, tail')
    p̓q̓əlqən   'mountain goat' (p̓əq̓ 'white' + -əlqən 'fur')
    ʔəxʷi:nəqən   'small container' (ʔəxʷi:n 'small' + -əqən 'container')

These function much like compounds where the lexical suffix serves as the head. The semantic head can be endocentric, where the meaning of the whole is a subset of the meaning of the head (e.g. English 'chapstick' is a subset of 'stick'; Halkomelem łiwiʔəłew̓txʷ 'church' is a subset of 'building'). The semantic head may alternatively be exocentric, where the head is non-compositional (e.g. English 'sabretooth' is a tiger, not a 'tooth'; Halkomelem təmələpsəm 'woodpecker' is a bird, not a 'neck', and laʔθən 'plate' is a something to lay food on, not a 'mouth'). These lexical suffixes behave in a manner typical of derivational affixes, each acting as the head and determining the noun word class for the whole.

In contrast, the lexical suffixes in the examples below do not determine the word class of the derived form. Rather the word class is determined by the category of the base.

(58) Halkomelem (Gerdts 2000: 337)
  a. V + N > V
    šk̓ʷəyəł   'bathe a baby' (šak̓ʷ 'bathe' + -əyəł 'baby')
    sq̓əlcəp   'split firewood' (səq̓ 'split' + -əlcəp 'firewood')

qʷseẏən 'set a net' (qʷəs 'submerge' + -eẏən 'net')
θəyeʔɬ 'make a bed' (θəy 'make' + -eʔɬ 'fabric')
ɬəlqətᶿeʔ 'dye wool' (ɬəlq 'soak' + -itᶿeʔ 'fibre')

b. ADJ + N > ADJ
xʷθiqən 'loud' (xʷ- 'prefix' + θi 'big' + qən 'throat/heat')
ʔiyəs 'happy' (ʔəẏ 'good' + -əs 'face')
ƛ̓əqtemət̓ᶿ 'tall' (ƛ̓eqt 'long' + -emət̓ᶿ 'long object')
ʔəẏaʔθ 'sharp' (ʔəẏ 'good' + -aʔθ 'edge')
ʔayəmšən 'slow (walking)' (ʔayəm 'slow' + šən 'foot')

In the case of verb-headed lexical suffix constructions (58a), the resulting verb functions as the main predicate of a clause, and the lexical suffix refers to the patient of a semantically transitive verb, which can be doubled with a free-standing oblique NP (Gerdts 2003; Gerdts & Hinkson 1996).

(59) Halkomelem (Gerdts 2010)
nem̓=č nəw̓-əlcəp ʔə kʷθə syaɬ.
go.AUX=2SG.SUB enter-firewood OBL DT wood
'Go bring in the firewood.'

With adjective-headed constructions (58b), the resulting adjective can be a predicate (60a) or the modifier in a noun phrase (60b).

(60) Halkomelem
a. nan ʔəw̓ ʔəẏ-aʔθ tᶿən̓ šəptən.
very LNK sharp DT-2POS knife.
'Your knife is very sharp.'

b. xʷəʔəw̓-cs-əm=č ʔə tᶿə ʔəẏaʔθ šəptən.
show-hand-MID=2SG.SUB OBL DT sharp knife
'Hand me the sharp knife.'

This function of lexical suffixes is sometimes referred to as classifying (Gerdts 2000, 2003), as they refer to some general property of an entity without actually naming it.[14]

Words formed by lexical suffixation appear with a full range of derivational and inflectional morphology. The examples in (61) show nominalizer prefixes.

(61) Halkomelem
a. nominalizer s-
scəqʷən̓ə 'earring' (s- + √čqa 'pierce' + ən̓ə 'ear')
scɬayθən 'upper lip' (s- + √cɬ 'above' + θən 'mouth')

---

[14] In addition, all Salish languages use a subset of their lexical suffix inventory as numeral classifiers (e.g. 30 in Halkomelem), attaching to numerals and quantifiers (Gerdts & Hinkson 2004: 27).

b. oblique nominalizer š-
    šƛ̓əšəṅəp   'plow' (š- + √ƛ̓se 'rip' + -ənəp 'ground')
                                 i.e. thing used to rip apart the earth <ipfv>
    šćeṅactən   'chair' (š- + √će? 'above' + nəc 'bottom' + -tən instrument)
                                   Lit.: 'the thing used when you locate your bottom on something'
    šƛ̓emq̓aləẃsheṅəm̓   'toenail clippers' (š- + t̓θəmq̓ 'cut end off' + -aləẃ 'appendage' + šen 'foot' + -m middle + imperfective)

The lexical suffix is followed by the redirective (benefactive), transitive, and object suffixes in (62).

(62) Halkomelem (Gerdts 2003: 348)
    šk̓ʷ-əyəɬ-əɬc-θamš.
    bathe-baby-RDR-TR:1OBJ
    'Bathe the baby for me.'

Words can have more than one lexical suffix, as seen in (63), where each lexical suffix is followed by the causative suffix.[15]

(63) Halkomelem (Gerdts 2003)
    sq̓-əlcəp-st-ənəq-stəxʷ
    split-firewood-CS-people-CS
    'make him have people cut firewood'

In sum, lexical suffixes can be considered derivational as they are used to form words with a change in meaning and sometimes also a change in word class. Like other morphology discussed above, lexical suffixation shows flexibility in the word class of the base, but also flexibility in the word class of the derived word.

29.4 ADJECTIVES

Based on the morphological and syntactic evidence as discussed above, it is now generally accepted that nouns and verbs are distinguished in Salish languages, 'albeit much more subtly than in languages like English' (Koch & Matthewson 2009: 126). Less attention has been paid to the word classes of adjective and adverb (section 29.5), but again we find that these concepts are relevant to Salish grammars. For example, Salish language grammars list morphology that turn nouns into adjectives, such as the combination of the prefix s- and the attributive suffix -aʔɬ.

---

[15] That lexical suffixes are truly suffixal is evidenced by the fact that they can be followed by other suffixes.

(64) Halkomelem (Hukari & Peter 1995)
xʷəlməxʷ   'First Nations person'   s-xʷəlməxʷ-aʔɬ   'pertaining to a First Nations person'
xʷənitəm̓   'white person'   s-xʷənitəm̓-aʔɬ   'pertaining to a white person'
q̓ʷəmiy̓iqən   Comiaken   s-q̓ʷəmiy̓iqən-aʔɬ 'Comiaken (from Comiaken)'

This creates a word that can serve as a modifier.

(65) Halkomelem
stem   tᶿə   s-xʷənitəm̓-aʔɬ   snes   tᶿə   šes?
what   DT   N-white.person-ATR   name   DT   sea.lion
'What is the English name of the *shes*?'

Two properties noted of adjectives are that, unlike verbs, they do not appear in the imperfective aspect (Van Eijk & Hess 1986; Suttles 2004: 219) and they do not select for auxiliaries (Montler 2003: 114).

Should a separate word class be proposed for adjectives, or should they be subsumed under the general label of predicate? Beck (1999a, 2002) says that 'there appear to be no grounds for distinguishing a lexical class of adjective, at least from among the words expressing semantic predicates. All of these words can be used both as unmarked modifiers and as unmarked syntactic predicates' (Beck 1999b: 48). He illustrates with the following examples showing that the word *haʔɬ* 'good' functions as a modifier in (66a) and as a predicate in (66b), and that the word *ləkʷəd* 'eat' functions as a predicate in (66a) and as a modifier in (66b).

(66) Lushootseed (Bates et al. 1994 cited by Beck 2002)
   a. ƛ̓u-ləkʷ-əd   tiʔəʔ   haʔɬ   sʔələd.
      HAB-eat-CS   DT   good   food
      'S/he would eat the good food.'

   b. haʔɬ   tiʔəʔ   sʔələd   ƛ̓u-ləkʷ-əd.
      good   DT   food   HAB-eat-CS
      'The food s/he would eat is/was good.'

In contrast, Montler (2003) and Davis (2011) among others offer evidence based on the behaviour of adjectives within noun phrases for the existence of adjectives as a word class.

29.4.1 Adjectives and agreement

A prototypical function of an adjective is to modify a nominal head (Hengeveld 1992a; Sasse 2015), and one type of evidence for modification is agreement between a modifier and a head noun within an NP. Montler (2003: 130–131) shows for Klallam that plain adjectives modify singular nouns (67a), and plural adjectives modify plural nouns (67b), but a plain adjective cannot modify a plural noun (67c):

(67) Klallam (Montler 2003: 130–131)
   a. k̓ʷənnəxʷ=cn   cə=čəq   swəy̓qaʔ.
      see:3OBJ=1SUB   DT=big   man
      'I see the big man/*men.'

b. k̓ʷənnəxʷ=cn   cə=čayq   sw̓wəy̓qaʔ.
   see:3OBJ=1SUB   DT=big<PL>   man<PL>
   'I see the big men.'

c. *k̓ʷənnəxʷ=cn   cə=čaq   sw̓wəy̓qaʔ.
   see:3OBJ=1sub   DT=big   man<PL>
   'I see the big men.'

Plural marking on nouns is optional in Klallam, as it is in many Salish languages, so an unmarked plural noun is possible, but the modifier must nevertheless be plural (68).

(68) Klallam (Montler 2003: 130)
     k̓ʷənnəxʷ=cn   cə=čayq   swəy̓qaʔ.
     see:3OBJ=1SUB   DT=big<PL>   man
     'I see the big men.'

Montler takes this as evidence that the word for 'big' and the word for 'man' are not of the same word class, so the logical conclusion is that *čaq* is an adjective and *swəy̓qaʔ* is a noun.

Data from plurals and diminutives in Halkomelem provide a second example. Halkomelem shows the opposite pattern from Klallam: the equivalent of (67c) is grammatical and (68) ungrammatical. In (the Island dialect of) Halkomelem, *swəy̓qeʔ* is in a class of nouns that obligatorily mark plural.[16] However, the adjective optionally agrees with the N it is modifying; the adjective can be uninflected (69) or inflected to match the head in both plural and diminutive (70).

(69) Halkomelem
     k̓ʷam̓k̓ʷəm̓ swəy̓qeʔ   strong man   'strong man'
     k̓ʷam̓k̓ʷəm̓ swiwiʔqeʔ   strong man<DIM>   'strong little man'
     k̓ʷam̓k̓ʷəm̓ səwəy̓qeʔ   strong man<PL>   'strong men'
     k̓ʷam̓k̓ʷəm̓ swəliwiʔqeʔ   strong man<PL.DIM>   'strong little men'

(70) Halkomelem
     k̓ʷam̓k̓ʷəm̓ swəy̓qeʔ   strong man   'strong man'
     k̓ʷaʔk̓ʷəm̓k̓ʷəm̓ swiwiʔqeʔ   strong<DIM> man<DIM>   'strong little man'
     k̓ʷaləm̓k̓ʷəm̓ səwəy̓qeʔ   strong<PL> man<PL>   'strong men'
     k̓ʷəlaʔk̓ʷəm̓k̓ʷə swəliwiʔqeʔ   strong<PL.DIM> man<PL.DIM>   'strong little men'

However, partial matching is also possible: a diminutive adjective can modify a plain noun, a plural diminutive adjective can modify a plural noun, and a plural adjective can modify a plural diminutive noun.

---

[16] In a study of plural marking in 800 Hul'q'umi'num' nouns, Gerdts (2012) shows that they divide into three classes: nouns whose plain form is (A) singular only (humans, bigger animals, some commonly occurring objects), (B) singular or plural (individuated objects, i.e. most animals and objects), or (C) non-individuated (collectives and mass nouns, type-shifted in the plural to kind, type, or containment readings).

(71) Halkomelem
k̓waʔk̓wəm̓k̓wəm̓ swəy̓qeʔ   strong<DIM> man   'strong little man'
k̓wəlaʔk̓wəm̓k̓wəm̓ səw̓əy̓qeʔ   strong<PL.DIM> man<PL>   'strong little men'
k̓wələm̓k̓wəm̓ swəliwiʔqeʔ   strong<PL> man <PL.DIM>   'strong little men'

That is, the modifier matches the head in number, but not necessarily in diminution. A plural adjective cannot modify a non-plural head.

(72) Halkomelem
* k̓wələm̓k̓wəm̓ swəy̓qeʔ   strong<PL> man   'strong man'
* k̓wəlaʔk̓wəm̓k̓wəm̓ swəy̓qeʔ   strong<DIM.PL> man   'strong man'
* k̓wələm̓k̓wəm̓ swiwiʔqeʔ   strong<DIM.PL> man<DIM>   'strong little man'
*k̓wəlaʔk̓wəm̓k̓wəm̓ swiwiʔqeʔ   strong<DIM.PL> man<DIM>   'strong little man'

In addition, plain diminutive forms entail singularity, and so plain diminutive adjectives cannot modify a plural noun without creating a mismatch in number.

(73) Halkomelem
* k̓waʔk̓wəm̓k̓wəm̓ səw̓əy̓qeʔ   strong<DIM> man<PL>   'strong men'
*k̓waʔk̓wəm̓k̓wəm̓ swəliwiʔqeʔ strong<DIM> man<PL.DIM>   'strong little men'

In sum, a modifier in Halkomelem does not have to be inflected for number, but when it is, it agrees in number with the noun it modifies.

29.4.2 Adjectives and word order

Arguing that adjectives are a distinct lexical class in Lillooet and other Interior Salish languages, Davis (2011: 13) shows that adjectives (such as *xzóm* 'big') can only appear as pre-head and not post-head modifiers.[17]

(74) Lillooet: St'á't'imcets (Davis 2011: 13)[18]
   a. wɛʔ   šeq̓w   kəntʔó   e=xzóm=ɛ   špəpzózɛʔ
      IPFV   fly   around.there   PL.DT=big=EXIS   birds
      'Some big birds are flying around over there.'

   b. *wɛʔ   šeq̓w   kəntʔó   e=špəpzózʔ=ɛ   xzom
      IPFV   fly   around.there   PL.DT=birds=EXIS   big

We find word order a useful diagnostic for distinguishing two types of modifiers in Halkomelem: a small class of around twenty true adjectives (75), describing inherent

---

[17] Davis (2011) argues that some apparent post-head modifiers are actually reduced clauses.
[18] /w/ in Lillooet examples represents a laryngeal rounded glide (Van Eijk 1997: 2).

qualities,[19] and an open-ended class of stative resultatives (76), which describe the result of an action.[20]

(75) Halkomelem
ʔəy̓ 'good', qəl 'bad', θi 'big', ʔəxʷi:n̓ 'little', x̌ew̓s 'new', tsas 'pitiful, poor', ƛ̓eqt 'long', ɬeqt 'wide', pɬet 'thick', θəʔit 'true'

The Hul'q'umi'num' dictionary (Hukari & Peter 1995) gives 474 stative-resultative forms, and a survey of 552 verb roots showed that 73% formed stative resultatives.

Adjectives and stative resultatives display syntactic differences. When modifying a noun, adjectives (e.g. θi 'big' and ʔəy̓ 'good') must occur before the noun they modify.

(77) Halkomelem
a. θə   θi   leləm̓   b. *θə leləm̓   θi
   DT   big   house   DT house   big
   'the big house'

(78) Halkomelem
a. θə   ʔəy̓   steniʔ   b. *θə steniʔ   ʔəy̓
   DT   good woman   DT woman   good
   'the good woman'

In contrast, stative resultatives can precede or follow the head noun.

(79) Halkomelem
a. tᶿə sq̓ʷəq̓ʷil̓ sce:ɬtən   b. tᶿə sce:ɬtən sq̓ʷəq̓ʷil̓
   DT   cooked   salmon   DT   salmon   cooked
   'the cooked salmon'   'the cooked salmon'

(80) Halkomelem
a. tᶿə syayək̓ʷ laʔθən   b. tᶿə laʔθən   syayək̓ʷ
   DT   broken   plate   DT   plate   broken
   'the broken plate'   'the broken plate'

In this respect, stative resultatives resemble nouns. When a noun is modified by another noun, either head-modifier order (81a)–(81c) or modifier-head order (81a')–(81c') is allowed.

(81) Halkomelem
a. q̓əwət k̓ʷələw̓   a' k̓ʷələw̓   q̓əwət   'hide drum'
   drum   hide   hide   drum

---

[19] This is not to imply that the 'true' adjectives are monomorphemic; the last four adjectives contain an old stative suffix -t.
[20] Work by Dixon (2004) and others has shown that the languages differ considerably in how many true adjectives they have; Salish languages would be examples of ones with fairly small inventories.

b.	x̣pey̓	kʷəmləxʷ	b.ʹ	kʷəmləxʷ		'x̣p̓eycedar root'
	cedar	root		root		cedar
c.	swəy̓qeʔ	meqeʔ	c.ʹ	meqeʔ		'swəy̓qeʔ snow man'
	man	snow		snow		man

When a noun is modified by a verb, the verb must precede the noun (82a); if a verb follows the noun, it is in fact a relative clause, as evidenced by the auxiliary verb ʔi (82b)–(82c).[21]

(82) Halkomelem
 a. θə t̓it̓ələm̓ steniʔ
  DT sing<IPFV> woman
  'the singing woman'

 b. θə steniʔ *t̓it̓ələm̓ / ʔi t̓it̓ələm̓
  DT woman sing<IPFV> / PROX.AUX sing<IPFV>
  'the woman (who is) singing'

 c. θə *t̓it̓ələm̓ / ʔi t̓it̓ələm̓
  DT sing<IPFV> / PROX.AUX sing<IPFV>
  'the (one) who is singing'

Stative resultatives can also appear in a post-head relative clause (83), but unlike verbs, this is not required of them, as seen in (82).

(83) Halkomelem
 nem̓=č səwq̓ ʔə kʷθə sce:ɬtən niʔ s-q̓ʷəq̓ʷiɬ.
 go.AUX=2SG.SUB look OBL DT salmon DIST.AUX ST-cook<RES>
 'Go look for the salmon that was cooked.'

In sum, adjectives are more verb-like, as they only occur before the head noun, and stative resultatives are more noun-like, in that they can occur before or after the head.

29.4.3 Adjectives and ellipsis

Davis (2011) shows that, in contrast to nouns (84a), adjectives may not be directly selected for by determiners (84b) in Lillooet.

(84) St'át'imcets (Lillooet, Davis 2011: 25)
 a. kʷénan-š=ken tɛ=šč̓óqʷɛẓ=ɛ
  get.caught-CS=1SG.SUB DT=fish=EXIS
  'I caught fish'

---

[21] Davis (2011) shows for Lillooet that all verbs used as modifiers are reduced relative clauses, whether they are pre-head or post-head.

b. *kʷénən-š=kɛn   tɛ=xzóm=ɛ
   get.caught-CS=1SG.SUB DT=big=EXIS
   'I caught a big.'

We see this in Halkomelem as well: adjectives in Halkomelem cannot stand alone by ellipsis of the head noun.[22]

(85) Halkomelem
   a. xʷəʔəẃ-cs-əm=č   ʔə   tᶿə   θi   šaptən.
      show-hand-MID=2SG.SUB OBL DT   big knife
      'Hand me the big knife.'
   b. *xʷəʔəẃ-cs-əm=č   ʔə   tᶿə   θi.
      show-hand- MID=2SG.SUB OBL DT   big
      'Hand me the big (one).'

In contrast, stative resultatives are interpretable without a head noun (86b):

(86) Halkomelem
   a. nem̓=č   səwq̓   ʔə   kʷθə   s-q̓ʷəq̓ʷil   sce:ɬtən.
      go.AUX=2SG.SUB look   OBL   DT   ST-cook<RES> salmon
      'Go look for the cooked salmon.'
   b. nem̓=č   səwq̓   ʔə   kʷθə   s-q̓ʷəq̓ʷil.
      go.AUX=2SG.SUB look   OBL   DT   ST-cook<RES>
      'Go look for the cooked (one).'
      [context: We are using different kinds of salmon in a recipe.]

Stative resultatives again resemble nouns, which follow determiners, rather than adjectives or verbs, which do not.

29.4.4 Types of adjectives

To sum up the Halkomelem evidence, adjectives are not verbs: verbs form imperfectives, but nouns and adjectives do not. Adjectives are not nouns: verbs, nouns, adjectives, and stative resultatives can serve as pre-head modifiers, but only nouns and stative resultatives serve as post-head modifiers. Adjectives show agreement effects with the head N and they cannot stand alone without an overtly expressed head. Evidence thus supports nouns, verbs, and adjectives as separate word classes in Salish languages (see Montler 2003; Suttles 2004: 219; Davis 2011).

The question remains: what word class are stative resultives? We see that, like participles and gerunds in English, they present as different word classes, depending on their function.

---

[22] Hukari (1978) points out that bare adjectives may not serve as relative clauses with eclipsed heads (section 29.2.2).

They are adjectives when they are modifiers, they are nouns when they head NPs, and they are verbs when they serve as predicates. One argument that they are verbs when they are predicates comes from their ability to take auxiliaries, for example the motion auxiliary *nem̓* 'go'.

(87) Halkomelem (MG 2811)
ʔiʔ nem̓ s-q̓əq̓aʔ tᶿə słánłeniʔ nem̓ k̓ʷiʔ ʔə tᶿə sme:nt.
CNJ go.AUX ST-be.added DT woman<PL> go.AUX climb OBL DT mountain
'And the women would go along together up the mountain.'

Stative resultatives are thus an example of a flexible word class, functioning as verbs, adjectives, and even nouns without further modification, a phenomenon that we claimed was otherwise not seen in Salish languages (see section 29.3).

29.5 ADVERBS

Taking the standard definition that adverbs are defined as modifiers of non-nominal heads (see Hengeveld 1992a), we find that in Salish languages such modification is largely accomplished by means of higher predicates, as well as a variety of clitics expressing the speaker's viewpoint.[23]

However, Halkomelem also has a small set of adverbs that can be divided into two types: those with no linker, and those with a linker (Bätscher 2014: 19). The first type (e.g. *qəĺet* 'again') exhibits flexibility in their placement, occurring either before (88) or after (89) the verb they modify.

(88) Halkomelem (Gerdts & Werle 2014)
nem̓ qəĺet q̓ʷəyiləš.
go.AUX again dance
'She went and danced some more.'

(89) Halkomelem (Gerdts & Werle 2014)
m̓i=ct=ceʔ səwq̓-t qəĺet.
come.AUX=1PL=FUT search-TR again
'We will come and look for him again.'

When they appear in clause-initial position, they host second position clitics:

(90) Halkomelem (Bätscher 2014: 21)
qəĺet=č=ceʔ čəl-cəs.
again=2SG.SUB=FUT switch-hand
'You will have to switch [hands] again.'

---

[23] See the list of 47 Halkomelem adverbial words given in Suttles (2004: 422).

Adverbs of the second type (e.g. x̣̌lim̓ 'really', cəlel 'almost') are typically connected to the constituent they modify with a linker, either the proclitic ʔəw̓, which is also used to introduce complement clauses, or the conjunctive particle ʔiʔ, which is also used to coordinate NPs, verbs, and clauses.

(91) Halkomelem (Bätscher 2014: 22)
x̣̌lim̓   ʔəw̓   łeliyəq̓   tᶿə   swiw̓ləs.
really   LNK   angry   DT   boy
'The young man is really angry.'

(92) Halkomelem
niʔ   wəł=cəlel   ʔiʔ   xʷə=təs   ʔə   tᶿə   yə=šxʷənəm̓is …
DIST.AUX   PRF=almost   LNK   INCH=arrive   OBL   DT   DYN=N.OBJ.go<IPFV>
'They had almost reached their destination …' (MJJ 3234)

The word order of these constructions is fixed; these adverbs immediately precede the word or phrase they modify, often appearing in clause initial position as in (93), again hosting second position clitics.

(93) Halkomelem
nan=cən   ʔəw̓   states   ʔə   θə   həy̓qʷ.
very=1SG.SUB   LNK   close.by   OBL   DT   fire
'I am too close to the fire.'

The choice of linker appears to be lexically determined by the adverb; see the Halkomelem list below (see Bätscher 2014: 26).

(94) Halkomelem
a. ʔəw̓:   b. ʔiʔ:
x̣̌lim̓   'really'   cəlel   'almost'
nan   'very, too (much)'   xʷeləq   'almost'
yaθ   'always'   q̓eq̓əl   'barely'
θəʔit   'truly'   x̌ʷəm   'can, able'
taxʷ   'exactly'

Montler (2003: 119) argues for the word class of adverb based on a similar set of adverbs in Klallam, with linkers ʔuʔ or ʔiʔ, cognate to the ones in Halkomelem, and in addition he was able to identify a semantically more robust form corresponding to each adverb that appears without a linker:

(95) Klallam (Montler 2003: 120)
              with linker   without linker
a. ʔuʔ   húy   'only'   'finish'
           łəŋ   'just like'   'detach'
           sə́łəŋ   'continuously'   'continue'
           cə́ʔət   'truly'   'tell the truth'

b. ʔi̓   ʔsɬáx̌ʷ   'definitely'   'be straight'
         čwín   'even (so)'   'not even (so)'
         túʔx̌ʷ   'exactly'   'be in the middle'
         čəyáy   'almost'   'barely'
         híc   'long since'   'long duration'
         x̌ʷəŋ   'possibly, might, can' 'quick, fast'

The historical development of adverbials from word classes such as verbs and adjectives is a common path of grammaticalization (Ramat 2011).

We see evidence that adverbs grammaticized from adjectives in Halkomelem as well. For example, x̌lim̓ 'really' comes from x̌əlim̓ 'right, straight', x̌ʷəm 'can' from x̌ʷəm 'fast', and θəʔit 'truly' from θəʔit 'be true', though for many adverbs there is no clear source. Montler (2003: 119) defines true adverbs as words that are predicate modifiers that do not function as predicates themselves.' Thus, we see syntactic differences between adverbs and the adjectives they derive from. Example (96a) is a single clause, and the adverb x̌ʷəm hosts the subject expressed by the second position clitic (cən), while in (96b) the adjective x̌ʷəm serves as a higher predicate hosting a nominalized clause, and the subject is expressed by possessive marking (nə-).

(96) Halkomelem (Bätscher 2014: 46)
  a. x̌ʷəm=cən   ʔi̓   x̌ʷčenəm.
     can=1SG.SUB LNK   run
     'I can run.'

  b. x̌ʷəm   kʷənəs   x̌ʷčenəm.
     fast   DT.1POS.N   run
     'I run fast.'

In (97) θəʔit 'truly' acts as an adverbial modifier of the verb statəl̓stəxʷ 'know', while in (98) θəʔit acts as a predicate adjective followed by a nominalized clause.

(97) Halkomelem
  kʷənəs   ʔəw̓   θəʔit   ʔəw̓   statəl̓-stəxʷ   kʷəw   mək̓ʷ   stem…
  DT.1POS.N   CN   truly   LNK   be.clear-CS   DT.CN   everything
  'That I truly know everything…' (ST 6856)

(98) Halkomelem
  ʔi̓   ʔəw̓   θəʔit   k̓ʷəs   kʷən-ət   tᶿey̓   ʔi̓   niʔ=č
  CNJ   CN   truly   DT.N   take-TR   DT   CNJ   DIST.AUX=2SG.SUB
  nem-əstəxʷ   ʔə   tᶿən̓   təl̓teləw̓…
  go-CS   OBL   DT.POS arm<PL>
  ʔi̓   ʔəwə   kʷs   q̓ik̓ʷ-əθamət.
  CNJ   NEG   DT.N   bite-TR:2OBJ
  'And it's true if you take it and rub it on your arms… the mosquitoes will never bite you.' (EW 26507)

We see then that Montler's expectation holds: adverbs are not higher verbs but rather modifiers.

As is typical of adverbs in many languages of the world, adverbs in Halkomelem can modify a variety of non-nominal categories. They can modify verbs, as θəʔit in (97), and taxʷ and cəlel the following.

(99) Halkomelem (WS 22265)
ʔiʔ   taxʷ   ʔəẃ   x̌ac-θət   kʷs   nem̓-s   ɬe:l...
CNJ   exactly   LNK   decide-REFL   DT.N   go.AUX-3POS   go.ashore
'And when he had absolutely decided to go ashore...'

(100) Halkomelem (EW 10604)
... niʔ   xʷə=s-x̌̓iʔ-s   θə   staləs   niʔ   cəlel   ʔiʔ   niʔ
DIST.AUX   INCH=N-like-3POS   DT   spouse   DIST.AUX   almost   LNK   DIST.AUX
q̓ay-t-əs.
kill-TR-3SUB
'...and he started loving his wife, whom he almost killed.'

Adverbs can modify adjectives (e.g. ʔəy̓), including predicate adjectives (101) and adjectives modifying a head noun (102):

(101) Halkomelem (ST 8335)
ʔiʔ   ʔəẃ   θəʔit   ʔəẃ   ʔəy̓.
CNJ   CN   truly   LNK   good
'And it truly is good.'

(102) Halkomelem
nan   ʔəẃ   ʔəy̓   nə=ćəwtən   tᶿəń   min̓ineʔ.
very   LNK   good   2POS=help   DT.POS   child <DIM>
'Your son is my very good helper.'

Adverbs can modify other adverbs, for example x̌̓lim̓ 'really' modifies cəlel 'almost' in (103).

(103) Halkomelem (EW 10010)
x̌̓lim̓-s   niẃ   cəlel   ʔiʔ   ćtem̓   θəẃniɬ   kʷis   wəɬ=həya-stəm.
really-3POS   AUX.LNK   almost   LNK   crawl   PRO.DT   DT.N   PRF=leave-CS.PAS
'She was really almost crawling when they took her out.'

Halkomelem adverbs can also modify nouns (e.g. sqʷəmey̓ 'dog') in predicate nominal position.

(104) Halkomelem (ST 7030)
šte:wən̓   yəxʷ   ʔə   k̓ʷənəs   ʔəẃ   θəʔit   ʔəẃ   sqʷəmey̓.
think   INFER   INQUIS   DT.N   CN   truly   LNK   dog
'Think they must that I am in truth a dog.'

In the debate about Salish word classes, much less attention has been paid to adverbs than to nouns and verbs, and this may be because they are less controversial. For example, Jelinek (1995: 510) posits three categories of words: predicates, particles, and a small class of adverbs. Even Salishanists who doubted the noun-verb distinction found reference to the word class of adverb to be useful.

29.6 Conclusion

We find in Salish languages classes of words that, in both form and function, have a lot in common with the traditional categories of noun, verb, adjective, and adverb. Nouns denote entities, verbs denote events, adjectives denote properties and can modify nouns (section 29.4), adverbs modify verbs, adjectives, and other adverbs (section 29.5). Nouns and verbs exhibit clear inflectional differences: nouns are inflected with determiners and possessors, while verbs are inflected with auxiliaries and subject/object markers (section 29.2.2).

Nevertheless, the concept of word class has been fairly controversial among Salish linguists. Some maintain the claim that there are only two kinds of words—predicates and particles (a cover term for the many clitics and small functional words). As Davis et al. (2014: 195) note, 'The issue of category neutrality arises for these languages because of what we term predicate–argument flexibility'. That is, words, and also phrases, of any class can function as predicates (section 29.2.1). Predicate nominals are intriguing because of the lack of copula verbs, the lack of determiners, and the positioning of second position clitics.

In addition, some inflectional morphology does not appear to select for lexical class (section 29.2.4). Inflections typically associated with verbs (e.g. tense) can appear on nouns, and those typically associated with nouns (e.g. plural, diminutive) can appear on verbs. On the other hand, although we find that these inflectional patterns are not restricted to particular lexical classes, they do not perform identical functions from one class to another. Tense clitics on nouns and adjectives have reduced scope, taking just the noun phrase rather than the entire clause. Plural and diminutive inflection on verbs can refer to plural or small (dear) verbal arguments, or doing something many times or a little bit, respectively. The occurrence of these inflections on various words classes in Salish languages does not constitute evidence for a lack of categorial distinctions, but it does raise interesting questions about the origin and semantic development of these morphemes.

The myriad of category-shifting morphemes raises a fundamental question about whether such morphology would be necessary if all lexical words are acategorical (section 29.3). We know of no Halkomelem words that can function both as a noun and a verb without some sort of modification, with the exception of stative resultatives (section 29.4). Each base (i.e. root or stem) is categorized as a noun (section 29.3.1.1), verb, adjective, or adverb and is used and inflected accordingly, and only with additional derivational morphology can a word shift functions. That being said, many of the derivational morphemes do not select for a specific base word class although the derived word regularly belongs to a specific lexical class, as evidenced by their inflection. Exceptions to this are the stative-resultative words, which function as verbs, adjectives, or nouns in appropriate environments, as do words formed with lexical suffixes (section 29.3.3).

Considering the distribution of information across words of different categories, we have come to understand the importance of word classes, as identified by the derivational and inflectional morphology, in conveying the information in discourse structure. Salish languages are often characterized as verb-centred languages compared to, for example, English, which is characterized as noun-centred (Hilpert & Östman 2016: 44). There are many reasons for a preponderance of verbs in natural speech in Salish languages. For example, pronominal subjects and objects are expressed by affixes and clitics, nouns are often omitted when they are recoverable from the context, and lexical suffixes can supply substantival meaning within the verb. The net effect is that much of the information about entities is encoded in the verb complex, as is typical of polysynthetic languages. We have seen for example that verbs, predicate adjectives, and even adverbs can encode semantic features of an entity, such as plurality and diminution. Nevertheless, nouns and verbs share the work of conveying the lexical information and anchoring the event in time and space (Gerdts & Schneider 2021). At the clause level, we see type-shifting: Salish languages make frequent use of nominalized clauses (section 29.2.3) and relative clauses with eclipsed heads resulting in a determiner followed by the VP (section 29.2.2).

In sum, most descriptions of morphological, syntactic, and even phonological phenomena in grammars of Salish languages make useful reference to lexical categories as well as to the syntactic categories of predicate/VP and NP. We conclude that categorial distinctions are relevant to the description and analysis of Salish languages at all levels: root, word, phrase, and clause.

Acknowledgements

Our heartfelt thanks to all—speakers, teachers, learners, and researchers—for their strength of purpose in carrying forward the Salish languages and for helping us in our Hul'q'umi'num' journey. Thank you to the elders who recorded stories and to Tom Hukari and Wayne Suttles for sharing them. The storytellers who are cited in this chapter are: Manson George (MG), Peter Mitchell (PM), Ellen Rice (aka Mrs. Jimmy Joe) (MJJ), Wilfred Sampson (WS), Samuel Tom (ST), and Ellen White (EW). We give our appreciation to all who helped with the transcriptions and translations of the stories—Arnold Guerin, Tom Hukari, Delores Louie, Ruby Peter, Theresa Thorne, Ellen White—and typing and editing them, including Elena Barreiro, Samara Channell, Rae Anne Claxton, Leona George-Peter, Sarah Kell, Zachary Gilkison, Kaoru Kiyosawa, and Zoey Peterson. A special thanks to Tom Hukari for sharing an electronic version of the Hul'q'umi'num' dictionary and the noun roots list, and to Bill Poser and especially Helen Zhang for creating and managing our databases. Donna would like to thank her colleagues in the verb class project, Arnold Guerin, Tom Hukari, Sarah Kell, Ruby Peter, and Theresa Thorne. Research on Hul'q'umi'num' was funded by the Social Sciences and Humanities Research Council, Simon Fraser University, and Jacobs Research Fund. Donna wishes to thank the scholars who have discussed the issue of word classes with her over the decades—David Beck, Henry Davis, Brent Galloway, Jan van Eijk, Nancy

Hedberg, Mercedes Hinkson, Tom Hukari, Peter Jacobs, Bill Jacobsen, Dale Kinkade, Paul Kroeber, Nancy Mattina, Tim Montler, Irina Presnyakova, Wayne Suttles, James Thompson, and others. We thank Nancy Hedberg, Marianne Huijsmans, and Charles Ulrich for their comments and suggestions on this chapter, and we thank the editors of this volume for their guidance and patience.

CHAPTER 30

WORD CLASSES IN IROQUOIAN LANGUAGES

KARIN MICHELSON

30.1 INTRODUCTION

A survey of contemporary grammatical descriptions of Iroquoian languages will leave readers without any doubt as to the parts of speech in these languages: nouns, verbs, and particles. Nouns and verbs are inflected while particles are uninflected and generally occur in only one form. There is an easily detected distinction between nouns and verbs, with verbs bearing the greatest number of inflections by far; stems expressing property concepts—adjectives in other languages—are also expressed by verbs. Yet, in some of the more typologically oriented literature, this inventory is not considered so clear-cut. On the one hand, the distinction between nouns and verbs has been denied, with all inflected words fundamentally claimed to be predications. This controversial claim was made in a number of publications by Sasse (1988; 1992). On the other hand, it has been claimed by Baker (2003) that Mohawk (and other Iroquoian languages) have not only the universal categories of nouns and verbs, but also the universal category of adjectives. What is uncontroversial, though, is that the Iroquoian languages are overwhelmingly verb-centric. This was noticed already by Jesuit and Sulpician scholars, who, in the nineteenth century, produced many excellent works on the languages. For example, Cuoq (1866: 87) states:

> Les Iroquois n'ont presque pas d'adjectifs; ... Ils manquent d'articles, et ils ne sauraient parer à ce défaut d'articles ni par des cas, ni par des prépositions, dont ils sont également dépourvus. Toutefois ils ont d'autres moyens d'y suppléer et de maintenir par là la clarté du discours.... Ils ne possèdent que peu d'adverbes et de conjonctions, mais ils sont d'une richesse étonnante en fait de verbes. Dans leur langue, presque tout est verbe ou peut le devenir.[1]

---

[1] 'The Iroquois have hardly any adjectives; ... They don't have articles, and they wouldn't know how to compensate for this lack of articles either with case or with prepositions, which they also lack. Nevertheless, they have other ways of establishing and maintaining clarity of discourse.... They have only a few adverbs and conjunctions, but in fact they have an astonishing richness of verbs. In their language almost everything is a verb, or can become one' (translation is from Chafe 2003, who also cites this passage).

Cuoq makes a similar comment in his Mohawk dictionary (1882: 206). Writing before Cuoq, Marcoux (1828: 22) remarks 'Le verbe est le mot par excellence de l'Iroquois puisque dans cette langue tout est verbe: noms, pronoms, adjectifs' (cited also in Pilling 1888: 115).[2] And Shea (n.d.) says 'every word is conjugated like a verb (p. 592), and then more eloquently: 'How different this noble, full and ancient language from our English; its grammatical structure rich beyond expression, has a form for every relation, while our verb, capable of only five or six inflections, limps with its crutches of auxiliaries' (p. 593). These comments can be interpreted in more than one way. They can be understood to mean that any word (or stem) can take verbal inflections, or any word can function as a verb, or verbs are the most frequent, or verbs have the most morphology. We shall see that all of these interpretations have some validity.

The bulk of the discussion that follows will be about nouns versus verbs. The issues that need to be resolved in order to posit a distinction between nouns and verbs include to what extent there are syntactic motivations for parts of speech, the morphological or paradigmatic criteria for distinguishing categories, the alignment (or in Iroquoian languages the frequent non-alignment) of ontological and formal categories, and finally the thorny issue of how predication and reference works in these languages. Section 30.2 provides some background on Iroquoian languages. The lack of syntactic evidence distinguishing parts of speech is discussed in section 30.3. Section 30.4 overviews the typical inflectional patterns of nouns and verbs. Reference and predication are tackled in section 30.5. Words that function to denote or refer to entities, but do not have the typical inflectional morphology of nouns are the topic of section 30.6. Section 30.7 is a brief summary of the status of adjectives. The final section is a brief conclusion.

30.2 IROQUOIAN LANGUAGES

The Iroquoian language family comprises two branches, The Northern branch includes Mohawk, Oneida, Onondaga, Cayuga, Seneca, and Tuscarora—the languages of the Six (originally Five) Nations—plus the Huron and Wendat, and a few other languages no longer spoken. Cherokee is the sole language in the Southern branch.

Iroquois-speaking people historically were located primarily in present-day New York State, the Canadian provinces of Ontario and Quebec, and in North Carolina, with their territory extending into Pennsylvania, Ohio, and Virginia. Due to colonization, territories in the form of reserves were established in Canada, and in the United States groups either moved or were forced to move to reservations established in places as distant as Wisconsin and Oklahoma. Today the Six Nations Iroquois or Haudenosaunee (literally, people of the extended lodge or dwelling) are fighting for their identity as sovereign nations. Since language is such an integral part of identity, intergenerational transmission of the languages has become a priority in every community. The languages are all considered endangered with some severely so. For example, reportedly there are only five first-language speakers of

---

[2] 'The verb is the word par excellence of the Iroquois since in this language everything is a verb: nouns, pronouns, adjectives.'

Onondaga (at the Six Nations of the Grand River in Ontario), and fewer than 40 of Oneida (all residing at the Oneida of the Thames settlement in Ontario); the last first-language speaker of Tuscarora died in 2018. Some innovative and excellent immersion programs have produced fluent second language speakers, and their (as well as their teachers') persistence and dedication must be acknowledged.

The data in this chapter comes mainly from Oneida and Mohawk, the languages the author has the most experience with. Grammars and dictionaries of Northern Iroquoian languages, written mostly as reference works by linguists who have researched the languages for decades are Abbott et al. (1996), Chafe (1967), Chafe (2015), Dyck et al. (2018), Michelson & Doxtator (2002), Michelson, Kennedy, & Doxtator (2016), Mithun & Henry (1982), Rudes (1999), Williams (1976), Woodbury (2003), and Woodbury (2018). Some works that provide more of an overview are Abbott (2000), Michelson & Price (2011), and Martin (2016), as well as works available on websites produced by the various nations. Montgomery-Anderson (2015) is a grammar of Oklahoma Cherokee; Cook (1979) is an unpublished dissertation primarily about Eastern Cherokee spoken in North Carolina. Mithun (2000) and Chafe (2012) specifically address controversies in the part-of-speech systems of Iroquoian, and many of the points made here echo generalizations made in these publications as well. When an example is from a language other than Oneida, the language is identified with the example. Oneida excerpts from Michelson, Kennedy, & Doxtator (2016) are identified by speaker and title of the text.

30.3 Syntactic criteria

Semantic arguments of verbs are realized inflectionally by obligatory, bound pronominal affixes, exemplified by the verb forms in (1) and (2). (In Oneida orthography, *ʌ* and *u* are nasalized vowels.)

(1) *wahakhnútlaneʔ*
 wa-hak-hnutlaʔ-neʔ
 FACT-3M.SG>1SG-catch.up.to-PNC
 'he caught up to me'

(2) *wahihnútlaneʔ*
 wa-hi-hnutlaʔ-neʔ
 FACT-1SG>3M.SG-catch.up.to-PNC
 'I caught up to him.'

As discussed by Koenig & Michelson (2014) in the context of Iroquoian languages, syntactic parts of speech are usually justified by the need to constrain combinations of words. The description and analysis of the syntax of most languages, within any number of formal syntactic frameworks, involves selection; the head selects a dependent expression and that dependent expression is external to the word that functions as the head. This relation of selection is based on several kinds of evidence: determination of the number and form of dependents, fixed ordering between head and dependent, binding relations between dependents, and valence alternations. But, as argued by Koenig & Michelson (2014, 2015) the syntax of Oneida is not 'selectional'. The verb is complete on its own and external expressions, as in the excerpts in (3) and (4), are adjoined to the verb.[3] The function of these external expressions is only to provide additional information about the argument referenced on the verb. Since the evidence for selection is absent in Oneida, there is no need to posit syntactic parts of speech and no need to distinguish between noun *words* and verb *words*.[4] (Underlining indicates devoicing, which occurs at the ends of utterances in Oneida.)

(3) *Nʌ kaʔikʌ́ kunukwé waʔtyonatuhútsyohseʔ ta·kutnuso·tʌ́·.*
 nʌ kaʔikʌ́ kun-ukwe waʔ-t-yon-atuhutsyohs-eʔ t-a·-ku-atnusot-ʌʔ
 then this 3FZ.PL.A-person FACT-DL-3FZ.PL.P-want,need-PNC CSL-OPT-3FZ.PL.A-squat-PNC
 'Then these girls needed to relieve themselves.' (Barbara Schuyler, 'A ghost on the tracks')

(4) *Nók tsiʔ yah kiʔ s thutahnéhtahkweʔ thikʌ́ aknulhá· khaleʔ lakeʔníha tsiʔ niyo·lé· thikʌ́ laulhá· lakeʔnihkʌ́ wahotétshʌʔ.*
 nók tsiʔ yah kiʔ kʌs th-u-t-a-hn-ehtahkw-eʔ thikʌ́
 but not in fact usually CONTR-OPT-CSL-OPT-3M.DU.A-believe-PNC that
 aknulhá· kháleʔ lakeʔníha tsiʔ niyo·lé· thikʌ́ laulhá· lakeʔnihkʌ́
 my mother and my father until that himself my late father
 wa-ho-atetshʌ-ʔ
 FACT-3M.SG.P-become.afraid-PNC
 'But my mother and father didn't believe it until my late father got scared himself.' (Rose Antone, 'What my brother Leo saw')

30.4 MORPHOLOGICAL STRUCTURE AND INFLECTION

There is clear agreement that Iroquoian languages have distinct word classes according to the *form* of inflectional affixes. This section presents an overview of the structure of nouns and verbs, following the traditional analysis going back to Lounsbury (1953). The function of these two formal classes is taken up in later sections.

30.4.1 Basic noun and verb structure

Minimally, the structure of verbs includes an obligatory pronominal prefix and an aspect suffix. In Northern Iroquoian, nouns generally include a noun suffix and, with the exception

---

[3] This includes demonstratives such as *thikʌ́* in (4); see section 30.5 for one of the functions of demonstratives. A particle glossed 'the', with various forms across the languages—*ne, neʔ, neh* for example—is sometimes, misleadingly, called a determiner. For extensive discussion of this particle in Seneca, see Chafe (1994: 153–156).

[4] Baker (1996) recognizes the inflectional marking of arguments but for him the realization of arguments is still syntactic and as a consequence requires reference to syntactic parts of speech.

of certain phonologically defined roots, a noun prefix. In Cherokee, most nouns for inanimate entities do not have any prefix or suffix. The example in (5) is a simple Oneida verb form, and a noun form, also Oneida, is given in (6).

(5) shakohlo·líheʔ
 shako-hloli-heʔ
 3M.SG>3-tell-HAB
 'he tells her or them'

(6) oyú·kwaʔ
 o-yuʔkw-aʔ
 3Z/N.SG.P-tobacco-NSF
 'tobacco'

In terms of internal structure, as suggested by the quotes above, verbs have by far the more elaborate structure. Table 30.1 identifies the categories and their linear sequence in a traditional position class arrangement of the verb (see Lounsbury (1953), Mithun (2017a)).

Table 30.1 The internal structure of verbs

Prepronominal prefixes						Pronominal prefix
Partitive Coincident Contrastive Negative	Trans- locative	Dualic	Factual Optative Future	Cislocative Repetitive	Factual Optative	Transitive Agent Patient
Reflexive	Noun stem	Verb root	Derivational suffixes			
Reflexive Reciprocal Semi-reflexive			Inchoative Reversative Nominalizer	Causative	Instrumental	Benefactive
Derivational suffixes		Aspect suffixes	Post-aspectual suffixes			
Distributive	Dislocative	Habitual Punctual Stative	Continuative Past Progressive			

The relative order of the derivational suffixes varies some; this can be seen from the attested combinations of suffixes laid out carefully in tabular form for Onondaga in Woodbury (2018). Some of the languages have additional derivational suffixes. The post-aspectual morphology also varies considerably from language to language, and due to the complex morphophonology, sometimes from analyst to analyst. What is particularly relevant here is that verb stems can combine with noun stems to form derived verb stems. This process of noun incorporation is productive in all the Northern Iroquoian languages; see Uchihara

(2014) for a recent analysis of incorporation in Cherokee, the sole Southern Iroquoian language. In the excerpt in (7) the noun *-hwist-* 'metal, money' has been incorporated into the verb *-u-* 'give'.

(7)   *nále? twenty-five cents wa?ukhwístu? aknulhá·,*
    nále?   twenty-five cents   wa?-yuk-hwist-u-?   aknulhá·
    then again   twenty-five cents   FACT-3>1SG-money-give-PNC my mother
    'then my mother would give me twenty-five cents,' (Olive Elm, 'Friday nights')

Noun incorporation is important in that noun stems always precede verb stems, and thus is a phenomenon that evidences a part-of-speech distinction between nouns and verbs. Sasse (e.g. 1988) acknowledges the role of noun incorporation in distinguishing different classes of roots, but for him syntactic criteria are critical (see Rauh 2010 for a different view).

30.4.2 The pronominal prefixes

We turn now to the inflectional patterns of nouns and verbs, beginning with the prefixes. There are three series: transitive, which reference two animate semantic arguments; intransitive Agent, which reference a single animate argument; and intransitive Patient, which also reference a single animate argument. The semantic categories distinguished by the prefixes are person (first, second, third, plus inclusive versus exclusive), number (singular, dual, plural), and gender (masculine, feminine, feminine-zoic). The feminine occurs only in the singular. An indefinite (or unspecified) person is syncretic throughout the system with the feminine, thus the traditional label 'feminine-indefinite'. Historically the feminine-zoic singular refers to some female persons, animals, and some inanimates in motion. Reference to single female persons with either feminine-zoic or feminine-indefinite is still active in Mohawk and Oneida but is mostly lost in the other languages and because of this the label 'neuter' sometimes is used in place of feminine-zoic (see Abbott 1984 or Michelson 2015 for what determines the choice of feminine-zoic versus feminine-indefinite in Oneida). All non-singular female persons are referred to with the feminine-zoic prefixes. Taken altogether there are from 58 to over 60 prefixes, depending on the language.

Verbs with two animate semantic arguments, and kinship terms, occur with the transitive series. The verb stems in (1) and (2) are inflected with transitive prefixes; these same prefixes occur on the kinship terms in (8) and (9).

(8) *lak-sótha*
    3M.SG>1SG-grandfather
    'my grandfather'

(9) *li-yáha*
    1SG>3M.SG-child
    'my son'

Agent prefixes occur with verbs whose meaning includes one animate semantic argument; the Agent category of prefixes also occurs with inalienably possessed body parts. Examples of Agent prefixes from Onondaga are (10) and (11). Patient prefixes also occur with verbs that have one animate semantic argument, and with alienably possessed nouns. Examples of Patient prefixes from Seneca are (12) and (13). Inanimate arguments are not referenced, except when they are the only argument and then the feminine-zoic singular prefix serves as the default (Koenig & Michelson 2015). Which verbs occur with the Agent category of prefix versus the Patient is semantically motivated but lexicalized. (There are additional factors that determine the selection of Agent versus Patient, such as aspectual category; see the works cited in section 30.2 for details.) Non-possessed nouns denoting inanimate entities occur with either a (default) Agent or a Patient feminine-zoic singular prefix (abbreviated Z/N), and which category occurs is simply lexicalized (examples of non-possessed noun forms are given in (14a) and (15a)).

(10) *hadatjí·nah* (Onondaga) (Woodbury 2018: 381)
 h-adat-jina-h
 3M.SG.A-REF-be.male-STV
 'he is a show-off'

(11) *hagahíʔge* (Onondaga) (Woodbury 2018: 361)
 ha-gahR-iʔ=ge
 3M.SG.A-eye-NSF=LOC
 'his eye'

(12) *hota:'* (Seneca) (Chafe 2015: 184)
 ho-thar-'
 3M.SG.P-talk-STV
 'he's talking'

(13) *hoënö'* (Seneca) (Chafe 2015: 187)
 ho-rën-a'
 3M.SG.P-song-NSF
 'his song'

The form of some of the prefixes can differ on verbs and nouns, and this is especially evident in Mohawk and Oneida. In these languages, the word-initial glides of the third person singular feminine-zoic/neuter Agent and Patient prefixes are absent on nouns, as shown by the following examples (in standard Mohawk orthography, the letter <i> before a vowel represents the glide *y*, and <en> and <on> are nasal vowels *ã* and *ũ*, respectively). The (a) examples give the noun form without an initial glide, and the (b) examples are verb forms with the initial glide.

(14) Mohawk
 a. *à:there'*
  a'ther-e'
  [3Z/N.SG.A]-basket-NSF
  'basket'

b. *wa'therowá:nen*
w-a'ther-owanen
3Z/N.SG.A-basket-large[STV]
'it's a large basket'

(15) Mohawk
a. *ora'wísta'*
o-ra'wist-a'
3Z/N.SG.P-peel-NSF
'peel, pancake'

b. *iora'wístatens*
io-ra'wist-a-tens
3Z/N.SG.P-peel-JOIN-thick[STV]
'the peel or skin is thick'

Mohawk and Oneida also have distinct Possessive Patient prefixes that occur with alienably possessed nouns (in the other languages the Patient prefixes occur with alienably possessed nouns). These lack word-initial glides throughout and, in addition, most of the third person possessive prefixes have a vowel sequence. A possessive form from Oneida is given in (16), and Table 30.2 gives Oneida verbal Patient prefixes, Possessive Patient prefixes, and so that the semantic distinctions can be compared, Agent prefixes for stems that begin in a consonant.

Table 30.2 Oneida noun prefixes (word-initial forms with stems beginning in a consonant)

	Patient prefixes	Possessive prefixes	Agent prefixes
1SG	wak-	ak-	k-
1EX.DU	yukni-	ukni-	yakni-
1IN.DU			tni-
1EX.PL	yukwa-	ukwa-	yakwa-
1IN.PL			twa-
2SG	sa-		
2DU	sni-		
2PL	swa-		
3M.SG	lo-	lao-	la-
3M.DU	loti-	laoti-	ni-
3M.PL			lati-
3FZ.SG	yo-	ao-	ka-
3FZ.DU	yoti-	aoti-	kni-
3FZ.PL			kuti-
3FI	yako-	ako-	ye-

(16) *laohwísta?*
 lao-hwist-a?
 3M.SG.POSS-money-NSF
 'his money'

Mithun (2000) points out an additional difference between the inflection on verbs and nouns with prefixes, and that is that animals (i.e. the 'zoic' in feminine-zoic), in the plural, are referred to with plural verbal prefixes, but the prefix that occurs on the noun word itself is always feminine-zoic *singular*. In (17), for example, the word for 'mosquito', based on a verb form (see section 30.6.2), has the singular prefix *o-*, while the verb has the plural prefix *hʌn-* (in this case masculine since animals are very often personified and then are referred to with masculine rather than feminine-zoic prefixes). However, singular prefixes on nouns may be due to the fact that the prefixes that occur with noun forms are lexicalized and do not vary.

(17) *kátsha? akwáh nú· nihʌ·né·se? thikʌ́ okalyahtá·ne?*
 kátsha? akwáh nú· ni-hʌn-e-?se? thikʌ́
 where exactly place PART-3M.PL.A-go,walk-HAB that
 o-kaly-a-ht-a-?ne?
 3Z/N.SG.P-bite-JOIN-CAUS-JOIN-AMB
 'where the mosquitoes are around' (Norma Kennedy, 'The legend of the mosquito')

30.4.3 Suffixes

Verbs fall into two major classes according to aspect distinctions. The largest class of verbs occurs in three aspects: the habitual (imperfective), punctual (perfective), and stative. Some of the verbs in this class, those that include in their meaning some sort of motion, have an additional aspect form, given various terms (e.g. purposive, present). The second class occurs only in the stative aspect. Most concepts that are expressed by adjectives in languages that have a distinct adjective class are expressed with verbs that belong to this stative-only class (see section 30.7). Aspect allomorphy is robust, so that typically stems are organized into 'conjugation classes' according to the aspect endings. Iroquoian languages are often classified as fusional, and the boundary between stem and suffix certainly justifies this label. Nouns mostly occur with a noun suffix, which also has several allomorphs, lexically selected by the noun stem. The noun form for 'peel' in (15a) has the suffix *-a'* while the form for 'basket' in (14a) has the suffix *-e'*. The noun suffix's only function is formal: to complete the inflection of the noun.

30.5 REFERENCE VERSUS PREDICATION

Among scholars of Iroquoian languages, there is consensus that words denoting entities and words denoting events, activities, or states can have different formal properties, in particular the form of noun prefixes and possessive prefixes. What has been a matter of considerable controversy is the proposal by Sasse (e.g. 1988, 1992) that words traditionally analysed as morphological nouns can by themselves (i.e. without a copula) have a predicating function. He introduces this idea with a discussion of the Oneida word *ohkwalí* 'bear', which he claims should be more aptly rendered into German as 'es ist ein Bär' (1988: 6) or even better 'es bärt ihn' (1988: 12), i.e. it is a thing that has the quality of a bear. He finds this unsurprising in light of his analysis of the Agent and Patient pronominal prefixes as basically belonging to the transitive series and, as such, fundamentally relational (but see, for example, Koenig & Michelson (2015) for arguments against such an analysis). This relational content is (for him) what one would expect of predication.

Mithun (2000) explicitly refutes this claim, citing decades of research and hundreds of hours of Mohawk narrations and conversations without once a bare noun form used in a predicative function. Likewise in Oneida, nouns by themselves do not assert. They do not constitute full propositions or sentences; for this they must occur together with certain particles, most often the so-called 'assertion' particle, *né·* (see Mohawk *né·* or *ne*, Onondaga *ná·yeʔ* or *naʔ*, Seneca *né:'*). These noun-particle patterns are discussed in the remainder of this section.

To identify a member of a category when the entity is in view of the speaker and hearer, the assertion particle occurs with a demonstrative. (Note that this structure occurs not only with words that are inflected nouns, but with any entity-denoting word; see section 30.6.)

(18) a. *Náhteʔ né· kaʔi·ká.*
    'What is this?'

   b. *Kanhóhaʔ né· kaʔi·ká.*
    'This is a door.'

Two entities can be equated and in this case too, the assertion particle *né·* occurs.[5] In (19) the narrative is about an ill-behaved little girl who has been raised, and spoiled, by her grandparents. They seek the advice of a fortune teller, who insists that what will cure her—her medicine—is a whipping with three red willow twigs. In (20) the story is about a vain and cocky young man; he is rendered speechless when he tries to flirt with a beautiful young woman who turns out to be a skeleton with bones for her face.

(19) *shekú yeksaʔshúha, né· kiʔ akonúhkwaʔt thiká onikwáhtalaʔ nikakwiló·tʌ.*
    shekú   ye-ksaʔ-shuha   né·   kiʔ   ako-nuhkwaʔt   thiká
    even   3FI.A-child-DISTR.PL   ASSRT in fact 3FI.POSS-medicine that
    onikwáhtalaʔ ni-ka-kwil-oʔtʌ
    red   PART-3Z/N.SG/A-twig-kind[STV]
    'even the children, it's their medicine the red [willow] whip.' (Mercy Doxtator, 'The spoiled child')

(20) *Óstyʌʔ né· yekuksne. Yéskʌn nʌʔ né·.*
    o-styʌ-ʔ   né·   ye-kuks-ne   ye-skʌn   nʌʔ né·
    3Z/N.SG.P-bone-NSF   ASSRT 3FI.A-face-LOC   3FI.A-skeleton   ASSRT
    'Her face was only bones. She was a skeleton.' (Georgina Nicholas, 'The flirt')

---

[5] The assertion particle should not be mistaken for a copula; as stated explicitly by Mithun (2000: 410) there are no copular verbs in Iroquoian.

Introduction of the name of a category of entities unknown to the hearer requires also the particle *né·n* (clearly related to the assertion particle). Before she utters the excerpt in (21) the narrator has been talking about her father's predictions about the future. He spoke about something noisy going by high above, and the narrator informs us that he is talking about airplanes. (This and the next example also have the frequent particles *kwí·* and *katiʔ wí·*, which speakers describe as functioning to connect discourse somehow; it is not always clear how best to translate such particles.)

(21)　*né· kwí· né·n airplane.*
　　　'It's an airplane.' (Margaret Antone, 'Forecasting things to come')

New discourse referents are frequently introduced in a presentational structure consisting of the assertion particle plus demonstrative; this structure is roughly equivalent to English 'there were these ...'. An example is the following excerpt:

(22)　*né· katiʔ wí· kaʔikʌ́ teknukwé*
　　　né·　　katiʔ wí·　　kaʔikʌ́　　te-kn-ukwe,
　　　ASSRT　well then　this　　　DL-3FZ.DU.A-person
　　　'well then there were these two ladies,' (Mercy Doxtator, 'Berries and bellies')

Finally, there is a residue of cases where just the inflected noun occurs. But in all of the cases that are attested in Oneida texts, the narrator is describing a category in someone's mind; she is not making an assertion. In (23) the narrator's father hears a strange noise in the house and he says (to himself) '(maybe) a mouse'. In (24) the narrator's friends get the urge to relieve themselves while they are walking along some railway tracks; she is supposed to be on the look-out for anyone coming. She sees someone and thinks to herself 'a man (male) maybe'.

(23)　*Né·n　　kwahikʌ́　wahotétshaʔ,　wahʌ́·luʔ, 'tá·t núwaʔ otsiʔno·wʌ́.'*
　　　so then　really　　he got scared　he said　maybe　a mouse
　　　'So he got really scared, he said, "maybe [it's] a mouse".' (Rose Antone, 'A night visitor')

(24)　*Wá·kelheʔ　kiʔ　　　ní·,　lukwé　uhte.*
　　　I thought　actually　me,　a man　probably
　　　'I thought, a man probably.' (Barbara Schuyler, 'A ghost on the tracks')

Negation patterns confirm the distinction between words that function referentially versus predicatively. Standard negation consists of a negative particle plus a prefix on the verb (not all the languages require both particle and prefix; see Michelson 2016). An example from Oneida is given in (25). Words that denote entities, regardless of morphological type (see section 30.6), are negated with a negative particle plus a separate word, *té·kʌ* in Oneida (26).

(25)　*yah teʔwakanúhteʔ*
　　　yah　　teʔ-wak-anuhte-ʔ
　　　not　　NEG-1SG.P-know-STV
　　　'I don't know.'

(26) Kwáh ok né· thiyutkalunyányu<u>he</u>ʔ. Yah tú·skeʔ té·kʌ.
 kwáh ok né· thi-yu-atkalunyanyu-heʔ yah tú·skeʔ té·kʌ
 just only ASSRT CONTR-3FI.A-tell.stories-HAB not true NEG
 'She's only making up stories. It's not the truth.' (Verland Cornelius, 'A lifetime of memories')

30.6 REFERRING EXPRESSIONS AND INFLECTIONAL STRUCTURE

Overwhelmingly, with only a handful of difficult cases, *roots* that denote entities have the inflectional structure of nouns and *roots* that denote situations (events, processes, states including properties) have the structure of verbs. But the relation between inflected noun and verb *words* and their classification as kinds of things in the world, specifically classes of entities versus situations (i.e. ontological category) is not nearly as unequivocal; indeed, what makes Northern Iroquoian truly remarkable is the extent to which fully inflected verbs (and sometimes even partially inflected verbs, as discussed below) function solely as referring expressions. In this section, we discuss entity-denoting words that are not derived from noun roots, namely: (1) words that denote entities but are fully inflected verb forms, (2) words derived from verb roots or stems that have the noun form of the pronominal prefixes or occur with possessive prefixes, (3) kinship terms, and (4) uninflected particles.

30.6.1 Inflected verbs

In Northern Iroquoian, fully inflected verbs are frequently lexicalized as referring to a particular category of entity. Examples are given in (27)–(30). (Mithun 1979 discusses the distinction between inflected verbs that function as predicates and lexicalized inflected verbs in Mohawk). Lexicalized inflected verbs cover a large range of vocabulary: tools and machinery, household appliances and furniture, items used as clothing and for adornment, maladies, names for plants and animals, celestial and other natural phenomena, foods, and so on. Often speakers can give a more literal translation of the form, and they talk about such forms as contributing to the idea that Iroquoian languages are particularly descriptive since these words identify the function of the entity, or characteristic appearance, and so on.

(27) latislanú·wehseʔ
 lati-sl-a-nuhwe-hseʔ
 3M.PL.A-smell-JOIN-like-HAB
 'gnats, picnic bugs'

(28) tekayaʔtanáhsuteʔ
 te-ka-yaʔt-a-nahsut-eʔ
 DL-3FZ.SG.A-body-JOIN-fasten,button-STV
 'wagon, bobsled'

(29) *tewatluhyayelúnyuheʔ*
 te-w-at-luhy-a-yelu-nyu-heʔ
 DL-3FZ.SG.A-SRF-sky-JOIN-deceive,display-DISTR-HAB
 'Northern Lights'

(30) *yakonyáktaʔ*
 yako-nyak-ht-haʔ
 3FI.P-get.married-CAUS-HAB
 'wedding cake'

In Michelson & Doxtator's (2002) dictionary of Oneida, there are close to 400 fully inflected, lexicalized, entity-denoting verbs, as compared with about 435 noun stems. This distribution, in addition to the fact that there is so little borrowing in these languages, has led some researchers (e.g. Woodbury 2018; Koenig & Michelson 2013, 2020) to claim that nouns are a closed class in Northern Iroquoian. When a new label for a concept is needed, typically an inflected verb form comes to be used to refer to it. But even categories of entities that we expect existed before Europeans arrived in America are lexicalized verbs, not just newly encountered or adopted objects or concepts, e.g. Mohawk *taonhtané:ken* or *tehahonhtané:ken* 'rabbit' (literally, 'he has ears side-by-side') or *anèn:taks* 'porcupine' (literally, 'evergreen eater'). Native names are also verbs, e.g. *Tharonhiakánere* 'he looks at the sky or heavens', the Mohawk name given to the missionary Joseph Marcoux, cited at the beginning of this chapter.

In addition to lexicalized words, verb forms that constitute internally headed relative clauses commonly function as referring expressions:

(31) *shakotinhá·u né· a·huwatikhúniʔ kaʔikʌ́ latiyʌtákwas.*
 shakoti-nhaʔ-u né· a·-huwati-khuny-ʌ-ʔ kaʔikʌ́
 3M.PL>3FI-hire-STV ASSRT OPT-3FI>3M.PL-cook-BEN-PNC this
 lati-yʌt-a-kw-as
 3M.PL-wood-JOIN-harvest-HAB
 'these woodcutters (lit. those who harvest wood) hired her to cook for them.'
 (Mercy Doxtator, 'Some woodcutters get a visitor')

Chafe (2003) attributes the common function of verbs as referring expressions to the fundamental nature of the verb. Because verb forms include bound pronominals that specify a participant in an event, it is not possible to describe an event without also evoking the participants in that event.[6] Chafe (2003: 46) states:

> It is quite common for Seneca verbs to express referents rather than events, a usage that throws a special light on the holistic nature of these verbs: the fact that the participants in the events are just as much a part of them as the events themselves, since the same verb can equally well express the idea of a participant.

---

[6] In later work, Chafe (e.g. 2015), as well as Mithun (e.g. 2017a), use the term *holophrastic* for this phenomenon.

30.6.2 Derivation

In Mohawk and Oneida, there are lexicalized forms that have the structure of verbs—an aspect suffix, incorporated noun, derivational suffixes, but take the nominal form of the prefix, either *o-* (when the verbal prefix is *yo-*) or zero (when the verbal prefix is *w-*). Examples with *o-* are the Oneida words for 'mosquito' (17) and 'soap' (32). An example with a zero form of the prefix is the Oneida word for 'key(s)' (33) or the Mohawk for 'suspenders' (35). Some of these lexicalizations are attested also with Patient Possessive prefixes; as in (34).

(32) *onohalé·thaʔ*
   o-nohale-ʔt-haʔ
   3FZ.SG.P-wash-CAUS-HAB
   'soap'

(33) *atenhotukwátha?*
   ate-nhotu-kw-a-ht-haʔ
   [3FZ.SG.A]-SRF-close.door-REV-JOIN-CAUS-HAB
   'key(s)'

(34) *akwatenhotukwátha?*
   akw-ate-nhotu-kw-a-ht-haʔ
   1SG.POSS-SRF-close.door-REV-JOIN-CAUS-HAB
   'my key(s)'

(35) *athnenhsotáhrhon* (Mohawk)
   at-hnenhs-otahrho-on
   [3FZ.SG.A]-SRF-shoulder-hook-STV
   'suspenders'

In addition, there is a small class of verb roots (half a dozen) that always occur with an incorporated noun and that are lexicalized with the noun form of the feminine-zoic/neuter singular prefix, i.e. the form without a word-initial glide. Oneida roots that fall into this category include *-kli-* 'liquid', *-kahtu-* 'raw', and *-osku-* 'majority'. Examples with *-kli-*, the root most often attested, and *-kahtu-* are given in (36) and (37).

(36) *ohyákliʔ*
   o-ahy-a-kli-ʔ
   3Z/N.SG.P-fruit,berry-JOIN-liquid-STV
   'fruit drink'

(37) *ohtehlakáhtuʔ*
   o-htehl-a-kahtu-ʔ
   3Z/N.SG.P-root-JOIN-raw-STV
   'radish'

Finally, all of the (Northern) languages also have one fairly productive overt nominalization process that derives noun stems from verb stems, and the derived noun stem is fully inflected like noun roots, i.e. takes both a noun prefix and a noun suffix. The output of this process is most often lexicalized; the word for 'butter' (38) is an example. Nominalized verb stems can undergo incorporation, which can also result in a form that has become lexicalized as denoting an entity. Examples are the Oneida word for 'rainwater' in (39) and the Mohawk word for 'playing cards' in (40). In Michelson & Doxtator (2002) there are 24 attested stems with the nominalizer (which suggests limited productivity).

(38) owistóhsli?
     o-wisto-hsli-?
     3Z/N.SG.P-cold-NMZR-NSF
     'butter'

(39) okʌnolehslákli?
     o-kʌnole-hsl-a-kli-?
     3Z/N.SG.P-rain-NMZR-JOIN-liquid-STV
     'rainwater'

(40) teiehiatónhseraientáhkhwa' (Mohawk)
     te-ie-hiaton-hser-a-ient-a-hkw-ha'
     DL-3FI.A-write-NMZR-JOIN-put.down-JOIN-INSTR-HAB
     'playing cards'

In recent work, Koenig & Michelson (2020) suggest these inflectional patterns are due to processes of conversion from elements that describe situations (traditionally, verbs) to ones that refers to entities (traditionally, nouns). For example, an overt process of derivation with the nominalizer suffix derives a stem that means 'butter' from a stem that means 'be cold'. Conversion, i.e. a process without an overt marker, applies to a constituent that consists of a verb stem plus aspect suffix to derive a stem that refers to an entity, 'key(s)' (33). Whole inflected 'verbs' can be converted into referential expressions, as is the case with the word for wagon, 'bobsled' (28).

While Northern Iroquoian has many words denoting entities that are fully inflected verb forms, Cherokee has many entity-denoting words that are derived from verbs and have overt nominalizers. In Cherokee verb forms have a modal suffix after the aspect suffixes, and in deverbal nouns, a nominalizer occurs instead of the modal suffix (see, for example, Barrie & Uchihara (2019)).

30.6.3 Kinship terms

Kinship terms, as described in detail for Oneida by Koenig & Michelson (2010), have formal properties of both verbs and nouns; see also Mithun (2010) for Mohawk, Chafe (2015) for Seneca, and Woodbury (2018) for Onondaga. Most terms take transitive pronominal prefixes, identifying the members in the relation. Because of their inflection with transitive prefixes, kinship terms were traditionally analysed as verbs. But certain prefixes lack word-initial glides and kinship terms do not end with aspect suffixes (instead most end with a diminutive ending). Semantically, also, the referential index of kinship terms is an entity, i.e. the term refers to a member of the kin relation (see also Chafe 2015). This is shown with the excerpt in (41).

(41) *Yah teʔwé·ne niyakonaʔkhwʌ́·u aknulhá·,*
 yah teʔ-w-eʔne ni-yako-naʔkhwʌ-ʔu wak-nulhá·
 not NEG-3Z/N.SG.A-evident[STV] PART-3FI.P-get.mad-STV 3FZ.SG>1SG-mother
 'It's incredible how mad my mother got,' (Olive Elm, 'Visits to my auntie's')

30.6.4 Uninflected particles

The large class of particles, upwards of 150 in most of the languages, express all kinds of meanings, including temporal and locational concepts; pronominal categories such as question words and indefinite expressions; negation; and a plethora of meanings that fall under discourse organization. Particles are defined as words that have neither the structure of nouns nor of verbs; any variation in their form is due to speech rate. For example, the Oneida particle *to·kʌ́ske?* 'truly, surely, in truth' is often pronounced *tú·ske?.*[7] A considerable number of animal names are also forms that occur in a single form and that do not have the typical inflectional structure of either nouns or verbs. There are 50 such Oneida entity-denoting particles in Michelson & Doxtator (2002). A few examples from Oneida are: *ʌtilú* 'raccoon', *kwaʔyʌ́ha* 'rabbit', *síksik* 'sheep', and *tsí·ks* 'fly'. Some of these are onomatopoetic, replicating either the sound made by the animal (e.g. *klíkli* 'bluejay' or *to·tís* 'spring frog') or the sound used to summon the animal (e.g. *kítkit* 'chicken'). A few uninflected particles are borrowings, such as *sotá·l* 'soldier', *kwénis* 'penny', *sílu* '25 cents' (from English 'shilling'), and *anikók* 'pancake'.

30.7 ADJECTIVES

The evidence for the absence of a class of adjectives in Northern Iroquoian has been presented in Chafe (2012). Focusing on Seneca, Chafe shows that roots that could be classified as adjectives based on their semantics have all of the morphology of other roots that occur only in the stative aspect. Two Oneida roots that occur only in the stative aspect are exemplified in (42) and (43), and two with more canonical adjectival meanings in (44) and (45).

(42) *lana·yé·*
 la-naye-ʔ
 3M.SG.A-vain-STV
 'he is vain, cocky'

---

[7] It may be noted though that etymologically it is not uncommon to discern a verb or noun root as the basis for a particle; again using *to·kʌ́ske?/tú·ske?* as an example, this particle clearly seems to come from a verb root *-tokʌ-*, which occurs in derived stems meaning 'find out about, become certain, holy'.

(43) loní·u
      lo-ni?-u
      3M.SG.P-stingy-STV
      'he is stingy'

(44) lahétkʌ?
      la-hetkʌ-?
      3M.SG.A-ugly-STV
      'he is ugly'

(45) lólehsʌ?
      lo-ale?sʌ-?
      3M.SG.P-fat-STV
      'he is fat'

Chafe discusses several phenomena that argue against a distinct category of adjectives: category of pronominal prefix, suffixation of the inchoative to derive a change-of-state meaning, the distribution of distributive suffixes, the meaning of the cislocative prefix, noun incorporation including the shift from a description of a state to reference to an entity, and some clitics with lexical meanings such as 'big, small, former, characteristic of, people of, genuine'. Lastly, he discusses the possibility of non-intersective interpretations of certain roots, which Baker (2003) claims is evidence for a class of adjectives in Mohawk. Chafe suggests that the relevance of non-intersective interpretations needs further study, and he demonstrates that Baker's two other arguments, gender agreement and noun incorporation, are flawed.

Cherokee has been argued to have innovated an adjective class, as first pointed out in (Lindsay & Scancarelli 1985). More recently though, Barrie & Uchihara (2019) point out that the properties attributed to the relatively small class of adjectives in Cherokee—no inflection for aspect, mode, and negation; pronominal prefixes are not obligatory; superhigh accent— are also characteristic of deverbal nouns; consequently it is questionable whether Cherokee has a distinct adjective class.

30.8 Conclusion

What is fascinating about Iroquoian is the extent to which referential expressions are words other than those with the inflectional properties of noun stems. The relation between roots that denote entities versus roots that denote situations (events, processes or states), and their inflectional paradigm is uncomplicated. But the relation between what inflections occur on *words* (as opposed to roots) and the meaning of words is very often not isomorphic. Using the corpus in Michelson, Kennedy, & Doxtator (2016), Koenig & Michelson (2013) report that only 1.9%–2.2% of words have the structure of inflected nouns (the differing percentages reflect exclusive noun morphology versus at least some noun morphology). The percentage of entity-denoting expressions is higher, 10.6%. Words that have a referential function can come from words that have all of the inflection of verbs, all of the inflection of nouns, some of the inflection of verbs and some of nouns, or no inflection at all. Expressions that are used in a referential function include particles, lexicalized inflected verb forms, internally headed relative clauses, kinship terms, independent pronouns, proper names that are English or borrowed from English, and English words (such as 'mattress'). So, Sasse (1988, 1992) was not entirely off the mark when he claimed that there was no natural class of entity-denoting words that could be given a privileged status of 'noun'. Sasse was mistaken, though, about the potential for predicative function by inflected noun stems. To use any entity denoting expression in a predicative function requires an explicit discourse structure.

Acknowledgements

The author would like to acknowledge the Oneida speakers whose stories were published in Michelson, Kennedy, & Doxtator (2016). Excerpts from that volume are cited here with the name of the narrator and the title of the recording. Thanks go also to Cliff Abbott, Samantha Cornelius, Jean-Pierre Koenig, Hiroto Uchihara, and Hanni Woodbury for helpful comments on an earlier draft.

CHAPTER 31

WORD CLASSES IN ESKIMO–ALEUT LANGUAGES

MARIANNE MITHUN

31.1 THE UNANGAN–YUPIK–INUKTITUT OR ESKIMO–ALEUT FAMILY

LANGUAGES of this family are spoken across the Arctic from Siberia to the east coast of Greenland. The family consists of two main branches, Aleut and Eskimoan. The Aleut branch consists of a single language, Unangan (Aleut). The Eskimoan branch consists of two major sub-branches: Yupik and Inuit-Iñupiaq. Relations are sketched in Figure 31.1, with languages in bold and dialects in italics.

Aleut branch
    Aleut
        Unangan = Aleut
            Western, Eastern dialects

Eskimoan branch
    Yupik
        Sirenikski
        Central Siberian Yupik
        Naukanski
        Central Alaskan Yup'ik
            Egegik, General Central Alaskan Yup'ik, Hooper Bay/Chevak, Nunivak, Norton Sound
        Alutiiq = Pacific Gulf Yupik
            Konag, Chugach
    Inuit-Iñupiaq
        Inuktitut
            Seward Peninsula, North Alaskan Iñupiaq, Western Canadian Inuktun, Eastern Canadian Inu ktut, Kalaallisut (Greenlandic) groups

FIGURE 31.1 The Eskimo–Aleut (Eskaleut) family (based on Fortescue et al. 2010)

Detailed descriptions of the languages and their locations are in Dorais (2010) and Fortescue et al. (2010). Unangan, also referred to as Unangax̂ or Aleut, is spoken on the Aleutian, Pribilof, and Commander Islands in the Bering Sea. Western and Eastern dialects are distinguished. Sirenikski was spoken until recently on the Chukchi Peninsula in Russia. It is not entirely clear whether it should be grouped within the Yupik sub-branch of Eskimoan or considered a sub-branch on its own. Central Siberian Yupik is spoken on St. Lawrence Island, off the coast of Chukotka but within the state of Alaska. Naukanski was spoken at East Cape on the Chukchi Peninsula in Russia. Central Alaskan Yup'ik is spoken over a wide area of south-western Alaska, with five main dialects: Egegik, General Central Alaskan Yup'ik, Nunivak, Hooper Bay/Chevak, and Norton Sound. Alutiiq is spoken by the Sugpiat people on the south coast of Alaska in two dialects: Koniag on Kodiak Island and the Alaska Peninsula, and Chugach around Prince William Sound and the southern Kenai Peninsula east and south of Anchorage. Inuktitut consists of a large dialect chain, with varieties spoken from north-western Alaska, across Canada in the Northwest Territories, Nunavut (Arctic Quebec), and northern Labrador, to the west and south-east coasts of Greenland. Neighbouring communities can generally understand each other, but those at the western and eastern edges cannot. Sixteen Inuktitut dialects, each with sub-dialects, have been grouped into five main dialect groups: Seward Peninsula Inuit, North Alaskan Iñupiaq, Western Canadian Inuktun, Eastern Canadian Inuktut, and Greenlandic Inuit (Kalaallisut).

Dorais (2010: 95–105) provides a detailed summary of current thought on the prehistory of the family, based on a combination of archaeological and linguistic evidence. Around 4,500 years ago, speakers of Proto-Eskaleut were living in what is now Alaska, their language having replaced those of earlier communities there. Around this time ancestors of the Unangan (Aleut) began migrating to the Aleutian Islands, resulting in the first split in the family. Between 3,000 and 2,000 years ago Eskimoans split into the major subgroups Sirenikski, Yupik, and Inuit-Iñupiaq. The first of these, the Sirenikski, ultimately crossed the Bering Strait to Chukotka. The second then spread out: the Sugpiat (Alutiit) migrated to south central Alaska, and the ancestors of the Central Siberian Yupiget and the Naukanski followed the Sirenikski to Chukotka. Between 1,000 and 800 years ago the third group began to expand, the Iñupiat moving into Yupik territory on the Seward Peninsula in Alaska, and others moving eastward on to the Canadian Arctic and Greenland.

It should be noted that the term *Eskimo* is no longer used among some groups to refer to the people and their language. The term *Yupiit* is used instead for the people by those in south-western Alaska, *Inuvialuit* in the Mackenzie region of the Northwest Territories, *Inuktun* in much of western Canada, *Inuit* ('human beings') in eastern Canada, and *Kalaallit* in Greenland. Other groups do not generally object to the term.

31.2 NOUNS AND VERBS

Lipscomb (1993) and Sadock (1999) address the hypothesis that Eskimoan languages contain no noun–verb distinction. In his delightful account of the history of the claims, Sadock traces the idea to the Eskimologist William Thalbitzer (1873–1958), citing a passage from Thalbitzer's chapter on Greenlandic in the *Handbook of American Indian Languages*:

> In the Eskimo mind the line of demarcation between the noun and the verb seems to be extremely vague, as appears from the whole structure of the language, and from the fact that the inflectional endings are, partially at any rate, the same for both nouns and verbs.
> (Thalbitzer 1911: 1057, cited in Sadock 1999: 383)

He observes that:

> every grammar and grammatical sketch of an Eskimo language is organized around the distinction between noun and verb ... even those descriptions that are written under the explicit assumption that no such distinction exists.
> (Sadock 1999: 384)

Crucially, Sadock also points to the fact that the two are inflected in distinct ways.

All languages of the family share similar basic grammatical structures. All are highly polysynthetic. Content words consist of a single initial root (often termed a base in work with languages in the family), optionally followed by one or more derivational suffixes (termed postbases), and an obligatory inflectional suffix complex (termed the ending). An important point is the fact that there is a clear formal distinction between roots and suffixes in all of the languages. All nouns and verbs begin with one and only one root. Roots appear only in word-initial position: there is no compounding. Suffixes, by contrast, never appear in initial position. The two categories are sharply delineated: members of each pattern as only one or the other.

For nouns, the inflectional ending specifies number, case, and optionally possession. The basic noun template can be seen in Figure 31.2.

ROOT = BASE	(DERIVATIONAL SUFFIXES) = (POSTBASES)	INFLECTIONAL SUFFIX NUMBER, CASE, (POSSESSION) = ENDING

FIGURE 31.2 Noun template

Most of the languages distinguish singular, dual, and plural number on nouns, though Kalaallisut has lost the dual. Cases distinguished include: absolutive, ergative (also called relative), genitive (= ergative in form), locative, allative (or terminalis), ablative (or modalis), instrumental (for some), vialis (or perlative), and equalis (or equative). Possessive suffixes on nouns identify both the possessor and possessed, normally third person. Examples are provided here in the conventional orthographies, which tend to differ more than the phonologies.

Nouns can be seen in (1)–(3). Examples are given from representative languages of each branch of the family.

(1) Unangan (Aleut) Nouns (Bergsland 1997: 54; 1994: 484; 1994: 482)
    a. *ula-x̂*   'house'
       ula-x   'two houses'
       ula-n   'three or more houses' (Eastern dialect)

       ula-ng   'my house'
       ula-a   'his/her house'
       ula-an   'his/her (own) house'

       ula-king 'my two houses' (Eastern dialect)
       ula-ning 'my (three or more) houses'
       ula-kin   'your two houses'   etc.

  b. *isuĝ-naaĝ-alu-x̂*
     seal-hunt-place-ABS
     'seal hunting place'

  c. *hani-ilgi-da-s*
     lake-DIM-DISTR-PL
     'lots of small lakes scattered around'

(2) Central Siberian Yupik (Jacobson 1979: 22; Nagai 2001: 168; de Reuse 1994: 56)
  a. *nunat*
     nuna-t
     land-PL
     'lands'

  b. *yugusimeggneng*
     yugusi-megg-neng
     carcass-3R.PL>3PL-ABL
     'from their bodies'

  c. *unangniightengughsaghqaq*
     unange-niigh-(s)te-(ng)ughte-yaghqaq
     seal.catch-HAB-NMLZ-become-FUT.NMLZ
     'One who ought to become a hunter.'

(3) Iñupiaq (MacLean 1986: 251, 165; 1995: 280)
  a. *kamik*
     'boot'

  b. *kammagni*
     kamik-k-ni
     boot-3SG>3DU-ABL
     'from his boots'

  c. *nukatpiagrusugruk*
     nukatpiaq-agruk-sugruk
     young.man-juvenile-large
     'a large young boy'

(4) Kalaallisut (Sadock 2003: 17)
   a. *nunamut*
      nuna-mut
      land-ALL
      'to the land'

   b. *nunaa*
      nuna-aa
      land-3SG>3SG
      'his/her land'

   c. *illugigaluarput*
      illu-gigaluaq-put
      house-previously.owned-1PL>3SG
      'our previous house' (Fortescue 1984: 317)

For verbs, the inflectional ending consists of what is termed a mood marker followed by a pronominal suffix identifying the core argument(s) of the clause. The verb template is shown in Figure 31.3.

ROOT = BASE	(DERIVATIONAL SUFFIXES) = (POSTBASES)	MOOD	PRONOMINAL SUFFIX
		= ENDING	

FIGURE 31.3 Verb template

Examples of verbs are in (5)–(8).

(5) Unangan (Aleut) (Bergsland 1997: 123)
   Ti-ng   adalu-usa -naaĝ-iiĝut-amasu-x̂ta-ku-x̂.
   PRONOUN-1SG   lie-toward-try-again-perhaps-apparently-PRES-3SG
   'Perhaps he tried to fool me again.'

(6) Central Siberian Yupik (de Reuse 1994: 81)
   Qimugsiqayugunaqnaqaquq
   qimugsigh-qayugu-naqe-aqe-u-q
   drive.dogteam-able-try-PROSP-PROG-INTR.IND-3SG
   'He intends to learn to drive a dogteam.'

(7) Iñupiaq (MacLean 1995: 364)
   Kavigluksiugaŋuluaqhiñiqsuq.
   kavigluksi-ugaq-ŋuluk-aqsi-ñiq-tu-q
   blush-REP-DIM-begin-CONFIRMATIVE-INTR.IND-3SG
   'It had begun to turn red.'

(8) Kalaallisut (Greenlandic) (Fortescue 1984: 128)
 Inuullua-qqu-ti-kkit.
 live.well-tell-CAUS-2SG>3PL.IMPER
 'Say hello to them.'

Nouns and verbs are easily identified by their inflectional endings. The categories generally correspond well to their syntactic functions: morphological nouns typically serve as arguments and their modifiers, and morphological verbs as predicates. They also correspond well to expected semantics: morphological nouns refer to persons, animals, objects, concepts, etc. while morphological verbs denote events and states.

Most scholars of these languages agree that there are no adjective or adverb categories. Concepts expressed with adjectives in other languages can be predicated with verbs.

(9) Unangan (Aleut) (Bergsland 1994: xiii, 381)
 Ula-x̂   tagada-ku-x̂.
 house-ABS be.new-PRES-3SG
 'The house is new.'

(10) Central Alaskan Yup'ik (Elizabeth Ali, speaker, p.c.)
 Assiqapiartua.
 assir-qapiar-tu-a
 be.good-very-INTR.IND-1SG
 'I'm very good.'

(11) Iñupiaq (MacLean 1980: 29)
 Nakuuruq.
 nakuu-ru-q
 be.good-INTR.IND-3SG
 'It is good.'

(12) Kalaallisut (Fortescue 1984: 104)
 Iniqunartuq.
 iniqunar-tu-q
 sweet-INTR.IND-3SG
 'She is sweet.'

Nominalized verbs may serve as attributive modifiers, appositives to nouns.

(13) Central Alaskan Yup'ik (Elena Charles, speaker, p.c.)
 neqpiayagat   qatellriit
 neqa-piaq-yagaq-t   qater-lria-t
 fish-real-little-ABS.PL be.white-NMLZ-ABS.PL
 'little fish that are white' = 'white fish'

(14) Kalaallisut (Fortescue 1984: 303)
 illuqarvik   *angisuujusuq*
 illuu-qar-vik   angisuuju-**suq**
 live-habitually-place   be.big-NMLZ
 'a **big** town'

More often, attributive modification is accomplished by derivational suffixes (termed postbases in the literature).

(15) Unangan (Aleut) (Bergsland 1994: 502)
 *sla**diga**x̂*
 sla-**diga**-x̂
 weather-**good**-ABS
 '**good** weather'

(16) Central Siberian Yupik (Nagai 2001: 77.40)
 *aghve-**ghllag**-et.*
 whale-AUG-ABS.PL
 '**big** whales'

(17) Central Alaskan Yup'ik (Elena Charles, speaker)
 *piipi**raurluq***
 piipi-**rurluq**
 baby-**poor.dear**
 '**poor dear** baby'

(18) Iñupiaq (MacLean 1995: 340.264)
 uluqpani
 ulu-**qpak**-ni
 ulo-**big**-3RSG>3SG.ABS
 'her **large** crescent-shaped knife'

There are substantial inventories of such suffixes with meanings corresponding to those of adjectives in other languages. For Central Alaskan Yup'ik, for example, Jacobson (2012) lists suffixes with such meanings as 'dilapidated', 'cute', 'ugly', 'late (deceased)', 'leftover', 'darned', 'former', 'shabby', 'authentic', 'poor quality', 'secret', 'imitation', 'weak, helpless', 'oldest', 'large', 'major', 'dear old', 'poor dear', and 'funny old' among others. Such constructions may have originated as compounds, but the modifying elements are no longer roots; they never occur in word-initial position nor form the basis of words on their own.

There is also not a separate adverb category. A wide variety of meanings expressed in other languages with adverbs are expressed with derivational suffixes.

(19) Unangan (Aleut) (Bergsland 1994: 547)
Umlasaaĝukux̂.
umla-**saaĝu**-ku-x̂
wake.up-**recently**-PRES-3SG
'He woke up **a while ago**.'

(20) Central Alaskan Yup'ik (George Charles, speaker p.c.)
Yuaryaaqelria   *nalkuteksaunani.*
yuar-**yaaqe**-lria   nalkute-**ksaite**-na-ni
search-**in.vain**-INTR.PARTICIPIAL.3SG   find-**not.yet**-SUBORDINATIVE-3SG
'He looked **in vain** but didn't find it.'

(21) Iñupiaq: MacLean 1995: 311.064
Tulauraagaqhiruq.
tulak-**uraaq**-aqsi-ru-q
come.to.shore-**slowly**-begin-INTR.IND-3SG
'He **slowly** begins to head back to shore.'

All of the languages contain large inventories of suffixes which contribute various kinds of adverbial meanings. Among the Central Alaskan Yup'ik suffixes listed by Jacobson (2012) are some meaning 'repeatedly', 'usually', 'immediately', 'quickly', 'in a small way', 'more and more', 'finally', 'suddenly and willfully', 'abruptly', 'hurriedly', 'well, enjoyably, beneficially', 'slowly', 'for a while', 'late', 'customarily', 'habitually a lot', 'chronically', 'to no particular end', 'no longer', 'almost', 'for the first time', 'intensely', 'well', 'only, merely', 'briefly', 'hard at intervals', 'back and forth', 'purposely', 'insufficiently', 'never'.

Various other adverbial meanings are expressed by nouns in locative, ablative, allative, vialis, or equalis cases.

(22) Central Alaskan Yup'ik (Elizabeth Ali, speaker p.c.)
  a. *Nunamnek*   *watua*   *avai.*
     nuna-**mnek**   watua   ava=i
     land-**ABL**   right.now over.there=EXCL
     'I just came from home.'

  b. *Elitnaurvigmi*   *uitaunga*
     elite-naur-vik-**mi**   uita-u-nga
     learn-habitually-place-**LOC**   be.situated-INTR.IND-1SG
     'I'm at the school.'

  c. *Kiarlua,*   *egalerkun.*
     kiarte-lu-nga   egaleq-**kun**
     look.around-SUBORD-1SG   window-**VIA**
     'I'm looking out the window.'

  d. *Qanemcilria*   *elli-gguq,*   *yugtun.*
     qanemci-lria   elli=gguq   yuk-**tun**
     talk-INTR.PARTICIPIAL   3SG.ABS=HRS   person-**AEQUALIS**
     'He spoke in Yup'ik.'

31.3 Flexibility?

A long-standing question has been whether major lexical categories are actually distinguished in all languages. Some recent surveys are in van Lier (2016, 2017), van Lier & Rijkhoff (2013), and chapters in Rijkhoff & van Lier (2013) and Vapnarsky & Veneziano (2017). Are there a-categorial or polycategorial entities in some languages, entities that take on category membership only when they occur in larger grammatical constructions? The discussion raises the further question of levels of structure, whether classification should take place at the stem or word level. (See also Chapter 3.) In Eskaleut languages, flexibility can be found at both the simplex (root) and complex (derived) stem levels, in both native and loan vocabulary. Thus, in example (21) *tulak-* 'come to shore', *tulak-uraaq-* 'slowly come to shore', and *tulak-uraaq-aqsu-* 'begin to slowly come to shore' are all stems. The first, *tulak-* is a root and simplex stem, and the second and third, *tulak-uraaq-* and *tulak-uraaq-aqsu-*, are derived or complex stems. Any of these could be followed by a mood marker (like the Indicative here) and a pronominal suffix (like the third person singular here).

As just seen, noun and verb words are easily identified by their inflectional endings. But all of the languages contain some pairs of homophonous stems, both simplex (roots) and complex (roots + derivational suffixes) that occur inflected as nouns and verbs.

31.3.1 Simplex stems: Roots

Some samples of roots that form the basis of both nouns and verbs are in (23)–(25).

(23) Unangan (Aleut) (Bergsland 1994)
  aqchu-   'bladder dance'
           'to dance, dragging the feet on the floor'
  di-   'soot, lampblack (from oil burning in a lamp or stuck on stove)'
           'to make sooty'
  gu-   'tube, tubular opening, nostril'
           'to penetrate, go through, pass through'
  x̂ani-   'red sky at dawn and sunset, afterglow'
           'to set (of the sun or moon)'
  hya-   'flood tide'
           'to be covered up by the tide'
  idma-   'content, what is in it, especially fetus, pregnancy'
           'to fill, put a content into (as a seal stomach with dried fish)'
  kachi- 'breast, chest, hiccup'
           'to choke, gag, have something stuck in one's throat, have the hiccups'
  qa-   'fish'
           'to eat' (TR, INTR), 'to bite' (of fish) (INTR)
  tagdu- 'dried grass'
           'to tie (grass) in bundles (for making roof)'
  yaĝi-   'skin thong for sewing the skin to the baidarka (Aleutian kayak) frame'
           'to sew (the skin) to the baidarka frame'

(24) Central Alaskan Yup'ik (Jacobson 2012)
 caruyag-   'bad thoughts, fornication, something evil'
            'to fornicate, be unchaste'
 egilra   'life's path'
            'to move, be in motion'
 engve-   'mucus'
            'to blow one's nose'
 kalngak   'bag made of reeds and used for carrying fish, knapsack'
            'to carry something in a knapsack'
 mallu-   'beached carcass'
            'to find a beached carcass'
 quseq   'cough, cold'
            'to cough, to have a cold'
 taangaq   'liquor'
            'to drink liquor'
 talu   'split sinew'
            'to split sinew'
 uspeq   'weight, pound'
            'to weigh'
 yuurqaq   'hot beverage, tea'
            'to drink by sipping (hot drink such as coffee, tea, hot chocolate)'

(25) Iñupiaq (MacLean 1980)
 amIq   'animal hide, peel of fruit; skin covering for a boat or kayak frame'
            'to put a hide covering on something' = 'boat frame'
 auk   'blood'
            'to melt, bleed'
 iła-   'addition, relative'
            'to add on to something'
 malukalI   'rabid animal'
            'to become rabid'
 misak   'wet ground, slush swamp'
            'to be damp, slushy, swampy'
 qaaq   'marijuana'
            'to explode, pop; to smoke marijuana, to pop something (as a balloon)'
 siġrI   'wax or scales in ear'
            'to remove wax from one's ear'
 taalutaq   'lampshade; windbreak'
            'to block someone's view, to shade someone, protect someone from wind'
 usiaq   'load, cargo'
            'to haul (someone or something) in a vehicle'
 yapu   'poor person; sick, weak, unhealthy, or crippled person or animal'
            'to become physically weak'

A Central Alaskan Yup'ik noun and verb that appear to be based on the same stem *qaner-* can be seen in (26).

(26) Central Alaskan Yup'ik (Jacobson 2012: 531)
   a. *qanqa*
      qaner-qa
      mouth-1SG>3SG
      'my mouth'

   b. *Qaneraa.*
      qaner-a-aa
      say-TR.IND-3SG>3SG
      'S/he said it.'

In fact, such stems are pervasive, but flexibility is not a general feature of these languages. In all of the languages, the majority of stems can be inflected only as nouns or only as verbs. Some samples are in (27)–(29).

(27) Unangan (Aleut) (Bergsland 1994)
   a. Nouns only
ana-	'mother'
chaĝna-	'outgoing surf'
igachi-	'sinew, tendon, stringy muscle, sinew thread'
kayu-	'muscle, strength, power'
lina-	'mat, old sealskin used as mat in baidarka and for building tent'
ni-	'paternal aunt'
sa-	'bird'
tana-	'land'
uxchu-	'tufted puffin'

   b. Verbs only
hachi-	'to get stuck'
chuux-	'to sizzle'
itmax̂-	'to peck, jump on one spot (as when fishing from land)'
la-	'to gather, pick, pluck, dig out (berries, eggs, limpets, grass, roots)'
niix̂-	'to swear'
ngaax-	'to be afraid, apprehensive'
sasxa-	'to be solid, in good condition (as of clothes)'
taqi-	'to turn around (of boat, person, etc.)'
udix̂-	'to sting, burn (of exterior body parts, e.g. lips, eyes)'
yag-	'to be charitable'

(28) Central Alaskan Yup'ik (Jacobson 2012)
   a. Nouns only
aniniq	'spawning blackfish'
caniryak	'separate extra point placed on shaft of an arrow behind main point'
egkuq	'corner or wall of house or room'

kanaqlak	'muskrat'
makuaq	'ice crystal suspended in water, dust particle suspended in air'
nauciq	'hair at nape of neck'
pagaq	'line of grain in wood'
qaliq	'top layer, type of traditional Yup'ik parka on Nelson Island'
taituk	'fog, mist'
ugtaq	'seal on an ice floe or shore'

b. Verbs only

aniqlaa-	'to curse, threaten with undesirable thing'
cavte-	'to feel or touch intentionally with one's hand'
ikuygur-	'to be destroyed by going into the hole in the ice along with unguarded animal bladders during the Bladder Feast'
kanari-	'to die in one's sleep'
malig-	'to take or bring along'
naive-	'to transfer from one container to another by pouring'
pai-	'to stay behind with, to babysit'
qakte-	'to breech (whale, fish)'
tage-	'to go up from a body of water, go up any gradual incline, move back from the center of attention'
ugayar-	'to strip bare, take off one's clothes, pillage, rob, plunder'

(29) Iñupiaq (MacLean 1980)

a. Nouns only

aaka	'mother, grandmother'
kauk	'walrus skin with blubber'
maktak	'whale skin with blubber'
mana-q	'hook and line for retrieving seals'
paa	'entry, doorway, river mouth'
qaalu	'dried or spoiled outside part of a piece of meat'
siku	'ice'
taktuk	'fog'
ui	'husband'
uglu	'bird's nest', perch on ship's mast, crow's nest'

b. Verbs only

avit	'to get a divorce, split one's pants, to divorce someone'
igit-	'for blubber to turn to oil'
iva-	'to bear a litter, to whelp, to lay eggs and sit on them'
kakaaq-	'to carry someone on one's shoulders'
maqu-	'to become spoiled; be destroyed, a human relationship to deteriorate'
nunu-	'to restrain oneself from saying something or expressing a desire'
pai-	'to stay behind while others depart, usually in care of another'
qaĝa-	'to take it easy, not do any work (while another does)'
taki-	'to be long'
uŋa-	'to act as if one wants to be loved and cuddled, esp. of a young child'

Homophonous pairs are the result of conversion or zero derivation. Conversion is productive in these languages, but it is a word formation process: it produces lexemes. Speakers know which forms exist in the language and which do not, and what the precise meanings and uses are of each. The meanings of the members of each pair are usually clearly related, but they are not fully predictable.

(30) Unangan (Aleut) (Bergsland 1994: 350)
    samga-   'snout' (of animal, seal; nose, whiskers, lips)
    samga-   'to fall forward, on the belly, to bow down (as in church), to worship'

(31) Central Alaskan Yup'ik (Jacobson 2012: 396)
    mecuq   'liquid part of something, spa, juice, green/waterlogged wood'
    mecur-   'get blood poisoning'

(32) Iñupiaq (MacLean 1980: 34)
    niu   'leg'
    niu-   'to get out of a conveyance or container' (INTR)
          'to take someone or something out of a container (TR)

Sadock (2003: 4) cites Bergsland (1955ms), who estimated that 'in Kalaallisut, about 200 out of 1500 roots had noun and verb homophones, the rest being roughly equally divided between the two classes, verbal roots preponderating slightly'. The Central Alaskan Yup'ik dictionary by Jacobson (2012), generally considered nearly exhaustive, contains 6,500 lexical entries. Of these, 35% of stems are nouns only, 53% are verbs only, and only 12% are doublets.

For some pairs, one might guess that the noun came into the language first and the verb is the result of conversion, while in others, it might appear that the verb was first. In still others, it is difficult to imagine which meaning might be more basic. As speakers have observed, any intuitions they might have about basic versus derived status most likely come from the order in which they themselves first encountered them.

(33) Unangan (Aleut) (Bergsland 1994)
    a. *cha-*   'hand'
       chadu-   'to pick (berries)'

       chadu-   'fat, oil (of seal, whale, fish), diesel, butter'
       chadu-   'to oil, smear, butter'

    b. *saxta-*   'to be lazy, idle'
       saxta-   'laziness'

       saĝa-   'to sleep, be asleep'
       saĝa-   'sleep'

(34) Central Alaskan Yup'ik (Jacobson 2012)
    a. *nangcar-*   'to tow'
       nangcaq   'towed thing'

       ngel'ar-   'to laugh'
       ngel'aq   'a laugh'

    b. *kalngak*   'bag made of reeds and used for carrying fish, knapsack'
       kalngag-   'to carry something in a knapsack'

       yuurqaq   'hot beverage, tea'
       yuurqar-   'to drink by sipping hot drink'

(35) Iñupiaq (MacLean 1980)
     a. *nasaq*   'hood'
        nasaq-   'to put one's hood up, to put someone's hood up'

       kuvraq   'fishnet'
       kuvra-   'to catch (it) with a fishnet'

     b. *qaaq-*   'to explode, pop; to smoke marijuana, to pop something (as a balloon)'
        qaaq   'marijuana'

       iła-   'to add on to something'
       iła   'addition, relative'

31.3.2 Loanwords

The languages contain varying numbers of loanwords, reflecting the intensity of contact with other cultures. For Alaskans, the first major European contact was with Russians. Some but certainly not all borrowed terms have also been subject to conversion, indicating that the process is productive. In general, more nouns have been borrowed than verbs, but in some cases the term was first borrowed as a verb.

(36) Unangan (Aleut) conversion (Bergsland 1994: 372, 286; xxxvii, 250, 371)
     struusza-   'a plane'   from Russian *struzh* 'plane'
     struuza-   'to plane (wood)'

     para-   'steam (as from volcano)'   from Russian *par* 'steam'
     para-   'to steam up, to dampen'

     kuri-   'to smoke (tobacco)'   from Russian *kuri-* 'to smoke'
     kuri-   'smoke, cigarette'

     stamita-   'to decorate with a design (e.g. flowers)'
     stamita-   'woolen tassels (for ornament)'
                                    prob. from Russian *stavit'* 'to put, apply'

(37) Central Alaskan Yup'ik conversion (Jacobson 2012: 423, 495, 991–995)
     kankiiq   'ice skate'   from Russian *kon'kí*
     kankiir-   'to ice skate'

apiataq	'lunch'		from Russian *obéd*
apiatar-	'to eat lunch'		
piaskaq	'piece in checkers'		from Russian *péshka* 'pawn'
piaskar-	'to play checkers'		
peluskaq	'snuff'		
peluskar-	'to take snuff'		from Russian *próshka*

31.3.3 Derived stems

Eskaleut languages have extraordinarily rich inventories of derivational suffixes (postbases) with varying productivity. The suffixes show clear categoriality in two ways. First, some attach only to noun stems, some attach only to verb stems, and some attach to both. Second, some form new noun stems, some form new verb stems, and some appear to form both. Those that appear to form both are more appropriately viewed as homophonous nominalizing and verbalizing suffixes, just like stems. Samples of each type are in (38) and (39).

(38)   Unangan derivational suffixes (Bergsland 1994)

-dgusi- 'container for N' (501)
  N > N   *qaqa-*   'food'   *qaqa-dgusi-*   'pantry'

-dug- 'suddenly, intensely V' (503)
  V > V   *kim-*   'to descend'   *kim-dug-*   'to pour down (of rain)'

-nu- 'to smell or taste of N' (538)
  N > V   *qa-*   'fish'   *qa-nu-*   'to smell of fish'

-gali- 'one who is going to V' (505)
  V > N   *tunu-*   'to speak'   *tunu-gali-*   'messenger'

-mag- 'big, real N, to V greatly' (528)
  N > N   *ala-*   'whale'   *ala-max*   'humpback whale'
  V > V   *tada-*   'to step'   *tada-mag-*   'to trample'

-diga- 'good N', 'V well' (502)
  N > N   *sla-*   'weather'   *sla-diga-*   'good weather'
  V > V   *ma-*   'to do'   *ma-diga-*   'to be lucky'
  N > V   *qachx̂(i)-*   'skin'   *qachx̂i-ciga-*   'to be smooth'

-li 'to remove, lose from N, to (in)to N, prepare N' (521)
  N > N   *uyu-*   'neck'   *nyu-li-*   'neckerchief, scarf'
  N > V   *qaagu-*   'dust, dirt'   *qaagu-li-*   'to clean (house)'
  N > V   *akayu-*   'strait'   *akayu-li-*   'to cross a strait'
  V > V   *chag-*   'to split'   *chag-li-*   'to cut out'

(39) Central Alaskan Yup'ik derivational suffixes (Jacobson 2012)
   -aq   'thing that resembes N'   (740)
       N > N   tutgaq   'bedmate'   tutgar-aq   'grandchild'

   -ciryar- 'be easily V-ed'   (753)
       V > V   iqair-   'to be washed' iqair-ciryar-tut 'it is easily washed'

   -ssur-   'to hunt, seek, check N'   (757)
       N > V   tuntu   'caribou'   tuntu-ssur-tuq 's/he is caribou hunting'

   -cuun   'device for V-ing'   (758)
       V > N   merter-   'to get water' mertar-cuun 'bucket for getting water'

   -cuk   'unpleasing, ugly old N, bad result of V-ing'   (755)
       N > N   putukuq   'big toe'   putuku-cuk   'sore toe, ingrown toenail'
       V > N   nau-   'to grow'   nau-cuk   'growth on body, tumor'

   -(q)ite- 'to encounter, experience N or V'   (769)
       N > V   mecak   'puddle'   mec-qit-uq   's/he stepped in a puddle'
       V > V   etgate-   'to be shallow' etgal-qit-uq 's/he reached a shallow spot'

   -lluk-   'no good N, no good one V-s'   (795)
       N > N   ui   'husband'   ui-lku-a   'her no-good husband'
       V-> V   ayag-   'to leave'   aya-lkug-tuq 'the darned one left'

   -mik-   'thing held in one's N, to put in one's N'   (807)
       N > N   uya-   'neck'   uya-mik   'necklace'
       N > V   qaneq   'mouth'   qaner-mig-aa 'he put it in his mouth'
       V > N   kegge-   'to bite'   kegg-mia-q   'thing held in the teeth'

   -nerraq 'new N, one recently V-ed, to have recently V-ed'   (820)
       N > N   ciku   'ice'   ciku-nerraq 'new ice'
       V > N   kassuute- 'to marry'   kassute-   'newlyweds'
                                          nerraak
       V > V   ayag-   'to leave'   aya-nerrar- 's/he just left'
                                          tuq

The lexical categories of stems can thus be distinguished by both the derivational and flectional suffixes that attach to them.

It should be noted again that though the translations of some of the derivational suffixes resemble those of roots in other languages like English, they differ both formally and semantically (Mithun 1989). They never occur word-initially and can never serve as the foundation of words on their own. Furthermore, their meanings tend to be more diffuse, general, and often abstract than roots with similar translations. The Yup'ik suffix -liur-, for example, might appear to mean 'brush', based on the stem keggute-liur- 'brush teeth' (noun keggun = 'tooth'). But the same suffix occurs in qusngi-liur- 'cook reindeer meat' (qusngiq 'reindeer'), *kipusvi-liur-* 'work at the store' (*kipusvik* 'store'), *eq-iur-* 'chop wood' (*equk* 'wood'), and *neqe-liur-* 'cut fish' (*neqa* 'fish'). It also occurs in nominalizations like *qanikc-iur-un* 'shovel' (*qanikcaq* 'snow') and *ciku-liur-un* 'ice pick' (*ciku* 'ice') (Jacobson 2012: 793–794) The suffix *-tur-* might appear to mean 'eat', based on the stem *akutar-tur-* 'eat Eskimo ice cream' (*akutaq* 'mixture, Eskimo ice cream'). This same suffix occurs in stems *atkug-tur-* 'wear a parka' (*atkuk* 'parka'), *puyur-tur-* 'to smoke' (*puyuq* 'smoke'), *umuyuar-tur-* 'think' (*umyuaq* 'mind'), *penar-tur-* 'cliff-hunt for birds' (*penaq* 'cliff'), and *aug-tur-* 'take Communion' (*auk* 'blood') (Jacobson 2012: 888) The development of more diffuse and general meaning is a typical result of grammaticalization. These constructions may have originated in noun incorporation, N–V compounds, long before the time of Proto-Eskimo–Aleut, but the second elements are no longer roots.

31.4 Lexical subcategories

As in most languages, subcategories can be distinguished within the major lexical categories. Groups of words share some but not all features of the major categories. Within the Eskaleut family, several subcategories are traditionally distinguished within nouns. Most prominent are demonstratives, pronouns, and numerals.

31.4.1 Demonstratives

Eskaleut demonstratives are formally like nouns in that they distinguish case and number, though the precise forms of the inflectional suffixes do not always match those on nouns. Absolutive and ergative demonstratives function like demonstrative pronouns, while those in oblique cases function as demonstrative adverbs. Thus, Central Siberian Yupik absolutive *aagna*, for example, is 'the one over there', while the ablative *agumeng* is 'from over there'. Unangan (Aleut) demonstrative pronouns distinguish singular, dual, and plural number, like regular nouns; in Central Alaskan Yup'ik there is only a two-way number distinction on demonstratives, though nouns show a three-way distinction; and in Kalaallisut there is also only a two-way number distinction, but it matches that on nouns. Bergsland (1997: 74) provides examples of Unangan demonstratives inflected for possession as well: *wa* 'this, this one', *waning* 'this one of mine', *wakuning* 'these ones of mine', etc.

The systems are rich. There are basic distinctions between extended (moving, long, or of large extent), restricted (stationary, localized, visible), and obscured (stationary, indistinct, or out of sight) forms. Central Alaskan Yup'ik, for example, has distinct demonstratives for 'this near the speaker', 'that near the listener', 'the one over there or going away', 'the one across a significant feature of topography', 'the one inside, inland, or upriver', 'the one outside', 'the one down towards the river or down below', 'the one downriver, towards the sea, or towards the exit (from inside)', 'the one up, back away from the river, or behind', 'the one up above', 'the aforementioned one', and 'the one approaching'. There are a few unsurprising paradigm gaps: 'this near the speaker' and 'that near the listener' do not have invisible forms, 'the aforementioned one' has only invisible forms, and 'the one approaching' has only 'extended (moving) forms (Jacobson 2012: 968–970).

Like nouns, demonstrative roots can be subject to derivation, though certain suffixes are more likely to occur than others. For Unangan, Bergsland provides examples of derived stems based on the basic proximal demonstrative *wa* 'this, here'.

(40) Ungangan (Aleut) demonstrative *wa* 'here, now' (Bergsland 1994: 459–460)
      wa   'this, here'
      wa-aĝa-   'to come here, arrive here, come back'
      wa-aĝachxi- 'to send here'
      wa-aĝax̂ta-   'to pay a visit here'
      wa-aĝaala-   'to be brought up here'
      wa-aĝani-   'to wait for (coming here)'
      wa-aĝaasa-   'to bring here, deliver, bring back'
      wa-aĝat-   'to arrive (here)'
      wa-lita-   'to come here, pay a visit here'
      wa-anu-   'to be on the way here'
      wa-ngudax̂-   'to come this way'
      wa-atxa-   'to be close to here'
      wa-atxat-   'to come near'
      wa-aĝi-   'the nearest, on this side'
      wa-hligan   'right here'

As throughout the languages, the suffixes attached to initial demonstrative roots never occur on their own or in word-initial position: they always follow a noun stem. The suffix *-aĝa-* 'arrive at' in the first word of (40), for example, can be seen after the noun root *tana-* 'dwelling place' in the verb *tana-aĝa-* 'return to his settlement', and after the noun *ukalĝa-* 'the village here' in *ukalĝa-âga-* 'come to this village' (Bergsland 1994: 476).

For Iñupiaq, MacLean provides a few derivational suffixes that can be added to oblique demonstrative adverbs. The verbalizing suffix *-aq* is attached to vialis case demonstratives to add the meaning 'go via', the suffix *-q* is attached to ablative demonstratives to add the meaning 'go from', and *-nmun* and *-nmuk* are added to allative demonstratives to add the meaning 'travel to'.

(41) Iñupiaq demonstrative with derivational suffix (MacLean 1986: 49)
      Unuunnaaqtuat
      un-uuna-aq-tu-at
      down.there.EXTENDED-VIALIS-VERBALIZER-INTR.IND-3PL
      'They (long line of people or group of animals) went via down there.'

(42) Iñupiaq demonstrative with derivational suffix (MacLean 1986: 51)
      Unuŋanmuksimaruat
      un-uŋa-nmuk-simar-u-at
      far.out.on.sea.EXTENDED-KNOWN-ALL-INTR.IND-3PL
      'They were travelling seawards.'

31.4.2 Independent pronouns

The functional counterparts of unstressed pronouns in languages like English are the pronominal suffixes on verbs. The languages also contain free pronouns used for special discourse functions and in contexts where verbs do not provide sufficient information. The free pronouns generally show the same number and case distinctions as regular nouns in each language, but first and second persons do not distinguish absolutive, ergative, and genitive cases, and the forms of the case suffixes on these pronouns differ from those on nouns.

The independent pronouns in Unangan are based on a root *t(x)i-/ti-* inflected for person.

(43)   Anangan (Aleut) pronouns (Bergsland 1994: 397)
   a. *ti-ng*
      PRONOUN-1SG
      'I, me'

   b. *txi-dix*
      PRONOUN-2–3R.DU
      'you two, they two'

Those in Central Alaskan Yup'ik are based on a root *wii/wang-* for first person, and *ell-* for other persons, again inflected for person.

(44)   Central Alaskan Yup'ik pronouns (Jacobson 2012: 256)
   a. *wangkuta*
      wang-kuta
      1-PL
      'we/us/our'   (ABSOLUTIVE, ERGATIVE, GENITIVE)

   b. *elpet*
      ell-pet
      PRONOUN-2SG
      'you'   (ABSOLUTIVE, ERGATIVE, GENITIVE)

   c. *elkegni*
      ell-kek-ni
      PRONOUN-3DU-LOC
      'in them two'

To a very limited extent, the pronouns serve as bases for some further derivation.

(45)   Anangan (Atkan) pronominal derivation (Bergsland 1994: 397)
   a. *tix̂siidang*
      ti-x̂siida-ng
      PRONOUN-pitiful-1SG
      'poor me'

b. *t(x)inax̂chx̂ikuchaan*
   t(x)i-nax̂chx̂i-kucha-an
   PRONOUN-damned-DIM-2SG
   'you damned little one'

(46) Central Alaskan Yup'ik pronominal derivation (Jacobson 2012: 256)
   Elpenguuq   tarenrami.
   ell-pet-ngu-u-q   tarenraq-mi
   PRONOUN-2SG-be-INTR.IND-3SG   image-LOC
   'It's you in the picture.'

31.4.3 Numerals

Numerals also behave much like nouns. They occur on their own as words or in initial position within the word. They show similar arrays of numbers and cases, though again the forms of the suffixes are not always precisely the same.

The Unangan numeral *ataqa-n* 'one' ends in the regular singular, and *aala-x* 'two' ends in the regular dual *-x*, but *qaan-kun* 'three' has a special plural which matches that on demonstratives. This plural suffix *-kun* can also yield words with special meanings.

(47) Unangan *ataqan* 'one' (Bergsland 1994: 106–107)
   ataqakun
   ataqa-kun
   one-PL
   'one set, alone (of several), continuous, direct course'

The Central Alaskan Yup'ik numeral *atauci-q* 'one' ends in the regular singular *-q*, and *malru-k* ends in the regular dual *-k*. But the regular plural suffix on nouns is *-t*, while that used in numerals 'three' through 'eight' is *-n*: *pingayu-n* 'three', *cetama-n* 'four', etc. (The numerals 'nine' and 'ten' are marked as singular.) Again, with the root for 'one', number marking can yield special meanings.

(48) Central Alaskan Yup'ik *atauciq* 'one' (Jacobson 2012: 148–149)
   a. *atauciik*
      atauci-k
      one-DU
      'one pair'

   b. *atauciin*
      atauci-n
      one-PL
      'one group, a single set'

The numerals serve as bases for a few derivational suffixes.

(49) Unangan *ataqan* 'one' (Bergsland 1994: 107)
 a. *ataqadim*
   ataqa-dim
   one-time
   'at one occasion, all of a sudden, at once'

 b. *ataqaasa-*
   ataqa-usa-
   one-give.as-
   'to provide with one, get one for'

 c. *ataqaanut-*
   ataqa-uunu-t-
   one-move.N-ward-start/CAUS
   'to unite, be united, put together in one place'

 d. *ataqasi-*
   ataqa-si-
   one-gather
   'to put together, to gather'

(50) Central Alaskan Yup'ik 'one' (Jacobson 2012: 149)
 a. *ataucikun*
   atauci-kun
   one-VIALIS
   'all together, at once, at the same time, simultaneously'

 b. *ataucitun*
   atauci-tun
   one-EQUALIS
   'like one, simultaneously, in unison'

 c. *ataucirqumek*
   atauci-rqu-mek
   one-times-ABL
   'once'

 d. *ataucitaar-*
   atauci-taar-
   one-act.or.be.acted.on.in.groups.of
   'to act on one at a time'

 e. *atauciuqaqe-*
   atauci-u-qaqe-
   one-be-one.after.another-
   'to act on one at a time'

The numerals, too, can be subject to conversion. Bergsland notes that all of the Unangan roots for lower numerals have verbal counterparts. Used intransitively they mean 'to make, score', and used transitively they mean 'to get (game)'.

(51) Unangan (Aleut) (Bergsland 1997: 64)
Aaykaaĝu-x̂   sichi-ku-qing
fox-ABS   four-PRES-1SG>3SG
'I got four foxes.'

31.5 BEYOND THE WORD

As seen so far, nouns and verbs are recognizable at the word level by their inflectional endings: nouns end with number, case, and optionally with possessive marking, while verbs end with a mood marker and pronominal suffix, as seen earlier in Figures 31.2 and 31.3.

But there is more to the story. The inflectional mood markers on verbs mark expected independent clause distinctions such as indicative, interrogative, and imperative. There are also a number of dependent mood markers, which form dependent clauses expressing manner, time, cause, etc. The exact inventories of moods, the labels used to designate them, their forms, and their functions are not identical across the languages, but overall they are similar. Examples of some of the moods in Central Alaskan Yup'ik can be seen in the excerpt from a narrative in (52), with the mood markers in bold.

(52) Central Alaskan Yup'ik moods (Elizabeth Ali, speaker p.c.)
Ak'a   ayagyuarullermni
ak'a   ayagyuar-u-ller-mni
past   teenager-be-**PAST.CONTEMPORATIVE**-1SG
'A long time ago **when** I was young.'

ayagallurrunga   yuilqumun
ayag-ar-llur-**u**-nga   yuilquq-mun
leave-continually-**PAST**-INTR.INDICATIVE-1SG   wilderness-ALL
'I **was** out travelling in the wilderness.'

ilank   paqeluki
ila-nka   paqete-lu-ki
relative-1SG>3PL   visit-**SUBORDINATIVE**-R>3PL
'**going** to see my relatives'

ilaka   tauna   kassuuteqatallerani.
ila-ka   tauna   kassuute-qatar-**ller-a**ni
relative-1SG>3SG   that   marry-FUT-**CONTEMPORATIVE**.1–3SG
'**When** one relative was going to get married.'

Angyakun   ayallruama
angyaq-kun   ayag-llru-a-ma
boat-VIA   leave-PAST-CONSEQUENTIAL-1SG
'Because I travelled by boat.'

unaa-- angun   malikluku.
unaa   angun   malike-lu-ku
this   man   take.along-SUBORDINATIVE-R>3SG
'This man took me along.'

Tua-i-ll   'ayainanemegni,
tuai=llu   ayag-inaner-megni
and=too   go-PRES.CONTEMPORATIVE-1DU
'And as we two were travelling.'

pellaangukuk,
pellaa-nge-u-kuk
lose.way-begin-INTR.INDICATIVE-1DU
'We began to lose our way.'

cunawa   tamalriakuk.
cunawa   tamar-lria-kuk
thus   lose-INTR.PARTICIPIAL-1DU
'getting lost'

31.5.1 The Subordinative mood

Among the dependent moods is one termed the Subordinative, seen in 'going to see my relatives' above. (Terminology used for the moods in the various languages varies somewhat.) Subordinatives can serve as adverbial clauses, as in (53), (54), and (55).

(53)   Central Siberian Yupik (Nagai 2001: 63.10)
   Nayug-lu-ki   *kine-ngh-ata*
   skin.an.animal-SUBORDINATIVE-3PL   be.dry-CONTEMP-3PL
   'After skinning (the seals) and when the sealskins get dry'

   aghi-s-lu-ki   *uspeq-aq-iit*
   be.wet-CAUS-SUBORDINATIVE->3PL   work.on-HAB-TR.IND.3PL>3PL
   'dampening them they work on them'

   yaataaghq-aq-iit.
   prepare-HAB-IND.3PL>3PL
   'to prepare them for containers'

(54) Iñupiaq (MacLean 1995: 313.083)
Nallallaktuk
nallaq-llak-tu-k
llie.down-gradually-IND-3DU
'They lie down'

kilunmun   saallutik,
kilu-t-mun   saat-lu-tik
near-toward-ALL   to.face-SUBORDINATIVE-2DU
'**facing** the rear of the house'

stitqutik   kasuqtillakɬugit
siitquq-tik   kasuq-tit-llak-lu-git
knee-R.DU>PL   contact-CAUS-gradually-SUBORDINATIVE->3PL
'**letting** their knees touch.'

(55) Kalaallisut (West Greenlandic) (Fortescue 1984: 63)
Qiqirtaq   tuqqar-lu-gu
island   head.for-SUBORDINATIVE>3SG

paa-lir-pu-q.
paddle-begin-INTR.IND-3SG
'He began to paddle, **heading for** the island.'

The Kalallisut Subordinatives in (56) and (57) set off complement constructions.

(56) Kalaallisut (West Greenlandic) (Fortescue 1984: 39)
Mianirsur-lu-ni   ajunngin-niru-ssa-a-q.
be.careful-SUBORDINATIVE-R   be.good-more-FUT-IND-3SG
'It would be best [**to be careful**].'

(57) Kalaallisut (West Greenlandic) (Fortescue 1984: 58)
Uuqattaa-ssa-vara   kalaallisut   allal-lu-nga
try-FUT-1SG>IND.3SG   Greenlandic   write-SUBORDINATIVE-1SG
'I shall try [**writing** Greenlandic].'

In all of these examples, the Subordinative clauses are syntactically dependent. Their subjects must be coreferential with those of the main clauses.

The diachronic source of this Subordinative mood marker is still clear: it is a nominalizer, which Fortescue et al. reconstruct as Proto-Eskaleut *-lu(R) (2010: 451). It has reflexes of the same shape in all of the languages of the family. It is no longer productive as a nominalizer, but it remains in words in all of the languages, particularly terms for body parts. A few samples are in (58)–(61).

(58) Proto-Eskaleut * tam-lu 'chin' (Fortescue et al. 2010: 358)
Aleut   cam-lu-x̂
Sirenikski   tam-lu
Central Siberian Yupik   tam-lu
Naukanski   tam-lu
Central Alaskan Yup'ik   tam-lu-q
Alutiiq   tam-lu-(q)
Seward Peninsula Inuit   tav-lu
North Alaskan Inuit   tav-lu
Western Canadian Inuit   tav-lu
Eastern Canadian Inuit   ta-llu
Kalaallisut   ta-ɬɬu

(59) Proto-Eskimoan *kum-lu 'thumb' (Fortescue et al. 2010: 199)
Sirenikski   kum-la
Central Siberian Yupik   kum-lu
Naukanski   kum-lu
Central Alaskan Yup'ik   kum-lu-q
Alutiiq   kum-lu-q
Seward Peninsula Inuit   kuv-lu
Northern Alaskan Inuit   kuv-lu
Western Canadian Inuit   kuv-lu
Eastern Canadian Inuit   ku-llu
Kalaallisut   ku-ɬɬu-q

(60) Proto-Eskimoan *alu(ʀ) 'sole of foot' (Fortescue et al. 2010: 22)
Central Siberian Yupik   a-lu-q   'blade of paddle or oar'
Naukanski   alu   'sole of foot'
Central Alaskan Yup'ik   a-lu-(q)   'sole of boot or foot'
Seward Peninsual Inuit   a-lu-(q)   'sole'
Northern Alaskan Inuit   a-lu   'sole'
Western Canadian Inuit   a-lu   'sole'
Eastern Canadian Inuit   a-lu-q   'sole, central runner or keel span of kayak,
                                      bottom of sea or lake'

(61) Proto-Eskimoan *qav-lu(ʀ) 'eyebrow' (Fortescue et al. 2010: 318, 310)
Naukanski   qav-lu-q
Central Alaskan Yup'ik   qav-lu-q
Alutiiq   aquy-lu-q
Seward Peninsula Inuit   qav-lu
Northern Alaska Inuit   qav-lu
Western Canadian Inuit   qav-lu
Eastern Canadian Inuit   qa-llu
Kalaallisut   qa-ɬɬu.

The bases to which the nominalizer -*lu* was attached are in many cases no longer clear, though there are possible candidates. Fortescue et al. trace the base of the noun **a-lu-(q)* 'sole of foot' to Proto-Eskaleut **at(ə)-* 'down, lower part' (2010: 51). The noun **qav-lu* 'eyebrow' might be based on a Proto-Yupik verb root **qaviʀ-* 'curve, be slanted' (2010: 310). A root similar to that in **tam-lu-* 'chin' is a verb **tamuʀ* 'chew' (Aleut *taamu-* 'lick') (2010: 359). The development of a dependent clause marker from a nominalizer is not altogether surprising. A common strategy cross-linguistically for forming dependent clauses is nominalization: these are clauses that function syntactically much like nouns.

The development has gone further in these languages, however. Subordinative verbs are now also used in grammatically independent sentences. Their function of signalling dependency has been extended from the domain of the sentence to that of discourse. Subordinative sentences can describe situations that constitute sequences of closely related events or parts of a larger whole (Mithun 2008).

(62) St. Lawrence Yupik (Nagai 2001: 77.41)
      Taaq-negh-megteki   nengighq-aq-lu-ki.
      quit-CONTEMP-3R.PL>3PL   divide.one's.catch-HAB-SUBORDINATIVE->3PL
      'When they finish it (butchering), they **divide** the meat.'

      Inpi-qugh-aq-lu-teng.
      distribute.sharees.of.catch-completely-HAB-SUBORDINATIVE-3PL
      'They **distribute** shares completely.'

(63) Central Alaskan Yup'ik Subordinatives (Elizabeth Ali, speaker p.c.)
      Kuigkun   anelrarluni,
      kuik-kun   anelrar-lu-ni
      river-VIA   go.downriver-SUBORDINATIVE-3SG
      'He went downriver.'

      Kusquqvamun   ayagluni,
      Kusquqvak-mun   ayag-lu-ni
      Kuskokwim.River-ALL   leave-SUBORDINATIVE-3SG
      '**went** towards the Kuskokwim River'

      tua-i-ll'   ayaumalllinilria,
      tuai=llu   ayag-uma-llini-lria
      then=also   leave-long.time-apparently-PARTICIPIAL.3SG
      'then travelling for a very long time'

      ayakcaaraluni.
      ayag-caarar-lu-ni
      go-endeavor-SUBORDINATIVE-3SG
      'he was travelling with pleasure'

In this use, there is no longer a matrix clause they would be a constituent of, and their subjects no longer need be coreferential with that of another clause.

31.5.2 The Participial mood

All of the languages contain additional dependent moods, though they have developed in somewhat different ways in the various languages. Many have also developed from nominalizations. Among these are the Participials of Sirenkski and the Yupik languages. There are separate forms for intransitives and transitives. Fortescue et al. (2010) reconstruct the sources of both to Proto-Sirenksi-Yupik and beyond.

(64) Proto-Sirenikski-Yupik Nominalizer/Participial *lri(C)a(q) (Fortescue et al. 2010: 450)
    Sirenikski   -ɬɹəX   'one that is -ing or has -ed'
    Naukanski   -lʀria   'one that is -ing'
    Central Alaskan Yup'ik -lʀia,   PL -lʀriit   'one who is -ing'
    Alutiiq   -lʀaa,   PL -lʀriit   'one who is -ing'
    Perhaps related to Aleut -la(a)ʀana-X   'one who recently -ed'

(65) Proto-Eskaleut Nominalizer/Participial (Fortescue et al. *-kə 2010: 443)
    Aleut   -ku-X   present/participial marker
    Sirenikski   -kə-   transitive participial (may be used for indicative)
    Central Siberian Yupik   -kə-   'something one is -ing', and participial mood
    Central Alaskan Yupik   -kə-   'that which one is -ing', transitive participial mood
    Alutiiq   -kə-   nominalizer, transitive past tense
    Seward Peninsula Inuit   -yi-   transitive indicative mood marker
    Northern Alaskan Inuit   -yi-
    Western Canadian Inuit   -yi-
    Greenlandic Inuit   -yi-   transitive participial mood marker

The nominalizers are still quite productive in the modern languages, forming nouns which refer to what would be the absolutives of the verbs they attach to. The transitives occur with the same possessive suffixes that occur on other nouns.

(66) Central Siberian Yupik Intransitive
    Nominalizer (Jacobson 1979: 58)
    neghelghii
    neghe-lghii
    eat-INTR.NOMINALIZER
    'the one who ate'

(67) Central Siberian Yupik Transitive
    Nominalizer (Jacobson 1979: 58)
    neghegkaka
    negheg-ka-ka
    eat-TR.NOMINALIZER-1SG>3SG
    'my eaten thing' = 'the thing I ate'

(68) Central Alaskan Yup'ik Intransitive
Nominalizer (George Charles, speaker p.c.)
qavalria
qavar-lria
sleep-INTR.NOMINALIZER
'the one sleeping'

(69) Central Alaskan Yup'ik Transitive
Nominalizer (George Charles, speaker p.c.)
nerkeka
nere-ke-ka
eat-TR.NOMINALIZER-1SG>3SG
'the thing I am eating'

As seen earlier in (13), nominalizations can be used in apposition to other nominals as modifiers. Clauses nominalized with these markers can function like relative clauses, adding information about a referent.

(70) Central Siberian Yupik (de Reuse 1994: 46)
Mekelghiighet   quyungighyaghnaqelghiit
mekelghiigh-t   quyngigh-yagh-naqe-lghii-t
boy-ABS.PL   reindeer-.go.after-PROSP-INTR.NOMINALIZER-PL

maliggnaqanka.
maligte-naqe-a-nka
follow-PROSPECTIVE-IND-1SG>3PL
'I am going to follow the boys **who were going after the reindeer**.'

Such nominalized clauses are also often used more generally to simply add additional information to the discussion.

(71) Central Alaskan Yup'ik Intransitive Participial (Elizabeth Ali, speaker p.c.)
Tauna	*nasaurluq,*	*piyualuni*	*cakneq...*
tauna	nasaurluq	piyua-lu-ni	cakneq
that	girl	walk-SUBORDINATIVE-3SG	very

'The girl walked very fast.'

avavet	*avatmun*	*ayalria, ...*
ava-vet	ava-tmun	ayag-lria
there-ALL	there-ward	go-INTR.PARTICIPIAL.3SG

'**going** this way and that ...'

The development of the Participial mood has followed a trajectory similar to that of the Subordinative. Nominalizers have been extended from their word-formation function of deriving noun stems, to a syntactic function of marking dependent clauses, then further to a discourse function marking relations among independent sentences.

As independent sentences, they still add supplementary information, typically off the event line.

(72) Central Siberian Yupik Intransitive Participial (Nagai 2001: 113)
'Long ago, they said some had real good houses just like us now.'
Ne-keg-sa-ghwaagh-aqe-lghii-t.
home-have.good-CAUS-thoroughly-HAB-INTR.PARTICIPIAL-3PL
'They used to maintain their houses very well and keep them tidy.'

(73) Central Siberian Yupik (Nagai 2001: 111.5)
'They used to keep on using seal oil lamps like that.'

Nani-m   puyuqe-rug-aqe-g-ka-ngi
seal.oil.lap-ERG.SG   become.sooty-AUG-HAB-EP-TR.PARTICIPIAL.3SG>3PL

puyuq-aqe-g-ka-ngi   entaqun.
become.sooty-HAB-EP-PARTICIPIAL.3SG>3PL   maybe
'Maybe the seal oil lamp used to make the houses very sooty.'

A departure from the event line can be seen in the remark in (74) when a speaker was telling a joke.

(74) Central Alaskan Yup'ik (George Charles, speaker p.c.)
Alartellrianga-tang.
alarte-lria-nga=tang
err-INTR.PARTICIPIAL-1SG=look
'Oh look, I made a mistake.'

31.5.3 The Indicative mood

One of the Indicative mood markers apparently followed a similar trajectory. As noted earlier, nominal possession is marked with suffixes on both the possessum and the possessor. The noun referring to the possession is marked with a transitive suffix identifying the possessor and the possessed: *angya-gka* 'boat-1SG>3DU' = 'my two boats'. Most of the pronominal suffixes on transitive Indicative verbs match these nominal possessive suffixes.

(75) Central Alaskan Yup'ik (Jacobson 1994: 113)
angyaq	'boat'	ner'-a-	'eat'
angya-qa	'my boat'	ner'-a-qa	'I am eating it'
angya-gka	'my two boats'	ner'-a-gka	'I am eating the two'
angya-nka	'my boats'	ner'-a-nka	'I am eating them'
angya-n	'your boat'	ner'-a-n	'you are eating it'
angya-ten	'your boats'	ner'-a-ten	'you are eating them'
angya-put	'our boat(s)'	ner'-a-put	'we are eating it/them'

angya-ci	'you all, your boat(s)'	ner'-a-ci	'you'll are eating it/them'
angya-a	'his/her boat'	ner-a-a	's/he is eating it'
angya-ak	'they two, their boat'	ner-a-ak	'they two are eating it'
angya-at	'their boat'	ner-a-at	'they are eating it'
angy-ak	'his/her two boats'	ner'-a-k	's/he is eating the two'
	etc.		etc.

(76) Kalaallisut (Greenlandic) (Sadock 1999: 400)

illug-a	'my house'	takuar-a	'I see it'
illuk-ka	'my houses'	takuak-ka	'I see them'
illu-t	'your house'	takua-t	'you see it'
illu-tit	'your houses'	takua-tit	'you see them'
ilu-a	'his/her house'	takua-a	's/he sees him/her/it'
illu-i	'his/her houses'	takua-i	's/he sees them'
etc.			etc.

Nouns referring to the possessor are marked with genitive case suffixes.

(77) Central Alaskan Yup'ik genitive (Elena Charles, speaker p.c.)
 arna-m pani-a
 arnaq-m panik-a
 woman-GEN.SG daughter-3SG>3SG
 woman's her daughter
 'the woman's daughter'

In transitive Indicative clauses, the ergative case suffix has exactly the same form as the genitive.

(78) Central Alaskan Yup'ik ergative (Elena Charles, speaker p.c.)
 Arnam payugtellrua.
 arnaq-m payugte-llru-a-a
 woman-ERG.SG bring.food.to-PAST-TR.IND-3SG>1SG
 'The woman brought her food.'

The Central Alaskan Yup'ik transitive Indicative suffix has exactly the same form as a nominalizer. It also shows the same complex idiosyncratic phonological behaviour, indicated by Jacobson with special symbols.

(79) Central Alaskan Yup'ik (Jacobson 2012: 739, 920)
 a. +'(g)aq- 'that which has been V-ed'
  iqair- 'to wash' iqair-a-q 'washed article of clothing'
  iqair-a-nka 'my washed things'
   = 'the things I washed'

 b. +(g)aq- Transitive Indicative mood
  iqair- 'to wash' iaqir-a-nka 'I washed them'

Further discussion of historical developments shaping modern ergative systems can be found in Bergsland (1989) and Fortescue (1995).

31.6 CONCLUSION

It was once hypothesized that there is no noun–verb distinction in Eskimo–Aleut languages: all inflected words are actually nouns. In fact, the distinction is clear at the root, derived stem, and word levels. Several factors could have led to such a hypothesis. One is that there is conversion (zero derivation) at both the root and derived stem levels, resulting in homophonous noun and verb stems. This is not polycategoriality. Speakers know which stems exist and which do not, and what their specific meanings are, meanings not necessarily obvious from the stem alone and its lexical category.

Adding further complexity to the issue is an extensive history throughout the family of forming dependent clauses by morphological nominalization of verbs. Some of these dependent clause constructions have been extended to use as independent sentences with special discourse functions. But their histories have left their mark, in matching forms for ergative and genitive cases on nouns, and matching forms for possessive suffixes on nouns and certain pronominal suffixes on verbs. As in so many cases, an understanding of the stages by which the structures have developed provides explanations for the modern configurations we find.

CHAPTER 32

WORD CLASSES IN MAYAN LANGUAGES

VALENTINA VAPNARSKY

32.1 INTRODUCTION

MAYAN languages present interesting properties that question word classes and the determination of lexical categories at the root and the stem level. Whereas Colonial descriptions analysed Mayan languages through the lens of Latin categories, grammarians of the 19th and early 20th centuries, struck by the similarities between Mayan nominal and verbal phrases, adopted a nominalist view. They saw nominal structures as primary, including for the reference to actions and events (see Lois & Vapnarsky 2003: 15). However, extensive studies carried out over the last decades have revealed significantly more complex word-class patterns. Studies have confirmed the existence of a clear N/V opposition, while showing the central role performed by verbo-nominal forms and nominalizations in the expression of events, both diachronically and synchronically. Works on linguistic acquisition have also shown that verbs are acquired earlier than nouns in Mayan languages (Brown 1998; de Leon 2001; Pfeiler 2006). Furthermore, convergent and divergent word-class patterns have been brought to light within the family that reveal the tension between rather strong lexical categorial determination, on the one hand (which may affect all levels, from roots to word forms, and from phonology to syntax), and, on the other hand, categorial flexibility and polyvalence. Such phenomena as well as the relation between root and stem word categories have led to different approaches to the analysis of Mayan word classes. Another point of interest of Mayan languages is a set of word classes (such as Positionals, Expressives/Ideophones, Classifiers) absent from the most studied languages of the world, despite their importance typologically (Evans & Levinson 2009).

In section 32.2, I present basic facts about Mayan languages and their grammar. Section 32.3 outlines the relation between roots, stems, and word classes, and provides an overview of the processes of word formation and their relations with word classes. In the following sections, I concentrate on the major word classes of Mayan languages, and the relations between them: Verbs (section 32.4), Nouns (section 32.5), Verbal nouns and verbo-nominals (section 32.6), Adjectives and participles (section 32.7), Positionals (section 32.8), Expressives (section 32.9), and Classifiers (section 32.10). Special attention is given to crossover phenomena between classes, as these represent productive dynamics in these languages.

Examples without references come from personal corpora collected during years of fieldwork with Yucatec Maya speakers in the state of Quintana Roo, Mexico, and with Itza' speakers in Guatemala. Examples from over a dozen other Mayan languages are given for comparison and to illustrate contrastive properties, but Yucatec is often preferred for expository purposes and to provide previously unpublished data. Yucatec also shows interesting patterns concerning word-class flexibility within the family. This chapter only intends to provide a general introduction to word classes in Mayan languages and to analytical issues related to them; more details on language specific patterns can be found in the references.

32.2 THE MAYAN LANGUAGES

32.2.1 The Mayan language family

The Mayan family numbers about 30 languages, many with significant dialectal variation. These are languages of Mesoamerica, now spoken in South-East Mexico, Guatemala, and Belize, and by migrants, mainly in the United States. In the past, the Maya area extended to what is today western Honduras and El Salvador. The Maya region is traditionally divided into two main geographical areas: Lowlands Maya, located in the lowlands of north Guatemala, Belize, southern Mexico and parts of Honduras, and Highlands Maya, along the Sierra Madre de Chiapas, from Chiapas in Mexico, across southern Guatemala and onwards into El Salvador. This division partially matches the linguistic branches of the family, with major diffusion patterns found within these vast areas (Campbell & Kaufman 1985; Campbell et al. 1986; Campbell 2017; Law and Stuart 2017). The term Classic Maya refers to the language attested in ancient Mayan hieroglyphic writing. Proto-Mayan refers to the hypothetical common ancestor of the language family. Mayan languages share a number of features with the other languages of Mesoamerica, with which they have been in contact for millennia (Campbell 2017; Law & Stuart 2017).

There are presently more than six million Maya speakers living in traditional Maya areas, and due to recent migrations, now also in northern parts of Mexico and the United States. Strong contrasts in linguistic vitality are observed within the family, ranging from highly endangered languages, such as Itza' and Mocho', with only a dozen speakers left, to much more living languages, such as Yucatec in Mexico with some 850,000 speakers, and Q'eqchi' and K'iche' in Guatemala with over one million speakers. However, in all languages, rapid socio-economic and technological changes have increasingly affected linguistic practices over the last decades, inducing more languages shifts towards non-Mayan languages (Spanish, and also English in Belize and the USA), and more lexical and structural influences and calques from these languages to Mayan languages.

32.2.2 Basic characteristics of Mayan languages grammar

Mayan languages are polysynthetic to various degrees. Mayan lexical roots have a general CVC format (about 90%–95% of the roots). Mayan phonological systems include series of plain voiceless and glottalized stops and coronal affricates. Vowels may also be glottalized, they show length contrasts in most languages and tone contrasts as an innovation in a few of them, including Yucatec, with lexical and grammatical functions (Bennett 2016; England & Baird 2017 and references therein). Words can be formed by bare roots, but more frequently they are complex combinations of compound roots, derivational and inflexional affixes and other morphophonological markings, such as vowel alternation and reduplication (see section 32.3.2).

Most words can function as predicates, a pattern analysed as omnipredicativity (Vapnarsky 2013). There is no equative copula for nominal and adjectival predication (but an existential predicate is needed for existential sentences). Predicates correspond to two main classes: verbal predicates, and non-verbal or stative predicates. The main distinctive property of verbal predicates is that they need to be marked for aspect.

All members of the Mayan family are ergative head-marking languages (a pattern reconstructed for Proto-Mayan), with obligatory indexation of the main arguments on the predicate. Morphologically, ergativity is expressed by person markers on the predicate, which do not require the presence of external NPs. In most languages, the sets of person markers used for verbs are shared with non-verbal predicates. Person indexes are traditionally tagged as set A and set B markers, which partially correspond to ergative and absolutive markers. Set A indexes the transitive subject, the nominal possessor, and the sole argument of intransitives in split ergativity constructions. Set B indexes the sole argument of intransitives and stative predicates (including nouns, adjectives, participles, deictics) as well as the transitive object. In (1), a second person set B marker (-*ech*) is used to index the sole argument of a nominal predicate in (a), the object of a transitive verbal predicate in (b), the sole argument of an intransitive verbal predicate in (c) and of an adjectival predicate in (d). In (2), a second person set A marker (*a-*) indexes the subject of a transitive predicate and the possessor of a nominal.

(1) Yucatec (a-d are parts of the same utterance)
    a. *tumen*   *teech=e'*   *jeeneral-ech*
        because PR2=TOP   general-B2SG
        'Because you, you are a general

    b. *yan*   *k-yáabil-t-(i)k-ech*   (…)
        DEON   A1-love-TRZER-IPFV.TR-B2
        'we must adore you   (…)'

    c. *teech*   *tun=e'*,   *le*   *ken*   *líik'-ech*   *tun*
        PR2   thus=TOP   DET   CONJ   rise-B3   thus
        'So you, when you'll stand up.'

    d. *te'*   *tu'ux*   *xool-okbal-ech*   *tun=o'*, (…)
        LOC   where   kneel-POSIT.PART-B2   thus=DEIC
        'from where you were kneeling (…)'

(2) Yucatec
     Yan   *a-ta-s-ik-ø*   *a-k'aan*
     DEON   A2-come-CAUS-IPFV.TR-B3   A2-hammock
     'You must bring your hammock.'

A few languages have developed verbal–non-verbal distinctions within the person index sets. Mam shows slight differences in set B markers between verbal and non-verbal predicates (England 1983, 2017: 503), whereas Ch'orti went a step further by creating a third set (set C), partially developed from set A, for the sole argument of intransitives in the imperfective (Edmonson 1988: 8; Becquey 2014: 229ff.).

Different types of split ergativity are observed across the family, triggered by a variety of factors depending on the language: aspect, clausal dependency, participant salience, and inherent features of the predicate, in particular +/− agentivity. Alternative alignment patterns depend on the triggering factor and the language: accusative, tripartite, neutral, inverse, or obviative, and active (see Zavala Maldonado 2017 for more details). Ergativity also governs some aspects of Mayan syntax with reflexes in constructions such as focus, relative clauses, information interrogatives, or control in subordinate clauses (Aissen 2017a; Zavala Maldonado 2017).

Word order in Mayan has been the object of much discussion. Yet, most researchers agree that it is Predicate initial, for non-verbal and verbal predicates alike. For the latter, it is VS for intransitives, and in transitives, rigid or more flexible VOS and VSO orders are found, depending on languages or within a language. However, it is rare that the two arguments are lexically represented together. When they are, one is often fronted with dedicated topic or focus constructions (see England 1991; Verhoeven and Skopeteas 2015; Clemens and Coon 2018, among others). For recent overviews on Mayan languages, see England and Zavala 2013, Bennett et al. 2016, Aissen et al. 2017, and Polian 2017a on morphology and lexical classes.

32.3 WORD CLASSES IN MAYAN LANGUAGES

32.3.1 Roots, stems, and word classes

Considering Mayan word classes requires us to distinguish the root from the stem level, since 'root classes do not map directly to surface lexical category ... but need the addition of functional morphology in order to form stems' (Coon 2019: 36). Roots of a particular class may often enter a variety of different surface stem forms, and the morphology required to form these stems may be used as diagnostic of root classes (see discussion in Haviland 1994; Lois & Vapnarsky 2006; Lois 2011; Coon 2019).

A number of roots can be used without derivation to form a surface word in one specific word-class category. Thus, in Yucatec, *LU'UM* 'earth, soil' is considered an N (Nominal root), because the bare form is used as a noun, and it requires derivation to form intransitive and transitive verbs such as *lu'um-tal* 'become earth', *lu'um-kíins* 'turn X into earth', *lu'um-bes* 'put earth into/onto X for a specific purpose', see ex. (3). By contrast, the root *XOK* 'count, read, study' is analysed as a Transitive root because it forms transitives without derivation, as in (4), contrary to, say, *OK* 'enter', which is considered an Intransitive root since it forms intransitives without derivation as in (5a), but requires a causativizer *-s* to form transitives, as in (5b).

(3) Yucatec'
a. *jach yan-ø* **lu'um** *way=e'*
very EXIST-B3 earth here=TOP
'There is a lot of earth here.'

b. *k-u-lu'um-tal*
ICP-A3-earth-INCH.ICP
'It's becoming earthy.'

c. *t-in-lu'um-bes-aj-ø   in-séemiya yo'osa   mun-la'ab-a(l)*
CP.TR-A1-earth-CAUS-PFV.TR-B3 A1-seed CONJ NEG.A3-damage.PASS-IPFV.INTR
'I put earth on my seeds so that they don't get damaged.'

(4) Yucatec
t-u-xok-aj-ø   uy-aalak'   k'eek'en
CP.TR-A3-count-PFV.TR-B3 A3-CLF.domestic_animal pig
'She counted her pigs.'

(5) Yucatec
a. *ka   j   ok-en*
CONJ CP.INTR enter-B1
'and I came in.'

b. *t-inw-ok-s-aj-ø   in-p'o'*
CP.TR-A1-enter-CAUS-PFV.TR-B3 A1-wash
'I took my washing in.'

In studies on Mayan languages, the stem category in which the bare root is used has been commonly taken as the basic categorial class of the root. Based on this criterion, Mayan grammars generally distinguish between the following main root classes: nominal roots (N), verbal roots: intransitive (Intr) or transitive (Tr), adjectival (Adj), and Classifier. Root classes may also present phonological contrasts. Whereas roots associated with verbal features are in general rigidly monosyllabic CVCs, other templates are also available to N and Adj roots (see sections 32.5 and 32.6).[1]

However, the relation between Mayan root classes and lexical category is often less straightforward. First, some roots always require derivation to form surface stems. This is the case in particular of Positional roots, developed in section 32.8. Second, a significant number of roots behave as roots from several classes. This is common with Transitive and Positional, but it is also found for other combinations, resulting in underived uses in different surface lexical categories. Thus, the root *p'o'* 'wash' in Yucatec is used as a nominal stem in its bare form in (6a) (see also (5a)), and also forms intransitive (6b) and transitive verbs (6c) with only the required inflection. This last pattern is especially representative of verbo-nominal roots in Yucatecan languages, related to Verbal Nouns (see section 32.6).

(6) Yucatec
a. *lel=a'   in-p'o'*
DET=DEIC A1-wash
'This is my washing (= what I have washed).'

b. *t-in-p'o'*
PROG-A1-wash
'I'm washing.'

c. *t-in-p'o'-ik-ø   nook'*
PROG-A1-wash-IPFV.TR cloth
'I'm washing clothes.'

---

[1] A significant number of nominal and adjectival disyllabic roots may result from frozen suffixation or reduplication patterns (for Yucatecan, see Lois & Vapnarsky 2003: 138).

All these patterns question the nature of the root determination regarding lexical categories. How should they be interpreted? Some authors describe these cases as *overlaps*, with a significant number of roots repeated in separated root classes (e.g. Mateo Toledo 2017 for Q'anjobal). Others suggest *polyvalence* (Smith-Stark 1983: 181ff.) or *mixed roots* (Haviland 1994), focusing on the ability of specific roots to combine properties of two (or more) root classes.[2] Still others believe that such flexibility has repercussions on the understanding of the very nature of lexical root classes. This idea was explored for Yucatecan, using the notion of *categorial polyvalence* or *polycategoriality* (Lois & Vapnarsky 2003, 2006; Vapnarsky & Veneziano 2017). A polycategorial item can be used in various lexical categories with an identical form. At the root level, categorial polyvalence is the ability for a root to be instantiated in different lexical categories without cross-category derivation. Coon (2019) elaborates a related view within a generative framework proposing that in Chuj, root class does not map directly to surface lexical category, but does determine which functional heads (i.e. valence morphology) may merge with the root (Coon 2019: 35). These analyses share some principles with certain theoretical frameworks, in particular Distributed Morphology (see Chapter 13), although they consider that Mayan roots are not acategorical in the strict sense.

32.3.2 Word-formation processes and word classes

Mayan languages have four main word-formation processes:

- affixation (prefixes, suffixes, rare infixes) for inflexion and derivation;
- vowel alternation (change of length, tone, rearticulation, e.g. Yucatec: *wuts*' 'fold' (TR) (active), *wuuts*' 'fold' (antipassive), *wu'uts*' 'be folded' (passive), *wúuts*' 'bend' (middle))
- reduplication (full/partial reduplications, often combined with fixed segments, e.g. Yucatec: *chokoj-chokoj* 'very hot', *wu'u-wu'uts*' 'folded in several places', *wuuts'-en-wuuts*' 'folded here and there (several objects)'
- compounding and incorporation (e.g. Yucatec: *wuts'-ju'un* 'fold-paper', *ka'-wuts*' 'fold again').

Conversion also occurs, although in some cases, alternative analysis in terms of categorial flexibility is possible.

Word-formation processes may affect word classes differently. Derivational affixation is mainly realized by suffixes and concerns all stem classes. Vowel alternation and reduplication (including fixed-segment reduplication) are clearly more productive in verbs (for transitivity/voice changes), classifiers, and ideophones, than in nouns.[3]

Compounding is more open, and forms a large variety of nouns, with the modifier element in first position (e.g. Ixil from Chajul, Adell 2019: *tch'u'.ka'* [breastN.stoneN] 'grindstone/

---

[2] It is also revealing that in major modern dictionaries of Mayan languages, which use the root as the main lexical entry, the lexical characterization of many roots includes at least two categorial groups, or is left as X 'undeterminable'. See in particular Bricker et al. 1998; Hofling 1997, 2014; Laughlin 1975. Polian 2018 avoids this difficulty by using the lexical word as the main entry. Smith-Stark (1983: 193) also signals many unclassified roots in Poqomam.

[3] For nouns, vowel alternation occurs as a vestige of a possession marking pattern, see section 32.5.1. Reduplication is possible in Tseltal for certain nouns to signal plural distributivity (Polian 2013a: 394).

mortar', *nim-la.q'ij* [bigAdj-attributive.dayN] 'celebration', *tchi'.k'u'l* [biteV.mindN] 'envy', etc.), as well as adjectives (e.g. Lacandon, Hofling 2014: *jujup-säk* [insertT.RED-whiteAdj] 'clear white', *ki'-b'ook* [tastyAdj-smell] 'tasty, smelling good'), expressives, numerals (Ixil *vinaq-ox-va'l* [person/tweenty-three-one] 'twenty-three'), and numeral expressions (see section 32.10). In the verbal domain, the most productive compounding is achieved by noun incorporation, in particular of the object (see for instance Gutierrez Bravo 2002 for Yucatec). Object incorporation (root/derived Vtr + N) shows an increasing degree of morphosyntactic integration in Eastern Mayan (7), Q'anjobalan and Yucatecan (8): compare the position of the incorporated N (underlined) in relation with the antipassive marker (in bold) in (7) and (8) (see also Polian 2017a: 207–208).

(7) Southern Mam (England 2017: 522)
    ex   ma   chin   k'aayi-**n**   <u>kxminch'il</u>=e'
    and   PROX   B1SG   sell-ANTIP   cherry=1SG
    'And I also sold cherries.'

(8) Yucatec
    kon-<u>xaak</u>-**n**-aj-en
    sell.TR-basket-ANTIP-INTR-B1
    'I sold baskets.'

In branches such as Cholan and Yucatecan, adverb incorporation is very productive with a small set of adverbs (maybe the only root adverbs in these languages). Less productively, verb compounds can also occur with instrument (Vtr–Nintr), positionals, adjectives, or as V–V compounds. For a more detailed overview of word-formation processes in Mayan languages, see Polian (2017a).

32.4 VERBS

32.4.1 General properties of Verbs

In Mayan languages, verbs are the most morphologically complex words. They carry inflexional affixes for person, aspect, mood, and transitivity; (9) gives the schematic structure of the VP (some cross-linguistic differences are mentioned below the structures, others may occur within specific languages).

(9) Verbal Phrase [without lexical arguments]
    (T)AM[i]—Absolutive [SetB][ii]—Ergative [SetA]—DIR[iii]/ ADV[iv]—**Root**—Compound Root[v]—Deriv [transcategorial, voice]—Status Suffixes—Absolutive [SetB][ii]
    [i] (T)AM: Depending on forms, (T)AM can be prefixed or function as an auxiliary or a pre-verbal predicate.
    [ii] [SetB]: Set B is originally pre-predicate, but Lowland languages and Ixil have developed a consistently post-predicate placement (Law 2009).

[iii] DIR: The position of directionals, before or after the root, varies cross-linguistically and even within a language, depending on verb class or mood.
[iv] ADV: A small set of adverbs can occur in this position in some languages.
v The order of the compounded roots depends on the type of compounding.

All Mayan languages share a general tense–aspect–mood (TAM) system, where aspect, mood, and occasionally tense information may be marked on two main positions, often in combination: pre-verbal (either as an aspectual prefix or a TAM auxiliary) and postverbal (called 'status' or 'thematic' suffix). Verbs are generally inflected with status suffixes which combine transitivity (transitive/intransitive), mood (indicative/subjunctive–optative/imperative), syntactic (independent/dependant), and often aspectual (imperfective/perfective) features. Status suffixes may also be sensitive to the contrast between root and derived forms (e.g. 'thematic vowels' in Poqomam, see Smith-Stark 1983), and to focus constructions (e.g. agent and manner adverb focus in Yucatec, Vapnarsky 2013). Status suffixes appear as reflexes of conjugation systems implying verb classes. The imperfective/progressive corresponds historically and sometimes synchronically to a complex clause where the aspect marker is the high predicate and the action is expressed by a nominal form. In some languages such as Yucatec, the grammaticalization of the aspect predicate led to the reanalysis of the nominal argument as the main verbal predicate of the clause (see Robertson 1980; Zavala Maldonado 2017: 234–235; section 32.6).

Derivational morphemes often co-occur, especially for different types of transitivization, voice, and pluractionality markers (Henderson 2017). Verbs may integrate objects, adverbs, or directionals.

To illustrate, the utterance in (10) includes two transitive verbs in the progressive (*tun* + imperfective status suffix *-ik*): (a) a simple underived transitive, (b) a derived transitive with adverb and instrument incorporation.

(10) Yucatec (a and b are parts of the same utterance)
  a. *tun-ts'iil-ik-ø*   yet   *u-k'ab*
     PROG.A3-peel-IPFV.TR-B3 with   A3-branch
     'he peels it with his hand,

  b. *tun-chan-jats'-k'a-t-ik-ø*   bin le   sojol   bin t=u-chun
     PROG.A1-small-hit-hand-TRZER-IPFV.TR-B3   REP DET   dead_leave REP PREP=A3-trunk
     DET tree=DEIC
     le che'=a',
     'he slightly pulls away with his hand the dead leaves from the tree trunk, they say'

The utterance in (11) includes two intransitive verbs in the completive: (a) an underived intransitive and (b) a derived passive with adverb incorporation. Verb stems can be formed from verbal roots as in (10), or they can be derived from a variety of word classes as in (11b).

(11) Yucatec
  a. *j*   *k'uch-ø*   *le*   *máak* *bey* *te'* *ichil* *le*   *kool* *bin=o'*,
     CP.INTR arrive-b3   det   person like LOC   in   DET   field   REP=DEIC
     'he arrived in the field like that, they say'

b. *ka   ki'-miis-t-a'ab-ø   u-sooj(o)l-il bin*
   CONJ tasty-sweep-TRVZER-PASS.PFV-B3   A3-fallen_leaves-REL REP
   'and the fallen leaves (of the place) were well swept away, they say'

32.4.2 Transitivity and agentivity

Among Mayan verbs, the most salient categorization pattern is transitivity. Transitive and intransitive verbs contrast in nearly all ways, from the root level, to the morphophonological and morphosyntactic levels. One expression of this contrast is the Mayan ergative pattern: the subject of transitive is indexed by Ergative A markers, and the subject of intransitives, with the Absolutive B marker (except when split occurs). Compare (12) transitive (a) vs intransitive (b).

(12) Yucatec
  a. *t-in-juch'-aj-ø*   b. *juuch'-n-aj-en*
     CP-A1-grind-PFV.TR-B3   grind.ANTIP-ANTIP-INTR-B1
     'I ground it'   'I ground' (antipassive)

Among intransitives, Yucatecan and Cholan languages have developed a further productive contrast between agentive (also described as 'active' or 'unergative' intransitives) and non-agentive (also labelled 'inactive' or 'unaccusative') roots and stems. At the root level, non-agentive roots correspond to intransitive proper, whereas agentive roots are treated as plain N roots (Cholan, Mopan) or as VN roots (Yucatec, Itza', Lacandon; see section 32.6). Compare in (13) the Mopan non-agentive intransitive root *JOK'* 'go out', which inflects directly with aspect, with the N root *XEJ* 'vomit(ing)' which requires a light verb. In (14) the cognate roots in Yucatec can both be inflected with aspect as verbs, but are distinguished by their status suffixes (*-ø* vs *-n-aj*). The same opposition extends to derived forms, e.g. passives and inchoatives are inflected similarly to non-agentive roots and antipassives like agentives, see (12b).

(13) Mopan (adapted from Danziger 1996: 392)
  a. *jok'-ø-ij*   b. *job'-ø-ij   u-xej*
     exit-INTR.CP-B3   LV.finish-INTR.CP-B3 A3-vomit
     'He came out.'   'He stopped vomiting.' (Lit. 'His vomiting ended')

(14) Yucatec
  a. *jok'-ij*   b. *xej-n-aj-ij*
     fall-B3   suck/kiss/smoke-ANTIP-INTR-B1
     'I fell.'   'I kissed/smoked.'

Among transitives, the contrast is mainly between root transitives and derived transitives (such as causatives, benefactives, applicatives), which often show distinct derivational (voice) and inflexional suffixes. Notice that some roots behave like derived transitives although they do not show overt derivation (e.g. Yucatec IL 'see' or U'UY 'hear, feel').[4]

32.4.3 Voice and verbal derivations

Voice derivations represent an elaborate system in all Mayan languages (Dayley 1981; Stiebels 2006; Coon 2019). The derivation, usually by means of affixes, may vary depending on the stem (root or derived) and specifics of the roles assigned to the agent, the object, or third participants such as recipients, bene-/malefactives or instruments, sometimes combined with aspectual or modal qualities of the action itself (active reflexive, canonical passive, middle voice, passives without agent, celeritive or 'unexpected' mediopassive, antipassives with or without agent incorporation, and the 'instrumental' or 'benefactive' voice as in (15)).

(15) Tzutujil (Dayley 1981, 1985: 125)
machat   x-in-r-choy-b'e-ej
machete   CP-B1-A3-cut-INSTR-MOD
'a machete is what he cut me with'

In a few languages of the Central K'ichean (K'iche', López Ixcoy 1994; Kaqchikel, Broadwell & Duncan 2002), Cholan (Coon 2017: 123–124) and Yucatecan branches, voice change is achieved with vowel alternations.[5] In Kaqchikel, transitive roots mark the passive by changing the vowel from lax to tense, see *chäy/ch'ay* in (16).[6] In the Yucatecan languages, vowel alternation governs a system of three or four voices and is associated with more general argument structure phonological templates. Voice vowel alternation only occurs on a class of CVC roots that form their transitive with a short vowel. These roots have been analysed as Transitive Verbal roots (Hofling 1997; Bricker et al. 1998) or as multivalent VN with the value of the CVC undetermined for certain phonological features (length, tone, and rearticulation in Yucatec and Lacandon, centrality of /a/ vs /ä/ in Itza', see ex. (17), and Lois & Vapnarsky 2003; Lois 2011). In parallel, all these languages also have a morphological passive for derived transitives (17c).

(16) Kaqchikel (Broadwell & Duncan 2002: 28)
a. *Ri   achin   x-u-chäy   ri   tz'i'*
   DET   man   CP-A3SG-hit   DET   dog
   'The man hit the dog.'

b. *Ri   tz'i'   x-ch'ay   r-oma'   ri   achin*
   DET   dog   CP-hit.PASS   A3SG-by DET   man
   'The dog was hit by the man.'

---

[4] In Yucatecan, this may be partly due to the non-canonical phonological template of these roots, which does not allow for voice vowel alternation, see section 32.4.3.
[5] This pattern may have originated in former <h> and <'v> infixations.
[6] This only occurs in forms having tense–lax contrasts. In other cases, the stem takes the same form in both active and passive, the only change concerning person indexation (Broadwell and Duncan 2002: 28, 29; McKenna Brown et al. 2006: 175).

(17) Yucatec
   a. t-u-**jep'**(-aj)-ø   u-suum-il
      CP-A3-tighten.TR-PFV.TR-B3   A3-string-REL
      'he tightened its string'

   b. kaj   **je'ep'**-en   yéetel   k'áan
      CONJ   tighten.PASS-B1   with   hammock
      'and I was tightly tied with a hammock'

   c. kaj wen-s-**a'ab**-en   ich   k'áan
      CONJ sleep-CAUS-PASS-B1   in   hammock
      'and I was put to sleep in a hammock'

Other verbal derivations include the productive inchoative derivation which forms predicates expressing change of state ('to become x') from nouns, adjectives, or positionals (18). There are multiple types of transitivization: e.g. causatives from adjective and positional roots 'to cause a particular state or quality [Adj] in X' (19); causatives from non-agentive root intransitives (suffixed with -Vs across the family) 'to cause X to do an action[V]', as in (17c); usatives 'to use a thing[N] on something', 'to take X for [N]', and applicatives from nouns or agentive intransitives (20), see also Bricker (1970, 2019: 171ff.). Transitivized forms can be further derived in passive and antipassive voices.

(18) Hooom! Tun-sáas-il-**tal**
     IDPH   PROG.A3-clear-ADJ-INCH.IPFV
     'Suddenly, it got luminous!'

(19) Ts'-u-taal   u-sáas-il-**kun**-t-ik-ø   to'on   in-yuum
     TERM-A3-come   A3-clear-ADJ-CAUS-TRVZER-IPFV.TR-B3   PR1PL   A1-father
     'He came to illuminate (this matter) for us, my father.'

(20) ma'ax   ken   u-pool-**int**-ej?
     who   PROS   A3-head-USAT-SBJ.B3
     'Who will be the head of it?' (= 'Who will lead it?')

Verbs in Mayan languages also derive many types of participles, varying depending on the valence of the base, and properties of the action involved (see section 32.7).

32.5 Nouns

32.5.1 General properties of nouns

Mayan languages have Nominal roots that in their bare form can be instantiated only as nouns and which require derivation to function as other categories. Nominal roots represent the most open class phonologically. Although most nouns share the dominant CVC phonological format of the Mayan lexicon (Ixil: *xu'k* 'basket' *b'aal* 'father', *ej* 'tooth'; Lacandon: *kib* 'candle, wax', *sáab* 'star'), contrary to other word classes, members of this class include a significant number of disyllabic (Ixil *potz'o'm* 'support beam', *k'oatch* 'banana', Poqomam *wahlaq* 'corncob', *ehcham* 'brother-in-law') and very rarely trisyllabic members (Ixil *txakmanch'el* 'rainbow', Itza' *pusik'al* 'heart'), most of the latter arguably resulting from old compositions or loan words (Yucatec *taak'in* 'money' > *ta'* 'excrement' *k'iin* 'sun'; Poqomam *tinamit* 'town' > Nahual *tenamitl*, *tuwaret* 'seat' > Spanish *taburete*). Nominal derivations are productive, though less than verbal derivations (see sections 32.5.2 and 32.6).

The main distinctions between nouns and verbs across the family are TAM inflexion—nouns cannot be inflected for aspect and/or mood—and N's ability to function as argument. The formula in (21) gives the schematic structure of the nominal phrase, in its maximal extension.

(21) Noun Phrase [Maximal extension]
DET + QUANT[i] + NC + Possessor [SetA]—Intens/Atten[ii] + Attributive Adj + Root—Compound Root[iii]—DERIV—REL—Plural/SetB (predicate subject) + possessor NP + Relative Clause + Topic enclitic/Deict/Evid[iv]

[i] Quant = quantifier, numeral or numeral + numeral classifier
[ii] The linear position of the Intensifier or Attenuative varies depending on language; it may precede (e.g. Yucatecan) or follow (e.g. K'iche') the adjective or appear in both positions (e.g. Mam).
[iii] The order of compound roots depends on the type of compounding.
[iv] These usually occur at the end of the intonational phrase.

Nouns are mainly inflected for person, number, and possession. They can be modified by quantifiers and adjectives, which generally precede the noun. Numeral expressions often trigger the use of numeral classifiers; some languages also have nominal and genitive classifiers (see section 32.10). To illustrate, (22) shows an unpossessed nominal used as a predicate (a), a nominal in a numeral + classifier expression and one with a possessor (b).

(22) Yucatec (a–b are parts of the same utterance)
a. *Teech **atan-tsil-ech**=e'*
   PR2 wife-ABS-B2=TOP
b. *yan a-bi-s-ik-ø **jun-ts'áap waaj** yéetel **uy-uk'-(u)l-i(l)***
   DEON A2-go-CAUS-IPFV.TR-B3 one-NUM.CLF tortilla with A3-drink-NOM-REL
   'You, you're a wife, you have to bring a pile of tortillas and its [accompanying] drink.'

Nominals can be introduced by determiners, which express various deictic and evidential dimensions (proximal/distal, symmetric/asymmetric access, sensory access, see Hanks 1990, 2005; Danziger 1994, for Yucatecan). Determiners and deictics can be realized by discontinuous forms; this is found in (at least) Tseltalan, K'ichean, and Yucatecan, see (23). The same determiners may be used to frame VPs and form relative clauses.

(23) Mopan (Danziger 1994: 896)
a   baal   a   lo'   yäj-ø!
DET thing DET DEIC.3.STAT.VIS be.ripe-B3
'That thing is ripe!' (Speaker is moving away from a plant she had inspected)

Plural marking on nouns (and plural indexation on verbal predicates) is optional and correlated with animacy. It is often used for humans and some animals, and is more optional, sometimes ungrammatical, on most other referents. In some languages, such as Yucatec and Mam, these are neat tendencies, with some flexibility, especially for inanimates (Lucy 1992; England 2011; discussion in Butler et al. 2014). This pattern seems to have become (quasi) grammaticalized in K'ichean languages, like in K'iche' where plural is obligatory for some animate nouns, especially humans (e.g. *ixoq-iib'* 'women', *iyom-aab'* 'midwives') optional with others (e.g. *chikop-iib'* 'animals', *amoly-iib'* 'flies') and agrammatical for inanimates, but also body parts, kinship terms, and most animals (Can Pixabaj 2017: 469–470).[7] A few Mayan languages have further developed contrasting plurals that may define noun subclasses (see Craig 1986: 246 for Jacaltek).

Mayan gender markers define two nominal classes. They have been reconstructed for PM (**ʔaj-* MASC, **ʔix-* FEM) and are still present in most Mayan languages, deriving agent nouns and demonyms. In the Yucatecan, Cholan, and Tseltalan branches, gender markers are still productive on nouns denoting humans and certain animal and vegetal terms. Itza' (and also Mopan, Hofling 2011) has a developed system, where gender markers function for personal names: *ix-Mariiyaj*, agent nouns: *aj-patz'-b'ak* [MASC-massage-bone] 'folk chiropractor', toponyms: *aj-p'ich-'ayim* [MASC-point/penis-crocodile] 'place of the penis of the crocodile', names of illnesses: *ix-jink'i'* 'whooping cough', and as relative operators, marking subclasses within classificatory sets (e.g. types of winds or stones: *aj-tok'-tunich* [MASC-flint_stone] 'flint stone') (Lois 1998). The *aj/ix* markers plus a neutral (unmarked) form are also used to distinguish animal and plant classes with taxonomic and cultural semantic correlates (Vapnarsky 1997).

Possession is often invoked as the main feature of Mayan noun–class distinctions. All Mayan languages distinguish between inalienable and alienable nouns, based on morphological patterns. Inalienable nouns bear no morphological marker if possessed, whereas their absolute use is generally morphologically marked. In contrast, alienable terms bear no morphological marker when unpossessed, and may be marked when possessed. Inalienable nouns include kin terms, body parts or parts of wholes and, in some languages, a set of objects or concepts conceived as extensions of the personal sphere (some clothes, instruments, food, and body productions/secretions). This is illustrated in (24) in K'iche'.

(24) K'iche' (Can Pixabaj 2017: 468)
nu-joloom [A1SG-head] 'my head'   *jolom-aaj* [head-UNPOSS] 'head'
nu-k'ajool [A1SG-man's.son] 'my son'   *k'ajol-axeel* [man's.son-UNPOSS] 'son of man'
nu-q'uu' [A1SG-blanket] 'my blanket'   *q'u'-aaj* [blanket-UNPOSS] 'blanket'
nu-k'aay [A1SG-sale] 'my sale'   *k'ay-iij* [sale-UNPOSS] 'sale'

---

[7] An intensified use of plural marking can also be an index of speech discourse registers.

From data available, marking of the absolute use seems to be always required for kin terms, but varies across languages for other subsets. For instance, in Ch'orti, body parts in the absolute use may be unmarked: compare *u-nya'r* 'her son-in-law' / *nya'r-tsir* 'son-in-law' with *u-b'ak(-er)* 'her bone' / *b'ak* 'bone, skeleton' (Becquey 2014: 259ff, see Lehmann 2002 for Yucatec). A few inalienable terms are inabsoluble (e.g. Yucatec *íits* 'resin', *otoch* 'home', Lehmann 2002: 54ff.).

Alienable words can occur unmarked in both possessed and unpossessed context. This large class includes most concrete nouns.

(25) Itza'
luuch	'gourd (to drink)'	*in-luuch*	'my gourd'
meyaj	'work'	*in-meyaj*	'my work'
k'ab'	'hand, arm'	*in-kab'*	'my hand/arm'

Some authors report intermediary classes between inalienable and alienable. For instance, in Yucatecan, there is a group of nouns that can occur with no suffix in absolute use but requires a suffix when possessed, e.g. Yucatec: *naj* 'house'/ *in-naj-il* 'my house' vs *inw-otoch* 'my home, my house'. This is also the case of a subset of body parts (mostly mass concepts, such as flesh, bone, blood, skin, hair, feathers, fat, veins, brain) that requires a specific suffix *-el/-al* when possessed in Yucatecan, Cholan, and less productively, K'ichean (e.g. Yucatec *chooch* 'tripes' / *in-chooch-el* 'my tripes/intestines', K'iche': *kik'* 'blood' / *nu-kik'-el* 'my blood', Lois & Vapnarsky 2003: 96; Can Pixabaj 2017: 468). In several cases, the property triggering possessive marking may be pragmatically determined, as a quality affecting the genitive relation in a given context, e.g. Ch'ol *i-b'uhk* 'her/his clothing'/ *b'uhk-äl* 'clothing' [related to someone] / *b'uhk* 'clothing' [generic], Becquey 2014: 261, 341).

Besides suffixation, the genitive relation can be marked by vowel alternations (e.g. tone change in Yucatec, Bricker et al. 1998: 360; vowel lengthening in Mam from Ixtahuacán, England 2017: 505), a few suppletive forms (e.g. Tojolabal: *waaj* 'tortillas' / *k-o'ot* 'my tortilla', Curiel Ramiréz del Prado 2017: 575) and genitive classifiers (see section 32.10). All these options are found in Mayan languages from different branches, although not in all of them.

32.5.2 Agent, instrument, and result nominalizations

Nominalizations in Mayan languages commonly produce deverbal agent, instrument, and result nouns, as well as deadjectival abstract nouns, place names, and demonyms. Event nominalizations and verbal nouns are discussed in section 32.6. It is common for nominalizations to involve a *-Vl/-el/-l/-r* suffix. This suffix may occur after argument structure modifier suffixes. In some cases, specific meanings require dedicated suffixes; in others, less frequent across the family, the same bare form can combine several meanings. This last pattern is notably productive in Yucatec, as part of the tendency of this language towards polycategoriality. Compare the noun formations from cognate roots in Tsotsil and Yucatec and their relation with verbal forms in (26) and (27).

(26) Tsotsil (Laughlin 1975)
   a. *tz'ib* 'ability to write', *tz'ib-a* [tr.v] 'write', *tz'ib-aj* [intr.v] 'write', *tz'ib-aj-el* 'writer, writing',
   b. *mes* [tr.v] 'sweep', *mes-ob* [n] 'broom', *j mes-om* [n] 'sweeper' (plus a dozen more intransitive affective formations)

(27) Yucatec
   a. *ts'íib* [n] 'writing (action, result)', [intr] 'write', *j ts'íib* 'writer', *ts'íib-t* [tr.v] 'write something'
   b. *míis* [vi.ag] 'sweep', [n] 'sweeping', 'broom', *j míis* 'sweeper' *míis-t* [tr.v] 'sweep something./place'

Agent nouns are derived from activity/action nouns, nominalizations, or antipassive stems (including compounds and object incorporated bases), often with the agentive/gender pre-clitic *(a)j* for masculine (or neutral) and *(i)x* for feminine (e.g. Chontal: *ah-ák'ot* 'dancer', Poqomchi: *aj muq'-an-eel* 'someone who buries', Chuj: *aj na'um* 'seer', *ix tz'isum* 'seamstress' [FEM], but *ilum kalnel* 'shepherd (lit. sheep caretaker)'). Agent nouns are also found with non-agentive roots, but less frequently (e.g. Tseltal: *chamel* 'sickness' > *j-chamel* 'sick person', Qeq'chi': *wark* 'sleep' > *war-inel* 'sleeping person', Tzul and Tzimaj Cacao 1997: 58). There are some dedicated derivational suffixes, with limited productivity, e.g. Yucatec and Itza' *-n(á)al*: *kool-n(á)al* 'farmer' > *kool* 'farm; corn field', *kaaj-n(á)al* 'inhabitant' > *kaaj* 'village, town', *poch'-náal* 'insulter' > *poch'* 'insult' (see Bricker 2019: 198–199). The gender clitics are also used to form demonyms with or without an additional suffix: Itza' *aj Motul-il* 'person from Motul'; Qeq'chi' *aj Kob'an* 'person from Coban'.

Instrument nouns are formed in all languages with a cognate suffix *–Vb*—reconstructed for PM—from a variety of roots, including compounds: e.g. Ixil *b'ix-ab'al* 'money paid for dancing' (instrument), 'dance hall' (location) > *b'ix* (INTR) 'to dance' (Ayres 1991: 53), Mam *chee'-b'l* 'instrument for grinding' (England 2017: 506), Chontal: *wäy-ibá* 'place for resting' > *wäy* (INTR) 'sleep', Ch'ol: *wäy-ib'-aläl* 'cradle' > *wäy* (INTR) 'sleep' + *aläl* (N) 'child' (Becquey 2014: 348, 352). In Mopan, the suffix presents variations depending on the root class that serves as the derivation base. Compare:

(28) Mopan (Ulrich & Ulrich 1976: 111; Hofling 2011)
   a. TR *juch'* 'grind' > *juch'-b'eeb'* 'mill'
   b. INTR *jok'* 'go out' > *jok'-eb'* 'exit'
   c. POSIT *kux* 'live' > *kux-l-eeb'al* 'something that gives life'.

In Yucatec, instrument nouns are often formed with the (gender) clitic *(i)x* (*x juch'-ub'* 'mill'), and in Itza' *aj* or *ix* (Lois 1998). The formation of instrument nouns is still very productive, especially with compounds, e.g. Yucatec *(x) pixchi'* (lit. 'cover-mouth', 'face masks'), a neologism that soon appeared during the Covid-19 pandemic.

Result nouns may take a dedicated suffix, as in the Cholan branch, e.g. Ch'orti': *b'on-emar* 'soiling, stain' > *b'on* (TR) 'paint, stain', Ch'ol: *lo{h}w-eñal* 'injury, wound' > *low* (TR) 'injure' (Becquey 2014: 355).

32.5.3 Relational Nouns

Relational Nouns form a class shared by all Mayan languages, they function roughly as the equivalent of English prepositions (Mayan languages only have one or two canonical prepositions each, with very broad functions). Formally, Relational Nouns are equivalent to possessed nouns, with the SetA marker indexing the argument introduced by the relational noun, and sometimes possession suffixes (-*Vl*, -*Vr*), e.g. *t = aw-éet-el* [PREP = A2-co/equal-REL] 'with you'.[8] They are often introduced by the preposition *ti/ta*, shared by all languages. Example (29) shows three relational nouns (in bold) with and without preposition and with and without -*Vl* suffix.

(29) Yucatec
t-u-men   táan-il-o'ob   yamar-t-a'an-ø   bolon jmeen
PREP=A3-do [=because] front-REL-3PL   call-TRZER-PART-B3   nine ritual.specialist
u-ti'-al   u-tsikbal-o'ob   **t-inw-éet-el**   xan
A3-PREP-REL   A3-talk-3PL   PREP=A1-co/equal-REL also
'**because** first nine ritual specialists were called **in order to** speak **with** me too'

Most Relational Nouns function as locative relators (30), others as syntactic relators introducing oblique arguments (such as agent and cause, especially in passive and middle constructions, comitative, benefactive), adjuncts, and subordinate clauses (29). Still others serve to form the reflexive (31), specify other types of personal involvement (e.g. Yucatec *tujunal* 'on its own', *tulakal* 'all') or, more rarely, introduce comparative adjectives (e.g. in Cajolá Mam, Pérez & Jiménez 1997: 227, England 2017: 521).

(30) Yucatec
k-u-ts'ab-a (l)   **yóo'** [>t=uy-óok'-ol]   meesa kaada finaados
ICP-A3-give.PAS-IPFV.INTR   **on** [PREP=A3-on-REL]   altar each   all.saints'day
'[the offerings] are put **on** the altar on each All Saints' Day'

(31) Yucatec
j-k-paaklan-áan-t-ik-ø   **in-baj-o'on**
ICP-A1PL-RECP-help-TRZER-IPFV.TR-B3   A1-REFL-1PL
'we mutually help **each other** now'

Whereas Classic Mayan appeared to have an open derivational class of grammatical relational nouns (also reconstructed for PM, Law & Stuart 2017: 165), today, they represent a closed class whose members show distinct stages of grammaticalization. These involve various types of erosion (loss of the initial preposition, of the relational suffix and/or the Set A marker, phonological reduction, and restriction to third person) that make relational nouns to resemble more canonical prepositions (contact with Spanish may have had some influence on this process): e.g. *tawéetel* 'with you' now also expressed as *éete tech* ['with' + PR2].

---

[8] Set A agrees in person and number with its complement, except when relational nouns are used as clause subordinators, in which case relational nouns are always in third person singular.

32.6 VERBAL NOUNS, VERBO-NOMINAL ROOTS, AND ACTION/EVENT NOMINALIZATIONS

Mayan so-called Verbal Nouns refer to nouns with an eventive meaning. Verbal nouns have been reported in grammars of most Mayan languages both at the root and stem levels, and reconstructed for Proto-Mayan. In surface forms, they may appear as bare roots or be nominalized by overt derivation (as action/eventive nouns). This class is related to agentivity distinctions and specific syntactic constructions.

Root Verbal Nouns refer to manner of motion (e.g. jump, dance, run), communication (e.g. cry, whistle, write) and other common activities (e.g. bathe, work, take care), or bodily excretions (e.g. sneeze, cough, urinate), e.g. PM *ahqot* 'dance', *tz'ihb* 'writing', *tze'* 'laugh' (Kaufman 1990: 103). Significant differences concerning the size of the root class and the morphosyntactic properties of its members are observed within the family. In languages from the Cholan and the Yucatecan branches, Verbal Noun roots have become an extended class of agentive intransitives—contrasting with non-agentive Intransitive roots—regularly used to form imperfective constructions. In this use, Mopan, Ch'ol, and Chontal members of this class require a light verb, see (32a), or a prepositional construction (32b), to be inflected for aspect, thus confirming their nominal nature (see Danziger 1996 for Mopan; Gutiérrez & Zavala 2005, Coon 2010, Becquey 2014 for Ch'ol and Chontal; Lois et. al 2017 for a comparative view).

(32) Chontal
    a. *mu'*   *u-che-n-ø*   *ts'ib*   b. *an-ø*   *tä*   *ts'ib*
        PROG   A3-LV-IPFV-B3   write/writing   EXIST-B3   PREP   write/writing
        'he is writing'   'he is writing'

In Yucatec and Itza', the imperfective construction has been reanalysed so that these roots can inflect for aspect with no light verb, as in (33). This new property has led authors to consider them as polycategorial verbo-nominal roots, with no synchronic derivation between the nominal (illustrated in a and b) and the verbal intransitive functions (c) (Lois & Vapnarsky 2003, 2006). Alternative analyses invoke conversion from N to V, maintaining a more univocal correlation between root classes and word classes (Lucy 1994; Bricker et al. 1998).[9] Interestingly, whereas most verbo-nominal roots are primarily intransitive, since they require derivation to form transitives, as in (33d), in Yucatec about 40 of these roots also form transitives without derivation, revealing recent developments of this language towards increasing lexical class flexibility (see Lois & Vapnarsky 2003: 53, 15ff.).[10]

---

[9] Another argument in favour of the verbo-nominal analysis is that Yucatec children first use the action nouns as verbs (Pfeiler 2006).

[10] The agentive VN class is also the open class, where we find all loanwords with an eventive meaning, especially those borrowed from verbs in Spanish, which are integrated in their Spanish infinitive form (Lois & Vapnarsky 2006: 108; Coon 2017: 657). As the other root Verbal Nouns, depending on the language, loanwords require a light verb construction to form verbal clauses, e.g. Chontal *u-ch[e]-i asepta(r)* [A3-LV-ACC[-3B] accept] 'He accepted' (Becquey 2014: 675ff.), or can inflect for aspect like verbs, e.g. Yucatec *k-u-reesar-o'* [ICP-A3-pray(ing)-3PL] 'they **pray**!'.

(33) Yucatec
    a. le   *maaya*   *ts'íib=o'*   *jach taalam*   b. *jats'-uts-ø*   *a-ts'íib*
       DET Maya   writing=DEIC   very complex   very-nice-b3   A2-writing
       'Mayan writing is very complex.'   'your writing is very nice'

    c. *k-a-ts'íib*   d. *ba'ax k-a-ts'íib-t-ik-ø?*
       ICP-A2-write   what ICP-A2-write-TRZER-IPFV.TR-B3
       'you write'   'What do you write?'

Besides Verbal Noun roots, most Mayan languages have action nouns resulting from overt nominalization of verbs (often also called 'verbal nouns' in Mayan studies), or more rarely from nouns: e.g. Ch'orti *pa'k-ma'r* 'action of sowing' (PAK' 'plant'[V]-*ma* [ANTIP]-*a'r* [NLZER]), Chol: *al-bäl* 'action of giving birth' (AL(N) 'woman's child'-*bäl* [NLZER]) (Becquey 2014; see also Lois et al. 2017: 115). Distinct suffixes may be required depending on the base, the most common being the general nominalizer -*Vl/-el/-l/-Vr*.

Derived action nouns are essentially intransitive, including passives, and antipassives with the dedicated morphology or voice alternation. They have two main functions: they are used either like ordinary nouns or in complement clauses. In the first function, they behave like nouns in distribution and syntactic properties, although they retain verbal properties, in particular as for argument structure (Can Pixabaj 2009). This is illustrated in K'iche': examples in (34) show a possessed action noun as a subject of a stative predicate (a), and an antipassive action noun (b) and a passive one (c) as subjects of transitive predicates.

(34) K'iche' (Can Pixabaj 2009: 46, 63, adapted)
    a. Ø$_i$ K'o   [*nu-war-aam*]$_i$
       b3sg exist a1S-sleep-vn
       'I am sleepy.' (lit: there is my sleepiness)

    b. *X-at-u$_i$-q'i'taj-isa-j*   [*ri*   *kem-on-eem*]$_i$
       CP-B2S-A3S-tire-cau-SUF   DET weave.ANTIP-VN
       'The weaving made you tired.'

    c. *X-in-u-q'i'taj-isa-j*   [*ri u-keem-ik*   *ri*   *po't*].
       CP-B1SG-A3SG-make.tire-CAU-SUF   DET A3SG-weave.PAS-VN   DET   blouse
       'The huipil weaving made me tired.'

The reanalysis of structures like (34a), in which the action noun functions as the subject of a stative predicate with aspectual meaning, has set the stage for the modern verbal imperfective constructions in Yucatecan and Cholan languages, mentioned above (ex. (32)–(33)).

In their second main function, which involve strong restrictions on the habitual nominal morphosyntactic properties, action nouns are required as the core of a wide variety of complement and purpose clauses (35), as well as event focus constructions, see (36).

(35) K'iche' (Can Pixabaj 2015: 107, adapted)
    x-ø-r-eta'ma-j   [*kuna-n-ik*]$_i$
    CP-B3S-A3S-know-ACT cure-AP-VN/SUF
    'She/he learned to cure.'

(36) Ch'orti (Becquey 2014: 474)
k'aywa'r war uche
k'ay-wi-a'r   war u-che
sing-INTR-VN PROG A3-LV[-B3]
'what he's doing is singing'

In these constructions—varying in type depending on the matrix predicate, the subordinate clause, semantic aspects, and the languages—action nouns function either as an internal or as an oblique argument of a matrix predicate. Constructions like (35) where neither aspect/tense nor person indexation can occur on the stem have been recently analysed as infinitives (Palancar and Zavala 2013; Aissen 2017b). In (35) the complement clause is indexed as third person on the matrix predicate, and the subject of the complement is coreferential with the subject of the matrix clause, where it is overtly indexed (see Can Pixabaj 2015).

Deverbal nominalizations forming action nouns are very productive with intransitives of various kinds in all Mayan languages. In contrast, there are strong restrictions on transitive nominalization. Aissen (2017) shows the range of detransitivation strategies that Mayan languages use to compensate for the incapacity of nominalizations to take fully fledged objects: object incorporation and antipassivization (e.g. Yucatec), restriction to bare generic objects (e.g. Mam, Tz'utujil, Q'anjobalan), demotion of the object to oblique (e.g. Mam), and passive-like constructions (e.g. Tz'utujil, K'iche', Tseltalan) (see also Polian 2013b, 2017b: 628 for Tseltal).

32.7 Adjectives and Participles

Mayan adjectives have semantic, functional, and a few morphosyntactic properties of their own which distinguish them from nouns and verbs. Besides root adjectives, adjectives as a surface lexical category form a rather heterogeneous class, which may be taken to include participles. Mayan so-called participles are deverbal words that behave like adjectives, although some are restricted to the predicative function. They express aspectual, argumental, and other semantic distinctions, many of which are not grammatically distinguished in Spanish or English.

The structure of the adjectival phrase is given in (37), and (38) shows adjectives in predicate ('is hungry') and attributive ('poor') uses.

(37) *Adjectival phrase*
Intens/Atten + **Root**—Deriv—Abs [SetB]

(38) Yucatec
wi'ij-ø   le   o'otsil   máak=a'
hungry-B3   DET   poor   person=DEIC
'this poor person is hungry'

Mayan languages have relatively small sets of root Adjectives; there are about 30 lexical roots in K'iche' (Can Pixabaj 2017: 472), 50 in Mam (England, 2004: 132), 51 in Tseltal (Polian

2013a: 538). In a few languages, however, they represent a bigger class: Smith-Stark (1983: 185) reports 98 in Poqomam, and Bricker et al. (1998: xvi) reports 143 in Yucatec. Like N roots, and contrary to V roots, root Adjectives are mainly monosyllabic CVC (e.g. Yucatec *chak* 'red', *pa'ap* 'spicy', *cheech* 'tearful'), but can also include disyllabic roots (e.g. Yucatec *ch'ujuk* 'sweet', *polok* 'big', *su'lak* 'shy'). Overall, the semantics of root Adjectives across Mayan languages maps onto semantic classes identified to be cross-linguistically the most likely to lexicalize as adjectives (Dixon 1982 and subsequent work, Martinez Cruz 2007, Coon 2018), such as dimension, basic colour, and physical property. Other classes (e.g. value, age, human propensity) are more variably represented (Kaufman 1990; Lehmann 1993; England 2004; Polian 2013a: 538).

In addition, there is a large number of distinct types of adjective-like derived and compound words that express property concepts (e.g. *úuch-be'en* 'old', *chi'ich-nak* 'restless', *ki'ich-pam* 'beautiful (woman)'), including participles illustrated below.

Attributive noun modification is a distinctive function of Mayan root Adjectives, since it is restricted to this word class. However, the most general and common function of adjective and adjective-like forms in Mayan languages is their use as stative predicates.

Mayan adjectives can be categorized into three basic classes (I–III), with intermediary subclasses (such as I') in certain languages.[11] These classes are partially correlated with semantic and morphological features.

I—Root full adjective: CVC or disyllabic, with unmarked attributive (39) (a) and predicative (b) functions.

(39) Yucatec
  a. *wáa   sajak   máak=e',   (...)   ma'   táan u-meeyaj-t-ik=o'*
     HYP   fearful   person=TOP   NEG   PROG A3-work-TRZR=DEIC
     'if he's a fearful person, (...) he doesn't do it'

  b. *pues   sajak-en   min=meet-ik-ø.*
     CONJ   fearful-B1   NEG.PROG.A1=do-IPFV.TR-B3
     'so I was frightened, I wasn't doing it'

I'—Root restricted adjective: e.g. monosyllabic CVC that requires suffixation for the attributive function (as in Tseltalan, Tojol-ab'al, K'iche'),[12] compare the Tojol-ab'al adjective *pim* as a predicate in (40a) and as an attributive adjective with -*Vl* in (40b).

(40) Tojol-ab'al (Gomez Cruz 2010: 162)
  a. *pim-ø   ja   k'ul=i'*
     thick-B3 DET   forest=TOP
     'The forest is thick/dense.'

---

[11] Gomez Cruz (2010) suggests a continuum between canonical and non-canonical adjectives.
[12] In Tojol-ab'al, Gomez Cruz (2010: 164–165) identifies 29 adjectives requiring suffixation for attributive use (referring to basic colours, dimensions, physical properties like cold, sweet, hard, dirty, stinky, and a few other semantic classes). According to Polian (2013a: 535ff.; 2017b: 618), in Tseltal there is no semantic correlate to the difference between marked and unmarked adjectives. For K'ichee', see Kaufman 1990: 73; Can Pixabaj 2017: 473.

b. *och-tikon y-oj **pim-il** k'ul*
   enter-B1PL.EXCL A3-interior thick-ATTR forest
   'We entered the dense forest.'

II—Derived full adjective: derived forms (including participles) with unmarked attributive, (41) (a), and predicative functions (b).

(41) Yucatec
   a. *Je'el le **póok-bi(l)** nal=a'!*
      OST DET toast-PART ear_of_corn=DEIC
      'Here is the toasted ear of corn!'

   b. *Yan a-póok-ik-ø ti'. Deporsi beey u-ts'aak=o'. **Póok-bi(l)-ø!***
      DEON A2-toast-IPFV.TR-B3 IPR3 CONJ MOD A3-cure=DEIC toast-PART-B3
      'You must toast it for her. That's how this cure is. It is to-be-toasted!'

III—Adjectives restricted to the predicative function: mostly participles, ex. (42).

(42) Yucatec
   a. *k'a'abéet-ø máak-o'ob xook-naj-a'an-o'ob*
      necessary-B3 person-B3PL study-ANTIPAS-PART-3BPL
      'Men who have studied are needed.'

   b. **k'a'abéet-ø xook-naj-a'an(-o'ob) máak-o'ob*

Adjectives in attributive use appear pre-nominally; they can be inflected for plural, and occur after the set A in possessive constructions, as in (43a), compared with (43b) where the predicative adjective precedes set A. The attributive adjective can be part of a NP predicate, in which case the noun bares the absolutive set B marker, as in (44).

(43) Yucatec
   a. *Ka bin t-u-wach'-a(j) (...) t=u-**polok** chun e che'=o'*
      CONJ REP CP-A3-untie-PFV.TR-B3 PREP=A3-big trunk DET tree=DEIC
      'and they say he untied (the rope) from the big tree trunk'

   b. ***polok**-ø u-chun e che'=o'*
      big-B3 A3-trunk DET tree=DEIC
      'the tree trunk is/was big'

(44) Yucatec
   Ts'ii-ts'iik máak-en *{ts'ii-ts'iik-en máak}
   RED-fierce person-B1 RED-fierce-B1 person
   'I'm a fierce person!'

Post-nominal attributive adjectives have been reported in a number of Mayan languages. However, this analysis has been challenged in languages where evidence supports considering them as relative clauses wherein the adjectives function as predicates (see

England 2004 for Mam: 134 and Coon 2018 for Chuj). In Chuj, the adjective position has been proposed as a criterion to distinguish between 'true' adjectives and other adjective-like words that only function as stative predicates, such as *way-nak* 'asleep':

(45) Chuj (Coon 2018: 6)
Ix-w-il   ix   {*way-nak}   nene   {way-nak-ø}
PFV-A1S-see CLF   sleep-PRF   baby   sleep-PRF-B3
'I saw the baby that was asleep.'

Like other non-verbal predicates, adjectives used as predicates do not require a copula, they are directly inflected for person with set B markers, and cannot be inflected for TAM (to receive aspectual marking, they must be derived into verbs).[13] They occur either pre-nominally, following the canonical word order Predicate–Subject of Mayan languages, see (40a) and (43a), or post-nominally (either as the head of relative clauses, as in (45) or when the subject of the adjective predicate is fronted). In Mam, most adjectives can also function as complement of an existential predicate, as in (46).

(46) Mam (England 2004: 132)
Puur   kyee'yex   yiin   t-od
very   excellent   ATT   EXIST-B1PL
'We are quite well.'

Adjectives can take dedicated affixes. This is the case with plural marking *-tak* in Yucatek, which is in turn restricted to the predicative function, ex. (47) (see also *-ik* in Tojol-ab'al, Curiel Ramírez del Prado 2017: 576).[14]

(47) Yucatec
a. ki'ichpam-tak   le   x   ch'upal-o'ob=o'
   beautiful-PL.ADJ   DET   F   woman-3PL=DEIC
   'the girls are beautiful'

b. le x ki'ichpam{*-tak} ch'upal-o'ob=o'
   'the beautiful girls'

Dedicated affixes may also function as adjective modifiers, as in Mam: *spiiky'an-ka* 'somewhat clear', *aq'na'n-maj* 'worked' [+emphasis], *naach-xax* 'very ugly' [intensity] (England 2004: 22). Syntactic combination of adjectives can occur, marginally. In Q'anjobal, for instance, this is only possible with adjectives of size and colour (Mateo Toledo, 2017: 545).

Adjectives can be derived from transitive and intransitive verbs (e.g. Yucatec participles from XOK 'read': *xoka'an* 'read', *xoknaja'an* 'having read (= being literate)', *xokbe'en* 'legible', *xokbil* '(to be) learned'; from WEN INTR 'sleep': *weenel* 'sleepy'), positional roots,

---

[13] Note, however, that in Mam, adjectives, and other non-verbal predicates, can take one aspectual (im)perfect marker which is shared with verbs (England 2004: 127).
[14] The cognates *-tyak* in Ch'ol and *-tak* in Chuj show the same restriction when occurring with adjectives, but are also used as nominal plurals in a non-predicative function (Vázquez Álvarez 2011; Becquey 2014; Coon 2018).

and adjectives. A significant number of derivations involve a variety of productive suffixation and reduplication patterns related to the Expressive formations (see section 32.9), e.g. in Yucatec, from K'I'IX N 'thorn': *k'ixlemak* 'stinging' (e.g. when feeling a speck in the eye), *k'ixinak* 'stinging' (e.g. rubbing the fur of a wild boar), *k'ixi(l)k'ix* 'several thorns on the bark of a tree close to one another', *k'ix-un-k'iix* 'several groups of thorns spread over'; from 'OP' V 'burst, break into pieces': *op'lemak* 'easily broken' (e.g. dried tortilla), *op'oknak* 'easily broken, fragile' (e.g. light bulb), *o'op'kil* 'fragile', *'o'o'op'* 'burst, broken in several places'.

Some adjective compounds are especially productive. This is the case of the multisensory colour adjectives found in Yucatec or Tseltal, which derive dozens of terms from each of the primary colours, combining root colour terms with words from various classes. The derived adjectives refer to a rich multisensory palette, with nuances of intensity and luminosity, but also including texture, size of the coloured area, or colour change (Laughlin 1975; Bricker 1999). For instance, among the many forms composed with *k'an* 'yellow' in Yucatec: *k'áan-ch'ay-e'en* 'watery yellow' (+ *ch'a'ay* Adj 'bloody'), *k'áan-jats'-e'en* 'shiny yellow' (+ *jats'* T 'whip, hit'), *k'áan-'ox-e'en* 'prickly yellow' (+ *'oox* N 'scab').

Adjectives, root or derived, can productively be used to derive intransitives ('inchoative' or 'versive') to form predicates expressing changes of state ('to become [quality]') and transitive causatives ('to cause a particular state or quality on X') (see section 32.4.3 and examples (18)–(19)). Mam has dedicated deajectival intransitive derivation (England 2004: 128), but in other languages this derivational morphology may be shared with or related to that of Nouns.[15] Adjectives can also derive abstract nouns, most often using a cognate of the general nominalizer -*Vl* (e.g. Yucatecan -*il*: *chokoj* 'hot'< *chokw-il* 'fever', *'eek'jo'ch'e'en-il* 'dark-ness'; Tz'utujil: *yaab'-iil*, 'ill-ness', *muun* 'glutton' < *muun-il* 'delicacy', Dayley 1985: 185). The abstract noun originates in a possessive construction.

A number of adjectives can be used adverbially with no change in form (England 2004). When modifying the verb, they often occur in the initial TAM auxiliary slot (48a) or with dependant forms of the verb (48b).

(48) Mam (England 2004: 138)
    a. *nim   x-ø-b'aj   w-aqna-'n-a*   b. *B'a'n t-b'ii-n-x.*
       many DEP-1>3SG-DIR A1SG-work-SUF-1SG   good A3SG-hear-AP-still
       'I worked a lot.'   'It still sounds good.'

Based on their morphophonological, derivational, and functional properties, adjectives show more similarities with nouns than with verbs (phonological template of adjectival roots, use as stative predicate, no TAM, often related derivation into verbs). Nevertheless, they share some properties with verbs, such as the ability to derive reduplicated forms. They are also linked to the Positional and Expressive classes, for which adjectival stems are often the privileged expression.

---

[15] For Tseltalan, see Polian (2017b: 617); for Yucatecan, see Bricker et al. (1998) or Lois & Vapnarsky (2003: 72ff.); for Tojolaban, see Curiel Ramírez del Prado (2017: 575).

32.8 Positionals

Mayan languages have a significant class of Positional roots, characterized by a paradigm of dedicated suffixes and with its own semantics, broadly referring to (dis)positions and conditions. In contrast with positionals in other Amerindian languages (see Foreman & Lillehaugen 2017; Kaufman 2013, among others), Mayan Positionals are very productive, generating hundreds of lexical forms. They also lexicalize a richer set of semantic dimensions (support/suspension/blockage of motion, orientation, and configuration of parts of an object with respect to each other). As illustrated in (49), each root often encodes distinctions on a number of these dimensions simultaneously, which are predicated as non-inherent properties; they are frequently used in locative descriptions as in (50) (Bohnemeyer & Brown 2007; Bohnemeyer 2017).[16]

(49) Tsotsil (from Haviland 1994: 694; Laughlin 1975)
   XOP   insert(ed) (object with a hole or a central cavity impaled on another object)
   TZ'AP   insert(ed) (pointed object inserted shallowly into surface without hole)
   PAJ   insert(ed), fix(ed) (long object inserted firmly into surface or medium)
   TIM   stretch(ed) taut, fix(ed) stretched taut (something flexible and long, cord, muscle)
   TEL   stretch(ed) out (something with a rigid structure: legs, loom, trunks, boa, body)
   XACH'   stretch(ed) lengthwise (leather, rope, burden, rubber, net)

(50) Yucatec
   ti'   **nik-ikbal-óo'**   bin   e   aj=kan-ul-o'b=o'.
   LOC   pile_up-STAT.POSIT-B3PL   REP   DET   M=guard-NOM-B3PL=DEIC
   'The guardian-spirits are there piled up.'

A unique property of Positionals is that they are always used as derived forms (Haviland 1994; Lois & Vapnarsky 2003; Coon 2016: 516), see Table 32.1. Positional roots are those roots that only take positional derivations. However, positional derivation patterns are open to many other roots, especially Transitive roots (Haviland 1994). Thus, the hundreds of Positionals reported in Mayan language (e.g. over 500 in Q'anjobal, Mateo Toledo 2017: 630) often include a significant proportion of items showing such 'mix' or polycategorial root pattern.[17] For instance, in the Tseltalan branch, only 40%–45% of the roots taking positional morphology can be considered 'pure positionals' (see Haviland 1994: 730 for Tsotsil; Polian 2017b: 630). In Yucatec only about a third of roots taking positional morphology are exclusively Positionals (Lois & Vapnarsky 2003). Compare in Table 32.1 the stem formations available for the exclusive Positional root CHIL 'lie down' with a small sample of the many forms available for JAW 'lie/turn face up', a non-exclusive Positional.

---

[16] For their multidimensional nature, Bonhmeyer & Brown (2007) suggest Mayan Positionals should be called 'Dispositional'. A few Positional roots encode other meanings e.g. Yucatec KUX 'live'. It may be argued that even in these cases, the meaning includes a spatial sense (e.g. in Yucatec 'existing' and 'living' involves 'being attached to a place', Hanks 1990).

[17] Mam, Tseltal, Tsotsil, and Yucatecan languages shows overlaps between Transitive, Positional, and Affect roots, whereas in Q'anjob'al, the overlap is mostly between Positionals and Affects (Mateo Toledo 2017: 543).

Table 32.1 Example of exclusive and non-exclusive Positional formations

	CHIL 'lie down' exclusive Positional root	JAW 'lie face up' polycategorial root
Positional formations	k-u-chiL-tal 'she lies down' k-u-chiL-kúun-s-ik-en 'she makes me lie down' chil-ikbal 'she is lying down' chíil-en-chíil 'lying down here and there'	k-u-jaw-tal 'she lies face up' k-u-jaw-kúun-s-ik-en 'she makes me lie face up' jaw-akbal 'she is lying face up' jáaw-en-jáaw 'lying face up here and there'
Transitive, intransitive, participial and classifier formations		k-u-jaw-ik 'she turns it face up' k-u-jáaw-al 'it turns face up' (middle) jaaw-al 'it is turned face up' jaw-a'an 'it is turned face up (as a result of an action)' ka'a-jáaw luuch 'two gourds (cut in half and positioned face up)' (use as Classifier) etc.

There are three main derivations shared by Positionals across Mayan languages: they form stative predicates ('be-in-position', 'have the property X'), inchoative intransitives ('get-into-position/shape/condition'), and causative transitives ('put-into-position/shape/condition). Variations are found in the specific derivational patterns applicable in each language. In K'iche', for instance, Can Pixabaj (2017: 480) reports that Positionals can receive up to 15 dedicated derivational affixes, only three of which are very productive (for stative (51) (a), inchoative (b), and causative (c); the rest generally deriving intransitive verbs with aspectual or manner connotations (d)).

(51) K'iche' (Can Pixabaj 2017: 480–481)
    a. *tzay-al-ik*
       hang-STAT.PRED-SUF
       'hung/ hanging'

    b. *x-ø-tzay-e'-ik*
       CP-B3SG-hang-INTR-SUF
       'it hung'

    c. *x-ø-u-tzay-ab'aa'*
       CP-B3SG-A3SG-hang-TV
       'she/he hung it'

    d. *ka-ø-tak'-ak'-ik*
       ICP-B3SG-stand.up-DER-SUF
       'stand up precipitously'

At the other extreme is Q'anjobal, where only two suffixes are exclusive of Positionals, forming adjectives and stative attributives (Martin 1977: 294; Mateo Toledo 2017: 542), while other 'Positional' affixes are shared with other classes, mainly with Expressives. In Yucatec, the stative suffix -*Vkbal* (V: vowel harmony with the root vowel) is the only one used exclusively with Positionals, see (50) and Table 32.1, while the morphology used to derive intransitive inchoatives is partly shared with adjectives (and with a subset of nouns) and causative derivation is fully shared with them (Lois & Vapnarsky 2003: 106, 123).

Depending on languages, stative positionals exclusively used as predicates coexist with adjective positionals (e.g. Kaqchikel, Henderson 2019), or stative positionals can function as attributives as well. When this is possible, semantic contrasts are often involved such as transitiory vs permanent quality (see Haviland 1994: 712 and Polian 2013a: 580 for Tseltalan). Some Positional and Transitive (polycategorial) roots have access to various stative formations with meaning contrasts involving agentivity (e.g. Tojol-ab'al: *jam-an* 'open (stative)' vs *jam-ub'al* 'opened (stative) by somebody' Gómez Cruz 2010: 134; Curiel Ramirez 2017: 588, see also Bohnemeyer & Brown 2007: 1116 for Yucatec).

For Kaqchikel, Henderson (2019) takes the fact that Kaqchikel Positional roots only share derivation with V roots as primary evidence for considering them as a subclass of V roots. However, given the specifics of the Positional roots and their close relations with other classes in Mayan languages as briefly overviewed in this section, the nature of the Positional root class still remains a subject for investigation.

32.9 Expressives

Expressives concern a part of the lexicon and the grammar that implies involvement and emotion from the speaker. They frequently refer to complex events involving more than one sensory modality and making productive use of sound symbolism and language iconicity (Hinton et al. 1994; Voeltz & Kilian-Hatz 2001).

(52) Tseltal (Polian 2017b: 631)
 X-*pum-pon*-∅ te *k'in=e.*
 IPFV-IDPH-EXPR-B3 DET party=DET
 'The party is resounding (music going boom-boom).'

As in most languages of the world, the grammar of Mayan Expressives has been underdescribed, despite its high significance in daily speech and the complex and productive nature of its systems in the family. Although reported in a number of Mayan grammars, only a few thorough analyses exist (see in particular Maffi 1990; Pérez González 2012; and Polian 2013a: 657ff for Tseltal; Baronti 2001 for K'iche'; Le Guen 2014 for Yucatec). First identified as 'Affect' constructions, roots or word class in the Mayan literature (Kaufman 1971), Mayan Expressives represent an open class which covers a wide range of dedicated word formations and forms derived from different root classes.

Traditionally, the label Affects was mainly used for Mayan derivational patterns that form regular verbs or adjectives, the peculiarity of these forms stemming from the complex sensory visualization of events or the spatial or temporal distributive/repetitive patterns they express, often associated with connotations of intensity, duration, repetition or suddenness, as in (53) (see in particular Kaufman 1971; Laughlin 1975 for Tsotsil; Bricker et al. 1998 for Yucatec). More recent work has brought to light a productive series of ideophone formations, and proposed a wider class of Expressives that would include them. All these forms have a highly pragmatic and multimodal nature, they are often accompanied with vocal effects, gestures and body postures; they are linked to emotional speech and often found in communicative contexts such as vivid narrations, gossip, teasing or scolding (Le Guen 2014; Maffi 1990).

(53) Yucatec [from a traditional tale]

*Ka jóop' ukuxkintkóo' bin le mejen muuch bin=o' [...] **p'itchaláankilóo'** bey-a'*,
'And he started reviving them, they say, the little toads, **they were making little jumps one after the other** like this
(...) *Ay dyoos kaj máanen sáamyake'*,
'My god, when I passed by a moment ago.'
*ti' máan **nakchaláankil** o'tsil mejen muuchóobo', laaj k'oja'antakóo'!*
'There they go, **leaning up against each other**, the poor little toads, they were all sick.'

Expressive words are mostly formed out of Transitive and Positional roots, but also from Nominal or Adjectival roots. Some are based on roots that can only derive expressive words, such as Yucatec KIL, used for experiences related to 'trembling', 'OL for those linked to 'softness', and JAL to 'slippery'. CVC roots which are exclusively dedicated to the formation of expressives have been categorized as 'Onomatopoeic roots' in Mayan dictionaries (see in particular Laughlin 1975) and recent studies (Le Guen 2014).

Main expressive formations involve derivational templates, which combine vowel change, reduplication patterns, and infixation (Le Guen 2014). For example in Yucatec: process changing (*kil-bal* 'tremble, quake', *jop-bal* 'catch fire'), repeated action (*jo'ojop* 'light several times'), repetitive cyclic action (*kikil-áankil* 'tremble (body)', *jojop-áankil* 'catch fire', *lóol-áankil* 'give flowers'), ideophones for short event/sound: *t'oj t'oj t'oj* [> T'ÓOJ 'strike, hit'] 'hits on wood/on an iron pot'), for staccato event/sound: *tsa'ah* [> TS'AJ 'fry'] (sound of a light animal passing) or *tso'oh* [> TSOJ 'crush'] (sound of heavier animal passing, e.g. peccary), etc. (see also section 32.7).

Besides their specific semantics and word formations, Expressives also have syntactic properties of their own. Expressive verbs, generally intransitive, may show aspectual restrictions (e.g. in Tseltal they only combine with the incompletive marker) and, apparently do not accept voice derivations. For Tseltal, Polian (2013a: 661) argues that Expressives lay somewhere between verbal and non-verbal predicates, sharing limited properties of each predicate class (e.g. aspect restriction, non-verbal negation). Ideophones appear without inflection, they function as secondary predicates—often in initial or final position of the utterance—and may be introduced by light verbs (K'iche') or quotatives (Yucatec), as in (54), showing a repeated ideophone formed on the root *nich'* 'bite', followed by the textual quotative *kij* (Le Guen: 2014: 6.4, see also Polian 2017a: 218).

(54) Yucatec (Le Guen 2014)
      kul-ukbal-en   Kaariyo,   níich'i'in   níich'i'in   kij   bey=a'
      seat-POSIT.STAT-B1   carrillo   IDPH.bite   IDPH.bite   CIT   like=DEIC
      'I was seated in Carrillo, "níich'i'in níich'i'in" it went like this.'
      [a woman talking about her experience of feeling her back itching 'as if a little ant was biting her']

32.10 CLASSIFIERS

Distinct classes of classifiers are found in Mayan languages: numeral, nominal, and genitive. Systems include forms ranging from a few grammaticalized root classifiers to productive processes of classifier formation.

The main class concerns Numeral Classifiers, required for counting things or actions. There are of the sortal (about a dozen), mensurative (the most productive), or action classifier types (Berlin 1968; Craig 1986; De Leon 1988; Grinevald 2000; Zavala 2000; Polian 2017a: 219–220). Numeral Classifiers are located right after the numeral, as in (55), the compound NUM + NUM.CLF can also be used pronominally like in (56).

(55) Yucatec
Yo'osal jun-*túul* a-chan paal=e', (...) jun-*túul* kaax,
For one-NUM.CLF[ANIM] A2-small child=TOP one-NUM.CLF[ANIM] chicken
óox-*ts'íit* kib, yéete(l) jum-*p'éel* sujuy nook',
three-NUM.CLF[LONG,THIN,RIGID] candle with one-NUM.CLF[INANIM] virgin cloth
'For one child of yours, (you need to bring) one chicken, three candles and a new garment.'

(56) Yucatec
ulaak'-o'ob púuts'-o'ob, ka'-*túul*-o'ob
other-B3PL escape-b3pl, two-NUM.CLF-B3PL
'the others escaped, they were two'

Numeral classifiers (reconstructed for PM) tend to be in obligatory use in Modern Lowland and Western Mayan languages, and more optional in Eastern languages (where they are usually described as 'enumeratives'). They have disappeared only in a few languages, leaving behind measure classifiers (e.g. Mam and Huastec, Edmonson 1988: 422–431).[18] The number of numeral classifiers varies from a few dozens to hundreds depending on languages. Only a small set of them are exclusive root Classifiers (10–20, most of them of the sortal type). Numeral classifiers are often derived from, or are polycategorial with, other root classes mainly Transitive or Positional (e.g. Tseltal: *jil* [> *jil* Tr V flat elongated] to count strip of clothes, *ch'ix* [> N 'thorn'] for thin, long objects). Some languages use a suffixed form identical to the positional adjective; this is regularly the case in Q'anjobalan (see Zavala 2000). Numeral classifiers may form complex words by reduplication and affixation, used as stative predicate as (57).

(57) Yucatec (Bricker et al. 1998: 53)
in-nal=e', *ts'íit-man-ts'íit* 'anil t=u-sak'b- il
A1-corn-TOP RED-SUF-NUM.CLF.long_rigid EXIST-MAF PREP=A3-corn_stalk-REL
'my corn is growing on the stalk one by one'

Noun classifiers are linked to specific syntactic uses and are independent from quantification; they precede nouns and numeral classifiers (58), and may be used as anaphoric pronoun.

(58) Akatek (Zavala 2000: 136)
yetoj eb' **naj** kaa-wan ox-wan w-uxhutaj=an
with HUM.PL NCLF two-NUM.CLF three-NUM.CLF A1-cousin=1SG
'with two or three cousins'

---

[18] Numeral classifiers can be used with Spanish numbers, but this often requires specific constructions (e.g. with a possessed numeral classifier in Yucatec, Briceño Chel 1996): *syeete u-tuul-u(l) kaax* [seven A3-NUM.CLF-REL chicken] 'seven chickens'.

Noun classifiers refer to social and natural/material classes or interactions (Craig 1990; Hopkins 2012). They are a relatively new development in Mayan that originates in the Great Q'anjobalan branch and has spread to several other languages, such as in Chuj, Tojol-ab'al, K'iche', and some Mam dialects (Craig 1986; Zavala 2000; Hopkins 2012; England 2017: 508). In the Q'anjobalan branch, languages have between 12 to 20 nominal classifiers (for humans M/F, animals, wood-plant, corn, thread, stone, salt, and water, etc., see Grinelvald 2000: 59; Zavala 2000: 134; Hopkins 2012: 415). Most nominal classifiers are transparently related to plain Nouns (e.g. in Tojol-ab'al the feminine classifiers *me'n* and *nan* are reductions of *me'jun* 'grandmother' and *nan* 'mother'). No overt derivation to form noun classifiers is attested; rather, nouns used in a polyfunctional way as noun classifiers undergo formal erosion and semantic changes (e.g. Chuj Hopkins 2012: 414).

Several Mamean languages have developed **genitive classifiers**, required in a limited portion of possessive constructions (after set A) for culturally salient relations (e.g. for fruit, food made with maize, meat, cooked vegetables) (England 1980, 2017: 508; Pérez Vail 2007). In Yucatec, the genitive classifier slot is open to other words, especially for actions of exchange or fabrication, and is actually syntactically productive with any derived antipassive that would fit the semantics (Lehmann 2002: 64ff.), as in (59), another facet of Mayan categorial flexibility.

(59)   Yucatec
        in-*siij* / *matan* / *bi'il*   *chamal*
        A1SG GEN.CL.offer/ receive_as_present/wrap   cigarette
        lit. 'my offered/received as present/wrapped cigarette'

32.11 Conclusion

Mayan languages show rich processes of word formation and derivation, characteristics of polysynthetic languages. Regarding word classes three main aspects are of particular interest: first, in terms of the complex relation between root classes and lexical categories at the stem level; second, in terms of the various patterns of cross-over between the word classes in each language, evident as a tension between lexical categorial determination and flexibility; third, in terms of the nature of their word classes, some of them unfamiliar in Indo-European languages. Mayan languages mostly share the same word classes but differ in the degree and form of flexibility between classes, as well as in the way categorial determination operates with respect to specific word-formation levels and processes. These variations raise important questions regarding how word-class configurations might change over time and vary cross-linguistically, even in closely related languages. New studies such as those language acquisition and Mayan Sign languages may also bring complementary evidence on the properties of word classes in the family (Haviland 2013; Safar & Petatillo 2020). Further research is required to explore these questions more thoroughly.

Acknowledgements

I thank Eva van Lier and two anonymous readers for their inspiring comments and helpful suggestions on an earlier version of this chapter, as well as Cédric Becquey and Telman Can Pixabaj for their help in clarifying some examples.

CHAPTER 33

WORD CLASSES IN MAWETI–GUARANI LANGUAGES

FRANÇOISE ROSE

33.1 INTRODUCTION

THE identification of word classes is one of the two central issues in Maweti–Guarani studies, along with the nature of their person indexation system on predicates. This question can be decomposed into two major issues: first, the distinction between nouns and verbs that is blurred by the fact that a large proportion of prototypical nouns can function as predicates without any derivational morphology, while sharing almost all the 'verbal' morphology; second, and related to the first issue, the identification of a class of lexemes with adjectival meaning as either verbal (as they most commonly occur as predicates in discourse), nominal (on the basis of their combination with person indexes which are also found on nouns) or adjectival (on the basis that they are neither prototypical nouns nor verbs). A third matter at hand is the fact that the three inflecting word classes (nouns, verbs, and postpositions) enter a similar construction with identical marking of their possessor/object/complement, in which a much debated 'relational' prefix plays a role. These issues in Maweti–Guarani linguistics essentially concern theoretical questions regarding the 'value' of various criteria used for determining word classes, rather than comparative issues that would be based on internal variation within the family. This group of languages is in general rather homogeneous for their word classes, but different authors of grammars answer these questions in diverging ways for similar datasets. This is not to deny any variation among those languages regarding word classes, but this variation is not central to the issues discussed in this chapter.

There is presently no consensus among specialists, on what the word classes of Maweti–Guarani languages are. Pioneer work on the question is that of Dietrich (1977, 2000). The identification of word classes in Maweti–Guarani languages became a research question essentially after the publication of a volume on nouns and verbs in Tupi–Guarani languages (Queixalós 2001a).[1] It is noteworthy that all grammars published after

---

[1] This volume collects proceedings from a conference on nouns and verbs in Tupi–Guarani languages organized in Cayenne (French Guiana) by the programme *Langues de Guyane* of the Institut de Recherche pour le Développement.

that date devote some discussion to the criteria used to define word classes, and most have a very lengthy chapter on word classes. However, this topic has not often been dealt with at the level of the Tupi-Guarani subgroup or the Maweti-Guarani group: for example, it is not addressed in comparative works, such as Jensen (1998) or Corrêa-da-Silva (2010: 175).

This chapter aims to account for the existing literature as neutrally as possible, rather than offer its own analysis of the data, essentially because there is no consensus regarding Maweti-Guarani word classes. The theoretical approach will be kept to the essential. First, it is important to specify that the discussion on so-called word classes actually deals with the categories of lexical roots, rather than words per se (that can be derived from roots). Criteria for word classes in the theoretical literature pertain to four levels of linguistic analysis (Croft 1991; Hengeveld 1992a): semantics, morphology, syntax, and discourse. For example, prototypical nouns and verbs can be defined very schematically on the level of semantics as items expressing objects vs actions; on the morphological level as taking for example determiners vs tense morphology; on the syntactic level as being the head of nominal phrases used as arguments in the clause vs the head of predicate phrases; and on the discourse level as being used for reference vs predication. The literature on Maweti-Guarani languages essentially uses criteria at two levels: the morphological one, and the syntactic/discourse one. In fact, these two criteria generally coincide, except for 'adjectives'.

This chapter will start with a short introduction to the language group (section 33.2). This chapter will then discuss at length three crucial problems regarding the identification of word classes in Maweti-Guarani that descriptivists face and may be of interest to both typologists and theoreticians working on word classes: the noun-verb distinction (section 33.3), the categorization of words with adjectival meaning (section 33.4), and the constructional parallelism between nouns, verbs, and postpositions with the so-called relational prefix (section 33.5). Once the identification of major word classes is settled, section 33.6 will describe each lexical word class with their major characteristics (not only those critical to word-class identification), with a focus on what may be typologically remarkable. It will start with the major word classes: verbs (section 33.6.1), nouns (section 33.6.2), and postpositions (section 33.6.3). It will then proceed to minor word classes such as adverbs (section 33.6.4), ideophones and interjections (section 33.6.5), and particles (section 33.6.6). Examples are taken from a large array of descriptions of Maweti-Guarani languages.

33.2 THE LANGUAGE GROUP

Maweti-Guarani is one of the seven branches of the Tupi family. It is the largest and best-described branch of the family, with 50 languages (Hammarström et al. 2020). The Maweti-Guarani branch itself has been established relatively recently and includes Mawé, Awetí, and the large Tupi-Guarani subgroup (Drude 2006; Rodrigues & Dietrich 1997). The Tupi-Guarani subgroup has traditionally been separated in eight branches (Rodrigues 1984; Rodrigues & Cabral 2002), while more recent lexical phylogenetic research has resulted in a more resolved internal structure (Michael et al. 2015). The Tupi family with its major subgroups is shown in Figure 33.1, with Tupi–Guarani language names in italics, and other Maweti–Guarani language names in bold.[2]

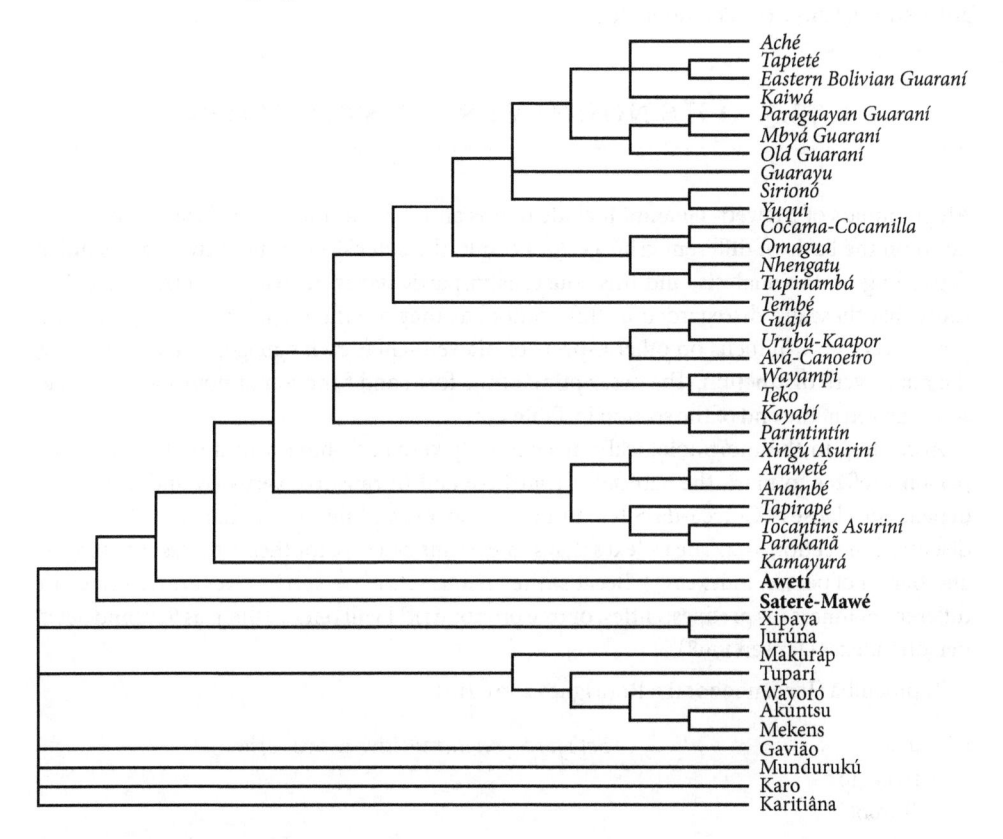

```
            Aché
            Tapieté
            Eastern Bolivian Guaraní
            Kaiwá
            Paraguayan Guaraní
            Mbyá Guaraní
            Old Guaraní
            Guarayu
            Sirionó
            Yuqui
            Cocama-Cocamilla
            Omagua
            Nhengatu
            Tupinambá
            Tembé
            Guajá
            Urubú-Kaapor
            Avá-Canoeiro
            Wayampi
            Teko
            Kayabí
            Parintintín
            Xingú Asuriní
            Araweté
            Anambé
            Tapirapé
            Tocantins Asuriní
            Parakanã
            Kamayurá
            Aweti
            Sateré-Mawé
            Xipaya
            Jurúna
            Makuráp
            Tuparí
            Wayoró
            Akúntsu
            Mekens
            Gavião
            Mundurukú
            Karo
            Karitiâna
```

FIGURE 33.1 The Tupi language family

Some comparative work has been published on Maweti–Guarani: Meira and Drude (2015) on phonology, Corrêa-da-Silva (2010) on phonology, morphology and syntax, and Corrêa-da-Silva (2013) on lexicon. Jensen (1998)'s comparative work on Tupi–Guarani has been for long a major source of information. The field has been greatly influenced by the Tupi specialist Aryon Rodrigues and his work on Tupinambá (Rodrigues 1953, 1996 among others).

Maweti–Guarani languages, and especially Tupi–Guarani languages, are 'noted for a high degree of lexical and morphological similarity in spite of their extensive geographical separation' (Jensen 1999: 128). They are agglutinating (i.e. concatenative and mono-exponential), with usually basic SVO or SOV order. Typologically salient features are the following: (i) nasality spreading at the word level (Drude 2009; Michael & Lapierre 2018); (ii) a hierarchical indexation system, whereby the person of both A and P counts in determining which argument is indexed on the verb (Birchall 2015; Jensen 1998: 562–576; Rose 2009, 2015b, 2018),

---

[2] This tree, kindly provided by Natalia Chousou-Polydouri, combines two trees resulting from phylogenetic analyses of lexicon, one for the whole Tupi family (Galucio et al. 2015) and a more specific one for the Tupi–Guarani branch (Michael et al. 2015). Nhengatu and Old Guaraní have been added manually.

once described as an inverse system (Payne 1994);[3] (iii) temporal modification of nouns (see section 33.6.2); and (iv) some genderlect distinctions (Pottier 1972; Drude 2002; Vallejos 2015; Rose & Chousou-Polydouri 2017).

33.3 THE NOUN–VERB DISTINCTION

All grammars of Maweti–Guarani include nouns and verbs as major word classes, but they do so on the basis of different criteria. As a result, the extension of these two classes differ depending on the analysis, and this concerns in particular roots with adjectival meaning (note that these are disregarded in this section, as they are the focus of section 33.4). The present section will focus on other aspects of Maweti–Guarani languages that are blurring the noun–verb distinction. The description of the form and function of nouns and verbs is summarized at the end of the section in Table 33.1.

According to the morphological criterion, only verbs combine with a particular set of person prefixes to mark the subject of transitive and intransitive verbs (A and S^A) in independent clauses (Corrêa-da-Silva 2010: 223), as exemplified in (1) and (2). S^P will be discussed in section 33.4. The indexes that some nouns can take for their possessor belong to another set of person indexes (3). Because the various sets of person indexes are described in different manners (as prefixes, clitics, or free pronouns),[4] I will refer to them as Set I and Set II person indexes (Jensen 1998).

Tupinambá (Jensen 1990: 117; Rodrigues 2001: 110)

(1) a-só   Set I for S_A on intransitive active verbs
     1SG.I-go
     'I went.'

(2) a-i-nupã   Set I for A on transitive verbs
     1SG.I-3.II-hit
     'I hit it.'

(3) syé=pɨ   Set II for Possessor on nouns
     1SG.II=foot
     'my feet'

It does not seem to matter that Set II, used on nouns for their possessors, is also found on verbs to refer to P as in (4) (see also section 33.6.1), even to A/S_A in some dependent clauses, and on words with 'adjectival' meaning when they predicate. What is generally taken as a crucial fact is that nouns can never take a Set I index.

---

[3] There is in fact no inverse marker in Maweti–Guarani verbs. The marker considered as an inverse marker by Payne (1994) is actually also found on nouns and postpositions. It is the so-called relational prefix r- discussed in section 33.5 (Rose 2009).
[4] This is so maybe partly because of differences in behaviour in different languages, but mostly because of authors' divergences in the criteria used to distinguish affixes, clitics, and words.

Tupinambá (Jensen 1990: 117)

(4)   *syé=nup ã*   *Set II for P*
     1SG.II=hit
     'He/she/they/you hit me.'

According to the syntactic/discourse criterion, the class of nouns comprises those items that are most often used as arguments in discourse, and that of verbs those most often used as predicates (along the lines of Hopper & Thompson 1984). This criterion has been considered necessary in Maweti–Guarani research due to the fact that 'there is no perfect superposition in these languages between nouns and arguments and verbs and predicates, i.e. between lexical categories and functional or syntactic categories'[5] (Corrêa-da-Silva 2010: 223). This situation is primarily based on the fact that even though nouns are most often used as arguments, they can be used as predicates without being first derived into verbs, a fact already discussed in Dietrich (1977). The type of nominal predication that is most often put forward is a construction within which possessible nouns can be used as possessive predicates, simply with a Set II marker for the possessor, just as in a noun phrase (see for example Vieira 2000; Rose 2002). In this possessive predicative construction, nouns can take the whole array of morphology used by verbs when they predicate (negation, TAM, causative, plural, see for example Vieira 2000; Rose 2002), with the exception of Set I prefixes. Examples (5) illustrate this with negation. This construction has often been analysed as an existential construction (Dietrich 2001; Rodrigues 2001; Rose 2002),[6] parallel to that involving non-possessible nouns like (6).[7]

Teko (Rose 2008: 449)

(5) a. *d-e-sapato-dʒi-ãhã.*
       NEG-1SG.II-shoe-NEG-only
       'I don't have any shoes.'

    b. *d-o-ʔu-dʒi*   *sautu.*
       NEG-3.I-eat-NEG   salt
       'She does not eat salt.'

Tapirapé (Praça 2007: 193)

(6) *xãwãr*   *tãj-pe*
     dog   village-LOC
     'There are dogs in the village'

---

[5] My translation for: 'não ocorre nessas línguas uma superposição exata entre nome e argumento e verbo e predicado, ou seja, entre categoria lexical e categoria funcional ou sintática'.

[6] Gerasimov (2016) argues against the hypothesis of a zero-copula in Paraguayan Guaraní. Vieira (2000) offers another analysis of these possessive clauses in Mbyá Guaraní as transitive, postulating a zero 'have'-verb.

[7] Note that no existential copula has been reconstructed for the whole language group (various languages have innovated different copulas), so that the noun is also the predicate in (6). It is not clear from the literature whether non-possessed nouns used as (copula-less) existential predicates share their morphology with verbs.

Another aspect of Tupi–Guarani morphosyntax that blurs the distinction between nouns and verbs in discourse is the curious -*a* suffix (not attested in Awetí and Mawé (Corrêa-da-Silva 2010: 203)). This suffix can be said to mark a referential expression (Queixalós 2001b).[8] Cabral (2001) draws a panorama of the use of -*a* in the Tupi–Guarani branch: it usually does not occur after a vowel, but has also been lost in many more contexts in various languages (Queixalós 2006). Across the Tupi–Guarani languages, its maximal distribution comprises nouns when used as arguments, possessors in adnominal possessive constructions and objects of postpositions (see example (7)), but not when they are used as vocative, citation form, in dislocated NPs, or as a predicate such as (8) (except for equative predication such as (9)). As a consequence, this -*a* suffix has been considered crucial in the distinction, not between nouns and verbs, but between the syntactic positions of argument and predicate. This distribution blurs the noun–verb distinction in two ways. First, as expected, nominal predicates do not carry this -*a* suffix. Its absence is an additional common feature of verbs and nouns (when used as predicates). Second, there is in many Tupi–Guarani languages a nominalizer -*a* as in (10), which is usually described as a morpheme distinct from the suffix found on nouns (except notably in Praça 2000; Rodrigues 2001). In the literature, verbs are usually judged as being able to be used as arguments with particular morphology only, i.e. with nominalizers, as in (11). If one considers this -*a* on a verb to be marking a referential argument, just as when found on a noun, then nouns and verbs can both fill in NP positions with the same -*a* morphology. By marking the syntactic/discourse functions of arguments and predicates, the -*a* suffix makes the distinction between nouns and verbs secondary.

Kamayurá (Seki 2001: 56, 161, 162)
(7) *kunu'um-a   ka'i-a   r-uwaj-a   w-ekyj*
    boy-*a*   monkey-*a*   REL-tail-*a* 3.I-pull
    'the boy is pulling the monkey's tail'

(8) *je=tutyr-a   morerekwat*
    1SG=uncle-*a*   chief
    'My uncle is (a) chief.'

(9) *je=tutyr-a   morerekwar-a*
    1SG=uncle-*a*   chief-*a*
    'My uncle is the chief.'

---

[8] It is called argumentative case (Rodrigues 2001 see for example), nominal case (Jensen 1998), or referencing suffix (Queixalós 2001b) among other terms. Examples show that the referential expressions can be semantically either definite or indefinite, even though this is not discussed explicitly in the literature.

Tupinambá (Rodrigues 2001: 108)
(10) né   kér-a   a-j-potár
      2SG.II   sleep-a   1SGI-3SG.II-want
      'I want you to sleep.'

Teko (Rose 2008: 450)
(11) o-kuwa-pa   o-manõ-maʔẽ
      3.I-know-COMPL   3.I-die-NZR
      'He (God) knows all the dead ones.'

On this basis, Queixalos (2001b, 2006) suggested that the Tupi–Guarani languages may have originated from an omnipredicative language (on omnipredicativity, see Launey 1994), in which all lexical word classes were predicative, and referring expressions are all derived from the predicates with the help of the *-a* suffix.[9] Interestingly, in the present state of these languages, there are many other morphological devices to derive arguments from verbs (Jensen (1998: 539–544) reconstructs seven nominalizers), while no verbalizer is ever mentioned.

As a conclusion, there is no one-to-one relation between the word classes and the syntactic/discourse functions. There are two major positions on the flexibility of nouns and verbs in Maweti–Guarani languages.[10]

- total flexibility of both nouns and verbs
  In this view, both nouns and verbs are flexible and can be used as referential phrases (with *-a*) or predicates (with 'verbal' morphology). They are nevertheless distinguished on the basis of their prime function (higher frequency of use in discourse).
- (partial) flexibility of nouns only
  In this view, verbs are not flexible because they need to be nominalized to be used as arguments. A (large) class of nouns (possessible ones) are flexible, and can be used both as referential phrases and as predicates. Nouns can be distinguished from verbs on the basis of two criteria (i) predication is not their prime function, if frequency in discourse is taken into account (ii) there are (non-possessible) nouns that are not used as predicates with 'verbal' morphology.

In the end, all authors converge in distinguishing nouns and verbs, because the morphological and syntactic/discourse criteria converge. Crucial facts for a distinction between nouns and verbs are summarized in Table 33.1. Sections 33.6.1 and 33.6.2 will present additional characteristics of verbs and nouns respectively.

---

[9] The languages show different stages of erosion of this initial stage, with a gradual loss of phonological and grammatical contexts associated with the appearance of *-a*.

[10] These two positions have been reconciled by Queixalós's (2001b, 2006) historical hypothesis for Tupi–Guarani languages, given that Tupinambá, where flexibility of both nouns and verbs is most visible, is considered a 'conservative' Tupi–Guarani language. There would be a historical trend from a more to less flexible parts-of-speech system.

Table 33.1 Function and morphology of verbs and nouns in Maweti–Guarani (generalization)

	Referential use	Predicative use
Verbs	Set I for S/A with -*a* or with nominalizers	Set I for S/A, Set II for P negation, TAME
Nouns	Set II for Poss with -*a*	Set II for S negation, TAME

33.4 WHERE HAVE ALL THE ADJECTIVES GONE?

Another ongoing debate among specialists of Maweti-Guarani concerns the issue of which part of speech 'descriptive' roots belong to (Dietrich 2000; Queixalós 2001a, 2006; Meira 2006, inter alia). This class of words with prototypical 'adjectival' meanings has often been described as stative verbs (Jensen 1998; Seki 2000). Nevertheless, some authors analyse them as nouns (Dietrich 1977; Couchili et al. 2002; Corrêa-da-Silva 2010). It is noticeable that frequently, authors working on the same language are on opposite sides of the debate as is the case with Urubú-Kaapor (Kakumasu 1986; Caldas & DaSilva 2002), Mawé (Franceschini 1999; Meira 2006), Tupinambá (Barbosa 1956; Rodrigues 1996), and Tapirapé (Leite 1990; Praça 2007). We are basically facing a problem of analysis, for which no consensus has been reached. For this reason, the semantic label 'descriptive roots' is commonly used in the Maweti-Guarani literature.

The class of descriptive roots is relatively stable semantically throughout the family, expressing physical states (permanent or temporary), and internal states (such as feelings). They take Set II indexes (12), like nouns do (13), but are typically used as predicates, as in (14) and (15). They can also modify a noun in their bare form as in (16) or after having been nominalized as in (17).[11] They are very rarely used as arguments, and then take the -*a* suffix as in (18) (in languages where it is used on arguments). One should nevertheless keep in mind that there are also real differences in the behaviour of the descriptive roots from one language to the other. Meira (2006: 200, 204) compares Kamayurá descriptive roots that take the same nominalizer -*(t)ap* as verbs (but not as nouns) with Mawé descriptive roots that are nominalized with -*hap*, that nominalizes either nouns or verbs. This criterion shows the verbal characteristics of Kamayurá descriptive roots but does not discriminate parts of speech in Mawé.

---

[11] Seki (2000: 70) indicates that in Kamayurá descriptive roots modify a noun more frequently through compounding or nominalization than as a bare form. There is no discussion about a difference in meaning between these modifying constructions.

Mawé (Meira 2006: 55–57)

(12) Maria   h-eera
      Maria   3-be.tired
      'Maria is tired.'

(13) Maria   h-et
      Maria   3-name
      'Maria has a name.'

(14) waipaka   i-hup
      chicken   3-be.red
      'The chicken is red.'

(15) aware   yt   i-wato   'i
      dog   NEG   3-be.big   NEG
      'The dog isn't big.'

Kamayurá (Seki 2000: 70)

(16) y'yw-a   katu   n=o-mopen-ite
      arrow-a   good   NEG=3-break-NEG
      'He did not break the good/straight arrow.'

(17) y'yw-a   i-katu-ma'e-a   n=o-mopen-ite
      arrow-a   3-good-NZR-a   NEG=3-break-NEG
      'He did not break the good/straight arrow.'

(18) awujete   i-powyj-a   ore-raha   ko=wa
      luckily   3-heavy-a   1EXCL-carry   PART=MS
      'Luckily we carried her heavy (load)'

The two major alternative analyses of descriptive roots as nouns or verbs rely on different criteria.[12] On the basis of the syntax/discourse criterion, descriptive roots should be described as a subclass of verbs because they are most frequently used as predicates. On the basis of the morphological criterion, they should be considered a subclass of nouns, because they are preceded by Set II indexes only. They function as predicates, in an existential construction, like possessible nouns do. In contrast to what has been discussed for nouns and verbs in the preceding section, here the two criteria do not coincide. Depending on the criteria used, descriptive roots are therefore considered as verbs (syntax/discourse criterion) or as nouns (morphological criterion). Other authors favour an analysis with a separate class of adjectives (Villafañe 2004; Magalhães 2007),[13] on the basis that these show simultaneously both verbal and nominal properties (on the syntactic and morphological levels, respectively). The crucial facts used for determining the part of speech of descriptive roots

---

[12] There is at least one author (Copin 2012) that splits this class of descriptive roots as descriptive verbs and descriptive nouns, the latter being those that can function as heads of an NP.
[13] Reiter (2011) also considers that there is an adjective class in Awetí, but it includes only two items.

are summarized in Table 33.2. Interestingly, this table shows that no word class is primarily used for modification in Maweti–Guarani languages. In the absence of a word class devoted to noun modification, a noun can be semantically specified by another noun used in apposition without particular morphology (Jensen 1998: 513), or by a nominalized verb (Rose 2011: 343–350).

Table 33.2 Comparison of Maweti–Guarani descriptive roots with nouns and verbs

	Morphology	Main syntactic/discourse function
Verbs	Set I for S/A	predication
Nouns	Set II for Poss	argument
Descriptive roots	Set II for S	predication

As a follow-up to his hypothesis of a former omnipredicative stage (see section 33.3), Queixalós (2006: 282) suggests that after the decline of omnipredicativity, 'it was the conservation, in this later stage, of its functional indistinction that allowed the class of states [FR: descriptive roots] to lean, in subsequent stages, either towards nouns […] or towards verbs'. There is actually one language with two clearly distinct classes of descriptive roots, Teko, a.k.a. Emerillon (Couchili et al. 2002).[14]

This section can be concluded with typological remarks regarding part of speech systems, and their interaction with syntax. First, the absence of adjectives in the presence of adverbs, at least in some Maweti–Guarani languages (see section 33.6.4), does not respect the parts-of-speech hierarchy given in Hengeveld (1992), that has been later updated to account for similar counterexamples (Hengeveld & van Lier 2010). Second, the flexibility of descriptive roots varies depending on their analysis. If descriptive roots are considered a subclass of verbs, word-class flexibility is then just partial: some verbs only (descriptive ones) can be used as noun modifiers without additional morphology. If descriptive roots are considered a subclass of nouns, word-class flexibility is again partial: many nouns (including descriptive ones), but not all, can be used as predicates without additional morphology. If descriptive roots are considered as a separate word class, its flexibility is not bidirectional: they can be used as predicates and (sometimes) noun modifiers without additional morphology, while verbs cannot be used as noun modifiers without additional morphology.

Another interesting typological remark is that noun modification using a lexical modifier is not very frequent in Maweti–Guarani languages. Published descriptions of noun phrases with descriptive modifiers are short and examples scarce. Other morphosyntactic means to modify nouns are sometimes mentioned, such as the use of augmentative and diminutive

[14] One of the descriptive root classes is comparable to the class of words discussed in this section, while the other includes roots that need additional morphology (specific to this class) to function as predicates and to be additionally nominalized to be used as modifiers or arguments.

morphology (Dietrich 2000: 256), or noun + noun and noun + verb compounding to create semantically more specific nouns (Jensen 1998: 511–512; Rodrigues 1951, 1996: 63–64).

A final typological remark is that the analysis of descriptive roots has a strong effect on the description of major aspects of the syntax of Maweti–Guarani languages. Most remarkably, it has an impact on the description of its alignment system (Corrêa-da-Silva 2010: 224). If descriptive roots are analysed as verbs, there is a split-intransitivity system between two classes of verbs, the active class taking Set I indexes and the descriptive class taking Set II indexes. If descriptive roots are analysed as nouns, verbs show a nominative–accusative system, with Set I for S^A and A, and Set II for P. Split intransitivity can then only be described at the level of predicates: verbal predicates take Set I indexes, while non-verbal predicates (i.e. nouns, including descriptive roots) take Set II indexes (Rose 2008: 453).

33.5 Construction parallelism with verbs, nouns, and postpostions as heads, and relational morphology

This section discusses how Maweti–Guarani postpositions share syntactic, morphological, and lexical behaviour with both nouns and verbs. Verbs, nouns and postpositions are often described as 'the three major lexical classes' or 'the three inflected parts of speech' (Corrêa-da-Silva 2010: 223). This section will also deal with 'relational prefixes', a topic of much debate.

Adpositions are treated in the typological literature as being syntactically more similar with verbs than with nouns (Jaworska 1999).[15] The literature on Maweti–Guarani instead regularly highlights some similarities between postpositions, verbs and nouns, in sharp contrast with adverbs, particles, and conjunctions. Below is a list of three features shared by these three word classes. In fact, the comparison targets all postpositions, but among verbs transitive verbs only and among nouns obligatorily possessed nouns only.

(i) The dependent of the three word classes is obligatory, although the object of transitive verbs is not always overtly expressed, but it is always semantically present (the referent is always recoverable), and is often inferred from the hierarchical indexation pattern on the verb, as in (34) (see section 33.6.1). It is then interpretable anaphorically.

(ii) The dependent of the three word classes is either expressed by a noun phrase as in (19) and (20) or a Set II index as in (21)–(23), and immediately precedes the head. This means that postpositions are inflected, as visible in (22) (see Jaworska 1999: 304, on the notion of inflected adposition). It is cross-linguistically common

---

[15] Jaworska (1999) notes that, in English for example, verbs and prepositions take an object noun phrase, while complements of nouns are introduced with 'of'. In Polish, only verbs and prepositions take accusative complements. This assertion is not explicitly dependent from the lexical origin of adpositions in serial verbs or relator nouns (see DeLancey (2005) on the sources of adpositions).

that possessed nouns, postpositions, and verbs mark their dependent element similarly (Bakker 2013).

Teko (Rose 2011: 162, 123, 66)
(19) *apam-a-baʔekʷər-a-kom*   NP + N
foreigner-*a*-custom-*a*-PL
'the customs of the foreigners'

(20) *Françoise   o-ho   **Surinam-a-pope**.*   NP + POSTP
Françoise   3.I-go   Surinam-*a*-in
'Françoise went to Surinam.'

(21) *e-mebir*   SetII-N
1SG.II-child
'my child'

(22) *o-naʔaŋ-tar   e-koti.*   SetII-POSTP
3.I-meet-FUT   1SG.II-at
'They meet at me (my place).'

(23) *zawar   e-suʔu.*   SetII-V
dog   1SG.II-bite
'A dog bit me.'

The situation with verbs is slightly different, with third person objects. Nouns and third person Set II index for objects may immediately precede the verb in some dependent clauses only, like (24) and (25). In independent clauses, verbs obligatorily take either a subject or an object index, within a so-called hierarchical indexation system (see section 33.6.1). This verbal morphosyntax differs from that of postpositions and nouns.

Teko (Rose 2011: 331)
(24) *o-zoka   **bokal-itʃig**.*   NP + V
3.I-break   jar-drop
'He broke the jar when dropping it.'

(25) *o-(w)eraho   ʔi-b   **i-mõbo**.*   SetII–V
3.I-carry   water-in   3.II-throw
'She carries (it) and throws it in the water.'

(3) Some items within these three classes of words are said to take a 'relational prefix' when immediately preceded by their dependent (either a noun phrase, or a first or second person index, but not when a third person index).

Teko (Rose 2011: 93, 95, 90)

(26) *teko-r-apidʒ-a-te.*   NP+r-N
Teko-REL-house-*a*-FOC
'It is the house of Teko.'

(27) *nõde-r-apidʒ-am*   SetII-r-N
2.II-REL-house-TRANSL
'for our houses'

(28) *o-sisig-a-r-ehe*   NP+r-POSTP
3.COREF-sister-*a*-REL-POSTP
'with his (own) sister'

(29) *de-r-ehe*   SetII-r-POSTP
2SG.II-REL-POSTP
'at/with you'

(30) *o-ho-tar*   **pureru-r-eka.**   NP+r-V
3.I-go-FUT   toad-REL-look_for
'He is going to look for the toad.'

(31) *d-e-r-aihi-dʒi.*   SetII-r-V
NEG-1SG.II-REL-like-NEG
'He does not like me.'

The subset of lexical items taking the relational prefix cannot be predicted on a semantic or a phonological basis, though all of the items taking it start with a vowel. This prefix has been reconstructed for Proto-Tupi (Rodrigues & Dietrich 1997; Corrêa-da-Silva 2010; Rodrigues & Cabral 2012). It has been much discussed (Payne 1994; Jensen 1998: 498–502, 557–562; Cabral 2000b) because its function is difficult to define: it is usually defined by its distribution, and is thus said to be marking the head–dependent relationship. There are two other analyses of the relational morpheme. Payne (1994) analyses it as a marker of inverse (see section 33.6.1), but this analysis does not account for its use on nouns and postpositions. Meira and Drude (2013) argue that it results from historical morphophonological changes undergone by the initial consonant of the root, conditioned by both the phonological context and the morphosyntactic structure. In their view, the relational morpheme should therefore not be reconstructed, since it is not a morpheme.

The three word classes are split in several inflectional classes depending on the allomorphs of the relational morpheme that they take (the distribution is only partly predictable on the basis of phonology). Because the same inflectional classes also seem to predict the form of the third person index for possessor, object, and object of postposition, most authors consider that third person indexes belong to a paradigm of four different relational prefixes (see for example Cabral 2000b; and Rose 2011: 97–103 for alternative analyses).

    (i) *r-* (or allomorphs) when the dependent (noun or first or second person index) immediately precedes the head;

(ii) *i-* (or allomorphs) when the dependent does not immediately precede the head. Elsewhere it is simply analysed as a third person Set II index.
(iii) *o-* when the dependent is coreferential with the subject. Elsewhere it is analysed as a third person index.
(iv) *t-* when the dependent is a non-specific human being. Elsewhere it is analysed as a dummy marker when an obligatorily possessed noun has no specific possessor.

The different constructions are illustrated in Table 33.3 with nouns of two different classes in Teko, *owa* 'face' that takes the relational prefix and *kija* 'hammock' that does not.

Table 33.3 Teko possessive constructions of nouns with or without the relational prefix

e-r-owa	*e-kija*	1st person
X-(a)-r-owa	*X-(a)-kija*	noun phrase
Ø-owa	*i-kija*	3rd person
o-owa	*o-kija*	3rd person coreferential
t-owa	*kija*	non-specific possessor

The common behaviour of nouns, verbs, and postpositions is summarized in Table 33.4. Postpositions share with some subclasses of nouns and verbs their syntax (they all enter a similar construction where they head a dependent), their morphology (Set II indexes, and relational prefixes for some), and their inflectional classes (determining which allomorph of the relational prefix they take). Additional information on postpositions will be given in section 33.6.3.

Table 33.4 Comparison of Maweti–Guarani postpositions with subclasses of nouns and verbs

	Morphology	Inflectional classes taking different allomorphs of the relational prefix	Syntactic construction with dependent expressed as an N
Transitive verbs	Set I for A, Set II for P	yes	N(-a-REL)-V in dependent clauses
Possessible nouns	Set II for Poss	yes	N(-a-REL)-N
Postpositions	Set II for Object	yes	N(-a-REL)-POSTP

33.6 Major features of lexical word classes

33.6.1 Verbs

As discussed in section 33.3, verbs in Maweti–Guarani are defined either as the class of roots that is most often used as predicates, or as the class of roots that can combine with Set I indexes. This section will discuss reduplication (a typical feature of Maweti–Guarani verbs), the hierarchical indexation system (a typologically remarkable characteristic of verb morphology), and finally the syntactic subclasses of verbs.

First, the process of reduplication expressing aspect has frequently been put forward as specific to verbs (Everett & Seki 1985; Rose 2005, 2007; Lima 2007; Cruz 2014; Dietrich 2014; Drude 2014). Jensen (1998: 538) reconstructs for Proto-Tupi-Guarani a distinction between monosyllabic reduplication, expressing event-internal plurality as in (32), and disyllabic reduplication, expressing event-external plurality as in (33), using here Cusic's (1981) terminology, distinguishing repetition within the limits of the event vs repetition of the event itself (see more details in Rose 2007). However, most modern Tupi (including Maweti–Guarani) languages do not clearly show this semantic distinction (Rose 2007; Dietrich 2014).

Tupinambá (Jensen 1990: 128–129)
(32) oro-pópór
1EXCL.I-jump.RED1
'We jumped, one after the other.'

(33) oro-poropór
1EXCL.I-jump.RED2
'We jumped frequently.'

Second, a feature of Maweti–Guarani verbs that is typological important (though not used in the definition of verbs) and plays a central role in the literature since Monserrat and Soares (1983) is the hierarchical person indexation system on transitive verbs. A first explicit definition of hierarchical indexing systems is found in Nichols (1992: 66): 'Access to inflectional slots for subject and/or object is based on person, number, and/or animacy rather than (or no less than) on syntactic relations.' In practice, this means that the participant that is higher on the hierarchy is favoured over the one that ranks lower. Inverse systems (a special case of hierarchical systems) indicate specifically whether the direction of the action respects the hierarchy or not. Maweti–Guarani languages are said to follow a person hierarchy, often 1>2>3, determining which of the two arguments of a transitive predicate is to be represented in the unique index slot of the predicate. There are two sets of person markers that qualify for this slot, Set I for A and Set II for P. When the A argument is the highest on the hierarchy, it is indexed on the verb with Set I. This is illustrated in (34) for 1 → 3 (X → Y stands for 'X is acting on Y'). When the P argument is the highest on the hierarchy, it is indexed on the verb with Set II. This is illustrated in (35) for 3 → 1. When two third persons interact, only the third person A argument is indexed on the verb (36).

Avá-Canoeiro (Borges 2006: 158–160)

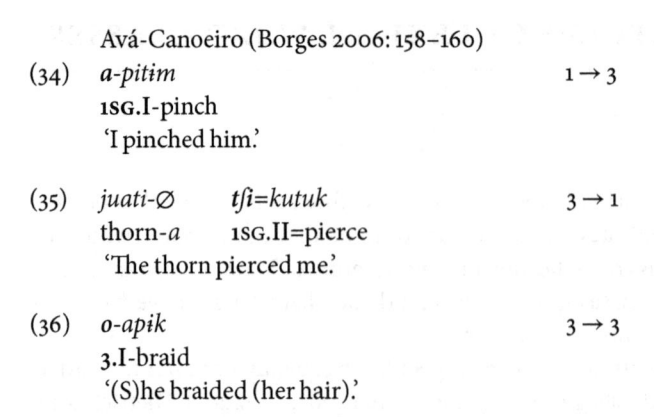

(34) a-pitim   1 → 3
     1SG.I-pinch
     'I pinched him.'

(35) juati-Ø   tʃi=kutuk   3 → 1
     thorn-a   1SG.II=pierce
     'The thorn pierced me.'

(36) o-apɨk   3 → 3
     3.I-braid
     '(S)he braided (her hair).'

The hierarchical indexing system is summarized in Table 33.5. Arguments against an analysis of this system as an inverse system (Payne 1994) have been given in Rose (2009).

Table 33.5 The 'canonical' hierarchical indexing system of Maweti–Guarani languages

	1P	2P	3P
1A		A	A
2A	P		A
3A	P	P	A

A survey of Tupi–Guarani languages (Rose 2015b) shows that only two languages out of 28 exemplify this canonical system, Avá-Canoeiro (Borges 2006) and Kayabí (Dobson 1997). The great majority of languages support a 1/2 > 3 hierarchy, but with a more complex encoding of configurations involving two speech act participants, that do not clearly support a robust 1>2 hierarchy. This can be seen, for example, in the detailed description of the Teko indexation system (Rose 2009). The hierarchy between the two speech act participants is in fact cross-linguistically debatable (Zúñiga 2006). It has also been argued that the person hierarchy has not been the functional motivation responsible for the creation of hierarchical systems, but that the latter basically result from independent historical morphological processes (Rose 2018). It is suggested that these systems originate from the absence of third person forms in the pronominal paradigms.

Finally, subclasses of verbs in Maweti–Guarani languages are not much discussed beyond the questions already presented above, i.e. the distinction between intransitive (37) and transitive (38) verbs, and that between two classes of intransitive verbs (see 'descriptive roots' in section 33.4). Two additional subclasses are sometimes discussed: first, extended intransitive verbs (39), which mark their subject with Set I and have a second obligatory argument marked with a postposition; second, ditransitive verbs (40), with a third obligatory argument, introduced by a postposition.

Araweté (Solano 2009: 184, 187, 186, 189)

(37) ere-ja   ku   ne   braziʎa-hɨ
     2.I-come   FOC   2   Brasilia-ABL
     'You come from Brasilia.'

(38) Iwaneru   ku   u-juka   mitu
     Iwaneru   FOC   3-kill   curassow
     'Iwaneru killed a curassow.'

(39) ere-maʔẽ   ku   kujĩ   r-ehe
     2.I-look   FOC   woman   REL-for
     'You look at the woman.'

(40) u-meʔẽ   ku   katfe   ure   r-e
     3.I-give   FOC   coffee   1EXCL   REL-for
     'He gives us coffee.'

33.6.2 Nouns

Beyond the issue of distinguishing nouns from verbs (and possibly adjectives), grammars of Maweti–Guarani languages usually discuss two issues concerning nouns: first, the scarce morphology that is specific to nouns, and second, the subclasses of nouns depending on possessibility.

As far as morphology is concerned, we have already seen that nouns can be distinguished from (most) verbs in that they do not take the 'subject person prefixes' (Set I indexes). They instead take Set II indexes for their possessor but these are also found on verbs, either for the object of transitive verbs or for the subject of stative intransitive verbs (often called descriptive).[16] Another type of morphology that distinguishes nouns and verbs, or rather nominal phrases and predicates, is negation (Chousou-Polydouri et al. 2016; Dietrich 2017), but it is actually extremely rarely invoked for distinguishing word classes (Reiter 2011 is an exception). Also, number marking is rarely invoked, probably because it varies a lot within the family (Gasparini 2011).

When considering the morphology specific to nouns, authors describing Tupi–Guarani languages usually discuss the -a suffix, cases and the so-called nominal tenses. The -a suffix that has already been discussed in section 33.3 is sometimes described as a case (e.g. 'argumentative case', 'nuclear case'). As mentioned before, the -a suffix is not really specific to nouns, since it is also used on verbs when they serve as arguments. There are four other case suffixes, three locative ones like -pe in (41), and a 'translative' one, expressing temporary

---

[16] This parallelism between transitive verb roots and their object and nouns and their possessor drove Dietrich (2001) as well as Cabral (2007a) to consider 'verbal roots' with a Set II index as forming a nominal phrase. According to them, the translation of '(s)he hits me' should in fact be analysed as '(there is) my action of hitting (= hitting that concerns me)'.

qualities as in (42). Nouns in Maweti–Guarani languages are supposed to be devoid of case suffixes only when used as vocatives, in compounds and as predicates, except that most languages are in the process of losing these suffixes, at least in some contexts (Rodrigues 2000). Only two of the locative cases are found in Mawé and Awetí, while the *-a*, the translative suffix and the third locative case are absent from these languages (Corrêa-da-Silva 2010: 203–207).

Asuriní do Tocantins (Cabral 2000a: 10, 13)
(41) más-a   ka?á-*pe*
      snake-*a*   forest-LOC.PUNCT
      'There are snakes in the forest.'

(42) sahý-a   sekwehé   akomaě-*ramo*   pané
      moon-*a*   in_the_old_days   man-TRANSL   FRUSTR
      'In the old days, the moon had been a man.'

Most Maweti–Guarani languages also show two nominal suffixes that are usually glossed 'past' and 'future' but are importantly never found on verbs. Tonhauser (2006, 2007) has studied this phenomenon in detail in Paraguayan Guaraní. She argues that Guaraní *-kue* and *-rã* do not locate the noun phrase in time like tense markers locate the state of affairs in time, but instead 'express a temporal precedence relation: they specify that the property (or relation) denoted by the nominal predicate is true of the individuals denoted by the noun phrase prior and subsequent to another time, respectively'. In (43), the woman whose existence is expressed in the noun phrase will be a wife in the future, while in (44), the possessive relation precedes the time at which the whole noun phrase is interpreted.

Paraguayan Guaraní (Tonhauser 2007: 833, 836)
(43) O-ho   peteĩ   arriéro   o-jeruré-vo   la   h-embireko-*rã*-re.
      3.I-go   one   man   3.I-ask.for-at   LA   3.II-wife-RA-RE
      'A man went to ask for his future wife.'

(44) Che   a-reko   peteĩ   lívro de medisína,   che-aguélo   mba'e-*kue*.
      PRO1SG   1SG.I-have   one   book of medicine   1SG.II-grandfather   thing-KUE
      'I have a medicine book, it was my grandfather's.'

All grammars similarly describe three classes of nouns, based on their behaviour in regard to adnominal possession. The relational nouns (also called obligatorily possessed, dependent or inalienable) are those that cannot appear without a possessor being expressed. In Wayampi, for example, relational nouns comprise parts of a whole (body or not) and bodily excretions, and kinship terms (Copin 2012: 37–38). The autonomous nouns (also called optionally possessed, possessible, or alienable) may appear with or without a possessor. In Wayampi, autonomous nouns comprise artefacts, social status, cyclic times of day or year, properties, natural phenomena, and food and drinks (Copin 2012: 41–42). Avalent nouns (also called non-possessible or absolute) cannot be expressed with a possessor. In Wayampi, these include human beings, ethnic names, and animals (Copin 2012: 44–45). The adnominal possession construction does not differ for those nouns that can or must be possessed, but the avalent nouns referring to animals can sometimes enter a different possessive construction, where they are possessed with the help of a relational noun for 'catch' or 'pet' in a construction reminiscent of possessive classifiers (Rose 2011: 163–166; Copin 2012: 45).

       Wayampi (Copin 2012: 45)
(45)   *e=lemija*   *ka'i*   *o-mo-kãẽ=ta*
       1SG.II=catch   monkey.sp   3.I-CAUS-be_smoked=FUT
       'She will smoke my brown capuchin monkey.' (lit. She will smoke my catch brown capuchin monkey)

33.6.3 Postpositions

Rodrigues (2000: 1) states that 'most languages of the Tupi–Guarani family mark dependent nouns with [case] suffixes as well as postpositions'.[17] In practice, it seems there is some confusion about these terms, for several reasons: first, postpositions may be seen as formal expressions of semantic cases (for example Cabral 2000a; Solano 2009: 164–173); second, postpositions may be described formally as suffixes (as for example in Dietrich 1986: 55–56; Villafañe 2004: 55) or as clitics (as in Vallejos 2010: 163), and last of all, there have probably been some historical changes which led to variation among Maweti-Guarani languages, and a less straightforward distinction in individual languages (da Cruz 2011: 222–224). Rodrigues (2000: 1) indeed suggests that 'it is possible that some of these languages have lost marking with case suffixes and have replaced them entirely with the use of postpositions'.[18]

A dozen of postpositions have been reconstructed for Proto-Tupi-Guarani (Jensen 1998: 514), but individual languages may have innovated new ones, either through compound postpositions or combinations of a relational (locative) noun with a case suffix or a postposition (see for example Copin 2012: 95–102). It has been shown in section 33.5 that Maweti-Guarani postpositions are inflected adpositions (Jaworska 1999: 304, on this notion): if the noun phrase they introduce is not overtly expressed, then it is indexed on the postposition with a Set II index.

Finally, in some languages like Awetí (Reiter 2011: 150) and Teko (Rose 2011: 368–370, 2013), some postpositions function as subordinators (see Rose 2006 for a typological investigation of formal identity between postpositions and subordinators), along more specific subordinating suffixes reconstructable to Proto-Tupi-Guarani (Jensen 1998: 528).

---

[17] My translation for: 'A maioria das línguas da família Tupi–Guarani marca os nomes dependentes por meio tanto de sufixos como de posposições'.
[18] My translation for: 'É possível que algumas dessas línguas tenham perdido a marcação por sufixos casuais e a tenham substituído inteiramente pelo uso de posposições'.

33.6.4 Adverbs

Central pieces of comparative work (Jensen 1998, 1999; Corrêa-da-Silva 2010) and the pioneering and influential description of a Maweti–Guarani language (Rodrigues 1953, on Tupinambá) do not mention a class of adverbs. Dietrich (2000: 255) asserts that there is no class of adverbs in Tupi–Guarani languages. Nevertheless, most descriptions of individual Maweti–Guarani languages do include a category of adverbs. These are described as non-inflected words, mainly used as modifiers of the predicate. They are easily distinguished from nouns, verbs, and postpositions by not taking person indexes. Two properties of adverbs are often put forward: (i) they can be nominalized with a specific de-adverbial nominalizer as in (46) (this also applies to postpositional phrases) and (ii) when in clause-initial position, they trigger a special form of the verb, differing from that of regular main verbs by taking a suffix and following a different person indexation pattern as in (47).[19]

Asuriní do Xingu (Pereira 2009: 163)
(46) karukame-war-a
yesterday-NZR-*a*
'the one of yesterday'

Kamayurá (Seki 2000: 76)
(47) ikue   rak   i-ker-i
yesterday   AT   3.II-sleep-CIRC
'Yesterday he slept.'

The usual subclasses of adverbs are temporal, locative, and manner adverbs. Note that in several grammars, numerals (often only three items) are considered adverbs, on the basis that they are often used to modify a predicate, can be nominalized with the de-adverbial nominalizer (48) and trigger the special (oblique-topicalized) verb form (49). In other languages, numerals are considered a separate word class, on the basis that they are generally used either as modifiers of a noun or as predicates; or they are considered as adjectives or nouns.

Asuriní do Xingu (Pereira 2009: 167)
(48) mukuj-war-a
two-NZR-*a*
'the two'

---

[19] This is called either Indicative 2 (following Rodrigues 1953: 132), circumstantial mood (see for example Pereira 2009: 162) or oblique-topicalized verb form (Jensen 1998: 526).

Kamayurá (Seki 2000: 80)
(49) *mokomokōj*   *i-porahaj-awa-i*
      two_by_two   3.II-dance-PL-CIRC
      They dance two by two

33.6.5 Ideophones and interjections

According to Dingemanse (2019: 13; see also Chapter 22 in this volume), 'a canonical ideophone is a member of an open lexical class of marked words that depict sensory imagery'. A class of ideophones has been identified in many Maweti–Guarani languages. They are often only briefly mentioned, but there are a few more detailed studies (Langdon 1994; Rose 2011: 400–409;) and an extraordinarily comprehensive and detailed investigation of ideophones in Awetí (Reiter 2011).

Leaving aside the phonosemantic and prosodic properties of ideophones, these can be distinguished from other parts of speech by their usual absence of morphological combinatorics except reduplication, and their variable syntactic integration. They can indeed be extra-clausal (50), introduced by a light verb (the same that introduces direct speech, *e'i* in (51)) or the sole predicate of a clause with its own arguments (52). They are often repeated in discourse, as in (51).

(50) Awetí (Reiter 2011: 338, 346, 337)
      Powowowo,   *o-to*   *a'yn.*
      IDEO.fly   3-go   PART
      'It flew off.' (lit.: '(There was) powowowo, it went off.')

(51) *Tyryk tyryk,*   *e'i*   *a'yt*   *ti*   *n=eko-tu*   *a'yn.*
      IDEO.limp   3.say   EMOT   EVID   3=walk-NZR   PART
      '"Tyryk tyryk", the poor (animal) does when it walks.'

(52) *Wej-t-atĩ*   *tsãn*   *a'yn.*   *Pywpywpyw*   *n-emi'ũkangut.*
      3-EPEN-wrap.up   3PL.PRO   PART[20]   IDEO.tie   3-rest.of.food
      'They wrapped it up. Pywpywpyw a leftover.'

In Yuqui (Villafañe 2004: 101–102) and Sirionó (Schermair 1949: 252), it is explicitly said that ideophones do not form a separate word class but are instead a subclass of verbs distinguished by their taking subject person suffixes. However, given that these 'suffixes' have a form similar to the conjugated verb 'say', it is at least reasonable to suggest that what has been analysed as verbal suffixes is at least historically the 'say' verb, postposed to ideophones in a light verb construction (Dahl 2014: 107, 114). The close study of Awetí lexicon also shows that some verbs may have been historically derived from ideophones (Reiter 2011: 454–455, 488–495). Also, Reiter (2011: 459) points to non-random correspondences between Awetí

---

[20] *a'yn* is a sentence-final particle.

and Teko ideophones, hinting at the reconstructability of some ideophones at the Proto-Maweti–Guarani stage.

Interjections are not often described in grammars as a separate word class, except for Awetí, where Reiter specifies how they differ from ideophones (Reiter 2011: 161–163). Interestingly, they can occur in this language with morphology and be used as a predicate with their own arguments. In many grammars, interjections are instead mentioned as a subclass of particles (see section 33.6.6). An interesting fact is that interjections are specified as being specific to men's and women's speech in several languages: Old Guaraní (Ruiz de Montoya 1640), Guarayu (Höller 1932), Tupinambá (Barbosa 1947) and Bolivian Guaraní (Ortiz & Caurey 2012). In South American languages in general (Rose 2015a) and Tupi languages in particular (Rose & Chousou-Polydouri 2017), a genderlect distinction is in fact often observed in various types of discourse markers (interjections or particles).

33.6.6 Particles

The term 'particle' is mentioned in most descriptions of Maweti–Guarani languages, with detailed accounts of the use and behaviour of this class of words in most grammars. Particles are defined as uninflected independent words. They are usually classified depending on their position: fixed in the clause, either in second (53) or final (54) position; or variable, following the constituent they have scope over (55). They cover a wide range of functions, with major functions being epistemicity/evidentiality as with the inferential in (53) (see the comparative study by Cabral 2007b), information structure as with the restrictive in (55), TAM as with *rã̃e* in (54), negation, interrogation as with *tã* in (54) and deixis. As the term 'particle' became associated with these functions and distribution, other authors call 'particles' items with similar functions, even though these are not considered words, but suffixes (as in Tapieté (González 2005)), clitics (as in Teko (Rose 2011)) or forms belonging to the same phonological word than the preceding element (as in Avá-Canoeiro (Borges 2006: 202)).

Tapirapé (Praça 2007: 163, 173, 177)
(53) marare-ø   pa   ã-wo   a-ka
     cow-refer   INFER   DEM-LOC   3.I-be
     'The cows are around (hearing the bellow of the cattle).'

(54) mayn   tã   ãkaj   ere-a   ãxe'i   rã̃e
     why   INTER   C.I.COM   2SG.I-go   yesterday   PST
     'Why did you go yesterday?'

(55) kotãtãi-wer-a   xe   rõ̃o   ke   ãkaj   'ã-wo   a-a   rã̃e
     girl-PL-a   REST   N.ASS   DUB   C.I.COM   DEM-LOC   3.I-go   PST
     'I think that only the girls went there.'

Example (55) shows five particles in one clause: *xe* with variable position, the second position particles *rõ̃o*, *ke*, and *ãkaj*, and clause-final *rã̃e*. They contribute to the expression of information structure (*xe* 'only'), tense (*rã̃e* 'past') and epistemicity (*rõ̃o*, *ke*, and *ãkaj* encode that the informational content of the clause is shared by the speaker and the addressee but non-asserted by the speaker that expresses some doubts towards it). Particles are in fact really frequent in spontaneous discourse, even though they are not obligatory (Borges 2006: 202). They are thus markers of native identity. In some languages, particles additionally show a genderlect distinction (Rose & Chousou-Polydouri 2017). For example, the affirmative particle of Mawé is *ta'i* for men and *hẽ* for women (da Silva 2010: 241).

33.7 CONCLUSION

This chapter has presented the major parts of speech of Maweti-Guarani languages. The central issue concerns the noun–verb distinction, a question that also concerns words with adjectival meaning. The noun–verb distinction in Maweti-Guarani is blurred by several facts: (i) the items that are most often used as arguments (i.e. nouns) can function as predicates without any additional morphology; (ii) verbs in some languages can function as arguments without any additional morphology (i.e. with the referential *-a* suffix only); (iii) transitive verbs, possessible nouns, postpositions, and descriptive roots (candidates for either the noun or verb class) share most of their morphology and syntax. Besides the issue of the noun–verb distinction, this chapter also presents the main characteristics of all major word classes: nouns, verbs, postpositions, adverbs, ideophones and interjections, and particles. It presents not only the features that are crucial in identifying these word classes, but also their subclasses and typical features, some of which are also typologically remarkable (such as the hierarchical indexation system on transitive verbs, or tense marking on nouns).

This chapter also gives an image of issues concerning word classes in South America in general, and Amazonia in particular. To start with, in many Amazonian languages various word classes can be used as predicates without additional morphology (Aikhenvald 2012: 136–137). A set of person indexes shared by nouns and verbs is also one of the features proposed in Dixon & Aikhenvald (1999: 9) for an 'Amazonian' profile, in contrast to an 'Andean' one. And the term 'particle' is part of the descriptive tradition of lowland South American languages (Dooley 1990). Also, South American languages rarely show an independent status of adjectives (Aikhenvald 2012: 139; Krasnoukhova 2012: 140). The function of words with adjectival meaning is noteworthy: few South American languages have a possibility of attributive modification by adjectives, whereas predicative use is always available (Krasnoukhova 2012: 158, 184, 2022). Many Maweti-Guarani languages adhere to this general South American profile. Finally, the parallel construction of possessible nouns, transitive verbs and postpositions with their arguments, including the use of a relational prefix, is one of the features for positing the historical relationship between the Tupi, Carib, and Macro-Jê families of Amazonia (Rodrigues 2009).

ACKNOWLEDGEMENTS

I would like to thank for their useful feedback on an earlier version of this chapter Natalia Chousou-Polydouri and Olga Krasnoukhova, as well as an external reviewer and the editor, Eva van Lier.

CHAPTER 34

WORD CLASSES IN QUECHUAN LANGUAGES

PIETER MUYSKEN

34.1 INTRODUCTION: THE LANGUAGE FAMILY

THE Quechuan languages are an important language family in South America for several reasons. The following overview is based on Adelaar with Muysken (2004); see also Cerrón-Palomino (1987).

First of all, it is a large family, with varieties spoken in (from north to south) Colombia, Ecuador, Peru, possibly Brazil, Bolivia, Chile, and Argentina. Undoubtedly, the heartland of the family is Peru. Here we find most variation between varieties, and the largest number of speakers. Speaker numbers are notoriously difficult to establish, with rapid language shift to Spanish in most areas, but an estimate could be somewhere around 8 million speakers, to give a first indication. It is mostly spoken in the Andean highlands, but there are increasing numbers of speakers in the Amazonian foothills as well. Historically, it is a fairly shallow family, with the Central Peruvian Andes as the most likely place of origin, datable to around 200 AD perhaps. Later, the languages split into two main branches, Quechua I and Quechua II. In many respects, the Quechuan languages are similar in major components of their morphosyntax. I will mostly comment on properties of Cuzco Quechua and Ecuadorian Quechua in this chapter (both Quechua II varieties), since these are the ones I have worked on myself.[1]

Second, it is historically and culturally an important language, since it was adopted by the Incas as the language of their empire, and later on used by the Spanish invaders and colonizers as a way of communicating with the indigenous populations. This has led to a large body of materials written in and about Quechuan languages. It has an important status as an official or semi-official language in Peru, Bolivia, and Ecuador, with many documents published in it even today.

---

[1] I have tried to cite as many examples as possible from Antonio Cusihuamán's excellent native speaker grammar (1976) of Cuzco Quechua, to honour this linguist who alas died much too young.

Third, the language has lexically influenced many languages in the region in recent times, and at the same time it has undergone influences from other languages such as the neighbouring Aymaran languages from the very beginning. In section 34.7, I will briefly place the Quechuan languages in the broader Andean context.

I will sometimes use the term 'Quechua' instead of 'the Quechuan languages' to illustrate features of the family as a whole, but for each individual example I will indicate the specific variety cited. The term 'Kichwa' refers to Ecuadorian varieties. Even though the Quechuan languages differ in many respects, I do not think they differ fundamentally in their categorical make up, except for some details pointed out below.

The Quechuan languages have a classical typological profile of accusative alignment, with generally verb–final (SOV), possessor–noun and adjective–noun (AN) constituent order. There are three vowels, combined with a richer inventory of consonants. Syllables may be C(C)VC, and word stress is on the penultimate syllable. There is rich suffixal, agglutinative morphology, both verbal and nominal. The languages have both head marking (with obligatory subject marking and object marking for first and second person human referents) and dependent marking (with a rich case system). Subordination is mostly marked morphologically, with a class of very productive nominalizer suffixes and with adverbial subordination suffixes marking switch reference.

This chapter will start with some comments on parts of speech, from the perspective of the Quechua lexicon, phonotactics, and morphology in section 34.2. In subsequent sections, specific categories are analysed: adjectives and adverbs (section 34.3), nominalizations (section 34.4), postpositions (section 34.5), and clitics (section 34.6). In section 34.7, an areal perspective is given, and section 34.8 contains some conclusions.

34.2 THE PARTS OF SPEECH: A BRIEF OVERVIEW

We can distinguish parts of speech in Quechua on various dimensions: syntax, morphology, and phonology. Here I will briefly survey these dimensions, and return to them at various points in subsequent sections where there is a more focused discussion.

34.2.1 Distinctions in the syntax

Grammatically, the parts of speech of Quechua are not very different from those of familiar European languages. There are nouns (underlined) that can form the nucleus of arguments and adjuncts, as in (1):

Salasaca Kichwa (fieldwork data)
(1) Ima   laya sumuk <u>tapis</u>   awa-na-da=ga   na yacha-n=chu chi <u>llakta</u>-bi.
    what way   pretty tapestry   weave-NMLZ-ACC=TOP not know-3=NEG that town-LOC
    'How to weave pretty tapestries they do not know in that town.'

Verbs form the nucleus of the clause; there is one finite verb per clause, such as the verb *yacha-* 'know' in (1). There can also be non-finite verbs in adverbial or complement clauses, such as nominalized *awa-* 'weave'.

Adjectives canonically directly precede the noun, as in the case of *sumuk* 'pretty' in (1). There may also be various kinds of adverbial expressions, derived in various ways (see section 34.3); they do not form a unified class, and have a relatively free position in the sentence, mostly determined by pragmatic and prosodic considerations. There are also postpositions and case markers, such as and *laya* 'kind, way' and *-bi* 'LOC' in (1).

Quechua has a number of subclasses of pronominal forms, numerals, and quantifiers. More details are given in section 34.2.3 for these categories.

There is also a small set of particles, separate words which do not have a categorical status and can only be suffixed with discursive suffixes, such as *na* (< *mana*) 'not' in (1). The precise inventory of this set varies across different Quechuan languages.

Special mention should be made of a class of exclamatives, which often have a specific fixed three-syllable /aCaCáw/ structure, as in (2).[2] These include:

(2)   Cuzco Quechua (Cusihuamán 1976: 287)
     achacháw   'damn!'
     alaláw   'how cold!'
     alhakáw   'how hot!'
     añañáw   'how rich (the food)!'
     atatáw   'how ugly!'

Their precise form and meaning varies, but they occur in many places in the Andes.

Much less common in the Quechuan languages, as far as is known, are ideophones. Nuckolls (1996) has extensively documented this category for Ecuador Amazonian Kichwa, and they may well be a feature shared with many languages in that area, such as Waorani, Barbacoan, and the Chicham languages. There are occasional examples in texts from other Quechuan varieties but not nearly with the same frequency and range. Ideophones show frequent reduplication and have many phonological properties of their own.

34.2.2 Distinctions in the morphology

From the perspective of parts of speech, several kinds of suffixes can be distinguished in Quechua. For the sake of the argument, I will take Cuzco Quechua as my point of departure here (with examples cited with page numbers from Cusihuamán 1976). The suffix classes are presented in Table 34.1, classified in terms of their base and their output.

---

[2] The specific form of these exclamatives varies somewhat, but they have a wide distribution across many Quechuan languages as well as neighbouring languages.

Table 34.1 Types of suffixes in Cuzco Quechua (using examples from Cusihuamán 1976)

class	suffixes	base N	base A	base V	base Prt	example	pp.
Output: nominal							
A	-kuna [PL]	x	x			mama-kuna [mother-PL] 'ladies'	70
	-ta [ACC]	x	x			allin-ta-n ri-sha-nchis [good-ACC go-PR-1PL.IN] 'we are going well'	128
	-cha [DIM]	x	x			sumaq-cha-ta [beautiful-DIM-ACC] 'something delicious[ACC]'	70
B	-y [INF]			x		kausa-y [live-INF] 'life'	219
Output: adjectival or nominal							
C	-q [AG]			x		puri-q [walk-AG] 'traveller'	73
Output: adjectival							
D	-yuq [POSS]	x				wasi-yuq [house-POSS] 'house owning'	72
	-sapa [AUG]	x				uma-sapa [head-AUG] 'big headed'	70
E	-karay [EXAG]		x			hatun-karay [big-EXAG] 'huge'	226
F	-mpa [POS]			x		t'ikra-mpa [turn.over-POS] 'inverted'	72
Output: verbal							
G	-cha [FAC]	x	x			alli-cha- [good-FAC-] 'to fix'	75
	-ya [DEV]	x	x			sipas-ya- [girl-DEV-] 'to become a girl'	75
H	-nki [2SG]			x		qarpa-nki [irrigate-2SG] 'you irrigate'	74
	-ysi [ASS]			x		llank'a-ysi- [work-ASS-] 'help work'	75
	-rqa [PST]			x		yanapa-rqa-yki [help-PST-1>2] 'I helped you'	169
I	-naya [DESI]	x				aycha-naya- [meat-DESI-] 'feel like (eating) meat'	197
				x		tusu-naya- [dance-DESI-] 'feel like dancing'	197
Output: neutral as to category							
J	-lla [DEL]	x	x	x		kuna-lla-n-ta-wan [now-DEL-3SG-ACC-with] 'only until today?'	70
K	-qa [TOP]	x		x		wasi-y=qa chay-pi-n ka-sha-n [house-1SG=TOP that-LOC-EVI COP-PR-3] 'my house is over there'	75
L	=mi/=n [EVI]	x	x	x	x	mana=n [NEG=EVI] 'not'	71
M	-y [1SG]	x	(x)	(x)		wasi-y [house-1SG] 'my house'	72

Of course, more complex and fine-grained analyses are possible, but Table 34.1 gives a first approximation of the types of suffixes in the language, where I assume Cuzco Quechua to be fairly typical of the family in this respect. I have ignored the important difference between syntactic and lexical uses of suffixes, but I do not think it makes a lot of difference here (see, e.g. Muysken 1981).

Class A consists of the highly frequent markers such as plural and case (there are around nine case markers) which are attached to either nouns or adjectives and with nominal expressions as the output. In class B, the infinitive marker turns verbs into nouns, while class C contains the nominalizers -*sqa* 'realized action', -*na* 'unrealized action' and -*q* 'agentive', which turn verbs into nouns or adjectives (if we take relative clauses to be adjectival).

Classes D–F involve different suffixes that derive adjectives. There are over half a dozen of these but they are only moderately productive. They can have various categories of words as their base. In class D, the suffix -*yuq* 'possessor/origin' (which may contain agentive -*q*) can be attached to nouns to form a noun or an adjective.

The suffixes in class G verbalize a noun or an adjective, while the very large class of suffixes in H are attached to verbs and yield verbs. This class includes a great many derivational suffixes, Tense/Aspect/Mood (TAM) suffixes and person markers. The desiderative suffix in class I -*naya* 'feel like', can take a verb or a noun as its base.

A special class of suffixes in Quechua does not change the class membership of its base. In J, the delimitative suffix -*lla* 'just' can be attached to nouns, verbs, and adjectives, but in contrast with the other 'class-free' suffixes it does not necessarily appear at the end of the word but often close to the root, as in the example given in Table 34.1. The topic marker -*qa* in K can occur on different constituents of the clause, including arguments, adjuncts, and the verb. The larger class in L includes evidentials and various other types of discourse particles. They can occur on nouns, verbs, adjectives, but also on particles, as in the example given in Table 34.1. Categories K and L are often analysed as enclitics (see section 34.7).

Category M (absent in Ecuador and Colombia), finally, comprises person markers that are often labelled nominal, since they can mark nominal possession, as in the example in Table 34.1. However, they can also occur on non-finite verbs in adverbial subordinate clauses, as -*yki* '2SG' in (3):

(3) Cuzco Quechua (Cusihuamán 1976: 222)
 Allin-ta yacha-qti-yki=qa astawan yacha-chi-sqayki.
 good-ACC learn-DS-2SG=TOP more learn-CAU-FUT.1>2
 'If you learn well, I will teach you more.'

The subordinate verb in (3) has no nominal characteristics, and cannot be marked for case, for instance. For this reason, Lefebvre and Muysken (1988) analyse this class as [-Main Tense] suffixes. Suffixes of class M can very marginally appear on adjectives, but it is difficult to find examples of this, and in the few cases found it is an adjective that heads a noun phrase, as in (4):

(4) (*Ollantay*, 18th-century Cuzco Quechua play)
 sumaq-ni-yki
 beautiful-EU-2SG
 'your beautiful one'

Summarizing, Quechua morphology suggests four parts of speech: nouns, verbs, adjectives, and particles. If we take shared morphological processes into account, we find the classification in Figure 34.1.

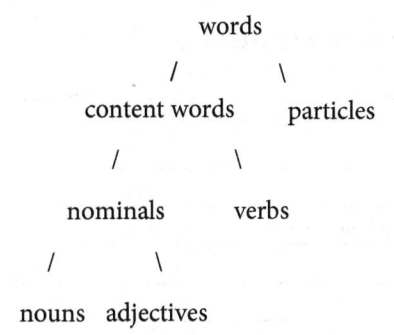

```
              words
             /      \
     content words   particles
        /    \
   nominals   verbs
    /    \
 nouns  adjectives
```

FIGURE 34.1 Classification of the parts of speech based on their suffixation possibilities

The morphological properties shared between nouns and adjectives have led to discussion in the literature about the status of adjectives, as we will see in section 34.4.

There is some reduplication in Quechua as well (Hannss & Muysken 2014), but categorical distinctions do not play a central role here, as far as I can see.

34.2.3 Distinctions in the phonology for word classes and suffixes

I will now turn to possible phonotactic distinctions between the parts of speech and suffixes. Except for the fact that all verbs must end in a vowel, there are no categorical restrictions on the phonotactics of the morphemes in Quechua.

The basic observations in terms of syllable structure are:

(a) All verb roots end in a vowel
(b) Nominal roots may end in a vowel (mostly) or a consonant
(c) Verbal suffixes end in a vowel, except for person markers and one nominalizer.
(d) Nominal suffixes end in a vowel (mostly) or a consonant

When a base ends in a consonant, a euphonic element *-ni-* intervenes (except in Ecuador and Colombia) between the base and a suffix.

In terms of syllable quantity, all nouns but one and all verbs but four are bisyllabic (overwhelmingly) or polysyllabic. Polysyllabic roots often are derived diachronically from bisyllabic ones. In Table 34.2, syllabicity is indicated for the different parts of speech and suffixes.

Table 34.2 Syllabic properties of parts of speech in Cuzco Quechua

	monosyllabic	bi- or polysyllabic
ROOTS		
nouns	ñan 'path'	others
verbs	ka- 'be', ri- 'go', qu- 'give', ñi- 'say'	others
adjectives		all
adverbs		all
postpositions		all
pronouns	qan [PRO.2SG], pay [PRO.3SG]	nuqa [PRO.1SG], ñuqanchis [PRO.1PL.IN], nuqayku [PRO.1PL.EX]
deictics	(an)kay [DEM.PROX], (an)chay [DEM.PROX]	(an)chahay [DEM.PROX]
interrogatives	may 'where', pi 'who',	ima 'what', mayqen 'which', mayna 'how', hayk'a 'how much', hayk'aq 'when'
quantifiers		kiki 'self', sapa 'alone', llapa~llipi 'all', wakin 'some'
numerals	huq '1'	iskay '2', kinsa '3', tawa '4', pisqa '5', suqta 'six', qanchis '7', pusaq '8', isqun '9', chunka '10'
particles	ña 'already'	ama [PROH], mana [NEG], yaqa 'perhaps'
ideophones	various	various
SUFFIXES		
case	-ta [ACC], -man [DIR], -pi [LOC]	-manta [ABL], -rayku 'reason', -kama 'until'
evidential	=mi [EVI], =si [HS], =cha [DUB]	
discourse	=taq [EMP], =raq [CNT], =pas [IND], =ri [CTR], ña 'already'	
verbal	-chi [CAU], -mu [CIS], -chis [PL], -ni [1SG]	-naya [DESI], -ykacha [HES]
nominal suffixes	-yuq [POSS]	-kuna [PL], -sapa [AUG],

Thus, there is an overwhelming tendency for lexical roots of all classes to be bisyllabic and end in an open syllable. More functional elements are either monosyllabic and bisyllabic.

34.3 ADJECTIVES AND ADVERBS

One of the issues that have been the topic of theoretical discussion is the status of adjectives and adverbs in Quechua. We saw in section 34.2.2 that Quechua nouns and adjectives should be grouped together morphologically, but at the same time also have different properties. The question is whether there really is a separate category of adjective, or whether adjectives should be conflated with nouns in a deep sense. While most Quechua specialists have assumed that they form separate categories, over the years, David Weber (1989) has argued that the traditional distinction between these categories does not hold for Quechua. Weber's analysis was given a wider distribution by one of his PhD supervisors at UCLA, Paul Schachter (1985), and Schachter's approach has been adopted by many typologists. Weber's argument rests on four distributional similarities between adjectives and nouns. I will present and discuss them one by one.

[1] Consider first (5), which shows that nouns and adjectives can both occur in object position:

(5) Huallaga Quechua (Weber 1989: 35–36)
  a. *Rumi-ta rikaa.*
     stone-ACC see.1SG
     'I see a stone.'

  b. *Hatun-ta rikaa.*
     big-ACC see.1SG
     'I see a big one.'

This argument is probably the one that persuaded most typologists who inspected Weber's original data to follow his and Schachter's analysis. Using Ecuadorian Quechua data, Floyd (2011) has argued against Schachter and Weber, however, showing that (5b) is contextually restricted, and only occurs when the entity that *hatun* 'big' refers to has been previously mentioned. I will not repeat Floyd's set of arguments here, but simply point out that my analysis parallels his critique. Presumably, his observations will carry over to other Quechuan varieties as well, but this remains to be demonstrated.

There is also a syntactic restriction on examples such as (5b), mentioned by Adelaar (2004: 208): the parallel between (5a) and (5b) does not hold in subject position. There we get a contrast in grammaticality. I do not have the data for Huallaga, but in the Cuzco Quechua example in (6) the adjective cannot occur by itself in subject position (6b),[3] but requires a modifying nominalized copula (6c):

(6) Cuzco Quechua (fieldwork data)
  a. *rumi llasa=n*[4]
     stone heavy=EVI
     'the stone is heavy'

  b. **hatun llasa=n*
     big heavy=EVI
     'the big one is heavy'

---

[3] The contrast between (5b) and (6b) calls to mind a seemingly very different contrast in Dutch, where adjectives may head a noun phrase only when they carry the agreement marker *-e*: *Ik zie een witte [ø]*. 'I see a white [ø]' (e.g. *koe* 'cow', non-neuter) versus **Ik zie een wit [ø]*. 'I see a white [ø]' (e.g. *paard* 'horse', neuter]. The only thing needed to license the construction is an inflection of some kind. This contrast was discussed in Muysken (1983) and Hinskens & Muysken (1986), and crucially requires the modifying element to be an adjective.

[4] In third person present singular contexts the copula is generally absent.

c. hatun   ka-q   llasa=n
   big   COP-AG heavy=EVI
   'the big one is heavy'

Admittedly Cuzco Quechua and Huallaga Quechua are from different branches of the family: Quechua I and II, but Adelaar's own observations are based on the Quechua I variety that he studied, Tarma Quechua. Most likely, the restriction on adjectives will apply to both varieties.

Case markers in Quechua can only attach to 'nominal' (in the sense of Figure 34.1) categories. They simply attach to the last element in the noun phrase or nominalized clause. There is one adjective that exceptionally is post-nominal, and it is this element that is marked with accusative *-ta*, as in (7), rather than the head noun itself:

(7) Cuzco Quechua (Lefebvre & Muysken 1988: 112)
    Wasi   hunt'a-ta   riku-ni.
    house   full-ACC   see-1SG
    'I see a full house.'

In (8) a perception complement is marked with *-ta*, as is the perceived referent:

(8) Cuzco Quechua (Lefebvre & Muysken 1988: 175)
    Xwancha-ta puri-q-ta   riku-ni.
    Juan-ACC   walk-AG-ACC see-1SG
    'I see Juan walking.'

A final consideration is that when an adjective is marked with *-ta*, but not in an elliptical noun phrase, it is interpreted as an adverb. Thus *allin-ta-n* 'good-ACC-EVI' is actually ambiguous:

(9) Cuzco Quechua (fieldwork data)
   a. allin-ta=n   ri-sha-nchis
      good-ACC=EVI go-PR-1PL.IN
      'we are going well'

   b. allin-ta=n   riku-sha-nchis
      good-ACC=EVI see-PR-1PL.IN
      'we are seeing the good one'

The transitivity of the verb (intransitive in (9a), transitive in (9b)) will contribute to our interpretation of *allin-ta-n* in these cases. Also recall the observation in (4) that when a person marker is attached to an adjective, this adjective is interpreted as heading an elliptical noun phrase.

Altogether the arguments given in Floyd (2011) and presented here in (6)–(9) speak against an analysis in which *hatun* 'big' in (5b) is seen as of the same category as *rumi* 'stone' in (5a), and in favour of an analysis in which in (5b) *hatun* modifies an absent referent and carries accusative case marking because it is the rightmost element in the noun phrase.

[II] The second argument given by Weber concerns the parallelism between (10a) and (10b):

(10) Huallaga Quechua (Weber 1989: 36)
 a. *rumi   wasi*
    stone   house
    'a stone house'
 b. *hatun   wasi*
    big   house
    'a big house'

If nouns and adjectives belong to the same category, they can both modify a noun, as if they were adjectives, as in (10a)–(10b). There are two problems with this argument. First of all, the class of nouns that can occur in pre-nominal position is restricted. It includes nouns that denote a material, as in (10a), but other combinations were rejected by consultants or only accepted with hesitations, such as (11).

(11) Cuzco Quechua (fieldwork data)
 ?? *wasi   qhari*
    house   man
    'a home-oriented man'

The parallel between the English translations of (10a)–(10b) is not used to argue that in English the class of adjectives corresponds to that of nouns, since there are restrictions in English as well.

The second problem regarding the argument in (10) is that there is a very productive process of noun–noun compounding in Quechua, which produces many noun–noun combinations. I am not familiar with detailed studies of Quechua compounding, but see Beck (2002) for some arguments from this area for the existence of an adjective class.

Cole (1982) claims that all compounds are noun–noun compounds. This is not correct. Table 34.3 shows the colour terms of Salasaca Kichwa, which are clearly adjectives. The

Table 34.3 Colour terms in Salasaca Kichwa (data from Agustín Jerez, cited from Muysken, 2019)

		white/light	black/dark
achuti	orange		
aurura	violet	*yuruk aurura*	*yana aurura*
chilka	yellow green	*yuruk chilka*	*yana chilka*
k'aura	colour of mature grains		
k'illu	yellow	*yuruk k'illu*	
muradu	purple		
puka	red	*yuruk puka*	*yana puka*
puzu	earth coloured	*yuruk puzu*	*yana puzu*
uki	grey	*yuruk uki*	*yana uki*
yana	black		
yuruk	white		

colour terms *yana* 'black' and *yuruk* 'white' can form a complex adjectival compound meaning 'dark X' or 'light X'.

It is not known whether we find compounds in other adjectival semantic domains. However, the compounding possibility suggests a parallel between adjectives and nouns.

[III] The third argument is that both adjectives and nouns can occur in predicate position preceding a copula, as in (12a)–(12b).

(12)　　Huallaga Quechua (Weber 1989: 36)
　　a.　*taqay　rumi　ka-yka-n*
　　　　that　stone　COP-PR-3
　　　　'that is a stone'

　　b.　*taqay　hatun　ka-yka-n*
　　　　that　big　COP-PR-3
　　　　'that is big'

This a bit of a strange argument, because in this pre-copula position any kind of non-verbal predicate can occur, including, e.g. locative expressions such as *kay-pi-qa* in (13) and *kay-pi-mi* in (14):

(13)　　Ayacucho Quechua (Soto Ruiz 1976: 51)
　　　　Achka-m　　kay-pi-qa　　sacha-kuna　　ka-n.
　　　　many-EVI　　this-LOC-TOP　tree-PL　　　COP-3
　　　　'There are many trees here.'

(14)　　Imbabura Kichwa (Cole 1982: 33)
　　　　Juan　kay-pi=mi　　ka-rka.
　　　　Juan　this-LOC=EVI　COP-PST
　　　　'Juan was here.'

Again, this argument could be used to assume that English nouns and adjectives also belong to the same class. Also bear in mind that (12a) does not mean 'that is stony/stone-like' and neither does (12b) mean 'that is the big one'; these interpretations would be expected if the categories of adjective and noun were non-distinct.

[IV] Weber's final argument is morphological, namely that both nouns and adjectives can be the base for derivation with *-ya-* 'become', as was already discussed in section 34.3.2.

(15)　　Huallaga Quechua (Weber 1989: 36)
　　a.　*rumi-ya-n*
　　　　stone-DEV-3
　　　　'it becomes a stone'

　　b.　*hatun-ya-n*
　　　　big-DEV-3
　　　　'it becomes big'

This type of example shows that there clearly are morphological features shared by nouns and adjectives in Quechua—case marking, compounding and verbalization—as pointed out in section 34.2.2, but that the other arguments adduced by Weber do not make the point he wants to establish. As pointed out by Floyd (2011), there are a host of distributional arguments against treating them as the same class. Thus, there are good reasons to assume that there are adjectives in Quechuan languages.

In contrast to adjectives, adverbs do not form a coherent morphological class in Quechua, although they are overwhelmingly nominal. There are various mono-morphemic adverbs in Cuzco Quechua such as *naha* 'before' and *hawa* 'outside' (Cusihuamán 1976: 64). These adverbs can be marked for case under specific circumstances, and are thus part of the nominal morphological class presented in Figure 34.1. There also is a subclass of lexicalized adjective + suffix combinations that have specific adverbial meanings:

(16) Cuzco Quechua (fieldwork data)
alli-lla-manta [good-DEL-ABL] 'slowly'
allin-ta [good-ACC] 'correctly'

34.4 Nouns and verbs and the issue of nominalizations

While nouns and verbs are clearly separate parts of speech, there are many larger constituents that have internal verbal characteristics such as allowing subjects and objects. Sometimes these subjects and objects receive special case marking, different from that in main clauses, suggesting that the structure of the embedded clause is partly nominal as well. Thus *wayra-q* 'wind-GEN' in (17) carries genitive case marking; in main clauses, it would not have a case marker. In (18) *runasimi* 'Quechua' is marked null rather than accusative; it would receive *-ta* 'ACC' if it were in a main clause (Lefebvre & Muysken 1988):

(17) Cuzco Quechua (Cusihuamán 1976: 221)
Ventana-ta kicha-y [wayra-q hayku-ri-mu-na-n-paq].
window-ACC open-IM [wind-GEN enter-INC-CIS-NMLZ-3-BEN]
'Open the window so that the air can come in.'

(18) Cuzco Quechua (Cusihuamán 1976: 220)
[Runasimi yacha-y=qa] mana-n sasa=chu.
[Quechua know-INF=TOP] NEG-EVI hard=NEG
'To learn Quechua is not hard.'

The precise distribution of case marking and other grammatical properties in nominalized clauses was discussed in Lefebvre and Muysken (1988). They show that there is an intricate mix of clausal and nominal properties in these nominalized clauses.

34.5 Postpositions

The question of postpositions in Quechua is a complicated one. Syntactically, there is good evidence for a class of PPs of location, time, manner, etc. which can occur in clause-initial, clause-final, and sometimes in pre-verbal position. An example was already given in (1). Other ones would be:

(19) Salasaca Kichwa (fieldwork data)
    a.   Ñuka   [turi   k'ipa]   shamu-sha.
        1SG.PRO brother back come-1SG.FUT
        'I will come after my brother.'

    b.   [Juanchu pudir]   María   shamu-nga.
        Juan   power   María   come-3.FUT
        'María will come instead of Juan.'

The etymology of these postpositions suggests that they are nominal. Also, *k'ipa* in (19a) may optionally be marked accusative: *k'ipa-da*, underlining its nominal status.

Many postpositions are spatial, often labelled relational nouns. They are like ordinary nouns, but not quite. Consider the following three-way contrast in Cuzco Quechua:

(20) Cuzco Quechua (Cusihuamán 1976: 148)
    a.   lliklla-q   pata-n-pi
        mantle-GEN   edge-3-LOC
        'at the edge of the mantle'

    b.   qucha   pata-pi
        lake   edge-LOC
        'at the border of the lake'

    c.   wasi   pata
        house   edge
        'above the house'

In (20a) we have a typical possessive construction with both possessor (genitive) and possessed element (3rd person) marked. This construction can be freely used to specify specific locations in Quechua, with an additional case marker. There are many nouns such as *chawpi* 'middle', *muyu* 'circle' (> 'around'), *qipa* 'back', *ukhu* 'inside', *siki* 'bottom', and *ura* 'lower side' (Cuzco Quechua, fieldwork data) that can be used to indicate precise location, more specific than the general locative case suffix *-pi*. Example (20b) is a compound, which can be used as a locative expression, again with case marking depending on its position in the clause. The word *pata* in (20a) and (20b) acts like an ordinary noun.

Example (20c) is the surprising one, since it is used without an additional case marker. This points to its status as a real postposition in the Quechuan languages. Notice that *pata* in (20c) has a different meaning from the noun in (20a)–(20b).

There is considerable variation in the locative postpositions or relational nouns. The most complex form would be (21a), the most simple (21c), with a frequent intermediary form (21b):

(21)   Cuzco Quechua (fieldwork data; see also (20b))
   a. [*wasi-q*   *ukhu-n-pi*]
      house-GEN   inside-3-LOC
      'inside the house'

   Imbabura Kichwa (fieldwork data)
   b. *Chai* [*yura uku-pi*] *kwitsa-ta   riku-ngi   xwillai-lla-gu=mi.*
      that   tree   inside-LOC girl-ACC   see-2SG   pretty-DEL-DIM=EVI
      'You see the girl under that tree, she is very pretty.'

   Tigua Kichwa (fieldwork data)
   c. *Xwana   chai-ri   cocina   uku   tiya-u-n.*
      Juana   DEM-CNT   kitchen   inside   sit-PR-3
      'Juana is still inside of the kitchen.'

In (21a) we have a canonical possessive noun phrase, in addition marked locative. In Ecuadorian Kichwa (represented here by Imbabura) there is no nominal possession marker and we only have the noun/postposition with locative *-pi*. In (21c), finally, the locative phrase from another Ecuadorian variety occurs without a case marker. I am not sure whether the genitive and the personal possessive are always either present or absent together in Peruvian varieties.

Altogether, a larger comparative study is needed of these postpositional nouns in the different Quechuan languages, and the degree to which they have developed into a separate class of postpositions, characterized by the absence of case, as in (21c). I think there is sufficient evidence, however, to assume that there are postpositional phrases in Quechua, even if the lexical items heading them derive from a nominal.

Another potential case of a postposition phrase is a specific serial verb construction in the Kichwa of Ecuador (Muysken 1977):

(22)   [*Pedro-ta   yalli*]   *yacha-n=mi.*
       Peter-ACC   exceed   know-3=EVI
       'S/he knows more than Pedro.'

In (22) the head of the adpositional phrase *yalli* 'exceed' appears to be a verb. Verbs always come with person (and optionally TAM) marking in Quechua, but in (22) *yalli* is bare. We know that it is a verb because it assigns accusative case, a property exclusive of verbs. The structure in (22) resembles that of serial verb constructions in many languages of the world, including Kwa and Caribbean Creole languages (Sebba 1987). However, the phrase *Pedro-ta yalli* has the property characteristic of adpositional phrases being freely movable to other positions in the clause in Kichwa, something which does not hold for verb phrases.

Finally, case markers are hard to distinguish from postpositions. In (23) *-rayku* 'because of' is traditionally viewed as an oblique case suffix.

(23) [Kan-rayku] shamu-n=mi.
 you-because come-3=EVI
 'S/he comes because of you.'

As noted in section 34.2.3, there are monosyllabic and bisyllabic case suffixes in Quechua. It is tempting to treat at least the bisyllabic case markers as (morphologically dependent) postpositions. Three things would speak for this: first, lexical roots tend to be polysyllabic in Quechua, and grammatical elements monosyllabic. Second, most monosyllabic case markers have a more grammatical, abstract meaning than the bisyllabic ones. Third, in relative clauses where the relativized element is not the subject of the relative clause, the monosyllabic case markers can generally be dropped, yielding phrases like [the house that I lived] or [the knife that I cut]. This does not hold for bisyllabic ones. We may assume that a grammatical element like case can be left out, but not a lexical postposition.

Nonetheless, there are good reasons not to take this road. First, the match between polysyllabicity and semantic concreteness is only partial. The bisyllabic element *-manta* 'ablative' is easily as abstract in meaning as the element *-paq* 'benefactive', for instance. Furthermore, *-paq* 'benefactive case' and *-wan* 'comitative case' cannot be omitted in relative clauses: [the girl I bought for book *(for)] and [the man I went to the movies *(with)]. Third, *-manta* seems composed of *-man* and *-ta*. In other Quechua languages, we also have *-pi-ta* and *-paq-ta*. This suggests that at least *-manta* is best analysed as a complex case marker rather than a postposition.

The distinction between postposition and case marker is something that could exist in an ideal world but may not correspond to the linguistic facts at hand. Semantic, phonological, syntactic, and morphological criteria do not always match as well as linguists would like.

If we assume that there is a category of postpositional phrase in Quechuan languages with a lexical head without a clear lexical identity as a postposition, this may help explain the considerable variation between the Quechuan languages in the use of postpositions.

34.6 CLITICS

In an ideal world, it would be possible to distinguish clitics from suffixes in Quechua (see, e.g. Muysken 1981). Clitics could be viewed as particles that are phonologically dependent, and sensitive to mostly pragmatic placement conditions. Criteria involved to distinguish these clitics from suffixes would be those in Table 34.4.

Table 34.4 Criteria to distinguish clitics from suffixes in Quechua (partly based on Muysken 1981)

	suffixes	clitics
A	closer to the root	at the end of the phonological word
B	sensitive to the category of the base	not sensitive to the category of the base
C	creates a word with a specific category	Leaves the category of the word it is attached to unmodified
D	can only be attached to content words	can be attached to content and non-content words alike
E	may have a more lexical meaning	generally has a discourse-related meaning
F	always triggers stress shift to the penultimate syllable	may or may not trigger stress shift to the penultimate syllable and sometimes carries independent stress
G	the shape of the suffix is not sensitive to prosodic properties of the base	the shape of the clitic may be sensitive to the prosodic properties of the base

I will briefly discuss these criteria, using prototypical examples such as (24).

(24) riku-*chi*-n=*mi*
      see-CAU-3=EVI
      's/he shows (it)'

(A) The causative suffix -*chi*- is closer to the root, while the evidential enclitic =*mi* is at the end of the word. (B) The causative suffix -*chi* can only be attached to verbs, while the evidential enclitic =*mi* can be attached to any category. (C) A word to which the causative suffix -*chi* is attached is clearly verbal, while attaching the evidential enclitic =*mi* does not create words of a specific category. (D) The causative suffix -*chi* can only be attached to a content word (and the same holds for nominal and adjectival suffixes), while the evidential enclitic =*mi* can also be attached to particles, as in *mana*=*n* [NEG=EVI]. (E) The causative suffix -*chi* may form a lexicalized combination with its root ('show' versus 'cause to see', 'teach' versus 'cause to know', etc.), while the evidential enclitic =*mi* only has a meaning at the level of the discourse structure. (F) It is possible to emphasize the clitic, as in *ri-ni* = *mí* 'indeed I am going'. (G) Finally the phonological form of evidentials in Cuzco Quechua depends on the phonotactics and probably prosody of the root: broadly speaking =*mi* after consonants, =*n* after vowels, e.g. *Pedro*=*n* [Pedro=EVI] versus *Xwan*=*mi* [Juan=EVI]. Suffixes do not show such alternations.

Consider now a brief overview in Table 34.5 of some morpheme classes with respect to these criteria, illustrated with particular morphemes.

Table 34.5 Status of some morphemes on the basis of the criteria in Table 34.4 (s = suffix, c = clitic)

		A internal/external	B base sensitive	C categorical signature	D content word	E lexicalized	F stress behaviour	G prosody sensitive
i	Evidential =mi/=n	c	c	c	c	c	c	c
ii	Indefinite -pas	c	c	c	c	c	s	s
iii	Delimitative -lla	s	c	c	s	s/c	s	s
iv	Genitive -pa/-q	s	s	s	s	s/c	s	c
v	Non-Main Tense person	s	c	c	s	c	s	s
vi	Desiderative -naya	s	c	s	s	s	s	s
vii	Causative -chi	s	s	s	s	s	s	s

While the two canonical cases (i) and (vii) were already discussed, there are four less straightforward items. The class in (ii) comprises discourse related suffixes or enclitics such as indefinite -pas that do not show any alternation depending on the prosodic context; there is maybe half a dozen of these, and possibly the difference with the evidentials is linked to their phonological make-up. The delimitative marker -lla 'just' (iii) behaves like a suffix in some respects: it is relatively close to the root and limited to content words, but not base sensitive and does not create a separate category. There appear to be some lexicalized combinations with -lla.

Genitive -pa/-q (iv) has many suffix properties but surprisingly enough shares with the evidentials the sensitivity in its shape to its prosodic environment. At least historically it could have had clitic status. Another unusual feature is that the genitive can be combined with another case marker, as in (25):

(25)   Xwancha-q-ta   riku-sha-ni=n.
       Juan-GEN-ACC   see-PR-1SG=EVI
       'I see Juan's/Juan's place.'

Here the genitive, when combined with a name, can have the lexicalized interpretation of 'X's place'.

The Non-Main Tense person markers (v), if they are analysed as such, can attach to any content word, and do not have a category of their own. In that sense, they are like clitics. Neither do they appear in lexicalized combinations. Desiderative -naya (vi) is clearly suffixal and creates a verb but can take both nouns and verbs as its base.

We can conclude that altogether there is reasonable evidence for a status of the category of clitics as separate from suffixes; there are some intermediate elements, suggesting that it is more a gradual than an absolute distinction.

34.7 THE ANDEAN AND SOUTH AMERICAN CONTEXT

The Quechuan languages have always formed part of a complex linguistic ecosystem involving a number of other languages, notably Aymara and Pukina. It may be useful therefore to place these languages in a slightly larger context. Are they exceptional in the region, or rather typical? Table 34.6 gives a brief overview of categories in the relevant languages (see also, e.g. Adelaar with Muysken 2004).

Table 34.6 First approximation of lexical categories in some Andean languages

	Quechua	Aymara	Pukina	Cholón	Leko	Chicham	Mochica	Chipaya	Barbacoan
Nouns	x	x	x	x	x	x	x	x	x
Verbs	x	x	x	x	x	x	x	x	x
Adjectives	*nom*	*nom*	x	*nom*	*nom*	*nom*	*nom?*	*nom*	x
Adverbs	*nom*	*nom*			x	*nom* *verb*		*nom*	x
Postpositions	*nom*	*nom*		x	*nom*		*nom*		*nom*
Particles	x	x	x					x	
Ideophones	(x)					x			x

Source: (Aymara based on Adelaar with Muysken 2004, Cerrón-Palomino and Carvajal 2009; Pukina based on Adelaar and van der Kerke 2009; Cholón based on Adelaar with Muysken 2004; Leko based on van der Kerke 2009; Chicham based on Saad in press; Mochica based on Adelaar with Muysken 2004; Chipaya based on Cerrón-Palomino 2009; Barbacoan based on Muysken, 2019); ***nom*** = has nominal features, ***verb*** = has verbal features

All languages are shown to clearly distinguish verbs from nouns. They have a separate category of adjective, and in many cases these adjectives have nominal features, as far as can be established. Many languages have postpositions as well, also often with a nominal character. In Chicham, a subclass of adverbs may be verbal in nature.

While Quechua may be fairly typical in its system of parts of speech when compared with other Andean languages, it is by no means representative of the languages of South America as a whole. As Krasnoukhova (2012) points out in her typological survey of noun phrase structures in South American languages, there is a big gap between the western region of the continent, including the Andes proper and the adjacent foothills, and the eastern region.

Property words are morphologically nominal in the Western languages (including the Andean languages), while the Eastern languages tend to have a small or no distinct adjective class, and verbal property words. In the Eastern languages, there may be gender in the noun phrase, there are classifiers, temporal/aspectual distinctions are marked on the noun and there is a class of inalienable nouns. These features are absent in Western languages such as Quechua. However, the broad Eastern-Western split does not imply that all 'Eastern' languages have similar category systems; there is quite a bit of diversity here.

As to word order in the noun phrase the Western languages have a pre-head position for modifiers (demonstratives, lexical possessors, numerals, property words), whereas the Eastern languages have a pre-head position for demonstratives, lexical possessors and numerals, and post-head property words.

34.8 CONCLUSIONS

This chapter argues that Quechua distinguishes a number of parts of speech syntactically: nouns, verbs, adjectives, adverbs, postpositions, and particles. However, in their morphological properties, there is only a broad nominal/verbal/particle split. Rich morphology allows lexical items to be part of larger constituents that belong to a different part of speech, as can be seen in nominalizations. There is a clitic–suffix distinction, but it is not watertight.

CHAPTER 35

WORD CLASSES IN AUSTRONESIAN LANGUAGES

ULRIKE MOSEL

35.1 INTRODUCTION

THE Austronesian languages form one of the largest language families both in terms of the number of its languages and its geographic extension from Taiwan and Hawaii in the North to New Zealand in the South and from Madagascar in the West to Easter Island in the East. There are about 1,200 languages, which are classified and subclassified in a complex tree of historical relationships. An overview of the typological features and historical relationships of Austronesian languages is given in the two handbooks *Oceanic Languages* by Lynch, Ross and Crowley (2002) and *The Austronesian Languages of Asia and Madagascar*, edited by Adelaar and Himmelmann (2005). Whereas the Oceanic languages form a fourth-level subgroup of the Austronesian Malayo-Polynesian Languages with about 500 languages, the languages of the second volume, also called Western Austronesian languages, belong to various subfamilies of Formosan and Malayo-Polynesian languages. For a comprehensive classification and a catalogue of research on Austronesian languages see Hammerström et al. (2017).[1] Rich linguistic and cultural data of Austronesian languages are provided by the DoBeS Archive, the Paradisec Archive, and La Collection Pangloss.[2]

Austronesian languages are configurational; the immediate constituents of clauses are phrases with clear-cut boundaries and a fixed order of functional particles and content words. Phrases are the basic unit for the discrimination of word classes and can formally be classified into predicate phrases with the subclasses of phrases with and without tense–aspect–mood (TAM) marking and referential phrases that function as arguments and complements of adpositions. Unmarked predicate phrases may have the same form as referential phrases.

---

[1] https://glottolog.org/resource/languoid/id/aust1307
[2] https://www.paradisec.org.au/collections/; https://dobes.mpi.nl/; https://pangloss.cnrs.fr/index.html

Special comparative studies on Oceanic word classes are Ross (1998a, 1998b) and van Lier (2016, 2017). Ross (1998a) analyses the morphosyntactic constructions of Oceanic property words in attributive and predicative function and finds 19 languages in which property words divide into a small and a larger class of Adjectives[3] with the small class mainly comprising property words of dimension, value, and age. His second article (Ross 1998b) focuses on attributive constructions of property words that are similar to possessive constructions.

On the basis of Croft's (2001) approach, van Lier (2016) compares the morphosyntactic behaviour and lexical flexibility of 'object/person words', 'event words', and 'property words' in a sample of 36 Oceanic languages with respect to the propositional functions of predication, reference, and modification[4])(see section 35.3.5. Using the same sample of languages and subgroups of property words van Lier's (2017) study discusses the morphosyntactic diversity of property words in and across Oceanic languages and in a worldwide typological perspective (section 35.4).

This chapter focuses on the classification of content words denoting objects (things and persons), events, and properties (including the properties of events), and describes what kind of morphological features and syntactic functions are diagnostic for the distinction of word classes. It first explicates lexicological concepts that are relevant for the categorization of Austronesian content words in section 35.2 and then analyses diagnostic features of Austronesian word classes in section 35.3; section 35.4 describes the heterogeneous classification of property words; section 35.5 presents a case study of word classes in the Philippine language Tagalog. The chapter concludes with a brief summary and a look at future research.

35.2 Lexicological concepts

35.2.1 Word classes and lexemes

In this chapter word classes are understood as grammatically established classes of lexemes whereby the term lexeme is used as defined by Cruse (1986: 80): 'a lexeme is a family of lexical units; a lexical unit is the union of a single sense with a lexical form; a lexical form is an abstraction from a set of word forms (or—alternatively—it is a family of word forms) which differ only in respect of inflections'.

Word classes are distinguished from semantic classes such as object, event, and property words, and from syntactic and propositional functions, because it cannot be assumed that any of these four types of category correlates in a one-to-one way with any of the other three types. Typical mismatches between these types of category are:

1. In Tagalog, Verbs can morphologically be defined as those lexemes that are marked for voice and inflected for aspect and mood. But the Verbs do not only head predicate phrases, but also referential phrases (section 35.5).

---

[3] The names of language-specific word classes are written with capital letters; see section 35.2.1.
[4] According to Croft's (2001: 66) theory van Lier's analysis does not consider the modification of event words by property words.

2. In many Austronesian languages, Nouns head referential and predicate phrases without copulas (examples (1)–(3)).
3. Property words often do not form a major lexeme class called Adjectives, but are members of the Verb or the Noun class, or fall into two or more subclasses (see section 35.4).

For reasons of space, the present description of word classes considers only the following categories:

1. three semantic classes: prototypical object, event, and property words, with object words including person and thing words, but not proper names;
2. four language-specific word classes: Nouns, Verbs, Adjectives, Manner Adverbs;
3. three syntactic functions: head of referential phrase; head of predicate phrase; modifier of object, event, or property words, or in case that these have been classified, modifier of Nouns, Verbs, Adjectives, and Manner Adverbs.[5]

35.2.2 Polysemy, homonymy, and the criterion of compositionality

Semantic criteria are necessary to distinguish polysemy from homonymy. If two lexical units of the same form, e.g. the Teop (PNG)[6] words *beera* 'big' and *beera* 'chief', denote concepts of radically distinct semantic categories, e.g. a property and a person, they are regarded as homonymous distinct lexemes (see section 35.2.3.3; Mosel 2017: 270–272).

But if the same lexical form, e.g. *beera* 'big' occurs in two distinct constructions, e.g. *a taba beera* (ART thing big) 'big thing', *paa beera* (TAM big) 'has become big', and the differences in meaning can be attributed to the constructions, the criterion of compositionality can be applied (Evans & Osada 2005: 367–375), so that in both constructions the form *beera* 'big' represents the same lexeme.

35.2.3 Multifunctionality, conversion, and lexical flexibility

In the analysis of Austronesian word-class systems three kinds of phenomena need to be distinguished: multifunctionality, conversion, and lexical flexibility.

---

[5] Hengeveld (2013) distinguishes between 'modifier of head of referential phrase' and 'modifier of head of predicate phrase'. This classification does not work for languages in which the form of a modifier is not determined by the syntactic function of the modified word, but by its word class (section 35.4).
[6] Language names are supplemented by the names of their location, e.g. PNG (abbr. of Papua New Guinea).

35.2.3.1 Multifunctionality

Multifunctionality is given when morphosyntactically established categories like Nouns and Verbs do not only occur in their prototypical functions, but also in some other function, without special marking. For example, in Tolai (PNG) Nouns are multifunctional as they head referential and predicate phrases. But Verbs are nominalized when functioning as the head of referential phrases, see (1).

(1) Tolai (Mosel 1984: 16, 36, 91)
  i *vana* (3SG.RLS go) 'went' a *vina-vana* (ART NMLZ-go) 'the going'
  i *tutana* (3SG.RLS man) 'became a man' a *tutana* (ART man) 'the man'

This kind of asymmetric multifunctionality is also found in other Oceanic and in Western Austronesian languages (Himmelmann 2005a: 127). Multifunctionality of Nouns and Verbs may also be symmetrical. In Teop (PNG) object and event words are divided into Nouns and Verbs, because Nouns are modified by Adjectives and Verbs by deadjectival Manner Adverbs (see section 35.4.3), but both function without any changes as the heads of referential and TAM-marked predicate phrases.

(2) Teop (Mosel 2017: 265, 266)
  a *aba*   (ART person)   'the person'
  paa aba   (TAM person)   'has become a person'
  paa paku a inu   (TAM make ART house)   'built a house'
  a *paku n=a inu*   (ART make 3SG.POSS=ART house)   'the making of a house'

35.2.3.2 Conversion

Conversion, also called zero derivation, is a process that without morphological changes derives a semantically related lexeme that belongs to a different word class. In the above mentioned Teop example, the Noun *beera*$_2$ 'chief' is considered as derived from *beera*$_1$ 'big; important' because of its semantic dependency, its less broad semantic scope, and its lower frequency.[7]

35.2.3.3 Lexical flexibility

The term lexical flexibility refers to multifunctional content words (section 35.2.3.1) and to content words that cannot be unequivocally affiliated with a single major word class on the basis of morphological or syntactic criteria. Such extremely flexible content words are found in Samoan (Polynesia), where object, event, and property words regularly head referential and TAM-marked predicate phrases and also function as modifiers. In contrast to Teop content words (section 35.2.3.1), Samoan object and event words select the same kind of property words as their modifiers, so that they cannot be divided into Nouns and Verbs, see (3) and section 35.4.3).

---

[7] See van Lier (2012); for Samoan examples, see Mosel & Hovdhaugen (1992: 82–83).

(3) Samoan (Mosel & Hovdhaugen 1992: 80, 540–541, 566)
   le teine   (ART girl)   'the girl'   sā teine   (TAM girl)   (she) was a girl
   le sau   (ART come)   'the coming'   'ua sau   (TAM come)   '(it) came'
   le pa'e'e (ART thin)   'the (being) thin' e lelei   (TAM good)   '(it) is good'

However, besides the presumably unclassifiable lexemes of (3), there are many lexemes marked by affixes that form subclasses like Causative Verbs and Deverbal Nouns, e.g. *fa'a-moe* (CAUS-sleep) 'put to sleep', *moe-ga* (sleep-NMLS) 'bed'. Furthermore, all Transitive Verbs are obligatorily marked by the so-called transitive suffix in certain environments, e.g. *fai, fai-a* 'to do, make', and at least 470 event and property words, but only 10 object words have plural forms of various kinds. Therefore the statement 'The categorisation of full words into nouns and verbs is not given a priori in the lexicon' (Mosel & Hovdhaugen 1992: 73) needs to be revised. Pawley's (1966) solution of this problem is to distinguish Nouns, Verbs, and additionally a class of Universals which share the distributional characteristics of Nouns and Verbs.

35.2.4 The principle of exhaustiveness

The principle of exhaustiveness (Evans & Osada 2005: 378) requires that statements on word classes 'need to hold for all relevant words in the lexicon that are claimed to have the same class'. It is impossible to apply this principle, but one can select a reasonable number of content words of diverse semantic domains and analyse their forms and distributions in an electronic corpus of texts, which may include elicited data (Mosel 2018). Ideally such analyses show how often the selected words are distributed across syntactic functions (Mosel 2017: 268). The few examples given in Table 35.1 illustrate that in Teop Verbs, Nouns, and Adjectives are most frequently used in their canonical functions, and that Adjectives are much more flexible than Nouns and Verbs.

Table 35.1 Frequencies of prototypical Teop event, object, and property words

Teop word	Basic meaning	Head of VC	Head of NP	Head of AP[1]
nao	'go'	882	6	—
paku	'do, make'	806	5	2
aba	'person'	6	356	—
moon	'woman'	8	559	—
beera, bebeera	'big, important'	95	1	310
mataa, matamataa	'good'	49	2	116

[1] Verb Complexes (VCs) are marked by TAM markers and only function as predicates. NPs are marked by articles and function as predicates, arguments, and complements of prepositions. Adjectival Phrases (APs) are marked by articles that agree in person and number with the NP they relate to. APs function as predicates and as modifiers. Modification of Nouns is also expressed by juxtaposed Nouns, Verbs, and Adjectives, see Table 35.6.

35.3 Diagnostic features for the identification of Austronesian word classes

35.3.1 Introduction

In grammars of Standard European Languages content words are divided into Nouns, Verbs, Adjectives, and Adverbs on the basis of morphological and corresponding syntactic characteristics. But Austronesian content words often lack such correlations between morphology and syntax as illustrated by the examples (1)–(3). The following description of diagnostics deals with category-establishing inflectional and derivational morphology (section 35.3.2, section 35.3.3), colligations, i.e. the co-occurrence restrictions within phrases (section 35.3.4), and the syntactic characteristics of event, object, and property words (section 35.3.5).

35.3.2 Inflectional morphology

While inflection for case is rare in Austronesian languages (section 35.3.2.1), inflection for TAM section 35.3.2.2) and subject agreement (section 35.3.2.3) is found in all areas of Austronesia. Property words may inflect for agreement in attributive and adverbial function (section 35.3.2.4). The various kinds of inflection are generally considered as a diagnostic for word–class distinctions. An exception is Mwotlap (Vanuatu), see section 35.3.2.2.

Whereas the inflection of content words is a diagnostic for their lexical classification, the co-occurrence of inflected functional words or clitics with content words is not necessarily a diagnostic. In Tolai (1) the subject indexing particle in the Verb Complex inflects for person and mood, but the head of the Verb Complex may be a Verb or a Noun, and in Teop (2) the article inflects for number, gender, and case, but the Referential Phrase may be headed by object, event, and property words (Mosel 2017: 262).

35.3.2.1 *Case inflection*

Nias (Indonesia) distinguishes two cases: an 'unmutated' citation form and a 'mutated form' which 'differs from the citation form in its initial segment, in accordance with a set of regular morphophonemic alternations' (Brown 2005: 567). A second example of case inflection is provided by Amis (Taiwan), which belongs to the symmetrical voice-marked languages (Bril 2017: 367–369). In other languages, the syntactic functions of arguments or adjuncts are either unmarked or marked by prepositions or articles as in Tagalog, see section 35.5.

35.3.2.2 *Inflection for* TAM

In the symmetrical-voice languages in Taiwan, Indonesia, and the Philippines (see section 35.3.3.1 and section 35.5) event words are distinguished from other content words as they are marked for voice and inflected for aspect and mood and are morphologically classifiable as

Verbs. But similar to other content words, they may head any kind of phrase (Himmelmann 2005a: 127; see also section 35.5).

In some Oceanic languages Verbs are inflected for the distinction of realis and irrealis mood, in others TAM categories are expressed by particles or clitics (Lynch et al. 2002: 44; see also section 35.3.4). An exceptional case seems to be Mwotlap (Vanuatu), where TAM inflection is not considered as a diagnostic for verbhood:

(4) Mwotlap (Vanuatu) (François 2005: 131)
 ... kē   ni-ēntē-yō   togolgol
 ... 3SG   AOR-child-3DU   straight,
 '(They adopted him, so that) he (became) their legitimate son.'

In (4) the TAM-inflected person word *ēntē* 'child' has a possessive suffix, which challenges its classification as a Verb. François (2005: 131) suggests 'that TAM inflection is just not a privilege of verbs, and can equally affect verbs, adjectives, or nouns in Mwotlap'.

35.3.2.3 *Inflection for subject agreement by person/number affixes*

Predicative content words with affixes that index the subject and simultaneously may indicate TAM are classified as Verbs. Such Verbs can denote events as well as properties as, for example, in Nias (Indonesia, Brown 2005: 570–572), Tukang Besi (Indonesia, Donohue 1999: 91), Biak (Indonesia, Steinhauer 2005), Mangap-Mbula (PNG, Bugenhagen 1995: 118–119; see also examples (11)–(12)), Jabêm (PNG, Lynch et al. 2002: 281–282); Mwotlap (Vanuatu, François 2005: 129–130); Paamese (Vanuatu, Crowley 1982: 69, 129).

35.3.2.4 *Agreement inflection of attributive content words*

Van Lier (2017: 1246–1248) lists three patterns of agreement of attributive property words and gives the following examples:

(1) agreement suffixes having the form of possessive suffixes as in Kokota (Solomon Islands), Lote (PNG) and Saliba (PNG);
(2) property words with reduplicated forms for plural agreement as in Rotuman (Fijii);
(3) property words with prefixes that index the semantic class of the Noun as in Kilivila, e.g. *to-* 'male', *na-* 'female', *ke* 'wooden'.[8]

In Samoan (Polynesia) number agreement is found with event and property words in attributive, adverbial and predicative function,[9] e.g. *tamaiti lāiti* (children.PL little.PL) 'little children', *mo-moe 'u-'umi* (RED sleep RED-long) 'sleep long' (section 35.2.3.3). In Māori (New Zealand) property words are marked by nominalizing and passive suffixes when they modify Nouns and Verbs that are marked by these suffixes:

---

[8] Senft (1986: 85–88); for a thorough analysis, see Lawton (1980).
[9] Mosel & Hovdhaugen (1992: 268, 297; 400, 442–444); Mosel and So'o (1997: 31–32).

(5) Māori (Bauer 1997: 516; 1993: 399)
    rahu-nga kino-tanga   (pull-NMLS bad-NMLS) 'pulling badly'
    aroha-ina nui-tia   (love-PASS big-PASS) 'be dearly loved'

35.3.3 Derivational morphology

Derivational morphology probably occurs in all Austronesian languages. Only the derivation of voice-marked forms and nominalizations are dealt with here. For further information, especially on reduplication, see Blust (2014).

35.3.3.1 Voice

The category voice is a diagnostic in so-called symmetrical voice languages which have two or more voices none of which is unmarked. These voice-marked lexemes are derived from unmarked bases and inflect for aspect and mood, e.g. Tagalog (Philippines) *nag-lutò* (AV.RLS. PRF-cook) '(somebody) cooked', *lutò* 'cooking, cuisine', and form a word class that is distinct from content words without voice marking, see Himmelmann (2005a: 112–113) and section 35.5. In contrast, some Western Austronesian languages and a few Polynesian languages have passive forms that are derived from active forms—see the Māori example in (5).[10]

35.3.3.2 Nominalization

Nominalization is a diagnostic for Noun–Verb distinction, if it is obligatory for event words when heading referential phrases.[11] In Toqabaqita (Solomon Islands) this is the case not only for event words, but with three exceptions also for property words, e.g. *qaranga-laa* (swim-NMLS) 'swimming'. *leqa-laa* (good-NMLS) 'goodness'.[12] Since event and property words are both preceded by subject markers in predicative function, they are classified as Verbs, see section 35.4.1. In Tolai (PNG), Verbs denoting events are nominalized by the affix *ni-/-in-/-un-* or by conversion, e.g. *m-in-omo* 'drinking'. Consequently, this affix is a diagnostic for a subclass of Nouns, but not for Noun–Verb distinction.

35.3.4 Colligations and (in)compatibilities

The exclusive co-occurrence with certain kinds of function and content words serves as a diagnostic for the distinction of Noun and Verbs:

1. Subject markers occur in predicate phrases and index the subject. They inflect for person and number and may additionally signify TAM or combine with TAM particles.

---

[10] Himmelmann (2005a: 167); Lynch et al. (2002: 44–45); Harlow (2007: 101, 104–105).
[11] For Nias (Indonesia) see Brown (2005: 587), for Tolai (PNG), see Foley (2014: 15–21); for South Efate (Vanuatu), see Thieberger (2006: 132–137).
[12] Lichtenberk (2008a: 421–444; 2008b: 159).

If they are incompatible with one or two of the three major categories of content words, they are a diagnostic as in Toqabaqita and South Efate[13] where only predicative event and property words, but not object words are marked by a subject marker, see (6).

2. The use of a copula with predicative object words is rare in Austronesian languages. It occurs, for example, in Biak (Indonesia, Steinhauer 2005: 804–805) and in the Vanuatu languages Paamese Crowley 1982: 169–172 and South Efate, see (6 below).
3. Negations are, for example, a diagnostic for the distinction of Nouns and Verbs in Sama/Balau (Philippines, Indonesia), Belait (Brunei Darussalam), and Tolai,[14] e.g. Belait *kay' blabiw* (NEG rat) '(is) not a rat', *ndeh nyeh melley* (NEG 3SG buy) 'he didn't buy'.
4. Plural determiners signifying the plurality of referents can be a diagnostic for the distinction of Nouns and Verbs. In Māori (New Zealand) both object and event words head singular referential phrases, but only object words occur with plural determiners, see (7) which also illustrates the difference between multifunctionality and conversion.

(6) South Efate (Vanuatu, Thieberger 2006: 85, 117, 271)
ga   i=pios   (he   3SG.RLS=call)   'he called out'
napu   i=sa   (road 3SG.RLS=bad)   'the road is bad'
Ga   i=pimarik ni… (he   3SG.RLS=be the man of)   'He is the husband of …'

(7) Māori (New Zealand, Harlow 2007: 102–103, 122; *Māori Dictionary*)[15]
tā	*rātou*	*waiata*	*tā*	*rātou*	*waiata*
3SG.POSS	3PL.PRON	song	3SG.POSS	3PL.PRON	sing
'their song'			'their singing'		

ā	*rātou*	*waiata*	*ngā*	*waiata*	
3PL.POSS	3PL.PRON	song	ART.PL	song	
'their songs'			'(the) songs, Psalms'		

But plural markers are not in general a diagnostic for Noun–Verb distinctions (see Mosel 2017: 275).

5. The quantification by cardinal numerals or frequentative numerals distinguishes Nouns and Verbs as in Kambera (Indonesia), e.g. *tau ma-dua* 'two persons/people' (lit. 'people that are two') and *unung pan-dua-ng* 'have a second drink' (lit. 'drink twice') and in Samoan, e.g. *vāiasu e tolu* (week TAM three) 'three weeks'; *tāumafa fa'a-tolu* (eat CAUS-three) 'eat three times'.[16]
6. The compatibility of event and object words with different kinds of modifiers is a diagnostic for the division of content words into Nouns and Verbs, Adjectives and Adverbs in Teop (PNG) (see Table 35.7).

---

[13] Lichtenberk (2005); Thieberger (2006: 78, 171–195).
[14] Mosel (1984: 111, 163); Clynes (2005: 435, 436); Himmelmann (2005a: 128); Jun (2005: 388).
[15] *Māori Dictionary* https://maoridictionary.co.nz
[16] Milner (1966: 275); Mosel & Hovdhaugen (1992: 116); Klamer (1998: 139, 94).

35.3.5 Syntactic functions

In many Western Austronesian languages, though not in symmetrical-voice languages, object, and event words are syntactically distinguished. In Nias (Indonesia), for example, Nouns head referential and predicate phrases, but Verbs only predicate phrases (Brown 2005: 568–572). In Oceanic languages object words are also to a greater degree multifunctional than event words. In predicative function, they either take the same position as event words and combine with subject markers and/or TAM markers (1), (2), or they head a phrase that has the same form as a referential phrase in so-called nominal clauses:[17]

(8) Teop (Mosel et al. 2007; Nah_2_CE)
     E   Bukimeasun   a   aba   ....
     ART   Bukumeasun   ART   person
     'Bukimeasun was a human, (but he had the tail of a snake).'

In (8) the object word *aba* 'person, human' functions as the head of the same type of phrase as in (2). From a descriptive perspective, this example does not show the multifunctionality of the content word *aba* 'person', but of the ART-marked phrase.

A different perspective is taken by van Lier (2016). She investigates the morphosyntactic behaviour of event words, object/person words and property words with respect to the three propositional functions of predication, reference, and modification. For each of the three semantic groups van Lier selects seven semantic subtypes as, for instance, monovalent and bivalent active event words, property words denoting dimensions and values, and object/person words denoting persons and artefacts. Her analysis 'shows that predication is the most flexible of propositional functions, accepting 92.1% of the 21 lexemes types in the 36 languages' without extra 'structural coding' like copulas (215–216), and that 52.4% of the 14 types of predicative object and property lexemes don't have extra structural codings as, for instance, *aba* in (2) and (8).

35.4 THE CLASSIFICATION OF PROPERTY WORDS

35.4.1 Introduction

In Austronesian languages, property words are accommodated in various word classes, depending on their forms in attributive and predicative function and on the linguists' evaluation of diagnostic criteria. In most Western Austronesian languages, property words seem to have the same syntactic distribution as Verbs, but they may be morphologically distinct. Tagalog

---

[17] Nominal clauses (also called equational clauses) are found in many Austronesian languages, see the indexes of Adelaar & Himmelmann (2005: 834, 837), Lynch et al. (2002: 917).

has two major morphologically distinct classes of property words called '*ma*-adjectives' e.g. *ma-lakí* 'big' (< *lakí* n.'size') and 'unaffixed adjectives' by Schachter & Otanes (1972). The unaffixed ones are derived by stress shift and often denote states resulting from a change of state, e.g. *baság* 'cracked, broken' (< *basag* n. 'crack').[18] In addition there are intensive and superlative forms derived by prefixes, e.g. *ma-gandá* 'beautiful', *napaka-ganda* 'very beautiful', *pinaka-ma-gandá* 'most beautiful'. Similar to event and object words, these property words are multifunctional.

In Oceanic languages, prototypical property words may belong to different word classes in predicative and attributive function (Ross 1998a, 1998b; van Lier 2017). Van Lier's statistical analysis of 36 languages shows that attributive property words are typically unmarked, whereas predicative ones are constructed like prototypical event words.

Table 35.2 shows that in 12 Oceanic languages the word-class affiliations of predicative and attributive property words form eight patterns. Three languages—Tawala, Mangap-Mbula, and Toqabaqita—use more than one pattern. The variation of word-class patterns suggests the hypothesis that if predicative and attributive property words belong to distinct word classes, they are Verbs in predicative function and Nouns or Adjectives in attributive function as, for example, in Mangap-Mbula (section 35.4.3).

Table 35.2 Word classes of property words in 12 Oceanic languages

Languages	Predicate	Attribute
Woleaian, Toqabaqita, South Efate	Verb	juxtaposed Verb
Kiribati, Mangap-Mbula	Verb	Verb in a relative clause
Mangap-Mbula, Saliba	Verb	Noun
Tawala	Verb	Adjective
Mangap-Mbula, Tolai	Noun	Noun
Toqabaqita	—	Noun
Takia, Tawala, Teop, Samoan	Adjective	Adjective
Toqabaqita	—	Adjective

Notes: location of the language and references: Kiribati: Micronesia, Ross (1998a); Mangap-Mbula: PNG, Bugenhagen (1995: 106–107, 171); Saliba: PNG, Margetts (1999: 21, 24–25, 86–87); Samoan: Polynesia, Mosel (2004), Mosel & So'o (1997: 22, 24); South Efate: Vanuatu, Thieberger (2006: 81–88); Takia: PNG, Ross (1998a); Tawala: PNG, Ezard (1997: 20–21, 51, 55–56); Teop: PNG, Mosel (2017, 2019); Tolai: PNG, Mosel (1984: 22–25); Toqabaqita: Solomon Islands, Lichtenberk (2005: 119–142); Woleaian: Micronesia, Ross (1998a)

[18] Schachter & Otanes (1972: 65, 118, 198–199); Rubino (2002: 22, 61, 147); Himmelmann (2008).

35.4.2 Mangap-Mbula and Toqabaqita

Mangap-Mbula has three types of property words, as shown in Table 35.3.

Table 35.3 Property words in Mangap-Mbula

Predicate	Attribute		Meaning
SM PW$_V$ N	PW-NMLS-PERS/NUM$_N$		physical property, colour, shape
	N REL SM PW$_V$		
PW$_V$	N PW-NMLS-PERS/NUM$_N$		'good', 'bad', 'huge', 'full' (a semantically diverse group)
PW$_N$	N PW$_N$		dimension, age

Predicative property words are classified as Verbs (PW$_V$), if the corresponding attributive property word is derived by a nominalizing affix, but as Nouns PW$_N$, if the corresponding attributive property word lacks the NMLS affix. The examples (19)–(11) illustrate the use of the Verbform *i-mbol* 'be strong' and its nominalized form *mbol-ŋa-na*:

(9) Mangab-Mbula (PNG, Bugenhagen 1995: 106)
 Iŋgi   i-mbol   som.
 this.one 3SG- be.strong NEG
 'This one is not strong.'

(10) Mangap-Mbula (PNG, Bugenhagen 1995: 107)
 Ka   koroŋ   ta   i-mbol   kat.
 2SG.get thing   REL   3SG-be.strong very
 'Get something that is really strong.'

(11) Mangap-Mbula (PNG, Bugenhagen 1995: 106)
 Kam   koroŋ   mbol-ŋa-na
 2SG.get thing   be.strong-NMLS-3SG
 'Get something strong.'

Toqabaqita has three classes of property words (see Table 35.4). The largest class are Verbs that in attributive function directly follow the Noun and do not form relative clauses as Lichtenberk's (2005) thorough analysis demonstrates. The second class consists of the two Nouns *thaama-* 'father' and *thaina-* 'mother' that are used in the sense 'large quantity', e.g. *teqe thaame-q qai* (one father-ASSOC tree) 'a big tree'. The third class has only one member meaning 'small', which is classified as an Adjective.

Table 35.4 Property words in Toqabaqita

	Predicate	Attribute	Meaning
Toqabaqita	SM PW$_V$	N PW$_V$	dimension, value, other kinds
	—	PW$_N$ -LNK N	only 'large quantity'
	—	PW$_{ADJ}$ N	only 'small'

35.4.3 Adnominal and adverbial modification

Most typological analyses of word-class systems only consider the syntactic functions of content words and neglect the fact that different types of content words may select different kinds of modifiers.[19] In languages in which property words seem to belong to the class of Verbs, one criterion to falsify this assumption is that property words may not be modified in the same way as event words forming the class of Verbs. This (in)compatibility criterion is a diagnostic for Samoan and Māori Adjectives[20] (Table 35.5).

Table 35.5 Modification in Samoan (Polynesia)

Construction	Example	Glossing	Translation
N Adj	mea leaga	thing bad	'bad thing'
N N	fale laupapa	house plank	'house (made of) planks'
N V	mea 'ai	thing eat	'food'
V Adj	nofo lelei	sit/stay good	'sit properly'
V N	tu'u 'apa	put tin	'put sth. into tins'
V V	ta-tipi fa'a-lāiti	PL-cut CAUS-small.PL	'cut sth. small'
	ta'ai fa'a-lelei	roll.up CAUS-good	'roll sth. up properly'
Adj N/V/Adj	—	—	—

In Teop (PNG) Manner Adverbs are regularly derived from Adjectives by the prefix va-, e.g. va-hata 'badly'. The selection of Manner Adverbs and other content words as juxtaposed modifiers depends on the word class of the modified word, irrespective of its syntactic function as the head of a referential or a TAM-marked predicate phrase (Table 35.6).

---

[19] Hengeveld (2013: 37); van Lier (2016, 2017); Ross (1998a).
[20] Mosel & Hovdhaugen (1992: 186, 294–313, 392–402); Bauer (1997: 301–316); Mosel (2004); Harlow (2001/2018: 37–42).

Table 35.6 Teop (PNG) content words with juxtaposed modifying content words

Construction	Example	Glossing	Translation
N Adj	*taba hata*	thing bad	'bad thing'
N N	*inu vasu*	house stone	'stone house'
N V	*taba ani*	thing eat	'food'
V Adv	*hio va-mataa*	sit ADVR-good	'sit properly'
V N	*hio-hio vaagum*	RED-sit group	'sit together in a group'
V V	*pee-pee va-ruta-rutaa*	RED-cut CAUS-RED-little	'cut something up into little pieces'
Adj Adv	*paru va-pereperee*	black ADVR-green	'greenish black'

Note: search the MWE structure field in https://dictionaria.clld.org/contributions/teop#twords for n–n, n–v, n–adj, v–n etc.

These distinct patterns of modification, which are independent of the syntactic function of the modified word, suffice to justify the classification of content words into Nouns, Verbs, Adjectives, and Manner Adverbs, as summarized in Table 35.7.

Table 35.7 Distribution of attributive and adverbial modifiers in Teop (Mosel 2017)

head word	Modifier			
	Verb	Noun	Adjective	Manner Adverb
Verb	+	+	–	+
Noun	+	+	+	–
Adjective	–	–	–	+
Manner Adverb	–	–	–	–

35.5 THE CLASSIFICATION OF TAGALOG EVENT AND OBJECT WORDS

Since the 19th century the Philippine language Tagalog has played a major role in the study of Austronesian word classes. It is a symmetrical-voice language,[21] in which inflected event and uninflected object lexemes may without any changes head predicates and referential phrases, compare (12) and (13):

---

[21] See section 35.3.3.1 and Himmelmann (2005a: 112–113; 2005b, 2008).

(14) Tagalog (Schachter & Otanes 1972: 84)
   <u>Nag-luto</u>[22]   ng   pagkain   ang   babae
   AV.RLS.PRF-cook GEN food NOM[23] woman
   'The woman cooked some food.'

(15) Tagalog (Schachter & Otanes 1972: 62)
   Artista   ang   <u>nag-luto</u>   ng   pagkain
   actress   NOM   AV.RLS.PRF-cook   GEN   food
   'The one who cooked some food (is) an actress.'

The event word-form *nagluto* '(one who) cooked' is an actor-voice form and inflected for perfective aspect and realis mood. In (14) it functions as the predicate and is followed by two case-marked referential phrases functioning as arguments; in (15) it heads the referential phrase marked by the case marker *ang*, whereas the unmarked object word *artista* 'actress' functions as the predicate. Most Tagalog voice-marked forms are related to monomorphemic lexemes denoting an entity which may be the instantiation or result of an event or a participant,[24] e.g. *nag-lutò* (AV.RLS.PRF-cook) 'cooked', *lutò* 'cooking, cuisine, cooked dish'.[25] Object words are either monomorphemic or derived by affixes, e.g. *taga-lutò* 'cook', i.e. 'person who cooks'.

The fact that inflected event words and uninflected object words equally function as predicates and heads of referential phrases and, second, that all event words are derived from bases denoting entities, e.g. *lutò* 'cooking, cuisine, cooked dish', has given rise to two kinds of classification. If the classification is based on morphological characteristics, object and event words are divided into two classes, but if syntactic criteria are given priority, they form a single class.

Schachter & Otanes (1972: 62) classify object and event words into Nouns and Verbs, but emphasize that their distribution is very different from English nouns and verbs, 'there is virtually no context in which a noun occurs in which it cannot be replaced by a verb or verb phrase'. Furthermore, they say 'that all Tagalog sentences … are essentially equational in nature', so that a literal translation of (12) would be 'the woman is the one who cooked'.

Himmelmann (2008: 285) shows that voice marking is derivational and that 'all voice-marked words in Tagalog, regardless of their base, are members of a single morpho-lexical class'. These 'V-words' are the only words that are derived from unaffixed bases and inflected for aspect and mood, whereby 'the aspect-mood marking and the voice making are formally inseparable'. Tagalog Nouns are either unmarked or derived by affixes of various kinds.[26]

One problem of this classification is that 'all V-words have two readings depending on the syntactic context. Used as predicates, they denote a specific instance of the action denoted by the root … Used as nominal expressions, however, V-words denote one of the participants involved in the ACTION denoted by the root' (Himmelmann 2008: 286–287), compare (12) *naglutò* 'cooked' and (13) *ang naglutò* 'the one who cooked'. As this semantic difference is

---

[22] Stress is not indicated in the examples from Schachter & Otanes (1972).
[23] The glossing NOM follows Kaufmann (2009); Himmelmann (2005b, 2008) uses SPEC.
[24] Himmelmann (2008: 275–284, 287); Kaufmann (2009: 11–14).
[25] Rubino (2002: 165); Kaufman (2009: 16).
[26] Schachter and Otanes (1972: 97–106); Rubino (2002: 18–20); Himmelmann (2005b: 373).

predictable, it can be attributed to the different constructions according to the criterion of compositionality (see section 35.2.2).

One of the first linguists who realized that the voice-marked words are derived from unaffixed basic words is Wilhelm von Humboldt who says that 'as a rule, the unaffixed basic word is a noun that with certain affixes is conjugabel' and that 'without any changes, every verbal expression ... can completely drop its verbal nature grammatically by simply preposing an article and a case marking preposition' (Humboldt 1838: 336, 348, my translation).

Bloomfield (1917) classifies the content words exclusively on the basis of their syntactic distribution so that all content words form the single word class of 'fullwords'.[27] This syntactic classification is also proposed by Kaufmann (2009:19) who presents a detailed analysis of unmarked and voice-marked forms in diverse contexts and concludes that 'apparent Verbs and Nouns such as *nag-íngay* ("made noise") and *áso* ("dog") in fact belong to a single (macro-) category'. Himmelmann (2009: 121) agrees with Kaufmann's (2009) 'nominalist hypothesis' and concludes 'that only in (standard) Tagalog almost all differences between nominal and verbal predicates have disappeared and given rise to the exclusive use of the equational clause type'.

To conclude, if the classification of Tagalog content words is based on their morphology, it is possible to distinguish voice and aspect–mood marked Verbs, unmarked and derived Nouns, and Adjectives (see section 35.4), whereas syntactically all content words form a single class.

35.7 Conclusion

In Austronesian languages, which are renowned for their lexical flexibility (section 35.2), the classification of prototypical event, object and property words relies on morphological features, restrictions of co-occurrences with particular other words, and syntactic functions (section 35.3). With respect to event and object words heading predicate and referential phrases, at least three kinds of language can be distinguished (see Table 35.8):

1. Languages like Nias, South Efate and Toqabaqita clearly distinguish Verbs and Nouns by the use of subject markers (SMS), i.e. subject indexing affixes and particles, TAM distinctions, case inflection or copulas (COPS), and nominalization affixes (NMLS) attached to event words heading referential phrases.
2. Languages like Tagalog morphologically distinguish Verbs and Nouns, but not with respect to their syntactic functions, so that syntactically they form a single class.
3. In languages like Teop and Samoan, neither the morphology of event and object words and nor their (in)compatibility with functional words divide them into the classes of Nouns and Verbs, though verbal and nominal subclasses such as Transitive Verbs, Causatives, or Deverbal Nouns can be established.

---

[27] Bloomfield (1917: 146–147); for further references to similar analyses see Himmelmann (2008: 258).

Table 35.8 The marking of event and object words in predicate and referential phrases

Language	predicate phrase		referential phrase	
	Event Words	Object Words	Event Words	Object Words
Nias	SM-EW	OW.CASE	NMLS-EW	OW.CASE
S. Efate	SM.TAM EW	COP OW	ART-EW-NMLS	OW
Toqabaqita	SM.TAM EW	OW	EW-NMLS	OW
Tagalog	TAM.VOICE-EW	OW	CASE TAM.VOICE EW	CASE OW
Tolai	SM.TAM EW	SM.TAM (TAM) OW	ART (NMLS)-EW	ART OW
Teop	TAM EW	TAM OW	ART EW	ART OW
Samoan	TAM EW	TAM OW	ART EW	ART OW

In Teop, Verbs, Nouns, Adjectives, and deadjectival Manner Adverbs can be distinguished by the selection of modifiers (section 35.4), whereas the analysis of the Samoan lexicon needs further research. A major problem is that groups of Samoan content words can morphologically be classified as subclasses of Verbs and Nouns, e.g. Transitive Verbs, Causatives, and Deverbal Nouns, whereas other content words seem to lack any diagnostics.

Property words are often affiliated with the Verb or the Noun class (section 35.4). In several languages, e.g. Mangap Bula, Tawala, and Toqabaqita, they are divided into subclasses that belong to different word classes. In Samoan—and probably other languages—property words form a distinct word class, because they are not modified by other content words, whereas both event and object words are modified by event, object, and property words.

The future research on Austronesian word classes will certainly be based on electronic corpora and apply corpus linguistic methods to analyse the usage of content words in context, explore co-occurrences with functional words and modifiers, and distinguish between conventional and sporadic, individual usages so that the nature of the so-called flexible content words can be better understood (section 35.2.4).

CHAPTER 36

WORD CLASSES IN TIMOR–ALOR–PANTAR AND THE PAPUAN REGION

MARIAN KLAMER

36.1 INTRODUCTION

THIS chapter describes the word classes of the Timor–Alor–Pantar (TAP) family of Papuan languages in eastern Indonesia, see Figures 36.1 and 36.2. The TAP languages are an outlier 'Papuan' group, located some 1,000 kilometres west of the New Guinea mainland. The term Papuan is used here as a cover term for the hundreds of languages spoken in New Guinea and its vicinity that are not Austronesian (Ross 2005: 15), it says nothing about the genealogical ties between languages in that area. The TAP family constitutes some 25 languages, which belong to a number of subgroups as indicated in Figure 36.3.

This chapter is based on a comparative study of a selection of TAP languages for which a descriptive grammar, or grammar sketch, exists. To ensure genealogical balance, I take into consideration languages from each of the subgroups in Figure 36.3. From left to right in Figure 36.3 (or West to East on the map in Figure 36.2), the languages investigated here are: Teiwa or Kaera of the Pantar-Straits subgroup, Adang and Abui of the Alor subgroup, Sawila or Wersing of the East Alor subgroup, and Bunaq or Makasae/Makalero[1] of the Timor subgroup.

The chapter is structured as follows. In sections 36.2–36.7, I discuss the salient characteristics of the verbs, nouns, adjectives, adpositions, adverbs, and numerals in TAP languages. In section 36.8, I report on the category-changing morphology and multifunctional words in TAP languages. In section 36.9, I show that despite the heavy dominance of the national language Indonesian, its influence on the lexicon of TAP languages remains limited. In section 36.10, I place the observations about word classes in TAP against the background of other Papuan language families, and section 36.11 presents a summary and conclusions.

[1] Makalero and Makasai are closely related to the extent that they can be considered dialects; only Makasae is represented in Figure 36.3.

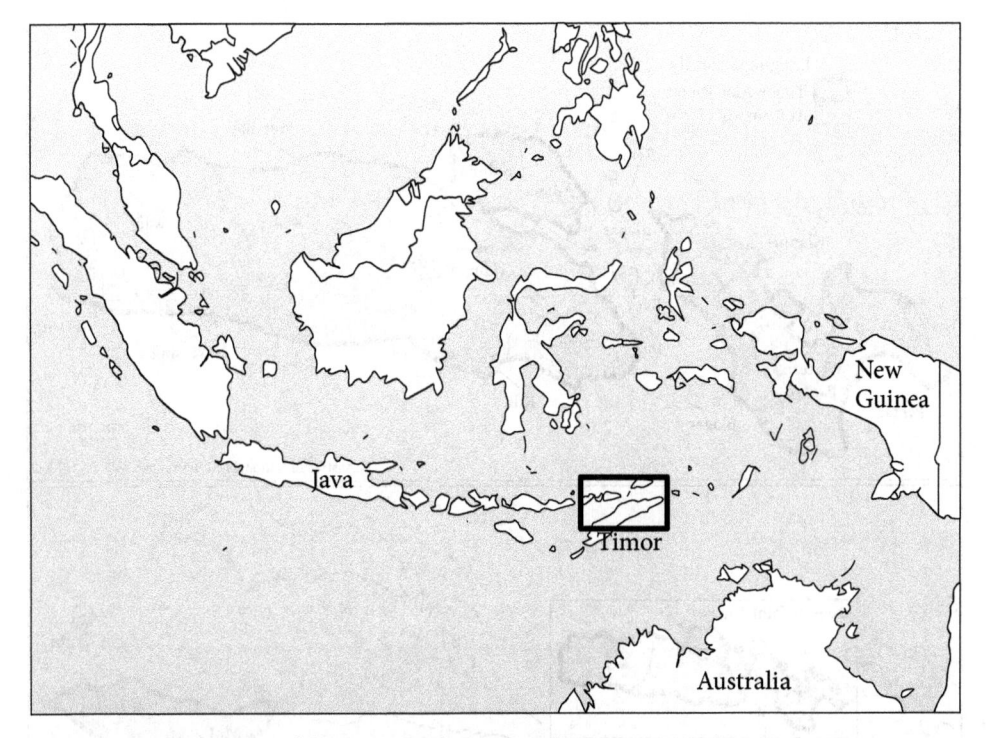

FIGURE 36.1 Location of the Timor–Alor–Pantar languages in Indonesia

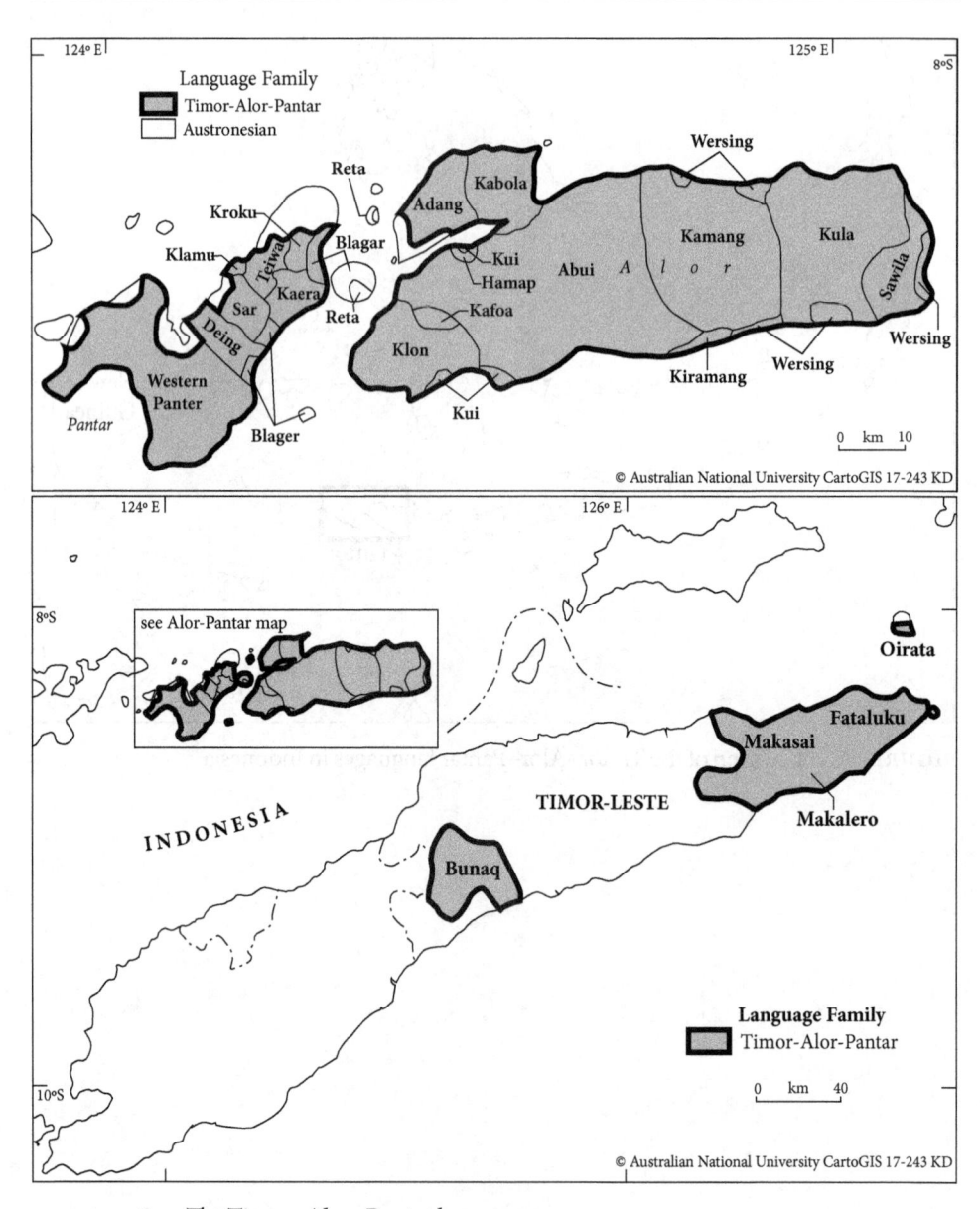

FIGURE 36.2 The Timor–Alor–Pantar languages

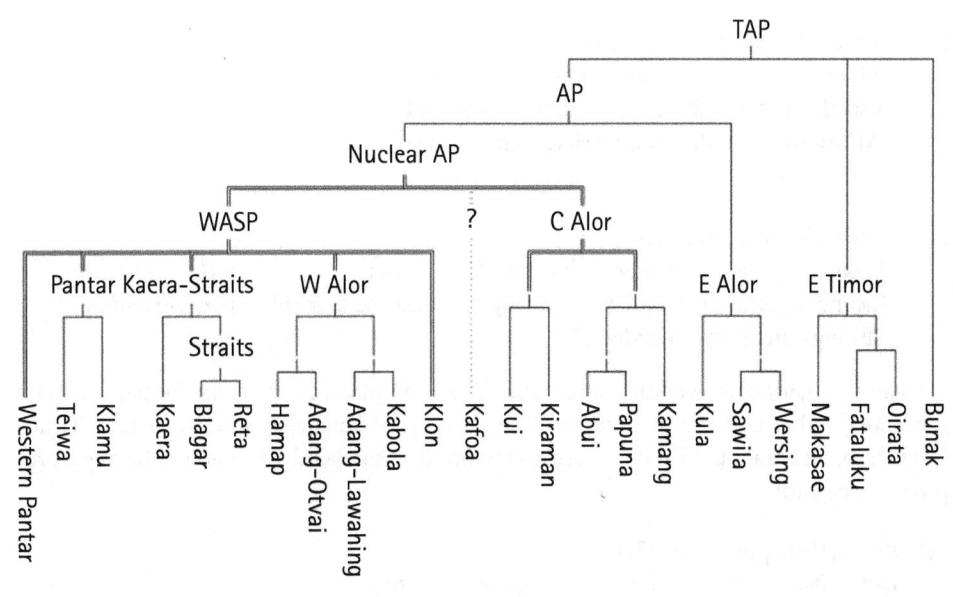

FIGURE 36.3 The internal structure of the Timor Alor Pantar family (Kaiping & Klamer 2022: 303)

36.2 VERBS

Across the TAP languages, verbs can be clearly distinguished from nouns by their functional–semantic, distributional, and morphological properties. Verbs canonically head VPs, function as predicates and take object prefixes, while nouns typically occur as heads of NPs, function as clausal arguments and take possessor prefixes. In (1), the verb *bun* 'answer' has a prefix that indexes the object *goqai* 'his child', and the object has a prefix indexing the person and number of the possessor *a* '3.SG'.

(1) Teiwa (Klamer 2010: 89)
　　A　　　g-oqai　　　ga-bun
　　3.SG　　3.SG.POSS　3SG.answer
　　'He answers his child.'

Word order in TAP is head-final: object NPs, adverbs, and adjunct phrases typically precede the verb which occurs in clause-final position. In (2), the adverb *di* 'still' precedes the object NP *patara ma* 'rice' (lit. 'edible corn'), which in turn precedes the clause-final verb. In (3), the adverb *user-user* 'quickly' precedes the serial verb *bir bleling* 'run open' in the first clause, while the locational adjunct phrase *gom mi* 'at/from inside' precedes the verb *eserit* 'exit' in the second clause.

(2) Sawila (Kratochvíl 2014b: 368)
 Ni-ya   di   patara   ma   maana.
 1.SG.II-mother still corn   edible FIN.cook
 'My mother is (still) cooking rice.' [N12.64]

(3) Kaera (Klamer 2014a: 111)
 Ilwang gang   user-user   bir   bleling   [g-om   mi]   eser-it...
 Ilwang 3.SG   RED-quick   run   open   3.SG.POSS-inside   LOC   exit-IPFV
 'Ilwang quickly ran outside ...'

Clausal negation is generally also final. The examples (4)–(5) from Bunaq illustrate a negated verbal and nominal clause. The other TAP languages spoken in East Timor (Makalero, Makasae, and Fataluku) are exceptions to the general TAP pattern, having a pre-predicate negator.

(4) Bunaq (Schapper 2009: 181)
 Hot   baq   no   zapal   ga-sasi   niq.
 sun   noon   OBL   folktale.AN   3.AN-say   NEG
 'During the day (we) don't tell folktales.' [Bk-70.102]

(5) Bunaq (Schapper 2009: 138)
 Nei   milisi   niq.
 1.PL.EXCL   militia   NEG
 'We are not militia.'

Besides negative particles, clauses may also be negated using negative verbs found across the TAP family. An illustration is the negative existential Bunaq verb *hobel* 'not exist' in (6).

(6) Bunaq (Schapper 2009: 204)
 En   waqen   mar   hobel.
 person   PART   garden   not.exist
 'Some people don't have gardens.'

Other negative verbs found in TAP languages include verbs denoting negative intention ('not want'), prohibition ('do not, should not, must not'), and disability ('not be able to, not know'). The latter is illustrated with *paat* 'not know' in (7).

(7) Teiwa (Klamer 2010: 263)
 Ha'an   tei   wrer-an   paat...
 you   tree   climb-REAL   not.know
 'You don't know how to climb a tree ...'

Note that TAP languages do not use copular verbs, neither for equative clauses with non-verbal predicates, as illustrated in (5), nor for existential clauses. To assert the existence of a referent in space or time, an existential verb is used, as illustrated in (8) (and a negative existential verb to negate such an existence—see (6)).

(8) Bunaq (Schapper 2009: 370)
Gewal   gene   ewi   hati.
Kewar   LOC   soldier   exist
'There are soldiers in Kewar.'

Across the TAP languages, the person and number of verbal arguments is expressed by free pronouns and/or verbal affixes. The examples (1)–(2) illustrate a pronominal and nominal subject and object. The typical pronoun paradigm in TAP languages distinguishes three persons and singular from plural, and also has a two-way distinction in the first person plural (exclusive/inclusive), which is expressed by pronouns containing the consonants <n> and <p>. Very commonly, we find a theme vowel <a> for singulars and <i> for plurals, and a 'distributive' pronoun that refers to a (non-collective) plurality of human referents.

The TAP languages are typologically unusual (Siewierska 2013) in that they show a preponderance to index the person and number of transitive objects (P) on verbs, more than transitive and intransitive subjects (A/S) (Holton & Klamer 2017; Klamer 2017), although some languages also index S under certain conditions (this is discussed below). The indexing of P on the verb is found across Alor and Pantar but is less frequent in the TAP languages of Timor. Bunaq indexes only the person (not the number) of P. In Makalero/Makasae only some fossilized forms of an earlier P-indexing system remain (Huber 2017: 329).

P-indexing in the TAP languages is determined by a number of factors, one of which is the animacy of the referent. The animacy of P may determine whether it is indexed with a prefix on the verb or expressed as a free lexical NP or free pronoun. Animacy may also play a role determining which of several possible prefixes is chosen to express the P in the specific context at hand. The role of animacy in the indexing of P is illustrated for Abui in (9). In (9a) the inanimate P *kanai do* 'these pili nut(s)' is not indexed on the verb *bol* 'to hit', while in (9b) the animate (human body part) P *netoku* 'my leg(s)' is indexed refixed on *bol* 'to hit'.

(9) Abui (Kratochvíl 2014a: 566)
  a. Di   kanai   do   bol   took.
     3.AGT   pili.nut   PROX   hit   drop
     'He was hitting pili nuts (and) dropping (them).'

  b. Baloka   ne-toku   he-bol   he-balasi   ba...
     k.o.grass 1.SG.POSS-leg   3.SG.LOC-hit   3.SG.LOC-beat.PFV   SIM
     'The *baloka* grass hit my legs slashing them ...'

Animacy is found as a condition on P-marking across the TAP family, and shows interesting variation in how it plays out in the individual languages (Fedden et al. 2013; 2014; Holton & Klamer 2017; Klamer & Kratochvíl 2018). In addition, in an individual TAP language, the marking of P may be sensitive to additional semantic conditions, such as the semantically more narrow distinction between human and non-human referents, or the affectedness of P (see Klamer & Kratochvíl 2018 for discussion).

Most TAP languages have more than one prefix to encode P, and the semantic role of the object can determine which prefix is used. In (10) it is illustrated how different Abui prefixes may roughly correspond to semantically different Ps (Klamer & Kratochvíl 2018: 83–84). The Abui prefixes differ in vowel quality and vowel length, and in (10) they express respectively: a patient (10a), a location (10b), a recipient (10c), a benefactive (10d), or a goal (10e).[2]

(10) Abui (Kratochvíl 2007: 592)[3]
    a. *Na   ha-ruidi.*
       1.SG.AGT   3.SG.PAT-wake.up.PFV
       'I woke him/her up.'

    b. *Di   palootang   mi   ne-l=bol.*
       3.AGT   rattan   take   1.SG.LOC-give=hit
       'He hit me with a rattan (stick).'

    c. *Fanmalei   no-k=yai.*
       Fanmalei   1.SG.REC-throw=laugh
       'Fanmalei laughed at me.'

    d. *Ma   na   ee-bol.*
       be.PROX 1.SG.AGT 2.SG.BEN-hit
       'Let me hit [it] for you.'

    e. *Simon   di   noo-dik.*
       Simon   3.AGT   1.SG.GOAL-prick
       'Simon is poking me.'

Although the examples in (10) show rather transparent relations between the prefix and the semantic role of the argument it encodes, in most instances where different prefixes are used to index P in TAP languages, the relation between the form of a prefix and the semantic role it encodes is vague or indirect; or the semantic relation is lexicalized. Part of the reason for this is that P-indexing in TAP languages is also heavily determined by inflection classes of verbs, and inflectional class assignments are mostly idiosyncratic (Fedden et al. 2013; 2014).

Verb classes reflecting different argument-indexing properties are found across the TAP family. For instance, Sawila has four inflectional verb classes (Kratochvíl 2014b: 407–418), of which classes I–III are relatively large and class IV is small, only containing about a dozen verbs. Class I verbs do not index their arguments, except when they are morphologically derived with an inverse or an applicative prefix. Class II verbs index their subject (S/A) argument. Class III index their P argument. Class IV verbs are monovalent but index their S in variable ways. Other TAP languages with verb classes that are distinguished by the way they index their arguments are Teiwa (Klamer 2010: 87), Abui (Fedden et al. 2013; 2014), Makalero (Huber 2017), and Bunaq (Schapper 2009: 338–352).

---

[2] Note also that some of the examples contain complex predicates that consist of two or more verbs forming a single phonological word, as in *l = bol* 'give=hit' in (10b) and *k = yai* 'throw=laugh' in (10c), where a verb may be shaped as just a single consonant (Klamer & Kratochvíl 2010).

[3] The 3SG object prefix in (10a) is erroneously glossed as 2SG in the source.

The synchronic pattern of the 'differential' marking of objects attested across the TAP family has led to a reconstruction of two classes of bivalent verbs for proto-Alor Pantar (the first order sub-branch of TAP encompassing all the Papuan languages of Alor and Pantar, not those of Timor). One class consists of bound verb forms (e.g. *-wel* 'bathe someone') which index P with a pronominal prefix; the other class consists of free verb forms (e.g. **nai* 'eat') which use a free form to index P (Klamer & Kratochvíl 2018).

In addition to the verbal indexing of P, the subject of a monovalent predicate (S) can also be indexed. When this is done, often a prefix is used that also functions as one of the P indexing prefix series, thus reflecting a 'semantic alignment' system (Mithun 1991; Donohue & Wichmann 2008; Klamer 2008). In such a system, the semantic features of the core argument (such as their more or less volitional involvement in the event encoded by the predicate) have an impact on the way they are marked (Holton & Klamer 2017: 598–599). Semantic alignment systems are found across Alor and Pantar, including Abui and Sawila (Klamer 2008; Kratochvíl 2011). Accusative alignment is confined to a smaller region covering parts of Alor and Pantar, including Teiwa and Adang; as well as the region of Timor (Klamer & Kratochvíl 2018). The Pantar language Kaera has accusative alignment in combination with some fossilized encoding of S of a small set of monovalent verbs, where a prefix is used that is otherwise used to index P (Klamer 2014a: 135–136). In (11), the intransitive verb *nimin* 'die' in the first clause has no subject prefix (as is the rule in Kaera), while the intransitive *waat* 'live' in the second clause is one of the verbs with an obligatory prefix indexing S. The prefix cannot be omitted, as shown by the ungrammatical example between brackets.

(11) Kaera (Klamer 2014a: 136)
   a. *N-uax   nimin-i   sei,   nang   yedi   n-waat.*   (**Nang yedi waat.*)
      1.SG-child die-PFV   COMPL   1.SG   still   1.SG-live   1.SG   still   live
      'My child is dead already, I still live.'

On the basis of the geographical spread and the fossilized state of these S-prefixes in Kaera it has been hypothesized that semantic alignment was the original system of the Alor Pantar languages, from which the accusatively aligning languages diverged (Klamer & Kratochvíl 2018).

Besides pronominal prefixes, verbal inflectional morphology in TAP languages also includes suffixes encoding aspect. For example, in (11), *nimin-i* 'die-PFV' in the first clause has a perfective suffix; compare the imperfective suffix of *eser-it* 'exit-IPFV' in (3). In Abui, the coding of aspect may also cause verb stem alternations, as the Abui examples above show. Mood distinctions are encoded by suffixes indicating a realis–irrealis distinction in Teiwa (Klamer 2011) and Sawila (Kratochvíl 2014b). Overall, however, TAM morphology is rather limited in TAP languages, and some languages, such as Adang and Bunaq, lack aspect and mood morphology altogether. Verbal markings of tense, active/passive voice morphology, and finiteness are lacking in all TAP languages.

Valency-changing verbal morphology is limited, and mostly confined to applicative prefixes, as illustrated in (12) (see the overview in Klamer 2018: 241). Most of the applicative prefixes historically derive from locational or deictic verbs in former serial verb constructions (see section 36.5), which would also explain why the applicative *u-* attaches outside of the object–verb combination in (12b).

(12) Adang (Robinson &Haan 2014: 270)
    a. *Sa   na-tan.*
       SG.SBJ   1.SG.OBJ-ask
       'S/he asked me.'

    b. *Uli lod   habar ho   u-na-tan.*
       Uli shirt new DEF   APPL-1.SG.OBJ-ask
       'Uli asked me about the new shirt.'

A few languages (including Adang and Kaera) have a causative prefix or suffix. All TAP languages express causation analytically, using serial verb constructions. Serial verb constructions are prevalent in TAP languages. Serial constructions are analysed here as in Klamer (2010: 27–28): two or more verbs that occur together in a single clause under a single intonation contour which share minimally one argument that is expressed maximally once.

In the TAP languages, serial verb constructions are 'core-layer' serializations (Foley & Olson 1985). They are distinguished from biclausal constructions by the presence of a clause boundary marker (which can be a conjunction-like element, or an intonational break). Verbs in serial verb constructions express notions such as purpose, manner, time, and direction; they encode modalities such as intention, obligation, imperative, hortative, and ability; they encode aspect such as continuous, imperfective, and perfective, and they function to introduce additional participants with semantic roles including goals, sources, locations, instruments, and displaced themes. Across the family, such participant-adding verbs in serial constructions have developed, or are currently developing into postpositions and/or valency-changing verbal prefixes. In this grammaticalization process some verbs are attested in an 'intermediate' stage of formal defectiveness: they are phonologically reduced, have lost some of the typical verbal properties such as the ability to take person or aspect/mood inflections, and/or have undergone semantic bleaching (see Klamer 2018; see also section 36.5).

As a result of the proliferation of verbs in many functional and semantic domains, classes of adverbs that express aspect, mood and manner adverbs are typically small in TAP languages. In case their etymology can be established it seems that historically, they often derive from verbs (see section 36.6).

Another salient feature of TAP verbs is that languages generally have intransitive and monotransitive verbs, but no ditransitive verbs; and in case they do have a ditransitive, it is usually only the verb 'give'. Most often, however, three-participant transfer events are in TAP languages are expressed as monoclausal serial verb constructions, illustrated in (13), where the first verb 'take' takes a theme P, and the second verb 'give' takes a recipient P. Alternatively, biclausal constructions involving two monotransitive verbs may be used, as illustrated in (14), where the conjunction *ba* links the two clauses.

(13) Abui (Klamer & Schapper 2012: 186–187)
    Hen   seng   hu   mi   he-l-e.
    3   money   DEM   take   3-give-IPFV
    'Give him just money.'

(14) Hen   mi   ba   Lius   la   he-l-e.
     3   take   CONJ   Lius   PART   3-give-IPFV
     'Just give that one to Lius.'

36.3 NOUNS AND PRONOUNS

Noun inflection in TAP languages is simple. All languages mark person and number of possessors with nominal prefixes, but lack inflection for case or gender. All TAP languages divide the class of common nouns into nouns with an 'alienable' possessor and nouns with an 'inalienable' possessor. The class of alienable nouns generally includes all nouns, except those referring to body parts and kinship terms—those are typically inalienable. In all TAP languages, alienable and inalienable nouns are formally distinguished by having an optional vs obligatory possessive prefix. This is illustrated in (15) where the possessor of the inalienable noun *fasu* 'skin' must be expressed either as a prefix (15a) or as a possessor noun (15b). In contrast, alienable nouns such as *sefar* 'dog' can occur with a possessor (16a) or without a possessor (16b).

(15)   Makalero (Huber 2017: 317–318)
   a.   *ki-fasu*
        3.POSS-SKIN
        '(its) skin, peel'

   b.   *muʔu   fasu*
        banana   peel
        'banana peel'

(16) a. *Kiloo   sefar=ee   pase.*
        3.SG   dog=DEF   hit
        'He hit the dog.'

     b. ... *ki-sefar   potil=ee   hai   mutu-puna*...
           3.POSS-dog   bottle=DEF   INITIAL   inside-look
           '... his dog is looking into the jar ...'

In most TAP languages, alienable and inalienable prefixes do not only differ in obligatoriness, but also occur in distinct configurations. For example, in Abui, the alienability distinction is encoded by a theme vowel in the possessor prefix: prefixes with the vowel *e* are alienable, as illustrated in (17a); prefixes with the vowel *a* are inalienable, as illustrated in (17b). Note that a third person possessor noun such as 'Daniel' in (17) precedes the possessed NP and forms a noun phrase with it. The order possessor–noun is universal in the TAP family.

(17) Abui (Saad, Klamer, & Moro 2019: 9)
   a. *Daniel   he-faling.*
      D.   3.AL-axe
      'Daniel's axe'

   b. *Daniel   ha-min.*
      D.   3.INAL-nose
      'Daniel's nose'

In some TAP languages, including Teiwa and Abui (Klamer & Kratochvíl 2006), the possessive prefix paradigm shows formal similarities with the object paradigm. For example, in Abui, the possessive prefix *he-* '3.SG.AL' in (17a) is formally identical to the object prefix *he* '3.SG.LOC' in (9b), and the same is true for possessive *ha-* in (17b) and object *ha-* '3.SG.PAT' in (10a). The formal similarity in the encoding of *objects* and nominal possessors observed in TAP languages contrasts with the cross-linguistically more commonly observed similarity in the marking of *subjects* and possessors (Bittner & Hale 1996: 60).

Number is morphologically expressed on nouns in the TAP languages of the Timor branch, but not in those of Alor Pantar. Makasae has a nominal plural suffix *-la* (Huber 2008: 14) (e.g. *asukai-la* 'man-PL'), while Makalero has different plural suffixes for kinship terms (*-raa*) and for other nouns (*-laa*) (Huber 2011: 236–237). Fataluku encodes plurality with an enclitic = *éré* on nouns (Heston 2015: 21). Bunaq nouns are generally unmarked for number, but nouns with human referents can be pluralized with = i 'HUM.PL', an enclitic that derives from the third person plural pronoun *hala'i* (Schapper 2009: 197–199). In the Alor–Pantar branch of the TAP family, the use of a plural word to encode nominal plurality is widespread (Klamer, Schapper, & Corbett 2017). There is good evidence to reconstruct a plural word *non for proto-Alor–Pantar (Klamer, Schapper, & Corbett 2017: 376–380). Some Alor–Pantar languages, such as Adang in (18), inherited both form and function from this proto-form, others innovated a new form for the plural word. The languages under investigation do not show restrictions on which referents can be marked plural with a plural word.

(18) Adang (Robinson & Haan 2014: 252)
   Pen ti   matɛ   nun   ʔa-bɔ-ʔɔi.
   P.   tree large   PL   3.INCL.OBJ-cut
   'Pen cut some large trees.'

For the expression of plural referents, TAP languages also use special sets of pronouns. Some, but by no means all, TAP languages have a set of dual pronouns alongside the singular and plural; languages with dual pronouns are Teiwa and Bunaq. The Bunaq free pronouns given in (19) distinguish singular, plural, and dual numbers, and have three persons, including an inclusive–exclusive distinction in both non-singular numbers. Instead of a 3SG personal pronoun Bunaq uses demonstratives (Schapper 2009: 90–91).

(19) Bunaq free pronouns

	SINGULAR	PURAL	DUAL
1.EXCL	neto	nei	neli
1.INCL		i	ili
2	eto	ei	eli
3	--	halaqi	halali

There are also languages with pronouns that refer to explicitly singular referents ('*x* alone'), illustrated with Adang *ilɔ* '2PL.ALONE' in 20). The paradigm of Teiwa '*x* alone' pronouns is given in (21). The Teiwa forms are derived from the root *qai* 'only, just' which is prefixed with a mix of object prefixes and short subject pronouns.

(20) Adang (Robinson & Haan 2014: 265)
    (I)   *ilɔ*   *sam*   *don.*
    2.PL.SUBJ 2.PL.ALONE go shop
    'You go shopping by yourselves.'

(21) Teiwa (Klamer 2010: 83–84)
    '*x* alone' pronouns in Teiwa
    1.SG-only   *na-qai*   'I alone'
    2.SG-only   *ha-qai*   'you (SG) alone'
    3.SG-only   *a-qai*   'he alone'
    1.PL.EXCL-only *ni-qai*   'we alone (excluding you)'
    1.PL.INCL-only *pi-qai*   'we alone (including you)'
    2.PL-only   *yi-qai*   'you (PL) alone'
    3.PL-only   *i-qai*   'they alone'

Teiwa also has pronouns referring to entities that are in the company of others ('*x* and they'), (22) (where the base *iqap* has no independent meaning), and pronouns referring to groups of particular numbers, (23) (where the base *man* also has no independent meaning). After a pronoun '*x* as a group of *y*', the number of *y* is given, as shown in (24) with *ut* 'four'.

(22) Teiwa (Klamer 2010: 83)

    '*x* and they' pronouns in Teiwa
    2.SG-and.they   *h-iqap*   'you (SG) and they'
    3-and.they   *ø-iqap*   's/he/they and they'
    1-and.they   *n-iqap*   'I/we (excluding you) and they'
    1.PL.INCL-and.they *p-iqap*   'we (including you) and they'
    2.PL-and.they   *y-iqap*   'you (PL) and they'

(23) Teiwa (Klamer 2010: 84)
    '*x* as a group of *y*' pronouns in Teiwa
    1.PL.EXCL   *ni-man y*   'we (excluding you) as group of *y* numbers'
    1.PL.INCL   *pi-man y*   'we (including you) as group of *y* numbers'
    2.PL   *yi-man y*   'you (pl) as group of *y* numbers'
    3.PL   *i-man y*   'they as group of *y* numbers'

(24) *Pi-man*   *ut*   *ina.*
     1.PL.EXCL-man four eat
     'The four of us (not including you) eat'

36.4 ADJECTIVES

In many TAP languages, property-denoting words are not distinguished as a class separate from intransitive stative verbs. This includes Adang (Robinson & Haan 2014: 249), Sawila (Kratochvíl 2014b: 381), Makalero (Huber 2017: 293), and Bunaq (Schapper 2009, 83). These TAP languages show similarity to Austronesian languages, where adjective-like words are also typically classed with stative verbs (Robinson & Haan 2014, 252). Among the TAP languages that do have adjectives, there are languages with a large class of adjectives, or a small class of adjectives to which no new members can be added. Languages like Teiwa have a large class of adjectives which can be used as modifiers and predicates, compare the use of *qa'an* 'black' in (26a)–(26b). Teiwa adjectives are distinct from verbs in that adjectival predicates do not take a realis suffix, as shown in (26c), while verbal predicates do (Klamer 2010: 116–121). Adjectives also frequently occur with a possessor prefix, (26d). Such formally derived nominals can be used as nominal attributes, (26d), and as independent nominal expressions, (26e) (see section 36.3). The use of possessive prefixes on adjectives is different from the use of possessive suffixes on nouns: on adjectives, the prefix functions to derive nominals and mark a 'part–whole' relation, as in constructions like (26d), while on underived nouns, the affix refers to possessors but is not used to encode 'part–whole' relations in nominal compounds, as shown in (27).

(25) Teiwa (Klamer 2010: 413, 120, 75)

    a.   *Mauqubar   qa'an.*
          frog   black
          'A black frog'

    b.   *Mauqubar   la   qa'an.*
          frog   FOC black
          'A frog that is black'

    c.* *Mauqubar la   qa'an-an.*
          frog   FOC black-REAL
          'A frog that is black' (constructed from field notes, cf. Klamer 2010: 120)

    d.   *Mauqubar   ga-qa'an.*
          frog   3.SG.POSS-black
          'Of the frogs the black one'

    e.   *Ga-qa'an.*
          3.SG.POSS-black
          'The black one'

(26) *batar   (*ga-)bag;   batar   (*ga-)kir*
       corn   (3.SG.POSS-)seed   corn   (3.SG.POSS-)ear
      'corn seed(s); corn cob(s)' (cf. Klamer 2014b: 145)

In Abui, there is a small class of six adjectives, *akan* 'black', *kul* 'white', *abet* 'young', *maek* 'young', *dakun* 'dirty', and *san* 'clean' (Kratochvíl 2007: 101–102). Abui adjectives are differentiated from the stative verbs by their distinct distributional properties: they may only occur as adnominal modifier and cannot head a predicate. Most other property-words in Abui are classified as stative verbs.

36.5 Adpositions

Overall, adpositions are rare in TAP languages. In most languages that have synchronic adpositions, the adpositions are etymologically related to verbs. This is illustrated for Adang in (29). In (29a), *mi* functions as a postposition, in (29b), *mi* is a transitive locational verb with the object *baang* 'house', and in (29c), the function of *mi* is ambiguous: it can either be analysed as the transitive locational verb *mi* in a serial verb construction with *ʔArabah* as its object, or as a postposition, as the gloss indicates.

(27) Adang (Robinson & Haan 2014: 235–236; Haan 2001: 403)
   a. *Aru   banary   mi.*
       deer   forest   in
       'There are deer in the forest.'

   b. *Roni ip-   l-   e   baang mi.*
       R.   go.down- DIR- DIST   house be.in
       'Roni is down there at the house.'

   c. *Na   ʔArabah   mi   mih.*
       1.SG.SUBJ Kalabahi   in   sit/live
       'I live in Kalabahi.'

Additional examples of transitive locational verbs are given in (27)–(28). In (28), the P is *itaʔa* 'where' and *uyan* 'mountain', in (29), the P is *lemari* 'closet'.

(28) Teiwa (Klamer 2010: 69)
     Lius   itaʔa   meʔ?   A   uyan   meʔ.
     Lius   where be.in 3.SG   mountain be.in
     'Where is Lius? He is in the mountains.'

(29) Kaera (Klamer 2014a: 118)
     Ne-na   xas-i   ula   lemari   ming.
     1.SG-thing split-PFV   FOC closet (IND) be.at
     'My clothes (lit. split things) are in the closet.'

Adang *mi*, Teiwa *meʔ* and Kaera *ming* are all modern reflexes of the proto-TAP locational verb **mi* 'be in, be at'. Reflexes of this proto-verb are found in ten languages across the TAP family, and these reflexes occupy different points on the continuum locative verb > locative postposition > applicative verbal prefix (Klamer 2018).

Another verb that has developed adpositional functions in some TAP languages is proto-TAP *ma 'come (here, to deictic centre)'. The verb has modern reflexes as main and serial verb in thirteen TAP languages, and evolved into a postposition/enclitic in three of them. The semantics of the original TAP verb *ma combine a motion with a deictic component. The Teiwa reflex of this verb is illustrated in (32).

(30) Teiwa (Klamer 2010: 326)
      Ha'an   la   Ma   le   na'an   la   wa?
      2.SG   FOC   come   or   1.SG   FOC   go
      'Are you coming (to me) or am I going (to you)?'

When the verb grammaticalizes into an adposition, the semantic motion component gets 'bleached' and only its deictic semantics survive (Klamer 2018: 246–249). Such forms developed adpositional functions that 'flag' oblique arguments such as goals, benefactives, sources, instruments, or themes; the Teiwa examples in (33)–(34) illustrate how *ma* 'come' flags a goal and a benefactive.

(31) Teiwa (Klamer 2010: 334)
      A   ta   war   upar   ma   ga-ayas.
      3.SG   TOP   rock   pebble   come   3.SG-throw.at
      'He throws pebbles at him.'

(32) Xa'a   ma   ha-bif   ga-mai.
      this.one   come   2.SG.POSS-younger.sibling   3.SG-save
      'Save this for your younger sibling(s).'

There are far fewer languages showing the grammaticalization continuum from verb to adposition for TAP *ma 'come' than there are showing this continuum for TAP *mi 'be in, be at'. The reason for this difference likely lies in the different semantic composition of the two verbs. It is easier to develop the original locational verb *mi 'be in, be at' into a locational adposition because it requires less semantic bleaching than the deictic verb *ma 'come'. The latter contains information on both movement and direction ('come' always involves a motion directed towards the speaker), and the entire movement component must be bleached from its verbal semantics in order for it to function as a goal/benefactive adposition.

The third example of grammaticalization of verbs in the TAP family is the development of the handling verb *med 'take'. Reflexes of this verb are found in 12 TAP languages. In all languages, the verb occurs frequently in SVCs that express 'give events' and consist of reflexes of *med 'take' and *-en(a/i) 'give', as shown for Abui in (13). In such constructions, both verbs are monotransitive; the verb 'take' takes the transferred object as its complement, and the verb 'give' has the recipient as complement.

Grammaticalization of verbs into postpositions and affixes is common in TAP languages because the grammar of the languages allows it: objects precede the predicate, locations and directions are typically expressed as arguments of locational and deictic verbs; locations, directions, instruments, goals, sources, and comitatives precede the major verb in a serial verb construction; and there is an overall prevalence for such serial verb constructions.

Furthermore, there is little verb morphology indicative of the categorical status of verbs, so that in a serial construction the first verb can easily be reinterpreted as an oblique marker and grammaticalize as a prefix on the V2, as was illustrated in (12b).

In sum, most TAP languages have only a few synchronic adpositions, and typically these are etymologically related to locational, deictic, or handling verbs. In addition, locations in TAP languages may also be expressed with locational nouns in possessive constructions. For example, in (30), the locational noun *siban* 'behind' is grammatically possessed by the 'ground' *axala*' 'his/its mother'.

(33) Teiwa (Klamer 2010: 118)
Bif   g-oqai   un   a-xala'   ga-siban   ma   o'on.
child   3.SG.POSS   PROG   3SG.POSS-mother   3SG.POSS-behind   come   hide
'Her child is hiding behind its mother.'

36.6 Adverbs

Since the class of verbs dominates many functional and semantic domains in TAP languages (section 36.2), classes of aspectual, modal and manner adverbs are typically small. The grammars and sketches currently available do not provide sufficient information on adverbs to describe patterns that apply across the TAP family.

36.7 Numerals

In the TAP family, the AP branch reflects a typologically rare combination of monomorphemic 'six' with quinary forms for numerals 'seven' to 'nine', a pattern which can be reconstructed to go back to proto-AP (Schapper & Klamer 2017). Illustrations are given in Table 36.1. A second strategy of creating numerals 'seven' through 'nine' found in the AP languages is subtraction (e.g. [10–3] for 'seven', [10–2] for 'eight', [10–1] for 'nine'). Adang applies this subtractive system (Schapper & Klamer 2017: 290–294) and is thus lacking from Table 36.1. The TAP languages of the Timor branch have a decimal system.

36.8 Category-changing derivation

Category-changing derivation is sparse in TAP languages. For Adang, Abui, Sawila, and Bunaq no category-changing morphology has been observed. In Teiwa, adjectives, adverbs, question words, and verbs can be nominalized with a possessor prefix (Klamer 2010: 29, 76, 86), but besides possessive prefixes, the language has no dedicated nominalizing morphology. In Makalero/Makasai a few unproductive derivational suffixes can be identified, illustrated in (35). Morphology deriving verbs from other word classes appears to be absent in the TAP languages.

(34) Makalero/Makasai (Huber 2017: 289)
    Makalero   *nua*   >   *nua-ini*   'food'
               eat   eat-NMLZ
    Makasai   *paʔ*   >   *paʔ-ini*   'everything related to sewing'
               sew   sew-NMLZ
    Makalero   *ʔuri*   >   *ʔuri-ʔ*   'to brush'
               brush(n.)   brush-VBLZ
    Makasai   *wali*   *wali-ʔ*   'to hear'
               ear   >   ear-VBLZ

Table 36.1 Numerals 'seven' to 'nine' in AP languages (Schapper & Klamer 2017: 288)

| | 'seven' | 'eight' | 'nine' |
	5 2	5 3	5 4
Teiwa	*jesraq*	*jesnerig*	*jesnaʔut*
Kaera	*jesrax-*	*jentug*	*jeniut*
Abui	*jetiŋajoku*	*jetiŋsua*	*jetiŋbuti*
Sawila	*jo:tiŋjaku*	*jo:tiŋtuo*	*jo:tiŋara:siiku*
Wersing	*wetiŋyoku*	*wetiŋtu*	*wetiŋarasoku*

36.9 RELATIVE FREQUENCY OF INDONESIAN LOANS ACROSS THE WORD CLASSES

All the TAP languages are currently under dominance of Indonesian, the national language of Indonesia used in education and the media. The dominance of Indonesian is a relatively recent phenomenon which started with the establishment of Indonesian schools in the 1960s and 1970s.[4] In East Timor, many adult speakers of TAP languages also speak Indonesian, as Indonesian was the language of education in Timor Leste since 1976 until it became independent from Indonesia in 2002. Today, Indonesian is still used in contacts between people from Timor Leste and people in West Timor and other parts of Indonesia. Given the

---

[4] Note that on Alor and Pantar, in places like the capital Kalabahi, a local variety of Malay referred to as Alor Malay was already spoken before the advent of Indonesian. Alor Malay is similar to the Malay variety spoken in the provincial capital of Kupang on Timor island. Malay has been the lingua franca in eastern Indonesia for centuries. Because of the lexical similarities between Malay and Indonesian, current speakers on Alor and Pantar consider Alor Malay as the colloquial variety of standard Indonesian, even though the two languages have very different histories.

dominant role of Indonesian in the TAP region over the last 40 years, the question can be asked whether, and, if so, how this contact has influenced the word classes of TAP languages. In particular, what is the relative frequency of Indonesian loans across the various word classes of the TAP languages?

Using the data in the lexical database LexiRumah (Kaiping & Klamer 2018; Kaiping, Edwards, & Klamer 2019) with word lists from 42 TAP varieties (i.e. both dialects and languages), we filtered the word lists of these TAP languages for those words that are identical or very similar to Indonesian words in both form and meaning. Such words we identified as Indonesian loans. Out of a total of 23,247 words, we found 212 possible Indonesian loans. The average number of items on each word list is 553 and the number of loans in each variety range from 1–20 loans per list, so on average the lists contain less than 3.6% Indonesian loans.

Among the loans, nouns are the majority. Indonesian nouns were borrowed 155 times, denoting 49 concepts; followed by 23 verbs denoting 12 concepts, and 16 adjectives denoting 8 concepts. Nouns that were borrowed in five or more language varieties are given in Table 36.2, verbs and adjectives that were borrowed in three or more varieties are given in Table 36.3.

Table 36.2 Indonesian nouns borrowed in five or more TAP varieties

(35)	English	Indonesian	Borrowed in N varieties
	cookhouse, kitchen	dapur	11
	jackfruit	nangka	12
	lamp	lampu (< orig. Dutch *lamp*)	7
	candle	lilin	7
	rope	tali	7
	market	pasar	8
	window	jendela (<orig. Portuguese *janela*)	8

Table 36.3 Indonesian verbs and adjectives borrowed in three or more TAP varieties

(36)	English	Indonesian	Borrowed in N varieties
	worship	bersembayang	6
	poor	miskin	5
	same	sama	4
	fold	lipat	3
	learn	belajar	3

Temporal expressions were borrowed in ten varieties (eight times *tahun* 'year', two times *jam* 'hour'), numerals in seven varieties (four times 'three' and three times 'five'), and the conjunction *kalau* 'if' was present in the word list of four varieties.

What this shows is that, overall, borrowing of Indonesian words appears to be very limited in the word lists of TAP languages. Of the content words, nouns are more frequently borrowed than verbs and adjectives, and only a few borrowed temporal nouns, numerals, and conjunctions occur. Given the low rate of lexical borrowing, we do not expect to see much Indonesian influence on the word classes of TAP languages.

36.10 Discussion: Word classes in TAP and other Papuan families

In this section, I place the word classes of TAP languages against the background of other Papuan languages. I compare the TAP features discussed above with those that have been suggested as characteristic for Papuan languages in general (Foley 2000; 2017; Aikhenvald & Stebbins 2007) or Trans New Guinea (TNG) in particular. The comparison with the TNG family is especially relevant because in earlier literature, the TAP family has been hypothesized to be a sub-branch of the TNG family (Wurm, Voorhoeve, & McElhanon 1975; Ross 2005). Historical comparative research has not yet found sufficient lexical evidence to support such an affiliation, so that in the absence of such evidence, the TAP languages are presently assumed to form an independent genealogical unit (Holton et al. 2012; Holton & Robinson 2017). In this section, I mostly use Foley (2017) as the reference to Papuan typology in general, and Fedden (to appear) as the most up-to-date survey of the properties of TNG languages. In what follows, I first discuss the commonalities between TAP languages and those of the TNG family, followed by a discussion of the differences.

In terms of syntax, TAP languages are right-headed, with SPV/AV word order and postpositions, as most other Papuan languages, including the TNG languages. TAP languages also agree with Papuan languages in general, and TNG languages in particular, by having a clear distinction between verbs and nouns, and having verbs as the morphologically most complex word class. Verbs in TNG languages are frequently sorted into inflection classes, just like we find for TAP languages.

Much of the verbal complexity in Papuan languages comes from inflections for modal distinctions like realis and irrealis, object and/or subject marking, and valency-increasing derivational processes, such as causatives and applicatives. Applicative constructions add arguments by making benefactive, comitative, locative, or temporal adjuncts into objects of the verb. This is also true for TAP languages. Besides using valency-increasing derivational morphemes, Papuan languages, including TNG and TAP, also express causative and applicative functions by verbs in serial verb constructions, or by using morphemes that are transparently derivable from such earlier verbal uses. Serial verb constructions are also employed to encode aspectual distinctions.

The great majority of the Papuan languages with pronominal agreement affixes for both subject and object arrange them according to an accusative alignment, though some Papuan languages have semantic alignment, an agreement system that is sensitive to the semantic notions of agent versus patient. In the TAP languages, we find accusative alignment, while semantic alignment may have been the original alignment system of the AP branch of the TAP family.

In many Papuan languages that have a verb meaning 'give', this verb is monotransitive. In constructions with three arguments, TNG languages in particular realize the theme (the object that is transferred) as the complement of another predicate in a serial verb construction, or as the complement of an adposition; and this is also observed in TAP languages. In those Papuan languages that have object agreement, it is the recipient that is expressed as the object affix on the 'give' verb, not the theme (cf. Reesink 2013).

Nouns in Papuan languages are commonly uninflected for number, as they are in most TAP languages. In TNG languages, nominal inflection for only the possessor can be found, and most TNG languages make a formal distinction between alienable and inalienable possession, where the inalienable nouns include kinship terms and body part nouns. As in TAP, the typical TNG pattern involves obligatory inflection of the possessed noun for the person and number of the possessor, while the forms used are often similar to the pronominal prefixes that index objects on verbs.

Turning now to the differences between TAP and other Papuan languages, including Trans New Guinea languages, we observe the following. The majority of Papuan languages has at least subject verbal agreement, which can be expressed as suffixes or (less frequently) as prefixes. Typical TNG languages have subject suffixes, while their objects can be either suffixes, prefixes, or not indexed on the verb. The pattern of TAP languages, with their pervasive object prefixes and only occasional subject prefixes is thus quite distinct from patterns in both TNG and Papuan languages in general. But TAP languages do share with TNG languages that if object affixes are used, these are typically associated with animate referents.

The typical Papuan and TNG pronoun paradigm distinguishes three persons, and singular from plural number. TAP pronoun paradigms are more elaborate, including a separate distributive pronoun, and pronouns distinguishing clusivity. An inclusive–exclusive distinction in pronouns is not commonly found in TNG languages.

Papuan languages, including the TNG family, can have elaborate tense systems. Particularly in past tenses one often finds multiple distinctions, for example a general past, a near past, a hesternal (yesterday's) past, a non-hodiernal (not today's) past, and a remote past (e.g. in Mian, Fedden 2011). In sharp contrast to this, TAP languages do not inflect for tense. Another difference is that in TNG languages, negation is often done by means of a verbal prefix or proclitic, while in TAP, clauses are negated by postverbal negators.

In the nominal domain, gender is a very common grammatical category in Papuan languages, with often a binary contrast between masculine and feminine. However, in both TNG as well as TAP languages, a gender distinction is uncommon, and languages often lack gender marking on nouns altogether. Papuan languages in general, and TNG languages in particular, mark core arguments with person indices on the verb, while using a range of case markers for peripheral arguments such as locations, goal, sources, and instruments. TAP languages generally lack case marking on nominal constituents.

Concerning the class of adjectives, no generalizations can be made that apply across the Papuan sphere: 'Some languages have a distinct class of adjectives, while others—subsuming the words denoting qualities and properties into the classes of nouns and verbs—do not' (Foley 2017: 896). TNG languages typically have sizable classes of adjectives, although languages with smaller sets of adjectives are also attested. In many of the TAP languages, there is no separate class of adjectives, and property concepts are expressed as stative verbs.

TNG languages show a wide range of numeral systems, but the most widespread type in TNG is a restricted system with numerals only for 'one' and 'two' (Pawley & Hammarström 2017: 128). In contrast, the most widespread numeral system in TAP is a quinary system.

In sum, the word classes in TAP languages share many morphological features with Papuan languages in general, and with TNG languages in particular. At the same time, there are also some significant differences between TAP languages and other Papuan languages. These differences relate to the position of subject and object affixes, the shape and place of negation, the form of pronominal paradigms, the lack of marking for tense, gender, and case, and the use of quinary numerals in TAP.

Acknowledgements

I would like to thank Hanna Fricke for her help in compiling data for the eight TAP languages discussed here and filtering out loans from Indonesian in the LexiRumah database, and the two reviewers for their insightful comments on a previous draft. This chapter was written as part of the VICI research project 'Reconstructing the past through languages of the present' at Leiden University, funded by the Netherlands Organisation for Scientific Research (NWO), project number 277-70-012.

CHAPTER 37

WORD CLASSES IN SIGN LANGUAGES

VADIM KIMMELMAN AND CARL BÖRSTELL

37.1 INTRODUCTION

SIGN languages are fully fledged, natural, human languages, found across the globe, within and around different communities of signing and speaking people. Sign languages are quite often referred to as a group of languages, although they constitute neither a genealogically nor a typologically uniform group (see, e.g., de Vos & Pfau 2015; de Vos & Nyst 2018). In fact, what unifies sign languages is the *modality*, being produced and perceived in a gestural–visual form rather than the vocal–auditory form of spoken languages. As such, the relevant contrast is one of modality—that is, between signed and spoken languages.

Nevertheless, in this chapter, we will attempt to summarize some of the key aspects of previous work on word classes (or *sign* classes) of languages in the signed modality. Our aim is to provide an overview of work done on individual languages without making any assumptions about the universality of any findings as applicable to *all* signed languages. It should also be noted that sign language linguistics is still a relatively young field of research, having emerged only in the 1960s–1970s, which also accounts for the fact that most if not all sign languages should still be considered under-studied (McBurney 2012).

This chapter consists of five parts, moving from considerations pertaining to the visual modality and signed language structure to theoretical definitions and applied methods for identifying and positing word classes in various sign languages, followed by a general summary. Section 37.2 will first introduce some key considerations concerning language as realized in the gestural–visual modality, indicating how these may affect the linguistic analysis of language structure. Section 37.3 will provide an overview of the word classes that have been postulated in individual sign languages, on the basis of both semantic and morphosyntactic criteria. Section 37.4 looks at the experimental and data-driven approaches used to find and label word classes using elicitation- and corpus-based methods. Section 37.5 concludes the chapter with a summary.

37.2 MODALITY AND STRUCTURE

In this section, we discuss how the modality and structure of signed languages give rise to cases that do not always fall into traditionally defined categories of neither words nor word classes. Section 37.2.1 introduces the general modality effects, focusing on simultaneity and information-stacking due to multiple articulators. Section 37.2.2 gives examples of expressions that are not always categorized as (lexical) signs and thus often fall outside of word-class discussions in the literature. Section 37.2.3 outlines language contact phenomena that also influence word-class categorizations. Finally, section 37.2.4 gives an interim summary, bridging into section 37.3, in which the more traditional and easily defined signs and word classes are discussed.

37.2.1 Sign language structure

Although there is no longer any doubt within the linguistics community that sign languages are fully fledged, natural human languages, the fact that they use a different modality has some consequences on their structural properties—part of *modality effects* (Meier 2012). One property of sign language structure that is clearly distinct from that of spoken language structure is, of course, phonology. By using the gestural–visual modality, basic units of linguistic building blocks look fundamentally different: there are no vowels or consonants, and signs are not formed by controlling air flow to produce sound waves. Sign languages are produced using a combination of individuated articulators—hands, torso, head, mouth, and facial gestures—that can move in a synchronized fashion or more or less separately. This allows sign language structure to encode a linguistic signal by stacking rather than sequencing information—that is, being more simultaneous than linear. A spoken signal may obviously express stacked information too, in the sense of adding suprasegmental features such as pitch on top of the phonemes, but signing is unique in the sense of also having paired, identical articulators in the two hands/arms as well as non-manual markers (gaze, eyebrows, posture, etc.), and thus the amount of simultaneity possible. Some features of the simultaneous potential of signed language will prove important in the discussion of word classes. This includes the use of non-manual marking, simultaneous use of a secondary hand, and the definition of morphological processes and syntactic structure in terms of sequential vs simultaneous modification.

37.2.2 What is (not) a sign?

An often debated topic in sign language linguistics involves the definition of a *sign*. This is mostly based on a debate around the definitions of signs vs gestures, but also whether there are some meaningful depicting constructions that should not be considered fixed sign forms but rather productive types of enactment (e.g. Liddell 2003; Hodge & Johnston 2014a, 2014b; Ferrara & Hodge 2018; Hodge & Cormier 2019). In this section, we summarize the main types of signs and expressions that have been discussed in the literature as potentially falling *outside* the core definition of (lexical) signs, which in turn complicates their categorization with regard to word classes. Here, we briefly describe gestures and pointing, depiction and enactment, and discourse-type elements researched within the field, along with discussions on how these relate to word classes.

When it comes to gestures, there are signs that are likely direct incorporations of *emblems*—that is, fixed, conventionalized, culture-dependent gestures that replace whole words, such as thumbs-up for 'good'—into sign languages (see Figure 37.1). This is because sign languages are often used as a minority language surrounded by a larger hearing non-signing community with its own gestural conventions and semiotic repertoire (see Kendon 2008). Since emblems can replace entire words or sentences, they can be difficult to categorize into word classes.

FIGURE 37.1 A sign variant meaning 'good' in Swedish Sign Language (Swedish Sign Language Dictionary online 2020: #12077)

This is a problem that pertains to their use in sign languages too, with the additional complication that they are linearly sequenced in the same modality and production stream/channel as other signs. Although easier for cases such as thumbs-up in Figure 37.1, it becomes far more complicated with forms such as the so-called palm(s)-up gesture (Figure 37.2). The palm-up gesture has been found to express a wide range of pragmatic discourse functions across both gesture and sign language communities, often associated with interrogative, epistemic, or turn-regulating functions (Cooperrider et al. 2018). In fact, this specific gesture has been found to occur across many sign languages, and with high lexical frequency at that (Börstell et al. 2016).

FIGURE 37.2 The palm(s)-up gesture/sign (Swedish Sign Language Dictionary online 2020: #18717)

Another obvious overlap in form across sign languages and gesture is the use of pointing signs. Pointing is prevalent across many cultures—although the form specifics may differ (as in which body part or configuration thereof is used for indication)—and also ubiquitous in sign languages, constituting the highest frequency signs in all corpus-based lexical frequency studies to date (Börstell et al. 2016; Fenlon et al. 2019). Fenlon and colleagues (2019) show that what appears to be obvious similarities in the use of pointing across sign and gesture exhibit form and distributional differences at closer inspection. This includes sign language pointing being more consistent in the use of some form parameters (one-handed pointing, and contact with the chest for self-points), suggesting that although pointing as a communicative strategy across sign languages and gesture have similar origin and function, the specifics get more detailed when adapted into a sign language as it becomes more entrenched in the linguistic system. Furthermore, pointing is used with equivalent functions to pronouns and demonstratives in sign languages, but especially the pronoun status has been questioned since pointing forms are context-dependent and theoretically infinite in number—that is, not listable, specified forms (see, e.g. Lillo-Martin & Klima 1990; Cormier et al. 2013; Johnston 2013; Hou & Meier 2018, for discussions).

Regarding depicting constructions, most, if not all, sign languages seem to use complex enactments—either embodied as taking on a character's physical being (called *character perspective*), or by mapping referents to different articulators of the body (called *observer perspective*). For many action-depicting signs, this is the iconic motivation behind the sign: showing how the action is being performed (e.g. 'to hammer, a hammer';

Figure 37.3). However, such constructions may also be much more elaborate, including several different referents mapped onto separate articulators (Dudis 2004), including adverbial/emotional information and complex manner descriptions (e.g. 'person angrily hammering a round object flat'). Some have argued that these types of *depicting* or *enacting* (Liddell 2003; Hodge & Johnston 2014a, 2014b; Ferrara & Hodge 2018; Hodge & Cormier 2019) would be outside the regular 'lexicon' in the sense that lexical sign forms, themselves initially formed on the basis of action depiction, revert back to a productive and modifiable iconic depiction in a sort of 'de-lexicalization' (Cormier et al. 2012, but see also Lepic & Occhino 2018 and Lepic 2019 for an alternative view). Bergman & Dahl (1994) argued that certain depicting constructions may better be described as a type of ideophones, with a visual sensory depiction. Analogously, Mesch and colleagues (2015) describe signing of sensory depictions with touch among signers using tactile signing—i.e. the tactile form of signing used primarily by deafblind signers. Although most linguists would probably agree on depicting constructions being closest to verb-like structures, there is clearly overlap with other word classes in the—often simultaneously layered—expression of property (adjective-like), manner (adverb-like), and 'sensory imagery' (ideophone-like; Dingemanse 2012: 655).

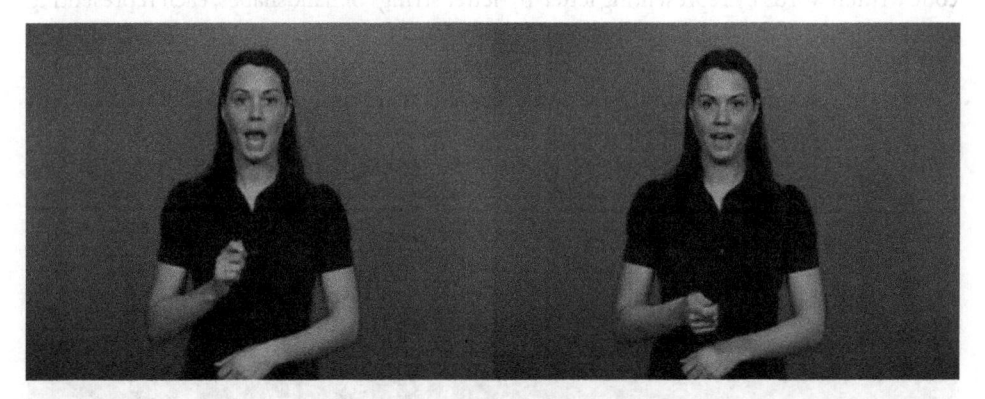

FIGURE 37.3 The sign HAMMER in Swedish Sign Language (Swedish Sign Language Dictionary online 2020: #03829)

Another category of simultaneous construction is the so-called *buoys* used across many sign languages. These are mainly discourse-regulating signs often articulated on the non-dominant hand simultaneously with the 'main' signing on the dominant hand. These signs are used for tracking individual referents or discourse topics, item-listing (Figure 37.4), or anchoring reference points in time and space (Liddell et al. 2007; Gabarró-López 2019). To the best of our knowledge, no one has attempted to classify buoys as falling into any traditionally defined word class, nor are they regularly listed in dictionaries. Nonetheless, they are similar in form to (demonstrative) pointing signs (topic- or referent-tracking) or numerals (item-listing), and may occur frequently in discourse.

FIGURE 37.4 A list buoy in Swedish Sign Language: three items listed on left hand; right hand points to each in turn before signing a comment about the associated listed referent (Swedish Sign Language Dictionary online 2020: #00074, phrase 2)

37.2.3 Language contact and borrowing

In many national sign languages, there is a manual alphabet in use. Manual alphabets encode written words by representing letter-by-letter strings of handshapes, each representing a written letter of the alphabet.[1] Although, in theory, any written word can be fingerspelled and thus borrowed into a sign language, one study on American Sign Language (ASL) showed that 70% of fingerspelled signs in discourse are nouns (evenly distributed between common and proper), followed by adjectives (10%) and verbs (6%) (Padden & Gunsauls 2003). Fingerspellings can also be part of word-formation processes, such as part of a compound together with a non-fingerspelled item (Padden & Gunsauls 2003), or by adding a borrowed derivational morpheme to a lexical sign, such as the H-E-T for Swedish—*het* ('-ity'), which can be added to verbs and adjectives to form nouns in Swedish Sign Language (see Figure 37.5).

FIGURE 37.5 The sign ACCESSIBLE^H-E-T ('accessible'+'-ity' = 'accessibility') in Swedish Sign Language (Swedish Sign Language Dictionary online 2020: #08617)

---

[1] Such manual alphabets may encode different writing systems, such as Latin script in most European-derived sign languages, Cyrillic for, e.g., Russian Sign Language, and kana-based characters for Japanese Sign Language.

Besides borrowing from a spoken language (in a written form), sign languages also borrow signs from other sign languages, for instance as a contact phenomenon between neighbouring languages (Quinto-Pozos 2008). Borrowing also happens through globalization and contact with geographically distant sign languages, for example often replacing exonymic toponyms with borrowed endonymic ones from the referenced region. However, the borrowing may lead to changes in meaning or function, such that it also affects the word class. One example is the sign WHAT'S.UP in ASL which is used as a question phrase 'what's up?', but has been borrowed into Swedish Sign Language with the meaning 'WhatsApp' (the messaging app) on the basis of mapping onto the (written/spoken/mouthed) *name* rather than the original *function* of the sign (Figure 37.6).[2]

FIGURE 37.6 The sign WHATSAPP in Swedish Sign Language, borrowed from the ASL phrase 'what's up?' (Swedish Sign Language Dictionary online 2020: #04672)

37.2.4 Interim summary

As shown in the sections above, sign languages contain several types of signs and expressions not easily categorized into traditional word classes, many of which are rarely even discussed in relation to word classes at all. In some cases, modality is part of the difficulty in categorizing signs—e.g. with buoys and other (partly) simultaneously articulated elements. In other cases, language contact situations—both signed-to-signed and spoken-to-signed languages— give rise to borrowings in which the source is altered in a way that changes the word-class assignment (e.g. WHATSAPP, Figure 37.6), or fingerspelling as a strategy for borrowing not only the form but also derivational patterns from another language (e.g. derivational suffixation, Figure 37.5). Although there are many types of signs across signed languages that have not yet been investigated with regard to word classes, others, such as nouns and verbs, have in fact been discussed extensively across relatively many languages: the categories and criteria established for word classes across sign languages are discussed in section 37.3.

---

[2] The use of WHAT'S.UP for the messaging app seems to be found among some signers of ASL too, albeit not very widespread (Lynn Hou, p.c.).

37.3 CATEGORIES AND CRITERIA

37.3.1 Categories

For most sign languages, a basic distinction between nouns and verbs (at least for a part of the lexicon, see section 37.3.3) has been proposed. Such claims have been made for ASL (Supalla & Newport 1978; Brentari et al. 2013; Abner 2017), Auslan (Australian Sign Language) (Johnston 2001), Austrian Sign Language (Hunger 2006), Catalan Sign Language (Ribera-Llonc et al. 2019), Israeli Sign Language (Tkachman & Sandler 2013), Russian Sign Language (Kimmelman 2009), Turkish Sign Language (Kubus 2008), and many others. A recent comparative handbook of sign languages of the world (Bakken Jepsen et al. 2015) contains short chapters on 33 sign languages, and although the issue of the distinction between nouns and verbs is not addressed explicitly in every chapter, the existence of these two word classes is acknowledged, at least in passing, for Argentine Sign Language, Austrian Sign Language, Danish Sign Language, Finnish Sign Language, Greek Sign Language, Malaysian Sign Language, and Spanish Sign Language. For French Sign Language and Norwegian Sign Language, it is claimed that this distinction does not apply (but note that these chapters do not offer detailed discussions of this issue). In other chapters, even when the difference between nouns and verbs is not mentioned, it is often implied by the inclusion of separate sections on nominal and/or verbal morphology (e.g. for Libras (Brazilian Sign Language), Chinese Sign Language, Hausa Sign Language, and others).

Adjectives is another word class that is often mentioned in sign language literature (see Loos 2014 for an overview). However, researchers quite often question whether adjectives form a separate word class, or whether they should instead be analysed as instances of nominal and verbal signs (e.g. Takkinen et al. 2015 for Finnish Sign Language).

Adverbs are even less studied than adjectives, and sometimes occur as part of more expressive depicting constructions as discussed above, and sometimes exclusively as non-manual features (e.g. Liddell 2003; Dudis 2004). Nevertheless, the label is still often used, even without a detailed motivation for the existence of this class.

Pronouns (which in sign languages are usually indexical/pointing signs) are usually discussed as a separate word class in most sign languages (e.g. in most chapters in Bakken Jepsen et al. 2015), as well as in the corpus-based studies discussed below. However, as discussed in section 37.2.2, they are not always considered to be fully lexical signs. This non-lexicalized or gestural view of pointing signs has often been motivated in terms of listability: the potentially infinite number of variations in context-dependent pointing would render these signs impossible to list in a 'lexicon', which would mean that they cannot be a part of a fixed, pronominal paradigm as assumed in the structuralist tradition. However, there are pointing signs with other pronominal-like functions across sign languages, such as possessive markers, which may use a different handshape than index points but are directed towards the location of the associated referent in the same manner (see Figures 37.7 and 37.8).

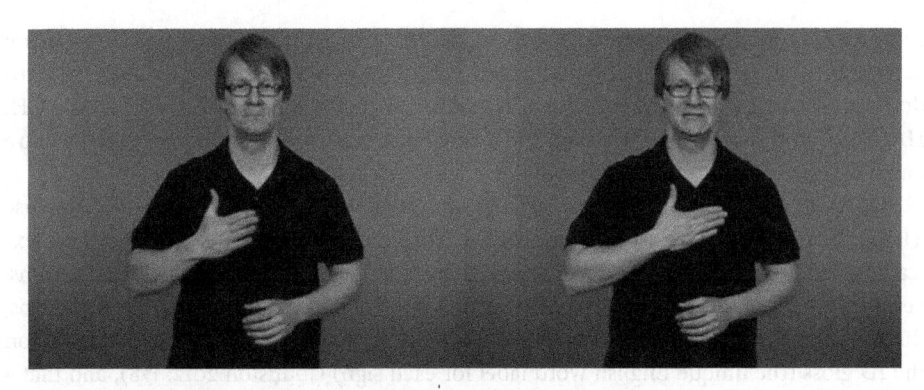

FIGURE 37.7 The sign POSS₁ ('my') in Swedish Sign Language (Swedish Sign Language Dictionary online 2020: #00187)

FIGURE 37.8 The sign POSS₂ ('your') in Swedish Sign Language (Swedish Sign Language Dictionary online 2020: #00275)

In some sign languages, mainly across the Nordic countries but also in the unrelated Israeli Sign Language, there are dedicated object pronouns in use. These appear to be cases of differential object marking and also exhibit some common features of a pronominal paradigm, such as making formal distinctions in both person and number. For example, in Swedish Sign Language, the object pronoun can be used with 2nd person plural but never 3rd person plural, which goes against this language only making a first vs non-first person distinction (Börstell 2019).

Another interesting category of signs across sign languages is proper nouns. Proper nouns can often be fingerspelled or initialized (using the first letter of the name as the handshape—see Padden & Gunsauls 2003), but may also be given a regular sign, most often referred to as a *name sign* (or *sign name*). Name sign conventions differ in form and motivation across sign languages (see Lutzenberger 2018 for an overview). Whereas some sign languages prefer arbitrary signs with initialization (common naming convention in the ASL community—see Supalla 1990), others prefer motivated signs based on property- or action-descriptive signs for individuals (common in the Swedish Sign Language community—see Börstell 2017). In Swedish Sign Language—and other sign languages—such descriptive signs can be chosen from various other word classes, such as adjectives (e.g. HAPPY), verbs denoting general actions (e.g. HORSE.RIDING, for a person who likes going horseback riding), or verbs depicting an action that the individual is known to perform habitually (e.g. SCRATCH. HAIR). Thus, signs that are motivated and formed into one word class can be transferred to a name sign (i.e. noun) function through this naming process.

Studies focused on creating and analysing sign language corpora and databases often use a larger number of word classes for annotation. For instance, in a corpus-based study of lexical frequency in Auslan, Johnston (2012) uses the following classes for 'lexical signs': nouns, verbs, adjectives, adverbs, auxiliaries, prepositions, wh-signs, conjunctions, interjections, discourse markers. At the same time, he notes that the classes are mostly defined based on the ID gloss (the unique English word label for each sign) (Johnston 2012: 178), and that a real analysis of word classes in Auslan would require further corpus-based research.

37.3.2 Semantics

In the literature on sign languages, it is commonly accepted that many of the same semantic categories and features are relevant across modalities. Therefore, major word classes are often defined using terms familiar from spoken language descriptions. Typically, nouns are associated with objects/entities, verbs with actions/events, and adjectives with properties.

One of the most detailed descriptions of the semantic basis of word classes in sign languages is provided in Schwager & Zeshan (2008), and applied to German Sign Language (DGS) and Kata Kolok. The authors argue that word classes should be defined in terms of semantic features, and assume these features to be universal. They define three major semantic classes (entity, event, and property), and further subdivide them into a large number of small categories defined by binary features (e.g. [±proper], [±concrete], [±count] for nouns; [±dynamic], [±agentive], [±telic] for verbs). They demonstrate that, for the semantic categories defined this way, they can find signs in both DGS and Kata Kolok. However, they do not discuss in any detail how they ascertained that the signs indeed have the ascribed semantic features.

In other studies, the common associations between word class and semantics is often assumed without detailed investigation.[3] In the majority of experimental studies, which we discuss below, the semantic basis for word classes is presupposed in the experimental design: stimuli depicting objects are expected to elicit nouns, and stimuli depicting actions/events are expected to elicit verbs.

---

[3] While the reliance on semantics is acceptable for purposes of cross-linguistic comparison (Haspelmath 2010), it is clearly not adequate for descriptions of word classes in specific languages, where word classes should be defined morphosyntactically.

37.3.3 Formal criteria of word classes

37.3.3.1 *Phonology of related noun–verb pairs*

Many sign languages investigated to date show a curiously similar pattern: there are some semantically related noun–verb pairs for which the nominal and the verbal signs are similar in form, but different in some phonological component (typically movement). This pattern, first described for ASL by Supalla & Newport (1978), is not only attested in the majority of sign languages for which this issue has been investigated, but also in so-called homesign systems (Abner et al. 2019).[4]

Consider the following example from Kimmelman (2009: 172–173). In Russian Sign Language (RSL), the signs LIGHTER and LIGHT.LIGHTER are very similar in form (Figure 37.9); however, they differ in a number of features. The nominal sign contains repeated movement (vs single movement in the verbal sign), the amplitude of the movement is smaller (more restrained) in the noun, and the more distal joints (e.g. finger joints instead of the elbow) are used in the nominal sign. Other RSL noun–verb pairs that show the same pattern include COMB ~ TO.COMB, HAMMER ~ TO.HAMMER, and BOOK ~ OPEN.BOOK. In addition, the nominal signs in RSL are more frequently accompanied by a mouthing (the silent miming of [part of] a spoken word on the mouth) than verbal signs, which often are accompanied by mouth gestures (mouth movements not related to spoken words). Other formal differences between related nouns and verbs in other sign languages include absence vs presence of movement, and the use of the non-dominant hand in verbs as reported for ASL, Nicaraguan Sign Language, and homesign by Abner et al. (2019). For some languages, including ASL and Italian Sign Language (LIS), it has been shown that there is a systematic handshape difference between related nouns and verbs, the nouns preferring the so-called object handshapes (related to the shape of the physical object/entity) and the verbs preferring the handling handshapes (related to the shape of the hand manipulating an object/entity) (Brentari et al. 2015; Goldin-Meadow et al. 2015; Padden et al. 2015).

The pattern of formally related noun–verb pairs has been described for ASL (Supalla & Newport 1978), Auslan (Johnston 2001), Turkish Sign Language (Kubus 2008), LIS (Pizzuto & Corazza 1996), Austrian Sign Language (Hunger 2006), Israeli Sign Language, (Tkachman & Sandler 2013), Nicaraguan Sign Language (Abner et al. 2019), and homesign (Hunsicker & Goldin-Meadow 2013, Abner et al. 2019). In the comparative handbook (Bakken Jepsen et al. 2015), this phenomenon is also mentioned for Danish Sign Language, Greek Sign Language, and Malaysian Sign Language. Note that the formal differences between nouns and verbs are not the same across different languages (see Abner et al. 2019: 232–233 for a comparison), and also within one language there is variation for different noun–verb pairs in terms of which of the features specifically distinguish between nouns and verbs (see, e.g. Johnston 2001; Kimmelman 2009).

---

[4] Isolated signed communication (e.g. within a single family) without an existing language model is sometimes referred to as 'homesign'—see Kusters & Hou (2020) for a critical discussion on labels for different ecologies of signing.

FIGURE 37.9 LIGHTER (2 frames) vs LIGHT.LIGHTER (2 frames) in RSL (from Kimmelman 2009: 172–173)

Two points are worth mentioning concerning these noun–verb pairs. First, no study has shown that all or even a majority of verbs in any sign language form such pairs. Most studies are focused only on nouns referring to concrete objects ('hammer', 'comb', 'door', etc.) and verbs describing activities involving these objects as instruments or themes ('to hammer', 'to comb', 'to open a door'). However, all studies also report that, for some concepts, the same sign can be used nominally or verbally without modification, and that for others verbal and nominal signs are unrelated. An exception is Abner (2017) who demonstrates that the systematic formal relation between nouns and verbs in ASL also applies to abstract verbs (e.g. ACCEPT, JOIN, SUPPORT), but no comparable findings are reported for any other sign language. Even for ASL, there is no large-scale lexical study showing what percentage of noun–verb pairs are indeed related but distinct in form.

Second, it is striking that formally similar and semantically related noun–verb pairs are found across a majority of sign languages for which this specific issue has been investigated, but even more striking that such pairs are also found in the first generation of an emerging sign language (Nicaraguan Sign Language), as well as in homesign—that is, in the absence of an accessible fully fledged language or even a language community (Hunsicker & Goldin-Meadow 2013; Abner et al. 2019). This has led various researchers to argue that the entity–event distinction is universal and cognitively important, which means that distinguishing the two semantic categories by grammatical means is indispensable in communication, and, in addition, that there is an iconic basis for such a distinction in sign languages. For instance, Kimmelman (2009) argues that verbs in such pairs are iconic depictions of the events, while nouns are less iconic (being reduced in size and details of articulation due to economic considerations). Abner et al. (2019) argue that the use of repetition for nouns (in comparison to verbs) is iconically linked to iterability of the event associated with the object. Recent experiments with non-signers categorizing gestures with handshape and/or movement distinctions as referring to either objects or actions have shown that the handshape distinction (instrument-depiction = noun; handling-depiction = verb) is stronger than movement distinctions (Lepic & Verhoef 2020; Emmorey & Pyers 2020). Although there may be language-specific preferences for encoding objects (nouns) and actions (verbs) systematically with, e.g. handshape distinctions, some patterns seem to extend also to the gestures of non-signers.[5] However, research on more sign languages and homesign systems is required to support this conjecture.

37.3.3.2 *Morphological modifications*

As discussed above, major word classes in sign languages have some morphological and syntactic properties that have been used to formally distinguish them from each other. In this and the following sections we discuss the main properties that have been associated with verbs, nouns, and adjectives in different sign languages.

However, two notes of caution are in order. First, as in the case in spoken languages, morphology and syntax vary between sign languages, so it is very likely that there is no single morphological or syntactic feature that would in all sign languages distinguish, e.g. nouns from verbs. For instance, Schwager & Zeshan (2008: 538) demonstrate that DGS and RSL have a large number of verbal morphological categories, but that Kata Kolok lacks most of these. Second, at least for morphological categories, they very often target only subclasses of the major word classes in sign languages. For instance, subject–object agreement (see below) is clearly a verbal category, but only a subclass of verbs (namely, agreeing verbs) shows such

---

[5] Recent work has also shown that handshape choices for action signs are driven by agent-(de)focusing (Rissman et al. 2020)—thus, this type of distinction may be more gradient as it is variable even within a proposed semantic category (i.e. actions).

agreement. In sign languages, as in spoken languages, the intensive modification (morphological or syntactic) of adjectives only applies to gradable adjectives (Loos 2014).

The most frequent verbal categories in sign languages are verbal agreement (Lillo-Martin & Meier 2011, but see also Schembri et al. 2018) and verbal aspect. Some verbs in most sign languages (but not all: Schwager & Zeshan 2008) can be modified in movement and/or orientation to indicate the subject and object referents. Referents can be associated with locations in the signing space, so the movement and/or orientation in agreeing verbs can use these locations to assign the subject/object syntactic functions to the referent. This is illustrated for the RSL verb HELP in Figure 37.10 for the 1st and 2nd person referents, but the same mechanism also applies to 3rd person referents.

FIGURE 37.10 The RSL signs $_1$HELP$_2$ 'I help you' and $_2$HELP$_1$ 'You help me'

This type of movement and/or orientation modification involving two locations is not found in nominal signs, not even in relational nouns that would have arguments with which they could potentially agree. However, as we discussed above, sign languages also have non-agreeing verbs (which cannot be modified) and spatial verbs (which are modified to describe movement of a referent), which do not show this double location type of agreement modification either.

In many sign languages, verbs can also be modified for aspect (e.g. iterative, habitual, inceptive, etc.) by altering movement and/or location in various ways, and/or by adding the second hand (Schwager & Zeshan 2008; Wilbur 2009). The simplest case is that iterative aspect is often marked by simple reduplication. Sometimes, however, formally identical modifications may also be applied to nominal signs to express collective or distributive plurality (Pfau & Steinbach 2006, 2016; Wilbur 2009; Kuhn 2019).[6] Therefore, the purely formal criterion of whether a certain type of reduplication is applicable to a sign does not distinguish word classes; one needs to consider the interpretation of the marker, which depends on the word class.

---

[6] The same is true for distributive marking, which is typically associated with verbal signs, but can often apply to nouns and numerals as well (Kimmelman 2017).

Some other morphological modifications that are word class-specific are negative affixes and clitics, which only attach to verbal signs mentioned by Schwager & Zeshan (2008),[7] intensive modification, restricted to scalar adjectives (Padden 1988), and—in between morphology and syntax—nominal classifiers that can accompany nouns (e.g. Pizzuto & Corazza 1996 for LIS; Tkachman & Sandler 2013 for Israeli Sign Language and Al-Sayyid Bedouin Sign Language; Safar & Petatillo Chen 2020 for Yucatec Maya Sign Languages). As for the latter, nouns in some sign languages can be accompanied by a Size-and-Shape Specifier (SASS) referring to the shape of the denoted entity—see examples (1) and (2). Figure 37.11 illustrates the RSL SASSs for rectangular.

(1)   LIPSTICK SMALL.OBJECT.SASS   [Israeli Sign Language]
      'A lipstick.' (Tkachman & Sandler 2013: 270)

(2)   BOX RECTANGULAR.SASS   [RSL]
      'A rectangular box.' (RSL corpus: http://rsl.nstu.ru/data/view/id/342/t/6370/d/7500)

FIGURE 37.11 The RSL sign RECTANGULAR.SASS

Similarly to SASSes, some sign languages have noun classifiers that are compound-like structures of a sign (of a lexical word class) and a free morpheme that functions as a derivational morpheme. Perhaps the most famous derivational morpheme is what has been referred to as an 'agentive marker' in ASL (e.g. Padden 1988) and a 'noun classifier' in Swedish Sign Language (Bergman & Wallin 2001, 2003). Although the forms differ between the two languages, the origin and use of the signs are similar, since both stem from a sign meaning 'person' and being added to nominalize and agentivize some meaning. For example, ASL TEACH^AGENTIVE = 'teacher', and Swedish Sign Language

---

[7] Negative affixes can only attach to verbs in the languages discussed by Schwager & Zeshan (2008); in other languages they can also attach to adjectives (Tomaszewski 2015), so this is a language-specific criterion—see also Wilkinson (2016) for a discussion on negation collocations, frequency, and chunking in ASL.

TO.TRAIN^PERSON = 'trainer, coach' (see Figure 37.12). In Swedish Sign Language, this sign is used to nominalize signs from various word classes, including agentivizing/individuating other nouns, such as its use with name signs for countries (i.e. toponyms) as a demonym (e.g. AMERICA^PERSON = 'an American'). In addition, it may have certain discourse functions, e.g. introducing referents (Bergman & Wallin 2001, 2003), and in several sign languages—e.g. DGS and Swedish Sign Language—it can be used to pluralize nouns with reduplicated and/or sideward movement (Pfau & Steinbach 2006).

FIGURE 37.12 The sign TO.TRAIN^PERSON ('trainer, coach') in Swedish Sign Language (Swedish Sign Language Dictionary online 2020: #13035)

37.3.3.3 Syntactic properties

The major word classes in sign languages are commonly associated with the major syntactic roles: nouns are typically subjects and objects, verbs are used as heads of clauses, and adjectives are nominal modifiers (Padden 1988; Schwager & Zeshan 2008; Loos 2014). Naturally, the order of the major constituents differs across different languages (see Leeson & Saeed 2012; Napoli & Sutton-Spence 2014), so the tests have to be language-specific.

Padden (1988) was probably the first to discuss syntactic tests for word classes in ASL. She argued that nouns can be modified by quantifiers, such as FOUR, while verbs and adjectives cannot, and that verbs cannot be preposed modifiers of other signs (*RUN SHOE), while nouns and adjectives can. Schwager & Zeshan (2008) use similar criteria for word classes in DGS and Kata Kolok. Pizzuto & Corazza (1996) argue that only nouns in LIS can be modified by possessives and adjectives. Johnston & Schembri (1999) argue that adjectives in Auslan can be distinguished as a separate class because only they can be preceded by modifiers like MOST and VERY. Abner et al. (2019) in an experimental study demonstrate that verbal signs in ASL and Nicaraguan Sign Language are more likely to be clause-final than nominal signs.

An important point discussed by Schwager & Zeshan (2008), as well as many others (e.g. Johnston & Schembri 1999; Johnston 2001; Loos 2014) is that many signs in different sign language appear to be flexible and can, for instance, appear both arguments and modifiers, as illustrated in (3)–(4) for RSL. This would mean that word order alone is not enough to distinguish word classes.

(3) DEAF ENTER [RSL]
'A deaf person enters.'

(4) AT₁ EXIST DEAF FRIEND [RSL]
'I have a deaf friend.'

Interestingly, Schwager & Zeshan (2008) show that, in Kata Kolok, most signs are not flexible, and can only serve one syntactic function; for instance the sign DEAF can be used as a noun but not as an adjective (5)–(6). This may be related to the fact that, as mentioned above, Kata Kolok lacks most of the morphological categories that other languages use to distinguish between word classes.

(5) DEAF COME [Kata Kolok]
'A deaf person came.' (Schwager & Zeshan 2008: 532)

(6) * FEMALE DEAF COME [Kata Kolok]
Intended meaning: 'A deaf woman came.' (Schwager & Zeshan 2008: 532)

For Swedish Sign Language, Bergman (1983) argued that many signs that could be thought of as adjectives, based on the fact that they describe properties, would form a class in-between 'true' adjectives and verbs. Bergman labelled these signs 'stative verbs', since they express a property but can only have a predicative function, and are never used as attributive modifiers within the noun phrase—e.g. the sign PREGNANT. However, these signs differ from prototypical verbs when negated, in that they would always follow the manual negator NOT (a property of adjective) rather than precede it (as one would expect for verbal signs): e.g. INDEX NOT PREGNANT ~ *INDEX PREGNANT NOT = 'she is not pregnant'.

37.3.4 Interim summary

In this section, we have discussed how a number of word classes have been suggested in several sign languages investigated. The visual modality has an effect on some (potential) categories, such as pointing signs being similar to pointing gestures but often functioning like pronouns (see also section 37.2.2), and adverbial functions often being expressed non-manually, by facial expressions. However, the most common word classes discussed for sign languages are nouns and verbs, unsurprisingly, suggesting a cognitively salient distinction between objects and actions/events. This distinction has been observed in several formal differences, such as changes in articulation (e.g. handshape and movement). Morphosyntactically, the basic noun–verb distinction also influences which type of modification is possible (e.g. spatial and repeated), available derivational elements (e.g. agentive or specifying classifiers), as well as the word order and syntactic function of the signs. In the next section (37.4), we will give an overview of how the categorization of signs into word classes has been applied—either in terms of experimental design in order to identify them, or in terms of practically labelling them in sign language databases (e.g. dictionaries and corpora).

37.4 Methods for categorization

37.4.1 Experimental approaches

Methodologically, word classes in sign languages have been investigated using several techniques. First, traditional descriptive approaches relying on elicitation of crucial (isolated) examples and acceptability judgments have been used (e.g. Abner 2017). Second, some relatively small-scale corpus-based investigations of word classes have been conducted (Voghel 2005).

Third, and most prominently for the studies focused on the phonological differences between nouns and verbs, a quasi-experimental approach has been applied in various studies (Johnston 2001; Kimmelman 2009; Tkachman & Sandler 2013; Abner et al. 2019, among others). Most such studies focus on production of nouns and verbs, while in some studies (Johnston 2001; Kimmelman 2009), perception is also investigated.

The basic method of production studies is to use visual stimuli (pictures and/or videos) of objects to elicit nouns, and visual stimuli of events when the same objects are manipulated to elicit formally related verbs. The nominal and verbal signs involving the same object are then compared to each other in order to establish the differences between formally similar signs. Using this method has the advantage that one can study whether all noun–verb pairs show the same differences, and also whether different signers of the same language are consistent. The method also has, however, some challenges: the concepts have to be predetermined and only signs for concrete objects can be elicited; in addition, some studies have shown that in natural discourse the differences found in the experimental condition disappear or become much weaker (Johnston 2001).

Perception studies typically involve native signers assigning the labels of nouns and verbs (or objects and events) to signs elicited in a production study, a methodology used in similar gesture experiments with hearing non-signers (e.g. Emmorey & Pyers 2020; Lepic & Verhoef 2020). In Kimmelman's (2009) study, for instance, the number of repetitions and the amplitude were useful for identifying both verbs and nouns, but the involvement of joints (e.g. the use of fingers vs the use of the elbow) was only useful for identifying nouns.

One of the most recent and the most advanced in terms of experimental design is the study reported in Abner et al. (2019). The authors used short video clips of objects manipulated in a typical way to elicit verbs (e.g. a man taking a picture with a camera) and in an atypical way to elicit nouns (e.g. a man dropping a camera into a trash can). They asked ASL signers, homesigners from Nicaragua, and signers from three different cohorts of Nicaraguan Sign Language to describe these clips. They statistically analysed the data and found that word order, the use of different joints, movement repetition, and the use of the non-dominant hand are all used to distinguish nouns from verbs in at least some of the groups. This study can be used as a template for future experimental studies of noun–verb distinction in sign languages.

37.4.2 Lexicography

Although sign language dictionaries have been around for a long time, longer than the field of sign language linguistics, many of them have assumed a close tie between a majority spoken/written language—and its word classes—and the sign language in question. Such assumptions may lead to inferring the categories and definitions of word classes of the spoken language. However, as more linguistically informed, sometimes corpus-based, lexical databases and dictionaries have been established, many questions have arisen as to how signs should be defined, categorized, and linked together. One main question in this domain is how to define sign lexemes and lemmas for use in lexicography and corpus work (Johnston & Schembri 1999; Johnston 2010, 2014b; Schembri & Crasborn 2010). Different lexicography projects have taken different routes in this matter, some opting for overarching, lemmatized forms being recorded (e.g. several of the Signbank projects: Fenlon et al. 2014; Johnston 2014a, 2014b; Crasborn et al. 2020), whereas others would separate slight form variations and derived/related signs into distinct sign entries (e.g. the Swedish Sign Language Dictionary online 2020). In many sign languages, the mouthing of a spoken language word may be used to distinguish manually identical forms, or specify related concepts or synonyms. This can be found in signs that are clearly based on a shared semantic motivation. An example of this is the Swedish Sign Language sign FLOOR in Figure 37.13, for which the manual part can similarly mean 'table', 'carpet', 'shelf', 'stage' if accompanied with the mouthing of the equivalent spoken word in Swedish, although all stemming from a depiction of a flat extended surface. In such cases, it is unclear which of these forms could be seen as a lemma form for all related meanings. Because of this, several Signbank projects have opted to conflate similar examples into a single sign entry, without mouthing specified, with a listing of possible translation equivalents in the spoken (written) language.

FIGURE 37.13 The sign FLOOR in Swedish Sign Language (Swedish Sign Language Dictionary online 2020: #12253)

However, there are cases for which it is unclear whether manually identical sign forms constitute polysemous or otherwise related forms with a similar derivation, or are accidental homonyms. One such example is found in Figure 37.14 illustrating the Swedish Sign Language sign DO, which can also (with appropriate mouthing) be used to mean 'verb', clearly related to 'doing, action' although used as a noun rather than verb, but also the question word 'why', in which case it is not obvious whether or not there is an association between the sign forms.

FIGURE 37.14 The sign DO in Swedish Sign Language (Swedish Sign Language Dictionary online 2020: #00563)

Thus, a constant conundrum for sign language lexicographers is whether to regard each *function* of manual sign forms as individual signs, or rather lump them together under a more abstract lemma, assuming that context will disambiguate. With the former approach, phonological detail (e.g. mouthing) and word-class status (e.g. noun or verb) would call for splitting into different entries, whereas the latter approach would favour an abstract conflation, later taking context into account for function or specified meaning and categorization of individual tokens.

37.4.3 Computational approaches

With the relatively recent emergence of true, machine-readable, large-scale sign language corpora, the question of what can be done automatically or semi-automatically with the help of big data has become relevant. Within the domain of natural language processing (NLP), automatic part of speech (word class) tagging is a large field with plenty of highly accurate taggers being applied to spoken/written languages. However, for sign languages this is not yet the case. An exception is Östling et al. (2015) who attempted to use an automatic word-class tagging of the Swedish translations of the Swedish Sign Language Corpus, later inferred and transferred to the Swedish Sign Language glosses by word alignment between words and sign glosses. This method proved to reach 77% accuracy in the automatic tagging compared to gold standard manual annotations of the same data, which shows that there is considerable overlap in word classes in Swedish and Swedish Sign Language that can be inferred from glosses (certainly aided by the fact that the Swedish Sign Language Corpus does not primarily lemmatize their gloss categories), but also that language-specific definitions and modelling are required. Furthermore, the manual annotation in Östling et al. (2015) was done on the type-level, which results in some sign glosses used for polysemous/homophonous signs potentially not being accurately tagged for each individual token (as context is ignored).

With sign language corpora growing ever larger, the prospects of building (semi-)automatic taggers—for word classes and other properties—increase. Through the advent of automatic recognition of sign forms—through tools like motion capture, 3D cameras, or post-production video recognition software—there is also a potential to recognize phonological cues such as repeated or larger movements, which could be useful for automatically recognizing such features argued to be associated with word classes (e.g. noun–verb distinction) in several sign languages.

37.4.4 Interim summary

In experimental approaches to identifying and establishing word classes for sign languages, the design has frequently been to use stimuli to elicit production based on the semantics of a viewed picture/event, later analysed for any observable formal differences in those elicited signs. In some cases, a reverse method has been used to investigate the perceptive side of word-class categorization. When developing lexical databases (e.g. dictionaries) and corpora of sign languages, word-class categorization is sometimes included in the process. Here, the categorization can be done partly based on form and meaning, such as taking distinguishing mouthings of manually identical forms into account (or not), and partly on function in context, such as the distribution and position in a corpus. As sign language corpora are still relatively small in size, few attempts have been made to categorize/induce word classes through automated methods.

37.5 SUMMARY

As mentioned at the beginning of this chapter, sign languages constitute a diverse set of languages defined by a shared modality. As such, it is ill-advised to assume cross-linguistic similarities in terms of categories or structure across different signed languages. Some of the methods applied in order to identify and describe word classes have been shared across sign languages, but the results differ between languages. Across many sign languages, a general distinction between nouns and verbs has been suggested—sometimes on the basis of semantics alone, but often based on formal differences in both basic and modified forms of signs. Other word classes (e.g. adjectives and pronouns) have been suggested for some sign languages, but not nearly to the extent of nouns and verbs. Furthermore, several additional types of categories deserve dedicated investigations, as the modality uniting sign(ed) languages may in fact give rise to forms and functions possibly unattested for any spoken language. This includes simultaneous articulation of a second hand (e.g. buoys) or non-manuals (e.g. facial adverbials), spatially dependent signs (e.g. pointing), and the re-encoding of borrowed material (e.g. fingerspelling and mouthings).

Much of the work that has been done on the structure of sign languages to date—be it word classes or any other linguistic phenomenon—is based on elicited data. Because of this, it is hard to judge whether findings and suggested features will be observable and relevant when looking at more natural, spontaneous, and contextualized language. However, as naturalistic data of sign languages are becoming increasingly more available—and in ever larger size—investigating word classes and their potential formal differences can eventually be done based on language use. In such cases, it has been suggested that proposed formal differences observed in more isolated contexts are much reduced and gradient. Furthermore, the development of large-scale lexical databases and corpora requires extensive decision processes in terms of labelling and categorizing the data, but will hopefully also result in a more data-driven approach to categories and patterns of language in use.

PART V

WORD CLASSES IN LINGUISTIC SUBDISCIPLINES

CHAPTER 38

WORD CLASSES IN CORPUS LINGUISTICS

NATALIA LEVSHINA

38.1 INTRODUCTION

IT is necessary to begin with a terminological note. The term 'word classes' is not widely used in corpus linguistics. Nouns, verbs, adjectives, and other categories are usually referred to as parts of speech (POS). The goal of POS annotation in corpus linguistics is to classify tokens (or wordforms) in context. The term parts of speech reflects this goal better than the term word classes because corpora represent *speech* as *parole*, where each unit plays a specific role determined by its context. For example, the word *play*, which can be regarded as a member of the NV word class, similar to words *love*, *walk*, or *change* (Hockett 1958: 225–227), is either a noun or a verb in a particular sentence (but see section 38.4 on how POS tags and syntactic dependencies can be used for studying the flexibility of word classes). Since most of the existing corpora represent written language rather than speech in the narrow sense, it might be even more precise to call POS 'parts of utterance', or POU.[1]

The other component of the term 'parts of speech', namely, the word 'parts', implies that we apply the tags to some speech segments. In most cases, these segments are tokens, or sequences of characters between spaces. They can be wordforms, symbols, digits, or punctuation marks. POS tags are usually assigned to these units. However, one can also assign POS tags below and above the level of tokens. For example, one can annotate a multiword expression *high school teacher* with one POS tag (noun). Alternatively, one can annotate the German orthographic word *im* as a combination of the preposition *in* and definite article *dem*. One could also use POS tags to annotate lemmas in a sentence-word in a polysynthetic language (e.g. Arkhangelskiy & Lander 2016). This is another reason why the term part of speech is better suited for corpus investigations than word classes.

The next section provides an overview of current practices in POS tagging and bottom-up induction of POS. There are many difficult decisions to make when choosing a POS tagset: the level of granularity, redundancy given the other layers of annotation, and so on.

---

[1] I thank Michael Cysouw for this idea.

These criteria are discussed in section 38.3. It also demonstrates how corpora can be used to model flexibility of word classes with the help of POS tags and syntactic dependencies. Section 38.4 provides the conclusions and an outlook.

38.2 CURRENT PRACTICES IN POS TAGGING

38.2.1 An overview of popular POS tagsets

This section describes several popular POS tagsets used by corpus linguists. The first tagsets were created for English, because English was the first language of contemporary corpus linguistics (Atwell 2008). The first POS-tagged corpora include the Brown corpus, the Lancaster–Oslo–Bergen (LOB) corpus, the Spoken English Corpus, the Polytechnic of Wales corpus (PoW), the University of Pennsylvania corpus (UPenn), the International Corpus of English (ICE) and the British National Corpus (BNC). The tagsets used in these corpora are not limited to traditional word classes. Since the applications of corpora were not known in advance, it was tempting to add as much linguistic information as possible (Atwell 2008). A good example of such a detailed tagset is CLAWS7[2] used in well-known English corpora developed at Brigham Young University:[3] the Corpus of Contemporary American English (COCA), COHA, iWeb and some others. It includes 137 tags, plus additional tags for elements of multiword expressions (e.g. *as soon as, in terms of*). They combine several types of information: morphological categories (e.g. separate tags for singular and plural nouns, third person present tense verbs), individual lexemes (e.g. particle *to*, preposition *of*, existential *there*), and fine-grained subclasses of traditional parts of speech (e.g. auxiliary verbs, comparative adjectives, and degree adverbs). CLAWS7 also includes lexicogrammatical classes based on distributional and semantic properties. For example, nouns have special tags if they represent measure units (*inch, feet*), location (*Street*), time (*day, year*) or direction (*north*). These nouns occur in various idiosyncratic constructions (such as adverbial uses with zero case marking, as in *go west, last year*). Also, separate labels are used for letters of the alphabet, foreign words, and formulas.

An example from COCA (Davies 2008–) is shown in (1). The first column represents the wordform. The second is the lemma, and the third one is the detailed POS tag. In the CLAWS7 tagset, *mc1* stands for a singular cardinal number, *nnt1* for a singular temporal noun, *y* for a punctuation mark, *pphs1* for the 3rd person singular subjective personal pronoun, *vvd* is the past tense form of a lexical verb, *appge* is the possessive prenominal pronoun, and *nn1* is a singular common noun.

(1)   One   one   mc1
       night   night   nnt1
       ,   ,   y
       he   he   pphs1
       attacked   attack   vvd

---

[2] http://ucrel.lancs.ac.uk/claws7tags.html
[3] https://www.english-corpora.org/

his	his	appge
wife	wife	nn1
.	.	y

After English, POS tagging has been performed for corpora in other languages, such as STTS (Stuttgart–Tübingen Tagset) for German with 54 tags[4] or the Estonian Treebank POS tagset with an impressive number of 579 tags.[5] There have been attempts to standardize corpus annotation in different languages. One should mention here an important initiative called EAGLES (Expert Advisory Group on Language Engineering Standards) supported by the European Union with the aim of developing comparable and interchangeable technologies for the multilingual European community. The experts' recommendation was to use an obligatory set of classes including noun, verb, adjective, pronoun/determiner, article, adverb, adposition, conjunction, numeral, interjection, unique/unassigned (for small and very specific categories, such as negative particles), residual (e.g. foreign words or mathematical formulae) and punctuation (Leech & Wilson 1999).

These categories are similar to tagsets used for multilingual corpora nowadays. For example, the Universal POS tags used in the Universal Dependencies corpora (Zeman et al. 2020), include six tags for open-class words: ADJ (adjective), ADV (adverb), INTJ (interjection), NOUN (common noun), PROPN (proper noun) and VERB (lexical verb). There are also eight tags for closed-class words: ADP (adpositions), AUX (auxiliaries and copulas), CCONJ (coordinate conjunctions), DET (determiners), NUM (numerals), PART (particles), PRON (pronouns) and SCONJ (subordinate conjunctions). Three remaining tags include PUNCT (punctuation), SYM (symbol) and X (other, including foreign words, URLs, etc.).[6] Morphological information is language-specific and provided in a separate layer.

Similarly, the Google tagset for cross-linguistic data includes 12 tags (Petrov et al. 2012): nouns, verbs, adjectives, adverbs, pronouns, determiners (including articles), adpositions, numerals, conjunctions, particles, punctuation marks and the category 'X', which is a catch-all for other categories such as abbreviations or foreign words. This tagset has been used for annotation of the Google Books Ngram Corpus in several major languages.[7]

Interestingly, these tagsets, which have been developed for NLP applications in diverse languages, are closer to the traditional parts of speech derived from traditional Latin grammatical categories (noun, verb, adjective, preposition, pronoun, adverb, conjunction, and interjection) than the first tagsets in corpus linguistics.

38.2.2 Methods of top-down automatic tagging and evaluation

One can annotate data by hand, but for large corpora this is not feasible. There exist diverse algorithms that provide POS tags automatically.

---

[4] https://www.ims.uni-stuttgart.de/forschung/ressourcen/lexika/germantagsets/#id-cfcbf0a7-0
[5] https://www.cl.ut.ee/korpused/morfliides/seletus/
[6] See https://universaldependencies.org/u/pos/index.html.
[7] https://books.google.com/ngrams

The main problem of POS tagging is disambiguation, or determining the POS of homographs like *play* (verb or noun) in the context. In the beginning of POS tagging in the 1950s and 1960s, one had to manually create rules for this purpose. For example, a token could not be a verb if it was immediately preceded by an article. According to Voutilainen (1999: 11), the first system was created at the University of Pennsylvania in the late 1950s. The tagging part contained a small disambiguator with 14 ordered context rules.

Nowadays, it is more common to use data-driven approaches, where one usually takes a manually annotated training corpus and creates a language model, which takes into account diverse statistical associations in the corpus. The tagger then uses this statistical model to select the tags with the highest probability in a given context. Already early implementations reached spectacular accuracy. For example, the first CLAWS parser (Constituent-Likelihood Automatic Word Tagging System, version 1) developed for the LOB corpus back in the 1980s had accuracy above 95% (Voutilainen 1999). Of course, the procedure is rarely fully automatic. One relies on lexicons, idioms lists, special rules, and other resources. Often, human annotators check manually the tokens that remain ambiguous.

Different surface cues can be useful for this purpose: n-grams (sequences of n words) preceding and following the target word (e.g. Brown et al. 1992); orthographic criteria, such as capital letters, digits, internal hyphens, apostrophes (e.g. Yatbaz et al. 2012); and morphological information (e.g. Clark 2003), where the algorithm tries to find suffixes or prefixes in words and combine the words that share common morphology. More sophisticated approaches like neural networks and hidden Markov models are able to take into account long-distance patterns. A combination of different criteria usually helps to improve the performance (Christodoulopoulos et al. 2010; Yatbaz et al. 2012). There are also successful approaches that are based on cluster prototypes (e.g. Haghighi & Klein 2006).

The performance of a tagger is usually evaluated on a test corpus with the help of several popular measures: correctness, ambiguity, precision and recall (van Halteren 1999). Correctness is simply the proportion of correct tags appropriate in the context relative to all tokens. Ambiguity is the average number of tags per token (see more in section 38.3.4). Precision shows how many tokens with a given tag (e.g. 'NOUN') are tagged correctly. Finally, recall is used to measure how many tokens that should have a certain tag are indeed tagged so. High performance numbers, however, do not necessarily mean that the tagging is useful because the usefulness also depends on the quality and quantity of information conveyed by the tags. One should also be aware that the tagger's performance may differ from one text type to another.

Many current taggers have performance with accuracy above 97% per token, which is at least as good as human interrater agreement (Manning 2011). This means that above 97% tokens are analysed correctly. However, if one computes the number of correctly analysed sentences, the same taggers have sentence accuracies around 55%–57%, a rather modest score, which has to do with the fact that some units are extremely frequent and ambiguous, e.g. *that*, which can function as a pronoun, determiner, complementizer, or even adverb, as in *She is not that crazy* (Manning 2011). In some cases, there may not be good conventions in linguistic descriptions. For example, the word *worth* has properties of both an adjective and a preposition governing a nominal phrase, as in *It's not worth the effort*. See section 38.3.4 on fuzzy boundaries between POS. Here, the prospects of POS tagging depend very much on improved descriptive linguistics (Manning 2011).

38.2.3 Bottom-up induction of POS

The approaches discussed above presuppose some 'gold standard', which is used to evaluate the accuracy of the labels. A different approach is induction of POS categories from the data in a bottom-up way. One such attempt is Wälchli (2008), who uses unlemmatized translations of the New Testament to perform unsupervised clustering based on Biemann's (2006) graph-theoretic method of Chinese whispers. Wälchli reports interesting crosslinguistic differences. Some languages yield few distributional classes, which emerge as a result of clustering (e.g. French has only 14 clusters), while others have hundreds (e.g. Finnish with 108 clusters). Some languages yield more formal classes, like French (e.g. finite verbs 3SG, auxiliaries, feminine nouns singular), whereas Vietnamese has 100 clusters with many semantic groups, such as body parts, animals and, surprisingly, even words related to doors and walls. It is pointed out that the distributional analysis based on the neighbouring words alone does not suffice for languages with rich morphology. For example, in synthetic languages some clusters represent case forms of nouns and pronouns or personal forms of verbs (e.g. Finnish, Hungarian, Latin, and Turkish). In particular, the accusative singular form *manum* 'hand' in Latin ends up in one cluster, and the ablative singular form *manu* in another. One needs some morphological information in order to improve the clustering.

The bottom-up approach to POS induction has been particularly important for theory of child language acquisition. More exactly, researchers usually use the term 'syntactic categories'. A fundamental question is how children perform induction of adult-like categories from the ambient language. Child language acquisition research was influenced strongly by Chomsky's (1972) idea known as the 'poverty of stimulus' argument: the data that children are exposed to is insufficient for learning grammar only from ambient language, therefore a large part of a child's grammar is innate.

However, there have been quite a few corpus-based studies showing that syntactic categories can be inferred from linguistic input data (see Diessel 2009). For example, Redington, Chater, & Finch (1998) use the CHILDES corpus (MacWhinney & Snow 1985) to perform hierarchical clustering of words based on the words that occur on the left and on the right. They obtained such interpretable classes, as proper nouns, adjectives, common nouns, prepositions, one large cluster of verbs, a cluster of determiners and possessive pronouns. They found that two words on the left and on the right together provide the clusters that are the most similar to the benchmark (12 classes from the Collins Cobuild Lexical Database). Similarly, Mintz, Newport, & Bever (2002) showed that co-occurrence patterns with surrounding words allow one to successfully categorize the majority of nouns and verbs. All this means that distributional information is a powerful cue for learning syntactic categories. In addition, Moran et al. (2018), who compare syntactic frames (frequently occurring nonadjacent sequences of words, e.g. *I X books*, as in *I read books*) and morphological frames (sequences of morphemes, e.g. *is Xing*, as in *is sleeping*), find that only the latter can serve as highly accurate cues cross-linguistically for learning of word classes. Therefore, morphological distributional information seems to be at least as relevant as the information about the surrounding words. This means that the term 'syntactic categories' is not very fortunate, and should be regarded as a manifestation of Anglocentrism in theoretical linguistics.

38.3 Part-of-speech annotation: Conflicting requirements and difficult Decisions

38.3.1 What makes a good part-of-speech annotation?

The goal of POS annotation is to maximize the usability of a corpus for its target users, who belong to different communities with diverse interests: from lexicographers and teachers to NLP researchers and software developers. Their needs should be reflected in the choice of POS tagsets. For example, the LOB corpus has a fine-grained, complex tagset because it was developed primarily for the purposes of English language teaching and research, while the UPenn (University of Pennsylvania) corpus has a smaller tagset, which is more convenient for Machine Learning applications (Atwell 2008).

The criteria of useful POS annotation include the following, which are often in conflict.

1. The level of granularity should allow for extraction of linguistic patterns of interest with maximal precision. As a result, annotation should be fine-grained. At the same time, the search for traditional broad categories, such as a noun or a verb, should be possible without too much effort. Moreover, the tags should be easy to remember. Therefore, the list of tags should be relatively short.
2. The distribution of linguistic information across different layers should be efficient. This means that POS annotation should not overlap with the other layers, such as morphological features and syntactic roles. At the same time, it should provide sufficient information for each layer to be used independently.
3. The annotation should strive for the ideal 'one token—one POS tag'. At the same time, it should be sufficiently flexible in order to take genuinely ambiguous uses into account.
4. POS annotation should reflect the existing standards and traditions in language description, if there are any, to make it easier for users to search for different categories. And yet, it should, ideally, be transferrable to other languages and varieties.

As one can already see from these contradictory desiderata, development of a perfect POS tagset is similar to attempts of squaring a circle. The remaining part of this section provides illustrations of how several well-known corpora deal with these challenges.

38.3.2 The level of granularity

As was discussed in section 38.2.1, there is substantial variation in the size of existing tagsets. The choice of tags depends on multiple factors, such as the application, the state of tagging algorithms and the performance expected by the tagger (Paroubek 2007). In particular, developers may simplify tags because they cannot achieve a required level of accuracy with the tools they have at disposal. For instance, the performance of a POS tagger for French could be only improved by excluding the gender information from the tags of nouns and adjectives (Chanod & Tapanainen 1995).

The large and detailed tagsets like CLAW7 are fine-tuned to the grammatical peculiarities of a language and help to search for specific words and constructions with high precision. For example, if one wants to find examples of *What a(n) NOUN!* (e.g. *What an idiot!*), one can use the wordform *What* followed by the indefinite article *at1* and a singular common noun *nn1*.

In most tagsets with detailed information, the first positions in the tags (e.g. *n* in *nn1* or *v* in *vvd*) represent the traditional parts of speech (i.e. nouns or verbs). In CLAWS7, each major part of speech begins with one unique letter. For example, we can find all adjectives by searching for a tag that starts with the letter 'J'.

Some tagsets are less convenient in that regard. For example, in the BNC the C5 tags of all nouns start with 'N'. However, if one wants to find adjectives, it is necessary to specify two letters, 'AJ'.[8] If one simply looks for 'A**', they will also get articles ('AT0') and adverbs ('AV*'). At the same time, the XML version of the BNC provides an additional layer of annotation, which corresponds to the traditional parts of speech. See an example in (2). Each word is on a separate line. The tags inside of the annotation XML tags <w...> before the wordform represent the coarse-grained POS tag 'pos' (e.g. pronoun, verb, substantive), the lemma 'hw', and the fine-grained POS tag from the 'c5' tagset, e.g. *PNP*—personal pronouns, *VVZ*—3rd person singular present tense of a verb, *NN1*—common singular noun, etc.

(2) Sentence: *She gazes at herself in wonder.* (FB0)
Annotation:
<s n='49'>
<w pos='PRON' hw='she' c5='PNP'>She </w>
<w pos='VERB' hw='gaze' c5='VVZ'>gazes </w>
<w pos='PREP' hw='at' c5='PRP'>at </w>
<w pos='PRON' hw='herself' c5='PNX'>herself </w>
<w pos='PREP' hw='in' c5='PRP'>in </w>
<w pos='SUBST' hw='wonder' c5='NN1'>wonder</w>
<c c5="PUN">.</c>
</s>

A more parsimonious way is to completely separate the fine-grained features such as number and person, from the major classes. This approach is implemented in the Universal Dependencies corpora (Zeman et al. 2020). An example from the English EWT corpus is provided in (3).[9] Each token is represented by several columns: token ID, token, lemma, Universal Part of Speech (UPOS), a finer-grained POS tag, morphological features, such as mood, tense, number, case, person, and degree of comparison, as well as the ID of the syntactic head, and finally the syntactic dependency relation (root, object, subordinator, etc.). Importantly, the UPOS tags are separated from the morphological features.

---

[8] http://www.natcorp.ox.ac.uk/docs/c5spec.html
[9] Some annotation layers, which are irrelevant for the discussion, are not shown.

(3) # sent_id = email-enronsent31_01-0012
text = Take care and hope to hear from you soon.

1	Take	take	VERB	VB	Mood=Imp|VerbForm=Fin	0	root
2	care	care	NOUN	NN	Number=Sing	1	obj
3	and	and	CCONJ	CC	_	4	cc
4	hope	hope	VERB	VBP	Mood=Ind|Tense=Pres|VerbForm=Fin	1	conj
5	to	to	PART	TO	_	6	mark
6	hear	hear	VERB	VB	VerbForm=Inf	4	xcomp
7	from	from	ADP	IN	_	8	case
8	you	you	PRON	PRP	Case=Acc|Person=2|PronType=Prs	6	obl
9	soon	soon	ADV	RB	Degree=Pos	6	advmod
10	.	.	PUNCT	.	_	1	punct

As mentioned, cross-linguistic tagsets, such as UPOS and Google tagsets, are coarse-grained. This is understandable, since the fine-grained categories are not (fully) applicable across different languages. It is not excluded that future development of tagsets beyond well-described European languages will result in even smaller and more general tagsets.

38.3.3 Distribution of information across different layers of annotation

As mentioned above, grammatical information can be distributed over several layers. This solves the problem of granularity. The user can combine information from different layers in any way to get more or less detailed descriptions. There is another problem here, however. Ideally, these layers should provide unique information, i.e. they should be orthogonal.

According to the famous account by Croft (2001: ch. 2), the core word classes (nouns, verbs, and adjectives) have two sides: semantics (e.g. objects, properties, and actions) and 'information packaging', such as reference, modification, and predication, which corresponds to syntactic constructions where they can be used. At the same time, because of their semantic component, they are not reduced to their syntactic roles.[10]

Croft et al. (2017) argue that semantics and information packaging should be disassociated in corpus annotation. They suggest to perform a simplification of the syntactic dependencies used in the UD corpora. The dependencies represent syntactic functions, such as subject, object, predicate, complement clause, etc.[11] One could group, for example, determiners, numeric modifiers, and adjectival modifiers of nouns under a more general tag 'modifier'. The differences between them can be captured by the Universal POS (UPOS) tags, which were discussed in sections 38.2.1 and 38.3.2. In that case, the annotation scheme would be more parsimonious.

---

[10] An additional source of entropy is the fact that the reference function performed primarily by nouns and pronouns is instantiated by different syntactic arguments (subject, direct object, indirect object, and oblique).

[11] See https://universaldependencies.org/u/dep/index.html.

However, this has not been implemented. The reason is practical. Some users (e.g. syntacticians) prefer using the dependencies, while some others use only the POS tags (which are perhaps more widely used in corpus linguistics). This annotation is therefore redundant, but practically useful.

But how serious is the problem of redundancy in actual corpus data? As an illustration, let us have a look at two layers in the Universal Dependencies corpora: UPOS and syntactic dependencies. According to Croft et al., these two types of information should not overlap, for the annotation schema to be maximally informative. One possible way of measuring this systematically is to compute Shannon's (1948) entropy for each UPOS tag in a corpus across different syntactic dependencies. If the entropy is high, we will not be able to predict the syntactic role from the part of speech. This means that each of the layers carries unique information. In contrast, if the entropy is low, this means that a particular UPOS tag is strongly associated with one or two syntactic functions, and the annotation has high redundancy.

Table 38.1 provides an illustration. It displays a subset of the frequencies of tokens annotated as NOUN in different syntactic roles in the corpus of Afrikaans in the Universal Dependencies corpora (version 2.5). These frequencies are divided by the total number of all tokens with a particular tag (here: NOUN) to obtain the probabilities.

Table 38.1 Some frequencies of common nouns as syntactic dependencies in the Afrikaans Universal Dependencies training corpus (v 2.5)

Universal POS	nsubj	obj	iobj	csubj	ccomp	xcomp	obl	vocative	expl
NOUN	903	1,573	42	0	0	1	1,557	0	0

The results averaged for each POS in the UD corpora are displayed in Figure 38.1. It shows that common nouns (NOUN) have the highest entropy on average. This means that they are the most diverse syntactically, and it is the most difficult to predict the syntactic role of a noun. They are followed by pronouns (PRON), lexical verbs (VERB) and proper nouns (PROPN). On the other end of the continuum are the subordinate (SCONJ) and coordinate (CCONJ) conjunctions, followed by adpositions (ADP). An examination of the syntactic dependencies reveals that these three Universal POS tags nearly always co-occur with the roles of subordination markers (*mark*), coordinating conjunctions (*cc*), and case markers (*case*), respectively. Adverbs (ADV) are often adverbial modifiers (*advmod*), whereas interjections (INTJ) are annotated as discourse elements (*discourse*). Auxiliaries (AUX) are syntactically annotated as auxiliaries (*aux*) and copulas (*cop*). Particles (PART) are adverbial modifiers (*advmod*), subordinating markers (*mark*) and discourse elements (*discourse*).

These results demonstrate that most function words are strongly associated with particular syntactic dependencies. This means a maximal overlap between UPOS and dependencies for these word classes. This is hardly surprising. Function words are defined by their syntactic role. Nouns, verbs, and adjectives have less redundancy. These POS are in

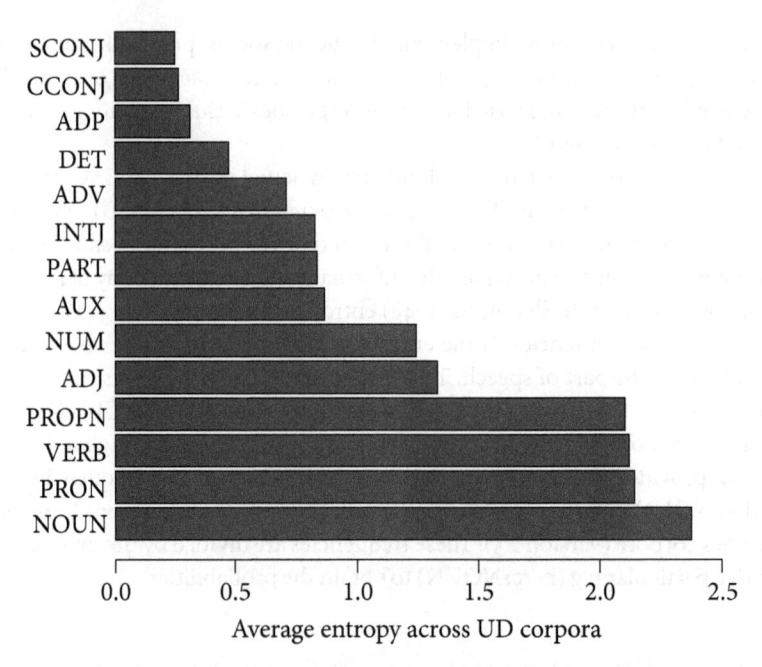

FIGURE 38.1 Average entropy scores of Universal POS tags regarding the syntactic dependencies in the Universal Dependencies corpora

fact doing well in comparison to the others. So, if one wanted to make any improvements in terms of redundancy, they would need to start with function words.

38.3.4 Fuzzy boundaries between parts of speech

Ideally, every token in a corpus should have one POS tag. This rule can be violated in three cases. First, the boundaries between parts of speech in a language can be fuzzy (e.g. Croft 2001: 103). A descriptively adequate POS annotation should be sufficiently flexible to take that fuzziness into account. Second, sometimes there is simply not enough contextual information for disambiguation between two categories. For example, it may be unclear whether the word *fire* in a short exclamatory sentence *Fire!* is a noun or a verb (Cloeren 1999: 48). The first and the second cases represent genuine ambiguity. Third, there can be not enough information for the automatic tagger to make a decision, but this ambiguity can be resolved by a human annotator.

Some well-known corpora, such as the BNC and COCA, have ambiguity tags. As an illustration, consider the BNC tagset (see section 38.3.2), which contains ambiguous tags, such as VVD-VVN. This means that the automatic tagger was unable to decide whether the word is a VVD (past tense verb) or a VVN (past participle). The two possibilities are left for the users to disambiguate.

Ambiguity tags constitute approximately 4.7% of the BNC tags (excluding punctuation tags). Table 38.2 displays the top ten most frequent ambiguity tags in the XML edition of the corpus. Which type of ambiguity do they represent?

Table 38.2 Top ten ambiguity tags in the British National Corpus

Tag	Meaning	Frequency	Example
NN1-VVB	Singular common noun or finite base form of lexical verb	528,014	*pay* cheques or slips
AJ0-NN1	General/positive adjective or singular common noun	421,584	the *chief* executive
NP0-NN1	Proper noun or common singular noun	347,428	I'm looking for *Bill*.
PRP-AVP	Preposition or general adverb	245,875	Put it *on* the reverse.
NN1-AJ0	Singular common noun or general/positive adjective	238,719	restrictive *patient* choice
VVB-NN1	finite base form of lexical verb or singular common noun	218,459	*Control* in this context has been defined by ...
VVN-VVD	past participle or past tense form of lexical verb	206,468	A survey *conducted* in the United States discovered ...
VVD-VVN	past tense or past participle form of lexical verb	190,747	Completely *ignored* it!
NN1-NP0	Common singular noun or proper noun	156,747	Any *Don* Juan can say he loves you.
VVG-AJ0	The -ing form of lexical verb or general/positive adjective	118,329	all seeming big and *threatening*

A closer look at the corpus data reveals some genuine cases of ambiguity. In particular, the adjective—noun choice is often very tricky. Examples are *its opposite, its excess population, some wild-eyed back-country messiah*, and *the protestant parts*. Another case of genuine ambiguity is VVG-AJ0, which represents an *ing*-participle or an adjective, e.g. *all these working people, developing countries, preceding and following period, measuring instruments, be terrifying*. These examples seem to illustrate the fuzzy boundaries between the semantic properties of POS. It is understandable that these words have ambiguity tags.

However, most of the examples in the corpus are simply due to problems with the automatic annotation. For example, the noun *mind* in *bearing in mind* is ambiguous with a verb (NN1-VVB) in one context. For a human annotator, these decisions are straightforward. Ideally, each of those tags should be manually checked and corrected, so that only the genuine cases remain. Unfortunately, the difference between genuine ambiguity and the algorithm's deficiency is rarely reflected in available corpora.[12]

One should also mention here a very different case, when the ambiguity of POS tags is less obvious. For example, in the EAGLES tags for Romance languages (see section 38.2.1), there is a value *C* for gender meaning 'either F or M'. Nouns like Spanish *estudiante* 'a male or

---

[12] Quite tellingly, a document with guidelines for EAGLES-style annotation says that dealing with genuine ambiguity is not a matter of great priority: https://home.uni-leipzig.de/burr/Verb/htm/LinkedDocuments/annotate.pdf (p. 17).

female student' are then annotated as having no gender, although in fact they do have a specific gender in a given context. The problem is that it is very difficult for a parser to annotate the gender correctly, which worsens the parser's performance.[13] Therefore, when evaluating POS ambiguity, one should also consider the level of detail provided by the tagset.

38.3.5 Cross-linguistic usability and traditional language-specific descriptions

Recently there has been strong interest in developing and applying uniform annotation schemas for different languages. The practical benefits of a standardized tagset are obvious: one can interchange and reuse resources and develop corpora and tools that can be used globally (Leech & Wilson 1999). Creating a tagset applicable to many diverse languages is a challenging task. The creators should strike a balance between the usefulness of the tagset for a maximum number of languages and its descriptive adequacy for any specific language. Let us consider these criteria in greater detail, using the Universal Dependencies corpora as an illustration.

The first criterion, the usefulness of the tagset for corpora in different languages, can be evaluated by counting the number of tags that are used in all corpora and those that are not used. Out of 150 corpora available at the moment of writing, 46 corpora contain all seventeen POS tags. 52 corpora contain all but one, and 30 corpora contain all but two, which means that more than 85% of the corpora have all or almost all tags. The total counts are shown in Table 38.3. Note that the missing tags are usually technical (see below).

Table 38.3 Number of unused tags (maximum: 17)

Number of unused tags	0	1	2	3	4	5	6	9
Number of corpora	46	52	30	13	5	5	1	1

Let us now look at the distribution of each individual Universal POS tag. Figure 38.2 displays the number of corpora in which a particular tag was not used. The tags VERB and NOUN are used in all corpora. They are followed by PRON (pronouns), ADP (adpositions), and ADJ (adjectives). The tags SYM (symbol), INTJ (interjections) and X (foreign words and other dubious cases) are the least commonly used, probably because they are on the periphery of a linguistic system, and do not receive much attention. Another reason may be that some corpora do not contain tokens representing these classes (e.g. one will not find many interjections in news reports, or symbols in spoken corpora). Among the traditional parts of speech, the ones that are used the least frequently are PART (particle), SCONJ (subordinate conjunctions), and DET (determiners). Some corpora do not annotate proper nouns (PROPN), AUX (auxiliaries), and PUNCT (punctuation).

---

[13] I thank Maarten Janssen for bringing up this important point.

Number of corpora NOT containing POS tags

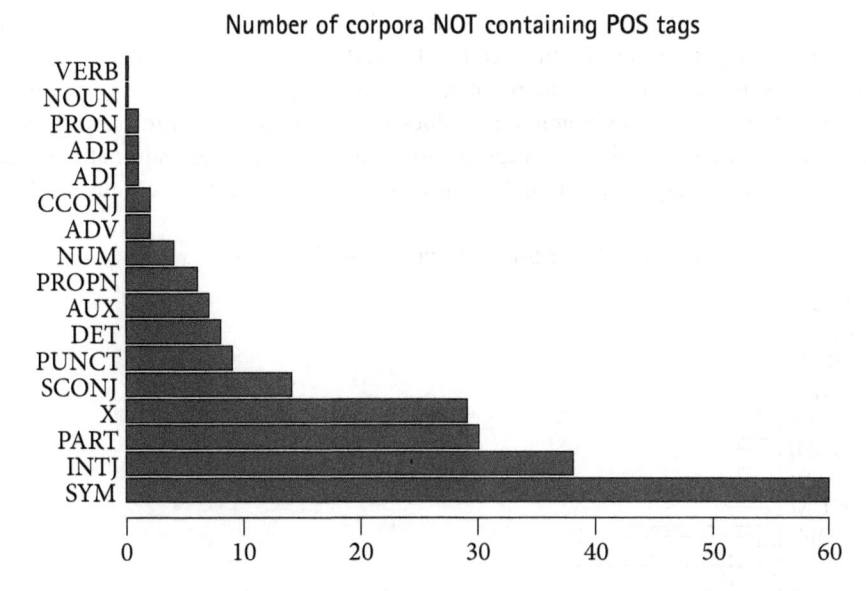

FIGURE 38.2 Number of corpora in the Universal Dependencies collection that do not have individual universal part-of-speech tags

The corpus with the largest number of unused tags is Warlpiri UFAL. It has nine categories that are not used. This may be at least partly due to data sparseness because the corpus is very small and contains grammar examples. The Tagalog corpus, which has five tags missing, is similar in that respect. For example, CCONJ (coordinate conjunctions) and NUM (numerals) are missing in the Warlpiri and Tagalog corpora, but these word classes are also missing in the English translations, which are provided in the files. This seems to be an artefact of the source data and is likely to change when more natural texts are added.

Some of the tags may be left out for a good reason. For example, the corpus of Swedish Sign Language does not contain tokens annotated with the punctuation tag PUNCT. ADP (adpositions) are missing in one of the Korean treebanks (the parallel treebank PUD), but the status of case and topic markers (particles), which can be interpreted as adpositions, is not straightforward in Korean. There are no ADJ (adjectives) in Classical Chinese (the treebank Kyoto). The functionally similar words are annotated as VERB. According to the corpus creators, 'adjective usages of verbs were not specialised as adjectives at that era' (https://universaldependencies.org/lzh/index.html).

Some missing tags are difficult to explain, however. For example, the Latin-Perseus corpus lacks PROPN (proper nouns), which are annotated as common nouns instead. PRON (pronouns) are absent in the Vietnamese VTB corpus. For some reason, they are coded as proper names. SCONJ (subordinate conjunctions) are missing in two Portuguese corpora, where they appear as CCONJ (coordinate conjunction) and in one Indonesian corpus, where they are annotated as adpositions. There is obviously room for improvement in such cases.

Overall, if we compare Indo-European with the other languages represented in the UD corpora, we will see that there are more non-Indo-European corpora with missing tags, as far as most traditional parts of speech are concerned. The frequencies of missing tags in

Indo-European and all other languages are shown in Figure 38.3. This difference becomes even more striking if we consider the fact that the total number of non-Indo-European corpora is almost twice as small as the number of Indo-European ones (only 57 vs 97). This means that the Universal POS annotation does have an Indo-European bias. There is a caveat, however. Many non-Indo-European corpora are very small and non-naturalistic, so some of these biases may disappear in the future, as more diverse texts become available.

Number of corpora NOT containing POS tags

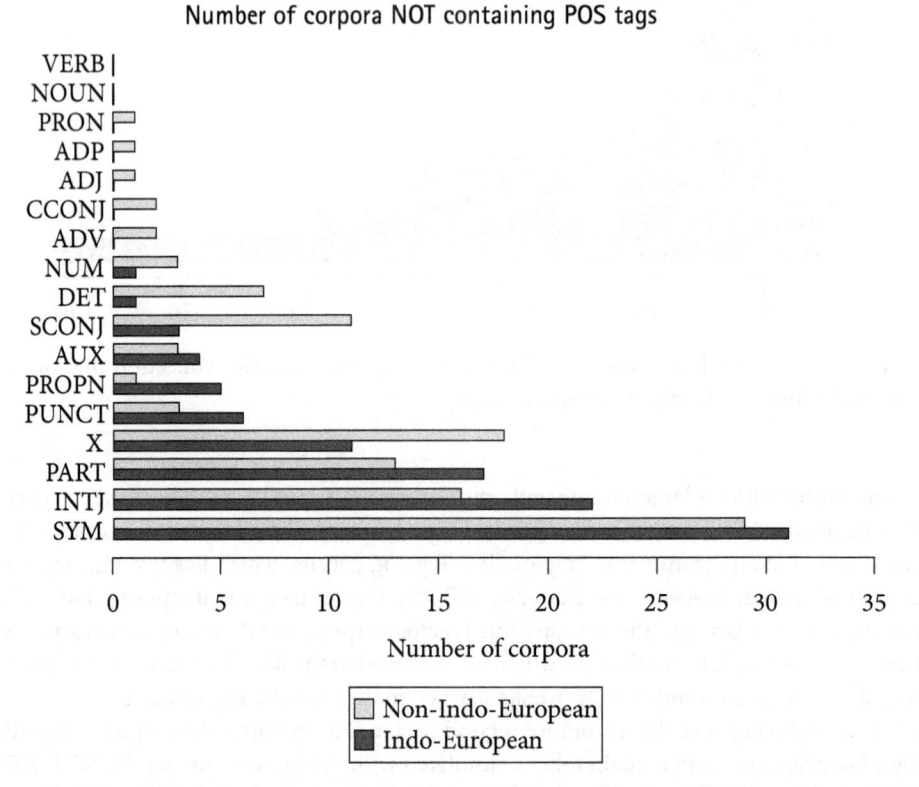

[Bar chart showing number of corpora without each POS tag, comparing Non-Indo-European and Indo-European languages, for tags: VERB, NOUN, PRON, ADP, ADJ, CCONJ, ADV, NUM, DET, SCONJ, AUX, PROPN, PUNCT, X, PART, INTJ, SYM]

FIGURE 38.3 Number of corpora in the Universal Dependencies collection without individual part-of-speech tags: Indo-European vs Non-Indo-European languages

The second criterion of POS tags usability is close correspondence between POS annotation and traditional language-specific descriptions. It is easier to search for constructions in a specific language when the tags are familiar from previous language descriptions. The Universal POS tags often deviate from this ideal. For example, cardinal numerals are annotated as numerals, but ordinal numerals are treated as adjectives because ordinal numerals are morphologically and syntactically similar to adjectives.

Another example is the annotation of particles (PART). For instance, Japanese has many function words that are traditionally called particles, but not all of them have the PART tag in the Universal Dependencies corpora of Japanese. Some of them do, e.g. the question particle *ka*. Others (e.g. *ni* and *no*) are parallel to adpositions in other languages and are tagged as ADP. Similarly, the Russian conditional/subjunctive particle *by* is coded as an auxiliary AUX because it accompanies the lexical verb of a verb phrase and expresses grammatical distinctions not carried by the lexical verb. This is very unconventional, since *by* is no longer perceived as a form of the verb *byt'* 'be' and has lost inflection and phonological substance. However, this choice makes sense from the cross-linguistic perspective.

In some cases, the cross-linguistic comparability is not achieved, as in the case of the boundary between determiners DET and pronouns PRON, which receives a lot of attention in the annotation guidelines.[14] In case of possessive pronouns, the developers advise annotation in accordance with language-specific properties of this subcategory. If possessive pronouns are more likely to be used attributively (modifying a noun phrase) than substantively (replacing a noun phrase), and if their inflection is similar to that of adjectives and distinct from nouns, they are annotated as DET. If they are more like normal personal pronouns (e.g. in the genitive case), they should be tagged PRON. One may wonder if this approach is optimal. It might be useful to make a clearer distinction between the Universal POS tags, which should be maximally universal, and language-specific tags, which are often available as a separate layer of annotation (i.e. as XPOS tags in the UD corpora).

Another question is how these guidelines are implemented. In most cases, the decisions are consistent with the rules. For example, possessive pronouns in the corpus English-EWT are annotated as PRON. This is reasonable because these words lack agreement with head nouns. In Czech-PDT and Russian-SynTagRus, possessive pronouns are annotated as DET. Again, this choice is justified because they are similar to adjectives in declension and agreement. At the same time, some annotation choices are difficult to explain, especially if different decisions are made for corpora representing the same language. For example, possessive pronouns are annotated as PRON in the Latin-Perseus corpus, but as ADJ in Latin-ITTB and PROIEL.

38.4 POS AND FLEXIBLE WORD CLASSES

The boundaries between content words (i.e. nouns, adjectives, verbs, and adverbs) vary cross-linguistically with regard to their morphosyntactic behaviour (Hengeveld 1992b; van Lier & Rijkhoff 2013; see Chapter 6 in this volume). For instance, Croft (2001: 69) points out that English exhibits substantial flexibility. Many lexemes, especially those belonging to the basic vocabulary, can be used in different functions (e.g. *a big house, a big* and *think big*). Another example is Tukang Besi, an Austronesian language spoken in Indonesia. In that language, words that can be used as adnominal modifiers can also be used freely, without additional coding, as arguments (the prototypical function of nouns) and as predicates (the main function of verbs) (Chapter 18 in this volume).

As was mentioned in the beginning of this chapter, POS are used to classify tokens and related syntagmatic units in context, rather than words as paradigmatic types. Therefore, POS, unlike word classes, cannot be flexible. In flexible languages, POS will be determined based on the syntactic roles. Each of the instances of big in *a big house, a big* and *think big* has

---

[14] See https://universaldependencies.org/u/pos/DET.html, https://universaldependencies.org/u/overview/morphology.html#pronominal-words.

a different POS tag (namely, adjective, noun, and adverb, using a coarse-grained annotation schema).

At the same time, POS tags can be easily aggregated across individual wordforms like *big*, so that one can obtain paradigmatic word classes for the purposes of studying word-class flexibility. The advantage of using corpora is that they can help us evaluate how systematic word-class flexibility is in a language. In other words, can the formal overlap be observed across the whole lexicon, or only in a few selected items? Below I show how this can be done for the adjective—adverb distinction based on the Universal Dependencies corpora of six languages.

The data were taken from the Universal Dependencies corpora of Chinese, Dutch, English, French, German, and Indonesian.[15] All tokens (wordforms) with POS tags ADJ (adjective) or ADV (adverb) were collected with the help of a Python script, and the frequencies of these tokens in the function of *amod* (adjectival modifiers of nouns, e.g. <u>hard</u> *work*) or *advmod* (adverbial modifiers of verbs or adjectives, e.g. *work <u>hard</u>*) were collected.

For each wordform, the log-odds ratio of being attracted towards the *amod* or *advmod* role was computed based on the following formula:

(4) $$\log OR = \log\left((amod_{token} / advmod_{token}) / (amod_{other} / advmod_{other})\right) =$$

$$= \log \frac{amod_{token} * advmod_{other}}{advmod_{token} * amod_{other}}$$

where $amod_{token}$ is the frequency of a token in the *amod* position, $advmod_{token}$ is the frequency of the same token in the *advmod* function, $amod_{other}$ is the frequency of occurrences of all other tokens in the *amod* position, and $advmod_{other}$ is the frequency of occurrences of all other tokens in the *advmod* position. By including the frequencies of the other tokens, we control for the differences between the corpora in the relative frequencies of *amod* and *advmod*. Log-odds ratio is a traditional measure of attraction between two categorical variables (Levshina 2015: ch. 9). Here, the variables are the token identity and the syntactic role. In order to deal with zero frequencies, which would cause division by zero, a small amount (0.05) was added to each of the frequencies. Taking the logarithm allows us to centre the value around zero, such that positive values mean attraction of the token towards the *amod* function, and negative ones towards the *advmod* function. The more extreme the values, the more specialized a form is in one or the other function.

Finally, I took absolute values of the *logOR* scores. The higher the absolute scores, the more in general the words are specialized in one or the other role, and the less flexible the language. The lower the scores, the more overlap there is between the *amod* and *advmod* tokens, and the more flexible the languages are, as represented by the corpora. Only the frequencies of the wordforms that occur ten times or more in either role were analysed, in order to avoid unjustifiably high scores that can arise due to data sparseness.

---

[15] The corpora were the following components from the UD collection Version 2.5: Chinese GSD, Dutch Alpino and LassySmall, English EWT and GUM, French GSD, German GSD, and Indonesian GSD. In Indonesian, an additional check was performed due to somewhat idiosyncratic annotation choices, e.g. *akan*, which is a future marker meaning 'will, going to', and *dapat*, *bias*, and *mampu*, which express modality 'can, be able to' are annotated as adverbs. These words were excluded with the help of the tag 'M' in the language-specific POS set.

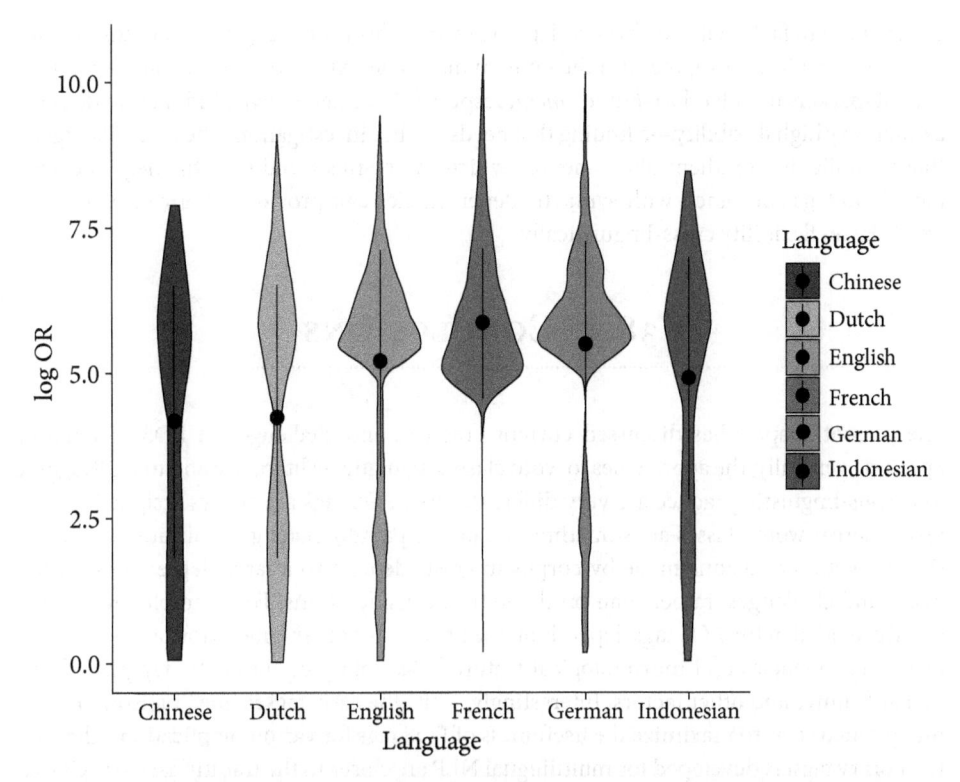

FIGURE 38.4 Absolute log-odds ratios of wordforms in six Universal Dependencies corpora, with the means (dots) and one standard deviation from the mean (black lines)

Figure 38.4 shows the distributions of the absolute log-odds ratios in the six corpora. The thickness of the figures represents the density (i.e. the number of tokens per interval of logOR values). The distributions are weakly bimodal. This means that the wordforms tend to be either flexible, or non-flexible. However, most wordforms seem to have high values, which means that they are attracted to one of the roles. The wordforms strongly attracted to *amod* are often adjectives representing size, novelty (old/new), nationality, as well as ordinal numerals, which are annotated in the UD as adjectives. Here also belong inflected adjectives, if they exist. As for the wordforms strongly attracted to *advmod*, they are highly frequent semi-function words *there, also, now, too,* or *then*. For example, in German the words with high scores are inflected adjectival forms, e.g. *gute, ehemaligen, verschiedene*, or highly frequent adverbs, such as *noch, auch, sehr, nur,* and *heute*.

Low scores mean that the relative frequencies of the wordforms as *amod* and *advmod* are similar to the total proportions of *amod* and *advmod* in the corpus. For example, in English, these include directions (e.g. *south*), dimensions (e.g. *wide, long*) and other properties (e.g. *hard, quick,* and *online*). In German, these are words like *nahe, super, unmittelbar, kurz, ganz, speziell,* which are often used as postnominally, e.g. *die Lage unmittelbar vor der Küste* 'the location directly in front of the coast'.

The distributions overlap greatly, which indicates that the flexibility is a matter of degree, although there are also subtle differences. As expected, Chinese and Dutch tend to have more wordforms with low scores and high flexibility. English, German, and particularly

French have in fact relatively few overlapping forms. This is not surprising, because French and German adjectives agree with the noun in many contexts, and English and French have special markers for adverbs (*-ly* and *-ment*, respectively). Interestingly, Indonesian does not exhibit very high flexibility—a finding that needs further investigation. These results suggest that flexibility is a gradient phenomenon, which can be measured with the help of corpus data. POS tags combined with syntactic dependencies can provide a source for studying word classes flexibility cross-linguistically.

38.5 Conclusions

The present chapter has discussed current practices and challenges in POS annotation. Speaking generally, the approaches to word classes in linguistic literature and to POS tagging in corpus-linguistic practice are very different. First, POS tags are always assigned in context, whereas word classes are sometimes treated as paradigmatic generalizations. Second, the annotation decisions made by corpus linguists depend to a large degree on practical needs and challenges, rather than on theoretical considerations. For example, the level of detail provided in the POS tags depends on the presence of other annotation layers (e.g. syntactic dependencies and morphological features), feasibility of automatic tagging of particular features and other factors. Interestingly, while the early tagsets for English were very fine-grained so as to maximize the usefulness of POS tags for various applications, the contemporary tagsets developed for multilingual NLP are closer to the traditional word classes. This suggests that the traditional categories reflect relevant properties, after all.

Bridging this gap would be beneficial to both communities. Corpora can provide a testing ground for pertinent theoretical issues, such as word classes flexibility, at the same time forcing linguists to formulate more precise, empirically testable hypotheses. On the other hand, annotation inconsistencies, especially in multilingual corpora, suggest room for improvement. Some nudging on the part of typologists may help to improve the comparability of cross-linguistic tagsets. As the interests of corpus developers expand to the languages that differ substantially from Standard Average European, thanks to such international initiatives as the Universal Dependencies project, we will soon see how universal the current 'universal' tagsets are in reality. We are living in exciting times.

CHAPTER 39

WORD CLASSES AND GRAMMATICALIZATION

K. AARON SMITH

39.1 INTRODUCTION

IN this chapter, I present an overview of grammaticalization in the light of word classes. In this way, grammaticalization may be thought of on one level as involving a word-class shift, in so far as it has been defined in traditional terms as the movement of words from the lexicon into the grammatical realm, as suggested in the earliest definition of that process by Antoine Meillet: 'l'attribution du caractère grammatical à un mot jadis autonome' ('the attribution of a grammatical character to a formerly autonomous word' (1912: 131).[1]

Grammaticalization has also been used to discuss the kinds of changes that occur to specific grammatical forms as they continue to develop in a gradual, overlapping, and stepwise manner. Such a characterization of grammaticalization, then, espouses the view that grammar is scalar, in so far as some forms are more grammatical than others, and gradual, in the sense that it does not involve wholesale movement of all instances of a given word/form ever further along a path (and see below on 'divergence'), instead resulting in layers or polysemies retaining younger (earlier grammatical) and older (later grammatical) meanings (examples below). The flowing character of grammaticalization has been expressed in the figure of clines of various sorts, such as that shown in (1).

(1)   content item > grammatical word > clitic > inflectional suffix
       (Hopper & Traugott 2003: 7)

While the cline in (1) attempts to capture the formal reflexes of grammaticalization (but as we will see below, it is an oversimplification of what is really going on), similarly arranged clines have been used to represent well-established, cross-linguistic 'paths' of semantic change that occur as forms move further into the grammatical realm. For instance, the figure

---

[1] For some time, there was some competition in terminology and some scholars preferred the term 'grammaticalization' and others, more rarely, 'grammation'. 'Grammaticalization' is the preferred term now.

in (2) captures the development of futures from earlier possession, obligation and intention meanings (adapted from Bybee, Perkins, & Pagliuca 1994: 263), and exemplified below.

(2) POSSESSION > { PREDESTINATION / OBLIGATION } > INTENTION > FUTURE

The metaphors of 'channel' and 'chains' (Heine, Claudi, & Hünnemeyer 1991: 67–86) have also been used to capture the kinds of gradient changes that occur to linguistic material as it is involved in grammaticalization.

The cross-linguistic validity of the types of clines seen in (1) and (2) have been supported through many independent studies by different researchers, often working with large databases of languages. Furthermore, many of those same studies have shown that the kinds of developments expressed in such formal and semantic clines are not independent of one another such that there is a correlation between reduction in form and reduction in meaning, i.e. semantic abstraction (Bybee et al. 1994: 104ff.). We will see many examples of just such a correlation in this chapter, although it is very important to mention at the outset that the formal effects of grammaticalization also show cross-linguistic variation such that in synthetic or agglutinating languages, affixation of the type suggested in (1) is likely, but not so in languages without much affixal material to begin with, e.g. Vietnamese (e.g. Bisang 2004). Another point to be made later in the chapter is that the relationship between changes in form and changes in meaning is sensitive to the effects of increased frequency of a certain type, which in turn may be a product of grammaticalization since, at least in languages in which such categories are obligatory, grammatical material is, all other things being equal, more frequent (and see section 39.6).

However, in this chapter I will also show an interesting case in which the formal effects of frequency (fusion of contiguous material in a construction), which have been showcased in the presentation of grammaticalizing constructions, like the *be going to* and *be fixing to* futures in English, can be seen to occur even before very advanced grammaticalization, underscoring the point that the mechanisms that drive that process also operate independently of it (see Smith 2009 on the history of *be fixing to*). The latter point then helps to situate grammaticalization within the larger study of language change.

39.1.1 Grammaticalization: A classic example

An example of grammaticalization, classic in the sense of being a long-standing and well-documented instance of that process, involves the development of the inflectional future in Romance, although here I will focus on that development in Spanish. The present-day Spanish inflectional future is signalled by the bold affixes shown in (3), which are attached to the infinitive of the lexical verb, i.e. the verb contributing the lexical content of the expression. Thus, reading downward in each column and then across, the forms may be translated into English as 'I will speak, you will speak, she/it/he will speak, we will speak, you (pl.) will speak, they will speak'.

(3)
	Singular	Plural
1st	hablaré	hablaremos
2nd	hablarás	hablaraís
3rd	hablará	hablarán

The origin of those affixes is traced to the Latin verb *habēre*, which had the lexical meaning of 'have/hold', although already in Classical Latin it was more regularly predicated of abstract possession, such as the example in (4), where the sense of *habēre* (qua *habeō*) is not about physical holding/possessing, but about something the speaker has in mind to tell.[2]

(4) habeo   etiam   dicere   quem...   de
    have:1ST.SING. PRES. even say:INF REL.PRO:ACC.SING   from
    ponte   in   Tiberim   deiecerit
    bridge:DAT.SING   into   Tiber:ACC.SING   throw:3RD.SING.PERF.SUBJ
    'I have even to tell of one whom he threw from a bridge into the Tiber' (from Cicero's [106–43 BC] *Pro Roscio Amerino*, cited in Fleishman 1982: 52, gloss and translation from Smith 2011: 368)

From such uses, more grammaticalized meanings with clearer future orientation begin to emerge, as in (5), also cited in Fleischman (1982: 58–59, translation and gloss again from Smith 2011: 368).

(5) Nazareus   vocari   habebat   secundum
    Nazarene:NOM.SING. call:PASS.INF.   have:3RD.SING.IMP.   in accordance with
    prophetiam
    prophecy:ACC.SING.
    'He was to be called the Nazarene in accordance with the prophecy' (Tertullian's [155–230 AD] *Adversus Marcionem* IV.)

Here *habēre* (qua *habebat*) may be thought of as indicating predestination (Benveniste 1968), involving too some obliging force (i.e. prophecy), and such uses have been analysed as expressing obligation (Fleischman 1982). By Old Spanish, reflexes of *habēre* expressing the meaning of intention, esp. with first person subjects, are regular, as in (6).

(6) si   yo   bivo   doblarvos   he   la soldada
    if   I   live   double: INF=PRO.2ND.SING.   aux:1ST.SG.PRES.   the rent
    'If I live I will/intend to double the rent for you.' (Poema de mio Cid, Cantar 1.6.80)

---

[2] As mentioned, one of the greatest contributions to the linguistic sciences afforded by studies on grammaticalization is scalarity, and such scalarity is apparent not only on the grammatical side of things but also on the lexical side as well in so far as the lexical material that becomes involved in grammaticalization is normally already somewhat abstract (Bybee et al. 1994: 9), and thus already moving towards mental storage as procedural rather than strictly propositional knowledge (and see Traugott & Trousdale 2013: 12).

From there, more central instances of futurity are apparent, as in (7), in which the speaker predicts what a third person will do, although meanings of intention are also apparent in that the speaker is making that prediction based on inference of the Campeador's intention.

(7) el Campeador   dexarlas   ha   en vuestra mano
    the Campeador leave:INF=PRO.3RD.PL.FEM.   AUX:3RD.SG.PRES.   in your hand
    'The Campeador will leave them in your hands.' (Poema de mio Cid 1.9.117)

Formally, we note that *habēre* now appears in quite reduced forms (*he/has*) as an unbound auxiliary separated from the lexical verb by intervening material, a possibility that diminished over time until the reduced forms of *habēre* eventually fused with the lexical verb (see the paradigm in (3)), thus traversing fully both the formal and semantic paths given in (1) and (2).

The examples illustrated so far might seem to suggest that, at least in its earliest stages, grammaticalization is a straightforward instance of a word-class shift of the type LEXICAL VERB > AUXILIARY VERB (and then later > AFFIX), but such a view is only true at a very abstract level and what has interested modern scholars working in the area of grammaticalization just as much as, if not more than, this kind of abstract characterization has been the role that context, both formal and semantic, plays in encouraging 'l'attribution du caractère grammatical'. Viewed in this way, it is not quite accurate to define grammaticalization in the traditional way as a type of language change focused on a lexical item but instead as affecting a lexical item as it occurs in a specific construction (see for example Traugott 2002; Brinton and Traugott 2005: 24). Viewed in this way, we can certainly say as an etymological exercise that *habēre* is the source of the Spanish inflectional future forms, but grammaticalization really involved *habēre* in a construction with an infinitive, an infinitive that provided no little input to the development of the future meaning of the entire construction given its prospective orientation.

Later in the chapter we will see further examples of the grammaticalization of expressions for future in some varieties of American English. Those examples will bring to light other concerns about grammaticalization and about the way material shifts between lexical and grammatical during that process.

39.1.2 Grammaticalization: Some further examples

Many of the examples and discussion points in this chapter involve auxiliation, that is the creation of auxiliary verbs for expression of tense, aspect, or mood (TAM systems), a process which may be thought of as a more specific sub-area within grammaticalization (Benveniste 1968; Heine 1993; Kuteva 2001). But it is hardly the case that grammaticalization is limited to the development of TAM systems and very regular, cross-linguistic patterns involving the shift of lexical material other than verbs into grammatical formants have been well documented. A good resource for such examples remains to be Bernd Heine & Tania Kuteva's *World Lexicon of Grammaticalization*, a resource that catalogues in alphabetical order hundreds of documented changes from lexical source to grammatical expression (as well as the movement of linguistic material from less grammatical to more grammatical categories) from many different authors and sources. The examples here are taken from Heine & Kuteva (2002), and for reasons of space have to be limited to just a few.

In some languages, nouns for parts of the body have developed over time into markers of various types (adverbs, prepositions, postpositions) expressing location and direction. Heine & Kuteva (2002: 140) give instances of the word for FOOT coming to express the semantic notion of 'down', as illustrated in Silacayoapan (Mixtecan, Mexico) in which the lexical noun sàʔà 'foot' is also used as a location marker as illustrated in (8).[3]

(8) kándúʔù   nà   sàʔà   yítò
    are:lying   they   foot   tree
    'They are lying [at] the base of the tree.' (quoted in Heine & Kuteva from Hollenbach 1995: 178 and Shields 1988: 317)

Other instances of body parts > locative/directional include BACK, BELLY, BUTTOCKS, EYE, FACE, HEAD, and NECK, among others.

Examples of grammaticalization such as those involving body parts coming to signal various locative or directional meanings underscore the fact that the grammaticalizing expression is hardly arbitrary in relation to the meaning of its lexical and constructional source (and see Bybee et al. 1994: 9ff. on the source determination hypothesis). In the next example, we find an instance in which a noun meaning 'boundary/limit' has come to express the adverbial notion of 'as long as/until' (Heine & Kuteva: 2001:194ff.). In Tamil the noun *varai* 'limit/end' inflected in the dative with the clitic *-um*, which is used to express inclusivity or entirety, has come to mark co-temporality in a construction that appears as the head of an adjectival clause, shown in (9).

(9) kumaar   veelai   cey-t-a   varai-kk-um   naan   kaattiru-nt-een
    Kumar   work   do-PAST-ADJV end-DAT-INCL   1:SG   wait-PAST-1SG
    'As long as Kumar worked, I was waiting.'   (cited from Lehmann 1989: 343)

Here again we see the importance of the construction in which such lexical material appears in that it is not merely the noun *varai* that becomes a temporal subordinating element, but the noun in use in a construction with the dative case marker and an enclitic (and see below).

As mentioned, once constructions containing material from lexical word classes shift into the grammatical realm, they may continue to develop further grammatical meanings. One common source for definite articles, for example, is from earlier demonstratives (Greenberg 1978, cf. Latin *ille/illa* 'that' > Spanish *el/la* 'the'). Heine & Kuteva (2001: 109ff.) list several examples, such as that involving the Chinook Jargon demonstrative, *úkuk* ('this/that'), which has developed in Grand Ronde Chinook Jargon into a prefixal definite article as shown in (10).

(10) uk-háya-haws
     this-big-house (from Grant 1996: 234)
     'this big house'

---

[3] While not universally agreed, many categories of adverb and those of pre- and postpositions, such as locative or directional, are taken in this tradition to be grammatical in nature due, at least in part, to their exponence by a sometimes large but nonetheless closed classed set of markers (see e.g. Heine, Claudi, & Hünnemeyer 1991: 3).

Another interesting example of a grammatical marker taking on different grammatical uses involves the development of third person personal pronouns becoming passive markers, as in (11a)–(11b).

(11)   Kimbundu (Heine & Kuteva 2001: 236, citing Givón 1979: 188, 211)
    (a)   Nzua   a-mu-mono
           John   3:PL-3:SG:OBJ-see
           'John, they saw him.'

    (b)   Nzua   a-mu-mono   (kwa meme)
           John   PASS-3:SG:SUBJ-see   (by me)
           'John was seen (by me).'

Such a development is not difficult to conceive of, particularly given the non-specific identity that 'they' may take on, as seen in English *They make a good pizza in New York*, with the focus on the predication (cf. *Good pizza is made in New York*).

39.2 GRAMMATICALIZATION: SOME HISTORY

The notion of grammaticalization is hardly restricted to modern linguistic thought nor to Western linguistics. Harbsmeier (1979: 159ff.) discusses the 13th-century Chinese grammarian Zhou Bo-qi who noticed the diachronic link between 'empty symbols' (grammatical words) and 'full symbols' (lexical items), and in the tradition of language philosophy out of which modern linguistics would grow, the relationship between lexical classes of words and the grammatical classes into which such words developed was discussed by no less a figure than Horne Took, who did not believe that grammatical and lexical words were equal in terms of their relationship to the origins of such words and that grammatical words were derivative of the former (Aarsleff 1983: 58). A century later, diachrony occupied the centre stage as linguistics grew into an independent science and many influential developers of that science figured grammaticalization at the centre of their theories, e.g. Bopp, Humboldt, Gabelentz, inter alia (see Hopper & Traugott 2003, and especially Heine, Claudi, & Hünnemeyer 1991 for more elaborate early histories of grammaticalization studies).

Given such promising attention to this particular area of word-class shift so early in the development of linguistic sciences, it is unfortunate that the dominant theories of the mid-20th century, so focused on synchronic description as they were, would largely ignore this earlier work and relegate contemporary scholarship concerning grammaticalization (and language change generally) to the margins of linguistics. Yet, some mid-20th-century scholars, such as Benveniste, Kuryłowicz, Watkins, inter alia, continued to refine our knowledge of what happens as material shifts from lexical to grammatical status, as they largely saw it. Grammaticalization was arguably reintroduced to mainstream theoretical linguistics by Talmy Givón, whose dictum 'today's morphology is yesterday's syntax' in his Chicago Linguistics Society paper, 'Historical Syntax & Synchronic Morphology: An Archeologist's Field Trip' (1971) sparked a renewed interest in the topic and since the mid-1980s, there have appeared several monograph treatments (Lehmann [1982] 1995; Bybee 1985; Dahl 1985; Heine, Claudi, & Hünnemeyer 1991; Hopper & Traugott [1993] 2003; Bybee, Perkins, & Pagliuca 1994, to name but some), conferences/workshops/symposia (Traugott and Heine 1991; Wischer & Diewald 2002; Fischer, Norde, & Perridon 2004; Hengeveld, Narrog, & Olbertz 2017, among many others), plus the *Oxford Handbook of Grammaticalization* (Narrog & Heine 2011), all of which have helped our understanding of what is happening when a 'formerly autonomous word' takes on grammatical characteristics.[4]

However, with fame also comes scrutiny and studies within the realm of grammaticalization have been met with criticism (see for example Campbell 2001, and the chapters therein). Among the greatest and most relevant of criticisms was the question of whether grammaticalization constituted an exceptional area of language change, the criticism relying often on the observation that what was seen to happen in grammaticalization could also be observed in other areas of language change. While sometimes framed as criticism of terms such as 'grammaticalization theory' (Janda 2005) or grammaticalization as a 'process' (Newmeyer 1998), or of hypotheses associated with grammaticalization, e.g. the unidirectionality hypothesis (see Haspelmath 2004 and Traugott 2002 for convincing support of the hypothesis), the resulting debates in fact helped to sharpen the field's knowledge of what constitutes grammaticalization and how various mechanisms work inside and outside of that process.

So for example, while early work in the 'grammaticalization renaissance' had regularly treated the development of the suffix *-mente* (< Lat. *mens* 'mind' in the ablative) which creates manner adverbs from adjectives in some varieties of Romance, cf. Spanish, *claramente* 'clearly' (*clara* 'clear') (e.g. Lehmann 1995: 87), the development is not so clearly grammatical, perhaps being better considered within the realm of derivational processes in the lexicon (Cowie 1995: 186–187); certainly less productive derivational material, even when traceable to full lexical items in compound constructions, e.g. *-dom* from OE *dom* 'judgement', are better considered cases of lexicalization (Brinton & Traugott 2005: 51). While the shift of *-mente* from a full lexical item to a derivational affix appears to satisfy the cline in (1), it is a good illustration that such formal changes are not definitional of grammaticalization because they are not limited to change of that type. This certainly may leave us with the question as to whether there is anything we should even call grammaticalization, and following Norde (2009: 31), I would suggest that the frequent clustering together of certain formal and semantic changes (and their interrelationship in some languages, and see below) in grammaticalization begs our attention. Furthermore given the important place that an understanding of grammar must occupy in linguistic theory, study of how that kind of knowledge develops is also of central interest for the field. I will return to questions concerning controversial aspects of grammaticalization and how grammaticalization fits more generally into a theory of language change at the end of the chapter.

---

[4] The works mentioned here are selective on the part of the author; the list could be proliferated greatly and does not even consider the very influential articles on the topic that have appeared in various journals of the field. A search in the Linguistics and Language Behavior Abstracts database from 1980 to the present turns up 6,369 results under the search term 'grammaticalization', a number that suggests the popularity of the topic over the last four decades.

39.3 THE CONSTRUCTION AS THE SITE OF GRAMMATICALIZATION

As mentioned, one way of seeing grammaticalization involves, at least in its initial stages (which we might call 'primary grammaticalization', Kuryłowicz [1965] 1975: 52; Traugott 2002), word-class shifts from lexical status to grammatical status, but as I also made clear, such a characterization is really only valid at a level of some abstraction. I suggested instead that the focus of grammaticalization should really be at the construction level. Now, let us consider the verbal periphrasis *be fixin(g) to + verb* found in some varieties of American English, in order to provide a more in-depth investigation into the importance of the construction as the site of grammaticalization. The history of the lexical verb *fix* is complex and begins with several likely points of borrowing into English, first from Medieval Latin and later from French (Smith 2009: 12). From about the 15th century, the lexical meaning of *fix* as 'make immobile' is established, and in subsequent centuries, the verb develops several extended and metaphorical meanings, among which is the expression of intention, as shown in the 1788 citation from the *Oxford English Dictionary* in (12), cited in Smith (2009).

(12)   He fix'd with some eclat to come to TOWN[5]

While the development of an intention meaning is undoubtedly important in setting up the conditions under which *fix* will become involved in the grammatical changes reviewed below, it is not sufficient for such change. Note that the use of *fix* in (12) is still analysable as a lexical verb with an infinitival complement, *to come*, separated by an adverbial prepositional phrase, *with some eclat*. The reanalysis of a verb's lexical status into that of auxiliary will only occur with formal and semantic support from the kinds of constructions that the lexical item occurs in. In this case, it was the occurrence of intention meanings of *fix* in the progressive that also encouraged reanalysis of the construction. Consider the sentence in (13).

(13)   and I **was a-fixing**[6] to move the family down in the basement, when suddenly my wife, Mrs. Arp, says she to me (Bill Arp, From the University of North Carolina electronic collection, First Person Narratives of the American South, From the Uncivil War to Date 1961–1903, p. 107. Published 1903. Electronic version retrievable at https://docsouth.unc.edu/fpn/arp/arp.html).

In such progressive constructions, the statement of intention is expressed with a future-oriented inference reinforced by a following infinitival complement that sets up the goal of that future intention (and see Hopper & Traugott 2003: 3 for a similar scheme in the development of the *be going to* future).[7] However, inferred meaning alone was not enough to

---

[5] All cited material in this chapter retains the original graphology, some of which is quite idiosyncratic.

[6] The *a-* prefix on the *-ing* form is a reduced from of the preposition *on* (~*an*) used within an earlier locative expression type exemplified in *and hii funde þane king; þar he was an hontyng* 'and they found the king where he was hunting' (quoted in Smith 2007).

[7] Comrie (1976b: 64–65) considers *be going to* as expressing 'prospective aspect'. Here I follow Hopper & Traugott's (2003) analysis of the construction as a future; see also Bybee et al. 1994: 244).

transform lexical *fix* within this construction into a futurate auxiliary, and an important part of that reanalysis involved instances in which there was no intervening lexical material between the participle *fixing* and the infinitival marker *to* in the progressive construction (contrast the intervening adverbial between *fix'd* and *to* in (12), albeit not in a progressive construction). That syntactic contiguity of the sort just described is an important factor in grammatical reanalysis is supported by the fact that of the 14 earliest instances of the *fixing to* construction, collected from mostly 19th-century southern American English in Smith (2009), not a single token shows any intervening material between *fixing* and *to*. Thus, the goal expressed by the infinitival *to* comes to be associated with the intention meaning of *fix*, which, together with their frequent textual collocation, supports fusion, a point I will return to below. Once *to* becomes associated with *fix*, however, the lexical verb in the erstwhile infinitival complement is reanalysed as the main verb and *fixing to* as orienting that lexical verb in future time.

The auxiliary status for *fixing to* is pushed further along the path to futurity through its eventual use with inanimate subjects, for which the speaker/writer cannot know intentions. Consider the example in (14).

(14) Usually, when it was fixing to storm, Elijay's mother would shut herself away in her room (Corpus of Contemporary American English)

In (10), intention (and volition) on the part of the subject is absent, and in such cases, then, the utterance is understood as a statement of prediction, with *fixing to* as a future marker.

While the example in (14) show the full form of *be fixing to* in its use as a future marker (i.e. grammatical meaning), other instances show formal evidence of reanalysis of *fixing* + *to* into a futurate auxiliary as the participial form fuses with the infinitival *to*, a point already alluded to above. In many varieties of American English in which *fixin' to* is frequent, several phonologically reduced and fused variants appear, cf. [fɪksɪŋtu], [fɪksɪntə], [fɪʔna], [fɪsə], [fɪnə], of which perhaps [fɪnə] (most often spelled <finna>), associated mostly with varieties of African American English (AAE) (Green 2002: 70–71; Smith 2009), is most familiar.

Such instances of fusion and phonological reduction have long been identified with grammaticalization and the assumption has been that fusion is facilitated by the kind of reanalysis seen with *fixing to*, and analogously with *going to* resulting in reduced/fused forms such as *gonna*, and even its extremely reduced variant [ə], shown in (15).[8]

(15) '... ima [ɑɪmə] have to disagree with you here' (COCA)[9]

The role of reanalysis and the importance of focus on the construction as the site of grammaticalization is underscored by the relationship between the persistent instances of lexical sources alongside grammaticalizing formants. In such cases we speak of 'split' in which some uses of a lexical item become grammatical while others remain lexical (Heine & Reh 1984: 57,

---

[8] Again it is important to recognize that the fusion of the type reviewed here in English is not a regular feature of grammaticalization in non-fusional languages and necessitates some revision of the hypothesis concerning the correlation of the reduction of form-meaning as developed in Bybee et al. (1994); see also section 39.6.

[9] The spelling <ima> is in the original; the phonetic representation is the regular one for that spelling in American English.

referred to as 'divergence' in Hopper 1991: 22). Thus, (16) shows the persistent use of lexical *fix* in the very sense that is the likely source of the grammaticalized variant. *Fix* did not grammaticalize into an auxiliary verb; *fixing to* in a specific construction did.

(16)   'I rejoiced to see it, as my mind was constantly roving and could fix upon nothing steady.' (Corpus of Contemporary American English).

This relationship between phonological reduction and grammaticalization can be seen in those instances in which the reduced forms of a grammaticalizing construction consistently represent grammatical use. For example, reduced forms of *be going to* do not occur with the lexical sense of *go* as denoting movement in space, as illustrated in (17). Similarly, *finna* (and other reduced forms of *fixing to*) do not represent lexical meanings.

(17)   'I'm gonna call the post office later this morning.'
       * I'm gonna post office later this afternoon. (to mean, '*I am going to the post office this afternoon.*')

While reanalysis likely has something to do with the formal results to be observed in the cases of *be going to* and *be fixing to*, frequency has also been offered as an explanation for the kinds of reduction and fusion observed in such instances of grammaticalization (Bybee 2006). Certainly it is true that as such constructions become grammatical formants they increase in frequency, but as will be suggested in the next sections, it is not simply increased frequency per se that encourages reduction/fusion, but the greater frequency of the collocation of the specific parts of a construction that brings about that result, a position supported by comparing the very recent development of yet another future in American English from the construction *be trying to*.

39.4 TRYING TO: RENEWAL AND LAYERING

Hopper (1991: 22) defines layering as: '[w]ithin a broad functional domain, new layers are continually emerging. As this happens, the older layers are not necessarily discarded, but may remain to coexist with and interact with the newer layers.' This scenario is certainly true of the expressions for future meaning in certain varieties of American English which show in addition to the grammaticalization of *be going to* and *be fixing to*, another very recent auxiliary development by which the lexical verb *try*, also in a progressive construction, *be trying to* (> <tryna> /[tʃɹɑɪnə]), has begun to show signs of movement along a path of grammaticalization similar to that of other futures reviewed in this chapter. The grammaticalization of *be trying to* (*tryna*) begins with the lexical meaning of 'attempt', illustrated in (18).[10]

---

[10] Currently *tryna* is mostly associated with AAE, but it is important to note that many of the recently developed futures in AAE, like *finna* from *fixing to*, are shared with other varieties of English. This chapter does not pretend to be sociolinguistic in scope or purpose, but collection of data on *tryna* has underscored in my mind the need for much more research to determine the social patterns in the use of this new auxiliary.

(18)   'I'm tryna get at you' (2007-19)[11]

The lexical sense of *try* as 'attempt' in (14) is underscored by its collocation with an accomplishment verb, thus 'attempting at some goal.'

Tryna also shows uses in which it appears to have moved towards auxiliary verb-like status with meanings of desire, which Bybee et al (1994: 255) consider under agent-oriented modality (and see Krug 2000: 239), and intention, illustrated respectively in (19) and (20).

(19)   'If they not tryna pay these college athletes then the nba should let them come straight outta HS' (2019-3) (cf. if they don't want to ...)

In (19), desire emerges as the central meaning of *tryna* because the time orientation is future or general, expressing the blogger's desire in the general present. Such uses are felicitously paraphrased with *want to/wanna*.

(20)   'Fuck my trainer'
       'I'm tryna get a hot dog' (2011-20)

However, the lyric in (20), 'I'm tryna get a hot dog' is not about the literal attainment of food, but may be interpreted as the speaker's (rapper's) intention to disobey the edicts of his trainer (presumably to eat right) and his desire to eat a hot dog.

Instances in which *tryna* takes on a more centrally futurate meaning (prediction) can be seen in (21).

(21)   'You fuck around with me, you tryna dodge bullets' (2015-43)

In this instance, the speaker (rapper) states a future situation in the form of a threat in a cause–effect relationship, paraphrased roughly as 'if you do X, Y will happen'. Here we even note that the paraphrasing of *tryna* with another future expression, like *will* or *be going to* (i.e. *you are going to be dodging bullets*) is wholly felicitous, suggesting future meaning in the form of predicted outcome.

Thus *tryna*, perhaps within just the last 20 years or so, follows the well-established path in (22) (and see Bybee et al 1994: 255, Coates 1983, Dahl 1985, inter alia, who identify similar paths from cross-linguistic data), which overlaps with that given in (2) given at the beginning of the chapter.

(22)   DESIRE > WILLINGNESS > INTENTION > PREDICTION

Tryna also illustrates that is not necessary that a grammatical domain, like futurity, be completely abandoned or that older material expressing some grammatical meaning need even be very eroded, semantically speaking, before newly grammaticizing constructions emerge in that same domain, although it is expected that older and newer material will express different parts of meaning within that area.

---

[11] The numbering of *tryna* examples reflects the coding scheme in Smith (in preparation) in the creation of a database of such tokens taken from the internet mostly from sites posting rap lyrics. Thus, 2017-19 is the 19th instance in the database from the year 2017. The examples can be found through a Google search.

The layering of *tryna* into a domain in which several other futures already exist may then be viewed as part of the ongoing drift of the English VP towards periphrasis. In a humorous passage, Narrog (2017: 169) says, 'individual languages, figuratively speaking, often cannot seem to get enough of specific categories, while they don't care at all about grammaticalizing other categories'. The development of *tryna* into a future auxiliary certainly supports such a scenario of grammatical gluttony, and it has been suggested that the existence of a grammatical category at one stage of a language may predict subsequent linguistic renewal of that same category (Smith 2006; Narrog 2017; and see below). *Tryna* is also an interesting case because it shows the effects of frequency on this construction even before grammaticalization gets very much underway in that the fusion of the participle and infinitive seems to have occurred when much lexical value was still present, a point that underscores the gradualness of the process and challenges the notion of a strict lexical–grammatical divide, an often repeated conclusion from grammaticalization studies (see Boye & Harder 2012 for an elaborated view).

39.5 Frequency and Grammaticalization

In section 39.3, I made the point that the reduced forms of *going to* (*gonna*) and *fixing to* (*finna*) do not express the lexical meanings out of which the grammatical formants develop and contrariwise that full forms of those constructions are still available to signal grammatical meanings, suggesting that fusion/reduction accompanied the grammaticalization of those constructions and that, perhaps, reanalysis may well have played some mechanistic role in the subsequent phonological changes.

However, the relationship between *trying to* and its reduced form *tryna* shows a different scenario in that reduced forms of *trying to*, e.g. [tʃɹaɪnə], often show lexical meaning, that is, express the meaning of 'attempt'. A preliminary analysis of 101 tokens of *tryna* collected from mostly rap lyrics spanning the last 20 years shows 34 of them to have 'attempt' meanings (Smith in preparation). In addition, full forms of *trying to* appear never to express grammatical meaning, and certainly not the most grammaticalized meanings (e.g. future). This suggests that *trying to* underwent fusion very early, when uses of the construction were still largely lexical. The explanation for such early fusion likely has to do with frequency. In the COCA database, the particple *trying* occurs 328,911 times, with 295,848 instances followed by *to*. Of those occurrences with *to*, only 2,827 involve prepositional *to*, while 286,758 instances of *trying* are followed by infinitival *to*. Thus in comparison to the overall frequency of the participle *trying*, the likelihood of *trying* with an infinitival complement is much higher than any other form. Contrastively, the participle *going* appears a whopping 1,222,681 times in COCA, of which only 485,013 are followed by an infinitival *to* (and 28,436 by prepositional *to*), showing less likelihood of *go* + an infinitival *to* in proportion to the total instances of *going to* or even simple *going*. Likewise out of 8,721 instances of *fixing*, only 387 are followed by an infinitival *to* and only 9 by prepositional *to*, again showing a not very strong probability of *fixing to* + verb in the light of *fixing* in other kinds of constructions.

While the exact role of frequency is not fully understood in changes such as phonological reduction and fusion of contiguous material, transitional probability appears to be an important factor (Jurafsky, Bell, Gregory, & Raymond 2001), that is the predictability of X following Y. But, even if it turns out that *trying to* did fuse into *tryna* in such a way that frequency and transitional probability played a more significant role than syntactic reanalysis, that fact would present no threat to the theoretical position regarding the importance of both frequency and reanalysis in grammaticalization, and would again underscore the fact that both operate outside of grammaticalization as well. In the case of *be going to* and *be fixing to* reanalysis encouraged split from other instances of its source material, and its increased frequency as an emerging grammatical expression distanced those constructions even further from their sources such that they gained a degree of autonomy (Bybee 2003) and increased a speaker's predictability of specific collocations with specific meanings.

That frequency and reanalysis are important in grammaticalization is certain, and while grammaticalization provides an instructive framework for the study of individual cases, it does not predict such changes per se. In the concluding sections that follow, I elaborate on this same point as I attempt to situate grammaticalization within the larger picture of language change.

39.6 SITUATING GRAMMATICALIZATION IN CURRENT LINGUISTICS: SOME FINAL POINTS

As mentioned earlier, in the history of grammaticalization studies, some scholars have, from time to time, spoken of 'grammaticalization theory', which in turn has invoked rather vehement objection (e.g. Janda 2005: 47, quoted in Norde 2009: 33–34). I don't see any particular benefit in rehashing the full set of the arguments, but it is important to mention that even though the patterns of formal and semantic change seen to occur in the process of grammaticalization are very regular and very regular across languages, no feature of it is predictive. For example, we have seen earlier that some examples of grammaticalization in Spanish and English involve phonological reduction and morphological fusion, but neither is a necessary outcome of that process.

Bisang (2004: 110ff.) argues that due to the lack of obligatory categories (obligatoriness often taken to be definitional of 'grammatical', e.g. Lehmann 1985: 139ff.) and a 'weak correlation between the lexicon and morphosyntax' in East and mainland South East Asian languages, morphological paradigms of the kind seen in the Spanish future example earlier do not emerge, and thus we do not find the same kinds of fusional or reductive tendencies in those languages as a result of grammaticalization. For example, *zài* in Chinese may occur as a full verb, as in (23a), an adposition, as in (23b) or a progressive marker as in (23c) (examples from Bisang 2004: 117).

(23)   Chinese
    (a)   tā   zài   túshūgŭan
            s/he   be.at   library
            'S/He is at the library.'

(b) tā   zài   yīyuàn   sĭ-le
    s/he   COV: be.at hospital   die-TAM
    'S/He died at the hospital.'[12]

(c) tā   zài   chuān   pixie
    s/he   TAM:be.at   put.on   leather.shoe
    'S/He is putting on her/his leather shoes.'

Regardless of its use in what we may think of as lexical in (23a) or grammatical, as in (23b) or (23c), the form *zài* is the same; grammatical uses do not appear more reduced (e.g. contra *be fixing to~finna* discussed earlier),[13] underscoring the point that grammaticalization and its effects are not deterministic (and see Newmeyer 1998: 239), but better suited to accounts in which product-oriented schemas (Bybee 2001: 126) are applied to explain emergent linguistic structure (and see Hopper 1987 for an early formulation), which probably accounts for its greater popularity among scholars working within functionalist/cognitive frameworks (pace e.g. Roberts & Roussou 1999; Van Gelderen 2011). As we continue testing the hypotheses of grammaticalization on language and language types we may well find further constraints that refine what grammaticalization (and indeed grammar) look like in cross-linguistic perspective (Bisang & Malchukov 2020) and within larger explanations/models of language change (Traugott & Trousdale 2013) and language structuration (Bybee 2010).

One exciting direction of future research, and one suggested earlier in this chapter, is whether and to what degree the inventory of existing grammatical categories attract additional lexical items to grammaticalize within the same (or closely related) domain. Narrog (2017: 169ff.) cites Chafe's (2000: 29) description of florescence in this regard to describe the proliferation of grammatical forms within a certain domain of a language. The multilayered expressions of *gonna*, *finna*, and *tryna* discussed above certainly suggest such a 'florescence' in those varieties of English in which they occur.

However, *tryna* also participates in a cluster of very similar formal developments in English in that it joins a list of lexical verbs in *-ing* that have fused with infinitival complements, i.e. *gonna, finna, wanna*.[14] Interestingly we also saw that such fusion in the case of *tryna* was precipitous, occurring quite early in its grammaticalization into a modal or future meaning. One hypothesis is that the prior existence of a cluster of similar constructions with future/modal meanings attracted *trying to* into that cluster, thus supporting specific formal developments within it. Such an explanation would also account for *hoping to*, which in casual speech may appear as [hoʊpɪnə], showing the same fusional tendencies as *gonna, wanna, finna, tryna*. While certainly already interesting as a fact of the history of English, it awaits much more cross-linguistic testing to see whether similar patterns of formal florescence might accompany grammatical florescence within specific languages (or language families/types).

---

[12] Quoted from Li & Thompson (1981: 221).

[13] It is also worth noting that according to Bisang (2004: 134), the lack of obligatory grammatical categories in such languages mitigates an increase in frequency.

[14] And consider non *-ing* forms that also show fusion with an infinitival complement and express some degree of TAM information in English: *wanna*, *liketa* (>like to), *gotta*, etc.

CHAPTER 40

WORD CLASSES IN FIRST LANGUAGE ACQUISITION

SABINE STOLL

40.1 INTRODUCTION

THE question of how infants categorize words takes centre stage in acquisition research. The reason for this is that word classes are the building blocks for a productive and creative use of syntactic structures. Composition and recursion are key in fuelling the creative power of language. A key aspect of this is our ability to substitute elements in syntactic structures. Take a simple sentence like 'The lake is green': we can substitute *lake* with *house* or *apple* etc., and this holds true for all the other word classes in this sentence as well. Using structure and being able to substitute words or linguistic units of the same category makes the human communication system so productive and creative. In other words, syntax is so potent because we can exchange the words of the same syntactic category and still create utterances that are immediately understood.

Given the importance of word classes, research on their acquisition, i.e. on how children generalize them, is of critical importance: do children have innate knowledge of word classes, independent of the target language? If yes, how do they build up language-specific categories under the constraints of innate parameters? Or are domain-general cognitive mechanisms—such as statistical learning or generalization abstraction—enough to explain this categorization process? This has been a long and ongoing dispute in acquisition research. However, innateness is usually underspecified and used in very diverse ways (Levinson 2003; Mameli & Bateson 2006). In response to this, it seems more promising to focus on empirical questions and testable hypotheses.

Empirical evidence shows that the process of generalization is slow and item-based, at least initially. Soon after producing their first words, around their first birthday, children start combining them to express new meaning. Initially, these combinations are very rudimentary and restricted to a confined number of constructions (Tomasello 1992; Lieven et al. 1997; Theakston et al. 2002; Tomasello 2003). Subsequently, they start to vary individual words within constructions, usually substituting them with words from the same word class e.g. 'want cookie, want milk, want teddy' (Lieven et al. 1997). This substitution process can be seen as the first step towards generalizing word classes. Only after accumulating a number of such constructions, do children move beyond individual combinations, learn their regularities, and end up being able to freely combine words and phrases into clauses and sentences. To get there, they need to extract patterns from the input to learn about the regularities behind possible substitutions. Only when children go beyond individual substitutions and use word classes in a construction-independent way, do we actually have empirical evidence for their full productive knowledge of word classes.

The acquisition of word classes has been the subject of a large amount of research, focusing both on the cognitive underpinnings of the learning process and the grammatical challenges individual languages provide. In this chapter, I mainly focus on the two major word classes: nouns and verbs. Nouns and verbs have been the focus of attention since they contribute largely to making language the powerful tool that it is.

The goal of the present chapter is to review the advances in research on the acquisition of nouns and verbs including studies on as wide a range of languages as possible. The chapter is structured as follows: section 40.2 reviews the cognitive preconditions, and discusses the theoretical assumptions underlying the categorization process. Section 40.3 focuses on category abstraction and what we actually know about when it happens. Here I focus mainly on experimental evidence. In section 40.4, I discuss the challenges provided by typologically diverse languages to survey the factors that can be involved in word-class categorization. In section 40.5, I ask how all this diversity can be learned. The ability to cope with such extreme variation as encountered in the languages of the world suggests that the learning process relies fundamentally on recurrent patterns and frequency distributions in the input. I present some potentially universal, recurrent patterns which would allow successful statistical learning. In section 40.6, I address the question how nouns and verbs are learned in typologically diverse contexts. Finally, Section 40.7 presents an outlook on future research.

40.2 Cognitive preconditions for category abstraction: Theoretical assumptions

A range of linguistic (e.g. Langacker 1987; Jackendoff 1992; Croft 2001; Talmy 2000), perception (Zacks et al. 2007) production (Levelt 1993), and developmental theories (Lakusta & Landau 2012; Ünal et al. 2021) assume a prelinguistic and universal conceptualization mechanism grounded in event cognition. The exact innate features of this mechanism are widely disputed across acquisition theories. What seems to be clear is that at least some species-wide event conceptualization potential has to be assumed if we want to explain the human ability to learn any language. Croft (2001) mentions three building blocks of human language as innate candidates: reference, predication, and modification. He assumes that this innate blueprint of event conceptualization corresponds to arguments, predicates, and modifiers in utterances, linguistically commonly expressed as nouns, verbs, and adjectives (Braine 1976; Maratsos 1988; Croft 2001). Conceptualization is thus taken to be mirrored in linguistic structure with nouns, verbs, and adjectives as universal categories (Croft (2001), but see section 40.2 on the universality of these categories).

With the exception of the most radical exemplar approaches, as advocated for instance by Ambridge (2017, 2020b; but see Ambridge 2020a for a reconsideration of this position), most theories of language acquisition (e.g. Valian 1986; Mintz 2002; Tomasello 2003) assume that abstract word classes are basic and actually a prerequisite of compositionality. The cognitive status of word classes, however, has been hotly debated and theories vary widely in the underlying mechanisms they assume. The main dispute is whether word classes are largely innate and their language-specific realization is constrained by innate principles and parameters of universal grammar (Chomsky 1981; Pinker 1984; Baker 2002), or whether they are only an epiphenomenon of general cognitive mechanisms such as statistical learning, associative learning, and abstraction (Braine 1987; Lieven et al. 1997; Mintz 2002; Tomasello 2003).

Theories which assume an innate set of word classes need to solve what is known as the linking problem. This means they need to provide evidence for how infants link the innate concepts with the idiosyncratic word classes and cues provided in their individual languages. A number of solutions have been proposed to solve this linking problem, relying on semantic or syntactic processes (Pinker 1984; Valian 1991, 2014). The semantic bootstrapping theory assumes semantic information as the motor in this linking process (Grimshaw 1981; Pinker 1984, 1987). The underlying assumption of this approach is that infants learn about the referential information of individual lexical items (e.g. verbs referring to actions). Cross-situational repetitions of this information then triggers the linking process with the innate categories. In the syntactic bootstrapping account the linking to innate categories is driven by syntactic distributions (see e.g. Gleitman 1990). Here children are hypothesized to mainly rely on regularities in word order and argument structure. Under this account, it remains unspecified how infants detect the relevant units without prior generalization of individual target language units.

Under either of these bootstrap accounts, the main reasoning behind the assumption of innate word classes is that children are unable to build up word classes on the basis of distributional cues alone because the input is notoriously underspecified. This assumption has not gone without challenges. For example, distributional cues alone have shown to be sufficient for children to build up the word classes of their native languages (Maratsos 1988; Braine 1992; Gómez & Gerken 2000; Naigles 2002). In line with this, empirical research suggests a domain general statistical learning mechanism which relies exclusively on language-specific distributional patterns. Such a general learning mechanism can account for category formation without necessitating any innate linguistic universals or rules. This general cue-detection mechanism allows for a slow generalization process that results in language-specific categories. The process is hypothesized to rely on a plethora of different correlational cues, including phonological (Gerken 1996; Kelly 1996; Shi et al. 1999; Monaghan et al. 2005, 2007), morphophonological (Gerken et al. 2005), morphological (Gerken 2001; Golinkoff et al. 2001), positional (Mintz 2003a, 2003b; Moran et al. 2018), prosodic (Gleitman et al. 1988), and semantic cues (Culbertson et al. 2019).

40.3 Category abstraction: When and how?

Being able to generalize word classes requires the ability of abstract categorization. A first step in understanding word-class categorization, therefore, is to find out whether and when infants are able to categorize.

Categorization involves the ability to extract form–category correlations from the input. Thus, infants need to be able to focus on cue correlations that then lead to generalizations and category formation (Braine 1987). Braine (1987) provided preliminary evidence that infants can form categories, first relying on either referential or other semantic cues and then generalizing this knowledge to previously unseen instances that exhibit these cues. Gómez & Lakusta (2004) tested this ability in 12-month-olds in an artificial language learning experiment. They showed that infants are capable of cue-based categorizations of nouns and verbs relying on probabilistic distributions of features. Infants were able to discriminate between legal and illegal marker–feature pairings, generalizing form–meaning correlations to novel test items in their syntactic environment. This shows that young infants are indeed able to categorize based on distributional features in their input. The most interesting result of this study is that this ability was not compromised under noisy conditions where only probabilistic correlations of markers were provided. In other words, children were able to disregard unreliable, infrequent cues and concentrate on the predominant patterns. This is an extremely important finding because it corresponds to the naturalistic learning environment, which is full of inconsistencies the learner has to be able to cope with. However, the categorization ability seems to develop with age and, presumably, is not yet fully in place at 12 months, i.e. their sensitivity to co-occurrence relations is not yet adult-like.

However, can infants categorize without relying on referential information? It turns out that children at age 1.5 years are able to do so by using distributional cues exclusively. Gerken et al. (2005) showed that 1.5-year-olds were able to make generalizations distinguishing grammatical from ungrammatical items of a foreign language without relying on referential information. This suggests that at that age the categorization process is already well developed and can rely on distributional information provided by the surrounding speech. There is convergent evidence that infants are able to extract cues and generalize them in a lab setting (see below). But when are children productive in their use of nouns and verbs? When do they go beyond the individual verb forms they have rote-learned?

In a number of experiments Tomasello and Olguin tested the productive use of novel nouns and verbs in 2-year-olds (Olguin & Tomasello 1993; Tomasello & Olguin 1993; Tomasello 2000). The goal was to find out whether children were able to apply novel words in spontaneous speech beyond the forms they have heard before. They found that nouns are generalized earlier than verbs. Children at age 23 months learning English as their native tongue were able to use nouns productively in new contexts (Tomasello & Olguin 1993). Most of the nouns tested in this experiment could be interpreted as proper names, and so far it is unresolved whether the findings also extend to other nouns. Even 25-month-old children, however, had difficulties in generalizing verbs and applying them productively to new contexts as tested in a similar experiment with verbs (see also Tomasello et al. 1997 for an experiment comparing the generalization of nouns and verbs in slightly younger children, age between 1;6-1;11). Findings by Akhtar & Tomasello (1997) showed that children up to age 3 are conservative in their production, using always the same argument frame, i.e. using the same word order with respect to agent and patient when confronted with novel verbs. Fisher (2002) supports these findings for comprehension.

The influence of the experimental settings on results, however, deserves some further exploration, as suggested in a study by Waxman et al. (2009). In contrast to the findings of Tomasello et al. (1997), Waxman and colleagues show that 24-month-old English learning infants can understand and distinguish both nouns and verbs in an experimental settings.

Infants were presented with dynamic scenes, and they were able to map verbs to events and nouns to objects.

Learning requirements might also be subject to cross-linguistic variation. A comprehension study with novel verbs by Arunachalam et al. (2013) testing 24-month-old Korean infants, takes a step into this direction. They show that the contexts in which nouns and verbs are learned differ across languages. Korean learning infants understand verbs better in linguistically sparser contexts, i.e. when arguments are omitted, as it is typically the case in Korean. The opposite holds for 24-month-old English learning infants who learned the verb meaning only in a richer linguistic context, i.e. when the verb is embedded in a lexical noun phrase indicating the referents of the event (Arunachalam & Waxman 2011). This shows that language-specific conditions can vary quite substantially, and infants learn better in contexts they are used to. In the following we look a bit more closely at the language-specific challenges, as they are exhibited across typologically diverse languages.

40.4 CHALLENGES IN DETECTING AND CATEGORIZING WORD CLASSES

Everything in human language needs to be learned: from phonemes and words to word classes, not to mention the combinatorics of these units. Learning word classes involves several steps, ranging from the detection and memorization of individual elements or units to the generalization of specific features of these units, ultimately leading to abstract categorization. The expression of linguistic units and categories, including the expression of word classes, however, varies enormously in the languages of the world. Yet children can learn any of them. This suggests that the underlying cognitive learning mechanism to detect these units must be highly flexible. It needs to be able to adapt to the diverse categorizations in the languages of the world.

So, how do children then actually generalize? The linking of language-specific word classes with underlying semantic notions such as objects, actions, and properties has been debated widely. There is wide consensus that even though semantics might be an initial facilitator in the word-class categorization process, morphosyntax provides more reliable linguistic cues (Maratsos 1988; Lieven et al. 1997; Croft 2001).

Typological research, however, has shown that there is huge variation in how the languages of the world realize word classes (see Chapter 2 in this volume). There seems to be a continuum of how languages express referents and predicates. Some languages clearly differentiate between nouns and verbs, others allow for some conversion for a few exemplars, others allow for free conversions and still others do not make a difference at all (Peterson 2010).

Languages which make a difference between nouns and verbs differ on a number of dimensions such as the number of category members and their formal expression. The number of actual members in the noun or verbs category differs strongly across languages. Some languages have only a very small number of verbs and rely on light verbs such as for instance the Mayan languages (De León 1999), while others have a very large inventory of verbs expressing intricate semantics (e.g. European languages).

Languages also exhibit extreme variation on the morphosyntactic level in how they express nouns and verbs. Usually, nouns are morphologically less complex than verbs, with verbs exhibiting more forms and grammatical information. To illustrate the range of variation, let us have a look at the two extremes of languages with respect to morphological marking, namely polysynthetic languages and analytic languages.

An example of a polysynthetic language is Chintang, a Sino-Tibetan language spoken in Eastern Nepal. Chintang has an extensive verbal paradigm. Each verb form is a complex composition of several affixes selected from a pool of 124 affixes. This results in a large number of verb forms, adding up to over 4,000 forms (Stoll et al. 2017). The Chintang noun paradigm is much less complex with 15 cases (Schikowski 2013) adding up to around 30 forms. Thus, verbs in Chintang are morphologically very different from nouns. The key learning challenge in this language consists in the generalization process of forms across stems. Children will hear each verb stem only in a restricted number of forms, and so the big question is how they generalize the grammatical marking of a specific stem to other stems. More generally, what are the underlying processes leading to verb categorization and paradigm building? Chintang is very transparent in its inflectional system, and this might help the learner (Stoll 2015). Children seem to be close to adult performance in their use of verb and noun forms by around age 3;6 (Stoll et al. 2012). However, there are other polysynthetic languages, such as Dëne (Athabaskan), with very opaque morphology (Cook 2004). Here, the generalization process from one stem to the other is even more complex, and here morphophonological generalizations would be key. Or, take, for instance, Archi (Nakh Dagestanian), for which more than one and a half million forms per verb are reported Kibrik (1998). Coping with such a system and learning it by merely extracting forms from the surrounding speech and generalizing the paradigm seems to be a task that goes beyond imagination. Whether learning these systems takes much longer than, say, learning English, or even Russian, is unclear so far. But we know that it is mastered by native speakers in their early years of development. There is some evidence, however, that very untransparent and irregular morphology can contribute to later acquisition. Blount (1988) found that in Luo (Nilotic, Kenya) some parts of the noun category namely plural marking are not learned before age 14. Whether this translates to the conceptualization of the category noun as a whole, however, is still unknown.

At the other end of the continuum are languages with impoverished morphology like English. In English, not many forms are to be learned, neither for nouns nor for verbs, and, in most cases, the word class is detectable from word order. But another complication arises: word classes are often fluid, words like *dispute, call, love, house*, to name only a few examples, can be used as nouns or verbs, depending on the context. Here, a child needs to learn to interpret identical forms in different contexts. Sometimes in these fluid forms there are phonological cues such as different stress that help in the categorization process, but this is not always the case. The generalization process of nouns and verbs in a language like English seems quite different from that in polysynthetic language. The task for English children is to generalize the same form to many contexts. By contrast, Chintang children are confronted with a one-to-one mapping of thousands of situations, with one form being used only for a very specific context as specified by grammatical markers providing important information on tense, aspect, spatial orientation, mood, person, number, etc.

However, variation gets even more extreme, as there are some languages, for which actually no categorical distinction is made between nouns and verbs, such as Strait Salish or

Kharia (Jelinek & Demers 1994; Peterson 2010). In Kharia for instance, the only formal distinction is between contentive morphemes and functional morphemes. Contentive morphemes can be used as referents, predicates, or adjectives (Peterson 2010), as specified by specific functional morphemes. The learning strategies and the underlying event conceptualizations in languages like Kharia seem again to be quite different from those of either English or Chintang. Do children who learn languages without a noun–verb distinction conceptualize referents and events differently from children who learn a language with separate categories? What seems to be clear is that children learning a language without such a distinction need to make different linguistic generalizations, since every content morpheme can take a different function depending on the context. Unfortunately, we neither know about the event conceptualization nor the linking to word classes of adult speakers of such languages. Neither do we know how learners behave in such a language. This remains a pressing question for future research.

These few examples illustrate that the challenges for learners in generalizing word classes vary extremely across languages. To understand how these word classes are learned within and beyond individual languages requires rigorous cross-linguistic research including as wide a range of word-class variation as possible (Stoll & Bickel 2013).

The main question in the acquisition of word classes is: how can all this diversity be learned? The ability to cope with such extreme variation suggests that the learning process relies fundamentally on recurrent patterns and frequency distributions in the input. It seems that most languages exhibit recurrent markers or patterns of the members of word classes or their surrounding elements which would allow such a statistical learning process to be successful. Thus, for the learner, patterns, and this includes phonological, prosodic, morphological, and syntactic regularities or cues, are key for extracting/generalizing categories from the individual words encountered in her native language. This is what I turn to in the following.

40.5 Patterns in the Input Infants Use to Generalize Nouns and Verbs

Nouns and verbs—or other word classes for that matter—are often not explicitly marked as such by grammatical morphemes. Thus, the identification of word classes usually relies on a complex correlational pattern-detection process provided by distributions of the members of the word classes and their surrounding units. There are two types of information that children can rely on in this process, called 'internal' and 'external' information by Monaghan et al. (2007): (i) internal information is the information provided by the word itself such as the presence of specific morphemes, prosodic, or phonological information; and (ii) external information is provided by the distribution of the immediate context in the utterance, such as the position of the unit. An additional yet under-researched type of external information is the extralinguistic presence of cues, i.e. semantic and referential information provided in situative contexts relying on the correlational patterns of these cues (Monaghan et al. 2007; You et al. 2021).

With respect to internal information, there are a number of language-specific acoustic patterns such as stress (Kelly 1988) and length (Cassidy & Kelly 2001) that could support children in the categorization process. Patterns of stress differ systematically in English nouns and verbs, and length is also a reliable cue. Nouns were found to be longer than verbs (Cassidy & Kelly 2001). Shi et al. (1999) showed that even newborns are sensitive to acoustic and phonological cues in distinguishing lexical from grammatical words. This shows that they take statistical phonological regularities into account. Shi and colleagues suggest that these abilities might be the perceptual basis for later categorization of grammatical categories. In a subsequent study on the acquisition of nouns and verbs in French children, Shi & Melançon (2010) found that 14-month-olds could categorize novel nouns but not verbs. Further, Gómez & Lakusta (2004) in an artificial language study on 12-month-old infants provide evidence that first steps in category abstraction are in place.

Regarding the categorization process itself, an experimental study by Gerken et al. (2005) suggests that children as young as 1;5 years can generalize a noun paradigm of a language unknown to them without relying on semantic cues. However, the relation and combination of cues still remains to be studied in more detail. In cross-linguistic research on the phonological factors of English, Dutch, French, and Japanese, Monaghan et al. (2007) found that both phonological and semantic cues interact. They conclude that the linguistic environment provides systematic cues, i.e. in this case the categorization of nouns and verbs benefits both from auditory and distributional cues. In a comparative study on the acquisition of word classes in Turkish and Mandarin (Shi et al. 1998) suggest that there are a number of overlapping phonetic cues that allow for a distinction between functional and lexical units. Interestingly, studies on adults using artificial language learning paradigms indicate that learning word classes was facilitated by the presence of a number of interrelated rules rather than only a single rule (Billman 1989). Related results were obtained by Monaghan et al. (2005) who provided evidence from an artificial language learning experiment that frequency was an important factor in determining which cue was more useful for category detection. For high-frequency non-words distributional cues were key, whereas for low-frequency items phonological information was more reliably used.

With respect to external cues, syntactic cues, such as the number of arguments in a sentence, seem to support verb learning (Fisher 2002). Further, as proposed by Maratsos & Chalkley (1980), the repetitive occurrence of the same adjacent words can serve as a cue for word categorization. Cartwright & Brent (1997) propose an incremental categorization of word classes based on distributional features, such as reoccurring bigrams in the input. A further pattern that has shown to be helpful for noun and verb categorization are frequent frames (Mintz 2002, 2003a). Frequent frames are repetitive patterns of linguistic units that frame an element, e.g. in *I like you*, the framed element is the verb, and the frame is what surrounds it: *I ... you*. If it is frequent, this frame readily predicts a verb, and a noun would not fit. Frequent frames have also been found on the morpheme level in typologically extremely diverse languages, and again they allow ready differentiation of nouns vs verbs (Moran et al. 2018). A further external pattern are pauses. In a recent cross-linguistic study of nine typologically diverse languages, Seifart et al. (2018) show a universal tendency of more pauses and slower articulation before nouns than before verbs. Seifart and colleagues suggest that this is an indicator of different processing demands imposed by nouns and verbs. The presence of such consistent patterns provides counterevidence for theories claiming that the input is too chaotic for children to extract grammar (Chomsky 1959; Pinker 1989).

The presence of such repetitive external cues or patterns, however, does not yet provide evidence that they are actually used by the learner. It is worth pointing out that the demonstration of pattern detection and generalization abilities in experiments does not necessarily translate to the use of these abilities in the naturalistic learning environment. There is some evidence, however, that infants actually make use of such patterns. In a recent study on the role of pauses and articulation before nouns and verbs in Chintang we found that these differences extend to both child-directed and child speech (Lester et al. 2019).

Further, Braine (1976) claims that children rely on a number of repetitive frames in their input in which specific words occur and then generalize across these patterns. Support for this approach was provided for instance by a longitudinal study on the acquisition of the English verb *go* and its various verb forms. Theakston et al. (2002) show that initially infants do not operate with a general understanding of the verb *go* but rather advance their knowledge in a step-by-step procedure of learning diverse constructions involving diverse verb forms of *go*. Even for an individual verb, there is no initial generalization; instead, children's understanding of different verb forms is rather restricted to individual constructions. Relations between these constructions were found to be a function of their frequency of occurrence.

40.6 Nouns or verbs: What's first and why?

This question has taken centre stage in research on the acquisition of word classes. The hope is to get insights into the underlying mechanisms of early language learning, potentially contributing to the bigger question: is language acquisition guided by universal principles or is it rather shaped by the structures of individual languages and social contexts? But why is it specifically the question about the lexical categories nouns and verbs that is relevant? The underlying reasoning is that the type and the use of early words can potentially provide insights into (i) early human event conceptualization as they relate to referents and predicates and (ii) the first steps into grammar development, i.e. argument structure and phrase structure.

Observations in a number of languages led to a long-standing dispute about whether nouns have a privileged position in early acquisition (Gentner 1982, 2006; Macnamara 1982; Gillette et al. 1999; Gentner & Boroditsky 2001). Supported by early findings in a cross-linguistic study of typologically unrelated languages (English, German, Kaluli, Mandarin, Japanese, and Turkish; Gentner 1982) collected with different methods, some have argued for a universal early noun preference. This noun bias was grounded in the assumption that nouns relate to more observable and concrete concepts which are more conducive to learning (Gentner 1982; Gentner & Boroditsky 2001; Gleitman et al. 2005; Golinkoff & Hirsh-Pasek 2008). Others have conjectured that this early noun preference correlates with the imageability of a word (McDonough et al. 2011). Verbs in this line of argumentation are taken to express events that are less observable or at least need more abstraction and relation to referents. This is taken as the reason for why verbs have been claimed to be more difficult to learn. This hypothesis has been proved to be too strong, however.

First, it has been shown that a large proportion of the nouns in the input to young English learning infants are not as concrete as it might seem; 40% of nouns in the input were found to denote non-concrete objects such as for instance 'morning' or 'kiss' (Nelson et al. 1993). This suggests that the underlying assumptions of Gentner's hypothesis about the concreteness of nouns would need some more empirical analyses of the actual use of nouns in the input to infants and their own use.

Second, to gain insight into early event conceptualization, it is useful to look at the very first words children utter. Here it turns out that nouns and verbs are not the only word class in early verbal communication. From early on, children use a wide range of non-referential words (Gopnik 1988; Kauschke & Hofmeister 2002). Further evidence comes from a systematic cross-linguistic study by Tardif et al. (2008) on English, Mandarin, and Cantonese using a questionnaire on the first ten words children use. Here, indeed, an early preference for a very specific type of nouns, namely kin terms was found in the three languages. However, inspecting object words and verbs in this very early phase of vocabulary acquisition, Tardif and colleagues found significant variation across these languages, i.e. not a clear preference for nouns. Even though most studies using questionnaires seem to suggest an early noun preference, this is not true for all languages. For children learning Ngas, a Chadic language spoken in Nigeria, Childers et al. (2007) do not report an early noun preference. In this language, an early verb preference in comprehension and no preference in production was observed (Childers et al. 2007). Similar results were obtained in a cross-linguistic study by Bornstein et al. (2004) studying the first 50 words of children learning seven different languages (English, Dutch, Spanish, French, Italian, Korean, Hebrew). Bornstein and colleagues did not find an overall early preferred usage of nouns. These results show that there is no universal noun preference in the earliest phase of vocabulary development. It rather seems that both pragmatic and language-specific factors determine distributions in early development. From an ontogenetic and pragmatic point of view, using names as an entry point into languages makes a lot of sense. The interaction with caretakers is the first and most important situation infants encounter and reference to caretakers is crucial. In fact, this early naming preference might be one of the few ontogenetic universals of early language development.

A third issue is how nouns and verbs are distributed in children's daily usage. The distribution of object words and verbs in the early vocabulary is expected to be influenced by the grammatical structures of individual languages and different cultural practices in talking to children. To understand early grammar development, it is exactly these distributions we need to learn more about, and they can be best studied in naturalistic data. For a wide range of languages such as French (Bassano et al. 1998; Bassano 2000), Wichi (Taverna & Waxman 2020), Chintang (Stoll et al. 2012), German (Kauschke & Hofmeister 2002) to name just a few, a higher noun-to-verb ratio was found in the production of children's early language. For other languages, there is conflicting evidence, for instance, Korean (Choi 1993, 1995) shows no preference for either nouns or verbs. Others still show a preference for verbs, as for instance Mandarin (Tardif 1996; Tardif et al. 1997), Tzeltal (Brown 1998), and Ttzotzil (de Léon 1999). Potential reasons for variation have been discussed extensively on a theoretical level (Gentner 1982; Waxman et al. 2013) focusing on saliency issues and cultural differences in talking to children. One feature, namely morphology, which is most susceptible to statistical learning, however, has been widely neglected in most studies. Stoll et al. (2012) hypothesized that morphology plays a key role for the asynchronic learning of nouns vs verbs. Both in Chintang and in Wichi, noun morphology is markedly simpler than verbal morphology (as in most languages in the world), and in both languages, verbs are more frequent in the input than nouns (Stoll et al. 2012; Taverna & Waxman 2020). Concomitantly with this, children in both languages show an early noun bias. Interestingly, both in Chintang (Stoll et al. 2012) and in Wichi (Taverna & Waxman 2020) the transition to the adult patterns correlates with morphological development.

40.7 Outlook

One of the main challenges in language acquisition research is to identify the underlying generalization processes which precondition productivity. Word classes are key in this process and nouns and verbs have been the main focus of attention here. There has been considerable progress in the last decades on how infants categorize word classes. Here I have focused on nouns and verbs since they have taken centre stage in most discussions of universal acquisition strategies. Adjectives and adverbs, however, are extremely relevant as well for our understanding of the acquisition of word classes. They play the key role in modification, one of the three core components of event conceptualization and cognition. Thus, in the future, we might want to put adjectives and adverbs more centre stage to get a broader picture about the interrelation of event conceptualization and word classes. However, this was beyond the focus of the present chapter.

Recent research has shifted in focus from a dispute about the linking problem to questions of what word classes children learn first and/or are productive with first. Even though there might be some universal tendencies there is considerable variation cross-linguistically. In most languages studied so far, children start out with nouns, but there are exceptions. These are actually the interesting cases. Studies on a typological large variety of languages such as Ngas (Childers et al. 2007), Mandarin (Tardif et al. 2008), and data provided in a large-scale cross-linguistic study by Bornstein et al. (2004) show that universal claims about a noun bias are more a tendency than a general rule. These studies illustrate a cross-linguistic variation in the acquisition process triggered by a multitude of possible factors such as variation in morphosyntax, input distributions, and cross-cultural interaction patterns.

This strongly suggests that we need a more fine-grained approach to take all these factors into our analyses rather than focusing on only one of them at a time. To do so, it might be useful to move away from questionnaires for these questions. Results on a noun bias can be strongly influenced by the method and the data we use (Stoll et al. 2012). Studies relying on questionnaires have often found a noun bias, this, however, could be partly due to the preponderance of nouns in questionnaires such as the MacArthur-Bates Communicative Development Inventories (MCDI) (Fenson et al. 1993).

These considerations suggest that there are potential biases which are not only induced by linguistic or cultural features but also by methodological choices. Only a multimethod approach will avoid such pitfalls.

Now that we have established that learning strategies vary significantly not only as a function of linguistic and cultural contexts but also as a function of methodological choices, it is high time to move away from simple questions of what is learned first. It is much more promising to dive into the question of how these factors actually interact in the learning process. Here naturalistic cross-linguistic data from as many languages as possible are key if we want to go beyond insights on the acquisition processes in individual languages.

CHAPTER 41

WORD CLASSES IN SECOND LANGUAGE ACQUISITION

SETH LINDSTROMBERG
AND FRANK BOERS

41.1 INTRODUCTION

IN this chapter, we examine the influence of word class—or, equivalently, part of speech—on the learnability of vocabulary in a second language, where the term learnability refers to how quickly and accurately a hitherto unfamiliar vocabulary item can be understood, remembered, and integrated into the lexicon of a second or foreign language (L2) learner. We focus here on post-childhood language learners (see Chapter 40 in this volume on first language acquisition) and our discussion of second language learning applies as well to additional languages that one might be learning (L3, L4, . . .).

We will first consider variables besides word class per se that may co-determine the learnability of L2 vocabulary items. It is necessary to examine these other variables because, as we shall see, when they are included in analyses of differential learning outcomes for words belonging to different word classes, an effect initially attributed to word class often shrinks or even disappears. This in fact led one authority in the field of second language vocabulary research already in the 1990s to suggest that word class is a factor 'with no clear effect' (Laufer 1997a: 154; see also Peters 2020). After reviewing the available literature decades later, we still have to concur with this assertion. So, before we evaluate research studies that appear to furnish evidence for independent word-class effects on the learnability of L2 vocabulary, let us briefly discuss some of these other variables, particularly ones that are likely to be unequally associated with the various word classes (e.g. nouns vs verbs vs adjectives) and which may therefore complicate detection of an effect of word class as such.

41.2 WORD-RELATED VARIABLES (OTHER THAN WORD CLASS) THAT AFFECT L2 WORD LEARNABILITY

Researchers of lexical processing and lexical memory have investigated a substantial number of potentially influential word-related variables (e.g. Rubin 1980; Taylor, Beith, & Sereno 2019). Among these are several that seem to be important in second language vocabulary acquisition. We begin with variables of meaning. The first of these is imageability, defined as the degree to which the referent of a lexical item is imageable. The imagery involved may be visual, motoric, or of some other perceptual modality. A related semantic dimension is concreteness, that is, the degree of physicality of what a lexical item refers to. Like imageability, concreteness is grounded in perception. Both are associated with open class words more than closed class words, with nouns showing the greatest tendency to be imageable and concrete; and both variables are strongly associated with greater learnability (e.g. Ellis & Beaton 1993; Tonzar, Lotto, & Job 2009; Pichette, De Serres, & Lafontaine 2012; Mestres-Missé, Münte, & Rodriguez-Fornells 2014). Concreteness and imageability are so highly correlated—$r \approx .80$ to $.90$, depending on the sample of vocabulary—that many researchers have used one or the other as a stand-in for both or have used the terms interchangeably (e.g. de Groot & Keijzer 2000).

Another semantic variable that may co-determine L2 vocabulary learnability is animacy, that is, the degree to which a word is understood as referring to a living rather than a non-living entity or substance. For example, VanArsdall, Nairne, Pandeirada, & Cogdill (2015) examined the learnability of Swahili–English pseudo translation equivalents (TEs) of nouns which had been assigned either animate or inanimate referents, and they found that the former were easier to learn. It is likely that the relevance of distinguishing living from non-living entities is deeply entrenched in human cognition (for instance, our prehistoric ancestors' survival must have depended on it).

Yet another meaning dimension, (emotional) valence, concerns the degree to which a word is felt to be pleasing, neutral, or displeasing (e.g. Kousta, Vigliocco, Vinson, Andrews & Del Campo 2011; Warriner, Kuperman, & Brysbaert 2013). For example, Ayçiçeği & Harris (2004) found that the learnability of L2 vocabulary is enhanced by extreme positive or negative valence (or arousal effects). As to word class, there is some evidence that the emotional content of adjectives and verbs is processed with more sustained attention than is the case for nouns, and that nouns are used to express emotional states or events less often than verbs and adjectives (Citron 2012). While imageability and concreteness are now often taken into consideration in studies on L2 vocabulary acquisition, this does not (yet) hold true for the other semantic variables just discussed.

It is worth noting that experiments on word learning almost invariably present participants with pairings of one word and one meaning. However, polysemy (and, to a lesser extent, homonymy) is very common in language and may pose additional challenges for learners (Hashimoto & Egbert 2019), not only owing to the fact that the various form–meaning pairings of a polyseme need to be acquired, but also because learners often mistakenly assume that a word they encounter in discourse has the meaning they have already learned for it, despite contextual clues to the contrary (Bensoussan & Laufer 1984). It stands to reason that some meanings of a polyseme or homophone will be easier to learn than others, because they may be more imageable or concrete (e.g. *board* in the sense of blackboard or whiteboard vs *board* in the sense of board of directors) and/or because they occur more frequently in the samples of language the learner is exposed to (see further below). The role of polysemy is under-explored in research on word-class effects, and yet it is relevant because members of different word classes are not equally likely to be polysemous. It has been reported, for example, that the average number of meanings for an English noun is about 2.10 as compared to 1.75 for an English verb (for references, see Elston-Güttler & Williams 2008: 183). Determining whether two uses of a word are sufficiently distinct to be treated as a case of polysemy is not always straightforward, however (and this is reflected in the fact that dictionaries often differ in the number of subentries they use to describe the meanings of the same word). What is largely undisputed, though, is that certain types of function word, such as prepositions, are extremely polysemous (e.g. Lindstromberg 2010).

Apart from semantic variables such as the above, phonological and orthographic factors are also believed to influence a word's learnability. One of these is length, which is most often measured in terms of the number of syllables, phonemes, or letters. On the one hand, longer L2 words may attract more attention, and, given the association between attention and uptake in memory (e.g. Godfroid, Boers, & Housen 2013), this can be expected to benefit subsequent recognition of these words when they are re-encountered. On the other hand, longer words tend to be harder to process in working memory, which makes it more challenging to reproduce them accurately. Experimental findings of an effect of length on the learnability of L2 vocabulary may therefore depend on whether receptive or productive knowledge is tested (Laufer 1997b). A related variable is pronounceability, where greater ease of pronunciation is associated with greater learnability (Ellis and Beaton 1993).

A third form-related variable often considered in experimental studies of word learning is phonological neighbourhood size, commonly operationalized as the number of same-language words that differ from a given word by one phoneme. Thus, *cat* has many phonological neighbours (e.g. *mat, cut, cap, scat, at*) while *bridge* has few (e.g. *ridge*). Unfamiliar words that show phonological resemblance to many other already known words appear to be easier to learn (e.g. Stamer & Vitevitch 2012). However, when a new word (e.g. *adopt*) has a single phonological neighbour that is already known by a learner (e.g. *adapt*), then the learner may be inclined to overlook the difference and attach the meaning of the already familiar word to the new word (Laufer 1997b).

Pronounceability, which we mentioned above, is to some extent an interlingual factor, as it involves interactions between the learner's L1 and the learner's L2. Another interlingual variable, degree of cognateness, refers to whether L2 vocabulary items can be matched to L1 items which are not only similar (or identical) in form but also similar (or identical) in meaning. Such similarities may exist because L2 and L1 have a common ancestor language or because of borrowings as a result of language contact. It is well documented that cognate L2 words are comparatively easy to learn (e.g. Lotto & de Groot 1998; de Groot & Keijzer 2000), and it is conceivable that some word classes in a given language contain more cognates than others whereby, for example, French learners of English may benefit from cognate effects much more when it comes to open class words (which are comparatively likely to be Latinate, like most French words) than when it comes to closed class words (which are comparatively likely to be Germanic). Whether verbs, nouns and adjectives might be differently susceptible to borrowings and thus potential cognate effects could be an interesting avenue of further inquiry in this context. In any case, a study aiming to isolate the effect (if any) of word class on word learnability will also need to take cognateness into consideration as a potential confounding variable.

Cognateness concerns both the form and the meaning of words. This also applies to the next variable worth considering. In many languages, an appreciable proportion of words are to some degree iconic; that is, they display a resemblance between meaning and form that individuals tend to agree about. This iconicity (or sound symbolism) can sometimes be strong enough to facilitate guessing the meanings of unfamiliar forms (e.g. Perry, Perlman, & Lupyan 2015; Winter, Perlman, Perry, & Lupyan 2017), and it has been found to facilitate L2 word learning (e.g. Imai, Kita, Nagumo, & Okada 2008; Kantartzis, Imai, & Kita 2011; Lockwood, Dingemanse, & Hagoort 2016; Deconinck, Boers, & Eyckmans 2017). To investigate differences in iconicity across word classes and sensory domains, Winter et al. (2017) recruited 1,593 native speakers to provide iconicity ratings for 3,001 English words (25–26 ratings per word). Replicating results of Perry et al. (2015), they found statistically significant levels of iconicity especially in onomatopoeic words and interjections but also in words of other types. Most highly rated for iconicity, in descending order, were verbs, adjectives, adverbs, and nouns. Unsurprisingly, function words received low ratings. These researchers also found that words referring to sensory experience, especially tactile and auditory experience, tend to be more iconic than words with abstract meanings.

All the previously mentioned variables are likely to influence the pace of acquisition of words in both intentional learning conditions (e.g. in experiments where participants are asked to try and memorize words) and incidental learning conditions (where words are picked up from ambient discourse, including reading, watching TV, and so on, without a deliberate effort on the part of the learner to acquire knowledge of these words). The last variable to be mentioned in this section matters especially for incidental learning. This variable is the frequency with which L2 vocabulary items are encountered in discourse.

A substantial body of research on the incidental learning of L2 open class words has demonstrated that encountering words multiple times facilitates their acquisition (for a meta-analytic review, see Uchihara, Webb, & Yanagisawa 2019). However, this effect does not operate across all word classes equally. For example, many L2 learners acquire extremely frequent L2 closed class words such as English articles comparatively late, if it at all. Reasons for this are complex. For example, closed class words are likely to undergo phonological reduction in natural speech, which makes them less noticeable. These words also tend to have abstract meanings, and, as discussed earlier, this makes learning harder. Learners may also experience words such as articles as non-essential to convey and comprehend messages.

Whether the benefits of frequent exposures might also vary between the open classes (e.g. nouns vs verbs. vs adjectives) merits investigation. Thanks to advances made in the discipline of corpus linguistics, this is becoming increasingly feasible. For example, in a list of the 5,000 most frequent lemmas occurring in the 450 million words of *Corpus of Contemporary American English* (COCA) (Davies 2008 to present), https://www.wordfrequency.info/free.asp, there are far fewer adjectives (838) than nouns (2,543). This is not surprising, since the function of adjectives is to modify nouns and so adjectives normally require the presence of a noun while nouns do not require the presence of an adjective. However, this does not necessarily mean that individual adjectives are on average less frequent than individual nouns. Although the average corpus frequency of the adjectives included in the above-mentioned list is 23,237, versus 26,602 for nouns, this difference is due mostly to a handful of highly frequent noun lemmas (e.g. *thing, man*). Excluding the 15 most frequent nouns, the average corpus frequency for the noun class drops to 24,258.

Turning to the verbs in the list of 5,000 most frequent lemmas, the average corpus frequency is a stunning 64,353. At first glance this suggests that verbs as a class enjoy a comparative advantage when it comes to incidental uptake from repeated encounters. Again, however, the high average is largely attributable to a small number of verbs (including *be, have*, and *do*), likely because some of these also serve as auxiliaries and thus as function words. Excluding the 15 most frequent verbs, the average drops to 34,125. However, beyond the 500 most frequent lemmas on the list (i.e. beyond 10% of the 5,000 highest-frequency word lemmas in the corpus, the average frequencies are more similar: 16,706, 18,525, and 18,374, for adjectives, nouns, and verbs, respectively. So, if incidental vocabulary acquisition is partly driven by frequency effects, then these effects can help to explain why, at the early stages of L2 acquisition, verbs might be picked up faster than nouns and adjectives. However, if the pace of incidental acquisition of these word classes were also found to differ for intermediate and advanced L2 learners (who have already acquired the most common words), then the frequency argument becomes less compelling.

It is necessary to note in this context that the above distributions concern a general language corpus; it is not clear to what extent these distributions are paralleled in materials developed for the purpose of L2 learning (e.g. textbooks) at various levels of proficiency or in teacher talk in the language classroom. The most direct examination of frequency effects requires analysis of frequency distributions in the language samples that a given learner is exposed to.

Examination of the frequency factor is further complicated by the variability of the forms in which a given lemma may occur. If a learner does not recognize *spoke* as another instance of the lemma *speak*, then this may reduce the benefits of repeated exposure. This may matter also with respect to word-class effects because the variability of forms in which words occur often differs from one class to another. Greater variability also entails a higher likelihood of errors. For instance, Källkvist (1999) found more inaccurate uses of English verbs (variable in tense, aspect, and subject–verb agreement) than of English nouns (variable just in plural marking) in writing samples collected from advanced learners of L2 English.

What emerges from the above review is that the learnability of L2 words is bound to be influenced by a panoply of variables besides, possibly, their word class. In the next section, we evaluate whether there is in fact any compelling experimental evidence for an independent effect of word class, or whether an effect attributed to word class might not rather be a side effect, so to speak, of one or more of the variables we have mentioned here.

41.3 ASSESSING THE EVIDENCE OF WORD-CLASS EFFECTS ON THE LEARNABILITY OF L2 VOCABULARY

41.3.1 Word class and the learnability of a word's form and meaning

Having indicated why a pure word-class effect is difficult to isolate in L2 vocabulary learning, it may not be surprising that only few attempts have been made to do so. We begin with four linked experiments carried out by Rodgers (1967). These experiments are of interest because they exemplify how an apparent word-class effect can vanish following a change in experimental procedure, how it can seem to reappear following another change, and how evidence for its existence can dissipate when a confounding variable is finally taken into account. The first two of these experiments involved Russian–English translation pairs that were to be memorized by L1 English speakers. During training and testing, the L2 Russian word was always the stimulus word and the measure of successful learning was the number of participants who could recall the L1 English translation. Scores from the first experiment seemed to Rodgers to show that word class is a determinant of word learnability because nouns were recalled markedly more often than words of other classes. For corroboration, Rodgers carried out a second experiment for which he created a new set of Russian–English word pairs. However, instead of using real TEs, he created fake TEs using Russian and English words of different word classes. Rodgers's expectation was that participants would assume that the paired words were genuine TEs and were therefore members of the same word class, whereby the results of the first experiment would be replicated. The actual outcome was very different. For instance, the English verbs—some of which had been paired with Russian nouns—were recalled far better than before. Speculating that the unanticipated results arose from wide variation in the pronounceability of the Russian stimulus words, Rodgers reran both experiments using supposedly easier-to-pronounce Japanese stimulus words. The hypothesized word-class effect seemed to have reappeared. However, possibly because of the unavailability of reliable concreteness ratings when he was conducting his research, Rodgers paid insufficient attention to concreteness. Drawing on concreteness ratings compiled by Brysbaert, Kuperman, & Warriner (2014), we were able to determine that a robust effect of concreteness is evident in the per word error counts given in Rodgers's tables VIII and IX. Specifically, the correlations between the concreteness ratings of the English response words and the error counts are $r = -.45$ ($p = .001$) for Russian and $r = -.49$ ($p = .0003$) for Japanese. It therefore seems possible that no independent word-class effect would be detectable in Rodgers's data if concreteness were systematically taken into account. Laufer (1997b: 149) has pointed out another problematic variable in Rodgers's study: the Russian verbs are substantially more complex, morphologically, than the nouns.

Whereas in Rodgers's experiments the learners were simply asked to memorize sets of L1–L2 translation pairs, Ellis & Beaton (1993) investigated variables influencing the effectiveness of a specific mnemonic procedure for L2 word learning, called the keyword method. The 'keyword' in this mnemonic procedure is a word in the learner's L1 that bears a formal resemblance to the L2 word to be remembered. It is then used as part of an image which creates an association with the L2 word, such that the L1 word will subsequently serve as a key to help the learner recall the L2 target word. For example, the target word might be the German word *schlagen* ('to hit') and the L1 English keyword might be *slug*. An image combining the two could then perhaps be a scene of someone hitting a giant slug. Learners may be encouraged to try this rather complex mnemonic method autonomously, but often the keywords and the images to create an association with the target words are chosen for them. This was the case in Ellis & Beaton's (1993) study. English learners of German studied sets of German nouns and verbs using the keyword method, and the researchers then examined a multitude of word-related variables as potential co-determinants of word learnability. One substantively significant variable appeared to be word class, because the nouns tended to be much better remembered than the verbs. However, the L2 target nouns used in the experiment were comparatively imageable and therefore likely to be comparatively easy to learn. Learning success was greater also when the L1 keywords were nouns than when they were verbs (note that a keyword need not share the same word class as the L2 target word), but overall these nouns were more imageable than the verbs as well. Ellis & Beaton nevertheless argued that 'there are good reasons to expect that there are independent effects of part of speech on learnability that are not mediated by imageability' (1993: 610), since more of the variance in the participants' learning success could be explained by including word class along with imageability in the statistical analyses.

Ellis & Beaton's study is impressive in that the potential influence of a wide range of word-related variables was examined. However, there may yet be additional variables which could help to explain why the keyword method worked better with some of the target words in their study than with others given that the precise application of the method varied from one word to the next. For example, for the German word *Messer* ('knife') the participants were told to imagine a knife in a mess of gravy, while for *laufen* ('to run') they were told to imagine bread loaves running down the street (1993: 580). In the former image, there is a prior semantic association with the target word's meaning (as a knife is a piece of cutlery and thus associated with food) whereas there is none in the latter image (as loaves of bread are not known for their inclination to start running down streets). A discussion of which type of image is likely to be mnemonically most effective is beyond the scope of this chapter. The point is that it cannot be ruled out that the mnemonic effectiveness of the images varied across the study materials that the learners were provided with, and by extension perhaps differently affected the success rates for the verbs and nouns.

One of the important conclusions drawn by Ellis & Beaton (1993: 610) is that 'a factorial experiment in which part of speech is crossed with imagery in its full range for both nouns and verbs is needed to properly disentangle effects of word class and imageability'. No large-scale study of this kind has been carried out in the area of L2 vocabulary learning so far as we are aware, even though close to three decades have passed since Ellis & Beaton's influential work.

Because there appears to be no certainty about word-class effects in L2 vocabulary learning, researchers wishing to investigate instructional interventions or rates of vocabulary uptake under various incidental learning conditions often select target words belonging to a single word class. Another option is to target members from multiple word classes, but then also to include information regarding other variables known to affect word learnability so as to avoid overestimation of a word-class effect. The latter has not always been done. For example, Horst & Meara (1999) traced one learner's vocabulary uptake from a comic strip (which the learner was asked to reread several times), and they found that particularly nouns tended to be picked up fast. No information is given about the concreteness of the words or about any of the other variables known to influence word learning. Besides, the illustrations accompanying the text probably helped the reader internalise especially the meaning of concrete nouns, whose referents were likely to figure in the illustrations. A more recent study of incidental vocabulary learning, but using listening texts as input material, did include concreteness ratings for the words (van Zeeland & Schmitt 2013). Although the primary topic of interest was the effect of repeated exposures to the same words, word class was included as a potentially influential factor. The words of interest included verbs, nouns, and adjectives (eight of each class). All 24 words had been rated for concreteness of meaning, and the three sets of words contained equal numbers of words with high and low concreteness ratings. As expected, concreteness emerged as a significant determinant of word learning, but so too did word class, with nouns being learned best. At first glance, this result supplements the earlier findings (Rodgers 1967; Ellis & Beaton 1993) in support of a word-class effect. It needs to be borne in mind, however, that van Zeeland & Schmitt's study (2013: 616) included only a small number of representatives per word class. Moreover, a close inspection of the recall data reveals that the better-than-average meaning recall for the set of nouns is entirely due to one specific item, the word denoting 'blood'. This word was recalled by 14 out of 20 participants while other words were recalled by only four participants at the very best. Among the relevant 24 English words, *blood* is exceptionally emotive (see the ratings list referred to by Warriner et al. 2013) and therefore likely to be especially memorable. The statistical evidence for a word-class effect in van Zeeland & Schmitt (2013) vanishes if this single item is removed from the analysis.

What this review suggests is that there is in fact little compelling evidence from experimental studies of an effect of word class on the learnability of open class L2 lexical forms and meanings, because oftentimes an observed trend indicative of a word-class effect may plausibly be attributed to other factors. When other variables are taken into account alongside word class, evidence of an independent word-class effect is unlikely to emerge. An example is a large-scale investigation by Puimège & Peters (2019) of English vocabulary knowledge among Flemish children (aged 10–12). The researchers used the children's test data relating to 60 nouns, 16 verbs, and 17 adjectives. Four lexical variables were included in the statistical modelling to predict word knowledge: cognateness, concreteness, corpus frequency, and word class. Cognateness was the most powerful predictor of what English words were known by the children, and only word class was found to play *no* statistically significant role. (For a similar study, but without inclusion of word class as a potential predictor of learning, see De Wilde, Brysbaert, & Eyckmans 2019).

41.3.2 Word class and the learnability of a word's usage patterns

Full knowledge of a word is multifaceted. So far, we have considered potential word-class effects regarding the acquisition of a word's form–meaning mapping. An additional facet of vocabulary knowledge regards the usage patterns of words. This includes their morphosyntactic and phraseological behaviour. As to the former, an important aspect is the word's part of speech (or knowledge of which word class it belongs to). The question we address next is how well learners—post-beginner learners in particular—assign encountered words to the correct classes. As one would expect, words lacking morphological clues are the most problematic (e.g. Odlin & Natalicio 1982).

Zyzik & Azevedo (2009) carried out a two-stage study involving university undergraduates (L1 English) studying Spanish as a second language. In the first stage of the study 74 participants were asked to write short topic-focused texts, which the researchers subsequently searched for word-class errors (i.e. uses of a word in an inappropriate syntactic frame). The errors that were identified were then placed in categories according to the word classes involved. Zyzik and Azevedo then produced a list of dual-choice sentences representing the three categories of error that their analysis had found to be especially common, with eight sentences for each error category, namely: Verb instead of Adjective, Verb instead of Noun, and Adjective instead of Noun. One of these sentences was: *Los hijos están (activos—activan) en deportes* ['The children are active in sports'], where it would be an error to use the verb *activan* rather than the adjective *activos*. In the second stage of the study these 24 sentences were presented to 240 undergraduate participants as forced choice test items. The participants did least well in distinguishing the forms of adjectives and nouns and best in distinguishing the forms of verbs and adjectives. While this seems to point to a word-class effect, Zyzik and Azevedo remarked that the relative difficulty of the three types of distinction may stem from features of Spanish and English and that a different pattern of relative difficulty might be observed in a study involving other languages. Besides, drawing firm conclusions about a word-class effect would have required experimental control of a daunting array of nuisance variables. For instance, some proportion of the categorization errors observed by Zyzik & Azevedo (2009) seem likely to have resulted from learners' inability to cope with the orthographic similarity of to-be-distinguished words (see Laufer 1997b on so-called synforms). The main finding, then, is that it cannot be taken for granted that learners can assign L2 word forms to the correct grammatical class. As Zyzik (2009: 161) remarked in her report of a related study, 'words can exist in the L2 lexicon for some time without specification of their category membership'.

Another facet of knowledge of the usage patterns of words concerns their phraseology. Indeed, were one to learn the meaning of every word of another language, still to be learned would be a vast multitude of multiword items of diverse types—situational clichés (*You're welcome*), figurative idioms (*bite the bullet*), compound nouns (*ballot box*), discourse markers (*in any case*), and more. Many of the factors affecting the learnability of L2 single words are at play also with respect to L2 multiword items. A prime example is imageability (Steinel, Hulstijn, & Steinel 2007). Degree of semantic transparency and availability of L1 form–meaning counterparts (cognates) also play an important part (Steinel, Hulstijn, & Steinel 2007). Likely to have effects as well are a number of form-related variables, such as length and the degree to which the components of a multiword items are fixed. One so far undiscussed form-related variable is the presence vs absence of potentially mnemonic patterns of sound repetition—for example, alliteration (*turn tail*), assonance (*save face*), and rhyme (*brain drain*), although it is not yet clear whether a learner needs to notice such patterns in order to benefit from a mnemonic effect (Boers, Lindstromberg, & Eyckmans 2014; Eyckmans, Boers, & Lindstromberg 2016).

A few studies about the learning of L2 multiword items have indicated an effect of word class in the sense that certain word constituents within multiword items appear harder to learn than others. In Peters (2016), for example, L1 Dutch university students studied 18 English expressions, which were adjective–noun combinations (e.g. *perishable goods*), verb–noun combinations (*exceed the budget*), or verb–preposition–noun combinations (e.g. *run up a deficit*). Peters estimated effects on learnability of two other variables besides syntactic structure: the length of the constituent words and the congruency of the whole item with L1 (i.e. whether the L1 translation of the given multiword item consists of translation-equivalent words). Post-study test results revealed that the adjective–noun expressions were learned the best. Word length was also a statistically significant predictor (its effect on productive recall being negative but its effect on passive recognition being positive), as was congruency with L1 counterpart expressions. An acknowledged limitation of this study is that other variables were left uncontrolled. For example, some of the constituents in the verb–noun combinations show a formal overlap (e.g. <u>ex</u>ceed and <u>ex</u>haust), which may have increased the likelihood of intra-item interference. In addition, the three sets of multiword items were not necessarily matched for concreteness or imageability of meaning. This could matter especially for the verb–preposition–noun combinations, as these contain an extra constituent of a comparatively abstract nature to be remembered. So, once again, we cannot be confident that the better learning of the adjective–noun phrases should be attributed to a word-class effect.

41.4 Conclusion

We have considered whether word class ever has a substantively important independent effect on the learnability of L2 vocabulary or whether effects of word class that have been reported are instead ascribable to psycholinguistic variables whose effects may be stronger or more fundamental. A major impediment to reaching a firm conclusion is that there are few published reports of directly relevant studies, especially in the literature on pedagogy-oriented L2 vocabulary acquisition. It is also worth acknowledging in this regard that, to our knowledge, the available literature on this topic concerns just a handful of languages (most notably English). As to psycholinguistics, it is as though there was wide agreement that the learnability of L2 vocabulary items can be accounted for quite well enough without recourse to word-class effects. Indeed, the question needs to be asked if there is any convincing rationale for expecting an independent word-class effect in the first place.

It is important to bear in mind, however, that our review concerns L2 vocabulary learning by post-childhood learners, for whom learning an L2 word seldom requires forming any entirely new concepts. Instead, it will often be a matter of attaching a new (L2) label to an already familiar concept. This, in fact, may help to explain why word-class effects (if any) are less likely to be observed in adults' L2 learning than in early L1 acquisition (see Chapter 40), where it has been suggested that young children acquire labels for objects (i.e. nouns) more easily than labels for processes (i.e. verbs) and labels for qualities (i.e. adjectives), owing to the fact that objects tend to be more clearly delineated and thus easier to conceptualize.

It is also worth bearing in mind that most of the studies on word-class effects reviewed here concerned open class words, mainly nouns, verbs, and adjectives. While we have found neither compelling nor consistent evidence for an effect at that level, we are not contesting that content words (open class words) and function words (closed class words such as determiners and prepositions) pose different challenges for L2 learners. This was briefly discussed in section 41.2 in connection with variables such as frequency, noticeability, and concreteness of meaning.

The comparison of the characteristics of content words and function words is a useful reminder that word-class membership does come with certain statistical probabilities regarding the member's relative length, imageability, valence, polysemy, and so on. As also mentioned in section 41.2, such statistical probabilities may well differ (albeit to a lesser degree) between the subclasses within the realm of content words. So, even if it is the case that independent word-class effects are too weak to matter much, or are undiscoverable for methodological reasons, or simply do not exist, the name of each word class could still usefully serve as a label for a set of probabilities associated with that word class—for example, a probability of being concrete to some degree, a probability of having a certain number of syllables, and so on. Thus, the name of each word class would represent a potentially useful *composite* variable. This could be an alternative approach especially in studies with very large sets of items drawn from different word classes, and where meticulous matching of the sets for the numerous word-related variables is not feasible. It seems, though, that much remains to be learned about many such statistical probabilities per word class.

CHAPTER 42

WORD CLASSES IN LANGUAGE CONTACT

YARON MATRAS AND EVANGELIA ADAMOU

42.1 INTRODUCTION

SINCE Whitney's (1881) pioneering discussion of the impact of language contact on structural change, studies have addressed the question whether structural categories differ in their susceptibility to borrowing and whether constraints can be identified on borrowability. In this contribution, we review key aspects of those discussions with a focus on the distinctive behaviours of different word classes. We begin with a brief survey of generalizations that have addressed the question of borrowing constraints on particular categories. We then examine individual word classes in respect of their contact behaviour and the processes of bilingual speech that initiate contact-induced language change. We conclude by addressing the implications for a theoretical and methodological appreciation of word-class categorization.

42.2 WORD CLASSES AND BORROWING HIERARCHIES

Whitney (1881) posited that word classes react differently to the pressure of language contact. He observed that nouns are more easily borrowed than adjectives and that adjectives in turn are more easily borrowed than verbs. Grammatical function words, he claimed, such as pronouns, articles, prepositions, conjunctions, and numerals, are even less likely to be borrowed and behave in that respect much like grammatical inflection, which tends to be exempted from language mixing (though it may accompany borrowed words, as in the case of the Latin plural ending in the English word *phenomena*). The founders of modern contact linguistics, Einar Haugen and Uriel Weinreich, both commented on the behaviour of categories in contact-induced language change. Haugen (1950: 224–225) refers to a scale of adoptability according to which borrowed nouns are more than three times more numerous than borrowed verbs while adjectives lag behind, followed by adverbs, prepositions, and interjections. Pronouns and articles do not appear among the list of borrowings, Haugen emphasizes. By way of explanation Haugen proposes that the prevalence of nouns and verbs is connected to vocabulary expansion over a speaker's lifetime (potentially linked to the cultural and technological development of a community) while grammatical items belong to a fixed inventory that is established in early childhood. An important distinction is made between importation of forms, which enriches the vocabulary, and substitution of pre-existing forms; the borrowing of nouns enriches the vocabulary by adding designations for new objects and routines that are specific to certain social and cultural settings. Weinreich (1953: 35) similarly argues that nouns show high borrowability because of their semantic function as designations of new things, the need for affective enrichment or euphemism, the need for differentiation, and a general need for renewal. The prominence of nouns over non-nouns is also noted by Moravcsik (1978b), who links borrowability to structural autonomy and semantic transparency; derivational morphology is also observed to be more borrowable than inflectional morphology and unbound elements more borrowable than bound elements. Poplack (2018: 48–50) remarks that the borrowing of nouns compared to other word classes by far exceeds their relative frequency in the receiving language and so the motivation to borrow nouns must be attributed to the richness of semantic content rather than frequency or the structural properties of nouns as potential stand-alone elements. This brief review already allows us to identify several issues that are involved in the distinct behaviours of word classes in borrowing: frequency issues (there are more nouns than words in other word classes), type-token issues (some classes such as interjections or connectors may have few items in the class but they occur more frequently in speech), specificity of semantic meaning, and the need for signifiers of cultural enrichment compared to substitution or doubling of existing words through loans.

Building on a discussion by Muysken (1981), Winford (2010: 176) offers the following hierarchy of borrowing by word class: nouns > adjectives > verbs > prepositions > coordinating conjunctions > quantifiers > determiners > free pronouns > clitic pronouns > subordinating conjunctions. Winford notes that this hierarchy has been confirmed by various studies. However, while the scale may reflect the frequency of loans across categories, it is not necessarily implicational. Moreover, some of the category designations are ambiguous. In particular, 'free pronouns' can be taken to include both indexical elements (deictic and anaphoric) and indefinites, which, however, behave quite differently in language contact situations. Thomason & Kaufman (1988: 74ff.) posit that the borrowing of structural categories is gradational and linked to the duration and intensity of social and cultural contacts. Their scale is formulated in general terms of structural properties but allows us to extract the following generalization in regards word classes: [content words] > conjunctions, adverbial particles > adpositions, personal and demonstrative pronouns, low numerals. While agreeing essentially with earlier observations, the scale does not offer an explanation as to why certain categories should be more resistant to borrowing, and what properties condition ease of borrowing. The link between intensity and duration of contact, and the ordering of categories, is thus associative or even corollary but not causal. This raises the point whether borrowing offers us an opportunity to rethink common categorizations of word classes: interrogating the precise relationship between categories that are more susceptible to borrowing and those that are less so has the potential to offer us insights into the reasons and motivations behind borrowing. But there is a risk that accepting sentence-based divisions into word classes in the more traditional sense may in fact hold us back in that process.

In his discussion of Hungarian loans in Selice Romani spoken in southern Slovakia based on the Loanword Typology Project elicitation list of 1,430 lexemes, Elšík (2009) identifies loans as constituting 63% of all nouns on the list, 50% of adverbs, 42% of adjectives, 41% of verbs, and 23% of function words. For the entire database of 41 sample languages considered in the Loanword Typology Project, the percentage of loans among nouns is 31.2, while among adjectives and adverbs it is 15.2, and for verbs it is 14.0 (Haspelmath & Tadmor 2009). This way of counting takes into consideration the relative frequency of word classes among lexemes that are deemed to be most salient in everyday speech. The category of 'function words' remains fuzzy and includes both elements that are observed to be highly borrowable such as connectors, particles, and indefinite expressions, and those that are rarely borrowed such as personal pronouns. In an overview assessment Tadmor (2009: 59–63) reports that the database shows twice as many content word borrowings as function words, though there are significant differences among the sample languages: At the far end of the scale, Imbabura Quechua shows a ratio of 14.4 loan content words to loan function words, while Kildin Sami and Selice Romani both show 2.1 and in Berber that ratio is 1.3. In terms of word-class frequency, twice as many nouns are borrowed across the corpus than adjectives and adverbs, with the latter closely followed by verbs. Here too there are significant differences: at the far end Takia shows a loan noun to loan verb ratio of 11.8, while in English that ratio is 1.4. The very high borrowers Selice Romani and Berber show loan noun to loan verb ratios of 1.7 and 1.3, respectively, while the very low borrowers Ket and Manange show 3.4 and 3.7, respectively, confirming that heavy borrowing makes the borrowing of verbs much more likely. The statistical comparison between the sample languages renders a borrowability score for each of the words on the elicitation list. Among the items that are least borrowable we find personal pronouns, demonstratives, and place adverbs ('there', 'here'), while interrogatives show a range of different scores: least borrowable are 'where', 'why', and 'which', with scores of 0.997, 0995, and 0.994, respectively; followed by 'how' (0.980), 'what' (0.971), 'when' (0.953), and 'how much' (0.946). This gives, in reverse, the following hierarchy representing the likelihood of interrogative borrowing: 'how much' > 'when' > 'what' > 'how' > 'where', 'why', 'which'.

The split among interrogatives in the Loanword Typology study shows that hierarchies of borrowability might be more meaningful when applied to individual values within a category rather than to the comparison between word classes. Matras (1998) postulates a universal tendency for contrastive connectors to show higher susceptibility to borrowing, followed by disjunctives and then additives ('but' > 'or' > 'and'). Examining a sample of Romani dialects in contact with a variety of different languages, Elšík & Matras (2006: 370–376) show that for some categories values that are 'unmarked' (more frequent, less complex) are more easily borrowed while for other categories the reverse applies. Borrowing is thus found to be linked not to frequency or formal composition but to the conceptual status of category values: lower accessibility and greater semantic-pragmatic complexity (e.g. contrast, free-choice indefinites, non-positive degree, peripheral localization) correlates with greater susceptibility to borrowing. Matras (2007) presents similar findings in a discussion of a cross-linguistic sample. The high borrowability of category values such as contrast, modality, obligation, and free choice indicates that susceptibility to borrowing is sensitive to the processing of presuppositions, in particular where a clash is anticipated between the expectations of the speaker and the listener and the speaker needs to exert greater control to manage the interaction (see also Matras 2020: 171ff.).

This interactional dimension is particularly relevant when it comes to the borrowing of function words. While earlier hierarchies based on quantitative impressions ranked function words low for borrowability, many studies have flagged the fact that particular kinds of function words are easily borrowed. Salmons (1990) discusses motivations for discourse–pragmatic operations to converge in bilingual speech leading to wholesale borrowing of discourse markers. Van Hout & Muysken (1994) report that Spanish items in Bolivian Quechua include frequently used words in Spanish and few items that are highly inflected, while items that are discourse-related are more susceptible to borrowing than those that belong to the structure of the clause. Stolz & Stolz (1996) examine borrowing in some 30 Mesoamerican languages in contact with Spanish and note the frequent borrowing of function words, in particular discourse markers and connectors. Matras (1998) postulates a functional category of 'utterance modifiers' including connectors, fillers, and tags, and phrasal adverbs, all of which are particularly prone to borrowing. As hinted above, these observations reinforce doubts as to whether an overall hierarchy of borrowability by word class is useful and indeed whether the distinctive features of sentence-based categories are at all aligned with the factors that drive or hinder borrowing. Matras (2020: 345–346) argues that the high susceptibility to borrowing of categories such as connectors and sequential adverbs, and to a lesser extent phasal adverbs, focus particles, indefinites, and modal particles, stems from their role in managing the interaction and processing gaps in presupposition, while at the opposite end of the scale categories such as personal pronouns, demonstratives, and place adverbs are less prone to borrowing precisely because they rely on the harmony between speaker and listener in mapping the presuppositional domain. Borrowing is thus regarded as the outcome of lapses in control over the selection and inhibition of structures by language, leading to convergence or 'fusion' of forms.

There thus appear to be at least two separate kinds of motivation for borrowing, affecting different categories in different ways: lexical borrowing is a process by which means of expressions are enriched. Nouns represent the most obvious way to enrich lexical expression even in the absence of full bilingual competence. Grammatical borrowing by contrast is motivated by the need to ease processing of propositions and the management of communicative interaction, by reducing the burden of having to sustain the selection and inhibition mechanism through which bilinguals make choices (see Green 1998; Bialystok et al. 2009). This latter motivation conditions the borrowability of non-lexical items or function words. This helps explain some features of postulated hierarchies of borrowing by word class, such as the prominence of nouns followed by other content words, and of connectors, while pronouns, determiners, and pronominal clitics appear low on the hierarchies. The precise interrelations among other categories, for example the position of adpositions or of subordinating conjunctions, is less clear and may be more worthwhile to investigate in regard to the relations between category values than word classes. It is important to note, however, that while some categories appear to be more immune when it comes to the direct transfer of forms or replication of 'matter', some may be more prone to replication of 'pattern'—the mapping of form and meaning (see Matras & Sakel 2007; Matras 2020). This is quite obvious for definite and to some extent indefinite articles, which are often found in areal clusters, that is, prone to convergence, yet are rarely transferred directly from one language to another. It also applies to clitics and modifiers of tense and aspect categories, and distinctions within pronoun paradigms such as inclusive/exclusive, while prepositions, subordinating conjunctions, complements, and relativizers can appear as either matter or pattern replicas. While above we have been dealing primarily with hierarchies that manifest themselves in the borrowability of linguistic matter, pattern borrowing also shows hierarchical behaviour, with some evidence that it progresses from the level of discourse to that of the clause, phrase, and word (Matras 2011: 154; see also discussion in Matras 2020: 264ff.).

A final note in connection with borrowability concerns the word-class distribution by etymology in cases of mixed languages (MLs). While opinions differ, by and large MLs are considered to be distinct from cases of borrowing in that they involve the abrupt emergence of a new variety of speech that draws more or less equally on two separate language components which the founder generation had at their disposal as a bilingual community. Bakker (1997, 2003) notes the predictability of structural intertwining in mixed languages, with the etymological split between lexicon and grammar, or nouns and verbs, and function words patterning in different ways, sometimes split between the two sources. According to Matras (2003), the ML 'prototype' is characterized primarily by a split between predication grammar and basic lexicon, while individual word classes can pattern either with the source language of the predication grammar or with that of core lexicon. For example, personal pronouns and demonstratives pattern in Michif with Cree, the donor language of verbs and verb inflection, and in Copper Island Aleut they pattern with Russian, the language of verb inflection; in Gurindji Kriol they pattern with Gurindji, the donor language of nominal inflection, while in Media Lengua they pattern with Spanish, the donor language of the lexicon. But structures involved in coordination, complementation, conditionals, causal relations, negation, and relativizing pattern overwhelmingly with the language of finite predication (Matras 2003: 165). This gives us a rough indication that the category of 'function words' is best divided at least between indexical devices (deixis and anaphora) on the one hand and operators that modify the predication on the other. Where there is a two-way etymological split between components, the first (indexical devices) can pattern with either of the donor languages while the second tend to pattern with the language of finite predication grammar.

42.3 THE INTEGRATION OF BORROWED WORD CLASSES

As discussed, nouns are prominent borrowings, representing a differentiated inventory of labels for concepts, practices, artefacts, products, human agents, and more. As Matras (2020: 188ff.) argues, it is the referentiality of nouns rather than their structural features that motivates the borrowing of nouns. 'Borrowability' should therefore be considered a direct product of communicative, social, and pragmatic motivations to borrow rather than a matter of formal constraint. Languages either treat borrowed nouns like native nouns and integrate them into native inflection patterns, or avoid integration and maintain a simplified representation of borrowed nouns. In some cases, nouns are integrated along with their original inflection from the source language, or else a special integration strategy is applied that marks out borrowed nouns as loans. Among the more common replications of source language inflection is the retention of plural marking (English *stimulus–stimuli*), often in addition to the indigenous or inherited plural inflection (Jerusalem Domari *zlām-e* 'men', from Arabic *zlām* 'men'; see Matras 2012), and the adoption of gender distinctions (Malay *putra* 'son' and *putri* 'daughter', from Sanskrit; see Tadmor 2007). In both cases the inflection is arguably derivational, thus referencing meaning rather than syntactic role. Swahili famously reinterprets segments of borrowed lexemes as grammatical markers of nominal class, as in *kitabu* 'book' from Arabic, reanalysed to form the Swahili plural *vi-tabu* 'books'. By contrast, in Algerian Arabic the French definite article can be reinterpreted as a plural marker, as in *kadu* 'gift', plural *likadu* 'gifts', while in Spanish the definite article in Arabic loans is reinterpreted as part of the lexical stem, as in **ar-roz* 'rice', **al-calde* 'mayor'. Romani dialects across Europe rely on nominal inflection endings borrowed from Greek during the Early Romani contact period with Byzantine Greek for the integration of both Greek and subsequent loan nouns, for example *doktor-os, doktor-is, doktor-o* 'doctor'.

Verbs show a variety of morphological integration strategies (Wichmann & Wohlgemuth 2008; Wohlgemuth 2009; Matras 2020: 191ff.). They can appear without modification of the original form of the verb ('direct insertion'), as in English *demand*; with morphological modification of the original form of the verb ('indirect insertion'), as in German *analysier-en* 'analyse', often drawing on derivational morphology used to create verbs from non-verbs (de-nominal or de-adjectival) or for intensification of an action, as in Hebrew *tilfén* 'to telephone'; in a compound construction where the verb stem or nominalized form is accompanied by an inherited verb ('light verb') as in Turkish *zann-etmek* 'to contemplate' (from Arabic *ẓann* 'think' and Turkish *etmek* 'to do'); or by replicating the original verb along with its original inflection ('paradigm transfer'), as in the replication of Turkish verbs such as *evlendim* 'I got married' in some Romani dialects of the Balkans or the replication of inflected modal and auxiliary verbs from Arabic such as *baqēt* 'I continued' in Jerusalem Domari (Matras 2012). Wichmann & Wohlgemuth (2008) propose that the various strategies represent a hierarchy of the intensity of contact, whereby increasing bilingualism requires less integration effort. Accordingly, light verbs represent the integration strategy that accompanies more casual contacts, followed by indirect insertion, while direct insertion and paradigm transfer are associated with more intense bilingualism. However, examining a database of some 800 examples of loan verbs from over 400 different languages, Wohlgemuth (2009: 286) concludes that the degree of bilingualism and contact intensity cannot fully explain the distribution of integration strategies. The question requires further investigation, but there are indications that the structure of the contact language may play a role. Thus, contemporary young speakers of Kurmanji in Turkey appear to favour a light verb integration pattern with loan verbs from Turkish, as in *beklemiş kir* '(I) waited', while the same generation of Kurmanji speakers in Syria favour indirect integration with Arabic loan verbs, as in *meṣîyam* 'I walked'; both groups are exposed to a similar level of bilingualism. Differences may in part be due to the fact that intensity of bilingualism is not constant over the lifespan of the contact situation, or indeed that of an individual user of language.

Adjectives tend to be integrated syntactically into the position of the attribute in the recipient language, thus Hebrew *yéled inteligénti* 'an intelligent boy', Yiddish *mešigene mentšn* 'crazy people' (from Hebrew **mešuga*). Like nouns, adjectives often adopt the agreement morphology of the recipient language, thus German *ein cool-er Typ* 'a cool guy', *die cool-en Typen* 'the cool guys'. By contrast, Urdu adopts English adjectives without integrating them into Urdu adjectival inflection, thus *final elān* 'final notice'. In Turkish, which lacks gender or number agreement, Arabic adjectives are replicated in the default masculine singular form: *ciddi bir plan* 'a serious plan' (Arabic *ğidd-ī* 'serious-M.SG'). Maltese integrates Italian adjectives into its own gender distinction in the singular, thus masculine *modern*, feminine *moderna*, where the inflectional endings of the two languages happen to coincide, but adopts the Italian inflectional ending in the plural, thus *toroq modern-i* 'modern roads'. Integration into the morphology of the host language usually also applies to comparative and superlative forms of adjectives, thus German *cool-er, am cool-sten* 'cooler', 'coolest'. But cases of wholesale borrowing of non-positive forms of adjectives are also attested: Jerusalem Domari for instance borrows non-positive forms from Arabic even for adjectives for which the language retains inherited positive forms, rendering in effect a system of adjective formation that is consistently suppletive, thus *tilla* 'big', *ákbar* 'bigger', *kištota* 'small', *ázġar* 'smaller' (Matras 2012).

The susceptibility of other word classes to borrowing is often explained by their sentence-peripheral or phrase-peripheral position and absence of inflection. While these may be facilitating factors, we have no evidence that the presence of morphology or morphological boundness actually constitute barriers to borrowing where there is a functional or language-processing motivation for borrowing, and sociolinguistic conditions are such that borrowing is allowed to propagate from isolated innovations in the speech of individuals to become a widespread pattern across a speech community. Thus, connectors and other utterance modifying particles such as focus particles and phasal adverbs ('still', 'already', etc.) are frequent borrowings in forms that are uninflected, unbound, and sentence peripheral. But Heath (1978: 100) reports on a number of bound affixes shared by unrelated languages in the Arnhem Land region of northern Australia, including *-ʔɲiriʔ* 'as well as, also', *-bugiʔ* 'only, still'. Jerusalem Domari borrows a direct object resumptive pronoun *iyyāh* from Arabic along with its Arabic inflection, which is used productively in Domari relative clauses, as in *ple illi torim iyyā-hum* 'the money that you have me'. The language also uses the Arabic-derived complementizer *inn-* and subordinating conjunction for cause/reason *li'ann-* along with their Arabic inflections (see Matras 2012), whereas in Syrian Kurmanji the same Arabic items are borrowed without Arabic inflection.

The borrowing of indefinites often shows a split between the marker of indefiniteness, which is borrowed, and an inherited ontological marker, thus Polish Romani *ni-so* 'nothing', *vare-kon* 'somebody', where *ni-* is Slavic and *vare-* originally Romanian. Here too borrowability correlates with category values and the tendency to borrow entire indefinite expressions prevails particularly with temporal indefinites wholesale, as in both Syrian Kurmanji and Jerusalem Domari *da'iman* 'always' and *abadan* 'never' from Arabic. As mentioned, split category values are also attested for interrogatives ('how much' and 'when' being highly borrowable); with prepositions, where facilitating semantic factors include distance complex reference points ('between', 'around'); and with contrastive meaning ('instead of', 'against', 'except for'; see e.g. Elšík & Matras 2006: 287–294).

The borrowing of numerals is sometimes explained as driven by a need to fill gaps in languages that have just rudimentary counting systems that distinguish relative quantities based on a highly presuppositional conceptualization of what constitutes 'many' or 'few'. But the replacive borrowing of numerals is not uncommon. Here too, category values play a key role, with borrowing more likely to affect higher and more abstract numerals. This is aligned with frequency and conceptual accessibility but also with sociolinguistic usage patterns, whereby borrowing appears in domains where counting is associated with interaction in the contact language such as negotiation of dates and business transactions (Matras 2020: 217–219). Williams-Van & Hajek (2018) confirm this for the Tetun Dili language of East Timor, where alongside the indigenous set of numerals there is wholesale borrowing of sets from

Indonesian and Portuguese. Speakers select sets by interaction domains such as dates and maths (Portuguese), education and prices (Indonesian) and domestic affairs and the family (Tetun Dili). Indonesian and Portuguese numerals, however, can only combine with nouns of the same respective etymology, and their morphosyntax follows the patterns of the respective source language. Jerusalem Domari borrows all numerals above '5' from Arabic and like Tetun Dili, it tends to select Arabic nouns when using Arabic numerals, apparently as a way of avoiding the typological clash among the two languages, as Domari numerals take singular nouns while Arabic numerals under '10' take plural nouns, thus *di wars* 'two year-Ø' but *talat snīn* 'three years' (Matras 2012).

Finally, it has been observed that personal pronouns are seldom borrowed (see Tadmor 2009). Exceptions noted in the literature are few and include primarily cases where a pronominal system was enriched in order to accommodate a new inclusive–exclusive distinction, or else cases where the 'pronoun' is in fact an honorific lexical expression rather than a deictic or anaphoric expression (Matras 2020: 219–225), particularly common in South East Asia. The distribution of pronouns and demonstratives in Mixed Languages was referred to above, as was the example of the Domari resumptive pronoun borrowed from Arabic as part of the template of organizing relative clauses. From this we can conclude that while there may not be an absolute constraint on the borrowability of pronouns, they tend not to fall among the categories around which bilingual language users are motivated to reduce processing load by eliminating the need for selection and inhibition among languages. This is connected to the fact that deictic and anaphoric elements operate on the basis of a harmonious mapping shared by speaker and listener of the presuppositional domain and so they do not trigger the kind of interaction tension that is associated with processing discontinuity or presuppositional gaps.

42.4 WORD CLASSES IN BILINGUAL SPEECH

The study of bilingual speech corpora offers a glimpse into the real-time phenomena that take place at the level of the speaker and may ultimately lead to borrowing at the level of the speech community. Summarizing research on borrowings based on corpora from several language pairs (e.g. French–English, English–Tamil, English–Japanese, English–Igbo), Poplack (2018) reaffirms that the great majority of other-language insertions are single words and that these are overwhelmingly content words like nouns, verbs, adjectives, adverbs, as well as interjections. In contrast, in these corpora, multi-word stretches are rare,[1] and there are no restrictions as far as word classes are concerned, with articles, pronouns, auxiliaries, prepositions, and conjunctions being used in addition to the other categories. Based on the analysis of corpora from less-studied languages like Romani, Balkan Slavic, and Ixcatec

---

[1] Alternational switching frequency may vary in other corpora. To compare the switching profiles of different corpora, Bullock et al. (2021) propose measures along the lines of burstiness (regularity of switching languages), Multilingual Index (ratio of words in each language), and Integration Index (probability of switching languages between any two tokens). Preliminary analyses show that in two Spanish–English conversation corpora from the USA, language switches are not only frequent but also consist of multi-word stretches.

(Otomanguean), Adamou (2016) finds that single-word insertions are the most frequent. A further correlation exists between word classes and the overall rates of contact words in bilingual speech corpora: those with over 20% contact words exhibit greater word-class variety while those with less than 5% contact words show a limited number of word classes, with nouns being the most prominent word class followed by verbs. More specifically, in two corpora with less than 5% contact words (Ixcatec-Spanish and Balkan Slavic Nashta-Greek) individual tokens from other word classes are used but their rate within their word class is very low. In comparison, in the Romani–Turkish–Greek corpus the analysis reveals that, in addition to nouns (40% in total from either Turkish or Greek, of which 27% from Turkish) and verbs (12% Turkish and 2% Greek) there is a significant number of adverbs (29% from Turkish and 6% from Greek), adjectives (19% Turkish and 10% Greek), and conjunctions (21% Turkish and 12% Greek), but there are no pronouns or determiners from the two current contact languages. In contrast, in the Finnish Romani–Finnish corpus, 72% of all conjunctions used are from Finnish, 27% of particles, 22% of adverbs, and 13% of nouns, 10% of verbs, and 5% of pronouns. In this corpus, it appears that Finnish Romani speakers who codeswitch the most do not use many Finnish nouns. Despite inter- and intra-speaker variability, which impact rates of use of individual word classes such as nouns, the statistics indicate that bilinguals conform to the patterns of codeswitching and borrowing that prevail in their bilingual community (see Adamou et al. 2016 on bilingual corpora from four Slavic minority languages).

Regarding morphological and syntactic integration, Poplack (2018) observes that single content words typically adopt the morphology of the recipient language. Determiner use and adjective placement also align with the grammar of the recipient language. This is not the case in multi-word stretches, where words are governed by the grammar of the donor language. Other corpus studies confirm that the choice of the determiner depends on the choice of the 'matrix language', defined by Myers-Scotton (2002) as the language that provides clause word order (Morpheme Order Principle) and morphemes such as case and verb agreement markers (System Morpheme Principle). Blokzijl, Deuchar, & Parafita Couto (2017) compare a bilingual corpus of Spanish–English from Miami, USA and a bilingual corpus of Spanish–English Creole from Nicaragua and report a tendency for Miami bilinguals to use Spanish determiners in mixed determiner phrases while Nicaraguan bilinguals use English Creole determiners consistently. Adamou & Granqvist (2015) note typologically rare patterns of mixing in two Romani corpora from Greece and Finland: Romani-Turkish speakers from Greece never use Romani verb morphology with the Turkish verbs even though Turkish verbs appear as single-word insertions into an otherwise Romani-dominant speech that includes nouns and pronouns with Romani case marking, Romani determiners, and Romani word order. A similar tendency is noted for Finnish verbs used by Finnish-Romani bilingual speakers.

From a cross-language perspective careful attention to methodological issues is therefore called for: some languages have definite and indefinite articles while others express definiteness through bare nouns; some languages rely more and others less on conjunctions, and some have more and others fewer adjectives; in some languages pronouns can be omitted in some environments or contexts while in others they are obligatory; languages that are morphologically isolating, agglutinative, or fusional can offer different opportunities and constraints on the borrowing of morphemes. At the same time, semantic–pragmatic and cognitive motivations may override constraints on the borrowability of bound morphemes, as in the case of the borrowing between Sakha (Yakut) and Lamunkhin Even alluded to above (Pakendorf 2019). Differences in word order can also play a role (affecting, for example, the borrowing of pre- and postpositions). Finally, the fuzziness of some word classes, alluded to above in relation to 'pronouns' and 'adverbs', makes cross-language comparability difficult. Indeed, Gomez Rendon (2008) argues based on a comparative study of three bilingual corpora from Latin America (Spanish with Quichua, Guaraní, and Otomí), that what ultimately determines the distribution of word classes in different language pairs are the particular characteristics of the bilingual communicative setting rather than the typology of parts of speech and morphology of the recipient language or source language.

To account for the differences in the word classes noted in bilingual speech corpora we now turn to discuss models of speech production. The classic model of monolingual speech production elaborated by Levelt (1989) involves three subsystems: A pre-linguistic conceptual system (Conceptualizer), a linguistic system at the lemma level (Formulator), and an output system at the word form level (Articulator). According to the bilingual version of this model proposed by de Bot (1992), the Conceptualizer first decides on the language that needs to be selected, based on the context. The intended meaning and the context then activate subsets of words belonging to one of the two languages. The Formulator then gains access to the lemma and lexeme levels as in the monolingual speech production model, before moving to the Articulator, which according to de Bot is not language specific; this can explain the variation in the phonetic–phonological integration of words in codeswitching observed in many bilingual speech studies.

Building on Levelt's model, Myers-Scotton and Jake (2017) propose the 4-M model to explain differences in the ways that various morpheme types are used in bilingual speech. The model distinguishes two types of morphemes: conceptually activated morphemes, which are activated early, at the level of the Conceptualizer, at the same time as content words ('early system morphemes'); and structurally assigned morphemes, which are activated later in this process, at the level of the Formulator ('late system morphemes'). Early system morphemes include determiners, derivational prepositions, particles in phrasal verbs, derivational and plural markers (the latter being the only kind of inflectional morphology to behave differently in codeswitching and borrowing), some tense and aspect markers, as well as subordinating and coordinating conjunctions. These morphemes can come either from the language of the content words or from the language that provides the grammar. Late system morphemes, in contrast, such as agreement and several case markers, are rarer in codeswitching and borrowing as they are not activated based on content but are accessed at a later stage in speech production.

Alternative models move beyond the word level and therefore in some sense and to some extent beyond word classes (e.g. the 'slot and insert' model in Dell et al. 1997; cognitive grammar in Langacker 2008a; naive discrimination theory in Baayen et al. 2013). According to usage-based approaches, in particular, speakers store larger units that can include a word together with its inflectional morphology or even entire lexicogrammatical constructions. Researchers investigating bilingual speech therefore note that some units, such as compound nouns, adjective–noun, and verb–object constructions (Backus 1996, 2003), nouns together with plural markers (Hakimov 2016), or verbs together with verb morphology (Adamou & Shen 2019) can also be stored as a whole in the mental lexicon and be accessible as such in bilingual speech production and comprehension, depending on their frequency.

Finally, researchers note that specific elements in a word class or subclasses are affected differently in bilingual speech production. For example, Backus (1996) observes that proper nouns differ from other nouns in that they have a more specific meaning, which makes them more susceptible to borrowing. Matras (1998) also notes that grammatical markers that are associated with interaction management and so with more intense language processing may be more prone to borrowing (e.g. the adversative marker 'but'). The reason for this, it is hypothesized, lies in the interaction-level tension surrounding the act of contradicting a shared presupposition, and the resulting increase in processing load, which can interfere with the language selection mechanism.

42.5 Conclusion

Studies in contact linguistics often make reference to word classes, both in respect of the likelihood that different word classes may be affected by borrowing or constitute points of language switching in conversation, and in respect of the characteristics of structural integration into a recipient language of items belonging to different word classes. The results of various observations are difficult to calibrate into overall generalizations, however. This is partly due to the great variety observed in different corpora, in particular those of bilingual speech. There are also obstacles that are of an epistemological nature. Thus, statistics may reflect different realities such as the overall quantity of borrowed or switched items of particular categories in a corpus, their frequency as a proportion of the overall number of borrowings or switches, their frequency in proportion to the overall count of items belonging to the same category, or the implicational arrangement in regard to the sequence of borrowing in the history of contact between two languages, to name but some. Then there is the potential ambiguity of some category labels and, in regard to attempts to derive an explanatory account from the data, the reasoning that is linked to the borrowability of certain categories when these are defined in terms of their sentence level and morphosyntactic characteristics as word classes. Indeed, one of the outcome observations is that language contact serves as a prompt to rethink the status of categories and of the relevance of the very notion of word classes. First, we find that the hierarchical nature of borrowing manifests itself particularly around different susceptibilities of single values within a category, alongside or perhaps even more so than among word-class categories. Furthermore, borrowing and switching both seem to illuminate links between categories that are anchored in their functional contribution to the management of interaction and the processing of discourse and thus do not strictly pertain to their status as word classes in the conventional sense. The general observation that content words are frequent borrowings, for example, has to do with their role in enriching content: nouns appear at the top of the list thanks to their contribution to naming objects and concepts, which are key elements of the process of cross-cultural exchange that is inherently involved when languages are in contact. Other elements, such as indefinites, discourse markers and connectors, interjections and greetings, phasal adverbs and fillers, appear high on the borrowing and switching scale due to the processing load that they impose on the speaker as part of the apparatus of 'managing and directing' the interaction and the link to broken presuppositional chains (for a discussion, see Matras 1998,

2020). This suggests that psycholinguistic dimensions rather than word-class affinity in the traditional sense are the motivating factors behind the behaviour of different categories in contact situations. An agenda for future research should therefore in our opinion see diachronic and corpus-based work supplemented by experimental research to investigate the interplay between speaker control over the selection and inhibition mechanism and longer-term redrawing of 'language boundaries' within speakers' repertoire of linguistic resources.

CHAPTER 43

WORD CLASSES IN PSYCHOLINGUISTICS

PAUL IBBOTSON

43.1 The psycholinguistic approach

Psycholinguistics is primarily concerned with how language is produced, comprehended, and acquired by the mind and brain. The psycholinguistic approach seeks to establish not only that language can be adequately described by any particular theory but also that people use language in a particular way. With respect to word classes, it asks what is the value added in predicting how people learn, behave, and change language, if we assume the categories of verb, noun and so on, exist? To that extent, psycholinguists are interested in word classes as a tool to investigate how the mind shapes and is shaped by their use; the learning mechanisms by which word classes become structured and knowledge about them becomes organized; the extent to which word classes behave differently from other linguistic and non-linguistic classes; and as a test case for the universality or otherwise of linguistic categories themselves.

43.2 If word classes are the solution, what is the problem?

Before we look at word classes in detail we might ask ourselves what is the payoff, psychologically speaking, of forming and maintaining a class or category of any type? By knowing some properties of a category, other *unobserved* properties can be inferred at a small computational cost, because of the way features of a category cluster together. For example, a dog encountered for the first time might be categorized as such, using the reasoning that this dog(x) is like the other dogs I've seen (y) in that it has four legs, barks, and has a furry coat(z). This best guess about its category membership can be used to hedge a bet about unobserved properties of that dog because the range of things a dog can be are not all equally likely; it probably also smells, chases cats, and fetches balls. And that information is useful in predicting behaviour and making smart behavioural responses. Likewise, knowing a word has the verb-like properties of referring to some action or state is also predicative how it behaves and coordinates with other linguistic properties such as tense, aspect, mood, voice, person, number, gender, or arguments. This is made possible because within languages these kinds of cues often work redundantly with one another as an insurance for recovering meaning in noisy or ambiguous communication. Category membership is also useful when trying to predict how a member of that category might behave when placed in a novel environment. For example, we can understand how the intransitive verb *sneeze* behaves transitively in the caused motion construction *Frank sneezed the napkin off the table*(x) because it is like *Mary sprayed paint onto the wall*(y) in the way A causes B to move C(z). This general kind of hierarchical classification structure—'x is like y in way z'—can be readily applied to word classes, for example, different sentential contexts make some word classes much more likely interpretations than others, as these examples from English (1a)–(1f) show (MacWhinney 2005):

(1) a. Here is a pum (count noun).
　　b. Here is Pum (proper noun).
　　c. I am pumming (intransitive verb).
　　d. I pummed the duck (transitive (causative) verb).
　　e. I need some pum (mass noun).
　　f. This is the pum one (adjective).

By knowing something of what different word classes mean, syntactic order can be inferred if there is some stable correspondence between the two, for example, agents of actions tend to be subjects of a sentence, patients and themes tend to objects and goals, locations and instruments tend to appear as oblique or indirect objects (Pinker 1984). Decades of psycholinguistic research have shown how sensitive adults and children are to the distributional patterns of word classes across a language and the frequency of items within word classes (Bloomfield 1938, 1973; Harris 1954; Finch & Chater 1992, 1994; Schütze 1993; Cartwright & Brent 1997; Redington, Chater, & Finch 1998; Mintz, Newport, & Bever 2002; Mintz 2003; Tomasello 2003; Goldberg 2006).

So, without categories, we would be doomed to treat each new object, action, experience, or word as an example of only itself; a class with a membership of one. That would make predicting, navigating, and thriving in the physical and social world extremely difficult and it would also rid language of much of its creative power. Word classes are essentially prediction engines that pump out best guesses—for example, verbs that I know about behave like this, knowing nothing else, I think this novel verb will also behave like this—and prediction is a general cognitive capacity that appears across domains, organized into a hierarchical cascade of forecasts at different levels of granularity across the brain (Rao & Ballard 1997, 1999; Bar 2007; Friston & Kiebel 2009; Lupyan & Clark 2015). Simulating the way that the world works is one of the big benefits of having a brain which costs so much to run (2% by weight, 25% of the calories; Leonard & Robertson 1992; Fonseca-Azevedo & Herculano-Houzel 2012). So, it seems to make good economics for different cognitive specializations—vision, hearing, language—to capitalize on the benefits that prediction can bring wherever they can; whether that is modelling the future trajectory of objects from visual input or predicting upcoming words in dialogue (Bar 2007; Adams, Friston, & Bastos 2015).

43.3 How word classes are constructed

An issue of central concern to psycholinguists is what kind of processes govern the formation of word classes? A modular theory of language would contend that language gets its own delimited mental processor, areas of which are encapsulated from other cognitive systems and furthermore, this area comes with content organized in advance of experience, designed to work exclusively on linguistic input. The implication is, word classes are built out of a fundamentally different sort of psychological structure than non-linguistic classes. Some of the most influential theorists in cognitive science have made the case 'that there is good reason to suppose that the functioning of the language faculty is guided by special principles specific to this domain' (Chomsky 1980: 44) and 'the structure of the sentence recognition system is responsive to universal properties of language and hence that the system works only in domains which exhibit these properties' (Fodor 1983: 50).

There is another theoretical framework that proposes language is special, not because it has processes hived off from the rest of cognition, but because of the forms it can take rather than the parts it is made of and because it could be an example par excellence of cognitive recycling and reuse (Tomasello 2003; Goldberg 2006; Bybee 2010; Ibbotson 2020). In comparison with the modular view, this deep integrationist account predicts general cognitive principles are at work right at the core of linguistic processes, including the very basics of grammar, word-class acquisition, comprehension, and production (e.g. Ibbotson, Theakston, Lieven, & Tomasello 2012; Ibbotson, Lieven, & Tomasello 2013; Ibbotson & Kearvell-White 2015). It also implies a more permeable boundary between language and cognition, higher plasticity (because language function is more substitutable with other cognitive areas) and greater developmental interdependence between these areas (Ibbotson 2020). Which view is right matters for psycholinguistic theory because it describes the cognitive resources available when constructing word classes. Under the developmental cognitive linguistics (DCL) account (Ibbotson 2020), the child can draw on a rich suite of domain-general processes including memory, attention, inhibition, categorization, analogy, and social cognition, before and during language acquisition and these are the processes that bear most heavily on the formation of word classes. Under the modular view (e.g. Chomsky 1980; Fodor 1983), domain-general cognition plays no serious role in constructing word-class structure itself, rather, developing cognition applies a filter through which the encapsulated (and largely non-dynamic) language system emerges.

In line with the DCL view we have already seen that both linguistic and non-linguistic word classes are motivated by the same functional pressure of prediction. We should expect, then, that many principles of class acquisition, processing, and comprehension are shared across the linguistic and non-linguistic domain. In this respect, the meaning or function that the word class serves is an important dimension over which people generalize a class and over which children form abstractions. What is functional or meaningful emerges from physical and social interaction with the world and the subsequent analogies people make to the scripts, events, and schemas in long-term memory (Tomasello 2003; Bar 2007, 2009). For example, in non-linguistic class formation, when 14- and 18-month-olds were presented with novel hybrid items made from parts of vehicles and animals (e.g. a cow body with wheels and a tractor chassis with cow legs) they resisted creating categories over these dimensions, even though they would have been 'statistically justified' in doing so from their distribution in the input (Rakison & Butterworth 1998). Instead they generalized over the dimensions they were familiar with because the children had no functional analogue in their experience to date (nor any from the experiment itself) that suggested forming categories of these hybrids had any predictive value about their behaviour. The cognitive cost of creating new categories for the hybrids was not offset by the predictive benefit they would bring and so they defaulted to the ones they knew were good predictors of behaviour (i.e. things that have legs tend to behave more like other things with legs and things with wheels tended to behave more like other things with wheels). The function of word classes too—how they behave, what they can do and not just their formal properties—deeply canalizes the possibilities over which generalizations are made.

For example, it has been extensively demonstrated that infants use intentional inference to constrain interpretations of conventionalized verb meanings and novel verbs (Tomasello 1995; Poulin-Dubois & Forbes 2002; Poulin-Dubois & Forbes 2006). Furthermore, children rely on intentional inference to map verbs to discrete actions (Tomasello & Barton 1994), map novel verbs to both concurrent and impending actions (Tomasello & Kruger 1992) and to actions that have occurred in the past (Akhtar, Carpenter, & Tomasello 1996). As well as internal perception and understanding of intentionality, the use of intentional-type language by others can provide a strong cue to meaning. For example, Carpenter, Akhtar, and Tomasello (1998) had an experimenter say *There!* or *Whoops!* after completing an action. Children were much more likely to imitate the action associated with intentional linguistic description than the accidental one. Likewise, words such as *Uh-oh*, or *Oops* reveal a speaker has not achieved their goal, and are used by 2-year-olds to abandon a possible association between a new noun and an object or a new verb and an action (Tomasello 1995). In general, toddlers' action re-enactments and verb-to-action mapping conform to the perceived intention of the agent executing the action (Tomasello & Barton 1994; Carpenter, Call, & Tomasello 2005).

For children to productively and normatively use these word–class distinctions depends on their acquisition of non-linguistic conceptual distinctions, namely, the types of things people are capable of believing, knowing, seeing, and so on. Despite the close integration of these systems, verbs still seem to represent a relatively difficult class of words to acquire, as there appears something about the nature of verbs that is a step removed from the perceptual availability of nouns, protracting the trajectory of their acquisition. For example, while *dog* and *cat* may remain stable referents throughout the duration of a scene, who is doing the 'chasing' and 'fleeing' may alternate. Even when between-speaker and inter-language variation are controlled for, we now know that nouns are easier to learn than verbs, not just for so-called noun friendly languages like English but also for 'verb-friendly' languages like Japanese (Ibbotson, Hartman, & Björkenstam 2018). Despite the formal differences between the Japanese and English language, Japanese and English children share the same underlying conceptual vocabulary, and this makes verbs harder to learn, not the nature of the language or the way their parents speak.

43.4 THE MENTAL STRUCTURE OF WORD CLASSES

A crucial source of evidence for the interconnectedness of word-class formation with general cognition comes from individual variation studies (Kidd, Donnelly, & Christiansen 2018). The general idea is that if two cognitive capacities share similar cognitive routines, skills, and resources, then being good at one ability should make somebody good at the other. For example, Konishi and colleagues (2016) established that the ability of 14-month-olds to categorize non-linguistic visualizations of an action's path (e.g. *around, through, over*) and manner (e.g. *spin, hop, jog*) predicted their verbal comprehension at 30 months, even after controlling for vocabulary levels. This is interesting because we know preverbal infants have the cognitive non-linguistic ability to discriminate both the direction of a figure and the way in which it moves with respect to the ground (Pulverman et al. 2008; Pulverman et al. 2013) and that they use knowledge for later categorization of path and manner when language is beginning to emerge (Pruden, et al. 2012; Pruden et al. 2013). Lakusta and colleagues showed English-speaking infants are able to categorize goal and source paths in dynamic motion events as early as 10 months of age—an age that precedes the acquisition of the relevant linguistic spatial terms *to, on*, and *in* (Lakusta, Spinelli, & Garcia 2017).

In order to use relational aspects of language like manner, path, and verbs in general, children first have to segment a continuous stream of action into meaningful units, then be able to categorize the same action in different contexts, and ultimately work out how their language expresses these categories (Hirsh-Pasek & Golinkoff 2010). So, while the preverbal action segmentation and recognition may proceed similarly cross-linguistically, by the time the child is learning to speak, this knowledge has to be packaged differently, as different languages have developed different solutions on how to divide the labour between manner and path within their morphosyntactic resources. For example, English packages manner within the main verb and puts path with a prepositional phrase while Spanish glues paths with the verb and outsources manner into optional gerunds (Talmy 2000). Likewise, different languages have come to different solutions as to how to mark the edge of event boundaries with verbs; with some languages happy with a basic separation between those verbs with built-in endpoints and those without; others like Russian and Bengali go further and make a distinction between changes that occur at the onset or at the end of an event (Malaia 2004; Basu & Wilbur 2010). The burden of communicating events at this level of granularity is either borne by phonology (as with American Sign Language and Japanese; Wilbur 2003; Fujimori 2012), morphology (as with Indonesian or Russian; Son & Cole 2008; Malaia & Basu 2013), or else by the interaction between the verbs, aspect, determiners, and quantifiers (as in many Germanic languages; Van Hout 2001; Ogiela, Schmitt, & Casby 2014).

Despite these differences, there are good reasons to suppose the same kinds of category-forming processes are a significant feature cross-linguistically in children's early comprehension and production of basic grammatical constructions including word classes (Ibbotson & Tomasello 2009). Evidence from English, German, Cantonese, and Polish shows that young children are slow to form abstract constructions because they fail to see the more general applicability of syntactic markers such as word order and case marking. Thus, the suggestion is that constructions redundantly marked with multiple cues could have a special status as a nucleus around which a prototype forms—which makes it difficult for them to isolate the functional significance of each cue. Introduced into the categorization literature by Rosch and colleagues, the basic idea of a prototype is that a concept, for example, *bird*, is not defined by a set of necessary and sufficient features—with all members that meet the criteria being equal. Rather, the concept has a graded structure, with fuzzy boundaries, in which some members play a privileged role and thus the prototypical bird is one that shares the most features with other birds and is maximally distinct from non-birds (Rosch

1983; Mervis & Rosch 1981). Since the introduction of the notion of a prototype into the categorization literature by Rosch and her colleagues (Rosch 1983; Mervis & Rosch 2003), the basic idea has been applied to explain the structure of word classes as well as more detailed aspects of lexical semantics (Lakoff 1987b); tense–aspect marking (Andersen & Shirai 1996; Shirai & Andersen 2006); relative clauses (Diessel & Tomasello 2005); questions with long-distance dependencies (Dąbrowska, Rowland, & Theakston 2009); subject auxiliary inversion (Goldberg 2006; Lambrecht 2012).

In the non-linguistic domain, sensitivity to the distribution of items in a category has been found to play a significant role in how quickly children form categories across a range of stimuli including shapes (Posner & Keele 1968), spatial relations (Casasola 2005), and social groups (Elio & Anderson 1984). In the early stages of language development, when the type–token ratio is low, the prototype will be closer to the most frequent item. As the type–token ratio increases, with more instances of that category, the average will begin to stabilize, and as the set approaches adulthood levels of exemplars, the prototype of that category will become increasing entrenched and insensitive to new members. If the type–token ratio remains low (as in the ditransitive), the prototype will remain skewed towards the mode. Another way of putting this is to say the prototype of a particular word class is weighted towards its most frequent members, so that children are unlikely to understand *read* or *pass* is as good an example of a ditransitive verb as *give*.

This prototype structure of word classes develops into a rich adult network of interrelated form–function associations, where words are organized in the brain more like a thesaurus of connections than a dictionary list of necessary and sufficient definitions. This predicts that upon hearing one word meaning, the hearer is primed for other similar meanings, as activation spreads through the complex network. Overall the psycholinguistic evidence supports the idea that knowledge of fairly specific (and sometimes idiosyncratic) aspects of usage patterns is available and recruited early in sentence processing. For example, sentences of the type *the boy heard the story was interesting* have structural ambiguity. *The story* could be the direct object (DO) of *heard* or it could be the subject noun of a sentential complement (SC), as it was in the above example. Hare et al. (2003, 2004) showed that it was possible to induce a DO or SC reading of the same verb on the basis of whether the preverbal context was associated with one reading or another (as determined from a corpus of natural speech). The general picture argues against a serial account of sentence processing where syntax proposes a structural interpretation for semantics to subsequently cash out (Clifton & Frazier 1989; Frazier 1987, 1989). Word-class knowledge is sensitive to contingencies (usage patterns) that hold across agents, aspect, instruments, event knowledge, and broader contextual discourse, so that altering any one may skew the construal of what is communicated. It seems unlikely then that syntactic knowledge is encapsulated from semantic, pragmatic, and world knowledge (e.g. Fodor 1995). Rather, the evidence is converging on the idea of word classes as probabilistic cues that point to a conceptual space of possibilities, which is revised and honed as the discourse unfolds between speakers.

43.5 WORD CLASSES SHAPING THOUGHT

The idea that language has a significant role in determining thought has been most intensively studied under the linguistic relatively hypothesis (Whorf 1956). In their insightful review on the topic, Wolff & Holmes (2011) find no support for the idea that language, including word classes, determines the basic categories of thought or that it overwrites pre-existing conceptual distinctions like motion, colour, number, space, time, objects, or actions. On empirical and conceptual grounds, they rule out two versions of the Whorfian hypothesis, namely that language and thought are the same thing or that there is a one-to-one mapping between language and thought. Instead, they argue that the evidence points towards language making some distinctions difficult to avoid—language as a 'spotlight' on cognition—as well as for the proposal that language can augment certain types of thinking (Wolff & Holmes 2011).

For example, if the language you use is constantly requiring you to carve the semantic space of the world in one way rather than another way it could have been carved, then it makes sense that these word-class boundaries themselves become foregrounded, privileged, and easier to access in memory, attention, and categorization, independent of whether language is being used to reason about these distinctions at the time (e.g. Van Bergen & Flecken 2017; Sakarias & Flecken 2019).

Turkish requires the speaker to take a stance on whether a past event was witnessed or not witnessed whereas English does not (Slobin 1996). Obviously, the witness–not witness class distinction is not made impossible to English speakers by not speaking Turkish, but it is made more salient to Turkish speakers when their language requires that they regularly engage with such a distinction. Likewise, for example, English speakers retain the ability to distinguish tight and loose fit, even though this distinction is not encoded with in their spatial preposition system, it is just more salient for Korean speakers who frequently must encode it (Hespos & Spelke 2004).

The permeable boundary between cognition and language also predicts that when the two conceptual systems align with each other, the speed and accuracy of judgements improve, and when they are in conflict, they reduce (Winawer et al. 2007). Boroditsky (2003) and her colleagues found support for this 'language as meddler' idea by showing that Spanish and German speakers' ability to learn associations between proper and common nouns (e.g. Tom and apple) showed interference when the grammatical gender of the common noun differed from the biological gender of the proper noun's referent. Papafragou found significant differences in the eye movements of native Greek and English speakers that corresponded to the differences in the way their language encoded manner and path. But when they watched the same videos with no expectation to engage their language the eye movements were largely the same (Papafragou, Hulbert, & Trueswell 2008).

Word classes can also push the boundaries of what cognition can do, for example there is evidence to suggest that exact magnitude calculation requires numeric language (Dehaene et al. 1999; Gordon 2004, 2010; Frank et al. 2008) as opposed to the numerosity that merely discriminates large and small quantities and that is present pre-linguistically and in non-human species (Gallistel 1990; Wynn 1995; Dehaene 1997). Mental-state verbs may also have a crucial role in exercising the mindreading ability to higher levels of flexibility. For example, de Villiers and colleagues have found that the language delays of deaf children have a very significant impact on their false belief reasoning even when the tasks are nonverbal: the more impoverished their language, the later is their false belief understanding with some children not passing the false belief until 8 years old (Peterson & Siegal 1995; de Villiers & de Villiers 2000; Woolfe, Want, & Siegal 2002; de Villiers 2005).

These findings are consistent with the idea of significant interaction between language and cognition and that the regular use of language can lead people to prefer one construal of the world, based on their word-class knowledge, over others. None of the findings imply that people are unable to use certain conceptual distinctions that are not afforded to them by their language. This means the conceptual playing field is wider than the area that language occupies—not the other way around. Second, note that for all the areas of cognition where language has been found to meddle with, highlight, or augment cognition—spatial categorization, intention-reading, colour perception—they are all beginning to emerge before language. It is language that first must accommodate to the landscape of cognition even if language then immediately responds by making future cognitive decision more or less likely.

A promising approach for understanding such complex interactions seems to be through theoretical frameworks like that of dynamic systems theory (DST) (Thelen & Smith 1994; Smith & Thelen 2003). It seeks to examine complex questions about the interrelatedness of the whole and its parts, particularly those relationships that are nested in some way into complex hierarchical feedback loops—in other words the kinds of relationships between word classes and cognition that psycholinguists are interested in (Bogartz 1994; Smith 2005). For example, this framework is useful in the debate as to whether increases in short-term verbal memory allow for greater vocabulary development (Adams & Gathercole 1995; Baddeley, Gathercole, & Papagno 1998; Avons et al. 1998; Leclercq & Majerus 2010) or vocabulary growth expands the boundaries of what short-term memory can do (Fowler 1991; Metsala 1999; Bowey 2006). This kind of transactional modelling is also evident in the social cognition–language interface: higher levels of perspective-taking motivate more sophisticated use of mental-state language and in turn, an expanding repertoire of mental state language repeatedly highlights different psychological perspectives.

43.6 The Universality or Otherwise of Word Classes

Before researchers get to put words under the psycholinguistic microscope, the sheer diversity of cultural forms that count as 'a word class' must be acknowledged. This point is made abundantly clear by the breath of typological variation under investigation in Part IV of this volume and in many previous works such as 'The Myth of Language Universals' by Evans and Levinson (2009). They note that it has widely been assumed the 'big four': nouns, verbs, adjectives, and adverbs will appear across all languages. Yet there are some languages that happily do without an open adverb class and modify actions, events, and states in other ways (Hengeveld 1992a); other languages like Lao have no adjective class but package the qualities of concepts as a kind of subclass of verb types (Enfield 2004) and perhaps there are even languages without a basic noun–verb distinction, although the leading contenders for this—like some of the languages of the Philippines and Pacific North-West Coast—remain controversial examples after a century of debate. There are also many classes of words outside the big four such as ideophones, positionals, and coverbs that are routinely employed but do not appear in the most-studied Indo-European languages.

The theoretical response to this cultural diversity has led some linguistics to use variation as their starting point when building theoretical frameworks rather than try to wrestle 'the big four' into a Procrustean bed. For example, Croft's Radical Construction Grammar (2001; and see Chapter 11 in this volume) begins with the assumption that different languages have different constructions, and, if word classes are defined by their distributional behaviour in those constructions, then it follows that the word classes that emerge from this are also unique to the language. To drive this point home, Croft uses examples showing the distinctiveness between the word classes of *different* languages and of different constructions *within* a language. Haspelmath (Chapter 2 in this volume) argues for the separation of any analysis of a particular language—which should remain a complete analysis of all a language's cross-cutting clauses, categories, and everything else—from analysis of the similarities between languages—which should remain partial because not everything in a language is comparable to something in other languages.

In the face of this diversity, does it make sense to talk of a general theory of word-class psycholinguistics that would go beyond a language-by-language inventory of descriptions, such as (1) people in language x use 'verb-like items' in construction p in this way (2) people in language y use 'verb-like items' in construction q in this way and so on? Croft acknowledges word classes *are* important for describing individual languages, though they are variable in usage and across time. Haspelmath, who as we have seen would warn against any cross-linguistic proliferation of word classes, is willing to say that all languages have roots denoting things and roots denoting actions, which behave in similar ways. Thus, we can meaningfully talk of comparative studies distinguishing nouns and verbs, however, comparison beyond this, he might argue, rapidly becomes problematic.

Acknowledging overlap between categories is not necessarily the same thing as acknowledging it is meaningless to talk of categories or that there is no inherent predictive value of having a category in the first place. For example, the overlapping bell curves of the men's and women's height shows it makes sense to talk of the typical man being taller than the typical woman (the peakiness of the distribution), while at the same time acknowledging there are some women taller than the average man and some men shorter than the average woman (the standard deviation of the distribution). In the absence of all other knowledge, gender is still a category for predicting height. Likewise, we can acknowledge that verbs and nouns exist on a huge typological spectrum of phonological, morphological, semantic, and syntactic variation. And yet it still might make sense to talk of something being more verb- or noun-like, especially if by doing so, we can predict the behaviour of how novel versions of these elements will behave in novel constructions across languages, based on the features that they share with members of their own class. The same goes for the classes of nouns, adjectives, adverbs, adpositions, and demonstratives that make Part III of this handbook possible.

So, while it is true the utility of forming a class remains universal—smart prediction—and the processes that form them psychologically similar, the *content* of those classes is best understood as an invitation to share a perspective on something meaningful to that culture. For example, Everett discusses the following example (2012: 194). When a concept is sufficiently prominent in a culture, that is part of the shared values, it can predict what is left unsaid, as in the case of Amele, a language spoken in New Guinea. It is an SOV language but when the meaning of 'giving' is expressed the verb is omitted. Roberts (1998) argues that there is no verb 'to give' because giving is so basic to Amele culture that this can be left backgrounded. For example:

(2)
> Jo   eu   ihaciadigen
> House   that   show
> 'I will show that house to you.'

The verb *ihac* means 'to show' but in the example below the verb is omitted:

(3) Naus   Dege   houten
     Name   name   Pig
     'Naus [gave] a pig to Dege.'

This shows us the extent to which word classes are often not given to us by the structure of the world or objective reality but choices we make to construe the situation from a particular perspective, quite often to adapt to the needs and/or expectations of the audience: I call a dandelion a flower if it's in a bouquet; I call it a weed if it's growing in the wrong place; I call it *Taraxacum officinale* if I'm a botanist; I call it food when feeding it to a pet guinea pig. Asking the question whether a dandelion is a flower or a weed just does not have the same truth-conditional relationship to reality as asking whether 2 + 2 = 4. So, our words and constructions are invitations to share our perspective on an object, event, or process and not always truth-conditional-bearing propositions about the world (Langacker 1987b, 1991).

Furthermore, psycholinguistics might be able to inform a more general theory of word-class acquisition, production, and comprehension if we regard word classes as behaving much like any other (non-linguistic) category. That means, regardless of the cultural form a word class might take, general cognitive process such as categorization, analogy, memory, attention, inhibition, and social cognition are at work on them. These processes, biases, bottlenecks, and constraints stand a much better chance of being generalized, precisely because they are not subject to the same cultural forces as language.

For example, cognition has responded to the challenge of a rapid stream of incoming linguistic information and a steep signal decay by quickly chunking the information and compressing it into a structured hierarchy (Christiansen & Chater 2016). Importantly, the same kind of perceptual pressure that creates this 'now-or-never' bottleneck is also in operation for cognitive domains other than language, such as vision, haptic stimuli, event cognition, and non-linguistic auditory stimuli (e.g. Miller, Galanter, & Pribram 1960; Ericcson, Chase, & Faloon 1980; Gobet et al. 2001). The kind of forward prediction that this kind of hierarchy buys the user, has been shown to be a common principle of computational design of motor control and wider cognition (Wolpert, Ghahramani, & Flanagan 2001; Clark 2013; Pickering & Garrod 2013a). The detail-rich bottom-up information is recoded, compressed, and passed up to the next level as a more abstracted and chunked representation. Language has evolved to fit this cognitive niche allowing linguistic chunks to exist at the same time across acoustic, phonological, word, and discourse levels (Christiansen & Arnon 2017). This chunk-and-pass solution allows cognition to capture the incoming information in a maximally distinct and efficient way, and reduces the chance of interference between overlapping representations (Christiansen & Chater 2016). Because this hierarchical structure is a domain-general format, language use shows the same practice effects as other domains, namely, repeated use of a chunk in the hierarchy leads to greater degrees of automaticity in a drive for cognitive efficiency (Newell & Rosenbloom 1981; Logan 1988; Heathcote, Brown, & Mewhort 2000; Bybee & McClelland 2005).

In the end, there must be room for both lumpers and splitters in the debate. We need both levels of analysis—those that celebrate the cultural diversity that word classes can take; seek to understand the historical roots of why some languages look the way they do when they could have looked differently (and yet still be cognitively possible); and remind us of all the ways language has evolved to get the communicative job done. We also need analysis that identifies when different languages have come to common solutions to the common engineering problems of acquisition, comprehension, and production, and identifying peaky distributions in cross-linguistic word-class data wherever they do occur. The conclusion is that, while the utility of forming a word class remains universal—behavioural prediction—and the processes that form them psychologically similar, the content of those classes is best understood as an invitation to share a perspective on something meaningful and specific to the culture from which language emerges.

CHAPTER 44

WORD CLASSES IN NEUROLINGUISTICS

DAVID KEMMERER

44.1 INTRODUCTION

GRAMMATICAL categories—also known as syntactic categories, lexical categories, word classes, and parts of speech—play important roles in human languages because they strongly influence the ways in which conceptual structures are packaged in lexical items and, even more importantly, the ways in which lexical items are combined to form complex expressions.[1] Across the roughly 6,500 languages of the world, the most basic and widely attested categories are nouns, verbs, and adjectives. They typically make up large open classes whose memberships constantly fluctuate as new items are added and old ones fade away. In contrast, other categories tend to be both small and closed, with memberships that do not change very quickly over time. Some familiar examples from English are prepositions, conjunctions, and articles, and some lesser-known examples from other languages are postpositions, classifiers, and focus markers. Although a great deal has been learned about the nature of grammatical categories during the past few decades, several competing accounts have been proposed by generative, cognitive, functional, and typological theorists, and many issues remain controversial (for a survey of approaches, see Rauh 2010; see also Hengeveld & van Lier 2010b; Haspelmath 2012a; Rijkhoff & van Lier 2013; Simone & Masini 2014; Blaszczak et al. 2015; Vapnarsky & Veneziano 2017).

Recent neurolinguistic research on grammatical categories has addressed a variety of phenomena, but the vast majority of studies have been devoted to a single topic of central importance, namely the noun–verb distinction. In fact, the cortical underpinnings of this distinction have been explored in countless investigations employing all of the major brain-mapping methods, including deficit–lesion correlations in brain-damaged patients, positron emission tomography (PET), functional magnetic resonance imaging (fMRI), transcranial magnetic stimulation (TMS), extracranial and intracranial electrophysiology, and magnetoencephalography (MEG) (for reviews and meta-analyses see Druks 2002; Black & Chiat 2003; Cappa & Perani 2003; Shapiro & Caramazza 2003b, 2004; Luzzatti et al. 2006;

---
[1] This chapter is a modified version of Kemmerer (2019b).

Berlingeri et al. 2008; Mätzig et al. 2009; Pillon & d'Honincthun 2010; Vigliocco et al. 2011; Crepaldi et al. 2011, 2013; Kemmerer 2014; Faroqi-Shah et al. 2018). As a consequence, the literature on this topic is now quite large and complex. But even though it contains a wealth of empirically solid, theoretically interesting, and clinically relevant material, there are still many unanswered questions. With the aim of providing a concise overview of the field, this chapter concentrates on some of the most prominent neurolinguistic issues regarding the noun–verb distinction. Towards the end, however, there is also a brief discussion of neurolinguistic research on adjectives and several types of closed-class items. The brain regions referred to in the text are illustrated in Figure 44.1.

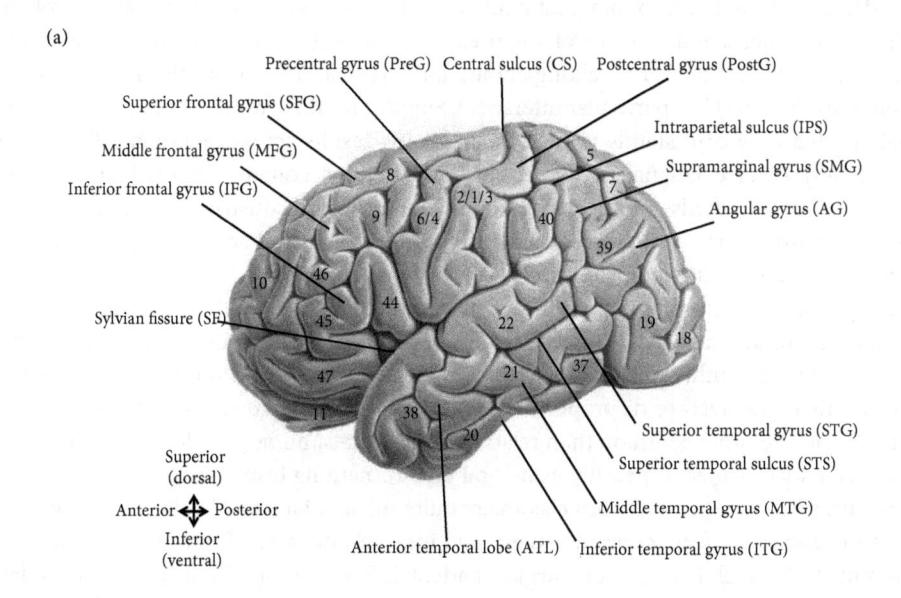

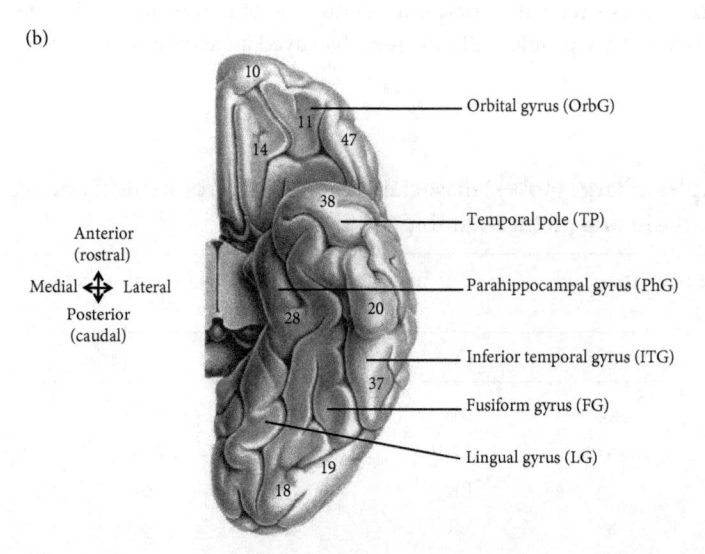

FIGURE 44.1 Major gyri, sulci, and Brodmann areas (numbered) of the human brain shown on left lateral (A) and ventral (B) surfaces

44.2 Nouns and verbs

44.2.1 Starting with the universal semantic prototypes

According to several linguistic frameworks, the most basic grammatical categories can be characterized partly in terms of universal prototypes that are grounded in meaning (Langacker 1987a; Anderson 1997; O'Grady 1997; Wierzbicka 2000; Croft 1991, 2000, 2007). For example, Croft (1991, 2000, 2007b) argues that prototypical nouns and verbs reflect certain default combinations of pragmatic function and semantic class, with nouns involving reference to objects and verbs involving predication of actions (for present purposes, 'reference' is what the speaker is talking about, and 'predication' is what the speaker asserts about the referent(s) in a particular utterance). Support for this proposal comes from corpus analyses that have consistently yielded the following results across geographically and genealogically diverse languages: referential constructions contain predominantly object words, and object words appear predominantly in referential constructions; similarly, predicative constructions contain predominantly action words, and action words appear predominantly in predicative constructions (Croft 1991, 2000, 2007b).

In light of these considerations, it is not surprising that the lion's share of neurolinguistic research on basic grammatical categories has focused on object nouns and action verbs. Some of the most influential studies have shown that each of these prototypical categories can be either selectively or disproportionately impaired by brain damage. Although relative verb deficits are more common than relative noun deficits, numerous double dissociations have been documented, especially using oral picture-naming tasks, and often the accuracy differences between the two word classes are quite substantial (see Mätzig et al. 2009, for a review of 240 previously reported patients and nine new ones; see Tomasino et al. 2019, for a recent study involving 99 neurosurgical patients). For example, Table 44.1 presents data from 20 representative cases—ten with worse oral production of nouns than verbs, and ten with the opposite performance profile—all of whom displayed an accuracy difference of at least 30%.

Table 44.1 Examples of large (30%+) dissociations between prototypical nouns and verbs in oral picture-naming tasks

Patients with worse noun than verb production			Patients with worse verb than noun production		
Case	Nouns	Verbs	Case	Nouns	Verbs
Mario	7	88	BW	98	60
HY	35	85	FDP	96	50
HF	49	83	LK	93	63
EA	42	82	LR	92	40
ZBL	41	78	EM	90	59

Table 44.1 Continued

Patients with worse noun than verb production			Patients with worse verb than noun production		
SK	47	77	TB	88	37
ML	38	75	UB	87	48
SF	27	73	FC	87	30
EBA	12	72	RE	83	35
RG	29	64	MB	83	35

Source: Cells indicate percent correct. (Data from Mätzig et al. 2009.)

For some patients with category-related deficits like these, the locus of the cognitive impairment appears to be at the level of conceptual knowledge, as indicated by the following forms of convergent evidence. First, the majority of errors are either omissions (i.e. 'don't know' responses) or semantic substitutions (e.g. calling a penguin a duck). Second, the relevant word class is disrupted not only during production tasks like picture naming, but also during comprehension tasks like word–picture matching. Third, the lesions affect brain regions that are likely to be involved in representing the relevant kinds of concepts. This last point is elaborated below (see also Kemmerer 2019a).

Patients who exhibit significantly greater noun than verb deficits usually have damage in the left temporal lobe due to either a stroke (Mätzig et al. 2009) or a degenerative disorder such as Alzheimer's disease (Cappa et al. 1998) or herpes simplex encephalitis (Damasio & Tranel 1993). These findings fit well with other literature regarding the neural substrates of the kinds of object concepts that tend to be encoded by prototypical nouns. When people process such concepts, they often retrieve various types of modality-specific object properties, including shape, colour, sound, smell, taste, and manipulability (Binder & Desai 2011). Among all of these features, however, the one that carries the most semantic weight is shape (Gainotti et al. 2013). It is well established that the posterior and middle portions of the ventral temporal cortex are essential for recognizing objects based on perceived shape (Damasio et al. 2004; Kriegeskorte et al. 2008). Additionally, a great deal of data suggests that some ventral temporal regions—partly overlapping, but mostly lying next to those involved in perception—also represent shape information when words for objects are processed (Martin 2007; Capitani et al. 2009). Moreover, compared to the comprehension of action words, the comprehension of object words engages the ventral temporal cortex quite rapidly, within about 200 ms (Pulvermüller et al. 1999a; Chan et al. 2011). Taken together, these discoveries support the hypothesis that the ventral temporal cortex implements the most important representational component, namely shape, of the meanings of prototypical nouns.

As for patients who exhibit significantly greater verb than noun deficits, their lesions are rather disparate, but usually one or more of the following left-hemisphere areas is affected: the inferior frontal gyrus (IFG), often together with nearby motor areas; the inferior parietal lobule, especially the supramarginal gyrus (SMG); and the posterior middle temporal gyrus (pMTG). These findings come primarily from studies of patients who have suffered either a stroke (Kemmerer et al. 2012; Desai et al. 2015; Alyahya et al. 2018; Riccardi et al. 2019) or a degenerative disorder such as progressive nonfluent aphasia (Hillis et al. 2006), amyotrophic lateral sclerosis (also known as motor neuron disease; Bak & Hodges 2004; York et al. 2014), or corticobasal degeneration (Silveri & Ciccarelli 2007; Cotelli et al. 2018). Such deficit–lesion correlations dovetail with other data suggesting that the implicated regions underlie the kinds of action concepts that tend to be encoded by prototypical verbs. Although the precise ways in which these regions contribute to action concepts are only beginning to be elucidated, some of the leading ideas are as follows. In the frontal lobe, the posterior IFG—in particular, Brodmann area (BA) 44—may subserve the sequential and hierarchical organization of action concepts (Clerget et al. 2009; Fazio et al. 2010), and precentral motor areas may subserve the body-part-specific motor features of action concepts (Pulvermüller 2013; Kemmerer 2015). In the parietal lobe, the SMG may subserve the spatial–relational and goal-directed aspects of action concepts (Hamilton & Grafton 2008; Goldenberg 2009). Moreover, in the temporal lobe, the pMTG may subserve the visual motion patterns specified by action concepts (Watson et al. 2013; Urgesi et al. 2014). It is noteworthy that all of these brain regions either overlap with or lie next to regions that are recruited during the execution and observation of actions (Molenberghs et al. 2012; see also Papitto et al. 2020). Furthermore, compared to the comprehension of object words, the comprehension of action words engages motor-related frontal regions very quickly, within about 200 ms (Pulvermüller et al. 1999a; Shtyrov et al. 2014). Overall, these findings support the hypothesis that the frontal, parietal, and temporal regions described above implement the core representational parameters of the meanings of prototypical verbs.

44.2.2 Category-related disorders involving the representation/retrieval of lexical forms

So far we have focused on semantic accounts of the sorts of noun–verb dissociations that are frequently displayed by brain-damaged patients when they perform picture-naming tasks. It is important to realize, however, that such dissociations can also arise from post-semantic impairments. This is revealed in a particularly striking way by patients who exhibit word production deficits that selectively or disproportionately affect not just one grammatical category—either nouns or verbs—but also just one output channel—either speaking or writing (Caramazza & Hillis 1991; Rapp & Caramazza 1998; Hillis et al. 2002, 2003; see also Rapp & Goldrick 2006).

For example, as shown in Figure 44.2, case MML, who suffered from progressive nonfluent aphasia, manifested steadily worsening spoken production of prototypical verbs over a 2.5-year period, while her written production of prototypical verbs, as well as her spoken and written production of prototypical nouns, remained fairly accurate (Hillis et al. 2002). MML's poor spoken production of prototypical verbs could not be due to impaired knowledge or processing of action concepts because her written production of the very same verbs was good. Instead, her remarkably specific deficit must reflect some kind of post-semantic problem.

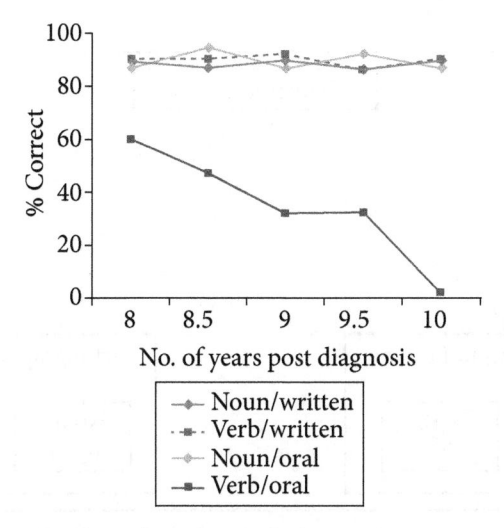

FIGURE 44.2 Longitudinal performance of the progressive nonfluent aphasic patient MML on tasks involving the spoken and written naming of objects and actions with nouns and verbs, from ~8 to 10.5 years following diagnosis. Spoken production of verbs deteriorated steadily (red plot), but written production of verbs, as well both spoken and written production of nouns, remained unaffected. (Reproduced with permission from Shapiro & Caramazza 2003; original data from Hillis et al. 2002)

Cases like this raise many intriguing questions about the relationships between meaning, grammar, and the modality-specific (i.e. phonological and orthographic) lexicons (for detailed theoretical discussion, see Caramazza & Miozzo 1998; Rapp & Caramazza 2002). Here, however, we will restrict our attention to the issue of whether the word forms in each lexicon are segregated according to grammatical category. On the one hand, the neuropsychological dissociations exhibited by patients like MML are clearly consistent with the hypothesis that the noun–verb distinction is respected at the level of lexical forms. For example, MML's own performance profile could be explained in terms of increasing damage to just one set of words—specifically, the verb compartment of the phonological lexicon (Figure 44.3a). On the other hand, the available data can also be accommodated by an alternative hypothesis that does not require nouns and verbs to be differentiated at the lexical level, but instead assumes that the connectional pathways between the meanings and forms of particular word classes can be independently disrupted. Applied to MML, such an account could be formulated as follows: (1) the meanings of prototypical nouns and verbs are represented in separate semantic subsystems, as discussed in the previous section; (2) each semantic subsystem projects to both of the modality-specific lexicons; and (3) MML's disorder involves increasing damage to just one route—specifically, the pathway that projects from action concepts to the corresponding verb forms in the phonological lexicon (Figure 44.3b).

(a)

[Diagram: Semantic System connecting to Phonological Output Lexicon (Nouns 'apple', Verbs 'bite' [crossed out]) and Orthographic Output Lexicon (Nouns 'apple', Verbs 'bite')]

(b)

[Diagram: Semantic System containing Object Concepts 'APPLE' and Action Concepts 'BITE', connecting to Phonoligical Output Lexicon and Orthographic Output Lexicon, with a cross on the link from Action Concepts to Phonological Output Lexicon]

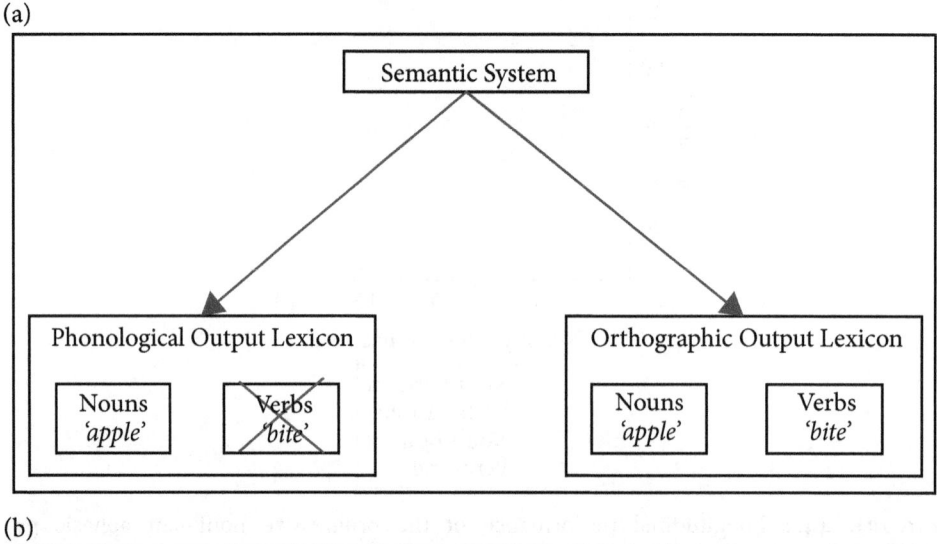

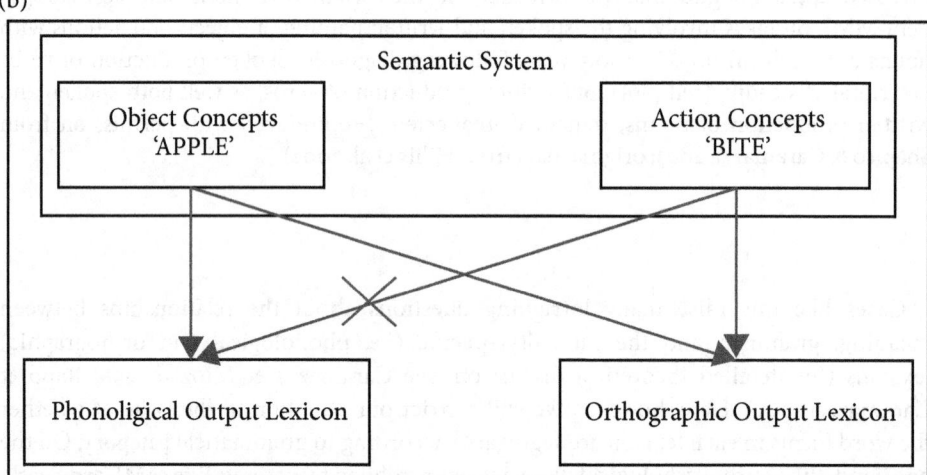

FIGURE 44.3 Two alternative accounts of the performance profile of patient MML depicted in 44.1. (A) An account that assumes segregation of nouns and verbs within the modality-specific output lexicons. (B) An account that assumes segregation of word meanings according to conceptual category within the semantic system. In each architecture, the cross indicates the site of progressive dysfunction

Thus, even though patients with combined grammatical category-specific and output channel-specific deficits support the view that the lexical forms of nouns and verbs are segregated in the brain, they certainly do not force such a conclusion. It is noteworthy, however, that the question of whether grammatical category distinctions are captured at the lexical level continues to be controversial, and it has been addressed from several other perspectives, as shown in the next section.

44.2.3 Efforts to overcome confounds between conceptual and grammatical factors

From a methodological point of view, there are both merits and shortcomings to deliberately designing some neurolinguistic studies so that they focus specifically on the most prototypical grammatical categories—i.e. object nouns and action verbs. On the positive side, such a strategy can shed light on how the brain implements the universal prototypes identified by typologically oriented linguists like Croft (1991, 2000, 2007b). On the negative side, however, conflating the conceptual distinction between objects and actions with the grammatical distinction between nouns and verbs makes it difficult if not impossible to discover the neural correlates of a much wider range of phenomena involving language-particular word classes. In an effort to overcome this limitation, an increasing number of researchers have begun to conduct studies in which conceptual–grammatical confounds are minimized. Two different approaches to doing this are summarized below. As we will see, however, both of them have generated mixed results, since some studies suggest that, *qua* lexical items, nouns and verbs are not systematically differentiated in the brain, whereas other studies suggest that they rely on at least partly separate neural networks.

44.2.3.1 *Strategy 1: Closely match the meanings and processing demands of nouns and verbs*

According to some studies, when nouns and verbs are well matched for semantic dimensions as well as processing requirements, they recruit essentially the same brain regions to the same degrees. For instance, in a PET study carried out in Italian, Vigliocco et al. (2006) asked subjects to simply listen to four sets of words. Crucially, all of the word lists were carefully created so as to allow the investigators to independently determine which patterns of brain activity were due to conceptual factors and which were due to grammatical factors:

- sensory nouns (SNs), i.e. nouns with rich sensory features (e.g. *lampi* 'lightning')
- motor nouns (MNs), i.e. nouns with rich motor features (e.g. *giravolta* 'twirl')
- sensory verbs (SVs), i.e. verbs with rich sensory features (e.g. *luccicano* 'shine')
- motor verbs (MVs), i.e. verbs with rich motor features (e.g. *scuote* 'shake')

Two contrasts were performed to identify the neural correlates of sensory words and motor words, irrespective of grammatical category, and both of these contrasts revealed activity in some of the expected areas. Specifically, with regard to sensory words, the contrast [(SNs + SVs)−(MNs + MVs)] revealed activity in the left ventral temporal cortex, and with regard to motor words, the opposite contrast [(MNs + MVs)−(SNs + SVs)] revealed activity in the left lateral motor cortex. In addition, and more importantly, two contrasts were performed to identify the neural correlates of nouns and verbs, irrespective of conceptual considerations; however, neither of these contrasts yielded any significant effects whatsoever, even when the investigators switched from whole-brain analyses to region-of-interest analyses. More precisely, no activity was revealed by the contrast [(SNs + MNs)−(SVs + MVs)], which was meant to identify regions unique to nouns, and likewise, no activity was revealed by the opposite contrast [(SVs + MVs)—(SNs + MNs)], which was meant to identify regions unique to verbs. What these findings suggest is that when conceptual–grammatical confounds are reduced, and when computational loads are also controlled, nouns and verbs are not segregated in the brain, but instead depend on shared neural resources (see also Siri et al. 2008, Barber et al. 2010, and Vigliocco et al. 2011, as well as Pulvermüller et al. 1999b, Collina et al. 2001, and Tabossi et al. 2010).

On the other hand, there is some recent evidence for the view that nouns and verbs do recruit at least partly separate neural networks, even when their meanings and processing demands are fairly similar. Focusing once again on Italian, Tsigka et al. (2014) conducted a MEG study in which participants silently read noun–verb homonyms in two syntactically minimal contexts that each had two variants (for a similar study in Spanish, only using event-related potentials, see Yudes et al. 2016):

- article + noun
  - singular (e.g. *il ballo* 'the dance')
  - plural (e.g. *i balli* 'the dances')
- pronoun + verb
  - first-person singular (e.g. *io ballo* 'I dance')
  - second-person singular (e.g. *tu balli* 'you dance')

The results of source analyses using Minimum Norm Estimates (MNE) are depicted in Figure 44.4 Looking first at the time windows for function word processing, it can be seen that the articles and pronouns activated essentially the same posterior bilateral areas; however, relative to the articles, the pronouns evoked greater activity at right parietal sites during the 88–108 ms window and at left prefrontal sites during the 232–251 ms window. Turning now to the more interesting time windows for content word processing, what stands out most clearly is that the verbs elicited more extensive and robust activity than the nouns over the entire course of measurement—initially in right parietal clusters during the 115–136 and 195–212 ms windows, then in bilateral central and midline regions during the 280–300 ms window, next in the left IFG during the 297–319 ms window, then in a large left parietal cluster during the 380–397 ms window, and finally again in the left IFG during the 393–409 ms window. Because the noun–verb homonyms were very close in meaning, the neurotopographic differences that emerged between them are unlikely to reflect conceptual factors. Hence, according to Tsigka et al. (2014: 95), the findings 'invite the conclusion that at least partly separable neural substrates are involved in processing grammatical class information and the corresponding morphosyntactic operations'. However, given that the homonymous nouns and verbs engaged many of the same regions, only with verbs activating them more strongly, the authors acknowledge that the data do not completely rule out the possibility that the two categories have some cortical underpinnings in common at the lexical level.

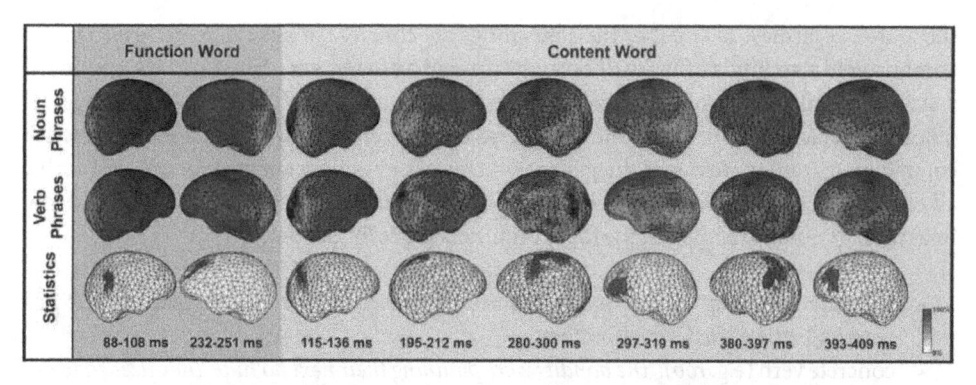

FIGURE 44.4 MEG-based Minimum Norm Estimates (MNEs) for the time windows during which significant differences between visually presented noun phrases (NPs) and verb phrases (VPs) were revealed by cluster analysis. The top and middle rows display the averaged MNEs of NP-and VP-related activity across the consecutive time slices for which cluster analysis revealed significant differences between NPs and VPs. The bottom row shows the extension of clusters which significantly differed between NPs and VPs. Significant clusters were defined as spatially and temporally contiguous brain regions (>10 vertices; >12 samples) whose spatial extent, however, could vary over time. To indicate the stability of the cluster, the percentage of samples with respect to overall temporal persistence of the cluster is coded by shading intensity. A value of 100% indicates that the corresponding vertex belonged to the cluster throughout the cluster's lifetime. Dark-grey and light-grey backgrounds indicate time windows corresponding to the presentation of function word and content word, respectively. (Reproduced with permission from Tsigka et al. 2014: 92.)

44.2.3.2 *Strategy 2: Investigate both concrete and abstract nouns and verbs*

Pursuing another approach to disentangling the conceptual and grammatical aspects of word classes, Moseley & Pulvermüller (2014) carried out an fMRI study in which participants silently read the following four types of stimuli:

- concrete nouns (e.g. *mouse*)
- concrete verbs (e.g. *chomp*)
- abstract nouns (e.g. *truce*)
- abstract verbs (e.g. *glean*)

Analyses of the imaging data revealed a significant interaction between conceptual (i.e. concrete vs abstract) and grammatical (i.e. noun vs verb) factors, especially in left frontocentral regions. Further exploration, however, indicated that although the concrete nouns and verbs triggered distinct patterns of cortical engagement, the abstract nouns and verbs did not. Based on these results, the authors concluded—in a manner similar to Vigliocco et al. (2006)—that when neurotopographic differences are observed between nouns and verbs in single-word processing tasks, they reflect semantic factors rather than lexical segregation.

On the other hand, an earlier study by Berndt et al. (2002) used neuropsychological methods to support the hypothesis that nouns and verbs have at least partly distinct neural substrates, regardless of whether their meanings are concrete or abstract. The investigators administered two kinds of tasks to seven brain-damaged patients. The first task employed a standard oral picture-naming paradigm to assess the patients' retrieval of prototypical object nouns and action verbs. The second task, however, employed an auditory sentence completion paradigm to assess the patients' retrieval of not only concrete nouns and verbs, all of which had high imageability, but also abstract nouns and verbs, all of which had low imageability. Some examples of the four conditions are as follows:

- concrete noun (e.g. *scale*): *Bonny had been following a strict diet. To find out if it was working, she weighed herself on the _____.*
- concrete verb (e.g. *rob*): *The bandits were planning their next holdup. They needed to decide which bank would be easiest to _____.*
- abstract noun (e.g. *fault*): *Jennifer was upset that she might be blamed for the accident. She hoped everyone knew that it wasn't her _____.*
- abstract verb (e.g. *stay*): *Andy found it difficult to visit his mother in the hospital. He wanted to get away, but she wanted him to _____.*

The seven patients exhibited several different kinds of performance profiles across the tasks, but for present purposes the most interesting case was RE. As shown in Figure 44.5, she manifested significantly worse production of verbs than nouns across the board, with no effect of imageability in the sentence completion task (for similar data from other patients, see Crepaldi et al. 2006). This demonstrates that, irrespective of conceptual considerations, verbs can be disproportionately impaired relative to nouns. And this in turn provides some leverage for the view that the neural substrates of word classes are determined to some extent by genuinely grammatical factors.

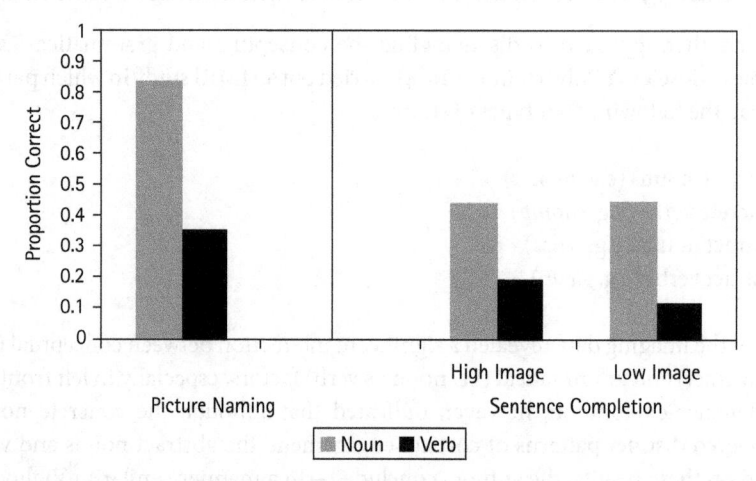

FIGURE 44.5 Proportion of correct responses by patient RE for nouns and verbs in a task involving object/action picture naming (left panel) and in a task requiring sentence completion with target words rated as having high or low imageability (right panel). Verb production was significantly worse than noun production in both tasks, and there was no effect of imageability in the sentence completion task. (Reproduced with permission from Berndt et al. 2002: 361.)

44.2.4 Focusing on inflection

Another way in which researchers have transcended the limitations of prototypical nouns and verbs is by investigating category-specific morphosyntactic operations that are not constrained by the conceptual distinction between objects and actions. So far, most of this work has attempted to elucidate the neural networks that underlie number inflection for count nouns (e.g. *I have two thoughts about that*) and tense–agreement inflection for main verbs (e.g. *Yesterday I developed a new plan*). Overall, the literature suggests that during production tasks these two types of category-specific morphosyntactic operations depend on neural networks that are partly shared and partly segregated (for reviews see Shapiro & Caramazza 2009; Kemmerer, in press, ch. 11). Broca's area (i.e. BAs 44 and 45 in the left IFG) seems to implement a relatively late stage of processing that occurs just before morphophonological encoding and that is essentially the same for the two classes of words (Sahin et al. 2006, 2009; Cappelletti et al. 2008). However, the computation of appropriate morphosyntactic features—i.e. number features for count nouns and tense–agreement features for main verbs—seems to take place during an earlier, higher-order stage of processing, and at this stage the operations for the two classes of words appear to have separate cortical underpinnings.

Some of the evidence for this view comes from neuropsychological studies that have revealed double dissociations between number inflection for count nouns and tense–agreement inflection for main verbs. For example, Shapiro et al. (2000) and Shapiro & Caramazza (2003a) reported two stroke patients, JR and RC, who were given two tasks that required them to complete sentence frames with the correctly inflected forms of words. In the first task, the key words were real noun–verb homonyms that had equivalent forms and closely related meanings (e.g. *a guide, to guide*). As shown below, two sentence frames called for singular and plural forms of count nouns, and two sentence frames called for third person plural and third person singular forms of main verbs:

- Inflection of real nouns
    - *These are guides; this is a* _____ *(guide-ø)*
    - *This is a guide; these are* _____ *(guides)*
- Inflection of real verbs
    - *This person guides; these people* _____ *(guide-ø)*
    - *These people guide; this person* _____ *(guides)*

In the second task, the key words were pseudo noun–verb homonyms (e.g. *a fleeve; to fleeve*), which gave the researchers even more assurance that if the patients responded differently to the two categories, it could not be due to either phonological or conceptual factors. As shown below, the sentence frames were identical to those employed in the first task:

- Inflection of pseudo nouns
    - *These are fleeves; this is a* _____ *(fleeve-ø)*
    - *This is a fleeve; these are* _____ *(fleeves)*
- Inflection of pseudo verbs
    - *This person fleeves; these people* _____ *(fleeve-ø)*
    - *These people fleeve; this person* _____ *(fleeves)*

The central finding was that the two patients manifested opposite performance profiles for the two types of inflection, and their dissociations were present for both real words and pseudo words. In particular, JR was significantly worse at inflecting count nouns for number than main verbs for tense–agreement, whereas RC was significantly worse at inflecting main verbs for tense–agreement than count nouns for number (for similar dissociations displayed by other patients, see Tsapkini et al. 2002; Laiacona & Caramazza 2004; Benetello et al. 2016). In their discussion of the complementary deficits exhibited by JR and RC, Shapiro & Caramazza (2003a: 1194) emphasize that in both cases the disrupted capacities are not only category-specific, but also 'seem to be grammatical, and not directly involved in retrieving stored information about word form or meaning; otherwise it is not clear how we might account for the observed deficits with pseudo words, which presumably have no memorized features'.

The discovery that certain morphosyntactic operations for count nouns and main verbs can be differentially impaired raises the question of which brain regions subserve those operations. Unfortunately, very little is known about the regions that underlie the computation of number features for count nouns, but there are some hints that this process may depend on cooperative interactions between the left mid/anterior fusiform gyrus, the left inferior parietal lobule, and the superior portion of Broca's area (Sahin et al. 2006; Shapiro et al. 2006, 2012; Shapiro & Caramazza 2009; see also Domahs et al. 2012). On the other hand, considerable progress has been made in identifying the regions that underlie the computation of tense–agreement features for main verbs, with most of the data pointing to a network involving the left pMTG and the left middle frontal gyrus (MFG). Here we will focus on the latter region and address the specific issue of whether its anterior or posterior sector is most critical.

Support for the importance of the *posterior* portion of the left MFG comes from case RC, since he was disproportionately impaired for verb inflection, and his lesion, but not JR's, extended into this territory. In addition, several fMRI studies suggest that, relative to noun inflection, verb inflection recruits the left posterior MFG immediately superior to BA44. For instance, Shapiro et al. (2006) obtained results along these lines in a study that used real and pseudo word tasks like those described above (see also Shapiro et al. 2012). When the verb conditions were contrasted against the noun conditions, one of the only activated areas was the left posterior MFG. The same region was also engaged significantly more by verb than noun inflection in an fMRI study by Willms et al. (2011), but these researchers went two steps farther than Shapiro et al. (2006): first, they employed tasks that required English–Spanish bilingual speakers to inflect words in both languages; and second, they used multivoxel pattern analysis to show that within the left posterior MFG the specific activation patterns elicited by the verb conditions, relative to the noun conditions, were virtually identical across the two languages. Finally, Kielar et al. (2011) recently found that both the overt (i.e. out loud) and covert (i.e. silent) production of tense–agreement morphology for English verbs recruited the left posterior MFG, together with the caudally adjacent precentral gyrus. Overall, then, there appears to be a fair amount of neuropsychological and fMRI data implicating the posterior sector of the left MFG in verb-specific morphosyntactic processing.

On the other hand, a recent fMRI study by Finocchiaro et al. (2010) generated results which suggest that the *anterior* portion of the left MFG also contributes to verb-specific morphosyntactic processing. The participants in this experiment performed tasks that required them to inflect Italian target words in ways that conformed to certain phrasal contexts. Some of the expressions involved count nouns (e.g. *uno starnuto* 'a sneeze'; *molti starnuti* 'many sneezes'), and others involved main verbs (e.g. *io taglio* 'I cut'; *tu tagli* 'you cut'). When the verb conditions were contrasted against the noun conditions, one of the only activated areas was the left anterior MFG, at the intersection of BAs 10, 46, and 47, immediately anterior to BA45. Surprisingly, the posterior portion of the left MFG was not engaged.

Given these inconsistencies, it makes sense to ask whether other brain-mapping methods have been used to address the same issues. In fact, a few TMS studies have yielded two relevant findings. First, Cappelletti et al. (2008) showed that, relative to sham stimulation, the application of repetitive TMS to the *posterior* portion of the left MFG did *not* interfere significantly with either verb or noun inflection. Second, both Cappelletti et al. (2008) and Shapiro et al. (2001) showed that, relative to sham stimulation, the application of repetitive TMS to the *anterior* portion of the left MFG *did* interfere significantly more with verb inflection than noun inflection (see also Finocchiaro et al. 2008). Taken together, these findings are at odds with the fMRI studies by Shapiro et al. (2006), Willms et al. (2011), and Kielar et al. (2011), and also with the neuropsychological data for patient RC; however, they are congruent with the fMRI study by Finocchiaro et al. (2010). Thus, there are still some uncertainties regarding the precise localization of the neural mechanisms that underlie tense–agreement inflection for main verbs, but these mechanisms most likely depend on *some* portion of the left MFG.

It should be clear from this brief review that neurolinguistic research on category-specific inflectional processes has been making significant headway. At the same time, however, it is important to realize that this line of work does not address the neural correlates of nouns and verbs in any sort of global (i.e. cross-constructional or construction-independent) sense; instead, it only addresses the neural correlates of the particular word classes that happen to occur in the inflectional constructions under investigation. This is why the classes discussed above are referred to rather narrowly as count nouns and main verbs. After all, other kinds of nouns, such as mass nouns, cannot easily be pluralized (e.g. compare *books* with *muds), and other kinds of verbs, such as modal verbs, are prohibited from taking tense markers (e.g. compare *walked* with *coulded). Furthermore, it bears mentioning that some languages, like Vietnamese, lack all inflection, and others, like Sirionó (Tupí–Guaraní, Bolivia), have inflection but employ it in peculiar ways, such as by applying tense to words that encode objects and serve as syntactic arguments of main verbs (Nordlinger & Sadler 2004a). Hence, caution is always warranted when using generic terms like 'noun' and 'verb' to describe the lexical categories that occur in certain constructions of certain languages (Kemmerer 2014).

44.2.5 Dissociations between subcategories

Continuing with the notion that the major parts of speech can be broken down into multiple subcategories, this last section deals with a few strands of neurolinguistic research that have begun to explore how such subcategories are implemented in the brain. Some of the most salient findings in this small but growing literature are briefly summarized below (see also Fieder et al. 2014a, 2014b).

44.2.5.1 Proper versus common nouns

In the domain of nominal constructions, one of the most fundamental distinctions is between proper and common nouns. These two classes of words differ both conceptually and grammatically. Proper nouns (e.g. *Roger Federer*) designate unique entities, and in accord with this function they typically do not allow either articles or adjectives (see Van Valin & LaPolla 1997: 59–60, for a brief discussion of cross-linguistic diversity and the special interpretive adjustments required by unusual expressions like *A tired Roger Federer completed Wimbledon once again*). In contrast, common nouns (e.g. *dog*) designate entire categories of entities, and for this reason they often co-occur with articles and adjectives.

Numerous neuropsychological studies have reported patients with significantly worse retrieval of proper nouns than common nouns, and a handful of studies have also documented the opposite dissociation (for reviews, see Rapp & Goldrick 2006; Semenza 2006, 2009). In at least one case, a selective deficit in both producing and comprehending the proper names of people has been traced to a highly circumscribed impairment at the level of concepts for unique individuals (Miceli et al. 2000; see also Gainotti et al. 2008). More often, however, patients with greater difficulties retrieving proper than common nouns have fairly well-preserved knowledge of the referents of the intended words. Interestingly, for some of these patients the selective or disproportionate deficit in generating proper nouns relative to common nouns is restricted to just one modality of output, either speaking or writing (Cipolotti et al. 1993; Kemmerer et al. 2005). And in keeping with the earlier discussion of patient MML (see Figures 44.2 and 44.3 and the associated text), such combined grammatical category-specific and output channel-specific disorders raise the intriguing possibility that proper nouns may be segregated from common nouns at the level of phonological and orthographic lexical forms. Further research is needed, however, to evaluate this hypothesis, since it is also possible that the two types of nouns are not systematically differentiated within each lexicon, but instead are accessed from distinct semantic subsystems via isolable projection pathways.

Turning to the brain, the neural basis of proper noun retrieval in oral picture-naming tasks has received a considerable amount of attention, and a sizable body of data from lesion studies, functional neuroimaging studies, and electrophysiological studies suggests that the left temporal pole plays an important role (for a review, see Tranel 2009; see also Ross et al. 2011; Abel et al. 2015). In fact, there is growing evidence that this region is essential not only for naming famous faces, but also for naming famous voices (Waldron et al. 2014), famous melodies (Belfi & Tranel 2014), and famous landmarks (Gorno-Tempini & Price 2001; Grabowski et al. 2001; Tranel 2006; see Figure 44.6). The left uncinate fasciculus, which interconnects the temporal pole with the orbitofrontal cortex, has also been implicated in proper noun retrieval (Papagno et al. 2011, 2016), and so have several other regions, including the temporo-occipital cortex and the inferior frontal cortex (for a review, see Semenza 2011; for fMRI data on the comprehension of proper versus common nouns, see Wang et al. 2016).

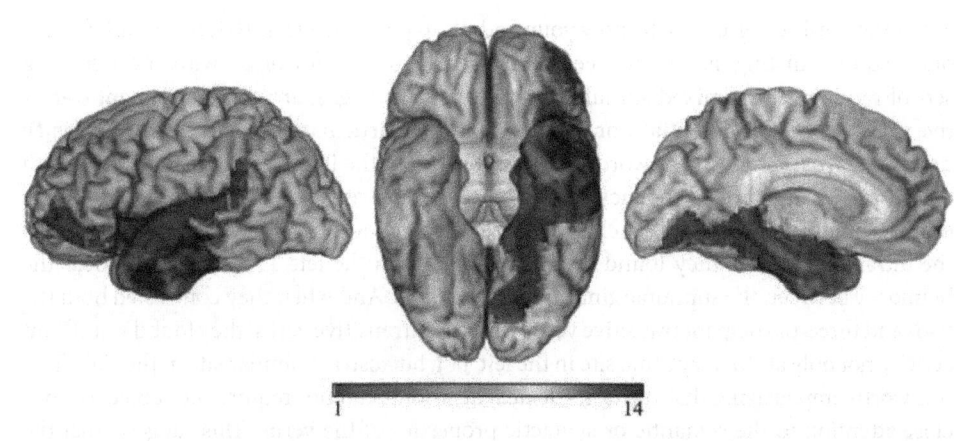

FIGURE 44.6 Lesion overlap map of patients with left temporal polar damage who have significantly impaired retrieval of proper nouns in tasks that require naming famous faces, voices, landmarks, and melodies. Images depict the overlap (from left to right) from the lateral perspective, ventral perspective, and mesial sagittal perspective. The darker shading depicts a higher number of lesion overlaps. (Reproduced with permission from Waldron et al. 2014: 53. See also Belfi & Tranel 2014.)

44.2.5.2 Transitive versus intransitive verbs

Turning to the realm of verbal constructions, perhaps the most general distinction is between transitive and intransitive verbs (Dixon 2010b: ch. 13). Transitive verbs designate events with two core participants, most often an 'actor' and an 'undergoer', with the actor being syntactically realized as a subject noun phrase and the undergoer being syntactically realized as an object noun phrase, at least in standard active-voice clauses (e.g. *The housewife kissed the mailman*). In contrast, intransitive verbs designate events with just one core participant, syntactically realized as a subject noun phrase. Usually this participant is a volitional actor (e.g. *The mailman bolted*), but sometimes it is a passive undergoer (e.g. *The mailman blushed*). It all depends on the nature of the verb. Transitivity itself also depends, ultimately, on the lexical specifications of particular verbs, not the real-world properties of the designated events. For example, the general notion of 'eating' is associated with the verbs *eat*, *devour*, and *dine*, but these three verbs exhibit different types of transitivity. The first verb, *eat*, is, technically speaking, ambitransitive, since it can be either transitive, as in *Bill ate the lasagne*, or intransitive, as in *Bill ate*. The second verb, *devour*, is strictly transitive, since one can say *Bill devoured the lasagne* but not **Bill devoured*. And the third verb, *dine*, is strictly intransitive, since one can say *Bill dined* but not **Bill dined the lasagne*. Despite these and other complications, there is still a strong overall tendency for two-participant verbs to be syntactically transitive and one-participant verbs to be syntactically intransitive.

Several recent fMRI studies suggest that transitive verbs depend more than intransitive ones on the temporoparietal junction (TPJ), a large territory that includes parts of the posterior superior and middle temporal cortices, the inferior SMG, and the anterior angular gyrus (for an overview of the TPJ, see Igelström & Graziano 2017). For instance, Thompson et al. (2007) asked a group of healthy young adults to perform a lexical decision task (which only requires distinguishing between real words and pseudowords) with the following sets of randomly intermixed stimuli: intransitive verbs (e.g. *soar*); two-participant transitive verbs (e.g. *hold*); potentially or obligatorily three-participant transitive verbs (e.g. *put*); nouns (e.g. *goat*); and pseudowords (e.g. *bromp*). All of the items were matched for length and (for the real words) frequency, and the three sets of verbs were also matched in terms of imageability. When the researchers contrasted the two-participant transitive verbs with the intransitive verbs, they found significant activity in the left TPJ, specifically near the boundary between the supramarginal and angular gyri. And when they contrasted both the two- and three-participant transitive verbs with the intransitive verbs, they found significant activity not only at the very same site in the left TPJ, but also at a similar site in the right TPJ. It is worth emphasizing that the task—lexical decision—did not require the subjects to pay close attention to the semantic or syntactic properties of the verbs. This suggests that the transitivity features of verbs are accessed automatically during comprehension.

These findings were subsequently replicated and extended in two other fMRI studies that also used lexical decision tasks. Meltzer-Asscher et al. (2013) focused on two types of verbs: transitives that can be converted to intransitives with undergoer subjects (e.g. *boil*, as in *Susan boiled the water* and *The water boiled*); and intransitives with actor subjects (e.g. *swim*, as in *The boy swam*). When they contrasted the first set of verbs with the second, they found bilateral activity in the TPJ, much like what Thompson et al. (2007) observed. Later on, Meltzer-Asscher et al. (2015) found activity in a slightly more inferior sector of just the left TPJ when they contrasted basic transitive verbs (e.g. *build*) with two types of intransitive verbs—those that have actor subjects (e.g. *swim*) and those that have undergoer subjects but cannot be made transitive (e.g. *fall*).

Taken together, the fMRI results described above demonstrate that the TPJ, especially in the left hemisphere, often responds more strongly to two-participant (or three-participant) verbs than to one-participant verbs, even when those verbs are perceived in isolation. These findings suggest that the TPJ is involved in representing the transitivity features of verbs (for a review that includes convergent data from other methods, see Thompson & Meltzer-Asscher 2014; and for recent neuropsychological support, see den Ouden et al. 2019). How, though, might we make more sense of this notion?

The following connection is definitely pertinent. The two core participants of transitive verbs—actor and undergoer—are frequently referred to by linguists as 'thematic relations' or 'thematic roles', and one part of the TPJ, namely the angular gyrus, not only appears to represent these grammatically relevant types of thematic relations, but has also been implicated in a much broader range of such relations. These more general thematic relations include the sorts of associations that tend to occur between certain entities and events in certain situations, like coffee, cups, mugs, cream, sugar, pouring, drinking, kitchens, cafes (for reviews, see Mirman et al. 2017; Davis & Yee 2019). Thus, the involvement of the angular gyrus in representing the transitivity features of verbs—which is to say, this region's specification of the roles that different participants play in lexically designated events—may simply be a particular manifestation of its more general job of serving as a transmodal semantic hub that forms spatiotemporally coherent representations of complex dynamic situations (for a similar observation, see Boylan et al. 2015).

It is important to note, though, that the overarching classes of transitive and intransitive verbs are by no means monolithic, since each of them can be broken down into many more fine-grained microclasses based on correspondences between semantic content and grammatical behaviour (Levin 1993; Malchukov & Comrie 2015). Hence it may be fruitful for future neurolinguistic research to take into account not only the general transitive–intransitive distinction, but also these more specific contrasts (Kemmerer 2000a, 2003, 2014; Kemmerer & Wright 2002; Kemmerer et al. 2008; Yang et al. 2017).

44.3 BEYOND NOUNS AND VERBS

The multifarious morphological and syntactic constructions that comprise the grammatical systems of individual languages distinguish not only between (subclasses of) nouns and verbs, but also between numerous other grammatical categories (Culicover 1999; Croft 2000; Haspelmath 2007; Pullum & Scholz 2007; Taylor 2012). None of these categories has received as much attention in neurolinguistics as nouns and verbs, but many of them have nevertheless been investigated in various ways.

In addition to nouns and verbs, most languages have two other open categories—namely, adjectives and adverbs (although the former category is sometimes closed, and the latter category is often ill-defined; see Dixon 2010b: ch. 12). Adverbs have not yet been carefully studied in neurolinguistics, but some aspects of adjectives have begun to be explored. For example, when multiple adjectives are strung together before a noun, their linear order must conform to certain constraints that are primarily semantic in nature (e.g. Bache 1978; Quirk et al. 1985; Frawley 1992; Feist 2011; Scontras et al. 2017; Trotzke & Wittenberg 2019). This is why it is fine to say *the other small inconspicuous carved jade idols* but not **the carved other inconspicuous jade small idols*. Interestingly, there is some evidence that brain damage—especially, but not exclusively, in Broca's area and/or the left inferior parietal lobule—can impair a person's knowledge of the positional restrictions on prenominal adjectives while leaving intact their knowledge of the idiosyncratic meanings of such adjectives (Kemmerer 2000b; Kemmerer et al. 2009; see also Kemmerer et al. 2007; Vandekerckhove et al. 2013). It is also noteworthy that in a neuropsychological study by Miozzo et al. (2014), two patients with lesion overlap in the left IFG manifested thematic role confusions for comparative adjectival constructions (e.g. *The glove is darker than the hat*) and spatial prepositional constructions (e.g. *The box is in the bag*), but not for simple transitive constructions (e.g. *The woman helps the man*). These patterns of association and dissociation suggest that non-verbal word classes, particularly adjectives and prepositions, may recruit different brain mechanisms for thematic role assignment than verbal word classes, particularly transitive verbs.

Whereas open-class categories provide most of the conceptual content of utterances, closed-class categories have relatively austere meanings and contribute more to the structural organization of utterances (Talmy 1988; see Chapter 4 in this volume). Some English examples include articles like *a* and *the*; demonstratives like *this* and *that*; auxiliary and modal verbs like *do, have, can, could, may, might, must, ought, should, would,* and *will*; prepositions like *in, on, over, under, across, through, for, of, until, during,* and *since*; and conjunctions like *and, or, but, because, therefore, moreover,* and *however*. During receptive language processing, closed-class words elicit different electrophysiological waveforms than open-class words, even when the two types of lexical items are matched for frequency and length (Pulvermüller et al. 1995). Moreover, within the sphere of closed-class elements, different categories have distinct electrophysiological signatures (Weber-Fox et al. 2006). As described below, dissociations have also been found during language production tasks, not only between the two large-scale domains of open- and closed-class words, but also between different types of closed-class words.

Most of the relevant data come from the syndrome of agrammatism (Menn et al. 1995). When attempting to formulate sentences, patients with this disorder can produce a wide range of open-class words, but they tend to have significant trouble generating closed-class words, with errors involving both omissions and substitutions. In addition, comparisons of the performance profiles of multiple patients have revealed a great deal of variability regarding both the kinds of closed-class words that are impaired and the degree to which they are affected. To take a rather striking example, consider preposition–particle homonyms that differ as to whether they are semantically or syntactically determined. In the sentence, *She ran up the stairs*, the preposition *up* denotes a specific direction of motion, but in the sentence *She called up her friend*, the particle *up* is just an obligatory ingredient of the verb–particle expression *call up* (hence, strictly speaking, it is lexically rather than syntactically determined, even though the latter term is used by Friederici 1982, and Friederici et al. 1982). Not surprisingly, these two instances of *up* have different grammatical behaviours. Although it would be fine to say *Up the stairs she ran*, it would be very odd to say **Up her friend she called*, and, conversely, one could never get away with **She ran the stairs up*, but there is nothing wrong with *She called her friend up*. Now, given such contrasts, it is especially interesting to note that semantically determined prepositions and syntactically determined particles can be impaired independently of each other by brain injury (Friederici 1982; Friederici et al. 1982; Kohen et al. 2011). This remarkable double dissociation suggests that the two types of closed-class words have at least partially separate neural substrates (for a similar dissociation between lexical and grammatical uses of pronouns, see Ishkhanyan et al. 2017).

Agrammatism is most often manifested by patients with stroke-induced Broca's aphasia, but the lesions in such patients are quite diverse, variably affecting all of the major sectors of the large left perisylvian zone, with Broca's area—which itself is poorly defined (Tremblay & Dick 2016)—sometimes being damaged and sometimes being spared (Mohr 1976; Vanier & Caplan 1990; Fridriksson et al. 2015). For these reasons, it has been challenging to use deficit–lesion correlations in agrammatic Broca's aphasics as a source of data about the neural underpinnings of closed-class items. On the other hand, agrammatism is also displayed by patients with progressive nonfluent aphasia, and the fact that their atrophy is typically centred in the left ventrolateral prefrontal territory provides some support for the view that Broca's area and the surrounding regions may actually be critically involved in the processing of closed-class items (Wilson et al. 2010). Further evidence for this view comes from a few PET and fMRI studies that have implicated Broca's area in some of the grammatical operations that take place during normal sentence production, including the generation of closed-class items (Indefrey et al. 2001, 2004; Haller et al. 2005). In addition, a meta-analysis of fMRI studies of receptive sentence processing found an association between closed-class items and activation in Broca's area (Zaccarella et al. 2017). Much more research is needed, however, to elucidate the many similarities and differences in how various categories of closed-class words are implemented in the brain.

44.4 Final Remarks

In closing, I would like to highlight two points that are especially important for future neurolinguistic research on word classes. First, as mentioned above, because many words in many languages are noun–verb homonyms, it is possible that their semantic properties are more prominent than their syntactic properties when they are processed in isolation, and that their syntactic properties only (or more frequently) come to the fore when they are processed in phrasal or sentential contexts. Although this point has been acknowledged and supported in some neurolinguistic studies (Tranel et al. 2005; Vigliocco et al. 2006; Tyler et al. 2008; Tsigka et al. 2014; Artoni et al. 2020), it warrants much more attention in the future.

The second point involves the criteria for defining word classes. As I argued in an earlier paper (Kemmerer 2014), if a given neurolinguistic study does not focus directly on the universal semantic–pragmatic aspects of prototypical nouns/verbs/adjectives (as specified, for example, by Croft 1991, 2000, 2007b), but instead deals with the idiosyncrasies of one or another language-particular word class, then it should be incumbent on the researchers to indicate, as precisely as possible, what makes that word class a coherent category that warrants a certain label. Now, some researchers do try to follow this practice, but others don't, preferring instead to work with what appear to be rather haphazardly assembled word lists that are assigned certain labels without clear theoretical justification. The reason this matters is because languages vary greatly with regard to which words can occur in which constructions, leading to substantial diversity in the nature of distributionally determined word classes. For instance, as noted above, some languages, like Sirionó (Tupí–Guaraní, Bolivia), apply tense–aspect–mood markers not only to what would ordinarily be called verbs, but also to what would ordinarily be called nouns and adjectives, which implies that in this language such markers cannot be used to distinguish between these traditional word classes (Nordlinger & Sadler 2004a). Findings like these have serious repercussions for neurolinguistics because they reveal the need for researchers in this field to be clear about the nature of the word classes that they are attempting to identify in the brain.

CHAPTER 45

WORD CLASSES IN COMPUTATIONAL LINGUISTICS AND ARTIFICIAL INTELLIGENCE

MELADEL MISTICA, EKATERINA VYLOMOVA, AND FRANCIS BOND

45. INTRODUCTION

COMPUTATIONAL *linguistics* is an overloaded term; it refers to the modelling of language by researchers who seek to process unstructured text to gain an understanding of the information that is encoded therein, as well as the computational modelling of languages in order to gain a better understanding of the linguistic phenomena exhibited within the text.

In this chapter, we refer to the former as natural language processing (NLP), and the latter as computational linguistics.[1] Largely, the difference lies in which field the research contributes to, and in this overview, we examine both. *Artificial intelligence* (AI) refers to the study and understanding of thought and intelligence and the embodiment of these qualities in machines.[2] Given that the probing of machines to access their embedded knowledge can involve natural language interactions; and the means by which common sense knowledge is injected into machines can derive from information gained from text, this field also overlaps substantially with NLP.

Although the title of this chapter only refers to computational linguistics, we also cover topics in NLP because of the common conflating of these terms. Word classes as employed, studied, and applied throughout these fields represent a spectrum of goals and methodologies. In section 45.2, we give an overview of how word classes are employed from a computational perspective. We look into how they are represented and how their

---

[1] The official Association for Computational Linguistics (2019) definition of *computational linguistics* encompasses both.

[2] As defined by Association for the Advancement of Artificial Intelligence (2019).

representation encodes different kinds of information at different granularities. In section 45.3, we discuss tools and resources based on words classes. Section 45.4 covers how word classes are determined computationally, their applications within the field of NLP in particular, and how we evaluate them within the discipline. Finally, we consider the current state of the art, where parts of speech (POS) are typically an implicit part of the model (section 45.4.3).

45.2 COMPUTATIONAL PERSPECTIVES ON WORD CLASSES

Word classes serve different purposes for different fields. Unlike in the fields of linguistics, in NLP and AI, word classes—their definition and separability—are mostly taken for granted as being universal. NLP systems use word classes as part of intermediate tasks or a step in the pipeline that allows us to gain further insight into a larger overall structure, for instance insight into syntactic structure.

The treatment of word classes varies in the computational domain depending on the application and task. The categories can be as fine-grained as specifying subcategorization frames and semantic subtypes, or as broad as simply specifying that tokens belong to a major word class. POS are a generalization of knowledge and in NLP a means of abstracting information so that generalizable patterns can emerge from the data. The more fine-grained the word classes are, the more informative, rich, and meaningful the categories. From a semantic perspective, it is commonplace for nouns to be categorized into certain types, such as the semantic distinction between proper nouns as being distinct from common nouns, or from a semantico-syntactic perspective of countable versus non-countable nouns.

This raises the question of how granular word classes should be. From a syntactic perspective, Clark (2002) employs supertags—each tag or class represents a very specific syntactic context, entailing more fine-grained categories of classes to improve parsing. These supertags are comparable to lexicalized subtrees (Schabes et al. 1988; Joshi & Srinivas 1994), which are syntactic parse tree fragments that include at least one leaf/terminal node (i.e. at least one word). Both supertags and lexicalized subtrees can define very a specific syntactic environment for a given word. On the other end of the spectrum are universal POS tags (Petrov et al. 2012; Ammar et al. 2016). This set of POS tags are designed to apply to a large range of languages and were derived from the common set of classes from 22 different languages (Petrov et al. 2012). They consist of 17 categories partitioned into three types: open word classes, closed word classes, and others.[3] However, it is uncertain whether a category across these different languages can be interpreted in the same way uniformly (Evans & Levinson 2009). Do nouns in English behave morphosyntactically in the way as nouns in French? Do they have the same features? In addition to the problem of what a noun could be applied to in one language and whether that label encompasses all the features that the label entails for a spectrum of languages, there is the issue of the practical applications of the classes.

---

[3] As of November 2019: https://universaldependencies.org/u/pos/

In NLP applications developed in the early 1990s to the early 2010s, POS tags were often employed as input features when building predictive models for a variety of tasks (see section 45.4.1). Therefore, words in the the input text used for training these applications would first have to be automatically labelled with the POS tags, which is essentially the word-class label for each item in the text. There is a trade-off between meaningfulness and widespread applicability of these word classes when applied as an intermediate step in these tasks. If the word class is too fine-grained, then they are more difficult to automatically (and manually) apply. However, the broader the categories are, the more likely it is for more frequent patterns to emerge, even if each category is less meaningful. For example, when automatically applying POS tags to text, if there is no distinction between plural count nouns, singular count nouns and mass nouns in a tag set, then when a trained automatic POS tagger encounters the word *fish* in sentences such as *We released the fish we caught*, or *I like fish*, then there is no having to decide whether *fish* in the first example is plural or singular, which without context would be very difficult. Furthermore, not having the count vs mass distinction in the POS inventory would mean we lose the ability to explain why certain nouns can replace the word *fish* in the latter sentence while others cannot.

45.2.1 Representations of word classes

Word classes can be represented as flat labels or collections of features. The label and the collection of features *can* mean the same thing, and having a collection of features simply makes explicit the characteristics of the class.

The most simple of the representations are labels such as those employed in POS tagging. One of the most widely used tagsets is the Penn Treebank (PTB), shown in Table 45.1. The PTB is a widely used text corpus that has syntactic parse information. The preterminal nodes of the parse trees in a treebank make up the tagset. These labels are one- to three-character symbols that were designed to provide distinct codings for each distinct grammatical behaviour (Marcus et al. 1993; Taylor et al. 2003, with many subsequent revisions.).

Table 45.1 The Penn Treebank

CC	Coordinating conj.	TO	infinitival *to*
CD	Cardinal number	UH	Interjection
DT	Determiner	VB	Verb, base form
EX	Existential there	VBD	Verb, past tense
FW	Foreign word	VBG	Verb, gerund/present pple
IN	Preposition	VBN	Verb, past participle
JJ	Adjective	VBP	Verb, non-3rd ps. g. present
JJR	Adjective, comparative	VBZ	Verb, 3rd ps. sg present
JJS	Adjective, superlative	WDT	Wh-determiner
LS	List item marker	WP	Wh-pronoun
MD	Modal	WP$	Possessive *wh*-pronoun

Table 45.1 Continued

NN	Noun, singular or mass	WRB	Wh-adverb
NNS	Noun, plural	#	Pound sign
NNP	Proper noun, singular	$	Dollar sign
NNPS	Proper noun, plural	.	Sentence-final punctuation
PDT	Predeterminer	,	Comma
POS	Possessive ending	:	Colon, semi-colon
PRP	Personal pronoun	(	Left bracket character
PP$	Possessive pronoun	)	Right bracket character
RB	Adverb	"	Straight double quote
RBR	Adverb, comparative	'	Left open single quote
RBS	Adverb, superlative	"	Left open double quote
RP	Particle	'	Right close single quote
SYM	Symbol	"	Right close double quote

Although the PTB's POS tags were designed to capture grammatical behaviour, they represent other functions too. For example FW (foreign word) does not represent a collection of terms that would have a distinct morphosyntactic behaviour because we would expect that a foreign word can be introduced not only to any open word class, but in some case closed class categories, for example *cum, à la* in English. In addition, this tag set exhibits many characteristics that point to the primary usage of these set of labels—they are designed especially to process text. For example the label LS (list item marker) ensures that text encoded as a list is processed as such. within the PTB is the noun distinction represented by the labels NN and NNS. However, singular and mass nouns are conflated into the one category, NN, with the main feature differentiator being number. This encoding reflects the expected surface form of the agreeing verb, rather than its syntactico-semantic type that would license its usage within a noun phrase.

Klein & Manning (2003) show that the PTB tags are in fact a little too coarse-grained for accurate parsing. They point out that the following types of words are all tagged indistinguishably: subordinating conjunctions (*while, as, if*); complementizers (*that, for*), noun-modifying prepositions (such as *of*); and other prepositions (*with, in, from*), which all get the tag IN—however, they state that distinguishing them increases parse accuracy by almost two percent. When we break down what a word class is or even what a POS tag label represents, we see that these labels are simply a convenient designation for a collection of common features. Within grammar engineering these features are made explicit, as shown in Figure 45.1 for common nouns and Figure 45.2 for non-past intransitive verbs exhibiting a certain kind of morphology. These attribute–value matrices, representing nouns and verbs, respectively, are akin to structures in the Lexical Functional Grammar (LFG) formalism. The implementation of grammars within this formalism aim to employ features that are cross-lingually applicable and as much as possible uniformly interpretable (Butt et al. 1999).

$$\begin{bmatrix} \text{PRED} & \text{'koala'} \\ \text{PERS} & 3 \\ \text{NUM} & \text{sg} \\ \text{NTYPE} & \text{common} \end{bmatrix} \quad \begin{bmatrix} \text{PRED} & \text{'leaf'} \\ \text{PERS} & 3 \\ \text{NUM} & \text{sg} \\ \text{NTYPE} & \text{common} \end{bmatrix} \quad \begin{bmatrix} \text{PRED} & \text{'fish'} \\ \text{PERS} & 3 \\ \text{NUM} & \text{sg-or-pl} \\ \text{NTYPE} & \text{common} \end{bmatrix}$$

FIGURE 45.1 Nouns

$$\begin{bmatrix} \text{PRED} & \text{'eats'} \\ \text{SUBJ} & \begin{bmatrix} \text{PERS} & 3 \\ \text{NUM} & \text{sg} \end{bmatrix} \\ \text{TNS-ASP} & \begin{bmatrix} \text{TENSE} & \text{pres} \end{bmatrix} \end{bmatrix} \quad \begin{bmatrix} \text{PRED} & \text{'drinks'} \\ \text{SUBJ} & \begin{bmatrix} \text{PERS} & 3 \\ \text{NUM} & \text{sg} \end{bmatrix} \\ \text{TNS-ASP} & \begin{bmatrix} \text{TENSE} & \text{pres} \end{bmatrix} \end{bmatrix}$$

FIGURE 45.2 Verbs

Grammar engineering involves the encoding of grammatical knowledge into a machine-readable description of a language for parsing. The types of grammatical descriptions produced are lexically driven and constraint-based. The parsing algorithms for these kinds of grammars that propagate complex features from the lexical entry ensure that these lexical features are unified in the process of obtaining a resulting complete and coherent parse. There are two major components that are produced in the process: a set of grammar rules and a lexicon. The broader the categories are in the lexicon, the more encompassing the rules are, but it also results in the greater possibility of overgeneration, leading to the additional production of ungrammatical sentences. For example, if there was only one broad category for nouns that did not distinguish between mass and count nouns in the lexicon, then there is no way to ensure that a sentence like *I sell table* is not an acceptable string according to the encoded grammar. These grammars are designed by computational linguists in a way that captures the nuances of variability within the language and as a means to capture grammatical behaviour.

These distinguishing features encoded in a lexicon for various word types can be collected up and coded as a macro or supertype, thereby giving a compositional representation of the word class (Flickinger 1987). For example, a representation of the NN class is shown in Figure 45.3.

$$\begin{bmatrix} \text{PERS} & 3 \\ \text{NUM} & \text{sg} \\ \text{NTYPE} & \text{common} \end{bmatrix}$$

FIGURE 45.3 Representing the word class NN with explicit features as an attribute–value matrix

Some representations lend themselves to encoding more detailed information. However, the representation itself, such as a flat single label rather than a collection of features, does not prevent the encoding of more information. Within grammar engineering, more fine-grained word classes are commonplace. These fine-grained classes represent syntactic types to define specific contexts in the prevention of overgeneration during parsing.

```
0.  S   → NP VP
1.  NP  → NN
2.  NP  → DT NN
3.  VP  → V NP
4.  NN:  water | leaf | koala
5.  DT:  the
6.  V :  drinks | eats
```

FIGURE 45.4 A toy grammar in Backus–Naur form (commonly referred to as BNF)

A toy grammar that defines rules shown in Figure 45.4 allows the parsing of the strings *the koala drinks water* as well as *the koala eats the leaf*. However, the broad definition of the noun category NN that encompasses both 'leaf' and 'koala' means that sentences such as **the koala eats leaf* is also produced by this grammar. A way to minimize the over-application of the dispreferred NP rule is to define more finer-grained morphosyntactic categories, which would preclude a count noun such as 'leaf' from being parsed by Rule 1 in Figure 45.4.

45.2.2 Universality of word classes: A computational perspective

Linguists need not get too excited about this section;[4] researchers in NLP have not yet solved the burning question of whether word classes are indeed universal, or which features all languages share in terms of their syntactico-semantic characteristics. The aims of NLP with respect to research in universality are quite different: to mitigate the problem of unavailable resources for (non-major) languages to fulfil certain tasks that are required in text processing and text understanding.

Many major languages such as French, German, English, and Spanish are fairly well resourced for NLP tasks, with resources about morphological, syntactic, and semantic information (such as lexicons, treebanks, and ontologies) as well as tools that deduce linguistic structure such as parsers and chunkers. However, not all languages have the basic inventory for off-the-shelf text processing. Given that in many instances the first step of an NLP pipeline is a means to provide some linguistic abstraction, such as POS tagging, chunking, or parsing, these resources and tools are indispensable. Universal word classes are a means of cross-language transfer with the assumption that shared POS tags enable cross-lingual model sharing and ultimately architectural simplicity for multi-language processing (Ammar et al. 2016). Typically, one can think of POS as having a universal, semantic definition: prototypical nouns refer to objects and entities; and then language-specific syntactic properties. In

---

[4] We refer to Haspelmath (2001) for a discussion on word classes from a typological perspective.

English, nouns are marked for number and take determiners, in Japanese nouns do not inflect and are followed by case markers, and so on. Initially, Petrov et al. (2012) propose an initial set of 12 POS tags which behave largely the same for 22 different languages. Since then the set of universal POS tags have only expanded slightly to include proper nouns and interjections in the open class categories. Within the closed word classes, adpositions, and verbal auxiliaries were added in addition to the conjunction category being split into coordinating conjunction and sentential conjunction. Finally, two extra tags—representing punctuation and symbols—were added to the miscellaneous 'other' category. These are shown in Table 45.2, along with the mapping to the PTB tags.

Table 45.2 Comparison of some universal parts of speech

WN	UPOS	Description	Frequency	Example	Penn
a	ADJ*	adjective	52,700	other	JJ, JJR, JJS
	ADP*	adposition	96,208	of	IN, TO
r	ADV*	adverb	48,409	not	PDT, RB, RBR, RBS, WRB
	AUX	auxiliary verb	30,494	had	MD, VAX
	CONJ*	coordinating conjunction	27,258	and	CC
	DET*	determiner	87,246	the	DT, WDT
	INTJ*	interjection	726	well	UH
n	NOUN*	noun	175,365	man	NN, NNP, NNPS, NNS
a,n	NUM	numeral	8,057	one	CD
	PRON	pronoun	95,170	I	EX, PRP, PRP$, WP, WP$
	PRT	particle	28,071	to	POS, RP, TO
	PUNCT	punctuation	17,202	,	" " '?' . ...
v	VERB*	verb	124,300	was	VB, VBD, VBG, VBN, VBP, VBZ
	V.PTCP**	participle (verbal adjective)			
	V.MSDR**	masdar (verbal noun)			
	V.CVB**	converb (verbal adverb)			
	X***	other	47	etc	FW

* Eight basic POS tags: subordinator and coordinator are both treated as CONJ
** Only in Unimorph
*** Not in Unimorph
Frequency and an example of most common word for each Universal POS is from the English part of the NTU Multilingual Corpus (Tan & Bond 2012).

These universal POS are now maintained with the Universal Dependencies (UD) (Nivre et al. 2016) and are being extended with morphological information in UniMorph (Sylak-Glassman et al. 2015). UniMorph, the Universal Morphological Feature Schema, aims at representing inflected word forms in any language in a universal format: each form is defined by its lexical meaning (expressed by its stem or lemma) and a set of cross-lingual morphosyntactic features. For instance, the Russian word 'skazal' is described as 'skazat' (to speak); V;FIN;IND;PFV;PST;SG;MASC'. The schema comprises 23 dimensions of meaning (such as person, tense, aspect, number) with over 212 features (such as singular, dual, past, perfect) that are attested in a range of typologically diverse languages. The features are similar to the annotation labels described in the Leipzig Glossing Rules. POS are universal features in the sense that all languages syntactically differentiate them, e.g. verbs and nouns are universally distinguished (Baker 2003). Both verbs and nouns are basic classes in the sense that they need not co-occur and are not a subclass of other POS. Adjectives, adverbs, and pronouns are rather cross-linguistically common. Adjectives modify nouns similar to how adverbs modify verbs. Pronouns and proper names are subclasses of nouns, although they present certain syntactic differences.[5]

The UniMorph schema follows the approach established by Croft (2000) that is based on the functionally motivated conceptual space. The space is defined as a cross-product of the concepts of object, property, and action with the functions of reference, modification, and predication. This allows for the following cross-linguistically common distinctions: nouns, adpositions, adjectives, verbs, masdars (verbal nouns), participles (verbal adjectives), converbs (verbal adverb), and adverbs, classifiers, articles, auxiliaries (subclass of verbs), complementizers, and conjunctions. Adpositions include pre- and postpositions, infixes, and circumfixes. Following the Universal Dependencies Project (Nivre et al. 2016), the schema also acknowledges less canonical classes such as numerals, particles, and interjections. The UniMorph and UD share most of their POS, which are shown in Table 45.2.

45.2.3 Granularity in word classes

Different applications call for different levels of granularity. At one extreme, we have resources like WordNet (Fellbaum 1998), which only has the four **open** class POS: noun, verb, adjective, and adverb. We then have the traditional grammarian's eight classes (Huddleston 1988: 22): An updated set of Verb, Noun, Adjective, Preposition, Determinative, Coordinator, and Subordinator. Interjections are also distinguished as a more peripheral class. These have been expanded further by the universal POS into 14 classes (17 including symbols, punctuation, and others). The PTB of English includes some morphology, and expands to over 25. Lexicons that encode subcategorization in the word classes end up with many more: the English Resource Grammar has over 1,400, including detailed information about subcategorization, modification, and constructions (Flickinger 2000). We show a comparison of some of the differences in granularity in Table 45.2. For example, in the PTB three adjective labels are specified: 'JJ', 'JJR', and 'JJS' for adjective, comparative adjective, and superlative adjective, respectively. While under 'UPOS' there is only one label 'ADJ'.

---

[5] For example, they are definite by default and, therefore, do not require articles.

45.2.4 Word classes and representation learning

In the 2010s, the pipeline approach we have discussed here began to be replaced by representation learning, where machine learning discovers not just the mapping from representation to output but also the representation itself (Goodfellow et al. 2016: 4). In the approach now known as deep learning, representations are expressed in terms of other, simpler representations and typically learned as part of a single end-to-end task. In these models, POS are not directly modelled, but instead are expected to be expressed as features inside the models, often a way that is non-transparent. These approaches take advantage of improvements in machine learning algorithms, faster computers, and more data.

POS are then mainly used only for (i) modelling languages for which there is limited data available (e.g. Anderson et al. 2021) or (ii) attempts to build explicit models that humans can understand (e.g. Kapanipathi et al. 2021). As this trend continues, it is likely that POS will become less important in both AI and NLP, with the generalizations they encode instead becoming implicit parts of larger models. We discuss this further in section 45.4.3.

45.3 TOOLS AND RESOURCES

45.3.1 POS taggers

POS taggers are sequential taggers that label words with their disambiguated word class for the given context. As mentioned previously, while only a handful of languages have a full suite of text processing tools and resources available, research in lower-resource languages is becoming ever more popular, particularly with the multilingual treebanks made available from UD (Nivre et al. 2016). While 114 languages[6] are included in the inventory for UD, it has given rise to methodologies that do not take the individual languages as separate resources, but as a whole collection (Straka & Straková 2017; Li et al. 2018; Nguyen & Verspoor 2018; Yasunaga et al. 2018). There is still, however, efforts into creating text processing tools for specific low-resourced languages, including Vietnamese (Nguyen 2019), Occitan (Vergez-Couret & Urieli 2014), Tamil (Thayaparan et al. 2018) and many other languages, but in reality these are very far away from being deployed as off-the-shelf tools that are employed within AI systems.

Although the most recent release of UD (version 2.8) presents 150 treebanks in 90 languages, it is still very sparse and might be insufficient to adapt a model to unfamiliar language. Therefore, Wang & Eisner (2016) released Galactic Dependencies 1.0, a dataset comprising 50,000 synthetic languages annotated in UD format. The synthetic treebanks are produced from existing UD treebanks (version 1.2) by reordering dependents of noun and/or verbs to follow the word order of other real languages.

The task of POS tagging, at least for English and other major languages, is largely seen as a solved problem with the state-of-the-art systems obtaining accuracy levels above 95% (Toutanova et al. 2003; Akbik et al. 2018).

---

[6] Version 2.8, released on 15 May 2021.

However, as pointed out by Manning (2011), POS tagging evaluation is done at the token level, so a 95% accuracy means that 1 in 20 tokens are incorrectly labelled! If we examine what sentence length is considered readable in English—which lies between 14 to 22 words (Islam et al. 2012)—then we can see that there is at least one tagging error per sentence on average. In fact, errors are not independent, so the sentence accuracy is 56% (Manning 2011), meaning almost half of the sentences have an error.

The task of improving POS taggers over the recent years was mainly tested and trained on the same data from the annotated portion of the *Wall Street Journal* of the PTB (Marcus et al. 1993). Researchers employed the exact same resources for this task, with the same split of data into training and testing sets (following Collins 2002) so that new methodologies could be fairly and directly compared with each other. However, this kind of rigour in maintaining the training and testing set-up may inadvertently produce systems that maximize the performance on the data set at hand, rather than improving on the task itself; Gorman & Bedrick (2019) claim that the accuracy of the figures that are reported on the standard splits cannot reliably be reproduced on random splits in the PTB corpus. This suggests that much of the incremental research in improving the task of POS tagging overfit to the standard splits rather than genuinely improving on the previous state-of-the-art methods (Gorman & Bedrick 2019). It is also the case that model trained on clean news data performs much less well on noisy data from other domains.

45.3.2 Knowledge resources

Many AI applications involve NLP techniques. One such example is employing text mining to augment knowledge resources for common sense reasoning. Common sense reasoning is required for AI agents in making decisions about situations in certain domains. Even navigation systems in cars use AI by making inferences when asked for a petrol station. There is no point in recommending the usual petrol station near your house when you are 100 miles away from home. Also, autonomous robots that are trained in various domains would require certain techniques depending on the task at hand. For example, a robotic culinary assistant would interpret the verb *peel* very differently depending on whether the object of the verbs was *banana* or *carrot*; one would require a tool while the other does not, and furthermore they would require a different set of actions.

Reasoning about the world and making decisions for a given context requires information about situations and actions taken in that domain. The kind of data that is often required in decision-making AI systems are domain ontologies, such as the objects and actions that are relevant to the domain. The second type of knowledge, which is a little different to an ontology is how these objects and actions are employed for the environment. For example, an ontology will encode information that both *a lamp* and *the lights* are similar because they are both objects that illuminate a room. However, an additional resource is required to know how these can be affected in the world; both these objects can be *switched on* and *off*, and as can be an *oven*, but unlike an oven, they do not have a temperature that is associated with them. This kind of knowledge can be hand-built, which is costly and time-consuming. The alternative is to try to extract that knowledge from the vast amount of unstructured text that we are surrounded with every day via text mining.

Text mining is the extraction of targeted knowledge from unstructured text. It is a means to harvest the knowledge from the written artefacts in the domain of interest. For example, Kaiser et al. (2014) define their corpus as a collection of recipes to acquire the knowledge needed for an autonomous robot designed for the kitchen environment. This kind of corpus would lend itself to the entities and actions that are commonplace in the preparation of food. In order to learn these vocabulary terms, Kaiser et al. (2014) extract the terms from a POS-tagged corpus, restricting the candidate set to those terms with tags that are either marked as noun or verb. The nouns are candidates for entities that are salient for the domain, and are filtered for 'concreteness' using WordNet. The verb candidates are filtered according to their type—if they are categorized according to WordNet as verbs of *change*, *contact*, *creation*, or *motion*, they are flagged as important actions for the kitchen domain. In terms of relation extraction, Kaiser et al. (2014) heavily rely on POS tags to find syntactic patterns within the text.

(#object, noun), (in, prep), (#location, noun)

FIGURE 45.5 Example of relation pattern based on POS tags

The aim of relation extraction is to define the syntactic relationship between symbols, and primarily involves discovering the argument patterns of the domain verbs. These hand-coded patterns define functions of the elements found in the text. An example of such a pattern is shown in Figure 45.5, which defines how two nouns can be related as well as their semantic type for this syntactic pattern.

45.4 APPLICATIONS AND METHODOLOGIES

45.4.1 Applications: Uses of word classes

45.4.1.1 NLP tasks

POS tagging is often considered as one of the first stages in many NLP applications. This section describes some of these applications and the way in which word classes are employed in such tasks.

Word sense disambiguation (WSD) is a subtask of natural language understanding (NLU) which entails determining the unique sense of a word as it is used in a particular piece of text, which can employ both semantic and syntactic strategies (Martinez 2004). The semantic context and the class of words surrounding a target lexeme are among the main factors in determining word sense (Agirre & Martinez 2001). Martínez et al. (2002) employ a trigram of POS tags as a means to emulate subcategorization frames that would differentiate the head words in a phrase, which is a more syntactic-based method. In addition, these word-class tags are combined as portmanteau classes, an amalgam of POS tags and other information such as surrounding surface words, to enrich the features extracted in the text as input into the machine learning algorithm. Recent state-of-the-art approaches for English use just neural net-based models with POS only implicitly modelled (Vial et al. 2019), but for languages without sense tagged data they remain extremely useful.

Lexical acquisition—up until the 2010s, the lexicon was deemed the chief 'bottleneck' of NLP (Briscoe 1991). With the surge of hybrid methods, incorporating linguistic knowledge with statistical methods that inferred knowledge from corpora, there was a growing need to create dictionaries and lexica with detailed information. Lexical acquisition is the automatic extraction of features of the lexeme, such as subcategorization information, selectional preference, semantic class, and other linguistic information regarding word usage. In much the same way as WSD above, lexical acquisition utilizes POS tags, or a sequence of POS tags, as a means to represent arguments of target words, as well as getting a general sense of the context in which words occurred. A general assumption in lexical acquisition is the idea that semantically similar words exhibit syntactically similar behaviour (Levin 1993). Based on this assumption, many semantically based lexical acquisition tasks, such as semantic class identification utilizes syntactic information as approximated by POS tags (Boleda et al. 2005). Specifically, Boleda et al. (2005) employ a sequence of POS tags in this very task as secondary features to morphological information.

Named Entity Recognition (NER) is the task of identifying relevant mention spans in a text. These identified mentions are classified as a particular entity types, such as *person* (PER), *organization* (ORG), *location* (LOC), *date* (DATE) (Tjong Kim Sang 2002; Tjong Kim Sang & De Meulder 2003). However, specific domains may require certain entities to be defined depending on the task at hand. For example, information extraction tasks for patents in the domain of chemistry, the task of NER involved identifying mentions of specific types of compounds such as *solvent, reaction_product, starting_material*, as well as important information about chemical reactions, such as *temperature, yield_percent*, and *time* (Zhai et al. 2019; Nguyen et al. 2020). NER is often framed as a sequence labelling task, where each word is labelled in sequence, and the marking-up of the data reflect this. The annotations, which indicate the span of the relevant mentions, typically specify whether an individual token or word is at the beginning of a named entity span (B), inside a span (I), or outside (O) any named entity spans. 'B' and 'I' are prefixed to the named entity type (e.g. 'ORG', 'PER') and both components combine to make up the label, for example 'B-LOC' indicates that a word is the beginning of a named entity span, where the named entity is classified as a *location*. Prior to the application of deep learning methods which became ubiquitous in NLP from the mid-2010s, POS tags were widely used as input features in non-neural methods. For instance, POS tags of the surrounding words have been used as one of the ways to insert information about context for the target word Takeuchi & Collier (2002); Florian et al. (2003).

Automatic summarization aims to convey the main ideas of a document or documents in less space, usually less than half the length of the original text (Radev et al. 2002). There are two major methods of creating summaries, either through extraction or abstraction. Extraction involves the identification of salient sentences or paragraphs from the original text to form a summary. Abstraction methods are those that do not involve sentences or paragraphs from the original text being reused. One such method is the compression method, which in the case of Knight & Marcu (2000) involves the compression of sentences using parse trees. The compression algorithm is deterministic. It comprises four types of actions: SHIFT transfers the next/first word onto a stack; REDUCE combines words in the stack to form a new phrase; DROP drops constituents or phrases from the input list; and ASSIGNTYPE is a relabeller. It reassigns the input words a new POS tag if necessary. Labelling the input word with the correct POS tag is crucial, particularly because it helps shape the form of the compressed sentence's parse tree.

Many recent deep learning methods to solve these NLP tasks do not utilize additional linguistic information such as POS (see section 45.4.3). This is because methods that employ pretrained word-based models such as BERT (Devlin et al. 2018) in the deep learning pipeline have been shown to learn a rich representation of language that incorporates semantic as well as syntactic information (Jawahar et al. 2019) (see section 45.4.1). POS tags are still used in some experiments, for example, Nallapati et al. (2016) who experiment with the addition of POS information in their deep learning pipeline utilizing as they do not employ the pretrained word-based model BERT but train their own Word2Vec (Mikolov et al. 2013b) word embeddings as their representation of language.

45.4.1.2 *AI and language applications*

Voice-enabled assistants and applications on mobile devices have become commonplace so that it is possible for anyone with a bit of time to develop their own with toolkits such as Dialogflow[7], Amazon Lex,[8] and wit.ai to name a few. These workbenches are fulfilling the very specific use of enabling voice commands in a narrow domain. The main idea around these workbenches is defining the possible goals and sub-goals pertaining to the domain at hand. These closed set of goals to fulfil are called *intents*, and each has associated with them arguments that need to be filled, called *slots*. For example, to build a voice interface for a smart home, one defines a set of intents such as a 'turn on' or 'turn off' intent which would require arguments such as an appliance or device, as well as a location or even type to uniquely identify what is being controlled. For example, the application could have the capability of turning the floor lamp in the bedroom on, or the light in the kitchen off. These arguments are called entities and in a sense the building of these voice interfaces entail defining a slot grammar, where the slots are filled with a subclass of nouns that are defined as the entities of interest.

These user friendly workbenches have their origins in the first types of dialogue systems designed in the 1970s. However, these systems took into consideration how people communicated and designed that as part of the communicative user experience. The task undertaken in building one of the first dialogue interaction systems, GUS (General Understanding System) (Bobrow et al. 1977), was not just significant because it was able to undertake a task ordinarily handled by human operators, but because it aimed to emulate some of the naturalistic features in human-to-human interactions. Some of these problems are still unsolved research questions, which include anaphora resolution; allowing for a mixed initiative conversation that allow for a more natural flow in the dialogue; and accommodating for indirect speech, which calls for an inference step and often knowledge of situational semantics.

In addition, these early systems introduced the notion of 'frame', 'slot', and 'filler' which are still relevant in modern slot filling tasks (Tür et al. 2010; Liu and Lane 2016; Zhang et al. 2019). A frame is a data structure in the GUS dialogue system, much like an 'intent' in more modern systems. The only difference is that a frame is a more general structure that can also hold meta information about dialogue flow, whereas intents usually just represents information that pertains to the sub-task within the overall goal that is to be achieved. The domain of

---

[7] https://dialogflow.com
[8] https://aws.amazon.com/lex/

GUS was restricted to the flight booking domain, and therefore the frames or intent pertain to steps in achieving a travel itinerary. For example, an intent or frame for 'TripLeg' specifies all the information that is required to book the outward-bound portion of the flight, which includes the slots 'FromPlace' and 'ToPlace', as well as information such as date and time. The exact number of slots varies from intent to intent depending on the sub-goal. The fillers can only fill a slot if it matches the particular semantic types allowed for that slot. For instance, only a proper noun that is a location can satisfy a 'FromPlace' slot as a filler.

Once the intents for a domain-specific system are defined, there are two main tasks for these kinds of dialogue systems: intent classification of the incoming user utterance; and slot filling to satisfy the information required for each intent. The identification of pos information is useful not only for the slot filling task, where nouns can identify entities of interest, but also in determining salient key terms. Furthermore, it was found that one of the causes of errors in intent classification stemmed from incorrect pos tagging (Tür et al. 2010). In such cases, as Tür et al. outlined, the surface word *arriving* in an utterance such as *I want to find the earliest arriving flight to Boston* is a cause for a false negative identification of an intent because in this case it is identified as an adjective rather than a verb.

These simple systems are still very widely deployed in industry.

45.4.2 Determining word classes

Determining words classes in computational linguistics often involves an unsupervised method referred to as word-class induction (Clark 2003a; Christodoulopoulos et al. 2010; Chrupala 2011; Mistica et al. 2013; Biemann 2014; Sirts et al. 2014; Lin et al. 2015). The word classes that are discovered through these methods are typically evaluated against attested or known classes.

In contrast, Biemann (2014) introduces a *Structure Discovery* paradigm. In this work, Biemann proposes an iterative framework that labels unstructured text with the structural information that is induced from patterns found in the text as a form of self-annotation. This is a move away from the *knowledge-intensive* approaches of NLP that relies upon the linguistically rich annotated resources, such as dictionaries, ontologies, and other information-rich lexica that are employed to drive learning. This *knowledge-free* method aims to exclude human intervention or the utilization of linguistic resources that require human effort to drive the learning process.

Word-class induction systems employ a method that results in a set of syntactic clusters, where the number of clusters induced may or may not be specified as a system parameter, depending on the induction method. The features employed in word-class induction tasks may involve contextual features, which is simply the surrounding words for our given target word. The idea in the design of this kind of feature captures the assumption that words which are of the same class should appear in the same environment. In a sense, these features broadly speaking model the syntactic environment of a word. In addition to context of a word within a phrase or a sentence being employed, the morphological profile of a word is also considered an important feature in these systems, with additional morphological information used as a means to prioritize clustered words that have similar morphological shapes (Clark 2003b; Higgins 2003; Mistica et al. 2013). These feature types are represented as an array of features called a vector representation.

These clustering methods that find similarities between words for their defined features are called unsupervised methods because the known gold labelled data[9] (the attested word class to which the item belongs) does not guide the learning process. The vector representation used in these word-class induction tasks utilize a *type* level characterization of a lexeme. This is in contrast to a *token* representation, which is simply one instance of usage or occurrence of a lexical form within a corpus. The type representation takes into consideration all the possible contexts in which the lexeme can occur and builds a up a profile as a vector representation of the word.

45.4.3 The evolution of word representations

Unlike earlier (more traditional) machine learning models that often relied on a set of manually designed features, representing morphological and syntactic information, contemporary models are trained to learn the features from raw data. These models brought significant improvement to many NLP tasks such as machine translation, language modelling, and POS tagging. In terms of this chapter, we will discuss two that are most relevant: language modelling and POS tagging.

Language modelling is the task of assigning a probability to a sequence of words (e.g. a sentence). Earlier models were mainly count-based, employing explicit token co-occurrence statistics. In the simplest case, each token was assigned a sparse vector with dimensionality equal to the total number of types. In order to reduce the high dimensionality, various methods such as Singular Value Decomposition (Golub & Reinsch 1971) were used to map the features to a smaller more general set.

More recent models, such as neural models, are prediction-based, and they replace word counts with a more sophisticated means of inference. The prediction-based models (such as Word2Vec (Mikolov et al. 2013a), Recursive Neural Nets, RNN (Elman 1990; Mikolov et al. 2013c) and Convolutional Neural Networks, CNN (LeCun & Bengio 1998; Kim et al. 2015)) are typically trained to predict a word out of context. The Word2Vec models inherently learn dense vector representations, often referred to as *word embeddings*. Both approaches are in line with the notion of distributional semantics (Harris 1954), which states that word meaning can be expressed as a distribution of the contexts the word appears in. Importantly, these models obtain a single embedding for a word that merges all its meanings and contextual usages. Although they share a training strategy, the models' architecture differ substantially. For instance, Word2Vec is a feedforward neural network that only allows for limited context: at each step, it only considers words that appear within a preset (sliding) *window*, which presets a limited context to the left and right. In addition, it is a *bag-of-words* in the sense that it does not take into account the order of the words within the window. RNNs, on the other hand, consist of recurrent units that gradually accumulate contextual information in hidden states (as a vector). Bengio et al. (1994) found that such an architecture does not work well on long sequences,[10] and various modifications of RNN units such

---

[9] Gold labelled data is hand-labelled data by domain experts that is designed to represent a reliable value.

[10] This is because of the problem of compounding calculations on ever-decreasing values called the 'vanishing gradient problem'.

as Long Short-Term Memory, LSTM (Hochreiter & Schmidhuber 1997) or Gated Recurrent Units. GRU (Cho et al. 2014) were proposed to remedy the issue.

A bidirectional[11] RNN-based model with LSTM cells proposed in Plank et al. (2016) was among best performing POS tagging systems achieving 96.5% average accuracy across 22 languages from the UD dataset and 97.2% on the PTB data. The model's architecture was based on the earlier work by Ling et al. (2015) who additionally showed the utility of character-level representations of words. Although various pos tagging models such as Bohnet et al. (2018) showed superior performance, Plank et al.'s approach still often serves as a jumping-off point to most architectures with recurrent units. Still, compressing a sentence-level meaning into a single vector seemed to be problematic, and Bahdanau et al. (2014) proposed enriching the RNN architectures with an *attention* mechanism, which marked a significant improvement in the performance of machine translation. The significance of the attention mechanism is that it allowed a sequence model to learn which part of the input sentence it should focus on at each inference step (instead of taking the whole sentence into account).

Vaswani et al. (2017) then presented a novel learning model, called the Transformer, that entirely relied on multiple self-attention mechanisms (without recurrent units). This contribution opened a new era in the field of NLP and has influenced how applications are designed by its practitioners. These Transformers were incorporated in a powerful language model, BERT (Bidirectional Encoder Representations from Transformers; Devlin et al. (2019)). As a language model, BERT is trained to predict a masked (hidden) word from its context, but more powerfully, it additionally performs the next sentence prediction task. The latter is a binary classifier that predicts whether Sentence A follows Sentence B. Unlike earlier language models that learned a single (type-level) representation for all word usages, BERT obtains contextual (token-level) representations which allows for WSD (see section 45.4.4.1). In addition, the authors released a multilingual BERT (M-BERT) that was trained on monolingual Wikipedia corpora from 104 languages. Experiments conducted in Pires et al. (2019) suggest that M-BERT is able to perform cross-lingual generalizations. Most recently, Heinzerling & Strube (2019) incorporated M-BERT representations into a POS tagger model achieving 96.77% average accuracy across 27 languages from the UD treebanks.

Some researchers studied representations learned by the models: what information do they capture and how well? In order to evaluate representations, Belinkov et al. (2017a) suggested feeding them into a simple feedforward neural network and training it for certain tasks, such as the prediction of POS or morphological tags. Such diagnostic methods were then referred to as *probes*. All the neural models consist of multiple layers that are analysed separately. By probing for linguistic structure, Belinkov et al. showed that lower layers capture more word-specific information (morphology) whereas higher layers model on semantics. Belinkov et al. (2017b) also found that the representations capture a significant amount of POS information. A classifier trained on these representations achieved over 90% accuracy on prediction of the PTB tags on languages such as Arabic, French, Spanish, Russian, and Chinese.

Furthermore, Hewitt & Manning (2019) developed a structural probe that evaluated whether syntax trees could be reconstructed from BERT representations. Results obtained

---

[11] Reading input sequences left to right and right to left.

on the PTB test set demonstrated that entire syntax trees are implicitly embedded into the vector space. Chi et al. (2020) continued the evaluation on ten languages using M-BERT and discovered syntactic subspaces that overlap between languages. This suggests that M-BERT stores syntactic features in a shared cross-lingual space. The clusters formed by representations of syntactic dependency labels mostly match the taxonomy used in UD. Finally, Pimentel et al. (2020) introduced an information–theoretic operationalization of probing showing that BERT encodes over 76% of POS information across 11 typologically diverse languages, which is at most 12% more information than in type-level representations. The information modelled by POS is an important part of the most effective models.

45.5 Conclusion

We have seen how POS tags can be used in the creation of knowledge bases, for example encoding actions and object for a robot assistant, where these AI applications often simplify entities and actions as largely mapping onto nouns and verbs. Of course, the world isn't just made up of nouns and verbs and we can't reliably categorize our world guided by only these word classes. However, this approximation serves us well in many AI applications. We have also showed how central the notion of the word class has been in NLP, with many tasks employing these features in their methodologies.

In this chapter, we have also discussed the ways that the representations of word classes vary in text processing, from the very detailed linguistically driven features used in grammar engineering to the flat labels which conflate language-specific characteristics into coarse-grained types, such as the word classes outlined as part of the UD labels, for the purpose of text processing. In addition, we have introduced the new ways in which words are represented by neural networks where the syntactic information modelled by POS and syntactic trees is implicitly represented within dense vector representations.

Although initially seen as a step on the way to syntactic analysis, POS tags have proved to be a useful level of extraction for many tasks, including primarily semantic ones. As the field of AI moves towards more complex models that capture a variety of information, probing has shown that the information on word classes is still an important part of these models. We expect POS tags to remain important in NLP and AI for the foreseeable future.

References

Aarsleff, Hans (1983). *The Study of Language in England, 1780–1860*. Minneapolis: University of Minnesota Press.

Aarts, Bas (2004a). Conceptions of gradience in the history of linguistics. *Language Sciences* 26: 343–389.

Aarts, Bas (2004b). Modelling linguistic gradience. *Studies in Language* 28: 1–50.

Aarts, Bas (2006). Conceptions of categorization in the history of linguistics. *Languages Sciences* 28: 361–385.

Aarts, Bas (2007). *Syntactic Gradience: The Nature of Grammatical Indeterminacy*. Oxford: Oxford University Press.

Aarts, Bas (2011). *Oxford Modern English Grammar*. Oxford: Oxford University Press.

Aarts, Bas, et al. (eds.) (2004). *Fuzzy Grammar: A Reader*. Oxford: Oxford University Press.

Abel, Taylor J., et al. (2015). Direct physiologic evidence of a heteromodal convergence region for proper naming in human left anterior temporal lobe. *Journal of Neuroscience* 35: 1513–1520.

Abbott, Clifford (1984). Two feminine genders in Oneida. *Anthropological Linguistics* 26: 125–137.

Abbott, Clifford, Amos Chirstjohn, & Maria Hinton (1996). *An Oneida Dictionary*. Oneida, WI: Oneida Tribe of Indians of Wisconsin.

Abbott, Clifford (2000). *Oneida*. (Languages of the World: Materials 301.) Munich: Lincom Europa.

Abbott, Edwin (1991). *Flatland: A Romance of Many Dimensions* (Princeton Science Library). Reprint. Originally published, 6th edn. New York: Dover Publications, 1953. Princeton, NJ: Princeton University Press.

Abeillé, Anne, et al. (2004). The syntax of French N' phrases. In Stefan Müller (ed.), *Proceedings of the 11th International Conference on Head-driven Phrase Structure Grammar*. Stanford, CA: CSLI Publications, 6–26.

Abner, Natasha (2017). What you see is what you get: Surface transparency and ambiguity of nominalizing reduplication in American Sign Language. *Syntax* 20(4): 317–352. https://doi.org/10.1111/synt.12147

Abner, Natasha, et al. (2019). The noun–verb distinction in established and emergent sign systems. *Language* 95(2): 230–267. https://doi.org/10.1353/lan.2019.0030

Abney, Stephen P. (1987). The English noun phrase in its sentential aspect. Dissertation, MIT.

Abusch, Dorit (1997). Sequence of tense and temporal de re. *Linguistics and Philosophy* 20: 1–50.

Acquaviva, Paolo (2008). *Lexical Plurals: A Morphosemantic Approach*. Oxford: Oxford University Press.

Acquaviva, Paolo (2009). Roots and lexicality in distributed morphology. *York Papers in Linguistics* 2(10): 1–21.

Adamou, Evangelia (2016). *A Corpus-Driven Approach to Language Contact: Endangered Languages in a Comparative Perspective*. Berlin: Mouton de Gruyter.

Adamou, Evangelia, et al. (2016). Borrowing and contact intensity: A corpus-driven approach from four Slavic minority languages. *Journal of Language Contact* 9(3): 515–544. https://doi.org/10.1163/19552629-00903004

Adamou, Evangelia & Kimmo Granqvist (2015). Unevenly mixed Romani languages. *International Journal of Bilingualism* 19: 525–47. https://doi.org/10.1177/1367006914524645

Adamou, Evangelia & Rachel X. Shen (2019). There are no language switching costs when codeswitching is frequent. *International Journal of Bilingualism* 23 (1): 53–70. https://doi.org/10.1177/1367006917709094

Adams, Anne-Marie & Susan E. Gathercole (1995). Phonological working memory and speech production in preschool children. *Journal of Speech & Hearing Research* 38(2): 403–414. https://doi.org/10.1044/jshr.3802.403

Adams, Karen Lee (1989). *Systems of Numeral Classification in the Mon-Khmer, Nicobarese, and Aslian Subfamilies of Austroasiatic*. Canberra: Australian National University.

Adams, Rick A., Karl J. Friston, & Andre M. Bastos (2015). Active inference, predictive coding and cortical architecture. In Manuel F. Casanova & Ion Opris (eds.), *Recent Advances on the Modular Organization of the Cortex*. Dordrecht: Springer, 97–121. https://doi.org/10.1007/978-94-017-9900-3_7

Adamson, Luke (2018). Denominal verbs: Past tense allomorphy, event frames, and zero-categorizers. *University of Pennsylvania Working Papers in Linguistics* 24(1): art. 2.

Adelaar, Willem & Simon van der Kerke (2009). Puquina. In Mily Crevels & Pieter Muysken (eds.), *Lenguas de Bolivia. Tomo I. Ambito Andino*. La Paz, Bolivia: Plural editores, 125–146.

Adelaar, Willem, in collaboration with Pieter Muysken (2004). *The Languages of the Andes*. Cambridge: Cambridge University Press.

Adell, Eric James (2019). The phonetics, phonology, and morphology of Chajul Ixil (Mayan). PhD dissertation. University of Texas at Austin.

Adger, David (2003). *Core Syntax*. Oxford: Oxford University Press.

Adger, David (2011). *A Syntax of Substance*. Cambridge, MA: MIT Press.

Adger, David & Peter Svenonius (2011). Features in minimalist syntax. In C. Boecks (ed.), *The Handbook of Linguistic Minimalism*. Oxford: Blackwell, 27–51.

Adrados, Francisco R. (1975). *Lingüística indoeuropea*. Madrid, Gredos.

Ahlner, Felix & Zlatev, Jordan (2010). Cross-modal iconicity: A cognitive semiotic approach to sound symbolism. *Sign Systems Studies* 38(1/4): 298–348.

Aikhenvald, Alexandra Y. (2000). *Classifiers: A Typology of Noun Categorization Devices*. Oxford: Oxford University Press.

Aikhenvald, Alexandra Y. (2004). *Evidentiality*. Oxford: Oxford University Press.

Aikhenvald, Alexandra Y. (2006). Classifiers and noun classes: Semantics. In Keith Brown (ed.), *Encyclopedia of Languages and Linguistics*. Oxford: Elsevier, 463–471.

Aikhenvald, Alexandra Y. (2007). Information source and evidentiality: What can we conclude? *Italian Journal of Linguistics* 19(1): 209–227.

Aikhenvald, Alexandra Y. (2011). Classifiers. Oxford Bibliographies Online. New York: Oxford University Press. doi:10.1093/obo/9780199772810-0007

Aikhenvald, A. Y. (2012). *The Languages of the Amazon*. Oxford: Oxford University Press.

Aikhenvald, Alexandra Y. (2017). A typology of noun categorization devices. In Alexandra Y. Aikhenvald (ed.), *The Cambridge Handbook of Linguistic Typology*. Cambridge: Cambridge University Press, 361–404.

Aikhenvald, Alexandra Y. & Tonya N. Stebbins (2007). Languages of New Guinea. In Osahito Miyaoka, Osamu Sakiyama, & Michael E. Krauss (eds.), *The Vanishing Languages of the Pacific Rim*. Oxford: Oxford University Press, 239–266.

Aissen, Judith (2017a). Correlates of ergativity in Mayan. In Jessica Coon, Diane Massam, & Lisa deMena Travis (eds.), *The Oxford Handbook of Ergativity*. Oxford: Oxford University Press, 665–689.

Aissen, Judith (2017b). Complement clauses. In Judith Aissen, Nora C. England, & Roberto Zavala Maldonado (eds.), *The Mayan Languages*. London/New York: Routledge, 259–292.

Aissen, Judith, Nora C. England, & Roberto Zavala Maldonado (eds.) (2017). *The Mayan Languages*. London/New York: Routledge.

Ajello, Roberto (1998). Armenian. In Anna Giacalone Ramat & Paolo Ramat (eds.), *The Indo-European Languages*. London: Routledge, 197–227.

Akhtar, Nameera & Michael Tomasello. 1997. Young children's productivity with word order and verb morphology. Developmental Psychology 33. 952–965.

Akhtar, Nameera, Malinda Carpenter, & Michael Tomasello (1996). The role of discourse novelty in early word learning. *Child Development* 67(2): 635–645. https://doi.org/10.1111/j.1467-8624.1996.tb01756

Akita, Kimi (2009). A grammar of sound-symbolic words in Japanese: Theoretical approaches to iconic and lexical properties of Japanese mimetics. PhD dissertation, Kobe University, Kobe. http://www.lib.kobe-u.ac.jp/handle_gakui/D1004724

Akita, Kimi (2020). A typology of depiction marking: The prosody of Japanese ideophones and beyond. *Studies in Language* 45 (4): 865–886. doi:10.1075/sl.17029.aki

Akita, Kimi & Prashant Pardeshi (eds.) (2019). *Ideophones, Mimetics and Expressives*. (Iconicity in Language and Literature vol. XVI.) Amsterdam: John Benjamins.

Albright, Adam (2008). How many grammars am I holding up? Discovering phonological differences between word classes. In Charles B. Chang & Hannah J. Haynie (eds.), *Proceedings of the 26th West Coast Conference on Formal Linguistics*. Somerville, MA: Cascadilla Proceedings Project, 1–20.

Alexeyenko, Sasha (2015). The syntax and semantics of manner modification: Adjectives and adverbs. PhD thesis, University of Osnabrück.

Alexiadou, Artemis (2001). *Functional Structure in Nominals*. Amsterdam: John Benjamins.

Alexiadou, Artemis (2004). On the formation and interpretation of derived nominals. Paper presented at the International Conference on Deverbal Nouns. Lille, September 2004.

Alexiadou, Artemis (2009). On the role of syntactic locality in morphological processes: The case of (Greek) derived nominals. In Anastasia Giannakidou & Monika Rathert (eds.) *Quantification, Definiteness and Nominalization*. Oxford: Oxford University Press, 253–280.

Alexiadou, Artemis & Chris Wilder (1998). *Possessors, Predicates and Movement in the Determiner Phrase*. Amsterdam: John Benjamins.

Allan, Keith (1977). Classifiers. *Language* 53(2): 277–311.

Allan, Keith (1980). Nouns and countability. *Language* 56(3): 541–567.

Allegranza, Valerio (1998). Determiners as functors: NP structure in Italian. In Sergio Balari & Luca Dini (eds.), *Romance in HPSG*. Stanford, CA: CSLI Publications, 55–107.

Allerton, D. J. (2002). *Stretched Verb Constructions in English*. London: Routledge.

Allwood, Jens, Joakim Nivre, & Elisabeth Ahlsén (1990). Speech management—On the non-written life of speech. *Nordic Journal of Linguistics* 13(01): 3–48. doi:10.1017/S0332586500002092

Alsharif, Ahmad & Louisa Sadler (2009). Negation in Modern Standard Arabic: An LFG approach. In Miriam Butt & Tracy Holloway King (eds.), *On-line Proceedings of the LFG2009 Conference*. Stanford, CA: CSLI Publications, 2–25.

Alyahya, Reem S. W., et al. (2018). The behavioural patterns and neural correlates of concrete and abstract verb processing in aphasia: A novel verb semantic battery. *NeuroImage: Clinical* 17: 811–825.

Armoskaite, Solveiga (2019). How to phraseologize nominal number. In Éric Mathieu, Myriam Dali, & Gita Zareikar (eds.), *Gender and Noun Classification*. Oxford: Oxford University Press, 268.

Ambridge, Ben. 2017. Syntactic categories in child language acquisition: Innate, induced, or illusory? In Handbook of categorization in cognitive science, 567–580. Elsevier.

Ambridge, Ben. 2020a. Abstractions made of exemplars or 'You're all right, and I've changed my mind': Response to commentators. First Language 40(5-6). 640–659.

Ambridge, Ben. 2020b. Against stored abstractions: A radical exemplar model of language acquisition. First Language 40(5-6). 509–559.

Ameka, Felix (1991). Ewe: Its grammatical constructions and illocutionary devices. PhD dissertation, Australian National University.

Ameka, Felix (1992a). Interjections: The universal yet neglected part of speech. *Journal of Pragmatics* 18(2–3): 101–118.

Ameka, Felix (1992b). The meaning of phatic and conative interjections. *Journal of Pragmatics* 18(2–3): 245–271.

Ameka, Felix (2001). Ideophones and the nature of the adjective word class in Ewe. In F. K. Erhard Voeltz & Christa Kilian-Hatz (eds.), *Ideophones*. Amsterdam: John Benjamins, 25–48.

Ameka, Felix & David Wilkins (2006). Interjections. In Jef Verschueren & Jan-Ola Östman (eds.), *Handbook of Pragmatics*. Amsterdam: John Benjamins, 1–19. doi:10.1075/hop.10.int12

Azeb Amha, (2001). *The Maale language*. Leiden: CNWS Publications.

Azeb Amha, & Gerrit Dimmendaal (2006). Converbs in an African perspective. In Felix K. Ameka, Alan Dench, & Nicholas Evans (eds.), *Catching Language: The Standing Challenge of Grammar Writing*. Berlin/New York: Mouton de Gruyter, 393–440.

Azeb Amha, (2010). Compound verbs and ideophones in Wolaitta revisited. In Mengistu Amberber, Brett Baker, & Mark Harvey (eds.), *Complex Predicates: Cross-linguistic Perspectives on Event Structure*. Cambridge: Cambridge University Press, 259–267.

Azeb Amha, (2012). Omotic. In Zygmunt Frajzyngier & Erin Shay (eds.), *The Afroasiatic Languages*. Cambridge: Cambridge University Press, 423–504.

Azeb Amha, (2013). Directives to humans and to domestic animals: The Imperative and some interjections in Zargulla. *Cushitic and Omotic Studies: Proceedings of the 5th International Conference on Cushitic and Omotic Languages, Paris, 16–18 April 2008*: 211–229.

Anderson, John M. (1997). *A Notional Theory of Syntactic Categories*. Cambridge: Cambridge University Press.

Andersen, R. & Yasuhiro Shirai (1996). The primacy of aspect in first and second language acquisition: The Pidgin-Creole connection. In William C. Ritchie & Tej K. Bhatia (eds.), *Handbook of Second Language Acquisition*. San Diego, CA: Academic Press, 527–570.

Anderson, Stephen R. (1992). *A-morphous Morphology*, Cambridge: Cambridge University Press.

Aoun, Joseph E., Elabbas Benmamoun, & Lina Choueiri (2009). *The Syntax of Arabic*. Oxford: Oxford University Press.

Arad, Maya (2003). Locality constraints on the interpretation of roots: The case of Hebrew denominal verbs. *Natural Language and Linguistic Theory* 21: 737–778.

Archangelskiy, Timofey & Yury Lander (2016). Developing a polysynthetic language corpus: Problems and solutions. *Computational Linguistics and Intellectual Technologies* 15(22): 40–49.

Aristotle (1984). *The Metaphysics*. In Jonathan Barnes (ed.), *The Complete Works of Aristotle*, rev. Oxford trans., vol. II, trans. W. D. Ross. Princeton, NJ: Princeton University Press, 1552–1728.

Arka, I. Wayan. (2013). Nominal aspect in Marori. In Miriam Butt & Tracy Holloway King (eds.), *On-line Proceedings of the LFG2013 Conference*. Stanford, CA: CSLI Publications, 27–47.
Arkadiev, Peter M. (2009). Differential argument marking in two-term case systems and its implications for the general theory of case marking. In Helen de Hoop & Peter de Swart (eds.), *Differential Subject Marking*. New York: Springer, 151–171.
Arkadiev, Peter M. (2016). Interaction of actionality, aspect and tense in Kuban Kabardian counterfactual conditionals. Handout for a talk at Thirteenth Conference in typology and grammar for young scholars. Saint-Petersburg.
Arnott, David W. (1970). *The Nominal and Verbal Systems of Fula*. Oxford: Clarendon Press.
Aronoff, Mark (1976). *Word Formation in Generative Morphology*. Cambridge, MA: MIT Press.
Aronoff, Mark (1994). *Morphology by Itself*. Cambridge, MA: MIT Press.
Aronoff, Mark (2007). In the beginning was the word. *Language* 83(4): 803–830.
Aronoff, Mark (2016). A fox knows many things but a hedgehog one big thing. In Andrew Hippisley & Gregory Stump (eds.), *The Cambridge Handbook of Morphology*. Cambridge: Cambridge University Press, 186–205.
Artoni, Fiorenzo, et al. (2020). High gamma response tracks different syntactic structures in homophonous phrases. *Scientific Reports* 10: 7537.
Arunachalam, Sudha & Sandra R Waxman. 2011. Grammatical form and semantic context in verb learning. Language Learning and Development 7(3). 169–184.
Arunachalam, Sudha, Erin M Leddon, Hyun-joo Song, Yoonha Lee & Sandra R Waxman. 2013. Doing more with less: Verb learning in Korean-acquiring 24-month-olds. Language Acquisition 20(4). 292–304.
Arutjunova, Nina D. & Evgenij Shirjaev (1983). *Russkoe predloženie. Bytijnyj tip* [Russian sentence. The existential type]. Moscow: Russkij jazyk.
Asbury, Anna. R (2008). The morphosyntax of case and adpositions. PhD dissertation. Utrecht, LOT.
Asudeh, Ash, Mary Dalrymple, & Ida Toivonen. (2013). Constructions with lexical integrity. *Journal of Language Modelling* 1(1): 77–130. http://jlm.ipipan.waw.pl/index.php/JLM/article/view/56
Atwell, Eric S. (2008). Development of tag sets for part-of-speech tagging. In Anke Lüdeling & Merja Kytö (eds.), *Corpus Linguistics: An International Handbook*. Berlin: de Gruyter, vol. 1, 501–526.
Audring, Jenny & Geert Booij (2016). Cooperation and coercion. *Linguistics* 54(4): 617–637.
Audring, Jenny, Sterre Leufkens, & Eva van Lier (2021). Small events: Verbal diminutives in the languages of the world. *Linguistic Typology at the Crossroads* 1 (1): 223–256.
Austin, Peter (1981). Switch-reference in Australia. *Language* 57(2): 309–334.
Austin, Peter (2013). *A Grammar of Diyari, South Australia*. 3rd edn. Cambridge: Cambridge University Press. https://www.academia.edu/2491078/A_Grammar_of_Diyari_South_Australia
Avery, C. Robert (1983). *Contemporary Turkish–English Dictionary*. Istanbul: Redhouse.
Avons, S. E., et al. (1998). Measures of phonological short-term memory and their relationship to vocabulary development. *Applied Psycholinguistics* 19(4): 583–601. https://doi.org/10.1017/S0142716400010377
Ayçiçeği, Ayse & Catherine Harris (2004). Bilinguals' recall and recognition of emotion words. *Cognition and Emotion* 8: 977–987.
Ayres, Glenn (1991). *La gramática ixil*. La Antigua, Guatemala: CIRMA.
Baayen, Harald R., Peter Hendrix, & Michael Ramscar (2013). Sidestepping the combinatorial explosion: An explanation of N-gram frequency effects based on naive discriminative

learning. *Language and Speech* 56(Pt 3): 329–347. https://dx.doi.org/10.1177/0023830913484896

Babalọla, Adeboye & Olugboyega Alaba (2003). *A Dictionary of Yoruba Personal Names*. Lagos: West African Book Publishers.

Bache, C. (1978). *The Order of Premodifying Adjectives in Present-Day English*. Odense: Odense University Press.

Backus, Ad (1996). *Two in One. Bilingual Speech of Turkish Immigrants in the Netherlands*. Tilburg: Tilburg University Press.

Backus, Ad (2003). Units in code switching: Evidence for multimorphemic elements in the lexicon. *Linguistics* 41: 83–132.

Baddeley, Alan, Susan Gathercole, & Costanza Papagno (1998). The phonological loop as a language learning device. *Psychological Review* 105(1): 158–173. https://doi.org/10.1037/0033-295X.105.1.158

Badenoch, Nathan & Toshiki Osada (eds.) (2019). *A Dictionary of Mundari Expressives*. Tokyo: Research Institute of Language and Cultures of Asia and Africa (ILCAA).

Badenoch, Nathan, Madhu Purti, & Nishaant Choksi (2019). Expressives as moral propositions in Mundari. *Indian Linguistics* 80(1–2): 1–17.

Bak, Thomas H. & John R. Hodges (2004). The effects of motor neurone disease on language: Further evidence. *Brain and Language* 89: 354–361.

Baker, Brett, et al. (2010). Putting it all together: Agreement, incorporation, coordination and external possession in Wubuy. In Miriam Butt & Tracy Holloway King (eds.), *On-line Proceedings of the LFG2010 Conference*. Stanford, CA: CSLI Publications, 64–84. http://web.stanford.edu/group/cslipublications/cslipublications/LFG/15/lfg10.toc.html

Baker, Mark C. (1996). *The Polysynthesis Parameter*. New York: Oxford University Press.

Baker, Mark C. 2002. The atoms of language. Oxford: Oxford University Press.

Baker, Mark C. (2003). *Lexical Categories: Verbs, Nouns, and Adjectives*. Cambridge: Cambridge University Press.

Baker, Mark C. (2008). *The Syntax of Agreement and Concord*. Cambridge: Cambridge University Press.

Baker, Mark C. & William Croft (2017). Lexical categories: Legacy, lacuna, and opportunity for functionalists and formalists. *Annual Review of Linguistics* 3: 179–197.

Bakken Jepsen, Julie, et al. (2015). *Sign Languages of the World: A Comparative Handbook*. Berlin/Boston: De Gruyter Mouton. https://doi.org/10.1515/9781614518174. https://www.degruyter.com/view/product/429986

Bakker, Dik (2013). Person marking on adpositions. In Matthew S. Dryer & Martin Haspelmath (eds.), *The World Atlas of Language Structures Online*. Leipzig: Max Planck Institute for Evolutionary Anthropology. http://wals.info/chapter/48

Bakker, Peter (1997). *A Language of Our Own. The Genesis of Michif—The Mixed Cree–French Language of the Canadian Métis*. New York: Oxford University Press.

Bakker, Peter (2003). Mixed languages as autonomous systems. In Yaron Matras & Peter Bakker (eds.), *The Mixed Language Debate: Theoretical and Empirical Advances*. Berlin: Mouton de Gruyter, 107–150.

Bakkerus, Astrid A., et al. (eds.) (2020). *Missionary Linguistic Studies from Mesoamerica to Patagonia*. Leiden: Brill.

Ball, Catherine N. (1977). Th-clefts. *Pennsylvania Review of Linguistics* 2: 57–64.

Bamyacı, Elif, Jana Häussler, & Barış Kabak (2014). The interaction of animacy and number agreement: An experimental investigation. *Lingua* 148: 254–277.

Banti, Giorgio (1986). 'Adjectives' in East Cushitic. In Marianne Bechhaus-Gerst & Fritz Serzisko (eds.), *Cushitic-Omotic. Papers from the International Symposium on Cushitic and Omotic Languages. Cologne, January 6-9 1986*. Hambourg: Helmut Buske, 203-259.

Banti, Giorgio & Moreno Vergari (2005). A sketch of Saho grammar. *Journal of Eritrean Studies* 4(1-2): 100-131.

Baptista, Marlyse (2013). Cape Verdean Creole of Brava structure dataset. In Susanne Maria Michaelis et al. (eds.), *Atlas of Pidgin and Creole Language Structures Online*. Leipzig: Max Planck Institute for Evolutionary Anthropology. https://apics-online.info/contributions/56

Bar, Moshe (2007). The proactive brain: Using analogies and associations to generate predictions. *Trends in Cognitive Sciences* 11(7): 280-289. https://doi.org/10.1016/j.tics.2007.05.005

Bar, Moshe (2009). The proactive brain: Memory for prediction. *Philosophical Transactions of the Royal Society B: Biological Sciences* 364(1521): 1235-1243.

Barber, Horacio A., et al. (2010). Event-related potentials to event-related words: Grammatical class and semantic attributes in the representation of knowledge. *Brain Research* 1332: 65-74.

Barbosa, A. Lemos (1947). Nova categoria gramatical tupi: A visibilidade e a invisibilidade nos demonstrativos. *Verbum* 4(2): 67-74.

Barbosa, A. Lemos. (1956). *Curso de Tupi Antigo: Gramática, Exercícios, Textos*. Livraria São José.

Barbu, Roxana & Ida Toivonen (2018). Romanian object clitics: Grammaticalization, agreement and lexical splits. In Miriam Butt & Tracy Holloway King (eds.), *On-line Proceedings of the LFG 2018 Conference*. Stanford, CA: CSLI Publications, 67-87. http://web.stanford.edu/group/cslipublications/cslipublications/LFG/LFG-2018/index.shtml

Barker, Chris (2010). Nominals don't provide criteria of identity. In Monika Rathert & Artemis Alexiadou (eds.), *The Semantics of Nominalizations across Languages and Frameworks*. Berlin: Mouton de Gruyter, 9-24.

Baronti, David S. (2001). Sound symbolism use in affect verbs in Santa Catarina Ixtahuacán. PhD dissertation, University of California at Davis, California.

Barrie, Michael & Hiroto Uchihara (2019). Iroquoian languages. In Daniel Siddiqi et al. (eds.), *The Routledge Handbook of North American Languages*. New York: Routledge, 424-451.

Barwise, Jon & John Perry (1983). *Situations and Attitudes*. Cambridge, MA: MIT Press.

Barwise, Jon & Robin Cooper (1981). Generalized quantifiers and natural language. *Linguistics and Philosophy* 4: 159-219.

Bassano, Dominique. 2000. Early development of nouns and verbs in French: exploring the interface between lexicon and grammar. Journal of Child Language 27. 521-559.

Bassano, Dominique, Isabelle Maillochon & Elsa Eme. 1998. Developmental changes and variability in the early lexicon: a study of French children's naturalistic productions. Journal of Child Language 25. 493-531.

Bastiaanse, Roelien & Hans Bennis (2018). Productie en begrip van voorzetsels bij sprekers met agrammatische en vloeiende afasie. [Production and comprehension of prepositions in speakers with agrammatic and fluent aphasia] *Nederlandse Taalkunde* 231: 3-22.

Bastiaanse, Roelien & Cynthia K. Thompson (eds.) (2012). *Perspectives on Agrammatism*. Brighton: Psychology Press.

Basu, Debarchana & Ronnie Wilbur (2010). *Complex Predicates in Bangla: An Event-based Analysis*. Rice Working Papers in Linguistics No. 2.

Bates, Dawn, Thom Hess, & Vi Hilbert (1994). *Lushootseed Dictionary*. Seattle: University of Washington Press.

Bätscher, Kevin (2014). Interclausal and intraclausal linking elements in Hul'q'umi'num' Salish. MA thesis, Simon Fraser University.

Bauer, Laurie (2013). Deriving locational nouns. *SKASE Journal of Theoretical Linguistics* 10(1): 1–11.

Bauer, Laurie (2017). *Compounds and Compounding*. Cambridge: Cambridge University Press.

Bauer, Laurie & Salvador Valera Hernández (eds.) (2005). *Approaches to Conversion/Zero-Derivation*. Münster: Waxmann.

Bauer, Winifred (1993). *Maori*. London/New York: Routledge.

Bauer, Laurie (2007). Derivational morphology. *Language and Linguistics Compass* 1:1–15.

Bauer, Winifred with William Parker, Te Kareongawai, & Te Aroha Noti Teepa (1997). *The Reed Reference Grammar of Māori*. Auckland: Reed Books.

Baunaz, Lena, et al. (2018). *Exploring Nanosyntax*. Oxford: Oxford University Press.

Bavelas, Janet B., Linda Coates, & Trudy Johnson (2000). Listeners as co-narrators. *Journal of Personality and Social Psychology* 79(6): 941–952. https://doi.org/10.1037/0022-3514.79.6.941

Baxter, William H. (1992). *A Handbook of Old Chinese Phonology*. Berlin: Mouton de Gruyter.

Baxter, William H. & Laurent Sagart (1998). Word formation in Old Chinese. In Jerome L. Packard (ed.), *New Approaches to Chinese Word Formation: Morphology, Phonology and the Lexicon in Modern and Ancient Chinese*. Berlin: Mouton de Gruyter, 35–76.

Baxter, William H. & Laurent Sagart (2014a). *Old Chinese: A New Reconstruction*. Oxford: Oxford University Press.

Baxter, William H. & Laurent Sagart (2014b). Baxter–Sagart Old Chinese reconstruction, version 1.1 (20 September 2014), William H. Baxter (白一平) and Laurent Sagart (沙加尔), order: by Mandarin and Middle Chinese. http://ocbaxtersagart.lsait.lsa.umich.edu/

Bažec, Helena (2019). Distribuzione areale degli articoli sloveni. Il caso dei dialetti del litorale. *Studi di linguistica slava*. Venezia: Ca' Foscari 20: 23–36.

Beard, Robert (1995). *Lexeme–Morpheme Base Morphology*. Albany, NY: SUNY Press.

Beaumont, Ronald C. (1985). *She shashishalhem: The Sechelt Language*. Penticton, BC: Theytus Books.

Beaumont, Ronald C. (2011). *Sechelt Dictionary*. Penticton, BC: Sechelt Indian Band.

Beck, David (1999a). The typology of parts of speech systems: The markedness of adjectives. PhD dissertation, University of Toronto.

Beck, David (1999b). Adjectives and the organization of lexical inventories. *Toronto Working Papers in Linguistics* 17: 18–57.

Beck, David (2000a). Bella Coola and North Wakashan: Convergence and diversity in the Northwest Coast Sprachbund. In Dicky Gilbers, John Nerbonne, & Jos Schaeken (eds.), *Languages in Contact: Studies in Slavic and General Linguistics* 28: 37–53.

Beck, David (2000b). Grammatical convergence and the genesis of diversity in the Northwest Coast Sprachbund. *Anthropological Linguistics* 42(2): 1–67.

Beck, David (2002). *The Typology of Parts of Speech Systems: The Markedness of Adjectives. Routledge Outstanding Dissertations in Linguistics*. New York: Routledge.

Beck, David (2008). Ideophones, adverbs, and predicate qualification in Upper Necaxa Totonac. *International Journal of American Linguistics* 74(1): 1–46.

Beck, David (2013). Uni-directional flexibility and the noun–verb distinction in Lushootseed. In Jan Rijkhoff & Eva van Lier (eds.), *Flexible Word Classes: A Typological Study of Underspecified Parts of Speech*. Oxford: Oxford University Press, 185–220.

Beck, Sigrid (2011). Comparison constructions. In Klaus von Heusinger, Claudia Maienborn, & Paul Portner (eds.), *Semantics: An International Handbook of Natural Language Meaning* (vol. II). Berlin: de Gruyter Mouton, 1341–1390.

Becker, Alton L. (1975). A linguistic image of nature: the Burmese numerative classifier system. *Linguistics* 165: 109–121

Becquey, Cédric (2014). *Diasystème, Diachronie: Études comparées dans les langues cholanes.* Utrecht: LOT.

Beghelli, Filippo & Tim Stowell (1997). Distributivity and negation: The syntax of *each* and *every*. In Anna Szabolcsi (ed.), *Ways of Scope Taking*. Dordrecht: Kluwer, 71–107.

Bekaert, Elisa & Renata Enghels (2019). On the edge between nouns and verbs: The heterogeneous behavior of Spanish deverbal nominalizations empirically verified. *Language Sciences* 73: 119–136.

Belfi, Amy M. & Daniel Tranel (2014). Impaired naming of famous musical melodies is associated with left temporal polar damage. *Neuropsychology* 28: 429–435.

Benetello, Annalisa, et al. (2016). The dissociability of lexical retrieval and morphosyntactic processes for nouns and verbs: A functional and anatomoclinical study. *Brain and Language* 159: 11–22.

Bennett, Ryan (2016). Mayan phonology. *Language and Linguistic Compass* 10: 469–514.

Bennett, Ryan, Jessica Coon, & Robert Henderson (2016). Introduction to Mayan linguistics. *Language and Linguistics Compass* 10: 453–454

Bennis, Hans, Ronald Prins, & Jan Vermeulen. (1983). Lexical–semantic versus syntactic disorders in aphasia: The processing of prepositions. *Publikaties van het Instituut voor Algemene Taalwerenschap* 40: 1–32.

Bensoussan, Marsha & Batia Laufer (1984). Lexical guessing in context in EFL reading comprehension, *Journal of Reading Research* 7: 15–32

Benton, Richard A. (1971). *Pangasinan Reference Grammar*. Honolulu: University of Hawaii Press.

Benveniste, Émile (1957). La phrase relative, problème de syntaxe générale. *Bulletin de la Societé Linguistique* 53: 39–53.

Benveniste, Émile (1968). Mutations of linguistic categories. In Winfred P. Lehmann & Y. Malkiel (eds.), *Directions for Historical Linguistics*. Austin: University of Texas Press, 85–94.

Benveniste, Émile (1971). *Problems in General Linguistics*. Coral Gables, FL: University of Miami Press.

Berger, Hermann (1998). Die Burushaski-Sprache von Hunza und Nager: Teil I: Grammatik. (Neuindische Studien, 13.) Wiesbaden: Otto Harrassowitz.

Berghäll, Liisa (2015). *A Grammar of Mauwake*. Berlin: Language Science Press.

Bergman, Brita (1983). Verbs and adjectives: Morphological processes in Swedish Sign Language. In Jim Kyle & Bencie Woll (eds.), *Language in Sign: An International Perspective on Sign Language*. London: Croom Helm, 3–9.

Bergman, Brita & Östen Dahl (1994). Ideophones in sign language? The place of reduplication in the tense–aspect system of Swedish Sign Language. In Carl Bache, Hans Basbøll, & Carl-Erik Lindberg (eds.), *Tense, Aspect and Action: Empirical and Theoretical Contributions to Language Typology*. Berlin: Mouton de Gruyter, 397–422.

Bergman, Brita & Lars Wallin (2001). The discourse function of noun classifiers in Swedish Sign Language. In Valerie Dively et al. (eds.), *Signed Languages: Discoveries from International Research*. Washington, DC: Gallaudet University Press, 45–61.

Bergman, Brita & Lars Wallin (2003). Noun and verbal classifiers in Swedish Sign Language. In Karen Emmorey (ed.), *Perspectives on Classifier Constructions in Sign Languages*. Mahwah, NJ: Erlbaum, 35–51.

Bergsland, Knut (1955) A grammatical outline of the Eskimo language of West Greenland [ms]. Oslo.

Bergsland, Knut (1989). Comparative aspects of Aleut syntax. *Aikakauskirja/Journal de la Société Finno-ougrienne* 82: 7–80.

Bergsland, Knut (1994). *Aleut Dictionary: Unangam Tunudgusii*. Fairbanks, AK: Alaska Native Language Center, University of Alaska.

Bergsland, Knut (1997). *Aleut Grammar: Unangam Tunuganaan Achixaasix*. Fairbanks, AK: Alaska Native Language Center.

Berlin, Brent (1968). *Tzeltal Numeral Classifiers: A Study in Ethnographic Semantics*. The Hague: Mouton.

Berlin, Brett & Paul Kay (1969). *Basic Color Terms: Their Universality and Evolution*. Berkeley: University of California Press.

Berlingeri, Manuela, et al. (2008). Nouns and verbs in the brain: Grammatical class and task specific effects as revealed by fMRI. *Cognitive Neuropsychology* 25: 528–558.

Berndt, R. S., et al. (2002). Grammatical class and imageability in aphasic word production: Their effects are independent. *Journal of Neurolinguistics* 15: 353–371.

Berners, Dame Juliana ([1486]; 1881 edn). *The Boke of Saint Albans, introduction by William Blades*. London: Elliot Stock. [the book is also known as *The Book of Hawking, Hunting, and Blasing of Arms*]

Berthele, Raphael (2003). The typology of motion and posture verbs: A variationist account. In Bernd Kortmann (ed.), *Dialectology Meets Typology. Dialect Grammar from a Crosslinguistic Perspective*. Berlin: Mouton de Gruyter, 93–126.

Bhat, D. N. Shankara (1994). *The Adjectival Category*. Amsterdam: John Benjamins.

Bialystok, Ellen, et al. (2009). Bilingual minds. *Psychological Science in the Public Interest* 10: 89–129.

Biber, Douglas, et al. (1999). *Longman Grammar of Spoken and Written English*. London: Longman.

Biberauer, Theresa (2017). Factors 2 and 3: A principled approach. *Cambridge Occasional Papers in Linguistics* 10: 38–65.

Billman, Dorrit. 1989. Systems of correlations in rule and category learning: Use of structured input in learning syntactic categories. Language and Cognitive Processes 4(2). 127–155.

Biberauer, Theresa & Ian Roberts (2015). Rethinking formal hierarchies: a proposed unification. *Cambridge Occasional Papers in Linguistics* 7: 1–31.

Bickel, Balthasar (2010). Capturing particulars and universals in clause linkage. In Isabelle Bril (ed.), *Clause Linking and Clause Hierarchy: Syntax and Pragmatics*. Amsterdam: John Benjamins, 51–101.

Bickel, Balthasar (2011). Grammatical relations typology. In Jae Jung Song (ed.), *The Oxford Handbook of Linguistic Typology*. Oxford: Oxford University Press, 399–444.

Bickel, Balthasar, Bernard Comrie, & Martin Haspelmath (2015). Leipzig glossing rules: Conventions for interlinear morpheme-by-morpheme glosses. http://www.eva.mpg.de/lingua/resources/glossing-rules.php

Bickel, Balthasar & Fernando Zúñiga (2017). The 'Word' in polysynthetic languages: Phonological and syntactic challenges. In Michael Fortescue, Marianne Mithun, & Nicholas Evans (eds.), *The Oxford Handbook of Polysynthesis*. Oxford: Oxford University Press, 158–185.

Biemann, Chris (2006). Unsupervised part-of-speech tagging employing efficient graph clustering. In *Proceedings of COLING ACL 2006*. Morristown, NJ, 7–12.

Bierwisch, Manfred (1988). On the grammar of local prepositions. In Manfred Bierwisch, Wolfgang Motsch, & Ilse Zimmermann (eds.), *Syntax, Semantik und Lexikon*. (Volume 29 of Studia Grammatica.) Berlin: Akademie Verlag, 1–65.

Binder, Jeffrey R. & Rutvik H. Desai (2011). The neurobiology of semantic memory. *Trends in Cognitive Sciences* 15: 527–536.

Birchall, Jane (2015). A comparison of verbal person marking across Tupían languages. *Boletim Do Museu Paraense Emílio Goeldi. Ciências Humanas* 10(2): 487–518.
Birjulin, Leonid A. & Viktor S. Khrakovskij (1990). *Funkcional'no-tipologičeskie aspekty analiza imperativa* [Functional typological aspects of analysis of imperative]. Leningrad: Institut jazykoznanija RAN
Bisang, Walter (1986). Die Verb-Serialisierung im Jabêm. *Lingua* 70: 131–162.
Bisang, Walter (1992). *Das Verb im Chinesischen, Hmong, Vietnamesischen, Thai und Khmer*. Tübingen: Narr.
Bisang, Walter (1995). Verb serialization and converbs—Differences and similarities. In Martin Haspelmath & Ekkehard König (eds.), *Converbs in Cross-linguistic Perspective. Structure and Meaning of Adverbial Verb Forms—Adverbial Participles, Gerunds*. Berlin/New York, Mouton de Gruyter, 137–188.
Bisang, Walter (1999). Classifiers in East and Southeast Asian languages: Counting and beyond. In Jadranka Gvozdanović (ed.), *Numeral Types and Changes Worldwide*. Berlin: Mouton de Gruyter, 113–185.
Bisang, Walter (2000). Finite vs. non-finite languages. In Martin Haspelmath, Ekkehard König, Wulf Oesterreicher, & Wolfgang Raible (eds.), *Language Typology and Language Universals*. Berlin: de Gruyter, vol. 2/2, 1400–1413.
Bisang, Walter (2004). Grammaticalization without coevolution of form and meaning: The case of tense–aspect–modality in East and mainland Southeast Asia. In Walter Bisang, Nikolaus P. Himmelmann, & Björn Wiemer (eds.), *What Makes Grammaticalization? A Look from Its Fringes and Its Components*. (Trends in Linguistics: Studies and Monographs.) Berlin: Mouton de Gruyter, 109–138.
Bisang, Walter (2006). From meaning to syntax—Semantic roles and beyond. In Ina Bornkessel et al. (eds.), *Semantic Role Universals and Argument Linking*. Berlin: Mouton de Gruyter, 191–236.
Bisang, Walter (2008a). Precategoriality and syntax-based parts of speech: The case of Late Archaic Chinese. *Studies in Language* 32: 568–589.
Bisang, Walter (2008b) Precategoriality and argument structure in Late Archaic Chinese. In Jaakko Leino (ed.), *Constructional Reorganization*. Amsterdam: John Benjamins, 55–88.
Bisang, Walter (2008c) Grammaticalization and the areal factor: The perspective of East and Mainland Southeast Asian languages. In María José López-Couso & Elena Seoane (eds.), *Rethinking Grammaticalization: New Perspectives*. Amsterdam: John Benjamins, 15–35.
Bisang, Walter (2009). On the evolution of complexity: Sometimes less is more in East and Mainland Southeast Asia. In Geoffrey Sampson, David Gil, & Peter Trudgill (eds.), *Language Complexity as an Evolving Variable*. Oxford: Oxford University Press, 34–49.
Bisang, Walter. (2010). Word classes. In Jae Jung Song (ed.), *The Oxford Handbook of linguistic Typology*. Oxford: Oxford University Press, 280–302.
Bisang, Walter (2012). Numeral classifiers with plural marking: A challenge to Greenberg. In Dan Xu (ed.), *Plurality and Classifiers across Languages of China*. Berlin/Boston: De Gruyter Mouton, 23–42.
Bisang, Walter (2013). Word class systems between flexibility and rigidity: An integrative approach. In Jan Rijkhoff & Eva van Lier (eds.), *Flexible Word Classes: Typological Studies of Underspecified Parts of Speech*. Oxford: Oxford University Press, 275–303.
Bisang, Walter (2014). Overt and hidden complexity: Two types of complexity and their implications. *Poznań Studies in Contemporary Linguistics* 50(2): 127–143.
Bisang, Walter (2015). Parts of speech. In J. D. Wright (ed.), *International Encyclopedia of the Social & Behavioral Sciences*, 2nd edn. Oxford: Elsevier, vol. XVII, 553–561.

Bisang, Walter & Andrej Malchukov (eds.) (2020). *Grammaticalization Scenarios: Cross-Linguistic Variation and Universal Tendencies*. Berlin: Mouton de Gruyter.

Bisang, Walter & Yicheng Wu (eds.) (2017). Numeral classifiers in East Asia. *Linguistics* 55(2) (special issue).

Biswas, Alexander (2017). Inflectional periphrasis in LFG. M.Phil. dissertation, University of Oxford.

Bittner, Maria & Ken Hale (1996). The structural determination of case and agreement. *Linguistic Inquiry* 27(1): 1–68.

Blachère, Régis & Maurice Gaudefroy-Demombynes (1975). *Grammaire de l'arabe classique (morphologie et syntaxe)*. Paris: Maisonneuve et Larose.

Black, Maria & Shuka Chiat (2003). Noun–verb dissociations: A multifaceted phenomenon. *Journal of Neurolinguistics* 16: 231–250.

Blake, Barry (1987). *Australian Aboriginal Grammar*. London: Croom Helm.

Blake, Barry (1993). Verb affixes from case markers: Some Australian examples. *La Trobe Working Papers in Linguistics* 6: 33–58.

Blake, Barry (1999). Nominal marking on verbs: Some Australian cases. *Word* 50(3): 299–317.

Blake, Barry (2001). The noun phrase in Australian languages. In Jane Simpson, et al. (eds.), *Forty Years on: Ken Hale and Australian Languages*. Canberra: Pacific Linguistics, 415–425.

Blakemore, Diane (1987). *Semantic Constraints on Relevance*. Oxford: Blackwell.

Blaszczak, Joanna, Dorota Klimek-Jankowska, & Krzysztof Migdalski (eds.) (2015). *How Categorical Are Categories? New Approaches to the Old Questions of Noun, Verb, and Adjective*. Mouton: De Gruyter.

Blecke (Thomas) 1996. *Lexikalische Kategorien and grammatische Strukturen im Tigemaxo (Bozo, Mande)*. Köln: Rüdiger Köppe.

Blokzijl, Jeffrey, Margaret Deuchar, & M. Carmen Parafita Couto (2017). Determiner asymmetry in mixed nominal constructions: The role of grammatical factors in data from Miami and Nicaragua. *Languages* 2: 20. https://doi.org/10.3390/languages2040020

Bloomfield, Leonard (1914). *An Introduction to the Study of Language*. New York: Holt.

Bloomfield, Leonard (1917/2018). *Tagolog Texts with Grammatical Analysis*. Urbana, IL: University of Illinois.

Bloomfield, Leonard (1933). *Language*. New York: Holt.

Bloomfield, Leonard (1938). Language or ideas? *Language* 12(2): 89–85. https://doi.org/10.2307/408751

Bloomfield, Leonard (1973). *Language*. London: George Allan & Unwin LTD.

Blount, Ben G. 1988. Cognition and phonology in acquisition of plurals and possessives by Luo children. Language Sciences 10. 225–240.

Blust, Robert (2014). Austronesian. In Rochelle Lieber & Pavol Štekauer (eds.), *The Oxford Handbook of Derivational Morphology*. Oxford: Oxford University Press, 545–557.

Boas, Franz (1911a). Introduction. In Franz Boas (ed.), *Handbook of American Indian languages: Part 1* (Bulletin of the Smithsonian Institution 40). Washington: Bureau of American Ethnology, 5–83.

Boas, Franz (1911b). Kwakiutl. In Franz Boas (ed.), *Handbook of American Indian Languages: Part 1* (Bulletin of the Smithsonian Institution 40). Washington, DC: Bureau of American Ethnology, 423–557.

Bobaljik, Jonathan (2012). *Universals in Comparative Morphology. Suppletion, Superlatives, and the Structure of Words*. Cambridge, MA: MIT Press.

Bobaljik, Jonathan & Höskuldur Thrainsson (1998). Two heads aren't always better than one. *Syntax* 1: 37–71.

Boers, Frank, Seth Lindstromberg, & June Eyckmans (2014). Is alliteration mnemonic without awareness raising? *Language Awareness* 23: 291–303.

Bogartz, Richard S. (1994). The future of dynamic systems models in developmental psychology in the light of the past. *Journal of Experimental Child Psychology* 58(2): 289–319. https://doi.org/10.1006/jecp.1994.1036

Bohnemeyer, Jürgen (2017). Organisation of space. In Judith Aissen, Nora C. England, & Roberto. Zavala Maldonado (eds.), *The Mayan Languages*. London/New York: Routledge, 327–347.

Bohnemeyer, Jürgen & Penelope Brown (2007). Standing divided: Dispositionals and locative predications in two Mayan languages, *Linguistics* 45: 1105–1151.

Bolinger, Dwight L. (1946). Thoughts on 'Yep' and 'Nope'. *American Speech* 21(2): 90–95. doi:10.2307/486479

Bolinger, Dwight L. (1961). *Generality, Gradience, and the All-or-None*. The Hague: Mouton.

Bolinger, Dwight L. (1963). It's so fun. *American Speech* 38(3): 236–240.

Bolinger, Dwight L. (1968). *Aspects of Language*. New York: Harcourt, Brace and World.

Bond, Oliver, et al. (2016). *Archi: Complexities of Agreement in Cross-Theoretical Perspective*. Oxford: Oxford University Press.

Bordet, Lucile & Denis Jamet (2010). Are English prepositions lexical or grammatical morphemes? *Cercles: Revue Pluridisciplinaire du Monde Anglophone*: 1–26.

Borer, Hagit (2003). Exo-skeletal vs. Endo-skeletal Explanations: Syntactic Projections and the Lexicon. In John Moore & Maria Polinsky (eds.), *The Nature of Explanation in Linguistic Theory*. Stanford, CA: Center for the Study of Language and Information, 31–67.

Borer, Hagit (2005a). *Structuring Sense. Volume 1: In Name Only*. Oxford: Oxford University Press

Borer, Hagit (2005b). *Structuring Sense. Volume 2: The Normal Course of Events*. Oxford: Oxford University Press.

Borer, Hagit (2013). *Structuring Sense. Volume 3: Taking Form*. Oxford: Oxford University Press

Borer, Hagit (2014). The category of roots. In Artemis Alexiadou, Hagit Borer, & Florian Schäfer (eds.), *The Syntax of Roots and the Roots of Syntax*. (Oxford Studies in Theoretical Linguistics 51.) Oxford: Oxford University Press, 112–148.

Borer, Hagit (2015). Wherefore roots? *Theoretical Linguistics* 40(3/4): 343–359.

Borges, M. V. (2006). Aspectos fonológicos e morfossintáticos do Avá-Canoeiro (Tupi-Guarani). Doctoral dissertation, Unicamp, Instituto de Estudos da Linguagem.

Börjars, Kersti, Safiah Madkhali, & John Payne (2015). Masdars and mixed category constructions. In Miriam Butt & Tracy Holloway King (eds.), *On-line Proceedings of the LFG2015 Conference*. Stanford, CA: CSLI Publications, 47–63. http://csli publications.stanford.edu/LFG/20/lfg15.html

Bornstein, Marc H, Linda R Cote, Sharone Maital, Kathleen Painter, Sung-Yun Park, Liliana Pascual, Marie-Germaine Pêcheux, Josette Ruel, Paola Venuti & Andre Vyt. 2004. Cross-linguistic analysis of vocabulary in young children: Spanish, Dutch, French, Hebrew, Italian, Korean, and American English. Child Development 75(4). 1115–1139.

Boroditsky, Lera (2003). Linguistic relativity. In Lynn Nadel (ed.), *Encyclopedia of Cognitive Science*. London: Macmillan, vol. II, 917–921.

Boroditsky, Lera, Lauren Schmidt, & Webb Phillips (2003). Sex, syntax, and semantics. In Dedre Gentner & Susan Goldin-Meadow (eds.), *Language in Mind: Advances in the Study of Language and Thought*. Cambridge, MA: MIT Press, 61–79.

Borsley, Robert & Jaklin Kornfilt. (2000). Mixed and extended projections. In Robert Borsley (ed.), *The Nature and Function of Syntactic Categories*. (Syntax and Semantics 32.) San Diego: Academic Press, 101–131.

Börstell, Carl (2017). Types and trends of name signs in the Swedish Sign Language community. *SKY Journal of Linguistics* 30: 7–34.
Börstell, Carl (2019). Differential object marking in sign languages. *Glossa: A Journal of General Linguistics* 4(1): 3. https://doi.org/10.5334/gjgl.780
Börstell, Carl, Thomas Hörberg, & Robert Östling (2016). Distribution and duration of signs and parts of speech in Swedish Sign Language. *Sign Language & Linguistics* 19(2): 143–196. https://doi.org/10.1075/sll.19.2.01bor
Bossong, Georg (1991). Differential object marking in Romance and beyond. In Dieter Wanner & Douglas A. Kibbee (eds.), *New Analyses in Romance Linguistics*. Amsterdam: John Benjamins, 143–170.
Bouchard, Denis (1995). *The Semantics of Syntax: A Minimalist Approach to Grammar*. Chicago/London: University of Chicago Press.
Boudelaa, Sami & William D. Marslen-Wilson (2001). Morphological units in the Arabic mental lexicon. *Cognition* 81: 65–92.
Boudelaa, Sami & William D. Marslen-Wilson (2011). Productivity and priming: Morphemic decomposition in Arabic. *Language and Cognition Processes* 26: 624–652.
Bowe, Heather J. (1990). *Categories, Constituents and Constituent Order in Pitjantjatjara: An Aboriginal Language of Australia*. New York: Routledge.
Bowerman, Melissa (2018). *Ten Lectures on Language, Cognition and Language Acquisition*. Leiden: Brill.
Bowerman, Melissa & Soonja Choi (2003). Space under construction: Language-specific spatial categorization in first language acquisition. In Dedre Gentner & Susan Goldin-Meadow (eds.), *Language in Mind: Advances in the Study of Language and Thought*. Cambridge, MA: MIT Press, 387–427.
Bowern, Claire (2008). The diachrony of complex predicates. *Diachronica* 25(2): 161–185.
Bowern, Claire (2010). The typological implications of Bardi complex predicates. *Linguistic Typology* 14(1): 45–61.
Bowern, Claire (2012). *A Grammar of Bardi*. (MGL, 57.) Berlin/Boston: Mouton de Gruyter.
Bowern, Claire (2014). Complex predicates in Australian languages. In Harold Koch & Rachel Nordlinger (eds.), *The Languages and Linguistics of Australia*. Berlin/Boston: Mouton de Gruyter, 263–294.
Bowern, Claire & Quentin Atkinson (2012). Computational phylogenetics and the internal structure of Pama–Nyungan. *Language* 88(4): 817–845.
Bowey, Judith A. (2006). Clarifying the phonological processing account of nonword repetition. *Applied Psycholinguistics* 27(4): 548–552. https://doi.org/10.1017.S0142716406060401
Boye, Kasper (2012). *Epistemic Meaning: A Crosslinguistic and Functional–Cognitive Study*. Berlin: Mouton de Gruyter.
Boye, Kasper (2018). Evidentiality: The notion and the term. In Alexandra Y. Aikhenvald (ed.), *The Oxford Handbook of Evidentiality*. Oxford: Oxford University Press, 261–272.
Boye, Kasper & Roelien Bastiaanse (2018). Grammatical versus lexical words in theory and aphasia: Integrating linguistics and neurolinguistics. *Glossa: A Journal of General Linguistics* 3(1): 29. http://doi.org/10.5334/gjgl.436
Boye, Kasper & Peter Harder (2012). A usage-based theory of grammatical status and grammaticalization. *Language* 88(1): 1–44.
Boye, Kasper & Peter Harder (2020). Dual processing in a functional–cognitive theory of grammar and its neurocognitive basis. In Alexander Haselow & Gunther Kaltenböck (eds.), *Grammar and Cognition: Dualistic Models of Language Structure and Language Processing*. Amsterdam: John Benjamins, 133–155.

Boylan, Christine, John C. Trueswell, & Sharon L. Thompson-Schill (2015). Compositionality and the angular gyrus: A multi-voxel similarity analysis of the semantic composition of nouns and verbs. *Neuropsychologia* 78: 130–141.

Bradshaw, Joel (1983) Dempwolff's description of verb serialization in Yabem. *Pacific Linguistics* C77: 177–198.

Bradshaw, Joel (1993). Subject relationships within serial verb constructions in Jabêm and Numbani. *Oceanic Linguistics* 32: 133–161.

Braine, Martin D. S. 1976. Children's first word combinations, vol. 41. Monographs of the Society for Research in Child Development.

Braine, Martin DS. 1987. What is learned in acquiring word classes—A step toward an acquisition theory.

Braine, Martin DS. 1992. What sort of innate structure is needed to "bootstrap" into syntax? *Cognition* 45(1). 77–100.

Braithwaite, Ben (2015). Nuu-chah-nulth nouns and verbs revisited: Root Allomorphy and the structure of nominal predicates. In Joanna Błaszczak, Dorota Klimek-Jankowska, & Krzysztof Migdalski (eds.), *How Categorical Are Categories? New Approaches to the Old Questions of Noun, Verb and Adjective*. Berlin: Mouton de Gruyter, 47–74.

Brala-Vukanović, Maja (2015). Communication and grammaticalization: The case of (Croatian) demonstratives. *Fluminensia* 27: 45–60.

Brame, Michael (1982). The head-selector theory of lexical specifications and the nonexistence of coarse categories. *Linguistic Analysis* 10(4). 321–325.

Branchereau, Laurance & Jean-Luc Nespoulous (1989). Syntactic parsing and the availability of prepositions in agrammatic patients. *Aphasiology* 3(5): 411–422.

Brems, Lieselotte (2003). Measure noun constructions: An instance of semantically-driven grammaticalization. *International Journal of Corpus Linguistics* 8–2: 283–312.

Brems, Lieselotte & Kristin Davidse (2010). The grammaticalisation of nominal type noun constructions with *kind/sort of*: Chronology and paths of change. *English Studies* 91: 180–202.

Brentari, Diane, et al. (2013). Acquiring word class distinctions in American Sign Language: Evidence from handshape. *Language Learning and Development* 9(2): 130–150. https://doi.org/10.1080/15475441.2012.679540

Brentari, Diane, et al. (2015). Cognitive, cultural, and linguistic sources of a handshape distinction expressing agentivity. *Topics in Cognitive Science* 7(1): 95–123. https://doi.org/10.1111/tops.12123

Bresnan, Joan (1978). A realistic transformational grammar. In Morris Halle, Joan Bresnan, & George A. Miller (eds.), *Linguistic Theory and Psychological Reality*. Cambridge, MA: MIT Press, 1–59.

Bresnan, Joan (1982a). Control and complementation. *Linguistic Inquiry* 13(3): 343–434. [reprinted in Bresnan (1982b: 282–390)]

Bresnan, Joan (ed.) (1982b). *The Mental Representation of Grammatical Relations*. Cambridge, MA: MIT Press.

Bresnan, Joan (1994). Locative inversion and the architecture of universal grammar. *Language* 70: 72–131.

Bresnan, Joan (1997). Mixed categories as head-sharing constructions. In Miriam Butt & Tracy Holloway King (eds.), *Proceedings of the LFG97 Conference, University of California, San Diego*. Stanford, CA: CSLI Publications. http://www-csli.stanford.edu/publications/

Bresnan, Joan (2001). *Lexical-Functional Syntax*. Oxford: Blackwell.

Bresnan, Joan & Sam A. Mchombo (1995). The lexical integrity principle: Evidence from Bantu. *Natural Language and Linguistic Theory* 13(2): 181–254.

Bresnan, Joan & John Mugane (2006). Agentive nominalizations in Gĩkũyũ and the theory of mixed categories. In Miriam Butt, Mary Dalrymple, & Tracy Holloway King (eds.), *Intelligent Linguistic Architectures: Variations on Themes by Ronald M. Kaplan*. Stanford, CA: CSLI Publications, 201–234.

Bresnan, Joan, et al. (2016). *Lexical-Functional Syntax* (2nd edn). Oxford: Wiley Blackwell.

Breunesse, Merlijn (2019). Demonstratives in space and discourse: A synchronic and diachronic analysis. PhD dissertation, University of Jena.

Briceño Chel, Fidencio (1996). De Gramaticalización y degramaticalización: Dos procesos en el maya yucateco actual. Tesis de Maestria en Lingüística, ENAH, México.

Bricker, Victoria R. (1970). Relationship terms with the usative suffix in Tzotzil and Yucatec Maya. Papers from the Sixth Regional Meeting of the Chicago Linguistic Society, Chicago, 75–86.

Bricker, Victoria R. (1999). Color and texture in the Maya language of Yucatan, *Anthropological Linguistics* 41: 283–307.

Bricker, Victoria (2019). *A Historical Grammar of the Maya Language of Yucatan, 1557–2000*. Salt Lake City: University of Utah Press.

Bricker, Victoria, Eleuterio Poʔot Yah, & Ofelia Dzul de Poʔot (1998). *A Dictionary of the Maya Language as Spoken in Hocobá, Yucatán*. Salt Lake City: University of Utah Press.

Bril, Isabelle (2017). Roots and stems in Amis and Nêlêmwa (Austronesian): Lexical categories and functional flexibility. In Eva van Lier (ed.), *Lexical Flexibility in Oceanic Languages: Studies in Language* (special issue) 41(2): 358–407.

Brinton, Laurel J. & Elizabeth C. Traugott (2005). *Lexicalization and Language Change*. Cambridge: Cambridge University Press.

Broadwell, George Aaron (2006). *A Choctaw Reference Grammar*. (Studies in the Anthropology of North American Indians.) Lincoln: University of Nebraska Press.

Broadwell, George Aaron & Lachlan Duncan (2002). A new passive in Kaqchikel. *Linguistic Discovery* 1(2): 1–16.

Broccias, Cristiano & Willem B. Hollmann (2007). Do we need summary and sequential scanning in (cognitive) grammar? *Cognitive Linguistics* 18: 487–522.

Broekhuis, Hans (2013). *Syntax of Dutch: Adpositions and Adpositional Phrases*. Amsterdam: Amsterdam University Press.

Broschart, Jürgen (1997). Why Tongan does it differently: Categorial distinctions in a language without nouns and verbs. *Linguistic Typology* 1(2): 123–165.

Brown, Lea (2005). Nias. In Alexander Adelaar & Nikolaus Himmelmann (eds.), *The Austronesian Languages of Asia and Madagaskar*. London: Routledge, 562–589.

Brown, Penelope (1998). Children's first verbs in Tzeltal: Evidence for an early verb category. *Linguistics* 36: 713–53.

Brown, Peter F., et al. (1992). Classbased n-gram models of natural language. *Computational Linguistics* 18(4): 467–479.

Bruening, Benjamin (2018). The lexicalist hypothesis: Both wrong and superfluous. *Language* 94(1): 1–42.

Brugmann, Karl (1904). *Demonstrativpronomina der indogermanischen Sprachen*. Leipzig: Teubner.

Brysbaert, M., A. Warriner & V. Kuperman (2014). Concreteness ratings for 40,000 generally known English word lemmas. *Behavior Research Methods* 46: 904–11.

Bugenhagen, Robert D. (1995). *A Grammar of Mangap-Mbula: An Austronesian Language of Papua New Guinea*. Canberra: Australian National University.

Bühler, Karl (1934). *Sprachtheorie: Die Darstellungsfunktion der Sprache.* Jena: Fischer.

Bullock, Barbara, et al. (2021). Processing multilingual data. In Evangelia Adamou & Yaron Matras (eds.), *The Routledge Handbook of Language Contact.* London: Routledge, 7–27.

Burenhult, Niclas & Majid, Asifa (2011). Olfaction in Aslian ideology and language. *Senses and Society* 6(1), 19–29.

Burling, Robbins (1961). *A Garo Grammar.* Poona: Deccan College.

Burling, Robbins (2003). *The Language of the Modhupur Mandi. Volume III: Glossary.* Ann Arbor, MI: University of Michigan Press.

Burling, Robbins (2004). *The Language of the Modhupur Mandi, Garo: Vol. I: Grammar.* Ann Arbor, MI: University of Michigan Press.

Bußmann, Hadumod (2002). *Lexikon der Sprahwissenschaft* (3rd edn). Stuttgart: Kröner. [Engl. trans. of 2nd edn, *Routledge Dictionary of Language and Linguistics.* London: Routledge 1996; Ital. rev. and enlarged version, ed. P. Cotticelli Kurras, *Lessico di linguistica.* Alessandria: Edizioni dell'Orso, 2007]

Butler, Lindsay K., Jürgen Bohnemeyer, & T. Florian Jaeger (2014). Syntactic constraints and production preferences for optional plural marking in Yucatec Maya. In Antonio Machicao y Priemer, Andreas Nolda, & Athina Sioupi (eds.), *Zwischen Kern und Peripherie (Studia Grammatica, Volume 75).* Berlin: Akademie-Verlag, 181–208.

Butt, Miriam (1997). Complex predicates in Urdu. In Alex Alsina, Joan Bresnan, & Peter Sells (eds.), *Complex Predicates.* Stanford, CA: CSLI Publications, 107–149.

Butt, Miriam (2001). Case, agreement, pronoun incorporation and pro-drop in South Asian languages. Konstanz Research Papers [ms].

Butt, Miriam & Tracy Holloway King (2004). The status of case. In Veneeta Dayal & Anoop Mahajan (eds.), *Clause Structure in South Asian Languages.* Dordrecht: Springer, 153–198.

Butt, Miriam & Tracy Holloway King (eds.) (2008). *On-line Proceedings of the LFG2008 Conference.* Stanford, CA: CSLI Publications. http://csli-publications.stanford.edu/LFG/13/lfg08.html

Butt, Miriam & Tracy Holloway King (eds.) (2018). *On-line Proceedings of the LFG2018 Conference.* Stanford, CA: CSLI Publications. http://web.stanford.edu/group/cslipublications/cslipublications/LFG/LFG-2018/index.shtml

Bybee, Joan (1985). *Morphology: A Study of the Relation between Meaning and Form.* Amsterdam: John Benjamins.

Bybee, Joan (2001). *Phonology and Language Use.* Cambridge: Cambridge University Press.

Bybee, Joan (2003). Mechanisms of change in grammaticization: The role of frequency. In Brian D. Joseph & Richard Janda (eds.), *The Handbook of Historical Linguistics.* Oxford: Blackwell, 602–623.

Bybee, Joan (2006). From usage to grammar: The mind's response to repetition. *Language* 82(4): 711–733.

Bybee, Joan (2010). *Language, Usage and Cognition.* Cambridge: Cambridge University Press. https://doi.org/10.1093/acprof:oso/9780195301571.001.0001

Bybee, Joan (2015). *Language Change.* Cambridge: Cambridge University Press.

Bybee, Joan, Revere Perkins, & William Pagliuca (1994). *The Evolution of Grammar: Tense, Aspect and Modality in the Languages of the World.* Chicago: University of Chicago Press.

Bybee, Joan & John L. McClelland (2005). Alternatives to the combinatorial paradigm of linguistic theory based on domain general principles of human cognition. *Linguistic Review* 22 (2–4): 381–410. https://doi.org/10.1515/tlir.2005.22.2-4.381

Byington, Steven T. (1942). Interjections of pain. *American Speech* 17(4): 277–279. doi:10.2307/487200

Bynon, James (1976). Domestic animal calling in a Berber tribe. In William McCormack & Stephen A. Wurm (eds.), *Language and Man: Anthropological Issues*. The Hague: Mouton, 39–65.
Cabral, Ana S. (2000a). Aspectos da marcação de caso no Asuriní do Tocantins. XIII Encontro Nacional da ANPOLL [CD Rom].
Cabral, Ana S. (2000b). Flexão relacional na família tupi-guarani. *ABRALIN, Boletim Da Associação Brasieira de Lingüística* 25.
Cabral, Ana S. (2001). Observações sobre a história do morfema -a da família tupí-guaraní. In F. Queixalós (ed.), *Des noms et des verbes en tupi-guarani: état de la question*. Munich: Lincom Europa, 133–162.
Cabral, Ana S. (2007a). As categorias nome e verbo em Zo'é. In Aryon Rodrigues & Ana S. Cabral (eds.), *Línguas e Culturas Tupí*. Campina: Editora Curt Nimuendajú, vol. I, 241–258.
Cabral, Ana S. (2007b). L'expression des notions de l'épistémique et de l'aléthique dans la famille tupi-guarani. In Z. Guentchéva & J. Landaburu (eds.), *L'énonciation médiatisée II. Le traitement épistémologique de l'information: illustrations amérindiennes et caucasiennes*. Leuven: Peeters Publishers, 267–292.
Caha, Pavel (2009). The nanosyntax of case. PhD dissertation, Tromso University.
Caha, Pavel & Guido Vanden Wyngaerd (2017). *ABA. *Glossa: A Journal of General Linguistics*.
Caldas, R. & DaSilva, T. (2002). Verbos de actividades mentais em Ka'apór e outras línguas da família Tupí-Guaraní. In Ana S. Cabral & Aryon Rodrigues (eds.), *Línguas Indígenas Brasileiras. Fonologia, Gramática e História. Atas do I Encontro Internacional do GTLI da ANPOLL*. Editoria Universitária UFPA, vol. I, 352–357.
Campbell, Akua Asantewaa (2017). A grammar of Gã. Doctoral thesis, Rice University.
Campbell, Lyle (2001). What's wrong with grammaticalization? *Language Sciences* 23: 113–161.
Campbell, Lyle (ed.) (2001). Grammaticalization: A critical assessment. *Language Sciences* 23(2–3): 113–161.
Campbell, Lyle (2017). Maya history and comparison. In Judith Aissen, Nora C. England, & Roberto Zavala Maldonado (eds.), *The Mayan Languages*. London/New York: Routledge, 43–62.
Campbell, Lyle & Terrence Kaufman (1985). Mayan linguistics: where are we now? *Annual Review of Anthropology* 14: 187–198.
Campbell, Lyle, Terrence Kaufman, & Thomas C. Smith-Stark (1986). Mesoamerica as a linguistic area. *Language* 62: 530–570.
Can Pixabaj, Telma (2009). Morphosyntactic features and behaviors of verbal nouns in K'ichee'. MA thesis, University of Texas, Austin.
Can Pixabaj, Telma (2015). Complement and purpose clauses in K'iche. PhD dissertation, University of Texas, Austin.
Can Pixabaj, Telma A. (2017). K'iche. In Judith Aissen, Nora C. England, & Roberto Zavala Maldonado (eds.), *The Mayan Languages*. London/New York: Routledge, 461–499.
Cantrell, Lisa & Linda B. Smith (2013). Set size, individuation, and attention to shape. *Cognition* 126(2): 258–267.
Capitani, Erminio, et al. (2009). Posterior cerebral artery infarcts and semantic category dissociations: A study of 28 patients. *Brain* 132: 965–981.
Cappa, Stefano F., et al. (1998). Object and action naming in Alzheimer's disease and frontotemporal dementia. *Neurology* 50: 351–355.
Cappa, Stefano F. & Daniela Perani (2003). The neural correlates of noun and verb processing. *Journal of Neurolinguistics* 16: 183–189.
Cappelletti, Marinalla, et al. (2008). Processing nouns and verbs in the left frontal cortex: A transcranial magnetic stimulation study. *Journal of Cognitive Neuroscience* 20: 707–720.

Caramazza, Alfonso & Argye E. Hillis (1991). Lexical organization of nouns and verbs in the brain. *Nature* 349: 788–90.

Caramazza, Alfonso & Michele Miozzo (1998). More is not always better: A response to Roelofs, Meyer, and Levelt. *Cognition* 69: 231–241.

Carnie, Andrew (2011). *Modern Syntax: A Coursebook*. Cambridge: Cambridge University Press.

Carnie, Andrew (2013). *Syntax: A Generative Introduction* (3rd edn). Chichester: Wiley-Blackwell.

Carlson, Gregory N. (1977). Reference to kinds in English. PhD thesis, University of Massachusetts at Amherst.

Carpenter, Malinda, Nameera Akhtar, & Michael Tomasello (1998). Fourteen- through 18-month-old infants differentially imitate intentional and accidental actions. *Infant Behavior and Development* 21(2): 315–330. https://doi.org/10.1016/S0163-6383(98)90009-1

Carpenter, Malinda, Josep Call, & Michael Tomasello (2005). Twelve- and 18-month-olds copy actions in terms of goals. *Developmental Science* 8(1): 13–20. https://doi.org/10.1111/j.1467-7687.2004.00385.x

Cartwright, Timothy A. & Michael R. Brent (1997). Syntactic categorization in early language acquisition: Formalizing the role of distributional analysis. *Cognition* 63(2): 121–170. https://doi.org/10.1016/S0010-0277(96)00793-7

Casasanto, Daniel & Lera Boroditsky (2008). Time in the mind: Using space to think about time. *Cognition* 106: 579–93.

Casasola, Marianella (2005). When less is more: How infants learn to form an abstract categorical representation of support. *Child Development* 76(1): 279–290. https://doi.org/10.1111/j.1467-8624.2005.00844.x

Cassidy, Kimberly Wright & Michael H Kelly. 2001. Children's use of phonology to infer grammatical class in vocabulary learning. Psychonomic Bulletin & Review 8(3). 519–523.

Castel, Ruth (2020). The structural possibilities of the nominal expression: A text study of the Australian languages Arabana and Garrwa. MA thesis, KU Leuven, Leuven.

Castro Zapata, Isabel María (2010). El camino hacia la preposición. Los procesos de gramaticalización de durante y mediante. *Interlingüística* 20: 11.

Caubet, Dominique (1993). *L'Arabe marocain. Tome I: Phonologie et Morphosyntaxe. Tome 2: Syntaxe et Catégories Grammaticales, Textes*. Leuven/Paris: Peeters.

Cazden, Courtney B. (1968). The acquisition of noun and verb inflections. *Child Development* 39(2): 433–448.

Cerrón-Palomino, Rodolfo (1987). *Lingüística Quechua*. Cuzco: Centro de estudios rurales andinos 'Bartolomé de las Casas'.

Cerrón-Palomino, Rodolfo (2009). Chipaya. In Mily Crevels & Pieter Muysken (eds.), *Lenguas de Bolivia. Tomo I. Ambito Andino*. La Paz, Bolivia: Plural editors, 29–78.

Cerrón-Palomino, Rodolfo & Juan Carvajal (2009). Aimara. In Mily Crevels & Pieter Muysken (eds.), *Lenguas de Bolivia. Tomo I. Ambito Andino*. La Paz, Bolivia: Plural editores, 169–214.

Chafe, Wallace (1967). *Seneca Dictionary and Morphology*. Washington, DC: Smithsonian Institution.

Chafe, Wallace (ed.) (1980). *The Pear Stories*. New York: Ablex.

Chafe, Wallace (1994). *Discourse, Consciousness, and Time*. Chicago: University of Chicago Press.

Chafe, Wallace (2000). Florescence as a force in grammaticalization. In Spike Gildea (ed.), *Reconstructing Grammar: Comparative Linguistics and Grammaticalization*. Amsterdam: John Benjamins, 39–64.

Chafe, Wallace (2003). The discourse effects of polysynthesis. In Carol Lynn Moder & Aida Martinovic-Zic (eds.), *Discourse across Languages and Cultures*. Amsterdam: John Benjamins, 37–52.

Chafe, Wallace (2012). Are adjectives universal? The case of Northern Iroquoian. *Linguistic Typology* 16: 1–39.

Chafe, Wallace (2015). *A Grammar of the Seneca Language* (University of California Publications in Linguistics, vol. 149). Oakland: University of California Press.

Chan, Alexander M., et al. (2011). First-pass selectivity for semantic categories in human anteroventral temporal lobe. *Journal of Neuroscience* 31: 18119–18129.

Chang, Anna Hsiou-chuan (2006). A reference grammar of Paiwan. Doctoral dissertation, Australian National University.

Chanod, Jean-Pierre & Pasi Tapanainen (1995). Creating a tagset, lexicon and guesser for a French tagger. In Evelyne Tzoukermann & S. Armstrong (eds.), *Proceedings of the ACL SIGDAT Workshop from Text to Tags: Issues in Multilingual Analysis*. University College, Dublin, Ireland, 58–64.

Chantraine, Pierre (1953). *Grammaire homérique*. Paris: Klincksieck.

Chao, Yuan Ren (1968). *A Grammar of Spoken Chinese*. Berkeley and Los Angeles: University of California Press.

Chappell, Hilary & William McGregor (eds.) (1996). *The Grammar of Inalienability. A Typological Perspective on Body Part Terms and the Part-Whole Relation*. Berlin: Mouton de Gruyter.

Chatzikyriakidis, Stergios & Zhaohui Luo (2020). *Formal Semantics in Modern Type Theories*. Chichester: Wiley.

Chaves, Rui (2013). Grammatical alignments and the gradience of lexical categories. In Philip Hofmeister & Elisabeth Norcliffe (eds.), *The Core and the Periphery: Data-driven Perspectives on Syntax Inspired by Ivan A. Sag*. Stanford, CA: CSLI Publications, 167–220.

Chen, Chengze. 陈承泽 (1922). 国文法草创 *Guówénfǎ cǎochuàng* [A Draft of Chinese Grammar]. Beijing: Commercial Press.

Cheng, Lisa Lai-Shen (2012). Counting and classifiers. In Diane Massam (ed.), *Count and Mass across Languages*. Oxford: Oxford University Press, 199–218.

Cheng, Lisa Lai-Shen & Rint Sybesma (1998). *Yi-wan tang, yi-ge Tang*: Classifiers and massifiers. *Tsing-Hua Journal of Chinese Studies, New Series* 28: 385–412.

Cheng, Lisa Lai-Shen & Rint Sybesma (1999). Bare and not-so-bare nouns and the structure of NP. *Linguistic Inquiry* 30(4): 509–542.

Chierchia, Gennaro (1998a). Reference to kinds across languages. *Natural Language Semantics* 6: 339–405.

Chierchia, Gennaro (1998b). Plurality of mass nouns and the notion of 'semantic parameter'. In Susan Rothstein (ed.), *Events and Grammar*. Dordrecht: Kluwer, 53–103.

Childers, Jane B, Julie Vaughan & Donald A Burquest. 2007. Joint attention and word learning in Ngas-speaking toddlers in Nigeria. Journal of Child Language 34(2). 199.

Childers, Jane B. (2014). Noun bias in word learning. In Patricia J. Brooks & Vera Kempe (eds.), *Encyclopedia of Language Development*. London: Sage, 416–417.

Childs, G. Tucker (1994). African ideophones. In Leanne Hinton & Johanna Nichols, & John J. Ohala (eds.), *Sound Symbolism*. Cambridge: Cambridge University Press, 178–204.

Childs, G. Tucker (2011). *A Grammar of Mani*. (Mouton Grammar Library, 54.) Berlin: Mouton de Gruyter.

Childs, G. Tucker (2014). Constraints on violating constraints: How languages reconcile the twin dicta of 'Be different' and 'Be recognizably language'. *Pragmatics and Society* 5(3): 341–354. doi:10.1075/ps.5.3.02chi

Cho, Young-Mee Yu & Peter Sells (1995). A lexical account of inflectional suffixes in Korean. *Journal of East Asian Linguistics* 4(2): 119–174.
Choi, Soonja. 1993. Development of Locative Case Markers in Korean. In Patricia M. Clancy (ed.), Japanese/Korean Linguistics, II, 205–22. Stanford, CA: Center for Study of Language and Information, Stanford University.
Choi, Soonja. 1995. The development of epistemic sentence-ending modal forms and functions in Korean children. In Joan L. Bybee & S. Fleischman (eds.), Modality in grammar and discourse, 165–204. John Benjamins.
Chomsky, Noam (1959). Review of verbal behavior. *Language* 35(1): 26–58. doi:10.2307/411334
Chomsky, Noam (1970). Remarks on nominalization. In Roderick A. Jacobs & Peter S. Rosenbaum (eds.), *Readings in English Transformational Grammar*. Waltham, MA: Ginn, 184–221.
Chomsky, Noam (1972). *Studies in Generative Semantics*. The Hague: Princeton.
Chomsky, Noam (1980). Rules and representations. *Behavioral and Brain Sciences* 3(1): 1–15. https://doi.org/10.1017/S0140525X00001680
Chomsky, Noam (1981). *Lectures on Government and Binding*. Dordrecht: Foris.
Chomsky, Noam (1986). *Knowledge of Language: Its Nature, Origin and Use*. New York: Praeger.
Chomsky, Noam (1995). *The Minimalist Program*. Cambridge, MA: MIT Press.
Chomsky, Noam (2000). *New Horizons in the Study of Language and Mind*. Cambridge: Cambridge University Press.
Chomsky, Noam (2001). Derivation by phase. In Michael Kenstowicz (ed.), *Ken Hale: A Life in Language*. Cambridge, MA: MIT Press, 1–53.
Chomsky, Noam (2014). *The Minimalist Program, 20th Anniversary Edition*. Cambridge, MA: MIT Press.
Chousou-Polydouri, Natalia, et al. (2016). *Reconstructing Negation Morphemes and Constructions in the Tupí-Guaraní Family*. Amazonicas VI, Leticia, Colombia.
Christensen, Marie H., et al. (2020). Grammar is background in sentence processing. *Language and Cognition* 13(1): 128–153. doi:10.1017/langcog.2020.30
Christiansen, Morten H. & Inbal Arnon (2017). More than words: The role of multiword sequences in language learning and use. *Topics in Cognitive Science* 9(3): 542–551. https://doi.org/10.1111/tops.12274
Christiansen, Morten H. & Nick Chater (2016). The now-or-never bottleneck: A fundamental constraint on language. *Behavioral and Brain Sciences* 39. https://doi.org/10.1017/S0140525X1500031X
Christodoulopoulos, Christos, Sharon Goldwater, & Mark Steedman (2010). Two decades of unsupervised POS induction: How far have we come? In Hang Li & Lluís Márquez (eds.), *Proceedings of the 2010 Conference on Empirical Methods in Natural Language Processing*. Cambridge, MA: MIT, 575–584.
Chumakina, Marina (2018). Atributiv v arčinskom jazyke [Атрибутив в арчинском языке]. *Rhema [Рема]* 4. https://doi.org/10.31862/2500-2953-2018-4-166-189
Chung, Sandra. 2012. Are lexical categories universal? The view from Chamorro. *Theoretical Linguistics* 38(1–2): 1–56. https://doi.org/10.1515/tl-2012-0001
Chung, Sandra & William A. Ladusaw (2003). *Restriction and Saturation*. Cambridge, MA: MIT Press.
Cikoski, John (1970). Classical Chinese word-classes. Dissertation, Yale University, New Haven, CT.
Cinque, Guglielmo (1999). *Adverbs and Functional Heads: A Cross-linguistic Perspective*. New York: Oxford University Press.

Cinque, Guglielmo (ed.) (2002). *Functional Structure in DP and IP: The Cartography of Syntactic Structures*. Oxford: Oxford University Press, vol. I.

Cinque, Guglielmo (ed.) (2006). *Restructuring and Functional Heads: The Cartography of Syntactic Structures*. Oxford: Oxford University Press, vol. IV.

Cinque, Guglielmo (2014). The semantic classification of adjectives: A view from syntax. *Studies in Chinese Linguistics* 35(1): 3–32.

Cinque, Guglielmo & Luigi Rizzi (2010). The cartography of syntactic structures. In Bernd Heine & Heiko Narrog (eds.), *The Oxford Handbook of Linguistic Analysis*. Oxford: Oxford University Press, 51–65.

Cipolotti, Lisa, Jane MacNeil, & Elizabeth K. Warrington (1993). Spared written naming of proper nouns: A case report. *Memory* 1: 289–311.

Citron, Francesca (2012). Neural correlates of written emotion word processing: A review of recent electrophysiological and hemodynamic neuroimaging studies. *Brain and Language* 122: 211–226.

Clancy, Patricia M., et al. (1996). The conversational use of reactive tokens in English, Japanese, and Mandarin. *Journal of Pragmatics* 26(3): 355–387. https://doi.org/10.1016/0378-2166(95)00036-4

Clark, Alexander (2003). Combining distributional and morphological information for part of speech induction. *Proceedings of the EACL 2003 Workshop on Evaluation Initiatives in Natural Language Processing*, 59–66.

Clark, Andy (2013). Whatever next? Predictive brains, situated agents, and the future of cognitive science. *Behavioral and Brain Sciences* 36(3): 181–204. https://doi.org/10.1017/S0140525X12000477

Clark, Eve V. & Herbert H. Clark (1979). When nouns surface as verbs. *Language* 55(4): 767–811.

Clark, Herbert H. (1996). *Using Language*. Cambridge: Cambridge University Press.

Clark, Herbert H. & Richard J. Gerrig (1990). Quotations as demonstrations. *Language* 66(4): 764–805.

Clark, Marybeth (1978). *Coverbs and Case in Vietnamese*. Pacific Linguistics B48.

Clemens, Lauren Eby & Jessica Coon (2018). Deriving verb initial order in Mayan. *Language* 94: 237–280.

Clerget, Emeline, et al. (2009). Role of Broca's area in encoding sequential human actions: A virtual lesion study. *NeuroReport* 20: 1496–1499.

Clift, Rebecca (2016). *Conversation Analysis*. Cambridge: Cambridge University Press.

Clifton, Charles & Lyn Frazier (1989). Comprehending sentences with long-distance dependencies. https://doi.org/10.1007/978-94-009-2729-2_8

Cloeren, Jan (1999). Tagsets. In Hans van Halteren (ed.), *Syntactic Wordclass Tagging*. Dordrecht: Kluwer, 37–54.

Clynes, Adrian (2005). Belait. In Karl A. Adelaar & Nikolaus Himmelman (eds.), *The Austronesian languages of Asia and Madagascar*. London: Routledge Press, 429–455.

Coates, Jennifer (1983). *The Semantics of the Modal Auxiliaries*. London: Croom Helm.

Cobbinah, Alexander & Friederike Lüpke (2009). Not cut to fit—Zero coded passives in African languages. In Matthias Brenzinger & Anna-Maria Fehn (eds.), *Proceedings of the 6th World Congress of African Linguistics*. Cologne: Köppe, 153–165.

Cobbinah, Alexander & Friederike Lüpke (2014). When number meets classification: The linguistic expression of number in Baïnounk languages. In Anne Storch & Gerrit J. Dimmendaal (eds.), *Number Constructions and Semantics: Case Studies from Africa, Amazonia, India and Oceania*. Amsterdam: John Benjamins, 199–220.

Coelho, Gail M. (2003). A grammar of Betta Kurumba. Doctoral dissertation, University of Texas at Austin.

Cohen, David (1973). La mutation aspective-temporelle dans quelques langues couchitiques et le système verbal chamito-sémitique. In Jacqueline M. C. Thomas & Lucien Bernot (eds.), *Langues et techniques, nature et société. Vol. 1 Approche linguistique*. Paris: Klincksieck, 57–63.

Cohen, David (1984). *La phrase nominale et l'évolution du système verbal en sémitique. Etude de syntaxe historique*. Leuven/Paris: Peeters.

Cohen, David (ed.) (1988a). *Les langues dans le monde ancien et moderne: Langues chamito-sémitiques*. Paris: Editions du CNRS.

Cohen, David (1988b). Introduction. In David Cohen (ed.), *Les langues dans le monde ancien et moderne: Langues chamito-sémitiques*. Paris: Editions du CNRS, 4–8.

Cohen, David (1988c). Chamito-sémitique. In David Cohen (ed.), *Les langues dans le monde ancien et moderne: Langues chamito-sémitiques*. Paris: Editions du CNRS, 9–30.

Cohen, David (1988d). Sémitique oriental: Akkadien. In David Cohen (ed.), *Les langues dans le monde ancien et moderne: Langues chamito-sémitiques*. Paris: Editions du CNRS, 40–55.

Cohen, David (1988e). Ougaritique. In David Cohen (ed.), *Les langues dans le monde ancien et moderne: Langues chamito-sémitiques*. Paris: Editions du CNRS, 58–67.

Cohen, David (1988f). Araméen. In David Cohen (ed.), *Les langues dans le monde ancien et moderne: Langues chamito-sémitiques*. Paris: Editions du CNRS, 84–104.

Cohen, David (1988g). Couchitique-Omotique. In David Cohen (ed.), *Les langues dans le monde ancien et moderne: Langues chamito-sémitiques*. Paris: Editions du CNRS, 243–269.

Cole, Peter. 1982. *Imbabura Quechua*. Lingua Descriptive Series. Amsterdam: North Holland.

Collier, Mark (1992). Predication and the circumstantial *sḏm(=f)/sḏm.n(=f)*. *Lingua Aegyptia* 2: 17–65.

Collina, S., P. Marangolo, & P. Tabossi (2001). The role of argument structure in the production of nouns and verbs. *Neuropsychologia* 39: 1125–1137.

Collins, Chris (2002). Multiple verb movement in ǂHoan. *Linguistic Inquiry* 33(1): 1–29.

Collins, Chris & Jeffrey S. Gruber (2014). *A Grammar of ǂHōä*. Cologne: Rüdiger Köppe Verlag.

Comrie, Bernard (1976). The syntax of action nominals: A cross-linguistic study. *Lingua* 40: 177–201.

Comrie, Bernard (1976b). *Aspect*. Cambridge: Cambridge University Press.

Comrie, Bernard & Sandra Thompson (1985). Lexical nominalizations. In Timothy Shopen (ed.), *Language Typology and Syntactic Description*. Cambridge: Cambridge University Press, vol. III, 349–398.

Constantinescu, Camelia (2015). Degree modification across categories: Nouns vs. adjectives. In Joanna Błaszczak, Dorota Klimek-Jankowska, & Krzysztof Migdalski (eds.), *How Categorical Are Categories? New Approaches to the Old Questions of Noun, Verb, and Adjective*. Berlin: De Gruyter, 155–195.

Contreras García, Lucía and Daniel Garcia Velasco (eds.) (2021). Interfaces in Functional Discourse Grammar: Theory and Applications. Berlin and New York: De Gruyter Mouton.

Cook, Anthony (1987). Wagiman Matyin: A description of the Wagiman language of the Northern Territory. Doctoral dissertation, Bundoora, La Trobe.

Cook, Eung-Do. 2004. A Grammar of Dëne Su̜ḷiné. Winnipeg: Algonquian and Iroquoian Linguistics.

Cook, William (1979). A grammar of North Carolina Cherokee. Doctoral dissertation, Yale University, New Haven, CT.

Coon, Jessica (2010). Rethinking split ergativity in Chol. *IJAL* 76: 207–53.

Coon, Jessica (2016). Mayan morphosyntax. *Language and Linguistics Compass* 10: 515–550.

Coon, Jessica (2017). Little-v agreement and templatic morphology in Ch'ol. *Syntax* 20: 101–137.

Coon, Jessica (2018). Distinguishing adjectives from relative clauses in Chuj (With help from Ch'ol). *McGill Working Papers in Linguistics* 25(1).

Coon, Jessica (2019). Building verbs in Chuj: Consequences for the nature of roots. *Journal of Linguistics* 55: 35–81

Cooperrider, Kensy, Natasha Abner & Susan Goldin-Meadow (2018). The palm-up puzzle: Meanings and origins of a widespread form in gesture and sign. *Frontiers in Communication* 3. https://doi.org/10.3389/fcomm.2018.00023.

Copin, François (2012). Grammaire wayampi. PhD dissertation, Paris 7.

Corbett, Greville G. (1991). *Gender*. Cambridge: Cambridge University Press.

Corbett, Greville G. (2000). *Number*. Cambridge: Cambridge University Press.

Corbett, Greville G. (2006). *Agreement*. Cambridge: Cambridge University Press.

Corbett, Greville G. (ed.) (2014). *The Expression of Gender*. Berlin: De Gruyter Mouton.

Corbett, Greville G. (2019). Pluralia tantum nouns and the theory of features: a typology of nouns with non-canonical number properties. *Morphology* 29, 51–108.

Cormier, Kearsy, et al. (2012). Lexicalisation and de-lexicalisation processes in sign languages: Comparing depicting constructions and viewpoint gestures. *Language & Communication* 32(4): 329–348. https://doi.org/10.1016/j.langcom.2012.09.004

Cormier, Kearsy, Adam Schembri, & Bencie Woll (2013). Pronouns and pointing in sign languages. *Lingua* 137: 230–247. https://doi.org/10.1016/j.lingua.2013.09.010

Corrêa-da-Silva, Beatriz C. (2010). Mawé/Awetí/Tupí–Guaraní: Relações Linguísticas e Implicações Históricas. PhD dissertation, Universidade de Brasília.

Corrêa-da-Silva, Beatriz C. (2013). O mundo a partir do léxico: Reconstruindo a realidade social Mawé-Awetí-Tupí-Guaraní. *Revista Brasileira de Linguística Antropológica* 5(2): 385–400.

Corris, Miriam (2006). A Grammar of Barupu: A Language of Papua New Guinea. PhD dissertation, University of Sydney.

Corver, Norbert & Henk van Riemsdijk (2001). *Semi-Lexical Categories: The Function of Content Words and The Content of Function Words*. Berlin: Mouton de Gruyter.

Costa, Joao & Naama Friedmann (2012). Children acquire unaccusatives and A-movement very early. In Martin Everaert, Marijana Marelj, & Tal Siloni (eds.), *The Theta System: Argument Structure at the Interface*. Oxford: Oxford University Press, 354–378.

Cotelli, Maria, et al. (2018). The role of the motor system in action naming in patients with neurodegenerative extrapyramidal syndromes. *Cortex* 100: 191–214.

Couchili, T., D. Maurel, & F. Queixalós (2002). Classes de lexèmes en émérillon. *Amerindia* 26/27: 173–208.

Couper-Kuhlen, Elizabeth & Margret Selting (2017). *Interactional Linguistics: An Introduction to Language in Social Interaction*. Cambridge: Cambridge University Press.

Cowie, Claire (1995). Grammaticalization and the snowball effect. *Language and Communication* 15: 181–193.

Craig, Colette G. (1986). Jacaltec noun classifiers: A study in language and culture. In Colette G. Craig (ed.), *Noun Classes and Categorization*. Amsterdam: John Benjamins, 263–293.

Craig, Colette G. (ed.) (1986). *Noun Classes and Categorization*. Amsterdam: John Benjamins.

Craig, Colette G. (1990). Clasificadores nominales: una innovación Q'anjob'al. In Nora England & Stephen R. Elliot (eds.), *Lecturas sobre la lingüística maya*. Antigua: CIRMA, 253–268.

Craig, Colette G. (1992). Classifiers in a functional perspective. In Michael Fortescue, Peter Harder, & Lars Kristoffersen (eds.), *Layered Structure and Reference in a Functional Perspective*. Amsterdam: John Benjamins, 227–302.

Crasborn, Onno, et al. (eds.) (2020). *Global Signbank*. Nijmegen: Radboud University. https://signbank.science.ru.nl

Creemers, Ava, Jan Don, & Paula Fenger (2018). Some affixes are roots, others are heads. *Natural Language and Linguistic Theory* 36(1): 45–84.
Creissels, Denis (1985). Les verbes statifs dans les parlers manding. *Mandenkan* 10: 1–32.
Creissels, Denis (1997). Postpositions as a possible origin of certain predicative markers in Mande. *Afrikanistische Arbeitspapiere* 50: 5–17.
Creissels, Denis (2015). Valency properties of Mandinka verbs. In Andrej Malchukov & Bernard Comrie (eds.), *Valency Classes in the World's Languages, Vol. 1*. Berlin: De Gruyter, 221–260.
Creissels, Denis (2017). The flexibility of the *noun* vs. *verb* distinction in the lexicon of Mandinka. In Valentina Vapnarsky & Edy Veneziano (eds.), *Lexical Polycategoriality: Cross-linguistic, Cross-theoretical and Language Acquisition Approaches*. Amsterdam: John Benjamins, 35–57.
Creissels, Denis (2018a). Current issues in the morphosyntactic typology of sub-Saharan languages. In Tom Güldemann (ed.), *The Languages and Linguistics of Africa*. Berlin: Mouton De Gruyter, 712–821.
Creissels, Denis (2018b). La catégorie des verbes statifs dans le système morphosyntaxique du soninké. *Mandenkan* 59: 3–30.
Creissels, Denis (2019). Grammatical relations in Mandinka. In Alena Witzlack-Makarevich & Balthasar Bickel (eds.), *Argument Selectors: A New Perspective on Grammatical Relations*. John Benjamins, 301–348.
Creissels, Denis. To appear. Evidence for a grammaticalization path from a verb 'do' to an antipassive marker and further to an event nominalization marker in Manding languages. In Sonia Cristofaro & Foong Ha Yap (eds.), *Nominalization in diachronic perspective*.
Creissels, Denis & Pierre Sambou (2013). *Le mandinka: phonologie, grammaire, textes*. Paris: Karthala.
Crepaldi, Davide, et al. (2006). Noun–verb dissociation in aphasia: The role of imageability and functional locus of the lesion. *Neuropsychologia* 44: 73–89.
Crepaldi, Davide, et al. (2013). Clustering the lexicon in the brain: A meta-analysis of the neurofunctional evidence on noun and verb processing. *Frontiers in Human Neuroscience* 7: art. 303.
Crepaldi, Davide, et al. (2011). A place for nouns and a place for verbs? A critical review of neurocognitive data on grammatical class effects. *Brain and Language* 116: 33–49.
Cresswell, M. J. (1976). The semantics of degree. In Barbara Partee (ed.), *Montague Grammar*. New York: Academic Press, 261–292.
Crevels, Mily & Pieter Muysken (eds.) (2009). *Lenguas de Bolivia. Tomo 1. Ambito Andino*. La Paz, Bolivia: Plural editores.
Cristofaro, Sonia (2003). *Subordination*. Oxford: Oxford University Press.
Croft, William (1990). A conceptual framework for grammatical categories (or: a taxonomy of propositional acts). *Journal of Semantics* 7(3): 245–279. doi:10.1093/jos/7.3.245
Croft, William (1991). *Syntactic Categories and Grammatical Relations: The Cognitive Organization of Information*. Chicago: University of Chicago Press.
Croft, William (1993). A noun is a noun is a noun—Or is it? Some reflections on the universality of semantics. *Proceedings of the Nineteenth Annual Meeting of the Berkeley Linguistics Society: General Session and Parasession on Semantic Typology and Semantic Universals*, 369–380.
Croft, William (2000a). *Explaining Language Change: An Evolutionary Approach*. Harlow, Essex: Longman.
Croft, William (2000b). Parts of speech as language universals and as language-particular categories. In Petra M. Vogel & Bernard Comrie (eds.), *Approaches to the Typology of Word Classes*. Berlin: Mouton de Gruyter, 65–102.

Croft, William (2001). *Radical Construction Grammar: Syntactic Theory in Typological Perspective.* Oxford: Oxford University Press. https://doi.org/10.1093/acprof:oso/9780198299554.001.0001

Croft, William (2003). *Typology and Universals* (2nd edn). Cambridge: Cambridge University Press.

Croft, William (2005a). Logical and typological arguments for radical construction grammar. In Mirjam Fried & Jan-Ola Östman (eds.), *Construction Grammar(s): Cognitive and Cross-Language Dimensions.* (Constructional Approaches to Language, 3.) Amsterdam: John Benjamins, 273–314.

Croft, William (2005b) Word classes, parts of speech and syntactic argumentation [Commentary on Evans and Osada, 'Mundari: The myth of a language without word classes']. *Linguistic Typology* 9: 431–441.

Croft, William (2007a). Beyond Aristotle and gradience: A reply to Aarts. *Studies in Language* 31: 409–430.

Croft, William (2007b). The origins of grammar in the verbalization of experience. *Cognitive Linguistics* 18: 339–382.

Croft, William (2009a). Methods for finding universals in syntax. In Sergio Scalise, Elisabetta Magni, & Antonietta Bisetto (eds.), *Universals of Language Today.* Dordrecht: Springer, 145–164.

Croft, William (2009b). Syntax is more diverse, and evolutionary linguistics is already here. *Behavioral and Brain Sciences* 32: 453–454.

Croft, William (2010a). Ten unwarranted assumptions in syntactic argumentation. In Kasper Bøye & Elisabeth Engberg-Pedersen (eds.), *Language Usage and Language Structure.* Berlin: Mouton de Gruyter, 313–350.

Croft, William (2010b). Pragmatic function, semantic classes and lexical categories [commentary on Smith, 'Pragmatic functions and lexical categories']. *Linguistics* 48: 787–796.

Croft, William (2010c). Relativity, linguistic variation and language universals. *CogniTextes* 4: 303 http://cognitextes.revues.org/303/

Croft, William (2010d). The origins of grammaticalization in the verbalization of experience. *Linguistics* 48: 1–48.

Croft, William (2013). Radical construction grammar. In Graeme Trousdale & Thomas Hoffmann (eds.), *The Oxford Handbook of Construction Grammar.* Oxford: Oxford University Press, 211–232.

Croft, William (2014). Comparing categories and constructions crosslinguistically (again): The diversity of ditransitives [review article on *Studies in Ditransitive Constructions: A Comparative Handbook,* ed. Andrej Malchukov, Martin Haspelmath, & Bernard Comrie]. *Linguistic Typology* 18: 533–551.

Croft, William (2016a). Comparative concepts and language-specific categories: Theory and practice. *Linguistic Typology* 20: 377–393.

Croft, William (2016b). Typology and the future of cognitive linguistics. *Cognitive Linguistics* 27: 587–602.

Croft, William (2019). Comparative concepts and practicing typology: On Haspelmath's proposal for 'flagging' and '(person) indexing'. *Te Reo* 62: 116–129.

Croft, William (2020a). *Ten Lectures on Construction Grammar and Typology.* Leiden: Brill. [revised version of *Ten Lectures on Construction Grammar and Typology.* Beijing: Foreign Language Teaching and Research Press, 2012]

Croft, William (2022a). *Morphosyntax: Constructions of the World's Languages.* Cambridge: Cambridge University Press http://www.unm.edu/~wcroft/WACpubs.html

Croft, William (2022b). On two mathematical representations of 'semantic maps'. *Zeitschrift für Sprachwissenschaft*, 41(1):67–88 special issue entitled 'Semantic maps', ed. Athanasios Georgakopoulos & Stéphane Polis, 41(1): 67–88. https://doi.org/10.1515/zfs-2021-2040.

Croft, William & D. Alan Cruse (2004). *Cognitive Linguistics*. Cambridge: Cambridge University Press.

Croft, William, et al. (2017). Linguistic typology meets universal dependencies. In Markus Dickinson, et al. (eds.), *Proceedings of the 15th International Workshop on Treebanks and Linguistic Theories (TLT15)*. CEUR Workshop Proceedings, 63–75.

Croft, William & Keith T. Poole (2008). Inferring universals from grammatical variation: Multidimensional scaling for typological analysis. *Theoretical Linguistics* 34: 1–37.

Croft, William & Eva van Lier (2012). Language universals without universal categories. *Theoretical Linguistics* 38(1–2): 57–72. https://doi.org/10.1515/tl-2012-0002

Crowley, Terry (1982). *The Paamese Language of Vanuatu*. Canberra: Australian National University.

Crowley, Terry (1985). Common noun phrase marking in Proto-Oceanic. *Oceanic Linguistics* 24: 135–193.

Cruse, D. Alan (1986). *Lexical Semantics*. Cambridge: Cambridge University Press.

Cruz, Aline da (2011). Fonologia e Gramática do Nheengatú. A língua geral falada pelos povos Baré, Warekena e Baniwa. PhD dissertation, Vrije Universiteit.

Cruz, Aline da (2014). *Reduplication in Nheengatu*. Leiden: Brill. https://brill.com/view/book/edcoll/9789004272415/B9789004272415_006.xml

Crysmann, Berthold & Olivier Bonami (2016). Variable morphotactics and information-based morphology. *Journal of Linguistics* 52: 311–374.

Crystal, David (1967). English. *Lingua* 17: 24–56.

Culbertson, Jennifer, Hanna Jarvinen, Frances Haggarty & Kenny Smith. 2019. Children's sensitivity to phonological and semantic cues during noun class learning: Evidence for a phonological bias. Language 95(2). 268–293.

Culicover, Peter W. (1999). *Syntactic Nuts: Hard Cases, Syntactic Theory, and Language Acquisition*. Oxford: Oxford University Press.

Culicover, Peter W. & Ray Jackendoff (2005). *Simpler Syntax*. Oxford: Oxford University Press.

Cuny, Albert & Michel Féghali (1924). *Du genre grammatical en sémitique*. Paris: Geuthner.

Cuoq, Jean-André (1866). *Études philologiques sur quelques langues sauvages de l'Amérique*. Montreal: Dawson.

Cuoq, Jean-André (1882). *Lexique de la langue Iroquoise avec notes et appendices*. Montreal: Chapleau & Fils.

Curiel Ramírez del Prado, Alejandro (2017). Tojolabal. In Judith Aissen, Nora C. England, & Roberto Zavala Maldonado (eds.), *The Mayan Languages*. London/New York: Routledge, 570–609.

Curnow, Timothy Jowan (1997). A grammar of Awa Pit (Cuaiquer). An indigenous language of South-West Columbia. PhD dissertation, Australian National University.

Cusic, David (1981). Verbal plurality and aspect. PhD dissertation, Stanford University, CA.

Cusihuamán G., Antonio (1976). *Gramática quechua Cuzco*. Lima: Instituto de Estudios Peruanos.

Cutfield, Sarah (2011). Demonstratives in Dalabon: A language of Southwestern Arnhem land. PhD dissertation, University of Melbourne, Melbourne.

Cuzzolin, Pierluigi, Ignazio Putzu, & Paolo Ramat (2006). The Indo-European adverb in diachronic and typological perspective. *Indogermanische Forschungen* 111: 1–38.

Czaykowska-Higgins, Ewa & M. Dale Kinkade (1998). Salish languages and linguistics. In Ewa Czaykowska-Higgins & M. Dale Kinkade (eds.), *Salish Languages and Linguistics: Theoretical and Descriptive Perspectives*. (Trends in Linguistics: Studies and Monographs 107.) Berlin: Mouton de Gruyter, 1–68.

Dabrowska, Ewa, Caroline Rowland, & Anna Theakston (2009). The acquisition of questions with long-distance dependencies. *Cognitive Linguistics* 20(3): 571–597. https://doi.org/10.1515/COGL.2009.025

Dahl, Östen (1985). *Tense and Aspect Systems*. London: Blackwell.

Dahl, Östen (2014). Siriono. In Mily Crevels & Pieter Muysken (eds.), *Lenguas de Bolivia*. La Paz: Plural Editores, 99–133.

Dahl, Östen (2015). How WEIRD are WALS languages? Talk given at Conference on Diversity Linguistics: Retrospect and Prospect, 1–3 May 2015, Leipzig. Slides available at: https://www.eva.mpg.de/fileadmin/content_files/linguistics/conferences/2015-diversity-linguistics/Dahl_slides.pdf

Dahl, Östen (2016). Thoughts on language-specific and crosslinguistic entities. *Linguistic Typology* 20: 427–437.

Dahl, Östen & Viveka Velupillai (2005). The future tense. In Martin Haspelmath et al. (eds.), *The World Atlas of Language Structures*. Oxford: Oxford University Press. https://wals.info/chapter/67

Dalrymple, Mary, et al. (eds.) (1995). *Formal Issues in Lexical-Functional Grammar*. Stanford, CA: CSLI Publications.

Dalrymple, Mary, Ronald M. Kaplan, & Tracy Holloway King (2004). Linguistic generalizations over descriptions. In Miriam Butt & Tracy Holloway King (eds.), *On-line Proceedings of the LFG2004 Conference*. Stanford, CA: CSLI Publications. http://web.stanford.edu/group/cslipublications/cslipublications/LFG/9/lfg04-toc.html

Dalrymple, Mary, John J. Lowe, & Louise Mycock (2019). *The Oxford Reference Guide to Lexical Functional Grammar*. Oxford: Oxford University Press.

Damasio, A. R., & D. Tranel (1993). Nouns and verbs are retrieved with differently distributed neural systems. *Proceedings of the National Academy of Sciences* 90: 4957–4960.

Damasio, H., et al. (2004). Neural systems behind word and concept retrieval. *Cognition* 92: 179–229.

Da Milano, Federica & Paolo Ramat (2011). Differenti usi di gerundi e forme affini nelle lingue romanze. *Vox Romanica* 70: 1–46.

Daniel, Michael & Yury Lander (2011). The Caucasian languages. In Bernd Kortmann & Johan van der Auwera (eds.), *The Languages and Linguistics of Europe*. Berlin: Mouton de Gruyter, 125–158.

Danziger, Eve (1994). Out of sight, out of mind: Person, perception, and function in Mopan Maya spatial deixis, *Linguistics* 32(4–5): 885–907.

Danziger, Eve (1996). Split intransitivity and active–inactive patterning in Mopan Maya. *International Journal of American Linguistics* 62: 379–414.

Darmon, Chloé (2017). A morphosyntactic description of Xamtanga. An Agaw (Central Cushitic) language of the northern Ethiopian highlands. PhD dissertation, Université Lumière Lyon 2 and Leiden University.

Darwin, Charles (1872). *The Expression of the Emotions in Man and Animals*. London: Murray.

da Silva, Raynice G. P. (2010). Estudo morfossintático da língua sateré-mawé. PhD, Unicamp.

Davidson, Donald (1967). The logical form of action sentences. In Nicholas Rescher (ed.), *The Logic of Decision and Action*. Pittsburgh: University of Pittsburgh Press, 81–95. [reprinted in D. Davidson, *Essays on Actions and Events*, Clarendon Press, London, 1980]

Davidson, Matthew (2002). Studies in Southern Wakashan (Nootkan) grammar. Unpublished PhD dissertation, State University of New York at Buffalo.

Davies, Mark (2004). BYU-BNC. [based on the British National Corpus from Oxford University Press] http://corpus.byu.edu/bnc/

Davies, Mark (2008). *The Corpus of Contemporary American English* (COCA): 600 million words, 1990–present. http://corpus.byu.edu/coca/

Davies, William & Stanley Dubinsky (2009). On the existence (and distribution) of sentential subjects. In Donna B. Gerdts, John C. Moore, & Maria Polinsky (eds.), *In Hypothesis A/Hypothesis B: Linguistic Explorations in Honor of David M. Perlmutter*. Cambridge, MA: MIT Press, 111–128.

Davis, Charles P. & Eiling Yee (2019). Features, labels, space, and time: Factors supporting taxonomic relationships in the anterior temporal lobe and thematic relationships in the angular gyrus. *Language, Cognition, and Neuroscience* 34: 1347–1357.

Davis, Henry (2000). Remarks on Proto-Salish subject-inflection. *International Journal of American Linguistics* 66: 499–520.

Davis, Henry (2011). Stalking the adjective in St'át'imcets. *Northwest Journal of Linguistics* 5(2): 1–60.

Davis, Henry (2020). Salish languages. In Daniel Siddiqi. et al. (eds.), *The Routledge Handbook of North American Languages*. New York: Routledge, 452–472.

Davis, Henry, Carrie Gillon, & Lisa Matthewson (2014). How to investigate linguistic diversity: Lessons from the Pacific Northwest. *Language* 90(4): 180–226.

Davis, Henry & Lisa Matthewson (1996). Subordinate clauses and functional projections in St'at'imcets. *Papers for ICSNL* 31.

Davis, Henry & Lisa Matthewson (1999). On the functional determination of lexical categories. *Revue québécoise de linguistique* 27: 27–69.

Davis, Henry & Lisa Matthewson (2009). Issues in Salish syntax and semantics. *Language and Linguistics Compass* 3(4): 1097–1166.

Dayal, Veneeta (2004). Number marking and (in)definiteness in kind terms. *Linguistics and Philosophy* 27(4): 393–450.

Dayal, Veneeta (2021). Reference to kinds and the notion of semantic parameter (a review of Chierchia 1998). Unpublished ms, to appear in Louise McNally & Zoltán Szabó (eds.), *A Reader's Guide to Classic Papers in Formal Semantics*. (Volume 100 of Studies in Linguistics and Philosophy.) Springer.

Dayal, Veneeta & Yağmur Săg (2020). Determiners and bare nouns. *Annual Review of Linguistics* 6: 173–194.

Dayley, John (1989). *Tümpisa (Panamint) Shoshone Grammar*. Berkeley, CA: University of California Press.

Dayley, Jon P. (1981). Voice and ergativity in Mayan languages. *Journal of Mayan Linguistics* 2(2): 3–82.

Dayley, Jon P. (1985). *Tz'utujil Grammar*. Berkeley, CA: University of California Press.

De Belder, Marijke (2011). *Roots and Affixes: Eliminating Lexical Categories from Syntax*. Utrecht: LOT Publications.

De Belder, Marijke (2019). Possible phonological cues in categorial acquisition. [lecture] Syntax Interface, Utrecht University 10.10.2019.

De Belder, Marijke & Jeroen van Craenenbroek (2014). How to merge a root. *Linguistic Inquiry* 46: 625–655.

de Bot, Kees (1992). A bilingual production model: Levelt's speaking model adapted. *Applied Linguistics* 13(1): 1–24.

Déchaine, Rose-Marie (1993). Predicates across categories. PhD thesis, University of Massachusetts, Amherst.

Deconinck, Julie, Frank Boers, & June Eyckmans (2017). Does the form of this word fit its meaning? The effect of learner-generated mapping elaborations on L2 word recall. *Language Teaching Research* 27: 31–53.

De Groot, Annette M. B. & Rieneke Keijzer (2000). What is hard to learn is easy to forget: The roles of words concreteness, cognate status, and word frequency in foreign-language vocabulary learning and forgetting. *Language Learning* 50: 1–56.

De Haan, Ferdinand (2010). *Typology of Tense, Aspect, and Modality Systems*. Oxford: Oxford University Press

Dehaene, Stanislas (1997). *The Number Sense*. New York: Oxford University Press.

Dehaene, Stanislas, et al. (1999). Sources of mathematical thinking: Behavioral and brain-imaging evidence. *Science* 284 (5416): 970–974. https://doi.org/10.1126/science.284.5416.970

Dehé, Nicole, et al. (2002). Introduction. In Nicole Dehé et al. (eds.), *Verb–Particle Explorations*. Berlin: Mouton de Gruyter, 1–20.

De Hoop, Helen & Peter de Swart (eds.) (2009). *Differential Subject Marking*. New York: Springer.

De Hoop, Helen & Joost Zwarts (2008). Case in formal semantics. In Andrej L. Malchukov & Adrew Spencer (eds.), *The Oxford Handbook of Case*. Oxford: Oxford University Press, 170–184.

DeLancey, Scott (1997). Grammaticalization and the gradience of categories. Relator nouns and postpositions in Tibetan and Burmese. In Joan Bybee, John Haiman, & Sandra A. Thompson (eds.), *Essays on Language Function and Language Type*. Amsterdam: John Benjamins, 51–69.

DeLancey, Scott (2005). Adpositions as a non-universal category. In Zygmunt Frajzyngier, Adam Hodges, & David Rood (eds.), *Linguistic Diversity and Language Theories*. Amsterdam: John Benjamins, 185–202.

de León, Lourdes (1988). Noun and numeral classifiers in Mixtec and Tzotzil: A referential view. PhD thesis, University of Sussex.

De León, Lourdes. 1999. Verbs in Tzotzil (Mayan) early syntactic development. International Journal of Bilingualism 3(2-3). 219–239.

de León, Lourdes (2001). Why Tzotzil (Mayan) children prefer verbs: The role of linguistic and cultural factors over cognitive determinants. In Margareta Almgren et al. *Proceedings of the 8th Conference of the International Association for the Study of Child Language*. Somerville: Cascadilla Press, 947–969.

Delfitto, Denis (2006). Bare plurals. In Martin Everaert & Henk van Riemsdijk (eds.), *The Blackwell Companion to Syntax*. New York: Wiley, 214–259.

Dell, Gary S., Lisa K. Burger, & William R. Svec (1997). Language production and serial order: A functional analysis and a model. *Psychological Review* 104: 123–147. http://dx.doi.org/10.1037/0033-295X.104.1.123

Demske, Ulrike (2019). Aspectual features and categorial shift: Deverbal nominals in German and English. *Language Sciences* 73: 50–61.

Dempwolff, Otto (1939). *Grammatik der Jabêm-Sprache auf Neuguinea. Abhandlungen aus dem Gebiet der Auslandskunde* 50. Hamburg: Friederichsen de Gruyter.

Demuth, Katherine, Nicholas Faraclass, & Lynell Marchese (1986). Niger–Congo noun class and agreement systems in language acquisition and historical change. In Colette G. Craig (ed.), *Noun Classes and Categorization*. Amsterdam: John Benjamins, 453–471.

Dench, Alan (1994). *Martuthunira: A Language of the Pilbara Region of Western Australia*. Canberra: Pacific Linguistics.

Dench, Alan & Nicholas Evans (1988). Multiple case-marking in Australian languages. *Australian Journal of Linguistics* 8(1): 1–47.

Denison, David (2001). Gradience and linguistic change. In Laurel J. Brinton (ed.), *Historical Linguistics 1999: Selected Papers from the 14th International Conference on Historical Linguistics*, Vancouver, 9–13 August 1999. Amsterdam: John Benjamins, 119–144.

Denison, David (2010). Category change in English with and without structural change. In Elizabeth C. Traugott & Graeme Trousdale (eds.), *Gradience, Gradualness and Grammaticalization*. Amsterdam: John Benjamins, 105–128.

Denison, David (2013). Parts of speech: Solid citizens or slippery customers? *Journal of the British Academy* 1: 151–185.

Denison, David (2017a). Ambiguity and vagueness in historical change. In Marianne Hundt, Sandra Mollin, & Simone E. Pfenninger (eds.), *The Changing English Language: Psycholinguistic Perspectives*. Cambridge: Cambridge University Press, 292–318.

Denison, David (2017b). Word classes in the history of English. In Mary Hayes & Allison Burkette (eds.), *Approaches to Teaching the History of the English Language: Pedagogy in Practice*. New York: Oxford University Press, 157–171.

Denny, J. Peter (1982). The semantics of the Inuktitut (Eskimo) spatial deictics. *International Journal of American Linguistics* 48: 359–384.

den Ouden, Dirk-Bart, et al. (2019). Cortical and structural-connectivity damage correlated with impaired syntactic processing in aphasia. *Human Brain Mapping* 40: 2153–2173.

Depraetere, Ilse (2003). On verbal concord with collective nouns in British English. *English Language and Linguistics* 7(1): 85–127.

Derbyshire, Desmond C. (1979). *Hixkaryana and Linguistic Typology*. Arlington, TX: University of Texas at Arlington: SIL Publication.

Derbyshire, Desmond C. (1985). *Hixkaryana*. Amsterdam: North Holland.

Derbyshire, Desmond C. & Doris L. Payne (1990). Noun classification systems of Amazonian languages. In Doris L. Payne (ed.), *Amazonian Linguistics: Studies in Lowland South American Languages*. Austin: University of Texas Press, 243–271.

Desai, Rutvik, et al. (2015). Concepts within reach: Action performance predicts action language processing in stroke. *Neuropsychologia* 71: 217–224.

De Smet, Hendrik (2008). Functional motivations in the development of nominal and verbal gerunds in Middle and Early Modern English. *English Language and Linguistics* 12: 55–102.

De Smet, Hendrik (2010). English -*ing*-clauses and their problems: The structure of grammatical categories. *Linguistics* 48(6): 1153–1193.

De Smet, Hendrik (2012). The course of actualization. *Language* 88: 601–633.

De Villiers, Jill C. (2005). Can language acquisition give children a point of view? In Janet Astington & Jodie Baird (eds.), *Why Language Matters for Theory of Mind*. New York: Oxford University Press, 186–219. https://doi.org/10.1093/acprof:oso/9780195159912.003.0010

De Villiers, Jill G. & Peter de Villiers (2000). Linguistic determinism and the understanding of false beliefs. In Peter Mitchell and Kevin Riggs (eds.), *Children's Reasoning and the Mind*. Hove: Psychology Press, 191–228.

de Vos, Connie & Victoria Nyst (2018). The time depth and typology of rural sign languages. *Sign Language Studies* 18(4): 477–487. https://doi.org/10.1353/sls.2018.0013

de Vos, Connie & Roland Pfau (2015). Sign language typology: The contribution of rural sign languages. *Annual Review of Linguistics* 1(1): 265–288. https://doi.org/10.1146/annurev-linguist-030514-124958

Devos, Maud (2008). *A Grammar of Makwe*. Munich: Lincom Europa.
De Wilde, Vanessa, Marc Brysbaert, & June Eyckmans (2019). Learning English through out-of-school exposure: How do word-related variables and proficiency influence receptive vocabulary learning. *Language Learning* (online early view).
Diakonoff, Igor M. (1988). *Afrasian Languages*. Moscow: Nauka.
Dialo, Amadou (1985). *Eléments expressifs du wolof contemporain: gestes, signaux oraux, unités significatives nasalisées, interjections, onomatopées, impressifs* (Langues Nationales Au Sénégal 27). Dakar: Centre de linguistique appliquée de Dakar.
Diesing, Molly (1992). Bare plural subjects and the derivation of logical representations. *Linguistic Inquiry* 23(3): 353-380.
Diessel, Holger (1999). *Demonstratives: Form, Function, and Grammaticalization*. Amsterdam: John Benjamins.
Diessel, Holger (2005). Pronominal and adnominal demonstratives. In Martin Haspelmath et al. (eds.), *The World Atlas of Language Structures*. Oxford: Oxford University Press, 174-179.
Diessel, Holger (2006). Demonstratives, joint attention, and the emergence of grammar. *Cognitive Linguistics* 17: 463-489.
Diessel, Holger (2009). Corpus linguistics and language acquisition. In Anke Luedeling & Merja Kytoe (eds.), *Corpus Linguistics. An International Handbook*. Berlin: Mouton de Gruyter, 1197-1212.
Diessel, Holger (2014). Demonstratives, frames of reference, and semantic universals of space. *Language and Linguistics Compass* 8: 116-132.
Diessel, Holger (2019). *The Grammar Network. How Linguistic Structure Is Shaped by Language Use*. Cambridge: Cambridge University Press.
Diessel, Holger & Merlijn Breunesse (2020). A typology of demonstrative clause linkers. In Åshild Næss, Anna Margetts, & Yvonne Treis (eds.), *Demonstratives in Discourse*. Leipzig: Language Science Press, 305-341.
Diessel, Holger & Kenny Coventry (2020). Demonstratives in spatial language and social interaction: An interdisciplinary review. *Frontiers in Psychology* 11.
Diessel, Holger & Michael Tomasello (2005). A new look at the acquisition of relative clauses. *Language* 81(4): 882-906. https://doi.org/10.1353/lan.2005.0169
Diewald, Gabriele (2010). On some problem areas in grammaticalization theory. In Katerina Stathi, Elke Gehweiler, & Ekkehard König (eds.), *Grammaticalization: Current Views and Issues*. Amsterdam: John Benjamins, 17-50.
Dietrich, Wolf (1977). Las categorías verbales (partes de la oración) en Tupí-Guaraní. *Indiana* 4: 245-261.
Dietrich, Wolf (1986). *El idioma chiriguano: gramática, textos, vocabulario*. ICI.
Dietrich, Wolf (2000). Problema de la categoría del adjetivo en las lenguas Tupí-Guaraníes. In Hein van der Voort & Simon van de Kerke (eds.), *Indigenous languages of Lowland South America*. Leiden: Universiteit Leiden, 255-263.
Dietrich, Wolf (2001). Categorias lexicais nas línguas tupi-guarani (visão comparativa). In F. Queixalós (ed.), *Des noms et des verbes en tupi-guarani: état de la question*. Munich: Lincom Europa, 21-37.
Dietrich, Wolf (2014). *Forms and Functions of Reduplication in Tupian Languages*. Leiden: Brill. https://brill.com/view/book/edcoll/9789004272415/B9789004272415_012.xml
Dietrich, Wolf (2017). Tipologia morfossintática da negação nas línguas do tronco Tupi. *LIAMES: Línguas Indígenas Americanas* 17(1): 7.
Diffloth, Gérard (1972). Notes on expressive meaning. *Chicago Linguistic Society* 8: 440-447

Diffloth, Gérard (1976). Expressives in Semai. *Oceanic Linguistics Special Publications* 13: 249–264.

Diffloth, Gérard (1979). Expressive phonology and prosaic phonology in Mon-Khmer. In Theraphan L. Thongkum (ed.), *Studies in Mon-Khmer and Thai Phonology and Phonetics in Honor of E. Henderson*. Bangkok: Chulalongkorn University Press, 49–59.

Diffloth, Gérard (2020). Foreword. In Nathan Badenoch & Nishaant Choksi (eds.), *Expressives in the South Asian Linguistic Area*. (Brill's Studies in South and Southwest Asian Languages 13.) Leiden: Brill, vii–x.

Dik, Simon C. (1978). *Functional Grammar*. Amsterdam: North-Holland.

Dik, Simon C. (1989). *The Theory of Functional Grammar*. Dordrecht: Foris.

Dik, Simon C. (1997). *The Theory of Functional Grammar* (2 vols.) (ed. K. Hengeveld). Berlin/New York: Mouton de Gruyter.

Dimmendaal, Gerrit (2011). *Historical Linguistics and the Comparative Study of African Languages*. Amsterdam: John Benjamins.

Dingemanse, Mark (2012). Advances in the cross-linguistic study of ideophones. *Linguistics and Language Compass* 6(10): 654–672. https://doi.org/10.1002/lnc3.361

Dingemanse, Mark (2019). 'Ideophone' as a comparative concept. In Kimi Akita & Prashant Pardeshi (eds.), *Ideophones, Mimetics, Expressives*. (Iconicity in Language and Literature 16.) Amsterdam: John Benjamins, 13–33. doi:10.1075/ill.16.02din

Dingemanse, Mark (2020a). Recruiting assistance and collaboration: A West-African corpus study. In Simeon Floyd, Giovanni Rossi, & N. J. Enfield (eds.), *Getting Others to Do Things: A Pragmatic Typology of Recruitments*. (Diversity Linguistics.) Berlin: Language Science Press, 369–421. doi:10.5281/zenodo.4018388

Dingemanse, Mark (2020b). Between sound and speech: Liminal signs in interaction. *Research on Language and Social Interaction* 53(1): 188–196. doi:10.1080/08351813.2020.1712967

Dingemanse, Mark & Kimi Akita (2017). An inverse relation between expressiveness and grammatical integration: On the morphosyntactic typology of ideophones, with special reference to Japanese. *Journal of Linguistics* 53(3): 501–532. doi:10.1017/S002222671600030X

Dingemanse, Mark & Andreas Liesenfeld (2022). From text to talk: Harnessing conversational corpora for humane and diversity-aware language technology. *Proceedings of the 60th Annual Meeting of the Association for Computational Linguistics*, 5614–5633. Dublin: Association for Computational Linguistics. doi: 10.18653/v1/2022.acl-long.385

Dingemanse, Mark, Francisco Torreira, & Nick Enfield (2013). Is 'Huh?' a universal word? Conversational infrastructure and the convergent evolution of linguistic items. *PLOS ONE* 8(11): e78273. doi:10.1371/journal.pone.0078273

Dixon, R. M. W. (1977). Where have all the adjectives gone? *Studies in Language* 1: 19–80.

Dixon, R. M. W. (1980). *The Languages of Australia*. Cambridge: Cambridge University Press.

Dixon, R. M. W. (1982). *Where Have All the Adjectives Gone? And Other Essays in Semantics and Syntax*. Berlin: Mouton de Gruyter.

Dixon, R. M. W. (1986). Noun classes and noun classification in typological perspective. In Colette G. Craig (ed.), *Noun Classes and Categorization*. Amsterdam: John Benjamins, 105–112.

Dixon, R. M. W. (1988). *A Grammar of Boumaa Fijian*. Chicago: University of Chicago Press.

Dixon, R. M. W. (2002). *Australian Languages: Their Nature and Development*. Cambridge: Cambridge University Press.

Dixon, R. M. W. (2003). Demonstratives: A cross-linguistic typology. *Studies in Language* 27: 61–122.

Dixon, R. M. W. (2004). Adjective classes in typological perspective. In R. M. W. Dixon & Alexandra Y. Aikhenvald (eds.), *Adjective Classes: A Cross-Linguistic Typology*. Oxford: Oxford University Press, 1–49.

Dixon, R. M. W. (2010a). *Basic Linguistic Theory: Volume 1*. Oxford: Oxford University Press.

Dixon, R. M. W. (2010b). *Basic Linguistic Theory, Volume 2: Grammatical Topics*. Oxford: Oxford University Press.

Dixon, R. M. W. ([1980] 2010). *The Languages of Australia*. Cambridge: Cambridge University Press.

Dixon, R. M. W. & Alexandra Y. Aikhenvald (1999). *The Amazonian Languages*. Cambridge: Cambridge University Press.

Dixon, R. M. W. & Alexandra Y. Aikhenvald (eds.) (2004). *Adjective Classes: A Cross-linguistic Typology*. Oxford: Oxford University Press.

Dobson, Rose (1997). *Gramática Prática Com Exercícios da Língua Kayabi*. Sociedade Internacional de Lingüística.

Doerfer, Gerhard (1982). Nomenverba im Türkischen. In Aldo Gallotta & Ugo Marazzi (eds.), *Studia turcologica memoriae Alexii Bombaci dicata*. Napoli: Istituto Universitario Orientale, Seminario di Studi Asiatici, 101–114.

Doetjes, Jenny (2012). Count/mass distinctions across languages. In Claudia Maienborn, Klaus von Heusinger, & Paul Portner (eds.), *Semantics: An International Handbook of Natural Language Meaning*. Berlin: De Gruyter Mouton, vol. III, 2559–2580.

Doetjes, Jenny (2017). The count/mass distinction in grammar and cognition. *Annual Review of Linguistics* 3: 199–217.

Döhler, Christian (2018). *A Grammar of Komnzo*. Berlin: Language Science Press.

Doke, Clement Martyn (1935). *Bantu Linguistic Terminology*. London: Longmans, Green, and Co.

Domahs, Frank, et al. (2012). Where the mass counts: Common cortical activation for different kinds of nonsingularity. *Journal of Cognitive Neuroscience* 24: 915–932.

Don, Jan & Marian Erkelens (2008). Possible phonological cues in categorial acquisition. *Studies in Language* 32(3): 670–682.

Don, Jan & Eva van Lier (2013). Derivation and categorization in flexible and differentiated languages. In Jan Rijkhoff & Eva van Lier (eds.), *Flexible Word Classes: Typological Studies of Underspecified Parts of Speech*. Oxford: Oxford University Press, 56–88.

Don, Jan, Petra Sleeman, & Thom Westveer (2015). Three types of suffixes in French, discarding the learned/non-learned distinction. In Björn Köhnlein & Jenny Audring (eds.), *Linguistics in the Netherlands 2015*. Amsterdam: John Benjamins, 32–46.

Donaldson, Tamsin (1980). *Ngiyambaa, the Language of the Wangaaybuwan*. Cambridge: Cambridge University Press.

Dong, Xiufang (董秀芳) (2016). 汉语的词库与词法 *Hànyǔ de cíkù yǔ cífǎ* [The lexicon and word formation in Chinese]. Beijing: University of Beijing Publisher.

Donohue, Mark (1999). *A Grammar of Tukang Besi*. Berlin/New York: Mouton de Gruyter.

Donohue, Mark (2008). Covert word classes: Seeking your own syntax in Tukang Besi. *Studies in Language* 32: 590–609.

Donohue, Mark & Søren Wichmann (eds.) (2008). *The Typology of Semantic Alignment*. Oxford: Oxford University Press.

Dooley, Robert (1990). The positioning of non-pronominal clitics and particles in Lowland South American Languages. In Doris Payne (ed.), *Amazonian Linguistics: Studies in Lowland South American languages*. Austin: University of Texas Press, 475–493.

Dorais, Louis-Jacques (2010). *The Language of the Inuit: Syntax, Semantics, and Society in the Arctic*. Montreal: McGill-Queen's University Press.
Doron, Edit (1983). Verbless predicates in Hebrew. PhD thesis, University of Texas at Austin.
Doron, Edit (2003). Bare singular reference to kinds. *Proceedings of Semantics and Linguistic Theory* 13: 73–90.
Doron, Edit (2013). Participle: Modern Hebrew. In Geoffrey Khan (ed.), *Encyclopedia of Hebrew Language and Linguistics*. Leiden: Brill. Available online at http://dx.doi.org/10.1163/
Downer, G. B. (1959). Derivation by tone-change in classical Chinese. *Bulletin of the School of Oriental and African Studies* 22: 258–290.
Drabbe, Petrus (1957). *Spraakkunst van het Aghu Dialect van de Awyu-taal*. The Hague: Martinus Nijhof.
Driem, George van (1987) *Grammar of Limbu*. Berlin: Mouton de Gruyter.
Drude, Sebastian (2002). Fala masculina e feminina em Awetí. In A. S. Cabral & Aryon Rodrigues (eds.), *Línguas Indígenas Brasileiras. Fonologia, Gramática e História. Atas do I Encontro Internacional do GTLI da ANPOLL*. Belém: Editora Universitária UFPA, 177–190.
Drude, Sebastian (2006). On the position of the Awetí language in the Tupí family. In W. Dietrich & H. Symeonidis (eds.), *Guaraní y 'Mawetí-Tupí-Guaraní'. Estudios históricos y descriptivos sobre una familia lingüística de América del Sur*. Münster: LIT Verlag, 11–45.
Drude, Sebastian (2009). Nasal harmony in Awetí and the Mawetí–Guarani family (Tupí). *Amerindia* 32: 239–276.
Drude, Sebastian (2014). Reduplication as a tool for morphological and phonological analysis in Awetí. In Gale Goodwin Gómez & Hein van der Voort (eds.), *Reduplication in South-American Languages*. Leiden: Brill, 185–215.
Druks, J. (2002). Verbs and nouns: A review of the literature. *Journal of Neurolinguistics* 15: 289–315.
Dryer, Matthew S. (1992). The Greenbergian word order correlations. *Language* 68: 81–138.
Dryer, Matthew S. (1997a). Are grammatical relations universal? In Joan Bybee, John Haiman, & Sandra A. Thompson (eds.), *Essays on Language Function and Language Type*. Amsterdam: John Benjamins, 115–143.
Dryer, Matthew S. (1997b). Why statistical universals are better than absolute universals. In Kora Singer, Randall Eggart, & Gregory Anderson (eds.), *CLS 33: Papers from the Panels*. Chicago: Chicago Linguistic Society, 123–145.
Dryer, Matthew S. (2007). Clause types. In Timothy Shopen (ed.), *Language Typology and Syntactic Description* (2nd edn). Cambridge: Cambridge University Press, vol. I, 224–275.
Dryer, Matthew. (2013a). Position of case affixes. In Matthew Dryer & Martin Haspelmath (eds.), *The World Atlas of Language Structures Online*. Leipzig: Max Planck Institute for Evolutionary Anthropology. Available online at http://wals.info/chapter/1
Dryer, Matthew S. (2013b). Order of adposition and noun phrase. In Matthew S. Dryer & Martin Haspelmath (eds.), *The World Atlas of Language Structures Online*. Leipzig: Max Planck Institute for Evolutionary Anthropology. Available online at http://wals.info/chapter/85
Dryer, Matthew S. & Martin Haspelmath (2013). *The World Atlas of Language Structures online*.
Dudis, Paul G. 2004. Body partitioning and real-space blends. *Cognitive Linguistics* 15(2): 223–238. https://doi.org/10.1515/cogl.2004.009
Dumestre, Gérard (2003). *Grammaire fondamentale du bambara*. Paris: Karthala.
Dunn, Michael J. (1999). A grammar of Chukchi. Doctoral dissertation, Canberra, Australian National University.

Dyck, Carrie, et al. (2018). Towards a grammar of Cayuga. Unpublished ms.
Eades, Diana (1979). Gumbaynggir. In R. M. W. Dixon & Barry Blake (eds.), *Handbook of Australian Languages*. Canberra: Australian National University Press, vol. 1, 244–361.
Eastman, Carol M. (1992). Swahili interjections: Blurring language-use/gesture-use boundaries. *Journal of Pragmatics* 18(2–3): 273–287. https://doi.org/10.1016/0378-2166(92)90055-G
Eberhard, David M., Gary F. Simons, & Charles D. Fennig (eds.). (2022). Ethnologue: Languages of the World (25th edn.). Dallas, Texas: SIL International.
Edmonson, Barbara Wedemeyer (1988). A descriptive grammar of Huastec (Potosino Dialect). PhD dissertation, Tulane University.
Edwards, Owen (2020). *Metathesis and Unmetathesis in Amarasi*. (Studies in Diversity Linguistics.) Berlin: Language Science Press. https://langsci-press.org/catalog/book/228
Ehlich, Konrad (1985). The language of pain. *Theoretical Medicine* 6(2): 177–187. doi:10.1007/BF00489662
Ehlich, Konrad (1986). *Interjektionen*. (Linguistische Arbeiten 111.) Tübingen: M. Niemeyer.
Ẹkundayọ, S. A. (1977). Restrictions on personal name sentences in the Yoruba noun phrase. *Anthropological Linguistics* 19(2): 55–77.
Elffers, Els (2007). Interjections: On the margins of language. In S. Matthaios & P. Schmitter (eds.), *Linguistische und epistemologische Konzepte—diachron*. Münster: Nodus, 114–138.
Elffers, Els (2008). Interjections and the language functions debate. *Newsletter—Henry Sweet Society for the History of Linguistic Ideas* 50: 17–29.
Elio, Renee & John R. Anderson (1984). The effects of information order and learning mode on schema abstraction. *Memory & Cognition* 12: 20–30. https://doi.org/10.3758/BF03196994
Ellis, Nick C. & Alan Beaton (1993). Psycholinguistic determinants of foreign language vocabulary learning. *Language Learning* 43: 559–617.
Elmendorf, William W. & Wayne Suttles (1960). Pattern and change in Halkomelem Salish dialects. *Anthropological Linguistics* 2(7): 1–32.
Elšík, Viktor (2009). Loanwords in Selice Romani, an Indo-Aryan language of Slovakia. In Martin Haspelmath & Uri Tadmor (eds.), *Loanwords in the World's Languages: A Comparative Handbook*. Berlin: Mouton de Gruyter, 260–303.
Elšík, Viktor & Yaron Matras (2006). *Markedness and Language Change: The Romani Sample*. Berlin: Mouton de Gruyter.
Elston-Güttler, Kerrie E. & John N. Williams (2008). First language polysemy affects second language meaning interpretation: Evidence for activation of first language concepts during second language reading. *Second Language Research* 24: 167–187.
Embick, David (2000). Features, syntax, and categories in the Latin perfect. *Linguistic Inquiry* 31(2): 185–230.
Embick, David (2014). Phase cycles, φ-cycles and phonological (in)activity. In Sabrina Bendjaballah et al. (eds.), *The Structure of Form and the Form of Structure*. Amsterdam: John Benjamins, 271–286.
Embick, David (2015) *The Morpheme: A Theoretical Introduction*. (Interface Explorations 31.) Boston/Berlin: De Gruyter Mouton
Embick, David & Rolf Noyer (2001). Movement operations after syntax. *Linguistic Inquiry* 32(4): 555–595.
Embick, David & Rolf Noyer (2007). Distributed morphology and the syntax–morphology interface. In Gillian Ramchand & Charles Reiss (eds.), *The Oxford Handbook of Linguistic Interfaces*. Oxford: Oxford University Press, 289–324.

Embick, David & Alec Marantz (2008). Architecture and blocking. *Linguistic Inquiry* 39(1): 1–53.

Emmorey, Karen & Jenny Pyers (2020). Is there an iconic motivation for the morphophonological distinction between noun–verb pairs in ASL? In Andrea Ravignani et al. (eds.), *The Evolution of Language: Proceedings of the 13th International Conference (EvoLang13)*. https://doi.org/10.17617/2.3190925. http://brussels.evolang.org/proceedings/paper.html?nr=132

Emonds, Joseph E. (1985). *A Unified Theory of Syntactic Categories*. Dordrecht: Foris.

Enfield, Nick J. (2004). Adjectives in Lao. In R. M. W. Dixon & Alexandra Y. Aikhenvald (eds.), *Adjective Classes: A Cross-linguistic Typology*. Oxford; Oxford University Press, 323–347.

Enfield, Nick. J. (2006). Heterosemy and the grammar–lexicon trade-off. In Felix K. Ameka, Alan Dench, & Nicholas Evans (eds.), *Catching Language: The Standing Challenge of Grammar Writing*. Berlin: Mouton de Gruyter, 297–320.

Enfield, Nick J. (2007). *A Grammar of Lao*. (Mouton Grammar Library, 38.) New York: Mouton de Gruyter.

Enfield, Nick J. (2014). *Natural Causes of Language: Frames, Biases and Cultural Transmission*. (Conceptual Foundations of Language Science 1.) Berlin: Language Science Press.

Enfield, Nick J., et al. (2013). Huh? What? A first survey in twenty-one languages. In Makoto Hayashi, Geoffrey Raymond, & Jack Sidnell (eds.), *Conversational Repair and Human Understanding*. Cambridge: Cambridge University Press, 343–380.

Enfield, Nick J. & Jack Sidnell (2015). Language structure and social agency: Confirming polar questions in conversation. *Linguistics Vanguard* 1(1): 131–143. https://doi.org/10.1515/lingvan-2014-1008

England, Nora C. (1980). Eating in Mam. *Journal of Mayan Linguistics* 1(2): 26–32.

England, Nora C. (1983). *A Grammar of Mam, a Mayan Language*. Austin: University of Texas Press.

England, Nora C. (1991). Changes in basic word order in Mayan languages. *International Journal of American Linguistics* 57: 446–486.

England, Nora C. (2004). Adjectives in Mam. In R. M. W. Dixon & lexandra Y. Aikhenvald (eds.), *Adjective Classes: A Cross-linguistic Typology*. Oxford: Oxford University Press, 125–146.

England, Nora C. (2011). Plurality agreement in some Eastern Mayan languages. *International Journal of American Linguistics* 77: 397–412.

England, Nora C. (2017). Mam. In Judith Aissen, Nora C. England, & Roberto Zavala Maldonado (eds.), *The Mayan Languages*. London/New York: Routledge, 500–532.

England, Nora C. & Brandon O. Baird (2017). Phonology and phonetics. In Judith Aissen, Nora C. England, & Roberto Zavala Maldonado (eds.), *The Mayan Languages*. London/New York: Routledge, 175–200.

England, Nora C. & Roberto Zavala (2013). Mayan languages. In Mark Aronoff (ed.), *Oxford Bibliographies in Linguistics*. Oxford: Oxford University Press.

Epstein, Samuel, et al. (1998). *A Derivational Approach to Syntactic Relations*. Oxford: Oxford University Press.

Epstein, Samuel & Daniel Seely (2002). *Derivation and Explanation in the Minimalist Program*. Oxford: Blackwell.

Ericcson, K. Anders, William G. Chase, & Steve Faloon (1980). Acquisition of a memory skill. *Science* 208(4448): 1181–1182.

Ernout, Alfred (1945). *Morphologie historique du latin*. Paris: Klincksieck.

Ernst, Thomas (2002). *The Syntax of Adjuncts*. Cambridge: Cambridge University Press.

Espinal, M.Teresa & Louise McNally (2011). Bare nominals and incorporating verbs in Spanish and Catalan. *Journal of Linguistics* 47(1): 87–128.
Evans, Nicholas (1992). 'Wanjh! bonj! nja!': Sequential organization and social deixis in Mayali interjections. *Journal of Pragmatics* 18(2–3). 225–244. https://doi.org/10.1016/0378-2166(92)90053-E
Evans, Nicholas (1995). *A Grammar of Kayardild with Historical-Comparative Notes on Tangkic*. Berlin: Mouton de Gruyter.
Evans, Nicholas (2000). Word classes in the world's languages. In Geert Booij, Christian Lehmann, & Joachim Mugdan (eds.), *Morphology: A Handbook on Inflection and Word Formation* (Handbücher zur Sprach- und Kommunikationswissenschaft). Berlin: Mouton de Gruyter, vol. I, 708–723.
Evans, Nicholas (2003a). *Bininj Gun-Wok: A Pan-dialectal Grammar of Mayali, Kunwinjku and Kune* (2 vols.). (Pacific Linguistics, 541.) Canberra: Research School of Pacific and Asian Studies, Australian National University.
Evans, Nicholas (2003b). Introduction: Comparative non-Pama–Nyungan and Australian historical linguistics. In Nicholas Evans (ed.), *The Non-Pama–Nyungan Languages of Northern Australia: Comparative Studies of the Continent's Most Linguistically Complex Region*. Canberra: Pacific Linguistics, 3–25.
Evans, Nicholas (2007). Insubordination and its uses. In Irina Nicolavea (ed.), *Finiteness: Theoretical and Empirical Foundations*. Oxford: Oxford University Press, 366–431.
Evans, Nicholas (2010). *Dying Words: Endangered Languages and What They Have to Tell Us*. Malden, MA: Wiley-Blackwell, 1–24.
Evans, Nick & Stephen C. Levinson (2009). The myth of language universals: Language diversity and its importance for cognitive science. *Behavioral and Brain Sciences* 32: 429–448. https://doi.org/10.1017/S0140525X0999094X
Evans, Nicholas & Rachel Nordlinger (2004). Extreme morphological shift: Verbal case in Kayardild. Abstract of talk presented at LFG2004 Conference, University of Canterbury. https://minerva-access.unimelb.edu.au/handle/11343/34558
Evans, Nicholas & Toshiki Osada (2005). Mundari: The myth of a language without word classes. *Linguistic Typology* 9(3): 351–390. doi:10.1515/lity.2005.9.3.351
Evans, Vyvyan (2009). Semantic representation in LCCM Theory. In Vyvyan Evans & Stephanie Pourcel (eds.), *New Directions in Cognitive Linguistics*. Amsterdam: John Benjamins, 27–55.
Everett, Daniel (2012). *Language: The Cultural Tool*. London: Profile Books.
Everett, Daniel & Lucy Seki (1985). Reduplication and CV Skeleta in Kamaiurá. *Linguistic Inquiry* 16(2): 326–330.
Eyckmans, June, Frank Boers, & Seth Lindstromberg (2016). The impact of imposing processing strategies on L2 learners' deliberate study of lexical phrases, *System* 56: 127–139.
Ezard, Bryan (1997). *A Grammar of Tawala: An Austronesian Language of the Milne Bay Area, Papua New Guinea*. Canberra: Australian National University.
Fabb, Nigel (2005). *Sentence Structure* (2nd edn). London: Routledge.
Fabb, Nigel (2007). Compounding. In Andrew Spencer & Arnold Zwicky (eds.), *The Handbook of Morphology*. London, Blackwell, 66–83.
Facundes, Sidney da Silva (2000). *The Language of the Apurinã People of Brazil (Maipure/Arawak)*. Buffalo: SUNY.
Faroqi-Shah, Yasmeen, Rajani Sebastian, & Ashlyn Vander Woude (2018). Neural representation of word categories is distinct in the temporal lobe: An activation likelihood analysis. *Human Brain Mapping* 39: 4925–4938.

Farrell, Patrick (2001). Functional shift as category underspecification. *English Language & Linguistics* 5(1): 109–130. doi:10.1017/S1360674301000156

Fassberg, Steven E. (2019). Modern Western Aramaic. In John Huehnergard & Na'ama Pat-El (eds.), *The Semitic Languages*. London: Routledge, 632–652.

Fazio, Patrik, et al. (2010). Encoding of human action in Broca's area. *Brain* 132: 1980–1988.

Fedden, Sebastian (2011). *A Grammar of Mian*. (Mouton Grammar Library, 55.) Berlin/Boston: Mouton de Gruyter.

Fedden, Sebastian (2020). The morphology of Trans New Guinea languages. In *Oxford Research Encyclopedia—Linguistics*. Oxford: Oxford University Press. https://doi.org/10.1093/acrefore/9780199384655.013.633

Fedden, Sebastian, et al. (2013). Conditions on pronominal marking in the Alor–Pantar languages. *Linguistics* 51(1): 33–74.

Fedden, Sebastian, et al. (2014). Variation in pronominal indexing: Lexical stipulation vs. referential properties in the Alor–Pantar languages. *Studies in Language* 38: 44–79.

Fedotov, M. L. (2017). Gban jazyk [The Gban language]. In Valentin Vydrin (ed.), *Jazyki mira: Jazyki mande* [The languages of the world: The Mande languages]. Sankt-Peterburg: Nestor-Istorija, 902–1000.

Fehn, Anne-Maria (2014). A grammar of Ts'ixa (Kalahari Khoe). Doctoral dissertation, Universität zu Köln.

Feist, Jim (2011). *Premodifiers in English: Their Structure and Significance*. Cambridge: Cambridge University Press.

Fenlon, Jordan, et al. (2014). *BSL Signbank: A Lexical Database of British Sign Language*. London: Deafness, Cognition and Language Research Centre, University College London. http://bslsignbank.ucl.ac.uk/dictionary/

Fenlon, Jordan, et al. (2019). Comparing sign language and gesture: Insights from pointing. *Glossa: A Journal of General Linguistics* 4(1): 2. https://doi.org/10.5334/gjgl.499

Fenson, Larry, Philip S. Dale, J. Steven Reznick, Donna Thal, Elizabeth Bates, Jeff Hartung, Stephen Pethick & Judy S. Reilly. 1993. The MacArthur communicative development inventories: user's guide and technical manual. Baltimore: Paul H. Brokes Publishing Company.

Fenwick, Rohan S. H. (2011). *A Grammar of Ubykh*. Munich: Lincom Europa.

Ferrara, Lindsay & Gabrielle Hodge (2018). Language as description, indication, and depiction. *Frontiers in Psychology* 9. https://doi.org/10.3389/fpsyg.2018.00716, https://www.frontiersin.org/articles/10.3389/fpsyg.2018.00716/full

Fieder, Nora, et al. (2014a). From 'some butter' to 'a butter': An investigation of mass and count representation and processing. *Cognitive Neuropsychology* 31: 313–349.

Fieder, Nora, Lyndsey Nickels, & Britta Biedermann (2014b). Representation of mass and count nouns: A review. *Frontiers in Psychology* 5: art. 589.

Fillmore, Charles J. (1997). *Lectures on Deixis*. Stanford, CA: CSLI Publications.

Fillmore, Charles J., Paul Kay, & Mary Catherine O'Connor (1988). Regularity and idiomaticity in grammatical constructions: The case of *let alone*. *Language* 64: 501–538.

Finch, Steven & Nick Chater (1992). Bootstrapping syntactic categories using statistical methods. In D. Daelemans and W. Powers (eds.), *Background and Experiments in Machine Learning of Natural Languages*. 229–236 Tilburg: Institute for Language Technology and Artificial Intelligence.

Finch, Steven & Nick Chater (1994). Distributional bootstrapping: From word class to proto-sentence. In Ashwin Ram & Kurt Eiselt (eds.), *Proceedings of the Sixteenth Annual Conference of the Cognitive Science Society*. New York: Routledge.

Findlay, Jamie Y. (2019). Multiword expressions and the lexicon. D.Phil. thesis, University of Oxford.

Finegan, Edward (2007). *Language: Its Structure and Use* (5th edn). Belmont, CA: Thomson Wadsworth.

Finocchiaro, Chiara, et al. (2008). When nominal features are marked on verbs: A transcranial magnetic stimulation study. *Brain and Language* 104: 113–121.

Finocchiaro, Chiara, et al. (2010). Morphological complexity reveals verb-specific prefontal engagement. *Journal of Neurolinguistics* 23: 553–563.

Fischer, Olga (2007). *Morphosyntactic Change: Functional and Formal Perspectives*. Oxford: Oxford University Press.

Fischer, Olga, Muriel Norde, & Harry Perridon (eds.) (2004). *Up and Down the Cline—The Nature of Grammaticalization*. Amsterdam: John Benjamins.

Fischer, Rafael & Kees Hengeveld (2023.). A'ingae (Cofán). In Patience Epps & Lev Michael (eds.), *Amazonian Languages: An International Handbook*. Berlin: de Gruyter Mouton, 65–124.

Fischer, Wolfdietrich (2002). *A Grammar of Classical Arabic*. New Haven, CT: Yale University Press.

Fisher, Cynthia. 2002. Structural limits on verb mapping: the role of abstract structure in 2.5?year?olds' interpretations of novel verbs. Developmental Science 5(1). 55–64.

Fleck, David W. (2003). A grammar of Matses. Doctoral dissertation, Rice University, Houston.

Fleck, David W. (2007). Evidentiality and double tense in Matses. *Language* 83(3): 589–614.

Fleishman, Suzanne (1982). *The Future in Thought and Language: Diachronic Evidence from Romance*. Cambridge: Cambridge University Press.

Fleming, Harold C. (1969). The classification of West Cushitic within Hamito-Semitic. In Daniel McCall et al. (eds.), *Eastern African History*. Boston University Studies in African History 3. New York: Praeger, 3–27.

Floyd, Simeon (2011). Re-discovering the Quechua adjective. *Linguistic Typology* 15(1): 25–63.

Fodor, István (1959). The origin of grammatical gender (I–II). *Lingua* 8: 1–41.

Fodor, Jerry A. (1983). *Modularity of Mind: An Essay on Faculty Psychology*. Cambridge, MA: MIT Press.

Fodor, Jerry (1995). Thematic roles and modularity. In Gerry T. M. Altmann (ed.), *Cognitive Models of Speech Processing*. Cambridge, MA: MIT Press, 434–456.

Foley, William A. (1991) *The Yimas Language of New Guinea*. Stanford: Stanford University Press.

Foley, William A. (1997). *Anthropological Linguistics: An Introduction*. Oxford: Blackwell.

Foley, William A. (2000). The languages of New Guinea. *Annual Review of Anthropology* 29: 357–404.

Foley, William A. (2014). A comparative look at nominalizations in Austronesian. In I. Wayan Arka & N. L. K. Maas Indrawati (eds.), *Argument Realisations and Related Constructions in Austronesian Languages*. Papers from 12-ICAL. Canberra: Australian National University, vol II, 1–51.

Foley, William A. (2017). The morphosyntactic typology of Papuan languages. In Bill Palmer (ed.), *The Languages and Linguistics of the New Guinea Area: A Comprehensive Guide*. Berlin/New York: Mouton de Gruyter, 895–937.

Foley, William A. & Mike Olson (1985). Clausehood and verb serialization. In Johanna Nichols & Anthony C. Woodbury (eds.), *Grammar Inside and Outside the Clause: Some Approaches to Theory from the Field*. Cambridge: Cambridge University Press, 17–60.

Foley, William & Robert van Valin (1984). *Functional Syntax and Universal Grammar.* Cambridge: Cambridge University Press.
Fonseca-Azevedo, Karina & Suzana Herculano-Houzel (2012). Metabolic constraint imposes tradeoff between body size and number of brain neurons in human evolution. *Proceedings of the National Academic Society USA* 109(45): 18571–18576
Fonteyn, Lauren (2019). *Categoriality in Language Change: The Case of the English Gerund.* Oxford: Oxford University Press.
Foolen, Ad (1997). The expressive function of language: Towards a cognitive semantic approach. In Susanne Niemeier & René Dirven (eds.), *The Language of Emotions: Conceptualization, Expression, and Theoretical Foundation.* Amsterdam: John Benjamins, 15–32.
Foolen, Ad (2004). Expressive binominal NPs in Germanic and Romance languages. In Gunter Radden & Klaus-Uwe Panther (eds.), *Studies in Linguistic Motivation.* Berlin: Mouton de Gruyter, 75–100.
Forchheimer Paul (1953). *The Category of Person in Language.* Berlin: Walter de Gruyter.
Ford, Lysbeth (1998). A description of the Emmi language of the Northern Territory of Australia. Doctoral dissertation, Australian National University, Canberra.
Foreman, John & Brook Danielle Lillehaugen (2017). Positional verbs in Colonial Valley Zapotec. *International Journal of American Linguistics* 83(2): 263–265.
Forker, Diana (2020). Elevation as a grammatical and semantic category of demonstratives. *Frontiers in Psychology* 11.
Forrester, Katerina (2015). The internal structure of the Mawng noun phrase. Thesis, University of Melbourne.
Forst, Martin, Tracy Holloway King, & Tibor Laczkó (2010). Particle verbs in computational LFGs: Issues from English, German, and Hungarian. In Miriam Butt & Tracy Holloway King (eds.), *On-line Proceedings of the LFG2010 Conference.* Stanford, CA: CSLI Publications, 228–248. http://csli-publications.stanford.edu/LFG/15/lfg10.html
Fortescue, Michael (1984). *West Greenlandic.* (Croom Helm Descriptive Grammars.) London: Croom Helm.
Fortescue, Michael (1995). The historical source and typological position of ergativity in Eskimo languages. *Études/Inuit/Studies* 19: 61–75.
Fortescue, Michael, Steven Jacobson, & Lawrence Kaplan (2010). *Comparative Eskimo Dictionary with Aleut Cognates* (2nd edn). Fairbanks, AK: Alaska Native Language Center.
Fortis, Jean-Michel (2018). Anderson's case grammar and the history of localism. In Roger Böhm & Harry van der Hulst (eds.), *Substance-based Grammar: The (Ongoing) Work of John Anderson.* Amsterdam: John Benjamins, 113–198.
Fortuin, Egbert & Jaap Kamphuis (2015). The typology of Slavic aspect: A review of the East-West theory of Slavic aspect. *Russian Linguistics* 39: 163–208.
Fortune, G. (1971). Some notes on ideophones and ideophonic constructions in Shona. *African Studies* 30(3): 237–258.
Fortuny, Jordi (2008). *The Emergence of Order in Syntax.* Amsterdam: John Benjamins.
Foucambert, Denis & Michael Zuniga (2012). Effects of grammatical categories on letter detection in continuous text. *Journal of Psycholinguistic Research* 41: 33–49.
Fowler, Anne E. (1991). How early phonological development might set the stage for phoneme awareness. In Susan A. Brady and Donald P. Shankweiler (eds.), *Phonological Processes in Literacy: A Tribute to Y. Liberman.* New York: Routledge, 97–117.
Frajzyngier, Zygmunt (2002). *A Grammar of Hdi.* Berlin: Mouton de Gruyter.
Frajzyngier, Zygmunt & Erin Shay (eds.) (2012). *The Afroasiatic languages.* Cambridge: Cambridge University Press.

Franceschini, Dulce (1999). La langue Sateré-Mawé: Description et analyse morphosyntaxique. PhD dissertation, Université Paris VII Denis Diderot.

Francez, Itamar & Andrew Koontz-Garboden (2017). *Semantics and Morphosyntactic Variation: Qualities and the Grammar of Property Concepts*. Oxford: Oxford University Press.

Franchetto, Bruna (2006). Are Kuikuro roots lexical categories? In Ximena Lois & Valentina Vapnarsky (eds.), *Lexical Categories and Root Classes in Amerindian Languages*. Berlin: Peter Lang, 33–68

Francis, Elaine J. & Stephen Matthews (2005). A multi-dimensional approach to the category 'verb' in Cantonese. *Journal of Linguistics* 41(2): 269–305. doi:10.1017/S0022226705003270

François, Alexandre (2005). A typological overview of Mwotlap, an Oceanic language of Vanuatu. *Linguistic Typology* 9: 115–146.

François, Alexandre (2017). The economy of word classes in Hiw, Vanuatu: Grammatically flexible, lexically rigid. *Studies in Language* 41(2): 294–357. doi:10.1075/sl.41.2.03fra

Frank, Michael C., et al. (2008). Number as a cognitive technology: Evidence from Pirahã language and cognition. *Cognition* 108: 819–824. https://doi.org/10.1016/j.cognition.2008.04.007

Frawley, William (1992). *Linguistic Semantics*. Mahwah, NJ: Erlbaum.

Frazier, Lyn (1989). Against lexical generation of syntax. In William D. Marslen-Wilson (ed.), *Lexical Representation and Process*. Boston: MIT Press, 505–528.

Frazier, Lyn (2016). Sentence processing: A tutorial review. In Max Coltheart (ed.), *Attention and Performance XII: The Psychology of Reading*. Hillsdale, NJ: Lawrence Elbaum Associates, 559–586. https://doi.org/10.4324/9781315630427

Frege, Gottlob ([1884] 1950). *The Foundations of Arithmetic* (*Die Grundlagen der Arithmetik*, trans. John L. Austin). Oxford: Blackwell.

Frege, Gottlob (1982). Über Sinn und Bedeutung. *Zeitschrift für Philosophie und philosophische Kritik* 100: 25–50. [English trans. in P. Geach & M. Black (eds.), *Translations from the Philosophical Writings of Gottlob Frege*. London: Blackwell, 1960, 566, 78]

Frege, Gottlob ([1903] 1997). *Grundgesetze der Arithmetik*. In Michael Beaney (ed.), *The Frege Reader*. Oxford: Blackwell, 258–289.

Freynik, Suzanne, Kira Gor, & Polly O'Rourke (2017). L2 processing of Arabic derivational morphology. *Mental Lexicon* 12(1): 21–50.

Friederici, Angela D. (1982). Syntactic and semantic processes in aphasic deficits: The availability of prepositions. *Brain and Language* 15: 249–258.

Friederici, Angela D., Paul Schönle, & Merill Garrett (1982). Syntactically and semantically based computations: Processing of prepositions in agrammatism. *Cortex* 19: 133–166.

Friedrich, Paul (1970). Shape in grammar. *Language* 46(2): 379–407.

Friedrich, Paul (1979). *Language, Context, and the Imagination*. Stanford, CA: Stanford University Press.

Fries, Charles C. & Kenneth L. Pike (1949). Coexistent phonemic systems. *Language* 25(1): 29–50.

Fridriksson, Julius, et al. (2015). Chronic Broca's aphasia is caused by damage to Broca's and Wernicke's areas. *Cerebral Cortex* 25: 4689–4696.

Friston, Karl & Stefan Kiebel (2009). Predictive coding under the free-energy principle. *Philosophical Transactions of the Royal Society B: Biological Sciences* 364: 1211–1221. https://doi.org/10.1098/rstb.2008.0300

Fujimori, Atsushi (2012). The association of sound with meaning. In A. M. Di Sciullo (ed.), *Towards a Biolinguistic Understanding of Grammar: Essays on Interfaces*. Amsterdam: John Benjamins, 141–166.

Gabelentz, von der, Georg (1881). *Chinesische Grammatik. Mit Ausschluss des niederen Stiles und der heutigen Umgangssprache*. Leipzig: T. O. Weigel.

Gabarró-López, Sílvia (2019). Describing buoys from the perspective of discourse markers: A cross-genre study of French Belgian Sign Language (LSFB). *Sign Language & Linguistics* 22(2): 210–240. https://doi.org/10.1075/sll.00034.gab

Gaby, Alice R (2017). *A Grammar of Kuuk Thaayorre*. Berlin: Mouton de Gruyter.

Gainotti, Guido, et al. (2008). Cross-modal recognition disorders for persons and other unique entities in a patient with right fronto-temporal degeneration. *Cortex* 44: 238–248.

Gainotti, Guido, et al. (2013). The evaluation of sources of knowledge underlying different conceptual categories. *Frontiers in Human Neuroscience* 7: art. 40.

Galand, Lionel (2010). *Regards sur le berbère*. Milan: Centro Studi Camito-Semitici.

Gallistel, Charles R. (1990). *The Organization of Learning*. Cambridge, MA: MIT Press.

Galloway, Brent (1993). *A Grammar of Upriver Halkomelem*. Berkeley: University of California Press.

Galucio, Ana, et al. (2015). Genealogical relations and lexical distances within the Tupian linguistic family. *Boletim Do Museu Paraense Emílio Goeldi. Ciências Humanas* 10(2): 229–274.

García Velasco, Daniel (1996). English manner satellites in Functional Grammar. *Atlantis* 18(1/2): 149–164.

García Velasco, Daniel (2016). A flexible lexicon for Functional Discourse Grammar. *Linguistics* 54(5): 907–945.

Gardner, Rod (2001). *When Listeners Talk: Response Tokens and Listener Stance*. (Pragmatics & Beyond.) Amsterdam: John Benjamins.

Garvin, Paul L. (1948). Kutenai III: Morpheme distributions (prefix, theme, suffix). *International Journal of American Linguistics* 14(3): 171–187. doi:10.1086/463999

Garvin, Paul L. (1951). Kutenai IV: Word classes. *International Journal of American Linguistics* 17(2): 84–97. doi:10.1086/464111

Garvin, Paul L. (1954). Delimitation of syntactic units. *Language* 30(3): 345–348.

Gasparini, Noé (2011). *L'expression du nombre dans les langues Tupí-Guaraní* [Master 1]. Université Lumière Lyon 2.

Gazdar, Gerald, et al. (1985). *Generalized Phrase Structure Grammar*. Oxford: Basil Blackwell.

Geach, Peter T. (1962). *Reference and Generality*. Ithaca, NY: Cornell University Press.

Geeraerts, Dirk (1988). Where does prototypicality come from? In Brygida Rudzka-Ostyn (ed.), *Topics in Cognitive Linguistics*. Amsterdam: John Benjamins, 207–229.

Geeraerts, Dirk (1989). Introduction: Prospects and problems of prototype theory. *Linguistics* 27: 587–612.

Geeraerts, Dirk (1997). *Diachronic Prototype Semantics: A Contribution to Historical Lexicology*. Oxford: Clarendon Press.

Geeraerts, Dirk (2008). Prototypes, stereotypes and semantic norms. In Gitte Kristiansen & René Dirven (eds.), *Cognitive Sociolinguistics: Language Variation, Cultural Models, Social Systems*. Berlin: Mouton de Gruyter, 21–44.

Geerts, Guido, et al. (1984). *Algemene Nederlandse Spraakkunst*. Groningen: Wolters-Noordhoff.

Geertz, Clifford (1973). *The Interpretation of Cultures*. New York: Basic Books.

Genee, Inge, Evelien Keizer, & Daniel García Velasco (2016). The lexicon in Functional Discourse Grammar: Theory, typology, description. *Linguistics* 54(5): 877–906.

Gennetti, Carol & Kristine Hildebrandt (2004). The two adjective classes in Manange. In R. M. W. Dixon & Alexandra Y. Aikhenvald (eds.), *Adjective Classes, A Cross-linguistic Typology*. Oxford: Oxford University Press, 74–96.

Gentner, Dedre. 1982. Why nouns are learned before verbs: linguistic relativity versus natural partitioning. In Stan A. Kuczaj (ed.), Language development, vol. 2, 38–62. Hillsdale, NJ: Lawrence Erlbaum Associates.

Gentner, Dedre (2001). Spatial metaphors in temporal reasoning. In Merideth Gattis (ed.), *Spatial Schemas in Abstract Thought*. Cambridge, MA: MIT Press, 203–222.

Georg, Stefan (2007). *A descriptive grammar of Ket (Yenisei-Ostyak): Part 1, Introduction, Phonology, Morphology*. (Languages of Asia series, 1.) Folkestone: Kent: Global Oriental.

Gentner, Dedre. 2006. Why verbs are hard to learn. In Kathryn Hirsh-Pasek & Roberta M. Golinkoff (eds.), Action meets words: how children learn verbs, 544–564. Oxford: Oxford University Press.

Gentner, Dedre & Lera Boroditsky. 2001. Individuation, relativity, and early word learning. In Melissa Bowerman & Stephen C. Levinson (eds.), Language acquisition and conceptual development, 215–256. Cambridge: Cambridge University Press.

Georgiev, Vladimir (1981). *Introduction to the History of the Indo-European Languages*. Sofia: Bulgarian Academy of Sciences.

Gerasimov, Dmitry (2016). *Predicative Possession in Paraguayan Guaraní: Against the Zero Copula Hypothesis*. Typology of Morphosyntactic Parameters 2016.

Gerdts, Donna B. (1977). A dialect survey of Halkomelem Salish. MA thesis, University of British Columbia.

Gerdts, Donna B. (1988). *Object and Absolutive in Halkomelem Salish*. New York: Garland.

Gerdts, Donna B. (2000). The combinatorial properties of Halkomelem lexical suffixes. In Steve S. Chang (ed.), *Proceedings of the Twenty-fifth Annual Meeting of the Berkeley Linguistics Society*. University of California, Berkeley, CA, 337–347.

Gerdts, Donna B. (2003). The morphosyntax of Halkomelem lexical suffixes. *International Journal of American Linguistics* 69(4): 345–356.

Gerdts, Donna B. (2010). Three doubling constructions in Halkomelem. In Donna B. Gerdts, John Moore, & Maria Polinsky (eds.), *Hypothesis A/Hypothesis B: Linguistic Explorations in Honor of David M. Perlmutter*. Cambridge, MA: MIT Press, 183–202.

Gerdts, Donna B. (2012). What agreement mismatches in Halkomelem tell us about NP architecture. Presented at LSA 86th Annual Meeting, Portland, OR.

Gerdts, Donna B. (2013a). The purview effect: Feminine gender on inanimates in Halkomelem Salish. *Berkeley Linguistics Society* 37: 417–426.

Gerdts, Donna B. (2013b). Salish languages. In *Oxford Bibliographies Online*. Oxford University Press.

Gerdts, Donna B. (2016). In-subordination and un-coordination in Hul'q'umi'num' (with some special attention to temporal adverbials), Presented at *SWL 7*.

Gerdts, Donna B. (2017). A deluge of diminutives: A study in Halkomelem morphosemantics. Presented at Linguistic Society of America Annual Meeting, Austin, TX.

Gerdts, Donna B. & Nancy Hedberg (2020). Demonstratives in Hul'q'umi'num' discourse. Presented at SSILA, New Orleans.

Gerdts, Donna B. & Mercedes Q. Hinkson (1996) Salish lexical suffixes: A case of decategorialization. In Adelee Goldberg (ed.), *Proceedings of the Conference on Conceptual Structure, Discourse, and Language, CSLI*. Stanford, CA, 163–176.

Gerdts, Donna B. & Mercedes Q. Hinkson (2004). The grammaticalization of Halkomelem 'face' into a dative applicative suffix. *International Journal of American Linguistics* 70(3): 227–250.

Gerdts, Donna B. & Thomas E. Hukari (1998). Inside and outside the middle. *Papers for the 33rd International Conference on Salish and Neighboring Languages*, Seattle, Washington, 166–220.

Gerdts, Donna B. & Thomas E. Hukari (2005). Multiple antipassives in Halkomelem Salish. In Lisa J. Conathan (ed.), *Proceedings of the Twenty-sixth Annual Meeting of the Berkeley Linguistics Society, University of California*. Berkeley, CA, 51–62

Gerdts, Donna B. & Thomas E. Hukari (2008). Halkomelem denominal verb constructions. *International Journal of American Linguistics* 74(4): 489–510.

Gerdts, Donna B. & Lauren Schneider (2021). Balancing act: A case study of the distribution of NPs and Vs in Hul'q'umi'num' texts. Presented at the 23rd Annual Workshop on American Indigenous Languages, hosted online by UC Santa Barbara.

Gerdts, Donna B. & Adam Werle (2014). Halkomelem clitic types. *Morphology* 24: 245–281.

Gerken, L. 2001. Signal to syntax. In Harald Clahsen & Lydia White (eds.), Approaches to bootstrapping: Phonological, lexical, syntact and neurophysiological aspects of early language acquisition, 147–166. John Benjamins Publishing.

Gerken, LouAnn. 1996. Phonological and distributional information in syntax acquisition. In Morgan James & Katherine A. Demuth (eds.), Signal to syntax: bootstrapping from speech to grammar in early acquisition, 411–425. Lawrence Erlbaum Mahwah, NJ.

Gerken, Louann, Rachel Wilson & William Lewis. 2005. Infants can use distributional cues to form syntactic categories. Journal of child language 32(02). 249–268.

Ghiselin, Michael T. (1974). A radical solution to the species problem. *Systematic Zoology* 23: 536–544.

Giacalone Ramat, Anna & Paolo Ramat (eds.) (1993). *Le lingue indoeuropee*. Bologna: Il Mulino. [Engl. trans., *The Indo-European Languages*. London: Routledge, 1998]

Gibson, Edward, et al. (2019). How efficiency shapes human language. *Trends in Cognitive Sciences* 23(5): 389–407. doi:10.1016/j.tics.2019.02.003

Gil, David (1993). Syntactic categories in Tagalog. *Pan-Asiatic Linguistics: Proceedings of the Third International Symposium on Languages and Linguistics Bangkok January 8–10 1991*, ed. Sudaporn Luksaneeyanawin. Bangkok: Chulalongkorn University Press, 1136–1150.

Gil, David (1996). Maltese 'collective nouns': A typological perspective. *Italian Journal of Linguistics* 8(1): 53–87.

Gil, David (2000). Syntactic categories, cross-Linguistic variation and Universal Grammar. In Petra M. Vogel & Bernard Comrie (eds.), *Approaches to the Typology of Word Classes*. Berlin: Mouton de Gruyter, 173–216.

Gil, David (2005). Adjectives without nouns. In Martin Haspelmath et al. (eds.), *The World Atlas of Language Structures*. Oxford: Oxford University Press. https://wals.info/chapter/61

Gil, David (2013a). Riau Indonesian: A language without nouns and verbs. In Jan Rijkhoff & Eva van Lier (eds.), *Flexible Word Classes: Typological Studies of Underspecified Parts of Speech*. Oxford: Oxford University Press, 89–130.

Gil, David (2013b). Para-Linguistic usages of clicks. In Matthew S. Dryer & Martin Haspelmath (eds.), *The World Atlas of Language Structures Online*. Leipzig: Max Planck Institute for Evolutionary Anthropology. http://wals.info/chapter/142

Gil, David (2013c). Word order without syntactic categories: How Riau Indonesian does it. In Andrew Carnie, Sheila Dooley, & Heidi Harley (eds.), *Verb First: On the Syntax of Verb-Initial Languages*. Amsterdam: John Benjamins, 243–263.

Gil, David (2015). The Mekong–Mamberamo linguistic area. In Nick J. Enfield & Bernard Comrie (eds.), *Languages of Mainland Southeast Asia: The State of the Art*. Berlin: De Gruyter Mouton, 266–355.

Gil, David (2016). Describing languoids: When incommensurability meets the language-dialect continuum. *Linguistic Typology* 20: 439–462.

Gillette, Jane, Henry Gleitman, Lila Gleitman & Anne Lederer. 1999. Human simulations of vocabulary learning. Cognition 73. 135–176.

Gillon, Carrie (2013). *The Semantics of Determiners: Domain Restriction in Skwxwu7mesh*. Cambridge: Cambridge Scholars Press.

Ginzburg, Jonathan & Ivan Sag. (2000). *Interrogative Investigations*. Stanford, CA: CSLI Publications.

Givón, Talmy (1971). Historical syntax and synchronic morphology: An archeologist's field trip. *Chicago Linguistics Society* 7: 394–415.

Givón, Talmy (1979). *On Understanding Grammar*. New York: Academic Press.

Givón, Talmy (1980). The binding hierarchy and the typology of complements. *Studies in Language* 4(4): 333–377.

Givón, Talmy (1984). *Syntax: A Functional-Typological Introduction*. Amsterdam: John Benjamins, vol. I.

Givón, Talmy (1986). Prototypes: Between Plato and Wittgenstein. In Colette Craig (ed.), *Noun Classes and Categorization*. Amsterdam: John Benjamins, 77–102.

Givón, Talmy (1990). *Syntax: A Functional-Typological Introduction*. Amsterdam: John Benjamins, vol. II.

Givón, Talmy (1995). *Functionalism and Grammar*. Amsterdam: John Benjamins.

Givón, Talmy (2001). *Syntax: An Introduction*. Amsterdam: John Benjamins, vol. I.

Glanville, Peter John (2018). *The Lexical Semantics of the Arabic Verb*. Oxford: Oxford University Press.

Glanzberg, Michael (2006). Quantifiers. In Ernest Lepore & Barry C. Smith (eds.), *The Oxford Handbook of Philosophy of Language*. Oxford: Oxford University Press, 794–821.

Gleitman, Lila R. 1990. The structural sources of verb meanings. Language Acquisition 1. 3–55.

Geitman, Lila R, Kimberly Cassidy, Rebecca Nappa, Anna Papafragou & John C Trueswell. 2005. Hard words. Language learning and development 1(1). 23–64.

Gleitman, Lila R, Henry Gleitman, Barbara Landau & Eric Wanner. 1988. Where learning begins: Initial representations for language learning.

Gobet, Fernand, et al. (2001). Chunking mechanisms in human learning. *Trends in Cognitive Sciences* 5(6): 236–243. https://doi.org/10.1016/S1364-6613(00)01662-4

Goddard, Cliff (1985). *A Grammar of Yankunytjatjara*. Alice Springs: Institute for Aboriginal Development.

Goddard, Cliff (2001). Universal units in the lexicon. In Martin Haspelmath et al. (eds.), *Language Typology and Language Universals: An International Handbook*. Berlin/New York: Walter de Gruyter, vol. II, 1192–1203.

Godfroid, Aline, Frank Boers, & Alex Housen (2013). An eye for words: Gauging the role of attention in incidental L2 vocabulary acquisition by means of eye-tracking. *Studies in Second Language Acquisition* 35: 483–517.

Goffman, Erving (1978). Response cries. *Language* 54(4): 787–815.

Göksel, Asli & Celia Kerslake (2005). *Turkish: A Comprehensive Grammar*. London/New York: Routledge.

Goldberg, Adele E. (1995). *Constructions: A Construction Grammar Approach to Argument Structure*. Chicago: University of Chicago Press.

Goldberg, Adele E. (2006). *Constructions at Work: The Nature of Generalization in Language*. Oxford: Oxford University Press. https://doi.org/10.1093/acprof:oso/9780199268511.001.0001

Goldenberg, Georg (2009). Apraxia and the parietal lobes. *Neuropsychologia* 47: 1449–14459.

Goldin-Meadow, et al. (2015). Watching language grow in the manual modality: Nominals, predicates, and handshapes. *Cognition* 136: 381–395. https://doi.org/10.1016/j.cognition.2014.11.029

Golinkoff, Roberta M., Kathryn Hirsh-Pasek & MA Schweisguth. 2001. A reappraisal of young children's knowledge of grammatical morphemes. In Harald Clahsen & Lydia White (eds.), Approaches to bootstrapping: Phonological, lexical, syntact and neurophysiological aspects of early language acquisition, vol. 1, 167–189. John Benjamins Publishing.

Golinkoff, Roberta Michnick & Kathy Hirsh-Pasek. 2008. How toddlers begin to learn verbs. Trends in Cognitive Sciences 12(10). 397–403.

Golla, Victor K. (1970). Hupa grammar. PhD dissertation, University of California at Berkeley.

Gómez, Rebecca L & LouAnn Gerken. 2000. Infant artificial language learning and language acquisition. Trends in Cognitive Sciences 4(5). 178–186.

Gómez, Rebecca L & Laura Lakusta. 2004. A first step in form-based category abstraction by 12-month-old infants. Developmental Science 7(5). 567–580.

Gómez Cruz, José (2010). Adjetivos en tojol-ab'al. MA thesis, CIESAS, Mexico.

Gómez Rendón, Jorge A. (2008). *Typological and Social Constraints on Language Contact: Amerindian Languages in Contact with Spanish*. Utrecht: LOT.

González, Hebe (2005). A grammar of Tapiete (Tupi–Guarani). PhD, University of Pittsburgh.

Goodman, Nelson (1966). *The Structure of Appearance* (2nd edn). Indianapolis: Bobbs-Merrill.

Goodwin, Charles (1986). Between and within: Alternative sequential treatments of continuers and assessments. *Human Studies* 9(2/3): 205–217.

Gopnik, Alison. 1988. Three types of early words: the emergence of social words, names and cognitive-relational words in the one-word stage and their relation to cognitive development. First Language 8. 49–69.

Gordon, Lynn (1986). *Maricopa Morphology and Syntax*. Berkeley: University of California Press.

Gordon, Peter (2004). Numerical cognition without words: Evidence from Amazonia. *Science* 306 (5695): 496–499. https://doi.org/10.1126/science.1094492

Gordon, Peter (2010). Worlds without words: Commensurability and causality in language, culture, and cognition. In Barbara Malt & Phillip Wolff (eds.), *Words and the Mind: How Words Capture Human Experience*. Oxford: Oxford University Press, 199–218. https://doi.org/10.1093/acprof:oso/9780195311129.003.0011

Görgülü, Emrah (2012). Semantics of nouns and the specification of number in Turkish. PhD dissertation Simon Fraser University (British Columbia, Canada).

Görgülü, Emrah (2018). Nominals and number neutrality in languages. *Language and Linguistics Compass* 12(10): e12301. https://doi.org/10.1111/lnc3.12301

Gorno-Tempini, M. L. & C. J. Price (2001). Identification of famous faces and buildings: A functional neuroimaging study of semantically unique items. *Brain* 124: 2087–2097.

Gotham, Matthew (2017). Composing criteria of individuation in copredication. *Journal of Semantics* 34(2): 333–371.

Gotham, Matthew (2021). Event-related readings and degrees of difference. In Luisa Martí, Hazel Pearson, & Yasutada Sudo (eds.), *Proceedings of Sinn und Bedeutung 25*. Konstanz: University of Konstanz.

Grabowski, Thomas J., et al. (2001). A role for the left temporal pole in the retrieval of words for unique entities. *Human Brain Mapping* 13: 199–212.

Grace, George (1987). *The Linguistic Construction of Reality*. London: Croom Helm.

Graczyk, Randolph (2007). *A Grammar of Crow: Apsáalooke Aliláau*. Lincoln: University of Nebraska Press.

Gragg, Gene & Robert Hoberman (2012). Semitic. In Zygmunt Frajzyngier & Erin Shay (eds.), *The Afroasiatic languages*. Cambridge: Cambridge University Press, 145–235.

Grant, Anthony P. (1996). The evolution of functional categories in Grand Ronde Chinook Jargon: Ethnolinguistic and grammatical considerations. In Philip Baker & Anand Syea (eds.), *Changing Meanings, Changing Functions: Papers Relating to Grammaticalization in Contact Languages*. (Westminster Creolistics Series, 2.) London: University of Westminster Press, 225–242.

Gravelle, Gloria (2010). A grammar of Moskona: An East Bird's Head language of West Papua, Indonesia. Doctoral dissertation, Vrije Universiteit Amsterdam.

Green, David W. (1998). Mental control of the bilingual lexico-semantic system. *Bilingualism: Language and Cognition* 1: 67–81. https://doi.org/10.1017/s1366728998000133

Green, Lisa J. (2002). *African American English: A Linguistic Introduction*. Cambridge: Cambridge University Press.

Greenberg, Joseph H. (ed.) (1963a). *Universals of Language*. Cambridge, MA: MIT Press.

Greenberg, Joseph H. (1963b). Some universals of grammar with particular reference to the order of meaningful elements. In Joseph H. Greenberg (ed.), *Universals of Language*. Cambridge, MA: MIT Press, 58–90.

Greenberg, Joseph H. (1963c). *The Languages of Africa*. Bloomington, IN: Indiana University Press.

Greenberg, Joseph H. (1966). Some universals of grammar with particular reference to the order of meaningful elements. In Joseph H. Greenberg (ed.), *Universals of Grammar* (2nd edn). Cambridge, MA: MIT Press, 73–113. [reprinted in Joseph H. Greenberg, *On language*, Stanford: Stanford University Press, 1990, 40–70]

Greenberg, Joseph H. (1972). Numeral classifiers and substantival number: Problems in the genesis of a linguistic type. *Working Papers on Language Universals* 9 (Stanford University): 2–39.

Greenberg, Joseph H. (1978). How does a language acquire gender markers? In Joseph H. Greenberg, Charles A. Ferguson, & Edith A. Moravcsik (eds.), *Universals of Human Language. Vol. 3: Word Structure*. Stanford: Stanford University Press, 48–82.

Greenberg, Joseph H. (1981). Nilo-Saharan moveable -*k* as a Stage III article (with a Penutian typological parallel). *Journal of African Languages and Linguistics* 3: 105–112.

Greenberg, Joseph H. (1991). The last stages of grammatical elements: Contrastive and expansive desemanticization. In Elizabeth Closs Traugott & Bernd Heine (eds.), *Approaches to Grammaticalization*. Amsterdam: John Benjamins, vol. I, 301–314.

Grégoire, Claire (1990). Etude comparative des items pour 'boire' et 'manger' dans les langues mandé. *Mandenkan* 19: 39–46.

Gregores, Emma & Jorge A. Suárez (1967). *A Description of Colloquial Guaraní*. The Hague: Mouton.

Grenoble, Lenore A. (2014). Verbal gestures: Toward a field-based approach to language description. In Vladimir A. Plungian, et al. (eds.), Язык, константы, переменные: памяти Александра Евгеньевича Кибрика: сборник статей = *Language, constants, variables: in memory of E. Alexander Kibrik*. Saint Petersburg: Алетейя, 105–118.

Grice, P. H. (1975). Logic and conversation. In Peter Cole & Jerry L. Morgan (eds.), *Speech Acts*. New York: Academic Press, 41–58.

Grimm, Scott (2012). Individuation and inverse number marking in Dagaare. In Diane Massam (ed.), *Count and Mass across Languages*. Oxford: Oxford University Press, 75–98.

Grimshaw, Jane. 1981. Form, function, and the language acquisition device. The logical problem of language acquisition 165: 178.
Grimshaw, Jane (1990). *Argument Structure*. Cambridge, MA: MIT Press.
Grimshaw, Jane (1991). Extended projection. Unpublished ms, Brandeis University, MA. [also appeared in J. Grimshaw, *Words and Structure*. Stanford: CSLI, 2005]
Grimshaw, Jane (1997). Projections, heads and optimality. *Linguistic Inquiry* 28: 373–442.
Grimshaw, Jane (1998). Locality and extended projection. In Peter Coopmans, Martin Everaert, & Jane Grimshaw (eds.), *Lexical Specification and Insertion*. Mahwah, NJ: Erlbaum, 115–133.
Grimshaw, Jane (2005). Extended projection. In Jane Grimshaw (ed.), *Words and Structure*. Stanford, CA: CSLI Publications, 1–74.
Grinevald, Colette (2000). A morphosyntactic typology of classifiers. In Gunter Senft (ed.), *Systems of Nominal Classification*. New York: Cambridge University Press, 50–92.
Grinevald, Colette (2005). Classifiers. In Geert Booij et al. (eds.), *Morphology: A Handbook on Inflection and Word Formation*. Berlin: Walter de Gruyter, vol. II, 1016–1031.
Grinevald, Colette (2007). The linguistic characterization of spatial entities: Classifiers and other nominal classification systems. In Michel Aurnague, Maya Hickmann, & Laure Vieu (eds.), *The Categorization of Spatial Entities in Language and Cognition*. Amsterdam: John Benjamins, 93–121.
Gross, Maurice (1979). On the failure of generative grammar. *Language* 55: 859–885.
Grossman, Eitan (2017). Targeting language contact in typological research: A case study on adposition borrowing. Paper delivered at TyLex.
Guérin, Valérie (2015). Demonstrative verbs: A typology of verbal manner deixis. *Linguistic Typology* 19: 141–199.
Guillaume, Antoine (2008). *A Grammar of Cavineña*. Vol. 44. Berlin: de Gruyter.
Güldemann, Tom (2008). *Quotative Indexes in African Languages: A Synchronic and Diachronic Survey*. Berlin: Mouton de Gruyter.
Güldemann, Tom (2018). Historical linguistics and genealogical language classification in Africa. In Tom Güldemann (ed.), *African Languages and Linguistics*. Berlin: DeGruyter Mouton, 58–444.
Gumperz, John J. & Stephen C. Levinson (eds.) (1996). *Rethinking Linguistic Relativity*. Cambridge: Cambridge University Press.
Guo, Rui (郭锐). (2018) [2002¹]. 现代汉语词类研究 *Xiàndài hànyǔ cílèi yánjiū* [Research on Parts of Speech in Modern Chinese], 3rd rev. edn. Shanghai: Commercial Press.
Guo, Yuqing, Josef van Genabith, & Haifeng Wang (2007). Treebank-based acquisition of LFG resources for Chinese. In Miriam Butt & Tracy Holloway King (eds.), *On-line Proceedings of the LFG2007 Conference*. Stanford, CA: CSLI Publications. http://web.stanford.edu/group/cslipublications/cslipublications/LFG/LFG-2007/index.shtml
Gupta, Anil (1980). *The Logic of Common Nouns: An Investigation in Quantified Modal Logic*. New Haven, CT: Yale University Press.
Gusev, Valentin Yu (2005). *Tipologija specializirovannyx form imperativa* [Typology of specialized imperative forms]. RAN candidate degree dissertation, Institut jazykoznanija, Moscow.
Gusev, Valentin Yu (2013). *Tipologija imperativnyx konstrukcij* [Typology of imperative constructions]. Moscow: Jazyki slavjanskoj kul'tury.
Gutiérrez Bravo, Rodrigo (2002). Formas verbales incorporadas transitivas en maya yucateco. In Paulette Levy (ed.), *Del cora al maya yucateco: Estudios lingüísticos sobre algunas lenguas indígenas mexicanas*. México City: UNAM, 131–178.

Gutiérrez Sanchez, Pedro & Roberto Zavala (2005). Chol and Chontal: Two Mayan languages of the agentive type. Paper presented at the Typology of Stative–Active Languages, MPI for Evolutionary Anthropology, Leipzig, Germany.

Haan, Johnson Welem (2001). The grammar of Adang: A Papuan language spoken on the Island of Alor East Nusa Tenggara—Indonesia. PhD thesis, University of Sydney, Sydney. http://www-personal.arts.usyd.edu.au/jansimps/haan/

Haegeman, Liliane (2012). The syntax of MCP: Deriving the truncation account. In Aelbrecht Lobke, Liliane Haegeman, & Rachel Nye (eds.), *Main Clause Phenomena: New Horizons* [Linguistik Aktuell/Linguistics Today 190]. Amsterdam/Philadelphia: Benjamins, 113–134.

Hagège, Claude (2010). *Adpositions*. Oxford: Oxford University Press.

Hagemeijer, Tjerk & Ota Ogie (2011). Edo influence on Santome: Evidence from verb serialization and beyond. In Claire Lefebvre (ed.), *Creoles, Their Substrates, and Language Typology*. Amsterdam: John Benjamins, 37–60.

Haghighi, Aria & Dan Klein (2006). Prototype-driven learning for sequence models. In *Proceedings of NAACL 2006*. Morristown, NJ, 320–327.

Hagman, Roy Stephen (1973). Nama Hottentot grammar. Dissertation, University of Columbia, New York.

Haig, Geoffrey (2006). Word-class distinctions and morphological type: Agglutinating and fusional languages reconsidered. Unpublished ms: https://www.academia.edu/9785467/Word_class_distinctions_and_morphological_type_agglutinating_and_fusional_languages_reconsidered

Haiman, John (2018). *Ideophones and the Evolution of Language*. Cambridge: Cambridge University Press.

Hakimov, Nikolay (2016). Explaining variation in plural marking of single German noun insertions in Russian sentences. In Harald Beherens & Stefan Pfänder (eds.), *Experience Counts: Frequency Effects in Language*. Berlin: Mouton de Gruyter, 21–260.

Hale, Ken (1982). Some essential features of Warlpiri verbal clauses. In Stephen Swartz (ed.), *Papers in Warlpiri Grammar: In Memory of Lothar Jagst*. Darwin: Summer Institute of Linguistics, 217–315.

Hale, Ken (1983). Warlpiri and the grammar of non-configurational languages. *Natural Language and Linguistic Theory* 1: 5–74.

Hale, Kenneth & Samuel J. Keyser (2002). *Prolegomenon to a Theory of Argument Structure*. Cambridge, MA: MIT Press.

Halle, Morris & Alec Marantz (1993). Distributed morphology and the pieces of inflection. In Kenneth Hale & Samual Keyser (eds.), *The View from Building 20, Essays in Linguistics in Honor of Sylvain Bromberger*. Cambridge, MA: MIT Press, 111–176.

Halle, Morris & Alec Marantz (1994). Some key features of distributed morphology. In Andrew Carnie & Heidi Harley (eds.), *Papers on Phonology and Morphology*, MITWPL 21, 275–288.

Haller, Sven, et al. (2005). Overt sentence production in event-related fMRI. *Neuropsychologia* 43: 807–814.

Hallonsten Halling, Pernilla (2018). Adverbs: A typological study of a disputed category. PhD thesis, Stockholm University, Stockholm.

Hamilton, Antonia F. & Scott T. Grafton (2008). The motor hierarchy: From kinematics to goals and intentions. In P. Haggard, Y. Rossetti, & M. Kawato (eds.), *Sensorimotor Foundations of Higher Cognition*. New York: Oxford University Press, 381–407.

Hammarström, Harald, et al. (2020). Glottolog 4.2.1. Jena: Max Planck Institute for the Science of Human History. Available online at http://glottolog.org

Han, Chung-hye (2000). *The Structure and Interpretation of Imperatives: Mood and Force in Universal Grammar*. New York: Garland.
Hanks, William F. (1990). *Referential Practice: Language and Lived Space among the Maya*. Chicago/London: University of Chicago Press.
Hanks, William F. (2005). Explorations in the deictic field. *Current Anthropology* 46(2): 191–220.
Hannss, Katja & Pieter Muysken. (2014) Reduplication in the languages of the Andes. In H. van der Voort & G. Goodwin Gómez (eds.), *Reduplication in South American Indian Languages*. Leiden: Brill, 39–76.
Harbour, Daniel (2020). Frankenduals. Their typology, structure and significance. *Language* 96(1): 60–93.
Harbsmeier, Christoph (1979). *Wilhelm von Humboldts Brief an Abel-Rémusat und die philosophische Grammatik des Altchinesischen*. Stuttgart: Friedrich Frommann Verlag.
Harbsmeier, Christoph (1998). *Science and Civilization in China* (Part I: Language and Logic). Cambridge: Cambridge University Press, vol. VII.
Harder, Peter (1996). *Functional Semantics: A Theory of Meaning, Structure and Tense in English*. Berlin: Mouton de Gruyter.
Harder, Peter (2010). *Meaning in Mind and Society*. Berlin: Mouton de Gruyter.
Hare, Mary, Ken McRae, & Jeffrey L. Elman (2003). Sense and structure: Meaning as a determinant of verb subcategorization preferences. *Journal of Memory and Language* 48(2): 281–303. https://doi.org/10.1016/S0749-596X(02)00516-8
Hare, Mary, Ken McRae & Jeffrey L. Elman (2004). Admitting that admitting verb sense into corpus analyses makes sense. *Language and Cognitive Processes* 19(2): 181–224. https://doi.org/10.1080/01690960344000152
Harley, Heidi (2006). *English Words: A Linguistic Introduction*. New York: Wiley.
Harley, Heidi (2014). On the Identity of Roots. *Theoretical Linguistics* 40(3): 225–276.
Harley, Heidi & Rolf Noyer (1998). Licensing in the non-lexicalist lexicon: Nominalizations, vocabulary items and the encyclopedia. In Heidi Harley (ed.), *MITWPL 32: Papers from the UPenn/MIT Roundtable on Argument Structure and Aspect*. Cambridge, MA: MITWPL, 119–137.
Harley, Heidi & Rolf Noyer (1999). State-of-the-article: Distributed morphology. *Glot-International* 4(4): 3–8.
Harley, Heidi & Elizabeth Ritter (2002). A feature-geometric analysis of person and number. *Language* 78: 482–526.
Harley, Heidi, Mercedes Tubino, & Jason D. Haugen (2017). Locality conditions on suppletive verbs in Hiaki. In Vera Gribanova & Stephanie S. Shih (eds.), *The Morphosyntax–Phonology Connection: Locality and Directionality at the Interface*. Oxford: Oxford University Press, 91–111.
Harlow, Ray (2007). *Māori: A Linguistic Introduction*. Cambridge: Cambridge University Press.
Harlow, Ray (2001/2018). *A Māori Reference Grammar*. Auckland: Pearson Education New Zealand Limited.
Harms, Phillip Lee (1994). *Epena Pedee Syntax*. Dallas: Summer Institute of Linguistics and University of Texas at Arlington.
Harriehausen, Bettina (1990). *Hmong Njua: syntaktische Analyse einder gesprochenen Sprache mithilfe datenverarbeitungstechnischer Mittel und sprachvergleichende Beschreibung des südostasiatischen Sprachraumes* [Linguistische Arbeiten 245]. Tübingen: Niemeyer.
Harris, Alice H. (2017). *Multiple Exponence*. Oxford: Oxford University Press.

Harris, Martin (1978). *The Evolution of French Syntax: A Comparative Approach.* London: Longman.

Harris, Zellig S. (1951). *Methods in Structural Linguistics.* Chicago: University of Chicago Press.

Harris, Zellig S. (1954). Distributional structure. *WORD.* https://doi.org/10.1080/00437956.1954.11659520

Hartmann, Stefan (2014). 'Nominalization' taken literally: A diachronic corpus study of German word-formation patterns. *Italian Journal of Linguistics* 26(2): 123–156.

Harvey, Mark (1986). Ngoni Waray Amungal-yang: The Waray language from Adelaide River. MA thesis, Australian National University, Canberra.

Harvey, Mark (2002). *A Grammar of Gaagudju.* Berlin: Mouton de Gruyter.

Harvey, Mark & Nicholas Reid (eds.) (1997). *Nominal Classification in Aboriginal Australia.* Amsterdam: John Benjamins.

Hashimoto, Brett J. & Jesse Egbert (2019). More than frequency? Exploring predictors of word difficulty for second language learners. *Language Learning* 69: 839–872.

Haspelmath, Martin (1993a). *A Grammar of Lezgian.* (Mouton Grammar Library 9.) Berlin: Mouton de Gruyter.

Haspelmath, Martin (1993b). Passive participles across languages. In Barbara Fox & Paul J. Hopper (eds.), *Voice: Form and Function.* Amsterdam: John Benjamins, 151–178.

Haspelmath, Martin (1993c). More on the typology of inchoative/causative verb alternation. In Bernard Comrie & Maria Polinsky (eds.), *Causatives and Transitivity.* Amsterdam: John Benjamins, 87–120.

Haspelmath, Martin (1995). The converb as a cross linguistically valid category. In Martin Haspelmath & Ekkehard König (eds.), *Converbs in Cross-Linguistic Perspective: Structure and Meaning of Adverbial Verb Forms—Adverbial Participles, Gerunds.* Berlin/New York: Mouton de Gruyter, 1–55.

Haspelmath, Martin (1998). Does grammaticalization need reanalysis? *Studies in Language* 22(2): 315–351.

Haspelmath, Martin (2003). The geometry of grammatical meaning: Semantic maps and cross-linguistic comparison. In Michael Tomasello (ed.), *The New Psychology of Language.* Mahwah, NJ: Erlbaum, vol. II, 211–242.

Haspelmath, Martin (2004). On directionality in language change with particular reference to grammaticalization. In Olga Fischer, Muriel Norde, & Harry Perridon (eds.), *Up and Down the Cline: The Nature of Grammaticalization.* Amsterdam: John Benjamins, 17–44.

Haspelmath, Martin (2007). Pre-established categories don't exist: Consequences for language description and typology. *Linguistic Typology* 11(1): 119–132.

Haspelmath, Martin (2005). Argument marking in ditransitive alignment types. *Linguistic Discovery* 3(1): 1–21.

Haspelmath, Martin (2007). Pre-established categories don't exist: Consequences for language description and typology. *Linguistic Typology* 11(1): 119–132.

Haspelmath, Martin (2010). Comparative concepts and descriptive categories in cross-linguistic studies. *Language* 86: 663–687.

Haspelmath Martin (2011). The indeterminacy of word segmentation and the nature of morphology and syntax. *Folia linguistica* 45(1): 31–80.

Haspelmath, Martin (2012a). How to compare major word-classes across the world's languages. In Thomas Graf et al. (eds.), *Theories of Everything: In Honor of Edward Keenan.* (UCLA Working Papers in Linguistics 17.) Los Angeles: UCLA, 109–130.

Haspelmath, Martin (2012b). Escaping ethnocentrism in the study of word-class universals. *Theoretical Linguistics* 38(1–2): 91–102. https://doi.org/10.1515/tl-2012-0004

Haspelmath, Martin (2014). Descriptive hypothesis testing is distinct from comparative hypothesis testing: Commentary on Davis, Gillon, and Matthewson. *Language* 90(4): e250–e257. doi:10.1353/lan.2014.0071

Haspelmath, Martin (2015). Ditransitive constructions. *Annual Review of Linguistics* 1: 19–41. https://doi.org/10.1146/annurev-linguist-030514-125204

Haspelmath, Martin (2016). The serial verb construction: Comparative concept and cross-linguistic generalizations. *Language and Linguistics* 17(3): 291–319.

Haspelmath, Martin (2018). How comparative concepts and descriptive linguistic categories are different. In Daniël Van Olmen, Tanja Mortelmans, & Frank Brisard (eds.), *Aspects of Linguistic Variation: Studies in Honor of Johan van der Auwera*. Berlin: De Gruyter Mouton, 83–113. https://zenodo.org/record/3519206

Haspelmath, Martin (2019). Indexing and flagging, and head and dependent marking. *Te Reo* 1: 93–115.

Haspelmath, Martin (2020). Human linguisticality and the building blocks of languages. *Frontiers in Psychology* 10: 3056.

Haspelmath, Martin (2021). Explaining grammatical coding asymmetries: Form–frequency correspondences and predictability. *Journal of Linguistics* 57(3): 605–633. doi:10.1017/S0022226720000535, https://ling.auf.net/lingbuzz/004531

Haspelmath, Martin & Andrea Sims (2010). *Understanding Morphology*, 2nd edn. London: Routledge.

Haspelmath, Martin & Ekkehard König (1995). *Converbs in Cross-linguistic Perspective: Structure and Meaning of Adverbial Verb Forms—Adverbial Participles, Gerunds*. Berlin: Mouton de Gruyter.

Haspelmath, Martin & Uri Tadmor (eds.) (2009) *Loanwords in the World's Languages: A Comparative Handbook*. Berlin: Mouton de Gruyter.

Hatfield, Adam (2016). A grammar of Mehek. Doctoral dissertation, State University of New York at Buffalo.

Hattnher, Marize Mattos Dall'Aglio & Kees Hengeveld (2016). The grammaticalization of modal verbs in Brazilian Portuguese: A synchronic approach. *Journal of Portuguese Linguistics* 15(1): 1, 1–14.

Haude, Katharina (2006). A grammar of Movima. PhD thesis, Radboud Universiteit Nijmegen.

Haude, Katharina (2009). Reference and predication in Movima. In Patience Epps & Alexandre Arkhipov (eds.), *New Challenges in Typology: Transcending the Borders and Refining the Distinctions*. Berlin: Mouton de Gruyter, 323–342.

Haudry, Jean (1981). *Les Indo-Européens*. Paris: Presses Universitaires de France.

Haug, Dag T. T. & Tatiana Nikitina (2016). Feature sharing in agreement. *Natural Language and Linguistic Theory* 34(3): 865–910.

Haugen, Einar (1950). The analysis of linguistic borrowing. *Language* 26: 210–231.

Haumann, Dagmar (2007). *Adverb Licensing and Clause Structure in English*. Amsterdam: John Benjamins.

Haviland, John B. (1994). 'Te xa setel xulem' [The buzzards were circling]: Categories of verbal roots in (Zinacantec) Tzotzil. *Linguistics* 32: 691–741.

Haviland, John B. (2013). The emerging grammar of nouns in a first generation sign language: Specification, iconicity, and syntax. *Gesture* 13: 309–353.

Haviland, John B. (2015). Hey! *Topics in Cognitive Science* 7(1): 124–149. https://doi.org/10.1111/tops.12126

Hawkins, John A. (1994). *A Performance Theory of Order and Constituency*. Cambridge: Cambridge University Press.

Hawkins, Johm A. (2004). *Efficiency and Complexity in Grammars*. Oxford: Oxford University Press.

Hayward, Richard (1979). Bayso revisited: Some preliminary linguistic observations—II. *Bulletin of the School of Oriental and African Studies* 42–1: 101–132.

He, QunXiong (1998). Chinese grammatical studies by Christian missionaries: Centering on those by the 19th century English protestants. *Hitotsubashi Research* 23(3): 27–36.

Heath, Jeffrey (1978). *Linguistic Diffusion in Arnhem Land*. Canberra: Australian Institute for Aboriginal Studies.

Heath, Jeffrey (1999). *A Grammar of Koyra Chiini: The Songhay of Timbuktu*. (Mouton Grammar Library, 19.) Berlin/New York: Berlin: Mouton de Gruyter.

Heath, Jeffrey (2003). Arabic derivational ablaut: Processing strategies, and consonantal roots. In Joseph Shimron (ed.), *Language Processing and Adquisition in Languages of Semitic, Root-Based Morphology*. Amsterdam & Philadelphia: John Benjamins, 115–129.

Heath, Jeffrey (2005). *A Grammar of Tamashek (Tuareg of Mali)*. (Mouton Grammar Library, 35.) Berlin/New York: Berlin: Mouton de Gruyter.

Heath, Jeffrey (2017). *A Grammar of Jalkunan (Mande, Burkina Faso)*. Ann Arbor, MI: University of Michigan.

Heath, Jeffrey (2019). The dance of expressive adverbials ('ideophones') in Jamsay (Dogon). *Folia Linguistica* 53(1): 1–24. https://doi.org/10.1515/flin-2019-2002

Heathcote, Andrew, Scott Brown, & D. J. K. Mewhort (2000). The power law repealed: The case for an exponential law of practice. *Psychonomic Bulletin and Review* 7: 185–207. https://doi.org/10.3758/BF03212979

Heim, Irene (2008). Features on bound pronouns. In Daniel Harbour, David Adger, & Susana Béjar (eds.), *Phi Theory: Phi-features across Modules and Interfaces*. Oxford: Oxford University Press, 35–56.

Heine, Bernd (1993). *Auxiliaries: Cognitive Forces and Grammaticalization*. Oxford: Oxford University Press.

Heine, Bernd & Mechtild Reh (1984). *Grammaticalization and Reanalysis in African Languages*. Hamburg: Buske.

Heine, Bernd, Ulrike Claudi, & Friederike Hünnemeyer (1991). *Grammaticalization: A Conceptual Framework*. Chicago/London: University of Chicago Press.

Heine, Bernd & Tania Kuteva (2002). *World Lexicon of Grammaticalization*. Cambridge: Cambridge University Press.

Heine, Bernd & Tania Kuteva (2007). *The Genesis of Grammar: A Reconstruction*. Oxford: Oxford University Press.

Hellwig, Birgit (2011). *A Grammar of Goemai*. (Mouton Grammar Library, 51.) Berlin: Mouton de Gruyter.

Henderson, Robert (2017). Pluractionality in Mayan. In Judith Aissen, Nora C. England, & Roberto Zavala Maldonado (eds.), *The Mayan Languages*. London/New York: Routledge, 362–377.

Henderson, Robert (2019). The roots of measurement. *Glossa: A Journal of General Linguistics* 4(1): 32.

Hengeveld, Kees (1989). Layers and operators in Functional Grammar. *Journal of Linguistics* 25(2): 127–157.

Hengeveld, Kees (1992a). Parts of speech. In Michael Fortescue, Peter Harder, & Lars Kristofferson (eds.), *Layered Structure and Reference in a Functional Perspective*. Amsterdam: John Benjamins, 29–56.

Hengeveld, Kees (1992b). *Non-verbal Predication: Theory, Typology, Diachrony*. Berlin: Mouton de Gruyter.

Hengeveld, Kees (1997). Adverbs in Functional Grammar. In Gerd Wotjak (ed.), *Toward a Functional Lexicology/Hacia una lexicología funcional*. Frankfurt: Peter Lang, 121–136.

Hengeveld, Kees (2004a). The architecture of a Functional Discourse Grammar. In J. Lachlan Mackenzie & María de los Ángeles Gómez-González (eds.), *A New Architecture for Functional Grammar*. Berlin/New York: Mouton de Gruyter, 1–21.

Hengeveld, Kees (2004b). Illocution, mood, and modality. In Geert Booij, Christian Lehmann, & Joachim Mugdan (eds.), *Morphology: A Handbook on Inflection and Word Formation,*. Berlin: Mouton de Gruyter, vol. II, 1190–1202.

Hengeveld, Kees (2007). Parts-of-speech systems and morphological types. *ACLC Working Papers* 2(1): 31–48.

Hengeveld, Kees (2013). Parts-of-speech system as a basic typological determinant. In Jan Rijkhoff & Eva van Lier (eds.), *Flexible Word Classes: Typological Studies of Underspecified Parts of Speech*. Oxford: Oxford University Press, 31–55.

Hengeveld, Kees & Eva van Lier. (2008). Parts of speech and dependent clauses in functional discourse grammar. *Studies in Language* 32: 753–785.

Hengeveld, Kees & Rafael Fischer (2018). A'ingae (Cofán/Kofán) operators. In Kees Hengeveld & Hella Olbertz (eds.), *Systems of Tense, Aspect, Modality, Evidentiality and Polarity in Functional Discourse Grammar*. Open Linguistics 4. Berlin: De Gruyter Mouton, 328–355.

Hengeveld, Kees & Marize Mattos Dall'Aglio Hattnher (2015). Four types of evidentiality in the native languages of Brazil. *Linguistics* 53(3): 479–524.

Hengeveld, Kees & J. Lachlan Mackenzie (2008). *Functional Discourse Grammar: A Typologically-Based Theory of Language Structure*. Oxford: Oxford University Press.

Hengeveld, Kees & J. Lachlan Mackenzie (2016). Reflections on the lexicon in Functional Discourse Grammar. *Linguistics* 54(5): 1135–1161.

Hengeveld, Kees, Heiko Narrog, & Hella Olbertz (2017). A functional perspective on the grammaticalization of tense, aspect, modality and evidentiality. In Kees Hengeveld, Heiko Narrog, & Hella Olbertz (eds.), *The Grammaticalization of Tense, Aspect, Modality and Evidentiality: A Functional Perspective*. Berlin: De Gruyter Mouton, 1–12.

Hengeveld, Kees, & Jan Rijkhoff (2005). Mundari as a flexible language. *Linguistic Typology* 9(3): 406–431.

Hengeveld, Kees, Jan Rijkhoff, & Anna Siewierska (2004). Parts-of-speech systems and word order. *Journal of Linguistics* 40(3): 527–570.

Hengeveld, Kees & Marieke Valstar (2010). Parts-of-speech systems and lexical subclasses. *Linguistics in Amsterdam* 3(1). http://www.linguisticsinamsterdam.nl/home?issue=31, 1–20

Hengeveld, Kees & Eva van Lier (2010a). Parts of speech and dependent clauses in Functional Discourse Grammar. In Umberto Ansaldo, Jan Don, & Roland Pfau (eds.), *Parts of Speech: Empirical and Theoretical Advances*. Amsterdam: John Benjamins, 253–285.

Hengeveld, Kees & Eva van Lier (2010b). An implicational map of parts-of-speech. *Linguistic Discovery* 8(1): 129–156.

Hengeveld, Kees & J. Lachlan Mackenzie (2021). Interfaces, mismatches, and the architecture of Functional Discourse Grammar. In Lucía Contreras García and Daniel García Velasco (eds.), *Interfaces in Functional Discourse Grammar: Theory and Applications*. Berlin & New York: De Gruyter Mouton, 15–57.

Henkin, Roni (1992). The three faces of the Arabic participle in Negev Bedouin dialects: Continuous, resultative, and evidential. *Bulletin of the School of Oriental and African studies* 55(3): 433–444.

Henkin, Roni (2021). Evidentiality and mirativity in traditional Negev Arabic. *Journal of Semitic studies* 66(1): 153–183.

Heny, Frank & Barry Richards (eds.) (1983). *Linguistic Categories: Auxiliaries and Related Puzzles*. Dordrecht: Reidel, vol. I.

Her, One-Soon & Chen-Tien Hsieh (2010). On the semantic distinction between classifiers and measure words in Chinese. *Language and Linguistics* 11–3: 527–551.

Herce, Borja (2017a). The diachrony of Spanish haber/hacer+time. *Journal of Historical Linguistics*, 7(3): 276–321.

Herce, Borja (2017b). Past–future asymmetries in time adverbials and adpositions: A crosslinguistic and diachronic perspective. *Linguistic Typology* 21(1): 101–142.

Hercus, Luise (1982). *The Baagandji Language*. Canberra: Pacific Linguistics.

Hercus, Luise (1994). *A Grammar of the Arabana-Wangkangurru Language, Lake Eyre Basin, South Australia*. Canberra: Pacific Linguistics.

Heritage, John (1984). A change of state token and aspects of its sequential placement. In J. Maxwell Atkinson & John Heritage (eds.), *Structures of Social Action: Studies in Conversation Analysis*. (Studies in Emotion and Social Interaction.) Cambridge: Cambridge University Press, 299–345.

Hespos, Susan J. & Elizabeth S. Spelke (2004). Conceptual precursors to language. *Nature* 430: 453–456. https://doi.org/10.1038/nature02634

Hess, Jean-Jacques (1897). Demotica. *Zeitschrift für Ägyptische Sprache* 35: 144–149.

Hess, Thom (1979). Central Coast Salish words for *deer*: their wavelike distribution. *International Journal of American Linguistics* 45: 5–16.

Heston, Tyler M. (2015). The segmental and suprasegmental phonology of Fataluku. PhD thesis, University of Hawaii at Manoa.

Hetzron, Robert (1980). The limits of Cushitic. *Sprache und Geschichte in Afrika* 2: 7–126.

Hewitt, Brian George (1979). *Abkhaz*. Lingua Descriptive Studies, vol. II. Amsterdam: North-Holland.

Heyvaert, Liesbet, Charlotte Maekelberghe, & Anouk Buyle (2019). Nominal and verbal gerunds in present-day English: Aspectual features and nominal status. *Language Sciences* 73: 32–49.

Hill, Clair (2018). *Person reference and interaction in Umpila/Kuuku Ya'u narrative*. Doctoral dissertation, Radboud Universiteit and KU Leuven.

Hill, Jane A. (2005). *A Grammar of Cupeño*. (University of California Publications in Linguistics, 136.) Berkeley and Los Angeles: University of California Press.

Hillis, Argye E., et al. (2003). Neural regions essential for writing verbs. *Nature Neuroscience* 6: 19–20.

Hillis, Argye E., et al. (2006). Naming and comprehension in primary progressive aphasia: The influence of grammatical word class. *Aphasiology* 20: 246–256.

Hillis, Argye E., Elizabeth Tuffiash, & Alfonso Caramazza (2002). Modality-specific deterioration in naming verbs in nonfluent primary progressive aphasia. *Journal of Cognitive Neuroscience* 14: 1099–1108.

Hilpert, Martin & Jan-Ola Östman (eds.) (2016). *Constructions across Grammars*. Amsterdam: John Benjamins.

Himmelmann, Nikolaus P. (1997). *Deiktikon, Artikel, Nominalphrase: Zur Emergenz syntaktischer Struktur*. Tübingen: Niemeyer.

Himmelmann, Nikolaus P. (2005a). The Austronesian languages of Asia and Madagaskar: Typological characteristics. In Alexander Adelaar & Nikolaus Himmelmann (eds.), *The Austronesian Languages of Asia and Madagascar*. New York: Routledge, 110–181.

Himmelmann, Nikolaus P. (2005b). Tagalog. In Alexander Adelaar & Nikolaus P. Himmelmann (eds.), *The Austronesian Languages of Asia and Madagascar*. New York: Routledge, 350–376.

Himmelmann, Nikolaus P. (2008). Lexical categories and voices in Tagalog. In Peter K. Austin & Simon Musgrave (eds.), *Voice and Grammatical Relations in Austronesian Languages*. Stanford, CA: CSLI Publications, 247–293.

Himmelmann, Nikolaus (2009). Notes on Tagalog nominalism. *Theoretical Linguistics* 35(1): 115–123.

Himmelmann, Nikolaus & Eva Schultze-Berndt (2005). Issues in the syntax and semantics of participant-oriented adjuncts: An introduction. In Nikolaus Himmelmann & Eva Schultze-Berndt (eds.), *Secondary Predication and Adverbial Modification: The Typology of Depictives*. Oxford: Oxford University Press, 1–67.

Hinkson, Mercedes Q. (1999). Salishan lexical suffixes: A study in the conceptualization of space. PhD dissertation, Simon Fraser University.

Hinskens, Frans & Pieter Muysken. 1986. Formele en funktionele verklaringen van dialektvariatie. In *Lexikon en Syntaxis, een bundel opgedragen aan Albert Sassen*. Dordrecht: Foris, 13–24.

Hinton, L., J. Nichols, & J. J. Ohala (1994). *Sound Symbolism*. Cambridge: Cambridge University Press.

Hirsh-Pasek, Kathryn A. & Roberta M. Golinkoff (2010). *Action Meets Word: How Children Learn Verbs*. Oxford: Oxford University Press. https://doi.org/10.1093/acprof:oso/9780195170009.001.0001

Hla Pe (1965). A re-examination of Burmese classifiers. *Lingua* 15: 163–185.

Hockett, Charles F. (1955). *A Manual of Phonology*. Baltimore: Waverly Press.

Hockett, Charles F. (1958). *A Course in Modern Linguistics*. New York: Macmillan.

Hodge, Gabrielle & Kearsy Cormier (2019). Reported speech as enactment. *Linguistic Typology* 23(1): 185–196. https://doi.org/10.1515/lingty-2019-0008

Hodge, Gabrielle & Trevor Johnston (2014). Points, depictions, gestures and enactment: Partly lexical and non-lexical signs as core elements of single clause-like units in Auslan (Australian Sign Language). *Australian Journal of Linguistics* 34(2): 262–291. https://doi.org/10.1080/07268602.2014.887408

Hoey, Elliott M. (2020a). *When Conversation Lapses: The Public Accountability of Silent Copresence*. New York: Oxford University Press.

Hoey, Elliott M. (2020b). Waiting to inhale: On sniffing in conversation. *Research on Language and Social Interaction* 53(1): 118–139. doi:10.1080/08351813.2020.1712962

Hoffmann, John (1903). *Mundari Grammar*. Calcutta: Secretariat Press.

Hoffmann, Sebastian (2005). *Grammaticalization and Complex Prepositions: A Corpus-based Study*. London: Routledge.

Hofling, Charles Andrew, with Félix Fernando Tesucún (1997). *Itzaj Maya–Spanish–English Dictionary*. Salt Lake City: University of Utah Press.

Hofling, Charles Andrew (2011). *Mopan Maya–Spanish–English Dictionary*. Salt Lake City: University of Utah Press.

Hofling, Charles Andrew (2014). *Lacandon Maya–Spanish–English Dictionary*. Salt Lake City: University of Utah Press.

Hofstede, Gerard (1999). De Interjectie als Illocutionaire Handeling. *Toegepaste Taalwetenschap in Artikelen*. John Benjamins 61(1): 127–135. doi:10.1075/ttwia.61.11hof

Hofstetter, Emily (2020). Nonlexical 'moans': Response cries in board game interactions. *Research on Language and Social Interaction* 53(1): 42–65. doi:10.1080/08351813.2020.1712964

Hollenbach, Barbara E. (1995). Semantic and syntactic extensions of body-part terms in Mixtecan: The case of 'face' and 'foot'. *International Journal of American Linguistics* 61(2): 168–190

Höller, A. (1932). *Guarayo-Deutsches Wörterbuch*. Guarayos, Bolivia: Verlag der Missionsprokura.

Hollmann, Willem B. (2012). Word classes: Towards a more comprehensive usage-based account. *Studies in Language* 36: 671–698.

Hollmann, Willem B. (2013). Nouns and verbs in Cognitive Grammar: Where is the 'sound' evidence? *Cognitive Linguistics* 24: 275–308.

Hollmann, Willem B. (2020). Word classes. In Bas Aarts, Jill Bowie, & Gergana Popova (eds.), *The Oxford Handbook of English Grammar*. Oxford: Oxford University Press, 281–300.

Holton, Gary, et al. (2012). The historical relations of the Papuan languages of Alor and Pantar. *Oceanic Linguistics* 51 (1): 86–122.

Holton, Gary & Marian Klamer (2017). The Papuan languages of East Nusantara and the Bird's Head. In Bill Palmer (ed.), *The Languages and Linguistics of the New Guinea Area*. Berlin/New York: Mouton de Gruyter, 569–640.

Holton, Gary & Laura C. Robinson (2017). The linguistic position of the Timor–Alor–Pantar Languages. In Marian Klamer (ed.), *The Alor–Pantar Languages: History and Typology* (2nd edn). Berlin: Language Science Press, 147–190.

Hopkins, Nicholas A. (2012). The noun classifiers of Cuchumatán Mayan languages: A case of diffusion from Otomanguean. *International Journal of American Linguistics* 78(3): 411–427.

Hopper, Paul J. (1987). Emergent grammar. *Berkeley Linguistics Society* 13: 139–157.

Hopper, Paul (1991). On some principles of grammaticalization. In Elizabeth C. Traugott & Bernd Heine (eds.), *Approaches to Grammaticalization, Vol. 1 Focus and Theoretical and Methodological Issues*. Amsterdam: John Benjamins, 17–36.

Hopper, Paul J. (2012). Emergent grammar. In James Gee & Michael Handford (eds.), *The Routledge Handbook of Discourse Analysis*. New York: Routledge, 301–312.

Hopper, Paul J. & Sandra A. Thompson (1980). Transitivity in grammar and discourse. *Language* 56: 251–299.

Hopper, Paul J. & Sandra A. Thompson (1984). The discourse basis for lexical categories in universal grammar. *Language* 60: 703–752.

Hopper, Paul J. & Elizabeth C. Traugott. (1993). *Grammaticalization*. Cambridge: Cambridge University Press.

Hopper, Paul J. & Elizabeth C. Traugott (2003). *Grammaticalization* (2nd edn). Cambridge: Cambridge University Press.

Horst, M., & P. Meara (1999). Test of a model for predicting second language lexical growth through reading. *Canadian Modern Language Review* 56: 308–328.

Hoskison, James T. (1983). A grammar and dictionary of the Gude language. PhD dissertation, Ohio State University.

Hou, Lynn & Richard P. Meier(2018). The morphology of first-person object forms of directional verbs in ASL. *Glossa: A Journal of General Linguistics* 3(1): 114. https://doi.org/10.5334/gjgl.469

Hough, Carole (ed.) (2016). *The Oxford Handbook of Names and Naming*. Oxford: Oxford University Press.

Houis, Maurice (1981). Les schèmes d'énoncé en bambara. *Mandenkan* 1: 17–24.

Hron, David (2005). On the derivation of Czech reflexive and reciprocal nouns. MA Thesis, Tel Aviv University.
Hualde, José Ignacio (2002). Regarding Basque postpositions and related matters. *Anuario del Seminario de Filología Vasca Julio de Urquijo*: 325–339.
Hualde, José I. & Jon Ortiz de Urbina (2003). *A Grammar of Basque*. (Mouton Grammar Library, 26.) Berlin: Mouton de Gruyter.
Huang, Chu-Ren & Kathleen Ahrens (2003). Individuals, kinds and events: classifier coercion of nouns. *Language Sciences* 25: 353–373.
Huber, Juliette (2011). *A Grammar of Makalero: A Papuan Language of East Timor*. Utrecht: LOT Publications.
Huber, Juliette (2017). Makalero and Makasae. In Antoinette Schapper (ed.), *The Papuan Languages of Timor, Alor, and Pantar*. Berlin: Mouton de Gruyter, vol. II, 268–351.
Huber, Juliette (2008). First steps towards a grammar of Makasae: A language of East Timor. (Languages of the World (Materials); Vol. 195). LINCOM.
Huddleston, Rodney (2002). Non-finite and verbless clauses. In Rodney Huddleston & Geoffrey K. Pullum (eds.), *The Cambridge Grammar of the English Language*. Cambridge: Cambridge University Press.
Huddleston, Rodney & Geoffrey K. Pullum (2002). *The Cambridge Grammar of the English Language*. Cambridge: Cambridge University Press, 1171–1272.
Hudson, Richard (2006). *Language Networks: The New Word Grammar*. Oxford: Oxford University Press.
Hudson, Richard (2010). *An Introduction to Word Grammar*. Cambridge: Cambridge University Press.
Huijsmans, Marianne (2015). Linearization and prosodic phrasing: The case of SENĆOŦEN second-position clitics. MA thesis, University of Victoria.
Huijsmans, Marianne (2023). Second-position clitics, from morphosyntax to semantics : the ʔayʔaǰuθəm (Comox-Sliammon) perspective. PhD dissertation, University of British Columbia.
Huijsmans, Marianne & Daniel K. E. Reisinger (2022). ʔayʔaǰuθəm determiners for women, animals, and small things. In Yixiao Song (ed.), *Proceedings of Semantics of Under-Represented Languages of the Americas (SULA)* 11: 111–126.
Huijsmans, Marianne, Daniel K. E. Reisinger, & Lisa Matthewson (2020). Evidential determiners in ʔayʔaǰuθəm. *Papers of the International Conference on Salish and Neighboring Languages (ICSNL)* 55: 165–182.
Huijsmans, Marianne & Gloria Mellesmoen (2021). How to distribute events: ʔayʔaǰuθəm pluractionals. *International Journal of American Linguistics* 87(3): 339–368.
Hukari, Thomas E. (1978). Halkomelem and configuration. *Papers for the 13th International Conference on Salish and Neighbouring Languages*. Omak, Washington, 214–238.
Hukari, Thomas E. (ed.) & Ruby Peter (assoc. ed.) (1995). *Hul'qumi'num' Dictionary*. Duncan, British Columbia: Cowichan Tribes.
Hull, David L. (1976). Are species really individuals? *Systematic Zoology* 25: 174–191.
Hull, David L. (1988). *Science as a Process: An Evolutionary Account of the Social and Conceptual Development of Science*. Chicago: University of Chicago Press.
Huls, Henrica Anna (1982). Taalgebruik in het gezin en sociale ongelijkheid: een interactioneel sociolinguïstisch onderzoek. PhD thesis, Katholieke Universiteit, Nijmegen.
Humboldt, Wilhelm von (1827). *Lettre à M. Abel-Rémusat sur la nature des formes grammaticales en général et sur le génie de la langue chinoise en particulier*.

Humboldt, Wilhelm von (1838). *Über die Kawi-Sprache auf der Insel Java*, zweiter Band. Berlin: Königliche Akademie der Wissenschaften.

Hundius, Harald & Ulrike Kölver (1983). Syntax and semantics of numeral classifiers in Thai. *Studies in Language* 7(2): 164–214.

Hundt, Marianne (2009). Concord with collective nouns in Australian and New Zealand English. In Pam Peters, Peter Collins, & Adam Smith (eds.), *Comparative Studies in Australian and New Zealand English: Grammar and beyond*. Amsterdam: John Benjamins, 207–224.

Hundt, Marianne (2016). Who is the/a/Ø professor at your university? A construction-grammar view on changing article use with single role predicates in American English. In Maria José López-Couso et al. (eds.), *Corpus Linguistics on the Move: Exploring and understanding English through corpora*. Amsterdam: Brill-Rodopi, 227–258.

Hurford, James R. (2012). *The Origins of Grammar: Language in the Light of Evolution*. Oxford: Oxford University Press.

Hunger, Barbara (2006). Noun/verb pairs in Austrian Sign Language (ÖGS). *Sign Language & Linguistics* 9(1/2): 71–94. https://doi.org/10.1075/sll.9.1.06hun

Hunsicker, Dea & Susan Goldin-Meadow (2013). How handshape type can distinguish between nouns and verbs in homesign. *Gesture* 13(3): 354–376. https://doi.org/10.1075/gest.13.3.05hun

Hyams, Nina & Robyn Orfitelli (2015). The acquisition of syntax. In Eva M. Fernandez & Helen S. Cairns (eds.), *Handbook of Psycholinguistics*. Hoboken, NJ: Wiley-Blackwell, 593–614.

Hyman, Larry M., Peter Jenks, & Emmanuel-Moselly Makasso (2013). Adjectives as nominal heads in Basa`a. In Olanike Ola Orie & K. Sanders (eds.), *Selected Proceedings of the 43rd Annual Conference on African Linguistics*. Cascadilla Proceedings Project, 151–162.

Iatridou, Sabine (1990). About AgrP. *Linguistic Inquiry* 21: 421–459.

Ibarretxe-Antuñano, Iraide (2017). Basque ideophones from a typological perspective. *Canadian Journal of Linguistics/La revue canadienne de linguistique* 62(2): 196–220.

Ibbotson, Paul (2020). *What It Takes to Talk: Exploring Developmental Cognitive Linguistics*. Berlin/New York: Mouton de Gruyter.

Ibbotson, Paul et al. (2012). Semantics of the transitive construction: Prototype effects and developmental comparisons. *Cognitive Science* 36(7): 1268–1288. https://doi.org/10.1111/j.1551-6709.2012.01249.x

Ibbotson, Paul, Rose Hartman, & Kristina Nilsson Björkenstam (2018). Frequency filter: An open access tool for analysing language development. *Language, Cognition and Neuroscience* 33(10): 1325–1339. https://doi.org/10.1080/23273798.2018.1480788

Ibbotson, Paul & Jennifer Kearvell-White (2015). Inhibitory control predicts grammatical ability. *PLoS ONE* 10(12). https://doi.org/10.1371/journal.pone.0145030

Ibbotson, Paul, Elena Lieven & Michael Tomasello (2013). The attention–grammar interface: Eye-gaze cues structural choice in children and adults. *Cognitive Linguistics* 24(3): 457–481. https://doi.org/10.1515/cog-2013-0020

Ibbotson, Paul & Michael Tomasello (2009). Prototype constructions in early language acquisition. *Language and Cognition* 1(1): 59–85. https://doi.org/10.1515/LANGCOG.2009.004

Idiatov, Dmitry (2008). Antigrammaticalization, antimorphologization and the case of Tura. In Elena Seoane & María José López-Couso (eds.), *Theoretical and Empirical Issues in Grammaticalization*. Amsterdam: John Benjamins, 151–169.

Idiatov, Dmitry (2010). Person–number agreement on clause linking markers in Mande. *Studies in Language* 34(4): 832–868.

Idiatov, Dmitry (2011). Review: Güldemann, Tom. 2008. Quotative indexes in African languages: A synchronic and diachronic survey. *Studies in Language* 35(2): 443–450.

Idiatov, Dmitry (2018). Isomorphism, conversion and lability in Mande verbal morphosyntax: big consequences of small changes. Paper presented at the conference Syntax of the World's Languages VIII. Paris.
Idiatov, Dmitry (2020). Perfective marking conditioned by transitivity status in Western Mande: constructional competition, specialization and merger. *Diachronica* 37(1): 43–82.
Igelström, Kajsa M. & Michael S.A. Graziano (2017). The inferior parietal lobule and temporoparietal junction: A network perspective. *Neuropsychologia* 105: 70–83.
Iljic, Robert (2001). The origin of the suffix -*men* 們 in Chinese. *Bulletin of the School of Oriental and African Studies* 64–1: 74–97.
Iljic, Robert (2005). Personal collective in Chinese. *Bulletin of the School of Oriental and African Studies* 68(1): 77–103.
Imai, Mutsumi, et al. (2008). Sound symbolism facilitates early verb learning. *Cognition* 109: 54–65.
Imai, Mutsumi & Dedre Gentner (1993). Linguistic relativity vs. universal ontology: Crosslinguistic studies of the object/substance distinction. In Katharine Beals et al. (eds.), *What We Think, What We Mean and How We Say It. Volume 2: Parasession on the Correspondence of Conceptual, Semantic and Grammatical Representations*. Chicago: Chicago Linguistic Society, 171–186.
Imai, Mutsumi & Dedre Gentner (1997). A cross-linguistic study of early word meaning: Universal ontology and linguistic influence. *Cognition* 62–2: 169–200.
Indefrey, Peter, et al. (2001). A neural correlate of syntactic encoding during speech production. *Proceedings of the National Academy of Sciences* 98: 5933–5936.
Indefrey, Peter, et al. (2004). Neural responses to the production and comprehension of syntax in identical utterances. *Brain and Language* 89: 312–319.
Inman, David (2018) The representation of predicates at the syntactic–semantic boundary in Nuuchahnulth. In Marianne Huijsmans et al. (eds.), *Proceedings of the Fifty-third International Conference on Salish and Neighbouring Languages. University of British Columbia Working Papers in Linguistics 47*. Vancouver: Department of Linguistics, University of British Columbia, 25–40.
Innes, Gordon (1971). *A Practical Introduction to Mende*. London: SOAS.
Isaksson, Bo (2000). Expression of evidentiality in two Semitic languages: Hebrew and Arabic. In Lars Johansson & Bo Utas (eds.), *Evidentials. Turkic, Iranian and Neighbouring Languages*. (Empirical Approaches to Typology 24.) Berlin/New York: Mouton de Gruyter, 383–399.
Ishkhanyan, Byurakn, et al. (2017). Grammatical and lexical pronoun dissociation in French speakers with agrammatic aphasia: A usage-based account and ERF-based hypothesis. *Journal of Neurolinguistics* 44: 1–16.
Ishkhanyan, Byurakn, Kasper Boye, & Jesper Mogensen (2019). The meeting point: Where language production and working memory share resources. *Journal of Psycholinguistic Research* 48(1): 61–79.
Ivanova, Elena Yu (2007). Unikal'na li russkaja konstrukcija *Mne ne rabotaetsja*' [Is the Russian construction *Mne ne rabotaetsja* unique?], *Filologija i čelovek* 3: 7–15.
Iwasaki, Noriko, Peter Sells, & Kimi Akita (eds.) (2017). *The Grammar of Japanese Mimetics: Perspectives from Structure, Acquisition, and Translation*. New York: Routledge.
Jackendoff, Ray S. (1973). The base rules for prepositional phrases. In Stephen R. Anderson & Paul Kiparsky (eds.), *A Festschrift for Morris Halle*. New York: Holt, Reinhart & Winston, 345–356.
Jackendoff, Ray (1977). *X' Syntax: A Study of Phrase Structure*. Cambridge, MA: MIT Press.
Jackendoff, Ray (1983). *Semantics and Cognition*. Cambridge, MA: MIT Press.

Jackendoff, Ray (1990). *Semantic Structures*. Cambridge, MA: MIT Press.
Jackendoff, Ray. 1992. Semantic structures, vol. 18. MIT press.
Jackendoff, Ray (2002). *Foundations of Language: Brain, Meaning, Evolution*. Oxford: Oxford University Press.
Jackendoff, Ray (2010). *Meaning and the Lexicon: The Parallel Architecture 1975–2010*. Oxford: Oxford University Press.
Jacobsen, William H. (1979). Noun and Verb in Nootkan. In Barbara S. Efrat (ed.), *The Victoria Conference on Northwestern Languages*. British Columbia Provincial Museum Heritage Record 4. Victoria, BC: British Columbia Provincial Museum, 83–153.
Jacobson, Steven A. (1979). *A Grammatical Sketch of Siberian Yupik Eskimo, as Spoken on St. Lawrence Island, Alaska* (2nd printing). Fairbanks, AK: Alaska Native Language Center.
Jacobson, Steven A. (1994). *A Practical Grammar of the Central Alaskan Yup'ik Eskimo Language*. Fairbanks, AK: Alaska Native Language Center.
Jacobson, Steven A. (2012). *Yup'ik Eskimo Dictionary* (2nd edn). Fairbanks, AK: Alaska Native Language Center.
Jagersma, Abraham Hendrik (2010). A descriptive grammar of Sumerian. PhD dissertation, Universiteit Leiden.
Jakobson, Roman (1959). Boas's view of grammatical meaning. In Walter R. Goldschmidt (ed.), *The Anthropology of Franz Boas: Essays in the Centennial of His Birth*. American Anthropology 61: 5, part 2.141.
Jakobson, Roman (1960). Linguistics and poetics. In Thomas A. Sebeok (ed.), *Style in Language*. Cambridge, MA: MIT Press, 350–377.
Jakobson, Roman & Linda R. Waugh (1979). *The Sound Shape of Language*. Bloomington: Indiana University Press.
Janda, Richard (2005). Morphemes grammatizing gradually vs theories scientizing glacially: On pushing grammaticalization studies along a path toward science. *Logos and Language* 6(2): 45–65.
Jaworska, Ewa (1999). Prepositions and prepositional phrases. In K. Brown & J. Miller (eds.), *Concise Encyclopedia of Grammatical Categories*. Oxford: Elsevier, 304–311.
Jefferson, Gail (1972). Side sequences. In David N. Sudnow (ed.), *Studies in Social Interaction*. New York: Macmillan/Free Press, 294–338.
Jefferson, Gail (2004). Glossary of transcript symbols with an Introduction. In Gene H. Lerner (ed.), *Conversation Analysis: Studies from the First Generation*. Philadelphia: John Benjamins, 43–59.
Jelinek, Eloise (1995). Quantification in Straits Salish. In Emmon Bach et al. (eds.), *Quantification in Natural Languages*. Dordrecht: Kluwer, 487–540.
Jelinek, Eloise & Richard Demers (1994). Predicates and pronominal arguments in Straits Salish. *Language* 70: 697–736.
Jenks, Peter, Andrew Koontz-Garboden, & Emmanuel-Moselly Makasso (2018). On the lexical semantics of property concept nouns in Basaá. In Robert Truswell et al. (eds.), *Proceedings of Sinn und Bedeutung* 21. Konstanz: University of Konstanz, 643–660.
Jenner, Philip N. & Saveros Pou (1980/1981). *A Lexicon of Khmer Morphology*. (Mon-Khmer Studies IX–X.) Honolulu: University of Hawaii Press.
Jensen, Cheryl (1990). Cross-referencing changes in some Tupí-Guaraní languages. In D. Payne (ed.), *Amazonian Linguistics: Studies in Lowland South American Languages*. Austin: University of Texas Press, 117–158.
Jensen, Cheryl (1998). Comparative Tupí-Guaraní Morpho-syntax. In Desmond Derbyshire & Geoffrey Pullum (eds.), *Handbook of Amazonian Languages: Vol. IV*. Mouton de Gruyter, 490–603.

Jensen, Cheryl (1999). Tupí-Guaraní. In R. M. W. Dixon & Alexandra Aikhenvald (eds.), *The Amazonian Languages*. Cambridge: Cambridge University Press, 125–163.

Jensen, Eva Skafte, Carsten Levisen, & Tina Thode Hougaard (2019). Interjections in Scandinavia and beyond: Traditions and innovations. *Scandinavian Studies in Language* 10(1): 1–6.

Jespersen, Otto (1922). *Language: Its Nature, Development and Origin*. London: George Allen & Unwin.

Johnson, Janet (2017). Compound nouns, especially abstracts, in Demotic. In Richard Jasnow & Ghislaine Widmer (eds.), *Illuminating Osiris: Egyptological Studies in Honor of Mark Smith*. Atlanta: Lockwood Press, 163–172.

Johnston, Trevor (2001). Nouns and verbs in Australian sign language: An open and shut case? *Journal of Deaf Studies and Deaf Education* 6(4): 235–57. https://doi.org/10.1093/deafed/6.4.235

Johnston, Trevor (2010). From archive to corpus: Transcription and annotation in the creation of signed language corpora. *International Journal of Corpus Linguistics* 15(1): 106–131. https://doi.org/10.1075/ijcl.15.1.05joh

Johnston, Trevor (2012). Lexical frequency in sign languages. *Journal of Deaf Studies and Deaf Education* 17(2): 163–193. https://doi.org/10.1093/deafed/enr036

Johnston, Trevor (2013). Formational and functional characteristics of pointing signs in a corpus of Auslan (Australian sign language): Are the data sufficient to posit a grammatical class of 'pronouns' in Auslan? *Corpus Linguistics and Linguistic Theory* 9(1): 109–159. https://doi.org/10.1515/cllt-2013-0012

Johnston, Trevor (2014a). *Auslan Signbank*. http://www.auslan.org.au/dictionary/

Johnston, Trevor. (2014b). The reluctant oracle: Adding value to, and extracting of value from, a signed language corpus through strategic annotations. *Corpora* 9(2): 155–189. https://doi.org/10.3366/cor.2014.0056

Johnston, Trevor & Adam Schembri (1999). On defining lexeme in a signed language. *Sign Language & Linguistics* 2(2): 115–185. https://doi.org/10.1075/sll.2.2.03joh

Joos, Martin (1950). Description of language design. *Journal of the Acoustical Society of America* 22: 701–708.

Jun, Akamine (2005). Sama (Bajau). In Alexander Adelaar & Nikolaus P. Himmelmann (eds.), *The Austronesian Languages of Asia and Madagascar*. Oxon/New York: Routledge, 377–396.

Jurafsky, Daniel (1996). Universal tendencies in the semantics of the diminutive. *Language* 72(3): 533–578.

Jurafsky, Daniel, et al. (2001). Probabilistic relations between words: Evidence from reduction in lexical production. In Joan Bybee & Paul Hopper (eds.), *Frequency and the Emergence of Linguistic Structure*. Amsterdam: John Benjamins, pp. 229–254.

Just, Marcel A. & Patricia A. Carpenter (1987). *The Psychology of Reading and Language Comprehension*. Boston, MA: Allyn & Bacon.

Kager, René & Wim Zonneveld (1986). Schwa, syllables, and extrametricality in Dutch. *Linguistic Review* 5(3): 197–221.

Kahr, Joan Casper (1975). Adpositions and locationals: Typology and diachronic development. *Working Papers on Language Universals* 19: 21–54.

Kaiping, Gereon, Owen Edwards, & Marian Klamer (2019). LexiRumah 3.0.0. Leiden University Centre for Linguistics. https://lexirumah.model-ling.eu/lexirumah/

Kaiping, Gereon & Marian Klamer (2018). LexiRumah: An online lexical database of theLesser Sunda Islands. *PLoS ONE* 13(10): e0205250. https://doi.org/10.1371/journal.pone.0205250

Kaiping, Gereo & Marian Klamer (2022). The dialect chain of the Timor-Alor-Pantar language family: A new analysis using systematic Bayesian phylogenetics. *Language Dynamics and Change* 12(2): 274–326.

Kakumasu, James (1986). Urubu-Kaapor. In Desmond Derbyshire & Geoffrey Pullum (eds.), *Handbook of Amazonian Languages*. Mouton de Gruyter, vol. 1, 326–403.

Kaljurand, Kaarel & Tobias Kuhn (2013). A multilingual semantic Wiki based on Attempto: Controlled English and grammatical framework. In Philip Cimiano et al. (eds.), *The Semantic Web: Semantics and Big Data. ESWC 2013*. Berlin: Springer, 427–441.

Källkvist, Marie (1999). *Form-Class and Task-Type Effects in Learner English: A Study of Advanced Swedish Learners*. Lund: Lund University Press.

Kantarovich, Jessica (2020). Argument structure in language shift: Morphosyntactic variation and grammatical resilience in modern Chukchi. PhD dissertation, Chicago University

Kantartzis, Katerina, Mutsumi Imai, & Sotaro Kita (2011). Japanese sound-symbolism facilitates word learning in English-speaking children, *Cognitive Science* 35: 575–586.

Kapeliuk, Olga (1988). Amharique. In David Cohen (ed.), *Les langues dans le monde ancien et moderne: Langues chamito-sémitiques*. Paris: Editions du CNRS, 146–159.

Kaplan, Ronald M. & Joan Bresnan (1982). Lexical-functional grammar: A formal system for grammatical representation. In Bresnan (1982b: 173–281). [reprinted in M. Dalrymple, et al. (eds.), *Formal Issues in Lexical-Functional Grammar*. Stanford, CA: CSLI Publications, 1995, 29–130]

Kaplan, Ronald M. & John T. Maxwell, III (1988). Constituent coordination in Lexical-Functional Grammar. In Coling Budapest 1988 volume 1: International Conference on Computational Linguistics, https://www.aclweb.org/anthology/C88-1061

Karcevski, Serge (1941). Introduction à l'étude de l'interjection. *Cahiers Ferdinand de Saussure* 1: 57–75.

Karlgren, Bernhard (1940). Grammata serica: Script and phonetics in Chinese and Sino-Japanese. *Bulletin of the Museum of Far Eastern Antiquities* 12: 1–471.

Karttunen, Frances (1992). *An Analytical Dictionary of Nahuatl*. Norman: University of Oklahoma Press.

Kastner, Itamar (2020). *Voice at the Interfaces: The Syntax, Semantics, and Morphology of the Hebrew Verb*. Berlin: Language Science Press.

Katamba, Francis (1993). *Morphology*. London: macMillan.

Kaufman, Daniel (2009). Austronesian nominalism and its consequences: A Tagalog case study. *Theoretical Linguistics* 35: 1–49.

Kaufman, Daniel (2017). Lexical category and alignment in Austronesian. In Lisa Travis, Jessica Coon, & Diane Massam (eds.), *Oxford Handbook of Ergativity*. Oxford: Oxford University Press, 589–630.

Kaufman, Daniel (2018). Austronesian predication and the emergence of biclausal clefts in Indonesian languages. In Sonja Riesberg, Asako Shiohara, & Atsuko Utsumi (eds.), *Perspectives on Information Structure in Austronesian Languages*. Berlin: Language Science Press, 207–245.

Kaufman, David (2013). Positional auxiliaries in Biloxi. *International Journal of American Linguistics* 79(2): 283–299.

Kaufman, Terrence (1971). *Tzeltal Phonology and Morphology*. Berkeley/Los Angeles: University of California Publications.

Kaufman, Terrence (1990). Algunos rasgos estrucurales de los idiomas Mayances con referenda especial al K'iche. In Nora C. England & Stephen R. Elliott (eds.), *Lecturas sobre la lingüística maya*. Guatemala: CIRMA, 59–114.

Kauschke, Christina & Christoph Hofmeister. 2002. Early lexical development in German: a study on vocabulary growth and vocabulary composition during the second and third year of life. Journal of Child Language 29. 735–757.

Kawachi, Kazuhiro (2007). A grammar of Sidaama (Sidamo), a Cushitic language of Ethiopia. PhD thesis, University at Buffalo.

Kayne, Richard (2000). *Parameters and Universals*. Oxford: Oxford University Press.

Kean, Marie-Louise (1979). Agrammatism: A phonological deficit? *Cognition* 7: 69–83.

Keen, Sandra (1983). Yukulta. In R. M. W. Dixon & Barry Blake (eds.), *Handbook of Australian Languages*. Canberra: Australian National University Press, vol. III, 190–304.

Keenan, Edward L. (1976). Towards a universal definition of subject. In Charles N. Li (ed.), *Subject and Topic*. New York: Academic Press, 303–333.

Keenan, Edward L. (1989). Semantic case theory. In Renate Bartsch, Johan van Benthem, & P. van Emde Boas (eds.), *Semantics and Contextual Expression*. Dordrecht: Foris, pp. 33–57.

Keenan, Edward L. (1996). The semantics of determiners. In S. Lappin (ed.), *The Handbook of Contemporary Semantic Theory*. Oxford: Blackwell, pp. 41–64.

Keenan, Edward L. & Bernard Comrie (1977). Noun phrase accessibility and universal grammar. *Linguistic Inquiry* 8: 63–99.

Keevallik, Leelo (2010). Bodily quoting in dance correction. *Research on Language & Social Interaction* 43(4): 401–426. doi:10.1080/08351813.2010.518065

Keizer, Evelien (2004). Postnominal PP complements and modifiers: A cognitive distinction. *English Language and Linguistics* 8(2): 323–350.

Keizer, Evelien (2007). The lexical–grammatical dichotomy in Functional Discourse Grammar. *ALFA: Revista di Linguística* 51(2): 35–56.

Keizer, Evelien (2015). *A Functional Discourse Grammar for English*. Oxford: Oxford University Press.

Keizer, Evelien (2018). Modal adverbs in FDG: Putting the theory to the test. *Open Linguistics* 4: 356–390.

Keizer, Evelien (2019). The problem of non-truth-conditional, lower-level modifiers: A Functional Discourse Grammar solution. *English Language and Linguistics* 24(2): 365–392.

Keizer, Evelien (2020). Modelling stance adverbs in grammatical theory: Tackling heterogeneity with Functional Discourse Grammar. *Language Sciences* 82.

Kelly, Michael H. 1988. Phonological biases in grammatical category shifts. Journal of Memory and Language 27(4). 343–358.

Kelly, Michael H. 1996. The role of phonology in grammatical category assignments. In James L. Morgan & Katherine Demuth (eds.), Signal to syntax: bootstrapping from speech to grammar in early acquisition, 249–262. Lawrence Erlbaum Associates Inc.

Kemmerer, David (2000a). Grammatically relevant and grammatically irrelevant features of verb meaning can be independently impaired. *Aphasiology* 14: 997–1020.

Kemmerer, David (2000b). Selective impairment of knowledge underlying prenominal adjective order: Evidence for the autonomy of grammatical semantics. *Journal of Neurolinguistics* 13: 57–82.

Kemmerer, David (2003). Why can you *hit someone on the arm* but not *break someone on the arm*? A neuropsychological investigation of the English body-part possessor ascension construction. *Journal of Neurolinguistics* 16: 13–36.

Kemmerer, David (2014). Word classes in the brain: Implications of linguistic typology for cognitive neuroscience. *Cortex* 58: 27–51.

Kemmerer, David (2015). Are the motor features of verb meanings represented in the precentral motor cortices? Yes, but within the context of a flexible, multilevel architecture for conceptual knowledge. *Psychonomic Bulletin and Review* 22: 1068–1075.

Kemmerer, David (2019a). *Concepts in the Brain: The View from Cross-linguistic Diversity*. New York: Oxford University Press.

Kemmerer, David (2019b). Grammatical categories. In Greig de Zubicaray & Niels Schiller (eds.), *The Oxford Handbook of Neurolinguistics*. New York: Oxford University Press, 769–795.

Kemmerer, David (2022). *Cognitive Neuroscience of Language: An Introduction* (2nd edn). New York: Routledge.

Kemmerer, David, et al. (2007). *Big brown dog* or *brown big dog*? An electrophysiological study of semantic constraints on prenominal adjective order. *Brain and Language* 100: 238–256.

Kemmerer, David, et al. (2008). Neuroanatomical distribution of five semantic components of verbs: Evidence from fMRI. *Brain and Language* 107: 16–43.

Kemmerer, David, et al. (2012). Behavioral patterns and lesion sites associated with impaired processing of lexical and conceptual knowledge of actions. *Cortex* 48: 826–848.

Kemmerer, David, Daniel Tranel, & Ken Manzel (2005). An exaggerated effect for proper nouns in a case of superior written over spoken word production. *Cognitive Neuropsychology* 22: 3–27.

Kemmerer, David, Daniel Tranel, & Cynthia Zdanscyzk (2009). Knowledge of the semantic constraints on adjective order can be selectively impaired. *Journal of Neurolinguistics* 22: 91–108.

Kemmerer, David & Saundra K. Wright (2002). Selective impairment of knowledge underlying *un*-prefixation: Further evidence for the autonomy of grammatical semantics. *Journal of Neurolinguistics* 15: 403–432.

Kemp, Lois (2018). English evidential -ly adverbs in main clauses: A functional approach. *Open Linguistics* 4: 743–761.

Kendon, Adam (2008). Some reflections on the relationship between 'gesture' and 'sign'. *Gesture* 8(3): 348–366. https://doi.org/10.1075/gest.8.3.05ken

Kenesei, István, Robert M. Vago, & Anna Fenyvesi (1998). *Hungarian*. (Descriptive Grammars Series.) London: Routledge.

Kennedy, Benjamin Hall (1871). *The Revised Latin Primer*. [edited and further revised by Sir James Mountford. Longman, 1930]

Kennedy, G. A. ([1956] 1964). *Selected Works of George A. Kennedy*. New Haven, CT: Far Eastern Publications.

Kennedy, Rod (1984). Semantic roles—The language speaker's categories in Kala Lagaw Ya. *Papers in Australian Linguistics* 16: 153–169.

Kettnerová, Václava & Marketa Lopatkova (2019). Towards reciprocal deverbal nouns in Czech: From reciprocal verbs to reciprocal nouns. *Journal of Linguistics/Jazykovedný casopis* 70(2): 434–443.

Kholodilova, Maria A. (2015). Finiteness of the head and finiteness of the argument: Some correlations. Unpublished ms.

Kibrik, Alexander (ed.) (1996). *Godoberi*. Munich: Lincom Europa.

Kibrik, Alexander E. 1998. Archi. In Andrew Spencer & Arnold M. Zwicky (eds.), The Handbook of Morphology, 455–476. Oxford: Blackwell Publishers.

Kibrik, Alexander, Sandro V. Kodzasov, & Irina A. Muravjeva (2000). *Jazyk i folklor alutorcev* [Language and folklore of Alutor people]. Moscow: Nasledie.

Kidd, Evan, Seamus Donnelly, & Morten H. Christiansen (2018). Individual differences in language acquisition and processing. *Trends in Cognitive Sciences* 22(2): 154–169. https://doi.org/10.1016/j.tics.2017.11.006

Kielar, Aneta, et al. (2011). Neural correlates of covert and overt production of tense and agreement morphology: Evidence from fMRI. *Journal of Neurolinguistics* 24: 183–201.

Kießling, Roland (2000). Some salient features of Southern Cushitic (Common West Rift). *Lingua Posnaniensis* 42: 69–89.

Kieviet, Paulus (2017). *A Grammar of Rapa Nui*. Berlin: Language Science Press.

Kilian-Hatz, Christa (2006). Ideophones. In Keith Brown (ed.), *Encyclopedia of Language & Linguistics*. Oxford: Elsevier, 508–512.

Killian, Don (2015). Topics in Uduk phonology and morphosyntax. PhD dissertation, University of Helsinki.

Kim, Jong-Bok & Peter Sells (2014). English binominal NPs: A construction-based perspective. Journal of Linguistics 51(1):41–73.

Kimmelman, Vadim (2009). Parts of speech in Russian Sign Language: The role of iconicity and economy. *Sign Language & Linguistics* 12(2): 161–186. https://doi.org/10.1075/sl

Kimmelman, Vadim (2017). Quantifiers in Russian Sign Language. In Denis Paperno & Edward L. Keenan (eds.), *Handbook of Quantifiers in Natural Language: Volume II*. (Studies in Linguistics and Philosophy vol. 97.) Cham: Springer, 803–855. https://doi.org/10.1007/978-3-319-44330-0_16, http://link.springer.com/10.1007/978-3-319-44330-0_16

Kinkade, Dale M. (1976). The copula and negatives in Inland Olympic Salish, *IJAL* 42: 17–23.

Kinkade, Dale M. (1982). Transitive inflection in Moses-Columbian Salish, *Kansas Working Papers in Linguistics* 7: 49–62

Kinkade, Dale M. (1983). Salish evidence against the universality of 'noun' and 'verb'. *Lingua* 60: 25–40.

Kinkade, Dale M. (1990). Sorting out third persons in Salishan discourse. *IJAL* 56: 341–360.

Kinkade, Dale M. (1991). Upper Chehalis dictionary. *University of Montana Occasional Papers in Linguistics 7*. Missoula: University of Montana.

Kinkade, Dale M. (1995). Transmontane lexical borrowing in Salish, *Papers for the 31st International Conference on Salish and Neighboring Languages*, 181–195.

Kinkade, Dale M. (1998). Is irrealis a grammatical category in Upper Chehalis? *Anthropological Linguistics (AL)* 40: 234–244.

Kiparsky, Paul (2014). New perspectives in historical linguistics. In Claire Bowern & Bethwyn Evans (eds.), *The Routledge Handbook of Historical Linguistics*. London: Routledge, 64–102.

Kirchhoff, Raina (2008). *Die Syncategoremata des Wilhelm von Sherwood: Kommentierung und historische Einordnung*. Leiden: Brill.

Kiss, Katalin (2002). *The Syntax of Hungarian*. Cambridge: Cambridge University Press.

Kittilä, Seppo (2002). *Transitivity: Towards a Comprehensive Typology*. Turku: University of Turku Editions.

Kiyosawa, Kaoru & Donna B. Gerdts (2010). *Salish Applicatives*. Leiden: Brill.

Klamer, Marian (1998). *A Grammar of Kambera*. Berlin/New York: Mouton de Gruyter.

Klamer, Marian (2008). The semantics of semantic alignment in Eastern Indonesia. In Mark Donohue & Søren Wichmann (eds.), *The Typology of Semantic Alignment*. Oxford: Oxford University Press, 221–251.

Klamer, Marian (2010). *A Grammar of Teiwa*. Berlin/New York: De Gruyter Mouton.

Klamer, Marian (2011). Reality Status in Teiwa (Papuan). *Language Sciences* 34 (2): 216–228.

Klamer, Marian (2014a). Kaera. In Antoinette Schapper (ed.), *The Papuan Languages of Timor, Alor and Pantar: Sketch Grammars*. Berlin: Mouton de Gruyter, vol. 1, 97–146.

Klamer, Marian (2014b). The history of numeral classifiers in Teiwa (Papuan). In Gerrit J. Dimmendaal & Anne Storch (eds.), *Number Constructions and Semantics: Case Studies from Africa, Amazonia, India and Oceania*. Amsterdam: John Benjamins, 135–166.

Klamer, Marian (2017). The Alor–Pantar languages: Linguistic context, history and typology. In Marian Klamer (ed.), *The Alor–Pantar Languages: History and Typology* (2nd edn). Berlin: Language Science Press, 1–48.

Klamer, Marian (2018). Typology and grammaticalization in the Papuan languages of Timor, Alor, and Pantar. In Heiko Narrog & Bernd Heine (eds.), *Grammaticalization from a Typological Perspective*. Oxford: Oxford University Press, 235–262.

Klamer, Marian & František Kratochvíl (2006). The role of animacy in Teiwa and Abui (Papuan). In *Proceedings of BLS 32*. Berkeley: Berkeley Linguistic Society, 59–70. http://dx.doi.org/10.3765/bls.v32i2.3492

Klamer, Marian & František Kratochvíl (2010). Abui tripartite verbs: Exploring the limits of compositionality. In Jan Wohlgemuth & Michael Cysouw (eds.), *Rara and Rarissima: Documenting the Fringes of Linguistic Diversity*. Berlin/New York: Mouton de Gruyter, 185–210.

Klamer, Marian & František Kratochvíl (2018). The evolution of differential object marking in Alor–Pantar languages. In Ilja Seržant & Alena Witzlack-Makarevich (eds.), *The Diachronic Typology of Differential Argument Marking*. Berlin: Language Science Press, 70–95.

Klamer, Marian & Antoinette Schapper (2012). 'Give' constructions in the Papuan languages of Timor–Alor–Pantar. *Linguistic Discovery* 10(3): 174–207.

Klamer, Marian, Antoinette Schapper, & Greville G. Corbett (2017). Plural number words in the Alor–Pantar languages. In Marian Klamer (ed.), *The Alor–Pantar Languages: History and Typology* (2nd edn). Berlin: Language Science Press, 365–402.

Klein, Henny (2001). Polarity sensitivity and collocational restrictions of adverbs of degree. In Jack Hoeksema et al. (eds.), *Perspectives on Negation and Polarity Items*. Amsterdam: John Benjamins, 223–236.

Klein, Raymond M. & Jean Saint-Aubin (2016). What a simple letter-detection task can tell us about cognitive processes in reading. *Current Directions in Psychological Science* 25(6): 417–424.

Klima, Gyula (2005). Syncategoremata. In Keith Brown (ed.), *Encyclopedia of language and linguistics* (2nd edn). Oxford: Elsevier, 353–356.

Koch, Harold (2014). Historical relations among the Australian languages: Genetic classification and contact-based diffusion. In Harold Koch & Rachel Nordlinger (eds.), *The Languages and Linguistics of Australia*. Berlin/Boston: Mouton de Gruyter, 23–89.

Koch, Harold & Rachel Nordlinger (2014). The languages of Australia in linguistic research: Context and issues. In Harold Koch & Rachel Nordlinger (eds.), *The Languages and Linguistics of Australia*. Berlin/Boston: Mouton de Gruyter, 3–21.

Koch, Karsten & Lisa Matthewson (2009). The lexical category debate in Salish and its relevance for Tagalog. *Theoretical Linguistics* 35(1): 125–137.

Kockelman, Paul (2003). The meanings of interjections in Q'eqchi' Maya: From Emotive reaction to social and discursive action. *Current Anthropology* 44(4): 467–497.

Koeneman, Olaf (2000). The flexible nature of verb movement. PhD dissertation, Utrecht University.

Koeneman, Olaf & Hedde Zeijlstra (2017). *Introducing Syntax*. Cambridge: Cambridge University Press.

Koenig, Jean-Pierre (1999). *Lexical Relations*. Stanford, CA: CSLI Publications.

Koenig, Jean-Pierre & Karin Michelson (2010). Argument structure of Oneida kinship terms. *International Journal of American Linguistics* 76: 169–205.

Koenig, Jean-Pierre & Karin Michelson (2013). Counting nouns is not always the right question. Paper presented at 'The relative frequencies of nouns, pronouns, and verbs in discourse: An international workshop', 12–13 August 2013, Max Planck Institute for Evolutionary Anthropology, Leipzig, Germany.

Koenig, Jean-Pierre & Karin Michelson (2014). Deconstructing SYNtax. In Stefan Müller (ed.), *Proceedings of the 21st International Conference on Head-Driven Phrase Structure Grammar*. Stanford, CA: CSLI Publications, 114–134.

Koenig, Jean-Pierre & Karin Michelson (2015). Invariance in argument realization: The case of Iroquoian. *Language* 91: 1–47.

Koenig, Jean-Pierre & Karin Michelson (2020). Derived nouns and structured inflection in Oneida. *Lingue e Linguaggio* 19(1): 9–33 [special issue on inflectional morphology].

Kohen, Francine, Gary Milsark, & Nadine Martin (2011). Effects of syntactic and semantic argument structure on sentence repetition in agrammatism: Things we can learn from particles and prepositions. *Aphasiology* 25: 736–747.

König, Ekkehard (2012). Le rôle des déictiques de manière dans le cadre d'une typologie de la déixis. *Bulletin de la Société de Linguistique de Paris* 107: 11–42.

König, Ekkehard (2017). The deictic identification of similarity. In Yvonne Treis & Martine Vanhove (eds.), *Similative and Equative Constructions: A Cross-linguistic Perspective*. Amsterdam: John Benjamins, 143–164.

König, Ekkehard & Peter Siemund (2000). Intensifiers and reflexives: A typological perspective. In Zygmunt Frajzyngier & Traci S. Curl (eds.), *Reflexives: Forms and Functions*. Amsterdam: John Benjamins, 41–74.

König, Ekkehard & Carla Umbach (2018). Demonstratives of manner, of quality and of degree: A neglected subclass. In Marco Coniglio et al. (eds.), *Atypical Demonstratives*. Berlin: Mouton de Gruyter, 285–328.

Konishi, Haruka, et al. (2016). Individual differences in nonlinguistic event categorization predict later motion verb comprehension. *Journal of Experimental Child Psychology* 151: 18–32. https://doi.org/10.1016/j.jecp.2016.03.012

Konoshenko, M. B. (2017). Kpelle jazyk [The Kpelle language]. In Valentin Vydrin (ed.), *Jazyki mira: Jazyki mande* [The languages of the world: The Mande languages]. Sankt-Peterburg: Nestor-Istorija, 284–342.

Koptjevskaja-Tamm, Maria (1993). *Nominalizations*. London: Routledge.

Koptjevskaja-Tamm, Maria (2001). 'A piece of the cake' and 'a cup of tea': Partitive and pseudo-partitive nominal constructions in the Circum-Baltic languages. In Østen Dahl & Maria Koptjevskaja-Tamm (eds.), *The Circum-Baltic Languages: Typology and Contact*. Amsterdam: John Benjamins, vol. II, 523–568.

Koptjevskaja-Tamm, Maria (2003). Action nominal constructions in the languages of Europe. In Frans Plank (ed.), *Noun Phrase Structure in the Languages of Europe*. Berlin: Mouton de Gruyter, 723–761.

Koptjevskaja-Tamm, Maria (2006). Nouns. In Keith Brown (ed.), *Encyclopedia of Languages and Linguistics* (2nd edn). Oxford: Elsevier, 720–724.

Kor Chahine, Irina & Marguerite Guiraud-Weber (2013). Impersonals and beyond in Slavic. In Irina Kor Chahine (ed.), *Current Studies in Slavic Linguistics*. (Studies in Language Companion Series 146.) Amsterdam: John Benjamins, 1–21.

Koriat, Asher & Seth N. Greenberg (1991). Syntactic control of letter detection: Evidence from English and Hebrew nonwords. *Journal of Experimental Psychology: Learning, Memory, and Cognition* 17(6): 1035–1050.

Kornfilt, Jaklin & John Whitman. (2011). Afterword: Nominalizations in syntactic theory. *Lingua* 121: 1297–1313.

Kortmann, Bernd (ed.) (2004). *Dialectology Meets Typology: Dialect Grammar from a Cross-Linguistic Perspective*. Berlin: De Gruyter Mouton.

Kortmann, Bernd & Ekkehard König (1992). Categorial reanalysis: The case of deverbal prepositions. *Linguistics* 30(4): 671–698.

Kousta, Stavroula-Thaleia, et al. (2011). The representation of abstract words: Why emotion matters. *Journal of Experimental Psychology: General* 140: 14–34.

Kövecses, Zoltan (2010). *Metaphor: A Practical Introduction. Second Edition*. Oxford: Oxford University Press.

Kramer, Ruth (2016). A split analysis of plurality: Number in Amharic. *Linguistic Inquiry* 47: 527–559.

Krasnoukhova, Olga (2012). *The Noun Phrase in the Languages of South America*. Utrecht: LOT.

Krasnoukhova, Olga (2022). *Attributive modification in South American indigenous languages*. Linguistics 60(3): 745–807. https://doi.org/10.1515/ling-2020-0133

Kratochvíl, František (2007). *A grammar of Abui: A Papuan language of Alor*. Utrecht: LOT Publications.

Kratochvíl, František (2011). Transitivity in Abui. *Studies in Language* 35(3): 588–635.

Kratochvíl, František (2014a). Differential argument realization in Abui. *Linguistics* 52(2): 543–602.

Kratochvíl, František (2014b). Sawila. In Antoinette Schapper (ed.), *Papuan Languages of Timor, Alor and Pantar: Sketch Grammars*. Berlin: De Gruyter Mouton, vol. I, 351–438.

Kratzer, Angelika (1996). Severing the external argument from its verb. In J. Rooryck & L. Zaring (eds.), *Phrase Structure and the Lexicon*. Berlin: Springer, 109–137

Kratzer, Angelika (2009). Making a pronoun: Fake indexicals as windows into the properties of pronouns. *Linguistic Inquiry* 40: 187–237.

Krejtz, Izabela, Agnieszka Szarkowska, & Maria Łogińska (2016). Reading function and content words in subtitled videos. *Journal of Deaf Studies and Deaf Education* 21(2): 222–232.

Kriegeskorte, Nikolaus, et al. (2008). Matching categorical object representations in inferior temporal cortex of man and monkey. *Neuron* 60: 1126–1141.

Krifka, Manfred (1990). Four thousand ships passed through the lock: Object-induced measure functions on events. *Linguistics and Philosophy* 13(5): 487–520.

Krifka, Manfred, et al. (1995). Genericity: An introduction. In Gregory N. Carlson & Francis J. Pelletier (eds.), *The Generic Book*. Chicago: University of Chicago Press, 1–124.

Kroeber, Paul D. (1999). *The Salish Language Family: Reconstructing Syntax*. Lincoln/London: University Nebraska Press.

Kroeger, Paul A. (1993). Phrase structure and grammatical relations in Tagalog. Stanford: CSLI Publications.

Krug, Manfred G. (2000). *Emerging English Modals: A Corpus-based Study of Grammaticalization*. Berlin: Mouton de Gruyter.

Kruspe, Nicole D. (1999). Semelai. PhD dissertation, University of Melbourne.

Kruspe, Nicole (2004). Adjectives in Semelai. In R. M. W. Dixon & Alexandra Y. Aikhenvald (eds.), *Adjective Classes: A Cross-linguistic Typology*. Oxford: Oxford University Press, 283–305.

Kubus, Okan (2008). An analysis of Turkish Sign Language (TİD) phonology and morphology. Master's thesis, Middle East Technical University, Ankara.

Kuhn, Jeremy (2019). Pluractionality and distributive numerals. *Language and Linguistics Compass* 13(2): e12309. https://doi.org/10.1111/lnc3.12309

Kuhn, Wilfried (1982). Formale Verfahren der Technik Kollektion. In Hansjakob Seiler & Franz Josef Stachowiak (eds.), *Apprehension: das Sprachliche Erfassen von Gegenständen. Teil II: Die Techniken und ihr Zusammenhang in Einzelsprachen*. Tübingen: Narr, 55–83.

Kuipers, Aert H. (1967). *The Squamish Language: Grammar, Texts and Dictionary.* The Hague: Mouton.

Kuipers, Aert H. (1968). The categories verb–noun and transitive–intransitive in English and Squamish, *Lingua* 21: 610–626.

Kulikov, Leonid & Nikolaos Lavidas (eds.) (2013). *Proto-Indo-European Syntax and Its Development.* Amsterdam/Philadelphia: Benjamins.

Kulikov, Leonid & Heinz Vater (eds.) (1998). *Typology of Verbal Categories Papers Presented to Vladimir Nedjalkov on the Occasion of his 70th Birthday.* Berlin: Max Niemeyer Verlag.

Kunene, Daniel P. (1965). The ideophone in Southern Sotho. *Journal of African Languages* 4: 19–39.

Kupfer, Peter (1979). Die Wortarten im modernen Chinesischen. Zur Entwicklung und Etablierung einer grammatischen Kategorie. PhD dissertation, University of Bonn.

Kuryłowicz, Jerz (1968). *Indogermanische Grammatik,* Band II: Akzent–Ablaut. Heidelberg: Winter.

Kuryłowicz, Jerzy. ([1965] 1976). The evolution of grammatical categories. *Diogenes* 13 (51). [reprinted in J. Kuryłowicz, *Esquisses linguistiques,* vol. II, 38–54. Munich: Fink]

Kusters, Annelies & Lynn Hou (2020). Linguistic ethnography and sign language studies. *Sign Language Studies* 20(4): 561–571. https://doi.org/10.1353/sls.2020.0018

Kuteva, Tania (1998). On identifying an evasive gram: Action narrowly averted. *Studies in Language* 22: 113–160.

Kuteva, Tania (2000a). TAM-auxiliation and the avertive category in Northeast Europe. In Jocelyne Fernandez-Vest (ed.), *Areal grammaticalization.* Louvain/Paris: Peeters, 27–41.

Kuteva, Tania (2000b). Areal grammaticalization: The case of the Bantu-Nilotic borderland. *Folia Linguistica* 34: 267–283

Kuteva, Tania (2001). *Auxiliation: An Enquiry into the Nature of Grammaticalization.* Oxford: Oxford University Press.

Kuteva, Tania, et al. (2019). *World lexicon of grammaticalization* (2nd edn). Cambridge: Cambridge University Press.

Kutsch Lojenga, Constance (1994). *Ngiti: A Central-Sudanic Language of Zaire.* (Nilo-Saharan: Linguistic Analyses and Documentation, 9.) Cologne: Rüdiger Köppe.

Kuznetsova, N. V. & O. V. Kuznetsova (2017). Guro jazyk [The Guro language]. In Valentin Vydrin (ed.), *Jazyki mira: Jazyki mande* [The languages of the world: The Mande languages]. Sankt-Peterburg: Nestor-Istorija. 765–876.

Labov, William (1973). The boundaries of words and their meaning. In Charles-James N. Bailey & Roger W. Shuy (eds.), *New Ways of Analyzing Variation in English.* Washington, DC: Georgetown University Press, 340–373.

Lacroix, René (2009). Description du dialecte laze d'Arhavi (caucasique du sud, Turquie): Grammaire et textes. Doctoral dissertation, Université Lumière Lyon 2.

Lahaussois, Aimée (2016). Where have all the interjections gone? A look into the place of interjections in contemporary grammars of endangered languages. In Carlos Assunção, Gonçalo Fernandes, & R. Kemmler (eds.), *Tradition and Innovation in the History of Linguistics.* Münster: Nodus Publikationen, 186–195. (https://hal.archives-ouvertes.fr/hal-01361106)

Lahaussois, Aimeé (2018). Ideophones in Khaling Rai. *Linguistics of the Tibeto-Burman Area* 40(2): 179–201. doi:10.1075/ltba.17005.lah

Laiacona, Marcella & Alfonso Caramazza (2004). The noun/verb dissociation in language production: Varieties of causes. *Cognitive Neuropsychology* 21: 103–123.

Lakoff, George (1987a). *Women, Fire and Dangerous Things: What Categories Reveal about the Mind.* Chicago: University of Chicago Press.

Lakoff, George (1987b). Cognitive models and prototype theory. In Ulric Neisser (ed.), *Concepts and Conceptual Development*. Cambridge: Cambridge University Press, 63–100.

Lakoff, George (1993). The contemporary theory of metaphor. In Andrew Ortony (ed.), *Metaphor and Thought*. Cambridge: Cambridge University Press, 202–251.

Lakoff, George ([1987] 1999). Cognitive models and prototype theory. In Eric Margolis & Stephen Laurence (eds.), *Concepts: Core Readings*. Cambridge, MA: MIT Press, 391–421.

Lakoff, George & Mark Johnson (1980). *Metaphors We Live By*. Chicago: University of Chicago Press.

Lakusta, Laura & Barbara Landau. 2012. Language and memory for motion events: Origins of the asymmetry between source and goal paths. Cognitive Science 36(3). 517–544.

Lakusta, Laura, Danielle Spinelli, & Kathryn Garcia (2017). The relationship between preverbal event representations and semantic structures: The case of goal and source paths. *Cognition* 164: 174–187. https://doi.org/10.1016/j.cognition.2017.04.003

Lamberti, Marcello (1991). Cushitic and its classification. *Anthropos* 86(4–6): 552–561.

Lambrecht, Knud (2012). *Information Structure and Sentence Form. Topic, Focus, and the Mental Representation of Discourse Referents*. Cambridge: Cambridge University Press. https://doi.org/10.1017/cbo9780511620607

Landar, Herbert (1985). Navajo interjections. *International Journal of American Linguistics* 51(4): 489–491.

Langacker, Ronald W. (1987a). Nouns and verbs. *Language* 63: 53–94.

Langacker, Ronald W. (1987b). *Foundations of Cognitive Grammar*, vol. 1, *Theoretical Prerequisites*. Stanford: Stanford University Press.

Langacker, Ronald W. (1990). *Concept, Image, and Symbol: The Cognitive Basis of Grammar*. Berlin/New York: Mouton de Gruyter.

Langacker, Ronald W. (1991). *Foundations of Cognitive Grammar*, vol. 2, *Descriptive Application*. Stanford: Stanford University Press.

Langacker, Ronald W. (1999). *Grammar and Conceptualization*. Berlin/New York: Mouton de Gruyter.

Langacker, Ronald W. (2002). *Concept, Image and Symbol: The Cognitive Basis of Grammar*. Second edition. Berlin/New York: Mouton de Gruyter.

Langacker, Ronald W. (2006). On the continuous debate about discreteness. *Cognitive Linguistics* 17–1: 107–151.

Langacker Ronald W. (2008a). *Cognitive Grammar: A Basic Introduction*. New York: Oxford University Press.

Langacker, Ronald W. (2008b). Sequential and summary scanning: A reply. *Cognitive Linguistics* 19: 571–584.

Langacker, Ronald W. (2009). *Investigations in Cognitive Grammar*. Berlin: Mouton de Gruyter.

Langdon, Margaret (1994). Noise words in Guaraní. In Leanne Hinton, Johanna Nichols, & John J. Ohala (eds.), *Sound Symbolism*. Cambridge University Press, 94–103.

Langendonck, Willy V. (2008). *Theory and Typology of Proper Names*. Berlin: Mouton de Gruyter.

LaPolla, Randy J. (2020). Forward to the past: Modernizing linguistic typology by returning to its roots. *Asian Languages and Linguistics* 1(1): 146–166.

Larsen, Darrell (2014). Particles and particle-verb combinations in English and other Germanic languages. Dissertation, University of Delaware, Newark, DE.

Larson, Richard K. (1998). Events and modification in nominals. *Proceedings of Semantics and Linguistic Theory* 8: 145–168.

Lasersohn, Peter (1995). *Plurality, Conjunction and Events*. Dordrecht: Springer.
Lasersohn, Peter (2000). Same, models and representation. *Proceedings of Semantics and Linguistic Theory* 10: 83–97.
Lasersohn, Peter (2011). Mass nouns and plurals. In Klaus von Heusinger, Claudia Maienborn, & Paul Portner (eds.), *Semantics: An International Handbook of Natural Language Meaning*. Berlin: De Gruyter Mouton, vol. II, 1131–1153.
Laufer, Batia (1997a). The lexical plight in second language reading: Words you don't know, words you think you know and words you can't guess. In James Coady & Thomas Huckin (eds.), *Second Language Vocabulary Acquisition: A Rationale for Pedagogy*. Cambridge: Cambridge University Press, 20–34.
Laufer, Batia (1997b). What's in a word that makes it hard or easy? Intralexical factors affecting the difficulty of vocabulary acquisition. In Norbert Schmitt, & Michael McCarthy (eds.), *Vocabulary: Description, Acquisition and Pedagogy*. Cambridge: Cambridge University Press, 140–155.
Laughlin, Robert M. (1975). *The Great Tzotzil Dictionary of San Lorenzo Zinacantan*. Washington, DC: Smithsonian Institution Press.
Launey, Michel (1994). *Une grammaire omniprédicative: Essai sur la morphosyntaxe du nahuatl classique*. Paris: CNRS Editions.
Laury, Ritva (1997). *Demonstratives in Interaction: The Emergence of a Definite Article in Finnish*. Amsterdam: John Benjamins.
Law, Danny (2009). Pronominal borrowing among the Maya. *Diachronica* 26: 214–52.
Law, Danny (2017). Language contacts with(in) Mayan. In Judith Aissen, Nora C. England, & Roberto Zavala Maldonado (eds.), *The Mayan Languages*. London/New York: Routledge, 112–127.
Law, Danny & David Stuart (2017). Classic Mayan: An overview of language in ancient hieroglyphic script. In Judith Aissen, Nora C. England, & Roberto Zavala Maldonado (eds.), *The Mayan Languages*. London/New York: Routledge, 128–172.
Lawton, Ralph S. (1980). The Kiriwian classifiers. MA thesis, Australian National University, Canberra.
Le Bruyn, Bert, Henriëtte de Swart, & Joost Zwarts (2017). Bare nominals. In *Oxford Research Encyclopedia of Linguistics*. https://doi.org/10.1093/acrefore/9780199384655.013.399
Leclercq, Anne-Lise & Steve Majerus (2010). Serial-order short-term memory predicts vocabulary development: Evidence from a longitudinal study. *Developmental Psychology* 46(2): 417–427. https://doi.org/10.1037/a0018540
Ledgeway, Adam & Roberts, Ian (eds.) (2017). *The Cambridge Handbook of Historical Syntax*. Cambridge: Cambridge University Press.
Lee, Jennifer (1987). *Tiwi Today: A Study of Language Change in a Contact Situation*. Canberra: Pacific Linguistics.
Leech, Geoffrey & Andrew Wilson (1999). Standards for tagsets. In Hans van Halteren (ed.), *Syntactic Wordclass Tagging*. Dordrecht: Kluwer, 55–80.
Leeson, Lorraine & John Saeed (2012). Word order. In Roland Pfau, Markus Steinbach, & Bencie Woll (eds.), *Sign Language: An International Handbook*. Berlin/Boston, MA: Mouton de Gruyter, 245–265.
Lefebvre, Claire & Pieter Muysken (1988). *Mixed Categories. Nominalizations in Quechua*. Dordrecht: Kluwer.
Le Guen, Olivier (2014). Expressive morphology in Yucatec Maya. In Jean-Léo Léonard & Alain Khim (eds.), *Patterns in Mesoamerican Morphology*. Paris: Houdiard, 178–221.
Lehmann, Christian (1985). Grammaticalization: Synchronic variation and diachronic change. *Lingua e Stile* 20: 303–318.

Lehmann, Christian (1988). Towards a typology of clause linkage. In John Haiman & Sandra Thompson (eds.), *Clause Combining in Grammar and Discourse*. Amsterdam: John Benjamins, 181–225.

Lehmann, Christian (1990). Towards lexical typology. In William Croft, Keith Denning, and Suzanne Kemmer (eds.), *Studies in Typology and Diachrony. Papers Presented to Joseph H. Greenberg on His 75th Birthday*. Amsterdam: John Benjamins, 161–185.

Lehmann, Christian (1993/1995). Predicate classes in Yucatec. Función 13–14: 195–272. http://www.uni-erfurt.de/sprachwissenschaft/personal/lehmann/CL_Publ/pred_classes_ym.pdf

Lehmann, Christian ([1982] 1995). *Thoughts on Grammaticalization*. Munich: Lincom Europa. [first published as *Thoughts on Grammaticalization: A Programmatic Sketch*. No. 48 in the series Arbeiten des Kölner Universalien Projekts, University of Cologne, Institut für Sprachwissenschaft, 1982]

Lehmann, Christian (1998). German abstract prepositional phrases. *Copenhagen Studies in Language* 22: 87–106.

Lehmann, Christian (2002). *Possession in Yucatec Maya* (2nd rev. edn). Erfurt: Seminar für Sprachwissenschaft der Universität.

Lehmann, Christian (2008). Roots, stems and word classes. *Studies in Language* 32(3): 546–567. doi:10.1075/sl.32.3.04leh

Lehmann, Christian (2010). On the function of numeral classifiers. In Franck Floricic (ed.), *Essais de typologie et de linguistique générale. Mélanges offerts à Denis Creissels*. Lyon: École Normale Supérieure. 455–445.

Lehmann, Christian (2013). The nature of parts of speech. *Sprachtypologie und Universalienforschung* 66: 141–177.

Lehmann, Christian (2015). *Thoughts on Grammaticalization* (3rd edn). Berlin: Language Science Press.

Lehmann, Christian (2020). Univerbation. *Folia Linguistica Historica* 41: 205–252.

Lehmann, Christian & Edith Moravcsik (2000). Noun. In Geert Booij, Christian Lehmann, & Joachim Mugdan (eds.), *Morphology: An International Handbook on Inflection and Word-Formation*. Berlin: Mouton de Gruyter, vol. I, 732–757.

Lehmann, Thomas (1989). *A Grammar of Modern Tamil*. Pondicherry: Pondicherry Institute of Linguistics and Culture.

Lehmann, Winfred P. (1974). *Proto-Indo-European Syntax*. Austin: University of Texas Press.

Lehmann, Winfred P. (1993). *Theoretical Bases of Indo-European Languages*. London/New York: Routledge.

Leikin, Mark (2002). Locative prepositions in language acquisition and aphasia. In Susanne Feigenbaum & Dennis Kurzon (eds.), *Prepositions in Their Syntactic, Semantic, and Pragmatic Context*. Amsterdam: John Benjamins, 283–299.

Leite, Yonne. (1990). Para uma tipologia ativa do Tapirapé. Os clíticos referenciais de pessoa. *Cadernos de Estudios Linguisticos* 18: 37–56.

Leonard, William R. & Marica L. Robertson (1992). Nutritional requirements and human evolution: A bioenergetics model. *American Journal of Human Biology* 4(2): 179–195.

Lepic, Ryan (2019). A usage-based alternative to 'lexicalization' in sign language linguistics. *Glossa: A Journal of General Linguistics* 4(1): 23. https://doi.org/10.5334/gjgl.840

Lepic, Ryan & Corrine Occhino (2018). A construction morphology approach to sign language analysis. In Geert Booij (ed.), *The Construction of Words: Advances in Construction Morphology*. (Studies in Morphology.) Cham: Springer, 141–172. https://doi.org/10.1007/978-3-319-74394-3_6, https://doi.org/10.1007/978-3-319-74394-3_6

Lepic, Ryan & Tessa Verhoef (2020). Gestural origins of verb and noun encoding in sign language emergence. In Andrea Ravignani et al. (eds.), *The Evolution of Language: Proceedings of the 13th International Conference (EvoLang13)*. https://doi.org/10.17617/2.3190925, http://brussels.evolang.org/proceedings/paper.html?nr=200

Letuchiy, Alexander B. (2015). Russian zero copulas and lexical verbs: similar or different? *Lingue e linguaggio* 2: 233–250.

Letuchiy, Alexander B. (2022). *Imperativ v roli glavnogo predikata* [Imperative as a main clause predicate]. Proceedings of the conference "Dialogue-2022". Moscow: RGGU Publishers. 1118-1130. https://www.dialog-21.ru/media/5738/letuchiyab101.pdf

Lester, Nicholas, Balthasar Bickel, Steven Moran, Sabine Stoll, Megan M Brown & Alexandra Kohut. 2019. Speech Rates Differentiate Nouns and Verbs in Child-Surrounding and Child-Produced Speech: Evidence from Chintang.

Letuchiy, Alexander B. (2021). *Russkij jazyk o situacijax: konstrukcii s sentencial'nymi aktantami* [Russian about situations: constructions with complement clauses]. Saint-Petersburg: Aletheia.

Letuchiy, Alexander B. & Anna V. Viklova (2020). Podjem i smežnye javlenija v russkom jazyke (preimuščestvenno na materiale interpretacii mestoimenij) [Raising and similar phenomena in Russian (mainly based on the pronoun interpretation)], *Voprosy jazykoznanija* 5: 31–60.

Levelt, Willem J. M. (1989). *Speaking: From Intention to Articulation*. Cambridge, MA: MIT Press.

Levelt, Willem JM. 1993. Speaking: From intention to articulation, vol. 1. MIT press.

Levin, Beth (1993). *English Verb Classes and Alternations*. Chicago: University of Chicago Press.

Levin, Beth & Malka Rappaport Hovav (2011). Conceptual categories and linguistic categories VIII: Nouns and individuation. Handout, *Conceptual Categories and Linguistic Categories*. Linguistics Institute Summer 2011, University of Colorado, Boulder, CO. Available at https://web.stanford.edu/~bclevin/lsa11nouns.pdf

Levine, Robert (2017). *Syntactic Analysis: An HPSG-based Approach*. Cambridge: Cambridge University Press.

Levinson, Stephen C. (2000). *Presumptive Meaning: The Theory of Generalized Conversational Implicature*. Cambridge, MA/London: MIT Press.

Levinson, Stephen C. (2003a). *Space in Language and Cognition*. Cambridge: Cambridge University Press.

Levinson, Stephen C. (2003b). Language and mind: Let's get the issues straight! In Dedre Gentner & Susan Goldin-Meadow (eds.), *Language in Mind: Advances in the Study of Language and Thought*. Cambridge, MA/London: MIT Press, 25–46. [also published in Susan D. Blum (ed.), *Making Sense of Language: Readings in Culture and Communication* (3rd edn) Oxford: Oxford University Press, 2016, 68–80]

Levinson, Stephen C. (2018). Demonstratives—Patterns of diversity. In Stephen C. Levinson, et al. (eds.), *Demonstratives in Cross-linguistic Perspective*. Cambridge: Cambridge University Press, 1–42.

Levinson, Stephen C. & Nicholas Evans (2010). Time for a sea-change in linguistics: Response to comments on 'The Myth of Language Universals'. *Lingua* 120: 2733–2758.

Levinson, Stephen C., Sérgio Meira, & the Language and Cognition Group (2003). 'Natural concepts' in the spatial topological domain—Adpositional meanings in crosslinguistic perspective: an exercise in semantic typology. *Language* 79: 485–516.

Levinson, Stephen C. & David Wilkins (2006). Appendix 4: 'Topological relations picture series'. In Stephen C. Levinson & David Wilkins (eds.), *Grammars of space: explorations in cognitive diversity*. Cambridge: Cambridge University Press, 570-585.

Levshina, Natalia (2015). *How to Do Linguistics with R: Data Exploration and Statistical Analysis*. Amsterdam: John Benjamins.

Levy, Paulette (1992). Adjectives in Totonac: Descriptive statement and typological considerations. *International Journal of American Linguistics* 58: 269-298.

Levy, Paulette (2004). Adjectives in Papantla Totonac. In R. M. W. Dixon & Alexandra Y. Aikhenvald (eds.), *Adjective Classes: A Cross-linguistic Typology*. Oxford: Oxford University Press, 147-176.

Lewis, David (1970). General semantics. *Synthese* 22: 18-67.

Lewis, Geoffrey L. (1967). *Turkish Grammar*. Oxford: Clarendon Press.

Lewis, Ioan M. (1958). The Gadabuursi Somali script. *Bulletin of the School of Oriental and African Studies* 21(1/3): 134-156.

Li, Charles N. & Sandra A. Thompson (1974). Co-verbs in Mandarin Chinese: Verbs or prepositions? *Journal of Chinese Linguistics* 2(3): 257-278.

Li, Charles N. & Sandra A. Thompson (1977). A mechanism for the development of copula morphemes. In Charles N. Li (ed.), *Mechanisms of Syntactic Change*. Austin: University of Texas Press, 419-444.

Li, Charles N. & Sandra A. Thompson (1981). *Mandarin Chinese: A Functional Reference Grammar*. Berkeley: University of California Press.

Li, Peggy, David Barner, & Becky H. Huang (2008). Classifiers as count syntax: Individuation and measurement in the acquisition of Mandarin Chinese. *Language Learning and Development* 4(4): 249-290.

Li, Peggy, Yarrow Dunham, & Susan Carey (2009). Of substance: The nature of language effects on entity construal. *Cognitive Psychology* 58: 487-524.

Libert, Alan (2006). *Ambipositions*. Munich: Lincom Europa.

Libert, Alan (2013). *Adpositions and Other Parts of Speech*. Bern: Peter Lang.

Lichtenberk, Frantisek (1991). Semantic change and heterosemy in grammaticalization. *Language* 67(3): 475-509. doi:10.2307/415035

Lichtenberk, Frantisek (2005). On the notion of 'adjective' in Toqabaqita. *Oceanic Linguistics* 44(1): 113-144.

Lichtenberk, Frantisek (2008a). *A Grammar of Toqabaqita*. Berlin/New York: Mouton de Gruyter.

Lichtenberk, Frantisek (2008b). *A Dictionary of Toqabaqita (Solomon Islands)*. Canberra: Australian National University.

Liddell, Scott K. (2003). *Grammar, Gesture, and Meaning in American Sign Language*. Cambridge: Cambridge University Press.

Liddell, Scott K., Marit Vogt-Svendsen, & Brita Bergman (2007). A crosslinguistic comparison of buoys. Evidence from American, Norwegian, and Swedish Sign Language. In Myriam Vermeerbergen, Lorraine Leeson, & Onno Crasborn (eds.), *Simultaneity in Signed Languages: Form and Function*. (Current Issues in Linguistic Theory vol. 281.) Amsterdam: John Benjamins, 187-215. https://doi.org/10.1075/cilt.281.09lid.

Lieber, Rochelle (1981). On the organization of the lexicon. PhD dissertation, MIT.

Lieber, Rochelle (2016). *English Nouns: The Ecology of Nominalization*. Cambridge: Cambridge University Press.

Lieber, Rochelle (2017). Derivational morphology. Online: *Oxford Research Encyclopedia of Linguistics*. doi:10.1093/acrefore/9780199384655.013.248

Liesenfeld, Andreas (2019). Cantonese turn-initial minimal particles: Annotation of discourse–interactional functions in dialog corpora. *Proceedings of the 33rd Pacific Asia Conference on Language, Information and Computation*. Waseda Institute for the Study of Language and Information, 471–479.

Lieven, Elena VM, Julian M Pine & Gillian Baldwin. 1997. Lexically-based learning and early grammatical development. Journal of Child Language 24. 187–219.

Liljegren, Henrik (2016). *A Grammar of Palula*. (Studies in Diversity Linguistics, 8.) Berlin: Language Science Press.

Lillo-Martin, Diane & Edward S. Klima (1990). Pointing out differences: ASL pronouns in syntactic theory. In Susan D. Fischer & Patricia Siple (eds.), *Theoretical Issues in Sign Language Research, Vol. 1: Linguistics*. Chicago: University of Chicago Press, 191–210.

Lillo-Martin, Diane & Richard P. Meier (2011). On the linguistic status of 'agreement' in sign languages. *Theoretical Linguistics* 37(3–4): 95–142. https://doi.org/10.1515/thli.2011.009

Lima, Suzie Oliveira de (2007). *Duplicação, Supleção, Afixação e Alternância Verbal em línguas Tupi: pluralidade de sintagmas nominais ou de eventos?* IX ENAPOL (Encontro dos Alunos de Pós-Graduação em Lingüística da Universidade de São Paulo), São Paulo.

Lima, Suzi Oliveira de (2018). New perspectives on the count–mass distinction: Understudied languages and psycholinguistics. *Language and Linguistics Compass* 12: e12303. https://doi.org/10.1111/lnc3.12303

Lindsey, Geoffrey & Janine Scancarelli (1985). Where have all the adjectives come from? The case of Cherokee. *Proceedings of the Berkeley Linguistics Society* 11: 207–215.

Lindstromberg, Seth (2010). *English Prepositions Explained*. Amsterdam: John Benjamins.

Lionnet, Florian (2014). Demonstratives and relative constructions in Ju. In Tom Güldemann & Anne-Maria Fehn (eds.), *Beyond 'Khoisan': Historical Relations in the Kalahari Basin*. Amsterdam: John Benjamins, 181–208.

Lionnet, Florian (2020). Paralinguistic use of clicks in Chad. In Bonny Sands (ed.), *Click Consonants*. Leiden: Brill, 422–437. doi:10.1163/9789004424357_015

Lipscomb, David Robert (1993). A critique of the nominal hypothesis for Eskimo. *Études/Inuit/Studies* 17(2): 127–140.

Littlefield, Heather (2005). Lexical and functional prepositions in acquisition: Evidence for a hybrid category. Boston University Conference on Language Development 29, Online Proceedings Supplement, Boston, MA.

Lobke, Aelbrecht, Liliane Haegeman, & Rachel Nye (eds.) (2012). *Main Clause Phenomena. New Horizons* [Linguistik Aktuell/Linguistics Today 190]. Amsterdam/Philadelphia: Benjamins.

Lockwood, Gwilym, Mark Dingemanse, & Peter Hagoort (2016). Sound-symbolism boosts novel word learning, *Journal of Experimental Psychology: Learning, Memory, and Cognition* 42: 1274–1281.

Lødrup, Helge (2012). In search of a nominal COMP. In Miriam Butt & Tracy Holloway King (eds.), *On-line Proceedings of the LFG2012 Conference*. Stanford, CA: CSLI Publications, 341–361. http://csli-publications.stanford.edu/LFG/17/lfg12.html

Logan, Gordon D. (1988). Toward an instance theory of automatization. *Psychological Review* 95(4): 492–527. https://doi.org/10.1037/0033-295X.95.4.492

Lohmann, Arne (2017). Phonological properties of word classes and the direction of conversion. *Word Structure* 10(2): 204–234. doi: 10.3366/word.2017.0108

Lois, Ximena (1998). Gender markers as 'rigid determiners' of the Itzaj Maya world. *International Journal of American Linguistics* 64: 224–282.

Lois, Ximena (2011). Roots and patterns in Yucatecan languages. In Kirill Shklovsky, Pedro Mateo, & Jessica Coon (eds.), *Proceedings of FAMLi: Formal Approaches to Mayan Linguistics*. Cambridge, MA: MIT Working Papers in Linguistics.

Lois, Ximena, et al. (2017). Polycategoriality across Mayan languages: Action nouns and ergative splits. In Valentina Vapnarsky & Edy Veneziano (eds.), *Lexical Polycategoriality: Cross-linguistic, Cross-theoretical and Language Acquisition Approaches.* Amsterdam: John Benjamins, 101–153.

Lois, Ximena & Valentina Vapnarsky (2003). *Polyvalence of Root Classes in Yukatekan Mayan Languages.* Munich: Lincom Europa.

Lois, Ximena & Valentina Vapnarsky (2006). Root indeterminacy and polyvalence in Yukatekan Mayan languages. In Ximena Lois & Valentina Vapnarsky (eds.), *Lexical Categories and Root Classes in Amerindian Languages.* Bern: Peter Lang, 69–116.

Longobardi, Giuseppe (1994). Reference and proper names: A theory of N-movement in syntax and logical form. *Linguistic Inquiry* 25(4): 609–665.

Longobardi, Giuseppe (2000). 'Postverbal' subjects and the mapping hypothesis. *Linguistic Inquiry* 31(4): 691–702.

Loos, Cornelia. A class of their own? Adjectives in ASL. Unpublished ms. Available at: https://www.academia.edu/37359021/A_class_of_their_own_Adjectives_in_ASL

López Ixcoy, Candelaria Dominga (Saqijiix) (1994). *Las vocales en K'ichee.* Nawal Wuj, Guatemala.

Loprieno, Antonio (1995). *Ancient Egyptian: A Linguistic Introduction.* Cambridge: Cambridge University Press.

Lord, Carol (1993) *Historical Change in Serial Verb Constructions.* Amsterdam: John Benjamins.

Lotto, Lorealla & Annette M. B. de Groot (2002). Effects of learning method and word type on acquiring vocabulary in an unfamiliar language. *Language Learning* 48: 31–69.

Louagie, Dana (2017). The status of determining elements in Australian languages. *Australian Journal of Linguistics* 37(2): 182–218.

Louagie, Dana (2020). *Noun Phrases in Australian Languages: A Typological Study.* Berlin/New York: Mouton de Gruyter.

Louagie, Dana (2022). Multiple construction types for nominal expressions in Australian languages: Towards a typology. *Studies in Language.* https://doi.org/10.1075/sl.21008.lou

Louagie, Dana (2023). Demonstratives. In Claire Bowern (ed.), *The Oxford Guide to Australian Languages.* Oxford: Oxford University Press 253–267. DOI: 10.1093/oso/9780198824978.003.0023.

Louagie, Dana & Jean-Christophe Verstraete (2015). Personal pronouns with determining functions in Australian languages. *Studies in Language* 39: 158–197.

Louagie, Dana & Jean-Christophe Verstraete (2016). Noun phrase constituency in Australian languages: A typological study. *Linguistic Typology* 20: 25–80.

Lounsbury, Floyd G. ([1953] 1976). *Oneida Verb Morphology.* New Haven, CT: Human Relations Area Files Press.

Lovestrand, Joseph (2018). Serial verb constructions in Barayin: Typology, description and Lexical-Functional Grammar D.Phil. thesis, University of Oxford. https://ora.ox.ac.uk/objects/uuid:39406562-02d3-46f5-abf3-180d22225925

Lovestrand, Joseph & John J. Lowe (2017). Minimal c-structure: Rethinking projection in phrase structure. In Miriam Butt & Tracy Holloway King (eds.), *On-line Proceedings of the LFG2017 Conference.* Stanford, CA: CSLI Publications. http://web.stanford.edu/group/cslipublications/cslipublications/LFG/LFG-2017/index.shtml.

Lowe, John J. (2015). The syntax of Sanskrit compounds. *Language* 91(3): 71–115.

Lowe, John J. (2016a). Clitics: Separating syntax and prosody. *Journal of Linguistics* 52(2): 375–419.

Lowe, John J. (2016b). English possessive 's: Clitic and affix. *Natural Language and Linguistic Theory* 34(1): 157–195.

Lowe, John J. (2017). *Transitive Nouns and Adjectives: Evidence from Early Indo-Aryan Oxford Studies in Diachronic and Historical Linguistics*. Oxford: Oxford University Press.

Lowe, John J. (2019). Mixed projections and syntactic categories. *Journal of Linguistics* 56(2): 315–357. https://doi.org/10.1017/S0022226719000100

Lowe, John J. & Joseph Lovestrand (2020). Minimal phrase structure: A new formalized theory of phrase structure. *Journal of Language Modelling* 8(1): 1–52.

Lowenstamm, Jean (2015). Derivational affixes as roots: Phasal spell-out meets English stress shift. In Artemis Alexiadou, Hagit Borer, & Florian Schäfer (eds.), *The Syntax of Roots and the Roots of Syntax*. Oxford: Oxford University Press, 230–259.

Lü, Shuxiang (吕叔湘) (1979). 汉语语法分析问题 *Hànyǔ yǔfǎ fēnxī wèntí* [Problems of grammatical analysis in Chinese]. Beijing: Commercial Press.

Lucy, John A. (1992). *Grammatical Categories and Cognition: A Case Study of the Linguistic Relativity Hypothesis*. Cambridge: Cambridge University Press.

Lucy, John A. (1994). The role of semantic value in lexical comparison: Motion and position in Yucatec Maya. *Linguistics* 32(4/5): 623–656.

Lucy, John A. (2010). Language structure, lexical meaning, and cognition: Whorf and Vygotsky revisited. In Barbara C. Malt & Phillip Wolff (eds.), *Words and the Mind: How Words Capture Human Experience*. Oxford: Oxford University Press, 266–286.

Lüpke, Friederike (2005). A grammar of Jalonke argument structure. PhD thesis, Nijmegen: Radboud University.

Lupyan, Gary & Andy Clark (2015). Words and the world: Predictive coding and the language–perception–cognition interface. *Current Directions in Psychological Science* 24(4): 279–284. https://doi.org/10.1177/0963721415570732

Lutzenberger, Hannah (2018). Manual and nonmanual features of name signs in Kata Kolok and sign language of the Netherlands. *Sign Language Studies* 18(4): 546–569. https://doi.org/10.1353/sls.2018.0016

Luzzatti, Claudio, Silvia Aggujaro, & Davide Crepaldi, D. (2006). Verb–noun double dissociation in aphasia: Theoretical and neuroanatomical foundations. *Cortex* 42: 872–883.

Lynch, John, Malcolm Ross, & Terry Crowley (2002). *The Oceanic Languages*. Richmond: Curzon.

Lyons, John (1968). *Introduction to Theoretical Linguistics*. Cambridge: Cambridge University Press.

Lyons, John (1977). *Semantics*. Cambridge: Cambridge University Press.

Ma, Jianzhong 马建忠 (1898). 马氏文通 *Mǎ shì wéntōng* [Ma's Grammar]. Shanghai: Commercial Press.

McBurney, Susan (2012). History of sign languages and sign language linguistics. In Roland Pfau, Markus Steinbach, & Bencie Woll (eds.), *Sign Language: An International Handbook*. Berlin/Boston, MA: Walter de Gruyter, 909–948.

McCawley, James D. (1976). *Grammar and Meaning. Papers on Syntactic and Semantic Topics*. New York: Academic Press.

McCawley, James D. (1995). Generative semantics. In Jef Verschueren, Jan-Ola Östman, & Jan Blommaert (eds.), *Handbook of Pragmatics*. Amsterdam: John Benjamins, 311–319.

McCawley, James D. (1998). *The Syntactic Phenomena of English* (2nd edn). Chicago: University of Chicago Press.

McDonald, David D. (1993). Internal and external evidence in the identification and semantic categorization of proper names. *Proceedings of the Workshop on Acquisition of Lexical Knowledge from Text*. Columbus, Ohio: Special Interest Group on the Lexicon of the Association for Computational Linguistics, 32–43.

MacDonald, Lorna (1990). *A Grammar of Tauya*. Berlin: Mouton de Gryuter.

McDonough, Colleen, Lulu Song, Kathy Hirsh-Pasek, Roberta Michnick Golinkoff & Robert Lannon. 2011. An image is worth a thousand words: Why nouns tend to dominate verbs in early word learning. Developmental Science 14(2). 181–189.

McGregor, William (1990). *A Functional Grammar of Gooniyandi*. Amsterdam: John Benjamins.

McGregor, William (2001). Ideophones as the source of verbs in Northern Australian languages. In F. K. Erhard Voeltz & Christa Kilian-Hatz (eds.), *Ideophones*. Amsterdam: John Benjamins, 205–221.

McGregor, William (2002). *Verb Classification in Australian Languages*. Berlin/New York: Mouton de Gruyter.

McGregor, William (2003). Aspect, time, and associative relations in Australian languages. *Tidsskrift for Sprogforskning* 1(1): 151–175.

McGregor, William (2004). *The Languages of the Kimberley, Western Australia*. London: RoutledgeCurzon.

McGregor, William (2005). Quantifying depictive secondary predicates in Australian languages. In Nikolaus Himmelmann & Schultze-Berndt (eds.), *Secondary Predication and Adverbial Modification: The Typology of Depictives*. Oxford: Oxford University Press, 173–200.

McGregor, William (2011). *The Nyulnyul language of Dampier land, Western Australia* (2 vols.). Canberra: Pacific Linguistics.

McGregor, William (2013). Lexical categories in Gooniyandi, Kimberley, Western Australia. In Jan Rijkhoff & Eva van Lier (eds.), *Flexible Word Classes: Typological Studies of Underspecified Parts of Speech*. Oxford: Oxford University Press, 221–246.

McGregor, William (2019a). Reported speech as a dedicated grammatical domain—And why defenestration should not be thrown out the window. *Linguistic Typology* 23(1): 207–219.

McGregor, William (2019b). Number in Gooniyandi. Unpublished ms, Dept. of Linguistics, Aarhus University (Denmark).

McGregor, William & Søren Wichmann (eds.) (2018). *The Diachrony of Classification Systems*. Amsterdam: John Benjamins.

Mackenzie, J. Lachlan (1987). Nominalization and basic constituent ordering. In Johan van der Auwera & Louis Goossens (eds.), *Ins and Outs of Predication*. Dordrecht: Foris, 93–106.

Mackenzie, J. Lachlan (2001). Adverbs and adpositions: the Cinderella categories of Functional Grammar. *Revista Canaria de Estudios Ingleses* 42: 119–136.

Mackenzie, J. Lachlan (2013). Spatial adpositions between lexicon and grammar. In J. Lachlan Mackenzie & Hella Olbertz (eds.), *Casebook in Functional Discourse Grammar*. Amsterdam: John Benjamins, 67-93.

Mackenzie, Laurel (2018). What's in a name? Teaching linguistics using onomastic data. *Language* 94(4): e293–e310.

McLaughlin, Fiona (2004). Is there an adjective class in Wolof? In R. M. W. Dixon & Alexandra Y. Aikhenvald (eds.), *Adjective Classes: A Cross-linguistic Typology*. Oxford: Oxford University Press, 242–262.

McLean, Bonnie (2020). Revising an implicational hierarchy for the meanings of ideophones, with special reference to Japonic. *Linguistic Typology* 25(3). doi:10.1515/lingty-2020-2063

MacLean, Edna Ahgeak (1980). *Iñpiallu Tanŋiḷḷu Uqaluŋisa Iḷaŋich: Abridged Iñupiaq and English Dictionary*. Barrow, AK: Iñupiat Language Commission, North Slope Borough, and Fairbanks, AK: Alaska Native Language Center, University of Alaska.

MacLean, Edna Ahgeak (1986). *North Slope Iñupiaq Grammar: First Year* (3rd edn). Fairbanks, AK: Alaska Native Language Center.

MacLean, Edna Ahgeak (1995). Inupiaq narratives: Interaction of demonstratives, aspect, and tense. PhD dissertation, Stanford University.

Macnamara, John. 1982. Names for things: a study of human learning. Cambridge, MA: Bradford Books.

MacWhinney, Brian (2005). Item-based constructions and the logical problem. *Proceedings of the Second Workshop on Psychocomputational Models of Human Language Acquisition*, 53–68.

MacWhinney, Brian, & Catherine Snow (1985). The child language data exchange system. *Journal of Child Language* 12: 271–295.

MacWhinney, Brian, Andrej Malchukov, & Edith Moravcsik (eds.) (2014). *Competing Motivations in Grammar and Usage*. Oxford: Oxford University Press.

Maekelberghe, Charlotte (2019). *The Present-day English Gerund System: A Cognitive-Constructionist Account*. Berlin: Mouton de Gruyter.

Maffi, Luisa (1990). Tzeltal Maya affect verbs: Psychological salience and expressive. *Functions of Language Proceedings of the Sixteenth Annual Meeting of the Berkeley Linguistics Society: Special Session on General Topics in American Indian Linguistics* (1990): 61–72.

Magalhães, Marina (2007). Sobre a morfologia e a sintaxe da língua Guajá (família Tupí-Guaraní). PhD dissertation, Universidade de Brasília.

Maienborn, Claudia (2011). Event semantics. In Claudia Maienborn, Klaus von Heusinger, & Paul Portner (eds.), *Semantics: An International Handbook of Natural Language Meaning*. Berlin: De Gruyter, vol. I, 802–829.

Maienborn, Claudia (2021). Revisiting Olga, the beautiful dancer: An intersective A-analysis. *Proceedings Semantics and Linguistic Theory* 30: 63–82.

Majid, Asifa & Stephen C. Levinson (2010). WEIRD languages have misled us, too. *Behavioral and Brain Sciences* 33(2–3): 103–103.

Majid, Asifa, Alice Gaby, & Lera Boroditsky (2013). Time in terms of space. *Frontiers in Psychology* 4: 554.

Malaia, Evie (2004). Event structure and telicity in Russian: an event-based analysis for telicity puzzle in Slavic languages. *Ohio State University Working Papers in Slavic Studies* 4.

Malaia, Evie & Debarchana Basu (2013). Verb–verb predicates in Bangla and Russian: Morpho-semantic event structure analysis. In *NINJAL International Conference on V–V complexes in Asian languages, Tokyo, Japan*.

Malchukov, Andrej (2004). *Nominalization/Verbalization: Constraining a Typology of Transcategorial Operations*. Munich: Lincom Europa.

Malchukov, Andrej (2006). Constraining nominalization: Function–form competition. *Linguistics* 44(5): 973–1008.

Malchukov, Andrej (2019). Verbalization of nominalizations: A typological commentary on the article by Nikki van de Pol. *Language Sciences* 73: 105–118.

Malchukov, Andrej & Anna Siewerska (2011). *Impersonal Constructions: A Cross-linguistic Perspective*. (Studies in Language Companion Series 124.) Amsterdam: John Benjamins.

Malchukov, Andrej & Bernard Comrie (eds.) (2015). *Valency Classes in the World's Languages*. Berlin: Mouton de Gruyter.

Maling, Joan (1983). Transitive adjectives: A case of categorial reanalysis. In Frank Heny & Barry Richards (eds.), *Linguistic Categories: Auxiliaries and Related Puzzles*. Dordrecht: Reidel, vol. I, 253–289.

Malinowski, Bronisław (1923). The problem of meaning in primitive languages. In C. K. Ogden & I. A. Richards (eds.), *The Meaning of Meaning: A Study of the Influence of Language upon Thought and the Science of Symbolism*. London: Kegan Paul, 296–336.

Malouf, Robert (2000a). *Mixed Categories in the Hierarchical Lexicon*. Stanford, CA: CSLI Publications.

Malouf, Robert (2000b). Verbal gerunds as mixed categories in HPSG. In Robert Borsley (ed.), *The Nature and Function of Syntactic Categories. Syntax and Semantics 32*. New York: Academic Press, 133–166.

Mameli, Matteo & Patrick Bateson. 2006. Innateness and the sciences. Biology and Philosophy 21(2). 155–188.

Manning, Christopher (2011). Part-of-speech tagging from 97% to 100%: Is it time for some linguistics? In Alexander F. Gelbukh (ed.), *Computational Linguistics and Intelligent Text Processing. CICLing 2011. Lecture Notes in Computer Science*, vol. 6608. Berlin: Springer, 171–189. https://doi.org/10.1007/978-3-642-19400-9_14

Manrique, Elizabeth (2016). Other-initiated repair in Argentine Sign Language. *Open Linguistics* 2(1): 1–34. doi:10.1515/opli-2016-0001

Manrique, Elizabeth & Nick J. Enfield (2015). Suspending the next turn as a form of repair initiation: Evidence from Argentine Sign Language. *Frontiers in Psychology: Language Sciences* 6: 1326. doi:10.3389/fpsyg.2015.01326

Marácz, László (1989). Asymmetries in Hungarian. PhD thesis, Rijksuniversiteit Groningen.

Marantz, Alec (1997). No escape from syntax: Don't try morphological analysis in the privacy of your own lexicon. In Alexis Dimitriadis et al. (eds.), *Proceedings of the 21st Annual Penn Linguistics Colloquium*. Penn Working Papers in Linguistics 4, 201–225.

Marantz, Alec (2001). Words. Paper presented at West Coast Conference of Formal Linguistics, UCLA.

Marantz, Alec (2007). Phases and words. In S. H. Choe (ed.), *Phases in the Theory of Grammar*. Seoul: Dong-In Publishing Co., 191–222.

Maratsos, Michael. 1988. Crosslinguistic Analysis, Universals, and Language. In Frank S. Kessel (ed.), The Development of Language and Language Researchers: Essays in Honor of Roger Brown, chap. 7, 121–152. Psychology Press.

Maratsos, Michael P. & Mary A. Chalkley. 1980. The internal language of children's syntax: the ontogenesis and representation of syntactic categories. In Katherine Nelson (ed.), *Children's Language*, vol. 2, 127–151. New York: Gardner Press.

Marcotte, Jean-Philippe (2014). Syntactic categories in the correspondence architecture. In Miriam Butt & Tracy Holloway King (eds.), *On-line Proceedings of the LFG2014 Conference*, Stanford, CA: CSLI Publications. http://csli-publications.stanford.edu/LFG/19/lfg14.html.

Marcoux, Joseph (1828). *Grammaire iroquoise ou la langue iroquoise reduite en principes fixes*. Manuscript kept in the St. Francis Xavier Mission Church. Kahnawake Mohawk Territory, Canada.

Mardale, Alexandru (2011). Prepositions as a semilexical category. *Bucharest Working Papers in Linguistics* 13: 35–50.

Margetts, Anna (1999). Valency and transitivity in Saliba, an Oceanic Language of Papua New Guinea. Radboud University dissertation, Nijmegen.

Marivate, Cornelius Tennyson Daniel (1983). The ideophone in Tsonga. PhD dissertation, University of South Africa.

Martin, Akwiratékha' (2016). *Iekawennahsonterónnion, Kanien'kéha Morphology*. Kahnawake, Mohawk Territory, Canada: Kanien'kehá:ka Onkwawén:na Raotitióhkwa.

Martin, Alex (2007). The representation of object concepts in the brain. *Annual Review of Psychology* 58: 25–45.

Martinet, André (1960). *Éléments de linguistique générale*. Paris: Armand Colin.

Martínez Cruz, Victoriano (2007). Los adjetivos y conceptos de propiedad en chol. MA thesis, CIESAS, Mexico.

Marvin, Tatjana (2002). Topics in the stress and syntax of words. PhD dissertation, MIT.

Maslova, Elena (2003). *A Grammar of Kolyma Yukaghir*. Berlin: Mouton de Gruyter.

Massam, Diane (ed.) (2012). *Count and Mass across Languages*. Oxford: Oxford University Press.

Mateo Toledo, Eladio (2017). Q'anjob'al. In Judith Aissen, Nora C. England, & Roberto Zavala Maldonado (eds.), *The Mayan Languages*. London/New York: Routledge, 570–609.

Mathiot, Madeleine (1967). The cognitive significance of the category of nominal number in Papago. In Dell Hymes & William Bittle (eds.), *Studies in Southwestern Ethnolinguistics*. (Studies in General Anthropology III.) The Hague: Mouton, 197–237.

Matras, Yaron (1998). Utterance modifiers and universals of grammatical borrowing. *Linguistics* 36: 281–331.

Matras, Yaron (2003). Mixed languages: Re-examining the structural prototype. In Yaron Matras & Peter Bakker (eds.), *The Mixed Language Debate: Theoretical and Empirical Advances*. Berlin: Mouton de Gruyter, 151–175.

Matras, Yaron (2007). The borrowability of grammatical categories. In Yaron Matras & Jeanette Sakel (eds.), *Grammatical Borrowing in Cross-Linguistic Perspective*. Berlin: Mouton de Gruyter, 31–74.

Matras, Yaron (2011). Explaining convergence and the formation of linguistic areas. In Osamu Hieda, Christa König, & Hirosi Nakagawa (eds.), *Geographical Typology and Linguistic Areas*. Amsterdam: John Benjamins, 143–160.

Matras, Yaron (2012). *A Grammar of Domari*. Berlin: Mouton de Gruyter.

Matras, Yaron (2020). *Language Contact* (2nd edn). Cambridge: Cambridge University Press.

Matras, Yaron & Jeanette Sakel (2007). Investigating the mechanisms of pattern-replication in language convergence. *Studies in Language* 31: 829–865.

Matthews, Peter H. (1981). *Syntax*. Cambridge: Cambridge University Press.

Matthews, Stephen & Virginia Yip (1994). *Cantonese: A Comprehensive Grammar*. London: Routledge.

Matthewson, Lisa (1998). *Determiner Systems and Quantificational Strategies: Evidence from Salish*. The Hague: Holland Academic Graphics.

Matthewson, Lisa (2000). On distributivity and pluractionality, *Semantics and Linguistic Theory* 10: 98–114.

Matthewson, Lisa & Hamida Demirdache (1995). Syntactic categories in St'at'imcets (Lillooet Salish). *North East Linguistics Society* 25(1): 69–75.

Mätzig, Simone, et al. (2009). Noun and verb differences in picture naming: Past studies and new evidence. *Cortex* 45: 738–758.

Mauri, Caterina (2010). The added value of the connectivity hypothesis for the map of parts of speech. *Linguistic Discovery* 8(1): 157–159.

Mayr, Ernst (1982). *The Growth of Biological Thought: Diversity, Evolution, Inheritance*. Cambridge, MA: Belknap Press.

Meakins, Felicity & Rachel Nordlinger (2014). *A Grammar of Bilinarra: An Australian Aboriginal Language of the Northern Territory*. Berlin: Mouton de Gruyter.

Mei, Tsu-Lin (梅祖麟) (1989). The causative and denominative functions of the *s- prefix in Old Chinese. In *Proceedings of the 2nd International Conference on Sinology: Section on Linguistics and Paleography*. Taipei: Academia Sinica, 33–51.

Mei, Tsu-Lin (梅祖麟) (2008). 上古汉语动词浊清别义的来源 *Shànggǔ hànyǔ dòngcí zhuó qīng biéyì de lái yuán* [Original differences in verbs with voice and voiceless initials in Ancient Chinese]. *Minzu Yuwen* 3: 3–20.

Mei, Tsu-Lin (梅祖麟) (2012). The causative *s- and nominalizing *-s in Old Chinese and related matters in Proto-Sino-Tibetan. *Language and Linguistics* 13: 1–28.

Meier, Richard P. (2012). Language and modality. In Roland Pfau, Markus Steinbach, & Bencie Woll (eds.), *Sign Language: An International Handbook*. Berlin/Boston, MA: De Gruyter Mouton, 574–601.

Meillet, Antoine (1912). L'évolution des formes grammaticales. *Scientia (Rivista di Scienza)* 12(26): 6.

Meillet, Antoine (1922). *Les dialects indo-européens* (2nd edn). Paris: Champion. [Engl. trans., *The Indo-European Dialects*. University of Alabama Press, 1967]

Meinard, Maruszka Eve Marie (2015). Distinguishing onomatopoeias from interjections. *Journal of Pragmatics* 76: 150–168. doi:10.1016/j.pragma.2014.11.011

Meira, Sergio (2006). Mawé stative verbs and predicate possession. In H. Symeonidis & W. Dietrich (eds.), *Guaraní y 'Mawetí-Tupí-Guaraní'. Estudios históricos y descriptivos sobre una familia lingüística de América del Sur*. Münster: LIT Verlag, 47–68.

Meira, Sergio & Sebastian Drude (2013). Sobre a origem histórica dos 'prefixos relacionais' das línguas Tupí–Guaraní. *Cadernos de Etnolingüística* 5(1): 1–30.

Meira, Sergio & Sebastian Drude (2015). A summary reconstruction of Proto-Maweti–Guarani segmental phonology. *Boletim Do Museu Paraense Emílio Goeldi. Ciências Humanas* 10(2): 275–296.

Melʹčuk, Igor A. (1995). Phrasemes in language and phraseology in linguistics. In Martin Everaert et al. (eds.), *Idioms: Structural and Psychological Perspectives*. Mahwah, NJ: Erlbaum, 167–232.

Melʹčuk, Igor A. (1998). *Kurs obščej morfologii*. Moskva: Jazyki russkoj kulʹtury, vol. II.

Melʹčuk, Igor A. (2006). *Aspects of the Theory of Morphology*. Berlin: Mouton de Gruyter

Mellesmoen, Gloria & Marianne Huijsmans (2019). Types of pluractionality and plurality across domains in ʔayʔajuθəm. *Proceedings of Semantics and Linguistic Theory Conference 29* (SALT): 103–116.

Melnik, Nurit, Tali Arad Greshler, & Shuly Wintner (2017). Seeking control in Modern Standard Arabic. *Glossa* 2(1): 1–41.

Meltzer-Asscher, Aya, et al. (2013). The neural substrates of complex argument structure representations: Processing 'alternating transitivity' verbs. *Language and Cognitive Processes* 28: 1154–1168.

Meltzer-Asscher, Aya, et al. (2015). How the brain processes different dimensions of argument structure complexity: Evidence from fMRI. *Brain and Language* 142: 65–75.

Menn, Lise, et al. (1995). *Nonfluent Aphasia in a Multilingual World*. Amsterdam: John Benjamins.

Merlan, Francesca (1982). *Mangarayi*. Amsterdam: North-Holland.

Merlan, Francesca (1983). *Ngalakan Grammar. Texts, and Vocabulary*. Canberra: The Australian National University.

Merlan, Francesca (1994). *A Grammar of Wardaman: A Language of the Northern Territory of Australia*. Berlin: Mouton de Gruyter.

Mervis, Carolyn B. & Eleanor Rosch (2003). Categorization of natural objects. *Annual Review of Psychology* 32: 89–115. https://doi.org/10.1146/annurev.ps.32.020181.000513

Mesch, Johanna (2016). Manual backchannel responses in signers' conversations in Swedish Sign Language. *Language & Communication* 50: 22–41. doi:10.1016/j.langcom.2016.08.011

Mesch, Johanna, Eli Raanes, & Lindsay Ferrara (2015). Co-forming real space blends in tactile signed language dialogues. *Cognitive Linguistics* 26(2): 261–287. https://doi.org/10.1515/cog-2014-0066

Messerschmidt, Maria, et al. (2018). Sondringen mellem grammatiske og leksikalske præpositioner. [The distinction between grammatical and lexical prepositions]. *Ny Forskning i Grammatik* 25: 89–106.

Mestres-Missé, Anna, Thomas Münte, & Antoni Rodriguez-Fornells (2014). Mapping concrete and abstract meanings to new words using verbal contexts. *Second Language Research* 30: 191–223.

Metsala, Jamie L. (1999). Young children's phonological awareness and nonword repetition as a function of vocabulary development. *Journal of Educational Psychology* 91(1): 3–19. https://doi.org/10.1037/0022-0663.91.1.3

Meyer, Ronny (2011). Amharic. In Stefan Weninger (ed.), in collaboration with Geoffrey Khan, Michael P. Streck, & Janet C. E. Watson, *The Semitic Languages: An International Handbook*. Berlin/Boston: De Gruyter Mouton, 1178–1212.

Miceli, Gabriele, et al. (2000). Selective deficit for people's names following left temporal damage: An impairment of domain-specific conceptual knowledge. *Cognitive Neuropsychology* 17: 489–516.

Michael, Lev, et al. (2015). A Bayesian phylogenetic internal classification of the Tupí-Guaraní family. *Liames* 15(2): 193–221.

Michael, Lev & Myriam Lapierre (2018). Nasal Harmony in Tupí-Guaraní: A Comparative Synthesis. Presented at SSLA II, UMass Amherst.

Michaelis, Susanne Maria & Rosalie, Marcel (2013). Seychelles Creole structure dataset. In Susanne Maria Michaelis et al. (eds.), *Atlas of Pidgin and Creole Language Structures Online*. Leipzig: Max Planck Institute for Evolutionary Anthropology. (https://apics-online.info/contributions/56)

Michel Lange, et al. (2017). Planning and production of grammatical and lexical verbs in multiword messages. *PLoS ONE* 12(11): e0186685. doi:10.1371/journal.pone.0186685

Michelson, Karin (1990). The Oneida lexicon. In David Costa (ed.), *Proceedings of the Sixteenth Annual Meeting of the Berkeley Linguistics Society: Special Session on General Topics in American Indian Linguistics (1990)*. University of California: Berkeley Linguistics Society, 73–85.

Michelson, Karin (2015). Gender in Oneida. In Marlis Hellinger & Heiko Motschenbacher (eds.), *Gender across Languages*. Amsterdam: John Benjamins, vol. IV, 277–301.

Michelson, Karin (2016). Iroquoian languages. In Mark Aronoff (ed.), *Oxford Research Encyclopedia of Linguistics*. Oxford: Oxford University Press.

Michelson, Karin & Mercy Doxtator (2002). *An Oneida–English/English–Oneida Dictionary*. Toronto: University of Toronto Press.

Michelson, Karin & Mercy Doxtator (2019). *An Oneida–English/English–Oneida Dictionary*. Toronto: University of Toronto Press.

Michelson, Karin, Norma Kennedy, & Mercy Doxtator (2016). *Glimpses of Oneida Life*. Toronto: University of Toronto Press.

Michelson, Karin & Catharine Price (2011). *Native Languages Resource Guide: Oneida, Cayuga, and Mohawk*. Ontario Ministry of Education.

Middleton, Erica L., et al. (2004). Separating the chaff from the oats: Evidence for a conceptual distinction between count noun and mass noun aggregates. *Journal of Memory and Language* 50(4): 371–394.

Mihas, Elena (2017). *Conversational structures of Alto Perené (Arawak) of Peru*. Amsterdam: John Benjamins.

Miller, George A., Eugene Galanter, & Karl H. Pribram (1960). *Plans and the Structure of Behavior*. New York: Holt, Rinehart & Winston.

Milner, G. B. (1966). *Samoan Dictionary*. London: Oxford University Press.

Mintz, Toben H. 2002. Category induction from distributional cues in an artificial language. Memory and Cognition 30(5). 678–686.

Mintz, Toben H. (2003a). Frequent frames as a cue for grammatical categories in child directed speech. *Cognition* 90(1): 91–117. https://doi.org/10.1016/S0010-0277(03)00140-9

Mintz, Toben H. 2003b. On the distribution of frames in child-directed speech as a basis for grammatical category learning. In Barbara Beachley, Amanda Brown & Frances Conlin (eds.), Proceedings of the 27th annual Boston University conference on language development, 545–555. Somerville, MA: Cascadilla Press.

Mintz, Toben H., Elissa L. Newport, & Thomas G. Bever (2002). The distributional structure of grammatical categories in the speech to young children. *Cognitive Science* 26: 393–424.

Miozzo, Michele, Kyle Rawlins, & Brenda Rapp (2014). How verbs and non-verbal categories navigate the syntax/semantics interface: Insights from cognitive neuropsychology. *Cognition* 133: 621–640.

Mirman, Daniel, Jon-Frederick Landrigan, & Allison Britt (2017). Taxonomic and thematic semantic systems. *Psychological Bulletin* 143: 499–520.

Mithun, Marianne (1979). The semantics of polysynthesis. In Adam Makkai (ed.), *The Fifth LACUS Forum*. (Linguistics Association of Canada and the United States.) New York: Hornbeam Press, 37–44.

Mithun, Marianne (1982). The synchronic and diachronic behavior of plops, squeaks, croaks, sighs, and moans. *International Journal of American Linguistics* 48(1): 49–58.

Mithun, Marianne (1984). The evolution of noun incorporation. *Language* 60(4): 847–894.

Mithun, Marianne (1989). The subtle significance of the locus of morphologization. *International Journal of American Linguistics* 55: 265–283.

Mithun, Marianne (1991). Active/agentive case marking and its implications. *Language* 67: 510–546.

Mithun, Marianne (1998). Yup'ik roots and affixes. In Osahito Miyaoka & Minoru Oshima (eds.), *Languages of the North Pacific Rim 4*. Kyoto: Kyoto University Graduate School of Letters, 63–76.

Mithun, Marianne (1999). *The Languages of Native North America*. Cambridge: Cambridge University Press.

Mithun, Marianne (2000). Noun and verb in Iroquoian languages: Multicategorisation from multiple criteria. In Petra M. Vogel & Bernard Comrie (eds.), *Approaches to the Typology of Word Classes*. Berlin: Mouton de Gruyter, 379–420.

Mithun, Marianne (2008). The extension of dependency beyond the sentence. *Language* 83: 69–119.

Mithun, Marianne (2009). Polysynthesis in the Arctic. In Marc-Antoine Mahieu & Nicole Tersis (eds.), *Variations on Polysynthesis: The Eskimo–Aleut Languages*. Amsterdam: John Benjamins, 3–18.

Mithun, Marianne (2010). The search for regularity in irregularity: Defectiveness and its implications for our knowledge of words. In Matthew Baerman, Greville Corbett, & Dunstan Brown (eds.), *Defective Paradigms: Missing Forms and What They Tell Us*. Oxford: British Academy and Oxford University Press, 125–149.

Mithun, Marianne (2017a). The Iroquoian language family. In Alexandra Aikhenvald & Robert Dixon (eds.), *The Cambridge Handbook of Linguistic Typology*. Cambridge: Cambridge University Press, 707–746.

Mithun, Marianne (2017b). Polycategoriality and zero derivation: Insights from Central Alaskan Yup'ik Eskimo. In Valentina Vapnarsky & Edy Veneziano (eds.), *Lexical Polycategoriality: Cross-linguistic, Cross-theoretical and Language Acquisition Approaches*. Amsterdam: John Benjamins, 155–174.

Mithun, Marianne (2019). Categorial shift: foundations, extensions and consequences. *Language Sciences* 73: 1–22.

Mithun, Marianne & Reginald Henry (1982). *Watęwayęstanih: A Cayuga Teaching Grammar*. Brantford, Canada: Woodland Indian Cultural Educational Centre.

Mittendorf, Ingo & Louisa Sadler (2008). NP would like to meet GF: A Welsh adjectival construction. http://csli-publications.stanford.edu/LFG/13/lfg08.html.

Mittwoch, Anita (1998). Cognate objects as reflections of Davidsonian event arguments. In Susan Rothstein (ed.), *Events and Grammar*. Dordrecht: Kluwer, 309–332.

Miyagawa, Shigeru (2009). *Why Move? Why Agree?* Cambridge, MA: MIT Press.

Miyagava, Shigeru (2012). Agreements that occur mainly in the main clause. In Aelbrecht Lobke, Liliane Haegeman, & Rachel Nye (eds.), *Main Clause Phenomena. New Horizons* [Linguistik Aktuell/Linguistics Today 190]. Amsterdam/Philadelphia: Benjamins, 79–112.

Miyaoka, Osahito (2012). *A Grammar of Central Alaskan Yupik: An Eskimo Language*. (Mouton Grammar Library.) Berlin: Mouton de Gruyter.

Mohr, Jay P. (1976). Broca's area and Broca's aphasia. In Haiganoosh Whitaker & Harry Whitaker (eds.), *Studies in Neurolinguistics*. New York: Academic Press, vol. I, 201–233.

Molenberghs, Pascal, Ross Cunnington, & Jason Mattingley (2012). Brain regions with mirror properties: A meta-analysis of 125 human fmri studies. *Neuroscience and Biobehavioral Reviews* 36: 341–349.

Moltmann, Friederike (2009). Degree structure as trope structure: A trope-based analysis of positive and comparative adjectives. *Linguistics and Philosophy* 32(1): 51–94.

Monaghan, Padraic, Nick Chater & Morten H Christiansen. 2005. The differential role of phonological and distributional cues in grammatical categorisation. Cognition 96(2). 143–182.

Monaghan, Padraic, Morten H. Christiansen & Nick Chater. 2007. The phonological-distributional coherence hypothesis: cross-linguistic evidence in language acquisition. Cognitive Psychology 55(4). 259–305.

Monserrat, Ruth & Marília Facó Soares (1983). Hierarquia referencial em línguas Tupi. *Ensaios de Linguística* 9: 164–187.

Montague, Richard (1973). The proper treatment of quantification in ordinary English. In J. Hin-tikka, J. Moravcsik, & P. Suppes (eds.), *Approaches to Natural Languages: Proceedings of the 1970 Stanford Workshop on Grammar and Semantics*. Dordrecht: Reidel, pp. 221–242. [reprinted in R. Thomason (ed.), *Formal Philosophy: Selected Papers of Richard Montague*, New Haven, CT: Yale University Press, 1974]

Montgomery-Anderson, Brad (2015). *Cherokee Reference Grammar*. Norman, OK: University of Oklahoma Press.

Montler, Timothy (1986). An outline of the morphology and phonology of Saanich, North Straits Salish, *Occasional Papers in Linguistics 4*. Missoula: University of Montana Press.

Montler, Timothy (2003). Auxiliaries and other categories in Straits Salishan. *International Journal of American Linguistics* 69: 103–134. doi:10.1086/379680

Moran, Steven, et al. (2018). A universal cue for grammatical categories in the input to children: Frequent frames. *Cognition* 175: 131–140. https://doi.org/10.1016/j.cognition.2018.02.005

Moravcsik, Edith (1978a). Reduplicative constructions. In Joseph H. Greenberg, Charles A. Ferguson, & Edith A. Moravcsik (eds.), *Universals of Human Language* vol. 3, *Word Structure*. Stanford, CA: Stanford University Press, 297–334.

Moravcsik, Edith (1978b). Universals of language contact. In Joseph H. Greenberg (ed.), *Universals of Human Language*. Stanford: Stanford University Press, 94–122.

Moravcsik, Edith (1997). Parts and wholes in the Hungarian noun phrase—A typological study. In Bohumil Palek (ed.), *Proceedings of LP '96. Typology—Prototypes, Item Orderings and Universals*. Prague: Charles University Press, 307–324.

Morphy, Frances (1983). Djapu, a Yolngu dialect. In R. M. W. Dixon & Barry Blake (eds.), *Handbook of Australian Languages*. Canberra: Australian National University Press, vol. III, 1–304.

Morzycki, Marcin (2016). *Modification*. Cambridge: Cambridge University Press.

Mosel, Ulrike (1984). *Tolai Syntax and Its Historical Development*. Canberra: Australian National University.

Mosel, Ulrike (2004). Complex predicates and juxtapositional constructions in Samoan. In Isabelle Bril & Francoise Ozanne (eds.), *Complex Predicates in Oceanic Languages*. Berlin: Mouton de Gruyter, 263–296.

Mosel, Ulrike (2017). Teop—An Oceanic language with multifunctional verbs, nouns and adjectives. In Eva van Lier (ed.), *Lexical Flexibility in Oceanic Languages. Studies in Language* 41(2): 255–293.

Mosel, Ulrike (2018). Corpus compilation and exploitation in language documentation projects. In Kenneth L. Rehg & Lyle Campbell (eds.), *The Oxford Handbook of Endangered Languages*. Oxford: Oxford University Press, 248–270.

Mosel, Ulrike (2019). *A Multifunctional Teop-English Dictionary*. Dictionaria 4. doi:10.5281/zenodo.3257580

Mosel, Ulrike, et al. (2007). *The Teop Language Corpus*. http://dobes.mpi.nl/projects/teop/

Mosel, Ulrike & Even Hovdhaugen (1992). *Samoan Reference Grammar*. Oslo: Scandinavian University Press.

Mosel, Ulrike & Ainslie So'o (1997). *Say It in Samoan*. Canberra: Australian National University.

Moseley, Rachel L. & Friedemann Pulvermüller (2014). Nouns, verbs, objects, actions, and abstractions: Local fMRI activity indexes semantics, not lexical categories. *Brain and Language* 132: 28–42.

Mous, Maarten (2008). Number as an exponent of gender in Cushitic. In Zygmunt Frajzyngier & Erin Shay (eds.), *Interaction of Morphology and Syntax: Case Studies in Afroasiatic*. Amsterdam: John Benjamins, 137–160.

Mous, Maarten (2012). Cushitic. In Zygmunt Frajzyngier & Erin Shay (eds.), *The Afroasiatic Languages*. Cambridge: Cambridge University Press, 342–422.

Mous, Maarten (2016). *Alagwa: A South Cushitic Language of Tanzania*. Cologne: Rüdiger Köppe.

Msimang, Christian T. & George Poulos (2001). The ideophone in Zulu: A re-examination of conceptual and descriptive notions. In F. K. Erhard Voeltz & Christa Kilian-Hatz (eds.), *Ideophones*. Amsterdam: John Benjamins, 235–249.

Mulder, Jean Gail (1994). *Ergativity in Coast Tsimshian (Sm'algyax)*. (University of California Publications in Linguistics, 124.) Berkeley: University of California Press.

Müller, Frank Ernst (1996). Affiliating and disaffiliating with continuers: Prosodic aspects of recipiency. In Elizabeth Couper-Kuhlen & Margret Selting (eds.), *Prosody in Conversation: Interactional Studies*. Cambridge/New York: Cambridge University Press, 131–176.

Müller, Henrik H., Kasper Boye, & Elisabeth A. Mørch (2020). Grammatikalisering af typekonstruktioner og pseudo-partitiver i dansk. [Grammaticalization of type constructions and pseudo-partitives in Danish]. *Ny Forskning i Grammatik* 27: 71–86.

Müller, Stefan (2018). The end of lexicalism as we know it? *Language* 94(1). e54–e66.

Munro, Pamela (1988). Diminutive syntax. In William Shipley (ed.), *In Honor of Mary Haas: From the Haas Festival Conference on Native American Linguistics*. Berlin: Mouton de Gruyter, 539–555.

Muravjeva, Irina A. (2004). Tipologija inkorporacii [Typology of incorporation]. Doctoral dissertation, RGGU, Moscow.

Mushin, Ilana (2012). *A Grammar of (Western) Garrwa*. Berlin: Mouton de Gruyter.

Muysken, Pieter (1977). *Syntactic Developments in the Verb Phrase of Ecuadorian Quechua*. Lisse: Peter de Ridder; Dordrecht: Foris; Berlin: Mouton de Gruyter.

Muysken, Pieter (1981). Quechua word structure. In Frank Heny (ed.), *Binding and Filters*. London/Cambridge, MA: Croom Helm/MIT Press, 279–327.

Muysken, Pieter (1983). Parasitic trees. *NELS* 13. Amherst: GLSA, 199–210.

Muysken, Pieter (2005). Quechua P-soup. In Hans Broekhuis et al. (eds.), *Festschrift for Henk van Riemsdijk*. Berlin: Mouton de Gruyter, 434–438.

Muysken, Pieter (2019). *El kichwa ecuatoriano: orígenes, riqueza, contactos*. Quito, Ecuador: Abya-Yala.

Myers-Scotton, Carol (2002). *Contact Linguistics: Bilingual Encounters and Grammatical Outcomes*. Oxford: Oxford University Press.

Myers-Scotton, Carol & Janice L. Jake (2017). Revisiting the 4-M Model: Codeswitching and morpheme election at the abstract level. *International Journal of Bilingualism* 21: 340–366. https://doi.org/10.1177/1367006915626588

Næss, Åshild (2007). *Prototypical Transitivity*. (Typological studies in language 72.) Amsterdam: John Benjamins.

Nagai, Kayo (2001). *Mrs. Della Waghiyi's St. Lawrence Island Yupik Texts with Grammatical Analysis*. Endangered Languages of the Pacific Rim A2-006. Kyoto: Nakanishi Printing Co.

Naigles, Letitia R. 2002. Form is easy, meaning is hard: resolving a paradox in early child language. Cognition 86. 157–199.

Nakayama, Toshihide (2001). *Nuuchahnulth (Nootka) Morphosyntax*. University of California Publications in Linguistics 134. Berkeley: University of California Press.

Napoli, Donna Jo & Rachel Sutton-Spence (2014). Order of the major constituents in sign languages: Implications for all language. *Frontiers in Psychology* 5: 1–18. https://doi.org/10.3389/fpsyg.2014.00376

Narrog, Heiko (2017). Typology and grammaticalization. In Alexandra Y. Aikhenvald & R. M. W. Dixon (eds.), *The Cambridge Handbook of Linguistic Typology*. Cambridge: Cambridge University Press, 151–177.

Narrog, Heiko & Bernd Heine (eds.) (2011). *The Oxford Handbook of Grammaticalization*. New York: Oxford University Press.

Navarro, Ia, & Albert Álvarez González (eds.) (2017). *Verb Valency Changes. Theoretical and Typological Perspectives*. Amsterdam: John Benjamins.

Nedjalkov, Igor (1997). *Evenki*. London: Routledge.

Nedjalkov, Vladimir P., Emma Š. Geniušienė, & Zlatka Guentchéva (eds.) (2007). *Reciprocal Constructions*. (Typological Studies in Language 71.) Amsterdam: John Benjamins.

Nedjalkov, Vladimir P. & Galina A. Otaina (2013). *A Syntax of the Nivkh Language: The Amur Dialect*. (Studies in Language Companion Series, 139.) Amsterdam: John Benjamins.

Nelson, Katherine, J Hampson & L.K. Shaw. 1993. Nouns in early lexicons: evidence, explanations, and extensions. Journal of Child Language 20. 61–84.

Newell, Allan & Paul S. Rosenbloom (1981). Mechanisms of skill acquisition and the law of practice. In John R. Anderson (ed.) *Cognitive Skills and Their Acquisition*. London: Routledge, 1–55.

Newman, Paul (1968). Ideophones from a syntactic point of view. *Journal of West African Languages* 5: 107–117.

Newman, Paul (1980). *The Classification of Chadic within Afroasiatic*. Leiden: Universitaire Pers.

Newman, Paul (2000). *The Hausa Language: An Encyclopedic Reference Grammar*. New Haven, CT: Yale University Press.

Newman, Stanley (1965). *Zuni Grammar*. (University of New Mexico Publications in Anthropology No. 14.) Albuquerque: University of New Mexico.

Newmark, Leonard, Philip Hubbard, & Peter Prifti (1982). *Standard Albanian: A Reference Grammar for Students*. Stanford, CA: Stanford University Press.

Newmeyer, Frederick J. (1998). *Language Form and Language Function*. Cambridge, MA: MIT Press.

Newmeyer, Frederick J. (2000). The discrete nature of syntactic categories: Against a prototype-based account. In Robert D. Borsley (ed.), *Syntax and Semantics: The Nature and Function of Syntactic Categories*. San Diego: Academic Press, 221–250.

Nicolas, Edith (1998). Etude du système verbal du bardi, langue du nord-ouest australien, avec une présentation contrastive du système bunuba. Doctoral dissertation, Université Paris VII-Denis Diderot, Paris.

Nicolle, Steve (1998). A relevance theory perspective on grammaticalization. *Cognitive Linguistics* 9: 1–35.

Nichols, Johanna. 1992. *Linguistic diversity in time and space*. Chicago: University of Chicago Press.

Nichols, Johanna (1986). Head-marking and dependent-marking grammar, *Language* 62: 56–119.

Nichols, Johanna (2011). *Ingush Grammar*. (University of California Publications Series.) Berkeley: University of California Press.

Nielsen, Sarah R., et al. (2019). The production of grammatical and lexical determiners in Broca's aphasia. *Language, Cognition and Neuroscience* 34(8): 1027–1040. doi:10.1080/23273798.2019.1616104

Nikitina, Tatiana (1985). Sintaksičeskij stroj drevnekitajskogo jazyka [Syntactic structure of Old Chinese]. Dissertation, Lerningradskij Universitet, Leningrad.

Nikitina, Tatiana (2007). Embedded clauses with nominal internal structure in Wan (Mande): Mixed syntax without class-changing morphology. *Acta Linguistica Petropolitana: Transactions of the Institute for Linguistic Studies* 3(3): 270–294.

Nikitina, Tatiana (2008). The mixing of syntactic properties and language change. Dissertation, Stanford University, Stanford, CA.
Nikitina, Tatiana (2009a). The syntax of postpositional phrases in Wan, an 'SOVX' language. *Studies in Language* 33(4): 907–930.
Nikitina, Tatiana (2009b). The function and form of action nominalization in Wan. *Mandenkan* 45: 17–28.
Nikitina, Tatiana (2011). Categorial reanalysis and the origin of the S–O–V–X word order in Mande. *Journal of African Languages and Linguistics* 32(2): 251–273.
Nikitina, Tatiana (2018). Transitivity in Wan. *Frankfurter Afrikanistische Blätter* 26: 107–123.
Nikitina, Tatiana & Dag T. T. Haug (2016). Syntactic nominalization in Latin: A case of non-canonical subject agreement. *Transactions of the Philological Society* 114(1): 25–50. doi:10.1111/1467-968X.12061
Nikolaeva, Irina. (2013) Unpacking finiteness. In Dunstan Brown, Marina Chumakina, & Greville G. Corbett (eds.), *Canonical Morphology and Syntax*. Oxford: Oxford University Press, 99–122.
Nikolaeva, Irina & Andrew Spencer (2019). *Mixed Categories: The Morphosyntax of Noun Modification*. Cambridge: Cambridge University Press.
Nikolaeva, Irina A. & Maria Tolskaya (2001). *A Grammar of Udihe*. Berlin/New York: Mouton de Gruyter.
Nilsen, Øystein (2003). Eliminating positions: syntax and semantics of sentential modification. PhD dissertation, Utrecht University.
Nilsson, Morgan (2016). Somali gender polarity revisited. In Doris L. Payne, Sara Pacchiarotti, & Mokaya Bosire (eds.), *Diversity in African Languages*. Berlin: Language Science Press, 451–466.
Noonan, Michael (1985). Complementation. In Timothy Shopen (ed.), *Language Typology and Syntactic Description*. Cambridge: Cambridge University Press, vol. II, 42–141.
Noonan, Michael (1992). *A Grammar of Lango*. Berlin: Mouton.
Noonan, Michael (2007). Complementation. In Timothy Shopen (ed.), *Language Typology and Syntactic Description* (vol. II *Complex Constructions*). Cambridge: Cambridge University Press, 52–150.
Norde, Muriel (2009). *Degrammaticalization*. Oxford: Oxford University Press.
Nordhoff, Sebastian (2013). Jack of all trades: The Sri Lanka Malay flexible adjective. In Jan Rijkhoff & Eva van Lier (eds.), *Flexible Word Classes: Typological Studies of Underspecified Parts of Speech*. Oxford: Oxford University Press, 247–274.
Nordlinger, Rachel (1998). *A Grammar of Wambaya, Northern Territory (Australia)*. Canberra: Pacific Linguistics.
Nordlinger, Rachel (2002). Non-finite subordinate verbs in Australian Aboriginal languages: Are nominalised verbs really nominalised? In Cynthia Allen (ed.), *Proceedings of the 2001 Conference of the Australian Linguistic Society*. 1–10.
Nordlinger, Rachel (2002). Non-finite subordinate verbs in Australian Aboriginal languages: Are nominalised verbs really nominalised? In Cynthia Allen (ed.), *Proceedings of the 2001 Conference of the Australian Linguistic Society*. 1–10.
Nordlinger, Rachel (2014). Constituency and grammatical relations. In Harold Koch & Rachel Nordlinger (eds.), *The Languages and Linguistics of Australia: A Comprehensive Guide*. Berlin: Mouton de Gruyter, 215–262.
Nordlinger, Rachel & Louisa Sadler (2004a). Nominal tense in crosslinguistic perspective. *Language* 80(4): 776–806.

Nordlinger, Rachel & Louisa Sadler (2004b). Tense beyond the verb: Encoding clausal tense/aspect/mood on nominal dependents. *Natural Language and Linguistic Theory* 22(3): 597–641.

Norman, Jerry (1988). *Chinese*. Cambridge: Cambridge University Press.

Norrick, Neal R. (2009). Interjections as pragmatic markers. *Journal of Pragmatics* 41(5): 866–891. doi:10.1016/j.pragma.2008.08.005

Nosofsky, Robert M. (1992). Exemplars, prototypes, and similarity rules. In Alice F. Healy, Stephen M. Kosslyn, & Richard M. Shiffrin (eds.), *Essays in Honor of William K. Estes: Vol. 1. From Learning Theory to Connectionist Theory*. Mahwah, NJ: Erlbaum, 149–167.

Nosofsky, Robert M., Brian J. Meagher, & Parhesh Kumar (2020). Comparing exemplar and prototype models in a natural-science category domain. *Proceedings for the 42nd Annual Meeting of the Cognitive Science Society*. Toronto, Canada. Available at https://cogs.sitehost.iu.edu/nosofsky/pubs/Nosofsky_CogSci2020.pdf

Nübling, Damaris (2004). Die prototypische Interjektion: Ein Definitionsvorschlag. *Zeitschrift für Semiotik* 26(1–2): 11–45.

Nuckolls, Janis B. (1996). *Sounds Like Life: Sound-Symbolic Grammar, Performance, and Cognition in Pastaza Quechua*. New York: Oxford University Press.

Nuckolls, Janis B. (2019). The sensori-semantic clustering of ideophonic meaning in Pastaza Quichua. In Kimi Akita & Prashant Pardeshi (eds.), *Iconicity in Language and Literature*. Amsterdam: John Benjamins, vol. 16, 167–198. doi:10.1075/ill.16.08nuc, https://benjamins.com/catalog/ill.16.08nuc

Nuckolls, Janis B., et al. (2016). The systematic stretching and contracting of ideophonic phonology in Pastaza Quichua. *International Journal of American Linguistics* 82(1): 95–116. doi:10.1086/684425

Nunberg, Geoffrey (1984). Individuation in context. In M. Cobler et al. (eds.), *Proceedings of the West Coast Conference on Formal Linguistics 2*. Stanford Linguistics Association, 203–217.

Nurmio, Silva (2015). Studies in grammatical number in Old and Middle Welsh. PhD dissertation, University of Cambridge, England, UK.

Nurmio, Silva (2017). Collective nouns in Welsh: A noun category or a plural allomorph? *Transactions of the Philological Society* 115(1): 58–78.

Nurmio, Silva & David Willis (2016). The rise and fall of a minor category: The case of the Welsh numerative. *Journal of Historical Linguistics* 6(2): 297–339.

Odlin, Terence & Diana Natalicio (1982). Some characteristics of word classification in a second language. *Modern Language Journal* 66: 34–8.

Ogden, Richard (2020). Audibly not saying something with clicks. *Research on Language and Social Interaction* 53(1): 66–89. doi:10.1080/08351813.2020.1712960

Ogiela, Diane A., Cristina Schmitt, & Michael W. Casby (2014). Interpretation of verb phrase telicity: Sensitivity to verb type and determiner type. *Journal of Speech Language and Hearing Research* 57(3): 865–875. https://doi.org/10.1044/2013_JSLHR-L-12-0271

Ogihara, Toshiyuki (1995). The semantics of tense in embedded clauses. *Linguistic Inquiry* 26: 663–679.

O'Grady, William (1997). *Syntactic Development*. Chicago: University of Chicago Press.

O'Grady, William, Michael Dobrovolsky, & Mark Aronoff (1997). *Contemporary Linguistics: An Introduction* (3rd edn). New York: St. Martin's Press.

O'Grady, William & Videa De Guzman (2011). Morphology: The analysis of word structure. In William O'Grady, John Archibald, & Francis Katamba (eds.), *Contemporary Linguistics: An Introduction*. London/New York: Pearson Longman, 116–144.

Ojeda, Almerindo E. (1998). The semantics of collectives and distributives in Papago. *Natural Language Semantics* 6(3): 245–270.

O'Keeffe, Anne & Svenja Adolphs (2008). Response tokens in British and Irish discourse: Corpus, context and variational pragmatics. In Klaus P. Schneider & Anne Barron (eds.), *Pragmatics & Beyond New Series*, vol. 178. Amsterdam: John Benjamins, 69–98. doi:10.1075/pbns.178.05ok

Okell, John (1969). *A Reference Grammar of Colloquial Burmese* (2 vols.). London: Oxford University Press.

Olguin, Raquel & Michael Tomasello. 1993. Twenty-five-month-old children do not have a grammatical category of verb. Cognitive Development 8(3). 245–272.

Olthof, Marieke (2020). Formal variation in incorporation: A typological study and a unified approach. *Linguistics* 58(1): 131–206.

Oltra-Massuet, Isabel (2013). Variability and allomorphy in the morphosyntax of Catalan past perfective. In Alec Marantz & Ora Matushansky (eds.), *Distributed Morphology Today*. Cambridge, MA/London: MIT Press, 1–20.

Ongaye, Oda Orkaydo (2013). *A Grammar of Konso*. Utrecht: LOT.

Oréal, Elsa (2014). Noun phrase syntax and definiteness marking: A new explanation for the morphology of earlier Egyptian participles. In Eitan Grossman et al. (eds.), *On Forms and Functions: Studies in Ancient Egyptian Grammar*. Hambourg: Widmaier, 173–200.

Oréal, Elsa (2017). Nominalizations as a source for verbal morphology. Grammaticalization paths of modality and information structure in Earlier Egyptian. *Lingua Aegyptia* 25: 1–33.

Oréal, Elsa. (2022). The negative existential cycle in Ancient Egyptian. In Ljuba Veselinova & Arja Hamari (eds.), *The Negative Existential Cycle from a Historical-Comparative Perspective*. Berlin: Language Science Press, 197–230.

Orkaydo, Ongaye Oda (2013). A grammar of Konso. PhD dissertation, Leiden University.

Ortiz, Elio García & E. Elías Caurey (2012). *Diccionario etimológico y etnográfico de la lengua guaraní hablada en Bolivia*. La Paz: Plural Editores.

Osada, Toshiki (1992). *A Reference Grammar of Mundari*. Tokyo: ILCAA, Tokyo University of Foreign Studies.

Osada, Toshiki, Madhu Purti, & Nathan Badenoch (2020). Expanding the model of reduplication in Mundari expressives. In Nathan Badenoch & Nishaant Choksi (eds.), *Expressives in the South Asian linguistic Area*. (Brill's Studies in South and Southwest Asian Languages 13.) Leiden: Brill, 78–99.

Östling, Robert, Carl Börstell, & Lars Wallin (2015). Enriching the Swedish Sign Language corpus with part of speech tags using joint Bayesian word alignment and annotation transfer. In Beáta Megyesi (ed.), *Proceedings of the 20th Nordic Conference on Computational Linguistics (NODALIDA 2015)*, NEALT Proceedings Series 23, 263–268. Vilnius: Linköping University Electronic Press, Linöpings universitet (ACL Anthology). http://www.ep.liu.se/ecp/109/ecp15109.pdf

Owens, Jonathan (1985). *A Grammar of Harar Oromo (Northeastern Ethiopia)*. Hamburg: Helmut Buske.

Padden, Carol (1988). *Interaction of Morphology and Syntax in American Sign Language*. New York: Garland.

Padden, Carol, et al. (2015). Tools for language: Patterned iconicity in sign language nouns and verbs. *Topics in Cognitive Science* 7(1): 81–94. https://doi.org/10.1111/tops.12121

Padden, Carol & Darline Clark Gunsauls (2003). How the alphabet came to be used in a sign language. *Sign Language Studies* 4(1): 10–33.

Paducheva, Elena V. (1996). *Semantičeskie issledovanija. Semantika vremeni i vida v russkom jazyke. Semantika narrativa* [Semantic studies. Semantics of tense and aspect in Russian. Semantics of narrative]. Moscow: Jazyki russkoj kul'tury.

Pakendorf, Brigitte (2019). Direct copying of inflectional paradigms: Evidence from Lamunkhin Even. *Language* 95: e364–80. https://doi.org/10.1353/lan.2019.0063

Palancar, Enrique L. (2006). Property concepts in Otomí. *International Journal of American Linguistics* 72: 325–366.

Palancar, Enrique L. (2009). *Gramática y textos de hñöñhö, Otomí de San Ildefonso Tultepec, Querétaro, vol. I: Gramática*. Mexico City: Plaza y Valdés.

Palancar, Enrique & Roberto Zavala (eds.) (2013). *Clases léxicas, posesión y cláusulas complejas en lenguas de Mesoamérica*. Mexico: CIESAS.

Palmer, Bill (2009). *Kokota Grammar*. (Oceanic Linguistics Special Publications, 35.) Honolulu: University of Hawaii Press.

Panagiotidis, Phoevos (2014). *Categorial Features: A Generative Theory of Word Class Categories*. Cambridge: Cambridge University Press.

Papafragou, Anna, Justin Hulbert, & John Trueswell (2008). Does language guide event perception? Evidence from eye movements. *Cognition* 108(1): 155–184. https://doi.org/10.1016/j.cognition.2008.02.007

Papagno, Costanza, et al. (2011). What is the role of the uncinate fasciculus? Surgical removal and proper name retrieval. *Brain* 134: 405–414.

Papagno, Costanza, et al. (2016). Long-term proper name anomia after removal of the uncinate fasciculus. *Brain Structure and Function* 221: 687–694.

Papitto, Giorgio, Angela D. Friederici, & Emiliano Zaccarella (2020). The topographical organization of motor processing: An ALE meta-analysis on six action domains and the relevance of Broca's region. *NeuroImage* 206: 116321.

Paroubek, Patrick (2007). Evaluating Part-of-Speech tagging and parsing. In Laila Dybkjær, Holmer Hemsen, & Wolfgang Minker (eds.)., *Evaluation of Text and Speech Systems: Text, Speech and Language Technology*. Springer, Dordrecht, vol. XXXVII, 99–124. https://doi.org/10.1007/978-1-4020-5817-2_4

Parsons, Terence (1990). *Events in the Semantics of English: A Study in Subatomic Semantics*. Cambridge, MA: MIT Press.

Partee, Barbara H. (2010). Privative adjectives: Subsective plus coercion. In R. Bauerle, U. Reyle, & T. E. Zimmermann (eds.), *Presuppositions and Discourse: Essays Offered to Hans Kamp*. Bingley, UK: Emerald, 273–285.

Patz, Elisabeth (2002). *A Grammar of the Kuku Yalanji Language of North Queensland*. Canberra: Pacific Linguistics.

Paul, Waltraud (2015). *New Perspectives on Chinese Syntax*. Berlin: Mouton de Gruyter.

Pawley, Andrew (1966). Samoan phrase structure: the morphology-syntax of a Western Polynesian Language. *Anthropological Linguistics* 8(5): 1–63.

Pawley, Andrew (1993). A language which defies description by ordinary means. In William A. Foley (ed.), *The Role of Theory in Language Description*. Berlin: De Gruyter, 87–129.

Pawley, Andrew & Harald Hammarström (2017). The Trans New Guinea Family. In Bill Palmer (ed.), *The Languages and Linguistics of the New Guinea Area: A Comprehensive Guide*. Berlin/New York: Mouton de Gruyter, 21–195.

Payne, Doris L. (1987). Noun classification in the Western Amazon. *Language Sciences* 9: 21–44. [special issue: *Comparative linguistics of South American Indian languages*, ed. Mary Ritchie Key]

Payne, Doris L. (1994). The Tupi-Guarani inverse. In Barbara Fox & Paul Hopper (eds.), *Voice: Form and Function.* Amsterdam: John Benjamins, 313-340.

Payne, John, Rodney Huddleston, & Geoffrey K. Pullum (2010). The distribution and category status of adjectives and adverbs. *Word Structure* 3: 31-81. http://dx.doi.org/10.3366/E17501 24510000486

Pehkonen, Samu (2020). Response cries inviting an alignment: Finnish huh huh. *Research on Language and Social Interaction* 53(1): 19-41. doi:10.1080/08351813.2020.1712965

Pereira, Antonio A. (2009). Estudo morfossintático do Asuriní do Xingu. PhD dissertation, UNICAMP.

Perekhvalskaya, Elena (2011). Nominalization in Mwan. *Mandenkan* 47: 57-75.

Perekhvalskaya, Elena & Valentin Vydrin (2019). Numeral systems in Mande languages. *Mandenkan* 61: 47-111.

Pérez, Eduardo & Odilio Jiménez (1997). *Ttxoolil qyool Mam: Gramática Mam.* Guatemala City: Cholsamaj.

Pérez González, Jaime (2012). Predicados expresivos e ideófonos en tseltal. MA thesis, CIESAS, Mexico.

Pérez Vail, José Reginaldo (2007). *Xtxolil Yool B'a'aj. Gramática Tektiteka.* Guatemala: Editorial Cholsamaj.

Perniss, Pamela, et al. (2012). Speaking of shape: The effects of language-specific encoding on semantic representations. *Language and Cognition* 4(3): 223-242.

Perry, Lynn, Marcus Perlman, & Gary Lupyan (2015). Iconicity in English and Spanish and its relation to lexical category and age of acquisition. *PLoS One* 10(9).

Pesetsky, David (1995). *Zero Syntax: Experiencers and Cascades.* Cambridge, MA: MIT Press.

Pesetsky, David & Esther Torrego (2007). The syntax of valuation and the interpretability of features. In Simin Karimi, Vida Samiian, & Wendy Wilkins (eds.), *Phrasal and Clausal Architecture: Syntactic Derivation, an Interpretation.* Amsterdam: John Benjamins, 262-294.

Peters, Elke (2016). The learning burden of MWIs: The role of interlexical and intralexical factors. *Language Teaching Research* 20: 113-138.

Peters, Elke (2020). The learning of single word items. In Stuart Webb (ed.), *The Routledge Handbook of Vocabulary Studies.* New York: Routledge, 125-142.

Peterson, Candida C. & M. Siegal (1995). Deafness, conversation and theory of mind. *Journal of Child Psychology and Psychiatry* 36: 459-474.

Peterson, John (2005). There's a grain of truth in every 'myth', or, why the discussion of lexical classes in Mundari isn't quite over yet. *Linguistic Typology* 9(3): 391-405. doi:10.1515/lity.2005.9.3.351

Peterson, John (2006). Kharia: A South Munda language. I: Grammatical analysis. II: Kharia texts. Glossed, translated and annotated. III: Kharia-English lexicon. Habilitationsschrift, Universität Osnabrück.

Peterson, John (2010). *A Grammar of Kharia: A South Munda Language. Brill's Studies in South and Southwest Asian Languages* 1. Leiden: Brill.

Petrov, Slav, Dipanjan Das, & Ryan McDonald (2012). A universal part-of-speech tagset. *Proceedings of the Eighth International Conference on Language Resources and Evaluation (LREC'12),* 2089-2096. ELRA. http://www.lrec-conf.org/proceedings/lrec2012/pdf/274_Paper.pdf

Pfau, Roland (2000). Features and categories in language production. PhD dissertation, Frankfurt am Main.

Pfau, Roland & Markus Steinbach (2006). Pluralization in sign and in speech: A cross-modal typological study. *Linguistic Typology* 10(2): 135-182. https://doi.org/10.1515/LINGTY.2006.006

Pfau, Roland & Markus Steinbach (2016). Modality and meaning: Plurality of relations in German Sign Language. *Lingua* 170: 69–91. https://doi.org/10.1016/j.lingua.2015.11.002

Pfeiler, Barbara (2006). Polyvalence in the acquisition of early lexicon in Yucatec Maya. In Ximena Lois & Valentina Vapnarsky (eds.), *Lexical Categories and Root Classes in Amerinidian Languages*. Frankfurt: Peter Lang, 319–341.

Pichette, François, Linda De Serres, & Marc Lafontaine (2012). Sentence reading and writing for second language vocabulary acquisition. *Applied Linguistics* 33: 66–82.

Pickering, Martin J. & Simon Garrod (2013). An integrated theory of language production and comprehension. *Behavioral and Brain Sciences* 36 (4): 329–347. https://doi.org/10.1017/s0140525x12001495

Pilling, James Constantine (1888). *Bibliography of the Iroquoian Languages*. Washington, DC: Government Printing Office.

Pillion, Betsy, et al. (2019). Verbal gestures in Cameroon. In Emily Clem, Peter Jenks, & Hannah Sande (eds.), *Theory and Description in African Linguistics*. Berlin: Language Science Press, 303–322. doi:10.5281/zenodo.3367128

Pillon, Agnesa & Peggy d'Honincthun (2010). The organization of the conceptual system: The case of the 'object versus action' dimension. *Cognitive Neuropsychology* 27: 587–613.

Pina-Cabral, João (2015). Names and naming. In James D. Wright (editor-in-chief), *International Encyclopedia of the Social and Behavioral Sciences* (2nd edn). Oxford: Elsevier, vol. XVI, 183–187.

Pinker, Steven (1984). *Language Learnability and Language Development*. Cambridge, MA: Harvard University Press.

Pinker, Steven. 1987. The bootstrapping problem in language acquisition. Mechanisms of Language Acquisition 399–441.

Pinker, Steven. 1989. Learnability and cognition: The acquisition of verbargument structure. Cambridge, MA: Harvard University Press.

Pinker, Steven & Paul Bloom (1990). Natural language and natural selection. *Behavioral and Brain Sciences* 13: 707–784.

Pinker, Steven & Ray Jackendoff (2009). The reality of a universal language faculty. *Behavioral and Brain Sciences* 32: 465–466. doi:10.1017/S0140525X09990720

Piwek, Paul, Robbert-Jan Beun, & Anita Cremers (2008). Proximal and distal language and cognition: Evidence from deictic demonstratives in Dutch. *Journal of Pragmatics* 40: 694–718.

Pizzuto, Elena & Serena Corazza (1996). Noun morphology in Italian Sign Language (LIS). *Lingua* 98(1–3): 169–196. https://doi.org/10.1016/0024-3841(95)00037-2

Plag, Ingo (1999). More on infinitives in creole: The nature of Sranan fu and its complements. In Pauline Christie et al. (eds.), *Studies in Caribbean Language II. Papers from the Ninth Biennial Conference of the Society for Caribbean Linguistics*, 1992. St. Augustine: Society for Caribbean Linguistics, 250–264.

Plag, Ingo & Laura Winther Balling (2020). Derivational morphology: An integrative perspective on some fundamental questions. In Vito Pirelli, Ingo Plag, & Wolfgang U. Dressler (eds.), *Word Knowledge and Word Usage*. Berlin/Boston: Walter de Gruyter, 295–335.

Plank, Frans (1994). Inflection and derivation. In Ronald E. Asher (ed.), *Encyclopedia of Language and Linguistics*. Oxford: Pergamon, 1671–1678.

Poggi, Isabella (2009). The language of interjections. *Multimodal Signals: Cognitive and Algorithmic Issues*, 170–186. doi:10.1007/978-3-642-00525-1_17

Polian, Gilles (2013a). *Gramática del tseltal de Oxchuc*. Tomos I y II. México: CIESAS.

Polian, Gilles (2013b). 'Infinitivos transitivos: innovaciones del tseltal en la familia maya'. In Enrique Palancar & Roberto Zavala (eds), *Clases Léxicas, Posesión y Cláusulas Complejas en Lenguas de Mesoamérica*. Mexico: CIESAS, 339–380.
Polian, Gilles (2017a). Morphology. In Judith Aissen, Nora C. England, & Roberto Zavala Maldonado (eds.), *The Mayan Languages*. London/New York: Routledge, 201–225.
Polian, Gilles (2017b). Tseltal and Tsotsil. In Judith Aissen, Nora C. England, & Roberto Zavala Maldonado (eds.), *The Mayan Languages*. London/New York: Routledge, 611–647.
Polian, Gilles (2018). *Diccionario multidialectal del tseltal tseltal—español*. México: Instituto Nacional de Lenguas Indígenas.
Polinsky, Maria (2013). Raising and control. In Marcel den Dikken (ed.), *The Cambridge Handbook of Generative Syntax*. Cambridge: Cambridge University Press, 577–606.
Polinsky, Maria (2015). *Tsez syntax: A description*. Manuscript. https://scholar.harvard.edu/files/mpolinsky/files/polinsky_15_tsez-syntax-a.5_2.pdf
Polinsky, Maria & Bernard Comrie (2009). Agreement in Tsez, *Folia Linguistica* 33(2): 33–109.
Pollard, Carl & Ivan Sag (1987). *Information-based Syntax and Semantics*. Stanford, CA: CSLI Publications.
Pollard, Carl & Ivan Sag (1994). *Head-driven Phrase Structure Grammar*. Stanford/Chicago: CSLI Publications and University of Chicago Press.
Pollock, Jean-Yves (1989). Verb movement, universal grammar, and the structure of IP. *Linguistic Inquiry* 20(3): 365–424.
Polotsky, Hans Jacob (1944). *Etudes de syntaxe copte*. Le Caire: Publications de la Société d'Archéologie Copte.
Poplack, Shana (2018). *Borrowing*. Oxford: Oxford University Press.
Posner, Michael I. & Steven W. Keele (1968). On the genesis of abstract ideas. *Journal of Experimental Psychology* 77(3, Pt.1): 353–363. https://doi.org/10.1037/h0025953
Pottier, Bernard (1972). Langage des hommes et langage des femmes en cocama (tupi). In Jacqueline Thomas & Lucien Bernot (eds.), *Langues et Techniques, Nature et Société*. Paris: Editions Klincksieck, vol. 1, 385–387.
Poulin-Dubois, Diane & James N. Forbes (2002). Toddlers' attention to intentions-in-action in learning novel action words. *Developmental Psychology* 38(1): 104–114. https://doi.org/10.1037/0012-1649.38.1.104
Poulin-Dubois, Diane & James N. Forbes (2006). Word, intention, and action: A two-tiered model of action word learning. In Kathy Hirsh-Pasek & Roberta M. Golinkoff (ed.), *Action Meets Word: How Children Learn Verbs*. New York: Oxford University Press, 262–285.
Praça, Walkíria N. (2000). Orações independentes com núcleos verbais e nominais em Tapirapé. *Universa*, 8(3).
Praça, Walkíria N. (2007). Morfossintaxe da língua Tapirapé [Tese de Doutorado]. Universidade de Brasilia, 553–570.
Prasad, Rashmi (2000). A corpus study of zero pronouns in Hindi: An account based on centering transition preferences. In *Proceedings of DAARC 2000, Discourse Anaphora and Reference Resolution Conference*. Lancaster: Lancaster University Press, 66–71.
Prasithrathsint, Amara (2000). Adjectives as verbs in Thai. *Linguistic Typology* 4: 251–271.
Ross, Malcolm (2002). Jabêm. In John Lynch, Malcolm Ross, & Terry Crowley (eds.), *The Oceanic Languages*. London: Routledge, 270–296.
Preminger, Omer (2014). *Agreement and Its Failures*. Cambridge, MA: MIT Press.
Prince, Alan & Paul Smolensky (2004). *Optimality Theory: Constraint Interaction in Generative Grammar*. Malden: Blackwell.

Pruden, Shannon M., et al. (2012). Find your manners: How do infants detect the invariant manner of motion in dynamic events? *Child Development* 83(3): 977–991. https://doi.org/10.1111/j.1467-8624.2012.01737.x

Pruden, Shannon M., et al. (2013). Infant categorization of path relations during dynamic events. *Child Development* 84(1): 331–345. https://doi.org/10.1111/j.1467-8624.2012.01843.x

Prunet, Jean François (2006). External evidence and the Semitic root. *Morphology* 16: 41–67.

Puimège, Eva & Elke Peters (2019). Learners English vocabulary knowledge prior to formal instruction: The role of learner-related and word-related variables. *Language Learning* 69: 943–977.

Pulleyblank, Edwin G. (1995). *Outline of Classical Chinese Grammar*. Vancouver, UBC Press.

Pullum, Geoffrey (1991). English nominal gerund phrases as noun phrases with verb-phrase heads. *Linguistics* 29: 763–799.

Pullum, Geoffrey K. & Rodney Huddleston (2002). Prepositions and prepositional phrases. In Rodney Huddleston & Geoffrey K. Pullum (eds.), *The Cambridge Grammar of the English Language*. Cambridge: Cambridge University Press, 597–661.

Pullum, Geoffrey K. & Barbara C. Scholz (2007). Systematicity and natural language syntax. *Croatian Journal of Philosophy* 7(21): 375–402.

Pulverman, Rachel, et al. (2008). Infants discriminate manners and paths in non-linguistic dynamic events. *Cognition* 108(3): 825–830. https://doi.org/10.1016/j.cognition.2008.04.009

Pulverman, Rachel, et al. (2013). Preverbal infants' attention to manner and path: Foundations for learning relational terms. *Child Development* 84(1): 241–252. https://doi.org/10.1111/cdev.12030

Pulvermüller, Friedemann (2013). How neurons make meaning: Brain mechanisms for embodied and abstract-symbolic semantics. *Trends in Cognitive Sciences* 17: 458–470.

Pulvermüller, Friedemann, Werner Lutzenberger, & Niels Birbaumer (1995). Electrocortical distinction of vocabulary types. *Electroencephalography and Clinical Neurophysiology* 94: 357–370.

Pulvermüller, Friedemann, Werner Lutzenberger, & Hubert Preissl (1999a). Nouns and verbs in the intact brain: Evidence from event-related potentials and high-frequency cortical responses. *Cerebral Cortex* 9: 497–506.

Pulvermüller, Friedemann, Bettina Mohr, & Hans Schleichert (1999b). Semantic or lexico-syntactic factors: What determines word-class-specific activity in the human brain? *Neuroscience Letters* 275: 81–84.

Pustejovsky, James (1995). *The Generative Lexicon*. Cambridge, MA: MIT Press.

Pustet, Regina (2003). *Copulas: Universals in the Categorization of the Lexicon*. Oxford: Oxford University Press.

Putzu, Ignazio & Paolo Ramat (2001). Articles and quantifiers in the Mediterranean languages: A typological–diachronic analysis. In Walter Bisang (ed.), *Aspects of Typology and Universals*. Berlin: Akademie Verlag, 99–132.

Queixalós, Francisco (2001a). *Des noms et des verbes en tupi-guarani: état de la question*. Munich: Lincom Europa.

Queixalós, Francisco (2001b). Le suffixe référentiant en émérillon. In F. Queixalós (ed.), *Des noms et des verbes en tupi-guarani: état de la question*. Munich: Lincom Europa, 115–132.

Queixalós, Francisco (2006). The primacy and fate of predicativity in Tupi-Guarani. In Ximena Lois & Valentina Vapnarsky (eds.), *Lexical Categories and Root Classes in Amerindian Languages*. Bern: Peter Lang, 249–287.

Quine, Willard (1960). *Word and Object*. Cambridge, MA: MIT Press.

Quinto-Pozos, David (2008). Sign language contact and interference: ASL and LSM. *Language in Society* 37(2): 161–189. https://doi.org/10.1017/S0047404508080251.
Quirk, Randolph (1965). Descriptive statement and serial relation. *Language* 41(2): 205–217.
Quirk, Randolph, et al. (1985). *A Comprehensive Grammar of the English Language*. London: Longman.
Rakison, David H. & George E. Butterworth (1998). Infants' use of object parts in early categorization. *Developmental Psychology* 34(1): 49–62.
Rákosi, György (2006). Dative experiencer predicates in Hungarian. Dissertation, Universiteit Utrecht.
Ramat, Paolo (1991). I costrutti assoluti nelle lingue indoeuropee. In F. Aspesi & M. Negri (a c. di), *Studia linguistica amico et magistro oblata. Scritti di amici e allievi dedicati alla memoria di Enzo Evangelisti*. Milan, UNICOPLI, 341–364.
Ramat, Paolo (1999). Linguistic categories and linguists' categorizations, *Linguistics* 37: 157–180.
Ramat, Paolo (2011). Adverbial grammaticalization. In Bernd Heine & Heiko Narrog (eds.), *The Oxford Handbook of Grammaticalization*. Oxford: Oxford University Press, 502–510.
Ramat, Paolo (2015). Language change and language contact. In Konstanze Jungbluth & Federica Da Milano (eds.), *Manual of Deixis in Romance Languages*. Berlin/Boston, de Gruyter, 581–596.
Ramat, Paolo & Davide Ricca (1998). Sentence adverbs in the languages of Europe. In Johan van der Auwera with Dónall P. Ó Baoill (eds.), *Adverbial Constructions in the Languages of Europe*. Berlin: Mouton de Gruyter, 187–275.
Ramchand, Gillian (1997). *Aspect and Predication: The Semantics of Argument Structure*. Oxford: Oxford University Press.
Ramchand, Gillian (2008). *Verb Meaning and the Lexicon: A First-Phase Syntax*. Cambridge: Cambridge University Press.
Ramchand, Gillian & Peter Svenonius (2014). Deriving the functional hierarchy. *Language Sciences* 46: 152–174.
Rao, Rajesh P. N. & Dana H. Ballard (1997). Dynamic model of visual recognition predicts neural response properties in the visual cortex. *Neural Computation* 9(4): 721–763. https://doi.org/10.1162/neco.1997.9.4.721
Rao, Rajesh P. N. & Dana H. Ballard (1999). Predictive coding in the visual cortex: A functional interpretation of some extra-classical receptive-field effects. *Nature Neuroscience* 2: 79–87. https://doi.org/10.1038/4580
Rapp, Brenda & Alfonso Caramazza (1998). A case of selective difficulty in writing verbs. *Neurocase* 4: 127–140.
Rapp, Brenda & Alfonso Caramazza (2002). Selective difficulties with spoken nouns and written verbs: A single case study. *Journal of Neurolinguistics* 15: 373–402.
Rapp, Brenda & Matthew Goldrick (2006). Speaking words: Contributions of cognitive neuropsychological research. *Cognitive Neuropsychology* 23: 39–73.
Ratcliff, Robert (2006). Analogy. In Kees Versteegh (ed.), *Encyclopedia of Arabic Language and Linguistics*. Leiden/Boston: Brill, vol. I, 74–82.
Ratliff, Martha (1991). *Cov*, the underspecified noun, and syntactic flexibility in Hmong. *Journal of the American Oriental Society* 111(4): 694–703.
Rauh, Gisa (1993). On the grammar of lexical and non-lexical prepositions in English. In Cornelia Zelinsky-Wibbelt (ed.), *The Semantics of Prepositions: From Mental Processing to Natural Language Processing*. Berlin: Mouton de Gruyter, 99–150.
Rauh, Gisa (2010). *Syntactic Categories*. Oxford: Oxford University Press.

Ravid, Dorit (2016). Word-level morphology: A psycholinguistic perspective on linear formation in Hebrew nominals. *Morphology* 16: 127–148.

Ravid, Dorit & Rachel Schiff (2006). Roots and patterns in Hebrew language development: Evidence from written morphological analogies. *Reading and Writing* 19: 789–818.

Redington, Martin, Nick Chater, & Steven Finch (1998). Distributional information: A powerful cue for acquiring syntactic categories. *Cognitive Science* 22: 435–469. https://doi.org/10.1207/s15516709cog2204_2

Reesink, Ger. Pieter (1987). *Structures and Their Function in Usan*. Amsterdam: John Benjamins.

Reesink, Ger (2013). Expressing the GIVE event in Papuan languages: A preliminary survey. *Linguistic Typology* 17(2): 217–66.

Refsing, Kirsten (1986). *The Ainu Language. The Morphology and Syntax of the Shizunai Dialect*. Århus: Aarhus University Press.

Regier, Terry, Naveen Khetarpal, & Asifa Majid (2013). Inferring semantic maps. *Linguistic Typology* 17: 89–105.

Reh, Mechthild (1985). *Die Krongo-Sprache (Nìinò Mó-dì)—Beschreibung, Texte, Wörterverzeichniss*. Berlin: Reimer.

Rehg, Kenneth L. (1981). *Ponapean Reference Grammar*. Honolulu: University of Hawaii Press.

Reisinger, Daniel K. E., Marianne Huijsmans, & Lisa Matthewson (2021). Evidentials in the Nominal Domain: A Speasian Analysis of ʔayʔajuθəm Determiners. *Proceedings of Sinn und Bedeutung* 25: 751–768.

Reiter, Sabine (2011). *Ideophones in Aweti*. PhD dissertation, Christian Albrechts University.

Ren, He (任荷) (2020). "名词动词"与上古汉语名词和动词的语义属性 *Míngcí dòngcí yǔ shànggǔ hànyǔ míngcí hé dòngcí de yǔyì shǔxìng* [Noun–verb conversion in Archaic Chinese: From the perspective of lexical semantic analysis]. Beijing: Chinese Academy of Social Sciences Press.

Reuse, Willem de (1994). *Siberian Yupik Eskimo: The Language and Its Contacts with Chukchi*. Salt Lake City, UT: University of Utah Press.

Rhodes, Richard (1990). Lexical hierarchies and Ojibwa noun derivation. In Savas L. Tsohatzidis (ed.), *Meaning and Prototypes: Studies in Linguistic Categorization*. London: Routledge, 151–158.

Ribera-Llonc, Eulàlia, M.Teresa Espinal, & Josep Quer (2019). The noun–verb distinction in Catalan Sign Language: An exo-skeletal approach. *Sign Language & Linguistics* 22(1): 1–43. https://doi.org/10.1075/sll.00027.rib

Riccardi, Nicholas, et al. (2019). Dissociating action and abstract verb comprehension post-stroke. *Cortex* 120: 131–146.

Richards, Norvin (2010). *Uttering Trees*. Cambridge, MA: MIT Press.

Richards, Norvin (2016). *Contiguity Theory*. Cambridge, MA: MIT Press.

Riehemann, Susanne (1998). Type-based derivational morphology. *Journal of Comparative Germanic Linguistics* 2: 49–77.

Rigby, C. P. (1877). Mr. J. M. Hildebrandt on his travels in East Africa. *Proceedings of the Royal Geographical Society of London* 22(6): 446–453.

Rijkhoff, Jan (1991). Nominal aspect. *Journal of Semantics* 8: 291–309. [an updated and improved version of this proposal is presented in Rijkhoff 2004: chs. 2 and 4]

Rijkhoff, Jan (1999). When can a language have adjectives? An implicational universal. In Petra M. Vogel & Bernard Comrie (eds.), *Approaches to the Typology of Word Classes*. Berlin: Mouton de Gruyter, 217–258.

Rijkhoff, Jan (2002): *The Noun Phrase*. Oxford: Oxford University Press.

Rijkhoff, Jan (2003). When can a language have nouns and verbs? *Acta Linguistica Hafniensia* 35: 7–38.
Rijkhoff, Jan (2004). *The Noun Phrase*. Oxford: Oxford University Press. [expanded paperback publication of the 2002 hb edn]
Rijkhoff, Jan (2007). Word classes. *Language and Linguistics Compass* 1(6): 709–726.
Rijkhoff, Jan (2008). On flexible and rigid nouns. *Studies in Language* 32(3): 727–752.
Rijkhoff, Jan (2009). On the (un)suitability of semantic categories. *Linguistic Typology* 13(1): 95–04.
Rijkhoff, Jan (2015). Word order. In James D. Wright (editor-in-chief), *International Encyclopedia of the Social and Behavioral Sciences (Second Edition)*. Oxford: Elsevier, vol. XXV, 644–656.
Rijkhoff, Jan (2016). Crosslinguistic categories in morphosyntactic typology: Problems and prospects. *Linguistic Typology* 20(2): 333–363.
Rijkhoff, Jan & Eva van Lier (eds.) (2013). *Flexible Word Classes: Typological Studies of Underspecified Parts of Speech*. Oxford: Oxford University Press.
Rini, Joel (1990). On the chronology of Spanish conmigo, contigo, consigo and the interaction of phonological, syntactic, and morphological processes. *Hispanic Review* 58(4): 503–512.
Rissman, Lilia, et al. (2020). The communicative importance of agent-backgrounding: Evidence from homesign and Nicaraguan Sign Language. *Cognition* 203: 104332. https://doi.org/10.1016/j.cognition.2020.104332
Rizzi, Luigi (1997). The fine structure of the left periphery. In Liliane Haegeman (ed.), *Elements of Grammar: Handbook in Generative Syntax*. Dordrecht: Kluwer, 281–337.
Rizzi, Luigi (2004). *The Structure of CP and IP. The Cartography of Syntactic Structures (volume 2)*. Oxford: Oxford University Press.
Roach, Peter (2009). *English Phonetics and Phonology*. Cambridge: Cambridge University Press.
Roberts, Ian & Anna Roussou (1999). A formal approach to 'grammaticalization'. *Linguistics* 37(6): 1011–1041.
Roberts, John R. (1998). Give in Amele. The linguistics of giving. In John Newman (ed.), *Typological Studies in Language* (36th edn). Amsterdam: John Benjamins, 1–33.
Robertson, John S. (1980). *The Structure of Pronoun Incorporation in the Mayan Verbal Complex*. New York: Garland.
Robins, R. H. (1952). Noun and verb in universal grammar. *Language* 28(3): 289–298. doi:10.2307/410101
Robinson, Laura C. & John Haan (2014). Adang. In Antoinette Schapper (ed.), *Papuan Languages of Timor, Alor and Pantar: Sketch Grammars*. Berlin: Mouton de Gruyter, vol. I, 221–284.
Rodgers, Theodore S. (1967). *Measuring Vocabulary Difficulty: An Analysis of Item Variables in Learning Russian-English and Japanese-English Vocabulary Pairs*. Technical report 124, Psychology series. Institute for mathematical studies in the social sciences. Stanford, CA: Stanford University.
Rodrigues, Aryon (1951). A composição em Tupi. *Logos* 6(14, separata): 1–8.
Rodrigues, Aryon (1953). Morfologia do verbo Tupi. *Letras, Separata* n°1: 121–152.
Rodrigues, Aryon (1984). Relações internas na família linguística Tupí-Guaraní. *Revista de Antropologia* 1: 33–53.
Rodrigues, Aryon (1996). Argumento e predicado em Tupinambá. *Boletim Da Associação Brasileira de Lingüística* 19: 57–66.
Rodrigues, Aryon (2000). Caso em Tupí-Guaraní, particularmente em Tupinambá. *Anais Do XIII Encontro Nacional Da ANPOLL*. XIII Encontro Nacional da ANPOLL, CD Rom.

Rodrigues, Aryon (2001). Sobre a natureza do caso argumentativo. In Francesc Queixalós (ed.), *Des noms et des verbes en tupi-guarani: état de la question*. Munich: Lincom Europa, 103–144.

Rodrigues, Aryon (2009). A case of affinity among Tupí, Karíb, and Macro-Jê. *Revista Brasileira de Linguística Antropológica* 1(1): 137–162.

Rodrigues, Aryon & Ana S. Cabral (2002). Revendo a classificação interna da família Tupí-Guaraní. In Ana S. Cabral & Aryon Rodrigues (eds.), *Línguas Indígenas Brasileiras. Fonologia, Gramática e História. Atas do I Encontro Internacional do GTLI da ANPOLL*. Belém: Editora Universitária UFPA, 327–337.

Rodrigues, Aryon & Ana S. Cabral (2012). Tupían. In Lyle Campbell (ed.), *The Indigenous Languages of South America*. Mouton De Gruyter, 495–574.

Rodrigues, Aryon & Wolf Dietrich (1997). On the linguistic relationship between Mawé and Tupí-Guaraní. *Diachronica* 14(2): 265–304.

Rogava, Georgi & Zaynab Kerasheva (1966). *Grammatika adygejskogo jazyka* [A grammar of Adyghe]. Krasnodar: Adygejskoe knižnoje izdatelʹstvo.

Rogers, Phillip (2016). Illustrating the prototype structures of parts of speech: a multidimensional scaling analysis. MA thesis, University of New Mexico.

Rojas-Berscia, Luis Miguel (2019). Nominalization in Shawi/Chayahuita. In Roberto Zariquiey, Masayoshi Shibatani, & David W. Fleck (eds.), *Nominalization in Languages of the Americas*. Amsterdam: John Benjamins, 491–514.

Romero-Figueroa, Andrés (1997). *A Reference Grammar of Warao*. Munich: Lincom Europa.

Rosch, Eleanor (1973). Natural categories. *Cognitive Psychology* 4: 328–350.

Rosch, Eleanor (1975). Cognitive reference points. *Cognitive Psychology* 7: 532–547.

Rosch, Eleanor (1978). Principles of categorization. In Eleanor Rosch & Barbara B. Lloyd (eds.), *Cognition and Categorization*. Mahwah, NJ: Erlbaum, 27–48.

Rosch, Eleanor (1983). Prototype classification and logical classification: The two systems. In Ellin Scholnick (ed.), *New Trends in Conceptual Representation: Challenges to Piaget's Theory?* Mahwah, NJ: Erlbaum, 73–86.

Rose, Françoise (2002). My hammock = I have a hammock. Possessed nouns constituting possessive clauses in Emérillon (Tupi-Guarani). In Ana S. Cabral & Aryon Rodrigues (eds.), *Línguas Indígenas Brasileiras. Fonologia, Gramática e História. Atas do I Encontro Internacional do GTLI da ANPOLL*. CNPQ & Universidade Federal do Pará, vol. I, 392–402.

Rose, Françoise (2005). Reduplication in Tupi-Guarani languages: Going into opposite directions. In B. Hurch (ed.), *Studies on Reduplication*. Mouton de Gruyter, 351–368.

Rose, Françoise (2006). Le syncrétisme adpositions/subordonnants. Proposition de typologie syntaxique. *Faits de Langues* 28 (Coordination et subordination: typologie et modélisation): 205–216.

Rose, Françoise (2007). Action répétitive et action répétée: aspect et pluralité verbale dans la réduplication en émérillon. *Faits de Langues* 29 (La réduplication): 125–143.

Rose, Françoise (2008). A typological overview of Emerillon, a Tupi-Guarani language from French Guiana. *Linguistic Typology* 12(3): 431–460.

Rose, Françoise (2009). A hierarchical indexation system: the example of Emerillon (Teko). In Patience Epps & Alexandre Arkhipov (eds.), *New Challenges in Typology. Transcending the Borders and Refining the Distinctions*. Mouton de Gruyte, 63–83.

Rose, Françoise (2011). *Grammaire de l'émérillon teko, une langue tupi-guarani de Guyane française*. Paris: Peeters.

Rose, Françoise (2013). Finitization. A shift of dependency-coding strategy from Proto-Tupi-Guarani to Emérillon. *Diachronica* 30(1): 27–60.

Rose, Françoise (2015a). On male and female speech and more. A typology of categorical gender indexicality in indigenous South American languages. *International Journal of American Linguistics* 81(4): 495–537.

Rose, Françoise (2015b). When 'you' and 'I' mess around with the hierarchy: A comparative study of Tupi-Guarani hierarchical indexation systems. *Boletim Do Museu Paraense Emílio Goeldi. Ciências Humanas* 10(2): 347–369.

Rose, Françoise (2018). Are the Tupi-Guarani hierarchical indexing systems really motivated by the person hierarchy? In Sonia Cristofaro & Fernando Zúñiga (eds.), *Typological Hierarchies in Synchrony and Diachrony*. Amsterdam: Benjamins, 290–307.

Rose, Françoise & Natalia Chousou-Polydouri (2017). *A Comparative Study of Genderlects in the Tupi family*. SSILA Annual Meeting, Austin.

Rose, Françoise (accepted). Teko Ideophones : description of a word class. *Linguistic Typology at the Crossroads*.

Ross, John Robert (1972). Endstation Hauptwort: The category squish. In Paul M. Peranteau et al. (eds.), *Papers from the Eighth Regional Meeting of the Chicago Linguistics Society*, 316–328.

Ross, John Robert (1973). Nouniness. In Osamu Fujimura (ed.), *Three Dimensions of Linguistic Research*. Tokyo: TEC, 137–257.

Ross, Lars A., et al. (2011). Improved proper name recall in aging after electrical stimulation of the anterior temporal lobes. *Frontiers in Aging Neuroscience* 3: art. 16.

Ross, Malcolm (1998a). Proto-Oceanic adjectival categories and their morphosyntax. *Oceanic Linguistics* 37(1): 85–119.

Ross, Malcolm (1998b). Possessive-like attributive constructions in the Oceanic languages of Northwest Melanesia. *Oceanic Linguistics* 37(2): 234–276.

Ross, Malcolm (2005). Pronouns as preliminary diagnostic for grouping Papuan languages. In Andrew Pawley et al. (eds.), *Papuan Pasts: Cultural, Linguistic and Biological Histories of Papuan-Speaking Peoples*. (Pacific Linguistics 572.) Canberra: Research School of Pacific & Asian Studies, Australian National University, 15–65.

Roth, Arlette (1975). *Le verbe dans le parler arabe de Kormakiti (Chypre)*. Paris: Geuthner.

Rothstein, Susan (2006). Predication. In Keith Brown (ed.), *Encyclopedia of Language and Linguistics*. Oxford: Elsevier, vol. x, 73–76.

Rothstein, Susan (2017). *Semantics for Counting and Measuring*. Cambridge: Cambridge University Press.

Roulon-Doko, Paulette (2001). Le statut des idéophones en Gbaya. In F. K. Erhard Voeltz & Christa Kilian-Hatz (eds.), *Ideophones*. Amsterdam: John Benjamins, 287–301.

Rovai, Francesco (2017). Tra verbo e aggettivo: il participio presente nel latino repubblicano. In Giovanna Marotta & Francesca Strik Lievers (eds.), *Strutture linguistiche e dati empirici in diacronia e sincronia*. Pisa: Pisa University Press, 83–110.

Rowlands, Evan Colins (1969). *Yoruba*. London: Hodder & Stoughton.

Roy, Isabelle (2013). *Nonverbal Predication: Copular Sentences and the Syntax–Semantics Interface*. (Oxford Studies in Theoretical Linguistics 45.) Oxford: Oxford University Press.

Rubin, David (1980). 51 properties of 125 words: A unit analysis of verbal behavior. *Journal of Verbal Learning and Verbal Behavior* 19: 736–55.

Rubino, Carl R. Galvez (2002). *Tagalog–English English–Tagalog Dictionary*. New York: Hippocrene Books.

Rubino, Carl (2005). Reduplication: Form, function, and distribution. In Bernhard Hurch and Veronika Mattes (eds.), *Studies on Reduplication*. New York: Mouton de Gruyter, 11–29.

Rudes, Blair A. (1999). *Tuscarora–English/English–Tuscarora dictionary*. Toronto: University of Toronto Press.

Rühlemann, Christoph (2020). Turn structure and inserts. *International Journal of Corpus Linguistics* 25(2): 185–214. doi:10.1075/ijcl.19098.ruh

Ruiz de Montoya, A. S. J. (1640). *Arte, y bocabulario de la lengua guarani*. Iuan Sanchez.

Rullmann, Hotze & Aili You (2006). General number and the semantics and pragmatics of indefinite bare nouns in Mandarin Chinese. In Klaus von Heusinger & Ken Turner (eds.), *Where Semantics Meets Pragmatics*. Oxford: Elsevier, 175–196.

Rüsch, Maren (2020). *A Conversational Analysis of Acholi: Structure and Socio-Pragmatics of a Nilotic Language of Uganda*. Leiden: Brill.

Russ, Charles (2013). *The Dialects of Modern German. A Linguistic Survey*. London: Routledge.

Russell, Bertrand (1923). Vagueness. *Australian Journal of Psychology and Philosophy* 1: 84–92.

Ryding, Katrin (2005). *A Reference Grammar of Modern Standard Arabic*. Cambridge: Cambridge University Press.

Ryding, Katrin (2014). *Arabic. A Linguistic Introduction*. Cambridge: Cambridge University Press.

Saad, George (in press). A grammar sketch of Shuar. In Mily Crevels & Pieter Muysken (eds.), *Grammatical Sketches of Four South American Languages*. Leiden: Brill.

Saad, George, Marian Klamer, & Francesca Moro (2019). Identifying agents of change: Simplification of possessive marking in Abui-Malay bilinguals. *Glossa: A Journal of General Linguistics* 4(1): 57. http://doi.org/10.5334/gjgl.846

Sadler, Louisa (2016). Agreement in Archi: An LFG perspective. In Oliver Bond et al. (eds.), *Archi: Complexities of Agreement in Cross-Theoretical Perspective*. Oxford: Oxford University Press, 150–183.

Sadler, Louisa (2019). Multiple controllers in nominal modification. *Argumentum* 15: 617–638.

Sadler, Louisa & Doug Arnold (1994). Prenominal adjectives and the phrasal/lexical distinction. *Journal of Linguistics* 30: 187–226.

Sadock, Jerrold (1999). The nominalist theory of Eskimo: A case study in scientific self-deception. *International Journal of American Linguistics* 65(4): 383–406. doi:10.1086/466400

Sadock, Jerrold (2003). *Grammar of Kalaallisut (West Greenlandic Inuttut)*. Languages of the World/Materials 162. Munich: Lincom Europa.

Safar, Josefina & Rodrigo Petatillo Chan (2020). Strategies of noun–verb distinction in Yucatec Maya Sign languages. In Olivier Le Guen, Josefina Safar, & Marie Coppola (eds.), *Emerging Sign Languages of the Americas*. Berlin/Boston, MA: De Gruyter Mouton, 155–202. https://doi.org/10.1515/9781501504884-004

Sag, Ivan (1997). English relative clause constructions. *Journal of Linguistics* 33: 431–484.

Sag, Ivan (2012). Sign-Based construction grammar: An informal synopsis. In Hans Boas & Ivan Sag (eds.), *Sign-Based Construction Grammar*. Stanford, CA: CSLI Publications, 69–202.

Sag, Ivan, Thomas Wasow, & Emily Bender (2003). *Syntactic Theory: A Formal Introduction* (2nd edn). Stanford, CA: CSLI Publications.

Sagart, Laurent (1993). L'infixe -r- en chinois archaique. *Bulletin de la Société de Linguistique de Paris* 88: 261–293.

Sagart, Laurent (1999). *The Roots of Old Chinese*. Amsterdam: John Benjamins.

Sagart, Laurent & William Baxter (2012). Reconstructing the *s- prefix in Old Chinese. *Language and Linguistics* 13: 29–59.

Sahin, Ned T., et al. (2009). Sequential processing of lexical, grammatical, and phonological information within Broca's area. *Science* 326: 445–449.

Sahin, Ned T., Steven Pinker, & Eric Halgren (2006). Abstract grammatical processing of nouns and verbs in Broca's area: Evidence from fMRI. *Cortex* 42: 540–562.

Sakarias, Maria & Monique Flecken (2019). Keeping the result in sight and mind: General cognitive principles and language-specific influences in the perception and memory of resultative events. *Cognitive Science* 43(1): 1–30. doi:10.1111/cogs.12708

Salmons, Joe (1990). Bilingual discourse marking: Code switching, borrowing, and convergence in some German-American dialects. *Linguistics* 28: 453–480.

Saltarelli, Mario (1988). *Basque*. London: Routledge.

Sanches, Mar & Linda Slobin (1973). Numeral classifiers and plural marking: An implicational universal. *Working Papers in Language Universals* 11 (Stanford University): 1–22.

Sanders, Gerald (1988). Zero derivation and the overt analogue criterion. In Michael Hammond & Michael Noonan (eds.), *Theoretical Morphology: Approaches in Modern Linguistics*. San Diego: Academic Press, 155–175.

Sands, Kristina (1995). Nominal classification in Australia. *Anthropological Linguistics* 37: 247–346.

Sapir, Edward (1921). *Language: An Introduction to the Study of Speech*. New York: Harcourt, Brace & Co.

Sapir, Edward (1922). The Takelma language of Southwestern Oregon. In Franz Boas (ed.) *Handbook of American Indian Languages, Volume Two. Smithsonian Institution Bureau of American Ethnology Bulletin* 40. Washington, DC: Government Printing Office, 1–296.

Sapir, Edward & Morris Swadesh (1939). *Nootka Texts: Tales and Ethnological Narratives with Grammatical Notes and Lexical Materials*. Philadelphia: Linguistic Society of America.

Sasse, Hans-Jürgen (1988). Der irokesische Sprachtyp. *Zeitschrift für Sprachwissenschaft* 7: 173–213.

Sasse, Hans-Jürgen (1992). *Das Nomen—eine universale Kategorie?* (Theorie des Lexikons Nr. 27.) Düsseldorf: Heinrich Heine Universität Düsseldorf.

Sasse, Hans-Jürgen (1993). Syntactic categories and subcategories. In Joachim Jacobs et al. (eds.), *Syntax: An International Handbook of Contemporary Research*. Berlin: De Gruyter, vol. II, 646–686.

Sasse, Hans-Jürgen (2015). Syntactic categories and subcategories. In Tibor Kiss & Artemis Alexiadou (eds.), *Syntax: Theory and Analysis* (Handbücher Zur Sprach- Und Kommunikationswissenschaft (HSK) 42). Berlin, Boston: De Gruyter, vol. I, 158–217.

Satzinger, Helmut & Ariel Shisha-Halevy (1999). The snark is dead. *Lingua Aegyptia* 6: 167–176.

Sauerland, Uli (2002). The present tense is semantically vacuous. *Snippets* 6: 12–13.

Sauerland, Uli (2008). On the semantic markedness of phi-features. In D. Harbour, D. Adger, & S. Béjar (eds.), *Phi Theory: Phi-features across Modules and Interfaces*. Oxford: Oxford University Press, 57–82.

Sauerland, Uli, Jan Anderssen, & Kazuko Yatsushiro (2005). The plural is semantically unmarked. In Stefan Kepser & Marga Reis (eds.), *Linguistic Evidence*. Berlin: De Gruyter, 409–430.

Saussure, Ferdinand de (1916). *Cours de linguistique générale*. Paris: Payot.

Sauvageot, Serge (1967). Note sur la classification nominale en baïnouk. In Gabriel Manessy (ed.), *La classification nominale dans les langues négro-africaines*. Paris: Éditions du CNRS, 225–236.

Schaaik, Gerjan van (1996). *Studies in Turkish Grammar*. Wiesbaden: Harrassowitz.

Schachter, Paul & Fe T. Otanes (1972). *Tagalog Reference Grammar*. Berkeley, CA: University of California Press.

Schachter, Paul (1985). Parts-of-speech systems. In Timothy Shopen (ed.), *Language Typology and Syntactic Description, Volume 1: Clause Structure*. Cambridge: Cambridge University Press, 3–61.

Schachter, Paul & Timothy Shopen (2007). Parts-of-speech systems. In Timothy Shopen (ed.), *Language Typology and Syntactic Description, Volume 1: Clause Structure*. Cambridge: Cambridge University Press, 1–60.

Schadeberg, Thilo (2001). Number in Swahili grammar. *Afrikanistische Arbeitspapiere* 68: 7–16.

Schaefer, Ronald P. (2001). Ideophonic adverbs and manner gaps in Emai. In F. K. Erhard Voeltz & Christa Kilian-Hatz (eds.), *Ideophones*. Amsterdam: John Benjamins, 339–354.

Schapper, Antoinette (2009). Bunaq: A Papuan language of Central Timor. PhD thesis, Australian National University, Canberra.

Schapper, Antoinette (2014). Elevation in the spatial deictic systems of Alor–Pantar languags. In Marian Klamer (ed.), *The Alor–Pantar Languages: History and Typology*. Berlin: Language Science Press, 247–284.

Schapper, Antoinette & Marian Klamer (2017). Numeral systems in the Alor–Pantar languages. In Marian Klamer (ed.), *The Alor–Pantar Languages: History and Typology* (2nd edn). Berlin: Language Science Press, 277–328.

Schegloff, Emanuel A. (1982). Discourse as interactional achievement: Some uses of 'uh huh' and other things that come between sentences. In Deborah Tannen (ed.), *Analyzing Discourse: Text and Talk*. Washington, DC: Georgetown University Press, 71–93.

Schegloff, Emanuel A. (2007). *Sequence Organization in Interaction: A Primer in Conversation Analysis*. Cambridge: Cambridge University Press.

Schegloff, Emanuel A., Gail Jefferson, & Harvey Sacks (1977). The preference for self-correction in the organization of repair in conversation. *Language* 53(2): 361–382.

Schembri, Adam, Kearsy Cormier, & Jordan Fenlon (2018). Indicating verbs as typologically unique constructions: Reconsidering verb 'agreement' in sign languages. *Glossa: A Journal of General Linguistics* 3(1): 89. https://doi.org/10.5334/gjgl.468

Schembri, Adam & Onno Crasborn (2010). Issues in creating annotation standards for sign language description. In Phillipe Dreuw et al. (eds.), *Proceedings of the 4th Workshop of the Representation and Processing of Sign Languages: Corpora and Sign Language Technologies*. Valletta: European Language Resources Association, 212–216. http://www.lrec-conf.org/proceedings/lrec2010/workshops/W13.pdf

Schermair, Anselmo E. (1949). *Gramática de la lengua sirionó*. Impresa en los Talleres Graficos de A. Gamarra

Schiering, René, Balthasar Bickel, & Kristine A. Hildebrandt (2010). The prosodic word is not universal, but emergent. *Journal of Linguistics* 46(3): 657–709.

Schikowski, Robert. 2013. Object-conditioned differential marking in Chintang and Nepali: Ph. D. dissertation, University of Zürich, Zürich PhD dissertation.

Schneider-Blum, Gertrud (2007). *A Grammar of Alaaba*. Cologne: Rüdiger Köppe.

Schroeder, Christoph (1999). *The Turkish Nominal Phrase in Spoken Discourse*. Wiesbaden: Harrassowitz.

Schultze-Berndt, Eva (2000). Simple and complex verbs in Jaminjung: A study of event categorisation in an Australian language. Doctoral dissertation, Katholieke Universiteit Nijmegen.

Schultze-Berndt, Eva (2001). Ideophone-like characteristics of uninflected predicates in Jaminjung (Australia). In F. K. Erhard Voeltz & Christa Kilian-Hatz (eds.), *Ideophones*. Amsterdam: John Benjamins, 355–373.

Schultze-Berndt, Eva (2003). Preverbs as an open word class in Northern Australian languages: Synchronic and diachronic correlates. In Geert Booij & Jaap van Marle (eds.), *Yearbook of Morphology 2003*. Dordrecht: Kluwer, 145–177.

Schultze-Berndt, Eva (2006). Secondary predicates in Australian Languages. In Martin Everaert & Henk van Riemsdijk (eds.), *The Blackwell Companion to Syntax*. Oxford: Blackwell, vol. IV, 180–208.

Schultze-Berndt, Eva (2017). Two classes of verbs in Northern Australian languages: Implications for the typology of polycategoriality. In Valentina Vapnarsky & Edy Veneziano (eds.), *Lexical Polycategoriality: Cross-linguistic, Cross-theoretical and Language Acquisition Approaches*. Amsterdam: John Benjamins, 243–271.

Schütze, Hinrich (1993). Part-of-speech induction from scratch. *Proceedings of the 31st Annual Meeting on Association for Computational Linguistics*. https://doi.org/10.3115/981574.981608

Schwager, Waldemar & Ulrike Zeshan (2008). Word classes in sign languages: Criteria and classifications. *Studies in Language* 32(3): 509–545. https://doi.org/10.1075/sl.32.3.03sch

Schwarze, Christoph (2001). On the representation of French and Italian clitics. In Miriam Butt & Tracy Holloway King (eds.), *On-line Proceedings of the LFG2001 Conference*. Stanford, CA: CSLI Publications, 280–304. http://csli-publications.stanford.edu/LFG/6/lfg01.html

Scontras, Gregory, Judith Degen, & Noah Goodman (2017). Subjectivity predicts adjective ordering preferences. *Open Mind: Discoveries in Cognitive Science* 1: 53–65.

Scorza, David (1985). A sketch of Au morphology and syntax. *Pacific Linguistics* A63: 215–273.

Sebba, Mark (1987). *The Syntax of Serial Verbs: An Investigation into Serialisation in Sranan and Other Languages*. Amsterdam: John Benjamins.

Segalowitz, Sidney J. & Korri C. Lane (2000). Lexical access of function vs content words. *Brain and Language* 75: 376–389.

Seifart, Frank (2010). Nominal classification. *Language and Linguistics Compass* 4(8): 719–736.

Seifart, Frank, et al. (2012). Nouns slow down speech across structurally and culturally diverse languages. *Proceedings of the National Academy of Sciences (PNAS)* 115(22): 5720–5725. http://www.pnas.org/content/pnas/115/22/5720.full.pdf

Seiler, Walter (1985). *Imonda, a Papuan Language*. Canberra: Australian National University.

Seki, Lucy (2000). *Gramática do Kamaiurá*. Editora da Unicamp.

Seki, Lucy (2001). Classes de palavras e categorias sintático-funcionais em Kamaiurá. In Francesc Queixalós (ed.), *Des noms et des verbes en tupi-guarani: état de la question*. Munich: Lincom Europa, 39–66.

Sells, Peter (1994). Subphrasal syntax in Korean. *Language Research* 30(2): 351–386.

Sells, Peter (1995). Korean and Japanese morphology from a lexical perspective. *Linguistic Inquiry* 26(2). 277–326.

Sells, Peter (2000). Negation in Swedish: Where it's not at. In Miriam Butt & Tracy Holloway King (eds.), *On-line Proceedings of the LFG2000 Conference*. Stanford, CA: CSLI Publications. http://csli-publications.stanford.edu/LFG/LFG5-2000/lfg00-toc.html

Selz, Gebhard J., Orly Goldwasser, & Colette Grinevald (2017). The question of Sumerian determinatives. Inventory, classifier analysis, and comparison to Egyptian classifiers from the linguistic perspective of noun classification, *Lingua Aegyptia* 25: 281–344.

Semenza, Carlo (2006). Retrieval pathways for common and proper names. *Cortex* 42: 884–891.

Semenza, Carlo (2009). The neuropsychology of proper names. *Mind and Language* 24: 347–369.

Semenza, Carlo (2011). Naming with proper names: The left temporal pole theory. *Behavioural Neurology* 24: 277–284.

Senft, Gunter (1986). *Kilivila. The Language of the Trobriand Islanders*. Berlin: Mouton de Gruyter.

Shā, Jiāěr (沙加尔, Laurent Sagart) and Yīpíng Bái (一平白, William H. Baxter) (2010). Shànggǔ Hànyǔ de N- hé m- qiánzhuì 上古汉语的 N- 和 m- 前缀 [The prefixes N- and m- in Old Chinese]. Hàn-Zàng yǔ xuébào 汉藏语学报 [Journal of Sino-Tibetan Linguistics] 4, 62-69.

Shagal, Ksenia (2019). *Participles: A Typological Study*. Berlin: Mouton de Gruyter.

Shannon, Claude E. (1948). A mathematical theory of communication. *Bell System Technical Journal* 27: 379-423, 623-656.

Shapiro, Kevin A., et al. (2001). Grammatical distinctions in the left frontal cortex. *Journal of Cognitive Neuroscience* 13: 713-720.

Shapiro, Kevin A. & Alfonso Caramazza (2003a). Grammatical processing of nouns and verbs in left frontal cortex? *Neuropsychologia* 41: 1189-1198.

Shapiro, Kevin A. & Alfonso Caramazza (2003b). The representation of grammatical categories in the brain. *Trends in Cognitive Sciences* 7: 201-206.

Shapiro, Kevin A. & Alfonso Caramazza (2004). The organization of lexical knowledge in the brain: The grammatical dimension. In Michael S. Gazzaniga (ed.), *The Cognitive Neurosciences* (3rd edn). Cambridge, MA: MIT Press, 803-814.

Shapiro, Kevin A. & Alfonso Caramazza (2009). Morphological processes in language production. In Michael S. Gazzaniga (ed.), *The Cognitive Neurosciences* (4th edn). Cambridge, MA: MIT Press, 777-788.

Shapiro, Kevind A., Lauren R. Moo, & Alfonso Caramazza (2006). Cortical signatures of noun and verb production. *Proceedings of the National Academy of Sciences* 103: 1644-1649.

Shapiro, Kevin A., Lauren R. Moo, & Alfonso Caramazza (2012). Neural specificity for grammatical operations is revealed by content-independent fMR adaptation. *Frontiers in Psychology* 3: art. 26.

Shapiro, Kevin A., Jennifer Shelton, & Alfonso Caramazza (2000). Grammatical class in lexical production and morphological processing: Evidence from a case of fluent aphasia. *Cognitive Neuropsychology* 17: 665-682.

Shea, John G. (1800). Caughnawaga, and the Rev. Joseph Marcoux, its late missionary. Archived at University of Alberta.

Shi, Rushen & Andréane Melançon. 2010. Syntactic categorization in Frenchlearning infants. Infancy 15(5). 517-533. 19

Shi, Rushen, James L. Morgan & Paul Allopena. 1998. Phonological and acoustic bases for earliest grammatical category assignment: a cross-linguistic perspective. Journal of Child Language 25. 169-201.

Shi, Rushen, Janet F Werker & James L Morgan. 1999. Newborn infants' sensitivity to perceptual cues to lexical and grammatical words. Cognition 72(2). B11-B21.

Shibatani, Masayoshi (2019). What is nominalization? Towards the theoretical foundations of nominalization. In Roberto Zariquiey, Masayoshi Shibatani, & David W. Fleck (eds.), *Nominalization in Languages of the Americas*. Amsterdam: John Benjamins, 15-167.

Shields, Janä K. (1988). A syntactic sketch of Silacayoapan Mixtec. In C. Henry Bradley & Barbara E. Hollenbach (eds.), *Studies in the Syntax of Mixtecan Languages* (Summer Institute of Linguistics Publications in Linguistics, 83.) Dallas: Summer Institute of Linguistics & University of Texas, Arlington, vol I, 305-449.

Shimelman, Aviva (2017). *A Grammar of Yauyos Quechua*. Berlin: Language Science Press.

Shipley, Elizabeth F. & Barbara Shepperson (1990). Countable entities: Developmental changes.*Cognition* 34: 109-136.

Shirai, Yasuhiro & Roger W. Andersen (2006). The acquisition of tense–aspect morphology: A prototype account. *Language.* https://doi.org/10.2307/415743

Shtyrov, Yuri, et al. (2014). Automatic ultrarapid activation and inhibition of cortical motor systems in spoken word comprehension. *Proceedings of the National Academy of Sciences* 111: E1918–1923.

Sicoli, Mark A. (2020). *Saying and Doing in Zapotec: Multimodality, Resonance, and the Language of Joint Actions.* (Bloomsbury Studies in Linguistic Anthropology.) London: Bloomsbury Academic.

Sidwell, Paul (2008). Issues in the morphological reconstruction of Proto-Mon-Khmer. In Claire Bowern, Bethwyn Evans, & Luisa Miceli (eds.), *Morphology and Language History. In Honour of Harold Koch.* Amsterdam & Philadelphia: John Benjamins, 251–265.

Siegel, Muffy E. A. (1976). Capturing *the Adjective*. PhD thesis, University of Massachusetts at Amherst. Published by Garland, New York.

Siewierska, Anna (1985). *The Passive: A Comparative Linguistic Analysis.* London: Croom Helm.

Siewierska, Anna (2013). Verbal person marking. In Matthew S. Dryer & Martin Haspelmath (eds.), *The World Atlas of Language Structures Online.* Munich: Max Planck Digital Library, ch. 102. http://wals.info/chapter/102.

Siewierska, Anna & Dik Bakker (2009). Case and alternative strategies: Word order and agreement marking. In Andrej Malchukov & Andrew Spencer (eds.), *The Oxford Handbook of Case.* Oxford: Oxford University Press, 290–303.

Silveri, Maria C. & Nicoletta Ciccarelli (2007). The deficit for the word-class 'verb' in corticobasal degeneration: Linguistic expression of the movement disorder? *Neuropsychologia* 45: 2570–2579.

Simone, Raffaele & Francesca Masini (eds.) (2014). *Word Classes. Nature, Typology and Representations.* Amsterdam/Philadelphia: Benjamins.

Simone, Raffaele & Francesca Masini (2014). On light nouns. In Raffaele Simone & Francesca Masini (eds.), *Word Classes. Nature, Typology and Representations.* Amsterdam: John Benjamins, 51–74.

Siri, Simona, et al. (2008). The neural substrate of naming events: Effects of processing demands but not of grammatical class. *Cerebral Cortex* 18: 171–177.

Shi, Rushen, Janet F. Werker, & Anne Cutler (2006). Recognition and representation of function words in English-learning infants. *Infancy* 10(2): 187–198.

Simpson, Jane (2005). Depictives in English and Warlpiri. In Nikolaus Himmelmann & Eva Schultze-Berndt (eds.), *Secondary Predication and Adverbial Modification: The Typology of Depictives.* Oxford: Oxford University Press, 69–106.

Skafte Jensen, Eva (2011). Et hamster. *Nyt fra Sprognævnet* 1: 1–4.

Skalička, Vladimar (1979). *Typologische Studien.* Braunschweig: Vieweg.

Skedsmo, Kristian (2020). Other-initiations of repair in Norwegian Sign Language. *Social Interaction. Video-Based Studies of Human Sociality* 3(2), 1–43. doi:10.7146/si.v3i2.117723

Skilton, Amalia (2023). Noun classes. In Bowern (ed.), *The Oxford Guide to Australian Languages.* Oxford: Oxford University Press, 205-216. DOI: 10.1093/oso/9780198824978.003.0019

Skinner, B. F. (1957). *Verbal Behavior.* New York: Appleton-Century-Crofts.

Slobin, Dan I. (1996). From 'thought and language' to 'thinking for speaking'. In John Gumperz & Stephen C. Levinson (eds.), *Rethinking Linguistic Relativity.* Cambridge, MA: Cambridge University Press, 70–96.

Slobin, Dan I. (1997). The origins of grammaticizable notions: Beyond the individual mind. In Dan I. Slobin (ed.), *The Crosslinguistic Study of Language Acquisition*, vol. v: *Expanding the Contexts.* Mahwah, NJ: Erlbaum, 265–323.

Smeets, Ineke (1989). A Mapuche grammar. PhD dissertation, University of Leiden.
Smeets, Ineke (2008). *A Grammar of Mapuche.* (Mouton Grammar Library, 41.) Berlin: Mouton de Gruyter.
Smeets, Rieks (1984). *Studies of West Caucasian Phonology and Morphology.* Leiden: Hakuchi Press.
Smit, Niels & Miriam van Staden (2007). Representational layering in Functional Discourse Grammar. *Alfa: Revista de Lingüística* 51(2): 143-164.
Smith, Carlota S. (1997). *The Parameter of Aspect. (Studies in Linguistics and Philosophy 43.)* Dordrecht: Foris.
Smith, Jennifer L. (1997). Noun faithfulness: On the privileged behavior of nouns in phonology. Ms, University of Massachusetts, Amherst. Available online at: Rutgers Optimality Archive #242.
Smith, Jennifer (2011). Category-specific effects. In Marc van Oostendorp et al. (eds.), *The Blackwell Companion to Phonology.* Malden MA: Wiley-Blackwell, 2439-2463.
Smith, K. Aaron (in preparation). The present-day grammatical status of *tryna*.
Smith, K. Aaron (2006). The universal tendency for renewal among grammatical expressions for anterior and related aspect. *Journal of Universal Language* 7(1): 139-160.
Smith, K. Aaron (2009). The history of be fixing to: Grammaticization, sociolinguisitc distribution and emerging literary spaces. *English Today* 12: 12-18.
Smith, K. Aaron (2011). Grammaticalization. *Language and Linguistics Compass* 5(6): 367-380.
Smith, Linda B. (2005). Cognition as a dynamic system: Principles from embodiment. *Developmental Review* 25(3-4): 278-298. https://doi.org/10.1016/j.dr.2005.11.001
Smith, Linda B. & Esther Thelen (2003). Development as a dynamic system. *Trends in Cognitive Science* 7: 343-348. https://doi.org/10.1016/S1364-6613(03)00156-6
Smith, Nicholas (2007). The development of the English progressive. *Journal of Germanic Linguistics* 19(3): 205-241.
Smith, Peter W. (2015). Feature mismatches: Consequences for syntax, morphology and semantics. PhD dissertation, University of Connecticut.
Smith, Wayne H. (1990). Evidence for auxiliaries in Taiwan Sign Language. In Susan D. Fischer & Patricia Siple (eds.), *Theoretical Issues in Sign Language Research.* Chicago: University of Chicago Press, vol. I, 211-228.
Smith Stark, Thomas C. (1983). Jilotepeque Pocomam phonology and morphology. PhD dissertation, University of Chicago.
Smits, Heleen (2017). *A Grammar of Lumun.* Utrecht: LOT.
Sohn, Ho-min (1994). *Korean.* London: Routledge.
Solano, Eliete de Jesus Bararuá (2009). *Descrição gramatical da língua Araweté.* PhD dissertation, Universidade de Brasilia.
Somesfalean, Stanca (2007). On the form and interpretation of clitics. Dissertation, Université de Québec à Montréal.
Son, Minjeong & Peter Cole (2008). An event-based account of kan-constructions in Standard Indonesian. *Language* 84(1): 120-160. https://doi.org/10.1353/lan.2008.0045
Song, Jae Jung (2001). *Linguistic Typology: Morphology and Syntax.* Harlow: Pearson.
Sonnenschein, Aaron Huey (2004). A descriptive grammar of San Bartolomé Zoogocho Zapotec. PhD dissertation, University of Southern California.
Sorace, Antonella & Frank Keller (2005). Gradience in linguistic data. *Lingua* 115: 1497-1524.
Soto Ruiz, Clotoaldo (1976). *Gramática quechua Ayacucho-Chanca.* Lima: Instituto de Estudios Peruanos.

Spencer, Andrew (2013). *Lexical Relatedness*. Oxford: Oxford University Press.
Spencer, Andrew & Arnold Zwicky (eds.). 2007. *The Handbook of Morphology*, London: Blackwell.
Sposato, Adam (2015). A grammar of Xong. Doctoral dissertation, State University of New York at Buffalo.
Spruyt, Joke (2011). Syncategoremata. In Henrik Lagerlund (ed.), *Encyclopedia of Medieval Philosophy: Philosophy between 500 and 1500*. Berlin: Springer, 1241–1245.
Staden, Miriam van (2000). Tidore: A linguistic description of a language of the North Moluccas. Doctoral dissertation, University Leiden.
Stamer, Melissa & Michael Vitevitch (2012). Phonological similarity influences word learning in adults learning Spanish as a foreign language. *Bilingualism: Language and Cognition* 15: 490–502.
Starke, Michael (2001). Move dissolves into merge: A theory of locality. PhD dissertation, University of Geneva.
Starke, Michal (2004). On the inexistence of specifiers and the nature of heads. In Adriana Belletti (ed.), *Structures and Beyond: The Cartography of Syntactic Structures*. Oxford: Oxford University Press, vol. III, 252–268.
Stassen, Leon (1997). *Intransitive Predication*. Oxford: Oxford University Press.
Steensig, Jakob & Søren Sandager Sørensen (2019). Danish dialogue particles in an interactional perspective. *Scandinavian Studies in Language* 10(1): 63–84.
Steinel, Margarita, Jan Hulstijn, & Wolfgang Steinel (2007). Second language idiom learning in a paired-associate paradigm: Effects of direction of learning, direction of testing, idiom imageability, and idiom transparency. *Studies in Second Language Acquisition* 29: 449–484.
Steinhauer, Hein (2005). Biak. In Alexander Adelaar and Nikolaus P. Himmelmann (eds.), *The Austronesian Languages of Asia and Madagascar*. Oxon/New York: Routledge, 793–823.
Stiebels, Barbara (2006). Agent focus in Mayan languages. *Natural Language and Linguistic Theory* 24: 501–570.
Stiebels, Barbara (2007). Towards typology of complement control. *ZAS Papers in Linguistics* 47: 1–80.
Stirling, Lesley & Brett Baker. 2007. Pronominal apposition and the status of 'determiner' in Australian languages. Paper presented at the Australian Linguistic Society Annual Conference, University of Adelaide.
Stivers, Tanya, et al. (2009). Universals and cultural variation in turn-taking in conversation. *Proceedings of the National Academy of Sciences* 106(26): 10587–10592. doi:10.1073/pnas.0903616106
Stoll, Sabine. 2015. Inflectional morphology in language acquisition. In Matthew Baerman (ed.), Handbook of inflectional morphology, Oxford University Press. Stoll, Sabine & Balthasar Bickel. 2013. Capturing diversity in language acquisition research. In Balthasar Bickel, Lenore A. Grenoble, David A. Peterson & Alan Timberlake (eds.), Language typology and historical contingency: studies in honor of Johanna Nichols, 195–260. Amsterdam: Benjamins Publishing Company.
Stoll, Sabine, Balthasar Bickel, Elena Lieven, Goma Banjade, Toya Nath Bhatta, Martin Gaenszle, Netra P. Paudyal, Judith Pettigrew, Ichchha P. Rai, Manoj Rai & Novel Kishore Rai. 2012. Nouns and verbs in Chintang: children's usage and surrounding adult speech. Journal of Child Language 39. 284-321.
Stoll, Sabine, Jekaterina Mazara & Balthasar Bickel. 2017. The acquisition of polysythetic verb forms in Chintang. In Michael Fortescue, Marianne Mithun & Nicholas Evans (eds.), Handbook of Polysynthesis, 495–517. Oxford UniversityPress.

Stolz, Christel & Thomas Stolz (1996). Funktionswortentlehnung in Mesoamerika Spanisch-amerindischer Sprachkontakt (Hispanoindiana II). *STUF—Language Typology and Universals* 49: 86–123.

Stolz, Thomas (2001). Singulative–collective: Natural morphology and stable classes in Welsh number inflexion on nouns. *Sprachtypologie und Universalienforschung* 54(1): 52–76.

Stoneham, John (2004). *Linguistic Theory and Complex Words: Nuuchahnulth Word Formation*. New York: Palgrave Macmillan.

Stowell, Timothy (1981). The origins of phrase structure. Dissertation, MIT, Cambridge, MA.

Stroomer, Harry (1987). *A Comparative Study of Three Southern Oromo Dialects in Kenya: Phonology, Morphology and Vocabulary*. (Cushitic Language Studies 6.) Hamburg: Buske.

Stroomer, Harry (1995). *A Grammar of Boraana Oromo (Kenya)*. Cologne: Rüdiger Köppe.

Stukenbrock, Anja (2015). *Deixis in der face-to-face-Interaktion*. Berlin: Mouton de Gruyter.

Stump, Gregory (2019). Theoretical issues in inflection. In Jenny Audring & Francesca Masini (eds.), *The Oxford Handbook of Morphological Theory*. Oxford: Oxford University Press, 56–84.

Sun, Linlin (2020). *Flexibility in the Parts-of-Speech System of Classical Chinese*. Berlin: Mouton De Gruyter.

Sundaresan, Sandhya (2012). *Context and (co)reference in the syntax and its interfaces*. PhD dissertation, University of Tromsø (CASTL)/Universität Stuttgart.

Supalla, Samuel J. (1990). The arbitrary name sign system in American Sign Language. *Sign Language Studies* 67: 99–126. https://doi.org/10.1353/sls.1990.0006

Supalla, Ted & Elissa L. Newport (1978). How many seats in a chair? The derivation of nouns and verbs in American Sign Language. In Patricia Siple (ed.), *Understanding Language through Sign Language Research*. New York: Academic Press, 91–132.

Suttles, Wayne (2004). *Musqueam Reference Grammar*. (First Nations Languages.) Vancouver: University of British Columbia Press.

Svenonius, Peter (2006a). The emergence of axial parts. In Peter Svenonius & Marina Pantcheva (eds.), *Nordlyd, Tromsø Working Papers in Language & Linguistics*: 33.1 [special issue on adpositions] Tromsø: University of Tromsø, 49–77.

Svenonius, Peter (2006b). uninterpretable features. *Linguistic Analysis* 33: 375–413.

Swadesh, Morris (1939) Nootka internal syntax. *International Journal of American Linguistics* 9: 77–109.

Swart, Henriëtte de & Joost Zwarts (2009). Less form—more meaning: Why bare singular nouns are special. *Lingua* 119: 280–295.

Szemerényi, Oswald (1989). *Einführung in die vergleichende Sprachwissenschaft*. Darmstadt, Wissenschaftliche Buchgesellschaft. (Ital. trans. *Introduzione alla linguistica indeuropea*. Milano, Unicopli 1985).

Szűcs, Péter (2018). A COMP-less approach to Hungarian complement clauses. In Butt & King (2018: 325–342). http://web.stanford.edu/group/cslipublications/cslipublications/LFG/LFG-2018/index.shtml

Tabor, Whitney & Elizabeth Closs Traugott (1998). Structural scope expansion and grammaticalization. In Anna G. Ramat & Paul Hopper (eds.), *The Limits of Grammaticalization*. Amsterdam: John Benjamins, 229–272.

Tadmor, Uri (2007). Grammatical borrowing in Indonesian. In Yaron Matras & Jeanette Sakel (eds.), *Grammatical Borrowing in Cross-Linguistic Perspective*. Berlin: de Gruyter, 301–328.

Tadmor, Uri (2009). Loanwords in the World's Languages: Findings and Results. In Martin Haspelmath & Uri Tadmor (eds.), *Loanwords in The World's Languages: A Comparative Handbook*. Berlin: Mouton de Gruyter, 55–75.

Takkinen, Ritva, Tommi Jantunen, & Outi Ahonen (2015). Finnish Sign Language. In Julie Bakken Jepsen et al. (eds.), *Sign Languages of the World: A Comparative Handbook*. Berlin/Boston, MA: De Gruyter Mouton, 253–272.

Talamo, Luigi (2017). Nominalizations of property concepts: Evidence from Italian. PhD dissertation, University of Bergamo and University of Pavia.

Talmy, Leonard (1985). Lexicalization patterns: Semantic structure in lexical forms. In Timothy Shopen (ed.), *Language Typology and Syntactic Description*. Cambridge: Cambridge University Press, 36–149.

Talmy, Leonard (1988). Force dynamics in language and cognition. *Cognitive Sciences* 12: 49–100.

Talmy, Leonard (2000). *Towards a Cognitive Semantics*. (Volume II Typology and Process in Concept Structuring). Cambridge, MA: MIT Press.

Talmy, Leonard (2007). Attention phenomena. In Dirk Geeraerts & Hubert Cuyckens (eds.), *The Oxford Handbook of Cognitive Linguistics*. Oxford: Oxford University Press, 264–293.

Tamm, Anne (2011). Cross-categorial spatial case in the Finnic nonfinite system: Focus on the absentive TAM semantics and pragmatics of the Estonian inessive m-formative nonfinites. *Linguistics* 49(4): 835–944.

Tamura, Suzuko (2000). The Ainu language. PhD dissertation, University of Tokyo.

Tang, Marc & One-Soon Her (2019). Insights on the Greenberg–Sanches–Slobin generalization: Quantitative typological data on classifiers and plural markers. *Folia Linguistica* 53-2: 297–331.

Tardif, Twila. 1996. Nouns are not always learned before verbs: evidence from Mandarin speakers' early vocabularies. Developmental Psychology 32. 492–504.

Tardif, Twila, Paul Fletcher, Weilan Liang, Zhixiang Zhang, Niko Kaciroti & Virginia A. Marchman. 2008. Baby's first 10 words. Developmental Psychology 44. 929–938.

Tardif, Twila, Marilyn Shatz & Letitia Naigles. 1997. Caregiver speech and children's use of nouns versus verbs: A comparison of English, Italian, and Mandarin. Journal of Child Language 24(3). 535–565.

Tatevosov, Sergej (2002). The parameter of actionality. Linguistic Typology 6(3): 317–401.

Taverna, Andrea S & Sandra R Waxman. 2020. Early lexical acquisition in the Wichi language. Journal of child language 47(5). 1052–1072.

Tayalati, Fayssal & Danièle Van de Velde (2014). Event nominalizations in French and Modern Standard Arabic: A parallel. *Brill's Annual of Afroasiatic Languages and Linguistics* 6: 119–155.

Taylor, Jack, Alistair Beith, & Sara Sereno (2019). LexOPS: An R Package and user interface for the controlled generation of word Stimuli. https://doi.org/10.31234/osf.io/7sudw

Taylor, John R. (1994). Fuzzy categories in syntax. The case of possessives and compounds. *Rivista di Linguistica* 7: 327–345.

Taylor, John R. (1996a). On running and jogging. *Cognitive Linguistics* 7(1): 2134.

Taylor, John R. (1996b). *Possessives in English: An Exploration in Cognitive Grammar*. Oxford: Clarendon Press.

Taylor, John R. (2002). *Cognitive Grammar*. Oxford: Oxford University Press.

Taylor, John R. (2003). *Linguistic Categorization* (3rd edn). Oxford: Oxford University Press.

Taylor, John R. (2008). Prototypes in cognitive linguistics. In Peter Robinson & Nick C. Ellis (eds.), *Handbook of Cognitive Linguistics and Second Language Acquisition*. New York & London: Routledge, 39–65.

Taylor, John R. (2012). *The Mental Corpus: How Language Is Represented in the Mind.* Oxford: Oxford University Press.

Taylor, John R. (2015). Prototype effects in grammar. In Ewa Dąbrowska & Dagmar Divjak (eds.), *Handbook of Cognitive Linguistics.* Berlin/New York: Mouton de Gruyter, 562–578.

Teng, Stacy Fang-Ching (2008). *A Reference Grammar of Puyuma, an Austronesian Language of Taiwan.* (Pacific Linguistics, 595.) Canberra: Australian National University.

Terrill, Angela (2003). *A Grammar of Lavukaleve.* Berlin: Mouton de Gruyter.

Testelets, Yakov G. (2008). Struktura predloženij s nevyražennoj svjazkoj v russkom jazyke [The structure of sentences with zero copulas in Russian]. In Galina I. Kustova & Raisa I. Rozina (eds.), *Dinamičeskie modeli: Slovo. Predloženie. Tekst. Sbornik statej v čest' E.V. Paduchevoj* [Dynamic models: Word. Sentence. Text. A festschrift for Elena V. Paducheva]. Moscow: Jazyki slavjanskix kul'tur, 773–789.

Thalbitzer, William (1911). Eskimo. In Frans Boas (ed.), *Handbook of American Indian Languages.* (Bureau of American Ethnology Bulletin 40.) Washington, DC: Smithsonian Institution, 967–1069.

Theakston, Anna L, Elena VM Lieven, Julian M Pine & Caroline F Rowland. 2002. Going, going, gone: The acquisition of the verb 'go'. Journal of Child Language 29(04). 783–811.

Theil, Rolf (2012). Omotic. In Lutz Edzard (ed.), *Semitic and Afroasiatic: Challenges and Opportunities.* Wiesbaden: Otto Harrassowitz, 369–383.

Thelen, Esther & Linda B. Smith (1994). *A Dynamical Systems Approach to the Development of Perception and Action.* Cambridge, MA: MIT Press.

Thieberger, Nicholas (2006). *A Grammar of South Efate. An Oceanic Languages of Vanuatu.* Honolulu: University of Hawaii Press.

Thomason, Sarah Grey & Terrence Kaufman (1988). *Language Contact, Creolization, and Genetic Linguistics.* Berkeley, CA: University of California Press.

Thompson, Cynthia K., et al. (2007). Neural correlates of verb argument structure processing. *Journal of Cognitive Neuroscience* 19: 1753–1767.

Thompson, Cynthia K. & Aya Meltzer-Asscher (2014). Neurocognitive mechanisms of verb argument structure processing. In Asaf Bachrach, Isabelle Roy, & Linnaea Stockall (eds.), *Structuring the Argument: Multidisciplinary Research on Verb Argument Structure.* Amsterdam: John Benjamins, 141–168.

Thompson, James (2003). Syntactic nominalization in Halkomelem Salish. PhD thesis, University of British Columbia.

Thompson, Laurence C. & M. Terry Thompson (1980). Thompson Salish//-xi//. *IJAL* 46: 27–32.

Thompson, Laurence C. & M. Terry Thompson (1992). The Thompson language. *Occasional Papers in Linguistics 8.* Missoula: University of Montana Press.

Thompson, Sandra (1988). A discourse approach to the cross-linguistic category 'adjective'. In John A. Hawkins (ed.), *Explaining Language Universals.* Oxford: Blackwell, 167–185.

Thompson, Sandra A. (2002). Object complements and conversation: Towards a realistic account. *Studies in Language* 26(1): 125–163.

Thompson, Sandra A., Joseph Sung-Yul Park, & Charles N. Li (2006). *A Reference Grammar of Wappo.* Berkeley: University of California Press.

Thumb, Albert & Robert Hauschild (1959). *Handbuch des Sanskrit,* II Teil., Heidelberg, Winter.

Tiersma, Peter (1982). Local and general markedness. *Language* 58(4): 832–849.

Timm, Jason (2020). MDS for Linguists. https://github.com/jaytimm/mds_for_linguists, accessed 1 September 2020.

Tjia, Johnny (2007). *A Grammar of Mualang.* Utrecht: LOT.

Tkachman, Oksana & Wendy Sandler (2013). The noun–verb distinction in two young sign languages. *Gesture* 13(3): 253-286. https://doi.org/10.1075/gest.13.3.02tka

Tobassi, Patrizia, et al. (2010). Speaking of events: The case of C.M. *Cognitive Neuropsychology* 27: 152-180.

Toivonen, Ida (2003). *Non-Projecting Words: A Case Study of Swedish Verbal Particles*. Dordrecht: Kluwer.

Tomasello, Michael. 1992. First verbs: a case study of early grammatical development. Cambridge: Cambridge University Press.

Tomasello, Michael & Michelle Barton (1994). Learning words in nonostensive contexts. *Developmental Psychology* 30(5): 639-650. https://doi.org/10.1037/0012-1649.30.5.639

Tomasello, Michael (1995). Joint attention as social cognition. In Chris Moore & Philip J. Dunham (eds.), *Joint Attention: Its Origins and Role in Development*. Mahwah, NJ: Erlbaum, 103-130.

Tomasello, Michael (1999). *The Cultural Origins of Human Cognition*. Cambridge, MA: Harvard University Press.

Tomasello, Michael. 2000. Do young children have adult syntactic competence? Cognition 74(3). 209-253.

Tomasello, Michael (2003). *Constructing a Language: A Usage-based Theory of Language Acquisition*. Cambridge, MA: Harvard University Press. https://doi.org/10.1017/CBO978110 7415324.004

Tomasello, Michael & Ann C. Kruger (1992). Joint attention on actions acquiring verbs in ostensive and non-ostensive contexts. *Journal of Child Language* 19(2): 311-333. https://doi.org/10.1017/S0305000900011430

Tomasello, Michael & Raquel Olguin. 1993. Twenty-three-month-old children have a grammatical category of noun. Cognitive Development 8(4). 451-464.

Tomasello, Michael, et al. 1997. Differential productivity in young children's use of nouns and verbs. Journal of Child Language 24. 373-387.

Tomasino, Barbara, et al. (2019). Noun–verb naming dissociation in neurosurgical patients. *Aphasiology* 33: 1418-1440.

Tomaszewski, Piotr (2015). Constraints on negative prefixation in Polish Sign Language. *PLOS ONE* 10(11): 1-29. https://doi.org/10.1371/journal.pone.0143574

Tomčina, S. I. (1978). *Vvedenie v sintagmatičeskuju morfologiju jazyka maninka* [Introduction to the syntagmatic morphology of the Maninka language]. Leningrad: State University of Leningrad.

Tonhauser, Judith (2006). The temporal semantics of noun phrases: Evidence from Guaraní. PhD dissertation, Stanford University.

Tonhauser, Judith (2007). Nominal tense? The meaning of Guaraní nominal temporal markers. *Language* 83(4): 831-869.

Tonzar, Claudio, Lorella Lotto, & Remo Job (2009). L2 vocabulary acquisition in children: Effects of learning method and cognate status. *Language Learning* 59: 623-646.

Tosco, Mauro (1991). *A Grammatical Sketch of Dahalo. Including Texts and a Glossary*. Hamburg: Helmut Buske.

Tosco, Mauro (1997). *Af Tunni. Grammar, Texts, and Glossary of a Southern Somali Dialect*. Cologne: Rüdger Köppe.

Tosco, Mauro (2001). *The Dhaasanac Language*. Cologne: Rüdiger Köppe.

Tosco, Mauro (2003). Cushitic and Omotic overview. In Marvin Bender et al. (eds.), *Afrasian: Selected Comparative-Historical Linguistic Studies in Memory of Igor M. Diakonoff*. Munich: Lincom Europa, 87-92.

Touré, Aboubacar (1994). Eléments de description de la langue soso. PhD thesis, Université Stendhal, Grenoble.
Tranel, Daniel (2006). Impaired naming of unique landmarks is associated with left temporal polar damage. *Neuropsychology* 20: 1–10.
Tranel, Daniel (2009). The left temporal pole is important for retrieving words for unique concrete entities. *Aphasiology* 23: 867–884.
Tranel, Daniel, et al. (2005). Effects of noun–verb homonymy on the neural correlates of naming concrete entities and actions. *Brain and Language* 92: 288–299.
Trap-Jensen, Lars (2007). Sprogligt kønsskifte. *Politiken* [Danish newspaper] of 31 October 2007. https://sproget.dk/raad-og-regler/artikler-mv/sprogligt-politikens-sprogklumme/31-oktober-2007
Traugott, Elizabeth Closs (2001). Legit counter examples to unidirectionality. Paper presented at Freiburg University, 17 October 2001.
Traugott, Elizabeth Closs (2002). From etymology to historical pragmatics. In Donka Minkova & Robert Stockwell (eds.), *Studies in the History of the English Language*. Berlin: Mouton de Gruyter, 19–49.
Traugott, Elizabeth Closs (2003). Constructions in grammaticalization. In Brian D. Joseph & Richard Janda (eds.), *The Handbook of Historical Linguistics*. Oxford: Blackwell, 624–647.
Traugott, Elizabeth & Bernd Heine (eds.) (1991). *Approaches to Grammaticalization* (2 vols.). Amsterdam: John Benjamins.
Traugott, Elizabeth & Graeme Trousdale (2013). *Constructionalization and Constructional Changes*. Oxford: Oxford University Press.
Treis, Yvonne (2008). *A grammar of Kambaata. Part 1: Phonology, morphology, and nonverbal predication*. Cologne: Rüdiger Köppe.
Treis, Yvonne (2012). Categorial hybrids in Kambaata, *Journal of African Languages and Linguistics* 33(2): 215–254.
Treis, Yvonne (2019). Similative and equative demonstratives in Kambaata. *Faits de Langues* 51: 175–202. [special issue 'Comparaisons d'égalité et de similitude et expression de la simulation']
Tremblay, Pascale & Anthony S. Dick (2016). Broca and Wernicke are dead, or moving past the classic model of language neurobiology. *Brain and Language* 162: 60–71.
Trotzke, Andreas & Eva Wittenberg (eds.) (2019). *Adjective Order through a German Lens*. [special issue of *Linguistics* 57(2)].
Trommelen, Mieke (1989). Lettergreepstruktuur en woordkategorie. *De Nieuwe Taalgids* 82: 64–77.
Trovesi, Andrea (2004). *La genesi di articoli determinativi. Modalità di espressione della definitezza in ceco, serbo-lusaziano e sloveno*. Milan: FrancoAngeli.
Tsapkini, Kyrana, Gonia Jarema, & Eva Kehayia (2002). A morphological processing deficit in verbs but not nouns: A case study in a highly inflected language. *Journal of Neurolinguistics* 15: 265–288.
Tsigka, Styliani, et al. (2014). Distinguishable neural correlates of verbs and nouns: A MEG study. *Neuropsychologia* 54: 87–97.
Tsunoda, Tasaku (2011). *A Grammar of Warrongo*. (Mouton Grammar Library, 53.) Berlin: Mouton de Gruyter.
Tsunoda, Tasaku, Sumie Ueda, & Yoshiaki Itoh (1995). Adpositions in word-order typology. *Linguistics* 33(4): 741–762.
Tucker, Matthew (2011). Even more on the anaphor agreement effect: when binding does not agree. Ms, UCSC.

Tufvesson, Sylvia (2011). Analogy-making in the Semai Sensory World. *Senses and Society* 6(1): 86–95. doi:10.2752/174589311X12893982233876

Tyler, Andrea & Vyvyan Evans (2001). The relation between experience, conceptual structure and meaning: Non-temporal uses of tense and language teaching. In Martin Pütz, Susanne Niemeier, & René Dirven (eds.), *Applied Cognitive Linguistics, vol. 1: Theory and Language Acquisition*. Berlin: Mouton de Gruyter, 63–105.

Tyler, Lorraine K., Billi Randall, & Emmanuel Stamatakis (2008). Cortical differentiation for nouns and verbs depends on grammatical markers. *Journal of Cognitive Neuroscience* 20: 1381–1389.

Tzul, Julio Alberto & Alfonso Tzimaj Cacao (1997). *Gramática del idioma Q'eqchi'*. Antigua Guatemala: Proyecto Lingüístico Francisco Marroquín.

Uchihara, Hiroto (2014). Noun incorporation in Cherokee revisited. *International Journal of American Linguistics* 80: 5–38.

Uchihara, Takumi, Stewart Webb, & Akifumi Yanagisawa (2019). The effects of repetition on incidental vocabulary learning: A meta-analysis of correlational studies. *Language Learning* 69: 559–599.

Ulrich, Mateo & Rosemary de Ulrich (1976). *Diccionario bilingüe maya mopán y español, español y maya mopán*. Guatemala: Impreso de los talleres del Instituto Lingüístico de Verano en Guatemala.

Ünal, Ercenur, Yue Ji & Anna Papafragou. 2021. From event representation to linguistic meaning. Topics in Cognitive Science 13(1). 224–242.

Underhill, Robert (1976). *Turkish Grammar*. Cambridge, MA: MIT Press.

Unterbeck, Barbara (1993). *Kollektion, Numeralklassifikation und Transnumerus*. Frankfurt am Main: Peter Lang.

Unterbeck, Barbara, et al. (eds.) (2000). *Gender in Grammar and Cognition: I Approaches to Gender. II Manifestations of Gender*. Berlin: Mouton de Gruyter.

Urban, Matthias (2012). Analyzability and semantic associations in referring expressions: A study in comparative lexicology. PhD dissertation, Leiden University. https://openaccess.leidenuniv.nl/handle/1887/19940

Urgesi, Cosimo, Matteo Candidi, & Alessio Avenanti (2014). Neuroanatomical substrates of action perception and understanding: An anatomical likelihood estimation meta-analysis of lesion-symptom mapping studies in brain-injured patients. *Frontiers in Human Neuroscience* 8: art. 344.

Ursini, Francesco-Alessio & Paolo Acquaviva (2019). Nouns for visual objects: A hypothesis of the vision–language interface. *Language Sciences* 72: 50–70.

Valian, Virginia. 1986. Syntactic categories in the speech of young children. Developmental psychology 22(4). 562.

Valian, Virginia. 1991. Syntactic subjects in the early speech of American and Italian children. Cognition 40(1-2). 21–81.

Valian, Virginia. 2014. Arguing about innateness. Journal of Child Language 41(S1). 78.

Vallejos, Rosa (2010). A grammar of kokama-kokamilla. PhD dissertation, University of Oregon.

Vallejos, Rosa (2015). La indexicalidad de género en kukama-kukamiria desde una perspectiva tipológica. In Ana Fernandez, Albert Alvarez, & Zarina Estrada (eds.), *Estudios de Lenguas Amerindias 3: contribuciones al estudio de las lenguas originarias de América*. Universidad de Sonora, 199–225.

VanArsdall, Joshua, et al. (2015). Adaptive memory: Animacy effects persist in paired-associate learning, *Memory* 23: 657–663.

Van Bergen, Geertje & Flecken, Monique (2017). Putting things in new places: Linguistic experience modulates the predictive power of placement verb semantics. *Journal of Memory and Language* 92: 26–42. doi:10.1016/j.jml.2016.05.003

Vandekerckhove, Bram, Dominiek Sandra, & Walter Daelemans (2013). Selective impairment of adjective order constraints as overeager abstraction: An elaboration on Kemmerer et al. (2009). *Journal of Neurolinguistics* 26: 46–72.

Van de Pol, Nikki (2019). A game of give and take: Category change on the border between adverbial verbal gerunds and augmented absolutes in English. *Language Sciences* 73: 91–104.

Van der Auwera, Johan & Vladimir Plungjan (1998). Modality's semantic map. *Linguistic Typology* 2: 79–124.

Van der Kerke, Simon (2009). Leko. In Mily Crevels & Pieter Muysken (eds.), *Lenguas de Bolivia*. Volume I. La Paz: Plural Editores. 287–332.

Van Driem, George (1997a). *A Grammar of Limbu*. Berlin: Mouton de Gruyter.

Van Driem, George. (1997b). A new analysis of the Limbu verb. In David Bradley (ed.), *Tibeto-Burman Languages of the Himalayas*. Canberra: Pacific Linguistics, 157–173.

Van Egmond, Marie-Elaine (2008). Incorporated adjunct classifiers in Anindilyakwa: An empirical challenge to LFG. http://csli-publications.stanford.edu/LFG/13/lfg08.html

Van Egmond, Marie-Elaine (2012). Enindhilyakwa phonology, morphosyntax and genetic position. Doctoral dissertation, University of Sydney.

Van Eijk, Jan P. (1997). *The Lillooet Language: Phonology, Morphology, Syntax*. Vancouver: UBC Press.

Van Eijk, Jan P. & Thom Hess (1986). Noun and verb in Salish. *Lingua* 69: 319–331.

Van Eynde, Frank (1998). The immediate dominance schemata of HPSG. In Peter-Arno Coppen, Hans van Halteren, & Lisanne Teunissen (eds.), *Computational Linguistics in the Netherlands 1997*. Amsterdam/Atlanta: Rodopi, 119–133.

Van Eynde, Frank (1999). Major and minor pronouns in Dutch. In Gosse Bouma et al. (eds.), *Constraints and Resources in Natural Language Syntax and Semantics*. Stanford, CA: CSLI Publications, 137–151.

Van Eynde, Frank (2004). Minor adpositions in Dutch. *Journal of Comparative Germanic Linguistics* 7, 1–58.

Van Eynde, Frank (2006). NP-internal agreement and the structure of the noun phrase. *Journal of Linguistics* 42: 139–186.

Van Eynde, Frank (2018). Regularity and idiosyncracy in the formation of nominals. *Journal of Linguistics* 54: 823–858. doi:10.1017/S0022226718000129

Van Gelderen, Elly (2011). *The Linguistic Cycle: Language Change and the Language Faculty*. Oxford: Oxford University Press.

Van Gijn, Erik (2006). A grammar of Yurakaré. PhD dissertation, Radboud University.

Van Halteren, Hans (1999). Performance of taggers. In Hans van Halteren (ed.), *Syntactic Wordclass Tagging*. Dordrecht: Kluwer, 81–94.

Van Hout, Angeliek (2001). Event semantics at the lexicon-syntax interface. In Carol Tenny & James Pustejovsky (eds.), *Events as Grammatical Objects*. Stanford, CA: CSLI Publications, 239–282.

van Hout, Roeland & Pieter Muysken (1994). Modeling lexical borrowability. *Language Variation and Change* 6: 39–62.

Vanhove, Martine (1993). *La langue maltaise. Etudes syntaxiques d'un dialecte arabe périphérique*. Wiesbaden: Harrassowitz.

Vanhove, Martine (2012). Roots and patterns in Beja (Cushitic): The issue of language contact. In Martine Vanhove et al. (eds.), *Morphologies in Contact*. Berlin: Akademie Verlag, 311–326.

Vanhove, Martine (2016). Refinitization of the manner converb in Beja (Cushitic). In Claudine Chamoreau & Zarina Estrada Fernández (eds.), *Finiteness and Nominalization*. Amsterdam, Philadelphia: Benjamins, 323–344.

Vanhove, Martine (2017). *Le bedja*. Leuven/Paris: Peeters.

Vanhove, Martine (2020). Grammaticalization in Cushitic, with special reference to Beja. In Andrej Malchukov & Walter Bisang (eds.), *Handbook on Grammaticalization Scenarios: Cross-linguistic Variation and Universal Tendencies*. New York: De Gruyter, vol. II, 659–694.

Vanier, Marie & David Caplan (1990). CT-scan correlates of agrammatism. In Lise Menn & Loraine K. Obler (eds.), *Agrammatic Aphasia: A Cross-language Narrative Sourcebook*. Amsterdam: John Benjamins, vol. I, 37–115.

Van Koppen, Marjo (2017). Complementizer agreement. In Martin Everaert & Henk van Riemsdijk (eds.), *The Wiley Blackwell Companion to Syntax* (2nd edn). Oxford: Wiley Blackwell, 923–962.

Van Langendonck, Willy (2007). *Theory and Typology of Proper Names*. Berlin: Mouton de Gruyter.

Van Lier, Eva (2009). *Parts-of-speech and dependent clauses*. Utrecht: LOT Publications. (LOT dissertation series 221)

Van Lier, Eva (2012). Reconstructing multifunctionality. *Theoretical Linguistics* 38(1–2): 119–135.

Van Lier, Eva (2016). Lexical flexibility in Oceanic languages. *Linguistic Typology* 20(2): 197–232.

Van Lier, Eva (2017). The typology of property words in Oceanic languages. *Linguistics* 55(6): 1237–1280.

Van Lier, Eva & Jan Rijkhoff (2013). Flexible word classes in linguistic typology and grammatical theory. In Jan Rijkhoff & Eva van Lier (eds.), *Flexible Word Classes: Typolopgical Studies of Underspecified Parts of Speech*. Oxford: Oxford University Press, 1–30.

Van Riemsdijk, Henk (1978). *A Case Study in Syntactic Markedness. The Binding Nature of Prepositional Phrases*. Dordrecht: Foris.

Van Riemsdijk, Henk (1990). Circumpositions. In Harm Pinkster & Inge Genee (eds.), *Unity in Diversity: Papers Presented to Simon Dik on his 50th Birthday*. Berlin: de Gruyter, 229–241.

Van Riemsdijk, Henk (1998). Categorial feature magnetism: The endocentricity and distribution of projections. *Journal of Comparative Germanic Linguistics* 2: 1–48.

Van Valin, Robert D. (2005). *Exploring the Syntax–Semantics Interface*. Cambridge: Cambridge University Press.

Van Valin, Robert D. & Randy J. LaPolla (1997). *Syntax: Structure, Meaning and Function*. Cambridge: Cambridge University Press.

van Zeeland, Hilde & Norbert Schmitt (2013). Incidental vocabulary acquisition through L2 listening: A dimensions approach. *System* 41: 609–624.

Vapnarsky, Valentina (1997). Du sexe des genres: relations entre classes grammaticales et classification du milieu naturel chez les Mayas Itzas. *Cahiers Art et Sciences*: 63–84.

Vapnarsky, Valentina (2013). Is Yucatec Maya an omnipredicative language? Predication, the copula and focus constructions. *STUF Language Typology and Universals*. Akademie Verlag, 40–86.

Vapnarsky, Valentina & Edy Veneziano (eds.) (2017). *Lexical Polycategoriality: Cross-linguistic, Cross-theoretical and Language Acquisition Approaches*. Amsterdam: John Benjamins.

Veikho, Sahiini Lemaina (2019). *A Grammar of Poumai Naga*. Bern: University of Bern.

Velde, Freek van de (2010). Ontwikkelingen in de linkerperiferie van de nominale constituent. *Nederlandse Taalkunde* 15: 220–237.

Vendler, Zeno (1957). Verb and times. *Philosophical Review* 66(2): 143–160.
Vendler, Zeno (1967). *Linguistics in Philosophy*. Ithaca, NY: Cornell University Press.
Verhoeven, Elisabeth & Stavros Skopeteas (2015). Licensing focus constructions in Yucatec Maya. *International Journal of American Linguistics* 81: 1–40.
Vernus, Pascal (1997). *Les parties du discours en Moyen Egyptien*. Genève: Société d'Egyptologie.
Verstraete, Jean-Christophe (2010). The noun phrase in Umpithamu. Presented at the Workshop on noun phrase structure, Aarhus Universitet.
Veselinova, Ljuba (2014). The negative existential cycle revisited. *Linguistics* 52(6): 1327–1369.
Vieira, Márcia D. (2000). *As sentenças possessivas em Mbyá-Guarani: evidência para a distinção nome e verbo*. Séminaire sur les langues tupi–guarani, Cayenne.
Vigliocco, Gabriella, et al. (2006). The role of semantics and grammatical class in the neural representation of words. *Cerebral Cortex* 16: 1790–1796.
Vigliocco, Gabriella, et al. (2011). Nouns and verbs in the brain: A review of behavioural, electrophysiological, neuropsychological and imaging studies. *Neuroscience and Biobehavioral Reviews* 35(3): 407–426.
Viljoen, Melanie Helen (2013). A grammatical description of the Buwal language. PhD dissertation, LaTrobe University, Melbourne.
Villafañe, Lucrecia (2004). *Gramática Yuki. Lengua Tupí-Guaraní de Bolivia*. Ediciones del Rectorado, Universidad Nacional de Tucumán.
Villar, Francisco (1991). *Los indoeuropeos y los orígenes de Europa. Lenguaje e historia*. Madrid, Gredos.
Visser, Eline (2020). A grammar of Kalamang: The Papuan language of the Karas Islands. PhD thesis Lund University. http://lup.lub.lu.se/record/0773ce4b-7791-4667-8dae-ca598532ba89
Visser, Willem (2011). Historical gender change in West Frisian. *Morphology* 21: 31–56.
Vittrant, Alice (2005). Classifier systems and noun categorization devices in Burmese. In Patrick Chew (ed.), *Proceedings of the Twenty-Eighth Annual Meeting of the Berkeley Linguistics Society: Special Session on Tibeto-Burman and Southeast Asian Linguistics* (BLS 28S). University of California: Berkeley Linguistics Society, 129–148.
Voeltz, F. K. Erhard & Christa Kilian-Hatz (eds.) (2001). *Ideophones*. (Typological Studies in Language 44.) Amsterdam: John Benjamins.
Vogel, Petra M. & Bernard Comrie (eds.) (2000). *Approaches to the Typology of Word Classes*. Berlin: Mouton de Gruyter.
Voghel, Amélie (2005). Phonologically identical noun–verb pairs in Quebec Sign Language (LSQ): Form and context. *Toronto Working Papers in Linguistics* 25: 67–75.
Völkel, Svenja (2017). Word classes and the scope of lexical flexibility in Tongan. *Studies in Language* 41: 445–495.
Volpe, Mark J. (2005). Japanese Morphology and its theoretical consequences: Derivational morphology in distributed morphology. PhD dissertation, Stoney Brook.
Vonen, Arfinn Muruvik (2000). Polynesian multifunctionality and the ambitions of linguistic description. In Petra M. Vogel & Bernard Comrie (eds.), *Approaches to the Typology of Word Classes*. Berlin: Mouton, 479–487.
Von Fintel, Kai & Lisa Matthewson (2008). Universals in semantics. *Linguistic Review* 25: 139–201.
Voorhoeve, Jan (1964). The structure of the morpheme in Bamileke (Bengangté dialect). *Lingua* 13: 319–334.
Voutilainen, Atro (1999). A short history of tagging. In Hans van Halteren (ed.), *Syntactic Wordclass Tagging*. Dordrecht: Kluwer, 9–21.

Vries, Hanna de (2021). Collective nouns. In Patricia Cabredo Hofherr & Jenny Doetjes (eds.), *The Oxford Handbook of Grammatical Number*. Oxford: Oxford University Press, 257–274.

Vydrine, Valentin (1990). Les adjectifs prédicatifs en bambara. *Mandenkan* 20: 47–89.

Vydrine, Valentin (1999). Les parties du discours en bambara: un essai de bilan. *Mandenkan* 35: 72–93.

Vydrin, Valentin (2009). On the problem of the Proto-Mande homeland. *Вопросы языкового родства—Journal of Language Relationship* 1: 107–142.

Vydrin, Valentin (2011). Ergative/absolutive and active/stative alignment in West Africa: The case of Southwestern Mande. *Studies in Language* 35(2): 409–443.

Vydrin, Valentin (2016). Towards a Proto-Mande reconstruction and an etymological dictionary. *Faits de Langues* 47: 109–123.

Vydrin, Valentin (2017). Dan jazyk [The Dan language]. In Valentin Vydrin (ed.), *Jazyki mira: Jazyki mande* [The languages of the world: The Mande languages]. Sankt-Peterburg: Nestor-Istorija, 469–582.

Wackernagel, Jacob (1920). *Vorlesungen über Syntax,* erste Reihe. Basel: Birkhäuser.

Wälchli, Bernhard (2008). Parts of speech (general perspective). Talk presented at the Uralic Typology Database Project Conference, Vienna, 26–27 September 2008.

Wälchli, Bernhard (2015). Co-compounds. In J. Darquennes & H. E. Wiegand (Hsgb.), *Handbücher zur Sprach- und Kommunikationswissenschaft*, vol. 1: *Word-Formation. An International Handbook of the Languages of Europe*. Berlin, de Gruyter, 707–727.

Waldron, Eric J., Kenneth Manzel, & Daniel Tranel (2014). The left temporal pole is a heteromodal hub for retrieving proper names. *Frontiers in Bioscience* S6: 50–57.

Walker, Neil Alexander (2013). A grammar of southern pomo: an indigenous language of California. Doctoral dissertation, University of California at Santa Barbara.

Wanders, Gerry (1993). Cómo actuar adverbialmente. MA thesis, Department of Spanish, University of Amsterdam.

Wane, Mohamadou Hamine (2017). *La grammaire du noon*. Utrecht: LOT.

Wang, Li (王力) (1958). 汉语史稿 Hànyǔ shǐgǎo [An Outline of the History of Chinese]. Beijing: Science Publishing House.

Wang, Li (王力) (1999). 古代汉语 Gǔdài Hànyǔ [Old Chinese]. 4 vols. Běijīng zhōnghuá shūjú [Beijing Zhonghua Book Company].

Wang, Xiaoying, Marius V. Peelen, Zaizhu Han, Alfonso Caramazza, & Yanchao Bi (2016). The role of vision in the neural representation of unique entities. *Neuropsychologia* 87: 144–156.

Ward, Nigel (2006). Non-lexical conversational sounds in American English. *Pragmatics & Cognition* 14: 129–182. doi:10.1075/pc.14.1.08war

Warriner, Amy B., Victor Kuperman, & Marc Brysbaert (2013). Norms of valence, arousal, and dominance for 13,915 English lemmas. *Behavior Research Methods* 45: 1191–1207. (Ratings list retrieved from: http://crr.ugent.be/archives/1003)

Watanabe, Honoré (2003). *A Morphological Description of Sliammon, Mainland Comox Salish with a Sketch of Syntax. Endangered Languages of the Pacific Rim*. ELPR Publications Series A2-040). Osaka, Japan.

Watanabe, Honoré (2007). Insubordination in Sliammon Salish. In Nicholas Evans & Honore Watanabe (eds.), *Insubordination [Typological Studies in Language, 115]*. Amsterdam: John Benjamins, 309–340.

Watkins, Calvert (1969). *Indogermanische Grammatik,* Band III: Formenlehre. Heidelberg, Winter.

Watson, Christine E., et al. (2013). Action concepts in the brain: An activation–likelihood estimation meta-analysis. *Journal of Cognitive Neuroscience* 25: 1191–1205.

Watson, Janet C. E. (2012). *The Structure of Mehri*. Wiesbaden: Harrassowitz.
Waxman, Sandra, Xiaolan Fu, Sudha Arunachalam, Erin Leddon, Kathleen Geraghty & Hyunjoo Song. 2013. Are nouns learned before verbs? Infants provide insight into a long-standing debate. Child Development Perspectives 7(3). 155–159.
Waxman, Sandra R, Jeffrey L Lidz, Irena E Braun & Tracy Lavin. 2009. Twenty four-month-old infants' interpretations of novel verbs and nouns in dynamic scenes. Cognitive Psychology 59(1). 67–95.
Weber, David John (1989). *A Grammar Huallaga (Huánuco) Quechua*. (University of California Publications in Linguistics, 112.) Berkeley, CA: University of California Press.
Weber-Fox, Christine, Laura J. Hart, & John E. Spruill (2006). Effects of grammatical categories on children's visual language processing: Evidence from event-related brain potentials. *Brain and Language* 98: 26–39.
Wechsler, Stephen & Larisa Zlatić (2000). A theory of agreement and its application to Serbo-Croatian. *Language* 76(4): 759–798.
Weinreich, Uriel (1953). *Languages in Contact*. The Hague: Mouton.
Weiss, Daniel (1993). Double verbs in Modern Russian (Dvojnye glagoly v sovremennom russkom jazyke). In P. Render (ed.), *Katyegorija skazuemogo v slavjanskih jazykah. Modal'- nost' i aktualizacija* ('The category of predicate in Slavonic languages. Modality and actualization.'). Slavistische Beiträge 306. München: Otto Sagner, pp. 67–97.
Weiss, Daniel (2013). Russian double verbs in the 1st pl imperative, *Wiener Slawistischer Almanach*, Sonderband 85: 165–175.
Werner, Heinrich (1997). *Die ketische Sprache*. Berlin: Harrasovitz Verlag.
Werning, Daniel (2008). Aspect vs. relative tense, and the typological classification of the Ancient Egyptian *sḏm.n=f*. Lingua Aegyptia 16: 261–292.
Wescoat, Michael T. (2002). On lexical sharing. Dissertation, Stanford University, Stanford, CA.
Wester, Ruth (2014). A linguistic history of Awyu-Dumut: Morphological Study and reconstruction of a Papuan language family. PhD dissertation, Free University of Amsterdam.
Wetzer, Harrie (1995). Nouniness and verbiness: a typological study of adjectival predication. PhD dissertation, University of Nijmegen.
Wetzer, Harrie (1996). *The Typology of Adjectival Predication*. (Empirical Approaches to Language Typology 17.) Berlin: Mouton de Gruyter.
Whaley, Lindsay J. (1997). *Introduction to Typology: The Unity and Diversity of Language*. Thousand Oaks, CA: Sage.
Wharton, Tim (2009). *Pragmatics and Non-Verbal Communication*. Cambridge: Cambridge University Press. http://dx.doi.org/10.1017/CBO9780511635649
Whitney, William Dwight (1874). Physei or thesei—natural or conventional? *Transactions of the American Philological Association* 6: 95–116.
Whitney, William D. (1881). On mixture in language. *Transactions of the American Philological Association* (1869–1896) 12: 1–26.
Whorf, Benjamin (1941). The relation of habitual thought and behaviour to language. In Leslie Spier (ed.), *Language, Culture, and Reality: Essays in the Memory of Edward Sapir*. Menasha: Sapir Memorial Publication Fund, 75–93.
Whorf, Benjamin L. (1956). *Language, Thought, and Reality: Selected Writings of Benjamin Lee Whorf*. (ed. J. B. Carroll). Cambridge, MA: MIT Press.
Wichmann, Soeren & Jan Wohlgemuth (2008). Loan verbs in a typological perspective. In Thomas Stolz, Dik Bakker, & Rosa Salas Palomo (eds.), *Aspects of Language Contact. New Theoretical, Methodological and Empirical Findings with Special Focus on Romanisation Processes*. Berlin: Mouton de Gruyter, 89–121.

Wiedenhof, Jeroen (2015). *A Grammar of Mandarin*. Amsterdam: John Benjamins.
Wierzbicka, Anna (1985). 'Oats' and 'wheat': The fallacy of arbitrariness. In John Haiman (ed.), *Iconicity in Syntax*. Amsterdam: John Benjamins, 311–342.
Wierzbicka, Anna (1986). What's in a noun? (or: how do nouns differ in meaning from adjectives?). *Studies in Language* 10–2: 353–389.
Wierzbicka, Anna (1991). *Cross-cultural Pragmatics: The Semantics of Human Interaction*. Berlin/New York: Mouton de Gruyter.
Wierzbicka, Anna (1992). The semantics of interjection. *Journal of Pragmatics* 18(2–3): 159–192. doi:10.1016/0378-2166(92)90050-L
Wierzbicka, Anna (2000). Lexical prototypes as a universal basis for crosslinguistic identification of 'parts of speech'. In Petra M. Vogel & Bernard Comrie (eds.), *Approaches to the Typology of Word Classes*. Berlin: Mouton de Gruyter, 285–317.
Wierzbicka, Anna (2003). *Cross-cultural Pragmatics: The Semantics of Human Interaction* (2nd edn). Berlin: Mouton de Gruyter.
Wierzbicka, Anna (2006). Shape in grammar revisited. *Studies in Language* 30(1): 115–177.
Wiese, Heike (2012). Collectives in the intersection of mass and count nouns: A cross-linguistic account. In Diane Massam (ed.), *Count and Mass across Languages*. Oxford: Oxford University Press, 54–74.
Wilbur, Ronnie B. (2003). Representation of telicity in ASL. Chicago: *Chicago Linguistic Society*.
Wilbur, Ronnie B. (2009). Productive reduplication in a fundamentally monosyllabic language. *Language Sciences* 31(2–3): 325–342. https://doi.org/10.1016/j.langsci.2008.12.017
Wilkins, David (1989). Mparntwe Arrernte (Aranda): Studies in the structure and semantics of grammar. Doctoral dissertation, Australian National University, Canberra.
Wilkins, David (1992). Interjections as deictics. *Journal of Pragmatics* 18(2–3): 119–158.
Wilkins, David (2000). Ants, ancestors and medicine: A semantic and pragmatic account of classifier constructions in Arrernte (Central Australia). In Gunter Senft (ed.), *Systems of Nominal Classification*. Cambridge: Cambridge University Press, 147–216.
Wilkinson, Erin (2016). Finding frequency effects in the usage of NOT collocations in American Sign Language. *Sign Language & Linguistics* 19(1): 82–123. https://doi.org/10.1075/sll.19.1.03wil
Wilkinson, Melanie (1991). *Djambarrpuyngu: A Yolngu variety of Northern Australia*. Doctoral dissertation, University of Sydney.
Wilkinson, Sue & Celia Kitzinger (2006). Surprise as an interactional achievement: Reaction tokens in conversation. *Social Psychology Quarterly* 69(2): 150–182. doi:10.1177/019027250606900203
Willems, Dominique (2012). Between construction and lexicon. In Myriam Bouveret & Dominique Legallois (eds.), *Constructions in French* [Constructional Approaches to Language 13]. Amsterdam, Philadelphia: Benjamins, 23–48.
Willett, Marie Louise (2003). A grammatical sketch of Nxa'amxcin (Moses-Columbia Salish). PhD dissertation, University of Victoria.
Williams, Marianne (1976). *A Grammar of Tuscarora*. New York: Garland.
Williams, Nicholas, Kristine Stenzel, & Barbara Fox (2020). Parsing particles in Wa'ikhana. *Revista Linguíʃtica* 16 (Esp.): 356–382. doi:10.31513/linguistica.2020.v16nEsp.a43715
Williams-Van Klinken, Catharina & John Hajek (2018). Mixing numeral systems in Timor-Leste. In Antoinette Schapper (ed.), *Contact and Substrate in the Languages of Wallacea Part 2*. NUSA 64: 65–94.

Willms, Joanna L., et al. (2011). Language-invariant verb processing regions in Spanish–English bilinguals. *NeuroImage* 57: 251–261.

Wilson, Jennifer (2017). *A grammar of Yeri: A Torricelli language of Papua New Guinea*. Doctoral dissertation, State University of New York at Buffalo.

Wilson, Patricia R. (1980). *Ambulas Grammar*. Ukarumpa, Papua New Guinea: Summer Institute of Linguistics.

Wilson, Stephen (1999). *Coverbs and Complex Predicates in Wagiman*. Stanford, CA: CSLI Publications.

Wilson, Stehpen M., et al. (2010). Connected speech production in three variants of primary progressive aphasia. *Brain* 133: 2069–2088.

Wiltschko, Martina (2012). Decomposing the mass/count distinction: Evidence from languages that lack it. In Diane Massam (ed.), *Count and Mass across Languages*. Oxford: Oxford University Press, 146–171.

Wiltschko, Martina (2014). *The Universal Structure of Categories. Towards a Formal Typology*. Cambridge: Cambridge University Press.

Winand, Jean (2007). Les formes verbales nominalisées en égyptien ancien, *Faits de langues* 30: 69–82.

Winawer, Jonathan, et al. (2007). Russian blues reveal effects of language on color discrimination. *Proceedings of the National Academy of Sciences* 104(19): 7780–7785. https://doi.org/10.1073/pnas.0701644104

Winford, Donald (2010). Contact and borrowing. In Raymond Hickey (ed.), *The Handbook of Language Contact*. Oxford: Wiley Blackwell, 170–187.

Winter, Bodo, Marcus Perlman, Lynn Perry, & Gary Lupyan (2017). Which words are most iconic? Iconicity in English sensory words. *Interaction Studies* 18: 433–454.

Winter, Yoad (2016). *Elements of Formal Semantics: An Introduction to the Mathematical Theory of Meaning in Natural Language*. Edinburgh: Edinburgh University Press. http://www.phil.uu.nl/~yoad/efs/main.html.

Winter, Yoad & Joost Zwarts (2012). Event orientated adnominals and compositionality. Unpublished in Proceedings of Annual Meeting of the Israeli Association of Theoretical Linguistics.

Wischer, Ilse & Gabriele Diewald (2002). *New Reflections on Grammaticalization*. Amsterdam: John Benjamins.

Wisniewski, Edward J. (2010). On using count nouns, mass nouns and *pluralia tantum*: What counts? In Francis Jeffry Pelletier (ed.), *Kinds, Things and Stuff: Mass Terms and Generics*. Oxford: Oxford University Press, 166–190.

Wittgenstein, Ludwig (1953). *Philosophical Investigations* (trans. G. E. M. Anscombe). Oxford: Blackwell.

Wnuk, Ewelina (2016). *Semantic specificity of perception verbs in Maniq*. PhD dissertation, Radboud University, Nijmegen.

Wohlgemuth, Jan (2009). *A Typology of Verbal Borrowings*. Berlin: Mouton de Gruyter.

Wojdak, Ruth (2001). An argument for categorial neutrality? In Karine Megerdoomian & Leora Anne Bar-el (eds.), *Proceedings of the Twentieth West Coast Conference on Formal Linguistics*. Somerville, MA: Cascadilla Press, 621–634.

Wolff, Philip & Kevin J. Holmes (2011). Linguistic relativity. *Wiley Interdisciplinary Reviews: Cognitive Science* 2(3): 253–265. https://doi.org/10.1002/wcs.104

Wolpert, Daniel M., Zoubin Ghahramani, & J. Randall Flanagan (2001). Perspectives and problems in motor learning. *Trends in Cognitive Sciences* 5(11): 487–494.

Woodbury, Anthony C. (1985). Noun phrase, nominal sentence, and clause in Central Alaskan Yupik Eskimo. In Johanna Nichols & Anthony C. Woodbury (eds.), *Grammar Inside and Outside the Clause*. Cambridge: Cambridge University Press, 61–99.

Woodbury, Hanni Joch (1975). Noun incorporation in Onondaga. PhD dissertation, Yale University.

Woodbury, Hanni (2003). *Onondaga–English/English–Onondaga Dictionary*. Toronto: University of Toronto Press.

Woodbury, Hanni (2018). *A Reference Grammar of Onondaga*. Toronto: University of Toronto Press.

Woods, Rebecca (2014). The syntax of orientation shifting: Evidence from English high adverbs. *ConSOLE XXII: Proceedings of the 22nd Conference of the Student Organization of Linguistics in Europe (8–10 January 2014, Lisbon)*, 205–230.

Woolfe, Tyron, Stephen C. Want, & Michael Siegal (2002). Signposts to development: Theory of mind in deaf children. *Child Development* 73(3): 768–778. https://doi.org/10.1111/1467-8624.00437

Wu, Denis H., Sara Waller, & Anjan Chatterjee (2007). The functional neuroanatomy of thematic and locative relational knowledge. *Journal of Cognitive Neuroscience* 19: 1542–1555.

Wunderlich, Dieter (1991). How do prepositional phrases fit into compositional syntax and semantics? *Linguistics* 29: 591–621.

Wurm, Stephen A., C. L. Voorhoeve, & Kenneth A. McElhanon (1975). The Trans-New Guinea Phylum in General. In Stephen A. Wurm (ed.), *New Guinea Area Languages and Language Study Vol 1: Papuan Languages and the New Guinea Linguistic Scene* [Pacific Linguistics, C 38]. Canberra: Research School of Pacific & Asian Studies, Australian National University, 299–322.

Wynn Karen (1995). Origins of numerical knowledge. *Mathematical Cognition* 1: 35–60.

Xing, Janet Zh. & Axel Schuessler (2020). Semantic extension in Old Chinese: Direction, transitivity, and voice. In Janet Zh. Xing (ed.), *A Typological Approach to Grammaticalization and Lexicalization*. Amsterdam: John Benjamins, 165–190.

Xu, Dan (ed.) (2012). *Plurality and Classifiers across Languages of China*. Berlin/Boston: De Gruyter Mouton.

Yakpo, Kofi (2019). *A Grammar of Pichi*. (Studies in Diversity Linguistics.) Berlin: Language Science Press.

Yang, Ying, et al. (2017). Sensorimotor experience and verb category mapping in human sensory, motor and parietal neurons. *Cortex* 92: 304–319.

Yap, Foong Ha, Karen Grunow-Hårsta, & Janick Wrona (2011). Introduction: Nominalization strategies in Asian languages. In Foong Ha Yap, Karen Grunow-Hårsta, & Janick Wrona (eds.), *Nominalization in Asian Languages: Diachronic and Typological Perspectives*. Amsterdam: John Benjamins, 1–60.

Yatbaz, Mehmet Ali, Enis Sert, & Deniz Yuret (2012). Learning syntactic categories using paradigmatic representations of word context. In *Proceedings of the 2012 Joint Conference on Empirical Methods in Natural Language Processing and Computational Natural Language Learning*. Jeju Island, Korea, 940–951

Ye, Jingtang (2021). Property words and adjective subclasses in the world's languages. PhD dissertation, Leipzig University.

Yliniemi, Juha (2019). A descriptive grammar of Denjongke (Sikkimese Bhutia). Helsinki: University of Helsinki. (PhD dissertation.)

Yngve, Victor (1970). On getting a word in edgewise. *Papers from the Sixth Regional Meeting, Chicago Linguistic Society*, 567–578.

York, Collin, et al. (2014). Action verb comprehension in amyotrophic lateral sclerosis and Parkinson's disease. *Journal of Neurology* 261: 1073–1079.

You, Guanghao, Moritz Daum, Balthasar Bickel & Sabine Stoll. 2021. Childdirected speech is statistically optimized for meaning extraction. Scientific Reports 11:16527.

Yuan, Renlin (袁仁林) (1710). 虛字說 *Xūzìshuō* [About empty words]. Peking Universiy Library. https://archive.org/details/02076148.cn/

Yudes, Carolina, et al. (2016). The time-course of processing grammatical class and semantic attributes of words: Dissociation by means of ERP. *Psicológica* 37: 105–126.

Zaccarella, Emiliano, Marianne Schell, & Angela D. Friederici (2017). Reviewing the functional basis of the syntactic Merge mechanism for language: A coordinate-based activation likelihood estimation meta-analysis. *Neuroscience and Biobehavioral Reviews* 80: 646–656.

Zacks, Jeffrey M, Nicole K Speer, Khena M Swallow, Todd S Braver & Jeremy R Reynolds. 2007. Event perception: a mind-brain perspective. Psychological Bulletin 133(2). 273.

Zadeh, Lotfi A. (1965). Fuzzy sets. *Information and Control* 8: 338–353.

Zádrapa, Lukáš (2011). *Word-Class Flexibility in Classical Chinese*. Leiden: Brill.

Zahn, Heinrich (1940). *Lehrbuch der Jabêmsprache (Deutsch-Neuguinea). Beihefte zur Zeitschrift für Eingeborenen-Sprachen* 21. Berlin: Reimer.

Zavala Maldonado, Roberto (2000). Multiple classifier systems in Akatek (Mayan). In G. Senft (ed.), *Systems of Nominal Classification*, Cambridge: Cambridge University Press, 114–146.

Zavala Maldonado, Roberto (2017). Alignment patterns. In Judith Aissen, Nora C. England & Roberto Zavala Maldonado (eds.), *The Mayan Languages*. London/New York: Routledge, 226–258.

Zeijlstra, Hedde (2004). Sentential negation and negative concord. PhD dissertation, University of Amsterdam.

Zeijlstra, Hedde (2008). On the syntactic flexibility of formal features. In Th. Biberauer (ed.), *The Limits of Syntactic Variation*. Amsterdam: John Benjamins, 143–174.

Zeijlstra, Hedde (2014). On the uninterpretability of interpretable features. In Peter Kosta et al. (eds.), *Minimalism and Beyond*. Amsterdam: John Benjamins, 109–129.

Zeijlstra, Hedde (2015) Let's talk about you and me. *Journal of linguistics* 51: 465–500.

Zeijlstra, Hedde (2020a). Labeling, selection, and feature checking. In Peter Smith, Johannes Mursell, & Katharina Hartmann (eds.), *Agree to Agree: Agreement in the Minimalist Programme*. Berlin: Language Science Press, 137–174

Zeman, Daniel, Joakim Nivre, & Mitchel Abrams (2020b). *Universal Dependencies 2.6*. LINDAT/CLARIAH-CZ digital library at the Institute of Formal and Applied Linguistics (ÚFAL), Faculty of Mathematics and Physics, Charles University, http://hdl.handle.net/11234/1-3226

Zhang, Wenguo (张文国) (2005). 古代汉语的名动词类转变及其发展 *Gǔdài hànyǔ de míng-dòng cílèi zhuǎnbiàn jí qí fāzhǎn* [Word-class transition between nouns and verbs in Old Chinese and their further developments]. Beijing: Zhonghua Book Company.

Zimmerman, Don H. (1999). Horizontal and vertical comparative research in language and social interaction. *Research on Language & Social Interaction* 32(1–2): 195–203. doi:10.1080/08351813.1999.9683623

Zimmermann, Klaus & Birte Kellermeier-Rehbein (eds.) (2015). *Colonialism and Missionary Linguistics*. Berlin/New York: De Gruyter.

Zipf, George Kingsley (1935). *The psycho-biology of Language: An Introduction to Dynamic Philology*. Cambridge, MA: MIT Press.

Zonneveld, Wim (1978). *A Formal Theory of Exceptions in Generative Phonology*. Lisse: Peter de Ridder Press.

Zúñiga, Fernano. (2006). *Deixis and Alignment: Inverse Systems in Indigenous Languages of the Americas*. John Benjamins.

Zwart, Jan-Wouter (2009). Prospects for top-down derivation. *Catalan Journal of linguistics* 8: 161–187.

Zwart, Jan-Wouter (2011). Structure and order: Asymmetric merge. In C. Boeckx (ed.), *Oxford Handbook of Linguistic Minimalism*. Oxford: Oxford University Press, 96–118.

Zwarts, Joost (1997). Vectors as relative positions: A compositional semantics of modified PPs. *Journal of Semantics* 14: 57–86.

Zwarts, Joost (2020). Formal semantics of spatial language. Unpublished ms, to appear in E. Pederson & J. Bohnemeyer (eds.), *The Expression of Space, The Expression of Cognitive Categories* (ECC), vol. VII, De Gruyter Mouton.

Zwicky, Arnold M. (1992). Jottings on adpositions, case inflections, government, and agreement. In Diane Brentari, Gary N. Larson, & Lynn A. MacLeod (eds.), *The Joy of Grammar: A Festschrift in Honor of James D. McCawley*. Amsterdam: John Benjamins, 369–383.

Zyzik, Eve (2009). Noun, verb, or adjective? L2 learners' sensitivity to cues to word class. *Language Awareness* 18: 147–64.

Zyzik, Eve & Clara Azevedo (2009). Word class distinctions in second language acquisition: An experimental study of L2 Spanish. *Studies in Second Language Acquisition* 31: 1–29.

Corpora, dictionaries, online resources

Commonwealth of Australia (2020). *National Indigenous Languages Report*. https://www.arts.gov.au/what-we-do/indigenous-arts-and-languages/national-indigenous-languages-report

Davies, Mark (2008). The corpus of contemporary American English (COCA). https://www.english-corpora.org/coca/

International Corpus of English, Great Britain (ICE-GB). Compiled by the Survey of English Usage, University College London.

Oxford English Dictionary Online (OED Online). Published by Oxford University Press.

RSL corpus (2020). *Russian Sign Language Corpus, 2012-2015*. Novosibirsk: Novosibirsk State Technical University. http://rsl.nstu.ru/

SIL International (2020). *Ethnologue*. https://www.ethnologue.com

Swedish Sign Language Dictionary (2020). *Swedish Sign Language Dictionary online*. Stockholm: Sign Language Section, Department of Linguistics, Stockholm University. teckensprakslexikon.su.se

Index of languages

For the benefit of digital users, indexed terms that span two pages (e.g., 52–53) may, on occasion, appear on only one of those pages.

N.B.
- Language varieties that are explicitly described as dialects are not listed, unless specific data (examples) are discussed.
- English is not listed separately.
- Language (sub-)families are not listed.
- Some chapters (especially those about language (sub-)families) contain language family trees or tables with many language names. These language names are listed only to the extent that they are also discussed in the body of the text.
- Languages that are only mentioned as being part of a typological sample, but not otherwise discussed, are not listed.
- Finally, languages mentioned in footnotes only are not listed.

Tables and figures are indicated by *t* and *f* following the page number

ǂHòã 452, 462
A'ingae 410–13, 411*t*, 412*t*
Abaza 321, 331
Abkhaz 92, 210*t*, 315, 324, 334
Abui 451–52, 788, 793–94, 795, 796, 797–98, 801, 802, 803
Acehnese 451–52
Adang 788, 795–96, 798, 799, 800, 801, 803
Adyghe 308, 313, 315, 324, 327, 334
Afar 509–11, 513–14
Afrikaans (Afr.) 841
Aghu 121–22
Ainu 447
Akatek 727
Akkadian 495, 496, 497–98, 503–5, 507, 508
Alagwa 509, 513–14
Alamblak 349
Albanian 411*t*, 412*t*, 416*t*, 580, 583, 588–89
Aleut *see* Unangan/Unangax̂
Al-Sayyid Bedouin Sign Language 823
Alutiiq 443, 692, 695
Ambulas 449
Amele 907–8

American Sign Language (ASL) 809–21, 823–24, 826
Amharic 261, 507, 508–9
Amis 776
Amorite 507
Ancient South Arabian 508
Anindilyakwa 544
Anywa 448–49
Arabana/Wangkangurru 553–55, 557
Arabic:
    Algerian Arabic 891–92
    Classical Arabic 312, 504–5, 507, 508
    Cypriot Arabic 508
    Mehri 507, 509
    Modern Standard Arabic 293, 323, 336, 337
    Moroccan Arabic
    Negev 320
    Soqotri 507
Aramaic:
    Biblical Aramaic 507, 508
    Western/Neo-Aramaic 26, 27
Araweté 744
Archi 26, 294–95, 870
Argentine Sign Language 487, 816

INDEX OF LANGUAGES

Armenian 580, 581, 583
Arrernte (Mparntwe) 558–59, 560, 562–63
Asuriní do Tocantins 745–46
Asuriní do Xingu 734, 748
Au 130, 131–32
Australian Sign Language (Auslan) 816, 818, 819, 824
Austrian Sign Language 816, 819
Avá-Canoeiro 743, 744, 750
Awa Pit 448, 454
Awetí 730–31, 734, 745–46, 747, 749–50
Aymara 769

Baïnounk 349
Bambara 349, 516, 518, 523, 527, 531–32, 533, 537
Bardi 551–52, 554, 556, 564–65, 569, 570
Barupu 410–13, 411t, 412t
Basaá 158
Basque 94, 210t, 315–16, 410, 411t, 413, 415t, 422, 423, 429–31, 435, 439, 441, 473, 474
Bayso 514
Beja 496, 509–12, 513–14
Belait 779
Belhare 453
Bella Coola 613–14
Bengali (Bangla) 754
Betta Kurumba 411t
Biak 777, 779
Bilinarra 555
Bininj Gun-Wok / Bininj Kunwok 411t, 547–48
Bisa 157t, 517t
Bobo 517t
Boko 517t
Bora 354–55
Brazilian Sign Language (Libras) 816
Breton 351–52
Bulgarian 308, 311, 320, 321, 335, 574, 580, 584, 585–86, 588–89
Bunaq (Bunak) 788, 792–93, 794, 795, 798, 800, 803
Burmese 352, 356
Burunge 513
Busa 517t
Buwal 22, 23

Cantonese 22, 228, 489, 874, 903–4
Cape Verdean Creole 17

Catalan 261, 585
Catalan Sign Language 816
Cavineña 435
Cayuga 59, 123, 124, 125–26, 133, 652
Central Alaskan Yupik 411t, 695
Central Siberian Yupik 670, 671, 673, 675, 685, 691, 692, 694, 695–97
Chamorro 37, 38, 145
Cherokee 37, 652, 653, 654–56, 665, 667
Chinese:
    Classical Chinese 590
    Mandarin Chinese 16, 22, 26, 27, 38, 39, 44–45, 129, 155, 156, 227–28, 345, 356–57, 360–61, 412t, 415t, 418, 482, 604–5, 611–12, 872, 873, 874–75
    Old Chinese 7–8, 67, 590
Chinese Sign Language 816
Chinook Jargon 855
Chintang 870–71, 872–73, 874–75
Chipaya 769
Choctaw 411t
Ch'ol 713, 714, 716
Cholón 769
Chontal 714, 716
Ch'orti 703, 713, 714, 716, 717
Chuj 705, 714, 720–21, 728
Chukchi 311, 411t, 464
Classical Nahuatl 2, 24–25, 48–50, 66, 68, 126
Coeur d'Alene 613–14
Columbian 613–14, 618, 621
Comox-Sliammon 613–15, 626, 627
Coptic 495, 496–97, 501
Cowlitz 613–14
Cree 891
Croatian / Serbo-Croat (Sb-Cr.) 454, 577, 584
Cupeño 389, 411t, 416t
Czech (Cze.) 319, 333, 577–78, 584, 587, 847

Dagaare 350
Dahalo 512, 513, 514
Dalabon 551
Dan 516–17, 528
Danish 74–75, 78–79, 80–81, 489
Danish Sign Language 816, 819
Dëne 870
Dhaasanac 512, 513
Dhuwal 570

Diegueño 93–94, 106
Ditidaht/Dididaht 115–16, 118
Diyari 553, 569
Djapu 550–51
Dom 451–52
Dutch (Du.) 479, 577–78, 581–83, 585–86, 805*t*, 848, 849*f*, 872, 874
Duun 517*t*
Dyirbal 453, 460, 562, 570

Edo 331
Egyptian 495, 496–503, 499*t*, 509, 514–15, 584
Emmi 555
Epena Pedee 460, 462
Eskimo *see* Greenlandic
Estonian 294, 835
Even 97, 103
Evenki 103, 449
Ewe 370–71, 469, 473–74, 484, 487–88

Fataluku 792, 798
Fijian 93–94, 100
Finnish 293–94, 446–47, 452, 485, 584, 837, 894–95
Finnish Sign Language 816
French (Fr.) 52–53, 78–79, 155–56, 158, 208, 216, 261, 266, 271–72, 276, 284–88, 289, 296–97, 307–8, 309–10, 318, 321, 324, 334, 335, 445, 448, 449, 451, 455, 457, 529, 532, 574, 575–78, 579, 580, 581–82, 583, 584, 585–86, 587, 632, 837, 838, 848, 849–50, 849*f*, 858, 871–72, 874–75, 878–79, 891–92, 894–95, 931, 935–36, 945
French Sign Language 816
Fula 93–94, 97

Gaagudju 411*t*
Gaelic (Gael.) 577
Garo 207, 209, 210*t*, 384, 389, 411*t*, 414, 415*t*
Garrwa 554
Gban 519–20, 534
Gbaya 473
Ge'ez 503, 504–5, 507, 508
Georgian 210*t*, 353
German 18, 24, 28, 29, 36, 44–45, 52–53, 130, 151–52, 179, 210*t*, 215–16, 219, 246, 266, 294, 311, 328, 333, 334, 346, 421, 431–32, 435, 439, 441–42, 445–46, 451, 453–54, 455, 456, 458, 479, 482, 575–76, 578, 581, 582, 833, 835, 848, 849–50, 873, 874–75, 881–82, 892–93, 903–4, 905, 935–36
German Sign Language (DGS) 818, 821–22, 823–24
Gĩkũyũ 299–300
Godoberi 29, 39
Goemai 386, 411*t*
Gooniyandi 545, 555, 556–57, 560–61, 563–64, 567
Greek:
    Classical/Ancient Greek 7, 110–11, 112, 115, 573, 574, 575–76, 579–80, 583, 584, 588
    Modern Greek 95–96, 261, 262, 272, 507, 587, 894–95, 905
Greek Sign Language 816, 819
Greenlandic (West Greenlandic/Greenlandic Inuit) 91, 92, 99, 101, 451, 670, 671, 674, 684–85, 692, 695, 697
Guaraní 749–50
Guarayu 750
Gumbaynggir 554, 556, 570
Gurindji 891
Gurindji Kriol 891
Guro 523

Halkomelem 8, 613
Hausa 157*t*, 158, 365, 368, 384
Hausa Sign Language 816
Hdi 446, 452
Hebrew 137–38, 145–46, 148–52, 251, 252, 261, 505–6, 507, 508, 874, 892–93
Hiaki 261
Hittite (Hitt.) 579–80, 581
Hiw 35
Hixkaryana 450–51
Hmong Njua 360–61
Hoan 331
Hopi 362
Huastec 727
Huitoto 157*t*
Hungarian 209, 210*t*, 293, 411*t*, 425–29, 439, 440–41, 451, 837, 889
Hupa 210*t*, 384, 411*t*

Icelandic (Ice.) 585–86, 587
Igbo 129, 469, 894–95

Ik 448–49
Imonda 451, 453
Indonesian 788, 804–6, 805*t*, 845, 848, 849–50, 893–94, 903
   Bahasa Indonesia 201
   Riau Indonesian 36, 237–38
Ingush 407*t*, 411*t*, 414, 416*t*
Inuktitut 459, 669–70
Iraqw 509, 513
Israeli Sign Language 816, 819, 823
Italian (It.) 16, 44, 102–3, 151–52, 156, 157, 177, 270, 272, 278, 299–300, 359, 455, 507, 574, 575, 576–77, 578, 579–80, 581–83, 584, 585–86, 587, 892–93, 917, 918, 922–23
Italian Sign Language (LIS) 819
Itza' 701, 708, 709, 710–11, 712, 713, 714, 716
Ixcatec 894–95
Ixil 705–6, 710–11, 714
Ixtahuacán 713

Jabêm 777
Jahai 474–75
Jalkunan 411*t*
Jalonke 516, 526, 529, 532–33, 538–39
Jaminjung 565, 566, 567, 570
Jamsay 469–72, 473
Japanese 34, 122, 130, 261, 354–55, 454, 466, 473, 475–76, 482, 846–47, 872, 873, 881, 894–95, 902, 903, 935–36
Jerusalem Domari 891–94
Jo 517*t*
Jogo 517*t*
Jula 517*t*

Ka'apor 736
Kabardian 306
Kaera 788, 792, 795, 796, 801, 804
Kalaallisut 91, 92, 99, 101, 451, 670–71, 673–74, 681, 685, 691–92, 697, *see also* Greenlandic
Kalam 342
Kalamang 485, 487–88
Kalispel 613–14
Kaluli 873
Kamaiurá 37, 734, 736, 748
Kambaata 449, 455, 460, 511, 512, 513
Kambera 210*t*, 779

Kaqchikel 709, 724–25
Kartvelian 353–54
Kata Kolok 818, 821–22, 824, 825
Kayabí 744
Kayardild 209, 210*t*, 549–50
Kemantney 510
Ket 91, 95, 100, 889
Khakas 308, 322
Khmer 42–43, 48, 57–59, 70, 600, 602
K'iche' 701, 709, 711, 712, 713, 717, 718–19, 724, 725, 726, 728
Kichwa *see also* Quechua
   Imbabura Kichwa 762, 765
   Salasaca Kichwa 753, 761–62, 764
Kilivila 777
Kimbundu 856
Kiribati 781*t*
Klallam 613–14, 618, 629, 638, 639, 645
Klamath 421, 422
Kokota 777
Kolyma Yukaghir 449, 460, 461, 462
Kono 517*t*
Konso 485
Korean 37, 91, 95, 105, 288, 390, 411*t*, 415*t*, 418, 447, 448, 452–53, 454, 601, 869, 874–75, 905
Kotiria 447
Koyra Chiini 386–87
Kpelle 521, 541
Krongo 210*t*
Kuikuro 261
Kuku Yalanji 550, 569
Kurmanji (also: Syrian Kurmanji) 892–93
Kuuk Thaayorre 549–50, 559, 570
Kxoe 452

Lacandon 705–6, 708, 709, 710–11
Lahu 217
Lak 130
Lango 210*t*, 215, 228, 343, 347, 350, 353, 359, 411*t*, 414, 415*t*, 416*t*, 448–49
Lao 35, 129, 388, 410, 411*t*, 447, 484, 485, 485*t*, 490, 906
Latin 7, 22, 24, 25, 28, 41–43, 44–45, 48, 55–60, 69, 72, 110–12, 115, 120–21, 123, 243, 246, 261, 266, 277, 293, 294, 299–300, 312, 326, 388, 437, 478, 572–73, 574, 575–76, 578, 579–80, 584, 585, 588, 835, 837, 845, 847, 853, 855, 858, 887–88

INDEX OF LANGUAGES

Latvian 584
Leko 769
Lezgian 17, 423–24, 435, 449, 454, 455, 456
Lillooet 22, 23, 25, 613–14, 616–18, 627, 629, 640, 642
Limbu 95, 103–4, 106, 311–12
Limilngan 544
Lithuanian (Lith.) 578, 582, 584, 585–86, 587
Loko 517t
Lote 777
Lower Chehalis 613–14
Lumun 411t
Luo 870

Macedonian 584
Makah 112, 115–16, 117, 118–19, 227–28, 238–39
Makasae/Makalero 788, 792, 793, 798
Malayalam 576–77
Malaysian Sign Language 816, 819
Maltese 507, 508, 892–93
Mam 130, 132, 703, 705–6, 712, 713, 714, 715, 718–19, 720–21, 722, 727, 728
Manange 368, 889
Mandinka 63, 516, 518, 519, 520, 522, 524, 525, 527–28, 529–37, 538, 539, 540
Mangap Mbula (/Mangap-Mbula) 777, 781, 781t, 782, 787
Mangarayi 93–94, 96–97
Maninka 516, 526, 541
Maniq 474–75
Maori/Māori 457–58, 777, 778, 779, 783
Mapudungun 411t, 416t, 417, 450, 460, 461
Maricopa 29
Marori 292–93
Martuthunira 547, 549–50, 560, 561, 563–64, 568–69
Matses/Matsés 329, 411t
Mauwake 460, 461
Mawé 730–31, 734, 736, 745–46, 750–51
Mawng 563–64
Media Lengua 891
Mehek 411t
Meithei 448–49
Menya 449
Mian 411t, 417, 807
Michif 891
Mochica 769

Mocho' 701
Mohawk 124–26, 313, 353–54, 629, 651, 652, 653, 656, 657, 658, 660, 662, 663, 664–66, 667
Mopan 708, 711, 712, 714, 716
Moskona 389, 411t
Movima 122
Mundari 207, 211, 237–38, 468–69
Musqueam 411t, 457–58, 460
Mwotlap 776, 777–524

Nama 91, 92, 349
Nenets 95–96
Neo-Syriac 505–6
Ngalakan 460
Ngas 874, 875
Ngiti 350, 386, 408t, 411t, 416t
Ngiyambaa 79, 93, 100
Nias 776, 777, 780, 786, 787t
Nicaraguan Sign Language 819, 821, 824, 826
Nihali 448–49
Nivkh 411t, 449, 460
Nooksack 613–14
Norwegian Sign Language 482, 483, 489, 816
Nunggubuyu 451, 452
Nuu-chah-nulth 23, 115–17, 118, 119–20, 133
Nyulnyul 557, 565–66, 568–69

Occitan 938
Ojibwe/Ojibwa 361–62, 363
Old Church Slavonic 584
Oneida 124, 279, 339, 341, 652–55, 656, 657, 658, 660, 661, 663, 664–66
Onondaga 652–53, 655–57, 660, 665–66
Oromo 352, 353–54, 511, 512, 513–14
Otomí 365, 372, 389, 895–96

Paamese 777, 779
Pacific Gulf Yupik *see* Alutiiq
Paiwan 410–13, 411t, 412t
Palula 411t
Pangasinan 450
Pentlatch 613–14
Persian 39
Pichi 411t, 419, 447
Pipil 210t
Pitjantjatjara 560

1080 INDEX OF LANGUAGES

Pitta Pitta 292
Pohnpeian 448–49, 456–58
Polish (Pol.) 313, 488, 579, 581, 584, 587, 903–4
Poqomam 707, 710–11, 718–19
Poqomchi 714
Portuguese (Port.) 574, 577–78, 581, 582, 584, 587, 805*t*, 845, 893–94
Pukina 769

Q'anjobal 705, 721, 723
Q'eqchi' 701
Quechua *see also* Kichwa
   Bolivian Quechua 890
Cuzco Quechua 752, 754–56, 755*t*, 758, 759–60, 761, 763, 764–65, 767
   Ecuadorian Quechua 759
   Huallaga Quechua 759, 760, 762
   Tarma Quechua 760
Quinault 613–14

Rapanui 411*t*, 416*t*
Romani:
   Finnish Romani 894–95
   Polish Romani 893
   Selice Romani 889
Rotuman 777
Rumanian (Rum.)/Romanian 574, 577–78, 581–82, 584, 893
Russian 16, 277, 305–6, 308–10, 311, 314, 315–16, 317, 319–20, 321, 322, 323, 324, 326, 327, 328, 329, 330, 331, 332, 333, 335, 336–37, 357–58, 422, 423, 457, 458, 488, 577, 580, 581, 593, 682, 846–47, 870, 881, 891, 903, 937, 945
Russian Sign Language (RSL) 816, 819, 821–22, 823, 824

Saho 509–10, 513–14
Sakha 896
Saliba 777, 781
Sama/Balau 779
Samoan 6–7, 53, 54, 59, 70, 210*t*, 237, 238, 339, 341, 352, 361, 572–73, 774, 777, 779, 781*t*, 783*t*, 786–87
San 517*t*
Sanskrit (Skr.) 299–300, 574, 575–78, 579–80, 581, 585–86
Santali 210*t*
Sawila 788, 791, 794, 795, 800, 803, 804

Sechelt 613–14, 627
Semai 473, 474–75
Seneca 129, 372–73, 652, 656–57, 660, 663, 665–66
Serbian(-Lusatian) 584
Sesotho 348, 349
Seychelles Creole 17, 26
Shona 473
Shuswap 613–14
Sicilian 507
Sidamo 509–10, 513–14
Silacayoapan 855
Sirenikski 670, 692, 695
Siriono/Sirionó 749–50, 923, 929
Siwu 476, 480, 481, 483, 489–490
Slave 602–3
Slovene (Slov.) 576–77, 584, 585
Somali 495, 509–11, 512, 513–14
Soninke 63, 518, 520, 522, 524, 529, 532–33, 536, 539, 540, 541–42
Soso 518, 529, 538–39, 541
South Efate 779, 781*t*, 786
Spanish 18, 19, 24, 25, 28, 36, 44–45, 48, 207, 276, 307, 354–55, 363–64, 376, 388, 389, 434–39, 442, 574, 588, 701, 710–11, 715, 718, 752, 843–44, 852, 853, 854, 855, 857, 863, 874, 884, 890, 891–92, 894–96, 903, 905, 918, 922, 935–36, 945
Spanish Sign Language 816
Squamish 613–14, 627
Sri Lanka Malay 22, 25
Straits Salish 211, 613–14, 621, 870–71
Supyire 452, 457–58
Swahili 877, 891–92
Swedish 33, 34, 288, 289, 845
Swedish Sign Language 479, 736, 814, 815, 817–18, 823–28

Taba 447
Tagalog 2, 6–7, 9, 16, 24, 25, 28, 42–43, 45–46, 48, 50–52, 65–66, 70–71, 122, 123, 133, 210*t*, 211, 772, 776, 778, 780–81, 784–86, 787*t*, 845
Takelma 130
Takia 781*t*, 889
Tamil 855, 894–95, 938
Tapieté 750
Tapirapé 733, 736, 750
Tauya 446–47, 452

INDEX OF LANGUAGES

Teiwa 788, 791, 792, 794, 795, 798–800, 801–2, 803, 804
Teko (/Emerillon) 733, 734, 738, 739, 740, 742, 744, 747, 749–50
Teop 773, 774–75, 776, 779, 781t, 783, 784, 784t, 786, 787, 787t
Tera 473
Tetun Dili 893–94
Thai 129, 344, 345, 346, 352, 354, 355, 357, 358, 359
Thompson 613–14, 617–18
Tidore 411t, 448–49, 453
Tillamook 613–14, 620
Tiwi 544
Tojolabal 713
Tolai 774, 776, 777, 779, 781t, 787t
Tongan 2, 42–43, 47, 48, 53–54, 59, 67, 69–71, 339, 361, 572–73
Toqabaqita 449, 778–79, 781, 781t, 782, 783t, 783, 786, 787, 787t
Trumai 449
Tsez 307
Tsonga 474
Tsotsil/Tzotzil 713, 723, 725
Tümpisa Shoshone 451, 457–58
Turkish 42–43, 44, 45, 47, 48, 55, 59, 61–62, 68, 69, 70, 122, 209, 210t, 347, 352, 387, 410–13, 411t, 412t, 415t, 449, 837, 872, 873, 892–93, 894–95, 905
Turkish Sign Language 816, 819
Tuscarora 210t, 652, 653
Tzeltal/Tseltal 711, 714, 718–19, 722, 725, 726, 727, 874–75
Tzimaj Cacao 714
Tzul 714
Tzutujil 709
Tz'utujil 718, 722

Udihe 389
Uduk 457–58
Ugaritic 507, 508, 509, 584
Ulwa 157t
Umpila 563–64
Unangan/Unangax̂ 669, 670, 671, 673, 674, 675, 677, 681–83, 685, 686, 687, 688, 690
Upper Chehalis 613–14, 634
Urdu 892–93
Usan 455

Vai 517t
Vietnamese 130–31, 447, 459, 837, 845, 852, 923, 938
Vinmavis 363–64

Wambaya 554
Wan 104, 517t, 522, 529
Waorani 754
Wappo 459, 460
Warao 204, 205, 206, 411t, 416t
Wardaman/Wagiman 451, 548, 570
Warlpiri 137–38, 140, 141–42, 283, 546–47, 557, 600
Warray 555
Warrongo 411t, 413, 415t
Watam 126–27
Wayampi 746–47
Wersing 788, 804
Wichi 874–75
Wolaytta/Wolaitta 449, 473
Woleaian 781t

Xamtanga 513–14
Xong 410–13, 411t, 412t, 415t, 416t

Yabem 130, 131
Yakkha 453
Yankunytjatjara 549–50, 560, 562–63, 568–69
Yeri 384, 410
Yiddish 892–93
Yimas 3, 61, 109, 112–16, 119, 120–21, 126–27, 128–29, 133
Yoruba/Yorùbá 33, 34, 42–43, 48, 60–61, 67, 68, 69, 70
Yucatec Maya 44–45, 310, 354–55, 357, 701–2, 703, 704, 705–6, 707–9, 710–12, 713–14, 715, 716, 718–19, 720, 721–22, 723, 724–26, 727, 728
Yucatec Maya Sign Languages 823
Yudja 362
Yukulta 549, 570
Yuracaré 460

Zapotec 447
Zargulla 487–88
Zuni 217, 349

Subject index handbook of word classes

For the benefit of digital users, indexed terms that span two pages (e.g., 52–53) may, on occasion, appear on only one of those pages.

N.B. Major word classes (noun, verb, adjective, adverb) are not listed, but some specific sub-types are, e.g. 'serial verb' and 'mass noun'. Some very common minor classes, such as demonstratives and adpositions, are also not listed. These word classes have their own dedicated chapter in Part III, but, of course, also appear in many other chapters, especially those in Part IV. Ideophones and interjections *are* listed here because, even though they also have each their own chapter, they are discussed less in the remainder of the book. The reader may therefore find it useful to know where else they are mentioned. Various other minor word classes, such as numerals, conjunctions, and personal pronouns, do not have their own chapter, but are often discussed and therefore also listed here.

As for linguistic theories/frameworks: many theories (though certainly not all; see Chapter 1) have a separate chapter dedicated to them in Part II, but are also mentioned elsewhere in the book and therefore listed below. Some other theories (e.g. Role and Reference Grammar) do not have a separate chapter, but do appear in the book and are therefore also listed.

Finally, extremely common and/or basic terms like 'predication/predicative' and 'derivation(al)' are not listed.

Tables are indicated by *t* following the page number.

acategorial/a-categorical /acategorical/ a-categorial 4, 22, 23, 24, 25, 26, 27, 28, 37, 64, 67, 111–12, 231, 236, 252, 627, 648–49, 677, 705, *see also* precategorial
agglutination/agglutinative 44, 208, 210, 312, 510, 731–32, 753, 852, 895–96
agrammatism 928
(in)alienable/(in)alienability 132, 230, 363, 603, 656–57, 658, 746–47, 770, 797–98, 807
Alzheimer('s) disease 913
animacy/animate 50, 53, 223, 230, 241, 311, 322, 350, 352, 363, 594, 654–55, 656–57, 659, 712, 743, 793, 807, 859, 877
aphasia 76, 78–79, 84, 913–14, 928
applicative 334, 517, 634, 708–9, 710, 794, 795, 801, 806
Aristotle/Aristotelian 3–4, 72, 76, 113, 114, 178, 179, 190, 572–73

article 24, 30, 36, 37–38, 54, 74–75, 78–79, 82, 85–86, 89–90, 93–94, 100, 138–39, 139*t*, 140, 155, 166–67, 176, 182–83, 230, 233, 237, 269, 272, 273, 274, 276–93, 310, 432, 438, 442, 450, 451, 463, 509, 511, 513, 524, 529, 563, 572, 574, 583–85, 618, 651, 775*t*, 776, 786, 833, 835, 836, 839, 855, 879, 887–88, 890–92, 894–96, 910, 918, 924, 927–28, 937
artificial language 868, 871–72
auxiliary xviii, 3, 7, 73–74, 78, 79, 81, 82, 95, 99, 103–4, 161–62, 175, 176–77, 181–82, 196, 205, 232–33, 298, 329–30, 392, 444, 470, 477–78, 498, 503, 518, 564–65, 606, 614, 615, 618, 620, 621, 628, 638, 642, 643–44, 648, 652, 706, 707, 722, 818, 834, 835, 837, 841, 844, 846–47, 854–55, 858–62, 880, 892, 894–95, 904, 927–28, 935–37

body part 132, 161, 538, 595, 596–97, 608–10, 630, 634, 656–57, 692, 712, 793, 797, 807, 837
borrowing 10, 207, 368, 389–90, 434–35, 565, 632, 633, 666, 667–68, 682, 805–6, 805t, 814–15, 829, 858, 878–79, 887–98
Broca's area 78–79, 921, 922, 927, 928

case marking 284, 292, 293–94, 358, 389, 445–46, 455, 500, 513, 545–46, 548, 550, 551–52, 568–69, 754, 756, 760, 763, 764, 765, 766, 768, 785, 807, 841, 895, 896, 903–4, 935
categoryless/category-less/category-neutral 36, 231, 234, 235, 236, 250, 616–17, 621
causative 61, 250, 308, 309, 318–19, 327, 329, 331, 497–98, 512, 517, 554, 592, 600, 603, 604, 607, 611–12, 632, 633, 634, 637, 655t, 708–9, 710, 722, 724, 733, 767, 768, 775, 786, 787, 796, 806, 899–900
classifier 6–7, 8, 78, 89–90, 93–94, 157, 157t, 181–82, 344–46, 352, 354–57, 358–59, 360–61, 363, 364, 447, 448, 452, 459, 496–97, 524, 545, 546, 552, 561, 562–64, 571, 606–7, 700, 704, 705, 711, 713, 726–28, 746–47, 770, 823–24, 825, 910, 937, 945
clitic 8, 24, 27, 37, 73, 74, 81, 116, 117, 118–19, 120, 122, 124–25, 287, 288, 289, 349, 366, 423, 430, 448–49, 470, 511, 513, 521, 524, 540, 614, 615, 616, 617–18, 620, 621, 622, 626, 644, 646, 648, 649, 711, 714, 732, 747, 750, 753, 756, 766–69, 770, 776, 777, 798, 802, 807, 823, 851, 855, 888, 890–91
cognate 51, 117, 145–46, 474–75, 497–98, 531, 627, 645, 708, 713, 714, 722, 878–79, 883, 884
Cognitive Grammar 3, 160, 193, 218–19
colour (terms) 127, 165–66, 180, 367–68, 379–80, 470, 509, 718–19, 721–22, 761–62, 781t, 904–5, 906, 913
common noun 10, 138–39, 233, 272, 508, 509, 525, 534, 536, 544, 561, 834, 835, 837, 839, 841t, 841, 843t, 845, 905, 924, 931, 933
comparative 38, 62, 102–3, 138–39, 185–86, 188, 190, 215, 242, 243, 574, 715, 834, 892–93, 927, 932t, 937

complement clause 92, 93–94, 209, 209t, 305, 319–20, 645, 717, 718, 754, 840
complementizer 196, 205, 236, 239, 263, 269, 274, 277–78, 294, 315, 332, 549, 628, 836, 893, 933, 937
compound(ing) 86, 145, 201, 310, 311, 342, 372, 377, 501, 517, 530, 536, 552, 568, 576–79, 580, 585–86, 605, 634, 635, 675, 684–85, 701–2, 705–6, 711, 714, 719, 722, 727, 738–39, 745–46, 747, 761–63, 764, 800, 814, 823–24, 857, 884, 892, 896, 941
concatenative 252, 510, 575–76, 731–32
conjunction 7, 30, 78, 138–39, 160–61, 172, 186, 269, 274, 277–78, 284, 305–6, 385, 386, 388, 396, 434, 500, 542, 545, 572, 586–87, 599, 606, 739, 796, 806, 818, 835, 841, 844, 845, 888, 890–91, 893, 894–96, 910, 927–28, 933, 935–36, 936t, 937
converb 102, 305, 313, 314, 315, 318–19, 384, 462, 473, 474, 497, 511, 587, 936t, 937
conversion 8, 36, 63–64, 65, 69–70, 111–12, 167, 189, 201, 211, 259, 260–61, 358, 371, 376–77, 526, 527, 528, 534, 556–57, 558, 665, 681–82, 690, 699, 705, 716, 773, 774, 778, 779, 869
copula 15, 16, 19, 21, 22–23, 25, 37–38, 39, 50, 52, 66, 99, 114, 115, 188, 201, 202, 204, 214, 215, 216, 308, 330, 336–38, 385, 445, 448, 456, 457, 459–60, 470, 474, 497–98, 499, 502, 503, 511, 530, 538–39, 540, 549–50, 560, 576–77, 586, 615, 617, 619, 648, 659–60, 702, 721, 759, 762, 773, 779, 780, 786, 792–93, 835, 841
count noun *see* mass noun/count noun
coverb 90, 545, 555, 906
(criterion of) exhaustiveness 47–503, 598, 775

definite(ness) 37, 38, 54, 66, 82, 85–86, 138–39, 141, 155, 176, 182–83, 230, 233, 272, 293, 340, 347–48, 387, 430, 432, 442, 448, 450, 451, 507, 509, 524, 529, 563, 583–84, 838, 890–91, 892, 895–96
dependent clause 103, 208, 209, 209t, 571, 687, 694, 696–97, 699, 732, 740, 744, *see also* embedded clause/subordinate clause
depictive 466–67, 470, 471–73, 475–76, 568–69

diminutive 621, 623t, 623–26, 625t, 633, 639–40, 648, 665–66, 738–39
discourse marker 189, 196, 434, 615, 750, 818, 884, 890, 897–98
Distributed Morphology (/DM) 4, 5, 43, 46, 67–69, 71, 231, 235, 236, 248, 705
ditransitive 20, 112–13, 161–62, 253, 519, 744, 796, 904

embedded clause 305–6, 317, 319–20, 321, 322, 325, 326–27, 329, 331, 336, 337, 547, 763, *see also* dependent clause/subordinate clause
equational/equative (construction) 45–46, 50, 51–52, 66, 456–57, 518–39, 671, 702, 734, 785, 786, 792–93
evidential/evidentiality xviii, 5, 61, 80–81, 240, 312, 313, 315, 320–21, 395, 401–2, 461, 581, 711, 750, 756, 758, 767, 768
expressive 8, 466, 467, 468–72, 474–76, 479–80, 485–86, 487–89, 490, 700, 705–6, 721–22, 724, 725–26, 816

finite/finiteness 5, 88, 92, 95, 97, 105, 106, 183, 233, 244, 245, 246, 266, 278, 315, 317, 319, 325–26, 331–32, 336, 337, 435, 441, 511, 566, 795, 837, 891, *see also* non-finite
flagging 20, 21, 520–21, 535
Functional Discourse Grammar (/FDG) 4, 6, 43, 65, 71, 196, 391, 410, 419
fusion/fusional 44, 208, 432, 524, 534, 659, 852, 858–59, 860–64, 890, 895–96

gender 29, 39, 56, 59, 66, 74–75, 88, 89–90, 121, 123–25, 131, 231, 270, 276, 292, 293, 294, 311, 316, 326, 328, 348, 363, 438, 445–46, 449, 458, 500, 501–2, 503–4, 505–6, 509, 510, 511, 513, 514, 558, 573, 583–84, 585, 618, 619, 656, 667, 712, 714, 770, 776, 807, 838, 843–44, 849–50, 891–93, 899–900, 905
generative grammar / generativist 3, 4–5, 33, 51–52, 79–80, 88, 90, 107, 181, 192, 213–14, 215, 219, 224–25, 231, 232, 234, 248, 262, 263, 265, 301, 391, 705, 910, *see* Minimalism
gerund 86, 87, 88, 95–96, 98, 103–4, 187, 194, 249–51, 263, 283, 291, 298–300, 323, 474, 588, 643–44, 903
(gestural-)visual modality 9, 809, 810, 825

Head-driven Phrase Structure Grammar (HPSG) 4–5, 107, 262
heterosemy/heterosemous 35–37
homesign(er) 819, 821, 826
homonym/homonymy 773, 827, 877–78, 918, 921, 928, 929

iconicity/iconic 95, 108, 317, 328, 466, 467, 472–73, 725, 812–13, 821, 879
ideophone 5, 6, 8, 390, 466, 477, 545, 546, 568, 700, 705, 725, 726, 730, 749–50, 751, 754, 758, 769, 812–13, 906
imageability 873, 877, 881–82, 884–85, 886, 919–20, 925–26
impairment 10, 82, 913, 914, 924
imperative 61, 81, 83, 317, 331, 566, 690, 707, 796
impersonal 316, 317
inchoative 61, 63–64, 127, 250–51, 264, 506, 547–48, 554, 580, 655t, 667, 708, 710, 722, 724
incorporation 85–86, 124–25, 127, 129, 145, 310, 311, 341–42, 363, 372–73, 655–56, 664, 667, 684–85, 705–6, 707, 709, 715, 718
indefinite(ness) 37, 62, 66, 119, 145–46, 151, 152, 155, 166–67, 176, 190, 205, 273, 276, 347–48, 450, 499, 500, 507, 511, 563–64, 583–84, 585, 656, 666, 768, 888–91, 893
infinitive 86, 92, 95–96, 284–85, 294, 298, 299–300, 305–6, 309–10, 315, 319–20, 326, 327–28, 338, 343, 435, 442, 474, 501, 505, 507, 575, 718, 756, 852, 854, 858–59, 862, 864
information structure 49, 281–82, 284, 497, 541, 750–51
innate(ness) 32, 40, 366–67, 837, 865, 866–67
intensifier 560, 586, 711
interjection 5, 6, 8, 30, 78, 82–83, 434, 466–68, 476, 477, 542, 545, 546, 572, 606, 615, 730, 750, 751, 818, 835, 841, 844, 879, 887–88, 894–95, 897–98, 932t, 935–36, 936t, 937
inverse 350, 671, 731–32, 741, 743, 744, 794
isolating 94, 109–10, 208, 210, 312, 895–96

kin(ship) term 630, 656, 662, 665–66, 667–68, 712, 713, 746–47, 797, 798, 807, 874

Lexical Functional Grammar (/LFG) 4–5, 107, 262, 281, 933
lexicography 629, 826–28
light verb 308, 510, 523, 708, 716, 726, 749–50, 869, 892
linguistic relativity 344, 354–55
loan word (loans) 9, 677, 682, 710–11, 804–6, 887–89, 891–92, *see also* borrowing

machine learning 938, 940, 944
machine translation 944, 945
masdar 92, 299–300, 323, 326, 507, 932*t*, 937
mass noun/count noun 6, 155–57, 159, 165–67, 170–71, 189, 232, 311, 340, 343, 346–54, 355, 357–59, 360, 361–63, 364, 639, 899–900, 921, 922–23, 932, 933–35
mass-count *see* mass noun/count noun
memory 877, 878, 901–2, 905, 906, 908
Minimalism/Minimalist 4, 107, 231
mixed category 2, 86–87, 98, 103, 104, 188, 291, 298–300, 323

Natural Language Processing 809, 835, 838, 850, 930
negation 54, 61, 243, 284–85, 288, 298, 311–12, 329–30, 333–15, 336, 337, 392*t*, 402, 437, 470, 473, 499, 500, 661, 666, 667, 733, 736, 745, 750, 779, 792, 807, 808, 891
neural net(work) 837, 838, 917, 918, 921, 940, 944–45, 946
nominalization 2, 8, 51, 57–58, 62, 63, 85, 112, 113, 125, 201, 204, 238–39, 249, 253, 283, 294, 299–300, 305–6, 308–9, 310, 315, 318–23, 331, 342, 497–98, 499–500, 527–32, 543, 549, 599, 601, 620–21, 628, 629, 665, 684–85, 694, 695–96, 699, 700, 713–14, 716–18, 753, 763, 770, 778, 786
nominalizer(s) xvii, 15–16, 16*t*, 18, 24, 25, 96, 447, 459, 599, 620, 627, 630, 636, 655*t*, 665, 692–94, 695–97, 698, 717, 722, 734, 735, 736, 748, 753, 756, 757
non-concatenative 55–56, 68, 496, 503, 509–11, 514, 631
non-finite xxii, 95–96, 112, 233, 284–85, 294, 305, 312, 315–16, 318, 319–21, 325–26, 328, 330, 337, 338, 498, 502, 512, 756

nonverbal predicate/predication / non-verbal predicate/predication 307, 328, 330, 333, 336, 341, 385, 538–39, 540, 580, 702, 703, 721, 726, 739, 762, 792–93
numeral 6, 9, 30, 78–79, 89–90, 93–94, 100, 217, 218, 223, 313, 341–42, 344, 345, 347–48, 349–50, 352–54, 358, 362–63, 364, 385, 396, 434, 513, 537, 542, 557, 563–64, 584, 685, 688–90, 705–6, 711, 727, 748, 754, 758, 770, 779, 788, 803, 804, 806, 807–8, 813, 835, 845, 846, 849, 887–88, 893–94, 936*t*, 937

omnipredicative/omnipredicativity 45–46, 48–50, 66
onomatopoeia/onomatopoeic 390, 466–67, 477, 666, 726, 879
Optimality Theory 2, 86–87, 104–7

participle 73, 92, 95–96, 102–3, 148–49, 187, 234, 265, 266, 299–300, 305–6, 313, 315, 316, 318–19, 320–21, 330, 474, 497–98, 500, 502, 505–6, 507, 509, 572, 573, 575, 579–80, 700, 702, 710, 718–22, 842, 843, 843*t*, 858–59, 862, 932*t*, 937
particle 4–5, 8, 27, 30, 78, 79, 81, 126, 205, 228, 287, 288–89, 385, 386, 410, 420, 449, 451–52, 457, 459, 477, 481, 487, 496–97, 499, 514, 542, 545, 551–52, 582, 586, 606, 614–15, 616, 645, 648, 651, 660–62, 666, 667–68, 730, 739, 750–51, 756, 758, 766–67, 769, 770, 771, 776, 777, 778–79, 786, 792, 834, 835, 844, 845, 846–47, 888, 889, 890, 893, 894–95, 896, 928, 932*t*, 936*t*, 937
person (on verbs):
    person agreement 48*t*, 131, 231, 281, 312, 777
    person index(ing) 16, 33, 37, 703, 718, 729, 731–32, 740–42, 742*t*, 743–44, 744*t*, 793, 807
    person inflection/marking 5, 41–42, 49, 56, 60, 61, 74, 88, 121, 124, 131, 149, 214–15, 241, 242, 244, 309, 310, 311–12, 313, 314, 316, 326, 331, 426, 430–31, 432, 437, 441, 460, 461, 503–4, 505, 506, 510, 511, 547, 564–65, 614, 617–18, 656, 702, –6, 721, 749–50, 751, 753, 756, 760, 765–66, 768, 776, 778–79, 793, 796, 837, 839, 870, 899–900, 918, 921, 937
personal pronoun 503–4, 550–51, 839, 847, 856, 889, 890, 891, 894, 932*t*
pluractional(ity) 512, 626, 707

polarity 7, 88, 390, 519–21, 525, 532–33, 540, 541–42
polycategorial(ity) 221, 525–26, 528, 537, 538, 541, 543, 607, 677, 699, 705, 713, 716, 723, 724, 725, 727
polysemy/polysemous/polyseme 181–82, 221, 593, 754, 773, 827, 828, 851, 877–78, 886
polysynthesis/polysynthetic 8, 92, 112, 113, 114, 123, 124, 312, 313, 614, 649, 671, 701–2, 728, 833, 870
POS tag(ging) 9–11, 833, 931–33, 935–36, 936t, 938–39, 940–42, 943, 944, 945, 946
possessive/possession 26, 38, 49, 51, 52, 62, 66, 86, 87, 89–90, 92, 93–94, 97–98, 99–100, 101, 106, 113, 114–15, 128, 132, 157t, 158, 181–82, 230, 274, 294, 298, 299, 322, 323, 363, 420, 435, 438, 442, 450, 451, 458, 498, 499, 524, 535–36, 538, 547–48, 563–64, 571, 583, 585, 599, 617, 619, 620, 628, 646, 648, 656–57, 658, 659–60, 662, 664, 671, 685, 695, 697, 698, 699, 702, 711, 712–13, 715, 717, 720, 722, 728, 729, 732–34, 735, 737–38, 739–40, 741–42, 745, 746–47, 751, 753, 756, 764, 765, 770, 772, 777, 795, 797–98, 800, 803, 807, 816, 824, 834, 837, 847, 851–52, 853
precategorial(ity) 36, 52, 53, 62, 598, 611, *see also* acategorial
pronunciation 590, 604–5, 878
proper name 32, 60–61, 67, 76–77, 80, 138, 139t, 224, 225, 343, 537, 542, 544, 553–54, 594, 667, 773, 845, 868, 924, 937, *see also* proper noun
proper noun 10, 38, 619, 817–18, 835, 837, 843t, 844, 845, 897, 899–900, 905, 924, 931, 932t, 935–36, 942–43
prototype:
  cognitive 3–4, 163, 174, 178, 180–82, 184–85, 190, 192–93, 903–4
  typological 33, 194, 912, 917

quantification 137–38, 147, 148, 159, 344, 392t, 394, 395, 398, 410, 414, 418, 727, 779, *see also* quantifier
quantifier(s) 30, 38, 176–77, 185–86, 187, 284, 342, 501–2, 557, 561, 571, 583, 636, 711, 754, 758, 824, 888, 900, 903, *see also* quantification
quotative 455, 471–73, 474, 540, 581, 726

Radical Construction Grammar 4, 43, 65, 160, 907
reciprocal 61, 325, 397, 507, 512, 655t
reduplication 120, 128–29, 350, 389, 413–14, 415t, 446, 469, 475, 496, 500, 509, 512, 553–54, 555, 560, 569, 582, 631, 701–2, 705, 721–22, 726, 727, 743, 749, 754, 757, 777, 778, 822, 823–24
reflexive 38, 57, 61, 92, 318–19, 323, 327, 328, 329, 333, 335, 497–98, 507, 570, 580, 585–86, 631, 631t, 633, 634, 655t, 705–6, 715
relative clause 17, 26, 27, 49, 60, 202, 207, 209, 214, 365–66, 370, 372, 462, 470, 473, 474, 511, 525, 579, 598, 599, 619, 628, 642, 649, 663, 667–68, 696, 703, 711, 720–21, 756, 766, 781t, 782, 893, 894, 903–4
resultative 320, 330, 500, 628, 640–44, 648–49
rigid (word class (system)) 4, 41, 112–15, 196, 206–8, 209–12, 372, 611
Role and Reference Grammar (RRG) 88–89, 90, 218–19, 595

semantic map 20, 228–29, 474
serial verb 5, 130–31, 288, 329, 331, 332, 389, 421, 423–24, 435, 765–66, 795–96, 801, 802–3, 806, 807
sound symbolism/sound symbolic 390, 568, 725, 879
statistical learning 10, 865, 866–67, 871, 874–75
stative verb 34, 129, 139t, 320, 357, 474–75, 514, 533, 536, 591, 592, 598, 601, 607, 736, 800, 801, 861
structuralism/structuralist 1, 179, 181, 213–14, 215, 216, 224–25, 616–17, 816
subordinate clause 315–16, 426, 435, 511, 548, 549, 566, 622, 703, 715, 718, 756, *see also* embedded clause/dependent clause
superlative 62, 129, 185–86, 188, 190, 215, 242, 243, 476, 509, 537, 574, 582, 780–81, 892–93, 932t, 937

TAM (Tense Aspect Mood) 7, 54, 61, 66, 90–91, 92, 95, 97, 292–93, 306, 499, 505–6, 510–11, 517–18, 519–20, 525, 532–33, 539, 540–42, 547–48, 549–50, 565, 570, 707, 711, 721, 722, 733, 736, 750, 756, 765–66, 795, 854–55

text mining 939
tone/tonal 350, 360–61, 467–68, 471, 512, 513, 516–17, 524, 604–5, 701–2, 705, 709, 713
toponym 581, 712, 815
transitivity 121, 308, 393–94, 420, 424, 520, 541, 570, 571, 614, 617–18, 705, 706, 707, 708, 760, 925–26

Universal Dependencies 835, 839, 841, 841*t*, 844, 846–47, 848, 850, 937
Universal Grammar 32–33, 40, 133, 220, 226, 236–37, 366–67, 866–67

valency/valence 5, 10, 61, 89, 90–91, 92, 94, 97, 101, 102, 103, 112–13, 197, 199, 217, 265, 266–67, 268, 269, 277–78, 305–6, 308, 309, 327, 334, 335, 337, 375, 517, 530, 531, 532–33, 535, 601, 632, 653–54, 710, 796, 806, 877, 886

verbalization (deriving verbs) 2, 86–87, 98–102, 107, 108
verbalizer(s) xxv, 99, 308, 686, 735
voice:
   antipassive 517, 522, 529, 532, 705–6, 708, 709, 714, 717, 728
   middle 95–96, 375, 506, 507, 512, 627, 628, 631*t*, 632, 636, 705, 709, 715, 724
   passive 55–56, 61, 218, 225, 246, 265, 305, 318–19, 323, 327, 330, 335, 497–98, 505, 507, 509, 512, 523, 530, 580, 705, 707, 708, 709, 715, 717, 718, 777, 795, 856, 884–85, 925
   symmetrical voice 776–77, 778, 780, 784, 785

Wernicke's area 78–79

zero-derivation/zero derivation 36, 55, 63–64, 69–70, 238, 460, 671, 699, 774

OXFORD HANDBOOKS IN LINGUISTICS

THE OXFORD HANDBOOK OF AFRICAN AMERICAN LANGUAGE
Edited by Sonja Lanehart

THE OXFORD HANDBOOK OF AFRICAN LANGUAGES
Edited by Rainer Vossen and Gerrit J. Dimmendaal

THE OXFORD HANDBOOK OF APPLIED LINGUISTICS
Second edition
Edited by Robert B. Kaplan

THE OXFORD HANDBOOK OF ARABIC LINGUISTICS
Edited by Jonathan Owens

THE OXFORD HANDBOOK OF CASE
Edited by Andrej Malchukov and Andrew Spencer

THE OXFORD HANDBOOK OF CHINESE LINGUISTICS
Edited by William S.-Y. Wang and Chaofen Sun

THE OXFORD HANDBOOK OF COGNITIVE LINGUISTICS
Edited by Dirk Geeraerts and Hubert Cuyckens

THE OXFORD HANDBOOK OF COMPARATIVE SYNTAX
Edited by Gugliemo Cinque and Richard S. Kayne

THE OXFORD HANDBOOK OF COMPOSITIONALITY
Edited by Markus Werning, Wolfram Hinzen, and Edouard Machery

THE OXFORD HANDBOOK OF COMPOUNDING
Edited by Rochelle Lieber and Pavol Štekauer

THE OXFORD HANDBOOK OF COMPUTATIONAL LINGUISTICS
Second Edition
Edited by Ruslan Mitkov

THE OXFORD HANDBOOK OF CONSTRUCTION GRAMMAR
Edited by Thomas Hoffman and Graeme Trousdale

THE OXFORD HANDBOOK OF CORPUS PHONOLOGY
Edited by Jacques Durand, Ulrike Gut, and Gjert Kristoffersen

THE OXFORD HANDBOOK OF DERIVATIONAL MORPHOLOGY
Edited by Rochelle Lieber and Pavol Štekauer

THE OXFORD HANDBOOK OF DEVELOPMENTAL LINGUISTICS
Edited by Jeffrey Lidz, William Snyder, and Joe Pater

THE OXFORD HANDBOOK OF ELLIPSIS
Edited by Jeroen van Craenenbroeck and Tanja Temmerman

THE OXFORD HANDBOOK OF ENDANGERED LANGUAGES
Edited by Kenneth L. Rehg and Lyle Campbell

THE OXFORD HANDBOOK OF ENGLISH GRAMMAR
Edited by Bas Aarts, Jill Bowie, and Gergana Popova

THE OXFORD HANDBOOK OF ETHIOPIAN LANGUAGES
Edited by Ronny Meyer, Bedilu Wakjira, and Zelealem Leyew

THE OXFORD HANDBOOK OF ERGATIVITY
Edited by Jessica Coon, Diane Massam, and Lisa Demena Travis

THE OXFORD HANDBOOK OF EVENT STRUCTURE
Edited by Robert Truswell

THE OXFORD HANDBOOK OF EVIDENTIALITY
Edited by Alexandra Y. Aikhenvald

THE OXFORD HANDBOOK OF EXPERIMENTAL SEMANTICS AND PRAGMATICS
Edited by Chris Cummins and Napoleon Katsos

THE OXFORD HANDBOOK OF EXPERIMENTAL SYNTAX
Edited by Jon Sprouse

THE OXFORD HANDBOOK OF GRAMMATICAL NUMBER
Edited by Patricia Cabredo Hofherr and Jenny Doetjes

THE OXFORD HANDBOOK OF GRAMMATICALIZATION
Edited by Heiko Narrog and Bernd Heine

THE OXFORD HANDBOOK OF HISTORICAL PHONOLOGY
Edited by Patrick Honeybone and Joseph Salmons

THE OXFORD HANDBOOK OF THE HISTORY OF ENGLISH
Edited by Terttu Nevalainen and Elizabeth Closs Traugott

THE OXFORD HANDBOOK OF THE HISTORY OF LINGUISTICS
Edited by Keith Allan

THE OXFORD HANDBOOK OF INFLECTION
Edited by Matthew Baerman

THE OXFORD HANDBOOK OF INFORMATION STRUCTURE
Edited by Caroline Féry and Shinichiro Ishihara

THE OXFORD HANDBOOK OF JAPANESE LINGUISTICS
Edited by Shigeru Miyagawa and Mamoru Saito

THE OXFORD HANDBOOK OF LABORATORY PHONOLOGY
Edited by Abigail C. Cohn, Cécile Fougeron, and Marie Hoffman

THE OXFORD HANDBOOK OF LANGUAGE AND LAW
Edited by Peter Tiersma and Lawrence M. Solan

THE OXFORD HANDBOOK OF LANGUAGE AND RACE
Edited by H. Samy Alim, Angela Reyes, and Paul V. Kroskrity

THE OXFORD HANDBOOK OF LANGUAGE AND SOCIETY
Edited by Ofelia García, Nelson Flores, and Massimiliano Spotti

THE OXFORD HANDBOOK OF LANGUAGE ATTRITION
Edited by Monika S. Schmid and Barbara Köpke

THE OXFORD HANDBOOK OF LANGUAGE CONTACT
Edited by Anthony P. Grant

THE OXFORD HANDBOOK OF LANGUAGE EVOLUTION
Edited by Maggie Tallerman and Kathleen Gibson

THE OXFORD HANDBOOK OF LANGUAGE POLICY AND PLANNING
Edited by James W. Tollefson and Miguel Pérez-Milans

THE OXFORD HANDBOOK OF LANGUAGE PROSODY
Edited by Carlos Gussenhoven and Aoju Chen

THE OXFORD HANDBOOK OF LANGUAGES OF THE CAUCASUS
Edited by Maria Polinsky

THE OXFORD HANDBOOK OF LEXICOGRAPHY
Edited by Philip Durkin

THE OXFORD HANDBOOK OF LINGUISTIC ANALYSIS
Second edition
Edited by Bernd Heine and Heiko Narrog

THE OXFORD HANDBOOK OF LINGUISTIC FIELDWORK
Edited by Nicholas Thieberger

THE OXFORD HANDBOOK OF LINGUISTIC INTERFACES
Edited by Gillian Ramchand and Charles Reiss

THE OXFORD HANDBOOK OF LINGUISTIC MINIMALISM
Edited by Cedric Boeckx

THE OXFORD HANDBOOK OF LINGUISTIC TYPOLOGY
Edited by Jae Jung Song

THE OXFORD HANDBOOK OF LYING
Edited by Jörg Meibauer

THE OXFORD HANDBOOK OF THE MENTAL LEXICON
Edited by Anna Papafragou, John C. Trueswell, and Lila R. Gleitman

THE OXFORD HANDBOOK OF MODALITY AND MOOD
Edited by Jan Nuyts and Johan van der Auwera

THE OXFORD HANDBOOK OF MORPHOLOGICAL THEORY
Edited by Jenny Audring and Francesca Masini

THE OXFORD HANDBOOK OF NAMES AND NAMING
Edited by Carole Hough

THE OXFORD HANDBOOK OF NEGATION
Edited by Viviane Déprez and M. Teresa Espinal

THE OXFORD HANDBOOK OF NEUROLINGUISTICS
Edited by Greig I. de Zubicaray and Niels O. Schiller

THE OXFORD HANDBOOK OF PERSIAN LINGUISTICS
Edited by Anousha Sedighi and Pouneh Shabani-Jadidi

THE OXFORD HANDBOOK OF POLYSYNTHESIS
Edited by Michael Fortescue, Marianne Mithun, and Nicholas Evans

THE OXFORD HANDBOOK OF PRAGMATICS
Edited by Yan Huang

THE OXFORD HANDBOOK OF REFERENCE
Edited by Jeanette Gundel and Barbara Abbott

THE OXFORD HANDBOOK OF SOCIOLINGUISTICS
Second Edition
Edited by Robert Bayley, Richard Cameron, and Ceil Lucas

THE OXFORD HANDBOOK OF TABOO WORDS AND LANGUAGE
Edited by Keith Allan

THE OXFORD HANDBOOK OF TENSE AND ASPECT
Edited by Robert I. Binnick

THE OXFORD HANDBOOK OF THE WORD
Edited by John R. Taylor

THE OXFORD HANDBOOK OF TRANSLATION STUDIES
Edited by Kirsten Malmkjaer and Kevin Windle

THE OXFORD HANDBOOK OF UNIVERSAL GRAMMAR
Edited by Ian Roberts

THE OXFORD HANDBOOK OF WORD CLASSES
Edited by Eva van Lier

THE OXFORD HANDBOOK OF WORLD ENGLISHES
Edited by Markku Filppula, Juhani Klemola, and Devyani Sharma